Example 5.5

Ratio	Formula	19X2	19X3	Trend
LIQUIDITY				
Working Capital	Current assets − current liabilities	60,000	64,600	I
Current Ratio	$\dfrac{\text{Current assets}}{\text{Current liabilities}}$	2.2	2.17	D
Quick Ratio	$\dfrac{\text{Cash + marketable securities + accounts receivable}}{\text{Current liabilities}}$	1.3	1.26	D
ACTIVITY				
Accounts receivable turnover	$\dfrac{\text{Net credit sales}}{\text{Average accounts receivable}}$	8.16	4.57	D
Average collection period	$\dfrac{365}{\text{Accounts receivable turnover}}$	44.7 days	79.9 days	D
Inventory turnover	$\dfrac{\text{Cost of goods sold}}{\text{Average inventory}}$	1.26	1.05	D
Average age of inventory	$\dfrac{365}{\text{Inventory turnover}}$	289.7 days	347.6 days	D
Operating cycle	Average collection period + average age of inventory	334.4 days	427.5 days	D
Total asset turnover	$\dfrac{\text{Net sales}}{\text{Average total assets}}$	.530	.381	D
LEVERAGE				
Debt ratio	$\dfrac{\text{Total debt}}{\text{Total assets}}$	.63	.62	I
Debt/equity ratio	$\dfrac{\text{Total liabilities}}{\text{Stockholders' equity}}$	1.67	1.60	I
Times interest earned	$\dfrac{\text{Earnings before interest and taxes}}{\text{Interest expense}}$	11 times	9 times	D
PROFITABILITY				
Gross profit margin	$\dfrac{\text{Gross profit}}{\text{Net sales}}$	.41	.38	D
Profit margin	$\dfrac{\text{Net income}}{\text{Net sales}}$	.12	.12	C
Return on total assets	$\dfrac{\text{Net income}}{\text{Average total assets}}$	.0623	.0457	D
Return on common	$\dfrac{\text{Net income}}{\text{Common equity}}$	.17	.1203	D
MARKET VALUE				
Earnings per share	$\dfrac{\text{Net income − preferred dividends}}{\text{Common stock outstanding}}$	$2.67	$2.13	D
Price-earnings ratio	$\dfrac{\text{Market price per share}}{\text{Earnings per share}}$	8.24	9.39	I
Book value per share	$\dfrac{\text{Stockholders' equity − preferred stock}}{\text{Common stock outstanding}}$	$16.67	$18.80	I
Market/book value ratio	$\dfrac{\text{Market price per share}}{\text{Book value per share}}$	1.319	1.063	D
Dividend yield	$\dfrac{\text{Dividends per share}}{\text{Market price per share}}$			
Dividend payout	$\dfrac{\text{Dividends per share}}{\text{Earnings per share}}$			

D = Deteriorated
I = Improved
C = Constant

ADVANCED ACCOUNTING

FOURTH EDITION

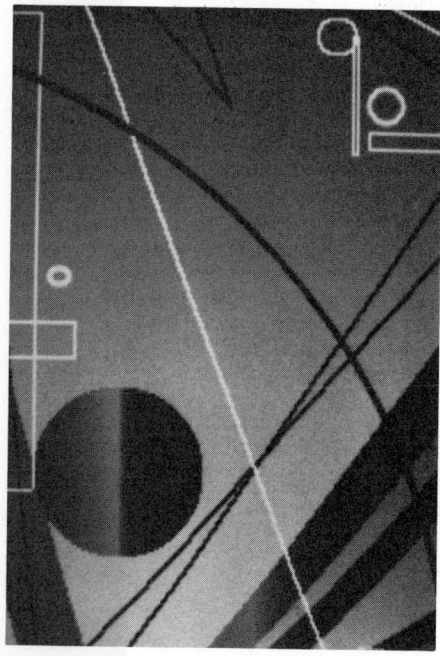

PAUL M. FISCHER, PhD, CPA

Professor of Accounting
University of Wisconsin, Milwaukee

WILLIAM JAMES TAYLOR, PhD, CPA

Assistant Professor of Accounting
University of Wisconsin, Milwaukee

J. ARTHUR LEER, MBA, CPA

Professor Emeritus of Accounting
University of Wisconsin, Milwaukee

AD90DA
PUBLISHED BY
SOUTH-WESTERN PUBLISHING CO.
CINCINNATI, OH   WEST CHICAGO, IL   DALLAS, TX   LIVERMORE, CA

2 3 4 5 6 7 8 Ki 3 2 1 0

Printed in the United States of America

COVER PHOTO: © Marjory Dressler

Material from the Uniform CPA Examination Questions
and Unofficial Answers, copyright © 1963, 1964, 1965, 1966,
1967, 1969, 1972, 1973, 1974, 1975, 1976, 1977, 1979, 1980,
1982, 1983, 1984, 1985, 1986, 1987, 1988 by the American
Institute of Certified Public Accountants, Inc., is reprinted
(or adapted) with permission.

Fischer, Paul M.
    Advanced accounting / Paul M. Fischer, William James Taylor, J.
Arthur Leer. - - 4th ed.
        p.   cm.
    Includes bibliographical references.
    ISBN 0-538-80315-0
    1. Accounting.   I. Taylor, William James. II. Leer, J. Arthur.
III. Title.
HF5635.F5389   1990
657'.046 - - dc20   89-38473
                                                                 CIP

PREFACE

Major revisions have been incorporated into the fourth edition of AD-VANCED ACCOUNTING, while retaining its emphasis on the relationship between theory and practice. The latest professional pronouncements available at the time of writing are embodied in the text, which continues to stress readability and understanding, thereby maximizing the productivity of the student's study time.

Questions at the end of each chapter encourage students to review important points. While exercises focus on limited areas of a topic, problems involve procedures covering a broader scope. Problems vary in difficulty, progressing from those requiring limited procedures to more challenging ones involving sophisticated skills to integrate concepts.

In the belief that placing lengthy consolidation worksheets within the chapter is disruptive to the flow of the narrative, we have placed such worksheets at the end of the chapter. A separate companion book with these consolidation worksheets is included with the text, permitting students to place worksheets and narrative side by side.

HIGHLIGHTS OF CHANGES IN THE FOURTH EDITION

The following changes from the third edition are the most notable:

1. In the first chapter, students are exposed to the standard-setting process affecting the accounting profession and to the various factors that influence this process.
2. Chapter 3 includes new tax accounting procedures that affect business combinations as required by FASB Statement No. 96, "Accounting for Income Taxes."
3. In accordance with common practice, consolidation terminology has been changed as follows: *Combined net income* is the undistributed net income amount on the consolidated income statement. *Consolidated net income* has been redefined as being the controlling interest's share of combined net income.

4. In Chapter 7, the elimination of intercompany bonds has been simplified through the use of a single worksheet procedure combined with a new supporting schedule.
5. A unique worksheet procedure is developed in Chapter 10 to assist in the preparation of a consolidated cash flows statement.
6. A new topic dealing with leveraged buyouts is introduced.
7. The area of multinational accounting has been expanded to two chapters (11 and 12). Additional emphasis has been placed on the equity method and consolidation procedures relating to foreign subsidiaries.
8. Chapter 14, a new chapter, discusses the Securities and Exchange Commission and its primary functions. Various reporting and disclosure requirements of the SEC also are presented.
9. GASB Statement No. 6, "Accounting and Financial Reporting for Special Assessments," eliminated the Special Assessments Funds. The resulting changes in accounting for special assessments are covered in Chapters 17 and 18.
10. In Chapter 18, the statement of cash flows reflects the influence of FASB Statement No. 95, "Statement of Cash Flows," on proprietary funds of a governmental unit.
11. Chapter 19 looks ahead to the influence of the new exposure draft, *Audits of Providers of Health Care Services*, which ultimately will supersede the *Hospital Audit Guide*.

ORGANIZATION OF THE BOOK

The fourth edition continues to offer flexibility in its use. The quantity of topics and depth of coverage offer ample material for two quarters or semesters. Where time is more limited, the instructor may select from the following topics to create a desirable course:

ACCOUNTING THEORY AND INCOME PRESENTATION (CHAPTERS 1 AND 2)

The introductory chapter sets forth a broad theoretical framework for better understanding of subsequent topics. Emphasis on the process by which accounting standards are established also contributes to the student's knowledge.

The second chapter contains concepts of income statement presentation and provides a thorough and straightforward analysis of earnings per share. These topics are included in preparation for the business combination chapters. For those students who have covered the details of the income statement and earnings per share in another course, this chapter will serve as a convenient reference.

BUSINESS COMBINATIONS

Basic Topics (Chapters 3–7). The mission of Chapter 3 is to build a strong theoretical foundation for the understanding of purchase and pooling of interests without being encumbered by the mechanical consolidation process. The chapter introduces an *equity transfer* chart for the distribution of combiner equity to the equity accounts of the issuer in a pooling. This chapter has been revised to include the new tax accounting procedures introduced in FASB Statement No. 96.

Chapters 4–10 explain consolidation procedures. The first of these chapters deals with consolidation procedures for only a balance sheet on the date of acquisition and introduces the *determination and distribution of excess schedule*. This analytical support schedule is used to ascertain the difference between the price paid in a purchase and the underlying subsidiary equity and to allocate that difference to various balance sheet accounts. This schedule has been a unique feature of this text since the first edition.

Chapter 5 deals with consolidation procedures subsequent to the date of acquisition. This chapter establishes procedures to be used in the remaining consolidation chapters. The primary method used to record the investment in a subsidiary is the *simple equity method,* which records the parent's share of subsidiary income but does not reduce the investment account for amortizations of excess of the price paid over the underlying equity acquired. There is no need to use the *sophisticated equity method* since the investment account is eliminated in the consolidation process. It is far easier to deal with amortizations of excess in the determination and distribution of excess schedule and on the consolidated worksheet. However, the chapter does include coverage of the sophisticated equity method for those desiring it. The text deals with the *cost method* through a worksheet conversion of the investment under cost to the simple equity method. This eliminates the need for separate cost method procedures for the entire worksheet.

The horizontal worksheet style continues to be the primary approach of this text. The format works from trial balances to develop columns for the consolidated income statement, minority interest, controlling retained earnings, and consolidated balance sheet. Since the horizontal style is used in intermediate accounting, students are familiar with it. In addition, it is the most common method in practice and is common on the CPA exam. The more cumbersome vertical style, which sometimes is used in the CPA exam, is included in the appendices of Chapters 5 and 6 and is supported by worksheet examples. Problems with requirements specifying the vertical format can be found in several of the chapters. Of course, either style may be used for any of the problems. The vertical format is not difficult to understand once the student has mastered the simpler horizontal format. Also introduced in Chapter 5 is the unique *income distribution schedule,* which is used to distribute combined net income to the minority and controlling interests.

Intercompany transactions are the focus of Chapters 6 and 7. The worksheet procedures for intercompany bonds have been simplified and aided with a new support schedule. Leasing has become one of the most common types of intercompany transactions, and the text has thorough coverage of this topic.

Specialized Topics (Chapters 8–10). Chapters 8 and 9 deal with complications involving the parent's investment account. Chapter 8 includes block purchases of a controlling interest, the sale of an investment in a subsidiary, and subsidiary preferred stock. Chapter 9 deals with subsidiary equity transactions and indirect and mutual holdings. Note that an appendix to Chapter 8 explains procedures for a consolidated balance sheet worksheet. Although not of concern in practice, this worksheet is a common testing format on the CPA exam.

Chapter 10 contains several vital topics. It begins with coverage of the consolidated cash flows statement, including a unique worksheet procedure for preparing the statement. Then coverage on the taxation of the consolidated firm is presented. The chapter includes details on the use of the sophisticated equity method for nonconsolidated investments. This topic, though complicated, is easy to teach when the students have a firm foundation in consolidation procedures. The chapter concludes with a newly introduced topic, leveraged buyouts. Again, this area is mastered easily once the student understands business combinations. Branch accounting has been moved to an appendix. Note that, where time is limited, Chapters 8 and 9 may be deleted from the study plan. Chapter 10 does not require their prior coverage.

MULTINATIONAL ACCOUNTING (CHAPTERS 11 AND 12)

The magnitude of our global economy is emphasized, along with the unique principles that are necessary to account for multinational operations. Principles relating to foreign currency transactions and hedging operations also are discussed. The translation of foreign financial statements into statements measured in dollars is illustrated. Accounting for investments in foreign subsidiaries is demonstrated through the use of the equity method and consolidation procedures.

SPECIAL REPORTING CONCERNS (CHAPTERS 13 AND 14)

The specialized areas of interim reporting and segmental disclosures are presented. The treatment of income taxes in interim reports is discussed in detail. The principles of segmental reporting are supported with a note from an actual annual report. Reporting and disclosure requirements of public companies are discussed in a new chapter focusing on the Securities and Exchange Commission.

PARTNERSHIPS (CHAPTERS 15 AND 16)

Major tax and nontax differences between partnerships and corporations are explained in order to identify the appropriateness of these alternative business forms. Equity theories previously discussed are employed to help the student understand the logic behind partnership accounting. The traditional topics of dissolution and liquidation are clearly and amply illustrated. Reference is made to the *Uniform Partnership Act* throughout the chapters in order to emphasize the influence of legal provisions on accounting for partnerships.

GOVERNMENTAL AND NOT-FOR-PROFIT ACCOUNTING (CHAPTERS 17–20)

Incorporated in the text material on governmental accounting are the latest pronouncements of the GASB. Its Statement No. 6, "Accounting and Financial Reporting for Special Assessments," eliminated the Special Assessments Funds. Henceforth, capital special assessments will be accounted for in the Capital Projects Funds, the General Fund, or the Enterprise Funds. The accounting treatment of special assessments for which the governmental unit is obligated for related debt is discussed in Chapter 18. The cash flows statement for proprietary funds follows the format detailed in FASB Statement No. 95, "Statement of Cash Flows." Interfund activities are emphasized.

The unsettled issue of whether or not to recognize depreciation for not-for-profit organizations is reviewed in Chapter 19. The text anticipates changes in hospital accounting as reflected in the exposure draft, *Audits of Providers of Health Care Services*, intended to supersede the *Hospital Audit Guide*. Issues related to accounting for malpractice claims are examined. Chapter 20 deals with the expanding field of voluntary health and welfare organizations.

FIDUCIARY ACCOUNTING (CHAPTERS 21 AND 22)

Estate planning is introduced in Chapter 21, with attention drawn to the proper use of the *unlimited marital deduction.* The use of gifts to reduce the impact of the unified tax is highlighted. Chapter 22 reviews the procedures available for companies that become insolvent, presenting a unique *accounting statement of affairs* on which to base decisions for possible action.

END-OF-TEXT MATERIALS

Present Value Tables
Index
Check Figures for Selected Problems

SUPPLEMENTARY MATERIALS

The materials supporting this text include a solutions manual, transparencies, and an examination book. A companion book accompanies the text, and consolidation templates, with solutions, for use with Lotus 1-2-3 are provided. For the student, a study guide and pre-printed consolidation working papers are available.

FOR THE INSTRUCTOR

Solutions Manual. The manual accompanying this text provides descriptions of all exercises and problems and their estimated completion time. The manual contains answers to all end-of-chapter questions and solutions to all exercises and problems, along with the logic for the solutions when appropriate. In particular, answers to multiple-choice questions include supporting explanations and computations.

Transparencies. The set of transparencies contains blank worksheets, solutions for all of the consolidation problems, and selected solutions from the remainder of the text.

Examination Book. The extensively revised test bank contains multiple-choice questions and examination problems for each chapter along with the solutions. These materials may be reproduced by the instructor.

Templates for Consolidation Chapters. Both student and solution templates for use with Lotus 1-2-3 are available. They are accompanied by problem instructions in ASCII form for easy conversion to most word processing programs. Many of the instructions are provided in both basic form (facts and basic requirements only) and full form (basic form plus guidelines for solving the problem and, when appropriate, complete supporting schedules). An additional choice for the instructor is provided, allowing selected problems to be worked assuming either the simple or the sophisticated equity method. General instructions and a complete summary of the problems are provided. The diskettes may be ordered for use with either IBM PC/Tandy 1000 or IBM PS/2 hardware. This software is provided free to instructors at educational institutions that adopt this text.

FOR THE STUDENT

Companion Book. This book, which accompanies the text, has removable pages to allow the student easy reference to the worksheets that appear at the end of Chapters 4–10 of the text. Thus, while studying the related narrative, the student may refer to each worksheet example concurrently. Included in this student aid are key terms (where appropriate) and highlights from each text chapter. These should enhance the understanding of the text material.

Study Guide. The study guide contains detailed chapter outlines, true/false and multiple-choice questions, and problems with solutions for self-evaluation of the mastery of subject areas.

Working Papers for Consolidations. The working papers for solving the consolidation problems in Chapters 4–10 and Chapter 12 contain pre-printed trial balances as a means of saving time. The pages are bound in a single volume and are perforated for easy removal. Two blank worksheets are included at the end for extra assignments. These may be duplicated if more are needed.

ACKNOWLEDGMENTS

To the American Institute of Certified Public Accountants, we are indebted for their permission to use selected questions and problems from the CPA exam and other materials.

Colleagues in the teaching profession have been generous in devoting their time and talent as reviewers. They have provided pertinent information for improving the text. In particular, we wish to acknowledge the contributions of Joseph H. Anthony, Michigan State University; John T. Burke, Western Michigan University; Stanley Y. Chang, University of Houston; Philip C. Cheng, East Carolina University; John E. Elsea, University of Northern Colorado; Hartwell C. Herring III, University of Tennessee; Walter L. Johnson, University of Central Florida; David W. Joy, Drake University; Hans E. Klein, Bentley College; Mary V. Parker, Metropolitan State College; Thomas F. Schaefer, Florida State University; Rudolph W. Schattke, University of Colorado; Sammie L. Smith, Stephen F. Austin State University; and W. T. Wrege, Ball State University.

We wish to thank the many individuals who, over the years, have provided valuable suggestions. Among these are the following faculty: Joyce C. Alman, Aquinas College; James R. Barnhart, Ball State University; Gary Berg, East Tennessee State University; Garth Blanchard, University of Puget Sound; Sylvia Boyd, Hope College; Pamela Brown, Drury College; Patricia Coplan, University of Texas at Tyler; James A. Davidson, Southeastern Oklahoma State University; H. Lawrence Dennis, North Georgia College; Donald Dockerty, Andrews University; Steven Fogg, Temple University; Howard Godfrey, University of North Carolina at Charlotte; William Grasty, Middle Tennessee State University; Richard Griffin, University of Tennessee at Martin; Emil J. Hensler, Seton Hall University; Jack Hudson, Lake Superior State College; Richard Johnson, Ferris State University; Stephen Jolly, University of North Carolina at Charlotte; Gerald Kruse, Siena Heights College; Victor Lomax, Savannah State College; Gale Newell, Western Michigan University; Roy Polley, University of Puget Sound; Dale Pulliam, West Texas State University; Jeffrey Ritter, St. Norbert's College; Warren Slagle, University of Tennessee; Ray Slager, Calvin College; Judson P. Stryker, Stetson University; Donald Swenson, National College; Roy Tuttle, University of Wisconsin — Madison; George Ulrich, Rio Grande College; Terry Unruh, Oral Roberts University; Roy Weatherwax, University of Wisconsin — Whitewater; and Shari Wescott, University of Houston.

Grateful acknowledgment is due to Karla Kubick, Drena LaPointe, and Laurel Rosien. Their meticulous proofing aided the revision of the text by detecting errors and inconsistencies.

To our families and friends for their understanding, support, and tolerance, we are truly thankful.

We invite users of the text to share their suggestions and comments with us.

Paul M. Fischer
William James Taylor
Jerry Leer

About the Authors

Paul M. Fischer is the Jerry Leer Professor of Accounting at the University of Wisconsin—Milwaukee. He teaches managerial and financial accounting and has received the Amoco Outstanding Professor Award and the School of Business Administration Advisory Council Teaching Award. He earned his PhD in Accounting from the University of Wisconsin—Madison and is a CPA. Previous books include *Financial Dimensions of Marketing Management* (with Crissy and Mossman) and *Cost Accounting: Theory and Applications* (with Frank). He also has authored journal articles and computer software.

Professor Fischer serves on committees of the American Accounting Association (AAA), the American Institute of CPAs, and the Wisconsin Institute of CPAs and is an officer of the Midwest AAA. He is involved in preparing candidates for the CPA exam and conducts several continuing education seminars for CPAs.

William James Taylor is involved in teaching advanced financial accounting topics and auditing at both the graduate and undergraduate levels. He has received several awards for teaching excellence, including the Amoco Outstanding Professor Award. He earned his PhD from Georgia State University. Other aspects of his professional career include work for Touche Ross & Co. and Arthur Andersen & Co. and extensive consulting in the areas of business valuation, litigation, and small businesses. He is active in teaching a CPA review program and conducting professional development programs.

Dr. Taylor is a member of the American Institute of CPAs and the AAA. He is also a member of the Wisconsin Institute of CPAs and is the chair of its Professional Conduct Committee.

J. Arthur Leer received a bachelor's degree from the University of Wisconsin—Madison in 1940, attended the Sorbonne from 1945–1946, and received an MBA with honors from Northwestern University in 1949. He joined the University of Wisconsin—Milwaukee in 1946 as an instructor, was promoted to associate professor in 1958 and to full professor in 1964. His areas of interest are financial accounting, not-for-profit and governmental accounting, and taxation. He designed the graduate program in taxation for the University of Wisconsin—Milwaukee. Upon his retirement in 1983, he was granted emeritus status.

Professor Leer has received the Amoco Outstanding Professor Award, the UWM Alumni Association Award for Teaching Excellence, the School of Business Administration Advisory Council Teaching Award, and the Alpha Kappa Psi Distinguished Professor Award.

For five years, Professor Leer served as a member of the advisory board for tax publications for Prentice-Hall Inc. He is co-author of *CPA Problems and Approaches to Solutions* (with Horngren). He is a member of the AAA and the Wisconsin Institute of CPAs. He was on the Board of Examiners of the AICPA, chaired the Grading Subcommittee, and was a member of the Accounting Practice Subcommittee, where he had primary responsibility for the governmental and not-for-profit areas of the CPA exam.

CONTENTS IN BRIEF

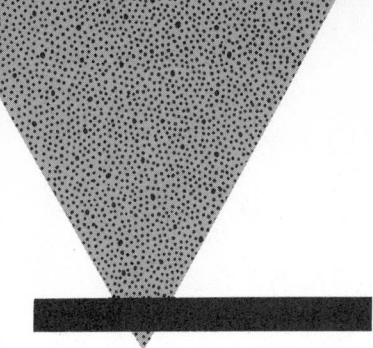

CONTENTS

PART ONE

ACCOUNTING THEORY AND INCOME PRESENTATION

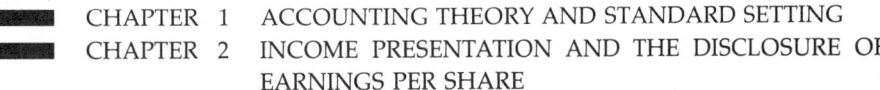

CHAPTER 1 ACCOUNTING THEORY AND STANDARD SETTING
CHAPTER 2 INCOME PRESENTATION AND THE DISCLOSURE OF
EARNINGS PER SHARE

The understanding of accounting is facilitated by relating principles and procedures to an underlying body of theory. The establishment of both accounting principles and their supporting theory is influenced by a standard-setting process. Knowledge of the role of the Financial Accounting Standards Board and other groups affecting standard setting is a basic part of comprehending accounting.

The income statement plays an important role in communicating financial data to a variety of users. Reported income is classified into components, such as continuing operations and discontinued operations, and is presented on an earnings per share basis that provides a useful common denominator for comparing financial statements. Understanding the characteristics of these components and earnings per share information is critical to a proper analysis of the income statement.

CHAPTER 1

ACCOUNTING THEORY AND STANDARD SETTING

Contemporary accounting is a service-oriented discipline concerned with measuring and communicating economic or financial data relating to the activities of economic entities. Accounting is a dynamic discipline which is influenced by numerous environmental factors and by an underlying theoretical structure. In general, accounting can be divided into the following functional areas: managerial, financial, tax, and governmental or not-for-profit accounting.

A major emphasis of this text is on financial accounting, which is concerned with measuring enterprise resources and obligations and subsequent changes in these items due to activities which affect the entity. Considerable attention is given to contemporary problems of income determination, accounting for special business entities, and accounting for financially troubled entities. Another area of emphasis is accounting for not-for-profit organizations, including governmental entities. Coverage of this area focuses on the unique accounting methods used to secure the control of the activities of such entities. Before attention is given to these basic areas of concern, however, a discussion of accounting and its supportive theory is in order. This discussion is not designed to be all-inclusive, but rather to present those aspects of accounting theory which relate to the topics contained in this text.

THE PURPOSE OF ACCOUNTING

The purpose of accounting is to measure and communicate relevant financial data to a variety of data users so that their decision-making processes are most effective. The identity or nature of the user and the type of decision process affect the resulting form of accounting. Therefore, financial accounting has been classified according to its applicability to business and not-for-profit organizations. The primary goal of the business organization is to provide goods and/or services for a profit, while the primary goal of the not-

3

for-profit organization is to discharge some social purpose. The not-for-profit organization receives a significant amount of its resources from parties who do not expect repayment or return of all or part of their investment. These resources are not represented by defined ownership interests and cannot be sold, transferred, or liquidated in return for the assets of the organization.

INFORMATIONAL NEEDS OF USERS

Although particular users may have specialized informational needs, their needs generally are traceable to certain broad needs. For example, information about resources and changes in resource levels must be provided to users for the purpose of deciding whether to allocate these resources to an entity, regardless of whether the entity is a business or not-for-profit organization. This informational need is basic, even though the reasons for allocating resources—financial reward or social purpose—may be diverse.

Information for assessing the operating performance of an entity must be provided as well. For a not-for-profit organization, performance data can be used to determine whether the entity is meeting its established social and service goals. For a business enterprise, potential cash flows may be suggested by performance data that focuses on measures of earnings. The importance of potential cash flows to a variety of users has been described as follows:

> Potential users of financial information most directly concerned with a particular business enterprise are generally interested in its ability to generate favorable cash flows because their decisions relate to amounts, timing, and uncertainties of expected cash flows . . . . Thus, investors, creditors, employees, customers, and managers significantly share a common interest in an enterprise's ability to generate favorable cash flows. Other potential users of financial information share the same interest, derived from investors, creditors, employees, customers, or managers whom they advise or represent or derived from an interest in how those groups (and especially stockholders) are faring.[1]

Furthermore, for both business and not-for-profit organizations, users must be provided information for assessing whether management has discharged its primary stewardship responsibilities for implementing the goals of the organization. This information may be more critical in a not-for-profit organization, which depends on resource providers rather than profit activities for continued operations.

---

[1]*Statement of Financial Accounting Concepts, No. 1,* "Objectives of Financial Reporting by Business Enterprises" (Stamford: Financial Accounting Standards Board, 1978), par. 25.

INFORMATION STANDARDS

For a financial reporting system to have maximum utility, given cost/benefit considerations and the needs of users, it should satisfy certain standards or qualitative criteria. These criteria, which provide a basis for evaluating alternative accounting and reporting methods, are concerned with the relevance, reliability, neutrality, and comparability of accounting information.[2]

Relevance. Accounting information is relevant if it pertains to the economic decisions or actions considered by users. Relevant data should influence or be capable of making a difference in the probabilities of occurrence surrounding an action or decision by the user, such as the decision to buy a security. The relevance or predictive value of data will be enhanced if the data are provided on a timely basis and in an understandable form. Of the various information standards, relevance is of extreme importance in that data which satisfy all the other standards will be only marginally useful if the data are not relevant to the needs of users.

Reliability. The overall utility of information is influenced by the information's reliability, defined as the ability of the information to represent or measure the attributes (conditions or events) of interest. Reliability is affected by the *verifiability* and *representational faithfulness* of the accounting measurement.

Verifiability refers to the bias or judgment required of the one measuring an attribute. Completely verifiable information means that, given identical measurement processes or models, independent measurers would reach the same conclusion regarding the attribute of interest. In statistical terms, verifiability is measured by the dispersion of independent measurements, which are derived from a common model, about the mean of the measurements. For example, the closing price of a security is much more verifiable than the expected value of the security six months hence, as evidenced by comparing the dispersion of the two sets of values which result from independent measurements.

Representational faithfulness refers not to the bias or judgment required of the measurer, but rather to the ability of the measurement model to portray what it purports to portray. Accuracy may be determined by measuring the difference between the mean value produced by the measurement model and the true (although perhaps unknown) value of the attribute. For example, the historical cost of an asset, even though more verifiable, may not be as representationally faithful with respect to measuring the asset's value as the net present value of cash flows traceable to the asset.

---

[2]*Statement of Financial Accounting Concepts*, No. 2, "Qualitative Characteristics of Accounting Information" (Stamford: Financial Accounting Standards Board, 1980).

Neutrality. Neutrality suggests that financial reporting should not favor one or more user groups or be designed to induce a particular behavior by biasing the selection of what is to be disclosed. Certainly, financial reporting should be expected to influence behavior and have a purpose, but it should not bias the output in order to achieve some predetermined goal.

Comparability. The comparability of financial data is a function of the differences between accounting methods used by various entities to record similar events. Such *interfirm comparability* suggests that the utility of financial data will be enhanced if the similarities and differences between entities are reflected over time. Comparability is influenced also by a single entity's changes in accounting methods used to measure similar events. This *intrafirm comparability*, which involves the consistent application of accounting methods within an entity over time, is an important criterion against which the utility of financial data should be assessed.

THE STANDARD-SETTING PROCESS

The process of setting financial accounting standards is extremely complex, demanding, and dynamic. A variety of organizations have been involved and remain involved to varying degrees in the process. To the student of accounting history, the process of standard setting provides interesting insights into the struggles and accomplishments of the accounting profession. A tremendous amount of information is available to detail the process of standard setting. Following is a brief overview of this information with an emphasis on the present environment in which accounting standards are established.

FACTORS AFFECTING THE DEVELOPMENT OF STANDARDS

Many factors have influenced how and when accounting standards and principles are established. The factors range from the significant contributions of certain individuals to the powerful forces exercised by large financial organizations. Some of the more significant factors which continue to influence standard setting are discussed next.

Securities and Exchange Commission. The Securities and Exchange Commission (SEC) was established in 1934 to administer the Securities Act of 1933 and the Securities Exchange Act of 1934. These acts are committed to insuring that full and fair financial disclosures are provided by any company whose securities are traded publicly. Both of the acts require the submission of audited financial statements which contain an opinion as to the reporting entity's conformity with generally accepted accounting principles (GAAP).

Beyond administering these acts, the SEC has adopted Regulation S-X, which sets forth the required form and content of financial statements filed with the Commission. More specifically, the SEC is empowered to establish accounting principles. However, over the years the SEC has elected to recognize the accounting profession itself as the primary arena in which accounting standards should be developed. Despite this shift of authority, the SEC maintains the role of critical evaluator of the profession and often prods the standard setters to take action.

The amount of resources and effort devoted to the standard-setting process is immense. The apparent difficulties for the SEC include:

1. Appropriating the resources necessary to carry on standard setting exclusively on its own behalf and
2. Imposing the responsibility of meeting the reporting requirements on corporate and public accountants without involving them in the standard-setting process.

These difficulties reinforce the idea that it makes sense for the profession to be involved actively in the process. Despite criticism, the results of the profession's efforts generally have been adopted and respected. In light of this, the SEC appears to be in no immediate need of reclaiming its position as the primary standard setter.

American Institute of Certified Public Accountants. The American Institute of Certified Public Accountants (AICPA) has been extremely active in standard setting almost since its founding in the 1930s. In 1934 the American Institute of Accountants (the predecessor of the AICPA) formally established six principles of accounting, primarily in response to some of the worst accounting practices of the time. Then, in 1938 the AICPA authorized the Committee on Accounting Procedure (CAP) to issue pronouncements on accounting principles. Until its termination in 1959, the CAP issued fifty-one Accounting Research Bulletins (ARBs). The ARBs were concerned mainly with formalizing existing practices but did little to reduce the number of alternatives available in financial reporting. In addition to not contributing to uniformity in accounting, the CAP did not attempt to develop any type of underlying conceptual framework from which additional principles could be formulated.

In 1959 the AICPA established the Accounting Principles Board (APB) as the primary organization responsible for promulgating accounting principles. The APB attempted to develop a conceptual framework and commissioned fifteen Accounting Research Studies. However, this process proved to be a disappointment, as several of the Studies were considered to be too radical to be of any major benefit. The APB continued to address problem areas but, like its predecessor, did little to improve uniformity in accounting. Furthermore, the APB was dealt a serious blow when the SEC decided not to accept the Board's position on accounting for an investment tax credit. Criticism of the APB continued to grow, and in the early 1970s two major studies were commissioned in response to the problems. One study, "Establishing Financial Accounting Standards" (referred to as the "Wheat Report"), became the foundation for today's standard-setting body. The other study, "Objectives of Financial Statements" (also known as the "Trueblood Report"), was the basis for a much needed conceptual framework upon which to establish accounting standards. The APB was dissolved finally in 1973 after having issued thirty-one authoritative opinions.

The AICPA has given support to established principles by incorporating into its Rules of Conduct an explicit requirement to follow principles promulgated by the authoritative bodies. More specifically, Rule 203 provides that an unqualified audit opinion cannot be rendered unless the reporting entity has complied with those pronouncements recognized as authoritative statements of GAAP. At present, Rule 203 encompasses Statements and Interpretations of the Financial Accounting Standards Board (FASB), Statements of the Government Accounting Standards Board (GASB), and, to the extent not superceded, Accounting Research Bulletins of the CAP and Opinions of the APB. The AICPA continues to be a major factor in the standard-setting process through the issuance of Statements of Position (SOPs) by its Accounting Standards Division.

Other Professional Organizations. A number of professional organizations have been involved in the standard-setting process and have influenced the content and direction of accounting standards. Some of the more significant organizations and the diverse interests they represent are as follows:

> American Accounting Association (AAA)—representing primarily accounting educators.
> Financial Analysts Federation—representing investment analysts and advisors.
> Financial Executives Institute (FEI)—representing reporting companies and their financial officers.
> Government Finance Officers Association (GFOA)—representing state and local government.
> National Association of State Auditors, Comptrollers and Treasurers—representing the internal audit and financial officers within state government.
> Securities Industry Association—representing stock associations and brokerage houses.
> Robert Morris and Associates—representing the banking industry.

Other Influencing Factors. A variety of other factors continue to influence the standard-setting process. For instance, elected officials have shown an interest in the "accounting establishment" and frequently have scrutinized the accounting profession and its responsiveness to current financial reporting problems. Of particular importance have been the investigations by Congressman John Moss, Senator Lee Metcalf, and most recently Congressman Dingell. These investigations have been critical of the process by which the accounting profession sets its standards and of what they perceive to be as control of the process by a select few. These congressional forces have resulted in increased pressure on the standard-setting process.

Specialized industries also have become involved in the process of developing standards. These industries often have unique accounting practices and are initiating new types of transactions which require the creation of new accounting principles. For example, recent principles have focused on several transactions unique to the banking and thrift industries. Given the diversity of interests influencing the formation of accounting principles, it is not surprising that politics and personal preferences also influence this process.

STRUCTURE OF THE FINANCIAL ACCOUNTING STANDARDS BOARD

The Financial Accounting Standards Board replaced the Accounting Principles Board in 1973 as the designated body to promulgate accounting principles. As previously stated, the FASB is concerned with narrowing the range of alternative accounting principles and with developing an underlying conceptual framework. Based largely on the recommendations of the Trueblood Report, the FASB has recognized the importance of a conceptual framework, and, to date, has issued six Statements of Financial Accounting Concepts. The AICPA, through Rule 203 of the Rules of Conduct, has recognized the Board as one of several authoritative sources of GAAP, while the SEC has designated the Board as the sole standard setter.

Financial Accounting Foundation. The Financial Accounting Foundation (FAF) is a not-for-profit organization which is concerned primarily with fund-raising and selecting members of the FASB and its Advisory Council. The FAF's Board of Trustees consists of 17 members, 14 of which are selected from the nominees put forth by sponsoring organizations and 3 of which are selected at large. (One of these latter 3 members is endorsed by banking associations.) The sponsoring organizations include the following: American Accounting Association; AICPA; Financial Analysts Federation; Financial Executives Institute; Government Finance Officers Association; National Association of Accountants; National Association of State Auditors, Comptrollers and Treasurers; and Securities Industry Association.

Financial Accounting Standards Advisory Council. The Financial Accounting Standards Advisory Council consists of at least 20 members. Its primary responsibility is to advise the FASB on policy and technical issues as well as project priorities. The Council also identifies task forces which provide project support.

Financial Accounting Standards Board. The FASB consists of 7 full-time members who are compensated for their services. Each member is appointed for a five-year term with possible reappointment for another term. Presently, pronouncements that are to be issued by the Board must receive a positive vote by a majority of the members. This requires a 4-to-3 vote, as compared to the earlier required 5-to-2 vote. Members of the Board are aware of trends in financial reporting and other developments, such as new legislation which may suggest topics to be considered. The members increase their awareness by maintaining contact with a number of the professional organizations listed above. In addition, in 1984 the Emerging Issues Task Force was created to help the FASB identify new issues and evolving alternative principles on a more timely basis. The Task Force accomplishes this by screening topics. If the Task Force reaches a consensus on an issue, the FASB does not add the item to its agenda. However, if consensus is not reached, the issue may receive further consideration by the FASB.

Major projects of the FASB, such as Statements of Financial Accounting Standards and Statements of Financial Accounting Concepts, are subject to a rigorous "due process" procedure. (Other pronouncements of the FASB, such as Interpretations and Technical Bulletins, are subject to a modified form of this "due process" procedure.) After the item is placed on the agenda, a task force is appointed to define the scope of the project and the nature of needed research as well as to assist the technical staff in the preparation of a discussion memorandum or document. In addition to outlining the scope of the project, the document presents possible alternatives along with their implications. The document is made public and becomes a basis for generating written and oral comments on the project, and notice is given at least 60 days before a public hearing is held. Comments received at the hearing, along with other written comments, are analyzed by the technical staff and presented to the Board. At this point the Board begins its deliberations on the topic and develops tentative conclusions. The staff is directed to prepare an exposure draft which sets forth the proposed standard and the basis for the Board's position. The draft has an exposure period of at least 60 days, after which time the Board considers further comments and begins its final deliberations. Ultimately, the final stance of the Board is voted on and adopted if a majority vote is received. Finally, the information generated by the due process procedure becomes part of the Board's public record.

STRUCTURE OF THE GOVERNMENTAL ACCOUNTING STANDARDS BOARD

Also in 1984, the Financial Accounting Foundation authorized the formation of the Governmental Accounting Standards Board, an independent board consisting of five members. The GASB establishes financial reporting standards for state and local governmental entities. Recognizing the importance of an underlying conceptual framework, the GASB has issued a conceptual statement entitled "Objectives of Financial Reporting". It applies to the financial statements of the governmental-type and business-type activities of governmental entities. The GASB has many similarities to the FASB, including the following:

1. Members are appointed by the Financial Accounting Foundation on a full-time and compensated basis.
2. Issuance of pronouncements follows the same "due process" procedure.
3. Activities are supported by the Governmental Accounting Standards Advisory Council.
4. A majority vote is required for adoption of a statement.
5. Its authority is recognized by the AICPA through Rule 203 of the Rules of Conduct.

THE ACCOUNTING ENTITY

The concept of an entity is indispensable to accounting because it defines the boundaries of accounting activity. An entity may be defined as a unit that controls the economic resources which are employed to produce a good or service. Although divisions, profit centers, and branches may be viewed as accounting entities in their own right, they also become a part of a larger entity. The boundaries of an entity are not confined to legal creations. For example, even though a parent corporation and its subsidiaries are separate and distinct legal entities, they may be viewed as one reporting entity for accounting purposes.

EQUITY CONCEPTS

When the entity has been defined, a decision must be made as to how it should be viewed theoretically, since the viewpoint adopted could affect the determination of net income, the valuation of assets, the definition of equity, and the requirements for disclosure. This need to define a viewpoint is not unique to the accounting profession. In the visual arts, for instance, given a distinct object, such as a tree, an artist develops an interpretation of the object. A realistic view would suggest different techniques and produce a different result than would a surrealistic or cubist viewpoint.

The theoretical framework of accounting consists, in part, of theories which explain the nature of the equities comprising a business unit and which also support the accounting principles applicable to that particular entity. This body of theory, often referred to as *equity theory*, consists of several mutually exclusive concepts. The difference between these concepts is in *the manner in which a particular entity is viewed*. For example, should the entity be viewed with regard to owners, creditors, management, all providers of capital, or some legal concept? Certainly, a choice of one of these viewpoints would influence the accounting principles used and the nature of the resulting financial statements.

Rarely can accounting for an entity be traced entirely to one equity theory. In fact, there are aspects of accounting within a particular organization that are traceable to more than one theory. Therefore, to understand the basis for applying specific accounting principles to a given entity, the student of accounting must understand the various equity theories. Of these theories, the *proprietary, entity,* and *fund theories* have had the most significant impact on the development of modern accounting thought.

Proprietary Theory. The proprietary theory elects to focus on the owners or proprietors of a business unit rather than viewing the unit as a distinct business entity in its own right. As one author stated:

> *According to the proprietary viewpoint, the standing and operations of a business firm are interpreted according to the manner in which they affect the proprietors or owners of the business. Whether the business be conducted in the form of an individual proprietorship, a partnership, or a corporation, the proprietary viewpoint looks at the business through the eyes of the owners. Thus, despite the fact that the corporation has a distinct legal identity, the proprietary viewpoint looks upon it essentially as a means whereby several individual entrepreneurs can conveniently carry on business together. At most, the corporation is regarded as an agent, representative, or arrangement through which the individual entrepreneurs or shareholders operate.* [3]

According to proprietary theory, the wealth and activity of a business unit are analyzed in terms of how they relate to the owners of the business. Assets are viewed as belonging to (or as the property of) the owners, and liabilities are viewed as obligations of the owners, or as "negative assets." This emphasis suggests the balance sheet equation of assets minus liabilities equals proprietorship ($A - L = P$). Income under the proprietary theory is an increase in the owner's wealth, versus the entity's wealth, in that revenues are viewed as increases in proprietorship, and expenses as decreases in proprietorship. Thus, the major objective of a business is that of increasing the proprietor's wealth; primary emphasis is placed on asset and liability measurement as a means of accurately measuring changes in the proprietary wealth.

The proprietary theory is one of the oldest equity theories supporting the development of accounting. It was discussed frequently in accounting textbooks of the nineteenth century and was relevant to the predominant business forms of that time (i.e., proprietorships and partnerships). The proprietary theory still is relevant, even though the corporate form of organization has become widespread. For example, the corporate concept of net

---

[3]John W. Coughlan, *Guide to Contemporary Theory of Accounts* (Englewood Cliffs: Prentice-Hall, Inc., 1965), 155.

income, which views interest and income taxes as expenses, represents the change in the wealth of the owners rather than that of all providers of capital. The inclusion in net income of the parent corporation's share of subsidiary net income also suggests a proprietary viewpoint emphasizing the wealth of the owners. The treatment of a sole proprietor's salary as a distribution of income, rather than as an expense, illustrates how the proprietary theory influences accounting for other forms of organizations.

Entity Theory. In direct contrast to the proprietary theory, the entity theory views the business unit as a separate and distinct entity which possesses its own existence apart from the owners. The capital structure of the firm is seen as being made up of creditors and stockholders (owners), both of whom are investors concerned with the success of the entity. Therefore, the entity theory suggests a balance sheet equation of assets equaling equities (A = E). The assets are viewed as rights which accrue to the entity, not the owners, while the equities are viewed as a common group of investors, often divided formally into the creditors' equity (liabilities) and the stockholders' equity. Normally, the liabilities of the entity can be valued more objectively and independently than the stockholders' equity and, thus, are viewed as the specific obligations of the entity. In addition, the creditors and stockholders have different rights with respect to income, risk, control, and liquidation. Nevertheless, both groups are viewed as being, in substance, members of a common equity element. According to the entity theory, the major objective of the business is generating income; therefore, primary emphasis is placed on the income statement and the determination of income available to all investors.

A strict interpretation of the entity theory would view income, excluding any charges representing cost of capital, as accruing to the entity, not the equities (owners). Paton and Littleton state:

> If the corporation were viewed as merely an aggregation of individual investors, it would be consistent to hold that the earnings of the enterprise belonged to the investors from the moment of original realization. Emphasis on the entity point of view, on the other hand, requires the treatment of business earnings as the income of the enterprise itself until such time as transfer to the individual participants has been effected by dividend declaration.[4]

The entity theory is most applicable to the corporate form of organization, which is characterized as a legal unit separate from its owners. This distinct identity is illustrated by the fact that unsatisfied creditors cannot seek recovery from the personal assets of the owners of the corporation, and that changes in the ownership structure of the corporation do not dissolve the entity. The classification of corporate owners' equity and the expensing

---

[4]W. A. Paton and A. C. Littleton, *An Introduction to Corporate Accounting Standards* (Iowa City: American Accounting Association, 1965), 8.

of salaries paid to employee-shareholders provide further evidence of the entity theory.

Fund Theory. The fund theory views the entity as consisting of economic resources (funds) and various restrictions or claims against the use of these resources, thus suggesting an accounting equation of assets equaling restrictions. Liabilities and owners' equity may be viewed as restrictions on the use of specific assets or assets in general. This asset-centered theory places primary emphasis on the administration and appropriate use of funds, rather than on the equity or proprietary interests of a particular group. Therefore, a statement of sources and uses of funds is one of the most important statements under this theory, while the income statement is viewed merely as a statement that describes a particular source of funds (i.e., operations).

Fund theory is most applicable to governmental and other not-for-profit organizations, where the profit motive is replaced by social goals which are achieved by the proper management of resources. The fund theory also is emphasized in accounting for bankruptcies as well as for estates and trusts, where attention is placed on funds available for liquidation and the restrictions on those funds.

ACCOUNTING MEASUREMENT

When the economic entity has been defined, its activity also must be measured. However, before measurement of its economic activities can proceed, three fundamental issues must be resolved. First, the relevant activities and attributes of the entity must be defined. Then, the unit of measure must be defined; finally, a measurement base must be selected.

Subject Matter of Measurement. As discussed earlier, a measurement process must measure those activities of an entity that are relevant to the needs of the intended recipients or users of the measurements. Thus, the general purpose of financial statements is to provide the data necessary for determining the allocation of scarce resources among competing entities.

This purpose suggests that existing levels of resources and changes in these levels should be measured by accounting. Therefore, the individual events and transactions affecting resources are of particular interest in accounting. However, accounting models do not capture all of the events or transactions affecting resources, but only those that satisfy certain criteria. In this screening process, events or transactions are evaluated against the criteria established by generally accepted accounting principles. For example, existing market conditions may suggest that an entity's inventory has become more valuable. However, this increase in value and resources will not be measured currently by accounting because the event fails to satisfy certain established revenue recognition criteria. Generally, only past or present transactions which may be quantified in a verifiable manner and which do not violate GAAP are measured.

Accounting measurement relates primarily to financial statements, which are part of a larger framework of financial reporting. Although financial statements and financial reporting have essentially the same objectives, financial reporting is not restricted to financial statements and is not as limited by the principles affecting the preparation of financial statements. For example, even though an increase in the value of inventory due to market conditions may not be recorded in financial statements, such information may be disclosed in financial reports.

Unit of Measure. The diversity of economic resources and obligations suggests the need for some common unit of measure which can be used to relate these items to each other. In nonbarter economies, the unit of measure for accounting purposes is money, which provides a common denominator for measuring certain attributes of the resources and obligations and for evaluating activities which influence entity wealth. These measured amounts then are combined or aggregated.

The significant characteristic of money is its purchasing power, or the quantity of goods and services which money can acquire. If the purchasing power of money has changed over time, however, the significance of combined monetary amounts may be questionable. For instance, if an economic resource measured in 1945 dollars is added to an identical resource measured in 1990 dollars, what meaning can be given to the combined total of the resources? Traditional accounting theory has dealt with this sort of question by establishing the *stable monetary assumption*, which states that the monetary unit is characterized by a stable purchasing power over time. This assumption is observed in current financial statements and is defended on the grounds that financial statements based on this assumption are well understood, compared to alternatives, and that such statements still have utility.

Although money serves as a unit of account or common denominator, serious concern has been expressed as to whether money can continue to serve in this role without adjusting certain nonmonetary assets and income statement elements so that they are expressed in terms of a constant purchasing power of the dollar (constant dollars). This conversion is accomplished by multiplying the historical cost basis by a conversion factor, defined as the current price index divided by the historical price index which existed when the nonmonetary item was acquired. To illustrate, assume that land costing $40,000 was acquired when the Consumer Price Index (CPI) was 100 and that the purchasing power of the dollar has decreased as evidenced by a current CPI of 120. In terms of the number of dollars, the land is measured at its original acquisition cost of $40,000, but in terms of the current purchasing power of the dollar (not to be confused with current replacement value), the land is measured at $48,000 ($40,000 × 120/100).

Monetary items (monetary assets and liabilities) represent sums of money which are fixed in amount or determinable without reference to changes in the purchasing power of the dollar. To illustrate, assume that at the beginning of the year a company held cash of $10,000 and incurred a long-term debt of $20,000 when the CPI was 100. At year end, when the CPI is 120, the cash and long-term debt still would be measured at $10,000 and $20,000, respectively. However, the company has experienced a loss in purchasing power due to holding a monetary asset in the form of cash. Cash which should have been worth $12,000 ($10,000 × 120/100) of current purchasing power is worth only the fixed amount of $10,000 of purchasing power. Also, the company has experienced a gain in purchasing power due to holding a monetary liability in the form of long-term debt. If the debt were not fixed in amount, it would take $24,000 ($20,000 × 120/100) of current purchasing power to repay the loan. However, because the debt can be satisfied for the fixed amount of $20,000, a $4,000 gain in purchasing power is experienced.

The following benefits may accrue to users of constant dollar data:

1. Comparisons over time will be more meaningful because data for different time periods will be expressed in terms of a uniform constant dollar.
2. The gain or loss arising from holding monetary items may serve as a partial measure of management's ability to manage assets and debts during inflationary times.
3. Accounting income will be a better measure of changes in wealth over time because certain expenses will be expressed in constant dollars. Also, accounting income will be a better measure of a company's ability to achieve real growth and maintain its operating capital.
4. When the changes in the purchasing power of the dollar approximate the changes in prices of the specific goods being restated, nonmonetary items expressed in constant dollars may be a better measure of wealth because their current economic values are approximated.

Selection of a Measurement Base. As discussed in the previous section, two possible units of measure currently are being used: the number of dollars as employed by the historical cost model and the purchasing power of the dollar as employed by the constant dollar model. Another major decision involves the concept of value to which the unit of measure should be applied. Alternative concepts of value or measurement bases represent differing views on how the value suggested by financial resources and obligations should be measured. Several measurement bases are used in accounting to various degrees. They are:

1. *Historical cost:* The most frequently employed base is historical cost, which measures value and changes in value in terms of the original or allocated acquisition (exchange) prices actually incurred. Changes in value subsequent to acquisition and prior to sale are not recognized, except in certain cases where there has been a decline in value.
2. *Current cost:* In contrast, current cost measures value in terms of current (present) money prices. For example, an economic resource is measured in terms of the current cost which would be incurred to acquire or replace the same service potential represented by the resource. Mea-

sures of changes in value would include increases or decreases in the current replacement value of economic resources and obligations. Presently, this measurement base is used to a limited extent, as evidenced by the accounting for certain current assets according to the valuation principle of lower of cost or market. However, current applications do not recognize movements in the current prices of items above their originally recorded costs.

3. *Exit value:* This measurement base expresses economic resources in terms of the current selling price which would be received if an exchange took place. Economic obligations are measured in terms of the current prices which would be paid to satisfy the obligations. Emphasis is placed on a selling market versus a buying (replacement) market, as is the case with the current cost measurement base. The exit value base is used rarely in current practice, except for instances involving the valuation of precious metals and agricultural commodities.

4. *Discounted cash flow:* Of increasing interest is discounted cash flow, a base which views the value of economic resources and obligations as being equal to the present value of expected future cash flows associated with the items. The interest factor used for discounting is revised periodically to reflect the timing of cash flows and their related risks. Discounted cash flow is applied on a limited basis in current practice. One such application is in the valuation of certain receivables and payables (see Accounting Principles Board Opinion No. 21). The capitalization of certain lease payments employs this measurement base as well.

The proper selection of a measurement base is dependent upon the informational needs of the identified users. Since it is unlikely that all users will have identical needs, the bases will vary among users. For instance, a short-term creditor may be concerned with exit values, while an equity investor may be interested in current costs. Not only should different measurement bases be available to different users, but a user should be able to use different bases to measure various economic resources and obligations. For example, a given user might prefer to have current assets measured in terms of exit values and noncurrent assets measured in terms of current cost. Therefore, the selection of a measurement base should consider the objectives of the financial report as suggested by the intended users.

Traditionally, accounting has accepted historical cost as the primary measurement base. A major defense of historical cost is that it represents prima facie evidence of the objectively determined value of a resource or obligation. At the time of acquisition, historical cost is the same as current market value and, therefore, measures value at a point in time as suggested by the arm's-length transaction. Because the measure of value is determined by the exchange, it can be measured independently (i.e., it is verifiable) and provides a degree of objectivity often lacking in other measurement bases. Thus, the emphasis on objectively determined values supports the historical cost concept of income determination, which generally recognizes changes in value only if they are evidenced by exchange transactions (i.e., a new historical cost or acquisition price is established).

Historical cost is supported also on the grounds that it has a utility for predictive purposes. The relevance of historical costs to certain types of future economic decisions, including those which involve predictions, is established in literature.[5] In addition, historical cost is supported as a satisfactory measure of management's stewardship function.

In spite of this support for historical cost, the accounting profession has recognized that the changing purchasing power of the dollar no longer can be ignored in financial reporting. In 1979, the Financial Accounting Standards Board issued a statement requiring certain companies to disclose supplementary information expressed in terms of constant dollars, using both historical costs and current costs. After significant research and development with both measurement bases, the FASB concluded that the historical cost/constant dollar information was less useful than the current cost/constant dollar information. Therefore, the FASB eliminated its requirement for the supplementary disclosure of historical cost/constant dollar information.[6] Then, in 1986 the FASB removed completely the requirement of disclosing current cost data (although such disclosure still is encouraged).[7] Even though no longer required, current cost disclosures may benefit users of financial reports in the following ways:

1. As compared to historical cost, measuring assets at current cost should present a more relevant measure of economic wealth at a point in time.
2. Including expenses measured at current cost in the determination of income should produce an income measure which more accurately gauges changes in real wealth over time and a firm's ability to maintain operating capital. In addition, such an income measure might serve as a basis for tax rate reductions and for negotiating price increases in order to allow firms to better maintain capital for expanded production and investment.
3. Comparability between entities would be enhanced by expressing assets and expenses of firms at current cost dollars rather than at dated historical costs.
4. Current cost measures of assets and income should provide users with an improved basis for predicting cash flows.
5. The standard of neutrality could be satisfied better by current cost data in that disclosure of such data may provide certain users with information that had previously been available only to more sophisticated users. Therefore, investment decisions and security valuations could become more efficient and equitable.

---

[5]Yuji Ijiri, *Theory of Accounting Measurement* (Sarasota: American Accounting Association, 1975), 88–90.
[6]*Statement of Financial Accounting Standards, No. 82*, "Financial Reporting and Changing Prices: Elimination of Certain Disclosures" (Stamford: Financial Accounting Standards Board, 1984).
[7]*Statement of Financial Accounting Standards, No. 89*, "Financial Reporting and Changing Prices: Elimination of Certain Disclosures" (Stamford: Financial Accounting Standards Board, 1986).

INCOME DETERMINATION

An important objective of accounting is to provide users with information regarding the economic entity's goal of maximizing the return on net economic resources employed. The ability of an entity to employ its resources to generate additional resources is referred to as *enterprise earning power.* The essence of earning power is to generate cash, which represents a return on invested capital. Over the life of an entity, the entity's earning power will equal its cash-generating ability. However, over shorter periods of time, earnings will not equal the cash generated because of lags between resource consumption and subsequent cash returns. But earnings for these shorter time periods will provide a basis for predicting the ultimate cash-generating ability of the entity. The periodic measurement of an entity's progress toward generating earnings represents a major factor which influences the allocation of scarce resources among entities and is of primary concern in accounting.

INCOME CONCEPTS

The measurement of earning power or income is influenced by different concepts of income and certain modifying conventions which are required to make a particular income concept operational. A discussion of various income concepts follows.

Psychic Income. Every individual is motivated by wants and, to varying degrees, every individual attempts to satisfy these wants. The extent to which wants are satisfied represents a measure of psychic income. This concept of income recognizes that human wants may be satisfied by noneconomic gratification as well as by economic resources in the form of goods and services. Measurement of psychic income is hindered by the dual forms of satisfaction, economic and noneconomic, and by the fact that the proportion of these satisfactions is changing constantly. To the extent that economic satisfaction can be identified as the dominant element of psychic income, measurements of such income become more objective. However, overemphasis of this element and a failure to consider the noneconomic elements of psychic income may result in socially undesirable economic activities.

Economic Income. To the extent that the subjective, noneconomic elements of income are not definable or measurable, other concepts of income which focus on the economic aspects can be defined. These concepts deal with the measurement of increases in economic wealth, as evidenced by the money value of goods and services.

Using the concept of economic income, only an increase in wealth beyond a beginning level of real capital represents income. Therefore, economic income represents the amount of consumption an individual can experience over time and be as well off at the end of the time period as at the beginning.[8] To be "as well off" means that the beginning level of real capital or wealth must be maintained. Thus, income is measured in real terms, and it is influenced by the changing purchasing power of the monetary unit and by changes in the current cost (specific prices) of the resources employed. The supplemental disclosure of constant dollar and current cost data is designed to provide users with a more direct measure of economic income than is achieved by traditional historical cost reporting. A simple example may serve to illustrate this point.

Facts:

At the beginning of the year, a company had four units of inventory costing $100 each. The general purchasing power of the dollar is evidenced by a Consumer Price Index of 100 at the beginning of the year and an index of 120 at year end. The specific cost to replace a unit of inventory at year end is $140. On the last day of the year, all four units of inventory were sold for $175 each.

Income Statement:

	Historical Cost	Constant Dollar	Current Cost
Revenue	$700[a]	$700	$700
Cost of goods sold	400[b]	480[c]	560[d]
Gross profit	$300	$220	$140

[a] 4 units × $175   [c] 4 units × ($100 × 120/100)
[b] 4 units × $100   [d] 4 units × $140

Analysis:

If the company is to maintain its beginning level of real capital represented by four units of inventory, it must replace the units at a current cost of $140 per unit, or $560. The historical cost gross profit of $300, if distributed to investors, would leave the entity with only $400 of capital, which would not be adequate to maintain the initial level of operating capital. The constant dollar gross profit, if distributed, would leave the entity with $480 of capital, which would have been adequate if the price of inventory only changed to the extent of the change in the purchasing power of the dollar as evidenced by the CPI. However, the specific price change of inventory suggests that $560 of capital would be required to maintain the beginning level of operating capital. Therefore, if the current cost gross profit of $140 were distributed, the firm would have the necessary $560 of remaining capital with which to maintain its beginning level of operating capital.

An alternative analysis would indicate that the firm had a beginning-of-the-year command over goods equal to four units of inventory. At year end, the current cost command over inventory would be equal to five units, or $700 of capital divided by the $140 current cost of inventory. Therefore, the firm's command over inventory would increase by one unit with a current value of $140. The gross profit per the current cost model would measure best the firm's increase in real wealth.

[8] J. R. Hicks, *Value and Capital* (Oxford: Clarendon Press, 1946), 172.

Accounting Income. Accounting income is referred to as *comprehensive income* in order to emphasize the various components contributing to income. Comprehensive income is defined as:

> . . . *the change in* equity *(net assets) of an entity during a period from transactions and other events and circumstances from nonowner sources. It includes all changes in equity during a period except those resulting from investments by owners and distributions to owners.* [9]

The measurement of the change in equity or return on capital resulting from comprehensive income is influenced by differing concepts of capital maintenance. Under the *financial capital concept,* capital is defined as "the monetary amount of net assets (stated in either units of money [dollars] or units of purchasing power)"[10] contributed to an entity. Income is the excess of dollars (or units of purchasing power) beyond the original dollars (or units of purchasing power) invested. When price changes on assets and liabilities are recognized, they are included in income. For example, assume that an item of inventory is purchased for $100 and then sold for $150, when the price to replace the inventory is $120. Under the financial capital concept, the amount of income is the $50 excess over the original financial capital of $100. Included in the income is the $20 price change on the inventory, as represented by the difference between the cost basis of $100 and the replacement cost of $120.

An alternative to the financial capital concept is the *physical capital concept.* Under this concept, capital is viewed as representing an amount of physical operating capacity that must be replaced before income is realized. Whether physical capital is measured in the number of dollars or by the purchasing power of the dollar, there is no income until the physical capacity consumed by an income-generating activity has been provided for or replaced. Changes in the physical capacity over time are not considered components of income. For example, in the inventory illustration, the amount of income is the $30 excess of the selling price over the replacement cost of the capacity consumed, since the $100 physical capacity consumed had to be provided for at a replacement cost of $120.

The change in equity measured by comprehensive income consists of several components: earnings, cumulative accounting adjustments, and other nonowner changes in equity. *Earnings* is a measure of the operational performance of an entity for a specific period. It is similar to net income as determined in present practice, except that cumulative accounting adjustments are excluded from earnings. *Cumulative accounting adjustments* represent the effect that current period adjustments or changes, such as the cumulative effect of changes in accounting principles, have on prior periods. Other nonowner changes in equity represent certain net asset changes that

---

[9]*Statement of Financial Accounting Concepts, No. 3,* "Elements of Financial Statements of Business Enterprises" (Stamford: Financial Accounting Standards Board, 1980), par. 56.
[10]W. W. Cooper and Yuji Ijiri, eds., *Kohler's Dictionary for Accountants,* 6th ed. (Englewood Cliffs: Prentice-Hall, Inc., 1983), 214.

are recognized as direct adjustments to owners' equity. For example, declines in the values of noncurrent marketable equity securities are accounted for as direct changes to owners' equity.[11]

The components of comprehensive income are measured by evaluating the effects of the various events or transactions that are recognized by an entity. *Recognition* is the process of formally recording and incorporating into financial statements the effect of any item that meets the following criteria, subject to a cost-benefit constraint:

> *Definitions — The item meets the definition of an element of financial statements.*
>
> *Measurability — The item has a relevant attribute which is measurable with sufficient reliability.*
>
> *Relevance — The information about the item is capable of making a difference in user decisions.*
>
> *Reliability — The information is representationally faithful, verifiable, and neutral.*[12]

Although the effects of some events will not be recognized, the effects of the basic types of transactions on revenues, expenses, gains, losses, assets, and liabilities will be recognized. The recognition criteria provide guidance that is especially critical to the recognition of revenues and expenses and ultimately comprehensive income.

REVENUE RECOGNITION

Revenue, which may be viewed as the "product" of an economic entity, is created by the sale of goods and/or services. However, revenue frequently has been defined from an inflow viewpoint:

> *Revenues are inflows or other enhancements of assets of an entity or settlements of its liabilities (or a combination of both) during a period from delivering or producing goods, rendering services, or other activities that constitute the entity's ongoing major or central operations.*[13]

Although definitions of revenue vary, all definitions trace revenue to the profit-directed activities of the enterprise. These activities generally take the form of providing goods and/or services to other entities. Therefore, changes in owners' equity resulting from the investment in assets by owners are excluded from the definition of revenue.

Increases in the net assets of an enterprise occur through gains as well, but these increases result from peripheral or incidental activities of an entity

---

[11]*Statement of Financial Accounting Concepts, No. 5*, "Recognition and Measurement in Financial Statements of Business Enterprises" (Stamford: Financial Accounting Standards Board, 1984), pars. 30–44.

[12]*Ibid.*, par. 63.

[13]*Statement of Financial Accounting Concepts, No. 3, op. cit.*, par. 63.

rather than from the entity's primary profit-directed activities. Precise distinctions between revenues and gains often are difficult from a practical standpoint. If necessary, however, distinctions should be made in order to improve the usefulness of comprehensive income calculations.

Revenue is measured by the exchange value of goods and/or services as represented by their cash-equivalent value. In those cases where cash equivalents are not involved, the fair market value of consideration to be received or given, whichever is more clearly evident, normally is viewed as the relevant measure of revenue.

Revenue is realized as a result of the production and/or marketing processes of an entity. The production process refers to the transformation of resources into products (goods) and/or services, and the marketing process involves the transfer of these goods and/or services to consumers.

In addition to the measurement of revenue, a determination must be made as to when revenue produced by these processes should be recognized. The recognition of revenue requires the consideration of two conditions: (1) being realized or realizable and (2) being earned.[14] Expanding slightly these two conditions suggests that the following criteria should be satisfied in order to recognize revenue:

1. The earning process must be complete or virtually complete.
2. An exchange (arm's-length transaction) has taken place.
3. The revenue-producing event or transaction must possess a high degree of permanence.

The first condition suggests the basic nature of revenue (i.e., increases in entity wealth arising from the profit-directed activities of the entity). Theoretically, profit-directed activities must be complete or virtually complete before the related wealth accrues to the entity. The second condition indicates that even if the earning process is complete, the goods and/or services must be transferred (sold) to a separate, distinct entity in exchange for cash or claims to cash. This condition emphasizes that wealth or value traceable to profit-directed activities is most accurately measured by an exchange transaction. In addition, the information standards of verifiability and representational faithfulness are inherent in the second condition. The condition of permanence requires that revenues traceable to the entity will not be reversed or reduced by subsequent conditions. For example, if, after an exchange transaction (sale), it becomes apparent that the purchaser of the goods is unable to pay, serious consideration should be given as to whether revenue from the sale should be recognized and, if so, to what extent. Permanence also influences the extent to which revenue measurement is considered to be verifiable.

A comprehensive current cost model would ignore at least the first two conditions for revenue recognition. Using this model, changes in current

---

[14]*Statement of Financial Accounting Concepts, No. 5, op. cit.,* par. 83.

cost that have accrued to date would be recognized as revenue, even if the earning process is not complete and an exchange has not taken place. For example, if the current cost of undeveloped land has increased, the increase in value would be recognized as income because it represents a change in wealth or "well offness" over time.

The previously discussed conditions are collectively viewed as the *revenue recognition principle*. This principle is applicable to the profit-directed activities of most entities. However, exceptions exist in those cases where an earlier recognition of revenue is warranted or where recognition should be delayed. These exceptions, which are traceable to a failure to completely or partially satisfy one or more of the conditions discussed, are found typically in the areas of long-term construction contracts, precious metals and agricultural commodities, and sales made on an installment basis.

Long-Term Construction Contracts. Recall that, theoretically, revenue may be earned throughout the production process. The correlation between earnings and production might suggest a preference for a production or activity basis of recognizing revenue, as opposed to a sales basis. With the production basis, emphasis is placed on the production effort, rather than on the marketing effort, as the major factor responsible for the creation of revenues and profits.

When the production basis is used, a proportionate amount of revenues and appropriate costs are recognized as construction progresses. This method is called the *percentage-of-completion method*, and progress on a project generally is measured in one of two ways. One procedure is to use engineering studies that indicate the level of completion. Another procedure is to compare costs incurred to date with the total costs to be incurred. This ratio of "costs-to-costs" suggests a level of completion. For example, an oil tanker is being constructed at a total estimated cost of $48 million and an established contract price of $60 million. The gross profit of $12 million will be recognized over the period of construction, based on stages of completion. If the costs incurred to date are $9.6 million, then, in comparison to the total estimated costs of $48 million, 20% (9.6 ÷ 48) of the gross profit will be recognized.

The production basis of revenue recognition is appropriate in those cases where all of the following conditions are satisfied:

1. The profit-directed activity (production) is expected to take place over several years.
2. The marketing or sales effort takes place prior to construction and is minor when compared to the production process.
3. Costs of construction, along with the degree of completion, can be reasonably estimated.

If these conditions are not satisfied, revenue must be recognized by the *completed-contract method*. This method defers the recognition of all revenues and costs until the project is completed. Regardless of which method is used, however, whenever the actual total costs exceed the contract price, a loss should be recognized immediately.

Precious Metals and Agricultural Commodities. In the case of precious metals and certain agricultural commodities, revenue may be recognized upon completion of the production process, but prior to sale, assuming that the following conditions are satisfied:

1. The production of these commodities, rather than their sale, is the primary determinant of revenue. Therefore, the production effort, not the marketing effort, is the critical event.
2. There is an established (assured) market price for these commodities. Thus, through an active market, the value of these goods can be determined objectively prior to sale.
3. The inventoriable costs associated with these goods cannot be determined easily. That is, production costs are not identified and allocated easily to the units produced.

Typically, those goods which have not been sold yet are inventoried at their net realizable value (estimated selling price less estimated costs to complete and market). The effect of this treatment is to carry inventory at a value greater than cost and to increase the gross profit by the difference between the net realizable value and the cost of the goods not sold.

Installment Sales. In most instances, the collectibility of credit or installment sales is less than certain. However, collectibility may be estimated, based on past experience and/or industry characteristics. Therefore, an allowance for collection losses usually is established, and estimated collection losses are matched against sales for the period. In certain extreme cases, collection of the sales price may be so uncertain that the condition of permanence and the standard of verifiability may not be satisfied. The deferral of gross profit recognition normally is not justified. However, such deferral has received official sanction in:

> . . . *exceptional cases where receivables are collectible over an extended period of time and, because of the terms of the transactions or other conditions, there is no reasonable basis for estimating the degree of collectibility. When such circumstances exist, and as long as they exist, either the installment method or the cost recovery method of accounting may be used.* [15]

Two methods are used frequently to defer the recognition of revenue beyond the point of sale. In the most extreme cases, the *cost recovery method* may be employed. This method initially treats all receipts of the sales price as a recoupment of the product costs. When the product costs have been re-

---

[15]*Opinions of the Accounting Principles Board*, No. 10, "Omnibus Opinion—1966" (New York: American Institute of Certified Public Accountants, 1967), footnote to par. 12.

covered, all additional receipts of the sales price are treated as gross profit. For example, if a major appliance costing $300 was sold for $500, with a $100 down payment and the balance payable over 24 months, the first $300 collected would be construed as a return of cost, with the balance being recognized as gross profit when collected.

In less extreme cases, the *installment method* may be appropriate. The installment method treats each receipt as a combination of cost recovery and realized gross profit, emphasizing the deferral of gross profit until collections are received. To illustrate, if an appliance costing $400 was sold for $600, with a $120 down payment and the balance payable in eight installments, each dollar of the collected selling price would be allocated as follows:

Recovery of cost............................. 400/600 or 2/3
Receipt of gross profit .... 200/600 or 1/3

Under the installment method, the profit to be recognized would be $40 ($120 × 1/3) upon receipt of the down payment and $20 ($60 × 1/3) upon receipt of each installment. In contrast, under the cost recovery method, no profit would be recognized until the $400 original cost had been received through collections.

In any case, if the cost of goods sold exceeds the selling price, the indicated loss should be recognized in the period of sale and not deferred to future periods.

EXPENSE RECOGNITION

Expenses represent the assumption of liabilities and the expiration of the service potential of resources resulting from the revenue-producing or profit-directed activities of an entity, explained as follows:

Expenses are outflows or other using up of assets or incurrences of liabilities (or a combination of both) during a period from delivering or producing goods, rendering services, or carrying out other activities that constitute the entity's ongoing major or central operations.[16]

The quality of financial reporting is improved if expenses are distinguished from losses. Losses are decreases in equity resulting from transactions that are not traceable to the entity's central operations. In addition, neither expenses nor these peripheral or incidental transactions include distributions to or withdrawals by owners.

Theoretically, the consumption or using up of service potentials occurs as the revenue-producing activities of the entity take place. For example, the service potential of shipping containers is consumed when goods are shipped to customers. The process of expiring service potentials is not always so direct, however. In the case of raw materials consumed in the productive pro-

---

[16]*Statement of Financial Accounting Concepts, No. 3, op. cit.*, par. 65.

cess, expense recognition usually is deferred until the resulting revenues are recognized. By this treatment, the transformation of service potentials into other forms (e.g., raw materials transformed into finished goods) does not represent the final expiration of the service potentials because the transformed items still have utility to the firm. However, when service potentials are sold (an exchange transaction takes place), they are viewed as expired and are recognized as expenses. Thus, the recognition of expenses is a function of the recognition of revenues. This relationship is the basis for the *matching principle,* which requires that revenues and the related expenses be recognized in the same accounting period.

In theory, the matching of revenues and expenses is based on the assumption that there is a connection between the incurrence of expenses and the production of revenue. Thus, a cause (incurrence of expense) and effect (production of revenue) relationship is suggested. There are many instances where this relationship is present, as in the case of the consumption of labor and raw materials and the resulting revenue from sales of the manufactured goods. However, there are instances where a strong correlation between revenues and expenses does not exist. For example, the salaries paid to general administrative personnel are not related to any specified revenues; nevertheless, such personnel contribute to the overall revenue-production ability of the entity.

Because of the nature of expenses, several principles of expense recognition influence the determination of entity net income. These principles, summarized below, provide a basic framework for handling the practical difficulties associated with the matching of expenses and revenues:

> *Associating cause and effect. Some costs are recognized as expenses on the basis of a presumed direct association with specific revenue.*
>
> *Systematic and rational allocation. In the absence of a direct means of associating cause and effect, some costs are associated with specific accounting periods as expenses on the basis of an attempt to allocate costs in a systematic and rational manner among the periods in which benefits are provided.*
>
> *Immediate recognition. Some costs are associated with the current accounting period as expenses because (1) costs incurred during the period provide no discernible future benefits, (2) costs recorded as assets in prior periods no longer provide discernible benefits or (3) allocating costs either on the basis of association with revenue or among several accounting periods is considered to serve no useful purpose.* [17]

The FASB acknowledges these principles of expense recognition in its conceptual statements.[18]

---

[17] *Accounting Principles Board Statements, No. 4,* "Basic Concepts and Accounting Principles Underlying Financial Statements of Business Enterprises" (New York: American Institute of Certified Public Accountants, 1971), pars. 157, 159, and 160.

[18] *Statement of Financial Accounting Concepts, No. 5, op. cit.,* par. 86.

QUESTIONS

1. Events or transactions affecting an economic entity are analyzed or screened to determine whether they will be measured by or comprehended in an accounting information model. By what criteria should the output of such a model be evaluated?

2. To measure a particular attribute, two measurement procedures are employed. Measurement procedure A produces a mean value of $70 and a standard deviation of $3. Measurement procedure B produces a mean value of $90 and a standard deviation of $7. The true value of the attribute being measured is $100. Indicate which measurement procedure has the greater degree of verifiability and which is more representationally faithful.

3. How is it possible that intrafirm comparability may not result in interfirm comparability?

4. Given an asset which is not held for resale, why would one expect that the "entry value" (historical cost) is less than or equal to the "value in use," which is greater than or equal to the "exit value"?

5. How do the entity theory and the proprietary theory differ in their views of income?

6. Given established information standards, how would you evaluate measures of income (a) based on the periodic change in the discounted value of future net cash receipts and (b) based on changes in value as evidenced by exchange transactions?

7. Business income may be viewed as the amount of assets a firm could distribute to its owners (i.e., dividends) and be as well off at the end of the period as it was at the beginning. Is it possible for a firm to have income even though the firm does not engage in any exchange transactions or production?

8. Explain how price changes in the replacement cost of inventory sold would be accounted for under the financial and the physical capital maintenance concepts.

9. What are some situations which may suggest a lack of permanence with respect to revenue recognition?

10. Why might costs to date divided by total estimated costs (costs-to-costs ratio) not provide a reasonable accounting for a long-term construction contract?

11. An entity holds an appreciated investment portfolio as its only productive asset. How might measures of economic and accounting income differ?

12. Why might the historical cost measurement base be considered more applicable to financial statement presentation than the discounted cash flow measurement base?

13. What official committees or organizations preceded the Financial Accounting Standards Board in the standard-setting process?

14. What is the primary purpose of the Governmental Accounting Standards Board, and how is it similar to the Financial Accounting Standards Board?

EXERCISES

Exercise 1. How would the following items be viewed under the proprietary theory? the entity theory?

(a) Interest on long-term debt.   (d) Net income.
(b) Cash dividends.   (e) Partners' salaries.
(c) Stock dividends.   (f) Long-term debt.

Exercise 2. For each of the following transactions, identify the appropriate revenue recognition method:

(1) A customer has a long outstanding liability to a company. The debt represents the purchase price of a piece of equipment. The customer begins to make infrequent payments after an extended period of time during which the payments were overdue.
(2) Highway Co. sells equipment on the installment payment basis. Cancellations and uncollectible amounts can be estimated.
(3) Steelbid Inc. has contracted to build a mine sweeper for the U.S. Navy.

Exercise 3. Before the Financial Accounting Standards Board issues a new statement, it must pass through a "due process" system. Discuss the basic steps in this process.

Exercise 4. Logan acquired inventory on January 1, 19X2, in exchange for (a) $20,000 in cash, (b) professional services valued at $8,000, and (c) land with a historical cost of $16,000 and a market value of $24,000.

(1) Explain how the inventory would be valued on February 1, 19X2, under each of the following measurement bases.
    (a) Historical cost.
    (b) Current cost.
    (c) Exit value.
    (d) Discounted cash flow.
(2) Assuming that financial statements are to be used by a bank lending officer, rank the measurement bases in (1) with respect to relevance, reliability, neutrality, and interfirm comparability.
(3) Which, if any, of the four measurement bases in (1) would be equal in value at the date of acquisition? Which would be equal two months after the acquisition?

Exercise 5. After the independent auditors' report on the examination of the financial statements is presented to the board of directors of Savage Publishing Company, one of the new directors is surprised that the income statement assumes that an equal proportion of the revenue is earned with the publication of every issue of the company's magazine. The director feels that the "crucial event" (i.e., the most difficult task) in the process of earning revenue in the magazine business is the cash sale of the subscription and does not understand why, other than for the smoothing of income, most of the revenue cannot be "realized" in the period of the sale.

Discuss the propriety of timing the recognition of revenue in Savage Publishing Company's accounts with:

(1) The cash sale of the magazine subscription.
(2) The publication of the magazine every month.
(3) Both events, by recognizing a portion of the revenue with the cash sale of the magazine subscription and a portion of the revenue with the publication of the magazine every month.   (AICPA adapted)

Exercise 6.   On July 1, 19X7, Growen Inc. contracted Holton Construction Co. to build an interstate pipeline to transport natural gas. It is estimated that the project will take three years to complete. Assume that the contract price is $1,800,000 and that Holton Construction has a calendar-year end. The following data applies to the construction period:

	19X7	19X8	19X9	19Y0
Annual cost..............................	$ 250,000	$600,000	$500,000	$150,000
Estimated cost to complete........	1,000,000	600,000	150,000	—
Annual billings.........................	400,000	760,000	440,000	200,000
Cash collections	350,000	675,000	525,000	250,000

(1) Using the completed-contract method, when would the income on the project be recognized?
(2) Compute the estimated income that would be recognized each year under the percentage-of-completion method.
(3) Assume at the end of 19X9, estimated costs to complete the pipeline were $600,000, making total costs greater than total revenue. Discuss the appropriate measures to take under the percentage-of-completion and completed-contract methods.

PROBLEMS

Problem 1–1.   The concept of the accounting entity, often considered to be the most fundamental of accounting concepts, pervades all of accounting.

Required:
(1) (a) What is an accounting entity? Explain.
    (b) Explain why the accounting entity concept is so fundamental that it pervades all of accounting.

(2) For each of the following, indicate whether the accounting concept of entity is applicable. Discuss and give illustrations.
(a) A unit created by or under law.
(b) The product-line segment of an enterprise.
(c) A combination of legal units and/or product-line segments.
(d) All of the activities of an owner or a group of owners.
(e) An industry.
(f) The economy of the United States.   (AICPA adapted)

Problem 1–2.   Brakeway Co. purchased 500 bikes for $45,000 in the beginning of 19X6. At midyear, Brakeway sold 300 bikes for $150 each, when the replacement value was $100 each. Year-end inventory consists of 200 bikes having a replacement value of $105 each. Brakeway wants to prepare supplemental constant dollar and current cost/constant dollar income statements for 19X6. The consumer price index used to measure the changing purchasing power of the dollar was 105 on January 1, 19X6, 110 at midyear, and 112 at year end.

Required:
(1) Calculate the 19X6 gross profit for Brakeway under the historical cost, constant dollar, and current cost/constant dollar methods. Note that the constant dollar and current cost/constant dollar data should be expressed in the year-end purchasing power of the dollar.
(2) Discuss which of the measures of income in (1) would be most useful for:
(a) establishing a level of dividend distributions.
(b) assessing a local income tax.
(3) Calculate the current cost of Brakeway's year-end inventory and indicate how much of this increase over historical cost is due to general price-level changes.

Problem 1–3.   Village Company is accounting for a long-term construction contract using the percentage-of-completion method. It is a three-year, fixed-fee contract that is presently in its first year. The latest reasonable estimates of total contract costs indicate that the contract will be completed at a profit. Village will submit progress billing to the customer and has reasonable assurance that collections on these billings will be received in each year of the contract.

Required:
(1) (a) What is the justification for the use of the percentage-of-completion method in accounting for long-term construction contracts?
(b) What facts in the situation above indicate that Village should account for its long-term construction contract using the percentage-of-completion method?
(2) How would the income recognized in each year of this long-term construction contract be determined, using the percentage-of-completion

method based on cost incurred to date compared to total estimated cost (the cost-to-cost method)?

(3) What is the effect on income, if any, of the progress billings and the collections on these billings?   (AICPA adapted)

Problem 1–4.   The earning of revenue by a business enterprise is recognized for accounting purposes when the transaction is recorded. In some situations, revenue is recognized approximately as it is earned in the economic sense. In most situations, however, accountants have developed guidelines for recognizing revenue by other criteria, such as the point of sale.

Required:
(1) Explain and justify why revenue often is recognized as earned at the time of sale.
(2) Explain in what situations it would be appropriate to apply the accretion concept (recognizing revenue as the productive activity takes place or as values increase).
(3) At what times, other than those included in (1) and (2), may it be appropriate to recognize revenue? Explain.   (AICPA adapted)

Problem 1–5.   Raysco Industries is a developer of gas-metering devices. To expand its development efforts, Raysco has entered into a partnership with two investors. Each of the investors will contribute $1,000,000; Raysco will contribute research technology. All of the research and development (R & D) work will be performed by Raysco.

If the R & D effort is successful, Raysco has an option to acquire exclusive rights in return for a $2,000,000 payment to the partnership. However, if the effort is not successful, Raysco is not obligated to repay either of the investors and may reacquire the partnership's research technology by paying $500,000.

Assume that Raysco is proposing to record the transfer of technology as a debit to the account Investment in Partnership and a credit to the account Gain on Sale of Technology in the amount of $500,000. The technology has a book basis for Raysco of zero because it represents past R & D which has been expensed.

Required:
(1) Evaluate Raysco's accounting for the transfer of technology.
(2) Evaluate how Raysco should account for the balance of the transaction.
(3) If the R & D effort is not successful after some time, how should it be accounted for?

Problem 1–6.   On May 5, 19X1, Sterling Corporation signed a contract with Stony Associates, under which Stony agreed (a) to construct an office building on land owned by Sterling, (b) to accept responsibility for procuring financing for the project and finding tenants, and (c) to manage the property for 50 years. The annual profit from the project, after debt service, was to be divided equally between Sterling Corporation and Stony Associates. Stony was to accept its share of future profits as full payment for its services in construction, obtaining finances and tenants, and managing the project.

By April 30, 19X2, the project was nearly completed, and tenants had signed leases to occupy 90% of the available space at annual rentals aggregating to $2,600,000. It is estimated that, after operating expenses and debt service, the annual profit will amount to $850,000. The management of Stony believed that the economic benefit derived from the contract with Sterling should be reflected on its financial statements for the fiscal year ended April 30, 19X2. In addition, Stony's management directed that revenue be accrued in an amount equal to the commercial value of the services Stony had rendered during the year, that this amount be carried in the contracts receivable account, and that all related expenditures be charged against the revenue.

Required:
(1) Explain the main difference between the economic concept of business income as reflected by Stony's management and the measurement of income under generally accepted accounting principles.
(2) Discuss the factors to be considered in determining when revenue is realized for the purpose of the accounting measurement of periodic income.
(3) Is the belief of Stony's management in accord with generally accepted accounting principles for the measurement of revenue and expense for the year ended April 30, 19X2? Support your opinion by discussing the application of the factors to be considered for asset measurement and revenue and expense recognition. (AICPA adapted)

Problem 1–7. Greenery Golf Course agrees to purchase 1,000 blue spruce trees from Leaves Nursery, to be delivered in 2 years. Prior to delivery, Leaves Nursery is to care for the trees and assume all related costs and responsibilities. Upon signing the agreement, Greenery transfers one acre of land to Leaves. The balance of the purchase price will be paid by Greenery in three annual payments of $6,000 beginning one year from the date of the agreement. The payments bear no interest. Any trees that do not survive 6 months after delivery will be replaced at a cost of $50 per tree. The original cost of each tree is $200.

Required:
(1) Determine how the land should be valued upon the signing of the agreement.
(2) Discuss how Leaves Nursery should account for the receipt of the land.
(3) Discuss when the warranty obligation should be recorded by Leaves Nursery.
(4) Discuss how installment payments received by Leaves Nursery prior to delivery should be accounted for.

Problem 1–8. Stern Inc. is a distributor of power boats. Meiser Co. purchases 60 boats from Stern for $540,000. In anticipation of this purchase, Meiser had made arrangements to secure the necessary financing. The participating bank required a commitment fee of $15,000. This fee is nonrefundable and entitles the borrower to secure a loan, with the specified terms, within 30 days of the commitment. If the loan is secured, Meiser must pay a loan origination fee of $5,000 as well. In a related transaction, Stern signs an agreement to repurchase the boats from Meiser and pay all storage and insurance costs associated with the boats. Stern also agrees to pay all interest and fees associated with Meiser's loan. The agreement requires Stern to repurchase the boats at a specified date for the original price of $540,000.

Required:
(1) Discuss how Stern Inc. should account for the sale of the boats to Meiser.
(2) Discuss how Stern Inc. should account for the loan origination fees.
(3) Discuss how Stern Inc. should account for the loan commitment fees.

Problem 1–9. An accountant must be familiar with the concepts involved in determining earnings of a business entity. The amount of earnings reported for a business entity is dependent on the proper recognition, in general, of revenues and expenses for a given time period. In some situations, costs are recognized as expenses at the time of product sale. In other situations, guidelines have been developed for recognizing costs as expenses or losses by other criteria.

Required:
(1) Explain the rationale for recognizing costs as expenses at the time of product sale.
(2) What is the rationale underlying the appropriateness of treating costs as expenses of a period, instead of assigning the costs to an asset? Explain.
(3) In what general circumstances would it be appropriate to treat a cost as an asset instead of as an expense? Explain.
(4) Some expenses are assigned to specific accounting periods on the basis of a systematic and rational allocation of asset cost. Explain the underlying rationale for this procedure.
(5) Identify the necessary conditions in which it would be appropriate to treat a cost as a loss.   (AICPA adapted)

CHAPTER 2

INCOME PRESENTATION AND THE DISCLOSURE OF EARNINGS PER SHARE

The goals and objectives of accounting discussed in Chapter 1 suggest the need for full and fair disclosure of information relevant to the needs of the various users of accounting data. The adequacy of disclosure is evaluated by the information standards of relevance, reliability, neutrality, and comparability. Like other forms of communication, accounting disclosures should report on various entity attributes which are definable and which are evaluated by authoritative criteria. The consistent application of understandable definitions and criteria will improve the utility and the comparability of the data reported by different entities.

Given established definitions and criteria, questions develop as to who should aggregate and classify data according to these definitions and criteria—management, independent auditors, or perhaps the intended user. Some have suggested that the utility of accounting data would be enhanced if it were presented in an unclassified form. For example, rather than management presenting earnings per share (EPS), investors could be provided with the unclassified data with which to develop their own EPS statistic.

This chapter focuses on specific areas of disclosure relating to the income statement format and to the reporting of earnings per share. Following the consolidations and foreign operations coverage (Chapters 3-12) are separate presentations on interim financial statement formulation, the disclosure of financial information by segments of a business, and Securities and Exchange Commission considerations.

INCOME PRESENTATION

Early in the twentieth century, the balance sheet or statement of financial position was viewed as the primary financial statement. In the 1930s, a gradual de-emphasis of the balance sheet began to occur. Currently, the income statement or statement of results of operations is viewed as the primary financial statement due to the importance of such information to security valuation theory and resource allocation decisions. This emphasis on the income statement has influenced the development of accounting principles to the extent that the propriety of accounting principles often is evaluated in terms of their potential effect on the determination of income. It is important to note that increased attention also has been placed on the reporting of cash flows. All business enterprises presently are required to have a statement of cash flows, rather than a statement of changes in financial position, as part of a full set of financial statements.[1]

CONCEPTS OF INCOME PRESENTATION

The income statement presents for a period of time the revenues, expenses, gains, losses, and resulting net income or net loss, recognized in accordance with generally accepted accounting principles. This statement emphasizes the calculation of periodic net income and the communication of relevant factors that influence income. Income statement presentation has been influenced by two competing concepts: the *current operating concept* and the *all-inclusive concept*. These concepts primarily have been concerned with the proper classification and disclosure of unusual or nonrecurring events affecting the determination of entity wealth.

Current Operating Concept. The current operating concept is based on the premise that the most relevant measure of net income is that which is attributable to normal operations. Therefore, only those revenues and expenses which are considered to be recurring in nature and are normal or dependable with respect to their incidence over time should be included in net income. Unusual or nonrecurrent items and corrections traceable to previously reported income should be excluded from the calculation of income and treated as direct charges or credits to retained earnings.

Proponents of the current operating concept argue that external users of income data are concerned mostly with events that are related directly to the normal business purpose or normal operations because such events reflect future earning power. If unusual and/or nonrecurrent revenues and expenses are included, the predictive ability of income statistics could be distorted significantly. Thus, to determine the more useful measure of operating net income, users of the income statement would be required to extract these data.

---

[1]*Statement of Financial Accounting Standards, No. 95,* "Statement of Cash Flows" (Stamford: Financial Accounting Standards Board, 1987), par. 1.

All-Inclusive Concept. The proponents of the all-inclusive concept argue that the summation of a series of income statements should reflect the change in entity wealth over time (excluding capital transactions and dividends), as measured by generally accepted accounting principles. Therefore, this concept focuses on the long-range operating performance of the entity and includes in net income the effects of unusual and/or nonrecurring revenues and expenses.

Supporting this viewpoint is the argument that the current operating concept revolves around a distinction between normal operational items and unusual, nonrecurring items. These items, therefore, may be subject to definitional interpretations, which may provide a basis for the manipulation or smoothing of income and which also may reduce the comparability between firms. Proponents of the all-inclusive concept suggest that unusual, nonrecurring data are relevant to the valuation of earning power and managerial efficiency, especially over a long period of time. Furthermore, the proponents point out that the disclosure of unusual, nonrecurring items is more visible in the income statement than in a retained earnings statement, which is given little attention by many external users.

Generally Accepted Income Presentation. In 1947, the American Institute of Accountants (later to become the American Institute of Certified Public Accountants) issued Accounting Research Bulletin (ARB) No. 32, which basically supported the current operating concept and identified five broad classifications of "material" items that should be excluded in the determination of income. At that time, the American Accounting Association and the Securities and Exchange Commission (SEC) strongly supported the all-inclusive concept. In 1966, in response to the varied interpretations given ARB No. 32, the Accounting Principles Board (APB) issued its Opinion No. 9, "Reporting the Results of Operations." This Opinion called for the inclusion in net income of all items of profit and loss except prior period adjustments. Extraordinary items included in net income were to be shown separately. The Opinion established criteria for both prior period adjustments and extraordinary items.

In 1973, the Accounting Principles Board issued Opinion No. 30, which confirmed the primarily all-inclusive concept of income presentation contained in APB Opinion No. 9. In addition, APB Opinion No. 30 provided guidance in the accounting for and presentation of discontinued operations of a business segment. In response to the difficulties associated with the meaning of extraordinary items, APB Opinion No. 30 also clarified the definition of such items. Furthermore, APB Opinion No. 30 observed the definition of prior period adjustments as established in APB Opinion No. 9 and continued to view these items as adjustments to beginning retained earnings balances and not income statement accounts. In 1977, the Financial Accounting Standards Board (FASB) Statement No. 16 redefined prior period adjustments to include only the following two items:

(a) *Correction of an error in the financial statements of a prior period and*

(b) *Adjustments that result from realization of income tax benefits of pre-acquisition operating loss carryforwards of purchased subsidiaries.*[2]

An analysis of APB Opinion No. 30 suggests the income statement format shown below. Following the income statement is an explanation of each of its components.

Income (loss) from continuing operations before income taxes, extraordinary items, and the cumulative effect of changes in accounting principles.....................................	$xxxx	
Provision for income taxes	xxxx	
Income (loss) from continuing operations before extraordinary items and the cumulative effect of changes in accounting principles...		$xxxx
Discontinued operations (Note _____):		
Income (loss) from operations of discontinued segment (less applicable income taxes of $_____)...........................	$xxxx	
Loss (gain) on disposal of segment, including provision of $_____ for operating losses (gains) during phase-out period (less applicable income taxes of $_____)................	xxxx	xxxx
Extraordinary items (less applicable income taxes of $_____) (Note _____)		xxxx
Cumulative effect on prior years of changes in accounting principles (less applicable income taxes of $_____) (Note _____)		xxxx
Net income (loss)		$xxxx

INCOME FROM CONTINUING OPERATIONS

Income from continuing operations before taxes and extraordinary items includes the following:

1. All items of revenue and expense that are traceable to the *normal* operations of *continuing* business segments should be included. These items are considered to be of a usual and recurring nature.

2. Items which are unusual in nature *or* which occur infrequently, but not both, should be included as well. These items are not extraordinary items, but should be disclosed in the body of the income statement as a separate component of income from continuing operations.

---

[2]*Statement of Financial Accounting Standards, No. 16,* "Prior Period Adjustments" (Stamford: Financial Accounting Standards Board, 1977), par. 11.

The taxes traceable to income from continuing operations should be shown as a single deduction from such income. Therefore, individual components of income from continuing operations are not shown net of tax. However, several critics of this presentation of taxes have stated that the utility of the income statement would be enhanced if certain items were shown net of tax, especially those items which are unusual or nonrecurring in nature, such as relocation expenses. Net-of-tax treatment would allow users to adjust reported income for these items, thereby making the income statement more useful for predictive and other purposes.

DISCONTINUED OPERATIONS

A separate component of net income is the income and losses traceable to a discontinued segment of a business. A segment of a business is defined as:

> ...a component of an entity whose activities represent a separate major line of business or class of customer. A segment may be in the form of a subsidiary, a division, or a department, and in some cases a joint venture or other nonsubsidiary investee, provided that its assets, results of operations, and activities can be clearly distinguished, physically and operationally and for financial reporting purposes, from the other assets, results of operations, and activities of the entity. ... The fact that the results of operations of the segment being sold or abandoned cannot be separately identified strongly suggests that the transaction should not be classified as the disposal of a segment of the business. The disposal of a segment of a business should be distinguished from other disposals of assets incident to the evolution of the entity's business, such as the disposal of part of a line of business, the shifting of production or marketing activities for a particular line of business from one location to another, the phasing out of a product line or class of service, and other changes occasioned by technological improvements.[3]

A segment that is discontinued is one that has been *sold, disposed of, spun off, or abandoned*. A segment that still is operating, but is the subject of a formal plan calling for its discontinuance, also should be viewed as a discontinued segment for reporting purposes. The following examples of disposals that either are or are not considered to be discontinued operations were identified by the Accounting Principles Board.[4]

Disposals Qualifying As Discontinued Operations

A sale by a diversified company of a major division which represents the company's only activities in the electronics industry. The assets and

---

[3]*Opinions of the Accounting Principles Board, No 30,* "Reporting the Results of Operations" (New York: American Institute of Certified Public Accountants, 1973), par. 13.

[4]*Accounting Interpretations,* "Reporting the Results of Operations: Accounting Interpretations of APB Opinion No. 30" (New York: American Institute of Certified Public Accountants, 1973), 9753–9754.

results of operations of the division clearly are segregated *for internal financial reporting purposes from the other assets and results of operations of the company.*

A sale by a meat packing company of a 25% interest in a professional football team which has been accounted for under the equity method. All other activities of the company are in the meat packing business.

A sale by a communications company of all its radio stations, which represent 30% of gross revenues. The company's remaining activities are three television stations and a publishing company. The assets and results of operations of the radio stations are physically, operationally, and for financial reporting purposes distinguishable *from the other assets and operating results of the company.*

A food distributor disposes of one of its two divisions. One division sells food wholesale primarily to supermarket chains, the other division sells food through its chain of fast food restaurants, some of which are franchised and some of which are company-owned. Both divisions are in the business of distributing food. However, the nature of selling food through fast food outlets is vastly different than that of wholesaling food to supermarket chains. Thus, by dealing with two major classes of customers, *the company has had two segments of business.*

Disposals Not Qualifying As Discontinued Operations

The sale of a major foreign subsidiary engaged in silver mining by a mining company which represents all of the company's activities in that particular country. Even though the subsidiary being sold may account for a significant percentage of gross revenue of the consolidated group and all of its revenues in the particular country, the fact that the company continues *to engage in silver mining activities in other countries would indicate that there has been a sale of only part of a <u>line of business</u>.*

The sale by a petrochemical company of a 25% interest in a petrochemical plant which has been accounted for as an investment in a corporate joint venture under the equity method. Since the remaining activities *of the company are in the* same *line of business as the 25% interest which has been sold, there has not been a sale of a major <u>line of business,</u> but rather a sale of only part of that line.*

A manufacturer of children's wear discontinues all of its operations in Italy which were composed of designing and selling children's wear for the Italian market. In the context of determining a segment of a business by class of customer, the nationality of customers or slight variations in product lines in order to appeal to particular groups are not determining *factors.*

A diversified company sells a subsidiary which manufactures furniture. The company has retained its other furniture manufacturing subsidiary. The disposal of the one subsidiary, therefore, is not a disposal of a segment of the business, but rather a disposal of only part of a <u>line of business.</u>

An apparel manufacturer sells all the assets (including the plant) related to the manufacture of men's woolen suits in order to concentrate activities in the manufacture of men's suits from synthetic products. This would represent a disposal of a product line *as distinguished from the disposal of a major line of business.*

Key Terms. The following terms and definitions are essential to the analysis of the presentation of discontinued operations:

1. *Measurement date*—The date on which management, given proper authority, commits itself to a formal plan of disposal, whether by sale or abandonment.
2. *Disposal date*—the date of closing if the segment is sold, or the date on which operations cease if the segment is abandoned.
3. *Plan of disposal*—a plan which includes, as a minimum, the following items: identification of the assets to be disposed of, the method of disposal (sale or abandonment), the time required to dispose of the segment, the means by which potential buyers of the disposed assets will be identified, the estimated operating results of the segment for the period from the measurement date to the disposal date, and the estimated proceeds to be realized from disposal.

Reporting Discontinued Operations. In the current period, financial information pertaining to discontinued operations must be classified as to: (A) that which is traceable to the period *prior to* the measurement date, and (B) that which is traceable to the period *beginning with* the measurement date. (See diagram on page 42.) As the earlier income statement illustrates, the activity relating to discontinued operations is divided into two line items. The income or loss from operations of the discontinued segment prior to the measurement date is shown as the first line item, "Income (loss) from operations of discontinued segment (less applicable income taxes of $_____)." This amount would include the realized elements of income or loss that currently accrue to the segment as well as the gain or loss resulting from the disposition of segment assets prior to the measurement date. When comparative financial data are presented, the net income for prior periods must be restated to reflect that portion of income traceable to operations which now are discontinued.

Activity of the discontinued segment between the measurement date and the disposal date must be disclosed separately in the income statement as part of the line item entitled "Loss (gain) on disposal of segment, including provision for operating losses (gains) during the phase-out period (less applicable income taxes of $_____)." Assuming that the measurement date and disposal date occur within the same accounting period, the segment's activity traceable to this time span would, as of year end, consist of the realized elements of income or loss from operations and realized gain or loss from the disposition of segment assets. If the measurement date and the disposal date do not occur within the same accounting period, the total gain or loss to be reported as of the fiscal year end prior to the year of disposal should include:

1. Net *realized* items for the period from the measurement date to the end of the fiscal period, consisting of:
    a. The realized income or loss from operations of the segment, net of taxes (part of Item R on the following diagram), and
    b. The realized gain or loss from the disposal or abandonment of segment assets, net of taxes (part of Item R on the following diagram), and
2. Net *expected* items for the period from the beginning of the new fiscal period to the disposal date, consisting of:
    a. The expected income or loss from operations of the segment, net of taxes (part of Item E on the diagram), and
    b. The expected gain or loss from the disposal or abandonment of segment assets, net of taxes (part of Item E on the diagram).

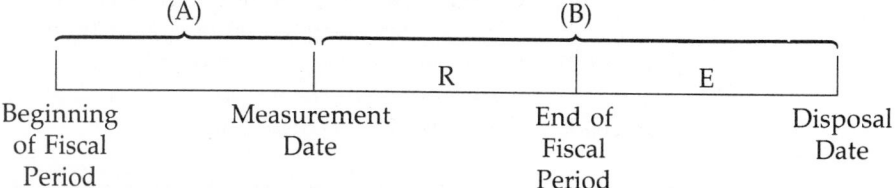

As of the end of the fiscal period, the reported gain or loss on disposal of the discontinued segment should consist of the net realized items (1.a and 1.b) plus the net expected items (2.a and 2.b), except that the final result *never* will be an overall *net expected gain*. This rule can be summarized as follows:

Given a net realized gain (1.a plus 1.b),
(a) a net expected gain is not recognized because revenues should not be anticipated;
(b) a net expected loss is recognized in total.

Given a net realized loss (1.a plus 1.b),
(a) a net expected gain can be recognized only to the extent of the net realized loss;
(b) a net expected loss is recognized in total.

Financial information regarding a discontinued segment is dependent upon estimates which may be revised in subsequent periods. According to APB Opinion No. 20, "Accounting Changes," subsequent adjustments of these estimates should be disclosed in the period of adjustment in the same manner as the original item.

Illustrations of Accounting for Discontinued Operations. The principles of accounting for discontinued operations are illustrated in Cases A, B, C, and D of Illustration 2–1.

5-1-67   12-1-67   4-30-68   11-30-68
Beg of FY   Measurement   End of FY   Disposal
            Date   Date

Illustration 2–1
Case A

1. The fiscal year end is April 30.
2. No extraordinary items or accounting changes occurred during the year ended April 30, 19X8.
3. On December 1, 19X7, management decided to dispose of a processing operation. This operation qualifies as a segment, and the disposition is expected to take place over the next 12 months.
4. The following information relates to the discontinued segment:

Income from operations of discontinued segment from May 1, 19X7, to measurement date, December 1, 19X7 (less applicable income taxes of $350,000)...			$380,000
Loss on disposal of segment:			
Realized loss from operations from measurement date to April 30, 19X8 (less applicable income tax benefits of $137,000)...................................	($152,000)		
Realized loss from asset disposals from measurement date to April 30, 19X8 (less applicable income tax benefits of $30,000).........	(40,000)	($192,000)	
Expected loss from operations subsequent to April 30, 19X8 (less applicable income tax benefits of $130,000).......................................	($139,000)		
Expected loss on disposal of segment assets subsequent to April 30, 19X8 (less applicable income tax benefits of $128,000).......................	(137,000)	(276,000)	(468,000)
Net loss from discontinued operations			($ 88,000)

Given a net realized loss of $192,000, the net expected loss of $276,000 is recognized in full, resulting in a total loss on disposal of $468,000. In the income statement for the year ended April 30, 19X8, the $380,000 income and the $468,000 loss would be reported as the two line items. Other information required by APB Opinion No. 30 would be disclosed in a footnote.

Case B

Assume the same facts as in Case A, except that the results of operations from December 1, 19X7, to April 30, 19X8 (less applicable income taxes of $325,000), were $356,000. The results of the disposal of the discontinued segment are combined as follows:

(continued)

Income from operations of discontinued segment from May 1, 19X7, to measurement date, December 1, 19X7 (less applicable income taxes of $350,000)...			$380,000
Gain on disposal of segment:			
Realized income from operations from measurement date to April 30, 19X8 (less applicable income taxes of $325,000)............	$356,000		
Realized loss from asset disposals from measurement date to April 30, 19X8 (less applicable income tax benefits of $30,000)	(40,000)	$316,000	
Expected loss from operations subsequent to April 30, 19X8 (less applicable income tax benefits of $130,000)...	($139,000)		
Expected loss on disposal of segment assets subsequent to April 30, 19X8 (less applicable income tax benefits of $128,000).........................	(137,000)	(276,000)	40,000
Net income from discontinued operations			$420,000

Given a net realized gain of $316,000, the net expected loss of $276,000 is recognized in its entirety.

Case C

Assume the same facts as in Case A, except that the expected income from operations from May 1, 19X8, to the disposal date (less applicable income taxes of $327,000) is $350,000. The results of the disposal of the discontinued segment are combined as follows:

Income from operations of discontinued segment from May 1, 19X7, to measurement date, December 1, 19X7 (less applicable income taxes of $350,000)...			$380,000
Loss on disposal of segment:			
Realized loss from operations from measurement date to April 30, 19X8 (less applicable income tax benefits of $137,000)...	($152,000)		
Realized loss from asset disposals from measurement date to April 30, 19X8 (less applicable income tax benefits of $30,000)...........	(40,000)	($192,000)	
Expected income from operations subsequent to April 30, 19X8 (less applicable income taxes of $327,000)...	$350,000		
Expected loss on disposal of segment assets subsequent to April 30, 19X8 (less applicable income tax benefits of $128,000).........................	(137,000)	213,000	—
Net income from discontinued operations			$380,000

Given a net realized loss of $192,000, a net expected gain can be recognized only to the extent of the realized loss. Therefore, $192,000 of the net expected gain is offset against the net realized loss of $192,000, resulting in no reported loss on disposal. The remainder of the aftertax net expected gain ($21,000) will be recognized when it becomes realized.

Case D

Assume the same facts as in Case A, except that the realized gain on the sale of segment assets from December 1, 19X7, to April 30, 19X8 (less applicable income taxes of $340,000), is $400,000 and that the expected gain on disposal of segment assets (less applicable income taxes of $90,000) is $360,000. The results of the disposal of the discontinued segment are combined as follows:

Income from operations of discontinued segment from May 1, 19X7, to measurement date, December 1, 19X7 (less applicable income taxes of $350,000)				$380,000
Gain on disposal of segment:				
Realized loss from operations from measurement date to April 30, 19X8 (less applicable income tax benefits of $137,000)	($152,000)			
Realized gain from asset disposals from measurement date to April 30, 19X8 (less applicable income taxes of $340,000)	400,000	$248,000		
Expected loss from operations subsequent to April 30, 19X8 (less applicable income tax benefits of $130,000)	($139,000)			
Expected gain on disposal of segment assets subsequent to April 30, 19X8 (less applicable income taxes of $90,000)	360,000	221,000	248,000	
Net income from discontinued operations				$628,000

Given a net realized gain of $248,000, the net expected gain of $221,000 is not recognized. The expected gain will be recognized when it becomes realized.

Illustration 2–2, pages 46 and 47, contains excerpts from the published financial statements of Fuqua Industries, Inc. which demonstrate the disclosure of discontinued operations as it relates to the income statement.

Illustration 2–2

Consolidated Statements of Operations
Fuqua Industries, Inc. and Subsidiaries
Years ended December 31,
(In thousands except per share amounts)

	1987	1986	1985
Net Sales (amounts charged for products sold)	$772,343	$701,194	$636,178
Equity in Pre-Tax Income of Georgia Federal..................	44,827	29,503	—
	817,170	730,697	636,178
Costs and Expenses			
Costs of products sold (includes materials, labor, plant overhead and depreciation, etc.)	520,253	469,092	427,645
Selling, general and administrative (costs of marketing, management and depreciation)................................	171,526	159,431	134,293
Provision for consolidation of manufacturing facilities...	4,300	—	—
Total operating expenses	696,079	628,523	561,938
Operating profit..	121,091	102,174	74,240
Interest (expense)..	(28,654)	(29,544)	(24,564)
Other income—net	6,704	5,894	9,933
Income before Income Taxes, Discontinued Operations and Extraordinary Item	99,141	78,524	59,609
Income taxes	36,191	31,651	27,684
Income from Continuing Operations	62,950	46,873	31,925
Discontinued Operations			
Income (loss) from operations	—	(2,120)	1,336
(Loss) on disposal of businesses...............................	—	(5,178)	(260)
	—	(7,298)	1,076
Income before Extraordinary Item........................	62,950	39,575	33,001
Extraordinary Item	—	—	219
Net Income...	$ 62,950	$ 39,575	$ 33,220
Earnings Per Share of Common Stock			
Primary			
Income from continuing operations..........................	$2.92	$2.20	$1.55
Discontinued operations...	—	(.34)	.05
Extraordinary item...	—	—	.01
Net income..	$2.92	$1.86	$1.61
Fully Diluted			
Income from continuing operations..........................	$2.87	$2.20	$1.54
Discontinued operations...	—	(.34)	.05
Extraordinary item...	—	—	.01
Net income..	$2.87	$1.86	$1.60

Notes to Consolidated Financial Statements
of Fuqua Industries, Inc. and Subsidiaries

Discontinued Operations

During 1986 Fuqua disposed of, or made the decision to dispose of, the businesses comprising its Seating segment. These businesses included operations in the areas of office systems and transportation seating, which were sold in July 1987, as well as manufactured housing, metal bar grating and retail farm stores, which were sold in 1986. During 1986 Fuqua also disposed of its investment in Triton Group Ltd. for a gain. (See Sale of Investment in Triton Group Ltd.) A pre-tax loss of $8,825,000 ($5,178,000 net of tax benefits) is included in discontinued operations in 1986 as a result of these dispositions. Included in this amount is a provision of $22,300,000 ($14,900,000 net of tax benefits) for the sale of the office systems and transportation seating operations. The 1987 sale of these operations produced results which were approximately equal to the provision made in 1986.

During 1985 Fuqua disposed of, or made the decision to dispose of, its businesses in the areas of boat trailers, bicycles and accessories, motorcycle parts and accessories and portable lighting and grain drying and storage. The sales of the boat trailer, bicycle and accessory and portable lighting businesses were completed in 1985. The motorcycle parts and accessories business and the grain drying and storage business were sold during the first quarter of 1986 on terms approximately equal to those provided for in 1985. A pre-tax loss of $954,000 ($260,000 net of tax benefits) resulting from the disposition of these businesses is reflected in discontinued operations in 1985.

The results of operations of all of the above businesses through the date of disposition or the decision to dispose have been reclassified from income from continuing operations to discontinued operations and are as follows for the two years ended December 31, 1986 (in thousands):

	1986	1985
Sales	$129,040	$287,120
Costs and expenses	132,637	283,845
Income (loss) before income taxes	(3,597)	3,275
Income taxes (benefit)	(1,477)	1,939
Net Income (Loss)	$ (2,120)	$ 1,336

The summary above includes certain costs and expenses relating to operations which had been discontinued prior to 1985.

EXTRAORDINARY ITEMS

In describing extraordinary items, APB Opinion No. 30 recognizes the attributes of unusual nature and infrequency of occurrence as the sole criteria for classifying such items. These attributes are defined as follows:

> (a) Unusual nature—*the underlying event or transaction should possess a high degree of abnormality and be of a type clearly unrelated to, or only incidentally related to, the ordinary and typical activities of the entity, taking into account the environment in which the entity operates.*

> (b) Infrequency of occurrence—*the underlying event or transaction should be of a type that would not reasonably be expected to recur in the foreseeable future, taking into account the environment in which the entity operates.*[5]

---

[5]*Opinions of the Accounting Principles Board, No. 30, op. cit.,* par. 20.

Extraordinary items must be *both* unusual in nature and infrequently occurring (nonrecurring). If one but not both of these attributes is present, the item in question should be included as a separate component of net income from continuing operations and should:

1. Not be disclosed net of taxes,
2. Not be disclosed in any manner which suggests that it is an extraordinary item, and
3. Not be listed as a separate component or determinant of earnings per share (EPS).

The criteria established in APB Opinion No. 30 are more restrictive and definitive than those established in APB Opinion No. 9, so that certain items formerly viewed as extraordinary no longer qualify. The following events, by themselves, should not be viewed as extraordinary items:

(a) *Write-down or write-off of receivables, inventories, equipment leased to others, deferred research and development costs, or other intangible assets.*

(b) *Gains or losses from exchange or translation of foreign currencies, including those relating to major devaluations and revaluations.*

(c) *Gains or losses on disposal of a segment of a business.*

(d) *Other gains or losses from sale or abandonment of property, plant, or equipment used in the business.*

(e) *Effects of a strike, including those against competitors and major suppliers.*

(f) *Adjustments of accruals on long-term contracts.*[6]

It is possible, however, for items (a) and (d) to be included as extraordinary items if they are the direct result of an event that otherwise qualifies as extraordinary (e.g., the write-down of inventory destroyed by a natural disaster that is unusual in nature and infrequent in occurrence).

Extraordinary items also include certain prescribed items that do not necessarily meet the standard criteria of unusual nature and infrequent occurrence. These items are few in number and receive special emphasis by virtue of their extraordinary classification. One example of such an extraordinary item is the subject of FASB Statement No. 4, "Reporting Gains and Losses from Extinguishment of Debt." This Statement, which was issued in 1975, concluded:

Gains and losses from extinguishment of debt that are included in the determination of net income shall be aggregated and, if material, classified as an extraordinary item, net of related income tax effect. That conclusion shall apply whether an extinguishment is early or at scheduled maturity date or later. The conclusion does not apply, however, to gains or losses

---

[6]*Ibid.*, par. 23.

from cash purchases of debt made to satisfy current or future sinking-fund requirements. Those gains and losses shall be aggregated and the amount shall be identified as a separate item.[7]

APB Opinion No. 30 emphasizes that only extraordinary items that are material "in relation to income before extraordinary items or to the trend of annual earnings before extraordinary items, or . . . by other appropriate criteria"[8] should be disclosed separately. To assess materiality, items should be considered individually and not in the aggregate. Therefore, it is possible that a series of unrelated, immaterial extraordinary items would not be disclosed, even though they may be material in the aggregate. However, a series of events or transactions that are related because they arise from a specific and identifiable extraordinary event should be aggregated to determine materiality.

The treatment of events or transactions that are unusual or nonrecurring, but not both, has been criticized on the basis that these events may be perceived as extraordinary. Furthermore, several members of the APB found the established criteria for an extraordinary event to be subjective, unworkable, and/or too narrow. Questions also have been raised as to whether the term "extraordinary" truly conveys the nature of items currently included in this category. Since the criteria for an extraordinary item have been changed from those established in APB Opinion No. 9, a new descriptive phrase might be appropriate.

CHANGES IN ACCOUNTING PRINCIPLES

A change in accounting principle is defined as a change from one generally accepted accounting principle to another or as a change in the method of applying a given principle, with the change justified on the basis that the newly adopted principle or method of application is preferable. In most cases, such a change should be disclosed separately in financial statements for the year of the change by showing the change's cumulative effect on income of prior periods, as well as certain other information.[9] APB Opinion No. 20 states:

The amount shown in the income statement for the cumulative effect of changing to a new accounting principle is the difference between (a) the amount of retained earnings at the beginning of the period of a change

[7]*Statement of Financial Accounting Standards, No. 4, "Reporting Gains and Losses from Extinguishment of Debt" (Stamford: Financial Accounting Standards Board, 1975), par. 8.
[8]*Opinions of the Accounting Principles Board, No. 30, op. cit.,* par. 24.
[9]Certain changes in accounting principles are not accounted for by showing its cumulative effect, but require the restatement of all prior periods presented. Changes accorded this treatment are: (a) a change from Lifo to some other method, (b) a change in the method of accounting for long-term construction contracts, and (c) a change to or from the full cost method of accounting used in the extractive industries.

and (b) the amount of retained earnings that would have been reported at that date if the new accounting principle had been applied retroactively for all prior periods which would have been affected and by recognizing only the direct effects of the change and related income tax effect. The amount of the cumulative effect should be shown in the income statement between the captions "extraordinary items" and "net income." The cumulative effect is not an extraordinary item but should be reported in a manner similar to an extraordinary item. The per share information shown on the face of the income statement should include the per share amount of the cumulative effect of the accounting change.[10]

If financial statements for those periods prior to the period of the change are presented, such statements and the related earnings per share statistics should not be restated to reflect the adoption of the new principle. However, pro forma income and EPS amounts are required. These pro forma amounts indicate what the income and EPS would have been in previous periods and the current period if the newly adopted principle had been in use for all these periods.

To illustrate the disclosure of a change in principle, assume that a company uses the straight-line method of depreciation for the years 19X1 through 19X2 and changes to the sum-of-the-years-digits method beginning in 19X3. The effect of changing to the new method must be computed for the years 19X1 through 19X2, and then this amount, net of tax, is included in the 19X3 income statement as a separate item. The complete treatment of the change is shown in Illustration 2–3.

Illustration 2–3
A Change in Accounting Principle

Facts:

1. The company acquired a plant asset on January 1, 19X1, at a cost of $15,000. The asset was estimated to have a useful life of 5 years and no residual value.
2. For the years 19X1 through 19X2, the asset was depreciated by the straight-line (SL) method. However, since the beginning of 19X3, the sum-of-the-years-digits (SYD) method has been used.
3. The effective tax rate for all years is 40%. The change in depreciation methods was for financial reporting purposes only.
4. Income statistics for years prior to the change in principle are as follows:

	19X1	19X2
Income from continuing operations before extraordinary items	$10,000	$17,500
Extraordinary items (net of taxes)	—	($2,500)
Earnings per share	$1.00	$1.50
Number of shares used to calculate EPS	10,000	10,000

---

[10]*Opinions of the Accounting Principles Board, No. 20,* "Accounting Changes" (New York: American Institute of Certified Public Accountants, 1971), par. 20.

5. 19X3 income from normal operations, based on the use of the new
    depreciation method, is $21,000. There are no extraordinary items in
    19X3.

Analysis of Depreciation:

	19X1	19X2	Total
Old method—SL..	$3,000	$3,000	$6,000
New method—SYD...	5,000	4,000	9,000
Cumulative effect	$2,000	$1,000	$3,000

The following entry records the change in principle:

Deferred Income Tax..	1,200	
Cumulative Effect of Change in Principle............................	1,800[a]	
Accumulated Depreciation...		3,000

[a]The cumulative effect of $3,000 less the tax of $1,200 (40% × $3,000).

Income Statement Presentation:

Comparative income statements and EPS data for 19X2 and 19X3 appear as
follows:

	19X2		19X3	
	Amounts	EPS	Amounts	EPS
Income from continuing operations before extraordinary items	$17,500	$1.75	$21,000	$2.10
Extraordinary items (net of taxes)	(2,500)	(0.25)	—	—
Cumulative effect of change in principle (net of taxes)	—	—	(1,800)	(0.18)
Net income.....................................	$15,000	$1.50	$19,200	$1.92

Pro Forma Data:

Pro forma amounts and EPS data also are shown on the income statements.
This pro forma information, based on the assumption that the new
depreciation method always had been used, appears as follows:

	19X2		19X3	
	Pro Forma Amounts	Pro Forma EPS	Pro Forma Amounts	Pro Forma EPS
Income from continuing operations before extraordinary items	$16,900[b]	$1.69	$21,000	$2.10
Extraordinary items (net of taxes).............	(2,500)	(0.25)	—	—
Net income...................	$14,400	$1.44	$21,000[c]	$2.10

[b]Based on SYD depreciation of $4,000, versus SL depreciation of $3,000, less the tax effect.
[c]Net income does not include the cumulative effect because it is assumed that the new principle always had been used.

EARNINGS PER SHARE

The determination of earnings per share of common stock has received considerable attention by both the accounting and financial communities because EPS is significant with respect to the evaluation of an entity's past and future operations. The importance of EPS also has been demonstrated by both theoretical analysis and empirical research dealing with security valuation and dividend policy.

Although some may feel that the calculation of EPS is an area best left to the various users of financial data, the AICPA has committed substantial effort to the establishment of principles to govern the calculation and disclosure of EPS data. For example, the calculation of EPS was the topic of Accounting Research Bulletin No. 49, issued in 1958, and Accounting Principles Board Opinion No. 9, "Reporting the Results of Operations," issued in 1966. However, the validity of the principles established in APB Opinion No. 9 was questioned to the extent that the APB issued Opinion No. 15, "Earnings per Share," in 1969. This Opinion has attempted to establish principles that can be applied consistently among various entities. To provide a more complete discussion of these principles, an interpretation of APB Opinion No. 15 was issued in 1970.

THE SUBSTANCE OF APB OPINION NO. 15

APB Opinion No. 15 requires on the face of the income statement the disclosure of EPS data that are consistent with the income statement presentation. Therefore, per share data normally are presented for each of the following levels of income: income from continuing operations, discontinued operations, extraordinary items, the cumulative effect of changes in principles, and net income.[11] The purpose of this per share disclosure is to show the potential or prospective effect that certain securities will have on EPS. These securities include common and preferred stocks, bonds, warrants, stock options, stock purchase contracts, stock subscriptions, and other agreements to issue stock.

Rather than focusing on earnings per share of outstanding stock, the per share calculation emphasizes a statistic that will have maximum predic-

---

[11]Mutual companies, registered investment companies, government-owned corporations, and nonprofit corporations are not subject to this requirement. Per share data also need not be prepared for parent company statements accompanying consolidated statements, for statements of wholly-owned subsidiaries, and for special purpose statements. *Statement of Financial Accounting Standards, No. 21,* has amended APB Opinion No. 15 to the extent that earnings per share disclosure for nonpublic enterprises no longer is required.

*See Item * on marked page 56.*

tive value. Therefore, attention is placed on determining what EPS would be if certain securities were converted into common stock and if the conversion effect would be dilutive (i.e., cause a decrease in EPS). This approach is conservative, since, in most cases, the disclosure of antidilutive effects on EPS (i.e., potential increases in EPS) is not permitted.

The extent of the EPS disclosure also is dependent upon whether the capital structure of an entity is viewed as simple or complex. A *simple* capital structure has no securities outstanding (or agreements to issue such securities) that, in the aggregate, could dilute earnings per outstanding common share. If there are securities outstanding which, in the aggregate, could dilute earnings per outstanding common share, but such dilution is less than 3%, this capital structure also is considered to be simple. A capital structure is *complex* if various securities outstanding could have a dilutive effect of at least 3%.

For simple capital structures, per share data should be labeled as *earnings per common share*. Corporations whose capital structures are complex are required to present two measures of EPS (dual presentation): primary earnings per share and fully diluted earnings per share.

Primary earnings per share (PEPS) is the amount of net income attributable to each share of common stock plus other securities which are in substance common stock and technically are referred to as *common stock equivalents*. The PEPS disclosure reflects the prospective viewpoint of APB Opinion No. 15. For example, a user of financial statements may be concerned with the following question: Given a constant level of income, if changes occur in the entity's capital structure, what would future EPS be? Such a question is significant particularly when agreements that could increase outstanding shares already exist. If EPS data are to serve predictive purposes, then the possible effect of common stock equivalents, which may or may not increase eventually the number of outstanding shares of common stock, must be disclosed. If EPS data were to serve only as an indicator of past operations, however, then the effect of common stock equivalents would be of little value.

Fully diluted earnings per share (FDEPS) is the amount of net income attributable to each share of common stock, common stock equivalent, and *other dilutive securities*. For the most part, the other dilutive securities influencing FDEPS will consist of securities that failed to meet the conditions established for common stock equivalents, and of common stock equivalents whose effect on FDEPS and PEPS is computed differently. The intent of disclosing FDEPS is to provide per share data that reflect the maximum potential dilution arising from securities which, upon conversion or exercise, would increase the number of common shares outstanding. PEPS may be described as a conservative measure, while FDEPS is an ultraconservative measure.

The basic starting point for the calculation of PEPS and FDEPS is determining earnings per common share. This latter per share statistic is computed as follows:

$$\text{Earnings per Common Share} = \frac{\text{Adjusted Net Income (ANI)}}{\substack{\text{Weighted Average Number of} \\ \text{Shares Outstanding During} \\ \text{the Period (S)}}}$$

The adjusted net income (ANI) represents reported net income, reduced by the amount of preferred dividends paid or declared this period or the current period dividends in arrears on cumulative preferred stock. In those capital structures where two or more classes of common stock exist, per share data are computed for the "ordinary" class of common stock. Therefore, net income must be adjusted also for the dividends paid (declared) or currently in arrears on other classes of common stock.

The computation of PEPS and FDEPS is a repetitive process for assessing the prospective effect of potentially dilutive securities on per share data. Each potentially dilutive security will have an assumed effect on the number of shares used to compute EPS and may have an assumed effect on the net income used in the computation. As each security is considered, a *share adjustment* (SA), representing the change in shares traceable to the security, and an *income adjustment* (IA), representing the change in income traceable to the security, must be determined. Again, all securities will have a share adjustment, but not all securities will have an income adjustment. For example, if a convertible preferred stock were considered the equivalent of common stock, the number of shares used to compute EPS would be increased by a share adjustment equal to the number of common shares that would have been issued upon conversion of the preferred stock. In addition, the earnings used to compute EPS would be increased by an income adjustment equal to the current dividends on preferred stock that would not have been declared if the preferred stock had been coverted into common stock.

The basic methodology for computing EPS, which is demonstrated in Illustration 2–4, involves the following steps:

1. For each security, calculate

$$\text{EPS}_i = \frac{\text{ANI}_{i-1} + \text{IA}_i}{\text{S}_{i-1} + \text{SA}_i} = \frac{\text{ANI}_i}{\text{S}_i}$$

where: ANI_{i-1} = the adjusted net income before considering security i.
IA_i = income adjustment traceable to security i.
S_{i-1} = the shares assumed to be outstanding before considering security i.
SA_i = the share adjustment traceable to security i.
ANI_i = the adjusted net income considering security i.
S_i = the shares assumed outstanding considering security i.

2. Determine the change in EPS, as follows:

$$\Delta EPS_i = EPS_i - EPS_{i-1}$$

where: ΔEPS_i = the change in EPS resulting from the evaluation of security i.

3. Consider whether security i is dilutive, as follows:

If ΔEPS_i is negative, then security i has a dilutive effect and should be considered.

If ΔEPS_i is positive, then security i has an antidilutive effect and usually should be ignored.

Although the sign of EPS will indicate whether or not a security is dilutive, other procedures can be used to identify antidilutive securities before the change in EPS actually is measured. These procedures are discussed in later sections of the chapter.

Illustration 2–4

Basic Methodology for Computing EPS

Assume that earnings per share of common stock is $2 $\left(\dfrac{ANI}{S} = \dfrac{\$200,000}{100,000}\right)$.

Assume that there are two common stock equivalents ($i = 1, 2$) with income adjustments (IA) and share adjustments (SA) as indicated in the following analysis:

	ANI_{i-1}	IA_i	ANI_i	S_{i-1}	SA_i	S_i	EPS_i
Earnings per common share	$200,000	—	$200,000	100,000	—	100,000	$2.00
$i = 1$	200,000	$20,000	220,000	100,000	20,000	120,000	1.83
$i = 2$	220,000	—	220,000	120,000	10,000	130,000	1.69*

*This amount will be reported as the EPS.

The earnings per common share (ANI ÷ S) is the basis upon which the potential dilutive effect of the first security is determined. It also may be necessary to compare EPS_{i-1} with the earnings per share for another level of income because a security may have a dilutive effect on one level of income (e.g., income from continuing operations) and an antidilutive effect on another level of income (e.g., an extraordinary loss). Since a security that has a dilutive effect on *any* level of income should be included in the computation of per share data for all other levels, the base EPS against which the dilutive effects of other securities is assessed should be the *highest* income figure (e.g., income from continuing operations or perhaps income after extraordinary gains).

To demonstrate this concept of assessing the dilutive effect of a common stock equivalent, assume the following:

Income from continuing operations	$100,000
Extraordinary loss	(20,000)
Net income	$ 80,000
Weighted average number of common shares outstanding	40,000

The earnings per common share is as follows:

Income from continuing operations per common share	$2.50
Extraordinary loss per common share	(.50)
Net income per common share	$2.00

Assuming that a common stock equivalent will result in a share adjustment of 10,000 shares and an income adjustment of $22,500 on income from continuing operations, the EPS considering the common stock equivalent is as follows:

Income from continuing operations per share	
[($100,000 + $22,500) ÷ (40,000 + 10,000)]	$2.45
Extraordinary loss per share [$20,000 ÷ (40,000 + 10,000)]	(.40)
Net income per share	$2.05

In this example, if net income is the base for evaluating potential dilution, the common stock equivalent would be ignored because it is antidilutive ($2.05 versus $2.00). However, if the base against which dilution is evaluated is the highest income figure, or income from continuing operations in this example, the common stock equivalent would be considered as dilutive ($2.45 versus $2.50). Therefore, in order to assess properly the dilutive nature of a common stock equivalent, its effect on the highest level of income should be the determining factor.

PRIMARY EARNINGS PER SHARE

As mentioned previously, primary earnings per share represents the earnings per share of common stock and common stock equivalents. The initial problem in calculating PEPS is to determine which securities are common stock equivalents. As defined in APB Opinion No. 15, a common stock equivalent is:

> ...a security which is not, in form, a common stock but which usually contains provisions to enable its holder to become a common stockholder and which, because of its terms and the circumstances under which it was issued, is in substance equivalent to a common stock. [12]

---

[12]*Opinions of the Accounting Principles Board*, No. 15, "Earnings per Share" (New York: American Institute of Certified Public Accountants, 1969), par. 25.

The designation of a security as a common stock equivalent is based on an evaluation of the security's substance rather than its form. Changes in the economic value of a common stock equivalent are largely a function of changing values resulting from earnings and earnings potential of the common stock to which they are equivalent. This functional relationship exists even if the common stock equivalent is not converted into the common stock or such conversion is not imminent. The various types of common stock equivalents are discussed in the following paragraphs.

Options and Warrants. Options and warrants represent rights to acquire shares of common stock in exchange for cash (exercise price) in accordance with underlying agreements. The following securities also are considered to be the equivalent of options and warrants: stock purchase contracts, stock subscriptions not yet fully paid, deferred compensation plans requiring the issuance of common stock,[13] and convertible securities allowing or requiring the payment of cash at conversion (regardless of yield). These securities derive their entire value from the right to acquire common stock and, therefore, are viewed automatically as common stock equivalents at all times. However, according to APB Opinion No. 15, a security will not be recognized as a common stock equivalent and will not be included in the calculation of PEPS unless the following criteria are satisfied:

1. The security must be exercisable within five years from the end of the current period.
2. The market price of the common stock obtainable upon exercise must be greater than the exercise price for substantially all of three consecutive months ending with the last month of any past or present period for which per share data are being presented. Once the three-month test is satisfied in any period, past or present, the security will be considered a common stock equivalent from that period on (assuming that the first criterion is satisfied as well).

The second criterion is established as a practical matter rather than as an absolute necessity. It prevents securities from being in and out of the EPS computation because of market price fluctuations above and below the exercise price.

Assuming that the two criteria have been met, the option or warrant will not enter into the calculation of PEPS unless the effect is dilutive. Such an effect will be experienced if, during the reporting period, the average market price of the common stock obtainable upon exercise is greater than the

---

[13]For a detailed discussion of the treatment of stock compensation plans in earnings per share computations, see *FASB Interpretation No. 31*, "Treatment of Stock Compensation Plans in EPS Computations" (Stamford: Financial Accounting Standards Board, 1980).

exercise price. The reporting period typically is three months; however, if a longer period is involved, a quarterly averaging technique may be employed.

Outstanding options or warrants that qualify as common stock equivalents are assumed to be exercised at the beginning of the period or at the issuance date, if later. The assumed exercise of these securities would result in the generation of funds in an amount equal to the *earliest* effective exercise price during the five-year period multiplied by the assumed number of shares to be obtained. These hypothetical funds could be employed in a variety of ways. For example, the funds could be used to reduce debt and, thereby, reduce interest expense, to purchase short-term government securities as an investment, or to expand the business and, thereby, earn the corporation's normal return on invested capital.

The APB recognized that some use of the funds had to be assumed, even though there was no certainty that the assumed use would approximate the actual use of funds received when options or warrants actually were exercised. Therefore, to achieve consistency, the APB recommended the use of the *treasury stock method*, which assumes that the generated funds are used to acquire common stock at the average market price for the period. This assumption is advantageous because the purchase of common stock does not result in an income adjustment. However, if a warrant allows or requires the tendering or retirement of debt, or if a convertible security requires the payment of cash upon conversion, an income adjustment would be necessary. This adjustment would be equal to the net-of-tax interest on debt or the dividend on convertible preferred stock.

For each option or warrant, the share adjustment under the treasury stock method is determined by using the following formula:

$$\text{Share Adjustment (SA)} = \frac{\text{Total Shares Obtainable}}{\text{Upon Exercise of Security}} - \frac{\text{Exercise Proceeds}}{\text{Average Market Price of Shares}}$$

The share adjustment always will be a positive number because options or warrants cannot influence PEPS unless the effect is dilutive, i.e., unless the average market price is greater than the exercise price. The share adjustment must be converted into a weighted average in those instances where the security was not outstanding during the entire period. If a security is exercised during the period, the number of treasury shares assumed to be acquired also is based on the average market price of the shares prior to exercise.

To demonstrate the treasury stock method, assume that options to acquire 4,000 shares of common stock were granted on January 1, 19X2, and still are outstanding as of December 31, 19X2. The options expire two years from the date of the grant and can be exercised at a price of $12 per share. EPS prior to considering the options is $2, based on 25,000 shares. Assuming an average annual market price of $13.25, EPS would be computed as follows:

Income adjustment (IA): Not applicable

Share adjustment (SA):

$$SA = \frac{\text{Total Shares Obtainable}}{\text{Upon Exercise of Security}} - \left[\frac{\text{Exercise Proceeds}}{\substack{\text{Average Market} \\ \text{Price of Shares}}} \right]*$$

$$= 4,000 - \frac{(\$12 \times 4,000 \text{ shares})}{\$13.25}$$

$$= 4,000 - 3,623$$

$$= 377 \text{ shares}$$

*The maximum number of treasury shares that could be acquired assuming all options are exercised and all treasury shares are purchased at the average market price.

EPS considering option (EPS_i):

$$EPS_i = \frac{ANI_{i-1} + IA_i}{S_{i-1} + SA_i}$$

$$= \frac{\$50,000 + 0}{25,000 + 377}$$

$$= \$1.97$$

When the reporting period is longer than three months and there are significant fluctuations in market values during the year, a *quarterly averaging technique* may be used in applying the treasury stock method. However, if market prices are relatively stable during the year, the treasury stock method may be applied on an annual basis using the annual average market price, as was done in the previous example. The quarterly averaging technique, as well as the concepts affecting the application of the treasury stock method for options and warrants to be considered in the computation of PEPS, are demonstrated in Illustration 2–5.

Illustration 2–5
Primary EPS Computations: Options and Warrants

1. At the beginning of 19X6, 250,000 shares of common stock were outstanding. The net income for 19X6 was $400,000.
2. During 19X6 the following stock warrants existed:
   Warrant X—10,000 warrants issued in 19X2, giving the holder of each warrant the right to purchase one share of common stock for $40. One thousand warrants were exercised on June 30, 19X6.
   Warrant Y—5,000 warrants issued in 19X4, giving the holder of each warrant the right to purchase one share of common stock for $50 anytime after December 31, 19Y2.
3. Both warrants X and Y previously had met the three-month test.

(continued)

4. Relevant market price information for 19X6 was as follows:

Quarter	Average Market Price
1	$41
2	43
3	49
4	53

Calculation of Income and Share Adjustments for PEPS

Stock Warrant X

This warrant is considered in the calculation of PEPS because it meets both the five-year and three-month tests.

9,000 Warrants Not Exercised

Income adjustment: Not applicable
Share adjustment:

Using the Quarterly Averaging Technique

Quarter	Shares Obtainable	Treasury Shares Acquired	SA
1	9,000	$\dfrac{\$360,000}{\$41} = 8,780$	220
2	9,000	$\dfrac{\$360,000}{\$43} = 8,372$	628
3	9,000	$\dfrac{\$360,000}{\$49} = 7,347$	1,653
4	9,000	$\dfrac{\$360,000}{\$53} = 6,792$	2,208
			4,709

Weighted average SA: 4,709 ÷ 4 = 1,177 shares

1,000 Warrants Exercised

Income adjustment: Not applicable
Share adjustment:

Using the Quarterly Averaging Technique

Quarter	Shares Obtainable	Treasury Shares Acquired	SA
1	1,000	$\dfrac{\$40,000}{\$41*} = 976$	24
2	1,000	$\dfrac{\$40,000}{\$43*} = 930$	70
3	Not applicable		-0-
4	Not applicable		-0-
			94

Weighted average SA: 94 ÷ 4 = 24 shares

*Average market price during the period prior to exercise.

Stock Warrant Y

This warrant is not considered in the calculation of PEPS because it fails to meet the five-year test.

Calculation of PEPS

	ANI_{i-1}	IA_i	ANI_i	S_{i-1}	SA_i	S_i	EPS_i
Earnings per common share	$400,000	—	$400,000	250,500*	—	250,500	$1.5968
X (not exercised)	400,000	—	400,000	250,500	1,177	251,677	1.5893
X (exercised)	400,000	—	400,000	251,677	24	251,701	1.5892
Y	Not a common stock equivalent — fails 5-year test						

*Weighted average of shares outstanding during the year: 250,000 shares + 1/2 of 1,000 shares issued on June 30 = 250,500.

The Special "20%" Rule. The treasury stock method is complicated further when the potential exercise of all options and warrants, whether dilutive or not, would result in the actual issuance of additional shares which, in the aggregate, exceed 20% of the outstanding shares of common stock at the end of the period. In this case, all options and warrants that meet the five-year and three-month criteria are assumed to be exercised, whether dilutive or not, and the aggregate exercise proceeds are applied as follows:

a. *As if the funds obtained were first applied to the repurchase of outstanding common shares at the average market price during the period (treasury stock method) but not to exceed 20% of the outstanding shares; and then*

b. *As if the balance of funds were applied first to reduce any short-term or long-term borrowings and any remaining funds were invested in U.S. government securities or commercial paper, with appropriate recognition of any income tax effect.* [14]

The results of these two steps are aggregated for all options and warrants, and if the net effect is dilutive, all options and warrants should enter into the determination of PEPS. With the 20% rule in effect, an income adjustment may result as well.

To demonstrate the 20% rule, assume that options to acquire 15,000 shares of common stock were granted on November 1, 19X0, and are outstanding at the end of 19X2. The options expire on December 31, 19X4, and may be exercised at $20 per share. In addition, on April 30, 19X1, warrants to acquire 10,000 shares of common stock were issued. These warrants are outstanding as of December 31, 19X2, expire on December 31, 19X6, and may be exercised at $25 per share. For the year 19X2, 100,000 shares of common stock were outstanding, net income was $450,000, and the only outstanding debt of the company was $200,000 in 5% bonds. The tax rate is 40%, and the average market price of common stock in all quarters was $22

---

[14]*Opinions of the Accounting Principles Board, No. 15, op. cit.,* par. 38.

per share. Because the total number of shares (15,000 + 10,000, or 25,000) obtainable by the options and warrants is greater than 20% of the outstanding common stock (20% × 100,000, or 20,000 shares), the 20% rule is applicable and would be applied to 19X2 as follows:

Total proceeds [(15,000 × $20) + (10,000 × $25)]	$550,000
Less proceeds used to purchase up to 20,000 shares at $22 each..........	440,000
Proceeds available to retire debt and interest......................................	$110,000

Share adjustment:
  SA = 25,000 shares − 20,000 shares = 5,000 shares
Income adjustment:
  IA = $110,000 × 5% interest rate × (1 − 40% tax rate) = $3,300

The PEPS is calculated as follows:

$$EPS_i = \frac{\$450,000 + \$3,300}{100,000 + 5,000} = \$4.32$$

If the market value of the common stock had been higher, it is possible that 20,000 shares of treasury stock would not have been acquired. For example, using the same assumptions, except that the average market price was $30 per share, the share and income adjustments would be as follows:

Share adjustment:
  SA = 25,000 shares − 18,333 shares ($550,000 ÷ $30) = 6,667 shares
Income adjustment:
  Not applicable because all available proceeds were used to acquire treasury stock in an amount not exceeding 20% of the outstanding common stock.

Contingent Shares. Contingent shares are shares that are issuable in the future, based upon the passage of time or upon the attainment of certain conditions which typically relate to the level of future income or future stock market values. For shares issuable upon the passage of time, there is no income adjustment, and the share adjustment should be based on the assumption that the shares involved have been outstanding since the inception of the contingent share agreement.

Shares that are issuable upon the attainment or maintenance of certain conditions should be included in PEPS only if the conditions have been currently met. Although the future issuance of shares is no longer contingent, PEPS must recognize this obligation to issue additional shares through a share adjustment. However, an income adjustment is not necessary because, to the extent that the contingency was based on income, the income must have occurred in order to be included in PEPS. Therefore, the reported net income already includes any income that may have been part of a contingent share agreement.

To illustrate, assume that Musketeer Inc. has 500,000 common shares outstanding for 19X9 and income of $750,000. In addition, Musketeer has an agreement to issue 75,000 shares to management in early 19Y0 if income is at least $700,000 in 19X9, and an additional 15,000 shares if income is in excess of $800,000. The calculation of PEPS would be as follows:

$$\text{EPS}_i = \frac{\$750,000 + 0}{500,000 + 75,000} = \$1.30$$

The 15,000 additional shares cannot be included in PEPS because the desired income level of more than $800,000 is not being met currently.

It is possible that a contingent share agreement may not be attained in the current year but rather in a subsequent year. This situation raises the question as to whether prior period EPS data should be restated to give retroactive effect to the shares subsequently issued. If the agreement was contingent upon the attainment of a certain income level or increase in income, the EPS data should not be restated. If the agreement was contingent upon the market price of the stock at a future date, however, retroactive treatment is appropriate. In the latter case, the number of shares issued or to be issued changes because of changes in the stock's market price.

It is also possible that a prior period calculation of PEPS included contingent shares which now will not be issued. For example, a contingency agreement may call for the maintenance of an earnings level for several periods. If the earnings level was attained in prior periods but the required earnings level has not been maintained, the shares would have been included in PEPS in prior periods, even though the shares now will not be issued. Therefore, prior period EPS data should be restated in order to remove the previously included shares.

Convertible Securities. A convertible security is one that can be converted into common stock at the option of the holder. Therefore, a portion of the security's value may be traceable to the value of the related common stock. At the time of original issuance, if a significant portion of the convertible security's value is traceable to this conversion feature, the security should be considered a common stock equivalent.

Effective Yield Test. The effective yield test is used for determining whether a convertible security is a common stock equivalent. According to this test, if the convertible security's effective yield, based on the market price at the time of issuance, is less than two-thirds of the then current average Aa corporate bond yield, the security should be considered a common stock equivalent. Satisfaction of the yield test suggests that the holder of convertible securities is willing to accept less than the current rate of return (as indicated by the average Aa corporate bond yield) because of the intrinsic value associated with the convertible securities being equivalent to common stock.

In applying the effective yield test, it should be noted that:

1. It is a one-time test, applied at issuance, and the security either is or is not classified as a common stock equivalent at that time. However, if an-

other convertible security, with the same terms as the security failing the yield test, exists or is issued later and is considered a common stock equivalent, then the security initially failing the test should be reclassified as a common stock equivalent.

2. The yield test using the Aa corporate bond yield is applicable to securities issued after February 28, 1982.[15] Securities issued prior to that date should use the bank prime interest rate rather than the bond yield for purposes of the test.

3. If the dividend or interest rate on the convertible security is scheduled to change over the next five-year period, the lowest scheduled rate during that period should be used for the yield test.

In addition to meeting the effective yield test, a convertible security must be convertible within five years from the end of the current reporting period if the security is to be considered a common stock equivalent.

The "If Converted" Method. For each outstanding convertible security that is determined to be a common stock equivalent, it is assumed that the security was converted into common stock as of the beginning of the period or the issuance date, if later.[16] Therefore, both a share adjustment and an income adjustment are necessary. The share adjustment is determined by calculating the weighted average number of common shares that would have been outstanding if conversion had taken place. If various conversion rates exist over the five-year period, the conversion rate in effect during the current period (or if not immediately convertible, the earliest effective conversion rate) should be used. The income adjustment is equal to the net-of-tax interest expense or the preferred stock dividend that would not have been paid or accumulated if the conversion had taken place. Furthermore, the aftertax effect of a premium or discount amortization must be eliminated from income. In the case of convertible bonds, the income adjustment should include *nondiscretionary* adjustments that were based on some measure of net income, e.g., bonus expense or royalty expense.

To illustrate, assume that $100,000, 4%, 20-year bonds were issued on July 1, 19X2, at a price of 98. Each $1,000 bond is convertible into 10 shares of common stock, beginning July 1, 19X3. Assuming that the effective yield test is satisfied and that the effective tax rate is 40%, the income adjustment and share adjustment for 19X2 would be computed as follows:

Income adjustment:
  Interest = [(4% × $100,000) + ($2,000 discount ÷ 20 years)] × 1/2 year
         = $2,050
  Interest after tax = $2,050 × (1 − 40% tax rate) = $1,230

---

[15]*Statement of Financial Accounting Standards,* No. 55, "Determining Whether a Convertible Security Is a Common Stock Equivalent" (Stamford: Financial Accounting Standards Board, 1982), pars. 7–8.

[16]When a common stock equivalent convertible security actually has been converted during a period, the "if converted" method is applied in the prior period. However, the results of applying this method are included in EPS calculations only if the effect is dilutive.

Share adjustment:
   Number of shares = 100 bonds × 10 shares = 1,000 shares
   Weighted average shares = 1,000 × 1/2 year = 500 shares

Dilutive Effect. When a convertible security is considered a common stock equivalent, it will be included in the PEPS calculation only if its effect is dilutive. To determine whether a convertible security is dilutive, an *incremental impact per share* test can be applied as follows:

1. Divide the income adjustment traceable to the convertible security by the share adjustment traceable to the convertible security. This amount is the incremental impact per share.
2. If the incremental impact per share is greater than EPS_{i-1}, then the new EPS_i will be greater than EPS_{i-1}. Therefore, if the incremental impact per share is greater than EPS_{i-1}, ignore the security because it is antidilutive.
3. If the incremental impact per share is less than EPS_{i-1}, the new EPS_i will be lower than EPS_{i-1}. Therefore, if the incremental impact per share is less than EPS_{i-1}, include the security because it is dilutive.

To insure that only the dilutive securities enter the per share computations, the following guidelines should be followed:

1. All other primary EPS dilution adjustments must be deducted first, i.e., consider convertibles last.
2. Each convertible security must be considered individually in the order of increasing incremental impacts per share, starting with the lowest. (This insures that no security is considered dilutive initially only to find that, due to the presence of more dilutive securities, it has a greater incremental impact than the final adjusted primary EPS.)[17]

To demonstrate these guidelines for determining whether securities are dilutive, assume the following information regarding convertible securities A and B:

1.

	Yield	Income Adjustment	Share Adjustment	Incremental Impact per Share
Security A	8%	$9,700	1,000	$9.70
Security B	4	4,000	1,500	2.67

2. EPS before considering the convertible securities is $10, based on 10,000 shares.

If the convertible securities are considered in the order presented, EPS would be as follows:

---

[17]Paul M. Fischer and Martin J. Gregorich, "Calculating Earnings per Share," *The Journal of Accountancy* (May 1973): 64.

	ANI$_i$	S$_i$	EPS$_i$
EPS before convertibles	$100,000	10,000	$10.00
Security A	109,700	11,000	9.97
Security B	113,700	12,500	9.10

However, if the convertible securities are considered individually in the order of increasing incremental impacts, as suggested by the guideline, EPS would be as follows:

	ANI$_i$	S$_i$	EPS$_i$
EPS before convertibles	$100,000	10,000	$10.00
Security B	104,000	11,500	9.04
Security A	113,700	12,500	9.10

In this case, security A is antidilutive. Therefore, the EPS should be reported as $9.04, rather than the $9.10 from the previous analysis.

FULLY DILUTED EARNINGS PER SHARE

The actual calculation of fully diluted earnings per share (FDEPS) generally is based on the weighted average of shares used to calculate PEPS, adjusted in certain instances, plus the effect of other dilutive securities.[18] Recall that FDEPS reflects the maximum dilution of EPS that would have resulted if all conversions, exercises of options and warrants, and issuances of contingent shares had taken place at the beginning of the period (or issuance date, if later). However, FDEPS sometimes may include the antidilutive effects of actual conversions and/or exercises.

Options and Warrants. The impact that options and warrants may have on FDEPS is determined by: (1) reconsidering options and warrants that were viewed as common stock equivalents for purposes of calculating PEPS and (2) considering for the first time options and warrants that did not qualify for purposes of calculating PEPS. The three-month test and the 20% test, which were discussed previously, are applicable to the calculation of FDEPS.

The reconsideration of options and warrants that were viewed as common stock equivalents for PEPS is necessary because of certain modifications governing the calculation of FDEPS. For options and warrants that have not been exercised, the share adjustment is based on the use of the market price at the end of the period or the average market price, whichever is greater. Unlike PEPS, the exercise proceeds are based on the lowest exercise price during the next ten years. Therefore, the share adjustment is determined as follows:

---

[18]Generally, a security that affects the calculation of PEPS also will influence the calculation of FDEPS. However, it is possible that a security will be dilutive for PEPS purposes but antidilutive, and thereby excluded, for FDEPS purposes.

$$\text{Share Adjustment (SA)} = \frac{\text{Total Shares Obtainable}}{\text{Upon Exercise of Security}} - \frac{\text{Exercise Proceeds}}{\substack{\text{Ending Market Price of Shares or} \\ \text{Average Market Price,} \\ \text{Whichever is Greater}}}$$

If options and/or warrants have been exercised during the period, the share adjustment for the time prior to exercise always is based on the market price at the date of exercise.

Certain options and warrants that did not qualify for purposes of calculating PEPS must be considered for purposes of calculating FDEPS. These options and warrants include those that:

1. Were not exercisable within five years from the end of the current period or
2. Met the five-year and three-month tests but would have had an antidilutive effect on PEPS.

Options and warrants that fail the five-year criterion for common stock equivalency will enter the calculation of FDEPS if the security is exercisable within ten years from the end of the period and if the higher of the average market price or the ending market price exceeds the lowest exercise price during the ten-year period. This rule will produce the maximum dilutive effect possible.

Another unique aspect of the fully diluted computation involves those securities that are omitted from the calculation of PEPS only because the average market price is less than the exercise price. If the ending market price is higher than the exercise price, even though the average market price is not, the security is included in the computation of FDEPS.

Although financially unattractive and antidilutive, options and/or warrants that were exercised during the period when the market price was less than the exercise price are included in the computation of FDEPS for that part of the period prior to exercise. For this calculation, it is assumed that the securities are exercised at the beginning of the period or at the date of issuance, if later, and the market price at the exercise date is used in the calculation of the share adjustment.

When there are significant variations between quarterly ending market prices and the annual ending market price, a quarterly averaging technique may be used when the share adjustment is computed for FDEPS. After each quarter is considered in the weighted average, using the higher of the quarter's average or the ending market price, the weighted average share adjustment is compared to the share adjustment calculated by using the actual market price at the end of the period or at the date of exercise, if earlier. The share adjustment used for FDEPS will be the *larger* of (1) the share adjustment derived by the quarterly averaging technique or (2) the share adjustment derived by use of the end-of-period market price.

For example, assume that EPS on a year-to-date basis is desired and that the following information is available:

		Quarter			
		1	2	3	4
(1)	SA based on the higher of the quarter's average or ending market price	1,250	1,320	1,690	2,000
(2)	Weighted average of year-to-date quarters	1,250	1,285[a]	1,420[b]	1,565[c]
(3)	SA at end of period, using the end-of-period market price	1,100	1,320	1,580	2,100
(4)	SA used for the year-to-date presentation (higher of 2 or 3)	1,250	1,320	1,580	2,100

[a]$(1,250 + 1,320) \div 2$
[b]$(1,250 + 1,320 + 1,690) \div 3$
[c]$(1,250 + 1,320 + 1,690 + 2,000) \div 4$

Special features affecting options and warrants in the calculation of FDEPS are summarized as follows:

1. The SA is based on the greater of the ending market price or the average market price.
2. The exercise proceeds are based on the lowest exercise price during the next ten years.
3. For options exercised during the year:
   a. The SA prior to exercise is based on the market price at date of exercise, and
   b. The security is included in FDEPS prior to exercise, even if the effect is antidilutive.
4. A quarterly averaging technique is used when there are significant variations between quarterly and annual ending market prices.

The quarterly averaging technique, as well as the concepts affecting the application of the treasury stock method for options and warrants to be considered in the computation of FDEPS, are demonstrated in Illustration 2–6. This illustration is based on the same facts as in Illustration 2–5, which was concerned with options and warrants in the calculation of PEPS. Illustrations 2–5 and 2–6 should be compared in order to note the differing treatment given options and warrants in the PEPS and FDEPS computations.

Illustration 2–6
Fully Diluted EPS Computations: Options and Warrants

In addition to the facts given in Illustration 2–5, relevant market price information for 19X6 was as follows:

Quarter	Market Price	
	Average	Ending
1	$41	$42
2	43	44
3	49	52
4	53	51

Calculation of Income and Share Adjustments for FDEPS

Stock Warrant X

This warrant was considered in the calculation of PEPS because it met both the five-year and three-month tests. However, 9,000 shares must be reconsidered for purposes of calculating FDEPS, using the market prices at the end of the period. The adjustments for the 1,000 shares exercised must be recalculated, using the market price on the exercise date.

9,000 Warrants Not Exercised

Income adjustment: Not applicable
Share adjustment: The greater number of shares according to the following
calculations:

Using the Quarterly Averaging Technique

Quarter	Shares Obtainable	Treasury Shares Acquired	SA
1	9,000	$\frac{\$360,000}{\$42} = 8,571$	429
2	9,000	$\frac{\$360,000}{\$44} = 8,182$	818
3	9,000	$\frac{\$360,000}{\$52} = 6,923$	2,077
4	9,000	$\frac{\$360,000}{\$53} = 6,792$	2,208
			5,532

Weighted average SA: 5,532 ÷ 4 = 1,383 shares

Using the Year-End Market Price

Shares Obtainable	Treasury Shares Acquired	SA
9,000	$\frac{\$360,000}{\$51} = 7,059$	1,941 shares

1,000 Warrants Exercised

Income adjustment: Not applicable
Share adjustment:

Quarter	Shares Obtainable	Treasury Shares Acquired	SA
1	1,000	$\frac{\$40,000}{\$44*} = 909$	91
2	1,000	$\frac{\$40,000}{\$44} = 909$	91
3	Not applicable		-0-
4	Not applicable		-0-
			182

Weighted average SA: 182 ÷ 4 = 46 shares

*Market price at date exercised.

(continued)

Stock Warrant Y

This warrant was excluded from the calculation of PEPS because it failed the five-year test; however, it is considered for FDEPS because it satisfies the ten-year test.

Income adjustment: Not applicable
Share adjustment: The greater number of shares according to the following calculations:

Using the Quarterly Averaging Technique

Quarter	Shares Obtainable	Treasury Shares Acquired	SA
1	Not applicable—antidilutive		-0-
2	Not applicable—antidilutive		-0-
3	5,000	$\dfrac{\$250,000}{\$52} = 4,808$	192
4	5,000	$\dfrac{\$250,000}{\$53} = 4,717$	283
			475

Weighted average SA: 475 ÷ 4 = 119 shares

Using the Year-End Market Price

Shares Obtainable	Treasury Shares Acquired	SA
5,000	$\dfrac{\$250,000}{\$51} = 4,902$	98 shares

Calculation of FDEPS

	ANI_{i-1}	IA_i	ANI_i	S_{i-1}	SA_i	S_i	EPS_i
Earnings per common share	$400,000	—	$400,000	250,500*	—	250,500	$1.5968
X (not exercised)	400,000	—	400,000	250,500	1,941	252,441	1.5845
X (exercised)	400,000	—	400,000	252,441	46	252,487	1.5842
Y	400,000	—	400,000	252,487	119	252,606	1.5835

*Weighted average of shares outstanding during the year: 250,000 shares + 1/2 of 1,000 shares issued on June 30 = 250,500.

Contingent Shares. As in the case of PEPS, contingent shares that are issuable upon the passage of time are included in FDEPS. For PEPS purposes, contingent shares that are issuable upon the attainment of certain conditions are not considered common stock equivalents prior to the current attainment of the conditions. However, these securities are included in the fully diluted computation if the effect is dilutive, even though the specified conditions have not been attained. In this case, it is assumed that the specified conditions were satisfied at the beginning of the period (or at the time the contingency arose, if later). As a result, the following adjustments are necessary:

1. If applicable, an income adjustment equal to the net-of-tax difference between reported income and the level of income stated as a specific condition, and
2. A share adjustment equal to the number of common shares needed to satisfy the contingency.[19]

Contingent shares that are issuable upon the attainment of certain conditions will be dilutive only if their incremental impact, as measured by the income adjustment divided by the share adjustment, is less than EPS prior to this calculation.

Shares also may be issuable contingent upon the level of future market prices per share of common stock. These contingent arrangements will not require an income adjustment. However, a share adjustment will be required, and it will be based on the number of shares that would be issuable using the actual end-of-period market price.

To demonstrate contingent share agreements, assume that Schrubbe Inc. had the following contingent agreements outstanding in 19X5:

Agreement A — To issue 5,000 shares to management if *aftertax* income reaches $1,000,000 by 19X8.

Agreement B — Former shareholders of another company were issued 20,000 shares of Schrubbe common stock as part of a business combination. If the actual total market value of the stock issued is less than $1,000,000 ($50 per share) on June 30, 19X6, the shareholders will be issued additional shares so that their total investment is then equal to $1,000,000.

During 19X5, *net* income was $950,000, and there were 50,000 common shares outstanding. The market price of the common stock was $48 per share on December 31, 19X5.

The calculations for PEPS are as follows:

	ANI_{i-1}	IA_i	ANI_i	S_{i-1}	SA_i	S_i	EPS_i
Earnings per common share	$950,000	—	$950,000	50,000	—	50,000	$19.00
Agreement A	Not a common stock equivalent — specified conditions not attained						
Agreement B	950,000	—[a]	950,000	50,000	833[b]	50,833	18.69

[a]Income adjustment: Not applicable
[b]Share adjustment:

$$SA = \frac{(20,000 \times \$50) - (20,000 \times \$48)}{\$48} = 833 \text{ shares}$$

If the $50 per share market price is attained by June 30, 19X6, no additional shares would be issued, and past EPS, which included the share adjustment, would be restated.

[19]*Opinions of the Accounting Principles Board, No. 15, op. cit.*, par. 62.

The calculations for FDEPS are as follows:

	ANI_{i-1}	IA_i	ANI_i	S_{i-1}	SA_i	S_i	EPS_i
Earnings per common share	$ 950,000	—	$ 950,000	50,000	—	50,000	$19.00
Agreement A	950,000	$50,000^c	1,000,000	50,000	5,000	55,000	18.18
Agreement B	1,000,000	—	1,000,000	55,000	833	55,833	17.91

^{c}Income adjustment:
   IA = $1,000,000 − $950,000 = $50,000

Convertible Securities. Convertible securities that satisfied the effective yield test for common stock equivalency will be considered in FDEPS. In addition, convertible securities that failed this test and/or the five-year test may be included in the calculation of FDEPS if both of the following conditions are satisfied:

1. The security must be convertible within ten years from the end of the current period. If the conversion rate varies during this time, the conversion rate most favorable to the holder of the security (i.e., the rate giving the holder the greatest number of common shares per convertible security) should be used.
2. The effect of the convertible security must be dilutive, as determined in calculating PEPS.

The "if converted" method also is used in the calculation of FDEPS. Therefore, the income adjustment and share adjustment are determined in the same manner as for PEPS. However, if a security was converted during the period, conversion is assumed to have occurred at the beginning of the period, and when the "if converted" method is employed, the conversion rate that existed at the date of the actual conversion is used, regardless of whether the effect is dilutive or antidilutive.

To illustrate the proper treatment of a conversion during the period, assume that on July 1, 19X2, $1,000,000 of 6% bonds were converted into 5,000 shares of common stock. The bonds originally were issued at par and the effective tax rate is 40%. The FDEPS prior to considering this security is $6.50.

The income and share adjustments for this security are as follows:

Income adjustment:
   IA = 6% × $1,000,000 × (1 − 40% tax rate) × 1/2 year = $18,000
Share adjustment:
   SA = 5,000 shares × 1/2 year = 2,500 shares

The effect of the income and share adjustments is antidilutive ($18,000 ÷ 2,500 shares = $7.20 per share) when compared to the preconversion FDEPS of $6.50. However, both the income and share adjustments would be included in the calculation of FDEPS because the security actually was converted during the period.

DISCLOSURE REQUIREMENTS

In addition to presenting both primary and fully diluted earnings per share on the face of the income statement, entities with complex capital structures are required to provide the following disclosures:

> ...a description, in summary form, sufficient to explain the pertinent rights and privileges of the various securities outstanding. Examples of information which should be disclosed are dividend and liquidation preferences, participation rights, call prices and dates, conversion or exercise prices or rates and pertinent dates, sinking fund requirements, usual voting rights, etc.
>
> A schedule or note relating to the earnings per share data should explain the bases upon which both primary and fully diluted earnings per share are calculated. This information should include identification of any issues regarded as common stock equivalents in the computation of primary earnings per share and the securities included in the computation of fully diluted earnings per share. It should describe all assumptions and any resulting adjustments used in deriving the earnings per share data. There should also be disclosed the number of shares issued upon conversion, exercise or satisfaction of required conditions, etc., during at least the most recent annual fiscal period and any subsequent interim period presented.[20]

In addition to this disclosure, it may be desirable to provide computations that indicate how the various EPS amounts were determined.

APB Opinion No. 15 also requires disclosure of the following supplementary EPS data:

1. EPS data based on the assumption that all significant conversions that occurred during the period took place at the beginning of the period. This disclosure would be provided regardless of whether or not the effect was dilutive.
2. EPS data reflecting subsequent period conversions that took place prior to the completion of the financial report.
3. EPS data reflecting the assumption that preferred stock or debt is retired at the beginning of the period (or date of issuance, if later) when the proceeds from an actual sale of common stock or equivalent occurring during the current period or shortly thereafter are used, or are intended to be used, to retire the preferred stock or debt.[21]

It is important to note that the supplementary disclosures are in addition to the normal disclosures required by APB Opinion No. 15 and that the supplementary disclosures are not to appear on the face of the income statement, but rather in its related notes.

---

[20]*Ibid.*, pars. 19–20.
[21]*Ibid.*, pars. 22–23.

GENERAL GUIDELINES

The following general guidelines summarize the basic aspects of computing and disclosing PEPS and FDEPS. Many of these aspects are demonstrated in Illustration 2–7, which is a comprehensive problem demonstrating both the PEPS and FDEPS computations.

1. Per share data should reflect only the potential dilution of EPS. Normally, securities whose conversion or exercise would increase EPS are not included in the computation of per share data. However, an antidilutive effect may result from options, warrants, and/or convertible securities that have been exercised during the year. For FDEPS, the SA calculation is based on the market price at date of exercise for options and warrants and the conversion rate at date of conversion for convertible securities. The SA for these securities is included in FDEPS, even if the effect is antidilutive.

2. Securities whose conversion or exercise would decrease a reported loss per share are not included in the computation of per share data if all levels of the income statement (e.g., net loss from continuing operations, extraordinary items, etc.) are losses. However, if at least one level of the income statement is not a loss, dilutive securities must be included in the computation of per share data for all levels of the income statement.

3. Except in certain instances involving contingent issuances, previously reported EPS are not to be restated retroactively when estimates that influence the calculation of per share data subsequently are revised. However, EPS data are restated retroactively for stock dividends, stock splits, and pooling agreements. When stock dividends and/or splits have taken place after the end of the period but before completion of the financial statements, EPS data for the period should give effect to the stock dividend and/or split.

4. The computation of the number of shares to be used as the denominator in the EPS statistic is based on a weighted average of shares rather than the number of shares outstanding at the end of the period. This refinement gives recognition to the fact that capital provided by equity investors may have been available for only a portion of the period. The weighted-average number of shares also is considered to be representative of the future number of shares to which earnings are traceable; therefore, the prospective nature of the per share calculation is emphasized. It is important to note that when a security is converted into common shares, it is included in the weighted average number of outstanding common shares automatically. For example, if a bond was converted at midyear into 1,000 shares of common stock, the shares of common stock would not be considered as outstanding in the first six months of the year but would be included as outstanding common stock for the last six months. Therefore, the 1,000 shares traceable to the convertible bond should not be added to outstanding shares in the last six months because the 1,000 shares are included already.

5. If either PEPS or FDEPS represent dilution that is at least three percent of simple earnings per common share, disclosure of both PEPS and FDEPS is required. Otherwise, only earnings per common share would be disclosed. However, if the current period is to be included in comparative financial statements, the disclosure of both PEPS and FDEPS always is recommended. This way the cumulative change in PEPS and FDEPS can be traced to specific years, even if the yearly change is less than three percent.

6. It is not common to consider options and warrants in either the PEPS or FDEPS computations until they meet the three-month test, although it is permissible to do so. All options and warrants in the illustrations, exercises, and problems in this text are assumed to have satisfied this test, unless data with which to apply the test are given.

Illustration 2–7
Demonstration of Primary and Fully Diluted Per Share Computations

1. Manchester Corporation's 19X2 income statement reflects the following:

Income from continuing operations before cumulative effect of changes in accounting principles	$88,100
Cumulative effect on prior years of changes in accounting principles	(7,300)
Net income	$80,800

2. As of January 1, 19X2, 20,000 shares of common stock were issued and outstanding. On May 1, 19X2, 10,000 shares of common stock were sold for $15 per share.

3. An analysis of securities relevant to the computation of earnings per share is as follows:

    Security A—consisting of 2,000 stock options granted in 19X1. Each option is exchangeable for one share of common stock at an option price of $13 per share up to October 1, 19X2, and $14 per share thereafter. The options expire on October 1, 19X6. One-half of the options were exercised on July 1, 19X2. The market price exceeded the exercise price for substantially all of the last three months in 19X1.

    Security B—consisting of 1,000 warrants, each exchangeable for one share of common stock at a price of $13 beginning after December 31, 19X9.

    Security C—consisting of a contingent share agreement (adopted on June 30, 19X2), whereby 4,000 shares of common stock will be issued to key personnel if pretax income increases by $3,000 in 19X3 and again in 19X4.

    Security D—consisting of 5%, $100,000 convertible bonds, issued on April 1, 19X2, at a price of 100. The average Aa corporate bond yield was 9% on April 1, 19X2. Each $1,000 bond is convertible into 20 shares of common stock beginning April 1, 19X4.

(continued)

Security E— consisting of 2,000 shares of 6% cumulative, convertible preferred stock, which was issued in 19X1 at par when the average Aa corporate bond yield was 8%. Each share of the preferred stock (par value, $10) is convertible into one share of common stock until the end of 19X5, after which time two shares of common stock would have been received. However, all of the preferred stock was converted on August 30, 19X2. During 19X2, dividends were paid on the preferred stock up to the date of conversion.

4. The corporate tax rate is 40%.

5. Daily market prices per share of common stock were as follows:

Date	Price	Date	Price
1/1/X2............................	$11.00	6/30/X2............................	$14.00
3/31/X2.........................	14.00	7/1/X2	14.50
5/1/X2...........................	15.00	9/30/X2............................	14.00
		12/31/X2.........................	16.00

6. Average market prices per share of common stock during 19X2 were as follows:

First quarter...	$12.00
Second quarter...	15.00
Third quarter...	14.50
Fourth quarter..	15.50

7. Since the illustration involves a complex capital structure, earnings per common share would not be presented in the financial statements; however, it must be computed as the basis for the computations of PEPS and FDEPS.

Calculation of Earnings per Common Share

An analysis of the common stock account reveals the following changes in the number of shares outstanding:

Date	Item	No. of Shares
1/1/X2	Beginning balance...............	20,000
5/1/X2	Additional sale....................	10,000
7/1/X2	Exercise of Security A..........	1,000
8/30/X2	Conversion of Security E......	2,000

The weighted average of shares outstanding is as follows:

Time Span	No. of Shares	Weight (in Months)	Share-Months
1/1/X2–4/30/X2	20,000	4	80,000
5/1/X2–6/30/X2	30,000	2	60,000
7/1/X2–8/29/X2	31,000	2	62,000
8/30/X2–12/31/X2	33,000	4	132,000
Total		12	334,000

Weighted average SA: 334,000 ÷ 12 = 27,833 shares

Earnings per common share would be as follows:

Income from continuing operations before cumulative effect of
   changes in accounting principles .... $3.14[a]
Cumulative effect on prior years of changes in accounting
   principles.. (0.26)
Net income.. $2.88

[a]Before computing EPS, the reported income has been appropriately reduced by the
19X2 preferred stock dividend of $800 (6% × $20,000 × 2/3 year). Therefore, the EPS
before the cumulative effect of changes in principles is based on income of $87,300.

Calculation of Primary Earnings per Share

The basic methodology presented in Illustration 2–4 is used to compute the
PEPS as follows:

	ANI_{i-1}	IA_i	ANI_i	S_{i-1}	SA_i	S_i	EPS_i
Earnings per common share	$87,300	—	$87,300	27,833	—	27,833	$3.14[b]
Security A	87,300	—	87,300	27,833	117[c]	27,950	3.12
Security B	Not a common stock equivalent—fails 5-year test						
Security C	Not a common stock equivalent—specified conditions not attained						
Security D	87,300	$2,250[d]	89,550	27,950	1,500[e]	29,450	3.04
Security E	Not a common stock equivalent—fails effective yield test						

[b]To insure that antidilutive securities would be identified properly, earnings per common share of $3.14
was used instead of the final per share figure of $2.88.
[c]Weighted average of quarters for Security A:

Quarter	Dilutive*	Shares Obtainable	Treasury Shares Acquired	SA
1	No	—	—	-0-
2	Yes	2,000	$\frac{\$26,000}{\$15} = 1,733$	267
3	Yes	1,000	$\frac{\$13,000}{\$14.50} = 897$	103
4	Yes	1,000	$\frac{\$14,000}{\$15.50} = 903$	97
				467

Weighted average SA: 467 ÷ 4 = 117 shares

*Dilutive if average market price is greater than exercise price.
[d]5% × $100,000 × 9/12 year = $3,750. Aftertax effect: 60% × $3,750 = $2,250.
[e]100 bonds × 20 shares = 2,000 shares assumed outstanding as of April 1, 19X2. Therefore, weighted
average = 2,000 × 3/4 year = 1,500 shares.

Primary earnings per share would be presented as follows:

Earnings per common share and common equivalent share:
   Income from continuing operations before cumulative effect
    of changes in accounting principles....................................... $3.04
   Cumulative effect on prior years of changes in
    accounting principles... (0.25)*
   Net income... $2.79

*The $7,300 cumulative effect divided by the final S_i of 29,450.

(continued)

Calculation of Fully Diluted Earnings per Share

The method shown in Illustration 2–6 is used to compute the FDEPS:

	ANI_{i-1}	IA_i	ANI_i	S_{i-1}	SA_i	S_i	EPS_i
Earnings per common share	$87,300	—	$87,300	27,833	—	27,833	$3.14
Security A (not exercised)	87,300	—	87,300	27,833	125[f]	27,958	3.12
Security A (exercised)	87,300	—	87,300	27,958	52[g]	28,010	3.12
Security B	87,300	—	87,300	28,010	187[h]	28,197	3.10
Security C	87,300	$3,600[i]	90,900	28,197	2,000[i]	30,197	3.01
Security E[j]	90,900	800[k]	91,700	30,197	1,333[l]	31,530	2.91
Security D	91,700	2,250[m]	93,950	31,530	1,500[m]	33,030	2.84

[f]The year-end market price is used for the entire period when it produces greater dilution than the quarterly average. Thus, the share adjustment is the 125 incremental shares resulting from use of the year-end market price, rather than the quarterly average of 108 shares. These amounts are computed as follows:

Quarter	Dilutive*	Shares Obtainable	Treasury Shares Acquired	SA
1	Yes	1,000	$\dfrac{\$13,000}{\$14} = 929$	71
2	Yes	1,000	$\dfrac{\$13,000}{\$15} = 867$	133
3	Yes	1,000	$\dfrac{\$13,000}{\$14.50} = 897$	103
4	Yes	1,000	$\dfrac{\$14,000}{\$16} = 875$	**125**
				432

Weighted average SA: 432 ÷ 4 = 108 shares

*Dilutive if the greater of the average or the end-of-period market price exceeds the exercise price.

[g]Weighted average of quarters for Security A—Exercised:

Quarter	Dilutive*	Shares Obtainable	Treasury Shares Acquired	SA
1	Yes	1,000	$\dfrac{\$13,000}{\$14.50} = 897$	103
2	Yes	1,000	$\dfrac{\$13,000}{\$14.50} = 897$	103
3	Not applicable			-0-
4	Not applicable			-0-
				206

Weighted average SA: 206 ÷ 4 = 52 shares

*Dilutive if the market price at the date of exercise is greater than the exercise price. The share adjustment for the time prior to exercise always is based on the market price at the exercise date, regardless of whether or not the result is dilutive. Note that securities exercised when the market price is less than the exercise price always are included in FDEPS, even if the effect is antidilutive.

[h]The year-end market price is used for the entire period when it produces greater dilution than the quarterly average. Thus, the share adjustment is the 187 incremental shares resulting from use of the year-end market price, rather than the quarterly average of 124 shares. These amounts are computed as follows:

Quarter	Dilutive*	Shares Obtainable	Treasury Shares Acquired	SA
1	Yes	1,000	$\dfrac{\$13,000}{\$14} = 929$	71
2	Yes	1,000	$\dfrac{\$13,000}{\$15} = 867$	133
3	Yes	1,000	$\dfrac{\$13,000}{\$14.50} = 897$	103
4	Yes	1,000	$\dfrac{\$13,000}{\$16} = 813$	**187**
				494

Weighted average SA: 494 ÷ 4 = 124 shares

*Dilutive if the greater of the average or the ending market price exceeds the exercise price.

[i]For purposes of computing FDEPS, it is assumed that the net-of-tax increases in 19X3 and 19X4 income [($3,000 + $3,000) × 60% = $3,600] have been realized. The weighted average number of shares would be 2,000 (4,000 × 1/2 year).

[j]Security E has a lower incremental impact than Security D and should be considered first.

[k]The preferred stock dividend is $800, computed as follows: 6% × $20,000 × 2/3 year = $800.

[l]When actual conversion of a security takes place during the period, conversion is assumed at the beginning of the period or at issuance, if later, for purposes of calculating FDEPS. Since the shares issued upon conversion already have been considered as outstanding, the SA is based on the period prior to conversion (2,000 × 8/12 = 1,333).

[m]The income and share adjustments for the convertible bonds are the same as they were in the PEPS computation.

Fully diluted earnings per share would be presented as follows:

Earnings per common share—assuming full dilution:
Income from continuing operations before cumulative effect of changes in
  accounting principles.. $2.84
Cumulative effect on prior years of changes in accounting principles .... (0.22)*
Net income.. $2.62

*The $7,300 cumulative effect divided by the final S_i of 33,030.

QUESTIONS

1. Why might the all-inclusive concept of income presentation be less useful in assessing the short-term performance of a company?

2. Why are the basic components of an income statement shown net of taxes rather than being combined to reflect a total amount of income before tax less a single tax amount?

3. Define the following two terms as they apply to the accounting for a discontinued segment: measurement date and date of disposition.

4. How do the results of a segment that has been discontinued in the current year affect the presentation of comparative financial data from prior years?

5. If the disposition of a segment results in a gain, under what circumstances may the gain be recognized before it is realized?

6. How would the current operating concept of income present the following items: extraordinary items, correction of an error, and discontinued operations?

7. Why do EPS calculations assume conversions of securities which in fact were not converted during the year? Is this valid? Why?

8. Explain why FDEPS is considered an ultraconservative measure of earnings per share.

9. When is the disclosure of PEPS and/or FDEPS required to be presented within financial statements?

10. When would the assumed exercise of options and/or warrants result in an income adjustment?

11. How do income taxes and an unamortized discount on convertible bonds affect the income adjustment when calculating earnings per share?

12. When is the quarterly averaging technique appropriate? Is the quarterly average always used for FDEPS?

13. How are contingent share agreements analyzed for purposes of computing primary EPS? Fully diluted EPS?

EXERCISES

Exercise 1.   Morgan Company grows various crops and then processes them for sale to retailers. Morgan has changed its depreciation method for its processing equipment from the double-declining-balance method to the straight-line method effective January 1 of this year. This change has been determined to be preferable.

   In the latter part of this year, Morgan had a large portion of its crops destroyed by a hailstorm. Morgan has incurred substantial costs in raising the crops destroyed by the hailstorm. Severe damage from hailstorms in the locality where the crops are grown is rare.

(1) How would Morgan calculate and report the effect of the change in accounting principle relative to the depreciation method in this year's income statement? Do not discuss earnings per share requirements.

(2) Where in its income statement should Morgan report the effects of the hailstorm? Why?

(3) How does the classification in the income statement of an extraordinary item differ from that of an operating item? Why? Do not discuss earnings per share requirements.

(AICPA adapted)

Exercise 2.   Computing Systems Inc. has two distinct segments: a software segment and a hardware segment. On June 15, 19X8, Computing Systems Inc. decided to dispose of its software segment and concentrate on computer hardware. Computing Systems' year end is December 31. Management expects final disposition of the segment to take place before July 1, 19X9. Prior to June 15, 19X8, the segment had a pretax operating loss of $500,000 and a separate pretax gain from the sale of segment assets of $270,000. During the remainder of 19X8, the software segment experienced a pretax gain of $1,050,000 and a pretax loss from the sale of segment assets of $780,000. Remaining segmental assets are expected to be disposed of during 19X9 at a gain of $1,200,000. Estimated pretax operating losses for 19X9 are $550,000. The effective tax rate is 34%.

(1) Prepare the portion of the 19X8 income statement that would reflect management's decision to discontinue the software segment.

(2) How would the answer to (1) differ if for 19X9 there was an unrealized loss on the disposal of assets of $300,000?

Exercise 3.   On May 1, 19X4, after serious consideration, the board of directors of Modern Electronics Inc. adopted a plan calling for:

1. The discontinuation of the satellite guidance operation and
2. The disposal of the transistor radio production operation.

Although the satellite guidance operation will be phased out, the company still will be involved actively in the development and manufacturing of other guidance systems, similar to satellite systems, to be used in missile and aircraft applications. Virtually all past and present activity in guidance systems has been undertaken on a government contract basis. The decision to dispose of the transistor radio operation is in response to increasing foreign competition and marks the end of Modern's involvement in any form of consumer-oriented communication devices.

Relevant pretax data relating to the satellite and radio operations for calendar years 19X4 and 19X5 are as follows:

	Satellite Guidance	Radio Production
Operating income (loss):		
1/1/X4 to 4/30/X4	($1,480,000)	($810,000)
5/1/X4 to 12/31/X4	(2,360,000)	(1,410,000)
Anticipated 19X5 as of 12/31/X4	(3,700,000)	(270,000)
Actual 19X5	(3,330,000)	(360,000)
Gain (loss) on disposal of assets:		
1/1/X4 to 4/30/X4	—	230,000
5/1/X4 to 12/31/X4	1,440,000	290,000
Anticipated 19X5 as of 12/31/X4	(1,260,000)	580,000
Actual 19X5	(835,000)	360,000

Assuming that the board of directors' plans are carried out completely by the end of April, 19X5, prepare that portion of the 19X4 and 19X5 income statements dealing with discontinued operations. During 19X4 and 19X5, the effective tax rate was 40%.

Exercise 4.   Brett Corporation has decided that in the preparation of its 19X3 financial statements, two changes will be made from the methods used in prior years:

1. *Depreciation.* Brett always has used the declining-balance method for tax and financial reporting purposes, but has decided to change during 19X3 to the straight-line method for financial reporting only. The effect of this change is as follows:

	Excess of Accelerated Depreciation Over Straight-Line Depreciation
Prior to 19X2.......	$1,300,000
19X2..................	101,000
19X3..................	99,000
	$1,500,000

   Depreciation is charged to cost of goods sold and to selling, general, and administrative expenses on the basis of 75% and 25%, respectively.

2. *Uncollectible accounts expense.* In the past, Brett has recognized uncollectible accounts expense equal to 1.5% of net sales. After careful review, a rate of 2% is determined to be more appropriate for 19X3. Uncollectible accounts expense is charged to selling, general, and administrative expenses.

The following information is taken from financial statements which were prepared before giving effect to the two changes:

Brett Corporation
Condensed Balance Sheet
December 31, 19X2 and 19X3

Assets	19X3	19X2
Current assets...	$43,561,000	$43,900,000
Property, plant, and equipment (at cost)..............	45,792,000	43,974,000
Less accumulated depreciation	(23,761,000)	(22,946,000)
	$65,592,000	$64,928,000

Equities		
Current liabilities	$21,124,000	$23,650,000
Long-term debt	15,154,000	14,097,000
Capital stock	11,620,000	11,620,000
Retained earnings...	17,694,000	15,561,000
	$65,592,000	$64,928,000

Brett Corporation
Income Statement
For Year Ended December 31, 19X2 and 19X3

	19X3	19X2
Net sales	$80,520,000	$78,920,000
Cost of goods sold...	54,847,000	53,074,000
	$25,673,000	$25,846,000
Selling, general, and administrative expenses	19,540,000	18,411,000
	$ 6,133,000	$ 7,435,000
Other income (expense)	(1,198,000)	(1,079,000)
Income before federal income tax	$ 4,935,000	$ 6,356,000
Federal income tax	2,368,800	3,050,880
Net income...	$ 2,566,200	$ 3,305,120

There have been no timing differences between any book and tax items prior to the above changes. The effective tax rate is 48%.

Based on APB Opinion No. 20, "Accounting Changes," compute for the following items the amounts which would appear on the comparative (19X3 and 19X2) financial statements of Brett Corporation after adjustment for the two accounting changes. Show amounts for both 19X3 and 19X2 and prepare supporting schedules as necessary.

(1) Accumulated depreciation
(2) Selling, general, and administrative expenses
(3) Retained earnings
(4) Deferred income tax expense at year end
(5) Pro forma net income   (AICPA adapted)

Exercise 5.   Chaplin Industries had net income of $1,950,000 for the year ended December 31, 19X8. As of January 1, 19X8, Chaplin had 550,000 shares of outstanding common stock. An additional 15,000 shares were issued on April 1, 19X8. Chaplin also had 200, 7%, 10-year, $1,000 convertible bonds outstanding which were issued on March 1, 19X7, to be converted after September 1, 19X7. On July 1, 19X8, 75 of these bonds were converted into 1,500 shares of common stock. The average Aa corporate bond yield was 12% on March 1, 19X7.

On September 15, 19X8, the board of directors declared a 2:1 stock split to be effective October 1, 19X8. The corporate tax rate is 34%.

Calculate PEPS for the year ended December 31, 19X8.

Exercise 6.   Throughout the last four years, Rough and Ready Wear Inc. has offered several different options and warrants to shareholders and employees. All are exercisable within five years of the current year end, 19X6, and have passed the three-month test in prior years. It has been determined that if all options and warrants had been exercised at the beginning of 19X6, 50,000 shares of stock would have been issued. However, none of the options or warrants were exercised in 19X6. The total proceeds from the options and warrants would have been $1,500,000 for PEPS and $1,450,000 for

FDEPS. There were 200,000 shares of common stock outstanding on December 31, 19X6.

On January 1, 19X6, the company had outstanding 15% interest-bearing bonds with a $100,000 face value and a $3,000 premium. The debt matured on June 1, 19X6. Government securities earned an average return of 12% throughout 19X6. The tax rate is 25%, and current-year average and ending market prices for the common stock are $33 and $34, respectively. No other outstanding securities existed in 19X6.

(1) Compute the income and share adjustments for both primary and fully diluted EPS for 19X6.
(2) What may be the reason for the lower total proceeds for FDEPS?
(3) Assuming that the income and share adjustments for PEPS are $11,000 and 10,000 shares, respectively, and that the weighted number of shares outstanding in 19X6 is 200,000, determine the minimum adjusted net income needed in order for dual disclosure to be required.

Exercise 7. Craig Manufacturing has various stock options outstanding during 19X9. All of the options were issued on January 1, 19X9, and are summarized as follows:

Option	Number of Options	Number of Shares per Option	Exercise Price per Option	Earliest Exercise Date
W	2,000	1	$39	19X9
X	4,000	1	34	19X9
Y	2,000	2	74	19Y6

At the beginning of 19X9, there were 50,000 common shares outstanding. However, on May 1, 19X9, one-half of the X options were exercised when the market price per share was $36. For 19X9, the average market price per share was $37, and the year-end market price per share is $38. Net income for 19X9 is $250,000.

Calculate the 19X9 primary and fully diluted earnings per share. Ignore the quarterly averaging technique.

Exercise 8. Dunphry Co. had net income of $775,000 after dividends for the fiscal year ending March 31, 19X9. Dunphry had 200,000 shares of common stock outstanding as of April 1, 19X8. The company issued 500, $200, 7%, 10-year convertible bonds on January 1, 19X7, at 103. The premium is being amortized by the straight-line method over a 10-year period. Each bond is convertible into two shares of common stock. Dunphry also had 10,000 convertible preferred shares outstanding on April 1, 19X8. Each preferred share has a quarterly dividend of $1.00 per share and is convertible into one share of common stock. However, after March 31, 19Y2, each preferred share may be converted into 1 1/2 shares. At the date of issue, the market price of the preferred stock was $58. The average Aa corporate bond yield was 12% when the convertible bonds and preferred stocks were issued. In addition, the company has a contingent share agreement with its officers to issue 25,000 shares of common stock if the earnings in any given year exceed $900,000. The market price of the common stock was $102 at year end and the average market price for the year was $80. The applicable tax rate is 38%.

Calculate the primary and fully diluted earnings per share for the year ended March 31, 19X9.

Exercise 9.   In 19X4, Cosmos Corporation purchased some Luna Corporation voting common stock from Luna's stockholders. As part of the agreement, Cosmos promised to issue 2,000 additional shares of its voting common stock to the Luna stockholders as soon as Cosmos realizes an annual net income of $40,000. The contingency consideration expires in 19X8. Net income in 19X4 and 19X5 was $15,000 and $6,000, respectively.

On March 1, 19X5, 400 options, each exercisable into 4 shares of Cosmos voting common stock, were issued. The exercise price is $36 per option. No options were exercised during 19X5. The market prices during the year were as follows:

Quarter	Average	Ending
1	$10	$10
2	7	7
3	10	12
4	11	10

The market price on March 1, 19X5, was $9.50. The tax rate is 40%. There were 20,000 weighted average shares outstanding in 19X5.

Calculate the 19X5 primary and fully diluted earnings per share.

Exercise 10.   Earth Corporation has net income of $900,000 for the fiscal year ending September 30, 19X9. The common stock account on October 1, 19X8, showed 240,000 shares outstanding. The company issued $2,000,000 of 6%, ten-year convertible bonds on June 1, 19X9, at 98. The bonds were dated June 1, 19X9, with interest payable on June 1 and December 1. The bond discount is amortized semiannually on a straight-line basis. Each $100 bond is convertible into one share of common stock. On August 1, 19X9, $500,000 of these bonds were converted. The remaining bonds should be considered common stock equivalents. The only other securities that the company had outstanding on October 1, 19X8, were 14,000 shares of convertible preferred stock, which returns a yearly dividend of $2.25 per share and is convertible into one share of common stock for each share of preferred. At date of issue, the market price of the preferred stock was $40, and the average Aa corporate bond yield was 9%. On December 1, 19X8, an additional 6,000 shares of the same convertible preferred stock were issued at a price of $60 per share when the average Aa corporate bond yield was 9.5%. All shares of preferred stock outstanding during the year received the full cash dividend. The tax rate applicable to Earth Corporation is 48%.

Present all EPS data required for Earth Corporation. Show all schedules and computations in good form.

PROBLEMS

Problem 2–1. The following comparative trial balances of Ranco Inc. at December 31, 19X8 and 19X7 have been adjusted except for accruing all of the 19X8 income tax expense.

	19X8	19X7
Cash..	612,000	550,000
Accounts Receivable (net).....................................	2,109,000	1,653,000
Inventory..	2,515,000	1,930,000
Property, Plant and Equipment (net)	8,935,000	8,240,000
Accounts Payable	(1,700,000)	(1,406,000)
Income Tax Payable...	(406,000)	(340,000)
Deferred Income Tax..	(298,000)	(275,000)
Common Stock...	(2,210,000)	(2,210,000)
Additional Paid-In Capital	(3,160,000)	(3,160,000)
Retained Earnings...	(4,982,000)	(4,025,000)
Net Sales—Metal Division	(11,800,000)	(10,020,000)
Net Sales—Glass Division...................................	(2,040,000)	(2,380,000)
Cost of Sales—Metal Division	6,012,000	5,950,000
Cost of Sales—Glass Division	1,790,000	1,630,000
Selling and Administrative Expense—Metal Division...	2,890,000	2,750,000
Selling and Administrative Expense—Glass Division...	585,000	550,000
Interest Income	(95,000)	(75,000)
Gain on Litigation Settlement	(260,000)	—
Depreciation Adjustment for Accounting Change....	375,000	—
Gain on Disposal of Glass Division.......................	(180,000)	—
Income Tax Expense	1,308,000	638,000
Total..	0	0

Other financial data for the year ended December 31, 19X8, includes the following:
(a) The tax rate on all types of income is 40%.
(b) The gain from litigation settlement is a taxable gain and is not considered infrequent.
(c) On September 30, 19X8, Ranco sold its Glass Division for $2,180,000 when the carrying amount was $2,000,000. The sale is considered to be a disposal of a segment. The measurement date was September 30, 19X8.
(d) On January 1, 19X8, Ranco changed to the straight-line method of depreciation from the 150%-declining-balance method for certain assets. The pretax cumulative effect of this accounting change was $375,000.

Required:
Prepare a formal comparative income statement for Ranco Inc. for the years ended December 31, 19X8 and 19X7.

Problem 2–2. Grant Corp. adopted a plan to discontinue a segment on March 31, 19X8. The date of disposal will be January 31, 19X9. Grant uses the calendar year for its fiscal period. The tax rate is 34%. For each of the following cases, results relating to the discontinued segment are:

	Pretax Income (Loss) from Operations			Pretax Gain (Loss) on Disposal of Assets	
	1/1/X8– 3/31/X8	4/1/X8– 12/31/X8	1/1/X9– 1/31/X9	4/1/X8– 12/31/X8	1/1/X9– 1/31/X9
(a)	$15,000	($22,000)	($7,000)	$ 6,000	($10,000)
(b)	12,000	32,000	5,000	(18,000)	(26,000)
(c)	8,000	(45,000)	(6,000)	15,000	38,000
(d)	(6,000)	5,000	(5,000)	(7,000)	6,000

Required:

For cases (a) through (d) above, present schedules of the detailed computation of the information needed for the section of the income statement dealing with discontinued operations. Assume that the tax benefits associated with any losses will be realized through offset against income from continuing operations.

Problem 2–3. XYZ Company decided in 19X9 to adopt the straight-line method of depreciation for equipment. The straight-line method will be used for new acquisitions as well as for previously acquired equipment for which an accelerated method had been used. The effect of this change on manufacturing overhead is not material. Other data concerning this change are presented in the following table:

Years	Accelerated Depreciation	Straight-Line
Prior to 19X5....................................	$67,290,000	$67,270,000
19X5...	257,600	177,600
19X6	275,400	205,400
19X7	309,000	259,000
19X8	289,000	259,000
19X9	332,000	322,000

The depreciation for 19X9 was recorded properly. The applicable income tax rate for XYZ Company is 48%. Income for years 19X8 and 19X9 was as follows:

	19X8	19X9
Income before extraordinary item and cumulative effect of change in accounting principle....................	$970,000	$1,106,000
Extraordinary item...	65,000	—

Required:

(1) Present computations, in good form, to compute the effect of the change in accounting principle.
(2) Present the method of reporting in the financial statements of XYZ Company this change.
(3) Write a footnote to disclose the change in principle in accordance with the requirements of APB Opinion No. 30.

Problem 2–4.   The condensed income and retained earnings statements of Shiloh Company for the years ended December 31, 19X4, and December 31, 19X3, are as follows:

Shiloh Company
Condensed Income and Retained Earnings Statements
For Years Ended December 31

	19X4	19X3
Sales..	$3,000,000	$2,400,000
Cost of goods sold..	1,300,000	1,150,000
Gross profit...	$1,700,000	$1,250,000
Selling, general, and administrative expenses	1,200,000	950,000
Income before extraordinary item	$ 500,000	$ 300,000
Extraordinary item..	(400,000)	—
Net income..	$ 100,000	$ 300,000
Retained earnings, January 1...................................	750,000	450,000
Retained earnings, December 31	$ 850,000	$ 750,000

The following are four unrelated situations involving accounting changes and classification of certain items as ordinary or extraordinary. Each situation is based on the previous income and retained earnings statements of Shiloh Company and requires revisions of these statements.

Situation A

On January 1, 19X2, Shiloh acquired machinery at a cost of $150,000. The company adopted the double-declining-balance method of depreciation for the machinery and has calculated this depreciation assuming an estimated life of ten years and no residual value. At the beginning of 19X4, a decision was made to adopt the straight-line method of depreciation for this machinery. Due to an oversight, however, the double-declining-balance method was used for 19X4. For financial reporting purposes, depreciation is included in selling, general, and administrative expenses.

The extraordinary item in the condensed income and retained earnings statement for 19X4 relates to shutdown expenses incurred by the company during a major strike by its operating employees in 19X4.

Situation B

At the end of 19X4, Shiloh's management decided that the estimated loss rate on uncollectible accounts receivable was too low. The loss rate used for the years 19X3 and 19X4 was 1% of total sales, and due to an increase in the write-off of uncollectible accounts, the rate has been raised to 3% of total sales. The amount recorded in uncollectible accounts expense under the heading of selling, general, and administrative expenses was $30,000 for 19X4 and $24,000 for 19X3.

The extraordinary item in the condensed income and retained earnings statement for 19X4 relates to a loss incurred in the abandonment of outmoded equipment formerly used in the business.

Situation C

The extraordinary item in the condensed income and retained earnings statement for 19X4 relates to a settlement agreement between Shiloh and the Internal Revenue Service in which Shiloh was assessed and agreed to pay additional income taxes of $60,000 for 19X3 and $340,000 for the four prior years.

Situation D

Late in 19X4, it was discovered that 19X2 administrative expenses did not include $90,000 of compensation expense associated with certain stock option plans. The extraordinary item in the condensed income and retained earnings statement for 19X4 relates to a loss incurred as the result of a flood. No floods previously had occurred in the area.

Required:

For each of the four unrelated situations, prepare revised condensed income and retained earnings statements of Shiloh Company on a worksheet for the years ended December 31, 19X4, and December 31, 19X3. Each answer should recognize the appropriate accounting changes and other items outlined in the situation. Ignore all earnings per share computations and all pro forma computations.

Problem 2–5. Tall Tales Publications Inc. is considering several contingent share agreements as part of its purchase of Real Romance Books Corporation. Tall Tales is concerned about the impact on its earnings per share for 19X5 and 19X6. As chief accountant, you must determine the expected income and share adjustments for PEPS and FDEPS for each agreement for both years and report to the board of directors. The agreement to purchase Real Romance is expected to go into effect on April 1, 19X5. Net incomes for the consolidated companies for 19X5 and 19X6 are expected to be $4,600,000 and $4,800,000, respectively. The contingent share agreements are as follows:

(a) Stockholders of Real Romance will receive 40,000 shares of Tall Tales voting common stock on May 1, 19X8.

(b) Tall Tales will issue 500 shares of its voting common stock to Real Romance shareholders for every $10,000 of net income over $4,250,000 in 19X5 and net income over $4,500,000 in 19X6.

(c) Tall Tales will issue 1,000 shares of its voting common stock to Real Romance shareholders for every $10,000 of net income between $4,500,000 and $5,000,000 for each of the next three years, 19X5, 19X6, and 19X7.

(d) When net income reaches $4,750,000, Real Romance shareholders will receive 40,000 shares of Tall Tales voting common stock. This agreement expires December 31, 19X8.

(e) When net income reaches $5,000,000, Real Romance shareholders will receive 40,000 shares of Tall Tales voting common stock. This agreement expires December 31, 19X8.

(f) The market value of Tall Tales stock on April 1, 19X5, is expected to be $35 per share. Tall Tales will issue 24,000 shares at that time and guarantees the original total stock value ($35 × 24,000) on December 31 of every year through 19X8. If the total value is not maintained, additional shares will be issued as necessary. The market value is $30 and $28 at the end of 19X5 and 19X6, respectively.

Required:

Present the effect on PEPS and FDEPS for each of the above agreements.

Problem 2–6.   Earnings per share is the single most featured financial statistic about modern corporations. Daily published quotations of stock prices for many securities recently have been expanded to include a times earnings figure that is based on EPS. Often the focus of analysts' discussions will be on the EPS of the corporation receiving their attention.

Required:

(1) Explain how dividends or dividend requirements on any class of preferred stock that may be outstanding affect the computation of EPS.
(2) One of the technical procedures applicable in EPS computations is the treasury stock method.
   (a) Briefly describe the circumstances under which it might be appropriate to apply the treasury stock method.
   (b) There is a limit to the extent to which the treasury stock method is applicable. Indicate what this limit is, and give a succinct indication of the procedures that should be followed beyond the treasury stock limits.
(3) Under some circumstances, convertible debentures would be considered common stock equivalents, while under other circumstances they would not.
   (a) When is it proper to treat convertible debentures as common stock equivalents? What is the effect on the computation of EPS in such cases?
   (b) If convertible debentures are not considered as common stock equivalents, explain how they are handled for purposes of EPS computations.   (AICPA adapted)

Problem 2–7.   Stopkin Inc. reported net income before dividends of $2,010,000 for 19X9. Stopkin had 900,000 shares of common stock outstanding as of January 1, 19X9, along with the following securities:

(a) 6% convertible bonds issued on March 15, 19X8, at 99. Each $150 bond is convertible into three shares of common stock. The discount is amortized over 5 years using the straight-line method. The 1,000 convertible bonds originally were issued when the Aa corporate bond rate was 10%.
(b) 7% convertible bonds issued on June 1, 19X6, at par. Each $45 bond is convertible into one share of common stock. The 5,000 bonds were issued when the Aa corporate bond rate was 12%.
(c) 9% convertible bonds, $100 par, issued on January 1, 19X7, at 103 when the Aa corporate bond rate was 10%. Each of the 2,000 bonds has a 1:2

conversion ratio. The premium is being amortized over 5 years using the straight-line method.

(d) $2.50 cumulative preferred stock, $50 par, each convertible into one share of common stock. The 8,000 preferred shares were issued in 19X7 at par when the Aa corporate bond yield was 8%. Dividends are in arrears for 19X8 and 19X9.

(e) 5,000 shares of $3 preferred stock, $45 par, each convertible into one share of common stock. The Aa corporate bond yield was 8% in 19X6 when the stock was issued.

On July 1, 19X9, 75% of the 7% convertible bonds were converted. The statutory tax rate for Stopkin is 34%.

Required:
Calculate primary earnings per share for 19X9.

Problem 2–8.   The following financial statements and additional information relate to Quin Industries:

Quin Industries
Partial Balance Sheet
June 30, 19X8

Current liabilities:	
Accounts payable	$ 70,000
15% note payable	75,000
Total current liabilities	$ 145,000
Long-term debt:	
15% note payable, net of current portion	$ 150,000
12% convertible $100 bonds, net of $4,800 premium,	
due 6/30/Y8 (in 10 years)	84,800
Total long-term debt	$ 234,800
Stockholders' equity:	
$4 cumulative preferred stock, $100 par, 25,000 shares	
authorized, 10,000 shares issued and outstanding	$1,000,000
Additional paid-in capital—preferred	100,000
Common stock, $10 par, 150,000 shares authorized,	
50,000 shares issued and outstanding	500,000
Additional paid-in capital—common	30,000
Total paid-in capital	$1,630,000
Retained earnings	4,000,000
Total stockholders' equity	$5,630,000
Total liabilities and stockholders' equity	$6,009,800

Quin Industries
Partial Income Statement
For Year Ended June 30, 19X8

Income from continuing operations before extraordinary loss	$1,000,000
Extraordinary loss, net of $50,000 tax benefit	(50,000)
Net income	$ 950,000

The following additional information applies:
(a) The 19X8 weighted average number of shares of common stock is 49,000.
(b) On January 1, 19X8, 200 of the $100 bonds were converted into common stock.
(c) The bond conversion schedule is:

Year of Conversion	Number of Shares per $100 Bond
19X8	10
19X9	12
19Y0	15

On the day the bonds were issued, the average Aa corporate bond yield was 15%. All bonds and notes were issued prior to July 1, 19X7. The premium on the 15-year bonds is being amortized on a straight-line basis.
(d) On May 1, 19X8, dividends of $1.25 per share were paid to common stockholders.
(e) Options and warrants: At the 19X8 year end, the following were outstanding:
   Option #1: Issued January 1, 19X6; exercise price, $25; 2,000 options exercisable into 2,000 shares of common stock.
   Option #2: Issued July 1, 19X6; exercise price, $30; 8,000 options exercisable into 8,000 shares of common stock.
   Warrant A: Issued July 1, 19X7; exercise price, $50; 1,000 warrants exercisable as 2 common stock shares per warrant.
   Warrant B: Issued December 31, 19X7; exercise price, $86; 300 warrants exercisable as 2 common stock shares per warrant.
   All options and warrants currently are exercisable. None were exercised in the current year.
(f) Quin Industries invests in corporate bonds yielding an annual return of 13%. Because of the costly interest rate related to the notes payable, Quin is anxious to retire that debt as quickly as possible.
(g) The market prices of the common stock were:

	Year Ended	
	6/30/X8	6/30/X7
Average common stock prices:		
First quarter	$26	$35
Second quarter	27	30
Third quarter	30	32
Fourth quarter	35	24
End of quarter price:		
First quarter	30	35
Second quarter	25	33
Third quarter	33	29
Fourth quarter	40	21
Annual average	29	30

For the treasury stock method, Quin uses quarterly averaging. For the 20% rule, Quin uses the annual average where appropriate.

(h) The tax rate is 50%.

Required:

(1) Using the above information, calculate PEPS and FDEPS for the year ending June 30, 19X8.

(2) Does Quin Industries have to disclose PEPS and FDEPS for the current fiscal year? Why or why not?

Problem 2–9.   Nexton Industries has the following securities outstanding as of June 30, 19X9:

Option A: Issued November 1, 19X6, exercise price is $32. The 2,500 options are exercisable into 2,500 shares of common stock beginning September 1, 19X8.

Option B: Issued January 30, 19X7, exercise price of $32 through March 31, 19X9, then $34. The 4,000 options are exercisable into 4,000 shares of common stock. On January 1, 19X9, 2,000 options were exercised when the market price was $35.

7% convertible preferred stock: $38 par, 5,000 shares issued and outstanding for the entire year. The shares were issued when the Aa corporate bond yield was 11%. Each preferred share is convertible into one common share.

8% convertible bonds: Issued on May 1, 19X6, at par. Each of the 2,000, $100 bonds was issued with a 1:3 conversion ratio, to be convertible after May 1, 19Y6. The Aa corporate bond yield at date of issue was 12.5%.

Contingent share agreement: Nexton has agreed to issue its officers 10,000 shares of common stock if net earnings exceed $600,000 in a year and will issue an additional 15,000 shares if net earnings exceed $700,000.

Nexton reported $650,000 of net income for the year ended June 30, 19X9. Common shares outstanding as of July 1, 19X8, were 250,000. The applicable tax rate is 35%. Common stock market price data is given as follows:

	Average Market Price	Ending Market Price
First quarter	$33	$33
Second quarter	34	35
Third quarter	37	36
Fourth quarter	37	38
Average for the year	35	

Required:

Calculate PEPS and FDEPS for the year ended June 30, 19X9.

Problem 2–10.   The controller of Midar Corporation has requested assistance in determining primary and fully diluted earnings per share figures for the company for the fiscal year ending on September 30, 19X1.

Working papers disclose the following beginning balances and transactions in the company's capital stock accounts during the 19X0–X1 fiscal year:

(a) Common stock (at October 1, 19X0, stated value $10, authorized 300,000 shares; effective December 1, 19X0, stated value $5, authorized 600,000 shares):

Balance, October 1, 19X0—60,000 shares issued and outstanding.

December 1, 19X0—60,000 shares issued in a 2-for-1 stock split.

December 1, 19X0—280,000 shares (stated value $5) issued at $39 per share.

(b) Treasury stock—common:

March 1, 19X1—purchased 40,000 shares at $38 per share.

April 1, 19X1—sold 40,000 shares at $40 per share.

(c) Stock purchase warrants, Series A (initially, each warrant, along with $60, was exchangeable for one common share; effective December 1, 19X0, each warrant became exchangeable for two common shares at $30 per share):

October 1, 19X0—25,000 warrants issued at $6 each.

(d) Stock purchase warrants, Series B (each warrant, along with $40, is exchangeable for one common share):

April 1, 19X1—20,000 warrants authorized and issued at $10 each.

(e) First mortgage bonds, 5-1/2%, due 19Y5 (nonconvertible; priced to yield 5% when issued):

Balance, October 1, 19X0—authorized, issued, and outstanding—the face value of $1,400,000.

(f) Convertible debentures, 7%, due 19Y9 (initially, each $1,000 bond was convertible at any time until maturity into 12-1/2 common shares; effective December 1, 19X0, the conversion rate became 25 shares for each bond):

October 1, 19X0—authorized and issued at their face value (no premium or discount) of $2,400,000.

The following table shows market prices for the company's securities and the assumed average Aa corporate bond yield during 19X0–19X1:

	Price (or Rate) at			Average for Year Ended September 30, 19X1
	October 1, 19X0	April 1, 19X1	September 30, 19X1	
Common stock	66	40	36 1/4	37 1/2*
First mortgage bonds	88 1/2	87	86	87
Convertible debentures	100	120	119	115
Series A warrants	6	22	19 1/2	15
Series B warrants	—	10	9	9 1/2
Average Aa corporate bond yield	8%	7 3/4%	7 1/2%	7 3/4%

*Adjusted for stock split

Required:

Compute the earnings per share data that the controller has requested, assuming that net income for the year is $540,000. Show all supporting schedules in good form. (Because of the relative stability of the market price for Midar Corporation common stock, the annual average market price may be used where appropriate in the calculations. Assume an income tax rate of 48%.)   (AICPA adapted)

Problem 2–11. The following information relates to PQB Corporation:

PQB Corporation
Partial Balance Sheets
December 31, 19X3 and 19X4

	19X4	19X3
Current liabilities:		
Accounts payable	$ 200,000	$ 200,000
Notes payable:		
8%, 3-month, due 2/1/X4	—	100,000
10%, 6-month, due 3/1/X5	100,000	—
Long-term liabilities:		
Bonds payable:		
10% stated rate, 20-year bonds, due 12/31/Y4 ..	4,000,000	5,000,000
8% stated rate, 15-year convertible bonds,		
due 12/31/Y6, net of discount	4,820,000	9,610,000
Total liabilities	$ 9,120,000	$14,910,000
Stockholders' equity:		
Preferred stock:		
6%, $100 par, 30,000 shares authorized;		
8,000 shares outstanding in 19X3	—	$ 800,000
10,000 shares outstanding in 19X4	$ 1,000,000	—
4% convertible, $100 par, 50,000 shares		
authorized;		
30,000 shares outstanding in 19X3	—	3,000,000
20,000 shares outstanding in 19X4	2,000,000	—
Common stock:		
$20 par, 5,000,000 shares authorized;		
1,000,000 shares issued, of which		
800,000 are outstanding in 19X3	—	20,000,000
1,306,000 shares issued, of which		
1,106,000 are outstanding in 19X4*	26,120,000	—
Total paid-in capital	$29,120,000	$23,800,000

*Note that 200,000 shares are held in treasury.

PQB Corporation
Partial Income Statement
For Year Ended December 31, 19X4

Income from continuing operations	$15,202,667
Extraordinary gain from early extinguishment of debt	
(net of $96,000 tax expense)	104,000
Net income	$15,306,667

Additional information:
(a) The average Aa corporate bond yields on selected dates were:

1/1/W1 — 10%	1/1/W5 — 14%	1/1/W9 — 5.75%
1/1/X2 — 12%	1/1/X3 — 8%	12/31/X3 — 9%
12/31/X4 — 10%		

(b) All preferred stock was issued at par on these dates:

6%	4%
1/1/W1 — 8,000 shares	1/1/W9 — 10,000 shares
1/1/X4 — 2,000 shares	1/1/X3 — 20,000 shares

(c) A 15% common stock dividend was issued to shares outstanding as of 5/1/X4.

(d) 4% preferred stock is convertible into three shares of common until 19X8, then into five shares of common. On August 31, 19X4, 10,000 shares of preferred stock were converted.

(e) The 8% bonds with an original face value of $10,000,000 were issued at 95-1/2 on January 1, 19X2. Each $1,000 bond is convertible into 30 shares of common stock. On June 30, 19X4, half of the bonds were converted. The discount is being amortized on a straight-line basis.

(f) The current tax rate is 48%.

(g) Common stock market price data:

	19X4	
	Average Market Price	Ending Market Price
First quarter..................	$46	$47
Second quarter..............	42	43
Third quarter.................	45	48
Fourth quarter...............	50	47
Average for the year......	46	

(h) Option A consists of 3,000 options, each of which may be used to acquire four shares of common stock at an exercise price of $180. Half of the options were exercised on June 30, 19X4. The balance of the options may be exercised within the next six years. The quarterly averaging technique is to be used.

Required:

Calculate PEPS for 19X4.

PART TWO

COMBINED CORPORATE ENTITIES AND CONSOLIDATIONS

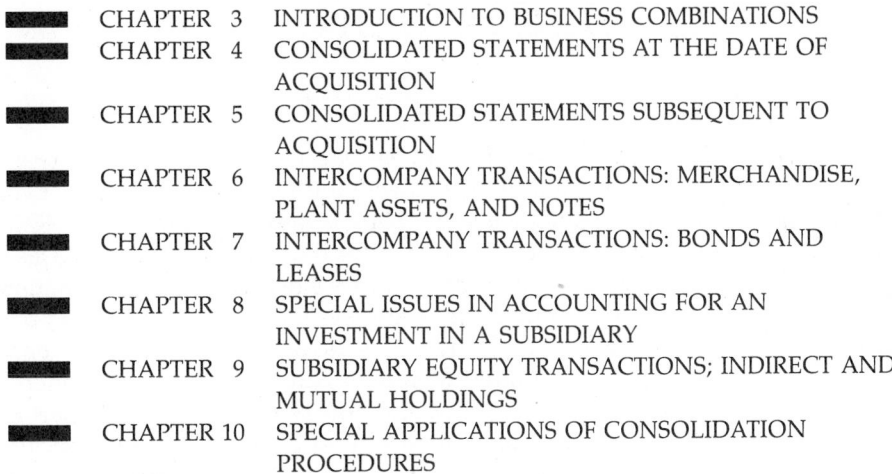
Business combinations have become a common occurrence for modern firms. Most of the publicly issued financial statements analyzed by accountants are consolidated statements. These statements are prepared by a firm that owns a controlling interest (over 50%) in one or more subsidiary firms. Control of another firm may be gained by acquiring directly all of that firm's assets or by purchasing a controlling interest in that firm's common stock shares. Control through stock ownership requires a worksheet process in order to prepare a single set of consolidated statements for a parent and its subsidiaries. Special procedures are applied to transactions between the related entities for preparation of both the consolidated earnings per share and a consolidated cash flows statement and for tax effects.

There are two methods of accounting for a business combination. Typically, the purchase method is used when the owners of the acquired firm are displaced by the owners of the purchasing firm. The pooling of interests method is used when the two shareholder groups combine their interests and the owners of the former firms retain an interest in the single surviving firm.

CHAPTER 3

INTRODUCTION TO BUSINESS COMBINATIONS

Business combinations make popular headlines. The purchase of American Motors by the Chrysler Corporation was national news. Even the acquisition of a local bank by a larger bank is important local news. Recently, state legislatures have considered statutes that would limit purchases of firms within a state by out-of-state firms. Fears exist that such combinations might cause a loss of jobs as operations are consolidated or moved to other states.

The last one hundred years have been marked by periods with an unusually high number of combinations. There were numerous combinations in the 1890s, the 1920s, and the 1960s as many prosperous firms pursued greater domination of their industry. The 1970s saw a decline in combination activity; this was probably the result of recessions, energy shortages, and inflation. But there has been a substantial resurgence in the number of combinations lately. Many of these recent combinations have been motivated by new concerns for diversification into other industries as a means of spreading risk. In other cases, smaller firms have had problems contending in a competitive international economy and have found it judicious to be purchased by a larger company that is more able to raise funds and modernize operations. Some writers have dubbed the recent years as a period of "merger mania" which, in part, has been fueled by relaxed anti-trust policies during the Reagan administration. There are concerns that the too-high prices often paid in acquisitions create a burden on the purchasing firms. In addition, there could be adverse impact on the economy brought about by lowered employment, reduced research and development activities, and an increased vulnerability to bad decision-making due to a reduced number of key executives.[1]

The accountant may be involved in various activities pertaining to business combinations. Accountants frequently aid a buyer or seller in arriving at a tentative price and may advise the firms on how to accomplish the com-

---

[1]Henry F. Myers, "The Outlook: Will Mergers Help or Hurt in the Long Run?", *Wall Street Journal*, 2 May 1988.

bination in view of tax and financial reporting implications. The accountant must record the combination in a manner that conforms to generally accepted accounting principles and must present the effects of the combination in the accounting statements of the current and subsequent periods.

TAX ADVANTAGES OF COMBINATIONS

Many business combinations are motivated, in large part, by tax issues. The stockholders of a small, privately held corporation may wish to retire from the active management of their corporation and/or convert their holdings into a more liquid investment. Through careful structuring of the transaction, they may be able to account for the sale of their interest as a tax-free exchange for tax purposes. The former owners would receive the stock of the purchasing company in exchange for their interest and would be able to assign the book value of their former investment to the shares received. No tax would be due until the shares received are sold.

Further advantages exist when the firm to be acquired has incurred losses in previous years. Section 172(b) of the Internal Revenue Code provides that operating losses can be carried back three years to obtain a refund of taxes levied in profitable years. Should the loss not be absorbed by income in the three previous years, the loss may be carried forward fifteen years to offset taxable income, thus eliminating or reducing taxes that otherwise would be payable. These tax loss maneuvers are of little value to the firm originating them if the firm has not had sufficient taxable income in past years and does not expect enough future income to offset the loss. However, since the tax loss is transferable in a business combination, it may have value for a profitable acquiring firm. Thus, by combining, the unprofitable absorbed firm is able to realize immediate value from its past tax losses by selling them to the acquiring firm. The acquiring firm benefits in that it seldom pays a price equal to the full tax value of the tax loss. However, the acquiring firm should exercise caution in anticipating the benefits of past tax losses, since the deductions may be disallowed if the primary purpose of acquiring a corporation is to receive tax benefits. Furthermore, the acquiring firm may obtain a tax advantage in subsequent years by filing a consolidated tax return for all corporations in the affiliated group. The operating losses of one corporation offset immediately the profits of another member of the affiliated group.

CONTROL

Control of another firm's assets is achieved by either an asset or a stock acquisition. In an *asset acquisition*, the assets of the firm are acquired directly from the owner. Payment might include cash, property, or securities issued by the acquiring firm. The use of debt or equity securities as a means of payment is popular, since it avoids depleting assets, particularly cash, that may be needed for future operations. From a legal perspective, a *statutory consolidation* refers to the combining of two or more previously independent legal entities into one new legal entity. Each of the previous firms is dissolved and is replaced by a single, continuing firm. By contrast, a *statutory merger* involves the absorption of one or more former legal entities by another firm that continues as the sole survivor. The absorbed firm ceases to exist as a legal entity, but it may continue as a division of the surviving firm.

In a *stock acquisition*, a controlling interest (more than 50%) of another company's voting common stock is acquired. The firm making the acquisition is termed the *parent*, and the firm controlled is termed a *subsidiary*. Both the parent and the subsidiary remain separate legal entities and maintain their own financial records and statements. However, for external financial reporting purposes, the firms usually will combine their individual financial statements into a single set of statements which are called *consolidated statements*. Thus, it occurs in practice that a consolidation may refer to a special type of combination or, more commonly, to the combined statements of a parent and its subsidiary.

There may be several advantages to obtaining control by purchasing a controlling interest in stock. Most obvious is the fact that the total cost is lower, since only a controlling interest in the assets, and not the total assets, must be acquired. In addition, control through stock ownership may be simpler to achieve since no formal negotiations or transactions with the acquired firm's management are necessary. Further advantages may result from maintaining the separate legal identity of the former firm. For example, risk is lowered because the legal liability of any one corporation is limited to its own assets. Separate legal entities may be desirable when only one of the firms is subject to government control. Lastly, there may be tax advantages resulting from the preservation of the legal entities.

ACCOUNTING RAMIFICATIONS

Control through asset acquisition results in the assets of the acquired firm being recorded on the books of the acquiring firm. All future transactions will be recorded in the combined set of accounts. The only skill required to master this type of combination is that of properly recording the acquisition when it occurs. Combined financial statements automatically will result for periods subsequent to the acquisition since all transactions of the newly combined firm will be recorded on one set of books.

Achieving control of a firm through the acquisition of its stock leads to more involved accounting procedures. Since the firms maintain their individual legal identities, they also maintain separate accounting records and prepare separate financial statements. Despite the existing segregation, accounting principles view most of these acquisitions as creating only one viable, economic entity. As a result, the financial statements of each firm involved are blended into one set of consolidated statements.

This chapter will discuss business combinations resulting from asset acquisitions, since the accounting principles involved are more easily understood in this context. Later chapters will treat the topic of accounting for business combinations where control is achieved through stock acquisition. Following is a discussion of the two basic theoretical models of accounting for business combinations, the *pooling of interests* and *purchase* methods. The theories and their resulting procedures apply to all combinations, whether achieved through asset or stock acquisition.

POOLING VS. PURCHASE

Current accounting practice is based on APB Opinion No. 16, "Business Combinations," which views most business combinations as a purchase of one firm by another for cash or other consideration. Purchase accounting requires that the assets acquired be recorded at their current market value or the value of the consideration given, whichever is more readily determinable. The combination is viewed as a group purchase of assets. The total price paid for the firm must be allocated to the individual assets, using their estimated market values as a guide. Should the price paid exceed the total market values of the identifiable assets, the excess is viewed as a payment for intangible future benefits and is captioned *goodwill* on the balance sheet. Subsequent income statements will include depreciation charges based on the market value of the depreciable assets and amortization deductions for goodwill. Where the acquiring firm issues securities as consideration, debt or equity accounts should reflect the market value of the securities issued. If that market value is not determinable, the market value of the assets acquired should be assigned to the securities.

According to APB Opinion No. 16 (par. 47), the only exception to accounting for a combination as a purchase may apply to situations in which the surviving company issues only voting common stock for all the assets or at least for 90% of the voting common stock of the acquired firm. The term "pooling of interests" is used to describe this fusion of previously separate stockholder groups. The proper structuring of such a combination supports the argument that no sale has occurred but rather that the stockholders of the acquired firm merely are exchanging their interest in the former firm for an interest in the combined corporation. The absence of a sale makes it unnecessary for the accountant to acknowledge the market values of the assets acquired and the securities issued. The acquiring firm combines the book values of the acquired company's assets and liabilities with its own. The total paid-in capital of the acquired firm is assigned to the securities issued by the surviving corporation. The retained earnings of the acquired firm, in most cases, is added to the retained earnings of the surviving company.

EFFECT ON FUTURE STATEMENTS

The consequences of the purchase versus pooling methods on the accounting statements may be very pronounced. The following chart compares the impact of the two accounting methods on future balance sheets:

Item	Purchase Method	Pooling Method
1. Recording of assets and liabilities.	At current market values with a possibility of goodwill.	At book value of acquired firm. No additional goodwill acknowledged. (a)
2. Equity securities issued.	Market value of shares issued added to paid-in capital.	Paid-in capital of acquired firm assigned as paid-in value of shares issued. (b)
3. Retained earnings of acquired firm.	Not acknowledged.	Added to retained earnings. (b)

See pages 107 and 128 page 132 on original

(a) Goodwill previously recorded by the acquired firm would be recorded at its remaining book value.

(b) The retained earnings of the acquired firm may be reduced to meet the issuer's par or stated value requirement.

Moreover, future income statements are affected by the values assigned to the assets of the acquired firm. Typically, *long-lived assets*[2] will have market values in excess of their book values. Therefore, recording a combination as a purchase will cause higher depreciation and amortization expense in future years. Note that any goodwill resulting from a purchase must be amortized over a period not to exceed 40 years,[3] thus burdening future income statements with a charge that would not have existed under the pooling method. Income statements for a period following a combination under the purchase and pooling methods would be prepared as follows:

	Purchase	Pooling
Revenue	$250,000	$250,000
Less:		
All expenses except depreciation on acquired firm's assets and amortization of goodwill	100,000	100,000
Depreciation of building acquired in combination:		
Purchase: 1/10 of $500,000 market value	50,000	
Pooling: 1/10 of $200,000 net book value.................		20,000
Goodwill amortization:		
Purchase: 1/40 of $200,000.............................	5,000	
Net income..	$ 95,000	$130,000

The only differences in the two income statements involve depreciation and goodwill amortization. The book value of the building acknowledged in

---

[2]The term "long-lived assets" will be used in this text to refer to all identifiable tangible and intangible noncurrent assets.

[3]*Opinions of the Accounting Principles Board, No. 17,* "Intangible Assets" (New York: American Institute of Certified Public Accountants, 1970), par. 29.

a pooling is assumed to be $200,000, while the market value acknowledged in a purchase is $500,000. In both cases, depreciation is calculated on a straight-line basis with a 10-year remaining life. In addition, the price paid for the firm exceeds the market values of the separate identifiable assets by $200,000. Thus the goodwill recorded under the purchase method is $200,000, and it is amortized on a straight-line basis with a maximum 40-year life. The added asset depreciation and goodwill amortization charges are particularly expensive since they usually are not tax deductible. Many combinations are structured as tax-free exchanges as to the seller, in which case the purchaser must base future depreciation charges on the selling firm's book value. Under no circumstances are goodwill amortization charges tax deductible. This means that, while other expenses are mitigated by tax deductibility, the goodwill amortization and added depreciation on assets caused by a purchase are not.

A common measure of a firm's profitability is the return on assets statistic. This is calculated by dividing net income by total assets. Return on assets can be doubly inflated for a pooling of interests. First, income is inflated by lower depreciation charges and a lack of goodwill amortization. Second, the asset values usually are understated since they are recorded at historical cost. The combination of greater income and lesser asset values may overstate severely the return on assets under a pooling as compared to the purchase method.

It is possible that current purchase accounting rules provide an advantage to foreign corporations that compete with domestic corporations to purchase U.S. companies. The United States is unique among major nations in that it requires the amortization of goodwill but does not allow a tax deduction for it. Other countries either allow a tax deduction for the amortization or do not require amortization. This puts domestic acquiring firms at a competitive disadvantage. Their future incomes from the acquired firm will be less than those of a foreign buyer; thus the price they can afford to pay for a firm may be less. This may help to explain why foreign acquisitions of U.S. corporations have increased from $5.9 billion in 1983 to $41.9 billion in 1987.[4]

The income statements of both the current and prior periods also are benefited by the retroactive application of the pooling concept. If a company purchases another firm midway through the year, it only may add the income of the firm purchased to its own income for the last half of the year. In a pooling, income may be added for the entire year no matter when during the year the combination occurred. When a purchase occurs, the prior years' comparative statements of the acquiring firm do not include the income of the acquired firm. In a pooling, prior years' comparative statements of the acquiring firm are restated to include the income of the acquired firm. Additional information on the effects of purchases and poolings on financial statements will be covered at the end of the chapter.

---

[4]Sanford Pensler, "Accounting Rules Favor Foreign Bidders," *Wall Street Journal*, 24 March 1988.

SUMMARY

If given a choice, most firms would choose to account for combinations under the pooling method. Where assets are undervalued and/or goodwill exists, the pooling method will produce higher incomes and a higher return on assets in future years. In addition, the balance sheet of the continuing firm is enhanced when the retained earnings of the acquired firm is added to existing retained earnings. The only likely disadvantage of the pooling method is that acquired assets may not be shown on the balance sheet at their full value. Therefore, the total worth of the combined firms may be considerably less than would have resulted under the purchase method. There are a limited number of cases where a firm may not prefer the pooling method. This may occur in acquisitions of firms with low or negative amounts of income and retained earnings.

Even with these advantages of the pooling method, it is difficult to justify its continued use. The distortions it causes, as compared to the purchase method, are disturbing to many accountants and financial analysts. It seems that the careful structuring of an acquisition to meet arbitrary criteria (see pages 122–126) is a shallow excuse for ignoring the true value of the assets over which control is achieved. It should be noted that the United States is the only country of the ten major industrial nations in the free world that allows the use of the pooling method for business combinations.[5]

Prior to the issuance of APB Opinion No. 16 in 1970, in most cases, firms chose the pooling method even though the transactions did not have the characteristics of a pooling. As a result, APB Opinion No. 16 provided very restrictive criteria for the use of the pooling method. All combinations not meeting the criteria must be accounted for as purchases. Thus there are no criteria for the use of the purchase method in accounting for combinations other than the failure to have the combinations qualify as poolings. If the pooling method is desired by the acquiring firm, the combination must be structured carefully in order to be classified as such. Currently, very few combinations meet the criteria. In recent years, only about 10% of the firms surveyed in *Accounting Trends and Techniques* used the pooling method.[6] Coverage of the application of the more popular purchase method is presented below and is followed by coverage of the criteria and application of the pooling method.

ASSET ACQUISITION AS A PURCHASE

When the acquisition of an existing company's assets is being considered, the current value of the firm's assets and the amount of its liabilities must be

---

[5]Choi and Mueller, *International Accounting* (New York: Prentice-Hall, 1984), 74.
[6]Jack Shohet and Richard Rikert, eds., *Accounting Trends and Techniques*, 41st ed. (New York: American Institute of Certified Public Accountants, 1987), 56.

appraised carefully. Such an evaluation usually precedes negotiations. Very likely, the prospective purchaser will seek permission to conduct a pre-acquisition audit to determine whether all assets and liabilities are recorded properly. The purchaser knows that, while book values may be indicative of the current value of some current assets, these values may not represent a reasonable market value for inventories, plant assets, or intangibles. Inventories priced on a Lifo basis will have little relationship to current market value. Inventories priced on a Fifo or average cost basis may be closer to market value but may still depart significantly when prices fluctuate quickly. Plant assets and intangibles are presented at historical cost less an arbitrary depreciation or amortization allowance, with no relationship to current market value. Even liabilities to be assumed may not be stated at their current market value in light of changes in market interest rates. For example, 10-year bonds issued at par 4 years ago when the prevailing interest rate was 8% now would sell at a discount if the current market rate of interest is 11%.

Acknowledging the limitations of book values, the purchaser may engage an independent consultant to estimate the current market values of the assets to be acquired and the liabilities to be assumed. Market values are an estimate of the price to which a willing buyer and seller would agree. These estimates provide only a guide to establishing the price to be paid for the entire firm.

Assume that Acquisitions Inc. is considering the purchase of Jacobs Company and has secured the following audited condensed balance sheet:

	Jacobs Company Balance Sheet December 31, 19X3		
Accounts receivable........	$ 20,000	Current liabilities	$ 20,000
Inventory........................	40,000	Capital stock	10,000
Land..............................	10,000	Paid-in capital in excess	
Buildings (net)................	40,000	of par	50,000
Equipment (net)..............	20,000	Retained earnings...........	50,000
Total assets....................	$130,000	Total liabilities and equity	$130,000

Aware of the deficiencies of book values, management obtains the following appraisal of market values:

Accounts receivable....................................	$ 20,000
Inventory...	45,000
Land...	10,000
Buildings	50,000
Equipment...	40,000
Current liabilities	(20,000)
Total market value of net assets	$145,000

If the market values are accurate, Acquisitions Inc. will expect to pay at least $145,000 for the net assets of Jacobs Company. The purchase of net assets means that Acquisitions Inc. will assume the liabilities of Jacobs Company. Perhaps a deal could be struck for less than $145,000, but, very likely, more will be paid. Acquisitions may be willing to pay a premium for Jacobs' assets, since Jacobs is a functioning firm with an established trade. If the assets were purchased individually from other sources, time would be required to combine them into a viable, profitable firm. The payment for this advantage is considered the purchase of goodwill. The amount of the payment depends on the expected future profitability of the assets to be acquired and the outcome of the negotiating process.

CALCULATING AND RECORDING GOODWILL

In addition to obtaining market values for other assets, the purchaser must try to appraise the value of potential goodwill. Typically, the appraisal is based on a comparison of estimated future income with normal income for the type and size of firm involved. Estimates of future income are likely to be based on an analysis of Jacobs income in the recent past. Normal income is calculated by applying an appropriate industry rate of return to the market value of the firm's total identifiable assets (which excludes previously recorded goodwill and the liabilities to be assumed). The following calculation of earnings in excess of normal might be made for Jacobs Company:

Expected average future income.......................................		$21,000
Less normal return on assets:		
Market value of total identifiable assets	$165,000	
Industry normal rate of return.......................................	10%	
Normal return on assets..		16,500
Expected annual earnings in excess of normal.....................		$ 4,500

There are several methods of using the expected annual earnings in excess of normal to estimate goodwill. A common approach is to pay for a given number of years' excess earnings. For example, Acquisitions might offer to pay for four years of excess earnings, which would total $18,000. Alternatively, the excess earnings could be viewed as an annuity. The most optimistic purchaser might expect the excess earnings to continue forever. If so, the buyer might capitalize the excess earnings as a perpetuity at the normal industry rate of return according to the following formula:

$$\text{Goodwill} = \frac{\text{Annual excess earnings}}{\text{Industry normal rate of return}}$$

$$= \frac{\$4,500}{.10}$$

$$= \$45,000$$

A more realistic purchaser might feel that the factors producing excess earnings are of limited duration, such as ten years, for example. This purchaser would calculate goodwill as follows:

Goodwill = discounted present value of a $4,500-per-year annuity for 10 years at 10%

= $4,500 × 10-year, 10% present value of annuity factor

= $4,500 × 6.145

= $27,653

Other purchasers might feel that the normal industry earning rate is appropriate only for tangible assets and not goodwill. Thus they might capitalize excess earnings at a higher rate of return to reflect the higher risk inherent in goodwill.

All calculations of goodwill are estimates used to assist in the determination of the price to be paid for a firm. For example, Acquisitions might add the $27,653 estimate of goodwill to the $145,000 market value of Jacobs' other net assets to arrive at a tentative maximum price of $172,653. However, estimates of goodwill may differ from actual negotiated goodwill. If the final agreed upon price for Jacobs' assets was $160,000, for example, the actual negotiated goodwill would be $15,000, which is the price paid less the market value of the net assets acquired.

RECORDING A PURCHASE

To continue the previous example, assume that the combining firms agree to a value of $160,000 for Jacobs Company's net assets, including goodwill. The *direct acquisition costs* of the business combination paid to third parties, such as audit fees and legal costs, are added to the agreed price to arrive at the total price paid for the net assets. *Indirect acquisition costs*, which are usually allocations of internal costs such as management time, may not be added to the price. Rather, they are expensed in the period of the purchase. Assume that Acquisitions paid $1,000 in direct legal costs. This would raise the price paid for the net assets of Jacobs to $161,000, and the following entry would be made by Acquisitions to record the net asset purchase:

Accounts Receivable (market value)	20,000	
Inventory (market value)	45,000	
Land (market value)	10,000	
Buildings (market value)	50,000	
Equipment (market value)	40,000	
Goodwill (price minus sum of net asset market values)	16,000	
Current Liabilities (market value)		20,000
Cash (includes direct acquisition costs)		161,000

Each identifiable asset and assumed liability is recorded at its estimated fair market value. Goodwill is recorded at the negotiated price, which, again, is always the excess of the total consideration given for the net assets ($161,000 in the example) over the sum of the values assigned to all identifiable net assets acquired. If an acquired firm already has goodwill on its books, such goodwill is ignored except as it is confirmed by the purchase price. For example, if Jacobs Company had previously recorded goodwill of $25,000, Acquisitions still would assign $145,000 to the net identifiable assets and assign the extra $16,000 paid to the goodwill. In this case, only $16,000 of the $25,000 recorded former goodwill would be confirmed by the current purchase price.

It should be noted that the selling firm's entries do not parallel those of the purchaser. The seller records the removal of net assets at their book values. The excess of the price received for the net assets by the seller ($160,000)[7] over the sum of the net asset book values ($130,000 assets − $20,000 liabilities = $110,000) is recorded as a gain on the sale. In this case, the gain is $50,000. The entry on Jacobs' books would be:

Cash	160,000	
Current Liabilities	20,000	
Accounts Receivable		20,000
Inventory		40,000
Land		10,000
Buildings (net)		40,000
Equipment (net)		20,000
Gain on Sale		50,000

RECORDING BARGAIN PURCHASES

Occasionally, a firm will be purchased at a "bargain" price. A bargain price is a price that is less than the sum of the estimated market values of a firm's separate identifiable assets and liabilities. Naturally, when this situation occurs, any goodwill existing on the books of the seller is ignored, since the price paid does not confirm it. The least reliable estimates of market values are assumed to be those applicable to long-lived assets, because a ready market often does not exist for such assets. Consequently, according to APB Opinion No. 16 (par. 87), *all current assets, long-term investments in marketable securities, and liabilities assumed are recorded at their full market value, regardless of the total price paid for the firm.* Any excess of the sum of the market values of the net identifiable assets over the price paid is to be deducted only from long-lived assets other than investments in marketable securities.

For example, assume that Acquisitions Inc. acquired Jacobs Company by paying $132,000 ($152,000 total asset value − $20,000 of liabilities) to the seller and $1,000 for direct acquisition costs. The excess of the market value of the net assets over cost would be determined as follows:

---

[7]Remember, the $1,000 in direct costs is paid by the purchaser to a third party, not to the seller.

Total estimated market value of separate net assets..	$145,000
Less price paid (including direct acquisition costs)...	133,000
Excess of market value over cost..............	$ 12,000

The excess must be deducted from the total estimated market value of the long-lived assets to arrive at the purchase cost assignable to these assets. The assignable cost then is allocated to the individual long-lived assets in proportion to their fair market values.

The total estimated market value of the long-lived assets and the percentage of the estimated market value of each of these assets to the total estimated market value are calculated first:

Asset	Estimated Market Value	Percent of Total Market Value
Land..	$ 10,000	10%
Buildings	50,000	50
Equipment..	40,000	40
Total market value......................................	$100,000	100%

The cost assignable to the long-lived assets is the $100,000 total market value less the $12,000 excess of market value over cost, or $88,000. This cost is assigned to the individual assets according to their relative market values as follows:

Asset	Percent of Total Market Value		Total Cost Assignable		Assigned Value
Land.....................................	10%	×	$88,000	=	$ 8,800
Buildings	50	×	88,000	=	44,000
Equipment...........................	40	×	88,000	=	35,200
	100%				$88,000

The entry to record the bargain purchase is:

Accounts Receivable (market value)................................	20,000	
Inventory (market value)..	45,000	
Land (assigned purchase cost)..	8,800	
Buildings (assigned purchase cost)	44,000	
Equipment (assigned purchase cost)................................	35,200	
Cash (includes direct acquisition costs)		133,000
Current Liabilities (market value)		20,000

Occasionally, some long-lived assets are given current asset status and recorded at net realizable value, regardless of the price paid for the firm. This situation occurs only when the purchaser intends to sell these assets soon after the date of the combination, as in the case of acquired assets that duplicate those already owned by the purchaser.

Though a rare occurrence, the price paid for a firm could be less than the market value of the current assets and any long-term investment in marketable securities less liabilities. Since accounts in these three categories must

It could be:

Excess of Market Value of Net Current Assets and Long-Term Investments in Marketable Securities Over Cost account.

be recorded at their market values, no value would remain to be assigned to long-lived assets. According to APB Opinion No. 16 (par. 91), the excess of the values assigned to the current assets, marketable securities, and liabilities over the price paid is to be recorded as a deferred credit in the account Excess of Market Value of Net Current Assets over Cost. The credit is to be amortized *to income* over a period not to exceed 40 years.

To illustrate this situation, assume that Acquisitions Inc. paid $30,000 for the net assets of Jacobs Company and paid $1,000 in direct acquisition costs. Since the market value of the net assets is $145,000, there is a bargain of $114,000 ($145,000 net assets at market − $31,000 total price for the net assets). The bargain exceeds the market value of the land, buildings and equipment by $14,000 ($114,000 bargain − $100,000 combined market value of land, buildings, and equipment accounts). The remaining $14,000 bargain may not be subtracted from the remaining assets which must be recorded at market value. Instead, the remaining bargain becomes the deferred credit which will be amortized to income in future periods. The entry would be as follows:

Accounts Receivable (market value)	20,000	
Inventory (market value)	45,000	
Land (no value available)	0	
Buildings (no value available)	0	
Equipment (no value available)	0	
Cash (includes direct acquisition costs)		31,000
Current Liabilities (market value)		20,000
Excess of Market Value of Net Current Assets over Cost		14,000

In summary, when a bargain purchase occurs:

1. Current assets, long-term investments in marketable securities, and liabilities assumed always are recorded at fair market value.
2. Previously recorded goodwill on the seller's books is reduced to zero and no new goodwill exists.
3. Long-lived assets are recorded at fair market value less a reduction for the bargain.
4. A deferred credit is recorded only after *all* long-lived assets are reduced to *zero*. The deferred credit is amortized over a period of 40 years or less.

ALLOCATING THE PURCHASE PRICE — SPECIAL CONCERNS

There are several situations that may complicate the recording of a purchase. There may be long-term liabilities that need to be revalued based on market values that differ from the recorded amounts on the books of the selling firm. Also, there may be lease agreements to which the seller was a party that must be recorded. In addition, tax law may require the purchasing firm to use the selling firm's book value for depreciation on future tax returns instead of the higher market value on the purchase date. Furthermore, the firm purchased may have tax loss carryovers available to the purchasing firm which become one of the assets being acquired. Lastly, there may be contingent assets, liabilities, or asset impairments that exist on the purchase date. Each of these situations is examined separately.

Revaluation of Long-term Liabilities. The market value concept must be applied to liabilities assumed in a purchase. The recorded book values of liabilities may not be indicative of their market values when prevailing interest rates have changed since the incurrence of the liabilities. When the debt instrument, such as bonds of a large corporation, is publicly traded, a quoted market value may be readily available. When such quotations are not available, the market value of a debt obligation must be estimated. The estimate is made by discounting all future cash flows required, using the current interest rate for debt issuances with similar risk and maturity. As an example, assume that the firm being acquired has outstanding $100,000 of 10% bonds that mature in 5 years. Assume further that interest is payable at the end of each of the next 5 years. If the current prevailing interest rate for similar issuances is 12%, the market value of the debt would be estimated as follows:

See page 107

Present value of interest payments at 12% ($10,000 annual interest × 5-year, 12% present value of annuity factor of 3.6048)	
Present value of principal ($100,000 × 5-year present value factor of .5674)	$36,048
Estimated market value of liability	56,740
	$92,788

Pls. see this. — How computed?

$36,048 = 3.6048 × 10,000.

56,740 = .5674 × 100,000.

The market value of the debt would be acknowledged in the purchase entry by recording a discount of $7,212 ($100,000 face value − $92,788 market value).

Lease Agreements. As mentioned earlier, special analysis of the purchase price in a business combination is necessary when the firm acquired in a purchase transaction is contractually bound by existing leases as either a lessee or lessor. In some cases, the terms of the lease may be modified as a result of the combination. These modifications would require the consent of a third party—either the lessor, when the selling firm is the lessee, or the lessee, when the selling firm is the lessor. When the terms of the lease are modified to the extent that a new lease is created, the new lease is classified and recorded according to the requirements of FASB Statement No. 13.[8] It is more common, however, to find that the contractual terms of a lease are not altered as a result of the purchase. In such cases it is necessary to record only the market value of the seller's existing rights and obligations under the lease.

---

[8]*Statement of Financial Accounting Standards, No. 13,* "Accounting for Leases" (Stamford: Financial Accounting Standards Board, 1976), par. 9.

When the firm acquired is a lessee under an operating lease, it has recorded rent as an expense but has not recorded any asset or long-term liability. Thus there is no existing recorded asset or liability to adjust. At acquisition if the contractual rent under the remaining lease term is materially below fair market rental value, an asset should be recorded equal to the value of the rent savings. The asset should be amortized over the lease term as an adjustment to rent expense. If the contractual rent exceeds the market rental value, a liability should be credited for the present value of the excess rent using an appropriate market interest rate. The liability should be amortized as a reduction of rent expense in future periods. Under both situations, future rent expense would reflect market rental value as of the date of the combination.[9]

When the acquired firm is a lessee under a capital lease, it has recorded the asset as well as the liability under that lease. At the time of the purchase, both the asset and the liability should be independently analyzed and recorded at their separate market values.

When the acquired firm is a lessor under an operating lease, it has recorded the cost of the leased asset less accumulated depreciation. In the purchase transaction, the asset should be recorded at its current market value. However, the market value may be based partly on the present value of the rents due under existing leases.

When the firm acquired is a lessor under a capital lease, it has recorded only a receivable due for future rents and perhaps an unguaranteed residual value. In the purchase transaction, the receivable should be recorded at its fair market value based on prevailing current interest rates. The unguaranteed residual value should be estimated and discounted to its present value, using the same current interest rate.

Nontaxable Exchanges. The selling firm may wish to structure the purchase so as to avoid a taxable gain at the time of the combination. This is accomplished by exchanging the common stock of the purchasing firm for the assets of the selling firm. The owners of the selling firm do not record a gain for tax purposes until the shares received are sold. The purchasing firm in a nontaxable exchange inherits the book values of the assets purchased for use in future tax calculations. This means that only the net book value on the books of the selling firm may be used as the tax basis of the assets acquired when they are sold or depreciated later. This results in the recording of a deferred tax liability for the added tax burden caused by the inability of the purchasing firm to deduct the excess of the value assigned to the assets over the selling firm's book value.[10]

---

[9]*Opinions of the Accounting Principles Board, No. 16*, "Business Combinations" (New York: American Institute of Certified Public Accountants, 1970), par. 88.
[10]*Statement of Financial Accounting Standards, No. 96*, "Accounting for Income Taxes" (Stamford: Financial Accounting Standards Board, 1987), par. 23.

As an example, assume that in a nontaxable exchange the tax basis of a given fixed asset is $50,000, and its fair market value at acquisition is $150,000. Depreciation on the $100,000 difference is not deductible on future tax returns. Therefore, if the purchasing firm is in a 35% tax bracket, there will be a $35,000 difference between what is recognized as tax expense and what is paid in taxes over the asset's depreciable life. The purchasing firm will record a deferred tax liability of $35,000 at the same time that it records the asset at $150,000. This tax liability will be reversed in future periods when taxable income exceeds financial ("book") income because of the lack of deductibility for the depreciation on the $100,000 excess of market over book value.

A deferred tax liability is not created with respect to any goodwill recorded in a purchase. A deferred tax liability is recorded with respect to only those asset values which normally would be available for tax deductions.

Tax Loss Carryovers. Tax law provides that a firm with a tax loss first may carry the loss back to the previous three years to offset income and thus receive a refund of taxes paid in the preceding years. If the loss exceeds income available in the prior three-year period, the loss can be carried forward up to fifteen years to offset future income and therefore reduce the taxes which otherwise would be paid. The selling firm may have unused tax loss carryovers which it has not been able to utilize due to an absence of sufficient income in prior years. This becomes a benefit for which the purchasing firm will pay. The purchaser is allowed to use the seller's tax loss carryovers to offset its own income in the current, prior, or if necessary, future periods. To the extent that the buyer can use the carryover to offset current income or income of the three prior years, the asset "tax refunds receivable" is recorded. If, however, the carryover is to be carried forward to offset future taxes, it becomes more difficult to record an asset. The asset "deferred tax expense" can be recorded only to the extent that the savings will be used in future periods to offset *existing* deferred tax liabilities.[11] For example, a tax loss carryforward could be recorded as an asset if it will offset future tax liabilities created by the earlier use of accelerated depreciation for tax and not financial reporting purposes. In later years the depreciation will be less for tax than for financial reporting purposes, and the deferred tax liability mounted in earlier years would be paid. The existence of the deferred tax expense then would be used as an offset.

There will be cases where the purchaser will pay for a tax loss carryforward that cannot be recorded because there are no deferred tax liabilities against which to offset it. The benefits of the tax loss carryforward cannot be realized until the future income materializes and the carryforward can offset

---

[11]*Statement of Financial Accounting Standards*, No. 96, "Accounting for Income Taxes" (Stamford: Financial Accounting Standards Board, 1987), pars. 17 and 50.

the earned income in order to reduce the taxes due. This presents a dilemma. The purchaser paid for an asset that cannot be recorded! The result is that the amount paid for the tax loss carryforward is included in the total price paid but cannot be assigned to the deferred tax expense account. Instead, the carryforward will end up in the general allocation of the price paid. Normally, the effect will be to increase the balance in the goodwill account. Then, when the benefits of the tax loss carryforward are realized, they will be recorded first as a reduction of the goodwill account, with any excess benefit being recorded as a reduction of tax expense in the period the credit is realized.

Consider an example of a purchase that includes both of the above tax ramifications. Farlow Inc. is purchasing Granada Company which has the following balance sheet on the purchase date:

Assets		Liabilities and Equity	
Inventory	$ 50,000	Liabilities	$180,000
Land	100,000	Common stock ($10 par)	100,000
Building	270,000	Retained earnings	70,000
Accum. depreciation	(70,000)		
Total assets	$350,000	Total liabilities and equity	$350,000

The market values of the land and the building are $120,000 and $300,000, respectively. Granada Company has a tax loss carryforward totaling $180,000 in operating losses. Farlow Inc. paid $325,000 for the net assets of Granada in a transaction structured as a nontaxable exchange. Farlow has an effective tax rate of 30% and has no future deferred tax liabilities against which the tax loss benefit can be offset. The price paid would be compared first to market values. The market values include the deferred tax liability caused by the excess of the building's market value over its book value.

Farlow would allocate its purchase price to the accounts in the following manner:

Price paid		$325,000
Market values of net assets:		
Inventory	$ 50,000	
Land	120,000	
Building	300,000	
Recorded liabilities	(180,000)	
Deferred tax liability, 30% × ($300,000 market value of building − $200,000 book value)	(30,000)	
Deferred tax expense (an asset), value of carryforward is 30% × $180,000 = $54,000; only the amount equal to the deferred tax liability recorded on the building may be recorded	30,000	290,000
Goodwill (includes the $24,000 unrecorded tax carryforward)		$ 35,000

The following entry would be made assuming that Farlow paid $325,000 cash:

Inventory	50,000	
Land	120,000	
Building	300,000	
Deferred Tax Expense	30,000	
Goodwill	35,000	
Liabilities		180,000
Deferred Tax Liability		30,000
Cash		325,000

Notice that the deferred tax expense and deferred tax liability are recorded separately, though they are offset in the statements. In future periods, the first $30,000 of the tax loss carryforward realized will be credited to the deferred tax expense account, and the excess will be credited to the goodwill account. If, at the time of realization, the goodwill balance is not able to absorb the entire credit, the remaining excess carryforward will reduce the tax expense of the period in which the carryforward is realized.

Contingencies. Special procedures should be followed when the seller has a contingent asset, liability, or asset impairment which exists on the date of the purchase. A contingency is "an existing condition, situation, or set of circumstances involving uncertainty as to possible gain or loss to an enterprise that will ultimately be resolved when one or more future events occur or fail to occur."[12] An example would be a lawsuit that existed before the purchase, or was filed shortly after the purchase but that involved an event that occurred prior to the purchase date.

When the existence of the contingent asset, liability, or asset impairment is probable and can be reasonably estimated, it should be recorded at the estimated amount as part of the allocation of the purchase price.[13] It is not necessary that the amount be probable and estimable on the date of the purchase. The assessments may be made subsequent to the purchase date during what is called the "allocation period," which is the time period when noncontingent assets and liabilities acquired in the purchase are quantified and valued. Normally, this period should not exceed one year. Amounts not recorded during the allocation period should be included in the income calculations for the period in which the amounts are determined.[14]

ISSUING SECURITIES AS CONSIDERATION

Many major business acquisitions involve the issuance of the purchaser's securities as payment. As previously stated, the use of securities preserves

---

[12]*Statement of Financial Accounting Standards, No. 5,* "Accounting for Contingencies" (Stamford: Financial Accounting Standards Board, 1975), par. 1.

[13]*Statement of Financial Accounting Standards, No. 38,* "Accounting for Preacquisition Contingencies of Purchased Enterprises" (Stamford: Financial Accounting Standards Board, 1980), par. 5.

[14]*Ibid.,* par. 6.

cash for the future operations of the buyer and may allow the transaction to qualify as a tax-free exchange for the seller. The principles for recording the purchase are not changed; only the recording of the consideration differs. The market value of the securities issued becomes the total consideration to be assigned to the acquired firm. The purchaser also must add the market value of the securities issued to its debt or paid-in capital. Using an earlier example which involved a $160,000 acquisition price for the net assets of Jacobs Company, assume that Acquisitions Inc. will issue its $2 par common stock as consideration. The total market value of the shares issued to Jacobs Company must equal the agreed upon net price of $160,000. Assuming a market value of $20 per share for its stock, Acquisitions Inc. must issue 8,000 shares ($160,000 ÷ $20). The following entry to record the purchase is identical to the entry on page 109, except that the addition to Acquisitions paid-in capital accounts is substituted for the cash payment.

Accounts Receivable (market value).................................	20,000	
Inventory (market value)...	45,000	
Land (appraised market value)	10,000	
Buildings (appraised market value).................................	50,000	
Equipment (appraised market value)	40,000	
Goodwill ($160,000 price minus sum of net market values		
plus $1,000 of acquisition costs).................................	16,000	
Current Liabilities (market value)		20,000
Common Stock (8,000 shares × $2 par)........................		16,000
Paid-In Capital in Excess of Par ($160,000 − $16,000		
par value)..		144,000
Cash (for acquisition costs)		1,000

Another form of consideration involves the issuance of the purchasing company's bonds for the assets of the acquired firm. Market values are recorded in the same manner as in the preceding entry. However, care must be taken to record properly the market value of the bonds issued. The applicable bond premium or discount must be recorded. For example, assume that Acquisitions Inc. plans to issue $1,000, 8% bonds in exchange for the $160,000 net assets of Jacobs Company. Normally, the purchaser would exchange 160 bonds ($160,000 ÷ $1,000 per bond) for the net assets of Jacobs Company. Assume, however, that on the settlement date the bonds have a market value of $990 each. Therefore, a discount of $1,600 ($10 per bond × 160 bonds) should be recorded. Assuming that the discount is settled by cash payment, the purchase would be recorded as follows:

Accounts Receivable...	20,000	
Inventory..	45,000	
Land...	10,000	
Buildings	50,000	
Equipment..	40,000	
Goodwill..	16,000	
Discount on Bonds Payable...	1,600	
Current Liabilities		20,000
Cash (acquisition cost plus discount on bonds)..............		2,600
Bonds Payable..		160,000

The resulting discount (or premium) must be amortized over the life of the bond issue. As an alternative to the cash payment, additional bonds could have been issued to compensate for the discount.

Any direct costs incurred to register and issue the securities are subtracted from the value assigned to the securities and are not treated as a direct acquisition cost. Had there been a $500 bond issuance cost in this example, a $2,100 deferred charge or increase in the discount would have been recorded.

[handwritten margin notes:]

Total of 160 bonds @ mkt $ 158,400 –
less: Issuance cost   500
Net market value   157,900
Bond par value   160,000
total discount $ 2,100 – * representing
                                       actual disc 1600
                                       plus direct costs

MIXING SECURITIES AS CONSIDERATION

The purchaser may exchange different types of securities in a single transaction. The differing securities may reflect the nature of the assets acquired. For example, the seller initially may desire debt or preferred equity securities equal to the market value of all assets, excluding goodwill. These securities provide a senior claim on earnings as well as on assets, should foreclosure become necessary. In this way, a preference in dissolution equal to the asset contribution of the purchased firm is provided. Typically, common stock is issued as payment for goodwill, reflecting the uncertainty involved in estimating this intangible asset.

Low-risk securities, however, have the disadvantage of lacking a long-run speculative appeal. Very likely, the seller will prefer to become a common stockholder if, at a later date, the acquiring firm prospers. Therefore, convertible debt or convertible equity securities may be used to satisfy both the seller's short-run security concern and long-run speculative interest. As an alternative to convertible securities, participating preferred stock may be used, since it offers a permanent preference on both assets and income by allowing full or limited participation with common stockholders in dividend distributions.

INCLUDING CONTINGENT CONSIDERATION IN A PURCHASE AGREEMENT

A purchase agreement may provide that the purchaser will transfer additional consideration to the seller, contingent upon the occurrence of specified future events or transactions. This consideration could involve the transfer of cash or other assets or the issuance of additional securities. During the period preceding the date on which the contingency is resolved, the purchaser has a contingent liability that is disclosed in a footnote to the financial statements but is not recorded.[15] On the date that the contingency is

---

[15]APB Opinion 16 (par. 78) provides that a liability is to be recorded if the amount of the contingent liability is determinable at the date of the acquisition. Of course, doing so would increase the price paid for the firm and would impact values assigned to the assets.

resolved, the contingent liability ceases, and the purchaser records any additional consideration as an adjustment to the original purchase transaction. The method used to make the adjustment is dependent upon the nature of the contingency.

Contingent Consideration Based on Earnings. A purchaser may agree to make a final payment contingent upon the earnings of the acquired firm during a specified future time period. If, during this period, the earnings of the acquired firm reach or exceed an agreed amount, further payment will be made at the end of the contingency period. In essence, the value of all or part of the goodwill is to be confirmed before full payment is made. Clearly, when an earnings contingency exists, the total price to be paid for the acquired firm is not known until the end of the contingency period. As is the case for the initial payment, the purchaser must record the fair market value of the consideration given, including the market value of additional securities issued. Normally, the amount of the additional payment will result in an increased amount of goodwill.[16] Adjustments to other assets would be made only if the contingency was based on their value.

To illustrate, assume that Company A acquires the assets of Company B on January 1, 19X2, in exchange for Company A common stock under conditions that require the acquisition to be recorded as a purchase. Also, Company A agrees to issue 10,000 additional common shares to the former stockholders of Company B on January 1, 19X5, if the acquired firm's average annual income before taxes for the three years reaches or exceeds $50,000. During the contingency period, Company A will disclose the contingent liability in the footnotes to its financial statements. If the earnings condition is met, Company A will record the final payment on January 1, 19X5 by increasing the goodwill account. Assuming that the 10,000 shares have a par value of $1 and a market value of $8 per share on January 1, 19X5, the following entry would be made:

Goodwill ($8 market value × 10,000 shares)	80,000	
Common Stock ($1 par × 10,000 shares)		10,000
Paid-In Capital in Excess of Par		70,000

Goodwill recorded as a result of a contingency payment must be amortized over the *remaining* life of the original goodwill. The period of amortization must end within 40 years of the original date of the combination. If, for example, a contingency involving goodwill is resolved 5 years after the original purchase, the added goodwill recorded can be amortized over a maximum of only 35 (40 − 5) years. No retroactive adjustment may be made for amortization applicable to prior periods.[17]

---

[16]When the contingency involves the value of an asset other than goodwill, that asset's value is to be adjusted as a result of the contingent payment. For example, with a contingency involving the value of a building, the value would be adjusted at the time the contingency was resolved and the added payment made.

[17]*Opinions of the Accounting Principles Board, No. 16,* "Business Combinations" (New York: American Institute of Certified Public Accountants, 1970), par. 80.

Contingent Consideration Based on Issuer's Security Prices. In exchange for its assets, a seller may be reluctant to accept the securities of the purchasing firm. This reluctance is caused by the seller's fear of a possible future decline in the market value of the securities. When a stock issuance is involved, the concern may be based, in part, on the dilutive effect of a significant increase in the number of shares outstanding. To combat this apprehension, the purchaser may guarantee the total value of the securities as of a given future date. The purchaser agrees to transfer additional assets or issue additional securities on that date for the amount by which the guaranteed value exceeds the market value on the date selected. For example, on January 1, 19X2, Company C issues 100,000 shares of its common stock, which has a $1 par value and a $12 market value per share, in exchange for the assets of Company D. The conditions of the exchange require the acquisition to be recorded as a purchase. The following summarized entry would be recorded:

Net Assets ($12 market value × 100,000 shares).......	1,200,000	
Common Stock ($1 par × 100,000 shares).............		100,000
Paid-In Capital in Excess of Par..........................		1,100,000

Company C guarantees the value of the stock at $12 per share as of January 1, 19X3. If necessary, additional consideration will be paid in cash. During the contingency period, Company C must disclose the contingent liability. Should the market price of the common stock be less than $12 per share on January 1, 19X3, additional consideration will be recorded.

Assume that on January 1, 19X3, the market value is $10 per share. Then $200,000 (100,000 shares × $2 per share deficiency) is the amount by which the guaranteed value of the shares exceeds the total market value. Company C will have to pay an additional $200,000 in cash. How should the payment be recorded? The payment is not based on a revaluation of the goodwill account, as is the case with an earnings contingency. Instead, the payment reflects the fact that the value assigned to the original security issuance was only an estimate, with the final amount to be determined later. To record the adjustment of the estimate, the original credit to Paid-In Capital should be decreased as shown by the following entry:

Paid-In Capital in Excess of Par.................................	200,000	
Cash...		200,000

In the preceding example, the value guaranteed was satisfied in cash. More often, the satisfaction will involve the issuance of additional securities. In that case, for example, Company C would issue 20,000 additional shares ($200,000 market value deficiency ÷ $10 current market value per share). Company C needs 120,000 shares to equate to the $1,200,000 original consideration, rather than the 100,000 shares previously issued. Accordingly, the $1,200,000 originally assigned to the 100,000 shares must be reassigned to 120,000 shares. The following entry will accomplish the reassignment:

Paid-In Capital in Excess of Par......................................	20,000	
Common Stock ($1 par × 20,000 shares).....................		20,000

Less frequently, price guarantees may apply to debt securities issued in a purchase transaction. Since bond prices react more to general money market conditions than to the operating performance of a particular firm, it is not common to guarantee their value. But when a price guarantee is used for bonds issued in a purchase, recording procedures parallel those used for stock. The settlement of a guarantee results in allocating the value assigned to the original bonds to a greater number of bonds. This allocation will decrease or eliminate an original premium and/or will increase or create a discount.

ASSET ACQUISITION AS A POOLING OF INTERESTS

A pooling of interests is a combination which must meet strict criteria to insure that there is a true fusion of existing interests. If the criteria are met, it is held that there is no basis for acknowledging market values since there has been no sale. Note that the terms of the exchange do consider the relative market values of the firms but that market values may not be acknowledged in accounting for the combination.

CRITERIA FOR THE USE OF THE POOLING METHOD

As previously mentioned, prior to the issuance of APB Opinion No. 16, many firms tended to ignore the then loosely defined criteria for the use of the purchase and pooling methods. A choice between the methods often was based on the impact of the methods on future financial statements. However, APB Opinion No. 16 states that the purchase and pooling methods are not alternative recording methods available for any given combination and that strict criteria have to be met in order for the combination to qualify as a pooling of interests. Any combination not meeting *all* of the criteria must be designated as a purchase. Thus the criteria seek to insure that only a true fusion of previous stockholder interests and assets will be accorded the pooling treatment. APB Opinion No. 16 classifies the criteria according to the attributes of the combining firms, the agreement as to how interests are to be combined, and the absence of planned subsequent transactions. The Opinion also introduces special terminology for referring to firms combining under the pooling method. The acquiring firm that will continue in existence is termed the *issuer*, while the acquired firm is termed the *combiner*. These terms will be used in subsequent discussions to avoid any connotation of a purchase-sale having occurred when the pooling method is appropriate.

Attributes of the Combining Firms. APB Opinion No. 16 (par. 46) provides two criteria that establish essential attributes of the combining firms.

Criterion 1. Each of the combining firms may not have been a subsidiary or division of another firm for two years preceding the date on which a plan of combination is initiated. The initiation date is the earliest date at which the stockholders of the combining firms are informed of the terms of the combination (including the stock exchange ratio) either through a public announcement or through written notification.

The intent of this condition is that a company should not be able to fragment a business enterprise and pool only part of it. For new firms created within the two years, this condition is applicable only to the firm's period of existence. For the purposes of this condition, a former subsidiary that was separated from the parent by government order is considered a "new" firm.

Criterion 2. Each of the combining firms must be independent of one another. On the date of initiation of the plan and until its consummation, no firm may own more than 10% of the voting common stock of any other combining firm. Shares acquired as a part of the plan of combination are exempted.

Agreement as to How Interests Are to be Combined. APB Opinion No. 16 (par. 47) provides seven criteria that relate to the manner in which interests are combined.

Criterion 1. The combination must be accomplished in a single transaction or in accordance with a specific plan, in which case the plan must be executed within one year of its initiation. One exception is allowed when there is a delay which is beyond the control of the combining firms. The only delays considered uncontrollable are (1) proceedings and deliberations of a federal or state regulatory agency on whether to approve or disapprove a combination where the combination cannot be effected without approval and (2) litigation aimed at prohibiting the combination.

The intent of this condition is to prevent a piecemeal, selective displacement of stockholders on possibly different terms.

Criterion 2. Subsequent to the initiation date, the issuer must issue its common stock for either all the assets of the combiner or at least 90% of the outstanding voting common shares of the combiner in a stock acquisition. The shares issued must have rights identical to those of the majority of the issuer's outstanding voting common shares.

For the purpose of the 90% provision, the computation of the combiner shares received excludes:

(a) Shares held by the issuer or its subsidiaries prior to the initiation date, and

(b) Shares acquired after the initiation date by giving any consideration other than the voting common shares of the issuer. Fractional shares acquired for cash cannot be considered in meeting the 90% provision.

To illustrate, assume that Company C (combiner) has 20,000 shares of voting common stock outstanding and that Company I (issuer) exchanges 8,500 shares of its voting common stock for 17,000 shares of Company C stock. Assume further that Company I, prior to the date of initiation, acquired 1,000 shares of Company C stock in exchange for its own shares. In addition, Company I paid cash for 500 shares of Company C stock as a part of the combination plan. Even though Company I holds 92.5% (18,500 ÷ 20,000) of Company C shares at the consummation date, the 90% rule is not met, and the combination must be accounted for as a purchase. The computations are as follows:

Shares owned by Company I.. 18,500
Less disqualified shares:
   Company C shares owned prior to initiation date 1,000
   Company C shares acquired after initiation date for cash..................... 500
Shares meeting the pooling requirement.................................... 17,000

Ownership interest for pooling criteria
(17,000 shares ÷ 20,000 outstanding shares).................................... 85%

The application of the 90% rule becomes more complex when the combiner holds shares of the issuer. To illustrate, assume that Company I issues 9,250 shares of its stock for 18,500 of the 20,000 shares of outstanding Company C stock subsequent to the initiation date of a plan of combination. In addition, assume that Company C previously acquired 500 shares of Company I stock. The following diagram summarizes the interfirm stock transactions:

	Company I	Company C
Prior to initiation date....................		Owns 500 shares of Company I stock
Subsequent to initiation date...........	Issues 9,250 shares of its stock to Company C ———————→ In exchange for 18,500 shares of ←——————— Company C stock	

According to the exchange ratio, 1 share of Company I stock is equal in value to 2 shares of Company C stock.[18] Thus, 1,000 (500 × 2) shares of Company C stock represent an equity in Company I. Viewed in another manner, the 1,000 shares of Company C stock support the investment in 500 shares of Company I stock. APB Opinion No. 16 would hold that on an equivalent share basis, 1,000 of the shares of Company C stock received by Company I are in essence a return of its own shares. Therefore, the equivalent shares must be subtracted from the total combiner shares held by the issuer on the consummation date. The 90% test is not met, and the combination must be accounted for as a purchase. The calculations are as follows:

---

[18]The exchange rate used is the actual resulting ratio at the consummation date. Any cash given for fractional shares will diminish the exchange rate.

Shares owned by Company I	18,500
Less disqualified shares:	
Equivalent number of Company C shares represented by Company C investment in Company I (500 × 2)	1,000
Shares meeting the pooling requirement	17,500

**Ownership interest for pooling criteria
(17,500 shares ÷ 20,000 outstanding shares)..................................... 87.5%**

If the combiner acquires shares of the issuer subsequent to the initiation date, these shares also are subtracted on an equivalent share basis from the total shares acquired by the issuer in determining compliance with the 90% rule.

The 90% criterion does allow partial payment using cash or other consideration for a minor portion of the shares. However, each combiner shareholder that is participating in the combination agreement must exchange *all* shares for those of the issuer. Cash or other consideration can be used only for fractional shares or for dissenting shareholders who will not be shareholders in the surviving firm.[19]

> *Criterion 3.* *The combining companies may not change their equity interests in contemplation of a combination for the period of time beginning two years before the intiation date and extending through the consummation date.*

The intent of this provision is to prevent a combiner from purchasing and reselling common shares in an attempt to create a group of shareholders who own 90% of the shares and who agree to combine. It is also the intent of the provision that the issuer be prevented from realigning its shareholders in an attempt to create a majority group who are willing to combine. Treasury stock purchases must be defended as normal and motivated by other purposes in order not to violate this condition. "Other purposes" would include, for example, acquisition of shares to satisfy employee stock option plans.

> *Criterion 4.* *Dividend distributions (other than in common stock) must be no greater than normal for two years before the initiation date through the consummation date.*

"Normal" is defined by reference to past dividend policy and earnings of the period. Greater than normal dividends would allow a firm to distribute part of its assets to shareholders and to pool only the residual. Thus, shareholders would receive part assets and part equity of the pooled firm, which is counter to the concept of pooling as a fusion of existing interests.

---

[19]*Opinions of the Accounting Principles Board, No. 16,* "Business Combinations" (New York: American Institute of Certified Public Accountants, 1970), par. 47b and *Accounting Interpretation No. 25 of APB Opinion No. 16,* "Business Combinations" (New York: AICPA, 1971).

Criterion 5. The voting common stockholders of the combiner must receive voting shares of the issuer proportionate to their holdings in the combiner.

For example, Mr. X., who owned 30% of Company Q voting common stock obtained by the issuer, must receive 30% of the issuer's voting common stock *in exchange* for shares of Company Q. In this way, the proportionate stockholder interests of the combiner are preserved.

Criterion 6. The voting rights of the resulting ownership interests are exercisable. There may be no deprivation or restriction of these rights for any time period.

An attempt to place the shares issued in a voting trust, for example, would violate this criterion.

Criterion 7. There can be no contingent consideration agreements based on events subsequent to the consummation date.

As addressed earlier, two types of contingent considerations are those involving future payments based on profits in subsequent periods and those involving an agreement which provides that the acquiring firm will compensate the acquired firm's shareholders for a decline in the value of the securities they receive as payment. Neither is allowed under the pooling criteria.

Absence of Planned Subsequent Transactions. Stipulations exist to prevent planned subsequent transactions that would counteract the conditions of a pooling of interests and allow a purchase to appear in the guise of a pooling. The pooling treatment is denied by APB Opinion No. 16 (par. 48) if any *one* of the following conditions is included explicitly or by intent in the negotiations and/or terms of the agreement to combine:

1. An agreement by which the issuer will retire or reacquire the common shares issued to effect the combination.
2. An agreement to aid financially a faction of the stockholders of the former combiner.
3. A plan to dispose of a significant part of the assets of the combining firms within two years of the consummation of the combination.[20]

POOLING OF INTERESTS ACCOUNTING

An asset acquisition deemed to be a pooling of interests requires that *all* of the assets and liabilities of the combiner be acquired in exchange for the is-

---

[20]APB Opinion No. 16 (par. 60) provides that if there is a material gain or loss on a sale of the assets of the previously separate firms within two years of a pooling, the gain or loss is shown as an extraordinary item.

suer common stock. Again, a pooling is viewed as a fusion of existing accounting entities, not as an exchange between entities. Assets, liabilities, and equities are combined at their existing book values. Adjustments to the accounts are allowed only to the extent that they would be proper for any firm in the course of normal operations. An example of a proper adjustment would be the write-down of inventory from cost to market value. Any adjustment to the assets or liabilities of the combiner also results in an adjustment to retained earnings for the impact of the change on the stockholders' equity of the combiner.

The combiner may have recorded a deferred tax expense for the benefits of a tax loss carryforward. If that is the case, the asset would be transferred to the issuer. In other cases, the combiner may have unrecorded tax loss carryforwards that did not qualify for recording as an asset since there were no future offsetting deferred tax liabilities. When the issuer does have the required offsetting deferred tax liabilities, the previously unrecorded tax loss carryforwards can be recorded as an asset, and the retained earnings of the combiner, which is being transferred to the issuer, is increased by the amount of that asset. *Dr. Deferred Tax Expense   Cr. Retained Earnings*

To illustrate the recording of a pooling of interests, the example used in an earlier purchase analysis is revised. Assume that Expansion Inc. (formerly Acquisitions Inc.) is going to pool with Jacobs Company by issuing common stock and that Expansion will be the surviving accounting entity. Expansion is the issuer, not the purchaser, and Jacobs is the combiner, not the seller. These terms emphasize that the firms are joint owners in a pooling and are not parties to an exchange. When the pooling is consummated, the *book values* of Jacobs Company will be recorded on the books of Expansion Inc.

The fact that market values are not recorded does not mean that they are ignored during negotiations preceding the combination. Both parties to a pooling must agree on the market values of the items involved in order to arrive at the number of issuer shares to be exchanged for the combiner's net assets.

Assume that the firms agree on the following values for the net assets of Jacobs Company:

	Book Value	Market Value
Accounts receivable	$ 20,000	$ 20,000
Inventory	40,000	45,000
Land	10,000	10,000
Buildings (net)	40,000	50,000
Equipment (net)	20,000	40,000
Current liabilities	(20,000)	(20,000)
Total	$110,000	$145,000

Expansion agrees that the value of goodwill is $15,000. To satisfy the $160,000 net asset value, Expansion will issue 8,000 shares of its common stock, with a par value of $2 and a market value of $20 per share. While negotiations and settlement are based on market values, these values are

ignored in recording the combination. If the combiner previously has recorded goodwill on its books, the goodwill is recorded also by the issuer at its book value. Book values of Jacobs Company are transferred to Expansion by recording the following entry:[21]

Accounts Receivable	20,000	
Inventory	40,000	
Land	10,000	
Buildings	40,000	
Equipment	20,000	
Current Liabilities		20,000
Common Stock (8,000 shares × $2 par)		16,000
Paid-In Capital in Excess of Par		44,000*
Retained Earnings		50,000

*($16,000 + $44,000 = $60,000, the total paid-in capital of Jacobs on the consummation date)

One difficult aspect of recording a pooling of interests is the combining of stockholders' equities. The total paid-in capital of the combiner must be carried as a unit to the total paid-in capital of the issuer. The composition of the combiner paid-in capital is ignored and is redistributed between the par or stated value and the additional paid-in capital of the issuer. In addition, recall that, in a pooling of interests, incomes of the combiner and issuer are combined retroactively for periods prior to the combination. This means that retained earnings balances of the combiner and issuer also are combined. Normally, the retained earnings of the combiner is added directly to the retained earnings of the issuer. The following chart summarizes the equity transfer of the previous entry:

Jacobs Company (combiner) Balances		Increase in Expansion Inc. (issuer) Balances	
Capital stock ($10 par)	$ 10,000	Capital stock ($2 par)	$ 16,000
Paid-in capital in excess of par	50,000	Paid-in capital in excess of par	44,000
Total paid-in capital	$ 60,000 →	Total paid-in capital	$ 60,000
Retained earnings	50,000 →	Retained earnings	50,000
Total equity	$110,000	Total equity	$110,000

Equity transfer rules must accommodate combinations in which the par or stated value of the shares issued exceeds the total paid-in capital of the combiner. This is a rare occurrence, since most firms have no par or very low par value shares. When this situation occurs, the issuer first must use its own paid-in capital in excess of par to cover the deficiency. Only when such an excess is depleted, or when it does not exist, may the combiner retained earnings be reduced. This is the only exception to the general rule that the retained earnings of the firms are combined. As an example, assume that in

---

[21]See Jacobs' balance sheet on page 107.

the previous situation Expansion was issuing $10 par stock and that all the other facts were unchanged. The issuer must add $80,000 (8,000 shares × $10 par) to its par value, while the total paid-in capital of the combiner is only $60,000. If the issuer has sufficient additional paid-in capital upon which to draw, the $20,000 deficiency would be met by reducing that account's balance as shown in the following chart:

Jacobs Company (combiner) Balances		Increase (Decrease) in Expansion Inc. (issuer) Balances	
Capital stock ($10 par).....................	$ 10,000	Capital stock ($10 par)...................	$ 80,000
Paid-in capital in excess of par..........	50,000	Paid-in capital in excess of par.........	(20,000)
Total paid-in capital......................	$ 60,000→	Total paid-in capital	$ 60,000
Retained earnings	50,000→	Retained earnings.........................	50,000
Total equity..............................	$110,000	Total equity	$110,000

Expansion's entry to record the pooling in this case would be:

Accounts Receivable..	20,000	
Inventory...	40,000	
Land..	10,000	
Buildings	40,000	
Equipment..	20,000	
Paid-In Capital in Excess of Par.....................................	20,000	
Current Liabilities		20,000
Common Stock ($10 par)..		80,000
Retained Earnings		50,000

If the issuer has no additional paid-in capital with which to meet the deficiency, the combiner retained earnings account would be used as shown in the following chart:

Jacobs Company (combiner) Balances		Reassignment	Increase in Expansion Inc. (issuer) Balances	
Capital stock ($10 par)..........	$ 10,000		Capital stock ($10 par)	$ 80,000
Paid-in capital in excess of par	50,000			
Total paid-in capital...........	$ 60,000	+20,000	Total paid-in capital	$ 80,000
Retained earnings	50,000	−20,000	Retained earnings..............	30,000
Total equity....................	$110,000		Total equity	$110,000

The entry to record the pooling then would be:

Accounts Receivable..	20,000	
Inventory...	40,000	
Land..	10,000	
Buildings	40,000	
Equipment..	20,000	
Current Liabilities		20,000
Common Stock ($10 par)..		80,000
Retained Earnings		30,000

In some cases, it may be necessary to consume all of the combiner retained earnings and draw upon the retained earnings of the issuer.

In a pooling, shareholders of the combiner must become shareholders of the continuing issuer. To accomplish the continuity of ownership, the combiner usually will dissolve itself by distributing the shares it receives from the issuer to its shareholders.

Pooling principles require that the assets of the combiner be recorded at book values and that combined assets may not be increased through the combination. Consequently, the direct costs of consummating the combination may not be capitalized as an asset. Similarly, the issuance cost of new securities may not be deducted from the value assigned to the securities. These expenditures, even though benefiting future periods, must be expensed entirely in the period that the acquisition occurs, according to APB Opinion No. 16 (par. 58). Assume that in the previous example Expansion paid $1,000 in direct acquisition costs. A separate entry would expense the cost as follows:

Professional Services Expense	1,000	
Cash		1,000

Another complication arises when an issuer uses previously issued and reacquired stock (treasury stock) to accomplish a pooling. In contemplation of the combination this treasury stock may not have been acquired in the two-year period preceding the business combination since such an acquisition of treasury shares would defeat a pooling criterion.[22] Pooling principles require that the book value of the combiner capital be assigned to stock issued in a pooling. Clearly, the issuer would violate these principles if it could reacquire previously issued shares and use their cost as the value assigned to the shares exchanged in the pooling. The problem that arises is: How does the issuer dispose of the difference between the price paid for the treasury shares and the value which must be assigned to them in a pooling of interests? The answer is: the treasury shares are treated as though they are retired. For instance, assume that Company E reacquired 10,000 shares of its common stock for $250,000 and later exchanged these shares for the assets of Company F. The summarized balance sheets of Companies E and F immediately prior to the pooling are as follows:

Company E (Issuer)

		Liabilities	$200,000
		Common stock (50,000 shares, $2 par)	100,000
		Retained earnings	700,000
		Less treasury stock at cost	(250,000)
Total assets	$750,000	Total liabilities and equity	$750,000

(10,000 sh @ $25-)

---

[22]*Accounting Interpretation No. 20 of Accounting Principles Board Opinion No. 16,* "Business Combinations" (New York: American Institute of Certified Public Accountants, 1971).

Company F (Combiner)

		Liabilities.........................	$ 50,000
		Common stock (20,000 shares, $1 par)..............	20,000
		Paid-in capital in excess of par	40,000
		Retained earnings	40,000
Total assets......................	$150,000	Total liabilities and equity...	$150,000

BOOK VALUE *60,000 ⊛*

In this case, the shares to be used in the combination were purchased for $25 each, but must carry a book value of $10 each (combiner equity of $100,000 ÷ 10,000 shares issued). *Since shares issued to accomplish a pooling must be treated as newly issued,* APB Opinion No. 16 (par. 54) requires that previously acquired shares be accounted for as though they were first retired. Therefore, Company E first should make a retirement entry for the 10,000 treasury shares as follows:

Treasury shares are retired

Common Stock (10,000 shares × $2 par)	20,000	
Retained Earnings	230,000	
Treasury Stock (at cost)		250,000

Then, the shares released to accomplish the pooling are recorded as newly issued:

Assets	150,000	
Liabilities		50,000
Common Stock (10,000 shares × $2 par)		20,000
Paid-In Capital in Excess of Par ($60,000 total paid-in − $20,000 par)		40,000
Retained Earnings		40,000

assignment See page 104

REPORTING REQUIREMENTS

As is true of all asset acquisitions, the purchase of another firm affects the financial statements of the purchaser only for periods following the purchase date. The comparability of current statements with statements of periods prior to the purchase is provided only by footnote disclosure of the estimation of what the financial information would have been had the purchase occurred at the beginning of the earliest period presented. Poolings of interests, however, require retroactive restatement, Thus all of the comparative financial statements are presented as they would have appeared had the pooled companies always been combined.

In a purchase or a pooling situation, the firms involved may have used different accounting principles to account for similar types of transactions. For example, one company might use Lifo inventory valuation, while the other may use Fifo. To achieve uniformity or to improve future reporting, it might be desirable to change the accounting principles of one or both members of the combination.

The following table summarizes the reporting requirements for business combinations:

Item	Purchase Method	Pooling Method
1. Change in accounting principles	Financial statements for previous periods restated retroactively. This procedure is an exception to the usual requirement to include in current income the cumulative effect of the change.[23]	Same as for a purchase.
2. Income earned in current year, prior to date of acquisition	Income of purchased firm included only as of purchase date. Disclose in footnote estimated income as if purchase had occurred at beginning of year. Estimate includes adjustments for asset and liability revaluations and goodwill amortization.	Income of both firms combined for entire period. Include in footnotes each firm's operating results for period prior to the combination.
3. Prior periods included in comparative statements	Only separate statements of parent shown. Disclose in footnote the estimated results as if purchase had occurred at the beginning of the comparative periods presented. Estimate includes adjustments for asset and liability revaluations and goodwill amortization.	Statements restated as if pooling occurred at beginning of the comparative periods presented. Intercompany transactions eliminated. Must disclose that statements of previously separate firms have been combined.

Let us study two examples of the impact of a business combination on comparative statements. Exhibit 1 on page 133 is a footnote from the 1985 financial statements of the Pennwalt Corporation. Notice that the terms of the purchase of the Turco-Purex business are disclosed, as is information concerning the allocation of the price paid to the assets acquired. Note also that disclosure is made of the impact that the purchase would have had on the current and previous period had it occurred at the start of the previous period. The footnote explains that the income of the acquired firm is not included in the body of the financial statements since the purchase occurred in

---

[23]*Opinions of the Accounting Principles Board*, No. 20, "Accounting Changes" (New York: American Institute of Certified Public Accountants, 1971), pars. 29 and 30.

the last month of the fiscal (calendar) year. Exhibit 2 on page 134 is a footnote from the 1985 financial statements of the Rubbermaid Corporation. The note explains that the statements of the periods presented have been restated to account retroactively for the pooling. The note then includes the separate operating results for the combiner and issuer for the portion of the year prior to the pooling and for two preceding years.

Exhibit 1

Pennwalt Corporation
Notes To Consolidated Financial Statements

3. Turco-Purex Acquisition

In December 1985, the Company acquired the Turco-Purex industrial business of Purex Industries Inc. ("Turco-Purex") for $34,500,000 in cash. Turco-Purex is a manufacturer of industrial cleaning products and aircraft maintenance chemicals and cleaners. The acquisition has been accounted for as a purchase transaction and the balance sheet of Turco-Purex has been consolidated with that of the Company effective December 31, 1985. No operating results of Turco-Purex are included in the Company's consolidated financial statements.

The purchase price was based on a preliminary determination of the net assets of Turco-Purex and may be adjusted subsequently upon final determination of such amount. The excess of the cost over the fair value of the net assets acquired is approximately $9,000,000 which will be amortized on a straight-line basis over 40 years or $225,000 annually. (Additionally, amortization of the Company's existing goodwill resulting from previous acquisitions amounted to approximately $225,000 in each of the years 1985, 1984 and 1983.)

Pro forma results of the Company's operations, assuming the acquisition had occurred at the beginning of 1984, are shown in the following table. These pro forma results have been prepared for comparative purposes only and do not purport to be indicative of what would have occurred had the acquisition been made at the beginning of 1984, or of results which may occur in the future.

	1985	1984
	(Millions of Dollars Except Per Share Amounts) (Unaudited)	
Net sales	$1,071.50	$1,042.2
Earnings from continuing operations	12.70	46.8
Net earnings (loss)	(18.20)	47.3
Per share:		
Earnings from continuing operations	$ .20	$ 3.41
Net earnings (loss)	(2.65)	3.45

Source: Jack Shohet and Richard Rikert, eds., *Accounting Trends and Techniques,* 40th ed. (New York: American Institute of Certified Public Accountants, 1986), 43.

Exhibit 2

Rubbermaid Incorporated
Notes To Consolidated Financial Statements
(Dollars in thousands except per share amounts)

2. (In Part): Acquisitions

In December 1985, 2,266,449 Common Shares were issued in exchange for all the outstanding Common Shares of Gott Corporation, a manufacturer of insulated chests, beverage coolers and other molded plastic products.

The acquisition has been accounted for as a pooling of interests, and accordingly the accompanying financial information has been restated to include the accounts of Gott Corporation for all periods presented. Gott Corporation financial information included in the accompanying consolidated financial statements has been converted from a fiscal year ending September 30 to the Company's calendar year basis of reporting.

Net sales and net earnings of the separate companies for the periods preceding the acquisition were:

	Eleven months ended November 30, 1985	Years ended December 31, 1984	Years ended December 31, 1983
Net sales:			
Rubbermaid	$570,337	$566,429	$479,584
Gott	55,996	42,706	32,124
Combined	$626,333	$609,135	$511,708
Net earnings:			
Rubbermaid	$ 50,466	$ 46,870	$ 39,575
Gott	3,358	2,558	2,222
Combined	$ 53,824	$ 49,428	$ 41,797

Source: Jack Shohet and Richard Rikert, eds., *Accounting Trends and Techniques,* 40th ed. (New York: American Institute of Certified Public Accountants, 1986), 40.

QUESTIONS

1. Income tax issues may be a motivation for firms to enter into a business combination. Suggest how income tax considerations may influence the desire of both parties in a combination.

2. Describe the two basic methods by which control of another firm's assets might be obtained. Which method would most likely involve a lower total cost? What are the ramifications of each method on accounting procedures in future periods?

3. Compare the balance sheet ramifications of a purchase versus a pooling of interests. Include the effects on assets, liabilities, and equity. Why

might a pooling of interests create a balance sheet with a more profitable appearance?

4. Explain why the asset values recorded in a pooling of interests will tend to result in higher future net incomes than if the combination were recorded as a purchase.

5. The firm being purchased has the total market values of $150,000 and $30,000 for its assets and liabilities, respectively. The acquiring firm issues 2,000 shares of common stock with a $10 par and a $60 market value per share for the net assets. What entry would be needed by the acquiring firm to record this transaction under the purchase method?

6. The firm being purchased has long-lived assets with a market value of $200,000. What are the accounting consequences of paying a price that is $50,000 in excess of the market value of the identifiable net assets? What happens if the price paid is $40,000 less than the value of the identifiable net assets?

7. Under the purchase method, which accounts always are recorded at full market value by the acquiring firm? Why are only these accounts given this priority? What procedure is used when the price paid for the firm is less than the total market value of these "priority" accounts?

8. What procedures should be followed in recording long-term bonds assumed in the purchase of another firm when interest rates have increased substantially since the bonds were issued?

9. A company that has been acquired is a party to several leases, in the capacity of both a lessee and a lessor. In each of the following situations, indicate which accounts should be used and state how to arrive at an amount:

   (a) The company is a lessee on a 2-year operating lease. The rent is below that which would be paid if currently negotiated.

   (b) The company is a lessee under a capital lease with a 6-year remaining term.

   (c) The company is a lessor under an operating lease with a remaining term of 3 years. The rents are below current rental value.

   (d) The company is a lessor under a direct financing (capital) lease with a 4-year remaining term. Title to the asset passes to the lessee at the end of the term.

10. A firm is contemplating the purchase of another company in a transaction that qualifies as a nontaxable exchange for tax purposes. The market values of the assets purchased are in excess of their book values. What are the accounting ramifications of purchasing this firm at a price high enough to result in the recording of goodwill?

11. The company being purchased has a tax loss carryover of $300,000 that it has not been able to utilize. The purchasing firm has an effective tax rate of 30%. The purchasing firm will be able to carryback $100,000 to obtain a tax refund, and the balance will be carried forward. How will the purchasing firm record the tax loss carryforward assuming that it (a) has deferred future tax liabilities available to offset and (b) has no deferred tax liabilities?

12. Company P acquired Company S at a price far in excess of the market value of its identifiable net assets. Pursuant to an earnings contingency, an additional payment is made 10 years later. How is this payment recorded, and what are the limitations concerning the allocation of the added amount to future periods?

13. An acquiring firm guaranteed that if the total market value of the 2,000 shares of $10 par stock issued in an acquisition fell below $120,000 on January 1, 19XX, additional shares would be issued to make up the deficiency. What entry would be made on January 1, 19XX, if the market value of the stock dropped to $40 per share?

14. How are the voting common stockholders of the combiner assured "equality of treatment" by the pooling of interests criteria?

15. One of the criteria to be met in order to use the pooling method is the 90% stock acquisition rule. Specifically, how and when must the stock of the combiner be obtained if it is to be included in the qualifying 90% of the combiner outstanding stock?

16. What uses are made of market values in a business combination accomplished through a pooling of interests versus a combination accomplished through a purchase?

17. Under the purchase and pooling methods, what recognition is given to previously recorded goodwill (goodwill already recorded on the books of the acquired firm) by the acquiring firm?

18. In a pooling of interests, how are the total paid-in capital and retained earnings of the combiner recorded on the books of the issuer? Describe the "basic equity transfer" rule.

19. How are direct acquisition costs, indirect acquisition costs, and issue costs recorded under (a) the purchase method and (b) the pooling method?

20. Assuming that a business combination occurs at midyear, contrast the reporting requirements of a purchase versus pooling concerning income earned during the year.

21. Company A is acquiring Company B on the last day of the fiscal reporting period of both firms. Company B has had substantial income in previous periods. What is the basic impact of the combination on the three years of comparative income and retained earnings statements to be provided if the combination is recorded as (a) a purchase and (b) a pooling? Include mention of related footnote disclosures.

EXERCISES

Present value tables are on pages 1178 and 1179.

Exercise 1. Ardell Company is contemplating the acquisition of Karns Corporation on January 1, 19X1, at which time it is anticipated that Karns Corporation will have the following balance sheet:

Karns Corporation
Pro Forma Balance Sheet
January 1, 19X1

Assets		Liabilities and Equity		
Current assets...........	$125,000	Current liabilities.......		$ 30,000
		Stockholders' equity:		
Property, plant, and		Common stock		
equipment:		($10 par)	$80,000	
Building (net)	80,000	Retained earnings ..	95,000	175,000
		Total liabilities		
Total assets...............	$205,000	and equity............		$205,000

Market values agree with book values, except for the building which has a market value of $220,000.

Ardell will issue 20,000 shares of its $5 par stock, with a market value of $22 per share, to acquire Karns. It has not been determined whether the transaction meets the criteria for a pooling of interests.

Ardell Company is concerned about the effect of a purchase versus a pooling on future income statements. An accountant has been asked to compare 19X1 income under both the pooling and purchase methods. For Ardell and Karns in 19X1 the accountant estimated combined revenues of $180,000 and combined expenses of $120,000, excluding depreciation of Karns' building and amortization of any goodwill resulting from the acquisition of Karns. Straight-line depreciation will be used for the building which has a 20-year remaining life. If any goodwill results, a 10-year amortization period would be assumed.

Compare the net incomes for the combined firm for 19X1 under the purchase and pooling methods. Prepare adequate support for all calculations. Ignore income tax consequences.

Exercise 2.   Apollo Company is considering the acquisition of Daphne Company. The following balance sheet of Daphne Company has been prepared:

Daphne Company
Balance Sheet
December 31, 19X1

Assets		Liabilities and Equity		
Current assets..........	$260,000	Total liabilities		$400,000
Property, plant, and		Capital stock		
equipment (net).....	650,000	($10 par)	$160,000	
		Retained earnings.....	350,000	510,000
Total assets..............	$910,000	Total liabilities and equity..........		$910,000

An appraisal has indicated that the market value of the current assets is approximately equal to their book value. The appraisal provided a market value of $740,000 for the property, plant, and equipment. Apollo Company predicts that Daphne Company will provide an average annual net income of $150,000 in future years. This income is above the 12% per year return on tangible assets which is considered normal for the industry.

(1) Prepare an estimate of goodwill, based on each of the following assumptions:
   (a) The purchaser paid for five years of excess earnings.
   (b) Excess earnings will continue for five years and should be capitalized at the normal industry rate of return.
   (c) Excess earnings will occur forever, but they should be capitalized at the higher rate of return of 20% due to the risk involved in such an asset.
(2) Determine the actual goodwill to be recorded if Apollo Company pays $800,000 cash and assumes the liabilities of Daphne Company.

Exercise 3. Borner Company is willing to pay $700,000 for the net assets of Nells Company, which has the following balance sheet on the purchase date:

Nells Company
Balance Sheet
December 31, 19X1

Assets			Liabilities and Equity		
Current assets:			Liabilities......................		$ 80,000
Accounts receivable...	$ 35,000		Stockholders' equity:		
Inventory..................	50,000	$ 85,000	Common stock		
Property, plant, and			($10 par)...............	$100,000	
equipment:			Paid-in capital in		
Land.........................	$ 40,000		excess of par..........	160,000	
Building (net)	250,000		Retained earnings......	245,000	505,000
Equipment (net).........	210,000	500,000	Total liabilities		
Total assets.................		$585,000	and equity		$585,000

The following market values have been secured for the assets and liabilities of Nells Company:

Inventory...	$ 60,000	10,000
Building and land	340,000	50,000
Equipment..	150,000	(60,000)
Liabilities (including unrecorded interest)....	81,200	1,200

To consummate the transaction, Borner must spend $10,000 to cover direct acquisition costs.
(1) On Borner's books, record the purchase of the net assets of Nells Company assuming Borner pays Nells $700,000 in cash.
(2) On Nells' books, record the sale of the net assets for $700,000.
(3) On Borner's books, record the purchase of all of the common stock of Nells Company for $700,000 plus acquisition costs.
(4) Assuming that all of the shares purchased in (3) were acquired from existing shareholders of Nells Company, what entry would be needed on the books of Nells Company to record Borner's purchase?

Exercise 4.   Thomas Company merged into Simonson Corporation on July 1, 19X1. The combination must be treated as a purchase because some of the pooling criteria were not met. Simonson exhanged 50,000 shares of its $5 par stock, with a market value of $22 per share, for the net assets of Thomas Company. Simonson Corporation paid cash for the following costs as a result of the transaction:

Direct acquisition costs	$10,000
Indirect acquisition costs............................	15,000
Costs to register and issue stock..................	20,000
Total costs	$45,000

Immediately prior to the merger, Thomas Company's balance sheet was as follows:

Thomas Company
Balance Sheet
July 1, 19X1

Assets			Liabilities and Equity		
Current assets..............		$340,000	Current liabilities..........		$ 70,000
Equipment under			Liability under capital		
capital lease (net)		175,000	lease		100,000
Property, plant, and equipment:			Bonds payable		300,000
Land........................	$200,000		Stockholders' equity:		
Buildings (net)...........	150,000	350,000	Common stock		
			($10 par)................	$200,000	
			Paid-in capital in		
			excess of par..........	100,000	
			Retained earnings......	95,000	395,000
			Total liabilities		
Total assets.................		$865,000	and equity		$865,000

The asset and liability under lease, the plant assets, and the bonds payable have market values that differ from book values. The appraised market values are:

Equipment under capital lease....................	$220,000
Land..	150,000
Buildings	300,000
Liability under capital lease	95,000
Bonds payable	285,000

Record the purchase of the net assets of Thomas Company by Simonson Corporation.

Exercise 5.   Santo Corporation has agreed to purchase the net assets of Barnet Corporation. Just prior to the purchase, Barnet's balance sheet was as follows:

Barnet Corporation
Balance Sheet
January 1, 19X1

Assets		Liabilities and Equity		
Current assets..........	$220,000	Current liabilities		$ 80,000
Equipment (net)........	100,000	Stockholders' equity:		
		Common stock		
		($10 par)	$100,000	
		Retained earnings..	140,000	240,000
		Total liabilities		
Total assets..............	$320,000	and equity.............		$320,000

Market values agree with book values except for the equipment which has an estimated market value of $40,000. Santo Corporation paid $10,000 in direct acquisition costs and $15,000 in indirect acquisition costs to consummate the transaction.

Record the purchase on the books of Santo Corporation assuming that the cash paid to Barnet Corporation was (a) $160,000 and (b) $90,000.

Exercise 6. Monty Company is about to purchase the net assets of Halgo Inc. On December 31, 19X6, Halgo had the following balance sheet:

Assets		Liabilities and Equity	
Current assets..................	$120,000	Liabilities.........................	$ 80,000
Land and buildings (net)....	200,000	Common stock ($10 par)....	200,000
Equipment (net)................	40,000	Retained earnings.............	140,000
Goodwill..........................	60,000		
Total assets.....................	$420,000	Total liabilities and equity..	$420,000

Monty has obtained the following market values for certain accounts of Halgo Inc.:

Current assets...	$100,000
Land and buildings..................................	150,000
Equipment..	100,000
Liabilities...	85,000

Prepare the entry by Monty Company to record the purchase of the net assets of Halgo Inc. on Dec. 31, 19X6, for $215,000 in cash.

Exercise 7. Arnold Company purchased the net assets of Blum Company in a business combination accounted for as a purchase. As a result, goodwill was recorded. For tax purposes, this combination was considered to be a nontaxable exchange.

One of Blum's assets that Arnold purchased was a building with an appraised value of $150,000 at the date of the business combination. This asset had a book value for Blum of $90,000, which was net of depreciation based on the sum-of-the-years-digits method used for financial reporting. The building is depreciated using the straight-line method for tax purposes and has a tax basis of $100,000. Based on this information and assuming a 30% income tax rate, state the accounts and the amounts that Arnold should record as related to the building? (AICPA adapted)

Exercise 8. Keefe Company had the following balance sheet on Dec. 31, 19X1, when it was purchased for $800,000 in cash by the Townsand Corporation:

Keefe Company
Balance Sheet
December 31, 19X1

Assets		Liabilities and Equity		
Current assets..........	$120,000	Current liabilities		$ 50,000
Equipment (net)........	160,000	Stockholders' equity:		
Building (net)	200,000	Common stock		
		($5 par)..............	$ 50,000	
		Retained earnings ..	380,000	430,000
		Total liabilities		
Total assets..............	$480,000	and equity.............		$480,000

The equipment has a market value of $200,000; all the other assets have market values equal to their book values. The combination is structured as a tax-free exchange. Keefe Company has a tax loss carryforward of $400,000 which it has not recorded. Townsand Corporation feels that it can use all of the carryover, $100,000 of which it can use to offset past income and generate a refund. Townsand is taxed at a rate of 30%.

Record the purchase assuming that Townsand Corporation (a) has $400,000 of prior deferred tax liabilities which is available for offset and (b) has no deferred tax liabilities prior to the combination.

Exercise 9. Kinn Corporation purchased Faber Company and properly recorded the following entry on January 1, 19X1:

Current Assets	120,000	
Equipment...	210,000	
Land and Building..	320,000	
Goodwill..	50,000	
Common Stock ($5 par)......		50,000
Paid-In Capital in Excess of Par................................		650,000

Record the appropriate entries on January 1, 19X4, assuming that 800 additional shares worth $65 each are issued (a) to satisfy a price guarantee relative to the value of the shares and (b) to satisfy an earnings contingency.

Exercise 10. Oak Corporation desires to pool with Elm Company. Elm has a total of 50,000 shares outstanding. Oak will issue three shares of its stock in exchange for five shares of Elm Company. On the initiation date, Oak owns 1,000 shares of Elm stock, and a wholly-owned subsidiary of Oak owns 1,400 shares of Elm stock.

One year after the initiation date, Oak issued 27,600 shares of its stock in exchange for additional shares in Elm Company according to the planned exchange rate. Oak also purchased 1,600 shares of Elm stock for cash.

Determine the number of shares of Elm stock that is eligible for meeting the 90% requirement necessary to treat the acquisition as a pooling of interests. Has the 90% requirement been satisfied?

Exercise 11. Company P holds 96,000 shares of Company S common stock on December 31, 19X6. Of these shares, 92,000 were acquired after the initiation date of the business combination by issuing one share of Company P stock in exchange for every five shares of Company S stock, 2,000 shares were purchased after the initiation date using cash, and 2,000 shares were acquired prior to the initiation date on the one-for-five exchange basis. On the initiation date, Company S held 500 shares of Company P stock. At all times, there were 100,000 shares of Company S common stock outstanding.

Analyze the combination to see if it qualifies as a pooling of interests.

Exercise 12. Imperial Corporation and Cisco Corporation have agreed to merge in a transaction that will qualify as a pooling of interests. Imperial Corporation will issue the required number of previously unissued shares of $5 par common stock in exchange for all of the net assets of Cisco Corporation. The number of shares issued will be based on the assumed market value of $48 per share of Imperial common stock and on the fair market value of Cisco Corporation.

Immediately prior to the pooling, Cisco Corporation prepared the following summarized balance sheet:

Cisco Corporation
Balance Sheet
December 31, 19X1

Assets		Liabilities and Equity	
Current assets................	$ 450,000	Current liabilities............	$ 100,000
Property, plant,		Bonds payable	800,000
and equipment............	2,000,000	Common stock ($10 par)..	250,000
Accumulated		Retained earnings...........	950,000
depreciation................	(500,000)		
Goodwill........................	150,000		
		Total liabilities	
Total assets....................	$2,100,000	and equity	$2,100,000

Current assets and liabilities are recorded at amounts approximating their market values. The following appraisals have been made:

Property, plant, and equipment................	$1,550,000
Goodwill..	200,000
Bonds payable	780,000

In consummating the transaction, Imperial Corporation spent $5,000 for direct acquisition costs and $15,000 for registering and issuing the shares of stock used to acquire Cisco Corporation.

(1) Determine the number of shares of stock that Imperial Corporation will issue.

(2) Record the pooling of interests on the books of Imperial Corporation.
(3) What entry would Cisco Corporation make to record the receipt of the shares and their distribution to shareholders in order to liquidate the corporation?

Exercise 13. Lakeside Company will be the issuer in a pooling of interests with Birchwood Company. The two firms had the following summarized balance sheets just prior to the pooling:

Assets		Lakeside		Birchwood
Current assets.........................		$ 50,000		$ 40,000
Property, plant, and equipment............................		750,000		312,500
Accumulated depreciation........		(250,000)		(62,500)
Other assets...........................		30,000		10,000
Total assets...........................		$580,000		$300,000
Liabilities and Equity				
Accounts payable....................		$ 40,000		$ 30,000
Accrued liabilities....................		10,000		—
Common stock........................	($20 par)	200,000	($10 par)	100,000
Paid-in capital in excess of par..		50,000		10,000
Retained earnings...................		280,000		160,000
Total liabilities and equity.........		$580,000		$300,000

Record the pooling of interests on Lakeside Company's books in each of the following situations:
(1) The pooling agreement requires Lakeside to issue 8,000 shares of its $20 par stock for the net assets of Birchwood Company.
(2) The pooling agreement requires Lakeside to issue 12,500 shares of its $20 par stock for the net assets of Birchwood Company. Lakeside also will pay $20,000 for stock registration and issuance costs.

Exercise 14. On December 31, 19X6, Cole Company and Bond Company entered into a business combination appropriately accounted for as a pooling of interests. A new company, Gold Corporation, was formed with 500,000 authorized shares of no-par, $1 stated-value common stock. The management of Gold did not intend to retain either Cole or Bond as subsidiaries.

On December 31, 19X6, Gold issued its common stock in exchange for all of the outstanding common stock of Cole and Bond as follows:

Cole: 300,000 shares of Gold common stock for all 10,000 outstanding shares of the $5 par common stock of Cole.

Bond: 200,000 shares of Gold common stock for all 4,000 outstanding shares of the $10 par common stock of Bond.

There were no intercompany transactions between these firms.

Following are the condensed financial statements of Cole and Bond for the year ended December 31, 19X6, prior to the pooling of interests.

Balance Sheets

Assets	Cole Company	Bond Company
Current assets..	$260,000	$235,000
Property, plant, and equipment (net)...........................	410,000	320,000
Other assets...	90,000	65,000
Total assets...	$760,000	$620,000

Liabilities and Stockholders' Equity

	Cole Company	Bond Company
Current liabilities	$167,000	$124,000
Long-term debt	300,000	—
Common stock..	50,000	40,000
Paid-in capital in excess of par...................................	10,000	160,000
Retained earnings...	233,000	296,000
Total liabilities and stockholders' equity.......................	$760,000	$620,000

Income and Retained Earnings Statement

	Cole Company	Bond Company
Net sales	$1,600,000	$2,200,000
Costs and expenses:		
Cost of goods sold..	($1,120,000)	($1,560,000)
Operating and other expenses	(330,000)	(480,000)
Total costs and expenses................................	($1,450,000)	($2,040,000)
Net income...	150,000	160,000
Retained earnings, January 1, 19X6.......................	83,000	136,000
Retained earnings, December 31, 19X6...................	$ 233,000	$ 296,000

Cole values its inventory using the Fifo method; Bond uses the Lifo method for its inventory. Bond agreed to change its method of inventory valuation from Lifo to Fifo prior to the business combination.

Bond began operations on January 1, 19X5, and data relevant to Bond's inventory account are as follows:

	Lifo	Fifo
Inventory, December 31, 19X5.......	$42,000	$62,000
Inventory, December 31, 19X6.......	55,000	85,000

(1) Prepare the adjusting journal entry to be made by Bond Company on December 31, 19X6, to change its inventory from Lifo to Fifo valuation. Income taxes should not be considered in the solution.
(2) Prepare a schedule computing pooled retained earnings of Gold Corporation as of December 31, 19X6.
(3) Prepare the December 31, 19X6 journal entry on the books of Gold Corporation to record the business combination as a pooling of interests.

(AICPA adapted)

Exercise 15. Ender Corporation has agreed to exchange 10,000 shares currently held as treasury stock for the net assets of Dopp Corporation. Just prior to the exchange, the two firms had the following summarized balance sheets:

Assets		Ender		Dopp
Current assets.........................		$ 350,000		$ 240,000
Property, plant, and equipment (net)		1,300,000		760,000
Total assets...........................		$1,650,000		$1,000,000
Liabilities and Equity				
Current liabilities		$ 170,000		$ 90,000
Common stock......................	($10 par)	1,000,000	($1 par)	30,000
Paid-in capital in excess of par................................		100,000		240,000
Retained earnings...................		460,000		640,000
Treasury stock at cost		(80,000)		—
Total liabilities and equity........		$1,650,000		$1,000,000

Prepare the journal entries for Ender Corporation to record the pooling of interests. (Prepare a retirement entry for the treasury stock prior to recording the pooling.)

Exercise 16. Northern Corporation acquired the net assets of West Company on January 1, 19X1, when West Company had the following summarized balance sheet:

West Company
Balance Sheet
January 1, 19X1

Assets		Liabilities and Equity		
Current assets......................	$ 40,000	Current liabilities		$ 40,000
Property, plant, and equipment (net).................	150,000	Stockholders' equity: Common stock ($10 par).....	$ 10,000	
Goodwill............................	60,000	Paid-in capital in excess of par..................	40,000	
		Retained earnings................	160,000	210,000
Total assets.........................	$250,000	Total liabilities and equity......		$250,000

Northern arrived at the following market values for the West Company's assets and liabilities:

Current assets...	$ 50,000
Property, plant, and equipment..................	200,000
Current liabilities	42,000

Northern agreed to issue 8%, $1,000, 10-year bonds in an amount equal to the market value of West's net assets other than goodwill. The bonds had a market value based on a current effective interest rate of 10% per year. Any fractional bond equivalent will be paid in cash. Northern also agreed to issue

500 shares of its $10 par common stock as additional consideration. The stock has a market value of $12 per share.

(1) Calculate the price paid for the net assets of West Company.
(2) Record the acquisition on the books of Northern Company.

PROBLEMS

Problem 3-1.   Link-Rich Company is being formed to consolidate the operations of the former separate Link Corporation and Rich Company. Prior to the consolidation, Link Corporation and Rich Company have the following balance sheets on December 31, 19X1:

Assets	Link	Rich
Current assets...	$ 140,000	$ 50,000
Long-term investment in marketable securities (at cost)...................................	220,000	35,000
Land..	120,000	50,000
Buildings (net)..	350,000	210,000
Equipment (net)...	410,000	125,000
Total assets..	$1,240,000	$470,000

Liabilities and Equity		
Current liabilities	$ 160,000	$ 55,000
Bonds payable	200,000	100,000
Common stock ($10 par).............................	400,000	180,000
Retained earnings.......................................	480,000	135,000
Total liabilities and equity...........................	$1,240,000	$470,000

The following market values are agreed upon by the two firms:

Assets	Link	Rich
Current assets..........................	$160,000	$ 50,000
Marketable securities	270,000	30,000
Land.......................................	100,000	60,000
Buildings	350,000	350,000
Equipment...............................	500,000	250,000
Goodwill..................................	170,000	45,000

Newly formed Link-Rich Company will issue 24,000 shares of its $10 par stock to acquire the net assets of Link Corporation and will issue 12,000 of the shares to acquire the net assets of Rich Company. The new company will incur $10,000 of direct acquisition costs and $15,000 of registration and stock issuance costs.

Required:
Record the acquisition on the books of Link-Rich Company, using purchase accounting principles.

Problem 3-2. Use the facts of Problem 3-1 for the creation of Link-Rich Company. Assume, however, that the pooling criteria are met. Be sure to record market values where they are less than recorded book values.

Required:
Record the combination on the books of Link-Rich Company, using pooling of interests principles.

Problem 3-3. Martin Company is planning to purchase the net assets of Companies A and B. The following balance sheets of the two firms on January 1, 19X8 were secured:

Assets	Company A	Company B
Current assets...	$ 150,000	$ 110,000
Property, plant, and equipment (net)......................	1,200,000	980,000
Goodwill...	100,000	90,000
Total assets...	$1,450,000	$1,180,000

Liabilities and Equity		
Current liabilities	$ 140,000	$ 120,000
Bonds payable, 10%...	400,000	—
Bonds payable, 9%	—	300,000
Common stock ($10 par)......................................	500,000	400,000
Retained earnings..	410,000	360,000
Total liabilities and equity...................................	$1,450,000	$1,180,000

Martin Company has agreed that market values equal book values, except for the goodwill and the bonds payable. For these accounts, the following information was found:

(a) The market rate of interest for bonds similar to those of Companies A and B is 12% on January 1, 19X8, the date of acquisition. The Company A 10% bonds are 10-year bonds that initially were issued on January 1, 19X3. The Company B 9% bonds are 20-year bonds that initially were issued on January 1, 19X6. Both bonds pay interest annually on December 31.

(b) The industry average rate of return for firms like A and B is 10% on tangible gross assets. In the past, Companies A and B have had the following net incomes:

Year	Company A	Company B
19X3	$120,000	$100,000
19X4	160,000	90,000
19X5	115,000	120,000
19X6	150,000	130,000
19X7	165,000	135,000

Martin will pay for average earnings in excess of the industry norm. Such excess earnings will be capitalized at 16% on the assumption of a 5-year life.

Required:

(1) Calculate the price paid for Company A and Company B. Include complete calculations for the present value of the bonds and for the estimate of the goodwill. (Note: Incomes may be used as recorded without adjustment for interest.)

(2) Using the values calculated in (1), prepare the journal entries recorded by Martin Company to account for the purchase.

Problem 3-4. Maynard Steel Company is considering the purchase of North Steel Company. At this point, Maynard is evaluating the accounting ramifications of alternative prices it might pay. The balance sheet of North Steel Company is as follows on Dec. 31, 19X1:

North Steel Company
Balance Sheet
December 31, 19X1

Assets			Liabilities and Equity		
Current assets:			Liabilities:		
Accounts receivable...	$ 80,000		Accounts payable		$ 20,000
Inventory	200,000	$280,000	Equity:		
			Common stock		
			($10 par)	$ 40,000	
Noncurrent assets:			Paid-in capital in		
Land........................	$ 20,000		excess of par..........	110,000	
Building (net)	40,000	60,000	Retained earnings......	170,000	320,000
			Total liabilities		
Total assets.................		$340,000	and equity		$340,000

The following market values differ from existing book values:

Inventory	$300,000
Land..	30,000
Building..	30,000

Required:

Record the purchase of North Steel Company at each of the following total prices paid in cash for its net assets:

(a) $480,000

(b) $400,000

(c) $340,000

Problem 3-5. Mittco Corporation is planning to acquire the net assets of Barns Company in a transaction that will not meet the pooling criteria.

Mittco Corporation will issue to Barns either common stock or bonds for the assets received. The balance sheet of Barns Company just prior to the acquisition is as follows:

Mittco Corporation
Balance Sheet
December 31, 19X1

Assets		Liabilities and Equity	
Cash.............................	$ 40,000	Accounts payable	$ 70,000
Marketable securities	80,000	Bonds payable	300,000
Accounts receivable..........	130,000	Common stock ($10 par)....	40,000
Inventory	110,000	Paid-in capital in excess	
Land..............................	40,000	of par	110,000
Buildings (net)..................	150,000	Retained earnings.............	210,000
Equipment (net)................	60,000		
Goodwill..........................	40,000		
Patents...........................	80,000		
Total assets.....................	$730,000	Total liabilities and equity..	$730,000

The following market values are secured for the assets of the Barns Company:

Marketable securities	$ 85,000
Accounts receivable....................................	130,000
Inventory	75,000
Land..	70,000
Buildings	140,000
Equipment...	105,000
Patent..	35,000

Required:
(1) Assume that Mittco Corporation will issue 20,000 shares of its common stock, with a par value of $2 and a market value of $18 per share, for the net assets, exclusive of cash, of Barns Company.
  (a) Prepare the entry to record the purchase on the books of Mittco Corporation.
  (b) Prepare the entry to record the sale on the books of Barns Company.
(2) Assume that Mittco Corporation will issue 200, $1,000 bonds, which currently are quoted at 98, for the net assets, exclusive of cash, of Barns Company.
  (a) Prepare the entry to record the purchase on the books of Mittco Corporation.
  (b) Prepare the entry to record the sale on the books of Barns Company.

Problem 3-6.   Sensor Inc. purchased for $1,800,000 in cash the net assets of All-Equipment Leasing Company. The purchase was made on December 31, 19X1, at which time All-Equipment had prepared the following balance sheet:

All-Equipment Leasing Company
Balance Sheet
December 31, 19X1

Assets		Liabilities and Equity	
Current assets............................	$ 100,000	Current liabilities	$ 150,000
Assets under operating leases	520,000	Obligation under capital	
Net investment in direct		lease of equipment..................	35,000
financing (capital) leases	730,000	Common stock ($5 par)...............	100,000
Leased equipment under		Paid-in capital in excess	
capital lease (net)	40,000	of par.....................................	400,000
Buildings (net)............................	200,000	Retained earnings......................	955,000
Land...	50,000		
Total assets..............................	$1,640,000	Total liabilities and equity............	$1,640,000

The following information is available concerning the assets and liabilities of All-Equipment:

(a) Current assets and liabilities are stated fairly. No payments resulting from leases are included in current accounts, since all payments are due each December 31 and payment for 19X1 has been made.

(b) Assets under operating leases have an estimated value of $580,000. This figure includes consideration of remaining rents and the value of the assets at the end of the lease terms.

(c) The net investment in direct financing leases represents receivables at their discounted present values. All leases are written at the current market interest rate of 12%, except one equipment lease requiring payments of $50,000 per year for 5 remaining years. The $50,000 payments include interest at 8%.

(d) The buildings and the land have appraised market values of $400,000 and $100,000, respectively.

(e) The leased equipment under the capital lease pertains to a computer used by All-Equipment. The obligation under the capital lease of equipment includes the present value of 5 remaining payments of $9,233 due at the end of each year and discounted at 10%. The current interest rate for this type of transaction is 12%. The market value of the equipment under the lease is $60,000.

(f) All-Equipment has been named in a $200,000 lawsuit involving an accident by a lessee using its equipment. It is likely that All-Equipment will be found liable in the amount of $50,000.

Required:

Record the purchase of All-Equipment Leasing Company by Sensor Inc. Carefully support your entry.

Problem 3-7. Ewald Corporation is purchasing the net assets of Vilter Company for an agreed price of $900,000 on December 31, 19X1. The purchase is structured to be a tax-free exchange as to the seller, meaning that Ewald Corporation will be able to deduct only the book value of the assets acquired in future tax returns. Ewald will issue its no-par common shares with a market value of $5 each to accomplish the purchase. The effective tax rate of Ewald Corporation is 30%. Vilter Company has the following balance sheet on the date of the purchase:

Vilter Company
Balance Sheet
December 31, 19X1

Assets			Liabilities and Equity		
Current assets:			Liabilities:		
Marketable					
securities..................	$ 30,000		Accounts payable	$ 50,000	
Accounts receivable...	90,000		Bonds payable, 10%...	200,000	$250,000
Inventory..................	300,000	$420,000	Equity:		
Property, plant,			Common stock		
and equipment:			($10 par)...............	$100,000	
Land.........................	$ 50,000		Paid-in capital in		
Building (net)............	350,000		excess of par..........	300,000	
Equipment (net).........	100,000	500,000	Retained earnings......	310,000	710,000
Intangible assets:					
Goodwill....................		40,000	Total liabilities		
Total assets.................		$960,000	and equity		$960,000

The following market values are not in agreement with book values:

Marketable securities	$ 50,000
Inventory...	400,000
Land..	60,000
Building...	400,000

The building has a 10-year life, the goodwill is amortized over 10 years, and the inventory was sold during 19X2.

Required:
(1) Record the purchase giving recognition to any tax issues.
(2) Provide the entry to adjust the deferred tax liability account at the end of 19X2.

Problem 3-8.   Pond Company is offering to purchase the net assets of Great Company, which has prepared the following summarized balance sheet as of December 31, 19X1:

Assets		Liabilities and Equity	
Current assets..................	$ 70,000	Current liabilities	$ 85,000
Property, plant,		Common stock ($10 par)....	100,000
and equipment (net)	220,000	Retained earnings.............	185,000
Goodwill.........................	80,000		
Total assets.....................	$370,000	Total liabilities and equity..	$370,000

The market value of the property, plant, and equipment is $250,000.

Pond Company has given Great Company two offers to consider:
(a) Pond will purchase the net assets for $400,000 cash. After three years, Pond will pay cash for average annual earnings of the former Great Company which are in excess of the industry average of 10% per year on gross assets. Pond will pay an amount equal to four years of average excess earnings.
(b) Pond will issue 10,000 shares of its common stock with a $5 stated value and $45 market value per share (December 31, 19X1) for the net assets of Great. One year later, Pond will issue additional stock to Great for any amount by which the value of the shares transferred falls below $42 per share. Fractional shares will be rounded to the nearest whole share.

Required:
(1) Assume that Great Company chooses offer (a) and that income of the former company is $61,000, $52,000, and $70,000 for the next three years.
   (a) Prepare the journal entry Pond Company would make on December 31, 19X1, to record the purchase.
   (b) Prepare the journal entry (if any) Pond Company would make on December 31, 19X4, to record contingent consideration.
(2) Assume that Great Company chooses offer (b) and that the market value of Pond Company stock falls to $35 per share on December 31, 19X2.
   (a) Prepare the journal entry Pond Company would make on December 31, 19X1, to record the purchase.
   (b) Prepare the journal entry (if any) Pond Company would make on December 31, 19X2, to record contingent consideration.

Problem 3-9.   Sullivan Company is offering to exchange 80,000 shares of its common stock on a one-to-one basis for the common stock of Rausch Corporation. The transaction will meet the criteria for a pooling of interests. The stockholders' equity of Sullivan Company on January 1, 19X1 is as follows:

Common stock ($2 par value, 250,000 shares outstanding)	$500,000
Paid-in capital in excess of par	150,000
Retained earnings	700,000

Rausch Corporation has the following summarized balance sheet on December 31, 19X1:

Assets		Liabilities and Equity	
Accounts receivable	$ 180,000	Accounts payable	$ 240,000
Inventory	410,000	Common stock ($5 par,	
Land	120,000	80,000 shares outstanding)	400,000
Building (net)	730,000	Paid-in capital in excess of par	200,000
		Retained earnings	600,000
Total assets	$1,440,000	Total liabilities and equity	$1,440,000

The building has been depreciated using the sum-of-the-years-digits method. Sullivan Company will use the straight-line method of depreciation to be consistent with its own policy. The cumulative effect of the change on previous periods is to decrease past depreciation charges by $60,000.

Required:

(Ignore tax effects.)

(1) Record the pooling of interests on the books of Sullivan Company.

(2) Assume, instead, that Sullivan Company has 83,333 shares of $6 par value common stock outstanding. Record the pooling of interests on the books of Sullivan Company.

(3) Assume, instead, that Sullivan Company has 50,000 shares of $10 par value common stock outstanding. Record the pooling of interests on the books of Sullivan Company.

Problem 3-10. Blunt Corporation merged into Acron Corporation on August 31, 19X6, with Blunt Corporation going out of existence. Both corporations had fiscal years ending on August 31, and Acron Corporation will retain this fiscal year. Prior to the merger, the following balance sheets were obtained:

Assets	Acron	Blunt
Current assets	$ 4,350,000	$ 3,200,000
Property, plant, and equipment (net)	18,500,000	11,100,000
Patents	450,000	200,000
Market research	—	40,000
Total assets	$23,300,000	$14,540,000

Liabilities and Equity	Acron	Blunt
Current liabilities	$ 2,650,000	$ 2,100,000
Common stock ($10 par) ..1,200,000 shares	12,000,000	—
Common stock ($5 par) ..750,000 shares	—	3,750,000
Paid-in capital in excess of par	4,200,000	3,200,000
Retained earnings	5,700,000	5,490,000
Treasury stock at cost ..100,000 shares	(1,250,000)	—
Total liabilities and capital	$23,300,000	$14,540,000

The following information was obtained as of the date of the merger:

(a) The fair market values of the assets and liabilities on August 31 were:

	Acron	Blunt
Current assets	$ 4,950,000	$ 3,400,000
Property, plant, and equipment	22,000,000	14,000,000
Patents	570,000	360,000
Market research	150,000	40,000
Total assets	$27,670,000	$17,800,000
Liabilities	(2,650,000)	(2,100,000)
Net assets	$25,020,000	$15,700,000

(b) Acron Corporation believes that its past market research has a value of $150,000; however, all past expenditures have been expensed as required by FASB Statement No. 2. Blunt Corporation spent $50,000 on September 1, 19X5, for research and development. The amount was capitalized and is being amortized over five years.

(c) Direct acquisition costs incurred because of the merger were $25,000 and are included in the current assets of Acron Corporation as a prepaid expense.

(d) There were no intercompany transactions during the year.
(e) Before the merger, Acron had 3,000,000 shares of common stock authorized, 1,200,000 shares issued, and 1,100,000 shares outstanding. Blunt had 750,000 shares of common stock authorized, issued, and outstanding.

Required:

(1) Assume that Acron Corporation exchanged 400,000 shares of previously unissued common stock and 100,000 shares of treasury stock for all of the outstanding common stock of Blunt Corporation. All of the conditions for a pooling of interests were met. Prepare a pro forma balance sheet to give effect to the merger.

(2) Assume that Acron Corporation purchased the assets and assumed the liabilities of Blunt Corporation by paying $3,400,000 in cash and issuing debentures of $16,900,000 at face value. Prepare a pro forma balance sheet to give effect to the merger.   (AICPA adapted)

Problem 3-11. In a business combination to be accounted for as a pooling of interests, Blazer Corporation will issue 40,000 shares of its common stock that has a market value of $20 ($10 par value) per share in exchange for the net assets, including cash, of Clinton Corporation on December 31, 19X6. Just prior to the exchange, Blazer and Clinton had the following balance sheets:

Assets	Blazer	Clinton
Cash..	$ 180,000	$ 80,000
Accounts receivable.................	400,000	200,000
Inventories.............................	475,000	190,000
Property, plant, and equipment (net)	1,100,000	600,000
Total assets.............................	$2,155,000	$1,070,000
Liabilities and Equity		
Current liabilities	$ 300,000	$ 140,000
Bonds payable	—	300,000
Common stock......................... ($10 par)	1,500,000 ($5 par)	200,000
Paid-in capital in excess of par..	—	150,000
Retained earnings....................	355,000	280,000
Total liabilities and equity.........	$2,155,000	$1,070,000

Blazer and Clinton, both of which were organized on January 1, 19X4, have agreed that Clinton's Accounts Receivable should be adjusted to give effect to uncollectibles on an aging basis. Clinton previously had used the direct write-off method. The two firms also decided that Clinton should change from the Fifo method of valuing inventory to the Lifo method. The board of directors of Clinton Corporation agreed that these adjustments will be made on a retroactive basis.

Additional data on Clinton Corporation follows:

Age of receivables (in months)...........	0–1	2–3	4–6	Over 6
Amount of receivables	$100,000	$60,000	$30,000	$10,000
Percent deemed uncollectible	1%	3%	5%	10%

End-of-the-year inventories:

	Fifo	Lifo
19X5	$180,000	$150,000	30,000
19X6	190,000	146,000	44,000 -

Income statement data before giving effect to the above information:

	19X5		19X6	
	Blazer	Clinton	Blazer	Clinton
Sales	$1,000,000	$600,000	$1,200,000	$650,000
Cost of sales	580,000	400,000	696,000	430,000
Operating expenses	150,000	100,000	200,000	110,000
	270,000	100,000	304,000	110,000

Required:
(1) Prepare a pro forma balance sheet to give effect to the business combination regarded as a pooling of interests.
(2) Prepare a comparative income statement for the years 19X5 and 19X6 for the combined corporation. (Ignore income taxes.)

Problem 3-12.   Financial statements of Dove Corporation and Martin Corporation appear as follows:

Balance Sheets
June 30, 19X6

Assets	Dove Corporation	Martin Corporation
Cash	$ 45,000	$ 1,500
Receivables (net)	33,000	10,000
Inventories	52,000	8,800
Due from Martin Corporation	7,600	—
Property, plant, and equipment (net)	69,500	35,800
Other assets	4,500	500
Total assets	$211,600	$56,600

Liabilities and Equity		
Accounts and notes payable	$ 50,600	$35,400
Due to Don Corporation	—	7,600
Accrued expenses	1,500	2,200
Federal income tax payable	9,500	—
Total liabilities	$ 61,600	$45,200
Capital stock ($10 par)	$ 50,000	—
Capital stock ($100 par)	—	$25,000
Paid-in capital in excess of par	30,000	32,000	57,000 -
Retained earnings, Dec. 31, 19X5	62,700	(38,600)
Net income (loss) from Jan. 1, 19X6, to June 30, 19X6	9,800	(7,000)	(45,600)
Dividends paid	(2,500)	—
Total equity	$150,000	$11,400
Total liabilities and equity	$211,600	$56,600

Income Statements
For Six Months Ended June 30, 19X6

	Dove Corporation	Martin Corporation
Sales...	$150,000	$60,000
Cost of goods sold...	(110,000)	(54,000)
Gross profit..	$ 40,000	$ 6,000
Operating expenses.......................................	(31,000)	(8,200)
Operating profit (loss)...............................	$ 9,000	$ (2,200)
Other income (deductions)	5,000	(4,800)
Income (loss) before tax..................................	$ 14,000	$ (7,000)
Provisions for income tax................................	(4,200)	—
Net income...	$ 9,800	$ (7,000)

On July 1, 19X6, Martin Corporation transferred to Dove Corporation all of its assets, subject to all liabilities, in exchange for unissued Dove Corporation capital stock. Since their inception in 19X0, both corporations have been owned by the same group of stockholders, although in different proportions as to individuals. The terms of the merger provided that the fair value of the stock in each case is to be its book value, except that an allowance is to be made for the value of any net operating loss carryovers. Obtaining the benefit of the tax loss carryover deduction was not the principal purpose for the merger. Dove Corporation is certain that any tax loss carryforward will be realized. (Assume a 30% tax rate.)

The income before income taxes and the losses that are available as tax loss carrybacks are as follows for the two corporations (income per books and taxable income are the same):

	Dove Corporation	Martin Corporation
19X3	$14,900	$(22,000)
19X4	31,200	(8,000)
19X5	28,900	(12,000)

Required:

(1) Compute the number of shares of Dove Corporation stock (a) to be distributed to the shareholders of Martin Corporation and (b) to be exchanged for each share of Martin stock.

(2) For the books of Dove Corporation, prepare the journal entry to record the merger with Martin as a pooling of interests. The acquisition should be recorded in a manner that will allow the combined income statement prepared for 19X6 to include the nominal accounts of both firms for the entire year.

(3) For the books of Martin Corporation, prepare the journal entries to record the merger with Dove, the distribution of Dove Corporation stock to the stockholders of Martin Corporation, and the dissolution of Martin Corporation.   (AICPA adapted)

Problem 3-13. P Corporation acquired all of the outstanding stock of S Corporation as of June 30, 19X7. As consideration for the acquisition, P Corporation gave the stockholders of S Corporation $550,000 and 500,000 shares of previously unissued common stock. P Corporation stock had a par value $500,000 of $1 and a quoted market value of $2.50 per share both before and after this transaction. $1,250,000

The balance sheet of S Corporation as of June 30, 19X7, was as follows:

Assets

Current assets:

Cash..	$120,000	
Accounts receivable..	240,000	
Inventories...	210,000	$ 570,000

Property, plant, and equipment:

	Cost	Accumulated Depreciation	Net	
Property A........................	$ 310,000	$160,000	$150,000	
Property B........................	370,000	170,000	200,000	
Property C........................	480,000	180,000	300,000	
Property D........................	250,000	150,000	100,000	
	$1,410,000	$660,000		750,000

Total assets...	$1,320,000

Liabilities and Stockholders' Equity

Accounts payable		$ 470,000
Stockholders' equity:		
Common stock, 500,000 shares authorized and outstanding ($1 par)	$500,000	3 600,000
Paid-in capital in excess of par................................	100,000	
Retained earnings...	250,000	850,000
Total liabilities and stockholders' equity......................		$1,320,000

All receivables are considered collectible. Inventories are stated at cost, which is also equivalent to replacement cost and is not in excess of market value. Properties B, C, and D have been appraised at $600,000, $800,000, and $200,000, respectively. Goodwill is not considered to be a significant factor in this business.

An engineer of P Corporation estimates that the properties of S Corporation will have a 10-year useful life from July 1, 19X7, with no salvage value at the end of that period. P Corporation uses the straight-line method of depreciating its assets.

On July 1, 19X7, S Corporation sold Property A for $500,000 and reported a net income of $450,000 for the six months ended December 31, 19X7. The net income included the gain from the sale of Property A and depreciation expense of $55,000.

The balance sheet of S Corporation at December 31, 19X7, was as follows:

Assets

Current assets:
Cash... $390,000
Accounts receivable... 355,000
Inventories.. 260,000 $1,005,000

Property, plant, and equipment:

	Cost	Accumulated Depreciation	Net
Property B	$ 370,000	$188,500	$181,500
Property C	480,000	204,000	276,000
Property D	250,000	162,500	87,500
	$1,100,000	$555,000	

PP&E net: 545,000

Total assets... $1,550,000

Liabilities and Stockholders' Equity

Accounts payable .... $ 250,000
Stockholders' equity:
Common stock.. $500,000
Paid-in capital in excess of par.............................. 100,000
Retained earnings... 700,000   1,300,000
Total liabilities and stockholders' equity...................... $1,550,000

On January 1, 19X8, S Corporation was dissolved, and all of its assets were transferred to and its liabilities assumed by P Corporation. The transaction is to be accounted for as a purchase and not as a pooling of interests.

Required:
(1) Prepare the journal entry of P Corporation to record its investment in S Corporation as of June 30, 19X7.
(2) Prepare the journal entries to record the accounts of S Corporation on the books of P Corporation upon the dissolution of S Corporation, and explain how the amounts were determined. (Disregard income tax implications.)   (AICPA adapted)

Note: This is a bargain purchase, such that long-lived assets will be recorded at less than full market value.

CHAPTER 4

CONSOLIDATED STATEMENTS AT THE DATE OF ACQUISITION

Accounting for business combinations where control is accomplished by an acquisition of assets was the concern of the preceding chapter. Control over another firm's assets also can be achieved indirectly by purchasing a controlling interest in the firm's voting common stock. Legally, the controlling parent firm has only an investment in the other firm, the subsidiary. However, the parent is able to control the subsidiary's operations, and the subsidiary's operations often will become integrated with those of the parent. When control through stock ownership exists, consolidated statements are necessary to erase the legal boundaries between the parent and subsidiary and to present the financial statements of the unified group as those of a single business entity. This chapter is the first of several which attempt to build a comprehensive set of principles and methods for the preparation of consolidated statements.

CONDITIONS FOR CONSOLIDATED STATEMENTS

Consolidated financial statements are designed to present the results of operations and the financial position of the parent and its subsidiaries *as if they were one firm.* Consolidated statements are more informative to the owners of the parent firm than are statements of the individual entities; but consolidated statements are not sufficient for the stockholders or the creditors of the individual entities. The rights of the minority stockholders extend only to the entity whose shares they hold. Creditors may look only to the legal entity that is indebted to them for satisfaction of their claims. Therefore, to be adequately informed, both minority shareholders and creditors require financial statements of the separate entities.

Generally, statements are consolidated when a parent firm owns, either directly or indirectly, over 50% of the voting common stock of another company. This means that if Company A owns 51% of the voting common stock of Company B and Company B owns 51% of the voting common stock of Company C, the statements of all three firms should be consolidated. The only exceptions to consolidating when control through stock ownership exists is if control of the subsidiary is only temporary or does not rest with the majority owner. Control would be assumed to not reside with a majority owner, for example, when the subsidiary is in bankruptcy or in legal reorganization, or when foreign exchange restrictions or foreign governmental controls cast doubt on the ability of the parent to exercise control over the subsidiary.

Prior to 1988, it was acceptable to exclude subsidiaries from consolidation when their operations were not homogeneous with those of the parent. For example, it was common for a manufacturing-based parent to exclude from consolidations those subsidiaries involved in banking, financing, or leasing activities. But this exception for "nonhomogeneity" came under criticism. Frequently, firms diversified and excluded varying subsidiaries from consolidation. This meant that a significant amount of assets, liabilities, and cash flows were not presented. The option of not consolidating subsidiaries was often a form of "off-balance sheet" financing. For example, a boat manufacturer could use a financing subsidiary to borrow funds from nonaffiliated lenders. The financing subsidiary then could loan funds to dealers and retail buyers in order to finance their boat purchases. By not consolidating the subsidiary under the nonhomogeneity exception, the accounts of the subsidiary, including the large debt, would not appear in the boat manufacturer's statements. Investors are interested in the total financial position of the corporation in which they own stock, regardless of how diversified its operations become. Based on these concerns and the divergence in practice as to consolidation policy, the nonhomogeneity exception was eliminated by FASB Statement No. 94.[1] In addition, the statement eliminated less commonly used exceptions for large minority interests and foreign locations.

Subsidiaries which are not consolidated because they are an exception to the requirement to consolidate are shown on the balance sheet as long-term investments. The accounting procedures for these investments are discussed in Chapter 10.

TECHNIQUE OF CONSOLIDATION

This chapter seeks to build an understanding of the techniques used to consolidate the separate balance sheets of a parent and its subsidiary immediately subsequent to the acquisition. The consolidated balance sheet as of the acquisition date is discussed first to focus on the combining of the balance sheet accounts, without the complication of subsequent operating results.

---

[1]*Statement of Financial Accounting Standards, No. 94,* "Consolidation of All Majority-owned Subsidiaries" (Stamford: Financial Accounting Standards Board, 1987).

The impact of consolidations on operating results is discussed in Chapters 5 through 10.

Chapter 3 pointed out that there are two basic means by which a company may gain control over the assets of another firm. A firm may acquire directly the assets of another firm, or it may purchase a controlling interest in the other firm's common stock. In an asset acquisition, the firm over which control is sought is dissolved. In a *stock* acquisition, the acquired firm is preserved as a *separate* legal and *accounting* entity. While initial accounting for the two types of acquisitions is significantly different, both types have the same practical effect of creating one larger reporting entity, and thus both should produce the *same* balance sheet. In the following discussion, the recording of the two types of acquisitions is compared, and the balance sheet that results from each type is presented.

REVIEWING AN ASSET ACQUISITION

Illustration 4–1 demonstrates an asset acquisition of Company S by Company P for cash. Part A of the exhibit presents the balance sheets of the two firms just prior to the acquisition. Part B shows the entry to record Company P's payment of $500,000 in cash for the net assets of Company S. The book values of the assets and liabilities acquired are assumed to be representative of their market values, and no goodwill is acknowledged. The assets and liabilities of Company S are added to those of Company P to produce the balance sheet for the combined firm, shown in Part C. Since account balances are combined in recording the acquisition, statements for the single combined reporting entity are produced *automatically*, and no consolidation process is needed.

Illustration 4–1

Asset Acquisition

A. Balance sheets of Companies P and S prior to acquisition:

Company P Balance Sheet

Assets		Liabilities and Equity	
Cash	$ 600,000	Current liabilities	$ 150,000
Accounts receivable	300,000	Bonds payable	300,000
Inventory	100,000	Common stock	100,000
Equipment (net)	150,000	Retained earnings	600,000
Total	$1,150,000	Total	$1,150,000

(continued)

Company S Balance Sheet

Assets		Liabilities and Equity	
Accounts receivable........	$200,000	Current liabilities	$100,000
Inventory.......................	100,000	Common stock...............	200,000
Equipment (net)	300,000	Retained earnings...........	300,000
Total	$600,000	Total...........................	$600,000

B. Entry to record acquisition of the net assets of Company S by Company P:

Accounts Receivable	200,000	
Inventory	100,000	
Equipment	300,000	
Current Liabilities...		100,000
Cash..		500,000

C. Balance sheet of Company P subsequent to asset acquisition:

Company P Balance Sheet

Assets		Liabilities and Equity	
Cash	$ 100,000	Current liabilities	$ 250,000
Accounts receivable......	500,000	Bonds payable	300,000
Inventory.....................	200,000	Common stock.............	100,000
Equipment (net)	450,000	Retained earnings.........	600,000
Total	$1,250,000	Total........................	$1,250,000

CONSOLIDATING A STOCK ACQUISITION

In a stock acquisition, the acquiring firm deals with existing stockholders only, not the firm itself. Assuming the same facts as those used in Illustration 4–1, except that Company P purchases all of the outstanding stock of Company S for $500,000, Company P would make the following entry:

Investment in Subsidiary S..	500,000	
Cash...		500,000

This entry does not acknowledge the underlying net assets over which control is achieved. Instead, the acquisition is recorded as an investment which represents controlling interest in the net assets. If no further action were taken, the investment in subsidiary account would appear as a long-term investment on the balance sheet of Company P. However, this presentation is permitted only if one of the rare exceptions to the requirement for consolidating statements exists.

Assuming that consolidated statements are required, the balance sheets of the separate firms must be combined into a consolidated balance sheet for the single resulting reporting entity. The consolidation process is a supplement to the existing accounting records of the firms. The process begins with the two firms' individual balance sheets from which the accounts representing the intercompany investment must be eliminated.

The consolidation process is demonstrated in Worksheet 4–1, pages 212–213. (Worksheets referred to in a chapter are at the end of the chapter and in the text's companion book.) The stockholders' equity accounts of the subsidiary are eliminated against the investment in subsidiary account of the parent. These accounts *do not appear* on a consolidated balance sheet. The equity accounts of the subsidiary have no economic substance, since the only common stock owned by parties outside the consolidated firm are the shares issued by the parent company. The investment in subsidiary account is not needed, as it will be replaced by the specific assets and liabilities of the subsidiary.

After the intercompany investment accounts are eliminated, the account balances of the two firms are combined. Worksheet 4–1 leads to the following formal consolidated balance sheet of Companies P and S:

Company P and Subsidiary Company S
Consolidated Balance Sheet
December 31, 19X1

Assets			Liabilities and Equity		
Current assets:			Current liabilities		$ 250,000
Cash..................	$100,000		Bonds payable		300,000
Accounts			Stockholders' equity:		
receivable.........	500,000		Common stock.....	$100,000	
Inventory.............	200,000	$ 800,000	Retained		
Equipment (net).......		450,000	earnings	600,000	700,000
			Total liabilities		
Total assets.............		$1,250,000	and equity		$1,250,000

This balance sheet is exactly the same as the balance sheet prepared for the asset acquisition in Part C of Illustration 4–1. This result is the objective of the consolidation process.

The format of Worksheet 4–1 should be analyzed carefully since it will be used in subsequent examples. It is acceptable to use a single line for like accounts of both firms. However, stockholders' equity accounts are shown on separate lines because the subsidiary equity is partially or entirely eliminated, while the equity of the parent survives as the controlling interest in the consolidated firm. Thus, separation of the equities will avoid confusion when the elimination entries are made.

It must be emphasized again that the consolidated financial statements are only a supplement to the statements of the separate firms. Eliminations are made *only* on the *worksheet* and are *not* recorded on the books of either firm. Since consolidation eliminations are *never recorded*, the consolidation process starts anew *each year* from the statements of the separate firms.

More detailed processes for preparing a consolidated balance sheet will be examined as follows in the remainder of this chapter:

Consolidating a purchase
  Parent owns 100% (no minority interest exists)
  Parent owns less than 100% (a minority interest exists)
Consolidating a pooling of interests

A STOCK ACQUISITION ACCOUNTED FOR AS A PURCHASE

The acquisition of a controlling interest in another firm must be analyzed before it can be recorded. When 90% or more of another firm's voting common stock is obtained and all other pooling criteria are met, the transaction must be recorded according to pooling procedures. All stock acquisitions not meeting the pooling criteria must be recorded under purchase procedures. Since most stock acquisitions do not qualify for the pooling treatment, the purchase treatment is discussed first.

When a stock acquisition is recorded as a purchase, the investment in the stock of the subsidiary is recorded at the fair market value of the property received or the securities issued, whichever is more readily determinable. The market value of the securities issued must be added to the total paid-in capital of the parent.

To illustrate, assume that Company P has the following balance sheet on December 31, 19X1, just prior to acquiring Company S:

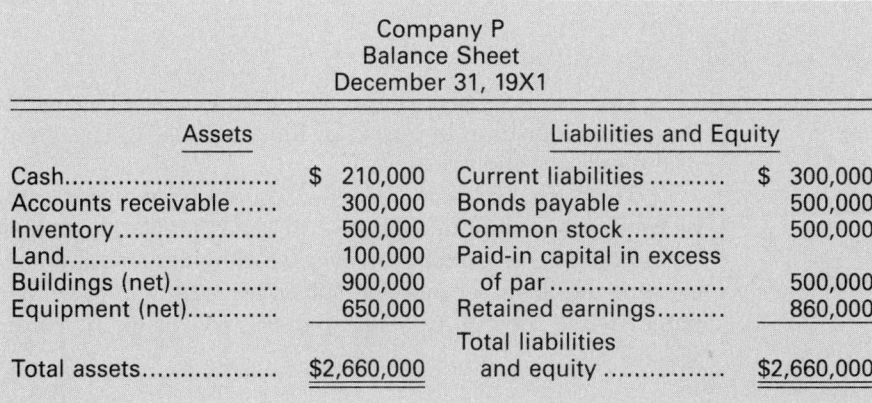

Company P Balance Sheet December 31, 19X1			
Assets		**Liabilities and Equity**	
Cash............................	$ 210,000	Current liabilities	$ 300,000
Accounts receivable......	300,000	Bonds payable	500,000
Inventory.....................	500,000	Common stock.............	500,000
Land............................	100,000	Paid-in capital in excess	
Buildings (net)..............	900,000	of par.......................	500,000
Equipment (net)............	650,000	Retained earnings.........	860,000
		Total liabilities	
Total assets..................	$2,660,000	and equity	$2,660,000

Par Value + Acg. cost = Total
$200,000 + $10,000 = $210,000

On December 31, 19X1, Company P issues 20,000 shares of its $10 par stock to acquire all the common stock of Company S and pays $10,000 in direct acquisition costs. Assuming that Company P shares have a market value of $50 each, the investment is recorded by the following entry:

Market Value
$1,000,000
10,000
$1,010,000

Investment in Subsidiary S (20,000 shares × $50 market value + $10,000 direct acquisition costs)	1,010,000	
Common Stock (20,000 shares × $10 par)................		200,000
Paid-In Capital in Excess of Par.............................		800,000
Cash (for acquisition costs)		10,000

This entry must acknowledge the market value of the shares exchanged, regardless of the underlying book value of the interest acquired in the subsidiary. As in the case of an asset acquisition, direct acquisition costs are considered part of the total cost of the interest acquired. Thus, in summary:

When deemed to be a purchase, the investment in a subsidiary always is recorded at the fair market value of the property received or the securities issued in exchange, plus the direct acquisition costs.

CONSOLIDATION OF THE PURCHASE OF 100% INTEREST

The example in Worksheet 4–1 portrayed a stock purchase in which the parent's payment for the interest in the subsidiary was equal to the book value of the equity acquired. The book value of the equity acquired may be expressed as either the subsidiary's net assets or its total stockholders' equity. The equality of the price paid and equity acquired is rare since market values and book values are seldom identical. As was true in the case of an asset purchase, the price paid for the stock will reflect the market value of the underlying net assets and possibly the existence of goodwill.

INVESTMENT EQUALS OR EXCEEDS THE MARKET VALUE OF THE SUBSIDIARY'S NET ASSETS

When the price paid for the stock of the subsidiary equals or exceeds the estimated market value of the subsidiary's net identifiable assets, it is necessary to adjust the recorded book value of these net assets to their market value as part of the consolidation process. Any excess of the price paid for the investment over the market value of these net assets is attributed to goodwill.

To provide guidance in making these worksheet adjustments, a supporting schedule is suggested for analyzing the excess of the price paid for the investment over the book value of the subsidiary stockholders' equity. The new schedule is termed the *determination and distribution of excess schedule.* Its function is (1) to calculate the difference between the price paid for the interest in the subsidiary and the recorded book value of the subsidiary equity and (2) to distribute this excess to those assets and liabilities of the subsidiary that require revaluation. To illustrate the schedule, assume that at the time of the purchase Company S has the following trial balance:

Cash	150,000	
Accounts Receivable	250,000	
Inventory	300,000	
Equipment (net)	400,000	
Current Liabilities		100,000
Bonds Payable		300,000
Common Stock ($5 par)		50,000
Paid-In Capital in Excess of Par		350,000
Retained Earnings		300,000
Total	1,100,000	1,100,000

The market values of Company S's inventory and equipment are estimated to be $350,000 and $550,000, respectively, and the accounts receivable will realize book value. The following determination and distribution of excess schedule compares the price paid for the investment in the subsidiary with the recorded book value of the interest acquired to arrive at an excess of cost over book value of $310,000.

Company P and Subsidiary Company S Determination and Distribution of Excess Schedule December 31, 19X1		
Price paid for investment in Co. S (including direct acquisition costs)		$1,010,000
Less interest acquired:		
Common stock ($5 par)	$ 50,000	
Paid-in capital in excess of par	350,000	
Retained earnings	300,000	
Total stockholders' equity	$700,000	
Interest acquired	100%	700,000
Excess of cost over book value		$ 310,000
Less undervaluation of current assets:		
Inventory		50,000
Excess of cost attributable to long-lived assets		$ 260,000
Less undervaluation of identifiable long-lived assets:		
Equipment		150,000
Goodwill		$ 110,000

As was true with an asset purchase, the excess of the cost of the investment over the subsidiary's book value must be used first to adjust the subsidiary's current assets, long-term investments in marketable securities, and liabilities. These accounts are to be adjusted to their market values for con-

solidated reporting, regardless of the price paid for the interest in the subsidiary. In this case, after the $50,000 undervaluation of the current assets is
deducted, the schedule shows that the long-lived assets are undervalued by
a total of $260,000, $150,000 of which is attributed to the equipment, with
the $110,000 balance reflecting goodwill.

The information contained in the determination and distribution of excess schedule is used in preparing the eliminations shown in Worksheet 4–2,
pages 214-215. Worksheet step (1) eliminates the stockholders' equity of the
subsidiary against the investment in subsidiary account, leaving an excess of
cost of $310,000. Step (2) distributes the excess to the inventory, equipment,
and goodwill accounts as prescribed by the determination and distribution
of excess schedule. After intercompany accounts are eliminated and the excess of cost is distributed, the account balances are added to arrive at the
consolidated balance sheet amounts. Note that if the price paid for a controlling interest equals the market value of the subsidiary's net identifiable assets, the procedures would parallel those of Worksheet 4–2, except that no
goodwill would be recognized.

INVESTMENT IS LESS THAN MARKET BUT MORE THAN RECORDED BOOK VALUE OF THE SUBSIDIARY'S NET ASSETS

As defined in the last chapter, a bargain purchase occurs when the price
paid for an interest in a subsidiary falls below the total market value of the
subsidiary's separate, identifiable net assets. However, the price paid in a
bargain purchase may exceed the recorded book value of those net assets. In
such a case, the determination and distribution of excess schedule still will
show an excess of the cost of the investment over the subsidiary's book
value. This situation is discussed next, followed by a discussion of the case
in which the bargain price paid for the investment is below the recorded
book value of the subsidiary's net assets.

In contrast to the preceding example assume that Company P issued
only 16,000 shares of its $50 market value ($10 par) common stock to acquire
its 100% interest in Company S and paid $10,000 in direct acquisition costs.
Company P's entry to record the acquisition would be:

Investment in Subsidiary S (16,000 shares × $50		
market value + $10,000 direct acquisition costs)	810,000	
Common Stock (16,000 shares × $10 par)..................		160,000
Paid-In Capital in Excess of Par................................		640,000
Cash (for acquisition costs)		10,000

The acquisition would lead to the following trial balances of Companies P
and S. Note that both the investment in subsidiary and the paid-in capital
accounts of Company P reflect the above entry.

	Company P		Company S	
Cash.........................	200,000		150,000	
Accounts Receivable..............	300,000		250,000	
Inventory........................	500,000		300,000	
Land............................	100,000			
Buildings (net)	900,000			
Equipment (net)..................	650,000		400,000	
Investment in Subsidiary S.......	810,000			
Current Liabilities		300,000		100,000
Bonds Payable.....................		500,000		300,000
Common Stock ($10 par)...........		660,000		
Common Stock ($5 par)...........				50,000
Paid-In Capital in Excess of Par....		1,140,000		350,000
Retained Earnings		860,000		300,000
Total	3,460,000	3,460,000	1,100,000	1,100,000

Assuming that Company S's recorded book values equal estimated market values, except for the inventory and the equipment which have market values of $350,000 and $550,000, respectively, the total market value of Company S is estimated to be $900,000 ($700,000 book value + $200,000 additional valuation for the inventory and the equipment). Since the $810,000 purchase price for Company S is less than Company S's total market value, a bargain purchase exists.

To facilitate the preparation of a worksheet for the consolidated statements, a determination and distribution of excess schedule should be prepared. The following schedule presents the calculation of the $110,000 excess of cost over book value and the required allocation of that excess:

Company P and Subsidiary Company S
Determination and Distribution of Excess Schedule
December 31, 19X1

Price paid for investment in Co. S (includes direct acquisition costs)............................		$810,000
Less interest acquired:		
Common stock ($5 par)...	$ 50,000	
Paid-in capital in excess of par..............................	350,000	
Retained earnings...	300,000	
Total stockholders' equity...................................	$700,000	
Interest acquired...	100%	700,000
Excess of cost over book value		$110,000
Less undervaluation of current assets:		
Inventory..		**50,000**
Excess of cost attributable to long-lived assets............		$ 60,000
Less increase in long-lived assets for MV* adjustments:		
Equipment..		**60,000**
Goodwill...		$ 0

*Market value

The excess always must be used first to increase the subsidiary's current assets, long-term investments in marketable securities, and liabilities to their full market values. As shown in this schedule, $50,000 is used to increase the value of the inventory, which is a current asset. The remaining $60,000 is used to increase the carrying value of the equipment, which is a long-lived asset. Since the price paid for the interest in the firm did not reflect fully the market value of the equipment ($550,000), that asset may be increased to only a portion of its market value.

In Worksheet 4–3, pages 216–217, step (1) eliminates the intercompany accounts, and step (2) distributes the excess of the cost of the investment over the book value of the subsidiary equity according to the determination and distribution of excess schedule. After these two steps are completed, the account balances can be added to arrive at the consolidated balance sheet amounts.

Note that the preceding example has been concerned with only one subsidiary long-lived asset; thus, the assignment of the $60,000 excess was straightforward. The preparation of the determination and distribution of excess schedule for a bargain purchase is complicated when there exist multiple long-lived assets. In such a case, the sum of the recorded book values of those assets plus the remaining excess of cost over book value attributable to the long-lived assets must be apportioned to each of them, since the price paid is not sufficient to increase all of the long-lived assets to their full market values. The following procedures are used:

1. The total assigned value of the subsidiary's long-lived assets will be the sum of their existing book values plus the remaining excess of cost attributable to long-lived assets.
2. Allocate this total assigned value to each long-lived asset in proportion to its share of the total market value of the long-lived assets.
3. Apportion to each long-lived asset the difference between its allocated assigned value and its existing book value.

Be sure to note that *all* long-lived assets are placed into the allocation process, including those that have equal market and book values. This is required since, when the allocation process is completed, all long-lived assets must be stated at the same percentage of their market values.

As an example, assume that the excess cost attributable to the long-lived assets of subsidiary Company S remains at $60,000, as shown in the determination and distribution of excess schedule on page 168, and that Company S has three long-lived assets with the following values:

	Book Value	Market Value
Land	$140,000	$206,250
Buildings (net)	180,000	275,000
Equipment (net)	80,000	68,750
Total	$400,000	$550,000

The following steps apportion the $460,000 of assigned value ($400,000 + $60,000 excess cost) to these long-lived assets:

1. Calculate the total assigned value:
   $400,000 book value + $60,000 excess cost = $460,000
2. Allocate the total assigned value:

	Market Value	Fraction of Market Value	×	Total Assigned Value	=	Allocated Assigned Value
Land.........	$206,250 (a.)	3/8*	×	$460,000	=	$172,500 (b)
Buildings ...	275,000	4/8	×	460,000	=	230,000
Equipment .	68,750	1/8	×	460,000	=	57,500
Total	$550,000					$460,000

*3/8 is calculated $206,250 ÷ $550,000.

3. Apportion to each asset the difference between its allocated assigned value and its book value:

	Allocated Assigned Value	−	Book Value	=	Increase (Decrease)
Land..................................	$172,500	−	$140,000	=	$32,500
Buildings	230,000	−	180,000	=	50,000
Equipment..........................	57,500	−	80,000	=	(22,500)
Total	$460,000	−	$400,000	=	$60,000

As a result of the allocation, the determination and distribution of excess schedule would conclude as follows:

Excess attributable to long-lived assets:
Land.....................................	$32,500	
Buildings	50,000	
Equipment.............................	(22,500)	$60,000

The following entry would be made on the worksheet to adjust the current asset, Inventory, to its full market value and to distribute the $60,000 excess attributable to long-lived assets:

Inventory (adjust to full market value)	50,000	
Land (partial adjustment to market)	32,500	
Building (partial adjustment to market)	50,000	
Equipment (partial adjustment to market)		22,500
Investment in Subsidiary S		
(excess after elimination of subsidiary equity).............		110,000

The procedure results in each long-lived asset sharing the same percentage of its market value. For example, each long-lived asset in the preceding illustration received 83.64% of its market value. It may be tempting to short-cut the procedure by allocating the $60,000 excess of cost by relative market values and then adding each asset's allocated portion of the excess to its recorded book value. The shortcut, however, will not result in each asset being recorded at the same percentage of its market value unless the original book value of each asset was an equal percentage of its market value. It is highly unlikely that book values would be so aligned.

Another complication occurs when the excess of cost over book value of the net assets is *less* than the amount required to adjust the current assets, long-term investments in marketable securities, and liabilities to market value. Remember that these accounts always are recorded at their market values on the acquisition date for consolidated reporting purposes. Since the excess of cost is insufficient for the entire write-up, the remainder of the write-up can be made only by decreasing the long-lived assets of the subsidiary below their recorded book values. For example, assume that the price paid in the immediately preceding example was $740,000. Even though the excess of cost over book value now would be $40,000, the inventory still would require an increase of $50,000, and thus the book values of the long-lived assets would have to be reduced by $10,000. If there was only one long-lived asset, the entire $10,000 would be credited to that asset in the eliminations on the worksheet. However, since there is more than one long-lived asset, the previously described allocation procedure must be followed. The one difference would be that the $10,000 reduction must be *subtracted* from the total recorded book values of the subsidiary's long-lived assets in order to determine the total assigned value.

[Handwritten margin notes: "assigned Values concept"]

[Handwritten right margin:]
BV
400,000.
10,000.
390,000 *

[Handwritten table:]

	MV	fraction	× TAV	= Allo. XV	Less BV	Increase (Decrease)
L	206,250	3/8 ×	390,000. =	146,250	-140,000	6,250.
B	275,000	4/8 ×	390,000 - =	195,000	-180,000	15,000.
E	68,750	1/8 ×	390,000 =	48,750	-80,000	(31,250)
	550,000			390,000	400,000	(10,000)

[Handwritten: 70.91 % % of sharing]

INVESTMENT IS LESS THAN RECORDED BOOK VALUE OF THE SUBSIDIARY'S NET ASSETS

An investment in a subsidiary amounting to less than the recorded book value of the subsidiary's net identifiable assets indicates that the recorded book value of the subsidiary's net assets or equity is overstated. To illustrate, assume that Company P acquired 100% of the common stock of Company S by issuing 12,000 shares of its $50 market value ($10 par) common stock and paying $10,000 in direct acquisition costs. The entry to record the acquisition would be:

Investment in Subsidiary S (12,000 shares × $50
    market value + $10,000 acquisition costs)............... 610,000
Common Stock (12,000 shares × $10 par)..................   120,000
Paid-In Capital in Excess of Par.................................   480,000
Cash (for acquisition costs)   10,000

This investment would lead to the following trial balances for Companies P and S. Note that both the investment in subsidiary and the paid-in capital accounts of Company P reflect the new lower acquisition cost.

	Company P		Company S	
Cash....................................	200,000		150,000	
Accounts Receivable..................	300,000		250,000	
Inventory..............................	500,000		300,000	
Land....................................	100,000			
Buildings (net)	900,000			
Equipment (net)......................	650,000		400,000	
Investment in Subsidiary S.........	610,000			
Current Liabilities		300,000		100,000
Bonds Payable........................		500,000		300,000
Common Stock ($10 par)...........		620,000		
Common Stock ($5 par).............				50,000
Paid-In Capital in Excess of Par....		980,000		350,000
Retained Earnings		860,000		300,000
Total	3,260,000	3,260,000	1,100,000	1,100,000

The recorded book values of Company S are assumed to equal market values, except for the inventory and the equipment which have market values of $350,000 and $300,000, respectively. In the following determination and distribution of excess schedule, a $90,000 *excess of book value* over the cost of the investment is calculated:

Company P and Subsidiary Company S
Determination and Distribution of Excess Schedule
December 31, 19X1

Price paid for investment in Co. S (including direct acquisition costs)............................		$610,000
Less interest acquired:		
Common stock ($5 par)...	$ 50,000	
Paid-in capital in excess of par.................................	350,000	
Retained earnings..	300,000	
Total stockholders' equity.......................................	$700,000	
Interest acquired...	100%	700,000
Excess of **book** value over cost....................................		$ 90,000
Add undervaluation of current assets:		
Inventory..		50,000
Excess of book value attributable to long-lived assets ..		$140,000
Decrease in long-lived assets for MV adjustments:		
Equipment...		140,000
Goodwill...		$ 0

As in previous schedules, the excess is first modified by the amount necessary to restate to full market value the current assets, long-term investments in marketable securities, and liabilities. In this example, the current asset, Inventory, is understated by $50,000 and is increased to market value. The excess book value attributable to long-lived assets is $140,000 ($90,000 excess of book value of all assets over cost + $50,000 write-up to market value for the inventory) and must be deducted from the equipment's original book value. Thus only $260,000 ($400,000 book value − $140,000) is assigned to the equipment acquired from Company S. Again, current assets, long-term investments in marketable securities, and liabilities always are adjusted to market value, regardless of the price paid for the interest in the subsidiary.

In Worksheet 4–4, pages 218–219, the subsidiary stockholders' equity is eliminated against the investment account in step (1). Step (2) distributes the resulting *credit* balance of the investment account to the specific subsidiary assets according to the determination and distribution of excess schedule. As in previous illustrations, the intercompany accounts are eliminated, and the consolidated balance sheet amounts are determined.

Two added complications may arise in handling an investment at a price below the book value of the subsidiary. First, there may be several subsidiary long-lived assets whose market values differ from their book values. In this case, the excess of book value attributable to long-lived assets must be apportioned among all long-lived assets. The procedure for apportionment is as follows:

1. The total assigned value of all long-lived assets will be the sum of the existing long-lived assets' book values *reduced* by the excess of *book value over the cost* of the investment attributable to the long-lived assets, as computed in the determination and distribution of excess schedule. The excess attributable to long-lived assets is the original excess of book value for the investment plus or minus any market value adjustment made for current assets, long-term investments in marketable securities, and liabilities.
2. Allocate this total assigned value to each long-lived asset in proportion to its share of the total market value of the long-lived assets.
3. Apportion to each long-lived asset the difference between its allocated assigned value and its existing book value.

As an example of this procedure, assume that in Worksheet 4–4 there were three long-lived assets with book and market values as follows:

	Book Value	Market Value
Land	$100,000	$ 75,000
Buildings (net)	250,000	175,000
Equipment (net)	50,000	50,000
Total	$400,000	$300,000

The following steps apportion the $140,000 excess of book value over cost attributable to long-lived assets:

1. Calculate the total assigned value:
    $400,000 book value − $140,000 excess book value = $260,000

2. Allocate the total assigned value:

	Market Value	Fraction of Market Value	×	Total Assigned Value	=	Allocated Assigned Value
Land	$ 75,000	3/12	×	$260,000	=	$ 65,000
Buildings	175,000	7/12	×	260,000	=	151,667
Equipment	50,000	2/12	×	260,000	=	43,333
Total	$300,000					$260,000

3. Apportion to each asset the difference between its allocated assigned value and its book value:

	Allocated Assigned Value	−	Book Value	=	Increase (Decrease)
Land	$ 65,000	−	$100,000	=	$ (35,000)
Buildings	151,667	−	250,000	=	(98,333)
Equipment	43,333	−	50,000	=	(6,667)
Total	$260,000	−	$400,000	=	$(140,000)

As a result of these computations, the following revised determination and distribution of excess schedule is prepared, based on the presence of the three long-lived assets:

Price paid for investment in Company S (including direct acquisition costs)		$610,000
Less interest acquired:		
Common stock ($5 par)	$ 50,000	
Paid-in capital in excess of par	350,000	
Retained earnings	300,000	
Total stockholders' equity	$700,000	
Interest acquired	100%	700,000
Excess of **book** value over cost		$ 90,000
Add undervaluation of current assets:		
Inventory		**50,000**
Excess of book value attributable to long-lived assets:		$140,000
Decrease in long-lived assets for MV adjustments:		
Land	$ 35,000	
Buildings	98,333	
Equipment	6,667	140,000
Goodwill		$ 0

The worksheet entry to write-up inventory and to distribute the excess attributable to long-lived assets would be as follows:

Investment in Subsidiary S (excess book value after elimination of subsidiary equity)	90,000	
Inventory (adjust to full market value)	50,000	
Land (partial adjustment)		35,000
Building (partial adjustment)		98,333
Equipment (partial adjustment)		6,667

A second complication occurs when the excess of book value over the cost attributable to long-lived assets *exceeds the total book value of the subsid-*

iary's long-lived assets. In such a case, the subsidiary long-lived assets are reduced to *zero.* The remaining excess is viewed as deferred income and carried on the consolidated balance sheet in the account *Excess of Market Value of Subsidiary Current Assets over Cost.* The deferred income account is amortized as an addition to consolidated income over a period of 40 years or less.

SUBSIDIARY WITH PREVIOUSLY RECORDED GOODWILL

It should be recalled from the discussion of direct asset acquisitions that goodwill on the books of an acquired firm is disregarded. In the case of a stock acquisition, however, a subsidiary's recorded goodwill is included in the subsidiary's balance sheet which is to be consolidated. But, *no goodwill should appear on the consolidated balance sheet until all long-lived assets are stated at full market value.* Thus the procedure will be to reassign the amount of existing goodwill to the extent that it is needed in order to bring long-lived assets to market value. Any portion of the previously recorded goodwill not required for the adjustment of other accounts will be extended to the consolidated balance sheet. To illustrate, assume that the purchased company has recorded goodwill of $60,000 and that the determination and distribution of excess schedule for this hypothetical case reads as follows:

Price paid for investment...		$800,000
Less interest acquired:		
Common stock ($5 par)...	$100,000	
Retained earnings..	500,000	
Total stockholders' equity......................................	$600,000	
Interest acquired...	100%	600,000
Excess of cost over book value		$200,000
Less undervaluation of current assets:		
Inventory..		**50,000**
Remaining excess..		$150,000
Add back goodwill needed to bring long-lived assets		
to market value ($60,000 available)		**50,000**
Excess available for long-lived assets		$200,000
Excess of cost attributable to long-lived assets:		
Buildings	**$150,000**	
Equipment..	**50,000**	**200,000**
Goodwill..		$ 0

The worksheet entry to write-up inventory and to distribute the excess attributable to long-lived assets would be as follows:

Inventory (adjust to full market value)	50,000	
Building (to market value)	150,000	
Equipment (to market value)	50,000	
Goodwill (reduced as needed)		50,000
Investment in Subsidiary S (excess cost after		
elimination of subsidiary equity)............................		200,000

see also page 110

On the worksheet, since $50,000 of the recorded $60,000 would be eliminated, only $10,000 of the goodwill would extend to the consolidated balance sheet. If the equipment and buildings accounts required a total write-up to market value of $210,000, all $60,000 of the goodwill would have been utilized.

PLANT ASSETS ACCOUNTING

Previous examples have used "net" values for depreciable assets to simplify explanations. In reality, the subsidiary will list original cost less accumulated depreciation. According to *purchase theory*, there is little justification for carrying to the consolidated balance sheet an amount for accumulated depreciation on a subsidiary's asset existing prior to the purchase. To do so would imply that the asset was used by the new owner prior to the purchase date. Thus, the preferable practice is to have the consolidated amounts reflect the market value, with no accumulated depreciation. Future depreciation charges on consolidated worksheets will be based on the new market value and the estimated remaining useful life.

To illustrate, assume that an acquired firm has a building on its books at an original cost of $600,000 less $400,000 accumulated depreciation. Assume further that the building has a $300,000 market value on the purchase date. The net write-up required is $100,000. The preferable procedure is to produce a net asset value of $300,000 as shown in the following partial worksheet:

	Partial Trial Balance		Eliminations & Adjustments		Consolidated Balance Sheet
	Co. P	Co. S	Dr.	Cr.	
Building		600,000		**300,000**	300,000
Accumulated Depreciation		(400,000)	**400,000**		—
Investment in Subsidiary S				100,000*	—

*The $100,000 is the balance remaining after the elimination of the subsidiary equity accounts.

A less theoretically correct but common procedure is to not eliminate all accumulated depreciation, but rather to adjust the plant asset by:

1. Increasing its net book value through a reduction of the existing accumulated depreciation or
2. Decreasing its net book value through a reduction of the original cost of the asset.

This practical approach tends to be used when the parent owns less than a 100% interest.

ADJUSTMENT OF ASSUMED LIABILITIES

Liabilities assumed in a purchase may have market values that are at variance with their recorded book values. This situation could exist as a result of failing to record accrued interest or as a result of changing interest rates. If interest rates decrease and the market value of the debt increases, the net assets of the firm are reduced, and the excess of cost available for long-lived assets increases. The impact on the remaining excess is the same as a decrease in the value of a current asset. On the other hand, if interest rates increase and the market value of the debt decreases, the net assets are adjusted upwards, and the excess available for long-lived assets decreases.

Remember, liabilities are adjusted to reflect their full market values, regardless of the price paid in a business combination. For example, assume that Company P pays $500,000 for all of the outstanding common stock of Company S at a time when Company S has the following balance sheet:

Assets		Liabilities and Equity	
Current assets..................	$250,000	Bonds payable	$200,000
Long-lived assets..............	350,000	Common stock.................	100,000
		Retained earnings.............	300,000
Total assets.....................	$600,000	Total liabilities and equity..	$600,000

Also, assume that the subsidiary's current assets have a book value equal to market value. However, certain equipment is undervalued by $40,000, and, due to a decrease in the interest rates, bond liability has a market value of $208,000. A determination and distribution of excess schedule would be prepared as follows:

Premium on Bonds Payable $8,000

Price paid for investment...		$500,000
Less interest acquired:		
Common stock..	$100,000	
Retained earnings...	300,000	
Total stockholders' equity.......................................	$400,000	
Interest acquired..	100%	400,000
Excess of cost over book value		$100,000
Add undervaluation of bonds payable		**8,000**
Excess of cost attributable to long-lived assets................		$108,000
Less undervaluation of identifiable long-lived assets:		
Equipment...		**40,000**
Goodwill..		**$ 68,000**

The worksheet entry to adjust the bonds to market value and to distribute the excess attributable to long-lived assets would be as follows:

Equipment (to market value)	40,000	
Goodwill (balance of excess)	68,000	
Premium on Bonds Payable (to market value)...............		8,000
Investment in Subsidiary S (excess cost after elimination of subsidiary equity)		100,000

TAX RELATED ADJUSTMENTS

Recall from Chapter 3 that a deferred tax liability results when the market value of an asset may not be used in future depreciation calculations for tax purposes. (This occurs when the purchase is a tax-free exchange as to the seller.) In this situation, future depreciation charges for tax purposes must be based on the book value of the asset, and a liability should be acknowledged in the determination and distribution of excess schedule by creating a deferred tax liability account. Consider the following determination and distribution of excess schedule for a subsidiary which has a building with a book value for tax purposes of $120,000 and a market value of $200,000. Assuming a tax rate of 30%, there is a deferred tax liability of $24,000 ($80,000 excess of market value over tax basis × 30%).

Price paid for investment..		$600,000
Less interest acquired:		
Common stock..	$100,000	
Retained earnings...	400,000	
Total stockholders' equity......................................	$500,000	
Interest acquired...	100%	500,000
Excess of cost over book value		$100,000
Less undervaluation of identifiable long-lived assets:		
Building...	**$ 80,000**	
Deferred tax liability, building..................................	**(24,000)**	**56,000**
Goodwill..		**$ 44,000**

The worksheet entry to distribute the excess of cost over book value would be as follows:

Building (to market value)	80,000	
Goodwill (balance of excess)	44,000	
Deferred Tax Liability (to market value)........................		24,000
Investment in Subsidiary S (excess cost after elimination of subsidiary equity)...		100,000

Worksheet eliminations will be simpler if each deferred tax liability is recorded below the asset to which it relates. It is possible that inventory could have a market value in excess of its book value used for tax purposes. This, too, would require the recognition of a deferred tax liability.

Recall the general rule that the market values of the liabilities are acknowledged in full even in a bargain purchase. There is an exception to this rule with respect to the deferred tax liability that results from recording the market value adjustments made in a purchase: *The deferred tax liability has the same priority as the asset to which it relates.* For instance, since inventory always is adjusted to full market value, the deferred tax liability related to inventory is recognized fully as well. In the case of a long-lived asset, only a portion of the difference between book and market value is recorded in a bargain purchase; thus the deferred tax liability is limited to the portion of the market-book value disparity that is recorded.

The need to recognize the deferred tax liability may complicate the distribution of the excess. Assume that we have an asset which has a market value estimated to exceed its book value by $150,000 but that there is only $70,000 of excess available to distribute to the asset. Assuming a 30% tax rate, the excess would be divided by 70%, or the net-of-tax percentage, to arrive at the amount to allocate to the asset itself—in this case $100,000 ($70,000 ÷ 70%)—and 30% of the $100,000 would be recognized as related deferred tax liability. The $70,000 excess of cost would be distributed as follows:

Excess of cost over book value available............................		$70,000
Distribute to:		
Asset..	$100,000	
Deferred tax liability..	(30,000)	70,000
		$ 0

A second tax complication arises when the subsidiary has tax loss carryovers. To the extent that the tax loss carryovers are not recorded by the subsidiary on its balance sheet, the carryovers may be an asset to be considered in the determination and distribution of excess schedule. If the parent has income in the prior three years which is available for offsetting some or all of the tax loss, a carryback is recognized as a current asset (Refund Receivable) which would receive its full value allocation even in a bargain purchase. Any remaining carryover is carried forward and recorded as an asset only when there are deferred tax liabilities available which may be offset. Assuming that these liabilities exist, the tax loss carryforward should be recognized as a current asset if it will be realized within one year; otherwise, it should be shown as a noncurrent asset. When the tax loss carryforward is a noncurrent asset, it should not be recorded at full market value in a bargain purchase. Instead, it should be one of several possible long-lived assets that is subject to the allocation procedure.

Let us consider the example of a subsidiary which has the following tax loss carryovers:

Tax loss carryback......................................	$200,000
Tax loss carryforward to be used	
within 1 year...	100,000
Tax loss carryforward to be used after 1 year..	50,000

Note:

Assume that the parent has deferred tax liabilities against which the tax loss carryforwards may be offset and has a 30% tax rate. A determination and distribution of excess schedule might appear as follows:

Price paid for investment...		$900,000
Less interest acquired:		
Common stock...	$300,000	
Retained earnings..	400,000	
Total stockholders' equity.......................................	$700,000	
Interest acquired...	100%	700,000
Excess of cost over book value		$200,000
Tax refund receivable (30% × $200,000)..........................	**$ 60,000**	
Current deferred tax expense (30% × $100,000)	**30,000**	**90,000**
Excess of cost attributable to long-lived assets................		$110,000
Less undervaluation of identifiable long-lived assets:		
Noncurrent deferred tax expense (30% × $50,000)		**15,000**
Goodwill...		$ 95,000

The worksheet entry would be as follows:

Tax Refund Receivable...	60,000	
Deferred Tax Expense — Current....................................	30,000	
Deferred Tax Expense — Noncurrent...............................	15,000	
Goodwill..	95,000	
Investment in Subsidiary S (excess after elimination		
of subsidiary equity)...		200,000

CONSOLIDATION OF THE PURCHASE OF LESS-THAN-100% INTEREST

When control of a firm is achieved through the purchase of common stock and consolidated statements are required, consolidation procedures are applied. Control may be secured by purchasing less than 100% but usually over 50% of the subsidiary's voting common stock. In those cases in which a less-than-100% interest is purchased, only a portion of the subsidiary stockholders' equity is eliminated against the parent's investment in subsidiary account. The remaining portion of the subsidiary common stock interest belongs to the minority interest, represented by stockholders of the subsidiary other than the parent. From a consolidated viewpoint, these shareholders are a special group of owners of the consolidated firm. However, their ownership rights are limited to their interest in the subsidiary as a separate legal entity. For example, minority stockholders receive only those dividends that are paid by the subsidiary. In liquidation, the only assets of the subsidiary available to minority stockholders are the assets remaining after creditor and preferred stockholder claims have been satisfied.

To illustrate, assume that Company P purchased an 80% interest in Company S for $400,000 in cash. The entry to record the purchase would be:

Investment in Subsidiary S	400,000	
Cash		400,000

Immediately following the acquisition, the account balances of Companies P and S would be as follows:

	Company P		Company S	
Cash	200,000			
Accounts Receivable	300,000		200,000	
Inventory	100,000		100,000	
Investment in Subsidiary S	400,000			
Equipment (net)	150,000		300,000	
Current Liabilities		150,000		100,000
Bonds Payable		300,000		
Common Stock		100,000		200,000
Retained Earnings		600,000		300,000
Total	1,150,000	1,150,000	600,000	600,000

In the following determination and distribution of excess schedule, the total subsidiary stockholders' equity is multiplied by the 80% ownership interest in calculating the interest acquired:

Company P and Subsidiary Company S Determination and Distribution of Excess Schedule December 31, 19X1		
Price paid for investment in Co. S		$400,000
Less interest acquired:		
Common stock	$200,000	
Retained earnings	300,000	
Total stockholders' equity	$500,000	
Interest acquired	**80%**	400,000
Excess		$ 0

In Worksheet 4–5, pages 220–221, the intercompany balances are eliminated. That portion of the subsidiary stockholders' equity not eliminated is extended to the Minority Interest column of the worksheet. The remaining balances are added to arrive at the amounts for the consolidated balance sheet. Thus, the worksheet is the source for the formal balance sheet.

The balance sheet illustration summarizes the total minority interest and includes it in stockholders' equity. As an alternative, the paid-in and earned elements of the minority interest may be shown. It is not common, however, to specify the composition of the ownership by minority groups when the parent controls several subsidiaries.

Company P and Subsidiary Company S
Consolidated Balance Sheet
December 31, 19X1

Assets

Current assets:		
Cash	$200,000	
Accounts receivable......................................	500,000	
Inventory...	200,000	$ 900,000
Equipment (net)		450,000
Total assets...		$1,350,000

Liabilities

Current liabilities...	$250,000	
Bonds payable	300,000	$ 550,000

Stockholders' Equity

Minority interest		**100,000**
Controlling interest:		
Common stock...	$100,000	
Retained earnings	600,000	700,000
Total liabilities and stockholders' equity..............		$1,350,000

The published financial statements of many consolidated firms exclude the minority interest from the stockholders' equity section of the balance sheet. These statements list the minority interest under noncurrent liabilities or place it between liabilities and equity. This exclusion of the minority interest from the stockholders' equity section of the balance sheet is a manifestation of the *proprietary theory* of consolidations, which emphasizes the controlling interest's position. Although the alternatives for disclosing the minority interest are generally accepted, this text will follow the *entity theory* format for statements, which focuses on the equity of all the owners and thus includes the minority interest as a part of the stockholders' equity.

INVESTMENT EXCEEDS MARKET VALUE OF THE CONTROLLING INTEREST IN THE SUBSIDIARY'S NET ASSETS

The purchase of an interest in a subsidiary at a price in excess of the book value of the subsidiary's net identifiable assets multiplied by the parent's ownership interest suggests that the subsidiary's net assets are undervalued. For consolidated reporting purposes, the carrying value of the net assets must be adjusted to reflect the price paid by the parent to acquire an interest in them. The only change from the previous 100% acquisition illustrations is that assets are adjusted on the worksheet by multiplying the parent's ownership percentage by the *difference* between the book and market values. For example, assume that a parent pays $40,000 above the book value for an 80% interest in the stockholders' equity of a subsidiary. Further assume that the subsidiary has one long-lived asset to which the excess is attributable. Logic might dictate that if a $40,000 excess was paid for an 80% interest in the asset, a $50,000 ($40,000 ÷ 80%) excess would be paid for a 100% interest. Even though the asset appears to be undervalued by $50,000, only the $40,000 increase is acknowledged. Again, the parent company's purchase confirms only its portion (80% in this example) of the difference between the book and market values. Thus, the worksheet adjustment acknowledges only the interest acquired. Recognition of the full increase, in essence, would require the recognition of a gain prior to its realization through a bargained exchange.

The purchase example on page 164 will be revised in order to apply what might be termed the "pro rata market value" adjustments. Assume that Company P purchases only an 80% interest in Company S and that all other facts, including the market value of the subsidiary's assets, remain the same. Since Company P was willing to issue 20,000 shares of its $50 market value ($10 par) common stock for a 100% interest in Company S, assume that it now issues 16,000 shares (80% × 20,000 shares) for the 80% interest and pays $10,000 in direct acquisition costs. The entry to record the acquisition would be:

Investment in Subsidiary S (16,000 shares × $50 market value + $10,000 direct acquisition costs)................	810,000	
Common Stock (16,000 shares × $10 par)..................		160,000
Paid-In Capital in Excess of Par................................		640,000
Cash (for acquisition costs)		10,000

The trial balance for each company immediately following the acquisition is as follows:

	Company P		Company S	
Cash......................................	200,000		150,000	
Accounts Receivable..................	300,000		250,000	
Inventory................................	500,000		300,000	
Land......................................	100,000			
Buildings (net)	900,000			
Equipment (net).......................	650,000		400,000	
Investment in Subsidiary S..........	810,000			
Current Liabilities		300,000		100,000
Bonds Payable..........................		500,000		300,000
Common Stock ($10 par)............		660,000		
Common Stock ($5 par)..............				50,000
Paid-In Capital in Excess of Par....		1,140,000		350,000
Retained Earnings		860,000		300,000
Total	3,460,000	3,460,000	1,100,000	1,100,000

The worksheet adjustments made on the basis of the following determination and distribution of excess schedule are shown in Worksheet 4–6, pages 222–223. The subsidiary's book values are assumed to be equal to market values, except for the inventory and the equipment which have market values of $350,000 and $550,000, respectively.

Company P and Subsidiary Company S
Determination and Distribution of Excess Schedule
December 31, 19X1

Price paid for investment in Co. S.............................		$810,000
Less interest acquired:		
Common stock ($5 par)...	$ 50,000	
Paid-in capital in excess of par...............................	350,000	
Retained earnings...	300,000	
Total stockholders' equity...................................	$700,000	
Interest acquired...	80%	560,000
Excess of cost over book value		$250,000
Less undervaluation of interest in current assets:		
Inventory ($50,000 total × 80%)		**40,000**
Excess of cost attributable to interest in		
long-lived assets..		$210,000
Less undervaluation of interest in identifiable		
long-lived assets:		
Equipment ($150,000 total × 80%).....................		**120,000**
Goodwill..		**$ 90,000**

Note the following unique features of a determination and distribution of excess schedule for a less-than-100% interest:

1. The excess of cost over book value is based on a comparison of the price paid and a pro rata share of the stockholders' equity of the subsidiary.
2. Current assets, long-lived assets, and assumed liabilities are adjusted by multiplying the ownership interest acquired by the difference between their book and market values.
3. Only the *parent's ownership interest* in the already recorded goodwill of the subsidiary is available for reassignment to long-lived assets.

The pro rata market value method of preparing consolidated worksheets is a feature of the proprietary theory of business combinations, which limits the adjustments of a subsidiary's assets to the interest purchased by the controlling firm. Some accounting theorists feel that the entire difference between market value and recorded book value should be acknowledged, regardless of the percentage interest purchased. Procedures for accomplishing this objective are discussed in the appendix found at the end of this chapter.

INVESTMENT FALLS BETWEEN MARKET AND RECORDED BOOK VALUE OF THE CONTROLLING INTEREST IN THE SUBSIDIARY'S NET ASSETS

A bargain purchase may occur when less than 100% of a subsidiary's outstanding voting common stock is purchased. For a bargain purchase to transpire, the total market value of the subsidiary's assets multiplied by the parent's ownership percentage must exceed the cost of the investment.

The following determination and distribution of excess schedule uses the same facts as those used in the schedule on page 168, except that an 80% interest is presented:

Price paid for 80% interest in Subsidiary S (including $10,000 direct acquisition costs)..................		$650,000
Less interest acquired:		
Common stock ($5 par)...	$ 50,000	
Paid-in capital in excess of par...................................	350,000	
Retained earnings...	300,000	
Total stockholders' equity..	$700,000	
Interest acquired...	80%	560,000
Excess of cost over book value		$ 90,000
Less undervaluation of current assets:		
Inventory (80% × $50,000)		**40,000**
Excess of cost attributable to long-lived assets................		$ 50,000
Increase in long-lived asset for MV adjustment:		
Equipment*		**50,000**
Goodwill...		$ 0

*The maximum increase would be $120,000 (80% × $150,000 excess of market value over book value). Since the excess available is less than this amount, all of the excess is added to the equipment account, leaving no excess for goodwill.

The worksheet entry to distribute the excess of cost over book value would be:

Inventory (80% of value difference)..	40,000	
Equipment (up to 80% of value difference)...............................	50,000	
Investment in Subsidiary S (excess after elimination of 80% of subsidiary equity).............................		90,000

Note that current assets, as well as long-term investments in marketable securities and all liabilities, are increased *by the amount of their undervaluation multiplied by the parent's ownership percentage,* regardless of the price paid for the interest.

In a bargain purchase, goodwill recorded by the subsidiary should be reassigned to long-lived assets. However, the *maximum* amount of goodwill available for reassignment is the subsidiary's previously recorded goodwill multiplied by the parent's ownership interest.

In those cases where there is a bargain purchase and several long-lived assets exist, the excess of cost attributable to those assets should be apportioned according to the procedure described on page 169. The market values of the separate long-lived assets still should be used as the weights for distributing the total assigned value of the long-lived assets. The assigned value is the parent company's share of the subsidiary book value plus the available excess. Suppose that in the above determination and distribution of excess schedule there were several long-lived assets with a total book value of $200,000. The assigned value to be allocated would be $160,000 (the parent's share of book value) plus the $50,000 excess available. The $40,000 of the long-lived assets' total book value applicable to the minority interest is *not* available for assignment since it has not been purchased. The difference between the assigned and book values of each long-lived asset should be entered in the determination and distribution of excess schedule. This difference is *not* multiplied by the controlling ownership percentage, since the assignable value includes only the excess applicable to the controlling interest.

INVESTMENT IS LESS THAN BOOK VALUE OF THE CONTROLLING INTEREST IN SUBSIDIARY'S NET ASSETS

An investment in a subsidiary at a price below the book value of the subsidiary stockholders' equity multiplied by the parent's ownership percentage necessitates a write-down of the recorded book values of the net assets to remove the overvaluation. However, as is true with write-ups, only the parent's ownership percentage of each account's total difference between book and market value is acknowledged. Also, the values of the subsidiary's current assets, long-term investments in marketable securities, and liabilities *always* must be adjusted by the full amount of the parent's ownership share of the difference between the book and market values of these accounts.

To illustrate the consolidation procedures applicable to acquisitions producing an excess of book value over cost, the determination and distribution of excess schedule on page 172 is restated to reflect an 80% acquisition as follows:

Price paid for 80% interest in Subsidiary S (including $10,000 direct acquisition costs)................		$490,000
Less interest acquired:		
Common stock ($5 par)...	$ 50,000	
Paid-in capital in excess of par..................................	350,000	
Retained earnings...	300,000	
Total stockholders' equity......................................	$700,000	
Interest acquired...	80%	560,000
Excess of **book** value over cost....................................		$ 70,000
Add undervaluation of interest in current assets:		
Inventory (80% × $50,000)		**40,000**
Excess of book value over cost attributable to interest in equipment		**$110,000***

*The maximum decrease would be $320,000 (80% × $400,000 book value).

The worksheet entry to distribute the excess of book value over cost would be:

Inventory (80% of value difference)...............................	40,000	
Investment in Subsidiary S (excess after elimination of 80% of subsidiary equity)	70,000	
Equipment (remaining excess of book value)................		110,000

If several long-lived assets exist, the previously illustrated apportionment procedure would be applied. Also, a special procedure is required if previously recorded goodwill appears on the subsidiary's books. As in the case of a 100% acquisition, previously recorded goodwill may have to be reassigned to identifiable long-lived assets on the determination and distribution of excess schedule. However, only a portion equal to the ownership percentage may be made available for reassignment; the minority portion of goodwill is not available for reassignment.

PUSH-DOWN ACCOUNTING

Thus far, it has been assumed that the subsidiary's statements are unaffected by the parent's purchase of subsidiary shares so that no asset or liability adjustment is reflected on the subsidiary's separate records. In all preceding examples, revaluations first occur on the consolidated worksheet. This method is the most common, but it is not the only generally accepted method.

Some accountants object to the inconsistency of using book values in the subsidiary's separate statements and using market-adjusted values where the same operations are included in the consolidated statements. These accountants advocate *push-down* accounting, whereby the subsidiary's records are adjusted to reflect the market value increases. In essence, it is argued that the purchase of a controlling interest gives rise to a new basis of accountability for the interest traded. It is argued further that the subsidiary retained earnings applicable to the controlling interest should be moved to paid-in capital.

If the push-down method were applied to the determination and distribution of excess schedule example on page 164, the following *entry* would be made by the subsidiary:

Inventory	50,000	
Equipment	150,000	
Goodwill	110,000	
Retained earnings (previous subsidiary balance)	300,000	
Paid-In Capital in Excess of Par (previous		
retained earnings plus revaluations)		610,000

This entry would raise the subsidiary total stockholders' equity to $1,010,000 and would mean a simple elimination of the $1,010,000 investment account, with no excess on the consolidated worksheet.

In the case of a less-than-100% purchase under the proprietary theory, adjustments would be limited to the controlling interest's percentage. Only the controlling interest's percentage of retained earnings would be transferred to paid-in capital.

Neither the FASB nor its predecessor, the Accounting Principles Board, has taken a stand on this issue. The SEC does require the push-down approach, however, for substantially wholly-owned subsidiaries, and it recommends this approach in other cases. The examples in the text will use the conventional approach, wherein the subsidiary's records are unaffected by the purchase. This approach is oriented toward the interest of minority shareholders, who are not impacted by the parent's stock purchase.[2]

AN INVESTMENT IN THE SUBSIDIARY ACCOUNTED FOR AS A POOLING OF INTERESTS

When the pooling criteria are met, as discussed in Chapter 3, the acquisition of a controlling interest in the common stock of another firm is recorded as a pooling of interests. Consolidated financial statements also will be required when the operations of the pooled firms are integrated.

CONSOLIDATING A 100% INTEREST UNDER POOLING

The recording and consolidation of a pooling achieved through a stock acquisition can be better understood by first reviewing the recording of a pooling achieved through an asset acquisition. Assume that Company C (the combiner) had the following balance sheet just prior to pooling with Company I (the issuer):

Company C Balance Sheet December 31, 19X1				
Current assets	$10,000	Liabilities		$10,000
Property, plant, and		Stockholders' equity:		
equipment (net).....	30,000	Common stock		
		($10 par)	$10,000	
		Retained earnings ..	20,000	30,000
		Total liabilities		
Total assets.............	$40,000	and equity............		$40,000

Assume also that Company I is willing to issue 3,000 shares of its stock for the $30,000 net assets of Company C. Company I stock has a par value of $2 and a market value of $15 per share. Since pooling principles ignore market values and combine book balances, the entry to record the pooling on Company I's books would be:

Current Assets	10,000	
Property, Plant, and Equipment (net)............................	30,000	
Liabilities		10,000
Common Stock ($2 per share × 3,000 shares)		6,000
Paid-In Capital in Excess of Par...................................		4,000
Retained Earnings		20,000

---

[2]For a further discussion of the issues, see Michael E. Cunningham, "Push-Down Accounting: Pros and Cons," *Journal of Accountancy* (June 1984): 72–77.

The original amount of the Company C total paid-in capital is preserved, although it is redistributed between the par value and paid-in capital in excess of par accounts of Company I. The full amount in the Company C retained earnings account is transferred to the Company I retained earnings account, since a reduction was not necessary to meet a par or stated value requirement of the issuer.

In this example which portrays a pooling through an asset acquisition, the combiner was dissolved and its accounts were merged with those of the issuer. Assume now that Company I exchanges its shares for the shares of Company C by dealing with stockholders and that all other pooling criteria are met. Assume further that Company I elects not to dissolve Company C but to let Company C continue as a separate legal entity with its own accounting records. In effect, a pooling through a stock acquisition occurs. Since the assets and liabilities of Company C remain on Company C's books, Company I can record only an investment in Company C. However, this investment must be recorded at the book value of the underlying net assets in order to comply with pooling principles. The market value of the securities exchanged is ignored. Normally, Company I must add to its paid-in capital an amount equal to the paid-in capital of Company C. The issuer must acknowledge as retained earnings its equity in the Company C retained earnings, unless it is needed to meet a par or stated value requirement and Company I has no additional paid-in capital available for redistribution. From these principles, the following entry is derived:

Investment in Subsidiary C..	**30,000**	
Common Stock ($2 per share × 3,000 shares)...............		6,000
Paid-In Capital in Excess of Par....................................		4,000
Retained Earnings		20,000

This entry would lead to the separate trial balances for Companies I and C shown in the first two columns of Worksheet 4–7, pages 224–225. In this worksheet, intercompany balances are eliminated, and the balance sheets of the parent and subsidiary are consolidated as of the date of the pooling.

When properly recorded, the investment in subsidiary account *always* will be eliminated against the stockholders' equity of the subsidiary *with no excess of any type* remaining after the elimination. This procedure must be followed, since the recorded value of the investment account equals the subsidiary stockholders' equity multiplied by the parent's ownership percentage (100% in this example). As a result of this equality, no determination and distribution of excess schedule is needed when pooling.

CONSOLIDATING A LESS-THAN-100% INTEREST UNDER POOLING

Often the issuer will not acquire 100% of the combiner stock, although it must acquire at least 90% to pool. In such a case, the issuer records only the pro rata book value acquired. If Company I of the previous example exchanges only 2,700 shares ($2 par) for 90% of Company C stock, the entry to record the investment would be:

Investment in Subsidiary C	27,000	
Common Stock ($2 per share × 2,700 shares)		5,400
Paid-In Capital in Excess of Par (90% × $4,000)		3,600
Retained Earnings (90% × $20,000)		18,000

Subsequent worksheet eliminations would cancel the investment in subsidiary account against 90% of the Company C equities, with a 10% minority interest remaining. Procedures for displaying the minority interest parallel those previously discussed.

If the parent firm later acquires all or part of the minority interest, the new acquisition is considered a purchase, since it could not possibly meet the pooling criteria. Such a situation would require a consolidated worksheet in which both pooling and purchase procedures are used. (Coverage of "piecemeal" acquisitions can be found in Chapter 8.)

RECOGNIZING AND CORRECTING THE IMPROPERLY RECORDED INVESTMENT ACCOUNT

Ordinarily, when a corporation issues stock, it must increase its total paid-in capital by the entire amount of consideration received. When it issues stock to acquire noncash assets, including shares of another firm's stock, the consideration received is the market value of the assets received or the shares given, whichever is more readily determinable. The only exception to these principles is an investment in a subsidiary to effect a pooling. In this case, only the net book value of the assets received should be recorded, as was previously illustrated. However, it is common to find a firm that ignores this exception. Such a firm will increase both its investment and paid-in capital accounts by an amount equal to the market value of the shares given or received. When this mistake is found, the issuer's accounts should be corrected prior to preparing the consolidated worksheet.[3]

To illustrate, assume that Company I made the following incorrect investment entry when it acquired 90% of the stock of Company C, although pooling criteria were met:

Investment in Subsidiary C ($15 per share market value × 2,700 shares)	40,500	
Common Stock ($2 per share × 2,700 shares)		5,400
Paid-In Capital in Excess of Par		35,100

---

[3]Some states require the investment to be recorded at market value. Where this is true, the "correction" entries would be made on the worksheet as part of the eliminations.

Prior to preparing the consolidated worksheet, the issuer's books would be corrected by reversing the original incorrect entry and recording the investment as a pooling. The following entries would be made:

Common Stock ($2 per share × 2,700 shares)	5,400	
Paid-In Capital in Excess of Par.......................................	35,100	
Investment in Subsidiary C		40,500
Investment in Subsidiary C (90% of Company C equity)......	27,000	
Common Stock ($2 per share × 2,700 shares)		5,400
Paid-In Capital in Excess of Par ($9,000 − $5,400)		3,600
Retained Earnings (90% × $20,000)............................		18,000

When these corrections have been made, the proper amounts have been recorded by the issuer, and subsequent worksheet eliminations would be identical to those for a less-than-100% interest pooling.

APPENDIX: ALTERNATIVE ASSET ADJUSTMENT METHODS FOR LESS-THAN-100% INTEREST

See also page 182

Preceding examples adjust the subsidiary's assets for only the parent's own-ership percentage multiplied by the difference between the recorded book value and the market value. This is appropriate under the proprietary the-ory. There are, however, alternative models known as the *entity theory* and the *parent company theory*.

THE ENTITY THEORY *See also page 184, proprietary theory.*

Under this approach, the entire entity over which control is achieved is re-valued. All of the subsidiary's assets, including goodwill, are to be restated at market value in preparing consolidated reports. Proponents of this ap-proach hold that all accounts of the subsidiary should reflect fair market value, regardless of the percentage of parent ownership. For example, they see no reason to list an asset at 80% market value plus 20% book value just because a 20% minority interest exists.

Let us return to the example of an 80% purchase as found on page 183 and illustrated in Worksheet 4–6. If the entity theory is applied to Company P's purchase of an 80% interest in Company S for $810,000, Company S would be worth $1,012,500 ($810,000 ÷ 80%). The determination and distribution of excess schedule would revalue the entire firm, not just the interest pur-chased, as follows:

Implied value of entire firm	$1,012,500
Less book value of subsidiary equity **(100%)**	700,000
Excess of market value over book value	$ 312,500[a]
Less undervaluation of inventory (100%)	**50,000**
Excess attributable to long-lived assets	$ 262,500
Less undervaluation of equipment (100%)	**150,000**
Goodwill applicable to entire firm	**$ 112,500**

The following worksheet entry would replace step (2) on Worksheet 4–6:

Inventory	50,000	
Equipment (net)	150,000	
Goodwill	112,500	
Investment in Subsidiary S		250,000
Appraisal Capital-Minority Interest		**62,500***

*$312,500[a] − [$810,000 price paid − ($700,000 total equity of subsidiary × 80% parent share = $560,000 book value acquired)]

The balance of the appraisal capital account would be amortized to the minority retained earnings account in future periods. The amortization would equal each period's extra depreciation or amortization charge caused by the write-up of assets applicable to the minority interest.

THE PARENT COMPANY THEORY

The approach in which all the subsidiary's assets are revalued is seldom used since it involves appraisal accounting. However, a compromise method, called the parent company theory, is sometimes used in practice. This method writes-up *identifiable* assets to 100% of market value, regardless of the parent's ownership percentage, and lets any remaining excess of cost flow to goodwill. Supporters of this method feel that consolidated statements are more meaningful when identifiable assets are stated at their full market value.

The following determination and distribution of excess schedule illustrates the compromise approach for the example on page 183:

Price paid for investment in Co. S	$810,000
Less book value of interest acquired **(100%)**	560,000
Excess of cost over book value	$250,000
Less undervaluation of inventory (100%)	**50,000**
Excess of cost attributable to long-lived assets	$200,000
Less undervaluation of equipment (100%)	**150,000**
Remaining excess to goodwill	**$ 50,000**

The distribution of excess contained in step (2) on Worksheet 4–6 would be replaced by the following worksheet entry:

Inventory	50,000	
Equipment (net)	150,000	
Goodwill	50,000	
Investment in Subsidiary S		250,000

Although this text uses the entity theory approach for financial statement format purposes, it otherwise will follow the pro rata market value approach derived from proprietary theory. This approach is more conservative and more consistent with current practice.

QUESTIONS

See page 160 { 1. What are the general conditions which require consolidated statements for two or more firms? What are the exceptions to these conditions?

2. A company may gain control over the assets of another firm by acquiring the assets of the firm or by purchasing a controlling interest in stock. Under which method is the acquired firm dissolved? Under which method is the acquired firm preserved as a separate legal and accounting entity?

3. What is the purpose of the consolidation process, and why does it start anew each year?

4. Are the eliminations that are made on a consolidated worksheet really journal entries that are recorded in the journals and ledgers? If not, what purpose do they serve?

5. Describe the two ways a stock acquisition may be recorded. At what value is the investment in the stock of the subsidiary recorded under each method?

6. What are the functions of the determination and distribution of excess schedule? Is it used for both a pooling and a purchase?

7. Under the purchase method, several accounts always are adjusted to their market value in consolidating, regardless of the price paid for the interest in the subsidiary. What are these accounts?

8. What is a bargain purchase, and what complications does it present to the consolidation process?

9. In a bargain purchase, describe how the value assigned to long-lived assets is determined when more than one long-lived asset exists.

10. Explain the meaning of the account Excess of Market Value of Subsidiary Current Assets over Cost. How does it arise in the consolidation process? Is it the same thing as negative goodwill? *See page 175 top.*

11. Explain the alternative methods for disclosing on the consolidated balance sheet the minority interest in the subsidiary stockholders' equity. Which method is best in theory?

12. Under the pooling method, the investment in subsidiary account should be eliminated against the parent's share of the subsidiary stock-

holders' equity, with no excess. If this result does not occur, what is the likely cause and how is it corrected?

EXERCISES

Exercise 1. The following balance sheets of Rose Company and Bench Company were prepared just prior to the purchase of a 100% interest in Bench by Rose.

Assets	Rose	Bench	Liabilities and Equity	Rose	Bench
Cash...........................	$500,000	$ 60,000	Current liabilities	$100,000	$100,000
Accounts receivable......	50,000	70,000	Bonds payable	300,000	100,000
Inventory.....................	50,000	100,000	Common stock		
Property, plant, and			($100 par)	200,000	150,000
equipment (net).........	200,000	300,000	Retained earnings.........	200,000	180,000
			Total liabilities		
Total assets..................	$800,000	$530,000	and equity	$800,000	$530,000

Rose paid $350,000 for a 100% interest in the net assets of Bench. The book values of Bench's assets and liabilities equal market values.
(1) Assume that the net assets are purchased directly from Bench Company.
   (a) Prepare the entry Rose would make to record the purchase.
   (b) Prepare a balance sheet for Rose Company immediately following the purchase.
(2) Assume that 100% of the outstanding stock of Bench Company is purchased from the former stockholders for a total of $350,000.
   (a) Prepare the entry Rose would make to record the purchase.
   (b) State how the investment would appear on Rose's unconsolidated balance sheet prepared immediately subsequent to the purchase.
   (c) Indicate how the consolidated balance sheet would appear.

Exercise 2. Pill Company purchased 100% of the outstanding stock of Sand Corporation for cash on January 1, 19X1. Just prior to the purchase, Sand Corporation prepared the following balance sheet:

Assets			Liabilities and Equity		
Current assets:			Current liabilities...........		$ 80,000
Cash........................	$70,000		Common stock ($5 par)..	$100,000	
Accounts receivable....	40,000		Retained earnings..........	190,000	290,000
Inventory..................	90,000	$200,000			
Property, plant, and					
equipment (net).........		170,000			
			Total liabilities		
Total assets..................		$370,000	and equity		$370,000

Pill feels that market values equal book values, except for the inventory, which is worth $110,000, and the property, plant, and equipment, which is appraised at $200,000.
(1) Assume that the price paid for the investment is $350,000 in cash.
    (a) Record the acquisition on the books of Pill Company.
    (b) Prepare a determination and distribution of excess schedule.
(2) Assume that the price paid for the investment is $300,000 in cash.
    (a) Record the acquisition on the books of Pill Company.
    (b) Prepare a determination and distribution of excess schedule.

Exercise 3. Donley Company purchased all of the outstanding stock of Andre Company for $110,000 and paid $5,000 for direct acquisition costs and $1,000 for management time (indirect costs). Just prior to the investment, the two firms had the following balance sheets:

Assets	Donley	Andre	Liabilities and Equity	Donley	Andre
Current assets..............	$120,000	$ 40,000	Current liabilities..........	$ 70,000	$ 35,000
Property, plant, and			Bonds payable	60,000	—
equipment (net).........	180,000	80,000	Common stock		
			($10 par)..................	70,000	30,000
			Retained earnings.........	100,000	55,000
			Total liabilities		
Total assets.................	$300,000	$120,000	and equity	$300,000	$120,000

Donley Company feels that the current assets and liabilities are valued correctly but that the property, plant, and equipment have a total market value of $90,000.
(1) Prepare the entry to record the purchase.
(2) Prepare a determination and distribution of excess schedule.
(3) Prepare the elimination entries that would be made on a consolidated worksheet.

Exercise 4. Black Company is contemplating the purchase of 8,000 shares of the outstanding stock of Wight Company, which has the following balance sheet just prior to acquisition:

Assets		Liabilities and Equity	
Cash................................	$ 20,000	Current liabilities..............	$250,000
Inventory..........................	280,000	Common stock ($5 par).....	50,000
Property, plant, and		Paid-in capital in excess	
equipment (net).............	400,000	of par...........................	130,000
Goodwill...........................	100,000	Retained earnings............	370,000
Total assets......................	$800,000	Total liabilities and equity..	$800,000

Black Company believes that the inventory has a market value of $400,000 and that the property, plant, and equipment is worth $500,000. For each of the following alternative purchase prices, prepare a determination and distri-

bution of excess schedule and the elimination entries that would be made on a worksheet subsequent to the purchase.
(1) The price paid per share acquired was $90.
(2) The price paid per share acquired was $74.
(3) The price paid per share acquired was $42.

Exercise 5.   Daryl Company is contemplating the purchase of 10,000 shares of the outstanding stock of Craig Company, which has the following balance sheet just prior to acquisition:

Assets		Liabilities and Equity	
Cash.................................	$ 50,000	Current liabilities..............	$ 70,000
Accounts receivable..........	90,000	Bonds payable	150,000
Inventory.........................	120,000	Common stock ($10 par)....	100,000
Plant and equipment (net) ..	240,000	Retained earnings.............	180,000
Total assets.....................	$500,000	Total liabilities and equity..	$500,000

Daryl Company paid $400,000 for its 100% investment in Craig Company. Inventory is estimated to have a market value of $140,000; the plant and equipment have an estimated total market value of $350,000. The purchase is considered a nontaxable exchange for the seller. The applicable tax rate is 30%.
(1) Record the purchase of the investment by Daryl Company.
(2) Prepare a determination and distribution of excess schedule for the investment.
(3) Prepare the elimination entries that would be made on the consolidated worksheet.

Exercise 6.   Lemming Company acquired 18,000 of the total 20,000 shares of Pursuit Company for $320,000. Immediately prior to the purchase, the balance sheets of the two firms were as follows:

Assets	Lemming	Pursuit	Liabilities and Equity	Lemming	Pursuit
Cash.........................	$ 600,000	$100,000	Current liabilities	$ 120,000	$200,000
Inventory..................	250,000	250,000	Common stock..........	400,000	200,000
Property, plant, and			Paid-in capital in		
equipment (net)......	450,000	300,000	excess of par..........	200,000	150,000
			Retained earnings......	580,000	100,000
			Total liabilities		
Total assets..............	$1,300,000	$650,000	and equity	$1,300,000	$650,000

Lemming Company feels that the inventory is worth $300,000 and that the property, plant, and equipment is worth $200,000. Based on these values:
(1) Record the investment.
(2) Prepare a determination and distribution of excess schedule.
(3) Prepare a consolidated balance sheet immediately subsequent to the purchase.

Exercise 7.   The balance sheet of Kozub Corporation on January 1, 19X3, was as follows:

Assets			Liabilities and Equity		
Current assets:			Current liabilities		$ 90,000
Cash......................	$ 80,000		Long-term liabilities:		
Accounts			Bonds payable	$300,000	
receivable...........	260,000		Deferred taxes........	50,000	350,000
Prepaid expenses ...	20,000	$ 360,000	Stockholders' equity:		
Property, plant,			Common stock		
and equipment:			($10 par).............	$300,000	
Land..................	$600,000		Retained earnings...	420,000	720,000
Building (net)	200,000	800,000			
			Total liabilities		
Total assets...............		$1,160,000	and equity		$1,160,000

On January 1, 19X3, Raabe purchased 27,000 shares of Kozub stock on the open market for $800,000. Raabe Company received the following appraisals supplementary to Kozub's balance sheet:

Accounts receivable.................................	$280,000
Land..	650,000
Bonds payable	280,000
Deferred taxes..	40,000

(1) Record the investment.
(2) Prepare a determination and distribution of excess schedule.
(3) Prepare the entries that would be made on the consolidated worksheet to eliminate the investment and to distribute the excess.

Exercise 8. Afram Company and Carlos Company are planning to combine their operations through a pooling of interests. Afram Company will exchange one share of its common stock for every two shares of Carlos Company stock. All of the Carlos shares will be exchanged by their owners for Afram shares. Immediately prior to the pooling of interests, the two firms have the following balance sheets:

Assets	Afram	Carlos	Liabilities and Equity	Afram	Carlos
Current assets..............	$250,000	$100,000	Liabilities	$120,000	$ 80,000
Property, plant, and			Common stock		
equipment (net).........	450,000	160,000	($10 par)...................	200,000	—
Goodwill......................	—	40,000	Common stock		
			($1 stated value)........	—	10,000
			Additional paid-in		
			capital	50,000	90,000
			Retained earnings.........	330,000	120,000
			Total liabilities and		
Total assets..................	$700,000	$300,000	equity.......................	$700,000	$300,000

(1) Prepare the entry to record the investment as a pooling of interests. Support your entry with an equity transfer schedule.
(2) Prepare a consolidated balance sheet immediately subsequent to the investment.

Exercise 9. Varsity Company and Top Company had the following balance sheets immediately prior to a pooling of interests:

Assets	Varsity	Top	Liabilities and Equity	Varsity	Top
Current assets...........	$ 500,000	$ 300,000	Liabilities............	$ 300,000	$ 500,000
Property, plant, and equipment (net)......	1,200,000	800,000	Common stock ($2 par)	400,000	—
			Common stock ($1 par)	—	150,000
			Paid-in capital in excess of par ...	150,000	50,000
			Retained earnings..........	850,000	400,000
			Total liabilities		
Total assets...............	$1,700,000	$1,100,000	and equity	$1,700,000	$1,100,000

Varsity will exchange its stock for all of the outstanding stock of Top Company. On Varsity's books, record the investment for each of the following situations. Support each entry with an equity transfer schedule.

(1) Varsity issues 80,000 shares.
(2) Varsity issues 100,000 shares.
(3) Varsity issues 150,000 shares.
(4) Varsity issues 250,000 shares.

Exercise 10. Jacob Company will issue shares of $5 par stock for all of the outstanding stock of Thorton Company. Jacob Company common stock has a current market value of $25 per share. Thorton Company prepared the following balance sheet just prior to the acquisition:

Assets		Liabilities and Equity	
Current assets..............	$80,000	Liabilities	$100,000
Property, plant, and equipment (net).........	250,000	Common stock ($2 par)	20,000
		Paid-in capital in excess of par	80,000
		Retained earnings.................	130,000
Total assets..................	$330,000	Total liabilities and equity......	$330,000

Jacob Company estimated the value of the current assets to be $100,000 and the value of the property, plant, and equipment account to be $400,000. Jacob agreed that the liabilities were correctly stated. Jacob issued sufficient shares of stock so that the market value of the stock equaled the market value of Thorton's net assets.

(1) Calculate the stock exchange ratio.
(2) Assuming that the criteria for a pooling of interests are met, record the investment in the stock of Thorton Company. Support your entry with an equity transfer schedule.
(3) Assuming that the criteria for a pooling of interests are not met, record the investment in the stock of Thorton Company.

Exercise 11. Subtra Inc. had the following balance sheet on December 31, 19X7:

Assets		Liabilities and Equity	
Current assets...........	$ 50,000	Liabilities................................	$150,000
Land.........................	70,000	Common stock ($10 par)	50,000
Buildings (net)...........	230,000	Retained earnings....................	400,000
Equipment (net).........	200,000		
Goodwill....................	50,000		
Total assets...............	$600,000	Total liabilities and equity.........	$600,000

Prior to a pooling of interests in which Parma was the issuer, Parma had the following stockholders' equity:

Common stock ($10 par)...........................	$ 500,000
Retained earnings....................................	2,000,000
	$2,500,000
Less treasury stock, 5,000 shares at cost...	300,000
Total stockholders' equity.....................	$2,200,000

Parma exchanged the 5,000 shares of treasury stock plus 5,000 new shares of common stock for 90% of the common stock of Subtra. $10,000 was paid in direct acquisition costs.

Record the acquisition of Subtra as a pooling of interests. Prepare an equity transfer schedule as support.

Exercise 12. Mittco Industries acquired 90% of the outstanding stock of Pardon Corporation by exchanging 20,000 shares of $35 market value ($5 stated value) stock directly with Pardon's stockholders on October 1, 19X6. On the exchange date, Pardon had the following stockholders' equity:

Common stock ($2 par)..............................	$ 50,000
Paid-in capital in excess of par...................	200,000
Retained earnings.....................................	250,000
Total equity...	$500,000

Mittco had the following balance sheet on December 31, 19X6:

Assets		Liabilities and Equity		
Current assets...............	$ 856,000	Liabilities		$ 900,000
Investment in Pardon		Common stock ($5 stated		
Corporation................	700,000	value)	$1,000,000	
Property, plant, and		Additional paid-in capital	700,000	
equipment (net)..........	2,150,000	Retained earnings...............	1,106,000	2,806,000
Total assets...................	$3,706,000	Total liabilities and equity....		$3,706,000

No entries have been made in the investment account since the inception of the pooling.

Prepare the necessary journal entry to correctly portray the above combination as a pooling of interests. Provide an equity transfer schedule as support.

Exercise 13. On January 1, 19X6, Trio Corporation exchanged 6,600 shares of its $5 par ($12 market value) common stock for 90% of the outstanding shares of Kling Corporation in a legitimate pooling of interests. Just prior to the combination, Kling Corporation had the following balance sheet:

Assets		Liabilities and Equity		
Current assets....................	$ 40,000	Current liabilities...................		$ 50,000
Property, plant, and		Common stock ($1 par)	$ 44,000	
equipment (net)..............	360,000	Paid-in capital in excess of		
Patents...........................	20,000	par	66,000	
		Retained earnings................	260,000	370,000
Total assets.......................	$420,000	Total liabilities and equity		$420,000

On December 31, 19X6, Trio Corporation purchased 3,000 shares of Kling Corporation common stock for $11 per share. By December 31, Kling's income for 19X6 was $200,000.

(1) Prepare the journal entry to record the investment acquired on January 1, 19X6, as a pooling of interests. Provide an equity transfer schedule as support.

(2) Prepare the journal entry to record the acquisition of the 3,000 additional shares on December 31, 19X6.

Appendix Exercise. Valco Company purchased 80% of the common stock of Brand Company for $200,000 when Brand had the following balance sheet:

Assets		Liabilities and Equity	
Cash.........................	$ 20,000	Liabilities................................	$110,000
Inventory..................	40,000	Common stock........................	50,000
Equipment (net).........	200,000	Retained earnings....................	100,000
Total assets...............	$260,000	Total liabilities and equity.........	$260,000

The inventory has a market value of $50,000, and the equipment has a market value of $260,000. Prepare determination and distribution of excess schedules to reflect each of the following approaches.

(1) The pro rata market value approach of the proprietary theory.

(2) The entity theory.

(3) The parent company (compromise) approach.

PROBLEMS

Present value tables are on pages 1178–1179.

Problem 4–1. Ricardo Company and Summer Company had the following balance sheets on June 30, 19X1:

Assets	Ricardo	Summer
Current assets......................................	$150,000	$ 70,000
Land..	100,000	40,000
Building (net)	340,000	100,000
Equipment (net)...................................	390,000	110,000
Goodwill..	—	30,000
Total assets.......................................	$980,000	$350,000

Liabilities and Equity		
Current liabilities	$160,000	$ 40,000
Common stock ($5 par).........................	400,000	200,000
Retained earnings.................................	420,000	110,000
Total liabilities and equity......................	$980,000	$350,000

On June 30, 19X1, Ricardo Company exchanged 400, $1,000 bonds for 100% of the outstanding stock of Summer Company. On July 1, 19X1, some of the former stockholders of Summer Company sold the bonds received at the quoted price of 97. Ricardo Company hired an independent appraiser, who found the land and the equipment to be undervalued by $70,000 and $20,000, respectively.

Required:
(1) Record the investment in Summer Company common stock.
(2) Prepare a determination and distribution of excess schedule.
(3) Prepare a consolidated balance sheet for July 1, 19X1, immediately subsequent to the acquisition.

Suggestion: In the determination and distribution of excess schedule, make the parent's share of the subsidiary's goodwill account available to adjust other assets.

Problem 4–2.   Balance sheets for Abbott Company, Bristol Company, and Costello Company on December 31, 19X1, are as follows:

	Abbott	Bristol	Costello
Cash...	$ 200,000	$100,000	$ 50,000
Inventory..	300,000	150,000	100,000
Property, plant, and equipment (net)........	500,000	200,000	150,000
Goodwill...	100,000	50,000	25,000
Total assets..	$1,100,000	$500,000	$325,000
Liabilities...	$ 300,000	$100,000	$150,000
Common stock ($10 par).........................	200,000	100,000	50,000
Paid-in capital in excess of par................	400,000	50,000	75,000
Retained earnings..................................	200,000	250,000	50,000
Total liabilities and equity.......................	$1,100,000	$500,000	$325,000

On this date, Abbott purchased all of the common stock of Bristol Company by issuing 600, 11% bonds with a face value of $1,000 each. (11% was the prevailing rate for similar bonds on the day of the sale.) Abbott also exchanged 5,000 shares of its common stock, with a market value of $30 each, for 80% of the common stock of Costello Company.

Required:

Prepare a determination and distribution of excess schedule and a consolidated balance sheet for December 31, 19X1, under each of the following assumptions.

(1) Bristol's inventory has a market value of $175,000, and its property, plant, and equipment is appraised at $325,000. Costello's inventory is understated by $50,000.

(2) Bristol's inventory is understated by $100,000, and the market value of its property, plant, and equipment is $500,000. Costello's liabilities are overstated by $10,000. Costello's inventory is grossly understated; its fair market value is $250,000.

Suggestion: Make goodwill available for reassignment in both determination and distribution schedules. Notice that it is needed in some cases and not in others.

Problem 4–3. Balance sheets for Delta Company and Essex Company on December 31, 19X1, are as follows:

Assets	Delta	Essex
Cash..	$ 800,000	$100,000
Inventory...	600,000	300,000
Property, plant, and equipment (net)...............	1,200,000	400,000
Total assets...	$2,600,000	$800,000
Liabilities and Equity		
Liabilities...	$ 500,000	$100,000
Common stock ($10 par)...............................	200,000	50,000
Paid-in capital in excess of par.......................	800,000	350,000
Retained earnings.......................................	1,100,000	300,000
Total liabilities and equity.............................	$2,600,000	$800,000

On this date, Delta purchased 80% of Essex Company common stock.

Required:

Record the investment, prepare a determination and distribution of excess schedule when needed, and prepare a consolidated balance sheet for December 31, 19X1, under each of the following assumptions.

(1) Delta issues 10,000 shares of its common stock in exchange for 4,000 shares of Essex common stock. The market values of Delta and Essex stock are not known since neither are traded publicly. Reliable market values are available for Essex's assets: the inventory and the property, plant, and equipment are valued at $400,000 and $500,000, respectively. Goodwill does not appear to exist.

(2) Delta issues 10,000 shares of its common stock, with a market value of $60 each, for 4,000 shares of Essex stock. Essex's assets and liabilities are stated fairly, except for property, plant, and equipment, which is undervalued by $100,000.

(3) Delta pays $360,000 in cash for the stock of Essex. Appraisals indicate that Essex's inventory is worth $400,000 and its property, plant, and equipment is worth approximately $100,000 due to its specialized nature.

Problem 4–4. Sparton Company had the following balance sheet on December 31, 19X1:

Assets		Liabilities and Equity	
Cash..............................	$ 70,000	Current liabilities	$120,000
Accounts receivable..........	60,000	Deferred rental income.....	50,000
Inventory.........................	150,000	Bonds payable, 10%.........	250,000
Property, plant, and		Common stock ($10 par)...	100,000
equipment (net).............	400,000	Paid-in capital in excess	
Long-term investment in		of par	200,000
marketable securities.....	150,000	Retained earnings............	210,000
Goodwill..........................	100,000		
Total assets......................	$930,000	Total liabilities and equity ..	$930,000

On that date, Port Company purchased an 80% interest in Spartan Company by exchanging 10,000 shares of its $20 par common stock for Spartan common stock. Port determined that, except for the assets with the following market values, all other assets and all liabilities of Spartan had market values equal to their book values:

> Inventory, $200,000 due to previous use of Lifo.
> Property, plant, and equipment, $500,000.
> Investment in marketable securities, $170,000.

The purchase was a tax-free exchange to the seller, which means that Port Company will use the book values of Sparton's assets for tax purposes. Sparton Company has $150,000 of tax loss carryovers. Port Company will be able to carry back $100,000 of losses to offset taxes paid. The balance of the carryovers will not be used within a year but will be used as an offset against deferred tax liabilities. The tax rate of both firms is 30%.

Required:
Record the investment and prepare a determination and distribution of excess schedule assuming the value given was $600,000.

Suggestion: The tax loss carryback is a current asset, and the tax loss carryforward is a long-lived asset. Asset adjustments other than goodwill should be accompanied by the appropriate deferred tax liability. Existing goodwill should be made available for assignment to other assets if needed.

Special Challenge: Solve this problem assuming the value given was $400,000. In valuing the assets, keep in mind the nondeductibility of the excess.

Problem 4–5. Dart Corporation had the following balance sheet on January 1, 19X3, the date that Spanwood Company purchased a controlling interest:

Assets		Liabilities and Equity		
Current assets...........	$ 190,000	Current liabilities		$ 180,000
Land........................	250,000	Bonds payable........................		400,000
Buildings (net)...........	150,000	Common stock ($2 par)	$100,000	
Equipment (net).........	400,000	Paid-in capital in excess of		
Goodwill...................	40,000	par	50,000	
		Retained earnings...................	300,000	450,000
Total assets...............	$1,030,000	Total liabilities and equity........		$1,030,000

Assets and liabilities that had market values different from cost are as follows:

	Market Value
Current assets...................................	$230,000
Land...	490,000
Buildings	160,000
Equipment...	350,000
Bonds payable	410,000

Spanwood purchased 45,000 shares of Dart common stock for $475,000. No tax ramifications need to be considered.

Required:
(1) Record the investment.
(2) Prepare a determination and distribution of excess schedule.
(3) Prepare the elimination entries that would be made on the consolidated worksheet.

Suggestion: This is a bargain purchase which will require allocation. Be sure to make the parent's share of the subsidiary's goodwill available for assignment to long-lived assets. The assigned value to be allocated should be only the parent's share of the subsidiary book values plus the remaining excess of market value.

Problem 4–6.   The balance sheets of Manor Company and Frome Company on December 31, 19X1, are as follows:

Assets	Manor	Frome
Current assets..	$ 300,000	$250,000
Property, plant, and equipment..............................	1,000,000	500,000
Accumulated depreciation	(300,000)	(200,000)
Total assets...	$1,000,000	$550,000

Liabilities and Equity		
Liabilities...	$ 200,000	$150,000
Common stock ($10 par)..	300,000	—
Common stock ($1 par)..	—	50,000
Paid-in capital in excess of par..............................	200,000	250,000
Retained earnings...	300,000	100,000
Total liabilities and equity......................................	$1,000,000	$550,000

On this date, Manor Company exchanged one share of newly issued common stock for every two shares of Frome Company common stock. Manor acquired all of the Frome stock outstanding. The market value of a share of Manor common stock is $25. Frome's assets are stated at values approximating market values, except for the property, plant, and equipment, which has a market value of $400,000.

Required:
(1) Assume that the acquisition does not meet the pooling criteria.
   (a) Record the investment in Frome Company stock.
   (b) Prepare a determination and distribution of excess schedule.
   (c) Prepare a consolidated balance sheet for December 31, 19X1, immediately subsequent to the investment.
(2) Assume that the acquisition does meet the pooling criteria.
   (a) Record the investment in Frome Company common stock.
   (b) Prepare a consolidated balance sheet for December 31, 19X1, immediately subsequent to the investment.

Suggestion: Use an equity transfer diagram to aid in the recording of the pooling of interests.

Problem 4–7. On December 31, 19X1, Mac Company purchased on the open market 60% of the outstanding shares of Van Company common stock and 75% of the outstanding shares of Dorn Company common stock. The following unconsolidated balance sheets of the companies were prepared immediately subsequent to the purchase:

	Mac	Van	Dorn
Cash...	$ 50,000	$ 30,000	$ 60,000
Inventory...	300,000	170,000	200,000
Property, plant, and equipment (net)............	500,000	200,000	340,000
Investment in Van Company........................	300,000	—	—
Investment in Dorn Company	350,000	—	—
Total assets...	$1,500,000	$400,000	$600,000
Current liabilities	$ 150,000	$ 50,000	$ 80,000
Common stock ($10 par).............................	500,000	—	—
Common stock ($5 par)..............................	—	100,000	—
Common stock ($1 par)..............................	—	—	10,000
Paid-in capital in excess of par....................	700,000	80,000	290,000
Retained earnings......................................	150,000	170,000	220,000
Total liabilities and equity..........................	$1,500,000	$400,000	$600,000

Mac Company feels that the inventory and property, plant, and equipment accounts of the subsidiaries do not reflect market values. Mac Company has secured the following market values:

	Van	Dorn
Inventory..................................	$220,000	$300,000
Property, plant, and equipment..	260,000	400,000

Required:

(1) Prepare a determination and distribution of excess schedule for each investment.

(2) Prepare a worksheet for a consolidated balance sheet for December 31, 19X1.

(3) Prepare the formal consolidated balance sheet for December 31, 19X1.

Problem 4–8. Yankee Corporation acquired 80% of the outstanding stock of Giant Corporation on December 31, 19X0 for $300,000 cash. The acquisition occurred on the last day of the fiscal year for both firms. Yankee paid $15,000 in direct acquisition costs to consummate the purchase. The following balance sheets of the parent and subsidiary were prepared immediately subsequent to the investment:

	Yankee	Giant
Cash.	$ 170,000	$ 80,000
Accounts receivable	360,000	140,000
Inventory	520,000	—
Land.	1,000,000	100,000
Building (net)	700,000	230,000
Equipment (net).	1,500,000	400,000
Investment in Giant	315,000	—
Total assets.	$4,565,000	$950,000
Current liabilities	$ 500,000	$ 85,000
Bonds payable, 10%, due December 31, 19X5	—	400,000
Discount on bonds payable	—	(7,270)
Common stock ($1 par)	600,000	50,000
Paid-in capital in excess of par	1,400,000	110,000
Retained earnings.	2,065,000	312,270
Total liabilities and equity	$4,565,000	$950,000

Giant Corporation's 10% bonds originally were issued on January 1, 19W6, at a discount of $14,540. The original discount has been amortized on a straight-line basis. Interest on the bonds is paid annually on December 31. Similar bonds are currently yielding 12% per annum.

On the purchase date, some of Giant Corporation's assets were recorded at book values not consistent with market values. The following market values were obtained:

Land.	$186,000
Building.	279,000
Equipment.	465,000

Required:

(1) Prepare a determination and distribution of excess schedule for the investment in Giant Corporation. The schedule should include a revaluation of the bonds based on the present value of the future cash flows at the current rate of interest.

(2) Prepare a worksheet for a consolidated balance sheet on December 31, 19X0.

(3) Prepare a formal consolidated balance sheet for December 31, 19X0.

Suggestion: Present value analysis is needed to calculate the market value of the bonds. In addition, this is a bargain purchase which requires allocation of available excess to the separate assets. The value to be assigned is the parent's interest in the subsidiary's recorded book values less the remaining excess of book value over cost of the investment.

Problem 4–9.   The balance sheets of Garth Company and Bowen Company as of December 31, 19X6, are as follows:

Garth Company

Cash............................	$ 30,000	Payables......................	$ 1,750,000
Receivables (net)	320,000	Accruals	450,000
Inventories...................	1,600,000	Common stock	
Prepayments...............	47,000	($100 par)	1,000,000
Property, plant, and		Retained earnings.........	800,000
equipment (net).........	2,003,000		
		Total liabilities	
Total assets..................	$ 4,000,000	and equity	$ 4,000,000

Bowen Company

Cash............................	$ 5,200,000	Payables......................	$ 7,992,000
Receivables (net)	2,400,000	Accruals	1,615,000
Inventories...................	11,200,000	Common stock	
Prepayments...............	422,000	($100 par)	10,000,000
Property, plant, and		Retained earnings.........	20,513,000
equipment (net).........	18,978,000		
Investment in Garth Co.	1,920,000		
		Total liabilities and	
Total assets..................	$40,120,000	equity......................	$40,120,000

An appraisal on December 31, 19X6, which was considered carefully and approved by the boards of directors of both firms, placed a total replacement value, less depreciation, of $3,203,000 on Garth's property, plant, and equipment.

Bowen Company offered to purchase all the assets of Garth Company, subject to its liabilities, as of December 31, 19X6, for $3,000,000. However, 40% of the stockholders of Garth Company objected to the price because it did not include any consideration for goodwill, which they believed to be worth at least $500,000. A counterproposal was made, and a final agreement was reached. In exchange for its own shares, Bowen acquired 60% of the common stock of Garth at the agreed upon market value of $320 per share. The purchase is structured as a tax-free exchange to the seller; thus Bowen will use the book value of the assets for future tax purposes. The tax rate for both firms is 30%.

Required:

Prepare a consolidated worksheet and a consolidated balance sheet as of December 31, 19X6.   (AICPA adapted)

Suggestion: Consider the deferred tax liability applicable to the asset revaluation.

Problem 4–10.   The balance sheets of Hellon Company and Vermat Company on December 31, 19X1, are as follows:

	Hellon	Vermat
Current assets	$ 800,000	$ 300,000
Property, plant, and equipment	2,700,000	1,700,000
Accumulated depreciation	(750,000)	(600,000)
Investment in Vermat Company	1,200,000	—
Total assets	$3,950,000	$1,400,000
Current liabilities	$ 600,000	$ 200,000
Common stock ($10 par)	1,400,000	—
Common stock ($2 par)	—	300,000
Paid-in capital in excess of par	800,000	400,000
Retained earnings	1,150,000	500,000
Total liabilities and equity	$3,950,000	$1,400,000

Just prior to the preparation of these balance sheets, Hellon and Vermat combined in a pooling of interests. Hellon issued 20,000 shares of its common stock for all the outstanding stock of Vermat. The investment was recorded properly.

Required:

(1) Prepare a worksheet for a consolidated balance sheet on December 31, 19X1.

(2) Prepare a formal consolidated balance sheet on December 31, 19X1.

Problem 4–11.   Knoll Company acquired 90% of the outstanding stock of Armon Corporation on April 15, 19X1, by exchanging three shares of its common stock for every five shares of Armon Corporation common stock. At this time, Knoll stock had a market value of $15 per share.

Immediately after this transaction, the two companies had the following balance sheets:

	Knoll	Armon
Current assets	$ 850,000	$ 200,000
Property, plant, and equipment	2,800,000	1,650,000
Accumulated depreciation	(900,000)	(500,000)
Investment in Armon Corporation	1,620,000	—
Total assets	$4,370,000	$1,350,000
Liabilities	$ 520,000	$ 440,000
Common stock ($5 par)	2,040,000	—
Common stock ($1 stated value)	—	200,000
Additional paid-in capital	1,180,000	650,000
Retained earnings	630,000	60,000
Total liabilities and equity	$4,370,000	$1,350,000

Knoll's investment account reflects the market value of the shares issued. The market value of Armon's property, plant and equipment is $1,500,000. Armon also has $200,000 of tax loss carryovers that can be used by Knoll to receive a refund of taxes already paid. The acquisition was structured as a tax-free exchange as to the seller, thus Knoll will be required to use Armon's book values for future tax purposes. Both firms have a 30% tax rate.

Required:
Prepare a consolidated worksheet and a consolidated balance sheet under each of the following assumptions:
(1) The combination is considered to be a purchase.
(2) The combination is considered to be a pooling of interests. (If necessary, correct the investment account prior to consolidating.)

Suggestion: In the purchase case, record the deferred tax liability applicable to the asset revaluation. The tax loss carryback should be recorded also. In the pooling case, the tax loss carryforward should be recorded and considered as a change in principle. This requires the adjustment of the subsidiary retained earnings prior to applying the equity transfer rules.

Problem 4–12. On April 30, 19X1, Petrofab Corporation acquired 95% of the outstanding stock of AMCO Industries in exchange for 20,000 shares of its previously unissued stock. Petrofab stock has a market value of $32 per share. Out-of-pocket costs of the business combination paid by Petrofab Corporation on April 30, 19X1, were as follows:

Direct acquisition costs	
(legal fees and finder's fees)	$18,500
Security and stock issuance costs.................	22,250

There were no intercompany transactions prior to the business combination. AMCO Industries will become a subsidiary of Petrofab Corporation.

Comparative balance sheets of the two companies just prior to the combination are as follows:

	Petrofab Corporation	AMCO Industries
Cash..	$ 300,000	$ 100,000
Marketable securities	80,000	40,000
Other current assets...	650,000	160,000
Property, plant, and equipment (net)........................	2,500,000	850,000
Patents	40,000	60,000
Total assets...	$3,570,000	$1,210,000
Current liabilities	$ 410,000	$ 340,000
Bonds payable	1,000,000	300,000
Common stock ($1 par)...	300,000	—
Common stock ($25 par)	—	25,000
Paid-in capital in excess of par...............................	1,200,000	275,000
Retained earnings..	660,000	270,000
Total liabilities and equity.......................................	$3,570,000	$1,210,000

On April 30, 19X1, AMCO's book values approximated market values, except for the following:

Marketable securities	$ 60,000
Property, plant, and equipment	910,000
Patents	80,000
Bonds payable	280,000

Required:

(1) Prepare the entry Petrofab would make on April 30, 19X1, to record the investment in the stock of AMCO Industries as: (a) a purchase and (b) a pooling of interests.

(2) Prepare a consolidated balance sheet for April 30, 19X1, immediately subsequent to the acquisition assuming that the acquisition is regarded as: (a) a purchase and (b) a pooling of interests.

(3) Compare the differences on the 19X1 fiscal year income statement that would occur as a result of the purchase versus pooling treatment.

Problem 4–13.   Comparative balance sheets of Edward Corporation and its subsidiary Hinkley Corporation on June 30, 19X7, are as follows:

	Edward Corporation	Hinkley Corporation
Cash	$ 153,200	$ 40,000
Accounts receivable	416,100	110,000
Prepayments	48,000	5,500
Land	750,000	160,000
Buildings	690,000	147,000
Accumulated depreciation	(50,000)	(12,000)
Delivery trucks	515,500	190,000
Accumulated depreciation	(35,000)	(10,000)
Investment in Hinkley Corporation	722,000	—
Total assets	$3,209,800	$630,500
Accounts payable	$ 152,210	$ 80,500
Accrued expenses	16,100	3,600
Bonds payable	400,000	—
Common stock ($2 par)	412,000	—
Common stock ($10 par)	—	400,000
Paid-in capital in excess of par	755,000	—
Retained earnings	1,474,490	146,400
Total liabilities and equity	$3,209,800	$630,500

On June 27, 19X7, Edward exchanged 18,000 of its shares, with a market value of $35 each, for 90% of the shares of Hinkley Corporation, using a one-for-two exchange rate. The transaction qualified as a pooling of interests. Edward Corporation paid $20,000 in direct acquisition costs which were capitalized in the investment account. Assume the Hinkley equity at the pooling was the same as shown above.

On June 30, 19X7, Edward acquired another 5% of Hinkley stock in exchange for 2,000 shares of Edward common stock which had a per share market value of $36 on that date.

Any payment in excess of book value is considered a payment for goodwill.

Required:

Prepare the correcting entries to be made on Edward's books and a work-sheet for a June 30, 19X7 consolidated balance sheet.

Suggestion: The first acquisition is a pooling of interests and requires a correction entry for the investment account. It should be supported by an equity transfer diagram. The second acquisition cannot meet the criteria for a pooling of interests and should be accounted for as a purchase. Be careful with the direct acquisition costs in the pooling.

Worksheet 4–1 (see page 163)

100% Ownership
Company P and
Worksheet for Consolidated
December

		Trial Balance	
		Company P	Company S
1	Debits:		
2	Cash	100,000	
3	Accounts Receivable	300,000	200,000
4	Inventory	100,000	100,000
5	**Investment in Subsidiary S**	**500,000**	
6	Equipment (net)	150,000	300,000
7	Total	1,150,000	600,000
8	Credits:		
9	Current Liabilities	150,000	100,000
10	Bonds Payable	300,000	
11	Common Stock, Co. P	100,000	
12	Retained Earnings, Co. P	600,000	
13	**Common Stock, Co. S**		**200,000**
14	**Retained Earnings, Co. S**		**300,000**
15	Total	1,150,000	600,000

Price Equals Book Value
Subsidiary Company S
Balance Sheet
31, 19X1

WORKSHEET 4–1

Eliminations & Adjustments				Consolidated Balance Sheet			
Dr.		Cr.		Dr.		Cr.	
							1
				100,000			2
				500,000			3
				200,000			4
		(1)	500,000				5
				450,000			6
							7
							8
						250,000	9
						300,000	10
						100,000	11
						600,000	12
(1)	200,000						13
(1)	300,000						14
	500,000		500,000	1,250,000		1,250,000	15

Eliminations and Adjustments:
(1) Eliminate the investment in subsidiary account against the subsidiary equity accounts.

Worksheet 4–2 (see page 167)

(see page 167)

100% Interest;
Company P and
Worksheet for Consolidated
December

		Trial Balance	
		Company P	Company S
1	Debits:		
2	Cash	200,000	150,000
3	Accounts Receivable	300,000	250,000
4	**Inventory**	500,000	**300,000**
5	Land	100,000	
6	Buildings (net)	900,000	
7	**Equipment (net)**	650,000	**400,000**
8	**Investment in Subsidiary S**	**1,010,000**	
9			
10	**Goodwill**		
11	Total	3,660,000	1,100,000
12	Credits:		
13	Current Liabilities	300,000	100,000
14	Bonds Payable	500,000	300,000
15	Common Stock ($10 par), Co. P	700,000	
16	Paid-In Capital in Excess of Par, Co. P	1,300,000	
17	Retained Earnings, Co. P	860,000	
18	Common Stock ($5 par), Co. S		50,000
19	Paid-In Capital in Excess of Par, Co. S		350,000
20	Retained Earnings, Co. S		300,000
21	Total	3,660,000	1,100,000

Price Exceeds Market Value
Subsidiary Company S
Balance Sheet
31, 19X1

WORKSHEET 4–2

Eliminations & Adjustments				Consolidated Balance Sheet			
Dr.		Cr.		Dr.	Cr.		
							1
				350,000			2
				550,000			3
(2)	50,000			850,000			4
				100,000			5
				900,000			6
(2)	150,000			1,200,000			7
		(1)	700,000				8
		(2)	310,000				9
(2)	110,000			110,000			10
							11
							12
					400,000		13
					800,000		14
					700,000		15
					1,300,000		16
					860,000		17
(1)	50,000						18
(1)	350,000						19
(1)	300,000						20
	1,010,000		1,010,000	4,060,000	4,060,000		21

Eliminations and Adjustments:

(1) Eliminate intercompany accounts. The investment in subsidiary account includes a 100% interest in the stockholders' equity of Company S. Therefore, the entire stockholders' equity of Company S is eliminated against the investment account. The balance of the investment account, $310,000, has no intercompany counterpart, but rather reflects the total undervaluation of Company S's assets. This balance is distributed in step (2).

(2) Distribute the $310,000 undervaluation of Company S's assets to the proper asset accounts. The following information for this distribution is taken from the determination and distribution of excess schedule:

Excess of cost over book value		$310,000
Distribute to:		
Inventory...	$ 50,000	
Equipment...	150,000	
Goodwill..	110,000	310,000
		$ 0

Worksheet 4–3 (see page 169)   **100% Interest; Price**
Company P and
Worksheet for
December

		Trial Balance	
		Company P	Company S
1	Debits:		
2	Cash	200,000	150,000
3	Accounts Receivable	300,000	250,000
4	**Inventory**	500,000	**300,000**
5	Land	100,000	
6	Buildings (net)	900,000	
7	**Equipment (net)**	650,000	**400,000**
8	Investment in Subsidiary S	810,000	
9			
10	Total	3,460,000	1,100,000
11	Credits:		
12	Current Liabilities	300,000	100,000
13	Bonds Payable	500,000	300,000
14	Common Stock ($10 par), Co. P	660,000	
15	Paid-In Capital in Excess of Par, Co. P	1,140,000	
16	Retained Earnings, Co. P	860,000	
17	Common Stock ($5 par), Co. S		50,000
18	Paid-In Capital in Excess of Par, Co. S		350,000
19	Retained Earnings, Co. S		300,000
20	Total	3,460,000	1,100,000

Between Book Value and Market Value   **WORKSHEET 4-3**
Subsidiary Company S
Consolidated Balance Sheet
31, 19X1

Eliminations & Adjustments				Consolidated Balance Sheet			
Dr.		Cr.		Dr.	Cr.		
							1
				350,000			2
				550,000			3
(2)	50,000			850,000			4
				100,000			5
				900,000			6
(2)	60,000			1,110,000			7
		(1)	700,000				8
		(2)	110,000				9
							10
							11
					400,000		12
					800,000		13
					660,000		14
					1,140,000		15
					860,000		16
(1)	50,000						17
(1)	350,000						18
(1)	300,000						19
	810,000		810,000	3,860,000	3,860,000		20

Eliminations and Adjustments:
(1) Eliminate intercompany accounts. The investment in subsidiary account includes a 100% interest in the stockholders' equity of Company S. Thus, the entire stockholders' equity of Company S is eliminated against the investment account.
(2) The balance of the investment account, $110,000, represents the total undervaluation of Company S's assets. Distribute the undervaluation amount to the proper asset accounts in the following manner, as prescribed by the determination and distribution of excess schedule:

Excess of cost over book value		$110,000
Distribute to:		
Inventory...	**$ 50,000**	
Equipment..	**60,000**	110,000
		$ 0

Worksheet 4–4 (see page 173)

100% Interest;
Company P and
Worksheet for Consolidated
December

		Trial Balance	
		Company P	Company S
1	Debits:		
2	Cash	200,000	150,000
3	Accounts Receivable	300,000	250,000
4	**Inventory**	500,000	**300,000**
5	Land	100,000	
6	Buildings (net)	900,000	
7	**Equipment (net)**	650,000	**400,000**
8	Investment in Subsidiary S	610,000	
9	Total	3,260,000	1,100,000
10	Credits:		
11	Current Liabilities	300,000	100,000
12	Bonds Payable	500,000	300,000
13	Common Stock ($10 par), Co. P	620,000	
14	Paid-In Capital in Excess of Par, Co. P	980,000	
15	Retained Earnings, Co. P	860,000	
16	Common Stock ($5 par), Co. S		50,000
17	Paid-In Capital in Excess of Par, Co. S		350,000
18	Retained Earnings, Co. S		300,000
19	Total	3,260,000	1,100,000

Cost Less Than Book Value
Subsidiary Company S
Balance Sheet
31, 19X1

WORKSHEET 4–4

Eliminations & Adjustments				Consolidated Balance Sheet			
Dr.		Cr.		Dr.		Cr.	
							1
				350,000			2
				550,000			3
(2)	50,000			850,000			4
				100,000			5
				900,000			6
		(2)	140,000	910,000			7
(2)	90,000	(1)	700,000				8
							9
							10
						400,000	11
						800,000	12
						620,000	13
						980,000	14
						860,000	15
(1)	50,000						16
(1)	350,000						17
(1)	300,000						18
	840,000		840,000	3,660,000		3,660,000	19

Eliminations and Adjustments:
(1) Eliminate intercompany accounts. Since the entire stockholders' equity of Company S is owned by Company P, it must be completely eliminated against the investment account. The negative or credit balance of $90,000 which results from the elimination represents the net overvaluation of Company S's assets.
(2) Distribute the credit balance of the investment account to the specific subsidiary accounts according to the determination and distribution of excess schedule. In this example, the net decrease in asset value is distributed so as to increase the inventory by $50,000 and decrease the equipment by $140,000.

Excess of **book** value **over cost**.....................................		$ 90,000
Distribute to:		
Inventory...	$ 50,000	
Equipment..	(140,000)	90,000
		$ 0

Worksheet 4–5 (see page 181)

80% Interest;
Company P and
Worksheet for Consolidated
December

		Trial Balance	
		Company P	Company S
1	Debits:		
2	Cash	200,000	
3	Accounts Receivable	300,000	200,000
4	Inventory	100,000	100,000
5	**Investment in Subsidiary S**	**400,000**	
6	Equipment (net)	150,000	300,000
7	Total	1,150,000	600,000
8	Credits:		
9	Current Liabilities	150,000	100,000
10	Bonds Payable	300,000	
11	Common Stock, Co. P	100,000	
12	Retained Earnings, Co. P	600,000	
13	**Common Stock, Co. S**		**200,000**
14	**Retained Earnings, Co. S**		**300,000**
15	**Minority Interest**		
16	Total	1,150,000	600,000

Price Equals Book Value
Subsidiary Company S
Balance Sheet
31, 19X1

WORKSHEET 4–5

Eliminations & Adjustments		Minority Interest	Consolidated Balance Sheet		
Dr.	Cr.		Dr.	Cr.	
					1
			200,000		2
			500,000		3
			200,000		4
	(1) 400,000				5
			450,000		6
					7
					8
				250,000	9
				300,000	10
				100,000	11
				600,000	12
(1) 160,000		40,000			13
(1) 240,000		60,000			14
		100,000		100,000	15
400,000	400,000		1,350,000	1,350,000	16

Eliminations and Adjustments:
(1)   Eliminate 80% of the subsidiary equity accounts against the investment in subsidiary account.

Worksheet 4–6 (see page 183)

(see page 183)

80% **Interest;**
Company P and
Worksheet for Consolidated
December

		Trial Balance	
		Company P	Company S
1	Debits:		
2	Cash	200,000	150,000
3	Accounts Receivable	300,000	250,000
4	**Inventory**	500,000	**300,000**
5	Land	100,000	
6	Buildings (net)	900,000	
7	**Equipment (net)**	650,000	**400,000**
8	**Investment in Subsidiary S**	**810,000**	
9			
10	**Goodwill**		
11	Total	3,460,000	1,100,000
12	Credits:		
13	Current Liabilities	300,000	100,000
14	Bonds Payable	500,000	300,000
15	Common Stock ($10 par), Co. P	660,000	
16	Paid-In Capital in Excess of Par, Co. P	1,140,000	
17	Retained Earnings, Co. P	860,000	
18	**Common Stock ($5 par), Co. S**		50,000
19	**Paid-In Capital in Excess of Par, Co. S**		350,000
20	**Retained Earnings, Co. S**		300,000
21	**Minority Interest**		
22	Total	3,460,000	1,100,000

Price Exceeds Market Value
Subsidiary Company S
Balance Sheet
31, 19X1

WORKSHEET 4–6

Eliminations & Adjustments		Minority Interest	Consolidated Balance Sheet		
Dr.	Cr.		Dr.	Cr.	
					1
			350,000		2
			550,000		3
(2) 40,000			840,000		4
			100,000		5
			900,000		6
(2) 120,000			1,170,000		7
	(1) 560,000				8
	(2) 250,000				9
(2) 90,000			90,000		10
					11
					12
				400,000	13
				800,000	14
				660,000	15
				1,140,000	16
				860,000	17
(1) 40,000		10,000			18
(1) 280,000		70,000			19
(1) 240,000		60,000			20
		140,000		140,000	21
810,000	810,000		4,000,000	4,000,000	22

Eliminations and Adjustments:
(1) Eliminate 80% of the subsidiary equity accounts against the investment account.
(2) Distribute the balance of the investment account, $250,000, to the specific subsidiary accounts according to the determination and distribution of excess schedule:

Excess of cost over book value		$250,000
Distribute to:		
Inventory..	**$ 40,000**	
Equipment..	**120,000**	
Goodwill...	**90,000**	250,000
		$ 0

Worksheet 4–7 (see page 189)

		Trial Balance	
		Company I	Company C
1	Debits:		
2	Current Assets	20,000	10,000
3	Property, Plant, and Equipment (net)	70,000	30,000
4	**Investment in Subsidiary C**	**30,000**	
5	Total	120,000	40,000
6	Credits:		
7	Liabilities	15,000	10,000
8	Common Stock, Co. I	56,000	
9	Paid-In Capital in Excess of Par, Co. I	4,000	
10	Retained Earnings, Co. I	45,000	
11	**Common Stock, Co. C**		**10,000**
12	**Retained Earnings, Co. C**		**20,000**
13	Total	120,000	40,000

Pooling of Interests
Subsidiary Company C
Balance Sheet
31, 19X1

WORKSHEET 4-7 ||||||||||||||||||||||||

Eliminations & Adjustments				Consolidated Balance Sheet				
Dr.		Cr.		Dr.		Cr.		
								1
				30,000				2
				100,000				3
	(1)		30,000					4
								5
								6
						25,000		7
						56,000		8
						4,000		9
						45,000		10
(1)	10,000							11
(1)	20,000							12
	30,000		30,000	130,000		130,000		13

Eliminations and Adjustments:
(1) Eliminate the investment account against the subsidiary equity accounts.

CHAPTER 5

CONSOLIDATED STATEMENTS SUBSEQUENT TO ACQUISITION

This chapter's mission is to teach the procedures needed to prepare consolidated income statements, retained earnings statements, and balance sheets in periods subsequent to the acquisition of a subsidiary. There are a variety of worksheet models to master. This variety is caused primarily by the alternative methods available to a parent for maintaining its investment in subsidiary account. Accounting principles do not address the method used by a parent to record its investment in a subsidiary which is to be consolidated. The method used is of no concern to standard setters since the investment account always is eliminated when consolidating. Thus, the method chosen to record the investment usually is based on convenience. This chapter does not deal with the income tax issues of the consolidated firm except to the extent that they are reflected in the original acquisition price (tax loss carryovers and deferred tax liabilities applicable to asset adjustments). A full discussion of tax issues in consolidations is included in Chapter 10.

In the preceding chapter, worksheet procedures for a combination deemed to be a purchase included asset and liability adjustments to reflect market values on the date of the purchase. This chapter discusses the subsequent depreciation and amortization of these asset and liability revaluations in conjunction with its analysis of worksheet procedures for preparing consolidated financial statements. Finally, the appendix found at the end of this chapter explains the vertical worksheet as an alternative approach to developing these consolidated statements.

RECORDING THE INVESTMENT IN A SUBSIDIARY

Two basic methods may be used by a parent to account for its investment in a subsidiary: the *equity method* or the *cost method*. The equity method records as income an ownership percentage of the reported income of the subsidiary, whether or not it was received by the parent. The cost method treats the investment in the subsidiary as a normal stock investment by recording income only when dividends are declared by the subsidiary.

EQUITY METHOD

In its simplest form, the equity method records as income the parent's ownership interest multiplied by the subsidiary reported income each period subsequent to the acquisition. The pro rata share of income is added to the investment account balance, while the pro rata share of a loss is subtracted. In addition, any dividends declared on the investment are viewed as a partial liquidation of the investment. Consequently, dividend declarations by the subsidiary reduce the investment balance as well. The investment account at any point in time can be summarized as follows:

Investment in Subsidiary (equity method)	
plus: Original cost Ownership interest × reported income of subsidiary since acquisition	less: Ownership interest × reported losses of subsidiary since acquisition less: Ownership interest × dividends declared by subsidiary since acquisition
equals: Equity-adjusted balance	

The *simple equity method* makes no adjustment to the parent's share of subsidiary income for any amortizations resulting from differences between the book and market values of the investment on the date of acquisition. There is no danger in omitting these amortizations from the investment account when consolidated statements are prepared since the investment account is eliminated entirely in the preparation of those statements. The real advantage of using the simple equity method when consolidating is that every dollar of change in the stockholders' equity of the subsidiary is recorded on a pro rata basis in the investment account. This method expedites the elimination of the investment account in the consolidated worksheets in future periods. It is favored in this text because of its simplicity.

For some unconsolidated investments, the *sophisticated equity method* is required by APB Opinion No. 18, "The Equity Method of Accounting for Investments in Common Stock." According to this Opinion, a firm's investment should be adjusted for amortizations when the investor has an "influential" investment of 20% or more of another firm's voting stock. For example, assume that the price paid for an unconsolidated and influential investment was in excess of its underlying book value and that the excess was attributed to goodwill. The investor would have to deduct the amortization of the goodwill from its percentage share of the investee firm's income. Thus, the investor must use the sophisticated equity method to account for an influential investment in an unconsolidated investee.[1] Such an investment is reported either in supplemental financial statements of the investor or in unconsolidated financial statements. The procedures for eliminating an investment recorded under the sophisticated equity method are more cumbersome than those of the simple equity method.

COST METHOD

When the cost method is used, the investment in subsidiary account is retained at its original cost-of-acquisition balance. No adjustments are made to the account for income as it is earned by the subsidiary. Income on the investment is limited to dividends received from the subsidiary. An exception is made for subsidiary dividends that are based on income *earned prior to the acquisition date.* Such dividends are viewed as a partial liquidation and are deducted from the original investment. For example, assume that an 80%-owned subsidiary which was acquired at the start of the year earned $10,000 and paid $15,000 in dividends. The parent would record dividend income of $8,000 (80% of the income earned) and would reduce its investment account by $4,000 (80% of the dividends in excess of income). The cost method is acceptable for subsidiaries that are to be consolidated since in the consolidation process the investment account is eliminated entirely.

EXAMPLE OF THE EQUITY AND COST METHODS

The simple equity, sophisticated equity, and cost methods will be illustrated by an example covering two years. This example, which will become the foundation for several consolidated worksheets in this chapter, is based on the following facts:

1. The following determination and distribution of excess schedule was prepared on the date of purchase. This schedule is similar to that of the preceding chapter but is modified to indicate the period over which adjustments to the subsidiary book values will be allocated. This expanded format will be used in preparing all future worksheets.

Price paid, January 1, 19X1...		$145,000
Less interest acquired:		
Common stock ($10 par)...	$100,000	
Retained earnings..	50,000	
Total stockholders' equity..	$150,000	
Interest acquired..	90%	135,000
Excess of cost over book value attributed to goodwill		
(10-year amortization)		$ 10,000

---

[1]The procedures for such influential investments are covered in Chapter 10.

2. Income during 19X1 was $30,000 for Company S; dividends declared by Company S during 19X1 were $10,000.
3. During 19X2, Company S had a loss of $10,000 and declared dividends of $5,000.

The journal entries and resulting investment account balances shown on pages 230 and 231 record this information on the books of Company P, using the simple equity, sophisticated equity, and cost methods. Note that the only difference between the sophisticated and simple equity methods is that the former reduces investment income each year for an amount equal to the amortization of goodwill.

The balance in the simple-equity-adjusted investment account of a parent easily can be tested for its correctness. Under the simple equity method, every change in the retained earnings account of the subsidiary leads to an equity adjustment in the investment account for an amount equal to the change multiplied by the ownership interest. *At any time, the balance in a simple-equity-adjusted investment account can be stated as follows:*

Cost + (Ownership interest
     × Change in subsidiary Retained Earnings since acquisition)

In the preceding example, the December 31, 19X2 balance in the simple-equity-adjusted Investment in Company S would be verified as follows:

Balance = Cost + (.90 × Change in Company S Retained Earnings since acquisition)

= $145,000 + [.90 × ($55,000 December 31, 19X2 balance

      − $50,000 January 1, 19X1 balance)]

= $145,000 + (.90 × $5,000)

= $149,500

This procedure will be valuable in checking the balance in an investment account prior to consolidating. Later in the chapter, this technique becomes the basis for converting investments recorded under the cost method to the simple equity method. If it is desired, the sophisticated equity balance can be obtained by adjusting the simple equity balance for the cumulative amortizations of excess.

Presentations of worksheet elimination procedures in subsequent chapters are based on the use of the simple equity method. Rather than mastering a separate set of procedures for investments carried at cost, such investments will be converted to the simple equity method prior to the application of elimination procedures.

Event	Simple Equity Method		
19X1			
Jan.1 Purchase of stock	Investment in Company S	145,000	
	Cash..............................		145,000
Dec. 31 Subsidiary income of $30,000 reported to parent	Investment in Company S	27,000	
	Subsidiary Income............		27,000
31 Dividends of $10,000 declared by subsidiary	Dividends Receivable...........	9,000	
	Investment in		
	Company S..................		9,000
	Investment balance, Dec. 31, 19X1		**$163,000**
19X2			
Dec. 31 Subsidiary loss of $10,000 reported to parent	Loss on Subsidiary		
	Operations..................	9,000	
	Investment in		
	Company S..................		9,000
31 Dividends of $5,000 declared by subsidiary	Dividends Receivable.........	4,500	
	Investment in		
	Company S..................		4,500
	Investment balance, Dec. 31, 19X2		**$149,500**

ELIMINATION PROCEDURES: EQUITY-ADJUSTED INVESTMENTS

Worksheet procedures necessary to prepare consolidated income statements, retained earnings statements, and balance sheets are examined in the following section. It must be recalled that the consolidation procedure is used each year as it is applied to each period's separate parent and subsidiary accounts. The consolidation process is performed independently each year since the worksheet eliminations of previous years are never recorded by the parent or subsidiary.

The illustrations that follow are based on the facts concerning the investment in Company S, as detailed in the previous example. The procedures for consolidating an investment maintained under the simple equity method will be discussed first, followed by an explanation of how procedures would differ under the sophisticated equity method.

Sophisticated Equity Method			Cost Method		
Investment in Company S ...	145,000		Investment in Company S	145,000	
Cash...........................		145,000	Cash...........................		145,000
Investment in Company S ...	26,000[a]		No entry.		
Subsidiary Income..........		26,000			
Dividends Receivable..........	9,000		Dividends Receivable..........	9,000	
Investment in			Subsidiary (Dividend)		
Company S.................		9,000	Income		9,000
Investment balance,			**Investment balance,**		
Dec. 31, 19X1		**$162,000**	**Dec. 31, 19X1 ....**		**$145,000**
Loss on Subsidiary			No entry.		
Operations.................	10,000[b]				
Investment in					
Company S.................		10,000			
Dividends Receivable..........	4,500		Dividends Receivable..........	4,500	
Investment in			Subsidiary (Dividend)		
Company S.................		4,500	Income		4,500
Investment balance,			**Investment balance,**		
Dec. 31, 19X2		**$147,500**	**Dec. 31, 19X2 ....**		**$145,000**

[a]Parent's share of subsidiary income less amortization of excess of $1,000 per year.
[b]Parent's share of subsidiary loss plus amortization of excess of $1,000 per year.

EFFECT OF SIMPLE EQUITY METHOD ON CONSOLIDATION

The trial balances of Company P and Company S at the end of 19X1 appear in the first two columns of Worksheet 5–1, pages 280–281. The balances reflect the simple equity adjustments for 19X1 which were illustrated on page 230. Be sure to pay close attention to step (1). It is this elimination step which creates what this text refers to as *date alignment*. On the trial balance, the investment account already has been adjusted to its year-end balance. However, the subsidiary retained earnings still reflects its beginning-of-the-year balance. Remaining eliminations may not proceed until the investment account and the subsidiary equity accounts, against which the former is eliminated, are at *the same point in time*. Step (1) eliminates the equity adjustments made and intercompany dividends declared during the year, thereby returning the investment account to its balance *at the start of the year*. Now that date alignment exists, the subsidiary equity at the start of the year can be eliminated against the investment account in step (2), and the excess cost can be distributed and amortized for the current year in steps (3) and (4), respectively.

The Consolidated Income Statement column follows the Eliminations and Adjustments columns. The adjusted nominal accounts of the constituent firms are used to calculate the *combined net income* of $69,000. This income is distributed to the controlling and minority interests. Note that the minority receives 10% of the $30,000 reported net income of the subsidiary, or $3,000. The controlling interest receives the balance of the combined net income, or $66,000, which this text terms *consolidated net income.*

The distribution of income is handled best by using *income distribution schedules* which appear at the end of Worksheet 5–1. The subsidiary income distribution schedule is a "T account" which begins with the reported net income of the subsidiary. This income is termed "internally generated net income" which connotes the income of only the firm being analyzed *without consideration of income derived from other members of the affiliated group.* Until Chapter 9, when the subsidiary owns an interest in the parent, the subsidiary's internally generated net income is the same as its net income. In Worksheet 5–1 the subsidiary net income is multiplied by the minority ownership percentage to calculate the minority interest in income. A similar T account is used for the parent income distribution schedule. The parent's share of subsidiary net income is added to the internally generated net income of the parent, and amortizations of excess are deducted. Goodwill amortization is borne entirely by the controlling interest. Note that this is true for *all* excess cost over book value situations. Only the portion applicable to the purchaser's interest is acknowledged, and thus the amortization of excess affects only the controlling interest. The balance in the parent T account is the controlling share of the combined net income. The income distribution is a self-check procedure since the sum of the income distributions should equal the combined net income on the worksheet.

The Minority Interest column of the worksheet summarizes the total ownership interest of the minority stockholders at the close of the period. The column includes the minority's interest in each of the following: subsidiary paid-in capital balance, subsidiary retained earnings balance at the beginning of the period, combined net income, and dividends declared by the subsidiary during the period.

The Controlling Retained Earnings column produces the controlling interest's retained earnings balance at the close of the period. The column includes the parent retained earnings balance at the beginning of the period plus the parent's share of combined net income. If the parent had declared dividends, the dividends would have been shown as a deduction in this column.

The Consolidated Balance Sheet column includes the combined asset and liability balances. The paid-in equity balance of the parent is extended as the consolidated paid-in capital balance. Usually, the net minority interest is extended to the balance sheet without enumeration of its components.

Also, the total of the Controlling Retained Earnings column is extended to the balance sheet.

Separate debit and credit columns may be used for the consolidated balance sheet. This arrangement may minimize errors and aid analysis. Single columns are not advocated, but are used to facilitate the inclusion of lengthy worksheets in a summarized fashion.

The information for the following formal statements is taken directly from Worksheet 5–1:

Company P and Subsidiary Company S
Consolidated Income Statement
For Year Ended December 31, 19X1

Revenue	$180,000
Expenses	(111,000)
Combined net income	$ 69,000
Minority interest	(3,000)
Consolidated net income	$ 66,000

Company P and Subsidiary Company S
Consolidated Retained Earnings Statement
For Year Ended December 31, 19X1

	Minority	Controlling
Retained earnings, January 1, 19X1	$5,000	$123,000
Distribution of combined net income	3,000	66,000
Dividends declared	(1,000)	—
Balance, December 31, 19X1	$7,000	$189,000

Company P and Subsidiary Company S
Consolidated Balance Sheet
December 31, 19X1

Assets		Stockholders' Equity		
Net tangible assets	$397,000	Minority interest		$ 17,000
Goodwill	9,000	Controlling interest:		
		Common stock	$200,000	
		Retained earnings	189,000	389,000
		Total stockholders'		
Total assets	$406,000	equity		$406,000

There are two features of these statements that deserve added attention. The first concerns the reporting procedures for consolidated net income. Technically, consolidated net income is the income available to both the parent and minority interests. However, it has become common practice to view consolidated net income as just the income available to the controlling interest. Unfortunately, this suggests that the minority interest in income is an expense which, of course, it is not. Many firms go so far as to show the minority interest in income as an expense. Exhibit 1 presents the minority interest in income as a deduction to arrive at consolidated net income. It is an implied expense by its location. Exhibit 2 includes an income statement and an accompanying footnote that show the minority interest in income as an expense. Showing the minority interest as an expense is a result of using the proprietary theory, which holds that the focus of the income statement should be on the income owned by the controlling interest. Any income not available to the controlling interest takes on the appearance of an expense to the controlling interest. This text uses the most common practice of subtracting the minority interest in the subsidiary's adjusted net income from the combined net income to arrive at the controlling firm's share of combined net income, or consolidated net income.

The second feature of the consolidated statements is that the balance sheet includes the minority shareholders' equity as a part of the total stockholders' equity. As was explained in Chapter 4, some firms treat the minority interest as a liability or place it in a separate category.

Exhibit 1

CBI Industries, Inc.

	1987	1986	1985
		Thousands	
Revenues			
Contracting Services	$ 580,452	$ 629,743	$ 611,238
Industrial Gases	491,970	450,827	439,177
Investments	87,312	85,825	69,234
Total revenues	1,159,734	1,166,395	1,119,649
Costs of services and products sold			
Contracting Services	(540,076)	(586,016)	(568,967)
Industrial Gases	(343,160)	(318,886)	(310,801)
Investments	(69,843)	(66,427)	(48,058)
Selling and administrative			
expense	(156,350)	(146,289)	(149,598)
Special credit/(charge)	31,890	—	(144,995)
Income/(loss) from operations	82,195	48,797	(102,770)
Other expenses			
Interest expense	(30,881)	(30,624)	(38,275)
Minority interest in subsidiaries	(2,032)	(2,390)	(6,053)
Total other expenses	(32,913)	(33,014)	(44,328)
Income/(loss) before income taxes	49,282	15,783	(147,098)

Source: Jack Shohet and Richard Rikert, eds., *Accounting Trends and Techniques*, 42nd ed. (New York: American Institute of Certified Public Accountants, 1988), 238.

Exhibit 2
Scott Paper Company

	1986	1985	1984
	(In millions)		
Sales...	$3,437.0	$3,049.5	$2,847.3
Costs and Expenses			
Product Costs...	2,264.8	2,019.1	1,905.1
Marketing and distribution	635.2	553.9	488.1
Research, administration and general......	182.0	170.0	149.8
Other	(13.4)	10.3	(1.9)
	3,068.6	2,753.3	2,541.1
Income from operations.............................	368.4	296.2	306.2
Interest expense..	122.0	81.4	64.2
Other income and (expense).......................	28.7	14.4	43.2
Income before taxes	275.1	229.2	285.2

Notes to Consolidated Financial Statements

Other Income and (Expense)

(Millions)	1986	1985	1984
Interest Income	$11.3	$ 7.7	$15.0
Dividend Income	.2	11.8	19.5
Equity Affiliate dispositions	19.0	(4.1)	(.2)
Legal Settlement	—	—	9.6
Minority Interest...	(1.8)	(1.0)	(.7)
	$28.7	$14.4	$43.2

In 1986 Other Income and Expense for 1985 and 1984 has been restated to exclude gains and losses due to asset restructurings affecting income from operations.

Interest and dividend income results primarily from investments in marketable securities and time deposits.

In 1986 equity affiliate dispositions include the sale of Scott's Interest in Amapá Florestal e Celulose S.A. (AMCEL) and the Company's indirect interest in British Columbia Forest Products Limited.

Minority interest represents that portion of earnings of the Company's consolidated international subsidiaries belonging to minority owners.

Source: Jack Shohet and Richard Rikert, eds., *Accounting Trends and Techniques,* 41st ed. (New York: American Institute of Certified Public Accountants, 1987), 268.

Now consider consolidation procedures for 19X2 as they would apply to Companies P and S under the simple equity method. This will provide added practice in preparing worksheets and will emphasize that, at the end of each year, consolidation procedures are applied to the separate statements of the constituent firms. In essence, *each year's consolidation procedures begin as if there never had been a previous consolidation.* However, reference to past worksheets is used commonly to save time.

The separate trial balances of Companies P and S are displayed in the first two columns of Worksheet 5–2, pages 282–283. The investment in subsidiary account includes the simple-equity-adjusted investment balance as calculated on page 230. Note that the balances in the retained earnings accounts of Companies P and S are calculated as follows:

Company P:	January 1, 19X1 balance	$123,000
	Net income, 19X1 (including Company P's share of subsidiary income)	67,000
	Balance, January 1, 19X2	$190,000
Company S:	January 1, 19X1 balance	$ 50,000
	Net income, 19X1	30,000
	Dividends declared	(10,000)
	Balance, January 1, 19X2	$ 70,000

Again, step (1) is used to create the needed date alignment. The equity adjustment made during the year and the intercompany dividends are eliminated. This returns the investment account to its balance at the start of the year so that the account is at a common point in time with the subsidiary equity accounts, against which the investment account is eliminated in step (2). Notice that step (4) amortizes the excess for both the current and past period. Be sure to understand that the amortization of excess done last year appeared only on that year's worksheet and *was not recorded* on either firms' accounting records. This emphasizes that consolidation starts from the separate statements of the two companies each year and that *the statements do not reflect the prior periods' consolidation procedures.*

Note that the original determination and distribution of excess schedule prepared on the date of acquisition becomes the foundation for *all* subsequent worksheets. Once prepared, the schedule is used *without modification.*

EFFECT OF SOPHISTICATED EQUITY METHOD ON CONSOLIDATION

A parent may desire to prepare its own separate statements as a supplement to the consolidated statements. In this situation, the investment in the subsidiary must be shown on the parent's separate statements at the sophisticated equity balance. This requirement may lead the parent to maintain its subsidiary investment account under the sophisticated equity method. Two ramifications occur when such an investment is consolidated. First, the current year's equity adjustment is net of excess amortizations; and second, the investment account contains only the remaining unamortized excess applicable to the investment.

The use of the sophisticated equity method complicates the elimination of the investment account in that the worksheet distribution and amortization

Excess amortizations refer to amortization of market value (see determination and distribution of excess schedule).

of the excess procedures are altered. However, there is no impact on the other consolidation procedures. To illustrate, the information given in Worksheet 5–2 will be used as the basis for an example. The trial balance of Company P will show the following changes as a result of using the sophisticated equity method:

1. The Investment in Company S will be carried at $147,500 ($149,500 simple equity balance less 2 years' amortization of excess at $1,000 per year).
2. The January 1, 19X2 balance for Company P Retained Earnings will be $189,000 ($190,000 under simple equity less 1 year's amortization of excess of $1,000).
3. The subsidiary loss account of the parent will have a balance of $10,000 ($9,000 share of the subsidiary loss plus $1,000 amortization of excess).

Based on these changes, a partial worksheet under the sophisticated equity method follows:

Company P and Subsidiary Company S

(Credit balance amounts are in parentheses.) Partial Worksheet for Consolidated Financial Statements For Year Ended December 31, 19X2

	Trial Balance		Eliminations & Adjustments			
	Company P	Company S	Dr.		Cr.	
Investment in Company S	147,500		(1)	10,000	(2)	153,000
			(1)	4,500	(3)	9,000
Goodwill			(3)	9,000	(4)	1,000
Retained Earnings, Jan. 1, 19X2, Co. P	(189,000)					
Common Stock ($10 par), Co. S		(100,000)	(2)	90,000		
Retained Earnings, Jan. 1, 19X2, Co. S		(70,000)	(2)	63,000		
Revenue	(100,000)	(50,000)				
Expenses	80,000	60,000	(4)	1,000		
Subsidiary Loss	10,000				(1)	10,000
Dividends Declared		5,000			(1)	4,500

Eliminations and Adjustments:
(1) Eliminate the current-year entries made in the investment account and the subsidiary loss account. The loss account now includes the $1,000 excess amortization.
(2) Using the balances at the beginning of the year, eliminate 90% of the Company S equity balances against the remaining investment account.
(3) Distribute the remaining unamortized excess on January 1, 19X2, ($10,000 on purchase date less $1,000 19X1 amortization) to the goodwill account.
(4) Amortize goodwill for the current year.

The sophisticated equity method is essentially a modification of simple equity procedures. The major difference in the consolidation procedures under the two methods is that, subsequent to the acquisition, the original excess calculated on the determination and distribution of excess schedule does not appear when the sophisticated equity method is used. Only the remaining unamortized excess appears. Since the investment account is eliminated in the consolidation process, the added complexities of the sophisticated method are not justified for most firms.

ELIMINATION PROCEDURES: COST-METHOD INVESTMENTS

Recall that a parent may choose to record its investment in a subsidiary under the cost method, whereby the investment is maintained at its original cost, with income from the investment recorded when dividends are declared by the subsidiary. The use of the cost method means that the investment account does not reflect changes in subsidiary equity. Rather than develop a new set of procedures for the elimination of an investment under the cost method, the cost method investment will be converted to its simple-equity balance at the beginning of the period to create date alignment. Then, the elimination procedures developed earlier can be applied.

Worksheet 5–3, pages 284–285, is a consolidated financial statements worksheet for Companies P and S for the first year of combined operations. The worksheet is based upon the entries made under the cost method, as shown on page 231. Reference to Company P's Trial Balance column in Worksheet 5–3 reveals that the investment in subsidiary account at year end still is stated at the original $145,000 cost and that the income recorded by the parent as a result of subsidiary ownership is limited to $9,000, or 90% of the dividends declared by the subsidiary. When the cost method is used, the account title *Dividend Income* may be used in place of Subsidiary Income.

At the end of the first year of operations, there would be no need for an equity conversion entry. Date alignment exists since the Company P investment account and the Company S equity accounts already are stated as of a common point in time, January 1, 19X1. For step (1), it is necessary to eliminate the intercompany dividends only. The remaining eliminations, steps (2) through (4), are identical to their corresponding entries in Worksheet 5–1. The last four columns of Worksheet 5–3 also are identical to their counterparts in Worksheet 5–1.

For periods subsequent to the first year of combined operations, an entry converting the investment in subsidiary account to its simple-equity-method balance will be needed on the consolidated worksheets in order to create date alignment. To illustrate, Worksheet 5–4, pages 286–287, covers the second year of operations for Companies P and S. This worksheet is identical to Worksheet 5–2 except that here the cost method is used to account for the investment in Company S. Thus the balance of the investment account is the original $145,000 cost as of the January 1, 19X1 purchase date. However, the

[handwritten margin note top: R/E begin 50,000. Add 1st yr inc. 30,000 & div. < 10,000 > 70,000]

[handwritten margin note right: or adjusted 12-31-X1 balance.]

retained earnings account of Company S carries the January 1, 19X2 balance. Because these accounts do not share a common point in time, eliminations cannot proceed. Note that in Worksheet 5–4 the balance of the parent retained earnings account is $18,000 less than its balance in Worksheet 5–2 since it does not include the undistributed income of the subsidiary. The conversion step, step (C) in Worksheet 5–4, converts the investment account to its simple-equity-method balance on January 1, 19X2, so that the account shares a common point in time with the subsidiary equity accounts against which the investment account now can be eliminated. The conversion entry simultaneously updates the Company P retained earnings account to its simple-equity-method balance as of January 1, 19X2. The dollar amount of the conversion is calculated by multiplying the ownership interest by the change in the subsidiary retained earnings account between the date of acquisition and the beginning of the current year. In this case, the adjustment is made as follows:

$$
\begin{aligned}
\text{Conversion} &= [.90 \times (\text{Company S Retained Earnings, January 1, 19X2} \\
&\quad - \text{Company S Retained Earnings, January 1, 19X1})] \\
&= [.90 \times (\$70,000 - \$50,000)] = .90 \times \$20,000 \\
&= \$18,000
\end{aligned}
$$

The simplicity of this technique of converting from the cost to the simple equity method should be appreciated. At any future date it is necessary to compare only the balance of the subsidiary retained earnings account on the worksheet trial balance with the balance of that account on the original date of acquisition (included in the determination and distribution of excess schedule) in order to convert to the simple equity method. Specific reference to income earned and dividends paid by the subsidiary in each intervening year is unnecessary. The only complications occur when stock dividends have been issued by the subsidiary or when the subsidiary has issued or retired stock. These complications are examined in Chapter 9.

After the conversion, the eliminations may proceed. Since the cost method is being used, the first elimination is confined to intercompany dividends. Steps (2) through (4) are identical to the corresponding steps in Worksheet 5–2. Note that step (2) is possible only after the conversion step brings the account balances to a common point in time.

COMPLICATED PURCHASE, SEVERAL CAUSES OF EXCESS

In Worksheets 5–1 through 5–4, it was assumed that the entire excess of cost over book value was attributable to goodwill. In reality, this assumption seldom will be true. The following example illustrates a more complicated purchase.

Paulos Company paid $790,000 to obtain 8,000 shares (80% interest) of Carlos Company on January 1, 19X1. In addition, $10,000 of direct acquisition costs were paid by Paulos Company. At the time of the purchase, Carlos Company had the following summarized balance sheet:

Carlos Company
Balance Sheet
January 1, 19X1

Assets			Liabilities and Equity		
Inventory........................		$ 75,000	Current liabilities...............		$ 50,000
Land...............................		150,000	Bonds payable, 6%, due		
Building...........................	$600,000		Dec. 31, 19X4.................		200,000
Less accumulated			Common stock ($10 par).....		100,000
depreciation..................	300,000	300,000	Paid-in capital		
Equipment.......................	$150,000		in excess of par..............		150,000
Less accumulated			Retained earnings		250,000
depreciation..................	50,000	100,000			
Goodwill...........................		125,000			
Total assets......................		$750,000	Total liabilities and equity ...		$750,000

The market values for Carlos Company's tangible assets and long-term liability on January 1, 19X1, are as follows:

	Market Values
Inventory...	$ 80,000
Land...	200,000
Building (20-year remaining life)	500,000
Equipment (5-year remaining life)	80,000
Bonds payable based on current 8% market interest rate as follows:	
Present value of interest payment at 8% ($12,000 annual interest × 4-year, 8% present value of annuity factor of 3.31213)..............	$ 39,746
Present value of principal ($200,000 × 4-year, 8% present value factor of .73503)	147,006 186,752

Based on these market values, the following determination and distribution of excess schedule is prepared. This schedule calculates an excess of cost of $400,000 on the interest acquired; $14,598 of this excess is consumed by the revaluation of the current assets and liabilities. Previously recorded goodwill was not added to the excess available for long-lived assets since only $184,000 was needed to adjust these assets to market value. The balance of the excess, $201,402, was allocated to additional goodwill.

Price paid (including $10,000 direct acquisition costs)......		$800,000
Less interest acquired:		
Capital stock ($10 par)...	$100,000	
Paid-in capital in excess of par..................................	150,000	
Retained earnings..	250,000	
Total stockholders' equity..	$500,000	
Interest acquired..	80%	400,000
Excess of cost over book value of subsidiary interest......		$400,000
Less adjustments to current assets and debt:		
Inventory undervalued $5,000; 80% × $5,000..............	$ 4,000	
Bonds payable overstated by $13,248;		
record discount of 80% × $13,248 (4-year life)..........	10,598	14,598
Excess available to adjust long-lived assets...................		$385,402
Land understated $50,000;		
increase land 80% × $50,000	$ 40,000	
Building (20-year life) understated $200,000; decrease		
accumulated depreciation 80% × $200,000...............	160,000	
Equipment (5-year life) overstated $20,000;		
reduce equipment 80% × $20,000	(16,000)	184,000
Balance of excess reflecting *additional* goodwill		
(10-year life)..		**$201,402**

Theoretically, the plant asset adjustments required by the determination and distribution of excess schedule should be made in a manner that would eliminate all accumulated depreciation applicable to the controlling interest as of the purchase date. This procedure would unduly complicate future worksheets. As a practical alternative when possible, the plant asset adjustments should be made in such a way as to reduce accumulated depreciation, and in no event should adjustments increase accumulated depreciation. Therefore, the increase in the net value of the building was accomplished by decreasing its accumulated depreciation account, not by increasing the asset account. The reduction in the equipment was accomplished by decreasing the asset account rather than increasing its accumulated depreciation account.

Worksheet 5–5, pages 288–291, is a consolidated financial statements worksheet for Paulos Company and Carlos Company one year after the acquisition. During the year, Carlos had a net income of $60,000 and declared $20,000 in dividends. Paulos Company shows the following simple-equity-adjusted balance for its investment in Carlos:

Original cost..	$800,000
80% of 19X1 income of $60,000..................	48,000
80% of $20,000 dividends	
declared by Carlos.................................	(16,000)
Investment balance,	
December 31, 19X1.............................	$832,000

The worksheet is completed by allocating the combined net income of $108,708 to the minority and controlling interests, with the minority interest receiving 20% of the subsidiary's reported $60,000 net income. Note once again that none of the amortizations resulting from revaluations affect the minority interest, because only the adjustments relating to the 80% controlling interest in the assets and liabilities were recorded initially. Therefore, all the amortizations pertain only to the controlling interest and are reflected only in the parent company income distribution schedule.

At this point it should be understood that the amortizations of excess cost applicable to long-lived assets could become more complex than they are in Worksheet 5–5. The amortization adjustments found in Steps (4c) and (4d) divide the applicable excess by the assets' remaining lives as shown in the determination and distribution of excess schedule. It was implicitly assumed that the amortization periods were the assets' remaining lives used by the subsidiary and that the subsidiary used straight-line depreciation. If the subsidiary had used an alternative depreciation method, that method would have been applied to the excess. It may occur that the parent company does not wish to use the subsidiary's depreciation method and/or remaining life. In this case, the parent would recompute depreciation, based on its ownership interest in the asset. The recomputed amount would be compared to the parent's ownership interest in the subsidiary's recorded depreciation expense, and the difference would become the amortization adjustment for the period.

Worksheet 5–6, pages 292–295, is the worksheet for the second year of combined operations for the purchase that was analyzed in Worksheet 5–5. The second year is included to emphasize that *each year the consolidation starts anew from the separate trial balances of the two firms.* None of the eliminations made on the previous period's worksheet are reflected in the 19X2 separate trial balances of Paulos Company and Carlos Company.

The following information may be inferred from the trial balance figures in Worksheet 5–6:

1. Carlos reported a net income of $100,000 for 19X2 and declared $20,000 in dividends. This income is based on the asset values maintained on Carlos' books, and does not reflect revaluations caused by the 80% purchase by Paulos.
2. The investment in Carlos account reflects:

Investment Balance, December 31, 19X1	$832,000
80% of 19X2 net income of $100,000...........	80,000
80% of $20,000 dividends declared	
by Carlos...	(16,000)
Balance, December 31, 19X2	$896,000

3. Paulos recorded subsidiary income of $80,000, which is 80% of Carlos' reported net income.
4. The January 1, 19X2 balance in the Paulos retained earnings account is derived as follows:

Balance, January 1, 19X1...	$700,000
19X1 income generated by Paulos Company.......................................	80,000
Subsidiary income under the equity method.......................................	48,000
Balance, January 1, 19X2...	$828,000

5. The $828,000 balance in the Paulos retained earnings account reflects 80% of the reported net income of Carlos and does not include adjustments resulting from the amortizations of the excess of the price paid for the 80% interest. These amortizations appear only on the consolidated worksheet.

TAX-RELATED ISSUES

Recall that there are two tax issues that may arise in a purchase. First, when the purchase is a tax-free exchange as to the seller, the parent must increase assets to their higher market value and must record a deferred tax liability for the nondeductible excess. As the excess of market value over cost of the asset is amortized in future periods, so must the deferred tax liability be reduced in future periods. The second issue is that the parent may have to acknowledge a deferred tax expense account when the price paid for its investment in the subsidiary reflects the purchase of a tax loss carryforward. The benefits of the tax loss carryforward must be allocated to the periods in which the benefits occur.

Assume that Paro Company purchased an 80% interest in Sunstran Corporation on January 1, 19X1, at which time the following determination and distribution of excess schedule was prepared:

Price paid (including $20,000 direct acquisition costs).....		$920,000
Less interest acquired:		
Capital stock ($10 par)...	$100,000	
Paid-in capital in excess of par................................	300,000	
Retained earnings..	400,000	
Total stockholders' equity......................................	$800,000	
Interest acquired..	80%	640,000
Excess of cost over book value		$280,000
Building (20-year life) understated $200,000 (decrease accumulated depreciation 80% × $200,000)...	$160,000	
Deferred tax liability (30% tax rate × $160,000)..........	(48,000)	
Deferred tax expense **(30% tax rate × 80% × $300,000 loss carryforward ...**	72,000*	184,000
Goodwill (10-year life)		$ 96,000

*For this example, assume that there is assurance of adequate 19X1 income to offset fully the tax loss carryforward. Without that assurance and without any already existing deferred tax liability on the books of the parent and/or subsidiary, the deferred tax expense would be limited in recognizable amount to the $48,000 deferred tax liability established in the determination and distribution of excess schedule. That limitation would require the remaining $24,000 to be contained in the goodwill amount until realized.

Worksheet 5–7, pages 296–299, is the consolidated worksheet for Paro Company and its subsidiary, Sunstran Corporation, at the end of 19X1. Unlike previous worksheets, the nominal accounts of both firms include a provision for tax. The calculation of the tax liabilities for affiliated firms is discussed in Chapter 10. For now, accept the amounts shown as given. It should be noted, however, that Paro has reduced its tax provision for the benefit of the tax loss carryforward of $72,000 that it purchased in the combination. The tax provision recorded by the subsidiary was calculated using the assets' book values as the bases for depreciation.

The procedures to eliminate the investment account are the same as for previous examples using the equity method. Notice that step (3a) distributes the excess to the accumulated depreciation account to increase the net value of the building by $160,000, and that step (3b) records the related deferred tax liability resulting from the inability to depreciate for tax purposes the increase. Step (3c) records the tax loss carryforward which was included in the determination and distribution of excess schedule. The goodwill resulting from the purchase is recorded in step (3d).

As a result of the increase in the net value of the building, step (4a) increases depreciation by $8,000 for the year. Given the 30% tax rate, step (4b) reduces the provision for tax account by $2,400 as a result of the depreciation adjustment. This step is not a reduction of the current taxes payable; instead, it is a reduction of the deferred tax liability recorded as part of the distribution of the excess cost. Remember that the deferred tax liability reflects the loss of future tax deductions caused by the difference between the building's higher market value and its lower book value on the date of purchase. Thus the net result of this entry is to record the tax provision as if the tax deductions were allowable without changing the tax payable for the year. Step (4c) reflects the fact that the tax loss carryforward is used to reduce the current year's tax liability. Paro reduced its provision for tax directly on its books when it reduced the taxes payable. Paro had no choice since the tax loss carryforward account did not exist on its separate books. Such an account is first acknowledged in the consolidation process. The tax loss carryforward account is established through the distribution of the investment excess (step 3c). Step (4c) eliminates the tax loss carryforward and increases the provision for tax for the current year to its position prior to the offsetting for the carryover amount. The parent company income distribution schedule reflects all the amortizations of the excess cost made on the worksheet as adjustments to the controlling interest's share of combined net income. This approach is consistent with previous worksheets.

INTRAPERIOD PURCHASE UNDER THE SIMPLE EQUITY METHOD

The accountant will be required to apply specialized procedures when consolidating a controlling investment in common stock that is acquired during the fiscal year. When such an acquisition is deemed to be a purchase, the determination and distribution of excess schedule must be based on the subsidiary stockholders' equity *on the interim purchase date, including the subsidiary retained earnings balance on that date.* A further complication under purchase accounting is that the combined net income of the consolidated firm, as derived on the worksheet, is to include only subsidiary income earned subsequent to the purchase date.

There are two options available for consolidating an intraperiod purchase. The first option is to require the subsidiary to close its books as of the purchase date. This procedure would make retained earnings on the acquisition date available for use in the determination and distribution of excess schedule and would mean that the consolidated worksheet would include only the operations of the subsidiary subsequent to the purchase date. The second and more realistic option is to modify the determination and distribution of excess schedule to include the purchased share of undistributed income for the portion of the year prior to the purchase. Then, it is possible to include the operations of the subsidiary for the entire fiscal year in the consolidated worksheet.

Option 1: Subsidiary Books Closed. Company S has the following trial balance on July 1, 19X1, the date of an 80% purchase by Company P:

Current Assets	68,000	
Equipment	80,000	
Accumulated Depreciation		30,000
Liabilities		10,000
Common Stock ($10 par)		50,000
Retained Earnings, January 1, 19X1		45,000
Dividends Declared	5,000	
Sales		90,000
Cost of Goods Sold	60,000	
Expenses	12,000	
Total	225,000	225,000

If Company P requires Company S to close its nominal accounts as of July 1, Company S would increase its retained earnings account by $13,000 with the following entries:

Sales	90,000	
Cost of Goods Sold		60,000
Expenses		12,000
Retained Earnings		18,000
Retained Earnings	5,000	
Dividends Declared		5,000

Assume that Company P pays $106,400 for its 80% interest in Company S. Assume also that the equipment is undervalued by $40,000 and has a 10-year remaining life. The determination and distribution of excess schedule would be as follows:

Price paid		$106,400
Less interest acquired:		
Common stock ($10 par)...	$ 50,000	
Retained earnings, July 1, 19X1	58,000	
Total stockholders' equity, July 1, 19X1.....................	$108,000	
Interest acquired..	80%	86,400
Excess of cost over book value attributed to equipment,		
10-year life (maximum asset increase would be		
80% × $40,000, or $32,000)...		$ 20,000

Proceeding to the end of the year, assume that the operations of Company S for the last six months result in a net income of $20,000 and that dividends of $5,000 are declared by Company S on December 31. Worksheet 5–8, pages 300–301, includes Company S nominal accounts for the second six-month period only, since the nominal accounts were closed on July 1. Company S Retained Earnings shows the July 1, 19X1 balance. The trial balance of Company P includes operations for the entire year. The subsidiary income listed by Company P includes 80% of the subsidiary's $20,000 second six-months' income. Company P's investment account balance shows:

Original cost...	$106,400
80% of subsidiary's second six-months' income of $20,000..................	16,000
80% of 5,000 dividends declared by subsidiary on Dec. 31...................	(4,000)
Investment balance, December 31, 19X1.......................................	$118,400

In conformance with purchase theory, the Consolidated Income Statement column of Worksheet 5–8 includes subsidiary income earned after the acquisition date only. Likewise, only subsidiary income earned after the purchase date is distributed to the minority and controlling interests. Income earned and dividends declared prior to the purchase date by Company S are reflected in its July 1, 19X1 retained earnings balance, of which the minority is granted its share. The notes to the statements would have to disclose what the income of the consolidated firm would have been had the purchase occurred at the start of the year.

Option 2: Subsidiary Books Not Closed. Usually, a subsidiary does not close its books as a result of the parent company securing a controlling interest in its stock. Normally the parent company is able to ascertain the income earned by the subsidiary between the beginning of the year and the date control is achieved. If the subsidiary already has declared dividends as of the time of the acquisition, these dividends would be deducted in arriving at the total subsidiary equity interest as of that date.

Assume that the parent had access to the Company S trial balance shown on page 245 but that Company S did not close its books as of July 1, 19X1. Company P would prepare its determination and distribution of excess schedule as follows:

Price paid		$106,400
Less interest acquired:		
Common stock ($10 par)...	$ 50,000	
Retained earnings, January 1, 19X1............................	45,000	
Income of Company S, January 1–July 1....................	**18,000**	
Dividends declared, January 1–July 1........................	**(5,000)**	
Total stockholders' equity, **July 1, 19X1**...................	$108,000	
Interest acquired...	80%	86,400
Excess of cost over book value attributed to the		
equipment, 10-year life (maximum asset increase		
would be 80% × $40,000, or $32,000)		$ 20,000

Since the subsidiary did not close its books as of July 1, 19X1, Worksheet 5–9 on pages 302–305 includes the Company S trial balance reflecting the entire year's operations. The Company S retained earnings account is dated January 1, 19X1. The Company P investment and subsidiary income accounts are identical to those in Worksheet 5–8.

In Worksheet 5–9, the nominal accounts of the subsidiary for the entire year are included in the consolidated income column. Since 80% of the income earned in the first half of the year belonged to outside interests (shareholders that are no longer members of the affiliated group), *Purchased Income* must be deleted to arrive at the combined net income that belongs to current members of the affiliated group. As with the income, 80% of the dividends declared by the subsidiary prior to the purchase also belonged to outside interests and must be eliminated. However, this elimination does *not* affect the consolidated income statement. Note that the minority interest existed for the entire year; thus it is permitted a *20% share* of subsidiary income for the *full* year. Worksheet 5–9 leads to the following unique income statement:

Company P and Subsidiary Company S Consolidated Income Statement For Year Ended December 31, 19X1	
Sales...	$682,000
Cost of goods sold...	(470,000)
Gross profit...	$212,000
Other expenses	(95,000)
Total net income of Company P and Company S for year 19X1....	$117,000
Income earned by outside interests existing prior	
to Company P purchase..	**(14,400)**
Combined net income..	$102,600
Minority interest..	(7,600)
Consolidated net income..	$ 95,000

The format of this income statement has the advantage of disclosing the total net income of the two firms for the year and the consolidated net income. The total net income for the year becomes the basis for a pro forma statement of what income would have been if the combination had occurred at the beginning of the year. This figure would need to be supplemented only by a disclosure that there would have been an additional $1,000 of equipment depreciation for the first six months of the year. The disclosure is required by APB Opinion No. 16 (par. 96) for intraperiod purchases.

Special care must be taken in consolidating an intraperiod purchase in subsequent periods. It is common to find that a firm has made an error by taking a full year's share of equity income in the period of acquisition rather than including only income earned after the date of acquisition. When this error is found, a correcting entry should be recorded by the parent.

INTRAPERIOD PURCHASE UNDER THE COST METHOD

There are only two variations of the procedures discussed in the preceding section if the cost method is used by the parent firm to record its investment in the subsidiary:

1. During the year of acquisition, the parent would record as income only its share of dividends declared by the subsidiary. Thus, eliminating entries would be confined to the intercompany dividends.
2. In subsequent years, the cost-to-equity conversion adjustment would be based on the change in the subsidiary retained earnings balance *from the intraperiod purchase date* to the beginning of the year for which the worksheet is being prepared.

POOLING OF INTERESTS: SUBSEQUENT TO ACQUISITION

In a pooling of interests, worksheet procedures in subsequent periods are simple if the original acquisition is recorded properly. Since there is no excess of cost over book value in a pooling, the cumbersome amortizations of the excess are not present. For example, assume that on January 1, 19X1 Company I issued 2,700 shares of its $2 par stock ($15 market value) for a 90% interest in Company C. As presented in the example on page 188, Company C had the following condensed balance sheet:

Assets		Liabilities and Equity	
Current assets	$10,000	Liabilities	$10,000
Property, plant, and		Common stock ($10 par)......	10,000
equipment (net)..............	30,000	Retained earnings..............	20,000
Total assets.......................	$40,000	Total liabilities and equity....	$40,000

The following net income figures were reported by Company C subsequent to the acquisition date:

19X1	$20,000
19X2	15,000
19X3 (current year)	25,000

Pooling rules require the issuer to record the investment at the book value of the underlying equity. Thus, Company I would have recorded the original acquisition as follows:

Investment in Company C (90% × $30,000 total Company C equity)	27,000	
Common Stock (2,700 shares × $2 par)		5,400
Paid-In Capital in Excess of Par (90% of Company C Paid-In Capital = $9,000, less $5,400 assigned to par)		3,600
Retained Earnings (90% × $20,000 Company C January 1, 19X1 Retained Earnings)		18,000

Worksheet 5–10, pages 306–307, is a consolidated financial statements worksheet for Companies I and C on December 31, 19X3. The balance in the investment in Company C account is the result of Company I's use of the equity method, as follows:

Original recorded value on January 1, 19X1	$27,000
90% × Company C 19X1 income of $20,000	18,000
90% × Company C 19X2 income of $15,000	13,500
90% × Company C 19X3 income of $25,000	22,500
Equity-adjusted balance, December 31, 19X3	$81,000

An investment might be recorded properly as a pooling initially and not be equity-adjusted in subsequent periods. When an investment deemed to be a pooling is maintained at cost, a simple equity conversion entry may be made to update the investment account to its beginning-of-the-period balance. After the conversion, eliminations proceed as under the simple equity method, except that the elimination entry is limited to the intercompany dividends. The conversion procedures follow those used in Worksheets 5–3 and 5–4 for an investment recorded at cost.

Also, it may occur that the investment originally was recorded incorrectly at market value. This complication was discussed in Chapter 4. If this situation is encountered, it is suggested that the investment account be corrected to reflect the book value of the investment prior to proceeding to the consolidated worksheet. The investment account should be adjusted to the correct balance under either the cost or equity method, depending on the issuer's desires.

INTRAPERIOD POOLING

Recall that under pooling theory, the incomes of the parent and the subsidiary are to be *consolidated at the beginning of the year, regardless of when control is achieved during the year.* Thus, there is no reason to close the subsidiary's books on the date control is achieved. Closing the books would, in fact, hinder the preparation of consolidated statements. Worksheets for consolidated financial statements must begin with a trial balance of the subsidiary that includes the entire year's operations and the beginning-of-the-year balance for the subsidiary retained earnings account. Since consolidation procedures are applied *retroactively to the beginning of the year*, the entire incomes of the parent and the subsidiary are distributed to the controlling and minority interests. No income is regarded as earned by outside interests. In summary, the consolidation procedures are identical to those used when the controlling investment has been made at the beginning of the year.

SUMMARY: WORKSHEET TECHNIQUE

At this point it is wise to review the overall mechanical procedures used to prepare a consolidated worksheet. It will help you to have this set of procedures at your side for the first few worksheets you do. Later, the process will become automatic. The following procedures are designed to provide for both efficiency and correctness:

1. When recopying the trial balances, always sum them before you proceed with the eliminations. At this point, you want to be sure that there are no errors in transporting figures to the worksheet. An amazing number of students' consolidated balance sheets are out of balance because their trial balances did not balance to begin with.
2. Carefully key all eliminations to aid future reference. It is suggested that a symbol, such as an asterisk, a line, or a circle, be used to identify each worksheet adjustment entry that affects combined net income. This identification will make it easier to locate the adjustments that must be posted later to the income distribution schedules. Recall that any adjustment to income must be assigned to one of the firm's income distribution schedules. This second step will become particularly important in the next two chapters where there will be many adjustments to income.
3. Sum the eliminations to be sure that they balance before you begin to extend the account totals.
4. Now that the eliminations are completed, horizontally determine account totals and then extend them to the appropriate worksheet column. Extend each account *in the order* that it appears on the trial balance. Do not select just the accounts needed for a particular statement. For example, do not work only on the income statement. This can lead to errors. There may be some accounts that you will forget to extend, and you may not be aware of the errors until your balance sheet column total fails to equal zero. Extending each account in order assures that none will be overlooked and allows careful consideration of the appropriate destination of each account balance.
5. Calculate combined net income.

6. Prepare income distribution schedules. Verify that the sum of the distributions equals the combined net income on the worksheet. Distribute the minority interest in income to the Minority Interest column and distribute the controlling interest in income to the Controlling Retained Earnings column.

7. Sum the Minority Interest column and extend that total to the Consolidated Balance Sheet column. Sum the Controlling Retained Earnings column and extend that total to the Consolidated Balance Sheet column as well.

8. Verify that the Consolidated Balance Sheet column total equals zero (or that the totals are equal if two columns are used).

APPENDIX: THE VERTICAL WORKSHEET

This chapter has used the *horizontal format* for its worksheets. Columns for consolidated income, minority interest, controlling retained earnings, and the balance sheet are arranged horizontally in adjacent columns. This arrangement makes it convenient to extend account balances from one column to the next. This format is similar to the trial balance working procedure used in prior principles and intermediate accounting textbooks. The horizontal format will be used for all illustrations in chapters that follow and in all worksheet problems unless stated otherwise.

There is, however, an alternative worksheet style, the *vertical format*, that may be used. Rather than beginning with the separate firm's trial balances, this format begins with the completed income statements, statements of retained earnings, and balance sheets of the separate firms. Worksheet 5–11, pages 308–309, illustrates this format by applying it to the same example used in Worksheet 5–6 (an equity method example for the second year of a purchase with a complicated distribution of excess cost). Worksheet 5–11 is based on the determination and distribution of excess schedule shown on page 241.

Note that the original separate statements are stacked vertically upon each other. Be sure to follow the *carry-down* procedure as it is applied to the separate statements. The net income from the income statement is carried down to the retained earnings statement. Then, the ending retained earnings balance is carried down to the balance sheet. Later, this same carry-down procedure is applied to the eliminations and to the consolidated statements.

Understand that there are *no* differences in the elimination and adjustment procedures as a result of this alternative format. Compare the elimination steps to those in Worksheet 5–6. Even though there is no change in the eliminations, there are two areas of caution. First, the order in which the accounts appear is reversed; that is, nominal accounts precede balance sheet accounts. This difference in order will require care in making eliminations.

Second, the eliminations to retained earnings must be made against the January 1 beginning balances, not the December 31 ending balances. The ending retained earnings balances are never adjusted but are derived after all eliminations have been made.

The complicated aspect of the vertical worksheet is the carry-down procedure used to create the retained earnings statement and the balance sheet. Arrows are used in Worksheet 5–11 to emphasize the carry-down procedure. Note that the net income line in the retained earnings statement and the retained earnings lines on the balance sheet are never available to receive eliminations. These balances are always carried down. The net income balances are derived from the same income distribution schedules used in Worksheet 5–6.

QUESTIONS

1. Discuss the difference between the simple equity method and the cost method of recording an investment in a subsidiary.
2. Why doesn't it matter whether the cost method or the equity method is used to account for an investment when the consolidation process is required?
3. Describe the difference between the simple and sophisticated equity methods of accounting for an investment in a subsidiary, and explain why the difference is irrelevant when consolidated statements are to be prepared.
4. Subsidiary Company paid dividends of $10,000 from income earned prior to the firm's acquisition by Parent Company. Parent acquired an 85% interest in Subsidiary at a cost of $178,000. Under the cost method, at what dollar value is the investment recorded after receipt of the dividend by Parent?
5. Describe the eliminations and adjustments to be made on the worksheet when the investment in a subsidiary is accounted for under the equity method.
6. Of what is the minority interest comprised? How is the minority interest presented on the consolidated balance sheet?
7. Describe the eliminations and adjustments to be made on the worksheet when the investment in a subsidiary is carried at cost.
8. In a purchase, the parent's share of the liabilities of the subsidiary is adjusted to reflect current market values at the time of acquisition. How are an undervalued and an overvalued subsidiary liability treated on the determination and distribution of excess schedule?

9. Under the proprietary theory approach, why is the minority's share of subsidiary income unaffected by amortizations that result from the revaluation of the subsidiary's assets and liabilities?
10. Prepare a skeleton outline of the parent company income distribution schedule for a parent that owns a 90% interest in a subsidiary. Assume that the price paid for the interest exceeded book value and that the excess is attributable to goodwill.
11. What effect does an intraperiod purchase have on the determination and distribution of excess schedule and on the worksheet covering the period of acquisition? What special disclosure is required on the consolidated income statement due to the intraperiod purchase?
12. In an intraperiod purchase, subsidiary income is allocated to three different interest groups in the year of acquisition. What are these groups?
13. How do the problems created by an intraperiod pooling differ from those created by an intraperiod purchase?

EXERCISES

Exercise 1. On January 1, 19X6, Barret Corporation purchased 80% of the outstanding stock of Warn Company for $248,000 in cash. Immediately prior to the purchase, Warn Company had the following balance sheet:

Assets		Liabilities and Equity	
Current assets.................	$ 70,000	Liabilities........................	$100,000
Land..............................	80,000	Common stock ($5 par).....	40,000
Building and		Paid-in capital	
equipment (net).............	190,000	in excess of par.............	60,000
		Retained earnings.............	140,000
Total assets.....................	$340,000	Total liabilities and equity..	$340,000

Book values approximated market values, except for the land which is worth $100,000. Any goodwill resulting from the purchase will be amortized over 10 years. Prepare a determination and distribution of excess schedule for this investment, and record the investment by Barret Corporation.

Exercise 2. Warn Company of Exercise 1 reports the following changes in its retained earnings account during 19X6 and 19X7:

Retained Earnings, January 1, 19X6...............................		$140,000
19X6 Net income..	$40,000	
19X6 Dividends	(24,000)	16,000
Balance, December 31, 19X6.......................................		$156,000
19X7 Net income..	$45,000	
19X7 Dividends	(21,600)	23,400
Balance, December 31, 19X7.......................................		$179,400

Prepare the journal entries that Barret Corporation would make to record this information relative to its 80% investment during 19X6 and 19X7 under (a) the simple equity method, (b) the sophisticated equity method, and (c) the cost method.

Exercise 3.   Aron Company purchased an 80% interest in Brewer Company for $230,000 in cash on January 1, 19X1, when Brewer Company had the following balance sheet:

Assets		Liabilities and Equity	
Current assets..................	$100,000	Current liabilities	$ 50,000
Property, plant, and		Common stock ($10 par)....	100,000
equipment (net).............	200,000	Retained earnings.............	150,000
Total assets.....................	$300,000	Total liabilities and equity..	$300,000

Any excess of the price paid over book value is attributable only to the plant assets, which have a 10-year remaining life. Aron Company uses the equity method to record its investment in Brewer Company.

The following trial balances of the two companies were prepared on December 31, 19X1:

	Aron	Brewer
Current Assets...	80,000	130,000
Property, Plant, and Equipment......................................	400,000	200,000
Accumulated Depreciation..	(106,000)	(20,000)
Investment in Brewer Company	246,000	—
Current Liabilities	(60,000)	(40,000)
Common Stock ($10 par)..	(300,000)	(100,000)
Retained Earnings, January 1, 19X1................................	(200,000)	(150,000)
Sales...	(150,000)	(100,000)
Expenses..	110,000	75,000
Subsidiary Income...	(20,000)	—
Dividends Declared..	—	5,000
Total..	0	0

(1) Prepare a determination and distribution of excess schedule for the investment.
(2) Prepare all the eliminations and adjustments that would be made on the 19X1 consolidated worksheet.
(3) Prepare the 19X1 consolidated income statement and its related income distribution schedules.
(4) Prepare the 19X1 consolidated balance sheet.

Exercise 4.   The trial balances of Aron and Brewer Companies of Exercise 3 for December 31, 19X2, are presented as follows:

	Aron	Brewer
Current Assets...	172,000	105,000
Property, Plant, and Equipment....................................	400,000	200,000
Accumulated Depreciation..	(130,000)	(40,000)
Investment in Brewer Company	242,000	—
Current Liabilities	(80,000)	—
Common Stock ($10 par)...	(300,000)	(100,000)
Retained Earnings, January 1, 19X2.............................	(260,000)	(170,000)
Sales..	(200,000)	(100,000)
Expenses..	160,000	95,000
Subsidiary Income..	(4,000)	—
Dividends Declared...	—	10,000
Total..	0	0

(1) Prepare all the eliminations and adjustments that would be made on the 19X2 consolidated worksheet.

(2) Prepare the 19X2 consolidated income statement and its related income distribution schedules.

Exercise 5. *(Note: read carefully. This is not the same as Exercise 3.)* Aron Company purchased an 80% interest in Brewer Company for $230,000 in cash on January 1, 19X1, when Brewer Company had the following balance sheet:

Assets		Liabilities and Equity	
Current assets...................	$100,000	Current liabilities	$ 50,000
Property, plant, and		Common stock ($10 par)....	100,000
equipment (net).............	200,000	Retained earnings.............	150,000
Total assets......................	$300,000	Total liabilities and equity..	$300,000

Any excess of the price paid over book value is attributable only to the plant assets, which have a 10-year remaining life. Aron Company uses the cost method to record its investment in Brewer Company.

The following trial balances of the two companies were prepared on December 31, 19X1:

	Aron	Brewer
Current Assets...	80,000	130,000
Property, Plant, and Equipment....................................	400,000	200,000
Accumulated Depreciation..	(106,000)	(20,000)
Investment in Brewer Company	230,000	—
Current Liabilities	(60,000)	(40,000)
Common Stock ($10 par)...	(300,000)	(100,000)
Retained Earnings, January 1, 19X1.............................	(200,000)	(150,000)
Sales..	(150,000)	(100,000)
Expenses..	110,000	75,000
Dividend Income (from Brewer Company)......................	(4,000)	—
Dividends Declared...	—	5,000
Total..	0	0

(1) If you did not solve Exercise 3, prepare a determination and distribution of excess schedule for the investment.

(2) Prepare all the eliminations and adjustments that would be made on the 19X1 consolidated worksheet.

(3) If you did not solve Exercise 3, prepare the 19X1 consolidated income statement and its related income distribution schedules.

(4) If you did not solve Exercise 3, prepare the 19X1 consolidated balance sheet.

Exercise 6. The trial balances of Aron and Brewer Companies of Exercise 5 for December 31, 19X2, are presented as follows:

	Aron	Brewer
Current Assets...	172,000	105,000
Property, Plant, and Equipment.....................................	400,000	200,000
Accumulated Depreciation...	(130,000)	(40,000)
Investment in Brewer Company	230,000	—
Current Liabilities	(80,000)	—
Common Stock ($10 par)..	(300,000)	(100,000)
Retained Earnings, January 1, 19X2..............................	(244,000)	(170,000)
Sales..	(200,000)	(100,000)
Expenses..	160,000	95,000
Dividend Income (from Brewer Company).......................	(8,000)	—
Dividends Declared...	—	10,000
Total..	0	0

(1) Prepare all the eliminations and adjustments that would be made on the 19X2 consolidated worksheet.

(2) If you did not solve Exercise 4, prepare the 19X2 consolidated income statement and its related income distribution schedules.

Exercise 7. Darrin Company purchased a 90% interest in Marcus Company on January 1, 19X1, when Marcus Company had the following balance sheet:

Assets		Liabilities and Equity	
Current assets..................	$200,000	Current liabilities	$100,000
Property, plant, and		Common stock ($10 par)....	150,000
equipment (net).............	300,000	Retained earnings.............	250,000
Total assets.....................	$500,000	Total liabilities and equity..	$500,000

Darrin Company paid $440,000 for the 90% interest and $10,000 in direct acquisition costs. At the purchase date, the property, plant, and equipment had a market value of $350,000 and a 10-year remaining life. Any excess attributable to goodwill is being amortized over the maximum allowable period. The investment is maintained under the cost method.

The following trial balances of the two companies were prepared on December 31, 19X2:

	Darrin	Marcus
Current Assets	278,000	320,000
Property, Plant, and Equipment	800,000	300,000
Accumulated Depreciation	(150,000)	(60,000)
Investment in Marcus Company	450,000	—
Current Liabilities	(140,000)	(90,000)
Common Stock ($10 par)	(400,000)	(150,000)
Retained Earnings, January 1, 19X2	(749,000)	(280,000)
Sales	(200,000)	(150,000)
Expenses	120,000	100,000
Dividend Income (from Marcus Company)	(9,000)	—
Dividends Declared	—	10,000
Total	0	0

(1) Prepare a determination and distribution of excess schedule for the investment.

(2) Prepare all the eliminations and adjustments that would be made on the 19X2 consolidated worksheet.

(3) Prepare the 19X2 consolidated income statement and its related income distribution schedules.

Exercise 8.   Mature Company paid $350,000 for a 90% interest in Spark Company on January 1, 19X1, at which time Spark Company had the following balance sheet:

Assets		Liabilities and Equity	
Accounts receivable	$ 70,000	Current liabilities	$ 70,000
Inventory	80,000	Common stock ($5 par)	100,000
Land	20,000	Paid-in capital in excess	
Building (net)	150,000	of par	130,000
		Retained earnings	20,000
Total assets	$320,000	Total liabilities and equity	$320,000

It was believed that the inventory and the building were undervalued by $20,000 and $50,000, respectively. The building had a 10-year remaining life; the inventory on hand January 1, 19X1, was sold during the year. The deferred tax liability associated with the asset revaluations was to be recorded by Mature. Spark Company also had $100,000 of tax loss carryforwards which were to be recorded by Mature. Each firm has an income tax rate of 30%. Goodwill, if any, would be amortized over 10 years.

The separate income statements of the two companies prepared for 19X1 are shown at the top of page 258.

(1) Prepare a determination and distribution of excess schedule for the investment.

(2) Prepare the 19X1 consolidated income statement and its related income distribution schedules.

	Mature	Spark
Sales..	$400,000	$150,000
Cost of goods sold....................................	(200,000)	(90,000)
Gross profit..	$200,000	$ 60,000
General expenses.....................................	(50,000)	(25,000)
Depreciation expense.................................	(60,000)	(15,000)
Operating income.....................................	$ 90,000	$ 20,000
Subsidiary income....................................	18,000	—
Net income before income tax........................	$108,000	$ 20,000
Provision for tax (does not include tax		
on subsidiary income)...............................	(27,000)	(6,000)
Net income...	$ 81,000	$ 14,000

Exercise 9.   Carns Company had the following balance sheet on January 1, 19X1:

Assets		Liabilities and Equity	
Current assets..................	$150,000	Current liabilities..............	$ 50,000
Equipment (net)................	300,000	Common stock ($10 par)....	100,000
		Retained earnings.............	300,000
Total assets.....................	$450,000	Total liabilities and equity..	$450,000

Between January 1 and July 1, 19X1, Carns Company estimated its net income to be $25,000. On July 1, 19X1, Abrams Company purchased 80% of the outstanding common stock of Carns Company for $300,000. Any excess of cost over book value was attributed to the equipment which had an estimated 5-year life. Carns Company did not close its books on July 1.

On December 31, 19X1, Abrams Company and Carns Company prepared the following trial balances:

	Abrams	Carns
Current Assets..	150,000	250,000
Equipment..	500,000	300,000
Accumulated Depreciation...........................	(140,000)	(20,000)
Investment in Carns Company	300,000	—
Current Liabilities	(150,000)	(70,000)
Common Stock ($10 par)............................	(200,000)	(100,000)
Retained Earnings, January 1, 19X1...............	(400,000)	(300,000)
Sales..	(300,000)	(200,000)
Cost of Goods Sold..................................	180,000	90,000
General Expenses....................................	60,000	50,000
Total...	0	0

(1) Prepare a determination and distribution of excess schedule for the investment.
(2) Prepare all the eliminations and adjustments that would be made on the December 31, 19X1 consolidated worksheet.

(3) Prepare the 19X1 consolidated income statement and its related income distribution schedules.

Exercise 10. Sharon Company had the following balance sheet on January 1, 19X1:

Assets		Liabilities and Equity	
Current assets.................	$ 80,000	Common stock ($5 par).....	$ 50,000
Property, plant, and		Paid-in capital in excess	
equipment....................	220,000	of par..........................	60,000
Accumulated		Retained earnings............	170,000
depreciation..................	(40,000)		
Goodwill.........................	20,000		
		Total liabilities	
Total assets.....................	$280,000	and equity...................	$280,000

On July 1, 19X1, Truman Company acquired 100% of the outstanding common stock of Sharon Company in a transaction that met the criteria for a pooling of interests. For the Sharon stock, Truman issued 14,000 shares of its $10 par common stock, with a market value of $50 each. Sharon estimated its first six months' income to be $20,000; the Sharon books were not closed. Sharon and Truman prepared the following trial balances on December 31, 19X1:

	Truman	Sharon
Current Assets..	120,000	132,000
Property, Plant, and Equipment....................................	1,950,000	220,000
Accumulated Depreciation...	(350,000)	(50,000)
Investment in Sharon Company....................................	700,000	—
Goodwill..	—	18,000
Common Stock ($10 par)..	(620,000)	—
Common Stock ($5 par)..	—	(50,000)
Paid-In Capital in Excess of Par...................................	(880,000)	(60,000)
Retained Earnings, January 1, 19X1.............................	(860,000)	(170,000)
Sales..	(120,000)	(80,000)
Expenses...	60,000	40,000
Total..	0	0

Prepare the consolidated income statement and balance sheet for December 31, 19X1.

Exercise 11. On January 1, 19X6, Pluto Inc. issued 200,000 additional shares of its voting common stock in exchange for 100,000 shares of the outstanding voting common stock of Sherry Company in a business combination appropriately accounted for by the pooling-of-interests method. The market value of the voting common stock of Pluto was $40 per share on the date of the business combination. Immediately prior to the acquisition, the balance sheets of Pluto and Sherry contained the following information:

Pluto Inc.

Common stock $5 par; authorized 1,000,000 shares;	
issued and outstanding 600,000 shares	$ 3,000,000
Additional paid-in capital	6,000,000
Retained earnings	11,000,000
Total stockholders' equity	$20,000,000

Sherry Company

Common stock, $10 par; authorized 250,000 shares;	
issued and outstanding 100,000 shares	$ 1,000,000
Additional paid-in capital	2,000,000
Retained earnings	4,000,000
Total stockholders' equity	$ 7,000,000

Additional information is as follows:

(a) Net income for the year ended December 31, 19X6, was $1,150,000 for Pluto and $350,000 for Sherry.

(b) During 19X6, Pluto paid $900,000 in dividends to its stockholders, and Sherry paid $210,000 in dividends to Pluto.

Prepare the consolidated stockholders' equity section of the balance sheet of Pluto Inc. and its subsidiary, Sherry Company, at December 31, 19X6.

(AICPA adapted)

PROBLEMS

Problem 5–1. Ace Company, Barns Company, and Charms Company had the following balance sheets on January 1, 19X1:

Assets	Ace	Barns	Charms
Current assets	$1,500,000	$100,000	$200,000
Property, plant, and equipment (net)	4,500,000	300,000	400,000
Total assets	$6,000,000	$400,000	$600,000
Equity			
Common stock ($10 par)	$2,000,000	$100,000	$200,000
Paid-in capital in excess of par	3,000,000	100,000	300,000
Retained earnings	1,000,000	200,000	100,000
Total equity	$6,000,000	$400,000	$600,000

Subsequent to the preparation of these balance sheets, Ace acquired 80% of the outstanding stock of Barns Company in exchange for 12,000 newly issued shares. Ace also acquired 90% of Charms Company stock in exchange for 16,000 newly issued shares. Each acquisition was deemed to be a purchase. The market value of the newly issued Ace Company shares was $30 each on the date of the acquisitions.

All the assets of Barns and Charms Companies were recorded at values approximating market values. All their plant assets had 10-year remaining lives. Any resulting goodwill is being amortized over the maximum allowable period.

During 19X1 and 19X2, the three companies reported the following:

	Ace Company		Barns Company		Charms Company	
	Income	Dividends	Income	Dividends	Income	Dividends
19X1	$200,000	$50,000	$50,000	$10,000	$10,000	$20,000
19X2	300,000	50,000	5,000	10,000	30,000	0

Required:
(1) Prepare determination and distribution of excess schedules for the investments.
(2) Record all entries pertaining to the investments for 19X1 and 19X2 under (a) the simple equity method, (b) the sophisticated equity method, and (c) the cost method.
(3) Assuming the use of the cost method, prepare the cost-to-equity conversion entries that would be made on the December 31, 19X2 consolidated worksheet.
(4) As of December 31, 19X2, calculate the minority and controlling interests in consolidated Retained Earnings.

Problem 5–2. The trial balances of Pence Company and its subsidiary, Bomberg Company, are as follows on December 31, 19X1:

	Pence Company	Bomberg Company
Current Assets..	295,000	160,000
Land...	100,000	135,000
Buildings (net)..	400,000	235,000
Equipment (net)..	60,000	140,000
Investment in Bomberg Company	650,000	—
Current Liabilities	(160,000)	(70,000)
Common Stock ($10 par)..	(400,000)	(100,000)
Paid-In Capital in Excess of Par.............................	(350,000)	(200,000)
Retained Earnings, January 1, 19X1........................	(500,000)	(250,000)
Sales..	(400,000)	(250,000)
Subsidiary Income...	(40,000)	—
Cost of Goods Sold..	250,000	150,000
Expenses..	95,000	50,000
Total..	0	0

Pence Company purchased an 80% interest in Bomberg Company on January 1, 19X1, paying $600,000 plus $10,000 in direct acquisition costs. The equity method is used to record the investment. At the purchase date, the market values of Bomberg's assets and liabilities agreed with their book values, except for the equipment which was undervalued by $70,000. The equipment had a 5-year remaining life on January 1, 19X1. Any remaining excess was attributed to goodwill and is being amortized over its maximum possible life.

Required:
(1) Prepare a determination and distribution of excess schedule for the investment.
(2) Prepare the consolidated statements for 19X1, including the income statement, retained earnings statement, and balance sheet. (A worksheet is not required.)

Problem 5–3.   On January 1, 19X4, Jack Inc. acquired 80% of the outstanding common stock of Jill Enterprises for $135,000. Jack Inc. also paid $5,000 in direct acquisition costs, which were added to the investment account. At the time of the acquisition, Jill Enterprises had the following stockholders' equity:

Common stock ($10 par)............................	$100,000
Paid-in capital in excess of par...................	30,000
Retained earnings.....................................	70,000
Total stockholders' equity.......................	$200,000

Any discrepancy between the price paid and the underlying book value was attributed to the equipment, which had a 10-year remaining life on January 1, 19X4.

Jack Inc. uses the sophisticated equity method to account for its investment in Jill Enterprises. The investment, retained earnings, and subsidiary income accounts of Jack Inc. include past- and current-year amortizations of excess book values.

The two companies prepared the following trial balances on December 31, 19X7:

	Jack Inc.	Jill Enterprises
Current Assets..	297,000	113,000
Equipment...	1,200,000	400,000
Accumulated Depreciation..	(310,000)	(174,000)
Investment in Jill Enterprises....................................	216,000	—
Liabilities..	(507,000)	(54,000)
Common Stock ($10 par)...	(400,000)	(100,000)
Paid-In Capital in Excess of Par................................	(20,000)	(30,000)
Retained Earnings, January 1, 19X7...........................	(410,400)	(120,000)
Sales..	(291,000)	(105,000)
Subsidiary Income...	(35,600)	—
Cost of Goods Sold...	145,000	38,000
Expenses...	100,000	25,000
Dividends Declared..	16,000	7,000
Total...	0	0

Required:

(1) Prepare a determination and distribution of excess schedule for the investment.
(2) Prepare the 19X7 consolidated statements, including the income statement, retained earnings statement, and balance sheet. (A worksheet is not required.)

Problem 5–4.   The trial balances of Errol Company and its subsidiary, Crystal Inc., are as follows on December 31, 19X3:

	Errol Company	Crystal Inc.
Current Assets...	530,000	130,000
Property, Plant, and Equipment...................................	1,805,000	440,000
Accumulated Depreciation..	(405,000)	(70,000)
Investment in Crystal Inc.	300,000	—
Liabilities...	(900,000)	(225,000)
Common Stock ($1 par)...	(220,000)	—
Common Stock ($5 par)...	—	(50,000)
Paid-In Capital in Excess of Par..................................	(880,000)	(15,000)
Retained Earnings, January 1, 19X3.............................	(230,000)	(170,000)
Revenues...	(460,000)	(210,000)
Investment Income	—	—
Expenses...	450,000	170,000
Dividends Declared...	10,000	—
Total...	0	0

On January 1, 19X1, Errol Company exchanged 20,000 shares of its common stock, with a market value of $15 per share, for all the outstanding stock of Crystal Inc. in a transaction that did not meet the criteria for a pooling of interests. Any excess of cost over book value was attributed to goodwill and is being amortized over a 40-year period. The stockholders' equity of Crystal Inc. on the purchase date was:

Common stock ($5 par).............................	$ 50,000
Paid-in capital in excess of par..................	15,000
Retained earnings.....................................	135,000
Total equity...	$200,000

Required:

(1) Prepare a determination and distribution of excess schedule for the investment.
(2) Prepare the 19X3 consolidated statements, including the income statement, retained earnings statement, and balance sheet. (A worksheet is not required.)

Problem 5–5.   On January 1, 19X1, Zelton Corporation exchanged 50,000 newly issued shares of common stock for all the outstanding stock of Ash Inc. The combination meets the criteria for a pooling of interests. Zelton Corporation maintains its investment in the subsidiary under the equity method.

The trial balances of the two companies on December 31, 19X1, are as follows:

	Zelton Corporation	Ash Inc.
Current Assets..	425,000	340,000
Property, Plant, and Equipment...............................	2,155,000	830,000
Accumulated Depreciation......................................	(355,000)	(90,000)
Investment in Ash Inc.	620,000	—
Liabilities..	(740,000)	(460,000)
Common Stock ($5 par)...	(1,000,000)	—
Common Stock ($10 par)..	—	(300,000)
Paid-In Capital in Excess of Par..............................	(560,000)	—
Retained Earnings, January 1, 19X1.........................	(490,000)	(280,000)
Revenues..	(440,000)	(210,000)
Subsidiary Income...	(70,000)	—
Expenses..	415,000	140,000
Dividends Declared..	40,000	30,000
Total...	0	0

Required:

Prepare the 19X1 consolidated statements, including the income statement, retained earnings statement, and balance sheet. (A worksheet is not required.)

Problem 5–6. Sauer Company prepared the following balance sheet on January 1, 19X1:

Assets		Liabilities and Equity	
Current assets............................	$ 50,000	Liabilities.....................................	$140,000
Land...	75,000	Common stock ($10 par)...............	100,000
Buildings	350,000	Paid-in capital in excess of par......	120,000
Accumulated		Retained earnings (deficit)............	(25,000)
depreciation—buildings............	(140,000)		
Total assets...............................	$335,000	Total liabilities and equity.............	$335,000

On this date, Roland Company purchased 8,000 shares of Sauer Company outstanding stock for a total price of $270,000. Also on this date, the buildings were understated by $40,000 and were felt to have a 10-year remaining life. Any remaining discrepancy between the price paid and book value was attributed to goodwill and estimated to have a 20-year life. Since the purchase, Roland Company has used the cost method to record the investment and its related income.

Roland Company and Sauer Company have the following separate trial balances on December 31, 19X1:

	Roland	Sauer
Current Assets...	100,000	110,000
Land..	150,000	75,000
Buildings	540,000	350,000
Accumulated Depreciation—Buildings.........................	(215,000)	(161,000)
Investment in Sauer Company	270,000	—
Liabilities..	(150,000)	(169,000)
Common Stock ($10 par)...	(200,000)	(100,000)
Paid-In Capital in Excess of Par...............................	—	(120,000)
Retained Earnings, January 1, 19X1.............................	(435,000)	25,000
Sales..	(320,000)	(90,000)
Cost of Goods Sold...	150,000	40,000
Expenses...	100,000	40,000
Dividends Declared...	10,000	—
Total...	0	0

Required:

(1) Prepare a determination and distribution of excess schedule for the investment.
(2) Prepare the 19X1 consolidated worksheet. Include columns for the eliminations and adjustments, the consolidated income statement, the minority interest, the controlling retained earnings, and the consolidated balance sheet. Prepare supporting income distribution schedules as well.
(3) Prepare the 19X1 consolidated statements, including the income statement, retained earnings statement, and balance sheet.

Problem 5–7. Roland Company and Sauer Company of Problem 5–6 have prepared the following separate trial balances as of December 31, 19X2:

	Roland	Sauer
Current Assets...	180,000	115,000
Land..	150,000	75,000
Buildings	590,000	350,000
Accumulated Depreciation—Buildings.........................	(265,000)	(182,000)
Investment in Sauer Company	270,000	—
Liabilities..	(175,000)	(133,000)
Common Stock ($10 par)...	(200,000)	(100,000)
Paid-In Capital in Excess of Par...............................	—	(120,000)
Retained Earnings, January 1, 19X2.............................	(495,000)	15,000
Sales..	(360,000)	(120,000)
Dividend Income (from Sauer Company).......................	(4,000)	—
Cost of Goods Sold...	179,000	50,000
Expenses...	120,000	45,000
Dividends Declared...	10,000	5,000
Total...	0	0

Required:

(1) Assuming the same facts applicable to the acquisition as used in Problem 5–6, prepare the 19X2 consolidated worksheet. Include columns for the eliminations and adjustments, the consolidated income state-

ment, the minority interest, the controlling retained earnings, and the consolidated balance sheet. Prepare supporting income distribution schedules as well.

(2) Prepare the 19X2 consolidated statements, including the income statement, retained earnings statement, and balance sheet.

Problem 5–8.   On January 1, 19X1, Fordum Corporation exchanged 90,000 shares of its $5 par stock, with a market value of $15 per share, for 90% of the outstanding common stock of Rice Corporation in a transaction qualifying as a pooling of interests. The account Investment in Rice Corporation reflects the market value of the shares exchanged and the issuance cost related to the common stock of Fordum Corporation.

Immediately prior to the exchange, Rice Corporation had the following owners' equity:

Common stock ($2 par)............................	$200,000
Paid-in capital in excess of par..................	400,000
Retained earnings (deficit)........................	(50,000)
Total equity...	$550,000

Since the exchange, Fordum has used the cost method to account for its investment in Rice. No intercompany transactions have ever occurred.

Fordum Corporation and Rice Corporation have the following trial balances on December 31, 19X3:

	Fordum Corporation	Rice Corporation
Current Assets...	840,000	360,000
Property, Plant, and Equipment............................	4,800,000	1,570,000
Accumulated Depreciation...................................	(1,600,000)	(520,000)
Investment in Rice Corporation...........................	1,400,000	—
Liabilities...	(1,830,000)	(790,000)
Common Stock ($5 par)......................................	(1,000,000)	—
Common Stock ($2 par)......................................	—	(200,000)
Paid-In Capital in Excess of Par...........................	(1,650,000)	(400,000)
Retained Earnings, January 1, 19X3......................	(900,000)	10,000
Sales...	(1,050,000)	(440,000)
Cost of Goods Sold..	600,000	250,000
Expenses...	350,000	160,000
Dividends Declared..	40,000	—
Total..	0	0

Required:
(1) Prepare the journal entries that should be made to reflect properly this investment on the books of the parent company.
(2) Prepare the 19X3 consolidated worksheet. Include columns for the eliminations and adjustments, the consolidated income statement, the minority interest, the controlling retained earnings, and the consolidated balance sheet. Prepare supporting income distribution schedules as well.

Problem 5–9. Stiles Corporation purchased the outstanding stock of Maybee Corporation for $50,000 in cash on January 1, 19X7. On the purchase date, Maybee Corporation had the following condensed balance sheet:

Assets		Liabilities and Equity	
Cash and receivables	$ 40,000	Liabilities.........................	$ 80,000
Inventory	20,000	Stockholders' equity	100,000
Land...............................	120,000		
Total assets.....................	$180,000	Total liabilities and equity..	$180,000

The land had lost significant value. The inventory was judged to have a market value of $10,000 at the time of the acquisition. For all other assets and all liabilities the book and market values were the same. During 19X7, half of the land and all of the inventory were sold by Maybee Corporation. However, none of these assets were sold to Stiles, and there were no other intercompany transactions during 19X7.

The trial balances of the two firms on December 31, 19X7, appear as follows:

	Stiles Corporation	Maybee Corporation
Cash and Receivables	150,000	20,000
Inventory	60,000	10,000
Land..	120,000	60,000
Buildings (net)..	600,000	—
Investrnent in Maybee Corporation........................	50,000	—
Liabilities...	(405,000)	(20,000)
Common Stock ($3 par).......................................	(300,000)	—
Common Stock ($.50 par)	—	(20,000)
Paid-In Capital in Excess of Par	(100,000)	(90,000)
Retained Earnings, January 1, 19X7.......................	(135,000)	10,000
Sales..	(210,000)	(40,000)
Costs of Goods Sold	120,000	35,000
Expenses	45,000	10,000
Loss on Sale of Land	—	25,000
Dividends Declared...	5,000	—
Total..	0	0

Required:
(1) Prepare a determination and distribution of excess schedule for the investment.
(2) Prepare the 19X7 consolidated worksheet. Include columns for the eliminations and adjustments, the consolidated income statement, the controlling retained earnings, and the consolidated balance sheet.
(3) Prepare the 19X7 consolidated statements, including the income statement, retained earnings statement, and balance sheet.

Suggestion: Half of the land was sold this year. Part of the market value adjustment made to the land at the purchase date may be realized now. This requires an adjustment to the loss on the sale of the land.

Problem 5–10. The trial balances of Canyon Corporation and Dawson Corporation as of December 31, 19X1, are as follows:

	Canyon Corporation	Dawson Corporation
Current Assets..	195,000	100,000
Land..	400,000	100,000
Building and Equipment (net)	900,000	240,000
Investment in Dawson Corporation.......................	417,600	—
Current Tax Liability...	(15,000)	(6,000)
Other Current Liabilities	(150,000)	(120,000)
Common Stock ($5 par).......................................	(500,000)	—
Common Stock ($50 par).....................................	—	(200,000)
Paid-In Capital in Excess of Par...........................	(550,000)	—
Retained Earnings, January 1, 19X1......................	(650,000)	(100,000)
Sales..	(309,000)	(150,000)
Subsidiary Income..	(12,600)	—
Cost of Goods Sold...	170,000	80,000
Expenses..	89,000	50,000
Provision for Tax	15,000	6,000
Total..	0	0

On January 1, 19X1, Canyon purchased 90% of the outstanding stock of Dawson Corporation for $405,000, including direct acquisition costs. The acquisition was a tax-free exchange as to the seller. At the purchase date, Dawson's equipment was undervalued by $100,000. All the other assets had book values that approximated their market values. Any resulting goodwill is being amortized over 40 years. A tax rate of 30% applies to both firms.

Required:
(1) Prepare a determination and distribution of excess schedule for the investment.
(2) Prepare the 19X1 consolidated worksheet. Include columns for the eliminations and adjustments, the consolidated income statement, the minority interest, the controlling retained earnings, and the consolidated balance sheet. Prepare supporting income distribution schedules as well.
(3) Prepare the 19X1 consolidated statements, including the income statement, retained earnings statement, and balance sheet.

Suggestion: A deferred tax liability results from the increase in the market value of the equipment. As the added depreciation is recognized on the equipment, the deferred tax liability becomes payable. Note that income distribution schedules record net-of-tax income. Therefore, be sure that any adjustments to the income distribution schedules consider tax where appropriate. Remember that goodwill amortizations are not tax deductible.

Problem 5–11.   Gray Steel Corporation purchased 80% of the outstanding stock of Pig Iron Company for $200,000 on January 1, 19X1, at which time Pig Iron Company had the following stockholders' equity:

Common stock ($5 par).............................	$150,000
Retained earnings.....................................	50,000
Total equity..	$200,000

The market values of Pig Iron's assets and liabilities agreed with the book values, except for the equipment, which was overdepreciated by $10,000 and was thought to have a 5-year remaining life. Any goodwill that results is being amortized over 20 years. Gray Steel uses the sophisticated equity method to record its investment.

Since the purchase date, both firms have operated separately and no intercompany transactions have occurred.

The separate trial balances of the firms on December 31, 19X2, are as follows:

	Gray Steel	Pig Iron
Current Assets..	380,000	90,000
Investment in Pig Iron Company	213,600	—
Land...	160,000	90,000
Building..	225,000	135,000
Accumulated Depreciation — Building	(100,000)	(50,000)
Equipment..	450,000	150,000
Accumulated Depreciation — Equipment	(115,000)	(60,000)
Liabilities...	(500,000)	(130,000)
Common Stock ($100 par)	(400,000)	—
Common Stock ($5 par)...	—	(150,000)
Paid-In Capital in Excess of Par...................................	(40,000)	—
Retained Earnings, January 1, 19X2.............................	(248,800)	(65,000)
Sales...	(460,000)	(120,000)
Subsidiary Income..	(4,800)	—
Cost of Goods Sold...	220,000	60,000
Expenses...	210,000	50,000
Dividends Declared..	10,000	—
Total...	0	0

Required:
(1) Prepare a determination and distribution of excess schedule for the investment.
(2) Prepare the 19X2 consolidated worksheet. Include columns for the eliminations and adjustments, the consolidated income statement, the minority interest, the controlling retained earnings, and the consolidated balance sheet. Prepare supporting income distribution schedules as well.

(continued)

(3) Prepare the 19X2 consolidated statements, including the income statement, retained earnings statement, and balance sheet.

Suggestion: The sophisticated equity method is used; this means that the remaining excess is net of prior years' amortizations. The parent retained earnings account does not need an adjustment for amortizations of excess since that has been recorded already on the parent's books.

Problem 5–12.   Michal Co. purchased 100% of the outstanding stock of Arron Inc. for $2,000,000 on January 1, 19X4. At the purchase date, the inventory, the equipment, and the patents of Arron Inc. had fair market values of $20,000, $44,000, and $50,000, respectively, in excess of their book values. The other assets and liabilities of Arron had book values that approximated their market values. The inventory was sold during the month following the purchase. The two companies agreed that the equipment had a remaining life of 8 years and the patents, 10 years. On the purchase date, the owners' equity of Arron was as follows:

Common stock ($10 stated value).............	$1,000,000
Additional paid-in capital.........................	300,000
Retained earnings...................................	400,000
Total equity...	$1,700,000

During the next two years, Arron had income and paid dividends as follows:

	Income	Dividends
19X4	$ 90,000	$30,000
19X5	120,000	30,000

The trial balances of the two corporations as of December 31, 19X6, are as follows:

	Michal Co.	Arron Inc.
Current Assets..	760,000	465,000
Equipment (net)...	1,290,000	940,000
Patents...	100,000	35,000
Other Assets	1,620,000	730,000
Investment in Arron Inc.	2,000,000	—
Liabilities...	(1,150,000)	(205,000)
Common Stock ($5 par)..	(2,000,000)	—
Common Stock ($10 stated value)	—	(1,000,000)
Additional Paid-In Capital	(1,200,000)	(300,000)
Retained Earnings, Jan. 1, 19X6	(1,255,000)	(550,000)
Sales...	(905,000)	(425,000)
Subsidiary (Dividend) Income	(30,000)	—
Cost of Goods Sold...	470,000	170,000
Expenses...	250,000	110,000
Dividend Declared	50,000	30,000
Total...	0	0

Required:

Assume that any resulting goodwill is being amortized over 20 years and that no intercompany transactions occurred.

(1) Prepare the original determination and distribution of excess schedule for the investment.

(2) Prepare the 19X6 consolidated worksheet for December 31, 19X6. Include columns for the eliminations and adjustments, the consolidated income statement, the controlling retained earnings, and the consolidated balance sheet.

Problem 5–13.   On July 1, 19X5, Punch Inc. purchased 90% of the common stock of Sun Inc. for $1,127,000 plus $16,000 in direct acquisition costs. Sun had the following stockholders' equity on January 1, 19X5:

Common stock ($10 par value)....................	$200,000
Paid-in capital in excess of par...................	300,000
Retained earnings.....................................	300,000
Total equity..	$800,000

Sun Inc. estimated income for the first 6 months of 19X5 was $40,000, including the $30,000 depreciation on the building, $20,000 depreciation on the equipment, and $1,000 goodwill amortization. Following is a summary of the book and market values of Sun's asset and liability accounts on July 1, 19X5. Book values include the above amortizations.

Account	Book Value	Market Value	Punch's Life Assumption
Cash...	$150,000	$150,000	
Accounts Receivable	200,000	200,000	Collected by year end
Inventory..	250,000	270,000	Sold by year end
Land..	100,000	200,000	
Building..	700,000	600,000	20-year life, no salvage, straight-line*
Accumulated Depreciation — Building	(300,000)	—	
Equipment..	300,000	250,000	5-year life, no salvage, straight-line*
Accumulated Depreciation — Equipment ...	(160,000)	—	
Goodwill...	50,000	?	25 years
Mortgage Payable...................................	(450,000)	(400,000)	10-year, straight-line amortization

*Life and method do not agree with those used by Sun Inc.

Sun's books were not closed on July 1, 19X5; thus, the following December 31, 19X5 trial balances of Punch and Sun include the results from operations for all of 19X5:

	Punch	Sun
Cash.	323,000	261,000
Accounts Receivable	200,000	230,000
Inventory	400,000	220,000
Land.	200,000	100,000
Building.	1,000,000	700,000
Accumulated Depreciation — Building	(500,000)	(330,000)
Equipment	400,000	300,000
Accumulated Depreciation — Equipment	(100,000)	(180,000)
Goodwill (net)	—	49,000
Investment in Sun Inc.	1,143,000	—
Mortgage Payable.	—	(450,000)
Common Stock.	(1,800,000)	(200,000)
Paid-In Capital in Excess of Par	—	(300,000)
Retained Earnings, Jan. 1, 19X5	(1,066,000)	(300,000)
Sales.	(2,000,000)	(900,000)
Cost of Goods Sold.	1,500,000	600,000
General Expense	100,000	98,000
Depreciation Expense.	200,000	100,000
Goodwill Amortization	—	2,000
Total.	0	0

Note that the Sun Depreciation Expense includes $60,000 on the building and $40,000 on the equipment.

Required:
(1) Prepare the original determination and distribution of excess schedule for the investment.
(2) Prepare the consolidated worksheet for December 31, 19X5. Include columns for the eliminations and adjustments, the consolidated income statement, the minority interest, the controlling retained earnings, and the consolidated balance sheet. Prepare supporting income distribution schedules as well.
(3) Prepare the 19X5 consolidated statements, including the income statement, retained earnings statement, and balance sheet.

Suggestion: Due to the minority interest, it is difficult to restate long-lived assets with no accumulated depreciation. It is recommended that the adjustments be made by decreasing accumulated depreciation. However, it is first necessary to recalculate what depreciation should be, using the parent's estimates. Remember that the parent, in this example, is using different life assumptions and depreciation methods from that of the subsidiary. The parent's estimate (for 90% of the asset's value) should replace 90% of the depreciation now recorded by the subsidiary.

Problem 5–14. On January 1, 19X1, Green Corporation purchased 80% of the outstanding common stock of Ivan Inc. for $6,000,000 in cash. The book and market values for Ivan Inc. were as follows:

	Recorded Book Value	Market Value
Cash and Receivables	$1,305,000	$1,305,000
Inventory	790,000	823,345
Land	2,500,000	3,900,000
Building	2,400,000	1,200,000
Accumulated Depreciation—Building	(1,600,000)	—
Equipment	2,750,000	1,700,000
Accumulated Depreciation—Equipment	(1,850,000)	—
Goodwill	120,000	200,000*
Current Liabilities	(580,000)	(580,000)
Bonds Payable, 6%	(2,000,000)	(1,730,845)
Common Stock ($5 par)	(3,000,000)	—
Retained Earnings	(835,000)	—
Total	0	

*Estimate, final value dependent upon total purchase price.

By the end of 19X1, the January 1, 19X1 inventory of Ivan Inc. had been sold. At the purchase date, the building and the equipment were judged to have remaining lives of 10 years and 6 years, respectively, and the resulting goodwill is being amortized over 10 years. As of January 1, 19X1, the 6% bonds had six years remaining to maturity. The fair market value of the bonds was based on the 9% prevailing interest rate on January 1, 19X1.

The trial balances of Green and Ivan on December 31, 19X1 are as follows:

	Green	Ivan
Cash and Receivables	2,400,000	1,581,800
Inventory	1,600,000	800,000
Land	4,000,000	2,500,000
Building	6,900,000	2,400,000
Accumulated Depreciation—Buildings	(3,400,000)	(1,680,000)
Equipment	10,000,000	2,750,000
Accumulated Depreciation—Equipment	(5,000,000)	(2,000,000)
Goodwill	200,000	108,000
Investment in Ivan Inc.	6,011,840	—
Current Liabilities	(2,000,000)	(610,000)
Bonds Payable	(6,000,000)	(2,000,000)
Common Stock ($5 par)	(13,000,000)	(3,000,000)
Retained Earnings, January 1, 19X1	(1,550,000)	(835,000)
Sales	(3,000,000)	(1,490,000)
Cost of Goods Sold	1,900,000	968,500
Expenses	900,000	476,700
Subsidiary Income	(35,840)	—
Dividends Declared	74,000	30,000
Total	0	0

Required:
(1) Prepare a determination and distribution of excess schedule for the investment.

(2) Prepare the 19X1 consolidated worksheet, include columns for the eliminations and adjustments, the consolidated income statement, the minority
interest, the controlling retained earnings, and the consolidated balance
sheet. Prepare supporting income distribution schedules as well.

(AICPA adapted)

Suggestion: The decrease in the value of the bonds payable consumes the
excess cost. The effective interest method should be used to amortize the
resulting discount.

Problem 5–15.   On April 1, 19X1, Jansen Inc. purchased 100% of the common stock of Murdock Company for $5,850,000. At the date of purchase, the
book and market values of Murdock's assets and liabilities were as follows:

	Book Value	Market Value
Cash..	$ 200,000	$ 200,000
Notes Receivable (net)	85,000	85,000
Accounts Receivable (net)......................................	980,000	980,000
Inventories...	828,000	700,000
Land..	1,560,000	2,100,000
Machinery and Equipment......................................	7,850,000	10,600,000
Accumulated Depreciation......................................	(3,250,000)	(4,000,000)
Other Assets	140,000	50,000
Total assets..	$8,393,000	$10,715,000
Notes Payable..	$ 115,000	$ 115,000
Accounts Payable	1,150,000	1,150,000
Subordinated Debentures (7%).............................	5,000,000	5,000,000
Common Stock ($10 par)..	1,000,000	
Paid-In Capital in Excess of Par..............................	122,000	
Retained Earnings..	1,006,000	
Total liabilities and equity..................................	$8,393,000	

By year's end, December 31, 19X1, the following transactions had
occurred:
(a) The balance of Murdock's net accounts receivable account at April 1,
19X1, had been collected.
(b) The inventory on hand at April 1, 19X1, had been charged to the cost of
goods sold. Murdock used a perpetual inventory system in accounting
for the inventories.
(c) Included in Jansen's investment account is $1,500,000 of Daley Corpora-
tion 7% subordinated debentures. These debentures mature on October
31, 19X7, with interest payable annually on October 31.
(d) As of April 1, 19X1, Jansen viewed the machinery and equipment as
having an estimated remaining life of six years. Murdock used the
straight-line method of depreciation and a different remaining life. Mur-

dock's depreciation expense calculation for the nine months ended December 31, 19X1, was based upon the old depreciation rates.

(e) The other assets consist entirely of long-term investments made by Murdock and do not include any investment in Jansen.

(f) Accrued interest on debt is recorded by both companies in their respective accounts receivable and accounts payable accounts.

(g) Jansen's policy is to amortize intangible assets over a 20-year period.

Murdock Company closed its books on April 1, 19X1. Therefore, the following December 31, 19X1 trial balances provide revenue and expense figures for 12 months for Jansen and 9 months for Murdock.

	Jansen Inc.	Murdock Company
Cash	972,000	530,000
Notes Receivable	—	85,000
Accounts Receivable (net)	2,758,000	1,368,400
Inventories	3,204,000	1,182,000
Land	4,000,000	1,560,000
Buildings	1,286,000	—
Accumulated Depreciation—Buildings	(372,000)	—
Machinery and Equipment	15,875,000	7,850,000
Accumulated Depreciation—Machinery and Equipment	(6,301,000)	(3,838,750)
Investments	7,350,000	—
Other Assets	263,000	140,000
Notes Payable	—	(115,000)
Accounts Payable	(1,364,000)	(954,000)
Long-Term Debt	(10,000,000)	—
Subordinated Debentures, 7%	—	(5,000,000)
Common Stock	(2,400,000)	(1,000,000)
Paid-In Capital in Excess of Par	(240,000)	(122,000)
Retained Earnings	(12,683,500)	(1,006,000)
Sales	(18,200,000)	(5,760,000)
Cost of Goods Sold	10,600,000	3,160,000
Selling, General, and Administrative Expenses	3,448,500	1,063,900
Depreciation Expense—Buildings	127,000	—
Depreciation Expense—Equipment	976,000	588,750
Interest Revenue	(105,000)	(1,700)
Interest Expense	806,000	269,400
Total	0	0

Required:

(1) Prepare a determination and distribution of excess schedule for the investment in the common stock of Murdock Company. Jansen Inc. desires that the consolidated statements reflect the replacement cost and related depreciation as shown in the market value information.

(2) Prepare a consolidated worksheet that converts the separate trial balances into a consolidated trial balance. This worksheet should have the following columns:

Trial Balance		Eliminations & Adjustments		Consolidated Trial Balance
Jansen Inc.	Murdock Co.	Dr.	Cr.	

(AICPA adapted)

Suggestion: This is a "short-cut" format that is often used on the CPA Exam. It is really the horizontal format, but it does not require the extension of amounts to the income statement, minority interest, controlling retained earnings, and balance sheet columns. This relieves you from having to allocate combined net income to the minority and controlling interests. Very likely, the grader of the exam will focus on the consolidated totals. This allows for variety in how an individual can make eliminations.

APPENDIX PROBLEMS

Problem 5A–1.   Bayfield Company purchased an 80% interest in LaPointe Company for $750,000 on January 1, 19X1. Bayfield Company also paid $10,000 in direct acquisition costs. On the purchase date, LaPointe Company had the following stockholders' equity:

Common stock ($10 par)............................	$150,000
Paid-in capital in excess of par...................	200,000
Retained earnings.....................................	350,000
Total equity...	$700,000

Also on the purchase date, it was determined that LaPointe's assets were understated as follows:

Inventory, sold during 19X1..........................	$20,000
Equipment, 10-year remaining life................	80,000

Any remaining excess of cost over book value was attributed to goodwill which is being amortized over 20 years.

The following summarized statements of Bayfield and LaPointe Companies are for the year ending December 31, 19X3:

(Credit balance amounts are in parentheses.)

	Bayfield	LaPointe
Income Statements:		
Sales	(610,000)	(310,000)
Cost of Goods Sold	260,000	140,000
Operating Expenses	170,000	80,000
Depreciation Expense	65,000	30,000
Subsidiary Income	(48,000)	—
Net Income	(163,000)	(60,000)
Retained Earnings Statements:		
Retained Earnings, Jan. 1, 19X3, Bayfield	(625,000)	—
Retained Earnings, Jan. 1, 19X3, LaPointe	—	(420,000)
Net Income	(163,000)	(60,000)
Dividends Declared	—	10,000
Retained Earnings, Dec. 31, 19X3	(788,000)	(470,000)
Balance Sheets:		
Cash	330,000	270,000
Inventory	135,000	340,000
Land	145,000	150,000
Building	900,000	500,000
Accumulated Depreciation — Building	(345,000)	(360,000)
Equipment	350,000	250,000
Accumulated Depreciation — Equipment	(135,000)	(90,000)
Investment in LaPointe Company	856,000	—
Current Liabilities	(248,000)	(40,000)
Bonds Payable	—	(200,000)
Common Stock, Bayfield	(1,200,000)	—
Common Stock, LaPointe	—	(150,000)
Paid-In Capital in Excess of Par, LaPointe	—	(200,000)
Retained Earnings, Dec. 31, 19X3	(788,000)	(470,000)
Balance	0	0

Required:

Using the vertical format, prepare a consolidated worksheet for December 31, 19X3. Precede the worksheet with a determination and distribution of excess schedule. Include income distribution schedules to allocate the combined net income to the minority and controlling interests.

Suggestion: Remember that all adjustments to retained earnings are to beginning retained earnings and that it is the beginning balance of the subsidiary retained earnings account which is subject to elimination. Carefully follow the "carry-down" procedure to calculate the ending retained earnings balances.

Problem 5A–2. Ixonia Company purchased a 90% interest in Sullivan Company for $700,000 on January 1, 19X1. The investment account includes $20,000 of indirect acquisition costs. The investment has been accounted for under the cost method. At the time of the purchase, a building owned by Sullivan was understated by $180,000; it had a 20-year remaining life on the purchase date. Any remaining excess was attributed to goodwill with a 10-year life. The stockholders' equity of Sullivan Company on the purchase date was as follows:

Common stock ($10 par).............................	$350,000
Retained earnings......................................	200,000
Total equity..	$550,000

The following summarized statements are for the year ending December 31, 19X2:

(Credit balance amounts are in parentheses.)

	Ixonia	Sullivan
Income Statements:		
Sales...	(580,000)	(280,000)
Cost of Goods Sold..	285,000	155,000
Operating Expenses..	140,000	55,000
Depreciation Expense...	72,000	30,000
Dividend Income	(9,000)	—
Net Income..	(92,000)	(40,000)
Retained Earnings Statements:		
Retained Earnings, Jan. 1, 19X2, Ixonia........................	(484,000)	—
Retained Earnings, Jan. 1, 19X2, Sullivan.....................	—	(320,000)
Net Income...	(92,000)	(40,000)
Dividends Declared..	20,000	10,000
Retained Earnings, Dec. 31, 19X2	(556,000)	(350,000)
Balance Sheet		
Cash...	330,000	170,000
Inventory..	260,000	340,000
Land...	99,000	150,000
Building..	800,000	500,000
Accumulated Depreciation — Building	(380,000)	(360,000)
Equipment...	340,000	250,000
Accumulated Depreciation — Equipment	(190,000)	(90,000)
Investment in Sullivan Company.................................	720,000	—
Current Liabilities	(123,000)	(60,000)
Bonds Payable	—	(200,000)
Common Stock, Ixonia	(800,000)	—
Paid-In Capital in Excess of Par, Ixonia.......................	(500,000)	—
Common Stock, Sullivan	—	(350,000)
Retained Earnings, Dec. 31, 19X2	(556,000)	(350,000)
Balance	0	0

Required:

Using the vertical format, prepare a consolidated worksheet for December 31, 19X2. Precede the worksheet with a determination and distribution of excess schedule. Include income distribution schedules to allocate the combined net income to the minority and controlling interests.

Suggestion: Remember that all adjustments to retained earnings are to beginning retained earnings and that it is the beginning balance of the subsidiary retained earnings account which is subject to elimination. One of the adjustments to the parent retained earnings account is the cost-to-equity conversion entry. Be sure to follow the carry-down procedure to calculate the ending retained earnings balances.

Worksheet 5–1 (see page 231)

Simple
Company P and
Worksheet for Consolidated
For Year Ended

(Credit balance amounts are in parentheses.)

		Trial Balance	
		Company P	Company S
1	**Investment in Company S**	163,000	
2			
3			
4	**Goodwill**		
5	Other Assets (Net of Liabilities)	227,000	170,000
6	Common Stock ($10 par), Co. P	(200,000)	
7	Retained Earnings, Jan. 1, 19X1, Co. P	(123,000)	
8	Common Stock ($10 par), Co. S		(100,000)
9	Retained Earnings, Jan. 1, 19X1, Co. S		(50,000)
10	Revenue	(100,000)	(80,000)
11	**Expenses**	60,000	50,000
12	**Subsidiary Income**	(27,000)	
13	**Dividends Declared**		10,000
14		0	0
15	**Combined Net Income**		
16	To Minority Interest (see distribution schedule)		
17	Balance to Controlling Interest (see distribution schedule)		
18	Total Minority Interest		
19	Retained Earnings, Controlling Interest, Dec. 31, 19X1		
20			

Eliminations and Adjustments:
(1) Eliminate the current-year entries made in the investment account and in the subsidiary income account. It should be noted that when this step is completed, the balance in the investment account is the balance *at the beginning of the year.* At this point, the investment account and the Company S equity accounts are *adjusted to a common point* in time and are ready for elimination. Only dividends paid to outside minority stockholders remain on the worksheet.
(2) Eliminate the pro rata share of Company S equity balances *at the beginning of the year* against the investment account. The elimination of the parent's share of subsidiary stockholders' equity leaves only the minority interest in each element of the equity.
(3) Distribute the $10,000 excess cost as required by the determination and distribution of excess schedule. In this example, Goodwill is recorded for $10,000.
(4) Amortize the resulting goodwill over the ten-year period. The current portion is $1,000 per year ($10,000 ÷ 10 years).

Equity Method
Subsidiary Company S
Financial Statements
December 31, 19X1

WORKSHEET 5–1

Eliminations & Adjustments Dr.	Eliminations & Adjustments Cr.	Consolidated Income Statement	Minority Interest	Controlling Retained Earnings	Consolidated Balance Sheet	
(1) 9,000	(1) 27,000					1
	(2) 135,000					2
	(3) 10,000					3
(3) 10,000	(4) 1,000				9,000	4
					397,000	5
					(200,000)	6
				(123,000)		7
(2) 90,000			(10,000)			8
(2) 45,000			(5,000)			9
		(180,000)				10
(4) 1,000		111,000				11
(1) 27,000						12
	(1) 9,000		1,000			13
182,000	182,000					14
		(69,000)				15
		3,000*	(3,000)			16
		66,000*		(66,000)		17
			(17,000)		(17,000)	18
				(189,000)	(189,000)	19
					0	20

Subsidiary Company S Income Distribution

Internally generated net income...	$30,000
Adjusted income	$30,000
Minority share............................	10%
Minority interest.........................	$ 3,000*

Parent Company P Income Distribution

Goodwill amortization ....**(4)** **$1,000**	Internally generated net income...	$40,000
	90% × Company S adjusted income of $30,000	27,000
	Controlling interest.....................	$66,000*

Worksheet 5–2 (see page 236)

Simple Equity
Company P and
Worksheet for Consolidated
For Year Ended

(Credit balance amounts are in parentheses.)

		Trial Balance	
		Company P	Company S
1	**Investment in Company S**	149,500	
2			
3	**Goodwill**		
4	Other Assets (Net of Liabilities)	251,500	155,000
5	Common Stock ($10 par), Co. P	(200,000)	
6	**Retained Earnings, Jan. 1, 19X2, Co. P**	**(190,000)**	
7	Common Stock ($10 par), Co. S		(100,000)
8	Retained Earnings, Jan. 1, 19X2, Co. S		(70,000)
9	Revenue	(100,000)	(50,000)
10	Expenses	80,000	60,000
11	**Subsidiary Loss**	**9,000**	
12	**Dividends Declared**		**5,000**
13		0	0
14	**Combined Net Income**		
15	To Minority Interest (see distribution schedule)		
16	Balance to Controlling Interest (see distribution schedule)		
17	Total Minority Interest		
18	Retained Earnings, Controlling Interest, Dec. 31, 19X2		
19			

Eliminations and Adjustments:
(1) Eliminate the current-year entries made in the investment account and in the subsidiary loss account. This step returns the investment in Company S account to its January 1, 19X2 balance. The investment account and the subsidiary equity accounts now are *stated at a common point in time,* which will facilitate their elimination.
(2) Using balances *at the beginning of the year,* eliminate 90% of the Company S equity balances against the remaining investment account.
(3) Distribute the $10,000 excess cost as indicated by the determination and distribution of excess schedule that was prepared on the date of acquisition.
(4) Amortize the goodwill over the selected 10-year period. It is necessary to record the amortization *for current and past periods,* because asset adjustments resulting from the consolidation process do not appear on the separate statements of the constituent firms. Thus, step (4) reduces Goodwill by $2,000 for the 19X1 and 19X2 amortization. The amount for the current year is expensed, while the cumulative amortization for prior years is deducted from the beginning controlling retained earnings account. The minority interest does not share in the adjustments, since the only goodwill originally acknowledged is that which is applicable to the controlling interest.

Method, Second Year
Subsidiary Company S
Financial Statements
December 31, 19X2

WORKSHEET 5–2

Eliminations & Adjustments			Consolidated Income Statement	Minority Interest	Controlling Retained Earnings	Consolidated Balance Sheet	
Dr.		Cr.					
(1) **9,000**	**(2)**	**153,000**					1
(1) **4,500**	**(3)**	**10,000**					2
(3) **10,000**	**(4)**	**2,000**				8,000	3
						406,500	4
						(200,000)	5
(4) **1,000**					(189,000)		6
(2) 90,000				(10,000)			7
(2) 63,000				(7,000)			8
			(150,000)				9
(4) **1,000**			141,000				10
	(1)	**9,000**					11
	(1)	**4,500**		500			12
178,500		178,500					13
			(9,000)				14
			(1,000)*	1,000			15
			10,000*		(10,000)		16
				(15,500)		(15,500)	17
					(199,000)	(199,000)	18
						0	19

Subsidiary Company S Income Distribution

Internally generated loss	$10,000	
Adjusted loss	$10,000	
Minority share...........................	10%	
Minority interest........................	*$ 1,000	

Parent Company P Income Distribution

Goodwill amortization..............(4)	$1,000	Internally generated net income...	$20,000	
90% × Company S adjusted loss of $10,000	9,000			
		Controlling interest.....................	**$10,000***	

Worksheet 5–3 (see page 238)

Cost
Company P and
Worksheet for Consolidated
For Year Ended

(Credit balance amounts are in parentheses.)

		Trial Balance	
		Company P	Company S
1	**Investment in Company S**	145,000	
2			
3	Goodwill		
4	Other Assets (Net of Liabilities)	227,000	170,000
5	Common Stock ($10 par), Co. P	(200,000)	
6	Retained Earnings, Jan. 1, 19X1, Co. P	(123,000)	
7	Common Stock ($10 par), Co. S		(100,000)
8	Retained Earnings, Jan. 1, 19X1, Co. S		(50,000)
9	Revenue	(100,000)	(80,000)
10	Expenses	60,000	50,000
11	**Subsidiary (Dividend) Income**	**(9,000)**	
12	**Dividends Declared**		**10,000**
13		0	0
14	Combined Net Income		
15	To Minority Interest (see distribution schedule)		
16	Balance to Controlling Interest (see distribution schedule)		
17	Total Minority Interest		
18	Retained Earnings, Controlling Interest, Dec. 31, 19X1		
19			

Eliminations and Adjustments:
(1) Eliminate intercompany dividends.
(2) Eliminate 90% of the Company S equity balances at the beginning of the year against the investment account.
(3) Distribute the $10,000 excess cost as indicated by the determination and distribution of excess schedule on page 228.
(4) Amortize the goodwill for the current year.

Method
Subsidiary Company S
Financial Statements
December 31, 19X1

WORKSHEET 5-3

Eliminations & Adjustments Dr.		Eliminations & Adjustments Cr.		Consolidated Income Statement	Minority Interest	Controlling Retained Earnings	Consolidated Balance Sheet	
		(2)	135,000					1
		(3)	10,000					2
(3)	10,000	(4)	1,000				9,000	3
							397,000	4
							(200,000)	5
						(123,000)		6
(2)	90,000				(10,000)			7
(2)	45,000				(5,000)			8
				(180,000)				9
(4)	1,000			111,000				10
(1)	**9,000**							11
		(1)	**9,000**		**1,000**			12
	155,000		155,000					13
				(69,000)				14
				3,000*	(3,000)			15
				66,000*		(66,000)		16
					(17,000)		(17,000)	17
						(189,000)	(189,000)	18
							0	19

Subsidiary Company S Income Distribution

Internally generated net income...	$30,000
Adjusted income	$30,000
Minority share............................	10%
Minority interest.........................	**$ 3,000***

Parent Company P Income Distribution

Goodwill amortization.................(4)	$1,000	Internally generated net income...	$40,000
		90% × Company S adjusted income of $30,000	27,000
		Controlling interest.....................	**$66,000***

Worksheet 5–4 (see page 238)

(Credit balance amounts are in parentheses.)

| | | Trial Balance | |
		Company P	Company S
1	**Investment in Company S**	**145,000**	
2			
3	Goodwill		
4	Other Assets (Net of Liabilities)	251,500	155,000
5	Common Stock ($10 par), Co. P	(200,000)	
6	**Retained Earnings, Jan. 1, 19X2, Co. P**	**(172,000)**	
7	Common Stock ($10 par), Co. S		(100,000)
8	Retained Earnings, Jan. 1, 19X2, Co. S		(70,000)
9	Revenue	(100,000)	(50,000)
10	Expenses	80,000	60,000
11	**Subsidiary (Dividend) Income**	**(4,500)**	
12	**Dividends Declared**		**5,000**
13		0	0
14	Combined Net Income		
15	To Minority Interest (see distribution schedule)		
16	Balance to Controlling Interest (see distribution schedule)		
17	Total Minority Interest		
18	Retained Earnings, Controlling Interest, Dec. 31, 19X2		
19			

Eliminations and Adjustments:
(C) Convert to simple equity method as of January 1, 19X2.
(1) Eliminate the current-year intercompany dividends.
(2) Eliminate 90% of the Company S equity balances at the beginning of the year against the investment account.
(3) Distribute the $10,000 excess cost as indicated by the determination and distribution of excess schedule on page 228.
(4) Amortize the goodwill for the current year and one previous year.

Second Year
Subsidiary Company S
Financial Statements
December 31, 19X2

WORKSHEET 5–4

Eliminations & Adjustments				Consolidated Income Statement	Minority Interest	Controlling Retained Earnings	Consolidated Balance Sheet	
Dr.		**Cr.**						
(C)	**18,000**	(2)	153,000					1
		(3)	10,000					2
(3)	10,000	(4)	2,000				8,000	3
							406,500	4
							(200,000)	5
(4)	1,000	**(C)**	**18,000**			(189,000)		6
(2)	90,000				(10,000)			7
(2)	63,000				(7,000)			8
				(150,000)				9
(4)	1,000			141,000				10
(1)	**4,500**							11
		(1)	**4,500**		500			12
	187,500		187,500					13
				(9,000)				14
				(1,000)*	1,000			15
				10,000*		(10,000)		16
				(15,500)			(15,500)	17
						(199,000)	(199,000)	18
							0	19

Subsidiary Company S Income Distribution

Internally generated **loss**	$10,000
Adjusted loss	$10,000
Minority share...........................	10%
Minority interest........................	*$ 1,000

Parent Company P Income Distribution

Goodwill amortization...............(4)	$1,000	Internally generated net income...	$20,000
90% × Company S adjusted loss of $10,000	9,000		
		Controlling interest.....................	**$10,000***

Worksheet 5–5 (see page 241)

Simple Equity
Paulos Company and
Worksheet for Consolidated
For Year Ended

(Credit balance amounts are in parentheses.)

		Trial Balance	
		Paulos	Carlos
1	Cash	100,000	50,000
2	Inventory	226,000	62,500
3	Land	200,000	150,000
4	Building	800,000	600,000
5	**Accumulated Depreciation — Building**	(80,000)	(315,000)
6	Equipment	400,000	150,000
7	**Accumulated Depreciation – Equipment**	(50,000)	(70,000)
8	**Investment in Carlos Company**	832,000	
9			
10			
11	Goodwill		112,500
12	Current Liabilities	(100,000)	
13	Bonds Payable		(200,000)
14	**Discount on Bonds**		
15	Common Stock, Paulos	(1,500,000)	
16	Retained Earnings, Jan. 1, 19X1, Paulos	(700,000)	
17	Common Stock ($10 par), Carlos		(100,000)
18	Paid-In Capital in Excess of Par, Carlos		(150,000)
19	Retained Earnings, Jan. 1, 19X1, Carlos		(250,000)
20	Sales	(350,000)	(200,000)
21	**Cost of Goods Sold**	150,000	80,000
22	**Expenses**	120,000	60,000
23			
24			
25	**Subsidiary Income**	(48,000)	
26	**Dividends Declared**		20,000
27		0	0
28	Combined Net Income		
29	To Minority Interest (see distribution schedule)		
30	Balance to Controlling Interest (see distribution schedule)		
31	Total Minority Interest		
32	Retained Earnings, Controlling Interest, Dec. 31, 19X1		
33			

Method, First Year
Subsidiary Carlos Company
Financial Statements
December 31, 19X1

WORKSHEET 5-5

Eliminations & Adjustments Dr.	Eliminations & Adjustments Cr.	Consolidated Income Statement	Minority Interest	Controlling Retained Earnings	Consolidated Balance Sheet	
					150,000	1
					288,500	2
(3e) 40,000					390,000	3
					1,400,000	4
(3d) 160,000	(4d) 8,000				(243,000)	5
	(3c) 16,000				534,000	6
(4c) 3,200					(116,800)	7
(1) 16,000	(1) 48,000					8
	(2) 400,000					9
	(3) 400,000					10
(3f) 201,402	(4f) 20,140				293,762	11
					(100,000)	12
					(200,000)	13
(3b) 10,598	(4b) 2,352				8,246	14
					(1,500,000)	15
				(700,000)		16
(2) 80,000			(20,000)			17
(2) 120,000			(30,000)			18
(2) 200,000			(50,000)			19
		(550,000)				20
(3a) 4,000		234,000				21
(4b) 2,352	(4c) 3,200	207,292				22
(4d) 8,000						23
(4f) 20,140						24
(1) 48,000						25
	(1) 16,000		4,000			26
913,692	913,692					27
		(108,708)				28
		12,000*	(12,000)			29
		96,708*		(96,708)		30
		(108,000)			(108,000)	31
				(796,708)	(796,708)	32
					0	33

(continued)

Eliminations and Adjustments:
(1) Eliminate the current-year entries made in the investment in Carlos Company account and in the subsidiary income account. The investment account now is adjusted to its January 1, 19X1 balance so that it may be eliminated.
(2) Eliminate the 80% ownership portion of the subsidiary equity accounts against the investment. A $400,000 excess cost remains.
(3) Distribute the $400,000 excess cost as follows, in accordance with the determination and distribution of excess schedule:
  (a) Increase the beginning inventory by $4,000. However, the beginning inventory has been closed to the cost of goods sold; thus, the cost of goods sold is increased by $4,000. If the inventory had not been sold, the inventory account would be adjusted. The cost of goods sold in the later period of sale then would be adjusted on a subsequent worksheet.
  (b) Record discount of $10,598 on the bonds payable.
  (c) Reduce the equipment by $16,000 by reducing the asset account directly.
  (d) Increase the building by $160,000 by decreasing its accumulated depreciation account.
  (e) Increase the land by $40,000.
  (f) Increase the goodwill by $201,402.
(4) Record amortizations resulting from the asset and liability revaluations of step (3). The adjustments are lettered (a) through (f) to correspond with the revaluations in step (3):
  (a) No amortization required; adjustment already charged to the cost of goods sold.
  (b) Amortize the discount as follows:
  Net present value of controlling interest in Carlos bonds, January 1, 19X1:

Face, 80% × $200,000	$160,000	
Discount	10,598	$149,402
Multiply by 8% effective interest rate		.08
Effective interest expense		$ 11,952
Nominal interest, 6% × $160,000		9,600
Discount amortization		$ 2,352

(c) Record annual decrease in equipment depreciation expense; $16,000 net decrease in the equipment divided by 5-year life equals $3,200.

(d) Record annual increase in building depreciation expense; $160,000 net increase in the building divided by 20-year life equals $8,000.

(e) No amortization results from adjustment of the land.

(f) Record additional annual amortization of the goodwill; $201,402 net increase in the goodwill divided by 10-year life equals $20,140. It is assumed that the previously recorded goodwill of $125,000 on January 1, 19X1, also is being amortized over 10 years.

Subsidiary Carlos Company Income Distribution

	Internally generated net income...	$60,000
	Adjusted income	$60,000
	Minority share............................	20%
	Minority interest.........................	**$12,000***

Parent Paulos Company Income Distribution

Inventory adjustment...............(3a)	**$ 4,000**	Internally generated net income...	$80,000
Discount amortization............. (4b)	**2,352**	80% × Carlos Company adjusted	
Building depreciation.............. (4d)	**8,000**	income of $60,000	48,000
Goodwill amortization.............. (4f)	20,140	**Equipment depreciation**......... (4c)	**3,200**
		Controlling interest....................	**$96,708***

Worksheet 5–6 (see page 242)

Simple Equity
Paulos Company and
Worksheet for Consolidated
For Year Ended

(Credit balance amounts are in parentheses.)

		Trial Balance	
		Paulos	Carlos
1	Cash	322,000	160,000
2	Inventory	210,000	120,000
3	Land	200,000	150,000
4	Building	800,000	600,000
5	Accumulated Depreciation — Building	(120,000)	(330,000)
6	Equipment	400,000	150,000
7	Accumulated Depreciation — Equipment	(100,000)	(90,000)
8	Investment in Carlos Company	896,000	
9			
10			
11	Goodwill		100,000
12	Current Liabilities	(150,000)	(40,000)
13	Bonds Payable		(200,000)
14	Discount on Bonds		
15	Common Stock, Paulos	(1,500,000)	
16	**Retained Earnings, Jan. 1, 19X2, Paulos**	**(828,000)**	
17			
18			
19			
20	Common Stock, Carlos		(100,000)
21	Paid-In Capital in Excess of Par, Carlos		(150,000)
22	Retained Earnings, Jan. 1, 19X2, Carlos		(290,000)
23	Sales	(400,000)	(300,000)
24	Cost of Goods Sold	200,000	120,000
25	Expenses	150,000	80,000
26			
27			
28	**Subsidiary Income**	**(80,000)**	
29	**Dividends Declared**		**20,000**
30		0	0
31	Combined Net Income		
32	To Minority Interest (see distribution schedule)		
33	**Balance to Controlling Interest** (see distribution schedule)		
34	Total Minority Interest		
35	Retained Earnings, Controlling Interest, Dec. 31, 19X2		
36			

Method, Second Year
Subsidiary Carlos Company
Financial Statements
December 31, 19X2

WORKSHEET 5–6

Eliminations & Adjustments				Consolidated Income Statement	Minority Interest	Controlling Retained Earnings	Consolidated Balance Sheet	
Dr.		Cr.						
							482,000	1
							330,000	2
(3e)	40,000						390,000	3
							1,400,000	4
(3d)	160,000	(4d)	16,000				(306,000)	5
		(3c)	16,000				534,000	6
(4c)	6,400						(183,600)	7
(1)	16,000	(1)	80,000					8
		(2)	432,000					9
		(3)	400,000					10
(3f)	201,402	(4f)	40,280				261,122	11
							(190,000)	12
							(200,000)	13
(3b)	10,598	(4b)	4,892				5,706	14
							(1,500,000)	15
(3a)	4,000	(4c)	3,200			(796,708)		16
(4b)	2,352							17
(4d)	8,000							18
(4f)	20,140							19
(2)	80,000				(20,000)			20
(2)	120,000				(30,000)			21
(2)	232,000				(58,000)			22
				(700,000)				23
				320,000				24
(4b)	2,540	(4c)	3,200	257,480				25
(4d)	8,000							26
(4f)	20,140							27
(1)	80,000							28
		(1)	16,000		4,000			29
	1,011,572		1,011,572					30
				(122,520)				31
				20,000*	(20,000)			32
				102,520*		(102,520)		33
				(124,000)			(124,000)	34
						(899,228)	(899,228)	35
							0	36

(continued)

Eliminations and Adjustments (the steps are keyed to correspond with those in Worksheet 5–5):
(1) Eliminate the current-year entries made in the investment in Carlos Company account and in the subsidiary income account. The investment account now is adjusted back to its January 1, 19X2 balance so that it may be eliminated.
(2) Eliminate the 80% ownership portion of the January 1, 19X2 subsidiary equity accounts against the investment. A $400,000 excess cost remains.
(3) Distribute the $400,000 excess cost as required by the determination and distribution of excess schedule. The distribution is identical to that shown in Worksheet 5–5, except for the January 1, 19X1 inventory adjustment of $4,000. The inventory adjustment now is carried to the purchaser's January 1, 19X2 retained earnings balance since it is an adjustment to 19X1 income.
(4) Record amortizations resulting from the asset and liability revaluations of step (3). The amortizations include those for the current and previous periods because the trial balances of the separate firms do not reflect the amortizations on the December 31, 19X1 consolidated worksheet. The adjustments are lettered (a) through (f) to correspond with the revaluations in step (3) of Worksheet 5–5:
    (a) No amortization required; adjustment already charged to January 1, 19X2 controlling retained earnings account.
    (b) Amortize the discount as follows:

Face, 80% × $200,000..	$160,000	
Discount, December 31, 19X1 (see Worksheet 5–5)....................	(8,246)	$151,754
Multiply by 8% effective interest rate		.08
Effective interest expense		$ 12,140
Nominal interest, 6% × $160,000		9,600
19X2 discount amortization.		$ 2,540
Add 19X1 discount amortization (from page 290)		2,352
Total amortization to date		$ 4,892

The current-year amortization is charged to expense, while the 19X1 amortization is charged to January 1, 19X2 controlling Retained Earnings.

(c)   Record $3,200 annual decrease in equipment depreciation for 19X1 and 19X2. The 19X1 portion is carried to January 1, 19X2 controlling Retained Earnings, while the 19X2 adjustment is reflected in current expense.

(d)   Record $8,000 annual increase in 19X1 and 19X2 building depreciation; the 19X1 adjustment reduces the January 1, 19X2 controlling retained earnings account; the 19X2 adjustment increases current expense.

(e)   No amortization results from adjustment of the land.

(f)   Amortize the goodwill for the current year by increasing expenses and for the past year by reducing the January 1, 19X2 controlling retained earnings account.

Subsidiary Carlos Company Income Distribution

	Internally generated net income..	$100,000
	Adjusted income	$100,000
	Minority share...........................	20%
	Minority interest.......................	**$ 20,000***

Parent Paulos Company Income Distribution

Discount amortization............. (4b)	**$ 2,540**	Internally generated net income..	$ 50,000
Building depreciation .... (4d)	8,000	80% × Carlos Company adjusted	
Goodwill amortization.............. (4f)	20,140	income of $100,000.................	80,000
		Equipment depreciation .... (4c)	3,200
		Controlling interest....................	**$102,520***

Worksheet 5–7 (see page 243)

(see page 243)

Equity Method,
Paro Company and Subsidiary
Worksheet for Consolidated
For Year Ended

(Credit balance amounts are in parentheses.)

		Trial Balance	
		Paro	Sunstran
1	Cash	300,000	60,000
2	Accounts Receivable (net)	376,000	65,000
3	Inventory, Dec. 31, 19X1	540,000	100,000
4	Investment in Sunstran Corporation	988,000	
5			
6			
7	Land	100,000	30,000
8	Building	1,300,000	950,000
9	Accumulated Depreciation	(400,000)	(300,000)
10	**Tax Loss Carryforward**		
11	Goodwill		
12	Accounts Payable	(248,000)	(20,000)
13	**Deferred Tax Liability**		
14	Common Stock, Paro	(510,000)	
15	Paid-In Capital in Excess of Par, Paro	(100,000)	
16	Retained Earnings, Jan. 1, 19X1, Paro	(1,750,000)	
17	Common Stock, Sunstran		(100,000)
18	Paid-In Capital in Excess of Par, Sunstran		(300,000)
19	Retained Earnings, Jan. 1, 19X1, Sunstran		(400,000)
20	Sales	(3,400,000)	(900,000)
21	Cost of Goods Sold	2,070,000	600,000
22	Selling and General Expense	530,000	150,000
23			
24	Subsidiary Income	(84,000)	
25	Provision for Tax	188,000	45,000
26	Dividends Declared	100,000	20,000
27		0	0
28	Combined Net Income		
29	To Minority Interest (see distribution schedule)		
30	Balance to Controlling Interest (see distribution schedule)		
31	Total Minority Interest		
32	Retained Earnings, Controlling Interest, Dec. 31, 19X1		
33			

Tax Issues
Sunstran Corporation
Financial Statements
December 31, 19X1

WORKSHEET 5-7

Eliminations & Adjustments				Consolidated Income Statement	Minority Interest	Controlling Retained Earnings	Consolidated Balance Sheet	
Dr.		Cr.						
							360,000	1
							441,000	2
							640,000	3
(1)	16,000	(1)	84,000					4
		(2)	640,000					5
		(3)	280,000					6
							130,000	7
							2,250,000	8
(3a)	160,000	(4a)	8,000				(548,000)	9
(3c)	**72,000**	**(4c)**	**72,000**					10
(3d)	96,000	(4d)	9,600				86,400	11
							(268,000)	12
(4b)	**2,400**	**(3b)**	**48,000**				(45,600)	13
							(510,000)	14
							(100,000)	15
						(1,750,000)		16
(2)	80,000				(20,000)			17
(2)	240,000				(60,000)			18
(2)	320,000				(80,000)			19
				(4,300,000)				20
				2,670,000				21
(4a)	8,000			697,600				22
(4d)	9,600							23
(1)	84,000							24
(4c)	**72,000**	**(4b)**	**2,400**	302,600				25
		(1)	16,000		4,000	100,000		26
	1,160,000		1,160,000					27
				(629,800)				28
				21,000*	(21,000)			29
				608,800*		(608,800)		30
					(177,000)		(177,000)	31
						(2,258,800)	(2,258,800)	32
							0	33

(continued)

Eliminations and Adjustments:
(1) Eliminate the current-year entries made in the investment in Sunstran Corporation account and in the subsidiary income account. The investment account is adjusted now to its January 1, 19X1 balance so that it may be eliminated.
(2) Eliminate the 80% ownership portion of the subsidiary equity accounts against the investment. A $280,000 excess cost remains.
(3) Distribute the $280,000 excess cost as follows, in accordance with the determination and distribution of excess schedule:
    (a) Increase the building by $160,000 by lowering its accumulated depreciation account.
    (b) Record the deferred tax liability relative to the building adjustment.
    (c) Record the tax loss carryforward.
    (d) Record the goodwill.
(4) Record amortizations resulting from the asset and liability revaluations of step (3). The adjustments are lettered (a) through (d) to correspond with the revaluations in step (3).
    (a) Record the annual increase in building depreciation; $160,000 net increase in the building divided by its 20-year life equals $8,000.
    (b) Reduce the provision for tax account by 30% of the increase in depreciation expense ($2,400).
    (c) The tax loss carryforward is used in the current period and is added to the provision for tax account. The parent company has already recorded the benefit of the tax loss carryforward by decreasing the liability and the provision for tax. This adjustment restores the amount of the decrease to the provision for tax account. The tax loss carryforward is the

result of the asset created in the consolidations process and not a reduction of the current provision for tax.

(d)   Amortize the goodwill for the current year ($96,000 ÷ 10-year life = $9,600).

Subsidiary Sunstran Corporation Income Distribution

	Internally generated net income..	$105,000
	Adjusted income	$105,000
	Minority share..........................	20%
	Minority interest.......................	$ 21,000*

Parent Paro Company Income Distribution

Increase in depreciation			Internally generated net income..	$612,000
expense...............................(4a)	$ 8,000		80% × Sunstran Corporation	
Increase in provision for tax .....(4c)	**72,000**		adjusted income of $105,000....	84,000
Goodwill amortization............. (4d)	9,600		**Decrease in provision**	
			for tax ....(4b)	**2,400**
			Controlling interest...................	**$608,800***

Worksheet 5–8 (see page 246)

Intraperiod Purchase; Subsidiary
Company P and
Worksheet for Consolidated
For Year Ended

(Credit balance amounts are in parentheses.)

		Trial Balance	
		Company P	Company S
1	Current Assets	187,600	87,500
2	**Investment in Company S**	**118,400**	
3			
4			
5	Equipment	400,000	80,000
6	Accumulated Depreciation	(200,000)	(32,500)
7	Liabilities	(60,000)	(12,000)
8	Common Stock, Co. P	(250,000)	
9	Retained Earnings, **Jan. 1, 19X1, Co. P**	(100,000)	
10	Common Stock, Co. S		(50,000)
11	Retained Earnings, **July 1, 19X1, Co. S**		(58,000)
12	Sales	(500,000)	(92,000)
13	Cost of Goods Sold	350,000	60,000
14	Expenses	70,000	12,000
15	**Subsidiary Income**	**(16,000)**	
16	Dividends Declared		5,000
17		0	0
18	Combined Net Income		
19	To Minority Interest (see distribution schedule)		
20	Balance to Controlling Interest (see distribution schedule)		
21	Total Minority Interest		
22	Retained Earnings, Controlling Interest, Dec. 31, 19X1		
23			

Eliminations and Adjustments:
(1) Eliminate the entries made in the investment in Company S account and in the subsidiary income account to record the parent's 80% controlling interest in the subsidiary's *second six-months' income* and the subsidiary *dividends,* restoring the investment account to its *balance as of the July 1, 19X1 investment date.*
(2) Eliminate 80% of the subsidiary's *July 1, 19X1* equity balances against the balance of the investment account.
(3) Distribute the excess of cost over book value of $20,000 to the accumulated depreciation account in accordance with the determination and distribution of excess schedule.
(4) Amortize *for one-half year* the excess attributable to the equipment.

Books Closed on Purchase Date
Subsidiary Company S
Financial Statements
December 31, 19X1

WORSHEET 5-8 ||||||||||||||||||||||||

Eliminations & Adjustments Dr.	Eliminations & Adjustments Cr.	Consolidated Income Statement	Minority Interest	Controlling Retained Earnings	Consolidated Balance Sheet	
					275,100	1
(1) 4,000	(1) 16,000					2
	(2) 86,400					3
	(3) 20,000					4
					480,000	5
(3) 20,000	(4) 1,000				(213,500)	6
					(72,000)	7
					(250,000)	8
				(100,000)		9
(2) 40,000			(10,000)			10
(2) 46,400			(11,600)			11
		(592,000)				12
		410,000				13
(4) 1,000		83,000				14
(1) 16,000						15
	(1) 4,000		1,000			16
127,400	127,400					17
		(99,000)				18
		4,000*	(4,000)			19
		95,000*		(95,000)		20
			(24,600)		(24,600)	21
				(195,000)	(195,000)	22
					0	23

Subsidiary Company S Income Distribution

Internally generated net income **second half of year**..................	**$20,000**
Adjusted income	$20,000
Minority share...........................	20%
Minority interest........................	$ 4,000*

Parent Company P Income Distribution

Equipment depreciation ....(4) $1,000	Internally generated net income...	$80,000
	80% × Company S adjusted income of $20,000 (last 6 mo.)..	16,000
	Controlling interest.....................	$95,000*

Worksheet 5–9 (see page 247)

(see page 247)

Intraperiod Purchase; Subsidiary
Company P and
Worksheet for Consolidated
For Year Ended

(Credit balance amounts are in parentheses.)

		Trial Balance	
		Company P	Company S
1	Current Assets	187,600	87,500
2	**Investment in Company S**	118,400	
3			
4			
5	Equipment	400,000	80,000
6	Accumulated Depreciation	(200,000)	(32,500)
7	Liabilities	(60,000)	(12,000)
8	Common Stock, Co. P	(250,000)	
9	Retained Earnings, **Jan. 1, 19X1, Co. P**	(100,000)	
10	Common Stock, Co. S		(50,000)
11	Retained Earnings, **Jan. 1, 19X1, Co. S**		(45,000)
12	Sales	(500,000)	(182,000)
13	Cost of Goods Sold	350,000	120,000
14	Expenses	70,000	24,000
15	**Subsidiary Income**	**(16,000)**	
16	**Dividends Declared**		**10,000**
17			
18	**Purchased Income**		
19		0	0
20	Combined Net Income		
21	To Minority Interest (see distribution schedule)		
22	Balance to Controlling Interest (see distribution schedule)		
23	Total Minority Interest		
24	Retained Earnings, Controlling Interest, Dec. 31, 19X1		
25			

Eliminations and Adjustments:
(1) Eliminate the entries made in the investment account and in the subsidiary income account (same as Worksheet 5–8). Notice that Company P's share of the subsidiary dividends declared are from those declared *after* the purchase.
(2) Eliminate 80% of the subsidiary equity balances at the beginning of the year plus 80% of Company S's income earned *as of July 1, 19X1,* against the investment account. The share of preacquisition income is entered as *Purchased Income* to emphasize that this income was

Books Not Closed on Purchase Date
Subsidiary Company S
Financial Statements
December 31, 19X1

WORKSHEET 5-9

Eliminations & Adjustments		Consolidated Income Statement	Minority Interest	Controlling Retained Earnings	Consolidated Balance Sheet	
Dr.	Cr.					
					275,100	1
(1) 4,000	(1) 16,000					2
	(2) 86,400					3
	(3) 20,000					4
					480,000	5
(3) 20,000	(4) 1,000				(213,500)	6
					(72,000)	7
					(250,000)	8
				(100,000)		9
(2) 40,000			(10,000)			10
(2) 36,000			(9,000)			11
		(682,000)				12
		470,000				13
(4) 1,000		95,000				14
(1) 16,000						15
	(1) 4,000		2,000			16
	(2) 4,000					17
(2) 14,400		14,400				18
131,400	131,400					19
		(102,600)				20
		7,600*	(7,600)			21
		95,000*		(95,000)		22
			(24,600)		(24,600)	23
				(195,000)	(195,000)	24
					0	25

earned prior to the date of purchase by Company P. For elimination purposes, this account may be viewed as a supplement to retained earnings. Since the subsidiary also declared dividends *prior to* July 1, 19X1, the controlling percentage of those dividends should be eliminated in this entry by crediting Dividends Declared.

(3) Distribute the $20,000 excess of cost over book value (same as Worksheet 5-8).
(4) Amortize for *one-half year* the excess attributable to the equipment (same as Worksheet 5-8).

(continued)

Subsidiary Company S Income Distribution

	Internally generated net income entire year	**$38,000**
	Adjusted income	$38,000
	Minority share...........................	20%
	Minority interest........................	$ 7,600*

Parent Company P Income Distribution

Equipment depreciation ....(4)	$1,000	Internally generated net income...	$80,000
		80% × Company S adjusted income of $20,000 **(last 6 mo.)**..	16,000
		Controlling interest.....................	$95,000*

Worksheet 5–10 (see page 249)

Pooling of
Company I and
Worksheet for Consolidated
For Year Ended

(Credit balance amounts are in parentheses.)

		Trial Balance	
		Company I	Company C
1	Current Assets	46,000	35,000
2	Property, Plant, and Equipment (net)	64,500	60,000
3	Investment in Company C	81,000	
4			
5	Liabilities		(5,000)
6	Common Stock ($2 par), Co. I	(55,400)	
7	Paid-In Capital in Excess of Par, Co. I	(3,600)	
8	Retained Earnings, Jan. 1, 19X3, Co. I	(60,000)	
9	Common Stock ($10 par), Co. C		(10,000)
10	Retained Earnings, Jan. 1, 19X3, Co. C		(55,000)
11	Sales	(150,000)	(100,000)
12	Cost of Goods Sold	70,000	50,000
13	Expenses	30,000	25,000
14	Subsidiary Income	(22,500)	
15		0	0
16	Combined Net Income		
17	To Minority Interest (see distribution schedule)		
18	Balance to Controlling Interest (see distribution schedule)		
19	Total Minority Interest		
20	Retained Earnings, Controlling Interest, Dec. 31, 19X3		
21			

Eliminations and Adjustments:
(1) Eliminate the current-year entries in the investment in Company C account and in the subsidiary income account, restoring the investment account to its January 1, 19X3 balance, so that it may be eliminated.
(2) Eliminate 90% of the balances in the Company C stockholders' equity accounts against the investment account. No excess results.

Interests
Subsidiary Company C
Financial Statements
December 31, 19X3

WORSHEET 5–10

Eliminations & Adjustments		Consolidated Income Statement	Minority Interest	Controlling Retained Earnings	Consolidated Balance Sheet	
Dr.	Cr.					
					81,000	1
					124,500	2
	(1) 22,500					3
	(2) 58,500					4
					(5,000)	5
					(55,400)	6
					(3,600)	7
				(60,000)		8
(2) 9,000			(1,000)			9
(2) 49,500			(5,500)			10
		(250,000)				11
		120,000				12
		55,000				13
(1) 22,500						14
81,000	81,000					15
		(75,000)				16
		2,500*	(2,500)			17
		72,500*		(72,500)		18
			(9,000)		(9,000)	19
				(132,500)	(132,500)	20
					0	21

Subsidiary Company C Income Distribution

Internally generated net income...	$25,000
Adjusted income	$25,000
Minority share............................	10%
Minority interest.........................	$ 2,500*

Parent Company I Income Distribution

Internally generated net income...	$50,000
90% × Company C adjusted income of $25,000	22,500
Controlling interest.....................	$72,500*

Worksheet 5–11 (see page 251)

(Credit balance amounts are in parentheses.)

Vertical
Paulos Company and
Worksheet for Consolidated
For Year Ended

		Financial Statements	
	Compare this worksheet to Worksheet 5–6. Note that eliminations and adjustments, explanations as well as the income distribution schedules are the same for Worksheet 5–11 as for Worksheet 5–6.	Paulos	Carlos
1	**Income Statement**		
2	Sales	(400,000)	(300,000)
3	Cost of goods sold	200,000	120,000
4	Expenses	150,000	80,000
5			
6			
7	Subsidiary income	(80,000)	
8	Net income	(130,000)	(100,000)
9	Minority interest (see distribution schedule)		
10	Controlling interest (see distribution schedule)		
11			
12	**Retained Earnings Statement**		
13	Retained earnings, Jan. 1, 19X2, Paulos	(828,000)	
14			
15			
16			
17	Retained earnings, Jan. 1, 19X2, Carlos		(290,000)
18	Net income (carrydown)	(130,000)	(100,000)
19	Dividends declared		20,000
20	Retained earnings, Dec. 31, 19X2	(958,000)	(370,000)
21	Retained earnings, minority interest, Dec. 31, 19X2		
22	Retained earnings, controlling interest, Dec. 31, 19X2		
23			
24	**Balance Sheet**		
25	Cash	322,000	160,000
26	Inventory	210,000	120,000
27	Land	200,000	150,000
28	Building	800,000	600,000
29	Accumulated depreciation—building	(120,000)	(330,000)
30	Equipment	400,000	150,000
31	Accumulated depreciation—equipment	(100,000)	(90,000)
32	Investment in Carlos	896,000	
33			
34			
35	Goodwill		100,000
36	Current liabilities	(150,000)	(40,000)
37	Bonds payable		(200,000)
38	Discount on bonds		
39	Common stock, Paulos	(1,500,000)	
40	Common stock, Carlos		(100,000)
41	Paid-in capital in excess of par, Carlos		(150,000)
42	Retained earnings, Dec. 31, 19X2 (carrydown)	(958,000)	(370,000)
43	Retained earnings, controlling interest, Dec. 31, 19X2		
44	Retained earnings, minority interest, Dec. 31, 19X2		
45	Total minority interest		
46	Total	0	0

Format, Equity Method
Subsidiary Carlos Company
Financial Statements
December 31, 19X2

WORSHEET 5–11

Eliminations & Adjustments				Minority Interest	Consolidated	
Dr.		Cr.				
						1
					(700,000)	2
					320,000	3
(4b)	2,540	(4c)	3,200		257,480	4
(4d)	8,000					5
(4f)	20,140					6
(1)	80,000					7
					(122,520)	8
				(20,000)		9
					(102,520)	10
						11
						12
(3a)	4,000	(4c)	3,200		(796,708)	13
(4b)	2,352					14
(4d)	8,000					15
(4f)	20,140					16
(2)	232,000			(58,000)		17
				(20,000)	(102,520)	18
		(1)	16,000	4,000		19
						20
				(74,000)		21
					(899,228)	22
						23
						24
					482,000	25
					330,000	26
(3e)	40,000				390,000	27
					1,400,000	28
(3d)	160,000	(4d)	16,000		(306,000)	29
		(3c)	16,000		534,000	30
(4c)	6,400				(183,600)	31
(1)	16,000	(1)	80,000			32
		(2)	432,000			33
		(3)	400,000			34
(3f)	201,402	(4f)	40,280		261,122	35
					(190,000)	36
					(200,000)	37
(3b)	10,598	(4b)	4,892		5,706	38
					(1,500,000)	39
(2)	80,000			(20,000)		40
(2)	120,000			(30,000)		41
						42
					(899,228)	43
				(74,000)		44
					(124,000)	45
	1,011,572		1,011,572	(124,000)	0	46

CHAPTER 6

INTERCOMPANY TRANSACTIONS: MERCHANDISE, PLANT ASSETS, AND NOTES

The accounting ramifications of consolidated statements do not end with procedures for eliminating the parent's investment in the subsidiary and the adjustments which stem from that elimination. It is common for the affiliated firms to engage in continuing business transactions with each other. The more integrated the firms are in terms of types of operations, the more numerous the intercompany transactions become. The most common of these transactions are intercompany sales of merchandise, services, and plant assets. In addition, it is common to find intercompany loan transactions that may result from or be independent of intercompany sales.

Consolidated statements become the single set of statements for the parent-subsidiary entity. Transactions between the separate legal entities should not be reflected in the consolidated statements. Instead, these statements should reflect only those transactions with firms outside the consolidated group. In other words, intercompany transactions must undergo elimination procedures. For each type of intercompany transaction, the applicable theory for elimination and resulting worksheet procedures are mastered by determining what evidence of the transaction should remain on the consolidated statements from the viewpoint of a consolidated entity.

INTERCOMPANY MERCHANDISE SALES

It is common to find that the goods sold by one member of an affiliated group have been purchased from another member of the group. One firm may produce component parts that are assembled by its affiliate, which sells the final product. In other cases, the product may be produced entirely by one member firm and sold on a wholesale basis to another member firm, which is responsible for selling and servicing the product to the final users. Taken as a whole, these different examples of merchandise sales represent the most common type of intercompany transaction and must be understood as a basic feature of consolidated reporting.

Sales between affiliated firms will be recorded in the normal manner on the books of the separate firms. Remember that each firm is a separate legal entity maintaining its own accounting records. Thus sales to and purchases from an affiliated firm are recorded as if they were transactions made with a firm outside the consolidated group, and the separate financial statements of the affiliated firms will include these purchase and sale transactions. However, when the statements of the affiliates are consolidated, such sales become transfers of goods within the consolidated entity. Since these sales do not involve parties outside the consolidated group, they cannot be acknowledged in consolidated statements.

Following are the procedures for consolidating affiliated firms engaged in intercompany merchandise sales:

1. The intercompany sale must be eliminated to avoid double counting. To understand this requirement, assume that Company P sells merchandise, which cost $1,000, to a subsidiary, Company S, for $1,200. Company S, in turn, sells the merchandise to an outside party for $1,500. If no elimination is made, the consolidated income statement would show the following with respect to the two transactions:

Sales	$2,700	($1,500 outside sale plus $1,200 sale to Company S)
Less cost of goods sold	2,200	($1,000 cost to Company P plus $1,200 purchase by Company S)
Gross profit	$ 500	(18.5% gross profit rate)

While the gross profit is correct, sales and the cost of goods sold are inflated. As a result, the gross profit percentage is understated, since the $500 gross profit appears to relate to $2,700 of sales. The intercompany sale must be eliminated from the consolidated statements. All that should remain on the consolidated income statement with respect to the two transactions is:

Sales	$1,500	(only the final sale to the outside party)
Less cost of goods sold	1,000	(only the purchase from the outside party)
Gross profit	$ 500	(33-1/3% gross profit rate)

When the goods sold between the affiliated firms are manufactured by the selling affiliate, the consolidated cost of goods sold includes only those costs that normally can be inventoried, such as labor, materials, and overhead, and may not include any profit.

The intercompany sale, though eliminated, does have an effect on the distribution of combined net income to the controlling and minority interests. This is true because the reported net income of the subsidiary reflects the intercompany sales price, and the subsidiary's separate income statement becomes the base from which the minority share of income is calculated. In effect, the intercompany transfer price becomes an agreement as to how a portion of combined net income will be divided. For example, if Company S is an 80%-owned subsidiary, the minority interest will receive 20% of the $300 profit made on the final sale by Company S, or $60. If the intercompany transfer price is increased from $1,200 to $1,300 and the final sales price remains at $1,500, Company S would earn only $200, and the minority interest would receive 20% of $200, or $40.

2. Often, intercompany sales will be made on credit. Thus, intercompany trade balances will appear in the separate accounts of the affiliated firms. From a consolidated viewpoint, intercompany receivables and payables represent internal agreements to transfer funds. As such, this internal debt has no effect on consolidated statements and must be eliminated. Only debt transactions with entities *outside* the consolidated group should appear on the consolidated balance sheet.

3. No profit on intercompany sales may be recognized until the profit is *realized by a sale to an outside party.* This means that any profit contained in the ending inventory of intercompany goods must be eliminated and its recognition deferred until the period in which the goods are sold to outsiders. In the example described in (1), assume that the sale by Company P to Company S was made on December 30, 19X1 and that Company S did not sell the goods until March of 19X2. From a consolidated viewpoint, there can be no profit recognized until the outside sale occurs in March of 19X2. At that time, consolidation theory will acknowledge a $500 profit, of which $200 will be distributed to Company P and $300 will be distributed to Company S as part of the 19X2 combined net income. However, until that time, the $200 profit on the intercompany sale recorded by Company P must be deferred. In addition, not only must the $1,200 intercompany sale be eliminated, but the inventory on December 31, 19X1 must be reduced by $200 (the amount of the intercompany profit) to its $1,000 cost to the consolidated firms.

Care must be taken in calculating the profit applicable to inventory. It is most convenient when the gross profit rate is provided so that it can be multiplied by the inventory value to arrive at the intercompany profit. In some instances, however, the profit on sales may be stated as a percentage of cost. For example, one might be told that the cost of units are "marked up" 25% to arrive at the intercompany sales price. If the inventory value is $1,000, it cannot be multiplied by 25% to calculate the intercompany profit because the 25% applies to the cost, and not the sales price, at which the inventory is stated. Instead, the gross profit rate, which is a percentage of sales price, must be calculated. The easiest method of accomplishing this is to pick the theoretical cost of $1 and mark it up by 25% (the given percentage of cost) to $1.25 and ask: "What is the gross profit percentage?" In this example, it is $.25 ÷ $1.25, or 20%. From this point, the $1,000 inventory cost can be multiplied by 20% to arrive at the intercompany profit of $200.

The worksheet procedures to eliminate the effects of intercompany sales are discussed in the following sections. In the first section, no intercompany goods remain in the ending inventory and none existed in the beginning inventory. In the second, which is the more common situation, some portion of the intercompany goods remains on hand at the end of the period. This example is expanded in the third section to show the additional worksheet procedures needed when intercompany goods are present in beginning inventory as well.

NO INTERCOMPANY GOODS IN PURCHASING FIRM'S INVENTORIES

In the simplest case, which is illustrated in Worksheet 6–1 on pages 360–361, all goods sold between the affiliates have been sold, in turn, to outside parties by the end of the accounting period. Worksheet 6–1 is based on the following assumptions:

1. Company S is an 80%-owned subsidiary of Company P. On January 1, 19X1, Company P purchased its interest in Company S at a price equal to its pro rata share of Company S book value. Company P uses the equity method to record the investment. Worksheet steps (1) and (2) eliminate the investment account.
2. Companies P and S had the following separate income statements for 19X1:

	Company P		Company S	
Sales		$700,000		$500,000
Less cost of goods sold:				
Beginning inventory..........	$ 60,000		$ 50,000	
Purchases.......................	520,000		340,000	
Ending inventory..............	(70,000)	510,000	(40,000)	350,000
Gross profit........................		$190,000		$150,000
Subsidiary income...............		60,000		—
Other expenses.................		(90,000)		(75,000)
Net income.......................		$160,000		$ 75,000

Note that under the equity method, Company P income includes 80% of the reported income of Company S.

3. Company S sold goods to Company P for $100,000. Company S recorded a 20% gross profit on the sales price. By the end of 19X1, Company P had sold all of the goods but had not yet paid for $25,000 of these purchases. That amount is included in the payables of Company P and the receivables of Company S.

Worksheet step (3) eliminates the intercompany "middle" sale. Step (4) eliminates the intercompany trade balances unpaid at year end. The combined net income of $175,000 is distributed to the minority and controlling interests using income distribution schedules. The profit on the intercompany sale, which is included in the subsidiary income of $75,000, is recognized, and no worksheet adjustment is required for the ending inventory, since the goods were resold to outside interests before year end. Note that these procedures would be identical if Company P were the seller of the intercompany goods.

INTERCOMPANY GOODS IN PURCHASING FIRM'S ENDING INVENTORY

Now assume that $20,000 of the goods purchased from Company S in the previous example still are unsold and are included in Company P's total ending inventory of $70,000. In Worksheet 6–2 on pages 362–363, elimination steps (1) through (4) are exactly the same as in Worksheet 6–1. However, step (5) must be added. This is because the ending inventory of Company P includes intercompany goods that must be inventoried at their cost to the consolidated entity, not at their cost to Company P. In addition, the $4,000 (20% gross profit rate × $20,000) profit recorded by Company S cannot be recognized until it is realized by a sale of the goods to an outside party. In arriving at the trial balance amount for cost of goods sold for Company P, the account was adjusted (decreased) for the ending inventory of intercompany goods at the intercompany price of $20,000. However, according to the consolidated view, the amount of the adjustment should be only the original cost ($16,000) of the goods. Thus, step (5) reduces the ending inventory and increases the cost of goods sold by $4,000 each. As a result, a lower combined net income is reported ($175,000 as reported in Worksheet 6–1 less the $4,000 internal profit in ending inventory equals $171,000).

In the income distribution schedules for Worksheet 6–2, the unrealized profit of $4,000 is deducted from the subsidiary's internally generated net income of $75,000. The adjusted net income of $71,000 is apportioned, with $14,200 (20%) distributed to the minority interest and $56,800 (80%) distributed to the controlling interest.

There is no change in worksheet elimination procedures if the parent is the seller and the subsidiary has intercompany goods in its ending inventory.

Only the distribution of combined net income changes. To illustrate, assume that the parent, Company P, is the seller of the intercompany goods. The income distribution schedules would be prepared as follows:

Subsidiary Company S Income Distribution

	Internally generated net income..................	$ 75,000
	Adjusted income	$ 75,000
	Minority share................	20%
	Minority interest.............	$ 15,000

Parent Company P Income Distribution

Unrealized profit in ending inventory....................(5) $4,000	Internally generated net income.......................	$100,000
	80% × Company S adjusted income of $75,000...................	60,000
	Controlling interest.........	$156,000

INTERCOMPANY GOODS IN PURCHASING FIRM'S BEGINNING AND ENDING INVENTORIES

When intercompany goods are included in the purchaser's beginning inventory, the inventory value includes the profit made by the seller. The intercompany seller of the goods has included in the prior period such sales in its separate income statement as though the transactions were consummated. Thus, the beginning retained earnings balance of the seller also includes the profit on these goods. While this profit should be reflected on the separate books of the affiliates, it should not be recognized when a consolidated view is taken. Remember, profit must not be recognized until it is realized in the subsequent period through the sale of goods to an outside party. Therefore, in the consolidating process, the beginning inventory of intercompany goods must be reduced to its cost to the consolidated firm. Likewise, the retained earnings of the consolidated entity must be reduced by deleting the profit that was recorded in prior periods on intercompany goods contained in the buyer's beginning inventory.

To illustrate, using the example of Company P and Company S from Worksheet 6–2, assume that the two companies have the following individual income data for 19X2:

	Company P		Company S	
Sales		$800,000		$600,000
Less cost of goods sold:				
Beginning inventory................	$ 70,000		$ 40,000	
Purchases.............................	600,000		450,000	
Ending inventory	(60,000)	610,000	(50,000)	440,000
Gross profit..............................		$190,000		$160,000
Subsidiary income......................		48,000		—
Other expenses		(120,000)		(100,000)
Net income..............................		$118,000		$ 60,000

Assume the following additional facts:

1. Company P's 19X2 beginning inventory includes $20,000 of the goods purchased from Company S in 19X1. The gross profit rate on the sale was 20%.
2. Company S sold $120,000 of goods to Company P during 19X2.
3. Company S recorded a 20% gross profit on these sales.
4. At the end of 19X2, Company P still owed $60,000 to Company S for the purchases. Company P also had $30,000 of the intercompany purchases in its 19X2 ending inventory.

Worksheet 6–3, pages 364–367, contains the 19X2 year-end trial balances of Company P and Company S. Steps (1) and (2) again eliminate the investment account. Step (3) *indirectly* removes from the 19X2 beginning inventory the $4,000 profit resulting from the 19X1 intercompany sale. Since the inventory was closed to the cost of goods sold, the cost of goods sold must be reduced by $4,000. The intercompany profit must be removed from beginning retained earnings as well. *Because the subsidiary made the sale,* the profit resides 20% with the minority interest and 80% with the controlling interest. This means the adjustment must be split 20/80 to the minority and controlling interests. Note that once the controlling share of subsidiary retained earnings is eliminated, there is a transformation of what was *subsidiary* retained earnings into what now is *minority interest* in retained earnings. Steps (4) through (6) eliminate the intercompany sales, trade accounts, and ending inventory in the same manner as was done in Worksheet 6–2. After all eliminations and adjustments are made, the combined net income of $128,000 is distributed as shown in the income distribution schedules. The adjustments for intercompany inventory profits are reflected in the *selling company's schedule.*

It might appear that the intercompany goods in the beginning inventory are assumed to be sold in the current period, since the deferred profit of the previous period is realized during the current period as reflected by the seller's income distribution schedule. That assumption need not be made, however. Even if the $20,000 beginning inventory is unsold at year end, it still would be a part of the $30,000 ending inventory, on which $6,000 of profit is deferred. The $4,000 profit from the previous period would be shown in the schedule as both realized beginning inventory profit and as unrealized ending inventory profit. Note that the use of the Lifo method for inventories could cause a given period's inventory profit to be deferred indefinitely. Unless otherwise stated, the examples and problems of this text will assume a Fifo flow.

Worksheet 6–3 assumed that the intercompany merchandise sales were made by the subsidiary. Procedures would differ as follows if the sales were made by the parent:

1. The beginning inventory profit would be subtracted entirely from the beginning controlling retained earnings since only the parent recorded the gain.
2. The adjustments for the beginning and ending inventory profits would be included in the parent income distribution schedule and not in the subsidiary schedule.

ELIMINATIONS FOR PERIODIC INVENTORIES

In Worksheets 6–1 through 6–3, the cost of goods sold was included in the trial balances, since both the parent and the subsidiary used a perpetual inventory system. However, in Worksheet 6–4 on pages 368–371, a periodic inventory system is used. In this illustration, which is based on the same facts as Worksheet 6–3, the following differences in worksheet procedures result from the use of a periodic inventory system:

1. The 19X2 beginning inventories of $70,000 and $40,000, rather than the ending inventories, appear as assets in the trial balances. The beginning inventories less the intercompany profit in Company P's beginning inventory are extended to the consolidated income statement column as a debit.
2. The purchases accounts, rather than the cost of goods sold, appear in the trial balances and, after adjustment, are extended to the consolidated income statement column.
3. The unadjusted ending inventories of $60,000 and $50,000 are combined and entered in both the debit and the credit eliminations columns as follows:

Inventory, Dec. 31 (balance sheet asset account)..........   110,000
   Inventory, Dec. 31 (reduction of cost of goods sold)...   110,000

The amount of the combined ending inventories less the intercompany profit in Company P's ending inventory is extended to the consolidated balance sheet column as a debit *and* to the consolidated income statement column as a credit, where it is deducted from purchases to arrive at the combined net income.

4. In the elimination process, adjustments are made directly to the beginning and ending inventories as well as to purchases.

EFFECT OF LOWER-OF-COST-OR-MARKET METHOD ON INVENTORY PROFIT

Intercompany inventory in the hands of the purchaser may have been written down by the purchaser to a market value below its intercompany transfer cost. Assume that for $50,000 Company S purchased goods that cost its parent company $40,000. Assume further that Company S has all the goods in its ending inventory but has written them down to $42,000, the lower market value at the end of the period. As a result of this markdown the inventory need be reduced by only another $2,000 to reflect its cost to the consolidated firm ($40,000). The only remaining issue is how to defer the $2,000 inventory profit in the income distribution schedules. As before, such profit is deferred by entering it as a debit on the intercompany seller's schedule. In the subsequent period, the profit will be realized by the seller.

It may seem strange that the $8,000 of profit written off is realized, in effect, by the seller, since it is not deducted in the seller's distribution schedule. This procedure is proper, however, since the loss recognized by the buyer is offset. Had the inventory been written down to $40,000 or less there would be *no need to defer the offsetting profit* in the consolidated worksheet or in the income distribution schedules.

LOSSES ON INTERCOMPANY SALES

Assume that a parent sells goods to a subsidiary for $5,000 and that the goods cost the parent $6,000. If the market value of the goods is $5,000 or less, the loss may be recognized in the consolidated income statement, even if the goods remain in the subsidiary's ending inventory. Such a loss can be recognized under the lower-of-cost-or-market principle that applies to inventory. However, if the intercompany sales price is below market value, the part of the loss that results from the price being below market value cannot be recognized until the subsidiary sells the goods to an outside party. Elimination procedures would parallel those used for unrealized gains.

INTERCOMPANY PLANT ASSET SALES

Any plant asset may be sold between members of an affiliated group, and such a sale may result in a gain for the seller. The buyer will record the asset at a price that includes the gain, and when the sale involves a depreciable asset, the buyer will base future depreciation charges on the price paid. While these recordings are proper for the firms as separate entities, they must not be reflected in the consolidated statements. Consolidation theory views the sale as an *internal transfer of assets*. In addition, there is no basis for recognizing a gain at the time of the internal transfer. Unlike the case of merchandise sales, however, recognition of the gain on the transfer does not have to await sale of the asset to an outside party. The buyer's intent is to use the asset, not to resell it. Since the asset is overstated by the amount of the intercompany gain, subsequent depreciation is overstated as well. The consolidation process reduces depreciation in future years so that depreciation charges in the consolidated statements reflect the cost of the asset to the consolidated firm. While the gain is deferred in the year of sale, it is realized later through the increased combined net income resulting from the reduction in depreciation expense in subsequent periods. The decrease in depreciation expense for each and every period is equal to the difference between the depreciation based on the intercompany sales price and the depreciation based on the book value of the asset on the sale date.

INTERCOMPANY SALE OF A NONDEPRECIABLE ASSET

One member of an affiliated group may sell land to another affiliate and record a gain. For consolidating purposes, there has been no sale; thus there is no cause to recognize a gain. Since the asset is not depreciable, the entire gain must be deferred until the land is sold to an outside party. This deferment may be permanent if there is no intent to sell at a later date. For example, assume that in 19X1 Company S (80% owned) sells land to its parent firm, Company P. The sale price is $30,000, and the original cost of the land to Company S was $20,000. Consolidation theory would rule that, until Company P sells the land to an outside party, recognition of the profit must be deferred. The following worksheet elimination is made in the year of sale:

| | Partial Trial Balance | | Eliminations & Adjustments | |
	Company P	Company S	Dr.	Cr.
Land	30,000			10,000
Gain of Sale of Land		(10,000)	10,000	

As usual, the selling firm's income distribution schedule would reflect the deferment of the gain.

In subsequent years, assuming that the land is not sold by Company P, the gain must be removed from the consolidated retained earnings. Since the sale was made by Company S, which is an 80%-owned subsidiary of Company P, the controlling interest must absorb 80% of the deferment, while the minority interest must absorb 20%. For example, the adjustments in 19X2 would be:

| | Partial Trial Balance | | Eliminations & Adjustments | |
	Company P	Company S	Dr.	Cr.
Land	30,000			10,000
Retained Earnings, Jan. 1, 19X2, Company P	(100,000)*		8,000	
Retained Earnings, Jan. 1, 19X2, Company S		(20,000)*	2,000	

*arbitrary balance

Now assume that Company P sells the land in 19X3 to an outside party for $45,000, recording a gain of $15,000. When this sale occurs, the $10,000 intercompany gain also is realized. The following elimination would remove the previously unrealized gain from the consolidated retained earnings and would add it to the gain already recorded by Company P. The retained earnings adjustment is allocated 80% to the controlling interest and 20% to the minority interest, since the original sale was made by the subsidiary.

	Partial Trial Balance		Eliminations & Adjustments	
	Company P	Company S	Dr.	Cr.
Gain on Sale of Land	(15,000)			**10,000**
Retained Earnings, Jan. 1, 19X3, Company P	(120,000)*		**8,000**	
Retained Earnings, Jan. 1, 19X3, Company S		(15,000)*	**2,000**	

*arbitrary balance

The income distribution schedule would add the $10,000 gain to the 19X3 internally generated net income of Company S. At this point, it should be clear that the gain on the intercompany sale was deferred, not eliminated. The original gain of $10,000 eventually is credited to the subsidiary. Thus, the gain does affect the minority share of combined net income at a future date. Any sale of a nondepreciable asset should be viewed as an agreement between the controlling and minority interests regarding the future distribution of combined net income.

When a parent sells a nondepreciable asset to a subsidiary, the worksheet procedures are the same, except that:

1. The deferment of the gain in the year of the intercompany sale and the recognition of the gain in the year of the sale of the asset to an outside party flow through only the parent company income distribution schedule.
2. In the years subsequent to the intercompany sale, the related adjustment is made exclusively through the controlling retained earnings.

INTERCOMPANY SALE OF A DEPRECIABLE ASSET

Returning to the case where a depreciable plant asset is sold between affiliates, the following example illustrates the worksheet procedures necessary for the deferment of a gain on the sale *over the asset's useful life*. Assume that the parent, Company P, sells a machine to a subsidiary, Company S, for $30,000 on January 1, 19X1. Originally, the machine cost $32,000. Accumulated depreciation as of January 1, 19X1 is $12,000. Therefore, the book value of the machine is $20,000, and the reported gain on the sale is $10,000. Further assume that Company S believes the asset has a 5-year remaining life and that it records straight-line depreciation of $6,000 annually.

The eliminations spread the gain over the 5-year life of the asset by reducing annual depreciation charges. For consolidated reporting purposes, depreciation is based on the asset's $20,000 book value to the consolidated firm. Worksheet 6–5, pages 372–373, is based on the following additional facts:

1. Company P owns an 80% investment in Company S. The amount paid for the investment was equal to the book value of Company S underlying equity. The simple equity method is used by Company P to record its investment. Steps (1) and (2) eliminate the investment account.
2. There were no beginning or ending inventories, and the firms had the following separate income statements for 19X1:

	Company P	Company S
Sales	$200,000	$100,000
Cost of goods sold	(150,000)	(59,000)
Gross profit	$ 50,000	$ 41,000
Depreciation expense	(30,000)	(16,000)
Gain on sale of machine	10,000	—
Subsidiary income (80%)	20,000	—
Net income	$ 50,000	$ 25,000

Step (3) eliminates the intercompany gain, restates the asset at cost, and restores the accumulated depreciation on the date of the intercompany sale as follows:

Gain on Sale of Machinery	10,000	
Machinery	2,000	
Accumulated Depreciation, Machinery		12,000

Step (4) reduces the depreciation expense for the year by the difference between depreciation based on:

- The original cost ($20,000 depreciable base ÷ 5 years = $4,000) and
- The intercompany sales price ($30,000 depreciable base ÷ 5 years = $6,000).

The following elimination results:

Accumulated Depreciation, Machinery	2,000	
Depreciation Expense, Machinery		2,000

The allocation of combined net income of $47,000 is shown in the income distribution schedules. Note that Company S (the buyer in this example) must absorb depreciation based on the agreed sales price and that it is the controlling interest which realizes the benefit of the reduced depreciation as the asset is used. Also note that the realizable profit for Company P (the seller) in any year is the depreciation absorbed by the buyer minus the depreciation for consolidating purposes. If the sale had been made by Company S, the profit deferment and recognition entries would flow through its income distribution schedule.

Worksheets for periods subsequent to the sale of the machine must correct the current-year nominal accounts and remove the unrealized profit in the beginning consolidated retained earnings. Worksheet 6–6, pages 374–377, portrays a consolidated worksheet for 19X2, based on the following separate income statements of Company P and Company S:

	Company P	Company S
Sales	$250,000	$120,000
Cost of goods sold	(180,000)	(80,000)
Gross profit	$ 70,000	$ 40,000
Depreciation expense	(20,000)	(16,000)
Subsidiary income (80%)	19,200	—
Net income	$ 69,200	$ 24,000

Step (3) in this worksheet corrects the asset's cost and restates the accumulated depreciation account as of the *beginning* of the year. The difference is the unrealized profit at the start of the year. Since the sale was by the parent, only the controlling interest in beginning retained earnings is adjusted. Had the sale been by the subsidiary, the adjustment would have been split 20/80 to the minority and controlling interests in beginning retained earnings.

Step (4) corrects the depreciation expense and the accumulated depreciation accounts for the current year. The resulting combined net income of $76,000 is distributed as shown in the income distribution schedules that follow Worksheet 6–6. During each year, Company S must absorb the larger depreciation expense that resulted from its purchase of the asset. Company P has the right to realize $2,000 more of the original deferred profit.

It may occur that an asset purchased from an affiliate is sold before it is depreciated fully. To illustrate this possibility, assume that Company S of the previous example sells the asset to a third party for $14,000 at the end of the second year. Since Company S's asset cost is $30,000, with $12,000 of accumulated depreciation, the loss recorded by Company S is $4,000 ($14,000 − $18,000 net book value). However, on a consolidated basis, the $4,000 loss becomes a $2,000 gain, determined as follows:

	On Books of Company S		For Consolidated Entity	
Selling price of machine sold by Company S		$14,000		$14,000
Less book value at end of second year following sale to Company S:				
Cost of machine	$30,000		$32,000	
Accumulated depreciation	(12,000)	18,000	(20,000)	12,000
Gain (loss)		$ (4,000)		$ 2,000

Worksheet 6–7, pages 378–379, is a revision of the previous worksheet so that Company S's subsequent sale of the depreciable asset at the end of the second year is included. Step (3) removes the $8,000 remaining intercompany profit on the asset sale from controlling retained earnings, adjusts current depreciation, and converts the $4,000 loss on the sale recorded by the subsidiary into a $2,000 gain on the consolidated statements.

The eliminations for the sale of a new asset purchased or manufactured by one affiliate and sold to another affiliate are less complicated than the eliminations for the sale of a used asset. In the previous examples involving the sale of a used asset, the adjustments were affected by the seller's depreciation that had accumulated before the sale and the resulting book value of the asset. When a new asset is sold, however, the seller has not depreciated the asset prior to its sale, and so the eliminations involve only restating the asset to its cost to the consolidated firm. Depreciation adjustments in subsequent years are made by allocating the gain on the sale over the asset's life.

A loss on an intercompany sale of a plant asset may be recorded at the time of the sale if the asset's fair market value is approximated by the sales price. This procedure is allowable because a plant asset should be written down to a market value below the asset's book value in the absence of a sale. However, when a sale results in a loss because the price is below fair market value, the part of the loss that results from the price being below market value is not recognized for consolidated reporting purposes. Instead, that loss must be deferred until the asset is used or the asset is sold to an outside party. The elimination procedures parallel those used for gains.

INTERCOMPANY LONG-TERM CONSTRUCTION CONTRACTS

One member of an affiliated group of companies may construct a plant asset for another affiliate over an extended period of time. The firm constructing the asset will record progress under the completed-contract method or the percentage-of-completion method. During construction, special adjustments may be necessary when consolidating, depending on which of the two methods is used to record the contract by the constructing affiliate. From a consolidated viewpoint such activity amounts to the self-construction of an asset to be used by the consolidated entity. Once the asset has been sold to an affiliate, consolidation procedures are similar to those used for a normal intercompany sale of a plant asset.

Completed-Contract Method. The constructing affiliate using the completed-contract method records no profit on the asset until it is completed and transferred to the purchasing affiliate. However, costs incurred to date on the contract are capitalized in a special account, such as *Cost of Construction in Progress.* This account will appear on the trial balance of the constructing affiliate. Since there is no intercompany profit included, the account requires no adjustment and is carried to the consolidated balance sheet.

The constructing affiliate may bill the purchasing affiliate for work done prior to the completion of the asset. When this occurs, the constructing affiliate will record billed amounts by debiting *Contracts Receivable* and crediting *Billings on Long-Term Contracts*. The billings account acts as a contra account to Cost of Construction in Progress. The purchasing affiliate would debit *Assets Under Construction* and credit *Contracts Payable* for billings received. Consolidation procedures require that the constructing affiliate's account Billings on Long-Term Contracts be eliminated against the purchaser's account Assets Under Construction, since only the costs incurred to date by the constructing affiliate should appear on the consolidated balance sheet. In addition, it is necessary to eliminate any remaining intercompany receivable and payable amounts recorded on the long-term contract.

Percentage-of-Completion Method. This method allows the constructing firm to recognize a portion of the total estimated profit on the contract as construction progresses. During the construction period, the contracting firm debits an account usually entitled *Construction in Progress* for costs that are incurred to outside firms. The contractor also debits Construction in Progress and credits *Earned Income on Long-Term Contracts* for the estimated profit earned during each accounting period. Thus, the construction in progress account includes *accumulated costs and estimated earnings.* When the purchaser is billed, the contractor will debit the amount billed to Contracts Receivable and credit Billings on Construction in Progress, while the purchaser will debit Assets Under Construction and credit Contracts Payable.

To illustrate the elimination procedures when the percentage-of-completion method is used, assume that a subsidiary, Company S, enters into a contract to construct a building for its parent firm, Company P, for $500,000 and that Company S estimates the cost of the building to be $400,000. During 19X1, the building is 50% completed and $200,000 of cost has been incurred as of December 31, 19X1, but only $150,000 has been billed. The contract is completed in 19X2 at an additional cost of $200,000. The entries on the books of the separate affiliates for December, 19X1 are as follows:

Company P

Assets Under Construction	150,000	
Contracts Payable		150,000
To record billing from subsidiary for amount due.		

Company S

Construction in Progress	200,000	
Payables (to outsiders)		200,000
To record costs incurred for the long-term contract under the percentage-of-completion method.		

Construction in Progress	50,000	
Earned Income on Long-Term Contracts.....................		50,000
To record pro rata share of estimated profit [50% × ($500,000 − $400,000)].		

Contracts Receivable	150,000	
Billings on Construction in Progress.........................		150,000
To record billing to parent for the portion of amount due under the contract.		

The subsidiary's balance sheet prepared at the end of 19X1 would list a net current asset of $100,000, as the $150,000 balance in Billings on Construction in Progress would be offset against the $250,000 balance in Construction in Progress. If billings exceed the amount recorded for construction in progress, a net current liability would be shown on the balance sheet.

The following partial consolidated worksheet for 19X1 shows the relevant accounts and the eliminations that would appear for this example. The elimination procedures are complex and involve answering the question: What should remain on the consolidated statements? From a consolidated viewpoint, a self-constructed asset is in progress and $200,000 has been spent to date. All that should remain on the consolidated statements is a $200,000 asset under construction and a $200,000 payable to outside interests. The income distribution schedule of the constructing affiliate would reflect the profit deferral through a debit for $50,000.

Company P and Subsidiary Company S
Partial Worksheet for Consolidated Financial Statements
For Year Ended December 31, 19X1

(Credit balance amounts are in parentheses.)

	Trial Balance		Eliminations & Adjustments	
	Company P	Company S	Dr.	Cr.
Assets Under Construction	150,000		**(3)** 50,000	
Contracts Receivable		150,000		**(1)** 150,000
Billings on Construction in Progress		(150,000)	**(3)** 150,000	
Construction in Progress		250,000		**(2)** 50,000
				(3) 200,000
Earned Income on Long-Term Contracts		(50,000)	**(2)** 50,000	
Contracts Payable	(150,000)		**(1)** 150,000	
Payables (to outsiders)		(200,000)		

Eliminations and Adjustments:
(1) Eliminate the intercompany debt and receivable resulting from the long-term contract.
(2) Eliminate the income recorded on the long-term intercompany contract and remove the profit from Construction in Progress.
(3) Eliminate the balances of Construction in Progress and Billings on Construction in Progress, and increase Assets Under Construction for the unbilled costs on the long-term intercompany contract.

As is true with all intercompany sales of plant assets, any intercompany profit is deferred until realized through the subsequent sale or use of the asset. Thus, the intercompany profit resulting from a long-term construction contract should be realized as the asset is depreciated. The unrealized profit will result in an adjustment to retained earnings in subsequent years.

INTERCOMPANY DEBT

Typically, a parent firm is larger than any one of its subsidiaries and can secure funds under more favorable terms. Because of this, a parent firm often will advance cash to a subsidiary. The parent may accept a note from the subsidiary as security for the loan, or the parent may discount a note that the subsidiary received from a customer. In most cases, the parent will charge a competitive interest rate for the funds advanced to the subsidiary.

In the examples that follow, the more common situation in which the parent is the lender is assumed. If the subsidiary were the lender, the theory and practice would be identical, with the only differences being the books on which the applicable accounts appear and the procedure for the distribution of combined net income.

INTERCOMPANY NOTES

Assume that on July 1, 19X1, an 80%-owned subsidiary, Company S, borrows $10,000 from its parent, Company P, signing a one-year, 8% note, with interest payable on the due date. This intercompany loan will cause the following accounts and their balances to appear on the December 31, 19X1 trial balances of the separate affiliated firms:

Parent Company P		Subsidiary Company S	
Notes Receivable	10,000	Notes Payable	(10,000)
Interest Income	(400)	Interest Expense	400
Interest Receivable	400	Interest Payable	(400)

While this information is required on the books of the separate firms, it should not appear on the consolidated statements. The procedures needed to eliminate this intercompany note and its related interest amounts are demonstrated in Worksheet 6–8 on pages 380–383. Step (3) eliminates the intercompany receivable and payable for the note and the accrued interest on the note. Step (4) eliminates the intercompany interest income and expense amounts. In this worksheet, it is assumed that the intercompany note is the only note recorded. However, it may occur that an intercompany note and its related interest expense, revenue, and accruals are commingled with notes to outside parties. Before the trial balances are entered on the worksheet and before consolidation is attempted, intercompany interest expense and revenue must be accrued properly on the books of the parent and subsidiary.

After all the necessary worksheet eliminations are made, the effect of the note on the distribution of combined net income must be considered. There might be a temptation to increase the minority share of combined net income by $400 as a result of eliminating the interest expense on the intercompany note, but it is not correct to do so. Even though the interest does not appear on the consolidated income statement, it is a legitimate expense for Company S as a separate entity and a legitimate revenue for Company P as a separate entity. In essence, Company S has agreed to transfer $400 to Company P for interest during 19X1, and the minority must respect this agreement when calculating its share of combined net income. Thus, the basis for calculating the minority share is the net income of Company S as a separate entity. The minority receives 20% of this $10,000 net income which includes the $400 of intercompany interest expense.

A parent receiving a note from a subsidiary may subsequently discount the note at a nonaffiliated financial institution in order to receive immediate cash. This results in a note receivable discounted being recorded by the parent. From a consolidated viewpoint, there is a note payable to outside parties. Consolidation procedures should eliminate the internal note receivable against the note receivable discounted. This elimination will result in the note, now payable to an outside party, being extended to the consolidated balance sheet. Intercompany interest accrued prior to the discounting is eliminated. Interest paid by the subsidiary subsequent to the discounting is paid to the outside party and is not eliminated. The net interest expense or revenue on the discounting of the note is a transaction between the parent and the outside party and thus is not eliminated. When consolidated statements are prepared, however, it is desirable to net the interest expense on the note recorded by the maker subsequent to the discounting of the note against the net interest expense or revenue on the discounting transaction.

INTERCOMPANY DISCOUNTING OF NOTES

A note received from a customer of the parent or its subsidiary is a valid asset from a consolidated viewpoint, and no adjustment or elimination is required. However, if the subsidiary discounts a customer's note with its parent, an internal contingent liability and asset are created. This internal transaction has no validity from a consolidated viewpoint and thus must be eliminated.

To demonstrate disclosure on the consolidated worksheet, a customer's note is traced through its receipt and the discounting process. Assume that a subsidiary, Company S, receives a one-year, 6%, $20,000 note from a customer on April 1, 19X1, and that on October 1, 19X1, Company S discounts the note with its parent, Company P, at an 8% discount rate. The proceeds are calculated as follows:

Principal of note...	$20,000
Interest due at maturity, 6% × $20,000..	1,200
Total maturity value	$21,200
Multiply maturity value by 8% discount rate for 1/2 year[1]	(848)
Net proceeds of note..	$20,352

The following entries are recorded on the separate books of Companies S and P as a result of the note and its discounting:

	Subsidiary Company S			Parent Company P		
1. Receipt of note on April 1, 19X1	Notes Receivable...... Sales	20,000	20,000			
2. Discounting of note on October 1, 19X1, at 8%, including accrual of interest earned for 6 months	Accrued Interest Receivable......... Interest Income	600	600			
	Interest Expense (loss on discounting)... Cash...................... Notes Receivable Discounted*....... Accrued Interest Receivable......... *or Notes Receivable	248 20,352	20,000 600	Notes Receivable..... Interest Receivable (6% cash interest for 6 months).... Cash .... Unearned Interest Income (net gain, interest in excess of 6% for 6 months)....	20,000 600	20,352 248
3. Year-end adjusting entry to record interest income, including amortization of one half of the unearned income recorded at time of discounting	None			Interest Receivable (6% cash interest for 3 months).... Unearned Interest Income .... Interest Income....	300 124	424

These entries would produce the trial balance figures shown in the following partial consolidated worksheet, which contains only the accounts relevant to the note. The elimination procedures have the effect of canceling the intercompany discounting transaction. The consolidated statements will include only the external note and interest related to it. The discounting transaction, however, is considered in the distribution of combined net income. The cost of discounting is included as an expense of the subsidiary and as revenue of the parent when combined net income is distributed.

---

[1]The discount rate is a percentage applied to maturity value. This is in contrast to an effective interest rate, which is applied to the original principal. In this case, the effective interest rate is 4.17% ($848 ÷ $20,352) for a half year (8.34% annual).

Company P and Subsidiary Company S
Partial Work Sheet for Consolidated Financial Statements
For Year Ended December 31, 19X1

(Credit balance amounts are in parentheses.)

	Trial Balance		Eliminations & Adjustments		Consolidated Income Statement	Consolidated Balance Sheet
	Company P	Company S	Dr.	Cr.		
Notes Receivable	20,000	20,000		(1) 20,000		20,000
Notes Receivable Discounted		(20,000)	(1) 20,000			
Interest Receivable	900					900
Interest Expense		248		(2) 248		
Interest Income	(424)	(600)	(2) 124		(900)	
Unearned Interest Income	(124)		(2) 124			

Eliminations and Adjustments:
(1) Eliminate the intercompany discounted note by removing the receivable on the books of Company P and the contingent liability account on the books of Company S. Only the external note receivable will be extended to the consolidated balance sheet. If Company S credited Notes Receivable rather than Notes Receivable Discounted, this elimination would not be necessary.
(2) To eliminate the expense on discounting reported by Company S as well as the realized and deferred gain on discounting reported by Company P, interest income for Company P is reduced to the 6% nominal rate.

Income Distribution:
Company P's internally reported net income is increased $124 in 19X1 and decreased $124 in 19X2. This procedure allows Company P to record the $248 net gain on the discounting on the date the transaction occurred, and parallels the recording of a $248 expense by Company S on the date of the discounting.

SOPHISTICATED EQUITY METHOD: INTERCOMPANY TRANSACTIONS

Chapter 5 demonstrated the use of the sophisticated equity method for the parent's recording of its investment in a subsidiary. Recall that one major difference between the simple and sophisticated equity methods was that the latter records subsidiary income net of amortizations of excess. In contrast, the simple equity method ignores amortizations and records as income for the parent the subsidiary reported income multiplied by the parent's percentage of ownership. Another major difference between the two methods is that the income recorded by the parent under the simple equity method is based on the subsidiary reported income without an adjustment for subsidiary-generated intercompany profits. The sophisticated equity method, however, first adjusts the subsidiary income for deferments and realizations of intercompany profits and then applies the parent's ownership percentage. In effect, this means that the parent must construct a subsidiary income distribution schedule before it can record its share of subsidiary income.

The added complexity of the sophisticated equity method is unwarranted when statements are to be consolidated since the subsidiary income and the investment in subsidiary accounts are eliminated entirely. However, this procedure must be used in the rare case when a subsidiary is not to be consolidated or when parent-only statements are to be prepared as a supplement to the consolidated statements.

UNREALIZED PROFITS OF THE CURRENT PERIOD

The case of intercompany profits generated only during the current period will be considered first. Although the same procedure applies to all types of subsidiary-generated unrealized intercompany profits and losses of the current period, the impact of the sophisticated equity method will be demonstrated assuming only the existence of inventory profits.

The following example is based on the information presented in Worksheet 6–2, but this time the parent is using the sophisticated equity method. Because of this fact, the parent has to prepare a subsidiary income distribution schedule before it can record its share of subsidiary income. This schedule is shown below. Note that instead of recording *on its books* a subsidiary income of $60,000, the parent would have recorded $56,800:

Equity Income: Subsidiary Company S

Unrealized profit in ending inventory $4,000	Internally generated net income.................. $75,000
	Adjusted income $71,000
	Controlling share............ 80%
	Controlling interest......... **$56,800***

*This is the same amount that is shown in the parent's income distribution schedule for Worksheet 6–2.

The only elimination procedure in this example that differs from Worksheet 6–2 is step (1), which eliminates the entry made by the parent to record its share of the subsidiary current period income. There is no impact on the other worksheet procedures, and the balance of Worksheet 6–2 would be unchanged. A portion of the revised worksheet follows:

Company P and Subsidiary Company S
Partial Worksheet
For Year Ended December 31, 19X1

(Credit balance amounts are in parentheses.)

	Trial Balance		Eliminations & Adjustments			
	Company P	Company S	Dr.		Cr.	
Accounts Receivable	110,000	150,000			(4)	25,000
Inventory, Dec. 31, 19X1	70,000	40,000			(5)	4,000
Investment in Company S	(b) 192,800				(1)	56,800
					(2)	136,000
Other Assets	314,000	155,000				
Accounts Payable	(80,000)	(100,000)	(4)	25,000		
Common Stock ($10 par), Co. P	(200,000)					
Retained Earnings, Jan. 1, 19X1, Co. P	(250,000)					
Common Stock ($10 par), Co. S		(100,000)	(2)	80,000		
Retained Earnings, Jan. 1, 19X1, Co. S		(70,000)	(2)	56,000		
Sales	(700,000)	(500,000)	(3)	100,000		
Cost of Goods Sold	510,000	350,000	(5)	4,000	(3)	100,000
Expenses	90,000	75,000				
Subsidiary Income	(a) (56,800)		(1)	56,800		
	0	0		321,800		321,800

Notes to Trial Balance:
  (a) See the previously prepared distribution schedule.
  (b) $136,000 beginning-of-year balance + $56,800 sophisticated equity-method income.

Eliminations and Adjustments:
  (1) Eliminate the entry recording the parent's share (80%) of the subsidiary net income under the sophisticated equity method.
  (2–5) Same as Worksheet 6–2.

UNREALIZED PROFITS OF CURRENT AND PRIOR PERIODS

The effect of the sophisticated equity method when there are intercompany profits from current and prior periods is demonstrated in the following example, which is based on the information given in Worksheet 6–3. The subsidiary income reported by the parent in 19X2 under the sophisticated equity method is calculated as follows:

Equity Income: Subsidiary Company S

Unrealized profit in ending inventory.......... $6,000	Internally generated net income....................	$60,000
	Realized profit in beginning inventory.......	4,000
	Adjusted income	$58,000
	Controlling share.............	**80%**
	Controlling interest...........	**$46,400**

The elimination procedures illustrated in the following partial worksheet are applicable to all types of subsidiary-generated intercompany profits and losses of prior and current periods. The differences in the parent's trial balance are explained in the notes that follow the partial worksheet.

(Credit balance amounts are in parentheses.)

Company P and Subsidiary Company S
Partial Worksheet
For Year Ended December 31, 19X2

	Trial Balance		Eliminations & Adjustments	
	Company P	Company S	Dr.	Cr.
Accounts Receivable	160,000	170,000		(5) 60,000
Inventory, Dec. 31, 19X2	60,000	50,000		(6) 6,000
Investment in Company S	(c) 239,200			(1) 46,400
				(2) 192,800
Other Assets	354,000	165,000		
Accounts Payable	(90,000)	(80,000)	(5) 60,000	
Common Stock ($10 par), Co. P	(200,000)			
Retained Earnings, Jan. 1, 19X2, Co. P	(b) (406,800)			
Common Stock ($10 par), Co. S		(100,000)	(2) 80,000	
Retained Earnings, Jan. 1, 19X2, Co. S		(145,000)	(Adj) 4,000	
			(2) 112,800	
Sales	(800,000)	(600,000)	(4) 120,000	
Cost of Goods Sold	610,000	440,000	(6) 6,000	(Adj) 4,000
				(4) 120,000
Expenses	120,000	100,000		
Subsidiary Income	(a) (46,400)		(1) 46,400	
	0	0	429,200	429,200

Notes to Trial Balance:
  (a) See the previously prepared distribution schedule.
  (b) $410,000 simple equity balance − (80% × $4,000 subsidiary beginning inventory profit).
  (c) $136,000 original balance + $56,800 sophisticated equity method income for 19X1 + $46,400 sophisticated equity method income for 19X2.

Eliminations and Adjustments:

(Adj) Eliminate the $4,000 beginning inventory profit from the cost of goods sold and the subsidiary beginning retained earnings accounts. This step replaces step (3) of Worksheet 6–2.

(1) Eliminate the entry recording the parent's share (80%) of the subsidiary net income under the sophisticated equity method.

(2) Eliminate 80% of the subsidiary equity balances against the investment account. The elimination of Retained Earnings is 80% of the adjusted balance of $141,000 ($145,000 − $4,000).

(4-6) Same as Worksheet 6–3.

When the sophisticated equity method is used, worksheet eliminations are complicated by the inconsistency between the parent and subsidiary trial balances. In the partial worksheet illustrated, the parent's investment and retained earnings accounts do not include the parent's share (80%) of the $4,000 subsidiary beginning inventory profit. The subsidiary's trial balance, however, does include the $4,000 profit in both the beginning inventory and the January 1, 19X2 Retained Earnings balance. This inconsistency is removed by an adjustment (Adj) that eliminates the entire intercompany profit from the subsidiary trial balance. This adjustment replaces step (3) of Worksheet 6–3.

Step (1) of the partial worksheet removes the subsidiary income as recorded by the parent. Step (2) reflects the adjustment of the subsidiary Retained Earnings. The remaining steps and worksheet procedures are identical to those in Worksheet 6–3.

APPENDIX: INTERCOMPANY PROFIT ELIMINATIONS ON THE VERTICAL WORKSHEET

In keeping with the overall worksheet format approach of this text, all previous examples in this chapter have been presented using the horizontal worksheet style. Worksheet 6–9, pages 384–387, provides the reader an opportunity to study the vertical worksheet when intercompany merchandise and plant asset transactions are involved. This worksheet is based on the following facts:

1. Company P purchased an 80% interest in Company S on January 1, 19X1. At that time the following determination and distribution of excess schedule was prepared:

Price paid		$500,000
Less interest acquired:		
Common stock ($5 par)......................................	$200,000	
Retained earnings, January 1, 19X1	350,000	
Total stockholders' equity	$550,000	
Interest acquired..	80%	440,000
Excess of cost over book value attributed to goodwill		
(40-year life)...		$ 60,000

2. Company P accounts for the investment under the simple equity method.
3. Company S sells merchandise to Company P at cost plus 25%. Sales totaled $150,000 during 19X2. There were $40,000 of such goods in Company P's beginning inventory and $50,000 of such goods in Company P's ending inventory. As of December 31, 19X2, Company P had not paid the $20,000 owed for the purchases.
4. On July 1, 19X1, Company P sold a new machine that cost $20,000 to Company S for $25,000. At that time both companies believed that the machine had a 5-year remaining life; both companies use straight-line depreciation.
5. Company S declared and paid $20,000 in dividends during 19X2.

Notice that the eliminations in Worksheet 6–9 are identical to those required for the horizontal format. Also, when working with the vertical format, keep in mind the cautions that are stated in the Chapter 5 appendix: (1) the nominal accounts are presented above the balance sheet accounts, and (2) the eliminations are made only to the *beginning* retained earnings accounts. The carry-down procedures for the vertical worksheet are the same as those presented in the Chapter 5 appendix.

QUESTIONS

1. After the elimination of the intercompany investment, additional adjustments are necessary to produce consolidated statements. Indicate several types of intercompany transactions that will require adjustments, and give reasons why the adjustments are needed.
2. A parent company sold to its subsidiary merchandise costing $15,000, at a 25% markup, for cash. The subsidiary company, in turn, sold 3/4 of the goods for $16,000. What adjustments are required in the consolidation process?
3. Explain why the intercompany sale of merchandise has an influence on the distribution of combined net income, even though the sale is eliminated on the consolidated statements.
4. A parent company sold to its subsidiary merchandise costing $75,000 for $100,000. Half of the goods were unsold at year end and had been written down to $40,000, the lower market value. What adjusting entries are required in the consolidation process?

5. Provide the worksheet entries needed to delete the unrealized profit on intercompany sales from beginning and ending inventories for the following situations, assuming that the parent has a 90%-ownership interest in the subsidiary:

   (a) Subsidiary's beginning inventory includes $20,000 of goods purchased from the parent company. Parent sells all merchandise at a 25% markup on cost. Subsidiary purchased goods at a price of $150,000 from Parent during the year and had $45,000 of the goods in ending inventory.

   (b) Parent's beginning inventory includes $36,000 of goods purchased from the subsidiary company. Subsidiary sells all merchandise at a 20% markup on cost. Parent purchased goods at a price of $280,000 from Subsidiary during the year and had $25,000 of the goods in ending inventory.

6. How does the deferral of a gain on an intercompany sale of a depreciable plant asset differ from the deferral of a gain on an intercompany sale of a nondepreciable plant asset?

7. What is the general treatment of losses on intercompany merchandise and plant asset sales?

8. Prepare parent and subsidiary income distribution schedules and enter each of the following items in the correct column: (a) intercompany profit on unsold ending inventory — parent seller; (b) realized intercompany profit on beginning inventory — subsidiary seller; (c) internally generated net income of parent; (d) internally generated net income of subsidiary; (e) unrealized gain on intercompany sale of depreciable asset — subsidiary seller; (f) gain on intercompany sale of depreciable asset realized through use — subsidiary seller; (g) realized intercompany profit on beginning inventory — parent seller; and (h) retirement loss on bonds — bonds issued by subsidiary, purchased by parent.

9. Hiller Construction Company is a 90%-owned subsidiary of Chain O'Lakes Properties Inc. Hiller is building an office complex for Chain O'Lakes and is accounting for the contract under the percentage-of-completion method. To date, Hiller has billed but not collected $1,450,000, recorded costs of $1,200,000, and recorded earned income of $250,000.

   No adjustments or eliminations were made concerning this transaction in the process of preparing the consolidated statements. What misstatements can be found on the consolidated income statement and balance sheet?

10. An accounting theorist once said "Intercompany gains and losses are never eliminated. They are just postponed." Discuss this statement.

11. Frequently, related firms will have outstanding intercompany loan balances. What effect do intercompany interest revenue and expense have on the consolidation process, including the distribution of combined net income?

EXERCISES

Exercise 1. Allcom Company is a wholly-owned subsidiary of Rasman Company. Both firms were newly organized on January 1, 19X1. Rasman sells all of its production to its subsidiary, which sells only goods it has purchased from the parent. The following facts apply to the 19X1–19X3 operations:

	Rasman Sales to Allcom	Rasman Gross Profit	Allcom Dec. 31 Inventory	Allcom Sales
19X1	$300,000	20%	$40,000	$350,000
19X2	340,000	25	35,000	375,000
19X3	400,000	30	60,000	425,000

The inventory on hand each December 31 is sold during the following year. Prepare a schedule in columnar form that states for each period:
(1) The gross profit recorded by Rasman Company,
(2) The gross profit recorded by Allcom Company, and
(3) The gross profit shown on the consolidated income statement.

Exercise 2. Gale Company, a wholly-owned subsidiary, sold all of its 19X5 output to its parent company for $40,000, which included a 25% markup on cost. Gale had not sold any output to the parent in prior years. The parent company sold 75% of the goods it purchased from Gale at a gross profit of 20%. The balance of the goods purchased from Gale was in the parent's December 31, 19X5 inventory. The value assigned to these goods under the lower-of-cost-or-market method was $8,500.
(1) Determine the gross profit on these sales recorded on the separate books of Gale Company and its parent.
(2) Calculate the gross profit shown as a result of these sales on the 19X5 consolidated income statement. Any write down of inventory is an adjustment to the cost of goods sold.

Exercise 3. Autoless Company is a 90%-owned subsidiary of Brewer Inc. The separate income statements of the two firms for 19X6 are as follows:

	Brewer Inc.	Autoless Company
Sales	$200,000	$100,000
Cost of goods sold	(140,000)	(75,000)
Gross profit	$ 60,000	$ 25,000
Other expenses	(40,000)	(15,000)
Other income	5,000	—
Operating income	$ 25,000	$ 10,000
Subsidiary income	9,000	—
Net income	$ 34,000	$ 10,000

The following additional facts apply to 19X6:
(a) Autoless sold $50,000 of goods to Brewer. The gross profits on sales to Brewer and to unrelated firms are equal and have not changed from previous years.
(b) Brewer held $10,000 of the goods purchased from Autoless in its beginning inventory and $15,000 of such goods in its ending inventory.
(c) Brewer billed Autoless $5,000 for consulting services. The charge was expensed by Autoless and treated as other income by Brewer.

Prepare the consolidated income statement for 19X6, including the distribution of the combined net income to the controlling and minority interests. The supporting income distribution schedules should be prepared as well.

Exercise 4. On January 1, 19X2, Furey Company sold a machine to Bardon Company for $20,000. The machine had an original cost of $24,000, and depreciation on the asset had accumulated to $9,000 at the time of sale. The machine has a 5-year remaining life and will be depreciated on a straight-line basis with no salvage value. Bardon Company is an 80%-owned subsidiary of Furey Company.
(1) Explain the adjustments that would have to be made to arrive at combined net income for the years 19X2 through 19X6 as a result of this sale.
(2) Prepare the elimination that would be required on the December 31, 19X3 consolidated worksheet as a result of this sale.
(3) Assuming that Bardon Company was the seller of the machine and that all the other facts remained constant, prepare the elimination that would be required on the December 31, 19X3 consolidated worksheet as a result of this sale.

Exercise 5. On July 1, 19X5, Biz Company sold a parcel of land to its 90%-owned subsidiary, Axel Company, for $90,000. Originally Biz had paid $50,000 for the land. On November 30, 19X6, Axel sold the land to Cline Corporation for $83,500.
(1) Prepare the eliminations relating to the land sale for the December 31, 19X5 consolidated worksheet.
(2) Prepare the eliminations relating to the sales for the December 31, 19X6 worksheet.

Exercise 6. Hilton Corporation sold a press to its 80%-owned subsidiary, Agri Fab Inc. for $5,000 on January 1, 19X2. The press originally was purchased by Hilton on January 1, 19X1, for $20,000, and $6,000 of depreciation for 19X1 had been recorded. The fair market value of the press on January 1, 19X2, was $10,000. Agri Fab proceeded to depreciate the press on a straight-line basis, using a 5-year life and no salvage value. On December 31, 19X3, Agri Fab, having no further need for the machine, sold it for $2,000 and recorded a loss on the sale.
(1) Explain the adjustments that would have to be made to the separate income statements of the two firms to arrive at the consolidated income statements for 19X2 and 19X3.

(2) Prepare the eliminations that would have to be made on the December 31, 19X3 consolidated worksheet as a result of the sales.

Exercise 7.   Donner Contractors, an 80%-owned subsidiary, is constructing a warehouse for its parent, Fast-Parts Corporation. The following information is available at December 31, 19X5:

Percent of completion	60%
Costs incurred to date	$120,000
Estimated costs to complete	80,000
Contract price	240,000
Amount billed to date (no amounts collected)	135,000

Donner uses the percentage-of-completion method to account for its long-term contracts.

Record the journal entries that each of the two firms would have made relative to the construction. Prepare a partial trial balance using the data from your entries, and show the eliminations relating to the contract for the December 31, 19X5 consolidated worksheet.

Exercise 8.   Petersen Shipbuilders constructs large vessels under the percentage-of-completion method. Shipfitters Inc. is a 90%-owned subsidiary of Petersen and produces marine hardware. Petersen's interest in Shipfitters was purchased for $670,000 on January 2, 19X1, when the total stockholders' equity of Shipfitters was $700,000. Any excess of cost was attributed to goodwill and is being amortized over a 40-year period.

The two firms had the following income statements for 19X5:

Petersen Shipbuilders		Shipfitters Inc.	
Earned income on long-term contracts	$800,000	Sales	$450,000
		Cost of goods sold	270,000
Cost of construction in progress	650,000		
Gross profit	$150,000	Gross profit	$180,000
Other expenses	90,000	Other expenses	140,000
Net income	$ 60,000	Net income	$ 40,000

Intercompany transactions were as follows:
(1) During 19X5, Petersen started and completed a display boat for Shipfitters. The boat was billed at $12,000 and had a cost of $10,000. The boat was to be depreciated over 5 years on a straight-line basis, with one-half year's depreciation being taken in the year of acquisition.
(2) During 19X5, Petersen started another display boat for Shipfitters to be delivered in 19X6. To date, Shipfitters has paid $15,000. The cost to date is $12,000, the estimated total cost is $24,000, and the sales price is $30,000.
(3) Shipfitters sells goods to Petersen to yield a gross profit of 30%. Sales to Petersen during 19X5 were $100,000. Petersen had $25,000 of goods purchased from Shipfitters in its beginning inventory and $10,000 of such goods in its ending inventory.

Prepare the 19X5 consolidated income statement and provide supporting calculations. Include income distribution schedules.

Exercise 9.   The separate income statements of Purin Company and its 90%-owned subsidiary, Jaines Company, for the year ended December 31, 19X3, are as follows:

	Purin Company	Jaines Company
Sales	$600,000	$250,000
Cost of goods sold	(400,000)	(170,000)
Gross profit	$200,000	$ 80,000
Expenses	(150,000)	(65,000)
Other income	—	18,000
Operating income	$ 50,000	$ 33,000
Subsidiary income	29,700	—
Net income	$ 79,700	$ 33,000

The following additional facts apply:
(a) On January 1, 19X2, Jaines purchased a building, with a book value of $100,000 and an estimated 25-year life, from Purin for $125,000. The building was being depreciated on a straight-line basis with no salvage value. On December 31, 19X3, Jaines sold the building to the nonaffiliated Fuera Corporation for $123,000.
(b) On January 1, 19X3, Jaines sold a machine with a book value of $50,000 to Purin for $60,000. The machine had an expected life of 4 years and is being depreciated on a straight-line basis with no salvage value.

Prepare the 19X3 consolidated income statement and the supporting income distribution schedules.

Exercise 10.   Preston Company owns a 90% interest in the Dakota Company. During 19X3, the following intercompany transactions were recorded by the separate firms:
(1) Dakota Company sold goods to Preston Company for $80,000 during 19X3, realizing the usual 30% gross profit. Preston Company had $10,000 of the Dakota Company goods in its beginning inventory and $20,000 of such goods in its ending inventory. The ending inventory was written down to $16,000 at year end. There is no outstanding trade debt.
(2) On January 1, 19X3, Preston Company gave a milling machine to Dakota at no cost. The machine originally cost $50,000, and had accumulated depreciation of $30,000 at the time of the gift. Also at the time of the gift, the machine had a market value of $5,000 and a 5-year remaining life. Dakota uses straight-line depreciation for similar machines.
Prepare all the eliminations (with explanations) that would be made for these intercompany transactions on the 19X3 consolidated worksheet.

Exercise 11.   Deck Company is a wholly-owned subsidiary of Bildge Company. On April 1, 19X1, Bildge loaned Deck $30,000 in exchange for a six-month, 8% note payable. Interest will be paid at maturity.

(1) Prepare the entries (including adjusting entries) that Bildge and Deck Companies would make concerning the note during the fiscal year ending June 30, 19X1.
(2) Prepare the eliminations that would be made on the June 30, 19X1 consolidated worksheet as a result of the note.

Exercise 12. Assume that Bildge Company discounted the note described in Exercise 11 to a bank on June 1, 19X1, and that the bank discounted the note at a 10% annual interest rate.
(1) Prepare the entries (including adjusting entries) that Bildge and Deck Companies would make concerning the note and its discounting during the fiscal year ending June 30, 19X1.
(2) Prepare the eliminations that would be made on the June 30, 19X1 consolidated worksheet as a result of the note and its discounting.

Exercise 13. Valco Company is a wholly-owned subsidiary of Rotunda Company. On April 1, 19X1, Valco accepted from a customer a $20,000, 10% one-year note with interest due at maturity. Being in need of cash, Valco Company discounted the note to its parent company on October 1, 19X1. A 12% annual discount rate was used by Rotunda Company.
(1) Prepare the entries (including adjusting entries) that Rotunda and Valco Companies would make to record the note and its discounting during the fiscal year ending December 31, 19X1.
(2) Prepare the eliminations that would be made on the December 31, 19X1 consolidated worksheet as a result of the note and its discounting.

PROBLEMS

Problem 6–1. On April 1, 19X1, Mooney Corporation purchased 80% of the outstanding stock of Tripper Company for $425,000. A condensed balance sheet of Tripper Company at the purchase date follows:

Assets		Liabilities and Equity	
Current assets..................	$180,000	Liabilities.........................	$100,000
Long-lived assets (net)	320,000	Equity..............................	400,000
Total assets......................	$500,000	Total liabilities and equity..	$500,000

All book values approximated market values on the purchase date. Mooney Corporation amortizes its intangibles over 20 years or their legal life, whichever is shorter.

The following information has been gathered pertaining to the first two years of operation since Mooney's purchase of Tripper Company stock:

(a) Intercompany merchandise sales are summarized as follows:

Date	Transaction	Sales	Gross Profit	Merchandise Remaining in Purchaser's Ending Inventory
April 1, 19X1 to	Mooney to Tripper	$35,000	15%	$9,000
March 31, 19X2	Tripper to Mooney	20,000	20	3,500
April 1, 19X2 to	Mooney to Tripper	32,000	22	6,000
March 31, 19X3	Tripper to Mooney	30,000	25	3,000

(b) On March 31, 19X3, Mooney owed Tripper $10,000 and Tripper owed Mooney $5,000 as a result of the intercompany sales.

(c) Mooney paid $25,000 in cash dividends on March 20, 19X2 and 19X3. Tripper paid its first cash dividend on March 10, 19X3, giving each share of outstanding common stock a $0.15 cash dividend.

(d) The trial balances of the two companies as of March 31, 19X3, follow:

	Mooney Corporation	Tripper Company
Cash...	216,200	44,300
Accounts Receivable (net)......................................	290,000	97,000
Inventory...	310,000	80,000
Investment in Tripper Company.............................	425,000	—
Land..	1,081,000	150,000
Building and Equipment...	1,850,000	400,000
Accumulated Depreciation......................................	(940,000)	(210,000)
Intangibles (net)	60,000	—
Accounts Payable	(242,200)	(106,300)
Bonds Payable	(400,000)	—
Common Stock ($.50 par)......................................	(250,000)	—
Common Stock ($1 par)..	—	(200,000)
Paid-In Capital in Excess of Par	(1,250,000)	(100,000)
Retained Earnings, April 1, 19X2	(1,105,000)	(140,000)
Sales...	(880,000)	(630,000)
Dividend Income (from Tripper Company)................	(24,000)	—
Cost of Goods Sold...	704,000	504,000
Other Expenses..	130,000	81,000
Dividends Declared...	25,000	30,000
Total..	0	0

Required:

(1) Prepare the worksheet necessary to produce the consolidated financial statements of Mooney Corporation and its subsidiary for the year ended March 31, 19X3. Include the determination and distribution of excess schedule and the income distribution schedules.

(2) Prepare the formal consolidated income statement for the fiscal year 19X2–19X3.

Problem 6–2. On January 1, 19X1, 100% of the outstanding stock of Smith Shoe Company was purchased by Paisley Inc. for $3,000,000. At that time the fair market and book values of Smith's net assets both equaled $2,800,000. The excess paid is being amortized as goodwill over 10 years. Throughout 19X1, sales to Paisley made up 20% of Smith's revenue and produced a 40% gross-profit rate. At year end, Paisley had sold 90% of the goods purchased from Smith and still owed Smith $18,000. None of the Smith products were in Paisley's January 1, 19X1 beginning inventory.

The following trial balances of Paisley Inc. and Smith Shoe Company were prepared on December 31, 19X1:

	Paisley	Smith
Cash..	1,250,000	250,000
Accounts Receivable	425,000	325,000
Investment in Smith Shoe Company.......................	3,250,000	—
Inventory..	600,000	275,000
Plant and Equipment (net).....................................	4,000,000	2,300,000
Accounts Payable	(235,000)	(100,000)
Common Stock ($10 par).......................................	(1,000,000)	(400,000)
Paid-In Capital in Excess of Par............................	(1,500,000)	(200,000)
Retained Earnings, Jan. 1, 19X1	(5,500,000)	(2,200,000)
Sales...	(12,000,000)	(1,000,000)
Cost of Goods Sold...	6,960,000	600,000
Selling and General Expenses...............................	4,000,000	150,000
Subsidiary Income..	(250,000)	—
Total..	0	0

Required:

Prepare the worksheet necessary to produce the consolidated income statement and balance sheet of Paisley Inc. and its subsidiary for the year ended December 31, 19X1. Include the determination and distribution of excess schedule.

Problem 6–3. On July 1, 19X4, Pluto Corporation acquired 100% of the outstanding stock of Star Ltd. in a one-for-one stock exchange that qualified as a pooling of interests. The stockholders' equity of Star Ltd. on that date showed:

Common stock ($10 par)............................	$ 50,000
Paid-in capital in excess of par...................	100,000
Retained earnings.....................................	300,000
Total..	$450,000

Since the acquisition, 45% of Pluto's ending inventories have been composed of goods purchased from Star, and 10% of Star's ending inventories have been composed of goods purchased from Pluto. The December 31, 19X5 inventories of Pluto and Star were $185,000 and $45,000, respectively.

Star has maintained a 30% gross profit on sales. Starting with 19X6 sales, Pluto increased its gross profit from 20% to 25% of sales. In 19X6, 50% of Star's sales and 10% of Pluto's sales were intercompany. Each company maintains its inventory under a Fifo flow assumption. On December 31, 19X6, $15,000 of Pluto's payable is owed to Star, and $3,000 of Star's payable is owed to Pluto.

The following trial balances of the two companies were prepared on December 31, 19X6:

	Pluto	Star
Cash...	78,750	43,000
Accounts Receivable...	135,000	95,000
Inventory...	220,000	50,000
Investment in Star Ltd.	590,000	—
Plant and Equipment (net).......................................	845,000	425,000
Accounts Payable..	(165,000)	(23,000)
Common Stock ($10 par)..	(625,000)	(50,000)
Paid-In Capital in Excess of Par..............................	(135,000)	(100,000)
Retained Earnings, Jan. 1, 19X6..............................	(700,000)	(400,000)
Sales..	(2,300,000)	(470,000)
Cost of Goods Sold...	1,725,000	329,000
Selling and General Expenses..................................	350,000	91,000
Subsidiary Income...	(50,000)	—
Dividends Declared..	31,250	10,000
Total...	0	0

Required:

Prepare the worksheet necessary to produce the consolidated income statement and balance sheet of Pluto Corporation and its subsidiary for the year ended December 31, 19X6.

Problem 6-4. Milwaukee Corporation purchased 80% of the common stock of Shorewood Ltd. on May 1, 19X1 for $552,000 in order to ensure its raw material supply would be consistently available. At the time of the purchase, Shorewood's net assets had a market value equal to the book value of $600,000. Also at that time, the Shorewood retained earnings account had a balance of $300,000. Milwaukee amortizes its intangible assets over 10 years.

Since the acquisition, Milwaukee has purchased 60% of Shorewood's production. Milwaukee's ending inventories on December 31, 19X1 and 19X2 contained $127,000 and $163,000, respectively, in goods purchased from Shorewood. Shorewood has maintained a 33 1/3% markup on cost. At the end of 19X1 and 19X2 Milwaukee's Accounts Payable contained $36,000 and $43,000, respectively, in liabilities to Shorewood for purchases of goods.

The December 31, 19X2 total inventories were $750,000 for Milwaukee and $100,000 for Shorewood.

Trial balances as of December 31, 19X2, are as follows:

	Milwaukee Corporation	Shorewood Ltd.
Cash..	323,000	60,000
Accounts Receivable (net).....................................	575,000	65,000
Inventory, Jan. 1, 19X2..	720,000	90,000
Investment in Shorewood Ltd.	552,000	—
Land..	100,000	30,000
Building and Equipment (net)	1,200,000	650,000
Accounts Payable	(280,000)	(72,500)
Bonds Payable, 10%, due Jan. 1, 19X8...................	—	(100,000)
Common Stock ($15 par).....................................	(510,000)	(180,000)
Paid-In Capital in Excess of Par............................	(100,000)	(120,000)
Retained Earnings, Jan. 1, 19X2	(1,750,000)	(375,140)
Sales...	(3,450,000)	(750,000)
Purchases..	2,100,000	572,640
Selling and General Expenses...............................	420,000	120,000
Interest Expense..	—	10,000
Dividends Declared...	100,000	—
Total..	0	0

Required:
(1) Prepare the worksheet necessary to produce the consolidated financial statements of Milwaukee Corporation and its subsidiary for the year ended December 31, 19X2. Include the determination and distribution of excess schedule and the income distribution schedules.
(2) Prepare the formal consolidated financial statements, including the income statement, retained earnings statement, and balance sheet.

Problem 6–5.   On January 1, 19X3, Lake Shore Corporation exchanged on a one-for-three basis common stock it held in its treasury for 70% of the outstanding stock of South Company. Lake Shore Corp. common stock had a stable market price of $40 per share at the exchange date.

On the date of the stock acquisition, the stockholders' equity section of South Co.'s balance sheet was as follows:

Common stock ($5 par)...........................	$ 450,000
Paid-in capital in excess of par.................	180,000
Retained earnings..................................	370,000
Total...	$1,000,000

Also on this date, South Co.'s book values approximated market values, except for the land, which was undervalued by $60,000. Any goodwill recognized from the acquisition is being amortized over 40 years.

Information regarding intercompany transactions for 19X5 follows:
(a) Lake Shore sells merchandise to South, realizing a 30% gross profit. Sales during 19X5 were $125,000. South had $30,000 of the 19X4 pur-

chases in its beginning inventory for 19X5 and $40,000 of the 19X5 purchases in its ending inventory for 19X5.
(b) South signed a 12%, 4-month, $10,000 note to Lake Shore in order to cover the remaining balance of its payables on November 1, 19X5. No new merchandise was purchased after this date.
(c) South wrote down to $30,000 the merchandise purchased from Lake Shore and remaining in its 19X5 ending inventory.

Trial balances of Lake Shore Corp. and its subsidiary, South Co., as of December 31, 19X5, are as follows:

	Lake Shore Corp.	South Co.
Cash	160,000	200,100
Interest Receivable	1,500	—
Notes Receivable	50,000	—
Accounts Receivable	395,000	110,000
Inventory	470,000	160,000
Investment in South Company	983,430	—
Land	350,000	300,000
Building and Equipment	1,110,000	810,000
Accumulated Depreciation	(500,000)	(200,000)
Intangibles	60,000	—
Liabilities	(611,500)	(175,000)
Interest Payable	—	(200)
Common Stock ($1 par)	(400,000)	—
Common Stock ($5 par)	—	(450,000)
Paid-In Capital in Excess of Par	(1,235,000)	(180,000)
Retained Earnings, Jan. 1, 19X5	(958,500)	(470,000)
Treasury Stock (at cost)	315,000	—
Sales	(1,020,000)	(500,000)
Interest Income	(1,500)	—
Subsidiary Income	(73,430)	—
Cost of Goods Sold	705,000	300,000
Other Expenses	200,000	95,100
Total	0	0

Required:

Prepare the worksheet necessary to produce the consolidated financial statements of Lake Shore Corp. and its subsidiary for the year ended December 31, 19X5. Include the determination and distribution of excess schedule and the income distribution schedules.

Problem 6–6. On September 1, 19X1, Glen Corporation purchased 80% of the outstanding common stock of Symba Corporation for $152,000. On that date, Symba's net book values equaled market values and there was no excess of cost or book value resulting from the purchase. Glen has been maintaining its investment under the simple equity method.

Over the next three years, the intercompany transactions between the firms were as follows:

(a) On December 1, 19X1, Symba sold its four-year old delivery truck to Glen for $12,200 in cash. At that time, Symba had depreciated the truck, which had cost $15,000, to its $5,000 salvage value. Glen estimated on the date of the sale that the asset had a remaining useful life of 3 years and an estimated salvage value of $200.

(b) On March 1, 19X3, Glen sold a building to Symba for $103,000. Glen originally paid $80,000 for the building and planned to depreciate it over 20 years, assuming a $10,000 salvage value. However, Glen had the property for only 10 years and carried it at a net book value of $45,000 on the sale date. Symba will use the building for 10 years, at which time Symba expects to sell the asset for $13,000.

Both companies use straight-line depreciation for all assets. One-half year's depreciation is taken for all assets in the year they are purchased and in the year they are sold.

Trial balances of Glen Corporation and Symba Corporation as of the August 31, 19X3 year end are as follows:

	Glen Corporation	Symba Corporation
Cash...	120,000	50,000
Accounts Receivable (net)....................................	115,000	18,000
Notes Receivable..	—	10,000
Inventory...	175,000	34,000
Investment in Symba Corporation..........................	217,440	—
Plant and Equipment...	990,700	295,000
Accumulated Depreciation....................................	(175,000)	(85,000)
Other Assets...	28,000	—
Accounts Payable...	(80,000)	(50,200)
Notes Payable...	(25,000)	—
Bonds Payable, 12%..	(300,000)	—
Common Stock ($10 par)......................................	(290,000)	(70,000)
Paid-In Capital in Excess of Par............................	(110,000)	(62,000)
Retained Earnings, Sept. 1, 19X2..........................	(498,850)	(118,000)
Sales...	(920,000)	(240,000)
Cost of Goods Sold...	598,000	132,000
Selling and General Expenses...............................	108,000	80,000
Investment Income...	(23,040)	—
Interest Income...	—	(800)
Interest Expense..	37,750	—
Gain on Sale of Building......................................	(58,000)	—
Dividends Declared...	90,000	7,000
Total..	0	0

Required:
Prepare the worksheet necessary to produce the consolidated financial statements of Glen Corporation and its subsidiary for the year ended August 31, 19X3. Include the income distribution schedules.

Problem 6–7.   On January 1, 19X5, Williams Industries acquired an 80% interest in Redline Corporation by exchanging, on a one-for-four basis, previously unissued common stock for outstanding common stock of Redline. The value per share of Williams Industries common stock immediately after the exchange was $50. At the purchase date, Redline Corporation book values approximated market values, and it had 200,000 shares of common stock outstanding with a total stockholders' equity of $2,225,000.

Redline constructed for its own use a special machine at a cost of $250,000, which was put into use on January 1, 19X1. The machine was sold to Williams on January 1, 19X5, for $250,000 when it had an estimated remaining life of 15 years and a book value of $190,000. Both the remaining life and the straight-line depreciation method will continue to be used by Williams.

Most of Redline Corporation's revenue is generated by long-term construction projects. Redline uses the percentage-of-completion method to account for all its long-term construction projects.

Redline started two long-term construction projects for Williams Industries. The first project was started in 19X6 and was completed on December 31, 19X6, at a total cost of $250,000. The total sales price to Williams for the completed project was $300,000, of which $60,000 still was unpaid on December 31, 19X6. The second project was started in 19X5 and was not completed as of December 31, 19X6. The following table presents the relevant information regarding this contract as of December 31, 19X6:

	19X5	19X6
Contract price...	$1,500,000	$1,500,000
Less costs:		
Actual costs to date	$ 300,000	$ 900,000
Estimated cost to complete....................................	900,000	310,000
Estimated total costs...	$1,200,000	$1,210,000
Estimated total income......................................	$ 300,000	$ 290,000
Apportionment of total income:		
19X5 ($300,000 ÷ $1,200,000 × $300,000)...................................		$ 75,000
19X6 ($900,000 ÷ $1,210,000 × $290,000)...................................		$ 215,702
Less income recognized to date		75,000
Income recognized in 19X6..		$ 140,702

Billings on this contract were $250,000 in 19X5 and $550,000 in 19X6, of which $100,000 was still uncollected as of December 31, 19X6. Amounts paid or owed by the parent are included in its property, plant, and equipment account.

Trial balances of Williams Industries and Redline Corporation as of December 31, 19X6, are as follows:

	Williams Industries	Redline Corporation
Cash...	1,140,000	180,000
Accounts Receivable (net).....................................	1,345,000	135,000
Construction Contracts Receivable.........................	—	830,000
Billings on Construction in Progress......................	—	(1,790,000)
Inventory...	1,500,000	215,000
Investment in Redline Corporation	2,236,000	—
Property, Plant, and Equipment.............................	6,800,000	3,800,000
Accumulated Depreciation....................................	(1,900,000)	(1,000,000)
Accounts Payable	(1,200,000)	(750,000)
Bonds Payable	(3,000,000)	(1,300,000)
Common Stock ($10 par).....................................	(5,000,000)	(2,000,000)
Retained Earnings, Jan. 1, 19X6...........................	(1,574,000)	(340,000)
Earned Income on Long-Term Contracts	—	(650,000)
Sales...	(3,900,000)	(390,000)
Other Income..	(205,000)	(28,000)
Construction in Progress.....................................	—	2,200,000
Cost of Goods Sold...	2,340,000	210,000
Other Expenses...	1,410,000	618,000
Subsidiary Income...	(192,000)	—
Dividends Declared..	200,000	60,000
Total...	0	0

Required:

Prepare the worksheet necessary to produce the consolidated financial statements of Williams Industries and its subsidiary for the year ended December 31, 19X6. Assume that all the necessary adjusting entries have been made, unless an obvious discrepancy exists. Any goodwill that could be attributed to William's acquisition of Redline Corporation should be amortized over 40 years. Include the determination and distribution of excess schedule and the income distribution schedules.

Problem 6–8. Pardon Inc. purchased 100% of the common stock of Slarno Corporation for $150,000 in cash on June 30, 19X6. At that date, Slarno's stockholders' equity was as follows:

Common stock ($1 par)............................	$100,000
Retained earnings....................................	50,000
Total...	$150,000

The fair market values of the assets and liabilities did not differ materially from their book values. Slarno has made no adjustments on its books to reflect the purchase by Pardon. On December 31, 19X6, Pardon and Slarno prepared consolidated financial statements.

The transactions that occurred between Pardon and Slarno during the next year included the following:

(a) On January 3, 19X7, land with a $10,000 book value was sold by Pardon to Slarno for $15,000. Slarno made a $3,000 down payment and signed an 8% mortgage note, payable in 12 equal quarterly payments of $1,135, including interest, beginning March 31, 19X7.

(b) Slarno produced equipment for Pardon under two separate contracts. The first contract, which was for office equipment, was begun and completed during the year at a cost to Slarno of $17,500. Pardon paid $22,000 in cash for the equipment on April 17, 19X7. The second contract was begun on February 15, 19X7, but will not be completed until May, 19X8. Slarno has incurred $45,000 of costs as of December 31, 19X7, and anticipates an additional $30,000 of costs to complete the $95,000 contract. Slarno accounts for all contracts under the percentage-of-completion method. Pardon has made no account on its books for this uncompleted contract as of December 31, 19X7.

(c) Pardon depreciates all of its equipment over a 10-year estimated economic life, with no salvage value. Pardon takes a half-year's depreciation in the year of purchase.

(d) Pardon sells merchandise to Slarno at an average markup of 12% on cost. During the year, Pardon charged Slarno $238,000 for merchandise purchased, of which Slarno paid $211,000. Slarno has $11,200 of this merchandise on hand on December 31, 19X7.

Trial balances of Pardon Inc. and its subsidiary as of December 31, 19X7, are as follows:

	Pardon Inc.	Slarno Corp.
Cash...	45,000	31,211
Accounts Receivable	119,000	73,500
Billings on Construction in Progress	—	(1,201,900)
Mortgage Receivable	8,311	—
Unsecured Notes Receivable....................................	18,000	—
Inventories..	217,000	117,500
Land..	34,000	42,000
Building and Equipment (net)	717,000	408,000
Investment in Slarno Corporation...........................	150,000	—
Accounts Payable	(203,000)	(147,000)
Mortgages Payable	(592,000)	(397,311)
Common Stock...	(250,000)	(100,000)
Retained Earnings, Jan. 1, 19X7	(139,311)	(70,000)
Sales..	(1,800,000)	—
Earned Income on Long-Term Contracts	—	(437,000)
Cost of Goods Sold...	1,155,000	—
Construction in Progress	—	1,289,000
Selling, General, and Administrative Expenses	497,000	360,000
Interest Income	(20,000)	—
Interest Expense..	49,000	32,000
Gain on Sale of Land	(5,000)	—
Total...	0	0

Required:

Prepare the worksheet necessary to produce the consolidated financial statements of Pardon Inc. and its subsidiary for the year ended December 31, 19X7. Assume that both companies have made all of the adjusting entries required for separate financial statements, unless an obvious discrepancy exists. Include the determination and distribution of excess schedule.

(AICPA adapted)

Problem 6–9.   Slue Company had the following balance sheet when it was acquired by Plane Company on January 2, 19X1:

Assets		Liabilities and Equity	
Inventory.........................	$ 50,000	Liabilities.........................	$ 60,000
Other current assets..........	40,000	Common stock ($10 par)...	120,000
Buildings........................	200,000	Retained earnings............	60,000
Accumulated depreciation...	(100,000)		
Net patent			
(5 years remaining)........	20,000		
Goodwill			
(20 years remaining)......	30,000		
Total assets................	$240,000	Total liabilities and equity...	$240,000

On January 2, 19X1, Plane Company issued and exchanged 10,000 shares of $2 par stock for 90% of the outstanding common stock of Slue in a transaction that qualified as a pooling of interests. On that date, the shares issued had a market value of $20 each. In addition, the book values of Slue's assets and liabilities agreed with market values, except for the patent which was undervalued by $20,000. All amortizations and depreciation are calculated on a straight-line basis by Slue Company.

The following intercompany transactions have occurred:

(1) On January 2, 19X2, Slue Company sold a machine, which cost $50,000, to Plane Company for $60,000. The asset had a 5-year remaining life and is being depreciated on a straight-line basis.

(2) Plane Company sold goods to Slue Company for $40,000 during 19X3. All sales were made to yield the usual 50% gross profit. Slue had $20,000 of such goods in its 19X3 beginning inventory and $30,000 of such goods in its 19X3 ending inventory.

(3) Slue Company borrowed $30,000 from Plane Company on a one-year note. Plane discounted the note at a bank. All interest expense and revenue is recorded in the account Other Expense.

The trial balances on page 351 were prepared on December 31, 19X3.

Required:

Prepare the worksheet necessary to produce the consolidated financial statements of Plane Company and its subsidiary for the year ended December 31, 19X3. Include the income distribution schedules.

Suggestion: Since Plane Company's combination with Slue Company is considered a pooling of interests, no excess should result. In addition, intercompany eliminations are unaffected by the fact that this is a pooling. Note that the cost method is used to record the investment in the subsidiary, and this requires you to make a cost-to-equity conversion.

	Plane Company	Slue Company
Notes Receivable...	30,000	—
Other Current Assets...	100,000	136,500
Inventory..	40,000	50,000
Buildings..	264,000	200,000
Accumulated Depreciation—Buildings........................	(100,000)	(130,000)
Equipment..	60,000	
Accumulated Depreciation—Equipment	(24,000)	—
Investment in Slue Company	162,000	—
Patents..	—	8,000
Goodwill...	—	25,500
Notes Payable..	—	(30,000)
Notes Payable Discounted	(30,000)	—
Common Stock..	(80,000)	(120,000)
Paid-In Capital in Excess of Par	(128,000)	—
Retained Earnings, Jan. 1, 19X3	(254,000)	(100,000)
Sales..	(200,000)	(150,000)
Cost of Goods Sold...	120,000	80,000
Other Expenses..	40,000	30,000
Total..	0	0

Problem 6–10. The following trial balances were prepared after completion of the examination of the December 31, 19X4 financial statements of Basic Corporation and its subsidiaries, Noah Corporation and Abel Corporation. The subsidiary investments are accounted for by the cost method.

	Basic	Noah	Abel
Cash...	82,000	11,000	27,000
Accounts Receivable	104,000	41,000	143,000
Inventories..	241,000	70,000	78,000
Investment in Noah Corporation	150,000	—	—
Investment in Abel Corporation....................	175,000	—	—
Investments (other).....................................	185,000	—	—
Property, Plant, and Equipment....................	375,000	58,000	99,000
Accumulated Depreciation............................	(96,000)	(7,000)	(21,000)
Cost of Goods Sold......................................	820,000	300,000	350,000
Operating Expenses.....................................	60,000	35,000	40,000
Accounts Payable	(46,000)	(33,000)	(24,000)
Sales..	(960,000)	(275,000)	(570,000)
Gain on Sale of Assets................................	(9,000)	—	—
Dividend Income	(18,000)	—	—
Common Stock ($20 par)..............................	(500,000)	(200,000)	(100,000)
Retained Earnings..	(563,000)	—	(12,000)
Appropriation for Contingency......................	—	—	(10,000)
Total..	0	0	0

The audit working papers provide the following additional information:
(a) Noah Corporation was formed by Basic Corporation on January 1, 19X4. To secure additional capital, 25% of the common stock of Noah was sold

at par value in the securities market. Basic purchased the remaining stock at par value for cash.

(b) On July 1, 19X4, Basic acquired from stockholders 4,000 shares of Abel Corporation common stock for $175,000. Any excess paid was attributed to goodwill and is being amortized over a 10-year period. A condensed trial balance of Abel Corporation at July 1, 19X4, was as follows:

Current Assets..	165,000
Property, Plant, and Equipment (net)	60,000
Current Liabilities	(45,000)
Common Stock ($20 par)..........................	(100,000)
Retained Earnings....................................	(36,000)
Sales..	(200,000)
Cost of Goods Sold..................................	140,000
Operating Expenses..................................	16,000
Total...	0

(c) The following intercompany product sales were made in 19X4:

	Sales	Gross Profit on Sales	Included in Purchaser's Inventory on December 31, 19X4, at Lower of Cost or Market
Basic to Abel.........................	$ 40,000	20%	$15,000
Noah to Abel.........................	30,000	10	10,000
Abel to Basic.........................	60,000	30	20,000
Total................................	$130,000		$45,000

In valuing Basic Corporation's inventory at the lower of cost or market, the portion of the inventory purchased from Abel Corporation was written down by $1,900.

(d) On January 2, 19X4, Basic Corporation sold a punch press to Noah Corporation. The machine originally was purchased on January 1, 19X2, and was being depreciated by the straight-line method over a 10-year life. Noah Corporation planned to compute depreciation by the same method based on the remaining useful life of the press. Details of the intercompany sale are as follows:

Sales price.................................		$24,000
Less book value of press:		
Cost of press.........................	$25,000	
Accumulated depreciation	(5,000)	20,000
Gain on sale.............................		$ 4,000

(e) Cash dividends were paid on the following dates in 19X4:

	Basic	Abel
June 30	$22,000	$ 6,000
December 31...............................	26,000	14,000
	$48,000	$20,000

(f) Basic Corporation billed $6,000 to each subsidiary at year end for executive services in 19X4. Basic treated it as a reduction of operating expense and the subsidiary recorded it as operating expense. The invoices were paid in January, 19X5.

(g) At year end, Abel Corporation appropriated $10,000 for a contingent loss in connection with a lawsuit that had been pending since 19X2.

Required:

Prepare the worksheet necessary to produce the consolidated financial statements of Basic Corporation and its subsidiaries for the year ended December 31, 19X4. Include any necessary determination and distribution of excess schedules and the income distribution schedules.

(AICPA adapted)

Problem 6–11. Penwick Company, a wholesaler, purchased 80% of the issued and outstanding stock of Sun Inc., a retailer, on December 31, 19X3, for $120,000. At that date, Sun Inc. had one class of common stock outstanding at a stated value of $100,000 and a retained earnings balance of $30,000. Penwick Company had a $50,000 deficit balance in its retained earnings account.

Penwick Company purchased the Sun Inc. stock from Sun's major stockholders primarily to acquire control of the signboard leases owned by Sun. The leases will expire on December 31, 19X8, and Penwick Company executives estimate that these nonrenewable leases were worth at least $25,000 more than their book value when the stock was purchased. Any remaining excess was attributed to goodwill and is being amortized over a 40-year period.

Penwick Company sells merchandise to Sun Inc. at the same price and terms that are used with other customers. During 19X7, Penwick's sales to Sun totaled $100,000. Sun had $30,000 of the merchandise purchased from Penwick on hand on December 31, 19X7, which was an increase of $10,000 over the previous year. Sun had not paid Penwick for $21,000 of the merchandise in inventory and also owed Penwick for a $10,000 cash advance that was in Sun's cash account on December 31, 19X7.

On July 1, 19X4, Sun purchased a parcel of land from Penwick for $15,000 in cash. A building on the land also was purchased from Penwick on the same date for $100,000. Sun paid $20,000 in cash and gave a mortgage note that called for four payments of $20,000 each, plus interest at 10 percent, to be paid annually on the anniversary of the sale. Penwick credits the interest earned from Sun to the expense account. The land originally cost Penwick $15,000 and Penwick's book value of the building was $80,000 at the date of the sale. Also on the sale date, Sun estimated that the building had a 20-year life and no salvage value and has computed depreciation on a monthly basis.

Sun declared a 9% cash dividend on December 20, 19X7, payable on January 16, 19X8, to stockholders of record on December 31, 19X7. Penwick carries its investment in Sun at cost and had not recorded this dividend on December 31, 19X7. Neither Penwick nor Sun paid a dividend during 19X6.

The trial balances of both companies for the year ended December 31, 19X7, follow:

	Penwick Company	Sun Inc.
Cash	14,200	19,300
Accounts Receivable	80,000	76,000
Inventories	54,800	85,600
Other Current Assets	15,000	10,200
Investment in Sun Inc.	120,000	—
Notes Receivable	20,000	—
Land	25,000	15,000
Building and Equipment	200,000	100,000
Accumulated Depreciation	(102,000)	(17,500)
Signboard Leases	—	42,000
Accumulated Amortization	—	(33,600)
Accounts Payable	(35,500)	(81,000)
Dividends Payable	—	(9,000)
Other Current Liabilities	(24,500)	(12,000)
Notes Payable	—	(20,000)
Common Stock	(300,000)	(100,000)
Retained Earnings, Jan. 1, 19X7	(27,000)	(59,000)
Sales	(420,000)	(300,000)
Cost of Goods Sold	315,000	240,000
Expenses	65,000	35,000
Dividends Declared	—	9,000
Total	0	0

Required:

Prepare the worksheet necessary to produce consolidated financial statements of Penwick Company and its subsidiary as of December 31, 19X7. Assume that both companies made all the adjusting entries required for separate financial statements, unless an obvious discrepancy exists. Include the determination and distribution of excess schedule and the income distribution schedules.   (AICPA adapted)

Problem 6–12.   *(Review of Chapters 5 and 6)* Pace Company purchased 80% of the common stock of Slow Ink Company for $380,000 on January 2, 19X1. At that time, Slow Ink had the following balance sheet:

Assets		Liabilities and Stockholders' Equity	
Cash	$ 50,000	Accounts payable	$ 50,000
Inventory	130,000	Bonds payable	200,000
Accounts receivable	70,000	Common stock ($5 par)	50,000
Land	50,000	Paid-in capital in excess of par	100,000
Buildings (net)	250,000	Retained earnings	200,000
Goodwill (net)	50,000		
Total assets	$600,000	Total liabilities and equity	$600,000

The following information was available for the accounts where market values differed from book values on the date of the acquisition:

Account	Market Value	Life at Jan. 2, 19X1
Inventory............................	$180,000	Sold in 19X1
Land..................................	100,000	
Buildings	400,000	25 years of 40-year original life
Bonds payable	190,000	5 years to maturity
Goodwill............................	?	20 years

The bond discount is to be amortized using the straight-line method.

The following transactions have occurred since the purchase and may be of concern in preparing the 19X3 consolidated financial statements:

(1) Pace's 19X3 beginning inventory includes $25,000 of the goods purchased from Slow Ink. Slow Ink always sells to Pace at cost plus 25%.

(2) Slow Ink made sales to Pace during 19X3 totaling $90,000. $10,000 was still unpaid at year end. Pace had $35,000 of such goods in its 19X3 ending inventory; however, the goods were adjusted to the lower market value of $31,000.

(3) Slow Ink sold a piece of equipment to Pace on January 2, 19X2 for $10,000. The equipment had a book value of $8,000 and a five-year remaining life at the time of the sale.

The following trial balances of Pace Company and its subsidiary were prepared on December 31, 19X3:

	Pace Company	Slow Ink Company
Cash..	60,000	100,000
Inventory..	180,000	120,000
Accounts Receivable...	120,000	100,000
Investment in Slow Ink Company.....................................	380,000	—
Land..	60,000	50,000
Building (net)...	340,000	230,000
Equipment (net)..	40,000	—
Goodwill (net)	—	42,500
Accounts Payable	(100,000)	(60,000)
Bonds Payable	—	(200,000)
Common Stock..	(300,000)	(50,000)
Paid-In Capital in Excess of Par......................................	—	(100,000)
Retained Earnings, Jan. 1, 19X3	(712,000)	(222,500)
Sales..	(300,000)	(120,000)
Cost of Goods Sold...	200,000	80,000
Other Expenses..	40,000	20,000
Dividends Declared...	—	10,000
Dividend Income (from Slow Ink Company)......................	(8,000)	—
Total...	0	0

Required:

Prepare the worksheet necessary to produce the consolidated financial statements of Pace Company and its subsidiary for the year ended December 31, 19X3. Include the determination and distribution of excess schedule and the income distribution schedules.

(continued)

Suggestion: Pace's acquisition of Slow Ink Company is a bargain purchase and will require an allocation of available market value to long-lived assets. Also, this is a cost-method problem that will require a cost-to-equity conversion.

Problem 6–13. Pelican Inc. purchased an 80% interest in Stork Company on January 1, 19X1, at which time the following determination and distribution of excess schedule was prepared:

Price paid		$600,000
Less interest acquired:		
Common stock ($10 par)..	$100,000	
Paid-in capital in excess of par....................................	250,000	
Retained earnings..	300,000	
Total stockholders' equity.......................................	$650,000	
Interest acquired..	80%	520,000
Excess of cost over book value		$ 80,000
Less excess attributable to building		
(10-year remaining life)		60,000
Goodwill (40-year life)...		$ 20,000

The building is depreciated and the goodwill is amortized on a straight-line basis. The two firms prepared the following trial balances on December 31, 19X3:

	Pelican	Stork
Current Assets..	480,000	215,000
Property, Plant, and Equipment.................................	1,200,000	900,000
Accumulated Depreciation...	(400,000)	(200,000)
Investment in Stork Company.....................................	693,300	—
Liabilities...	(200,000)	(120,000)
Common Stock ($20 par)—Pelican.............................	(300,000)	—
Common Stock ($10 par)—Stork................................	—	(100,000)
Paid-In Capital in Excess of Par	(700,000)	(250,000)
Retained Earnings, Jan. 1, 19X3	(625,000)	(380,000)
Sales..	(1,000,000)	(600,000)
Cost of Goods Sold..	750,000	450,000
Expenses...	150,000	80,000
Investment Income	(48,300)	—
Dividends Declared..	—	5,000
Total..	0	0

The following additional information is applicable:
(a) Pelican prepares separate parent-only statements as a supplement to its consolidated statements. To facilitate their preparation, the investment account is maintained under the APB Opinion No. 18 (sophisticated) equity method.
(b) Stork sells goods to Pelican at a price to yield a 25% gross profit. There were $50,000 of such sales during 19X3. Pelican had $10,000 of goods purchased from Stork in its 19X3 beginning inventory and $16,000 of these goods in its 19X3 ending inventory.

Required:
Prepare the worksheet necessary to produce the consolidated financial statements of Pelican Inc. and its subsidiary for the year ended December 31, 19X3. Include the income distribution schedules.

APPENDIX PROBLEMS

Problem 6A–1.   Arther Corporation acquired all of the outstanding $10 par voting common stock of Trent Inc. on January 1, 19X2, in exchange for 50,000 shares of its $10 par voting common stock. On December 31, 19X1, the common stock of Arther had a closing market price of $15 per share on a national stock exchange. The retained earnings balance of Trent Inc. was $156,000 on the date of the acquisition. The acquisition was accounted for appropriately as a purchase. Both companies continued to operate as separate business entities maintaining separate accounting records with years ending December 31.

On December 31, 19X4, after year-end adjustments but before the nominal accounts were closed, the companies had the following condensed statements:

	Arther Corporation	Trent Inc.
Income Statement:		
Sales	(1,900,000)	(1,500,000)
Dividend Income (from Trent Inc.)	(40,000)	—
Cost of Goods Sold	1,180,000	870,000
Operating Expenses (includes depreciation)	550,000	440,000
Net Income	(210,000)	(190,000)
Retained Earnings:		
Retained Earnings, Jan. 1, 19X4	(250,000)	(206,000)
Net Income	(210,000)	(190,000)
Dividends Paid	—	40,000
Balance, Dec. 31, 19X4	(460,000)	(356,000)
Balance Sheet:		
Cash	285,000	150,000
Accounts Receivable (net)	430,000	350,000
Inventories	530,000	410,000
Land, Plant, and Equipment	660,000	680,000
Accumulated Depreciation	(185,000)	(210,000)
Investment in Trent Inc. (at cost)	750,000	—
Accounts Payable and Accrued Expenses	(670,000)	(544,000)
Common Stock ($10 par)	(1,200,000)	(400,000)
Additional Paid-In Capital	(140,000)	(80,000)
Retained Earnings, Dec. 31, 19X4	(460,000)	(356,000)
Total	0	0

Additional information is as follows:

(a) There have been no changes in the common stock and additional paid-in capital accounts since the one necessitated in 19X2 by Arther's acquisition of Trent Inc.

(b) At the acquisition date, the market value of Trent's machinery exceeded book value by $54,000. This excess is being amortized over the asset's estimated average remaining life of six years. The fair market values of Trent's other assets and liabilities were equal to book values. Any goodwill resulting from the purchase is being amortized over a 20-year period.

(c) On July 1, 19X2, Arther sold a warehouse facility to Trent for $129,000 in cash. At the date of sale, Arther's book values were $33,000 for the land and $66,000 for the undepreciated cost of the building. Trent allocated the $129,000 purchase price to the land for $43,000 and to the building for $86,000. Trent is depreciating the building over its estimated five-year remaining useful life by the straight-line method with no salvage value.

(d) During 19X4, Arther purchased merchandise from Trent at an aggregate invoice price of $180,000, which included a 100% markup on Trent's cost. At December 31, 19X4, Arther owed Trent $75,000 on these purchases, and $36,000 of the merchandise purchased remained in Arther's inventory.

Required:

Complete the vertical worksheet necessary to prepare the consolidated income statement and retained earnings statement for the year ended December 31, 19X4, and a consolidated balance sheet as of December 31, 19X4, for Arther Corporation and its subsidiary. Formal consolidated statements and journal entries are not required. Include the determination and distribution of excess schedule and the income distribution schedules.

(AICPA adapted)

Problem 6A–2. Peters Corp. purchased a 90% interest in Suma Inc. for $750,000 on January 1, 19X4, when the stockholders' equity of Suma was as follows:

Common stock ($10 par)............................	$200,000
Retained earnings......................................	500,000
Total stockholders' equity.......................	$700,000

On this date, it was determined that Suma's plant assets were undervalued by $80,000 and had an 8-year remaining life. Any remaining excess purchase price was attributed to goodwill. Peters Corp. uses the maximum write-off period for its intangibles.

Suma sold a machine to Peters Corp. for $20,000 on July 1, 19X4. The machine originally cost Suma $30,000, and $20,000 of accumulated depreciation had been recorded as of the sale date. Also on the sale date, the machine had a 10-year remaining life and no salvage value. Peters uses straight-line depreciation.

Peters Corp. sells merchandise to Suma at cost plus 50%. Sales totaled $300,000 during 19X5. Suma had $90,000 of such goods in its ending inventory, which was an increase of $30,000 from the previous year. Suma had not paid Peters for $25,000 of the purchases made during the year.

Peters Corp. uses the simple equity method to record its investment in Suma. At December 31, 19X5, Peters Corp. and its subsidiary, Suma Inc., had the following trial balances:

	Peters Corp.	Suma Inc.
Sales...	(822,000)	(500,000)
Cost of Goods Sold..	300,000	200,000
Other Expenses...	60,000	50,000
Depreciation Expense...	20,000	40,000
Subsidiary Income..	(189,000)	—
Dividends Declared...	20,000	10,000
Retained Earnings, Jan. 1, 19X5	(900,000)	(800,000)
Cash...	150,000	125,000
Accounts Receivable...	115,000	180,000
Inventory..	135,000	175,000
Plant Assets..	600,000	1,000,000
Accumulated Depreciation....................................	(189,000)	(150,000)
Investment in Suma Inc.	1,200,000	—
Accounts Payable...	(50,000)	(30,000)
Other Liabilities..	(150,000)	(100,000)
Common Stock ($5 par)..	(300,000)	—
Common Stock ($10 par)	—	(200,000)
Total..	0	0

Required:

Complete the vertical worksheet necessary to prepare the consolidated income statement and retained earnings statement for the year ended December 31, 19X5, and consolidated balance sheet as of December 31, 19X5, for Peters Corp. and its subsidiary. Formal consolidated statements and journal entries are not required. Include the determination and distribution of excess schedule and the income distribution schedules.

Suggestion: This problem is to be solved using the vertical format for worksheets. However, the information is arranged in the traditional trial balance format which lends itself to the horizontal format for worksheets. Your challenge is to rearrange the information into the three statement format which is needed for the vertical format.

Worksheet 6–1 (see page 313)

Worksheet 6–1 (see page 313)

Intercompany Sales;
Company P and
Worksheet for Consolidated
For Year Ended

(Credit balance amounts are in parentheses.)

		Trial Balance	
		Company P	Company S
1	**Accounts Receivable**	110,000	150,000
2	Inventory, Dec. 31, 19X1	70,000	40,000
3	Investment in Company S	196,000	
4			
5	Other Assets	314,000	155,000
6	**Accounts Payable**	(80,000)	(100,000)
7	Common Stock ($10 par), Co. P	(200,000)	
8	Retained Earnings, Jan. 1, 19X1, Co. P	(250,000)	
9	Common Stock ($10 par), Co. S		(100,000)
10	Retained Earnings, Jan. 1, 19X1, Co. S		(70,000)
11	**Sales**	(700,000)	(500,000)
12	**Cost of Goods Sold**	510,000	350,000
13	Expenses	90,000	75,000
14	Subsidiary Income	(60,000)	
15		0	0
16	Combined Net Income		
17	To Minority Interest (see distribution schedule)		
18	Balance to Controlling Interest (see distribution schedule)		
19	Total Minority Interest		
20	Retained Earnings, Controlling Interest, Dec. 31, 19X1		
21			

Eliminations and Adjustments:
(1) Eliminate the entry recording the parent's share of subsidiary net income.
(2) Eliminate against the investment in Company S account the pro rata portion of the subsidiary equity balances (80%) owned by the parent. To simplify the elimination, there is no discrepancy between the cost and book values of the investment in this example. Also note that the worksheet process is expedited by always eliminating the intercompany investment first.
(3) Eliminate the intercompany sales to avoid double counting. Now only Company S's original purchase from third parties and Company P's final sale to third parties remain in the consolidated income statement.
(4) Eliminate the $25,000 intercompany trade balances resulting from the intercompany sale.

No Intercompany Goods in Inventories

WORSHEET 6–1

Subsidiary Company S
Financial Statements
December 31, 19X1

Eliminations & Adjustments				Consolidated Income Statement	Minority Interest	Controlling Retained Earnings	Consolidated Balance Sheet	
Dr.		Cr.						
		(4)	25,000				235,000	1
							110,000	2
		(1)	60,000					3
		(2)	136,000					4
							469,000	5
(4)	25,000						(155,000)	6
							(200,000)	7
						(250,000)		8
(2)	80,000				(20,000)			9
(2)	56,000				(14,000)			10
(3)	100,000			(1,100,000)				11
		(3)	100,000	760,000				12
				165,000				13
(1)	60,000							14
	321,000		321,000					15
				(175,000)				16
				15,000*	(15,000)			17
				160,000*		(160,000)		18
					(49,000)		(49,000)	19
						(410,000)	(410,000)	20
							0	21

Subsidiary Company S Income Distribution

Internally generated net income..	$ 75,000
Adjusted income	$ 75,000
Minority share...........................	20%
Minority interest........................	$ 15,000*

Parent Company P Income Distribution

Internally generated net income..	$100,000
80% × Company S adjusted income of $75,000	60,000
Controlling interest....................	$160,000*

Worksheet 6–2 (see page 314)

Intercompany Goods
Company P and
Worksheet for Consolidated
For Year Ended

(Credit balance amounts are in parentheses.)

		Trial Balance	
		Company P	Company S
1	Accounts Receivable	110,000	150,000
2	**Inventory, Dec. 31, 19X1**	**70,000**	**40,000**
3	Investment in Company S	196,000	
4			
5	Other Assets	314,000	155,000
6	Accounts Payable	(80,000)	(100,000)
7	Common Stock ($10 par), Co. P	(200,000)	
8	Retained Earnings, Jan. 1, 19X1, Co. P	(250,000)	
9	Common Stock ($10 par), Co. S		(100,000)
10	Retained Earnings, Jan. 1, 19X1, Co. S		(70,000)
11	Sales	(700,000)	(500,000)
12	**Cost of Goods Sold**	**510,000**	**350,000**
13	Expenses	90,000	75,000
14	Subsidiary Income	(60,000)	
15		0	0
16	Combined Net Income		
17	To Minority Interest (see distribution schedule)		
18	Balance to Controlling Interest (see distribution schedule)		
19	Total Minority Interest		
20	Retained Earnings, Controlling Interest, Dec. 31, 19X1		
21			

Eliminations and Adjustments:
(1) Eliminate the entry recording the parent's share of subsidiary net income.
(2) Eliminate 80% of the subsidiary equity balances against the investment in Company S account. There is no excess of cost or book value in this example.
(3) Eliminate the intercompany sale.
(4) Eliminate the intercompany trade balances.
(5) Eliminate the profit in the ending inventory.

in Ending Inventory
Subsidiary Company S
Financial Statements
December 31, 19X1

WORKSHEET 6–2

Eliminations & Adjustments		Consolidated Income Statement	Minority Interest	Controlling Retained Earnings	Consolidated Balance Sheet	
Dr.	Cr.					
	(4) 25,000				235,000	1
	(5) 4,000				106,000	2
	(1) 60,000					3
	(2) 136,000					4
					469,000	5
(4) 25,000					(155,000)	6
					(200,000)	7
				(250,000)		8
(2) 80,000			(20,000)			9
(2) 56,000			(14,000)			10
(3) 100,000		(1,100,000)				11
(5) 4,000	(3) 100,000	764,000				12
		165,000				13
(1) 60,000						14
325,000	325,000					15
		(171,000)				16
		14,200*	(14,200)			17
		156,800*		(156,800)		18
			(48,200)		(48,200)	19
				(406,800)	(406,800)	20
					0	21

Subsidiary Company S Income Distribution

Unrealized profit in ending inventory..................(5) **$4,000**	Internally generated net income.. $ 75,000
	Adjusted income .... $ 71,000
	Minority share........................... 20%
	Minority interest....................... $ 14,200*

Parent Company P Income Distribution

	Internally generated net income.. $100,000
	80% × Company S adjusted income of $71,000 56,800
	Controlling interest.................... $156,800*

Worksheet 6–3 (see page 316)   **Intercompany Goods in**
                                                        Company P and
                                                Worksheet for Consolidated
(Credit balance amounts are in parentheses.)   For Year Ended

		Trial Balance	
		Company P	Company S
1	Accounts Receivable	160,000	170,000
2	**Inventory, Dec. 31, 19X2**	**60,000**	**50,000**
3	Investment in Company S	244,000	
4			
5	Other Assets	354,000	165,000
6	Accounts Payable	(90,000)	(80,000)
7	Common Stock ($10 par), Co. P	(200,000)	
8	**Retained Earnings, Jan. 1, 19X2, Co. P**	**(410,000)**	
9	Common Stock ($10 par), Co. S		(100,000)
10	**Retained Earnings, Jan. 1, 19X2, Co. S**		**(145,000)**
11			
12	Sales	(800,000)	(600,000)
13	**Cost of Goods Sold**	**610,000**	**440,000**
14			
15	Expenses	120,000	100,000
16	Subsidiary Income	(48,000)	
17		0	0
18	Combined Net Income		
19	To Minority Interest (see distribution schedule)		
20	Balance to Controlling Interest (see distribution schedule)		
21	Total Minority Interest		
22	Retained Earnings, Controlling Interest, Dec. 31, 19X2		
23			

Eliminations and Adjustments:
(1) Eliminate the entry recording the parent's share of subsidiary net income.
(2) Eliminate 80% of the subsidiary equity balances against the investment account. There is no
     excess of cost or book value in this example.
(3) Eliminate the intercompany profit of $4,000 (20% × $20,000) in the beginning inventory by
     reducing both the cost of goods sold and the beginning retained earnings accounts. 20% of
     the decrease in retained earnings is shared by the minority interest, since, in this case, *the
     selling firm was the subsidiary.* If the parent had been the seller, only the controlling interest
     in retained earnings would be decreased. It should be noted that the $4,000 profit is shifted

Beginning and Ending Inventories
Subsidiary Company S
Financial Statements
December 31, 19X2

WORKSHEET 6–3

Eliminations & Adjustments			Consolidated Income Statement	Minority Interest	Controlling Retained Earnings	Consolidated Balance Sheet	
Dr.		Cr.					
	(5)	60,000				270,000	1
	(6)	**6,000**				104,000	2
	(1)	48,000					3
	(2)	196,000					4
						519,000	5
(5)	60,000					(110,000)	6
						(200,000)	7
(3)	**3,200**				(406,800)		8
(2)	80,000			(20,000)			9
(2)	116,000						10
(3)	**800**			(28,200)			11
(4)	120,000		(1,280,000)				12
(6)	**6,000**	(3) 4,000					13
		(4) 120,000	932,000				14
			220,000				15
(1)	48,000						16
	434,000	434,000					17
			(128,000)				18
			11,600*	(11,600)			19
			116,400*		(116,400)		20
				(59,800)		(59,800)	21
					(523,200)	(523,200)	22
						0	23

from 19X1 to 19X2, since, as a result of the entry, the 19X2 consolidated cost of goods sold balance is reduced $4,000. This procedure emphasizes the concept that intercompany inventory profit is not eliminated but only deferred until inventory is sold to an outsider.

(4) Eliminate the intercompany sales to prevent double counting.

(5) Eliminate the intercompany trade balances.

(6) Eliminate the intercompany profit of $6,000 (20% × $30,000) recorded by Company S for the intercompany goods contained in Company P's ending inventory, and increase the cost of goods sold balance by this same amount.

(continued)

Subsidiary Company S Income Distribution

Unrealized profit in ending inventory, 20% × $30,000 ....(6) $6,000	Internally generated net income.. $ 60,000
	Realized profit in beginning inventory, 20% × $20,000 ...(3) 4,000
	Adjusted income .... $ 58,000
	Minority share........................... 20%
	Minority interest........................ $ 11,600*

Parent Company P Income Distribution

Internally generated net income..	$ 70,000
80% × Company S adjusted income of $58,000	46,400
Controlling interest....................	$116,400*

Worksheet 6–4 (see page 317)   **Intercompany Goods in Beginning and**
                                                              Company P and
                                                     Worksheet for Consolidated
(Credit balance amounts are in parentheses.)   For Year Ended

		Trial Balance	
		Company P	Company S
1	Accounts Receivable	160,000	170,000
2	**Inventory, Jan. 1, 19X2**	**70,000**	**40,000**
3	Investment in Company S	244,000	
4			
5	Other Assets	354,000	165,000
6	Accounts Payable	(90,000)	(80,000)
7	Common Stock ($10 par), Co. P	(200,000)	
8	**Retained Earnings, Jan. 1, 19X2, Co. P**	**(410,000)**	
9	Common Stock ($10 par), Co. S		(100,000)
10	**Retained Earnings, Jan. 1, 19X2, Co. S**		**(145,000)**
11			
12	Sales	(800,000)	(600,000)
13	Purchases	600,000	450,000
14	**Inventory, Dec. 31, 19X2**		
15			
16	Expenses	120,000	100,000
17	Subsidiary Income	(48,000)	
18		0	0
19	Combined Net Income		
20	To Minority Interest (see distribution schedule)		
21	Balance to Controlling Interest (see distribution schedule)		
22	Total Minority Interest		
23	Retained Earnings, Controlling Interest, Dec. 31, 19X2		
24			

Eliminations and Adjustments:
(1) Eliminate the entry recording the parent's share of subsidiary net income.
(2) Eliminate 80% of the subsidiary equity balances against the investment account. There is no
excess of cost or book value in this example.
(3) Eliminate the intercompany profit of $4,000 (20% × $20,000) in the beginning inventory by
reducing both the January 1 inventory and the beginning retained earnings balances. 20%
of the decrease in retained earnings is shared by the minority interest, since, in this case,
the selling firm was the subsidiary. If the parent had been the seller, only the controlling interest in retained earnings would be decreased. It should be noted that the $4,000 profit is

Ending Inventories; Periodic Inventory
Subsidiary Company S
Financial Statements
December 31, 19X2

WORKSHEET 6–4

Eliminations & Adjustments Dr.	Eliminations & Adjustments Cr.	Consolidated Income Statement	Minority Interest	Controlling Retained Earnings	Consolidated Balance Sheet	
	(5) 60,000				270,000	1
	(3) 4,000	106,000				2
	(1) 48,000					3
	(2) 196,000					4
					519,000	5
(5) 60,000					(110,000)	6
					(200,000)	7
(3) 3,200				(406,800)		8
(2) 80,000			(20,000)			9
(2) 116,000						10
(3) 800			(28,200)			11
(4) 120,000		(1,280,000)				12
	(4) 120,000	930,000				13
(Inv) 110,000	(6) 6,000				104,000	14
(6) 6,000	(Inv) 110,000	(104,000)				15
		220,000				16
(1) 48,000						17
544,000	544,000					18
		(128,000)				19
		11,600*	(11,600)			20
		116,400*		(116,400)		21
			(59,800)		(59,800)	22
				(523,200)	(523,200)	23
					0	24

shifted from 19X1 to 19X2, since, as a result of the entry, 19X2 consolidated cost of goods sold will be reduced $4,000. This procedure emphasizes the concept that intercompany inventory profit is not eliminated but only deferred until inventory is sold to an outsider.

(4) Eliminate the intercompany sales to prevent double counting of purchases and sales.

(5) Eliminate the intercompany trade balances.

(Inv) Enter the combined ending inventories of Company P and Company S, $60,000 and $50,000, respectively.

(6) Eliminate the intercompany profit of $6,000 (20% × $30,000) recorded by Company S for the intercompany goods contained in Company P's ending inventory.

(continued)

Subsidiary Company S Income Distribution

Unrealized profit in ending inventory, 20% × $30,000 ....(6) **$6,000**	Internally generated net income..	$ 60,000[a]
	Realized profit in beginning inventory, 20% × $20,000 ...(3)	**4,000**
	Adjusted income	$ 58,000
	Minority share..........................	20%
	Minority interest.......................	$ 11,600*

[a][$600,000 − ($40,000 + $450,000 − $50,000) − $100,000 = $60,000]

Parent Company P Income Distribution

	Internally generated net income..	$ 70,000[b]
	80% × Company S adjusted income of $58,000	46,400
	Controlling interest	$116,400*

[b][$800,000 − ($70,000 + $600,000 − $60,000) − $120,000 = $70,000]

Worksheet 6–5 (see page 321)

Intercompany Sale
Company P and
Worksheet for Consolidated
For Year Ended

(Credit balance amounts are in parentheses.)

		Trial Balance	
		Company P	Company S
1	Current Assets	15,000	20,000
2	**Machinery**	50,000	(a) 230,000
3	**Accumulated Depreciation — Machinery**	(25,000)	(b) (100,000)
4	Investment in Company S	120,000	
5			
6	Common Stock ($10 par), Co. P	(100,000)	
7	Retained Earnings, Jan. 1, 19X1, Co. P	(10,000)	
8	Common Stock ($10 par), Co. S		(50,000)
9	Retained Earnings, Jan. 1, 19X1, Co. S		(75,000)
10	Sales	(200,000)	(100,000)
11	Cost of Goods Sold	150,000	59,000
12	**Depreciation Expense**	30,000	(b) 16,000
13	**Gain on Sale of Machine**	(10,000)	
14	Subsidiary Income	(20,000)	
15		0	0
16	Combined Net Income		
17	To Minority Interest (see distribution schedule)		
18	Balance to Controlling Interest (see distribution schedule)		
19	Total Minority Interest		
20	Retained Earnings, Controlling Interest, Dec. 31, 19X1		
21			

Notes to Trial Balance:
(a) Includes machine purchased for $30,000 *from Company P* on January 1, 19X1.
(b) Includes $6,000 depreciation on machine purchased from Company P on January 1, 19X1.

Eliminations and Adjustments:
(1) Eliminate the entry recording the parent's share of subsidiary net income for the current year.
(2) Eliminate 80% of the subsidiary equity balances against the investment account. There is no excess to be distributed.
(3) Eliminate the $10,000 gain on the intercompany sale of the machine. In addition, adjust the machine to $32,000 and restore its related accumulated depreciation to $12,000 in order to reflect the book value of the asset to the consolidated firm on January 1, 19X1.
(4) Reduce the depreciation expense and accumulated depreciation accounts to reflect the depreciation ($4,000 per year) based on the consolidated book value of the machine, rather than the depreciation ($6,000 per year) based on the sales price.

of Depreciable Asset
Subsidiary Company S
Financial Statements
December 31, 19X1

WORKSHEET 6–5

| Eliminations & Adjustments | | Consolidated Income Statement | Minority Interest | Controlling Retained Earnings | Consolidated Balance Sheet | |
Dr.	Cr.					
					35,000	1
(3) 2,000					282,000	2
(4) 2,000	(3) 12,000				(135,000)	3
	(1) 20,000					4
	(2) 100,000					5
					(100,000)	6
				(10,000)		7
(2) 40,000			(10,000)			8
(2) 60,000			(15,000)			9
		(300,000)				10
		209,000				11
	(4) 2,000	44,000				12
(3) 10,000						13
(1) 20,000						14
134,000	134,000					15
		(47,000)				16
		5,000*	(5,000)			17
		42,000*		(42,000)		18
			(30,000)		(30,000)	19
				(52,000)	(52,000)	20
					0	21

Subsidiary Company S Income Distribution

	Internally generated net income...	$25,000
	Adjusted income	$25,000
	Minority share...........................	20%
	Minority interest........................	$ 5,000*

Parent Company P Income Distribution

Unrealized gain on sale of machine............................ (3) $10,000	Internally generated net income (including sale of machine).......	$30,000
	80% × Company S adjusted income of $25,000	20,000
	Gain realized through use of machine sold to subsidiary....(4)	**2,000**
	Controlling interest	$42,000*

Worksheet 6–6 (see page 322)

Intercompany Sale
Company P and
Worksheet for Consolidated
For Year Ended

(Credit balance amounts are in parentheses.)

		Trial Balance	
		Company P	Company S
1	Current Assets	85,000	60,000
2	**Machinery**	50,000	(a) **230,000**
3	**Accumulated Depreciation — Machinery**	(45,000)	(b) **(116,000)**
4			
5	Investment in Company S	139,200	
6			
7	Common Stock ($10 par), Co. P	(100,000)	
8	**Retained Earnings, Jan. 1, 19X2, Co. P**	**(60,000)**	
9	Common Stock ($10 par), Co. S		(50,000)
10	Retained Earnings, Jan. 1, 19X2, Co. S		(100,000)
11	Sales	(250,000)	(120,000)
12	**Cost of Goods Sold**	180,000	80,000
13	**Depreciation Expense**	20,000	(c) **16,000**
14	Subsidiary Income	(19,200)	
15		0	0
16	Combined Net Income		
17	To Minority Interest (see distribution schedule)		
18	Balance to Controlling Interest (see distribution schedule)		
19	Total Minority Interest		
20	Retained Earnings, Controlling Interest, Dec. 31, 19X2		
21			

Notes to Trial Balance:
(a) Includes machine purchased for $30,000 *from Company P* on January 1, 19X1.
(b) Includes $12,000 accumulated depreciation ($6,000 per year) on machine purchased from Company P on January 1, 19X1.
(c) Includes $6,000 depreciation on machine purchased from Company P on January 1, 19X1.

Eliminations and Adjustments:
(1) Eliminate the entry recording the parent's share of subsidiary net income for the current year.
(2) Eliminate 80% of the subsidiary equity balances against the investment account. There is no excess to be distributed.
(3) Eliminate the gain on the intercompany sale as it is reflected in beginning retained earnings on the parent's trial balance. This entry adjusts the machine account to $32,000 and restates

of Depreciable Asset
Subsidiary Company S
Financial Statements
December 31, 19X2

WORKSHEET 6–6

Eliminations & Adjustments Dr.	Eliminations & Adjustments Cr.	Consolidated Income Statement	Minority Interest	Controlling Retained Earnings	Consolidated Balance Sheet	
					145,000	1
(3) 2,000					282,000	2
(3) 2,000	(3) 12,000					3
(4) 2,000					(169,000)	4
	(1) 19,200					5
	(2) 120,000					6
					(100,000)	7
(3) 8,000				(52,000)		8
(2) 40,000			(10,000)			9
(2) 80,000			(20,000)			10
		(370,000)				11
		260,000				12
	(4) 2,000	34,000				13
(1) 19,200						14
153,200	153,200					15
		(76,000)				16
		4,800*	(4,800)			17
		71,200*		(71,200)		18
			(34,800)		(34,800)	19
				(123,200)	(123,200)	20
					0	21

accumulated depreciation as of the *beginning* of the year. Thus, the adjustment to accumulated depreciation includes a $12,000 increase in order to acknowledge the $12,000 balance on the sale date and a $2,000 reduction for the profit element of the 19X1 depreciation. Since the sale was made by the *parent,* Company P, the entire unrealized gain at the beginning of the year (now $8,000) is removed from the controlling retained earnings beginning balance. If the sale had been made by the subsidiary, the adjustment of beginning retained earnings would be split 80% to the controlling interest and 20% to the minority interest.

(4) Reduce the depreciation expense and accumulated depreciation accounts to reflect the depreciation based on the consolidated book value of the asset on the date of sale. This entry will bring the accumulated depreciation account to its correct consolidated year-end balance.

(continued)

Subsidiary Company S Income Distribution

	Internally generated net income...	$24,000
	Adjusted income	$24,000
	Minority share............................	20%
	Minority interest........................	$ 4,800*

Parent Company P Income Distribution

Internally generated net income...	$50,000
80% of Company S adjusted income of $24,000	19,200
Gain realized through use of machine sold to subsidiary....(4)	**2,000**
Controlling interest	$71,200*

Worksheet 6–7 (see page 323)   **Intercompany Sale of Depreciable Asset, Subsequent**
                                                      Company P and
                                              Worksheet for Consolidated
(Credit balance amounts are in parentheses.)   For Year Ended

		Trial Balance	
		Company P	Company S
1	Current Assets	85,000	74,000
2	Machinery	50,000	200,000
3	Accumulated Depreciation—Machinery	(45,000)	(104,000)
4	Investment in Company S	136,000	
5			
6	Common Stock ($10 par), Co. P	(100,000)	
7	**Retained Earnings, Jan. 1, 19X2, Co. P**	**(60,000)**	
8	Common Stock ($10 par), Co. S		(50,000)
9	Retained Earnings, Jan. 1, 19X2, Co. S		(100,000)
10	Sales	(250,000)	(120,000)
11	Cost of Goods Sold	180,000	80,000
12	**Depreciation Expense**	20,000	**16,000**
13	**Loss on Sale of Machine**		**4,000**
14	Subsidiary Income	(16,000)	
15	**Gain on Sale of Machine**		
16		0	0
17	Combined Net Income		
18	To Minority Interest (see distribution schedule)		
19	Balance to Controlling Interest (see distribution schedule)		
20	Total Minority Interest		
21	Retained Earnings, Controlling Interest, Dec. 31, 19X2		
22			

Eliminations and Adjustments:
(1) Eliminate the entry recording the parent's share of subsidiary net income for the current year.
(2) Eliminate 80% of the subsidiary equity balances against the investment account. There is no excess to be distributed.
(3) Eliminate the gain on the intercompany sale as it is reflected in the parent's beginning retained earnings account, adjust the current year's depreciation expense, and revise the recording of the sale of the equipment to an outside party to reflect the net book value of the asset to the consolidated firm.

Subsidiary Company S Income Distribution

Internally generated net income...	$20,000
Adjusted income	$20,000
Minority share............................	20%
Minority interest........................	$ 4,000*

Sale of Asset to an Outside Party
Subsidiary Company S
Financial Statements
December 31, 19X2

WORKSHEET 6–7

Eliminations & Adjustments		Consolidated Income Statement	Minority Interest	Controlling Retained Earnings	Consolidated Balance Sheet	
Dr.	Cr.					
					159,000	1
					250,000	2
					(149,000)	3
(1) 16,000						4
(2) 120,000						5
					(100,000)	6
(3) 8,000				(52,000)		7
(2) 40,000			(10,000)			8
(2) 80,000			(20,000)			9
		(370,000)				10
		260,000				11
	(3) 2,000	34,000				12
	(3) 4,000					13
(1) 16,000						14
	(3) 2,000	(2,000)				15
144,000	144,000					16
		(78,000)				17
		4,000*	(4,000)			18
		74,000*		(74,000)		19
			(34,000)		(34,000)	20
				(126,000)	(126,000)	21
					0	22

Parent Company P Income Distribution

Internally generated net income...	$50,000
80% × Company S adjusted income of $20,000	16,000
Gain realized on sale of machine ....(3)	**8,000**[a]
Controlling interest.....................	**$74,000***

[a]$10,000 original gain − $2,000 realized in 19X1

Worksheet 6–8 (see page 326)

(Credit balance amounts are in parentheses.)

		Trial Balance	
		Company P	Company S
1	Cash	35,000	20,400
2	**Note Receivable from Company S**	**10,000**	
3	**Interest Receivable**	**400**	
4	Property, Plant, and Equipment (net)	140,000	150,000
5	Investment in Company S	128,000	
6			
7	**Note Payable to Company P**		**(10,000)**
8	**Interest Payable**		**(400)**
9	Common Stock, Co. P	(100,000)	
10	Retained Earnings, Jan. 1, 19X1, Co. P	(200,000)	
11	Common Stock, Co. S		(50,000)
12	Retained Earnings, Jan. 1, 19X1, Co. S		(100,000)
13	Sales	(120,000)	(50,000)
14	**Interest Income**	**(400)**	
15	Subsidiary Income	(8,000)	
16	Cost of Goods Sold	75,000	20,000
17	Other Expenses	40,000	19,600
18	**Interest Expense**		**400**
19		0	0
20	Combined Net Income		
21	To Minority Interest (see distribution schedule)		
22	Balance to Controlling Interest (see distribution schedule)		
23	Total Minority Interest		
24	Retained Earnings, Controlling Interest, Dec. 31, 19X1		
25			

Eliminations and Adjustments:
(1) Eliminate the parent's share (80%) of subsidiary net income.
(2) Eliminate the controlling portion (80%) of the Company S January 1, 19X1 stockholders' equity against the investment in Company S account. No excess results.

Notes
Subsidiary Company S
Financial Statements
December 31, 19X1

WORKSHEET 6–8

Eliminations & Adjustments				Consolidated Income Statement	Minority Interest	Controlling Retained Earnings	Consolidated Balance Sheet	
Dr.		Cr.						
							55,400	1
		(3)	10,000					2
		(3)	400					3
							290,000	4
		(1)	8,000					5
		(2)	120,000					6
(3)	10,000							7
(3)	400							8
							(100,000)	9
						(200,000)		10
(2)	40,000				(10,000)			11
(2)	80,000				(20,000)			12
				(170,000)				13
(4)	400							14
(1)	8,000							15
				95,000				16
				59,600				17
		(4)	400					18
138,800		138,800						19
				(15,400)				20
				2,000*	(2,000)			21
				13,400*		(13,400)		22
					(32,000)		(32,000)	23
						(213,400)	(213,400)	24
							0	25

(3) Eliminate the intercompany note and accrued interest applicable to the note. This step removes the *internal note* from the consolidated balance sheet.

(4) Eliminate the intercompany interest expense and revenue. Since an equal amount of expense and revenue is eliminated, there is no change in the combined net income as a result of this step.

(continued)

Subsidiary Company S Income Distribution

Internally generated net income...	$10,000
Adjusted income	$10,000
Minority share............................	20%
Minority interest........................	$ 2,000*

Parent Company P Income Distribution

Internally generated net income...	$ 5,400
80% × Company S adjusted income of $10,000....................	8,000
Controlling interest.....................	$13,400*

Worksheet 6–9 (see page 333)

(Credit balance amounts are in parentheses.)

		Financial Statements	
		Company P	Company S
1	**Income Statement**		
2	Sales	(600,000)	(530,000)
3	Cost of goods sold	400,000	280,000
4			
5	Depreciation expense	40,000	50,000
6	Other expenses	60,000	70,000
7	Subsidiary income	(104,000)	
8	Net income	(204,000)	(130,000)
9	Minority interest (see distribution schedule)		
10	Controlling interest (see distribution schedule)		
11			
12	**Retained Earnings Statement**		
13	Retained earnings, Jan. 1, 19X2, Co. P	(600,000)	
14			
15			
16	Retained earnings, Jan. 1, 19X2, Co. S		(400,000)
17			
18	Net income (carrydown)	(204,000)	(130,000)
19	Dividends declared		20,000
20	Retained earnings, Dec. 31, 19X2	(804,000)	(510,000)
21	Minority interest, retained earnings, Dec. 31, 19X2		
22	Controlling interest, retained earnings, Dec. 31, 19X2		
23			
24	**Balance Sheet**		
25	Inventory	300,000	250,000
26	Accounts receivable	120,000	180,000
27	Plant assets	236,000	400,000
28	Accumulated depreciation	(100,000)	(60,000)
29			
30	Investment in Company S	628,000	
31			
32			
33	Goodwill		
34	Current liabilities	(80,000)	(60,000)
35	Common stock ($5 par), Co. S		(200,000)
36	Common stock ($10 par), Co. P	(300,000)	
37	Retained earnings (carrydown)	(804,000)	(510,000)
38	Retained earnings, controlling interest, Dec. 31, 19X2		
39	Retained earnings, minority interest, Dec. 31, 19X2		
40	Total minority interest		
41	Total	0	0

WORSHEET 6-9

Worksheet Alternative
Subsidiary Company S
Financial Statements
December 31, 19X2

Eliminations & Adjustments Dr.		Eliminations & Adjustments Cr.		Minority Interest	Consolidated	
						1
(6)	150,000				(980,000)	2
(8)	10,000	(6)	150,000			3
		(5)	8,000		532,000	4
		(10)	1,000		89,000	5
(4)	1,500				131,500	6
(1)	104,000					7
					(227,500)	8
				(25,600)*		9
					(201,900)*	10
						11
						12
(4)	1,500					13
(5)	6,400					14
(9)	4,500				(587,600)	15
(2)	320,000					16
(5)	1,600			(78,400)		17
				(25,600)	(201,900)	18
		(1)	16,000	4,000		19
						20
				(100,000)		21
					(789,500)	22
						23
						24
		(8)	10,000		540,000	25
		(7)	20,000		280,000	26
		(9)	5,000		631,000	27
(9)	500					28
(10)	1,000				(158,500)	20
		(1)	88,000			30
		(2)	480,000			31
		(3)	60,000			32
(3)	60,000	(4)	3,000		57,000	33
(7)	20,000				(120,000)	34
(2)	160,000			(40,000)		35
					(300,000)	36
						37
					(789,500)	38
				(100,000)		39
					(140,000)	40
	841,000		841,000	(140,000)	0	41

(continued)

Eliminations and Adjustments:

(1) Eliminate the current year entries recording the parent's share (80%) of subsidiary net income and the dividends declared.

(2) Eliminate the pro rata portion of the subsidiary equity balances owned by the parent (80%) against the balance of the investment account.

(3) Distribute the excess to the goodwill account according to the determination and distribution of excess schedule.

(4) Amortize the goodwill at $1,500 per year for the past year and current year.

(5) Eliminate the intercompany profit in the beginning inventory, 20% (.25 ÷ 1.25) multiplied by $40,000. Since it was a subsidiary sale, the profit is shared 20% by the minority interest.

(6) Eliminate the intercompany sales made during 19X2.

(7) Eliminate the intercompany trade balances.

(8) Eliminate the intercompany profit (20%) applicable to the $50,000 of intercompany goods in the ending inventory.

(9) Eliminate the intercompany gain remaining on January 1, 19X2, applicable to the sale of the machine by Company P ($5,000 original gain less one-half year's gain of $500).

(10) Reduce the depreciation expense and accumulated depreciation accounts ($1,000 for the current year) in order to reflect depreciation based on the original cost.

Subsidiary Company S Income Distribution

Unrealized profit in ending inventory (20% × $50,000)...... (8)	$10,000	Internally generated net income..		$130,000
		Realized profit in beginning inventory (20% × $40,000)...(5)		8,000
		Adjusted income		$128,000
		Minority share...........................		20%
		Minority interest........................		$ 25,600*

Parent Company P Income Distribution

Goodwill amortization............... (4)	$ 1,500	Internally generated net income..		$100,000
		Gain realized on sale of machine....................... (10)		1,000
		80% × Company S adjusted income of $128,000................		102,400
		Controlling interest....................		$201,900*

CHAPTER 7

INTERCOMPANY TRANSACTIONS: BONDS AND LEASES

This chapter focuses on intercompany transactions that create a long-term debtor-creditor relationship between the members of a consolidated group. First, intercompany bond holdings will be analyzed. Here, one member of the consolidated group, usually the subsidiary, has issued bonds which appear on its balance sheet as long-term liabilities. Another member may purchase the bonds and list them on its balance sheet as an investment. However, when consolidated statements are prepared, the intercompany purchase, in effect, should be viewed as a retirement of the bonds. Following the bond coverage will be the consideration of intercompany leasing of assets. In this case, one member of the consolidated group purchases the asset and leases it to another member. While the leasing transaction is recorded as such on the separate books of the affiliates, the lease has no substance from a consolidated viewpoint. Only a lease which involves a nonaffiliated firm may survive to the consolidated statements.

INTERCOMPANY INVESTMENT IN BONDS

To secure long-term funds, one member of a consolidated group may sell its bonds directly to another member of the group. Clearly, such a transaction results in intercompany debt which must be eliminated from the consolidated statements. On the worksheet, the investment in bonds recorded by one firm must be eliminated against the bonds payable of the other. In addition, the applicable interest expense recorded by one affiliate must be eliminated against the applicable interest revenue recorded by the other affiliate. Interest accruals recorded on the books of the separate firms also must be eliminated.

There are situations where one affiliate (usually the subsidiary) has outstanding bonds which have been purchased by parties that are not members of the affiliated group, and a decision is made by another affiliate (usually the parent) to obtain these bonds. The simplest way to accomplish the removal of subsidiary bonds from outsiders is for the parent to advance funds to the subsidiary so that the subsidiary may retire the bonds. From an accounting standpoint, this transaction is easy to record. The former debt is retired and a new, long-term intercompany debt originates. The only procedures required on future consolidated worksheets involve the elimination of the resulting intercompany debt.

A more complicated method is to have the parent purchase the subsidiary bonds from the outside parties and to hold them as an investment. This method creates an intercompany investment in bonds, where each affiliate continues to accrue and record interest on the bonds. While the intercompany bonds are treated as a liability on one set of books and as an investment on the other set, from a consolidated viewpoint the bonds have been retired, and the debt to outside parties has been liquidated. The purchase of intercompany bonds has the following ramifications when consolidating:

1. Consolidated statements will show *an extraordinary gain or loss* on the retirement of the bonds in the period of their purchase by the affiliated firm whenever the price paid by the affiliate does not agree with the book value of the bonds on the issuer's records.
2. Consolidated statements must not include the intercompany investment, the bond liability, interest accruals, or interest expense and revenue applicable to the intercompany bonds.

BONDS ORIGINALLY ISSUED AT FACE VALUE

The complexity of the elimination procedures for intercompany bonds depends on whether a discount or premium exists as a result of the original issuance to outside parties. When bonds are sold at face value by a subsidiary to outside parties, contract (nominal) interest agrees with the effective, or market, interest, and no amortizations of issuance premiums or discounts need to be recorded. However, subsequent to the issuance, the market rate of interest most likely will deviate from the contract rate. Thus, while there is no original issuance premium or discount, there will be what could be termed an *investment premium or discount* resulting from the intercompany purchase of the bonds.

To illustrate the procedures required for intercompany bonds originally issued at face value, assume that a subsidiary, Company S, issued 8%, 5-year bonds at face value of $100,000 to outside parties on January 1, 19X1. Interest is paid on January 1 for the preceding year. On January 2, 19X3, the parent, Company P, purchased the bonds from the outside parties for $103,600.

Company S will continue to list the $100,000 bonded debt and to record interest expense of $8,000 during 19X3, 19X4, and 19X5. However, Company P will record a bond investment of $103,600 and will amortize $1,200 per year by reducing the investment account and adjusting interest revenue. (Though the interest method of amortization is preferable, the straight-line method is permitted if results are not materially different. This initial example and most others in this chapter use the straight-line method in order to simplify analysis. A summary example is used to demonstrate the interest method of amortization.)

Although the investment and liability accounts continue to exist on the separate books of the affiliated firms, retirement has occurred from a consolidated viewpoint. Debt with a book value of $100,000 was retired by a payment of $103,600, and there is a $3,600 extraordinary loss on retirement. If a consolidated worksheet is prepared on the day the bonds are purchased, Bonds Payable would be eliminated against Investment in Company S Bonds, and an extraordinary loss on retirement would be reported on the consolidated income statement. The following abbreviated worksheet displays the procedures used to retire the bonds as part of the elimination process:

	Partial Trial Balance		Eliminations & Adjustments	
	Company P	Company S	Dr.	Cr.
Investment in Company S Bonds	103,600			**103,600**
Bonds Payable		(100,000)	**100,000**	
Loss on Bond Retirement			**3,600**	

This partial worksheet is only hypothetical, since, in reality, there will be no consolidated worksheet prepared until December 31, 19X3, the end of the period. During 19X3, Companies P and S will record the transactions for interest as follows:

Company P		
Interest Receivable......................	8,000	
Investment in Company S Bonds..		1,200
Interest Income.........................		6,800
To record interest revenue net of $1,200 per year premium amortization.		

Company S		
Interest Expense	8,000	
Interest Payable........................		8,000
To record interest expense.		

On the December 31, 19X3 consolidated worksheet shown in Worksheet 7–1 on pages 426–429, these entries will be reflected in the trial balances. Note that Investment in Company S Bonds reflects the premium amortization, since the balance is $102,400 ($103,600 original cost − $1,200 amortization). In this worksheet, it is assumed that Investment in Company S

Stock reflects a 90% interest purchased at a price equal to the book value of the underlying equity and that the simple equity method is used by Company P to record the investment in stock.

Steps (1) and (2) eliminate the intercompany stock investment. Step (3) eliminates the intercompany bonds at their year-end balances and the intercompany interest expense and revenue recorded during the year. The loss at the start of the year is the sum of the remaining loss reflected in the year-end balances of the intercompany bonds and that portion of the loss that was amortized by the firms during the year. The loss at the start of 19X3 is verified in the explanation to step (3). Step (4) eliminates intercompany accrued interest.

As a result of the elimination steps, the consolidated income statement will include the extraordinary retirement loss but will exclude intercompany interest payments. The consolidated balance sheet will not list the intercompany bonds payable or investment in bonds accounts.

The only remaining problem is the distribution of combined net income to the controlling and minority interests. The income distribution schedule shows Company S absorbing all of the retirement loss. It is most common to view the purchasing affiliate as a mere agent of the issuing affiliate. Therefore, it is the issuer, not the purchaser, that must bear the entire gain or loss on retirement. Even though the debt is retired from a consolidated viewpoint, it still exists internally. Company P has a right to collect the interest as part of its share of Company S's operations. Based on the value of the debt on January 2, 19X3, the interest expense/revenue is $6,800. The interest cost of $8,000 recorded by Company S must be corrected to reflect the internal interest expense of $6,800. The income distribution schedule increases the operating income of Company S to reflect the adjustment ($1,200) to interest expense. It should be noted that the retirement loss borne by Company S will offset entirely the adjustments to interest expense by the time the bonds mature. If the parent, Company P, had issued the bonds to outside parties and if the subsidiary, Company S, later had purchased them, the only change would be that the income distribution schedule of Company P would absorb the loss on retirement and the interest adjustment.

The worksheet procedures that would be needed at the end of 19X4 are shown in Worksheet 7–2 on pages 430–433. The interest revenue and expense have been recorded on the books of the separate firms. The investment in Company S bonds account on the parent's books reflects its book value at the end of 19X4. Step (3) eliminates the intercompany bonds at their year-end balances and the intercompany interest expense and revenue. Step (4) eliminates intercompany interest accruals.

The 19X4 consolidated income statement will not include intercompany interest. The income distribution schedules for Worksheet 7–2 reflect the fact that the debt still existed internally during the period. However, the interest expense recorded by Company S is reduced to reflect the interest cost based on the January 2, 19X3 purchase price.

If Company S was the purchaser and Company P the issuer of the bonds, Worksheet 7–2 would differ as follows:

1. The January 1, 19X4 retained earnings adjustment would be absorbed completely by the controlling Retained Earnings, since the parent company would be the issuer absorbing the loss.
2. The income distribution schedule of the parent would contain the interest adjustment.

BONDS NOT ORIGINALLY ISSUED AT FACE VALUE

The principles of eliminating intercompany investments in bonds are not altered by the existence of a premium or discount stemming from original issuance. The numerical calculations just become more complex. To illustrate, assume that Company S issued $100,000 of 5-year, 8% bonds on January 1, 19X1. The market interest rate approximated 9% and, as a result, the bonds sold at a discount of $3,890. Interest is paid each December 31. On each interest payment date, the discount is amortized $778 ($3,890 ÷ 5 years) by decreasing the discount and by increasing interest expense. On December 31, 19X3, the balance of the discount is $1,556 [$3,890 − (3 × $778 annual amortization)].

The parent, Company P, purchased the bonds for $103,600 on December 31, 19X3, after interest had been paid. The parent will amortize $1,800 of the investment each subsequent December 31, reducing the parent's interest income to $6,200 ($8,000 cash–$1,800 amortization) for 19X4 and 19X5.

The following abbreviated December 31, 19X3 (date of purchase) worksheet lists the investment in Company S bonds account, the bonds payable account, and the remaining issuance discount. Eliminating the $103,600 price paid for the bonds by Company P against the book value of $98,444 ($100,000 − $1,556) creates a retirement loss of $5,156 that is carried to combined net income.

	Partial Trial Balance		Eliminations & Adjustments	
	Company P	Company S	Dr.	Cr.
Investment in Company S Bonds	103,600			**103,600**
Bonds Payable, 8%		(100,000)	**100,000**	
Discount on Bonds Payable		1,556		**1,556**
Loss on Bond Retirement			**5,156**	
Interest Expense		8,778*		

*$8,000 cash + $778 straight-line amortization

Interest expense on the books of Company S is extended to the consolidated income statement, since this interest was incurred as a result of transactions with outside parties. There would be no interest adjustment for 19X3, since the bonds were not purchased by the parent until December 31, 19X3. The income distribution schedules accompanying the worksheet would assess the retirement loss against the issuer, Company S.

The implications of these intercompany bonds on the 19X4 consolidated worksheet are reflected in Worksheet 7–3 on pages 434–437. Assume that Company P acquired a 90% interest in the common stock of Company S at a price equal to the book value of the underlying equity. The simple equity method is used by the parent to record the investment in the stock of Company S. The trial balances include the following items:

1. The Investment in Company S Bonds at its amortized December 31, 19X4 balance of $101,800 ($103,600 − $1,800 amortization),
2. Interest revenue (adjusted for amortization) of $6,200 on the books of Company P,
3. The discount on bonds account at its amortized December 31, 19X4 balance of $778, and
4. Interest expense (adjusted for discount amortization) of $8,778 ($8,000 cash + $778 amortization) on the books of Company S.

Step (3) eliminates the investment in bonds against the bonds payable and the applicable remaining discount. Step (3) also eliminates interest expense and revenue. Be sure to understand the calculation of the adjustment to beginning retained earnings which is explained in the step (3) information.

Again, the consolidated income statement does not include intercompany interest. However, the Company S income distribution schedule does reflect the adjustment of Company S's interest expense. The original $8,778 interest expense has been replaced by a $6,200 expense, based on the purchase price paid by Company P. The smaller interest expense compensates the subsidiary for the retirement loss absorbed in a previous period.

INTEREST METHOD OF AMORTIZATION

The procedures used to eliminate intercompany bonds are not altered by the interest method of amortization; only the dollar values change. To illustrate the calculations, assume that Company S issued $100,000 of 5-year, 8% bonds on January 1, 19X1. The market interest rate on that date was 9%, so that the bonds sold at a discount of $3,890. Interest on the bonds is paid each December 31. The discount amortization for the term of the bonds follows:

Year	Balance January 1	Effective Interest	Nominal Interest	Discount Amortization
1	$96,110	$8,650 (.09 × $96,110)	$8,000	$ 650
2	96,760 ($96,110 + $650)	8,708 (.09 × $96,760)	8,000	708
3	97,468 ($96,760 + $708)	8,772 (.09 × $97,468)	8,000	772
4	98,240 ($97,468 + $772)	8,842 (.09 × $98,240)	8,000	842
5	99,082 ($98,240 + $842)	8,918* (.09 × $99,082)	8,000	918
*Includes $1 rounding error				$3,890

On December 31, 19X3, after interest had been paid, the bonds were purchased by parent Company P at a price to yield 6%. Based on present value computations, $103,667 was paid for the bonds. The premium on the bonds would be amortized by Company P as follows:

Year	Investment Balance, January 1	Effective Interest	Nominal Interest	Premium Amortization
4	$103,667	$6,220 (.06 × $103,667)	$8,000	$1,780
5	101,887 ($103,667 − $1,780)	6,113 (.06 × $101,887)	8,000	1,887
				$3,667

The abbreviated December 31, 19X3 (date of purchase) worksheet at the top of the following page lists the investment in Company S bonds account, the bonds payable account, and the remaining issuance discount. Eliminating the $103,667 price paid by Company P against the book value of $98,240 ($100,00 − $1,760) creates a retirement loss of $5,427 that is carried to combined net income.

The differences in the 19X4 consolidated worksheet caused by the interest method of amortization are shown in Worksheet 7–4 on pages 438–441. Note particularly the change in the Company S income distribution schedule. The original 9% interest, totaling $8,842, has been replaced by the $6,220 of interest calculated using the 6% rate.

	Partial Trial Balance		Eliminations & Adjustments	
	Company P	Company S	Dr.	Cr.
Investment in Company S Bonds	103,667			**103,667**
Bonds Payable, 8%		(100,000)	**100,000**	
Discount on Bonds Payable		1,760		**1,760**
Loss on Bond Retirement			**5,427**	
Interest Expense		8,772*		

*See preceding discount amortization schedule for issuer.

INTERCOMPANY LEASES

Intercompany leases have become one of the most frequently encountered types of transactions between affiliated firms. It is particularly common for parent firms with substantial financial resources to acquire major assets and to lease the assets to their subsidiaries. This action may occur because the financially stronger parent may be able to both purchase and finance assets on more favorable terms. Also, the parent company may desire close control over plant assets and may prefer centralized ownership and management of assets. Leasing becomes a mechanism through which the parent can convey the use of centrally-owned assets to subsidiaries. Some firms achieve centralized asset management by forming separate leasing subsidiaries whose major function is to lease assets to affiliated firms. When such subsidiaries exist, their accounts are consolidated automatically with those of the parent.[1]

OPERATING LEASES

Consolidation procedures for intercompany leases depend on the original recording of the lease by the separate firms. When an operating lease exists, the lessor has recorded the purchase of the asset and depreciates the asset. The lessor records rent revenue, while the lessee records rent expense. In such cases, it is necessary to eliminate in the consolidation process the intercompany rent expense/revenue and any related rent receivable/payable. The lessor's asset and related accumulated depreciation should be reclassified as a normal productive asset rather than as property under an operating lease. As an example, assume that the parent, Company P, has both productive equipment used in its own operations and equipment that is under operating lease to a subsidiary, Company S. The following partial worksheet may be used to analyze required consolidation procedures:

[1]*Statement of Financial Accounting Standards, No. 13,* "Accounting for Leases" (Stamford: Financial Accounting Standards Board, 1976), par. 31.

	Partial Trial Balance		Eliminations & Adjustments	
	Company P	Company S	Dr.	Cr.
Equipment	800,000		(3) 100,000	
Accumulated Depreciation — Equipment	(300,000)			(3) 40,000
Equipment Under Operating Lease	100,000			(3) 100,000
Accumulated Depreciation — Equipment Under Operating Lease	(40,000)		(3) 40,000	
Rent Receivable	1,200			(2) 1,200
Rent Payable		(1,200)	(2) 1,200	
Rental Income	(14,400)		(1) 14,400	
Rent Expense		14,400		(1) 14,400
Depreciation Expense	50,000			

Eliminations and Adjustments:
(1)   Eliminate intercompany rent expense and revenue of $1,200 per month.
(2)   Eliminate one month's accrued rent.
(3)   Reclassify the asset under the intercompany operating lease and its related accumulated depreciation as a normal productive asset.

No adjustments are made in the income distribution schedules as a result of operating leases. The eliminations made on the worksheet do not change the amount of income or the distribution of income between the minority and controlling interests.

CAPITALIZABLE LEASES

Consolidation procedures become more complicated when the lease is recorded as a capital lease by the lessee and as a direct-financing or sales-type lease by the lessor. The lessee records an asset and recognizes intercompany long-term debt. Generally, the criteria for determining when a lease requires such accounting treatment are the same for affiliated firms as for independent firms. However, when the terms of the lease are significantly affected by the fact that the lessee and lessor are affiliates, the usual criteria for classification of leases do not apply. Lease terms could be considered "significantly affected" when they could not reasonably be expected to occur between independent firms.[2] For example, a parent might lease to its subsidiary at a rent far below the market rate, or a parent might rent a highly specialized machine to its subsidiary on a month-to-month basis. Typically, such specialized machinery would be leased only on a long-term lease promising a full recovery of cost to the lessor, since there would be no use for the machine by other lessees if it were returned to the lessor. The month-to-month lease is possible only because the parent's control of the

---
[2]Ibid., par. 29.

subsidiary assures a continued flow of rent payments. When, in the accountant's judgment, the terms of the lease are affected significantly by the parent-subsidiary relationship, the normal criteria are not used, and the transaction is recorded so as to reflect its true economic substance.[3] Usually in these circumstances, the lessee is viewed as having purchased the asset using funds borrowed from the lessor.

Consolidation Procedures for Direct-Financing Leases.

A direct-financing lease is viewed as a unique type of asset transfer by the lessor, who accepts a long-term receivable from the lessee as consideration for the asset received by the lessee. There is no profit or loss to the lessor on the transfer; only future investment revenue as payments become due.

Prior to studying consolidated worksheet procedures, the entries made by the affiliated lessee and lessor will be analyzed. In its simplest form, a direct-financing lease is recorded by the lessee as an asset, and debt is recorded to recognize the lease obligation. The lessor records the lease as a receivable from the lessee. If all payments to be received by the lessor will come from or are guaranteed by the original lessee, the present value of the net receivable recorded by the lessor will equal the present value of the payable recorded by the lessee, and the interest rates used to amortize the debt will be equal.

To illustrate, assume that Company S is an 80%-owned subsidiary of Company P. On January 1, 19X1, Company P purchased a machine for $5,851 and leased it to Company S. The terms of the direct-financing lease provide for rental payments of $2,000 per year at the beginning of each period and allow the lessee to exercise an option to purchase the machine for $1,000 at the end of 19X3. The $1,000 purchase option is considered a bargain purchase option that will be exercised. The implicit interest rate (which equates all payments, including the bargain purchase option, to the lessor's purchase cost) is 16%. The lessee will depreciate the capitalized cost of the machine over 5 years, using the straight-line method. The lessee may use a 5-year life, despite the 3-year lease term, because it is assumed that the bargain purchase option will be exercised and that the asset will be used for 5 years.

The amortization of the debt at the implicit 16% interest rate is as follows:

Date	Payment	Interest at 16% on Previous Balance	Reduction of Principal	Principal Balance
Jan. 1, 19X1	$2,000	—	$2,000	$3,851*
Jan. 1, 19X2	2,000	$ 616	1,384	2,467
Jan. 1, 19X3	2,000	395	1,605	862
Dec. 31, 19X3	1,000	138	862	—
Total	$7,000	$1,149	$5,851	

*Purchase price of $5,851 − $2,000 initial payment

---

[3]*Ibid.*

The journal entries for the separate firms would be as follows for the first two years:

Date	Company S (Lessee)			Company P (Lessor)		
19X1						
Jan. 1	Assets Under Capital Lease	5,851		Minimum Lease Payments		
	Obligations Under Capital			Receivable........................	5,000	
	Lease.............................		3,851	Cash	2,000	
	Cash.................................		2,000	Unearned Interest Income......		1,149
				Accounts Payable (for asset)...		5,851
Dec. 31	Interest Expense......................	616		Unearned Interest Income.........	616	
	Interest Payable....................		616	Interest Income...................		616
	Depreciation Expense					
	(1/5 × $5,851)	1,170				
	Accumulated					
	Depreciation—Assets					
	Under Capital Lease		1,170			
19X2						
Jan. 1	Interest Payable......................	616		Cash	2,000	
	Obligations Under Capital			Minimum Lease Payments		
	Lease.............................	1,384		Receivable......................		2,000
	Cash.................................		2,000			
Dec. 31	Interest Expense......................	395		Unearned Interest Income.........	395	
	Interest Payable....................		395	Interest Income...................		395
	Depreciation Expense	1,170				
	Accumulated					
	Depreciation—Assets					
	Under Capital Lease		1,170			

At the end of each period, consolidation procedures would be needed to eliminate the intercompany transactions. In substance, there appears on the separate records of the affiliates an intercompany transfer of a plant asset with resulting intercompany debt. The intercompany debt, related interest expense/revenue, and interest accruals must be eliminated. Also, it is necessary to reclassify the assets under capital leases as productive assets owned by the consolidated group. The adjusted partial worksheets shown on pages 399 and 400 illustrate consolidation procedures at the end of 19X1 and 19X2.

A review of the worksheet eliminations and adjustments reveals that combined net income is not changed because equal amounts of interest expense and revenue were eliminated. Therefore, *no adjustments are required in the income distribution schedules.*

Some capital leases will designate a portion of the annual rent as being applicable to executory costs, such as property taxes or maintenance, incurred by the lessor. Such payments for executory costs are not included in the obligation of the lessee or the minimum lease payments receivable recorded by the lessor. Instead, such payments are recorded as rent expense and revenue in each period. In the consolidation process, that portion of rent applicable to executory costs is eliminated like any other charge for intercompany services.

Partial Worksheet
For Year Ended December 31, 19X1

	Trial Balance		Eliminations & Adjustments			
	Company P	Company S	Dr.		Cr.	
Assets Under Capital Lease		5,851			(3)	5,851
Accumulated Depreciation— Assets Under Capital Lease		(1,170)	(3)	1,170		
Property, Plant, and Equipment	200,000	120,000	(3)	5,851		
Accumulated Depreciation— Property, Plant, and Equipment	(80,000)	(50,000)			(3)	1,170
Obligations Under Capital Lease		(3,851)	(2)	3,851		
Interest Payable		(616)	(2)	616		
Minimum Lease Payments Receivable	5,000				(2)	5,000
Unearned Interest Income	(533)		(2)	533		
Interest Expense		616			(1)	616
Interest Income	(616)		(1)	616		

Eliminations and Adjustments:
(1) Eliminate intercompany interest expense/revenue of $616.
(2) Eliminate the intercompany debt recorded by the lessee (obligation under capital lease plus accrued interest payable) against the net intercompany receivable of the lessor (minimum lease payments receivable less unearned interest income).
(3) Reclassify the asset under capital lease and its related accumulated depreciation as a productive asset owned by the consolidated firm.

The lessor may have an *unguaranteed residual value* in a lease at the end of the lease term. As a result, some of the expected cash flow from a leased asset may come from parties other than the original lessee. The original lessee, therefore, is contractually bound to provide only part of the total cash flow expected by the lessor. The lessee records the asset and the resulting obligation under the capital lease at the present value of the minimum lease payments to be made by the lessee. The present value is computed using the lessee's incremental borrowing rate unless the lessor's implicit interest rate in the lease is known or is reasonably estimable and is lower, in which case the lessor's implicit rate is used.[4] Usually, the lessor's implicit rate should be available or estimable since the lessee and the lessor are members of the same consolidated group. Therefore, the lessor's implicit rate will be used for leases between affiliates of the consolidated group. Leases recorded using any other rate would be adjusted prior to consolidating.

_____

[4]When the present value of the minimum lease payments using the incremental borrowing rate exceeds the market value of the asset, the asset and the obligation are recorded at the market value of the asset. The interest rate that equates the present value of the payments to the market value of the asset is used then to amortize the debt.

Partial Worksheet
For Year Ended December 31, 19X2

| | Trial Balance | | Eliminations & Adjustments | |
	Company P	Company S	Dr.	Cr.
Assets Under Capital Lease		5,851		(3) 5,851
Accumulated Depreciation— Assets Under Capital Lease		(2,340)	(3) 2,340	
Property, Plant, and Equipment	200,000	120,000	(3) 5,851	
Accumulated Depreciation— Property, Plant, and Equipment	(100,000)	(60,000)		(3) 2,340
Obligations Under Capital Lease		(2,467)	(2) 2,467	
Interest Payable		(395)	(2) 395	
Minimum Lease Payments Receivable	3,000			(2) 3,000
Unearned Interest Income	(138)		(2) 138	
Interest Expense		395		(1) 395
Interest Income	(395)		(1) 395	

Eliminations and Adjustments:
(1)   Eliminate intercompany interest expense/revenue of $395.
(2)   Eliminate intercompany debt and net receivable.
(3)   Reclassify the asset under capital lease and its related accumulated depreciation as a productive asset owned by the consolidated firm.

The lessor records the gross investment in the lease, which is the sum of the minimum lease payments receivable and the unguaranteed residual value. Unearned interest income is recorded as a contra account at an amount that reduces the gross investment to the market value of the asset at the inception of the lease. Unearned interest is amortized using the implicit rate of the lessor. The implicit rate of the lessor thus equates the present value of all payments expected, including the unguaranteed residual value, to the market value of the asset.

The recording methods used by the lessee and lessor for leases with an unguaranteed residual value present a complication to the consolidation process. The amount of the asset under the capital lease recorded by the lessee will be less than the asset's market value, since the present value of the lease payments recorded by the lessee will not include the asset's unguaranteed residual value. To understand this complication, the previous example may be used with one change. Instead of the $1,000 bargain purchase option that was included in the set of minimum lease payments, assume that there is a $1,000 unguaranteed residual value. Since the residual value is not guaranteed, it is not part of the minimum lease payments. The revised facts are as follows:

1. Cost of asset to lessor: $5,851
2. Lease terms: Three annual payments of $2,000 due at the start of each year. Unguaranteed residual value of $1,000 to lessor at the end of 19X3.
3. Lessor implicit rate: 16% equates the three $2,000 payments plus the unguaranteed residual value to $5,851.
4. Lessee interest rate: 16% (lessor implicit rate) which, when applied to only the lease payments, results in a present value of $5,210.
5. Depreciation: Straight-line over the 3-year lease term, since the contractual use of the asset is for three years.
6. Amortization tables:

Lessor (16%)

Date	Payment	Interest at 16% on Previous Balance	Reduction of Principal	Principal Balance
Jan. 1, 19X1	$2,000	—	$2,000	$3,851*
Jan. 1, 19X2	2,000	$ 616	1,384	2,467
Jan. 1, 19X3	2,000	395	1,605	862
Dec. 31, 19X3	1,000	138	862	—
Total	$7,000	$1,149	$5,851	

*Purchase price of $5,851 − $2,000 initial payment

Lessee (16%)

Date	Payment	Interest at 16% on Previous Balance	Reduction of Principal	Principal Balance
Jan. 1, 19X1	$2,000	—	$2,000	$3,210**
Jan. 1, 19X2	2,000	$514	1,486	1,724
Jan. 1, 19X3	2,000	276	1,724	—
Total	$6,000	$790	$5,210	

**Present value of $5,210 − $2,000 initial payment

The journal entries for the separate firms would be as follows for the first two years:

Date	Company S (Lessee)			Company P (Lessor)		
19X1						
Jan. 1	Assets Under Capital Lease	5,210		Minimum Lease Payments		
	Cash		2,000	Receivable	4,000	
	Obligations under			Unguaranteed Residual Value	1,000	
	Capital Lease		3,210	Cash	2,000	
				Unearned Interest Income		1,149
				Accounts Payable (for asset)		5,851
Dec. 31	Interest Expense (at 16%)	514		Unearned Interest Income	616	
	Interest Payable		514	Interest Income (at 16%)		616
	Depreciation Expense					
	(1/3 × $5,210)	1,737				
	Accumulated					
	Depreciation—Assets					
	Under Capital Lease		1,737			

Date	Company S (Lessee)			Company P (Lessor)		
19X2						
Jan. 1	Obligations Under			Cash	2,000	
	Capital Lease.....................	1,486		Minimum Lease Payments		
	Interest Payable......................	514		Receivable.......................		2,000
	Cash.................................		2,000			
Dec. 31	Interest Expense (at 16%)	276		Unearned Interest Income........	395	
	Interest Payable...................		276	Interest Income (at 16%)		395
	Depreciation Expense	1,737				
	Accumulated					
	Depreciation—Assets					
	Under Capital Lease		1,737			

A comparison of the lessor's and lessee's amortization tables shows the following difference between the lessee's interest expense and the lessor's interest income each period:

Year Ending December 31	16% Lessor Implicit Interest	16% Lessee Interest	Difference
19X1	$ 616	$514	$102
19X2	395	276	119
19X3	138	—	138
Total	$1,149	$790	$359

The difference is the interest on the unguaranteed residual value, which is recorded only by the lessor. This can be demonstrated as follows:

Date	16% Implicit Interest	Difference in Principal Balances
January 1, 19X1		$ 641*
December 31, 19X1	$102	743
December 31, 19X2	119	862
December 31, 19X3	138	1,000
Total	$359	

*$5,851 − $5,210

In the consolidation process, the intercompany debt and all interest applicable to the lease are eliminated. Even the interest income recorded on the unguaranteed residual value is eliminated, since it is a ramification of a lease which, from a consolidated viewpoint, does not exist. The asset recorded by the lessee and the unguaranteed residual value recorded by the lessor are eliminated and replaced by a productive asset recorded by the consolidated firm.

Worksheet 7–5, pages 442–445, contains the detailed steps for the elimination of the intercompany lease at the end of 19X1. In this worksheet, it is assumed that the interest in the 80%-owned subsidiary was purchased at its book value. Steps (1) and (2) eliminate the investment. Step (3) eliminates the $616 of interest income against the $514 of interest expense. The

$102 disparity reflects the interest applicable to the unguaranteed residual value and is returned to unearned interest income. Step (4) eliminates the intercompany debt applicable to the lease. The $359 disparity reflects the interest applicable to the unguaranteed residual value over the life of the lease. This amount is used to reduce the unguaranteed residual value to its original present value of $641. The $641, combined with the $5,210 asset under capital lease, is eliminated and replaced by an owned asset and recorded at the $5,851 original cost to the consolidated firm. Step (5) adjusts the depreciation to reflect the cost and the residual value of the asset to the consolidated firm. The accumulated depreciation also is reclassified as that applicable to an owned asset.

In Worksheet 7–6 on pages 446–449, the consolidation procedures for the second year of the lease term are illustrated.

Consolidation Procedures for Sales-Type Leases.

Under a sales-type lease, a lessor records a sales profit or loss at the inception of the lease. The sales profit or loss is the difference between the fair market value of the asset at the inception of the lease and the cost of the asset to the lessor. Consolidation procedures do not allow recognition of this profit or loss at the inception of the lease. Instead, the profit or loss is deferred and then amortized over the lessee's period of usage. This period will be the lease term unless there is a bargain purchase or bargain renewal option, in which case the asset's useful life would be used.

To illustrate, assume that in the previous example the asset leased to Company S had a cost to Company P of $4,951. Company P would have recorded the following entry at the inception of the sales-type lease:

Minimum Lease Payments Receivable	4,000	
Unguaranteed Residual Value	1,000	
Cash	2,000	
Unearned Interest Income		1,149
Asset (cost of asset leased)		4,951
Sales Profit on Leases		900

This entry differs from that of the previous example only to the extent of recording the gain and transferring an existing asset. None of the lessor's subsequent entries recording the earning of interest and the payment of the receivable would change. The lessee's entries are unaffected by the existence of the sales profit.

Consolidation procedures for a sales-type lease, however, do require added steps to those already illustrated. The sales profit is similar to a profit on the sale of a plant asset. The $900 profit in this example must be deferred over the three-year lease term. Thus, the asset and its related depreciation accounts must be adjusted to reflect the original sales profit.

The following added adjustments on Worksheet 7–5 would be needed for the original $900 sales profit:

Sales Profit on Leases	900	
Property, Plant, and Equipment...		900
To reduce cost of asset for gain on sales-type lease.		

Accumulated Depreciation—Property, Plant, and Equipment	300	
Depreciation Expense		300
To reduce depreciation expense at the rate of $300 per year.		

The income distribution schedule of the parent (lessor) would reflect the deferral of the original $900 profit in the year of the sale and would recognize $300 per year during the asset's life.

On Worksheet 7–6, the following added adjustments would be required if a sales-type lease was involved:

Retained Earnings—Controlling Interest...................................	600	
Accumulated Depreciation—Property, Plant, and Equipment	300	
Property, Plant, and Equipment...		900
To adjust the remaining sales profit at the beginning of the period.		

Accumulated Depreciation—Property, Plant, and Equipment	300	
Depreciation Expense		300
To reduce depreciation expense at the rate of $300 per year.		

INTERCOMPANY TRANSACTIONS PRIOR TO BUSINESS COMBINATION

It is possible that the firms involved in a business combination may have had dealings with each other prior to the consummation of the acquisition. The ramifications of such dealings on the consolidation process depend on whether the combination is a purchase or a pooling of interests.

When the acquisition is a purchase, there is no need to be concerned with intercompany sales occurring prior to the acquisition. It is assumed that the sales were arm's-length transactions between unrelated parties. *Even though assets containing the profit are on the balance sheet on the acquisition date, no adjustments are needed when consolidating.* When one affiliate previously purchased the other affiliate's bonds, a complication does arise. The bonds become an intercompany debt as of the purchase date and thus are *viewed as retired* on the purchase date when consolidating.

Acquisitions deemed to be a pooling of interests create a need for eliminating intercompany transactions occurring prior to the acquisition date. Recall that poolings are retroactive to the entire current period and to earlier periods. This means that all intercompany transactions during the period in which a pooling occurs must be eliminated, no matter when the pooling occurs. In essence, consolidated statements for the period during which a pooling occurs are the same as they would appear if the pooling had occurred at the beginning of the period. When comparative statements are prepared, pooling is retroactive for all such statements. This means that transactions between the firms during those previous periods must be eliminated. In summary, consolidation procedures are applied as they would be if the firms had been pooled from their inception.

QUESTIONS

1. What are the alternative methods of extinguishing debt in the hands of outside parties, and how is the consolidation process affected by each method? When the parent purchases bonds issued by the subsidiary from an outside party, why is the resulting gain or loss borne entirely by the issuer?

2. What is the effect on combined net income in the year of acquisition and in subsequent periods of the following parent purchases of 8% subsidiary bonds?
   (a) Issued at 9%, purchased to yield 7%
   (b) Issued at 7%, purchased to yield 9%
   (c) Issued at 9%, purchased to yield 10%
   (d) Issued at 10%, purchased to yield 9%

3. Why would the amounts of interest expense and revenue recorded by affiliated firms relative to intercompany bondholdings not agree? How is the disparity dealt with in the consolidation process?

4. Assume that a subsidiary company's outstanding bonds are purchased at a gain by the parent company.
   (a) Explain why a gain on bond retirement appears on the consolidated statements, even though the subsidiary has not retired the bonded debt.
   (b) The income distribution schedule for the subsidiary company shows internally generated net income and adjusted income. As-

suming no other intercompany transactions, compare these two income figures:

(1) In the year of bond acquisition,

(2) Each succeeding year until maturity, and

(3) In the aggregate for the periods during which the bonds are outstanding.

Briefly justify each answer.

5. Company P purchased Company S's $50,000, 5-year, 6% bonds three years after issuance. The bonds originally were issued at face value and later purchased by Company P at a market rate of 5% for $50,928. Using the straight-line method of amortization, compute the income distribution schedule interest adjustments over the remaining term of the bonds and explain their relationship to the original consolidated gain or loss on retirement. On whose income distribution schedule do these items appear?

6. What are the benefits of leasing among affiliated firms?

7. Why are no adjustments made on the income distribution schedules of controlling and minority interests as a result of operating and direct-financing leases?

8. Distinguish between a direct-financing lease and a sales-type lease from the standpoint of the lessor.

9. Company X is leasing several plant assets from its parent firm, Company T. Which of the following items should Company X include in minimum lease payments if the lease is classified as an operating lease? As a capital lease?

(a) Annual rental payments

(b) Amounts reimbursing the lessor for executory costs, such as insurance, maintenance, and taxes

(c) Guaranteed residual value

(d) Unguaranteed residual value

(e) Penalties paid for failure to renew

(f) Bargain purchase option

10. Designate whether the following accounts normally are recorded on the books of the lessor or the lessee. Indicate which accounts are eliminated, reclassified, or adjusted in the consolidation process.

(a) Equipment Under Operating Lease

(b) Rent Expense — Executory Costs

(c) Accounts Payable (for asset)

(d) Unguaranteed Residual Value

(e) Depreciation Expense — Operating Lease

(f) Depreciation Expense — Capital Lease

(g) Unearned Interest Income

(h) Assets Under Capital Lease

11. Parent Company purchased an asset for $30,850 and has agreed to lease the asset to its subsidiary over a 5-year period. The fair market value at

the inception of the lease term was $32,000. Record the adjustments pertaining to the sales profit on the lease that would be made on the consolidated worksheet for the first and final years of the lease term.

EXERCISES

Exercise 1.   Estran Corporation is an 80%-owned subsidiary of Biza Fittings Company. Estran has $800,000 of 10% bonds outstanding, which originally were sold at face value and mature on June 30, 19X9. Interest is paid semi-annually on June 30 and December 31. On January 1, 19X5, the market rate for similar bonds is 10%. Compare the effects on the consolidated statements under the following alternative possibilities:
(1) Biza loans Estran the funds necessary to retire the bonds on January 1, 19X5, at 10% interest.
(2) Biza purchases the bonds in the market on January 1, 19X5.

Exercise 2.   Handy Distributing Company is an 80%-owned subsidiary of Grand Global Industries. On January 1, 19X2, Handy issued $200,000 of 10-year, 10% bonds payable at face value. Interest is paid annually on January 1. On January 1, 19X8, Grand purchased the bonds for $196,000; the resulting discount is being amortized on a straight-line basis. For the years ending (a) December 31, 19X8, and (b) December 31, 19X9, determine the effects of this transaction:
(1) On combined net income.
(2) On the distribution of income to the parent and the subsidiary.

Exercise 3.   Konkel Ltd. is an 80%-owned subsidiary of Peters Construction Company. Konkel issued $100,000 of 10%, 8-year bonds for $101,600 on January 1, 19X1. Annual interest is paid on January 1. Peters purchased the bonds on January 2, 19X5, for $100,400. Both firms are using the straight-line method to amortize the premium on these bonds.
(1) Prepare the eliminations and adjustments that would be made on the December 31, 19X5 consolidated worksheet as a result of this purchase.
(2) Prepare the eliminations and adjustments that would be made on the December 31, 19X6 consolidated worksheet.

Exercise 4.   On January 1, 19X4, Dornfield Corporation, an 85%-owned subsidiary of German Industries, received $46,208 for the $50,000 of 8%, five-year bonds it issued when the market rate was 10%. When German purchased these bonds for $45,197 on January 2, 19X6, the market rate was 12%. Given the following amortization schedules for both firms, calculate the gain or loss on retirement and the interest adjustments to the issuer income distribution schedules over the remaining term of the bonds.

Dornfield (issuer)

Date	Effective Interest (10%)	Nominal Interest	Discount Amortization	Balance
1/1/X4	—	—	—	$46,208
1/1/X5	$4,621	$4,000	$621	46,829
1/1/X6	4,683	4,000	683	47,512
1/1/X7	4,751	4,000	751	48,263
1/1/X8	4,826	4,000	826	49,089
1/1/X9	4,911*	4,000	911	50,000

*$2 rounding error

German (purchaser)

Date	Effective Interest (12%)	Nominal Interest	Discount Amortization	Balance
1/1/X6	—	—	—	$45,197
1/1/X7	$5,424	$4,000	$1,424	46,621
1/1/X8	5,594	4,000	1,594	48,215
1/1/X9	5,785	4,000	1,785	50,000

Exercise 5. Real Veal Products is an 80%-owned subsidiary of Foremost Veal Packers Inc. On January 1, 19X8, Real Veal sold $100,000 of 10-year, 9% bonds for $95,000. Interest is paid annually on January 1. The market rate for this type of bond was 12% on January 1, 19Y0, when Foremost purchased 40% of the Real Veal bonds for $34,000. Discounts may be amortized on a straight-line basis.
(1) Prepare the eliminations and adjustments required for this bond purchase on the December 31, 19Y0 consolidated worksheet.
(2) Prepare the eliminations and adjustments required on the December 31, 19Y1 consolidated worksheet.

Exercise 6. Largo Industries, a 90%-owned subsidiary of Shallow Incorporated, issued $150,000 of 12-year, 13% bonds on January 1, 19X5, to yield 12% interest. Interest is paid annually on January 1. The interest method is used to amortize the premium. Shallow purchased the bonds for $175,915 on January 2, 19X8, when the market rate of interest was 10%. On the purchase date, the remaining premium on the bonds was $7,999. Largo's 19X8 net income was $500,000.
(1) Prepare the eliminations and adjustments required for this purchase on the December 31, 19X8 consolidated worksheet.
(2) Prepare the 19X8 income distribution schedule for the minority interest.

Exercise 7. Warren Company is an 80%-owned subsidiary of Kingway Industries. On January 1, 19X2, Warren signed a five-year operating lease with Kingway for a small building with a 15-year life and a book value of $150,000. Warren's payments under the contract are $2,000 each, payable the first of each month. The separate books of the two firms provide the following information for 19X3:

	Kingway	Warren
Sales...	$700,000	$300,000
Cost of goods sold...	460,000	190,000
General expenses..	160,000	60,000
Depreciation expense (including leased assets)...............	27,000	9,000

Rental revenue and expense are not included in the preceding amounts.

Prepare a partial worksheet showing the partial trial balances, the eliminations and adjustments, and the consolidated income statement for 19X3. Include the distribution of income to the controlling and minority interests.

Exercise 8. On January 1, 19X0, Adams Company, an 80%-owned subsidiary of Beatrix Electronics Inc., signed a 4-year direct-financing lease with its parent for the rental of electronic equipment. The lease agreement requires a $6,000 payment on January 1 of each year, and Adams may purchase the equipment under a bargain purchase option for $2,000 on January 1, 19X4. The equipment originally cost $21,682 and had an estimated remaining life of six years at the start of the lease term. The lessor's implicit interest rate is 12%. The lessee also uses the 12% rate to record the transaction.

(1) Prepare the eliminations and adjustments required for this lease on the December 31, 19X0 consolidated worksheet.

(2) Prepare the eliminations and adjustments for the December 31, 19X1 consolidated worksheet.

Exercise 9. Penn Company leased a production machine to its 80%-owned subsidiary, Smith Company. The lease agreement, dated January 1, 19X1, requires Smith to pay $18,000 each January 1 for three years. There is an unguaranteed residual value of $5,000. The machine cost $50,098. The present value of the machine at Penn's 16% implicit interest rate was $50,098 on January 1, 19X1. Smith also uses the 16% lessor implicit rate to record the lease. The machine is being depreciated over 3 years on a straight-line basis with a $5,000 salvage value. Lease payment amortization schedules are as follows:

Penn (16%)

Date	Payment	Interest at 16% on Previous Balance	Reduction of Principal	Principal Balance
Jan. 1, 19X1	$18,000	—	$18,000	$32,098
Jan. 1, 19X2	18,000	$5,136	12,864	19,234
Jan. 1, 19X3	18,000	3,078	14,922	4,312
Jan. 1, 19X4	5,000	688	4,312	—
Total	$59,000	$8,902	$50,098	

Smith (16%)

Date	Payment	Interest at 16% on Previous Balance	Reduction of Principal	Principal Balance
Jan. 1, 19X1	$18,000	—	$18,000	$28,894
Jan. 1, 19X2	18,000	$4,623	13,377	15,517
Jan. 1, 19X3	18,000	2,483	15,517	—
Total	$54,000	$7,106	$46,894	

(1) Prepare the eliminations and adjustments required for this lease on the December 31, 19X1 consolidated worksheet.
(2) Prepare the eliminations and adjustments for the December 31, 19X2 consolidated worksheet.

Exercise 10. Marshfield Clinic is an 80%-owned subsidiary of King Diagnostic Equipment. On January 1, 19X3, Marshfield signed a 3-year lease with King for the rental of diagnostic equipment. Under the terms of the lease, Marshfield is to pay $12,000 each January 1, with a bargain renewal option for the following 2 years at $3,000 per year. Each payment includes $1,000 for maintenance to be provided by King. The present value of the minimum payments, net of executory costs, at the 10% lessor implicit rate was $32,960 on January 1, 19X3. The equipment cost King $30,000. It is being depreciated on a straight-line basis over its 5-year expected life, with no anticipated salvage value.

Prepare the eliminations and adjustments required for this lease on the December 31, 19X3 consolidated worksheet.

Exercise 11. Merrill Department Stores Inc. is leasing specialized display fixtures from its 80%-owned subsidiary, Kris Promotions. Lease payments are $20,000 per year, payable at the beginning of each year. The lessor paid $52,000 for the asset, which had a market value of $57,717 at the start of the lease term. The lessor estimates that the fixtures will have a residual value (unguaranteed) of $5,500 at the end of the 3-year lease. The lessor's implicit interest rate is 12%. The 12% rate also is used by the lessee to record the lease. Lease amortization schedules are as follows:

Kris (12%)

Date	Payment	Interest at 12% on Previous Balance	Reduction of Principal	Principal Balance
Jan. 1, 19X5	$20,000	—	$20,000	$37,717
Jan. 1, 19X6	20,000	$4,526	15,474	22,243
Jan. 1, 19X7	20,000	2,669	17,331	4,912
Jan. 1, 19X8	5,500	588	4,912	—
Total	$65,500	$7,783	$57,717	

Merrill (12%)

Date	Payment	Interest at 12% on Previous Balance	Reduction of Principal	Principal Balance
Jan. 1, 19X5	$20,000	—	$20,000	$33,802
Jan. 1, 19X6	20,000	$4,056	15,944	17,858
Jan. 1, 19X7	20,000	2,142	17,858	—
Total	$60,000	$6,198	$53,802	

Prepare the eliminations and adjustments required for this lease on the December 31, 19X5 consolidated worksheet.

PROBLEMS

Problem 7–1. Since its 100% acquisition of Owen Corporation stock on December 31, 19X2, Kelly Corporation has maintained its investment under the simple equity method. At the time of the purchase, the fair market value of Owen's assets equaled their book value. However, due to Owen's earning potential, the price included a $15,000 payment for goodwill to be amortized over 5 years.

On January 2, 19X5, Owen Corporation issued 10-year, 9% bonds with a face value of $50,000 for $44,576. These bonds pay interest each December 31. Owen amortizes the discount using the straight-line method. On January 2, 19X6, Kelly purchased one-half of Owen Corporation's outstanding bonds for $25,000. They have been included in Kelly's long-term investment in bonds account.

Below are the trial balances of both firms on December 31, 19X6:

	Kelly Corporation	Owen Corporation
Cash	100,000	60,000
Accounts Receivable (net)	450,000	75,000
Inventory	200,000	65,000
Investment in Owen Corporation	347,339	—
Investment in Bonds	45,000	—
Plant and Equipment (net)	2,420,000	196,000
Accounts Payable	(275,000)	(18,000)
Bonds Payable, 9%	—	(50,000)
Discount on Bonds Payable	—	4,339
Common Stock ($10 par)	(1,000,000)	(100,000)
Paid-In Capital in Excess of Par	(750,000)	(130,000)
Retained Earnings, Jan. 1, 19X6	(728,531)	(77,381)
Sales	(2,500,000)	(540,000)
Cost of Goods Sold	1,000,000	405,000
Interest Income	(3,850)	—
Selling and General Expenses	720,000	105,000
Subsidiary Income	(24,958)	—
Interest Expense		5,042
Total	0	0

Required:

Prepare the worksheet necessary to produce the consolidated balance sheet and income statement of Kelly Corporation and its subsidiary for the year ended December 31, 19X6.

Problem 7–2. On December 31, 19X1, Apparent Winds Inc. purchased 90% of the common stock of Square Rigging Ltd. for $250,000. On that date, there was no significant difference between the book value and market value of Square Rigging's net assets. Since then, Apparent Winds has maintained its investment in the subsidiary using the simple equity method.

Square Rigging issued $100,000, 10%, 8-year bonds on January 2, 19X3. The bonds pay interest semiannually on July 1 and January 2 and were sold to yield 9%. Effective interest amortization is used by Square Rigging.

On October 31, 19X5, Apparent Winds purchased all of Square Rigging's bonds for $97,830 plus accrued interest of $3,333. Apparent Winds is using the straight-line amortization method.

The trial balances of the two firms on December 31, 19X6, are presented below:

	Apparent Winds	Square Rigging
Cash	95,000	45,000
Accounts Receivable (net)	97,500	78,000
Inventory, 12/31/X6	88,000	58,860
Investment in Square Rigging Ltd.	326,392	—
Investment in Bonds	98,320	—
Plant and Equipment (net)	642,000	346,096
Accounts Payable	(102,500)	(62,000)
Bonds Payable, 10%, due 1/2/Y1	—	(100,000)
Premium on Bonds Payable	—	(3,298)
Common Stock (no par)	(450,650)	(75,000)
Retained Earnings, 1/1/X6	(683,750)	(260,000)
Sales	(800,000)	(305,000)
Cost of Goods Sold	525,000	183,000
Selling and General Expenses	100,000	85,000
Interest Income	(10,420)	—
Subsidiary Income	(24,892)	—
Interest Expense	—	9,342
Dividends Declared	100,000	—
Total	0	0

Required:

Prepare the worksheet necessary to produce the consolidated financial statements of Apparent Winds Inc. and its subsidiary for the year ended December 31, 19X6. Include income distribution schedules.

Problem 7–3. DeWitt Diversified Industries acquired an 80% interest in Janden Corporation on January 1, 19X0, by purchasing 96,000 shares of its $5 par common stock for $970,000. Direct acquisition costs were $5,000. Janden stockholders' equity accounts at that date showed a balance of $260,000 in Paid-In Capital in Excess of Par and $140,000 in Retained Earnings. It also was determined that Janden's inventory was undervalued by $8,000, that its land was undervalued by $70,000, and that its equipment with an 8-year life was undervalued by $80,000. Any goodwill is to be amortized over six years.

On July 1, 19X0, Janden issued $80,000 of 8-year, 11% bonds at face value. Interest payment dates are January 1 and July 1. DeWitt purchased these bonds in the market for $83,087 on July 2, 19X3, when the market rate was 10%. The purchase premium is being amortized on the straight-line basis.

The following trial balances were prepared by the two companies on December 31, 19X3:

	DeWitt Diversified Industries	Janden Corporation
Cash...	130,088	80,000
Receivables (net)	190,000	140,000
Inventory...	98,000	75,000
Investment in Janden Corporation........................	1,119,000	—
Investment in 11% Bonds	82,778	—
Land..	220,000	240,000
Buildings and Equipment	1,350,000	1,060,000
Accumulated Depreciation.................................	(651,000)	(230,000)
Accounts Payable	(210,000)	(105,000)
Bonds Payable, 11%.....................................	—	(80,000)
Common Stock ($5 par)...................................	(975,000)	(600,000)
Paid-In Capital in Excess of Par...........................	(724,375)	(260,000)
Retained Earnings, Jan. 1, 19X3...........................	(463,400)	(260,000)
Sales...	(1,940,000)	(1,020,000)
Interest Income	(4,091)	—
Subsidiary Income...................................	(76,000)	—
Cost of Goods Sold..................................	1,010,000	610,000
Interest Expense....................................	—	8,800
Other Expenses....................................	769,000	306,200
Dividends Declared..................................	75,000	35,000
Total..	0	0

Required:

Prepare the worksheet necessary to produce the consolidated financial statements of DeWitt Diversified Industries and its subsidiary at December 31, 19X3. Include the determination and distribution of excess and income distribution schedules.

Problem 7–4. On January 1, 19X3, Warehouse Outlets had the following balances in its stockholders' equity accounts: Common Stock ($10 par), $800,000; Paid-In Capital in Excess of Par, $625,000; and Retained Earnings, $450,000. General Appliances purchased 64,000 shares of Warehouse Outlets common stock for $1,700,000 on that date. Any excess of cost over book value was attributed to goodwill and given a 10-year life.

Warehouse Outlets issued $500,000 of 8-year, 11% bonds on December 31, 19X2. The bonds sold for $476,000. General Appliances purchased one-half of these bonds in the market on January 1, 19X5, for $259,000. Both firms use the straight-line method of amortization of premiums and discounts.

On July 1, 19X6, General Appliances sold to Warehouse Outlets an old building with a book value of $167,500, remaining life of 10 years, and $30,000 salvage value, for $195,000. The building is being depreciated on a straight-line basis. Warehouse Outlets paid $20,000 in cash and signed a mortgage note with its parent for the balance. Interest, at 11% of the unpaid balance, and principal payments are due annually beginning July 1, 19X7. (For convenience, the mortgage balances are not divided into current and long-term portions.)

The trial balances of the two firms at December 31, 19X6, are as follows:

	General Appliances	Warehouse Outlets
Cash..	401,986	72,625
Accounts Receivable (net).................................	752,500	105,000
Interest Receivable...	9,625	—
Inventory..	1,950,000	900,000
Investment in Warehouse Outlets........................	1,700,000	—
Investment in 11% Bonds	256,000	—
Investment in Mortgage	175,000	—
Property, Plant, and Equipment..........................	9,000,000	2,950,000
Accumulated Depreciation.................................	(1,695,000)	(940,000)
Accounts Payable	(670,000)	(80,000)
Interest Payable..	(18,333)	(9,625)
Bonds Payable, 11%..	(2,000,000)	(500,000)
Discount on Bonds Payable	10,470	12,000
Mortgage Payable..	—	(175,000)
Common Stock ($5 par).....................................	(3,200,000)	—
Common Stock ($10 par)	—	(800,000)
Paid-In Capital in Excess of Par..........................	(4,550,000)	(625,000)
Retained Earnings, Jan. 1, 19X6	(1,011,123)	(770,000)
Sales...	(9,800,000)	(3,000,000)
Gain on Sale of Building	(27,500)	—
Interest Income	(35,625)	—
Dividend Income	(48,000)	—
Cost of Goods Sold..	4,940,000	1,700,000
Depreciation Expense.......................................	717,000	95,950
Interest Expense...	223,000	67,544
Other Expenses..	2,600,000	936,506
Dividends Declared..	320,000	60,000
Total..	0	0

Required:

Prepare the worksheet necessary to produce the consolidated financial statements of General Appliances and its subsidiary for the year ended December 31, 19X6. Include the determination and distribution of excess and income distribution schedules.

Problem 7–5. On January 1, 19X2, Linskey Company purchased 60% of the outstanding stock of Yankee Inc. for $400,000. Yankee had the following stockholder's equity at that time:

Common stock ($.50 par)...........................	$ 25,000
Paid-in capital in excess of par....................	225,000
Retained earnings.....................................	300,000
Total equity...	$550,000

On the date of the purchase, Yankee's book values approximated market values, except for the patents, which were undervalued by $10,000.

During 19X2, Yankee Inc. sold merchandise to Linskey Company at cost plus 40%. These merchandise sales totaled $77,000, of which $25,000 remained unpaid at December 31, 19X2. Linskey Company has $14,000 worth of this merchandise remaining in its ending inventory.

Linskey purchased $100,000 of Yankee's 10%, 10-year bonds on January 2, 19X2, for $105,535. These bonds originally were issued at face value on January 1, 19X0, and pay interest on January 1 of each year. The price paid reflects a 9% annual interest rate. The interest method of amortization is used.

Trial balances of the two firms as of December 31, 19X2, are as follows:

	Linskey Company	Yankee Inc.
Cash..	51,465	90,500
Receivables (net)	80,000	74,000
Accrued Interest Receivable.......................................	10,000	—
Inventory...	270,000	100,000
Prepaid Expenses	16,000	3,500
Investment in Yankee Inc.	400,000	—
Investment in 10% Bonds	105,033	—
Land.................:..	600,000	193,000
Building and Equipment...	1,750,000	850,000
Accumulated Depreciation...	(800,000)	(350,000)
Patents and Other Intangibles...................................	60,000	50,000
Accounts Payable..	(170,000)	(107,000)
Accrued Interest Payable	—	(30,000)
Bonds Payable, 10%..	—	(300,000)
Common Stock ($5 stated value)...............................	(500,000)	—
Common Stock ($.50 par)...	—	(25,000)
Paid-In Capital in Excess of Par................................	—	(225,000)
Retained Earnings, Jan. 1, 19X2	(1,830,000)	(300,000)
Sales..	(800,000)	(300,000)
Interest Income	(9,498)	—
Dividend Income	(3,000)	—
Cost of Goods Sold...	480,000	150,000
Interest Expense...	90,000	30,000
Other Expenses...	180,000	91,000
Dividends Declared...	20,000	5,000
Total...	0	0

Required:

(1) Prepare the worksheet necessary to produce the consolidated financial statements of Linskey Company and its subsidiary for the year ended December 31, 19X2. Any intangibles associated with the stock purchase should be amortized over 10 years. Include the determination and distribution of excess and income distribution schedules.

(2) Prepare the formal consolidated statements, including the income statement, retained earnings statement, and balance sheet.

Problem 7–6. *(Note: This problem is designed to be worked using the vertical worksheet format introduced in the appendix to Chapter 5.)* In a transaction that meets the pooling rules, Prince Company acquired 90% of the outstanding common stock of Sand Company on January 1, 19X0. Sand stockholders' equity on January 1, 19X0, consisted of $200,000 in Common Stock and $120,000 in Retained Earnings.

Sand issued $100,000 of 8-year, 10% bonds for $90,066 on January 1, 19W9, when the market rate was 12%. The market rate for this type of bond declined substantially. The discount remaining on January 1, 19X3, was $6,073.

On January 2, 19X2, Prince purchased 60% of Sand's bonds for $64,792, to yield 8%. Prince purchased the remaining bonds for $45,544 on January 2, 19X3, when the market rate was 6%.

Prince routinely sells merchandise inventory to Sand at a price to yield a gross profit of 30%. Intercompany merchandise sales in 19X3 were $100,000. Purchases from Prince accounted for $20,000 of Sand's beginning inventory and $15,000 of its ending inventory.

Separate trial balances prepared by the two firms at December 31, 19X3, showed the following information:

	Prince Company	Sand Company
Sales	(900,000)	(390,000)
Interest Income	(7,851)	—
Cost of Goods Sold	580,000	210,000
Interest Expense	—	11,271
Other Expenses	234,850	136,729
Subsidiary Income	(28,800)	—
Cash	25,031	40,000
Accounts Receivable (net)	68,800	58,000
Inventory	70,000	67,000
Investment in Sand Company	390,600	—
Investment in 10% Bonds	107,370	—
Property, Plant, and Equipment	700,000	500,000
Accumulated Depreciation	(210,000)	(92,000)
Accounts Payable	(70,000)	(43,802)
Bonds Payable, 10%	—	(100,000)
Discount on Bonds Payable	—	4,802
Common Stock ($10 par)	(300,000)	—
Common Stock ($2 par)	—	(200,000)
Paid-In Capital in Excess of Par	(425,000)	—
Retained Earnings, Jan. 1, 19X3	(265,000)	(202,000)
Dividends Declared	30,000	—
Total	0	0

Required:

Prepare the worksheet necessary to produce the consolidated financial statements of Prince Company and its subsidiary for the year ended December 31, 19X3. Use the vertical format. Include income distribution schedules.

Problem 7–7. On January 1, 19X4, Kaeppler Corporation purchased 80% of the outstanding stock of Hacker Company for $1,000,000 in cash.

A condensed January 1, 19X4 Hacker Company balance sheet follows:

Assets		Liabilities and Stockholders' Equity	
Current assets	$ 450,000	Liabilities, net	$ 760,000
Property, plant,		Common stock ($8 par)	640,000
and equipment (net)	1,100,000	Retained earnings	200,000
Other assets	50,000		
Total assets	$1,600,000	Total liabilities and equity	$1,600,000

At the purchase date, Hacker Company's inventory and land accounts were understated by $25,000 and $100,000, respectively. Any remaining excess was attributed to goodwill and given a 40-year life. The inventory on hand January 1, 19X4, was sold during 19X4.

On January 1, 19X1, Hacker Company issued $500,000 of 8%, 20-year bonds. The bonds, which sold at a price to yield 7%, pay interest on each December 31. The premium on these bonds was $47,233 on January 1, 19X5.

On January 1, 19X5, Kaeppler Corporation purchased $200,000 (face value) of these bonds for $168,705, to yield 10%.

Trial balances of the two firms as of December 31, 19X5, are as follows:

	Kaeppler Corporation	Hacker Company
Cash...	386,024	147,789
Accounts and Notes Receivable (net)......................	495,000	225,000
Inventory...	510,000	235,000
Investment in 8% Bonds......................................	169,576	—
Investment in Hacker Company...............................	1,146,000	—
Land..	1,000,000	400,000
Building and Equipment......................................	3,650,000	1,400,000
Accumulated Depreciation....................................	(1,400,000)	(650,000)
Other Assets...	—	40,250
Accounts and Notes Payable..................................	(475,000)	(230,000)
Bonds Payable, 7%..	(2,000,000)	—
Bonds Payable, 8%..	—	(500,000)
Premium on Bonds Payable....................................	—	(45,539)
Common Stock ($5 stated value)..............................	(2,500,000)	—
Common Stock ($8 par).......................................	—	(640,000)
Retained Earnings, Jan. 1, 19X5	(705,000)	(300,000)
Sales..	(2,400,000)	(1,050,000)
Subsidiary Income...	(90,000)	—
Other Income..	(46,600)	(12,000)
Cost of Goods Sold..	1,560,000	693,000
Other Expenses..	600,000	256,500
Dividends Declared..	100,000	30,000
Total...	0	0

Interest income and expense related to Hacker Company's bonds are included in the other income and other expenses accounts. Amounts included reflect amortization of premiums or discounts, using the interest method of amortization.

Required:
Prepare the worksheet necessary to produce the consolidated financial statements of Kaeppler Corporation and its subsidiary for the year ended December 31, 19X5. Support should be provided for amounts pertaining to interest on Hacker Company's 8% bonds. Include the determination and distribution of excess and income distribution schedules.

Problem 7–8. Paro Company acquired a 90% interest in Sandman Company on January 1, 19X1, for $660,000. Any excess of cost over book value was due to goodwill, which is being amortized over the maximum period.

Capital balances of Sandman Company on January 1, 19X1, were:

Common stock ($10 par)............................	$200,000
Paid-in capital in excess of par...................	100,000
Retained earnings.....................................	300,000
Total equity...	$600,000

Sandman Company sold a machine to Paro for $30,000 on January 1, 19X4. It cost Sandman $20,000 to build the machine, which had a 5-year remaining life on the date of the sale and is subject to straight-line depreciation.

Paro purchased one-half of the outstanding 9% bonds of Sandman for $89,183 (to yield 12%) on December 31, 19X5. The bonds were sold originally by Sandman to yield 10% to outside parties. The discount on the bonds was $7,586 on December 31, 19X5. The effective interest method of amortization is used.

During 19X6, Paro Company sold merchandise to Sandman for $50,000. Paro recorded a 30% gross profit on the sales price. $20,000 of the merchandise purchased from Paro remains unsold at the end of the year.

The trial balances of Paro and its subsidiary, Sandman, are as follows on December 31, 19X6:

	Paro Company	Sandman Company
Inventory...	40,000	80,000
Equipment..	371,193	1,522,414
Accumulated Depreciation.............................	(200,000)	(600,000)
Investment in Sandman Stock........................	660,000	—
Investment in Sandman Bonds	90,885	—
Bonds Payable, 9%	—	(200,000)
Discount on Bonds Payable	—	6,345
Common Stock ($10 par)...............................	(200,000)	(200,000)
Paid-In Capital in Excess of Par....................	(300,000)	(100,000)
Retained Earnings, Jan. 1, 19X6	(401,376)	(500,000)
Sales..	(300,000)	(260,000)
Cost of Goods Sold.......................................	100,000	72,000
Interest Income	(10,702)	—
Other Expenses...	150,000	160,000
Interest Expense...	—	19,241
Total..	0	0

Required:

Prepare the worksheet necessary to produce the consolidated financial statements of Paro Company and its subsidiary for the year ended December 31, 19X6. Include the determination and distribution of excess and income distribution schedules.

Problem 7–9. Symple Corporation, a wholly-owned subsidiary of Paratec Corporation, leased equipment from its parent company on August 1, 19X6. The terms of the agreement clearly do not require the lease to be accounted for as a capital lease. Both entities are accounting for the lease as an operating lease. The lease payment is $12,000 per year paid in advance each August 1.

Paratec purchased its investment in Symple on December 31, 19X1. The investment is maintained under the simple equity method. Included in the original purchase price was a $50,000 premium attributable to Symple's history of exceptional earnings. Intangible assets are amortized over a 10-year period.

The December 31, 19X8 trial balances of Paratec and its subsidiary are presented below:

	Paratec Corporation	Symple Corporation
Cash..	190,000	40,000
Accounts Receivable (net).....................................	1,160,000	142,000
Inventory..	500,000	75,000
Prepaid Rent on Equipment.................................	—	7,000
Investment in Bonds...	250,000	65,000
Investment in Symple Stock	647,000	—
Bond Sinking Fund	400,000	—
Land...	250,000	85,000
Plant and Equipment...	1,950,000	295,000
Accumulated Depreciation—Plant and Equipment....	(250,000)	(60,000)
Equipment Under Operating Lease........................	120,000	—
Accumulated Depreciation—Assets Under Operating Lease	(36,000)	—
Patents...	155,000	—
Accounts Payable	(385,000)	(52,000)
Deferred Rent Revenue	(7,000)	—
Bonds Payable, 10%...	(1,000,000)	—
Discount on Bonds Payable	23,350	—
Common Stock (no par).......................................	(2,000,000)	(200,000)
Retained Earnings, Jan. 1, 19X8	(1,236,350)	(310,000)
Sales..	(4,720,000)	(500,000)
Rent Income..	(12,000)	—
Cost of Goods Sold...	3,068,000	300,000
Rent Expense	—	12,000
Other Expenses...	725,000	101,000
Subsidiary Income..	(87,000)	—
Dividends Declared...	295,000	—
Total...	0	0

Required:

Prepare the worksheet necessary to produce the consolidated income statement and balance sheet of Paratec Corporation and its subsidiary for the year ended December 31, 19X8.

Problem 7–10. On January 1, 19X1, Tucker Distributing Company acquired an 80% interest in Wong Warehousing Inc. for $1,198,000. Wong's Retained Earnings at that date was $320,000. Its book values approximated market values, and any excess was attributed to goodwill and given a 5-year life.

Tucker is leasing a warehouse from Wong that originally cost Wong $825,000. On July 1, 19X1, the date the lease agreement was signed, the warehouse had an estimated remaining life of 20 years, a salvage value of

$50,000, and accumulated depreciation of $155,000 under the straight-line method. The terms of the 10-year lease require a $5,000 rental payment on the first of each month, including executory costs of $300 per month.

In conjunction with its warehousing operations, Wong purchases and sells merchandise to distributors. Sales to Tucker, at the usual 25% above cost, totaled $260,000 for 19X2. At year end, Tucker owed $15,000 on these purchases. Tucker's beginning inventory balance included $60,000 in merchandise purchased from Wong, and its ending inventory balance included $45,000.

The following trial balances were prepared by the separate firms on December 31, 19X2:

	Tucker Distributing Company	Wong Warehousing Inc.
Cash	63,000	40,000
Receivables (net)	106,600	85,000
Inventory	180,000	100,000
Investment in Wong Warehousing Inc.	1,302,000	—
Property, Plant, and Equipment	2,580,000	2,000,000
Accumulated Depreciation—Property, Plant, and Equipment	(1,249,000)	(1,550,000)
Assets Under Operating Lease	—	1,975,000
Accumulated Depreciation—Assets Under Operating Lease	—	(990,000)
Accounts Payable	(125,000)	(70,000)
Bonds Payable, 10%	(400,000)	—
Common Stock ($10 par)	(1,000,000)	—
Common Stock ($5 par)	—	(600,000)
Paid-In Capital in Excess of Par	(720,000)	(540,000)
Retained Earnings, Jan. 1, 19X2	(526,000)	(380,000)
Sales	(2,400,000)	(1,000,000)
Rent Income	—	(150,000)
Cost of Goods Sold	1,390,000	600,000
Rent Expense	60,000	—
Interest Expense	40,000	—
Other Expenses	698,400	450,000
Subsidiary Income	(80,000)	—
Dividends Declared	80,000	30,000
Total	0	0

Required:

Prepare the worksheet necessary to produce the consolidated financial statements of Tucker Distributing Company and its subsidiary for the year ended December 31, 19X2. Include the determination and distribution of excess and income distribution schedules.

Problem 7–11. Plessor Industries acquired 80% of the outstanding common stock of Slessee Company on January 1, 19X1, for $320,000. On that date, Slessee's book values approximated market values, and the balance of its retained earnings account was $80,000. Any excess was attributed to goodwill and given a five-year life. Slessee's net income was $20,000 for 19X1 and $30,000 for 19X2. No dividends were paid in either year.

On January 1, 19X2, Slessee signed a 5-year lease with Plessor for the rental of a small factory building with a 10-year life. Payments of $25,000 are due each January 1, and Slessee is expected to exercise the $5,000 bargain purchase option at the end of the fifth year. The market value of the factory was $103,770 at the start of the lease term. Plessor's implicit rate on the lease is 12%.

A second lease agreement, for the rental of production equipment with an 8-year life, was signed by Slessee on January 1, 19X3. The terms of this 4-year lease require a payment of $15,000 each January 1. The present value of the lease payments at Plessor's 12% implicit rate was equal to the market value of the equipment, $52,298, when the lease was signed. The cost of the equipment to Plessor was $45,000, and there is a $2,000 bargain purchase option. Eight-year, straight-line depreciation is being used, with no salvage value.

The following trial balances were prepared by the separate firms at December 31, 19X3:

	Plessor Industries	Slessee Company
Cash	60,000	40,745
Accounts Receivable	97,778	76,000
Inventory	140,000	120,000
Minimum Lease Payments Receivable	127,000	—
Unearned Interest Income	(14,417)	—
Investment in Slessee Company	320,000	—
Assets Under Capital Lease	—	156,068
Accumulated Depreciation—Assets Under Capital Lease	—	(27,291)
Property, Plant, and Equipment	1,900,000	310,000
Accumulated Depreciation—Property, Plant, and Equipment	(1,077,000)	(72,000)
Accounts Payable	(148,000)	(45,065)
Obligations Under Capital Lease	—	(100,520)
Common Stock ($10 par)	(700,000)	(300,000)
Paid-In Capital in Excess of Par	(325,000)	—
Retained Earnings, Jan. 1, 19X3	(295,000)	(130,000)
Sales	(1,400,000)	(600,000)
Sales Profit on Leases	(7,298)	—
Interest Income	(12,063)	—
Cost of Goods Sold	780,000	380,000
Interest Expense	—	12,063
Other Expenses	510,000	165,000
Dividend Income	(12,000)	—
Dividends Declared	56,000	15,000
Total	0	0

Required:

Prepare the worksheet necessary to produce the consolidated financial statements of Plessor Industries and its subsidiary for the year ended December 31, 19X3. Include the determination and distribution of excess and income distribution schedules.

Problem 7–12. Steven Truck Company has been an 80%-owned subsidiary of Paulz Heavy Equipment since January 1, 19X3, when Paulz purchased 128,000 shares of Steven common stock for $832,000, an amount equal to the book value of Steven's net assets at that date. Steven's net income and dividends paid since acquisition are as follows:

Year	Net Income	Dividends
19X3	$70,000	$25,000
19X4	75,600	25,000
19X5	81,650	30,000

On January 1, 19X5, Paulz leased a truck from Steven. The 3-year financing-type lease provides for payments of $10,000 each January 1. On January 1, 19X5, the present value of the truck at Steven's 8% implicit rate, including the unguaranteed residual value of $6,000 at the end of the third year, was $32,596. Paulz also has used the 8% implicit rate to record the lease. The truck is being depreciated on a straight-line basis.

On January 1, 19X6, Steven signed a 4-year financing-type lease with Paulz for the rental of specialized production machinery with an 8-year life. There is a $7,000 purchase option at the end of the fourth year. The lease agreement requires lease payments of $30,000 each January 1 plus $1,500 for maintenance of the equipment. It also calls for contingent payments equal to 10% of Steven's cost savings through the use of this equipment, as reflected in any increase in net income (excluding gains or losses on sale of assets) above the previous growth rate of Steven's net income. The present value of the equipment on January 1, 19X6, at Paulz's 10% implicit rate was $109,388.

On October 1, 19X6, Steven sold Paulz a warehouse having a 20-year remaining life, book value of $135,000, and estimated salvage value of $20,000. Paulz paid $195,000 for the building, which is being depreciated on a straight-line basis.

The trial balances at the top of page 423 were prepared by the separate firms on December 31, 19X6.

Required:

Prepare the worksheet necessary to produce the consolidated financial statements of Paulz Heavy Equipment and its subsidiary for the year ended December 31, 19X6. Include income distribution schedules.

	Paulz Heavy Equipment	Steven Truck Company
Cash...	90,485	123,307
Accounts Receivable (net).............................	228,000	120,000
Inventory...	200,000	140,000
Minimum Lease Payments Receivable	97,000	10,000
Unguaranteed Residual Value	—	6,000
Unearned Interest Income	(9,673)	(444)
Assets Under Capital Lease	27,833	109,388
Accumulated Depreciation—Assets Under Capital Lease..	(18,556)	(13,674)
Property, Plant, and Equipment......................	2,075,000	1,145,000
Accumulated Depreciation—Property, Plant, and Equipment...	(713,000)	(160,000)
Investment in Steven Truck Company.............	1,045,800	—
Accounts Payable	(100,000)	(85,000)
Interest Payable...	(740)	(7,939)
Obligations Under Capital Lease	(9,260)	(79,388)
Common Stock ($5 par)................................	(1,800,000)	(800,000)
Retained Earnings, Jan. 1, 19X6	(864,834)	(387,250)
Sales..	(3,200,000)	(1,400,000)
Gain on Sale of Assets................................	—	(60,000)
Interest Income	(7,939)	(1,152)
Rent Income..	(2,182)	—
Cost of Goods Sold.....................................	1,882,000	770,000
Interest Expense..	740	7,939
Depreciation Expense..................................	135,000	45,000
Other Expenses..	924,326	483,213
Subsidiary Income......................................	(124,000)	—
Dividends Declared.....................................	144,000	35,000
Total..	0	0

Problem 7–13. Pankow Inc. purchased an 80% interest in Sampson Company for $480,000 on January 1, 19X1, when Sampson had the following stockholders' equity:

Common stock ($10 par)............................	$100,000
Additional paid-in capital...........................	300,000
Retained earnings.....................................	100,000
Total equity...	$500,000

Any excess was attributed to goodwill and given a 40-year life.

The trial balances of Pankow Inc. and Sampson Company at the top of page 424 were prepared on December 31, 19X5.

The following intercompany leases have been written by Sampson since the acquisition:

1. On January 1, 19X3, Sampson purchased for $140,000 land and a building, which it leased to Pankow Inc. under a 5-year operating lease. Payments

	Pankow Inc.	Sampson Company
Cash..	91,273	26,050
Inventory..	70,000	20,000
Property, Plant, and Equipment...	320,000	50,000
Accumulated Depreciation—Property, Plant, and Equipment..................	(70,000)	(20,000)
Assets Under Capital Lease	37,782	—
Accumulated Depreciation—Assets Under Capital Lease........................	(11,056)	—
Assets Under Operating Lease..	—	420,000
Accumulated Depreciation—Assets Under Operating Lease	—	(80,000)
Minimum Lease Payments Receivable	—	350,000
Unguaranteed Residual Value (leases)	—	62,000
Unearned Interest Income on Leases...	—	(4,000)
Investment in Sampson Company...	480,000	—
Accounts Payable...	(130,000)	(180,000)
Obligations Under Capital Lease	(21,666)	—
Interest Payable...	(3,861)	—
Common Stock ($10 par)..	(200,000)	(100,000)
Paid-In Capital in Excess of Par...	(300,000)	(300,000)
Retained Earnings, Jan. 1, 19X5...	(278,333)	(226,610)
Sales...	(300,000)	(130,000)
Rent Income..	—	(34,000)
Interest Income—Capital Lease	—	(4,440)
Depreciation Expense...	41,000	23,000
Interest Expense...	3,861	—
Selling and General Expense	70,000	38,000
Cost of Goods Sold..	190,000	90,000
Rent Expense...	11,000	—
Total..	0	0

of $11,000 per year are required at the beginning of each year. The $120,000 building cost is being depreciated over 20 years on a straight-line basis.

2. On January 1, 19X4, Sampson purchased a machine for $14,000 and leased it to Pankow Inc. The 4-year lease qualifies as a capital lease. The rentals are $5,000 per year, payable at the beginning of each year. There is a bargain purchase option whereby Pankow will purchase the machine at the end of 4 years for $2,000.

The market value of the machine was $17,560 at the start of the lease term. The lease payments, including the purchase option, yield an implicit rate of 15% to the lessor. Pankow is depreciating the machine over 7 years on a straight-line basis with no salvage value.

3. On January 1, 19X5, Sampson purchased a truck for $23,116 and leased it to Pankow Inc. under a 3-year capital lease. Payments of $8,000 per year are required at the beginning of each year. There was no dealer's profit for Sampson. The truck has an estimated unguaranteed residual value of $5,000 at the end of 3 years. Based on the rents and the salvage value, the lease has a lessor implicit rate of 20%. Pankow Inc. has an incremental borrowing rate of 12%, but has recorded the lease based on the 20% rate.

4. Pankow Inc. has accrued interest in 19X5 on its capital lease obligations. Sampson has recognized earned interest for the year on its capital leases.

Required:

Prepare the worksheet necessary to produce the consolidated financial statements of Pankow Inc. and its subsidiary for the year ended December 31, 19X5. Include the determination and distribution of excess and income distribution schedules.

Worksheet 7–1 (see page 390)   **Intercompany Investment in Bonds, Year of Acquisition;**
                                                            Company P and
                                                     Worksheet for Consolidated
(Credit balance amounts are in parentheses.)   For Year Ended

		Trial Balance	
		Company P	Company S
1	Other Assets	56,400	220,000
2	**Interest Receivable**	**8,000**	
3	Investment in Company S Stock (90%)	100,800	
4			
5	**Investment in Company S Bonds (100%)**	**102,400**	
6	**Interest Payable**		**(8,000)**
7	**Bonds Payable, 8%**		**(100,000)**
8	Common Stock ($10 par), Co. P	(100,000)	
9	Retained Earnings, Jan. 1, 19X3, Co. P	(120,000)	
10	Common Stock ($10 par), Co. S		(80,000)
11	Retained Earnings, Jan. 1, 19X3, Co. S		(20,000)
12	Operating Revenue	(100,000)	(80,000)
13	Operating Expense	70,000	60,000
14	**Interest Income**	**(6,800)**	
15	**Interest Expense**		**8,000**
16	Subsidiary Income	(10,800)	
17	**Loss on Bond Retirement**		
18		0	0
19	Combined Net Income		
20	To Minority Interest (see distribution schedule)		
21	Balance to Controlling Interest (see distribution schedule)		
22	Total Minority Interest		
23	Retained Earnings, Controlling Interest, Dec. 31, 19X3		
24			

Eliminations and Adjustments:
(1) Eliminate the entry recording the parent's share of subsidiary net income for the current year. This step returns the investment in Company S stock account to its January 1, 19X3 balance to aid the elimination process.
(2) Eliminate 90% of the subsidiary equity balances of January 1, 19X3, against the investment in stock account. No excess results.
(3) Eliminate intercompany interest revenue and expense. Eliminate the balance of the investment in bonds against the bonds payable. Note that the investment in bonds is at its end-of-year amortized balance. The loss on retirement at the date the bonds were purchased is calculated as follows:

Straight-Line Method of Amortization **WORKSHEET 7-1**
Subsidiary Company S
Financial Statements
December 31, 19X3

Eliminations & Adjustments			Consolidated Income Statement	Minority Interest	Controlling Retained Earnings	Consolidated Balance Sheet	
Dr.		Cr.					
						276,400	1
	(4)	8,000					2
	(1)	10,800					3
	(2)	90,000					4
	(3)	102,400					5
(4)	8,000						6
(3)	100,000						7
						(100,000)	8
					(120,000)		9
(2)	72,000			(8,000)			10
(2)	18,000			(2,000)			11
			(180,000)				12
			130,000				13
(3)	6,800						14
		(3)	8,000				15
(1)	10,800						16
(3)	3,600		3,600				17
	219,200	219,200					18
			(46,400)				19
			960*	(960)			20
			45,440*		(45,440)		21
				(10,960)		(10,960)	22
					(165,440)	(165,440)	23
						0	24

Loss remaining at year end:
  Investment in bonds at Dec. 31, 19X3 .... $102,400
  Carrying value of bonds at Dec. 31, 19X3 .... 100,000 $2,400
Loss amortized during year:
  Interest expense eliminated 8,000
  Interest revenue eliminated... 6,800   1,200
    Loss at Jan. 2, 19X3 .... $3,600

(4) Eliminate intercompany interest payable and receivable.

(continued)

Subsidiary Company S Income Distribution

Retirement loss on bonds ....(3) $3,600	Internally generated net income, **including interest expense**........ $12,000
	Interest adjustment **($3,600 ÷ 3)**.........................(3) **1,200**
	Adjusted income .... $ 9,600
	Minority share........................... 10%
	Minority interest........................ $ 960*

Parent Company P Income Distribution

Internally generated net income, **including interest revenue**........	$36,800
90% × Company S adjusted income of $9,600......................	8,640
Controlling interest......................	$45,440*

Worksheet 7–2 (see page 391)

**Intercompany Investment in Bonds,
Straight-Line Method**
Company P and
Worksheet for Consolidated
For Year Ended

(Credit balance amounts are in parentheses.)

		Trial Balance	
		Company P	Company S
1	Other Assets	94,400	242,000
2	Interest Receivable	8,000	
3	Investment in Company S Stock (90%)	120,600	
4			
5	**Investment in Company S Bonds (100%)**	**101,200**	
6	Interest Payable		(8,000)
7	Bonds Payable, 8%		(100,000)
8	Common Stock ($10 par), Co. P	(100,000)	
9	**Retained Earnings, Jan. 1, 19X4, Co. P**	**(167,600)**	
10	Common Stock ($10 par), Co. S		(80,000)
11	**Retained Earnings, Jan. 1, 19X4, Co. S**		**(32,000)**
12			
13	Operating Revenue	(130,000)	(100,000)
14	Operating Expense	100,000	70,000
15	Subsidiary Income	(19,800)	
16	Interest Expense		8,000
17	Interest Income	(6,800)	
18		0	0
19	Combined Net Income		
20	To Minority Interest (see distribution schedule)		
21	Balance to Controlling Interest (see distribution schedule)		
22	Total Minority Interest		
23	Retained Earnings, Controlling Interest, Dec. 31, 19X4		
24			

Eliminations and Adjustments:
(1) Eliminate the entry recording the parent's share of subsidiary net income for the current year.
(2) Eliminate the pro rata share of subsidiary equity balances against the investment in stock account. There is no excess to be distributed.
(3) Eliminate intercompany interest revenue and expense. Eliminate the balance of the investment in bonds against the bonds payable. Note that the investment in bonds is at its end-of-year amortized balance. The remaining unamortized loss on retirement at the start of the year is calculated as follows:

Year Subsequent to Acquisition; of Amortization
Subsidiary Company S
Financial Statements
December 31, 19X4

WORKSHEET 7–2

Eliminations & Adjustments Dr.	Eliminations & Adjustments Cr.	Consolidated Income Statement	Minority Interest	Controlling Retained Earnings	Consolidated Balance Sheet	
					336,400	1
	(4) 8,000					2
	(1) 19,800					3
	(2) 100,800					4
	(3) **101,200**					5
(4) 8,000						6
(3) 100,000						7
					(100,000)	8
(3) **2,160**				(165,440)		9
(2) 72,000			(8,000)			10
(2) 28,800			(2,960)			11
(3) **240**						12
		(230,000)				13
		170,000				14
(1) 19,800						15
	(3) 8,000					16
(3) 6,800						17
237,800	237,800					18
		(60,000)				19
		2,320*	(2,320)			20
		57,680*		(57,680)		21
			(13,280)		(13,280)	22
				(223,120)	(223,120)	23
					0	24

Loss remaining at year end:
    Investment in bonds at Dec. 31, 19X4... $101,200
    Carrying value of bonds at Dec. 31, 19X4 .... 100,000 $1,200

Loss amortized during year:
    Interest expense eliminated 8,000
    Interest revenue eliminated... 6,800   1,200
        Remaining loss at Jan. 1, 19X4... $2,400

The remaining unamortized loss of $2,400 on January 1, 19X4 is allocated 90% to the controlling retained earnings and 10% to the minority retained earnings since the bonds were issued by the subsidiary.

(4) Eliminate intercompany interest payable and receivable. *(continued)*

Subsidiary Company S Income Distribution

Internally generated net income, including interest expense	$22,000
Interest adjustment ($3,600 ÷ 3) ....(3)	1,200
Adjusted income	$23,200
Minority share	10%
Minority interest.....................	$ 2,320*

Parent Company P Income Distribution

Internally generated net income, including interest revenue.............................	$36,800
90% × Company S adjusted income of $23,200................	20,880
Controlling interest.................	$57,680*

Worksheet 7–3 (see page 393)

Intercompany Bonds, Subsequent Period;
Company P and
Worksheet for Consolidated
For Year Ended

(Credit balance amounts are in parentheses.)

		Trial Balance	
		Company P	Company S
1	Other Assets	59,400	259,082
2	Investment in Company S Stock	143,874	
3			
4	Investment in Company S Bonds	101,800	
5	Bonds Payable		(100,000)
6	**Discount on Bonds**		**778**
7	Common Stock, Co. P	(100,000)	
8	**Retained Earnings, Jan. 1, 19X4, Co. P**	**(160,000)**	
9	Common Stock, Co. S		(40,000)
10	**Retained Earnings, Jan. 1, 19X4, Co. S**		**(110,000)**
11			
12	Sales	(80,000)	(50,000)
13	**Interest Income**	**(6,200)**	
14	Cost of Goods Sold	50,000	31,362
15	**Interest Expense**		**8,778**
16	Subsidiary Income	(8,874)	
17		0	0
18	Combined Net Income		
19	To Minority Interest (see distribution schedule)		
20	Balance to Controlling Interest (see distribution schedule)		
21	Total Minority Interest		
22	Retained Earnings, Controlling Interest, Dec. 31, 19X4		
23			

Eliminations and Adjustments:
(1) Eliminate the entry recording the parent's share of subsidiary net income for the current year.
(2) Eliminate 90% of the January 1, 19X4 subsidiary equity balances against the January 1, 19X4 investment in Company S stock balance. No excess results.
(3) Eliminate intercompany interest revenue and expense. Eliminate the balance of the investment in bonds against the bonds payable. Note that the investment in bonds and the discount on bonds are at their end-of-year amortized balances. The remaining unamortized loss on retirement at the start of the year is calculated as follows:

WORKSHEET 7–3

Straight-Line Method of Amortization
Subsidiary Company S
Financial Statements
December 31, 19X4

Eliminations & Adjustments			Consolidated Income Statement	Minority Interest	Controlling Retained Earnings	Consolidated Balance Sheet	
Dr.		Cr.					
						318,482	1
	(1)	8,874					2
	(2)	135,000					3
	(3)	101,800					4
(3)	100,000						5
	(3)	778					6
						(100,000)	7
(3)	4,640				(155,360)		8
(2)	36,000			(4,000)			9
(2)	99,000			(10,484)			10
(3)	516						11
			(130,000)				12
(3)	6,200						13
			81,362				14
	(3)	8,778					15
(1)	8,874						16
	255,230	255,230					17
			(48,638)				18
			1,244*	(1,244)			19
			47,394*		(47,394)		20
				(15,728)		(15,728)	21
					(202,754)	(202,754)	22
						0	23

Loss remaining at year end:
Investment in bonds at Dec. 31, 19X4..	$101,800	
Bonds payable at Dec. 31, 19X4..	100,000	
Discount on bonds at Dec. 31, 19X4...	(778)	$2,578
Loss amortized during year:		
Interest expense eliminated	8,778	
Interest revenue eliminated..	6,200	2,578
Remaining loss at Jan. 1, 19X4...		$5,156

The remaining unamortized loss of $5,156 on January 1, 19X4 is allocated 90% to the controlling retained earnings and 10% to the minority retained earnings since the bonds were issued by the subsidiary.

(continued)

Subsidiary Company S Income Distribution

Internally generated net income, including interest expense	$ 9,860
Interest adjustment ($8,778 − $6,200) ....(3)	2,578
Adjusted income......................	$12,438
Minority share	10%
Minority interest......................	$ 1,244*

Parent Company P Income Distribution

Internally generated net income, including interest revenue..............................	$36,200
90% × Company S adjusted income of $12,438	11,194
Controlling interest..................	$47,394*

Worksheet 7–4 (see page 395)

Intercompany Bonds;
Company P and
Worksheet for Consolidated
For Year Ended

(Credit balance amounts are in parentheses.)

		Trial Balance	
		Company P	Company S
1	Other Assets	59,333	259,082
2	Investment in Company S Stock	144,000	
3			
4	**Investment in Company S Bonds**	**101,887**	
5	**Bonds Payable**		**(100,000)**
6	**Discount on Bonds**		**918**
7	Common Stock, Co. P	(100,000)	
8	Retained Earnings, Jan. 1, 19X4, Co. P	(160,180)	
9	Common Stock, Co. S		(40,000)
10	Retained Earnings, Jan. 1, 19X4, Co. S		(110,200)
11			
12	Sales	(80,000)	(50,000)
13	**Interest Income**	**(6,220)**	
14	Cost of Goods Sold	50,000	31,358
15	**Interest Expense**		**8,842**
16			
17	Subsidiary Income	(8,820)	
18		0	0
19	Combined Net Income		
20	To Minority Interest (see distribution schedule)		
21	Balance to Controlling Interest (see distribution schedule)		
22	Total Minority Interest		
23	Retained Earnings, Controlling Interest, Dec. 31, 19X4		
24			

Eliminations and Adjustments:
(1) Eliminate the entry recording the parent's share of subsidiary net income for the current year.
(2) Eliminate 90% of the January 1, 19X4 subsidiary equity balances against the January 1, 19X4 investment in Company S stock balance. No excess results.
(3) Eliminate intercompany interest revenue and expense. Eliminate the balance of the investment in bonds against the bonds payable. Note that the investment in bonds and the discount on bonds are at their end-of-year amortized balances. The remaining unamortized loss on retirement at the start of the year is calculated as follows:

Interest Method of Amortization
Subsidiary Company S
Financial Statements
December 31, 19X4

WORKSHEET 7–4

Eliminations & Adjustments		Consolidated Income Statement	Minority Interest	Controlling Retained Earnings	Consolidated Balance Sheet	
Dr.	Cr.					
					318,415	1
	(1) 8,820					2
	(2) 135,180					3
	(3) 101,887					4
(3) 100,000						5
	(3) 918					6
					(100,000)	7
(3) 4,884				(155,296)		8
(2) 36,000			(4,000)			9
(2) 99,180			(10,477)			10
(3) 543						11
		(130,000)				12
(3) 6,220						13
		81,358				14
	(3) 8,842					15
						16
(1) 8,820						17
255,647	255,647					18
		(48,642)				19
		1,242*	(1,242)			20
		47,400*		(47,400)		21
			(15,719)		(15,719)	22
				(202,696)	(202,696)	23
					0	24

Loss remaining at year end:
Investment in bonds at Dec. 31, 19X4... $101,887
Bonds payable at Dec. 31, 19X4... 100,000
Discount on bonds at Dec. 31, 19X4.. (918) $2,805

Loss amortized during year:
Interest expense eliminated 8,842
Interest revenue eliminated... 6,220   2,622

Remaining loss at Jan. 1, 19X4.. $5,427

The remaining unamortized loss of $5,427 on January 1, 19X4 is allocated 90% to the controlling retained earnings and 10% to the minority retained earnings since the bonds were issued by the subsidiary.   *(continued)*

Subsidiary Company S Income Distribution

Internally generated net income, including interest expense	$ 9,800
Interest adjustment ($8,842 − $6,220) ....(3)	2,622
Adjusted income	$12,422
Minority share	10%
Minority interest......................	$ 1,242*

Parent Company P Income Distribution

Internally generated net income, including interest revenue............................	$36,220
90% × Company S adjusted income of $12,422................	11,180
Controlling interest..................	$47,400*

Worksheet 7–5 (see page 402)

(Credit balance amounts are in parentheses.)

		Trial Balance	
		Company P	Company S
1	Accounts Receivable	30,149	44,793
2	**Minimum Lease Payments Receivable**	**4,000**	
3	**Unguaranteed Residual Value**	**1,000**	
4	**Unearned Interest Income**	**(533)**	
5	**Assets Under Capital Lease**		**5,210**
6	**Accumulated Depreciation—Assets Under Capital Lease**		**(1,737)**
7	Property, Plant, and Equipment	200,000	120,000
8	Accumulated Depreciation—Property, Plant, and Equipment	(80,000)	(50,000)
9	Investment in Company S	87,634	
10			
11	Accounts Payable	(21,000)	(5,000)
12	**Obligations Under Capital Lease**		**(3,210)**
13	Interest Payable		(514)
14	Common Stock ($10 par), Co. P	(50,000)	
15	Retained Earnings, Jan. 1, 19X1, Co. P	(120,000)	
16	Common Stock ($5 par), Co. S		(40,000)
17	Retained Earnings, Jan. 1, 19X1, Co. S		(50,000)
18	Sales	(120,000)	(70,000)
19	**Interest Income**	**(616)**	
20	Subsidiary Income	(15,634)	
21	Operating Expense	65,000	38,207
22	**Interest Expense**		**514**
23	Depreciation Expense	20,000	11,737
24		0	0
25	Combined Net Income		
26	To Minority Interest (see distribution schedule)		
27	Balance to Controlling Interest (see distribution schedule)		
28	Total Minority Interest		
29	Retained Earnings, Controlling Interest, Dec. 31, 19X1		
30			

Capital Lease
Subsidiary Company S
Financial Statements
December 31, 19X1

WORKSHEET 7–5

| Eliminations & Adjustments | | Consolidated Income Statement | Minority Interest | Controlling Retained Earnings | Consolidated Balance Sheet | |
Dr.	Cr.					
					74,942	1
	(4) 4,000					2
	(4) 1,000					3
(4) 635	(3) 102					4
	(4) 5,210					5
(5) 1,737						6
(4) 5,851					325,851	7
	(5) 1,617				(131,617)	8
	(1) 15,634					9
	(2) 72,000					10
					(26,000)	11
(4) 3,210						12
(4) 514						13
					(50,000)	14
				(120,000)		15
(2) 32,000			(8,000)			16
(2) 40,000			(10,000)			17
		(190,000)				18
(3) 616						19
(1) 15,634						20
		103,207				21
	(3) 514					22
	(5) 120	31,617				23
100,197	100,197					24
		(55,176)				25
		3,908*	(3,908)			26
		51,268*		(51,268)		27
			(21,908)		(21,908)	28
				(171,268)	(171,268)	29
					0	30

(continued)

Eliminations and Adjustments:
(1)   Eliminate the parent company's entry recording its share of Company S net income. This step
      returns the investment account to its January 1, 19X1 balance to aid the elimination process.
(2)   Eliminate 80% of the January 1, 19X1 Company S equity balances against the investment in
      Company S balance.
(3)   Eliminate the interest income recorded by the lessor, $616, and the interest expense recorded
      by the lessee, $514. The $102 disparity reflects the interest recorded on the unguaranteed
      residual value. This amount is returned to the unearned interest income.
(4)   Eliminate the intercompany debt and the unguaranteed residual value. Eliminate the asset
      under capital lease and record the owned asset. The amounts are reconciled as follows:

Disparity in recorded debt:	
Lessor balance, $4,000 − $635 unearned interest income...................................	$3,365
Lessee balance, $3,210 + $514 accrued interest	3,724
Interest applicable to unguaranteed residual value	**$ (359)**
Unguaranteed residual value..	1,000
Net original present value of unguaranteed residual value...................................	**$ 641**
Asset under capital lease	5,210
Owned asset at original cost..	$5,851

(5)   Reclassify accumulated depreciation and adjust the depreciation expense to acknowledge
      cost of asset. The adjustment to depreciation expense is determined as follows:

Capitalized cost by lessee		$5,210
Depreciable cost:		
Cost..	$5,851	
Less residual (salvage) value..	1,000	4,851
Decrease in depreciable cost..		$ 359
Adjustment to depreciation expense ($359 ÷ 3-year lease term)...............		$ 120

Subsidiary Company S Income Distribution

Internally generated net income, **including interest on lease**	$19,542
Adjusted income	$19,542
Minority share	20%
Minority interest.....................	$ 3,908*

Parent Company P Income Distribution

Interest eliminated.....................**(3)**	**$102**	Internally generated net income, **including interest income on lease**...................	$35,616	
		80% × Company S adjusted income of $19,542	15,634	
		Decrease in depreciation.......**(5)**	**120**	
		Controlling interest..................	$51,268*	

Worksheet 7–6 (see page 403)

Intercompany Capital
Company P and
Worksheet for Consolidated
For Year Ended

(Credit balance amounts are in parentheses.)

		Trial Balance	
		Company P	Company S
1	Accounts Receivable	102,149	82,925
2	**Minimum Lease Payments Receivable**	**2,000**	
3	**Unguaranteed Residual Value**	**1,000**	
4	**Unearned Interest Income**	**(138)**	
5			
6	**Assets Under Capital Lease**		**5,210**
7	**Accumulated Depreciation—Assets Under Capital Lease**		**(3,474)**
8	Property, Plant, and Equipment	200,000	120,000
9	Accumulated Depreciation—Property, Plant, and Equipment	(100,000)	(60,000)
10	Investment in Company S	102,129	
11			
12	Accounts Payable	(41,000)	(15,000)
13	**Obligations Under Capital Lease**		**(1,724)**
14	Interest Payable		(276)
15	Common Stock ($10 par), Co. P	(50,000)	
16	**Retained Earnings, Jan. 1, 19X2, Co. P**	**(171,250)**	
17	Common Stock ($5 par), Co. S		(40,000)
18	Retained Earnings, Jan. 1, 19X2, Co. S		(69,542)
19	Sales	(150,000)	(80,000)
20	**Interest Income**	**(395)**	
21	Subsidiary Income	(14,495)	
22	Operating Expense	100,000	49,868
23	**Interest Expense**		**276**
24	Depreciation Expense	20,000	11,737
25		0	0
26	Combined Net Income		
27	To Minority Interest (see distribution schedule)		
28	Balance to Controlling Interest (see distribution schedule)		
29	Total Minority Interest		
30	Retained Earnings, Controlling Interest, Dec. 31, 19X2		
31			

Lease, Subsequent Period
Subsidiary Company S
Financial Statements
December 31, 19X2

WORKSHEET 7–6

Eliminations & Adjustments		Consolidated Income Statement	Minority Interest	Controlling Retained Earnings	Consolidated Balance Sheet	
Dr.	Cr.					
					185,074	1
	(5) 2,000					2
	(5) 1,000					3
(5) 359	(3) 119					4
	(4) 102					5
	(5) 5,210					6
(6) 3,474						7
(5) 5,851					325,851	8
	(6) 3,234				(163,234)	9
	(1) 14,495					10
	(2) 87,634					11
					(56,000)	12
(5) 1,724						13
(5) 276						14
					(50,000)	15
(4) 102	(6) 120			(171,268)		16
(2) 32,000			(8,000)			17
(2) 55,634			(13,908)			18
		(230,000)				19
(3) 395						20
(1) 14,495						21
		149,868				22
	(3) 276					23
	(6) 120	31,617				24
114,310	114,310					25
		(48,515)				26
		3,624*	(3,624)			27
		44,891*		(44,891)		28
			(25,532)		(25,532)	29
				(216,159)	(216,159)	30
					0	31

(continued)

Eliminations and Adjustments:

(1) Eliminate the parent company's entry recording its share of Company S net income.

(2) Eliminate 80% of the January 1, 19X2 Company S equity balances against the investment in Company S balance.

(3) Eliminate the interest income recorded by the lessor, $395, and the interest expense recorded by the lessee, $276. The $119 disparity reflects the interest recorded on the unguaranteed residual value. This amount is returned to the unearned interest income.

(4) Adjust the unearned income and the parent's retained earnings for the $102 interest recorded in 19X1 on the unguaranteed residual value.

(5) Eliminate the intercompany debt and the unguaranteed residual value. Eliminate the asset under capital lease and record the owned asset. The amounts are reconciled as follows:

Disparity in recorded debt:	
Lessor balance, $2,000 − $359 unearned interest income..................................	$1,641
Lessee balance, $1,724 + $276 accrued interest	2,000
Interest applicable to unguaranteed residual value	**$ (359)**
Unguaranteed residual value..	1,000
Net original present value of unguaranteed residual value...................................	**$ 641**
Asset under capital lease	5,210
Owned asset at original cost..	$5,851

(6) Reclassify accumulated depreciation. Adjust the depreciation expense for the current year and the controlling retained earnings for the preceding year to acknowledge cost of asset. The adjustment to the depreciation expense and the retained earnings is determined as follows:

Capitalized cost by lessee		$5,210
Depreciable cost:		
Cost..	$5,851	
Less residual (salvage) value..	1,000	4,851
Decrease in depreciable cost...		$ 359
Adjustment to depreciation expense and retained earnings		
($359 ÷ 3-year lease term)..		$ 120

Subsidiary Company S Income Distribution

	Internally generated net income, **including interest on lease**	$18,119
	Adjusted income	$18,119
	Minority share	20%
	Minority interest	$ 3,624*

Parent Company P Income Distribution

Interest eliminated............(3) **$119**	Internally generated net income, **including interest income on lease**	$30,395
	80% × Company S adjusted income of $18,119	14,495
	Decrease in depreciation.......(6)	**120**
	Controlling interest	$44,891*

CHAPTER 8

SPECIAL ISSUES IN ACCOUNTING FOR AN INVESTMENT IN A SUBSIDIARY

This chapter deals with special issues resulting from the various methods by which the parent company acquired its controlling interest in the subsidiary. The chapter first considers the procedures used when a parent acquires its controlling interest in subsidiary stock directly from the subsidiary. The special procedures needed to consolidate subsidiary investments that have been acquired in a piecemeal manner at different points in time then are analyzed.

This chapter also discusses special procedures needed to consolidate subsidiaries that have preferred stock as well as common stock outstanding. Additional consolidation procedures are needed to segregate the preferred stockholders' interest in the subsidiary equity accounts. Further analysis is needed when the parent owns subsidiary preferred stock, since all intercompany investments must be eliminated in the process of consolidating.

In addition, the chapter presents the theory and the recording of a sale of all or a portion of the parent's investment in a subsidiary. The procedures used vary substantially, depending on the relative proportion of the investment sold.

The chapter concludes with an appendix which studies the worksheet procedures needed to produce a consolidated balance sheet only. So far, all of the worksheets prepared subsequent to the acquisition date have been based on trial balances which were used to produce consolidated income and retained earnings statements and a balance sheet. Knowing how to prepare just a consolidated balance sheet is a topic which is of concern to those who plan to take the Uniform CPA exam, since it is a popular testing format.

PARENT ACQUISITION OF STOCK DIRECTLY FROM SUBSIDIARY

A parent firm may organize a new corporation and supply all of the common stock equity funds in exchange for all of the newly organized firm's common stock. Since the newly formed corporation receives the funds directly, there will be no difference between the price paid for the shares and the equity in assets acquired. Thus, the determination and distribution of excess schedule will show no excess of cost over book value or excess of book value over cost.

In other cases, the parent firm will allow the newly organized subsidiary to sell a portion of the shares to persons outside the consolidated group. If the shares are sold to outsiders at a price equal to the price paid by the parent, the cost and book value again will be equal. However, if a price greater or less than the price paid by the parent is charged to outside parties, an excess of cost or book value will result. This excess occurs because the total price paid by the parent will not equal its ownership interest multiplied by the total subsidiary common stockholders' equity. Normally, the excess of cost is recorded as goodwill, and an excess of book value is recorded as a deferred credit, since the only asset held by a newly organized firm is cash, which is not subject to adjustment. If noncash assets are given in exchange for the subsidiary shares, these assets would be adjusted according to the normal distribution of excess procedures.

An existing corporation might sell a sufficient number of new shares to grant a controlling interest to the buying firm. For example, assume that Company S had the following equity balances prior to a sale of shares to Company P:

Common stock, $10 par, 10,000 shares..........	$100,000
Paid-in capital in excess of par......................	150,000
· Retained earnings	220,000
Total stockholders' equity.........................	$470,000

Assume that Company S sells 30,000 additional shares directly to Company P at $50 per share, for a total of $1,500,000. Subsequent to the sale, the equity balances of Company S appear as follows:

Common stock, $10 par, 40,000 shares........	$ 400,000
Paid-in capital in excess of par...................	1,350,000
Retained earnings	220,000
Total stockholders' equity......................	$1,970,000

The fact that the payment was made directly to the subsidiary does not alter the need to analyze the difference between the price paid and the book value of the newly acquired controlling interest. The determination and distribution of excess schedule still must compare the price paid with the portion of the total subsidiary equity acquired. The excess, as determined in the following schedule, then would be distributed according to purchase rules.

Price paid		$1,500,000
Less interest acquired:		
Common stock ($10 par)...	$ 400,000	
Paid-in capital in excess of par.............................	1,350,000	
Retained earnings...	220,000	
Total stockholders' equity..................................	$1,970,000	
Interest acquired...	75%	1,477,500
Excess of cost over book value		$ 22,500

Any adjustment of existing accounts would be limited to 75% of the difference between book and market values since only a 75% interest has been purchased.

PIECEMEAL ACQUISITION OF INTEREST IN SUBSIDIARY

Past examples of combinations in this text have involved an acquisition of a controlling interest in a subsidiary through a single purchase of stock. A parent also may acquire a controlling interest as a result of a series of purchases of subsidiary stock. There will likely be a different excess of cost or book value for each block, and *the causal factors for the differences may vary at the time of each acquisition.* Each block acquired must be accompanied by a separate determination and distribution of excess schedule. The excess of cost or book value must be distributed and amortized separately for each block.

CONTROL ACHIEVED UPON INITIAL INVESTMENT

When control is achieved with the initial investment, consolidation procedures already are in effect when subsequent blocks are purchased. Thus, no major change in accounting methods is required. Another determination and distribution of excess schedule must be prepared for each new investment, and additions to the existing consolidated worksheet procedures must be acknowledged.

Assume that Company P purchases on the open market its original 60% interest in Company S on January 1, 19X1, for $126,000, when Company S has the following balance sheet:

Assets		Liabilities and Equity	
Current assets	$ 50,000	Liabilities	$ 40,000
Equipment (net)................	150,000	Common stock ($10 par)....	100,000
		Retained earnings.............	60,000
Total assets.....................	$200,000	Total liabilities and equity ...	$200,000

Further assume that the current assets require no adjustment, and that the equipment has a net market value of $180,000 and a 5-year remaining life. Goodwill resulting from the purchase of the stock will be amortized over a 10-year period. The following determination and distribution of excess schedule would be prepared on *January 1, 19X1*, for the first acquisition:

Price paid		$126,000
Less interest acquired:		
Common stock..	$100,000	
Retained earnings...	60,000	
Total stockholders' equity......................................	$160,000	
Interest acquired	**60%**	96,000
Excess of cost over book value		$ 30,000
Excess of cost attributable to equipment: 60% × $30,000		
undervaluation (to be amortized over 5 years)		**18,000**
Goodwill (10-year amortization)......................................		**$ 12,000**

On January 1, 19X3, Company P purchases on the open market an additional 20% interest in Company S by paying $50,000. The following balance sheet of Company S on January 1, 19X3, reflects two years of continued operations:

Assets		Liabilities and Equity	
Current assets...................	$ 80,000	Liabilities.........................	$ 50,000
Building (net)	80,000	Common stock ($10 par)....	100,000
Equipment (net)................	90,000	Retained earnings.............	100,000
Total assets......................	$250,000	Total liabilities and equity ...	$250,000

Company P's analysis on January 1, 19X3, indicates that the equipment listed on Company S's balance sheet now is undervalued by $24,000 and has a 3-year remaining life. The current assets and the building appear to have market values equal to their book values. Goodwill is assumed to have a 10-year life. Based on this analysis, the following determination and distribution of excess schedule would be prepared for the *January 1, 19X3* investment:

Price paid		$50,000
Less interest acquired:		
Common stock..	$100,000	
Retained earnings...	100,000	
Total stockholders' equity......................................	$200,000	
Interest acquired	**20%**	40,000
Excess of cost over book value		$10,000
Excess of cost attributable to equipment: 20% × $24,000		
undervaluation (to be amortized over 3 years)		**4,800**
Goodwill (10-year amortization)......................................		**$ 5,200**

Note that this determination and distribution of excess schedule is *free standing*, in that it is completely independent of the appraisals made for the January 1, 19X1 schedule.

The additional worksheet procedures that arise from this piecemeal acquisition are shown in Worksheet 8–1 on pages 506–509. The trial balances of Companies P and S are shown as they would appear on December 31, 19X3. The investment in Company S account is based on the use of the simple equity method during the current and previous years. The December 31, 19X3 balance was determined as follows:

Cost of 60% investment (January 1, 19X1)		$126,000
Add equity share of change in Company S retained earnings as of January 1, 19X3:		
Balance, January 1, 19X3..	**$100,000**	
Balance, January 1, 19X1..	**60,000**	
Increase in retained earnings..	**$ 40,000 × 60% =**	24,000
Cost of 20% investment (January 1, 19X3)...............................		50,000
Add equity share of Company S 19X3 net income:		
80% × $35,000		28,000
Investment account balance, December 31, 19X3.....................		**$228,000**

The combined net income of $78,080 is distributed to the controlling and minority interests as shown in the income distribution schedules that accompany Worksheet 8–1. *Since only the parent's share of excesses of cost or book value is recorded,* all amortizations of excess resulting from parent company purchases are deducted *only* from the controlling interest.

When investment blocks are carried *at cost,* each block must be converted separately to its simple equity balance as of the *beginning* of the year. For each block, the adjustment is based on the change in subsidiary retained earnings between the date of acquisition of the individual block and the beginning of the current year.

Suppose that the subsidiary of the previous example sold merchandise to the parent during 19X2, and that a $2,000 subsidiary profit is included in the parent's ending inventory of merchandise and in the subsidiary retained earnings. *In theory,* the determination and distribution of excess schedule prepared for the 20% investment purchased on January 1, 19X3, should reflect the unrealized gross profit on sales applicable to the 20% interest purchased. Thus, the determination and distribution of excess schedule would be revised to distribute the excess as follows:

Excess of cost over book value	$10,000
Deferred gross profit on inventory sale (20%)...................................	400
Excess of cost attributable to equipment (3-year life).........................	(4,800)
Goodwill (10-year life)	$ 5,600

The deferred gross profit on the inventory sale means that the minority interest just acquired is overstated since the profit is included already in retained earnings. The decrease in the equity acquired increases the excess of cost over book value, thereby making more excess available to remaining assets.

The following entry would distribute the revised excess on the 19X3 worksheet:

Accumulated Depreciation—Equipment............................	4,800	
Goodwill..	5,600	
Deferred Gross Profit on Inventory Sale		400
Investment in Company S..		10,000

The following elimination for the $2,000 profit in the beginning inventory then would be made:

Retained Earnings—Controlling Interest (60% interest at time		
of original sale)	1,200	
Retained Earnings—Minority Interest (20%).........................	400	
Deferred Gross Profit on Inventory Sale	400	
Cost of Goods Sold (beginning inventory)		2,000

In practice, the concept of materiality often will prevail, and the above procedure will not be followed. The determination and distribution of excess schedule will not recognize the unrealized profit; thus the excess cost available for other assets will be less. Worksheets for periods subsequent to the second purchase will ignore the deferred gross profit existing on the purchase date and will distribute the retained earnings adjustments according to the ownership percentages prevailing at the time each worksheet is prepared. The 19X3 elimination would be:

Retained Earnings—Controlling Interest (80%)......................	1,600	
Retained Earnings—Minority Interest (20%).........................	400	
Cost of Goods Sold (beginning inventory)		2,000

This practical approach corrects the controlling interest for unrealized profits existing at the time of the second purchase and is consistent with the practice of charging all excess amortizations to the controlling interest. The procedures discussed are applicable also to retained earnings adjustments resulting from intercompany sales of plant assets and intercompany investments in subsidiary bonds.

CONTROL NOT ACHIEVED UPON INITIAL INVESTMENT

When an initial investment in the stock of another firm represents less than a 50% interest, ordinarily it is improper to prepare consolidated statements. Such an investment is carried under the cost or the sophisticated equity method, depending upon the percentage of interest acquired. APB Opinion No. 18 generally requires the use of the sophisticated equity method when the interest equals or exceeds 20% of the outstanding common shares of an investee corporation.[1] If a second block of stock is purchased, resulting in an interest that exceeds 50%, consolidation becomes appropriate. It will be necessary to treat separately each block of stock acquired when the determination

---

[1]*Opinions of the Accounting Principles Board, No. 18,* "The Equity Method of Accounting for Investments in Common Stock" (New York: American Institute of Certified Public Accountants, 1971), par. 17.

and distribution of excess schedule and the worksheet are prepared. Added complications arise because the original investment must be subjected to the consolidation process retroactively. The complexities involved depend on whether the original investment was recorded under the sophisticated equity or the cost method.

Original Interest Under the Equity Method. The sophisticated equity method of APB Opinion No. 18, described in Chapter 5, requires that the original excess of cost over book value be amortized as an adjustment of investment income in subsequent years. The amortization pattern depends on the underlying nature of the excess. The Opinion admits that it may be difficult to ascertain the nature of the excess, and thus goodwill may be assumed to be the *inferred* cause of the entire excess of cost over book value of an investment.

To illustrate the sophisticated equity method, assume that Company P purchases on the open market a 20% interest in Company S on *January 1, 19X1,* for $48,000. The balance sheet of Company S on January 1, 19X1, is:

Assets		Liabilities and Equity	
Current assets..................	$ 50,000	Liabilities.........................	$ 50,000
Buildings and equipment		Common stock ($10 par)....	50,000
(net)...........................	150,000	Retained earnings.............	100,000
Total assets.....................	$200,000	Total liabilities and equity ...	$200,000

Assuming that the excess of cost is attributable to goodwill, the determination and distribution of excess schedule would be prepared as follows:

Price paid		$48,000
Less interest acquired:		
Common stock..	$ 50,000	
Retained earnings...	100,000	
Total stockholders' equity......................................	$150,000	
Interest acquired	**20%**	30,000
Excess of cost attributed to goodwill (to be amortized		
over 20 years)		$18,000

This schedule requires that the investor reduce the investment account $900 ($18,000 ÷ 20) per year. Since goodwill cannot be recorded in the absence of consolidation and merely is buried in the investment account, the amortization required must be accomplished indirectly *through the investment account.* If Company S reports income of $15,000 for 19X1, for example, Company P would record the following sophisticated equity adjustment to the $48,000 recorded investment cost:

Investment in Company S..	2,100	
Investment Income		2,100
To recognize 20% of Company S reported income less		
amortization of goodwill [(20% × $15,000) − $900].		

Continuing this example, assume that on January 1, 19X2, Company P acquires an additional 60% interest in Company S on the open market for a price of $130,000. The balance sheet of Company S appears as follows on January 1, 19X2:

Assets			Liabilities and Equity	
Current assets......................		$ 70,000	Liabilities.............................	$ 40,000
Building and equipment........	$150,000		Common stock ($10 par)	50,000
Less accumulated			Retained earnings	115,000
depreciation.....................	15,000	135,000		
Total assets.........................		$205,000	Total liabilities and equity	$205,000

If it is assumed that the current assets have book values equal to their market values and that the equipment with a 9-year remaining life is undervalued by $9,000, the determination and distribution of excess schedule for the 60% acquisition on *January 1, 19X2,* would be prepared as follows:

Price paid		$130,000
Less interest acquired:		
Common stock..	$ 50,000	
Retained earnings..	115,000	
Total stockholders' equity.......................................	$165,000	
Interest acquired	**60%**	99,000
Excess of cost over book value		$ 31,000
Excess of cost attributable to equipment: 60% × $9,000		
undervaluation (amortized over 9 years)		5,400
Goodwill (to be amortized over 20 years)........................		$ 25,600

Assuming that Company S reports net income of $20,000 for 19X2, Company P would make the following *simple equity* adjustment for its entire investment:

Investment in Company S..	16,000	
Subsidiary Income..		16,000
To adjust for **80%** of Company S reported income of $20,000.		

Since control now has been achieved, it is appropriate to use the simple equity method. It no longer is necessary to amortize the excess resulting from the January 1, 19X1 and January 1, 19X2 investments through the investment account, since the amortizations will be recorded on the consolidated worksheet as shown in Worksheet 8–2 on pages 510–513. The balance in the investment account results from the investments and income adjustments, which are summarized as follows:

Cost of January 1, 19X1 20% investment..	$ 48,000
19X1 sophisticated equity adjustment..	2,100
Cost of January 1, 19X2 60% investment..	130,000
19X2 simple equity adjustment for 80% interest................................	16,000
Investment balance, December 31, 19X2...	$196,100

If the parent wished for consistency in the recording of the investment, it could elect to remove the previous year's amortization of excess adjustments from the investment account and restore them to the parent's retained earnings. This would mean that the worksheet could include all amortization adjustments, not just those subsequent to obtaining control.

Original Interest Under the Cost Method. When the investment acquired prior to obtaining control is recorded under the cost method, the easiest procedure is to convert the investment account to its simple equity balance, if the later investment in the subsidiary is to be recorded under the simple equity method in future periods. Conversion to the simple equity method thus will make the prior investment compatible with the later investment made to secure control. The conversion preferably should be made directly *on the parent's books*.

Assume that Company P in the previous illustration originally purchased only a 10% interest for $24,000 on January 1, 19X1, and used the cost method to record its investment in Company S. The following determination and distribution of excess schedule would be prepared as of *January 1, 19X1*:

Price paid		$24,000
Less interest acquired:		
Common stock..	$ 50,000	
Retained earnings..	100,000	
Total stockholders' equity.......................................	$150,000	
Interest acquired	**10%**	15,000
Excess of cost attributed to goodwill (to be amortized		
over 20 years)		$ 9,000

When Company P acquires controlling interest on January 1, 19X2, it would convert the 10% interest to the simple equity method *on its books* as follows:

Investment in Company S...	1,500	
Retained Earnings		1,500
To adjust for 10% of the $15,000 increase in the		
subsidiary retained earnings during 19X1.		

It would not be necessary to amortize the $450 ($9,000 ÷ 20 years) of goodwill through the investment account, since that amortization can be done in the normal manner on the 19X2 worksheet for consolidated statements. The conversion process simplifies eliminations and adjustments because the entire original excess of cost of $9,000 will appear on the worksheet.

If the parent does not make the conversion entry on its books, a cost conversion entry should be made on the worksheet. Worksheet 8–3, pages 514–517, is similar to Worksheet 8–2, except that Company P used the *cost* method on an original *10%* investment in Company S and did not convert to the simple equity method on January 1, 19X2. Note that the balance in the investment account would be:

Cost of original **10%** investment	$ 24,000
Cost of 60% investment	130,000
Simple equity adjustment for 19X2	
(**70%** × Company S income of $20,000)...	14,000
Investment balance, December 31, 19X2......................................	$168,000

Alternative Procedure for Cost Method Investment.

When control is not achieved on the first purchase, ARB No. 51 permits a parent to use the date control is achieved as the date of acquisition for both blocks.[2] Thus, a parent is excused from analyzing the cause of excess for a prior-to-achieving-control investment and is allowed to let the original investment remain under the cost method up to the date control is achieved if the result of doing so is not material. In the previous case of Companies P and S, the original 10% interest purchased for $24,000 could be added to the $130,000 cost of the second investment to produce the following determination and distribution of excess schedule on January 1, 19X2:

Price paid (January 1, 19X1 plus January 1, 19X2 investments, $24,000 + $130,000)...............................		**$154,000**
Less interest acquired:		
Common stock..	$ 50,000	
Retained earnings..	115,000	
Total stockholders' equity.......................................	$165,000	
Interest acquired	**70%**	115,500
Excess of cost over book value		$ 38,500
Excess of cost attributable to equipment: **70%** × $9,000 undervaluation (amortized over 9 years)		6,300
Goodwill (to be amortized over 20 years)........................		$ 32,200

The procedure of lumping investments together *cannot* be recommended on theoretical grounds, since the facts surrounding the separate investments are ignored. Also, when the original investment meets or exceeds 20% of the shares of the subsidiary, this procedure would be a direct violation of APB Opinion No. 18.

The parent may use the cost method for blocks that are acquired prior to achieving control and continue to use it for blocks acquired after achieving control. In this situation, each block would be *independently converted* to the equity method as of the beginning of the year, prior to making any elimination entries. The cost-to-equity conversion technique was described in Chapter 5.

---

[2]*Accounting Research Bulletin No. 51*, "Consolidated Financial Statements" (New York: American Institute of Certified Public Accountants, 1959), par. 10.

SUBSIDIARY PREFERRED STOCK

The existence of preferred stock in the capital structure of a subsidiary complicates the calculation of a parent's claim on subsidiary retained earnings, both at the time of acquisition and in the preparation of subsequent consolidated statements. In previous examples the subsidiary had only common stock outstanding, so that all retained earnings were associated with common stock, and the parent had a claim on subsidiary retained earnings in proportion to its ownership interest. When a subsidiary has preferred stock outstanding, however, the preferred stock also may have a claim on retained earnings. This claim may be caused by a liquidation value in excess of par value and/or by participation and cumulative dividend rights. When these conditions exist, the retained earnings must be divided between the preferred and common stockholder interests.

Once retained earnings are allocated between the common and preferred stockholders, the intercompany investments can be eliminated. The investment in subsidiary common stock account will be eliminated against the total equity claim of the common stockholders. If there is an investment in subsidiary preferred stock account, it will be eliminated against the preferred stockholders' total equity.

DETERMINATION OF PREFERRED SHAREHOLDERS' CLAIM ON RETAINED EARNINGS

The allocation of the retained earnings to the preferred and common stockholder interests is accomplished by employing the procedures used to calculate the book value of preferred and common stock. Although typically covered in intermediate accounting, the topic will be reviewed briefly in the following paragraphs.

The preferred shareholders' claim on retained earnings equals the claim they would have if the firm was dissolved. In addition to the par value of the preferred shares, there may be a stipulated liquidation value in excess of par and/or dividend preferences. In the rare case of a liquidation value in excess of par, an amount equal to the liquidation bonus (liquidation value less par value) must be segregated from retained earnings as a preferred shareholder claim. Liquidation values should not be confused with paid-in capital in excess of par which results from the sale of preferred shares. Such paid-in capital is not available to preferred shareholders in liquidation and is not part of the book value of preferred shares. Instead, it becomes part of the total paid-in capital that is available to common shareholders.

In addition to a liquidation bonus, there must be an analysis of any cumulative and/or participation clauses applicable to the preferred stock. Other than the effect of a liquidation bonus, if the preferred stock is noncumulative and nonparticipating, the preferred stockholders would have no claim, and all the retained earnings attach to the common stock. However, if there are preferred shareholder claims resulting from cumulative and/or participation clauses, these claims reduce the retained earnings applicable to the common stock. For example, if the preferred stock is noncumulative but fully participating, the retained earnings are allocated pro rata according to the total par or stated values of the preferred and common stock. If the preferred stock is cumulative but nonparticipating and, for example, has two years' dividends in arrears, a claim on retained earnings equal to the two years of dividends exists, although there is no liability to pay the preferred dividends until a dividend is declared.

When preferred stock is both cumulative and fully participating, the arrearage for prior periods is met first. The remaining retained earnings are allocated pro rata according to the total par values of the preferred and common stock. When preferred stock is cumulative and participating but no dividends are in arrears, the analysis is the same as if the preferred stock were noncumulative but participating.

When preferred stock is cumulative and limited in participation to a percentage of par value, the arrearage for prior periods is met first and is excluded from the limited participation. The lesser of a pro rata share of the remaining retained earnings or the limiting percentage of the preferred stock's par value is allocated to the preferred claim. Any retained earnings remaining after this allocation are assigned to the common stock.

APPORTIONMENT OF RETAINED EARNINGS

Additional procedures are required when a subsidiary with preferred stock that has liquidation and/or dividend preferences is consolidated, even if none of the preferred shares are owned by the parent. In this situation, allocation of retained earnings to the preferred and common stock is as follows:

1. The determination and distribution of excess schedule prepared as of the date of the parent's investment in common stock must include only that portion of retained earnings that is allocable to the common stock on the purchase date.
2. Periodic equity adjustments for the parent's investment in common stock are made only for the common shareholders' claim on income. The preferred shareholders' claim on the current year's income, including dividends paid or accumulated and any participation rights for the current year, must be deducted to arrive at income available to common shareholders. When the cost method is used, the worksheet simple equity conversion adjustment is made for the parent's share of change in the retained earnings applicable to common stock since the date of acquisition.
3. Subsidiary retained earnings must be allocated between preferred and common stockholders on consolidated worksheets. The parent's invest-

ment in common stock account then is eliminated against the parent's pro rata share of only the equity attaching to common stock.

To illustrate these procedures, assume that Company S has the following stockholders' equity on January 1, 19X3, the date on which Company P purchases an 80% interest in the common stock for $150,000:

Preferred stock, $100 par, 6% cumulative.......	$100,000
Common stock, $10 par	100,000
Retained earnings	80,000
Total equity...	$280,000

The preferred stock has a liquidation value equal to par value, and dividends are two years in arrears as of January 1, 19X3. Company S assets have a market value equal to book value. Any excess purchase price is attributable to goodwill with a 10-year life. The determination and distribution of excess schedule would be prepared as follows:

Price paid			$150,000
Less interest acquired:			
Common stock ($10 par).....................................		$100,000	
Retained earnings:			
Balance, Jan. 1, 19X3.....................................	**$80,000**		
Less preferred dividends in arrears (2 years × $6,000)	**12,000**	**68,000**	
Total equity applicable to common stock		$168,000	
Interest acquired..		80%	134,400
Excess of cost attributed to goodwill (10-year amortization)			$ 15,600

Assume that income is exactly $25,000 per year in future years and that no dividends are paid. Each year, the following entry would be made by Company P using the simple equity method of accounting for its subsidiary investment:

Investment in Common Stock of Company S....................	15,200	
Subsidiary Income...		15,200
To adjust for 80% of Company S income applicable to common stock ($25,000 reported income − $6,000 cumulative claim of preferred stock).		

Worksheet 8–4, pages 518–521, is a consolidated financial statements worksheet for the year ended *December 31, 19X5* (3 years subsequent to the purchase). The investment in common stock account includes the original cost of the investment plus 3 years (3 × $15,200 = $45,600) of simple equity adjustments for income and dividends. The worksheet is unique in that it subdivides the subsidiary retained earnings into two parts: one for the common portion and one for the preferred portion of retained earnings. This is done only for analytical purposes; there is still only one subsidiary retained earnings account.

After the eliminations and adjustments are completed, the resulting combined net income of $173,440 is allocated as shown in the income distribution schedules. Since none of the preferred stock is owned by controlling shareholders, the minority interest receives all applicable preferred income plus 20% of the income allocable to common stock. It should be observed that the Minority Interest column, as well as the minority interest shown on a formal balance sheet, includes the minority interest in both preferred and common shares.

The worksheet just analyzed can handle all types of subsidiary preferred stockholder claims. Once the claim is determined, with supporting calculations, it can be isolated in a separate worksheet account, *Retained Earnings Allocated to Preferred Stock.*

When a parent uses the cost method to record its investment in a subsidiary, slightly different worksheet procedures are used. In the previous illustration, if Company P had used the cost method, the investment account still would be at the $150,000 original cost. In addition, there would be no subsidiary income shown, and the January 1, 19X5 Retained Earnings of Company P would not reflect the 19X3 and 19X4 simple equity adjustments. As described earlier, a conversion to the simple equity method is made on the worksheet. Since the beginning-of-the-period investment balance is needed for elimination, the equity adjustment converts the investment account to the January 1, 19X5 balance, as follows:

Retained earnings, Company S, January 1, 19X5	$130,000	
Less 4 years' arrearage of preferred dividends	24,000	
Retained earnings applicable to common stock, January 1, 19X5		**$106,000**
Retained earnings, Company S, January 1, 19X3	$ 80,000	
Less 2 years' arrearage of preferred dividends	12,000	
Retained earnings applicable to common stock, January 1, 19X3		**68,000**
Increase in common stock portion of retained earnings		$ 38,000
Controlling interest (80%)		$ 30,400

The conversion entry for $30,400 would debit the investment account and credit the Company P retained earnings account. The investment account now would be stated at its simple-equity-adjusted, January 1, 19X5 balance. Worksheet steps (1), (3), (4), and (5) would be made just as in Worksheet 8–4. Only step (2) would be omitted, since it is not applicable to the cost method. The partial worksheet on page 464 includes the conversion and subsequent eliminations and adjustments under the cost method. All remaining procedures for this example would be identical to those used in Worksheet 8–4.

PARENT INVESTMENT IN SUBSIDIARY PREFERRED STOCK

A parent company may purchase all or a portion of the preferred stock of a subsidiary. *Such an investment is not considered in determining whether the parent owns a controlling interest.* Controlling interest for purposes of consolidated

	Partial Trial Balance		Eliminations & Adjustments			
	Company P	Company S	Dr.		Cr.	
Investment in Common Stock of Co. S	150,000		**(C)** 30,400		(3)	164,800
					(4)	15,600
Goodwill			(4)	15,600	(5)	4,680
Retained Earnings, Jan. 1, 19X5, Co. P	(309,600)		(5)	3,120	**(C)**	30,400
Preferred Stock ($100 par), Co. S		(100,000)				
Retained Earnings Allocated to Preferred Stock, Jan. 1, 19X5, Co. S					(1)	24,000
Common Stock ($10 par), Co. S		(100,000)	(3)	80,000		
Retained Earnings, Jan. 1, 19X5, Co. S		(130,000)	(1)	24,000		
			(3)	84,800		
Expenses	100,000	25,000	(5)	1,560		

Eliminations and Adjustments:

(C) The cost-to-equity conversion entry was explained prior to the partial worksheet.

(1) Distribute the beginning-of-the-period subsidiary retained earnings into the portions allocable to common and preferred stock. The typical procedure would be to consider the stated subsidiary retained earnings as applicable to common and to remove the preferred portion. This distribution reflects 4 years of arrearage (as of January 1, 19X5) at $6,000 per year.

(3) Eliminate the pro rata subsidiary common stockholders' equity at the beginning of the period against the investment account. This step includes elimination of the 80% of subsidiary retained earnings applicable to common stock.

(4) Distribute the excess of cost according to the determination and distribution of excess schedule.

(5) Amortize the goodwill for the past two years and the current year.

statements applies only to the parent's interest in voting common stock, since preferred stock generally is nonvoting. Thus, a 100% ownership of preferred stock and a 49% interest in common stock normally would not require the preparation of consolidated statements.

From a consolidated viewpoint, the parent's purchase of subsidiary preferred stock usually is viewed as a retirement of the stock.[3] The amount paid is compared to the sum of the original proceeds resulting from the issuance of the shares and any claim the shares have on retained earnings, and an increase or decrease in equity as a result of the retirement is calculated. When the price paid is less than the preferred equity retired, the resulting increase in equity is credited to the controlling paid-in capital account, not the retained earnings account, since it results from a transaction with the

---

[3]It also would be possible to view the investment as treasury shares, in which case they would appear as a contra account to the preferred stock in the minority interest section of the consolidated balance sheet. This approach, however, does not have popular support. It could be justified only if there is an intent to reissue the shares.

consolidated firm's shareholders. A decrease in equity, which occurs when the price paid exceeds the preferred equity, would offset against the paid-in capital applicable to the preferred stock. If not enough of the preferred stock paid-in capital exists, the remaining decrease would be taken from the controlling retained earnings and viewed as a retirement dividend.

To illustrate this type of investment, assume that Company P in the previous example purchased 600 shares (60%) of Company S preferred stock on January 1, 19X3, for $65,000. The increase or decrease in equity resulting from the retirement would be calculated as follows:

Price paid		$65,000
Less preferred interest acquired:		
Preferred stock ($100 par)..	$100,000	
Claim on dividends (2 years in arrears × $6,000 per year) ...	12,000	
Total preferred interest..	$112,000	
Interest acquired..	60%	67,200
Increase in equity (credit Paid-In Capital)........................		**$ 2,200**

Though viewed as retired, the preferred stock investment account will continue to exist on the books of the parent in subsequent periods. At the end of each period, the investment must be "retired" on the consolidated worksheet. The procedures used depend on whether the parent accounts for the investment in preferred stock under the equity method or the cost method. Under the equity method, the parent adjusts the investment in preferred stock account each period for any additional claim on the subsidiary retained earnings, including any continued arrearage or participation privilege. In this example, the arrearage of dividends would be recorded each year, 19X3 to 19X5, as follows:

Investment in Company S Preferred Stock...........................	3,600	
Subsidiary Income..		3,600
To acknowledge 60% of the annual increase in		
the Company S preferred stock dividend arrearage.		

Assuming that the equity adjustments are made properly, any original discrepancy between the price paid for the preferred shares and their book value would be maintained. The equity method also acknowledges that, even though the shares are viewed as retired in consolidated reports, the controlling interest is entitled to its proportionate share of combined net income based on both its common and preferred stock holdings.

Worksheet 8–5, pages 522–525, displays the consolidation procedures that would be used for the ownership interest in preferred stock described above. This worksheet parallels Worksheet 8–4 except that the parent owns 60% of the subsidiary preferred stock. The investment is listed at its $65,000 cost plus three years of equity adjustments to reflect the increasing dividend arrearage.

Combined net income is distributed as shown in the income distribution schedules that accompany the worksheet. The distributions respect the controlling/minority ownership of both common and preferred shares. The common and preferred equity interests of the minority again are summarized on the worksheet and for presentation on the formal balance sheet.

If a parent uses the cost method for its investment in subsidiary preferred stock, the investment should be converted to its equity balance as of the beginning of the period. In this example, if the cost method is used for the investment in preferred stock, the following conversion adjustment would be made on the worksheet:

Investment in Company S Preferred Stock............................ 7,200
    Retained Earnings (January 1, 19X5, Co. P)........................   7,200

The adjustment reflects two years of arrearage at $6,000 per year times the 60% ownership interest. Eliminations and adjustments would proceed as in Worksheet 8–5, except that there would be no need for step (6).

This example contains only cumulative preferred stock. However, the same principles would apply to participating preferred stock, and the allocation procedures outlined earlier in this chapter would be used. Only the subdivision of the subsidiary retained earnings and the amounts of the equity adjustments would differ.

SALE OF PARENT'S INVESTMENT IN COMMON STOCK

A parent may sell all of its subsidiary interest or enough shares to fall below the greater-than-50% interest generally required for consolidated reporting. Such an action makes it unnecessary to continue consolidated reporting and requires that a gain or loss on the sale of the investment be recorded. There may be other situations in which a parent sells a part of its shares of subsidiary common stock but still retains a greater-than-50% interest after the sale. When such an event occurs, subsequent financial reports still would be prepared on a consolidated basis. In theory, the consolidated, single-firm viewpoint could be applied to such a stock sale. This view holds that the consolidated firm has sold shares to the minority interest and that no gain or loss should be reflected on the consolidated income statement as a result of the intercompany transaction. It has become common practice, however, to record a gain or loss on such sales. This treatment is based on the concept that there has been a sale of a corporate asset (an investment) and that the purchaser was an outside party (not an existing minority interest) at the time of the sale. The new ownership interest, of course, does become a minority shareholder subsequent to the purchase.

SALE OF ENTIRE INVESTMENT

The sale of the entire investment in a subsidiary terminates the need for consolidated financial statements. In fact, when a sale occurs during the parent's fiscal year, the results of the subsidiary operations prior to the sale date typically are not consolidated. Instead, the net results of the subsidiary operations up to the sale date are shown as a separate line item on the parent's statements. In recording the sale of the investment in a subsidiary, the accountant's primary concern is to adjust the carrying value of the investment so that the correct gain or loss on the sale can be recorded.

The accountant also must determine if the sale of the investment in a subsidiary constitutes a disposal of a segment of a business as defined by APB Opinion No. 30. The Opinion states: "... the term *segment of a business* refers to a component of an entity whose activities represent a separate major line of business or class of customer."[4] The Opinion indicates that a segment can be in the form of a subsidiary. However, an interpretation of the Opinion makes it clear that not all subsidiaries qualify as segments of a business. For example, a parent may own several subsidiaries engaged in mining coal. If one subsidiary is sold, that would not constitute a sale of a major line of business, since the parent still is involved in coal mining. When the sale of a subsidiary qualifies as a disposal of a business segment, both the gain or loss on the sale and the results of operations for the period are shown net of tax in a separate discontinued-segment section of the income statement (see Chapter 2). When the sale does not qualify as a disposal of a business segment, the gain or loss and the results of operations for the period usually are shown on the income statement as a part of the normal recurring operations.

The complexities of properly recording the sale of an entire subsidiary investment are shown in the following example. Suppose that Company P purchased an 80% interest in Company S on January 1, 19X1, for $250,000, and the following determination and distribution of excess schedule was prepared.

Price paid		$250,000
Less interest acquired:		
Common stock ($10 par)...	$100,000	
Retained earnings, January 1, 19X1.............................	150,000	
Total stockholders' equity..	$250,000	
Interest acquired..	80%	200,000
Excess of cost over book value		$ 50,000
Excess of cost attributable to equipment (5-year life)........		20,000
Goodwill (10-year life)...		$ 30,000

Company S earned $40,000 in 19X1 and $25,000 in 19X2. Company P sells the entire 80% interest on January 1, 19X3, for $320,000. Assuming the use of the simple equity method, Company P's separate statements reflect the following:

---

[4]*Opinions of the Accounting Principles Board, No. 30,* "Reporting the Results of Operations" (New York: American Institute of Certified Public Accountants, 1973), par. 13.

Purchase price..	$250,000
Share of subsidiary income, 19X1, 80% × $40,000.............................	32,000
Share of subsidiary income, 19X2, 80% × $25,000.............................	20,000
Investment in Co. S, December 31, 19X2......................................	$302,000

The investment account and the parent's January 1, 19X3 retained earnings balance reflect a $52,000 increase as a result of subsidiary operations in 19X1 and 19X2. On this basis, it appears that there is an $18,000 gain on the sale of the investment ($320,000 selling price less $302,000 simple-equity-adjusted cost). This result does not agree, however, with the consolidated financial statements prepared for 19X1 and 19X2, which included as expenses the amortizations of excess required by the determination and distribution of excess schedule. The parent's share of subsidiary income appeared as follows in the consolidated statements:

	19X1	19X2	Total
Share of subsidiary income to Company P (80%)..........................	$32,000	$20,000	$52,000
Less amortization of excess of cost of investment over book value:			
Adjustment for depreciation on equipment:			
$20,000 ÷ 5 = $4,000 per year...	(4,000)	(4,000)	(8,000)
Adjustment for amortization of goodwill:			
$30,000 ÷ 10 = $3,000 per year	(3,000)	(3,000)	(6,000)
Net increase in Company P income due to ownership of			
Company S investment...	$25,000	$13,000	$38,000

Thus, while Company P's separate books show a $52,000 share of Company S income, the consolidated statements reflect only $38,000, the difference being caused by the $14,000 of amortizations indicated by the determination and distribution of excess schedule. Clearly, the recording of the sale of the parent's interest must be based on the $38,000 share of income, since that amount of income is shown on the prior income statements of the consolidated firm. Before recording the sale of the investment, Company P must adjust its books to be consistent with prior consolidated statements. The entry needed will adjust the January 1, 19X3 retained earnings account on the separate books of the parent to the December 31, 19X2 balance of the controlling interest in retained earnings shown on the consolidated statements. The adjusting entry on the books of Company P is:

Retained Earnings (January 1, 19X3)................................	14,000	
Investment in Company S...		14,000
To adjust the investment account and Company P retained earnings account for amortizations made on past consolidated statements.		

If the sophisticated equity method was used, the amortizations would be reflected already in the investment account and no adjustment would be needed. Under either method, the entry to record the sale then would be:

Cash..	320,000	
Investment in Company S ($302,000 − $14,000)..........		288,000
Gain on Disposal of Subsidiary....................................		32,000
To record the gain on the sale of the 80% interest in Company S.		

Note that the $14,000 adjusting entry for the past years' amortizations of excess normally would have been made on the consolidated worksheet for 19X3. However, since there will be no further consolidations, the adjustment must be made directly on Company P's books. The gain (net of tax) on the disposal of the subsidiary will appear as a separate item on the income statement for 19X3 if the sale of the subsidiary meets the criteria for a disposal of a business segment.

In this example, if Company P had used the cost method, the investment account still would be shown at the original cost of $250,000. It then would be necessary to update the investment and retained earnings accounts on the separate books of Company P to include its $38,000 (net of amortizations) share of subsidiary income for 19X1 and 19X2. This adjustment would allow the accounts of the parent on January 1, 19X3, to conform to past consolidated statements. The following entries would be made on the books of Company P to record the sale of the parent's 80% interest:

Investment in Company S..	38,000	
Retained Earnings (January 1, 19X3).........................		38,000
To record the parent's share of subsidiary income as shown on prior years' consolidated statements.		

Cash..	320,000	
Investment in Company S ($250,000 + $38,000).......		288,000
Gain on Disposal of Subsidiary.................................		32,000

Assume that the investment in the previous example was sold for $320,000 on July 1, 19X3, and that Company S reported income of $12,000 for the first six months of 19X3. Since Company S will not be a part of the consolidated group at the end of the period, the results of its operations will not be consolidated with those of the parent. Therefore, the parent must record its share of subsidiary income for the current period to the date of disposal. The parent's net share of subsidiary income would be calculated on a basis consistent with past consolidated statements, as follows:

Share of subsidiary income for first six months to Company P (80%)	$9,600
Less amortizations of excess of cost over book value that would have been made on consolidated statements:	
Equipment depreciation adjustment, $4,000 per year × 1/2 year.........	(2,000)
Amortization of goodwill adjustment, $3,000 per year × 1/2 year........	(1,500)
Net share of subsidiary income...	$6,100

The parent would proceed to record the July 1, 19X3 sale of its subsidiary investment as follows:

1. Assuming the past use of the simple equity method, the parent's investment account on January 1, 19X3, is adjusted to reflect the amortizations made on past consolidated statements (as calculated on page 468).

   Retained Earnings (January 1, 19X3) 14,000
      Investment in Company S   14,000

2. The parent's share of subsidiary income for the partial year is recorded. This amount is the $6,100 income net of amortizations (as calculated on page 469).

   Investment in Company S 6,100
      Operating Income of Subsidiary Disposed of During
        Year   6,100

3. The sale of the investment for $320,000 is recorded.

   Cash 320,000
      Investment in Company S   294,100
      Gain on Disposal of Subsidiary   25,900

   The adjusted cost of the investment is determined as follows:

Original cost (January 1, 19X1)	$250,000
Simple equity income adjustments for 19X1 and 19X2	52,000
Amortization of excess (entry 1)	(14,000)
Share of Company S income for six months (entry 2)	6,100
Net cost, July 1, 19X3	$294,100

SALE OF PORTION OF INVESTMENT

The sale of a portion of an investment in a subsidiary requires unique treatment, depending on whether effective control is lost as a result of the sale. Special procedures also must be used when a sale of a partial interest occurs during a reporting period.

Loss of Control. A parent may sell a portion of its investment in a subsidiary, so that its remaining interest falls below 50%. This situation may occur for foreign subsidiaries when the foreign government passes a law forbidding control of its firms by nonresidents. Such a sale also may be made to avoid consolidating an affiliated firm. This may occur as a reaction to FASB Statement No. 94, which now requires the consolidation of nonhomogeneous subsidiaries which previously did not have to be consolidated.[5] If an interest is reduced below 50%, consolidation procedures no longer will apply. This situation would require that the parent company books be adjusted to make them consistent with prior consolidated statements. Exactly the same adjusting entries as in the immediately preceding section are needed to ad-

---

[5]*Statement of Financial Accounting Standards, No. 94,* "Consolidation of All Majority-owned Subsidiaries" (Stamford: Financial Accounting Standards Board, 1987), par. 9.

just the parent's investment account. Note that the adjustments are made for the entire interest previously owned, not just the portion sold. If in the preceding example Company P sells one-half instead of all of its 80% interest, the investment account should be adjusted for the entire 80% interest in past and current years' subsidiary income, net of amortizations. The 40% interest sold must be adjusted to record the sale properly, and the 40% interest retained also must be adjusted, since it no longer will be consolidated. Past adjustments that would be handled as part of the annual consolidation process now must be made directly to the investment account, so that the investment remaining conforms with APB Opinion No. 18. The sophisticated equity method described in APB Opinion No. 18 should be applied to remaining interests of 20% or more.

If one-half of Company P's investment of the preceding section is sold for $160,000 on July 1, 19X3, the following entries would be recorded:

1. Assuming the past use of the simple equity method, the parent's investment account on January 1, 19X3, is adjusted to reflect the amortizations made on past consolidated statements.

   Retained Earnings (January 1, 19X3)............................. 14,000
       Investment in Company S....................................... 14,000

2. The parent's share of subsidiary income for the partial year is recorded. This amount is the $6,100 income net of amortizations.

   Investment in Company S.. 6,100
       Subsidiary Income.. 6,100

   Note that this income is no longer from a disposed-of subsidiary.

3. The sale of one-half of the investment for $160,000 is recorded.

   Cash.. 160,000
       Investment in Company S (1/2 of $294,100 adjusted
         cost calculated on page 470)............................. 147,050
       Gain on Sale of Investment................................... 12,950

   Note that the sale of a partial interest *will not qualify* as a discontinued segment. Thus, the operating results on the investment to the sale date and the gain or loss on the sale would be shown as a part of ordinary income from continuing operations.

Control Retained. A parent company may sell a portion of its investment in a subsidiary but still have an interest that exceeds 50% after the sale. For example, assume that on January 1, 19X1, a parent purchased from outside parties 8,000 of the total 10,000 shares of a subsidiary. On January 1, 19X3, the parent sold 2,000 shares and thereby lowered its percentage of ownership to 60%. Since the parent still had control, the 2,000 shares were sold, in essence, to minority shareholders. According to the entity theory of business combinations, which focuses on the position of the entire combined entity, this transaction should be viewed as a treasury stock transaction that occurred strictly between members of a consolidated group. Thus, any change in equity due to the resale of the stock should be treated as an adjustment to paid-in capital.

According to the proprietary theory, which focuses on only the position of the controlling interest, the sale of a portion of an interest in a subsidiary should be viewed as producing a gain or loss to be reported on the income statement. This treatment is common in practice and is required by the SEC, unless the sale is part of a broader corporate reorganization. Therefore, this treatment will be used in this text.

To illustrate the recording of such a partial sale, return to the example for which a determination and distribution of excess schedule was prepared on page 467. Assume that on January 1, 19X3, Company P sells 2,000 subsidiary shares to lower its total interest to 60%. Only the portion of the investment account sold is to be adjusted to the sophisticated equity method to allow the proper recording of the sale. The 60% retained need not be adjusted on Company P's books, since all amortization adjustments on the 60% interest will be made on future consolidated statements. The adjustment of the 20% interest on the separate books of Company P must agree with the treatment of that interest in prior consolidated statements. Assuming the use of the simple equity method, the portion of the investment sold must be adjusted for its share of the past amortizations made on consolidated statements. Since the 19X1 and 19X2 amortizations on page 468 totaled $14,000 for an 80% interest, the amortizations for the 20% interest sold would be one-fourth of $14,000, or $3,500. The parent would make the following entry:

Retained Earnings (January 1, 19X3)	3,500	
Investment in Company S		3,500
To adjust for amortizations made on previous consolidated statements for the portion of the subsidiary investment sold.		

To record the sale of the investment, the parent would remove from its books one-fourth of the simple-equity-adjusted cost of January 1, 19X3 (calculated at $302,000 on page 468), which along with the previous $3,500 adjustment nets to $72,000. If the sale price is less than $72,000, a loss would be recorded. If the sale price is greater than $72,000, a gain would be recorded, as shown in the following entry to record the sale of the investment for $80,000:

Cash	80,000	
Investment in Company S [(1/4 × $302,000) − $3,500 amortization adjustment]		72,000
Gain on Sale of Subsidiary Stock		8,000

If the parent in the previous example had used the cost method, only the portion of the investment sold would be adjusted to the sophisticated equity method on the parent's books. The analysis on page 468 shows that the parent's 80% share of income for 19X1 and 19X2 was $38,000 on a consolidated basis, net of amortizations. The 20% interest sold must be adjusted by one-fourth of $38,000, or $9,500. The remaining 60% will be adjusted in future worksheets. The entry to adjust the 20% interest would be:

Investment in Company S..	9,500	
Retained Earnings (January 1, 19X3)..............................		9,500
To adjust for the parent's share of past consolidated income pertaining to the interest sold.		

The parent then would proceed to record the sale of the investment for $80,000 as follows:

Cash..	80,000	
Investment in Company S (1/4 of original $250,000 cost + $9,500 equity income).......................................		72,000
Gain on Sale of Subsidiary Stock.................................		8,000

Intraperiod Sale of a Partial Interest. When a sale of an interest during the reporting period does not result in loss of control, careful analysis is needed to insure that the worksheet adheres to consolidation theory. Referring to the situation on page 467, assume that Company P sells one-fourth of its 80% interest for $80,000 on July 1, 19X3, and that subsidiary income for the first half of the year is $12,000. Assuming the use of the simple equity method, the parent would adjust its own investment and the beginning-of-the-year retained earnings accounts for one-fourth of the amortizations of excess cost recorded on the prior years' consolidated worksheets. The adjustment would be recorded as follows:

Retained Earnings (January 1, 19X3)..................................	3,500	
Investment in Company S...		3,500
To record one-fourth of the $14,000 amortizations (shown on page 468) for 19X1 and 19X2.		

A parent using the cost method would adjust the retained earnings for the subsidiary income, net of amortizations, for 19X1 and 19X2 (20% × $38,000 income on a consolidated basis).

Next the parent would calculate its share of subsidiary income for the first half of 19X3 applicable to the 20% interest sold and adjusted for partial-year amortizations of excess relating to that portion of the investment as follows:

Income on 20% interest in Company S sold (20% × $12,000)..................	$2,400
Less amortizations of excess of cost over book value that would be necessary on consolidated statements:	
Equipment depreciation adjustment,	
$4,000 per year × 1/2 year × 1/4 interest sold...........................	(500)
Amortization of goodwill adjustment,	
$3,000 per year × 1/2 year × 1/4 interest sold...........................	(375)
Net share of income on interest sold..	$1,525

The parent then would make a sophisticated equity method adjustment for this income and record the sale as follows:

Investment in Company S...	1,525	
Subsidiary Income...		1,525

To record share of first six months' subsidiary income applicable to the 20% interest sold and adjusted for partial-year amortizations of excess relating to that portion of the investment.

Cash...	80,000	
Investment in Company S [(1/4 × $302,000) − $3,500 amortizations + $1,525 income]		73,525
Gain on Sale of Subsidiary Stock.................................		6,475

To record sale of 20% interest in subsidiary.

The sale of a partial interest that does not result in loss of control requires special procedures on the consolidated worksheet for the period in which the sale occurs. Worksheets of later periods would not include any complications resulting from the sale. In Worksheet 8–6 on pages 526–529, the following should be noted:

1. The investment in Company S account reflects its simple equity balance on December 31, 19X3, for the remaining 60% interest held. The balance is computed as follows:

December 31, 19X2 balance applicable to remaining (60%) interest held at year end, 3/4 × $302,000.................................	$226,500
Add 60% of subsidiary reported income of $30,000	18,000
Simple equity balance, December 31, 19X3	$244,500

2. The balance in Gain on Sale of Subsidiary Stock is the gain resulting from the 20% interest sold.
3. The balance in Subsidiary Income includes 60% of the subsidiary's $30,000 19X3 income, plus the $1,525 earned on the 20% interest prior to its sale.
4. The income applicable to the interest sold, $2,400, is transferred to the minority interest. Thus, income was earned by the controlling interest but has been sold to the minority interest. The income transferred is without deduction for amortizations of excess cost since such excesses only apply to the parent company.

The income distribution schedules that accompany Worksheet 8–6 show the distribution of combined net income according to the ownership interests in effect during the period.

If the parent, Company P, had used the cost method, there would be few changes in Worksheet 8–6. Step (1) would be unchanged; however, an entry would be needed to convert the remaining 60% interest to the simple equity method at the beginning of the year. Step (2) would not be applicable, since there would be no current-year equity adjustment to reverse. Steps (3) through (6) would remain the same.

Complications Resulting from Intercompany Transactions. When a sale of subsidiary stock results in loss of control, the parent should adjust its investment account on the date of the sale for its share of unrealized subsidiary gains and losses resulting from intercompany transactions. When control is not lost as the result of a sale of subsidiary shares, the adjustment on the consolidated worksheet for unrealized gains and losses resulting from previous intercompany transactions need be recorded only as it applies to the interest sold. The remaining controlling interest's share of these gains and losses can be adjusted on subsequent consolidated worksheets. On these worksheets, retained earnings adjustments for unrealized gains and losses would be distributed according to the relative ownership interests existing on the dates the worksheets are prepared.

APPENDIX: WORKSHEET FOR A CONSOLIDATED BALANCE SHEET

Previous chapters displayed procedures applicable to worksheets that produced a consolidated income statement, retained earnings statement, and balance sheet. However, there may be occasions when only consolidated balance sheets are required, and the separate balance sheets of the affiliates form the starting point for consolidation procedures. Such occasions are rare in practice, but are of concern to students desiring to take the CPA examination. Past examinations have used balance-sheet-only consolidation problems as an expedient method for testing purposes. This type of problem requires less time to solve while still testing the candidates' knowledge of consolidations.

A balance sheet worksheet requires only adjustments to balance sheet accounts. No adjustments for nominal accounts are required. Your past experience often will lead you to consider the impact of an elimination on the nominal accounts, but you must adjust your thinking to cover only the remaining impact of an elimination on the balance sheet. For example, intercompany merchandise sales no longer will require an elimination of the sales and cost of goods sold relative to the transaction. The following sections examine the simplified procedures that are used on a consolidated balance sheet worksheet.

INVESTMENT ACCOUNT

When the investment account is maintained under the simple equity method, it will reflect the same point in time as do the subsidiary equity balances. There is no need to eliminate the parent's entry for its share of subsidiary income. Instead, the pro rata share of subsidiary equity balances may be eliminated directly against the investment account.

Investments maintained under the sophisticated equity method are also at a common point in time and thus can be eliminated directly against the underlying subsidiary equity. The distributable excess, however, will be only that which remains net of the amortizations made in the current and previous periods.

Investments maintained at cost should be converted to the simple equity method as of the end of the year to agree in time with the subsidiary equity balances. The entire conversion adjustment is carried to the controlling retained earnings.

Excesses are distributed according to the determination and distribution of excess schedules. Once distributed, the excesses are amortized to the balance sheet date, and the entire amortization is carried to the controlling retained earnings.

MERCHANDISE SALES

Only the intercompany profit in the ending inventory needs adjustment. The profit is eliminated from the inventory and from retained earnings. The adjustment to retained earnings is allocated according to the minority/controlling ownership percentages in effect when the subsidiary made the intercompany sale. If the parent made the sale, the adjustment is made only to the controlling retained earnings. The intercompany profit in the beginning inventory either has been realized through the subsequent sale of the merchandise to an outside party or, if the units in the beginning inventory are still on hand at year end, they would be included in the adjustment for intercompany profit in the ending inventory.

PLANT ASSET SALES

The only matter for concern in the case of intercompany plant asset sales is the adjustment of the asset and retained earnings accounts for the undepreciated portion of the intercompany gain or loss as of year end. The asset account is adjusted to its cost to the consolidated firm; accumulated depreciation is adjusted for all periods to date; and retained earnings is adjusted for the undepreciated profit or loss that is to be deferred to future periods. If the subsidiary sold to the parent, the retained earnings adjustment is allocated to the minority and controlling interests that existed at the time of the sale.

INVESTMENT IN BONDS

The amortized balance in Investment in Company S Bonds is eliminated against the bonds payable and any related discount or premium balance. The net disparity in amounts is the net retirement gain or loss remaining at year end, which is carried to retained earnings. When the subsidiary is the issuer, the retained earnings adjustment is allocated to the minority and controlling interests.

To illustrate the procedures used for the balance sheet worksheet, assume that Company P purchased an 80% interest in Company S on January 1, 19X1. Company P uses the cost method to record its investment in Company S. The determination and distribution of excess schedule prepared for this purchase is as follows:

Price paid		$750,000
Less interest acquired:		
Common stock ($10 par)..	$200,000	
Retained earnings, January 1, 19X1..................................	600,000	
Total stockholders' equity...	$800,000	
Interest acquired..	80%	640,000
Excess of cost over book value		$110,000
Excess of cost attributable to building (10-year remaining life)		30,000
Goodwill (20-year life)..		$ 80,000

The facts pertaining to intercompany sales by Company S to Company P are as follows:

	19X3	19X4
Intercompany sales	$80,000	$100,000
Gross profit..	30%	40%
Intercompany sales in ending inventory.............................	20,000	40,000
Unpaid balance, end of the year.......................................	30,000	35,000

On January 1, 19X2, Company P sold a new piece of equipment that cost $10,000 to Company S for $15,000. Company S is depreciating the equipment over five years on a straight-line basis.

Company S has outstanding $100,000 of 5%, 20-year bonds due January 1, 19X9. Interest is payable on January 1 for the previous year. The bonds originally were sold to yield 6%. On January 1, 19X3, Company P purchased the bonds on the open market at a price to yield 8%.

Worksheet 8–7, pages 530–531, contains the balance sheets and eliminations and adjustments for Companies P and S on December 31, 19X4. After the worksheet steps are completed, the amounts are combined to produce the consolidated balance sheet. The time saving of the balance sheet worksheet results from the fact that there is no combined net income to calculate and distribute.

QUESTIONS

1. Under what circumstances is a determination and distribution of excess schedule needed when a parent acquires its controlling interest in stock directly from the subsidiary?

2. What is a piecemeal purchase? Describe the accounting consequences of such an acquisition as they affect the determination and distribution of excess schedules and worksheet procedures.

3. Is it possible that a piecemeal acquisition could include a transaction that qualifies as a pooling of interests? If so, explain the ramifications.

4. Explain how the equity method investment account balance generally can be recalculated to verify its correctness when an investment in a subsidiary has been acquired in more than one purchase.

5. What special consolidation procedures are required when a subsidiary has preferred stock outstanding?

6. If a parent company owns 80% of the preferred stock and 45% of the common stock of a subsidiary, would the parent company normally have a controlling interest in the subsidiary? Explain.

7. What are the consolidation procedures required when a parent owns subsidiary preferred stock?

8. What factors determine whether the sale of a parent's entire interest in a subsidiary qualifies as a disposal of a segment?

9. Parent Company sold its entire 75% interest in Subsidiary Company for $100,000. May it be said that the parent realized a $20,000 gain on the sale (a) assuming a correct simple equity method investment account balance of $80,000? (b) assuming a correct cost method investment account balance of $80,000? Explain.

10. Describe the adjustments required when a parent sells enough of its ownership interest in a subsidiary to lose control. How do these adjustments differ when the parent sells part of its ownership interest, but not enough to lose control?

EXERCISES

Exercise 1. On January 2, 19X3, Pablo Company and Samual Company had the following balance sheets:

Assets	Pablo Company	Samual Company
Current assets	$ 650,000	$ 60,000
Land	100,000	40,000
Property, plant, and equipment (net)	600,000	300,000
Total assets	$1,350,000	$400,000

Liabilities and Equity				
Liabilities		$ 200,000		$150,000
Equity:				
Common stock ($10 par)	$500,000		$100,000	
Retained earnings	650,000	1,150,000	150,000	250,000
Total liabilities and equity		$1,350,000		$400,000

Samual Company issued 15,000 additional shares of stock on January 2, 19X3, for a price of $40 per share. All 15,000 shares were purchased with cash by Pablo Company. On this date, the market value of Samual's land was $50,000, and the market value of the property, plant, and equipment was $400,000. Any remaining excess is attributable to goodwill.

Prepare the determination and distribution of excess schedule for Pablo's purchase of Samual Company shares, and prepare the consolidated balance sheet immediately subsequent to the purchase.

Exercise 2. On January 1, 19X1, Paller Company purchased a 70% interest in Total Company common stock for $120,000. Paller purchased another 20% of Total common stock on December 31, 19X2, for $42,000. Immediately prior to the second purchase, Paller Company and Total Company had the following balance sheets:

Assets	Paller Company		Total Company	
Current assets...	$230,000		$ 50,000	
Investment in Total Company	141,000		—	
Property, plant, and equipment (net)......................	600,000		150,000	
Total assets...	$971,000		$200,000	
Liabilities and Equity				
Liabilities...	$300,000		$ 50,000	
Equity:				
Common stock ($10 par)...................................	$500,000		$100,000	
Retained earnings...	171,000	671,000	50,000	150,000
Total liabilities and equity...................................		$971,000		$200,000

Any excess of cost over book value on either purchase is to be attributed to goodwill and given a 10-year life. The investment in Total Company account is adjusted correctly for the simple equity method as of December 31, 19X2.

Prepare the consolidated balance sheet of Paller Company and its subsidiary immediately subsequent to the purchase of the additional 20% block by Paller.

Exercise 3. The following determination and distribution of excess schedule was prepared by Siedle Company on January 1, 19X4, the date it acquired a 60% interest in Todd Company:

Price paid		$200,000
Less interest acquired:		
Common stock ($1 par)...	$ 20,000	
Paid-in capital in excess of par...................................	220,000	
Retained earnings...	60,000	
Total stockholders' equity...	$300,000	
Interest acquired..	60%	180,000
Excess of cost over book value		$ 20,000
Excess of cost attributable to machine: 60% × $20,000		
undervaluation (to be amortized over 4 years)..............		12,000
Goodwill (20-year life)...		$ 8,000

On January 1, 19X6, Siedle Company purchases another 20% interest in Todd Company for $80,000. Immediately prior to this purchase, Todd Company had the following balance sheet:

Assets		Liabilities and Equity		
Current assets......................	$100,000	Liabilities		$ 60,000
Land....................................	30,000	Equity:		
Buildings (net)......................	150,000	Common stock ($1 par)	$ 20,000	
Machinery (net)	120,000	Paid-in capital in excess		
		of par	220,000	
		Retained earnings..............	100,000	340,000
Total assets.........................	$400,000	Total liabilities and equity......		$400,000

Siedle Company's analysis on January 1, 19X6, indicates that the machinery on Todd's balance sheet is undervalued by $8,000, with a 2-year remaining life, and that the land is undervalued by $10,000.

Prepare the determination and distribution of excess schedule for the 20% purchase.

Exercise 4.   Gunwale Corporation acquired a 10% interest in Tidecraft Company for $30,000 on January 1, 19X1. The following determination and distribution of excess schedule was prepared at that time:

Price paid		$30,000
Less interest acquired:		
Common stock ($20 par)	$250,000	
Retained earnings (deficit)...	(50,000)	
Total stockholders' equity.......................................	$200,000	
Interest acquired..	10%	20,000
Excess of cost over book value		$10,000
Excess of cost attributed to equipment: 10% × $30,000		
undervaluation (to be amortized over 10 years)		3,000
Goodwill (20-year life)...		$ 7,000

From January 1, 19X1, through December 31, 19X5, Tidecraft Company paid no dividends on common stock and earned the following annual incomes:

19X1................	$10,000	19X4................	$20,000
19X2................	5,000	19X5................	30,000
19X3................	20,000		

On January 1, 19X6, Gunwale purchased 6,250 additional shares of Tidecraft common stock for $180,000. This purchase increased Gunwale's ownership interest in Tidecraft to 60%. Tidecraft had the following balance sheet immediately prior to Gunwale's second purchase:

Assets		Liabilities and Equity		
Current assets......................	$110,000	Liabilities		$ 65,000
Building (net)	140,000	Equity:		
Equipment (net)...................	100,000	Common stock ($20 par).....	$250,000	
		Retained earnings..............	35,000	285,000
Total assets.........................	$350,000	Total liabilities and equity......		$350,000

At the time of the second purchase, Gunwale determined that Tidecraft's equipment was undervalued by $30,000 and had a 5-year remaining life. All other book values approximated market values.

(1) Prepare the determination and distribution of excess schedule for the second purchase. Any goodwill is assumed to have a 20-year life.
(2) Record the investment made on January 1, 19X6.
(3) Since control now has been achieved, Gunwale will use the simple equity method for its investment in Tidecraft. Assuming that the cost method was used for the original 10% investment, convert the 10% block to the equity method as of January 1, 19X6.

Exercise 5. Cleft Company purchased a 20% interest in Key Industries on January 1, 19X2, for $100,000 and another 60% interest on January 1, 19X4, for $360,000. Key had the following stockholders' equity balances immediately prior to each purchase:

Stockholders' Equity	Jan. 1, 19X2	Jan. 1, 19X4
Common stock ($7 par)...	$350,000	$350,000
Paid-in capital in excess of par.............................	100,000	100,000
Retained earnings...	20,000	100,000
Total equity..	$470,000	$550,000

Cleft's analysis on the two purchase dates revealed the following: (1) On January 1, 19X2, Key's equipment was undervalued by $10,000 and had a remaining life of 5 years. (2) On January 1, 19X4, Key's equipment was undervalued by $9,000, with a 3-year remaining life. (3) Any excess attributable to goodwill is to be amortized over 10 years.

Key had income of $30,000 in 19X4 and $50,000 in 19X5 and paid its first dividend, a $.20 per share dividend to common stock, on December 30, 19X5.

(1) Prepare a determination and distribution of excess schedule for each investment.
(2) Assuming that the cost method is used for both investments, prepare the calculations necessary to convert the investment account to its simple-equity-adjusted balance on December 31, 19X5.

Exercise 6. On January 1, 19X2, Boelter Company purchased 80% of the outstanding common stock of Miller Corporation for $280,000. On this date, Miller Corporation stockholders' equity was as follows:

6% preferred stock (1,000 shares, $100 par).....................................	$100,000
Common stock (20,000 shares, $10 par)	200,000
Retained earnings...	90,000
Total stockholders' equity..	$390,000

Prepare a determination and distribution of excess schedule under each of the following situations (any excess of cost over book value is attributable to goodwill with a 10-year life):

(a) The preferred stock is cumulative, with dividends one year in arrears at January 1, 19X2, and has a liquidation value equal to par.
(b) The preferred stock is noncumulative, but fully participating.
(c) The preferred stock is cumulative, with dividends two years in arrears as of January 1, 19X2, has a liquidation value equal to par, and is 10% (limited) participating.

Exercise 7.   Ace Construction Company had the following stockholders' equity on January 1, 19X1, the date on which Ressel Company purchased a 60% interest in the common stock for $600,000:

8% cumulative preferred stock (5,000 shares, $100 par)	$ 500,000
Common stock (40,000 shares, $20 par)	800,000
Retained earnings	100,000
Total stockholders' equity	$1,400,000

Ace Construction Company did not pay preferred dividends in 19X0.
(1) Prepare a determination and distribution of excess schedule. Assume that the preferred stock's liquidation value is equal to par and that any excess of cost is attributable to goodwill with a 20-year life.
(2) Assume that Ace Construction has the following net income (loss) for 19X1 and 19X2 and does not pay any dividends:

19X1	$50,000
19X2	(10,000)

Prepare the entries necessary on Ressel's books to adjust its investment account to the simple equity balance at the end of 19X1 and 19X2.

Exercise 8.   Lineman Corporation purchased 1,000 shares of the preferred stock of Lakeshore Corporation on January 1, 19X1, for $98,000. Lakeshore issued a total of 2,000 preferred shares. Dividends on preferred stock were paid in 19X1 and 19X2, but not in subsequent years. Lineman accounts for its investment using the cost method.

On December 31, 19X4, Lineman purchased an 80% interest in the common stock of Lakeshore Corporation for $300,000. The stockholders' equity of Lakeshore on December 31, 19X4, was as follows:

8% cumulative preferred stock (2,000 shares, $100 par)	$200,000
Common stock ($10 stated value)	300,000
Retained earnings	80,000
Total stockholders' equity	$580,000

Any excess of cost over book value was attributed to goodwill and given a 20-year life. The common stock investment is accounted for under the cost method.

During 19X5 and 19X6, Lakeshore paid no dividends and its retained earnings balance on December 31, 19X6, was $120,000. Lakeshore income during 19X7 was $40,000.

(1) Calculate the preferred and common stockholders' equity claim on Lakeshore Company retained earnings balance at January 1, 19X7.

(2) Prepare the cost-to-simple-equity conversion and the elimination that would be made on the December 31, 19X7 consolidated worksheet for the investment in preferred stock.

(3) Prepare the cost-to-simple-equity conversion and the elimination that would be made on the December 31, 19X7 consolidated worksheet for the investment in common stock. Provide a determination and distribution of excess schedule as support.

Exercise 9.   Rieger Company purchased a 90% interest in Sander Company for $350,000 on January 1, 19X3. Any excess of cost over book value was attributed to goodwill, which is being amortized over the maximum period. Both companies end their reporting periods on December 31. Since the investment in Sander Company is consolidated, Rieger has chosen to use the cost method to maintain its investment.

On July 1, 19X6, Rieger sold its entire investment in Sander for $620,000. The following stockholders' equity balances of Sander are available:

	January 1, 19X3	January 1, 19X5
Common stock......................................	$100,000	$100,000
Retained earnings..................................	200,000	400,000
Total equity..	$300,000	$500,000

Sander earned $50,000 during the first 6 months of 19X6.

Prepare a determination and distribution of excess schedule and record the sale of the investment. Include supporting calculations.

Exercise 10.   Duckler Company has the following balance sheet on December 31, 19X5:

Assets		Liabilities and Equity		
Current assets......................	$140,000	Liabilities		$100,000
Investment in Bolt Company ...	140,000	Equity:		
Property, plant, and		Common stock ($10 par).....	$500,000	
equipment (net).................	420,000	Retained earnings..............	100,000	600,000
Total assets........................	$700,000	Total liabilities and equity		$700,000

The investment in Bolt Company account reflects the original cost of an 80% interest (40,000 shares) purchased on January 1, 19X2. On the date of the purchase, Bolt stockholders' equity had a book value of $150,000. Bolt's other book values approximated market, except for a machine with a 5-year remaining life that was undervalued by $10,000. Any additional excess was attributed to goodwill and given a 10-year life.

A review of Bolt's past financial statements reveals the following:

	Income	Dividends Paid
19X2	$ 20,000	$ 3,000
19X3	25,000	3,000
19X4	30,000	4,000
19X5	35,000	4,000
Total	$110,000	$14,000

Duckler sold 2,000 shares of Bolt common stock on January 1, 19X6, for $15,000.

Prepare the necessary entries on Duckler's books to account accurately for the sale of the 2,000 Bolt shares. Provide a determination and distribution of excess schedule along with all other necessary computations as support.

Exercise 11.   On July 1, 19X8, Dynamo Company sold 4,500 shares of Stibbins Company stock to reduce its investment from 60% to 45%. Stibbins Company is a foreign firm. The sale was in response to a recent change in law in Stibbins' country, which prohibits the ownership of a controlling interest by a nonresident. Dynamo received $150,000 from the sale of Stibbins stock.

Dynamo originally had purchased the 60% interest on January 1, 19X5, at which time the following determination and distribution of excess schedule was prepared:

Price paid		$450,000
Less interest acquired:		
Common stock ($15 par)	$450,000	
Retained earnings	150,000	
Total stockholders' equity	$600,000	
Interest acquired	60%	360,000
Excess of cost over book value		$ 90,000
Excess of cost attributable to building: 60% × $50,000		
undervaluation (to be amortized over 15 years)		30,000
Goodwill (20-year life)		$ 60,000

Stibbins Company reported net income of $35,000 for the six months ended July 1, 19X8. Dynamo's simple-equity-adjusted investment balance was $498,000 as of December 31, 19X7.

Prepare all the entries necessary on Dynamo's books to account for the partial sale of its investment in Stibbins Company. (Control is assumed to be lost with the sale.)

PROBLEMS

Problem 8–1. The following determination and distribution of excess schedule was prepared on January 1, 19X2, the date on which Paddle Company purchased a 60% interest in Sardon Company:

Price paid		$100,000
Less interest acquired:		
Common stock ($10 par)..	$ 75,000	
Retained earnings...	50,000	
Total stockholders' equity.....................................	$125,000	
Interest acquired..	60%	75,000
Excess of cost over book value attributable to goodwill (20-year life)..		$ 25,000

On December 31, 19X3, Paddle Company purchased an additional 20% interest in Sardon Company for $60,000. Sardon stockholders' equity was determined to be the following at that date:

Common stock	$ 75,000
Retained earnings...................................	75,000
Total stockholders' equity......................	$150,000

Any excess of cost over book value was attributed to goodwill and given a 20-year life.

On December 31, 19X5, the following trial balances are available:

	Paddle Company	Sardon Company
Current Assets..	210,000	50,000
Investment in Sardon Company	215,000	—
Property, Plant, and Equipment (net)	450,000	170,000
Current Liabilities	(110,000)	(20,000)
Common Stock ($10 par)...	(500,000)	(75,000)
Retained Earnings, Jan. 1, 19X5	(154,000)	(85,000)
Sales...	(400,000)	(110,000)
Subsidiary Income..	(36,000)	—
Cost of Goods Sold...	200,000	50,000
Other Expenses..	100,000	15,000
Dividends Declared...	25,000	5,000
Total...	0	0

Required:

(1) Prepare the determination and distribution of excess schedule for the second purchase of Sardon stock by Paddle Company.

(2) Prepare the worksheet necessary to produce the consolidated financial statements of Paddle Company and its subsidiary as of December 31, 19X5. Include income distribution schedules.

Problem 8–2. The following balance sheets were condensed from past annual reports of Loeb Corporation:

Assets	Jan. 1, 19X1	Jan. 1, 19X4
Current assets...	$ 70,000	$ 80,000
Land...	30,000	30,000
Buildings (net)...	80,000	65,000
Equipment (net)...	70,000	105,000
Total assets...	$250,000	$280,000

Liabilities and Equity		
Liabilities...	$100,000	$ 90,000
Equity:		
Common stock ($2.50 par)...............................	$ 25,000	$ 25,000
Paid-in capital in excess of par.........................	55,000	55,000
Retained earnings...	70,000	110,000
Total equity...	$150,000	$190,000
Total liabilities and equity....................................	$250,000	$280,000

Mrazek Company purchased a 70% interest in Loeb Corporation on January 1, 19X1, for $125,000 and an additional 10% interest on January 1, 19X4, for $25,000. An analysis of Loeb's accounts on each of the purchase dates indicated:

(a) On January 1, 19X1, Loeb's land was undervalued by $10,000.

(b) On January 1, 19X4, Loeb's land was undervalued by $15,000; the equipment was undervalued by $15,000 and had an estimated remaining life of 5 years.

(c) Any other excess of cost over book value on either investment is attributed to goodwill and given an estimated future life of 10 years.

On December 31, 19X5, the trial balances of the two firms, shown at the top of the next page, are secured.

Loeb income and dividends paid for 19X1–19X5 were as follows:

	Income	Dividends Paid
19X1.................................	$20,000	$10,000
19X2.................................	40,000	20,000
19X3.................................	30,000	20,000
19X4.................................	30,000	20,000
19X5.................................	50,000	20,000

Required:

(1) Prepare a determination and distribution of excess schedule for each purchase of Loeb stock by Mrazek Company.

	Mrazek Company	Loeb Corporation
Current Assets..	200,000	60,000
Land..	100,000	30,000
Buildings	400,000	120,000
Accumulated Depreciation—Buildings....................	(150,000)	(40,000)
Equipment..	500,000	200,000
Accumulated Depreciation—Equipment	(200,000)	(90,000)
Investment in Loeb Corporation...........................	150,000	—
Liabilities..	(329,000)	(50,000)
Common Stock ($20 par)...................................	(300,000)	—
Common Stock ($2.50 par)	—	(25,000)
Paid-In Capital in Excess of Par...........................	—	(55,000)
Retained Earnings, Jan. 1, 19X5	(305,000)	(120,000)
Sales..	(500,000)	(150,000)
Subsidiary Income (dividend)...............................	(16,000)	—
Cost of Goods Sold..	250,000	60,000
Other Expenses..	150,000	40,000
Dividends Declared..	50,000	20,000
Total..	0	0

(2) Prepare the worksheet necessary to produce the consolidated financial statements of Mrazek Company and its subsidiary as of December 31, 19X5. Include income distribution schedules.

Problem 8–3.   On January 1, 19X4, Madden Company purchased a 20% interest in Clayton Company for $100,000. Two years subsequent to this purchase, Madden Company acquired an additional 45% interest in Clayton Company for $250,000.

Balance sheets of Clayton Company immediately prior to these purchases were as follows:

Assets	Jan. 1, 19X4	Jan. 1, 19X6
Current assets...	$150,000	$120,000
Land...	150,000	150,000
Equipment (net)..	200,000	300,000
Total assets..	$500,000	$570,000

Liabilities and Equity		
Liabilities..	$100,000	$110,000
Equity:		
Common stock ($5 par)...................................	$100,000	$100,000
Paid-in capital in excess of par..........................	150,000	150,000
Retained earnings..	150,000	210,000
Total equity..	$400,000	$460,000
Total liabilities and equity...................................	$500,000	$570,000

On January 1, 19X4, and January 1, 19X6, Clayton's book values approximated market values, except for the land, which was undervalued by $50,000. Any resulting goodwill is being amortized over 10 years.

The original 20% investment had been maintained under the sophisticated equity method. Since it now will be necessary to prepare consolidated statements, the simple equity method is in use for 19X6.

On December 31, 19X6, Madden's investment in Clayton Company was determined as follows:

Original cost of 20% investment..	$100,000
19X4–X5 equity adjustment, net of excess amortization	10,000
Original cost of 45% investment..	250,000
65% of income, January 1, 19X6—December 31, 19X6.....................	26,000
Investment in Clayton Company...	$386,000

The following trial balances were prepared on December 31, 19X6:

	Madden Company	Clayton Company
Current Assets...	250,000	225,000
Investment in Clayton Company.................................	386,000	—
Land..	240,000	150,000
Building (net)	480,000	—
Equipment (net)...	400,000	220,000
Other Assets	20,000	5,000
Liabilities..	(340,000)	(100,000)
Common Stock ($10 par)..	(1,000,000)	—
Common Stock ($5 par)..	—	(100,000)
Paid-In Capital in Excess of Par................................	—	(150,000)
Retained Earnings, Jan. 1, 19X6	(350,000)	(210,000)
Sales...	(900,000)	(350,000)
Subsidiary Income...	(26,000)	—
Cost of Goods Sold..	540,000	180,000
Other Expenses...	250,000	130,000
Dividends Declared..	50,000	—
Total...	0	0

Required:

Prepare the worksheet necessary to produce the consolidated financial statements of Madden Company and its subsidiary as of December 31, 19X6. Include the determination and distribution of excess and income distribution schedules.

Problem 8–4.   On January 1, 19X7, Palmer Corporation paid $284,000 for a 20% interest in Johnson Company common stock. Any excess of cost is attributed to goodwill. This investment was in addition to the 60% interest in common stock that Palmer bought on January 1, 19X5, for $640,000, when Johnson had a retained earnings balance of $300,000. The 19X5 purchase included an excess cost of $40,000 which was attributed to goodwill. It is estimated that the benefits of all goodwill will not extend past December 31, 19Y4.

Throughout 19X6 and 19X7, Johnson has been Palmer's sole supplier of stainless steel cleats. Palmer's 19X7 beginning and ending inventories contained $9,000 and $12,000, respectively, of goods purchased from Johnson. Johnson sells goods to realize a 45% gross profit. Intercompany sales were $35,000 in 19X6 and $50,000 in 19X7. On December 31, 19X7, Palmer owed Johnson $10,000 for unpaid purchases.

On December 31, 19X7, the two firms had the following trial balances:

	Palmer Corporation	Johnson Company
Cash..	190,000	205,000
Accounts Receivable (net).....................................	260,000	150,000
Inventory, Dec. 31, 19X7......................................	200,000	100,000
Investment in Johnson Company............................	924,000	—
Plant and Equipment..	3,800,000	1,555,000
Accumulated Depreciation.....................................	(934,000)	(325,000)
Accounts Payable	(120,000)	(55,000)
Bonds Payable, 8%, due 12/31/X9........................	—	(200,000)
Common Stock (no par)..	(1,000,000)	(700,000)
Retained Earnings, Jan. 1, 19X7	(3,000,000)	(600,000)
Sales...	(2,500,000)	(900,000)
Cost of Goods Sold...	1,500,000	495,000
Selling and General Expenses...............................	480,000	225,000
Interest Expense...	—	50,000
Dividends Declared..	200,000	—
Total..	0	0

Required:

Prepare the worksheet necessary to produce the consolidated financial statements of Palmer Corporation and its subsidiary for December 31, 19X7. Include the determination and distribution of excess and income distribution schedules.

Suggestion: In distributing the excess cost from the second investment, allocate part of the excess to the deferred profit on inventory account. The amount should be the beginning inventory profit applicable to the interest purchased on January 1, 19X7. The deferred profit account will be eliminated when the elimination is made for the beginning inventory profit.

Problem 8–5. The following information is available regarding the investments of Broderick Corporation in Chesewick Company for the years 19X1–19X5:

Date	Transaction	Interest	Price
1/1/X1	Purchased common	10%	$ 20,000
1/1/X2	Purchased preferred	60	30,000
1/1/X3	Purchased common	50	140,000
1/1/X5	Purchased common	20	60,000
12/31/X5....................................	Sold common	20	70,000

The stockholders' equity section of Chesewick Company's balance sheet has not changed since the January 1, 19X0 original sale of preferred stock to the public, except for the balance in the retained earnings account. The stock-holders' equity as of January 1, 19X5, is as follows:

6% cumulative preferred stock ($50 par, liquidation value equals par value)	$ 50,000
Common stock ($10 par)...	100,000
Paid-in capital in excess of par..	20,000
Retained earnings...	150,000
Total stockholders' equity...	$320,000

Other relevant facts are as follows:

(a) On January 1, 19X1, Chesewick had a $60,000 retained earnings balance, and there were no dividends in arrears on the preferred stock.

(b) The excess of cost over book value on each investment in common stock was viewed as goodwill with a 10-year life.

(c) The 20% interest sold on December 31, 19X5, was the interest purchased on January 1, 19X5.

(d) Income and dividends were as follows for 19X1–19X5:

	Net Income	Preferred Dividends	Common Dividends
19X1......................	$25,000	$3,000	None
19X2......................	30,000	3,000	$6,000
19X3......................	30,000	3,000	5,000
19X4......................	25,000	None	None
19X5......................	20,000	None	None

Broderick's investment account balances for its interests in Chesewick Company were calculated as follows on December 31, 19X5:

Investment in preferred stock:

Original cost	$ 30,000
Plus dividends in arrears for 19X4...................................	1,800
Balance, December 31, 19X5.......................................	$ 31,800

Investment in common stock:

January 1, 19X1 purchase...	$ 20,000
January 1, 19X3 purchase...	140,000
19X3 Chesewick income, $30,000 × 60%.........................	18,000
19X3 Chesewick dividends, $5,000 × 60%	(3,000)
19X4 Chesewick income, $25,000 × 60%.........................	15,000
January 1, 19X5 purchase...	60,000
19X5 Chesewick income, $20,000 × 80%.........................	16,000
December 31, 19X5 sale	(70,000)
Balance, December 31, 19X5.......................................	$196,000

Required:

Assume that the investment accounts are to be maintained properly under the simple equity method. Prepare all necessary correcting entries on the books of Broderick Corporation as of December 31, 19X5. (Assume that nominal accounts are open.) All supporting computations and schedules should be in good form.

Problem 8–6.   Barns Corporation purchased an 80% interest in the common stock of Transam Corporation on December 31, 19X3, for $700,000, when Transam had the following condensed balance sheet:

Assets		Liabilities and Stockholders' Equity	
Current assets...........................	$ 400,000	Liabilities....................................	$ 600,000
Land..	200,000	Preferred stock (8% cumulative,	
Building (net)	400,000	$100 par)	100,000
Equipment (net)........................	500,000	Common stock ($20 par)	750,000
		Retained earnings.......................	50,000
Total assets.............................	$1,500,000	Total liabilities and equity............	$1,500,000

On the December 31, 19X3 purchase date, the dividends on the preferred stock were two years in arrears. Also on this date, the book values of Transam's assets approximated market values, except for the building which was undervalued by $30,000 and had a 20-year remaining life. Any resulting goodwill is being amortized over a 10-year life.

For 19X4–19X6, earnings and dividends for Transam Corporation were as follows:

	Income	Preferred Dividends	Common Dividends
19X4..............................	$30,000	—	—
19X5..............................	50,000	$16,000	—
19X6..............................	90,000	24,000	$26,750

The following trial balances of the two firms were prepared on December 31, 19X6:

	Barns Corporation	Transam Corporation
Current Assets..	826,400	473,250
Investment in Transam Corporation........................	700,000	—
Land..	400,000	200,000
Building...	950,000	500,000
Accumulated Depreciation — Building	(200,000)	(160,000)
Equipment..	1,500,000	740,000
Accumulated Depreciation — Equipment	(400,000)	(200,000)
Liabilities...	(800,000)	(550,000)
Preferred Stock, 8%	—	(100,000)
Common Stock ($20 par)..	(2,000,000)	(750,000)
Retained Earnings, Jan. 1, 19X6	(860,000)	(114,000)
Sales...	(2,100,000)	(1,000,000)
Subsidiary Dividend Income	(21,400)	—
Cost of Goods Sold..	1,155,000	600,000
Other Expenses...	650,000	310,000
Dividends Declared..	200,000	50,750
Total..	0	0

Required:

Prepare the worksheet necessary to produce the consolidated financial statements of Barns Corporation and its subsidiary as of December 31, 19X6.

(continued)

Include the determination and distribution of excess and income distribution schedules.

Problem 8–7. On January 1, 19X1, Krug Company purchased an 80% interest (8,000 shares) directly from Bohrman Company on the day Bohrman was organized.

On April 1, 19X5, Krug Company purchased 1,000 additional shares of Bohrman Company for $38,900. Bohrman had an exceptional first quarter with income of $9,000. No dividends had been paid. Any excess of cost is considered to be goodwill with a 10-year life. Unrealized gains and losses applicable to the 10% interest are ignored on the basis of materiality.

The subsidiary sells merchandise to the parent at cost plus 50%. Intercompany sales were $60,000 during 19X5; $20,000 was unpaid at year end. There were $9,000 of such goods in the beginning inventory of Krug Company and $15,000 of such goods in the ending inventory. However, the ending inventory had been adjusted down to its market value of $12,000.

The parent sold a machine with a book value of $10,000 to the subsidiary for $15,000 on January 1, 19X4. The machine had a 5-year life as of January 1, 19X4, and is being depreciated on a straight-line basis.

Bohrman Company issued $100,000 of face value, 6%, 5-year bonds on January 1, 19X3. The bonds sold at a premium of $4,329 since the market rate of interest was 5%. On January 1, 19X4, when the market rate was 8%, Krug Company purchased all of these bonds for $93,375.

Bohrman Company paid a $1 per share cash dividend on December 31, 19X5.

The following trial balances were prepared as of December 31, 19X5:

	Krug Company	Bohrman Company
Cash.........	8,155	103,722
Accounts Receivable	80,000	40,000
Inventory	43,100	63,000
Plant and Equipment.........	400,000	300,000
Accumulated Depreciation.........	(200,000)	(80,000)
Investment in Bohrman Company Stock	198,900	—
Investment in Bohrman Company Bonds	96,433	—
Liabilities.........	(60,000)	(40,000)
6% Bonds Payable.........	—	(100,000)
Premium on Bonds Payable.........	—	(1,858)
Common Stock ($10 par)	(200,000)	(100,000)
Paid-In Capital in Excess of Par.........	—	(100,000)
Retained Earnings, Jan. 1, 19X5	(300,000)	(80,000)
Sales.........	(250,000)	(120,000)
Cost of Goods Sold.........	150,000	80,000
Other Expenses.........	50,000	20,000
Subsidiary Income.........	(9,000)	
Dividends Declared.........	—	10,000
Interest Income	(7,588)	—
Interest Expense.........	—	5,136
Total.........	0	0

Required:

Prepare the worksheet necessary to produce the consolidated financial statements of Krug Company and its subsidiary as of December 31, 19X5. Include the determination and distribution of excess and income distribution schedules.

Suggestion: Determine what method Krug Company is using to maintain its investment in Bohrman Company stock account (i.e., cost, simple equity, or sophisticated equity) before attempting the requirements of this problem.

Problem 8–8.   On January 1, 19X3, Horton Corporation purchased 90% (18,000 shares) of the outstanding common stock of Neff Company for $468,000. Just prior to Horton Corporation's purchase, Neff Company had the following stockholders' equity:

Common stock ($5 par)	$100,000
Paid-in capital in excess of par	300,000
Retained earnings	100,000
Total stockholders' equity	$500,000

At this time, Neff Company's book values approximated market values. Any excess of cost was attributed to goodwill and given a 20-year life.

On January 1, 19X7, Neff Company retained earnings balance amounted to $200,000. No changes had taken place in the paid-in capital accounts since the original sale of common stock on July 10, 19X0.

On July 1, 19X7, Horton Corporation sold 2,000 of its Neff Company shares to Welch Corporation for $75,000. At the time of this sale, Horton had no intention of selling the balance of its holding in Neff Company.

In an unexpected move on December 31, 19X7, Horton Corporation sold its remaining 70% interest in Neff Company to Welch Corporation for $500,000.

Neff Company reported income and dividends for 19X7 are as follows:

	Income	Dividends
January 1, 19X7 — July 1, 19X7	$25,000	$.50/share
July 1, 19X7 — December 31, 19X7	35,000	.50/share

Required:

Prepare the determination and distribution of excess schedule for Horton Corporation's purchase of Neff Company common stock on January 1, 19X3. Then prepare all the entries on Horton's books needed to reflect the changes in its investment account from January 1, 19X7, to December 31, 19X7. (Assume that Horton uses the cost method to report its investment in Neff Company.)

Problem 8–9.   During 19X7, Away Company acquired a controlling interest in Stallman Inc. Trial balances of the companies at December 31, 19X7, are as follows:

	Away Company	Stallman Inc.
Cash......	100,000	78,000
Notes Receivable......	100,000	—
Accounts Receivable......	200,000	100,000
Interest Receivable......	3,000	—
Dividends Receivable......	4,500	—
Inventories......	924,000	125,000
Investment in Stallman Inc.	470,500	—
Property, Plant, and Equipment......	1,250,000	500,000
Accumulated Depreciation......	(500,000)	(150,000)
Deferred Charges......	25,000	—
Patents and Licenses......	—	50,000
Accounts Payable......	(425,000)	(80,000)
Notes Payable......	—	(75,000)
Dividends Payable......	—	(5,000)
Capital Stock......	(300,000)	(100,000)
Retained Earnings, Jan. 1, 19X7......	(1,605,000)	(400,000)
Sales and Services......	(1,800,000)	(750,000)
Subsidiary Income......	(45,000)	—
Interest Income......	(3,000)	—
Cost of Goods Sold......	1,350,000	525,000
Administrative and Selling Expenses......	251,000	174,000
Interest Expense......	—	3,000
Dividends Declared......	—	5,000
Total......	0	0

The following information is available regarding the transactions and accounts of the two companies:

(a) An analysis of the investment in Stallman Inc. account follows:

	Description	Amount	Interest Acquired
January 1, 19X7......	Investment	$325,000	70%
September 30, 19X7......	Investment	105,000	20%
Total......		$430,000	90%
December 31, 19X7......	90% of Stallman income for 19X7	45,000	
December 31, 19X7......	90% of Stallman dividends for 19X7	(4,500)	
Total......		$470,500	

The net income of Stallman Inc. for the nine months ended September 30, 19X7, was $25,000.

(b) The price paid by the parent on January 1, 19X7, to achieve control reflects uncertainty as to the future value of the patents. The remaining amortization is 10 years.

(c) On September 30, 19X7, Away Company loaned its subsidiary $100,000 on a one-year, 12% note. Interest and principal are payable in quarterly installments beginning December 31, 19X7. The December 31, 19X7 payment was made by Stallman but was not received by Away. Away Company has no other notes receivable outstanding.

(d) Stallman Inc. sales principally are engineering services billed at cost plus 50%. During 19X7, Away Company was billed for $40,000, of which $16,500 was treated as a deferred charge at December 31, 19X7.

(e) During the year, parent company sales to the subsidiary totaled $60,000, of which $10,000 remained in the inventory of Stallman Inc. at December 31, 19X7.

(f) In 19X7, Away constructed certain tools at a cost of $15,000 and sold them to Stallman Inc. for $25,000. Stallman Inc. depreciates such tools using the straight-line method over a 5-year life. One-half year's depreciation is taken in the year of acquisition.

Required:

Prepare the worksheet necessary to produce the consolidated financial statements of Away Company and its subsidiary for the year ended December 31, 19X7. Include the determination and distribution of excess and income distribution schedules.

(AICPA adapted)

Problem 8–10. The following information pertains to Titan Corporation and its two subsidiaries, Boat Corporation and Motor Corporation:

(a) The three corporations are all in the same industry and their operations are homogeneous. Titan Corporation exercises control over the boards of directors of Boat Corporation and Motor Corporation and has installed new principal officers in both.

(b) Boat Corporation had a retained earnings balance of $92,000 at January 1, 19X7, and had income of $15,000 for the first three months of 19X7 and $20,000 for the first six months of 19X8.

(c) Titan Corporation acquired 250 shares of fully participating Motor preferred stock for $7,000 and 14,000 shares of Motor common stock for $196,000 on January 2, 19X8. Motor Corporation had a net income of $20,000 in 19X8 and did not declare any dividends.

(d) Motor Corporation's inventory includes $22,400 of merchandise acquired from Boat Corporation subsequent to July, 19X8, for which no payment has been made. Boat Corporation marked up the merchandise 40% on cost.

(e) Titan Corporation acquired in the open market twenty-five $1,000, 6% bonds of Boat Corporation of $21,400 on January 1, 19X5. Boat Corporation bonds mature December 31, 19Y0. Interest is paid each June 30 and December 31. Straight-line amortization is allowed on the basis of materiality.

(f) The 19X8 year-end balance in the investment in Boat Corporation stock account is composed of the items shown in the following schedule:

Date	Description	Amount
4/1/X7	Cost of 5,000 shares of Boat Corp. stock..	$ 71,400
12/31/X7	20% of the dividends declared in December, 19X7, by Boat Corp.	(9,000)
12/31/X7	20% of the 19X7 annual net income of Boat Corp.	12,000
7/1/X8	Cost of 15,000 shares of Boat Corp.	226,200
12/31/X8	80% of the dividends declared in December, 19X8, by Boat Corp.	(24,000)
12/31/X8	80% of the 19X8 annual net income of Boat Corp.	32,000
12/31/X8	Total	$308,600

(g) The December 31, 19X8 trial balances for the three corporations appear as follows:

	Titan Corporation	Boat Corporation	Motor Corporation
Cash..	100,000	87,000	95,000
Accounts Receivable	158,200	210,000	105,000
Inventories....................................	290,000	90,000	115,000
Advance to Boat Corporation...........	17,000	—	—
Dividends Receivable	24,000	—	—
Property, Plant, and Equipment........	777,600	325,000	470,000
Accumulated Depreciation...............	(180,000)	(55,000)	(160,000)
Investment in Boat Corporation:			
6% Bonds	23,800	—	—
Common Stock...........................	308,600	—	—
Investment in Motor Corporation:			
Preferred Stock...........................	7,400	—	—
Common Stock...........................	207,200	—	—
Notes Payable	(45,000)	(14,000)	(44,000)
Accounts Payable	(170,000)	(96,000)	(86,000)
Bonds Payable	(285,000)	(150,000)	(125,000)
Discount on Bonds Payable	8,000	—	—
Dividends Payable	(22,000)	(30,000)	—
Preferred Stock ($20 par)................	(400,000)	—	(50,000)
Common Stock ($10 par)................	(600,000)	(250,000)	(200,000)
Retained Earnings, Jan. 1, 19X8	(154,600)	(107,000)	(100,000)
Sales..	(1,050,000)	(500,000)	(650,000)
Other Revenue	(2,100)	—	—
Subsidiary Income:			
Common Stock (Boat)...................	(32,000)	—	—
Preferred Stock (Motor)................	(400)	—	—
Common Stock (Motor)................	(11,200)	—	—
Cost of Goods Sold.........................	650,000	300,000	400,000
Other Expenses.............................	358,500	160,000	230,000
Dividends Declared.........................	22,000	30,000	—
Total..	0	0	0

Required:

Prepare the worksheet necessary to produce the consolidated financial statements of Titan Corporation and its subsidiaries as of December 31, 19X8. Consolidated retained earnings should be allocated to Titan Corporation, and the minority interests should be shown separately in the consolidated balance sheet column. The consolidation is to be accounted for as a purchase. All supporting computations and schedules should be in good form.   (AICPA adapted)

Problem 8–11.   On January 1, 19X7, Davis Corporation purchased all of the preferred stock and 60% of the common stock of Baldwin Company for $60,000 and $50,000, respectively. Immediately prior to the purchases, Baldwin Company had the following stockholders' equity:

8% cumulative preferred stock ($100 par, 3 years in arrears)	$ 50,000
Common stock ($10 par)..	100,000
Paid-in capital in excess of par (common stock)............................	20,000
Retained earnings (deficit)	(20,000)
Total stockholders' equity...	$150,000

The June 30, 19X8 trial balances of the two firms are as follows:

	Davis Corporation	Baldwin Company
Cash..	47,400	10,000
Accounts Receivable (net)......................................	120,000	26,000
Inventories...	230,000	44,000
Other Current Assets..	20,000	8,000
Investment in Baldwin Company:		
Preferred Stock...	58,000	—
Common Stock..	61,400	—
Property, Plant, and Equipment..............................	1,450,000	122,000
Accumulated Depreciation.....................................	(420,000)	(25,000)
Liabilities...	(350,000)	(18,000)
Preferred Stock ($100 par)	—	(50,000)
Common Stock ($10 par)	(1,000,000)	(100,000)
Paid-In Capital in Excess of Par (common stock)........	—	(20,000)
Retained Earnings, Jan. 1, 19X8	(195,000)	9,000
Sales..	(420,000)	(96,000)
Subsidiary Income (preferred)................................	(2,000)	—
Subsidiary Income (common)	(4,800)	—
Cost of Goods Sold..	300,000	60,000
Other Expenses...	80,000	26,000
Dividends Declared..	25,000	4,000
Total...	0	0

Additional information:
(a) On January 1, 19X7, Baldwin Company's only plant asset, equipment, had a book value equal to market value, as did all its other assets and liabilities. The equipment had an estimated remaining life of seven years and is being depreciated on a straight-line basis.
(b) On both December 31, 19X7, and June 30, 19X8, Baldwin Company paid preferred stock dividends of $8 per share.
(c) Baldwin Company had a net income of $15,000 in 19X7 and earnings of $10,000 for the first half of 19X8.
(d) Davis Corporation sold a piece of equipment with a book value of $8,000 to Baldwin Company for $11,000 on January 2, 19X7. The machine had

an estimated future life of five years, and straight-line depreciation is being used.

(e) Information regarding intercompany merchandise sales follows:

	Davis Corporation	Baldwin Company
Merchandise in beginning inventory of purchaser, January 1, 19X8	$ 1,200	$2,800
Sales, January 1, 19X8—June 30, 19X8..............	20,000	8,000
Merchandise in purchaser's inventory, June 30, 19X8...	1,600	7,000
Merchandise not paid for as of June 30, 19X8.....	2,000	6,000
Markup on cost...	40%	60%

(f) On July 1, 19X8, Davis Corporation sold its 60% interest in Baldwin Company common stock for $70,000.

Required:
(1) Prepare the worksheet necessary to produce the consolidated financial statements of Davis Corporation and its subsidiary for the six months ended June 30, 19X8. Include the determination and distribution of excess and income distribution schedules.
(2) Prepare the entries on Davis' books to reflect the sale of its investment in Baldwin Company common stock on July 1, 19X8.

Problem 8–12.   Condensed (unconsolidated) statements of income and retained earnings statements for the year ended December 31, 19X5, and the balance sheets as of December 31, 19X5, of Pace Company and its subsidiary, Smith Company, are as follows:

Condensed Statements of Income	Pace Company	Smith Company
Sales...	$4,000,000	$1,700,000
Cost of goods sold..	(2,982,000)	(1,015,000)
Operating expenses...	(400,000)	(377,200)
Dividend income	75,000	—
Subsidiary income..	232,000	—
Interest expense	—	(7,800)
Net income...	$ 925,000	$ 300,000

Retained Earnings Statements		
Balance, January 1, 19X5......................................	($2,100,000)	$ (640,000)
Net income..	(925,000)	(300,000)
Dividends declared	170,000	100,000
Balance, December 31, 19X5...................................	($2,855,000)	$ (840,000)

Balance Sheets

Assets

Cash..	$ 486,000	$ 249,600
Accounts receivable..	235,000	185,000
Inventories..	475,000	355,000
Machinery and equipment (net)	2,231,000	530,000
Investment in stock of Smith Company..................	954,000	—
Investment in bonds of Smith Company	58,000	—
Total assets..	$4,439,000	$1,319,600

Liabilities and Stockholders' Equity

Accounts payable	$ (384,000)	$ (62,000)
Bonds payable	—	(120,000)
Unamortized discount on bonds payable	—	2,400
Common stock, Pace Company............................	(1,200,000)	—
Common stock, Smith Company..........................	—	(250,000)
Paid-in capital in excess of par...........................	—	(50,000)
Retained earnings (carried down).........................	(2,855,000)	(840,000)
Total liabilities and stockholders' equity................	($4,439,000)	($1,319,600)

Additional information:

(a) On January 3, 19X3, Pace acquired from the sole stockholder of Smith Company a patent valued at $40,000 and 80% of the outstanding common stock of Smith. Pace's total cost of the transaction was $440,000 in cash. The net book value of Smith stock on the date of acquisition was $500,000, and the book values of the individual assets and liabilities were equal to their fair market values. Pace charged the entire $440,000 to the account, Investment in Stock of Smith Company. The patent, for which no amortization had been charged, had a remaining legal life of four years as of January 3, 19X3.

(b) On July 1, 19X5, Pace reduced its interest in Smith Company stock to 75% by selling shares for $70,000 to an unaffiliated company at a profit of $16,000. Pace recorded the proceeds as a credit to its investment account.

(c) For the six months ended June 30, 19X5, Smith had a net income of $140,000. Pace recorded 80% of this amount on its books of account prior to the time of sale.

(d) During 19X4, Smith sold merchandise to Pace for $130,000, which was at a markup of 30% over Smith's cost. On January 1, 19X5, $52,000 of this merchandise remained in Pace's inventory. This merchandise subsequently was sold by Pace in February, 19X5, at a profit of $8,000.

(e) In November, 19X5, Pace sold merchandise to Smith for the first time. Pace's cost for this merchandise was $80,000, and the sale was made at 120% of cost. Smith's inventory at December 31, 19X5, contained $24,000 of the merchandise that was purchased from Pace.

(f) On December 31, 19X5, there was a $45,000 payment in transit from Smith Company to Pace Company. Accounts Receivable and Accounts Payable include intercompany receivables and payables.

(g) In December, 19X5, Smith declared and paid cash dividends of $100,000 to its stockholders.

(h) On December 31, 19X5, Pace purchased, for $58,000, 50% of the outstanding bonds issued by Smith. The bonds mature on December 31, 19X9, and originally were issued at a discount. On December 31, 19X5, the balance in Smith's account, Unamortized Discount on Bonds Payable, was $2,400. It is the intention of the management of Pace to hold these bonds until their maturity.

Required:

Prepare the worksheet in vertical format for the consolidated financial statements of Pace Company and its subsidiary as of December 31, 19X5. Include the determination and distribution of excess and income distribution schedules. (AICPA adapted)

APPENDIX PROBLEMS

Problem 8A–1. The December 31, 19X6 post-closing trial balances of Pym Corporation and its 90%-owned subsidiary, Sy Corporation, are as follows:

	Pym Corporation	Sy Corporation
Cash..	75,000	15,000
Accounts and Other Current Receivables................	410,000	120,000
Merchandise Inventory...	920,000	670,000
Plant and Equipment (net)	1,000,000	400,000
Investment in Sy Corporation	1,200,000	—
Accounts Payable and Other Current Liabilities.......	(140,000)	(305,000)
Common Stock ($10 par)......................................	(500,000)	(200,000)
Retained Earnings...	(2,965,000)	(700,000)
Total...	0	0

Additional information is as follows:

(a) Pym's investment in Sy was purchased for $1,200,000 in cash on January 1, 19X6, and is accounted for by the cost method.

(b) The excess of cost over book value of Pym's investment in Sy was identified appropriately as goodwill and is being amortized over 10 years.

(c) On January 1, 19X6, Sy retained earnings balance was $600,000, and its common stock balance was $200,000.

(d) Sy declared a $1,000 cash dividend in December, 19X6, payable in January, 19X7.

(e) As of December 31, 19X6, Pym had not recorded any portion of Sy 19X6 income or dividend declaration.

(f) Sy borrowed $100,000 from Pym on June 30, 19X6, with the 10% note maturing on June 30, 19X7. Correct accruals have been recorded by both companies.

(g) During 19X6, Pym sold merchandise to Sy at a total invoice price of $300,000, which included a profit of $60,000. At December 31, 19X6, Sy had not paid Pym for $90,000 of this merchandise, and 5% of the total merchandise purchased from Pym still remains in Sy's inventory.

Required:

Prepare the worksheet necessary to produce the consolidated balance sheet of Pym Company and its subsidiary as of December 31, 19X6. Include the determination and distribution of excess schedule.   (AICPA adapted)

Problem 8A–2.   The December 31, 19X9 post-closing trial balances of Encanto Corporation and its subsidiary, Norris Corporation, are as follows:

	Encanto Corporation	Norris Corporation
Cash..	167,250	101,000
Accounts Receivable...	178,450	72,000
Notes Receivable..	87,500	28,000
Dividends Receivable..	36,000	—
Inventories..	122,000	68,000
Property, Plant, and Equipment.............................	487,000	252,000
Accumulated Depreciation...................................	(117,000)	(64,000)
Investment in Norris Corporation	240,800	—
Accounts Payable	(222,000)	(76,000)
Notes Payable...	(79,000)	(89,000)
Dividends Payable	—	(40,000)
Common Stock ($10 par)	(400,000)	(100,000)
Retained Earnings...	(501,000)	(152,000)
Total...	0	0

The following additional information is available:

(a) Encanto initially acquired 60% of the outstanding common stock of Norris in 19X7. There was no difference between the cost and book value of the net assets acquired. As of December 31, 19X9, the percentage owned is 90%. An analysis of the investment in Norris Corporation account is as follows:

	Description	Amount
December 31, 19X7	Acquired 6,000 shares	$ 70,800
December 31, 19X8	60% of 19X8 net income of $78,000	46,800
September 1, 19X9	Acquired 3,000 shares	92,000
December 31, 19X9	Subsidiary income for 19X9	67,200*
December 31, 19X9	90% of dividends declared	(36,000)
Investment balance, December 31, 19X9		$240,800

*Subsidiary income for 19X9:

60% × $96,000...	$57,600	
30% × $96,000 × 33-1/3%...............................	9,600	
Total	$67,200	

Norris net income is earned ratably during the year. Amortization of the excess of cost over the net assets acquired is being recorded over sixty months.

(b) On December 15, 19X9, Norris declared a cash dividend of $4 per share of common stock, payable to shareholders on January 7, 19Y0.

(c) During 19X9, Encanto sold merchandise to Norris. Encanto's cost for this merchandise was $68,000, and the sale was made at 125% of cost. Norris's inventory at December 31, 19X9, included merchandise purchased from Encanto at a cost to Norris of $35,000.

(d) In December, 19X8, Norris sold merchandise to Encanto for $67,000, which was at a markup of 35% over Norris's cost. On January 1, 19X9, $54,000 of this merchandise remained in Encanto's inventory. This merchandise subsequently was sold by Encanto at a profit of $11,000 during 19X9.

(e) On October 1, 19X9, Encanto sold excess equipment to Norris for $42,000. Data relating to this equipment are as follows:

Book value on Encanto's records... $36,000
Method of depreciation .... Straight-line
Estimated remaining life on October 1, 19X9 .... 10 years

(f) Near the end of 19X9, Norris reduced the balance of its intercompany account payable to zero by transferring $8,000 to Encanto. This payment still was in transit on December 31, 19X9.

Required:
Prepare the worksheet necessary to produce the consolidated balance sheet of Encanto Corporation and its subsidiary as of December 31, 19X9. Include the determination and distribution of excess schedule for Encanto's purchase of Norris common stock on September 1, 19X9. (AICPA adapted)

Problem 8A–3. Case Inc. acquired all of the outstanding $25 par common stock of Frey Inc. on June 30, 19X4, in exchange for 40,000 shares of its $25 par common stock. The business combination meets all the criteria for a pooling of interests. On June 30, 19X4, Case Inc. common stock closed at $65 per share on a national stock exchange. Both corporations continued to operate as separate businesses, maintaining separate accounting records with years ending December 31.

Additional information is as follows:

(a) Case Inc. uses the equity method to account for its investment in Frey. The investment account has not been adjusted to reflect intercompany transactions.

(b) On June 30, 19X4, Frey's assets and liabilities had market values equal to book values, except for the land which had a market value of $550,000.

(c) On June 15, 19X4, Frey paid cash dividends of $4 per share on its common stock.

(d) On December 10, 19X4, Case paid a cash dividend totaling $256,000 on its common stock.

(e) On June 30, 19X4, immediately before the combination, the stockholders' equities were:

	Case Inc.	Frey Inc.
Common stock.....................	$2,200,000	$1,000,000
Additional paid-in capital......	1,660,000	190,000
Retained earnings................	3,036,000	980,000
Total..............................	$6,896,000	$2,170,000

(f) Frey's long-term debt consisted of 10%, ten-year bonds issued at face value on March 31, 19W8. Interest is payable semi-annually on March 31 and September 30. Case had purchased Frey's bonds at the face value of $320,000 in 19W8, and there has not been any change in ownership.

(g) During October, 19X4, Case sold merchandise to Frey at a total invoice price of $720,000, which included a profit of $180,000. At December 31, 19X4, one-half of the merchandise remained in Frey's inventory, and Frey had not paid Case for the merchandise purchased.

(h) The 19X4 net income amounts per the separate books of Case and Frey were $890,000 (exclusive of equity in Frey earnings) and $580,000, respectively.

(i) The retained earnings balances at December 31, 19X3, were $2,506,000 and $820,000 for Case and Frey, respectively.

(j) On December 31, 19X4, the companies had the following post-closing trial balances:

	Case Inc.	Frey Inc.
Cash...	825,000	330,000
Accounts and Other Current Receivables...................	2,140,000	835,000
Inventories..	2,310,000	1,045,000
Land...	650,000	300,000
Depreciable Assets (net)..	4,575,000	1,980,000
Investment in Frey Inc.	2,430,000	—
Long-Term Investments and Other Assets.................	865,000	385,000
Accounts Payable and Other Current Liabilities..........	(2,465,000)	(1,145,000)
Long-Term Debt	(1,900,000)	(1,300,000)
Common Stock ($25 par)..	(3,200,000)	(1,000,000)
Additional Paid-In Capital	(1,850,000)	(190,000)
Retained Earnings..	(4,380,000)	(1,240,000)
Total...	0	0

Required:

(1) Prepare the worksheet necessary to produce the consolidated balance sheet of Case Inc. and its subsidiary for the year ended December 31, 19X4.

(2) Prepare the formal consolidated statement of retained earnings for December 31, 19X4.   (AICPA adapted)

Problem 8A–4.   Wiley Corporation acquired 10% of the 100,000 shares of $2.50 par common stock outstanding of Dole Company on December 31,

19X7, for $38,000. An additional 70,000 shares were acquired for $331,600 on June 30, 19X9 (at which time there was no material difference between the market values and book values of Dole's assets and liabilities). Wiley uses the equity method of accounting for its investment in Dole.

The following information also is available:

(a) An analysis of Investment in Dole Company Stock:

Date	Description	Amount
December 31, 19X7	Investment	$ 38,000
June 30, 19X9	Investment	331,600
December 31, 19X9	80% of net increase in retained earnings of Dole Corporation during 19X9	36,000
	Balance...	$405,600

(b) An analysis of the retained earnings accounts of the two companies:

	Wiley Corporation	Dole Company
Balance, December 31, 19X7	$540,000	$101,000
Net income for 19X8	55,000	40,000
Cash dividends in 19X8	—	(5,000)
Balance, December 31, 19X8	$595,000	$136,000
Net income:		
January 1–June 30, 19X9	31,000	23,000
June 30–December 31, 19X9.........................	40,800	33,000
Dividends declared, December 15, 19X9..............	(20,000)	(11,000)
80% of net increase in retained earnings of Dole Company during 19X9......................................	36,000	—
Balance, December 31, 19X9.............................	$682,800	$181,000

(c) Dole's other equity accounts have not changed since 19X3.

(d) Data on 19X9 intercompany sales and ending inventories were as follows:

	Wiley Corporation	Dole Company
Intercompany sales:		
January 1–June 30	$39,000	$24,000
July 1–December 31	41,600	41,000
Gross profit on sales...	30%	25%
Intercompany payables at year end	12,000	7,000
Year-end inventory of intercompany purchases at fifo cost..	26,000	22,000

(e) Wiley Corporation acquired $30,000 of Dole Company 6% bonds on August 31, 19X9, for $30,588 plus accrued interest. Dole Company issued the 20-year bonds on January 1, 19X0, at 90 and has been paying the interest on each January 1 and July 1 due date. Straight-line amortization has been used on the issuer's bond discount and the premium paid by the investor.

(f) On September 1, 19X9, Wiley Corporation sold equipment with a cost of $40,000 and accumulated depreciation of $9,300 to Dole Company for $20,200. Dole Company recorded the equipment as having a cost of $29,500 with accumulated depreciation of $9,300. At that date, the equipment had a market value of $35,000, an estimated salvage value of $500, and an estimated remaining life of 10 years.

(g) Included in Wiley Corporation's Notes Receivable are $2,000 in noninterest-bearing notes of Dole Company.

The post-closing trial balances of both companies on December 31, 19X9, are as follows:

	Wiley	Dole
Cash	130,000	60,000
Marketable Securities	31,240	9,700
Notes Receivable	15,000	12,200
Accounts Receivable	160,000	75,000
Interest Receivable	2,100	1,600
Dividends Receivable	8,800	—
Inventories	180,000	96,000
Advance to Dole Company	32,000	—
Investment in Dole Company Stock	405,600	—
Investment in Dole Company Bonds	30,560	—
Property, Plant, and Equipment	781,500	510,000
Accumulated Depreciation	(87,000)	(85,000)
Unamortized Bond Discount	—	7,500
Notes Payable	(5,500)	(3,800)
Accounts Payable	(34,500)	(16,000)
Dividends Payable	(20,000)	(11,000)
Interest Payable	(18,000)	(13,000)
Accrued Liabilities	(15,000)	(1,200)
Advance from Wiley Corporation	—	(32,000)
Bonds Payable	(400,000)	(150,000)
Capital Stock	(500,000)	(250,000)
Paid-In Capital in Excess of Par	(14,000)	(29,000)
Retained Earnings	(682,800)	(181,000)
	0	0

Required:

Prepare the worksheet necessary to produce the consolidated balance sheet of Wiley Corporation and its subsidiary as of December 31, 19X9. Include the determination and distribution of excess schedules. Any amortization required by APB Opinion No. 17, "Intangible Assets," is to be computed by the straight-line method over a 40-year period.

(AICPA adapted)

Worksheet 8–1 (see page 454)

Worksheet 8–1 (see page 454)

Investment Acquired in Blocks;
Company P and
Worksheet for Consolidated
For Year Ended

(Credit balance amounts are in parentheses.)

		Trial Balance	
		Company P	Company S
1	Current Assets	60,000	130,000
2	Investment in Company S	228,000	
3			
4			
5			
6	Building	400,000	80,000
7	Accumulated Depreciation — Building	(100,000)	(5,000)
8	Equipment		150,000
9	**Accumulated Depreciation — Equipment**		**(90,000)**
10			
11	Goodwill		
12			
13	Liabilities	(100,000)	(30,000)
14	Common Stock, Co. P	(200,000)	
15	**Retained Earnings, Jan. 1, 19X3, Co. P**	**(210,000)**	
16			
17	Common Stock, Co. S		(100,000)
18	Retained Earnings, Jan. 1, 19X3, Co. S		(100,000)
19	Sales	(400,000)	(200,000)
20	Cost of Goods Sold	300,000	120,000
21	**Expenses**	**50,000**	**45,000**
22			
23			
24			
25	Subsidiary Income	(28,000)	
26		0	0
27	Combined Net Income		
28	To Minority Interest (see distribution schedule)		
29	Balance to Controlling Interest (see distribution schedule)		
30	Total Minority Interest		
31	Retained Earnings, Controlling Interest, Dec. 31, 19X3		
32			

Immediate Control
Subsidiary Company S
Financial Statements
December 31, 19X3

WORKSHEET 8–1

Eliminations & Adjustments Dr.		Eliminations & Adjustments Cr.		Consolidated Income Statement	Minority Interest	Controlling Retained Earnings	Consolidated Balance Sheet	
							190,000	1
		(1)	28,000					2
		(2)	160,000					3
		(3a)	30,000					4
		(4a)	10,000					5
							480,000	6
							(105,000)	7
							150,000	8
(3a)	18,000	(3b)	10,800				(79,600)	9
(4a)	4,800	(4b)	1,600					10
(3a)	12,000	(3c)	3,600				13,080	11
(4a)	5,200	(4c)	520					12
							(130,000)	13
							(200,000)	14
(3b)	7,200					(200,400)		15
(3c)	2,400							16
(2)	80,000				(20,000)			17
(2)	80,000				(20,000)			18
				(600,000)				19
				420,000				20
(3b)	3,600			101,920				21
(3c)	1,200							22
(4b)	1,600							23
(4c)	520							24
(1)	28,000							25
	244,520		244,520					26
				(78,080)				27
				7,000*	(7,000)			28
				71,080*		(71,080)		29
					(47,000)		(47,000)	30
						(271,480)	(271,480)	31
							0	32

(continued)

Eliminations and Adjustments:
(1)   Eliminate the parent's entry recognizing 80% of the subsidiary net income for the current year. This step restores the investment account to its balance at the beginning of the year, so that it can be eliminated against Company S beginning-of-the-year equity balances.
(2)   Eliminate the 80% controlling interest in beginning-of-the-year subsidiary equity accounts against the investment account. The 60% and 20% investments could be eliminated separately if desired.
(3a)   The $30,000 excess of cost on the original 60% investment is distributed to the accumulated depreciation and goodwill accounts according to the determination and distribution of excess schedule prepared on January 1, 19X1.
  (b)   Since the equipment has a 5-year remaining life on January 1, 19X1, the depreciation should be increased $3,600 per year for 3 years. This entry corrects the controlling retained earnings for the past 2 years by $7,200 and corrects the current depreciation expense by $3,600.
  (c)   The $12,000 original goodwill is to be amortized $1,200 per year for 3 years. The controlling retained earnings must be corrected for 2 past years ($2,400), and the current year's expenses are increased by $1,200.
(4a)   The $10,000 excess of cost on the 20% block is distributed to the accumulated depreciation and goodwill accounts according to the determination and distribution of excess schedule prepared on January 1, 19X3.
  (b)   The $4,800 excess attributable to the equipment is to be depreciated over 3 years. Therefore, current expenses are increased by $1,600.
  (c)   The $5,200 increase to the goodwill account is to be amortized over 10 years, requiring current expenses to be increased by $520.

Subsidiary Company S Income Distribution

	Internally generated net income...	$35,000
	Adjusted income	$35,000
	Minority share...........................	20%
	Minority interest........................	$ 7,000*

Parent Company P Income Distribution

Equipment depreciation:			Internally generated net income...	$50,000
Block 1, 60% ....**(3b)**	$3,600		80% × Company S adjusted	
Block 2, 20% ....**(4b)**	1,600		income of $35,000	28,000
Goodwill amortization:				
Block 1, 60% ....**(3c)**	1,200			
Block 2, 20% ....**(4c)**	520			
			Controlling interest.....................	$71,080*

Worksheet 8–2 (see page 457)

Investment Acquired in Blocks;
Company P and
Worksheet for Consolidated
For Year Ended

(Credit balance amounts are in parentheses)

		Trial Balance	
		Company P	Company S
1	Current Assets	69,900	85,000
2	Investment in Company S	196,100	
3			
4			
5			
6	Building and Equipment	300,000	150,000
7	**Accumulated Depreciation—Building and Equipment**	**(200,000)**	**(30,000)**
8	**Goodwill**		
9			
10	Liabilities		(20,000)
11	Common Stock, Co. P	(100,000)	
12	Retained Earnings, Jan. 1, 19X2, Co. P	(200,000)	
13	Common Stock, Co. S		(50,000)
14	Retained Earnings, Jan. 1, 19X2, Co. S		(115,000)
15	Sales	(300,000)	(100,000)
16	Cost of Goods Sold	200,000	60,000
17	**Expenses**	**50,000**	**20,000**
18			
19			
20	Subsidiary Income	(16,000)	
21		0	0
22	Combined Net Income		
23	To Minority Interest (see distribution schedule)		
24	Balance to Controlling Interest (see distribution schedule)		
25	Total Minority Interest		
26	Retained Earnings, Controlling Interest, Dec. 31, 19X2		
27			

Control Achieved with Second Block
Subsidiary Company S
Financial Statements
December 31, 19X2

WORSHEET 8-2

WORKSHEET 8-2

Eliminations & Adjustments				Consolidated Income Statement	Minority Interest	Controlling Retained Earnings	Consolidated Balance Sheet	
Dr.		Cr.						
							154,900	1
		(1)	16,000					2
		(2)	132,000					3
		(3a)	17,100					4
		(4a)	31,000					5
							450,000	6
(4a)	5,400	(4b)	600				(225,200)	7
(3a)	17,100	(3b)	900				40,520	8
(4a)	25,600	(4c)	1,280					9
							(20,000)	10
							(100,000)	11
						(200,000)		12
(2)	40,000				(10,000)			13
(2)	92,000				(23,000)			14
				(400,000)				15
				260,000				16
(3b)	900			72,780				17
(4b)	600							18
(4c)	1,280							19
(1)	16,000							20
	198,880		198,880					21
				(67,220)				22
				4,000*	(4,000)			23
				63,220*		(63,220)		24
					(37,000)		(37,000)	25
						(263,220)	(263,220)	26
							0	27

(continued)

Eliminations and Adjustments:

(1)   Eliminate the parent's entry recognizing the 80% interest in subsidiary net income under the simple equity method. This step restores the investment account to its balance at the beginning of the year.

(2)   Eliminate the 80% controlling interest in the beginning-of-the-year subsidiary equity accounts against the investment account. If desired, the two investment blocks may be eliminated separately.

(3a)   The remaining excess of cost over book value on the original 20% investment is $17,100 ($18,000 less 1 year of $900 amortization). It must be remembered that under the sophisticated equity method, amortization entries prior to securing control reduce the investment account. Always remember that *only the unamortized original excess remains.* The remaining $17,100 excess is carried to the goodwill account according to the determination and distribution of excess schedule prepared on January 1, 19X1.

(b)   Goodwill amortization of $900 is recorded for the current year. Recall that no amortization is needed for periods prior to achieving control, since that amortization was recorded previously through the parent's investment account. Thus, the controlling retained earnings is reduced already.

(4a)   The excess attributable to the January 1, 19X2 60% acquisition is distributed to the accumulated depreciation and goodwill accounts according to the determination and distribution of excess schedule for this second acquisition.

(b)   Depreciation for the current year is increased $600 according to the January 1, 19X2 determination and distribution of excess schedule.

(c)   Goodwill amortization of $1,280 increases expenses for the current year as required by the January 1, 19X2 determination and distribution of excess schedule.

Subsidiary Company S Income Distribution

Internally generated net income...	$20,000
Adjusted income	$20,000
Minority share............................	20%
Minority interest.........................	$ 4,000*

Parent Company P Income Distribution

Equipment depreciation:			Internally generated net income...	$50,000
Block 2, 60% ....**(4b)**	$ 600		80% × Company S adjusted	
Goodwill amortization:			income of $20,000	16,000
Block 1, 20% ....**(3b)**	900			
Block 2, 60% ....**(4c)**	1,280			
			Controlling interest......................	$63,220*

Worksheet 8–3 (see page 458)

Investment Acquired in Blocks; Control
Cost Method on
Company P and
Worksheet for Consolidated
For Year Ended

(Credit balance amounts are in parentheses.)

		Trial Balance	
		Company P	Company S
1	Current Assets	93,900	85,000
2	**Investment in Company S**	**168,000**	
3			
4			
5			
6	Building and Equipment	300,000	150,000
7	**Accumulated Depreciation — Building and Equipment**	**(200,000)**	**(30,000)**
8	**Goodwill**		
9			
10	Liabilities		(20,000)
11	Common Stock, Co. P	(100,000)	
12	**Retained Earnings, Jan. 1, 19X2, Co. P**	**(197,900)**	
13	Common Stock, Co. S		(50,000)
14	Retained Earnings, Jan. 1, 19X2, Co. S		(115,000)
15	Sales	(300,000)	(100,000)
16	Cost of Goods Sold	200,000	60,000
17	Expenses	50,000	20,000
18			
19			
20	Subsidiary Income	(14,000)	
21		0	0
22	Combined Net Income		
23	To Minority Interest (see distribution schedule)		
24	Balance to Controlling Interest (see distribution schedule)		
25	Total Minority Interest		
26	Retained Earnings, Controlling Interest, Dec. 31, 19X2		
27			

Achieved with Second Purchase;
First Investment
Subsidiary Company S
Financial Statements
December 31, 19X2

WORKSHEET 8-3

Eliminations & Adjustments Dr.	Eliminations & Adjustments Cr.	Consolidated Income Statement	Minority Interest	Controlling Retained Earnings	Consolidated Balance Sheet	
					178,900	1
(C) 1,500	(1) 14,000					2
	(2) 115,500					3
	(3a) 9,000					4
	(4a) 31,000					5
					450,000	6
(4a) 5,400	(4b) 600				(225,200)	7
(3a) 9,000	(3b) 900				32,420	8
(4a) 25,600	(4c) 1,280					9
					(20,000)	10
					(100,000)	11
(3b) 450	(C) 1,500			(198,950)		12
(2) 35,000			(15,000)			13
(2) 80,500			(34,500)			14
		(400,000)				15
		260,000				16
(3b) 450		72,330				17
(4b) 600						18
(4c) 1,280						19
(1) 14,000						20
173,780	173,780					21
		(67,670)				22
		6,000*	(6,000)			23
		61,670*		(61,670)		24
			(55,500)		(55,500)	25
				(260,620)	(260,620)	26
					0	27

(continued)

Eliminations and Adjustments:

(C)   Convert the original 10% investment to the simple equity method: 10% × $15,000 change in Company S Retained Earnings.

(1)   Eliminate the parent's entry recognizing the 70% interest in subsidiary net income under the simple equity method. This step restores the investment account to its balance at the beginning of the year.

(2)   The 70% controlling interest in the beginning-of-the-year subsidiary equity accounts is eliminated against the investment account.

(3a)   The original excess of cost on the 10% investment ($9,000) still is contained in the investment account and now can be recognized as goodwill according to the January 1, 19X1 determination and distribution of excess schedule.

(b)   Goodwill for the past year and current year is amortized at $450 per year. Note that the Company P beginning-of-the-year retained earnings is corrected for the prior year's goodwill amortization. Amortization was not recorded previously since the cost method was in use.

(4a)   The excess attributable to the January 1, 19X2 60% acquisition is distributed to the accumulated depreciation and goodwill accounts according to the determination and distribution of excess schedule prepared for the 60% block on January 1, 19X2.

(b)   Depreciation for the current year is increased $600.

(c)   Goodwill of $1,280 is amortized for the current year.

Subsidiary Company S Income Distribution

Internally generated net income..............................	$20,000
Adjusted income	$20,000
Minority share...........................	30%
Minority interest.........................	$ 6,000*

Parent Company P Income Distribution

Equipment depreciation:			Internally generated net income..............................	$50,000
Block 2, 60% ....(4b)	$ 600		70% × Company S adjusted income	
Goodwill amortization:			of $20,000...............................	14,000
Block 1, 10%...........................**(3b)**	**450**			
Block 2, 60% .... (4c)	1,280		Controlling interest......................	$61,670*

Worksheet 8–4 (see page 462)

(Credit balance amounts are in parentheses.)

Subsidiary Preferred Stock,
Company P and
Worksheet for Consolidated
For Year Ended

		Trial Balance	
		Company P	Company S
1	Current Assets	259,600	150,000
2	Property, Plant, and Equipment (net)	400,000	250,000
3	Investment in Common Stock of Company S	195,600	
4			
5			
6	Goodwill		
7	Liabilities	(150,000)	(45,000)
8	Common Stock, Co. P	(200,000)	
9	Retained Earnings, Jan. 1, 19X5, Co. P	(340,000)	
10	Preferred Stock ($100 par), Co. S		(100,000)
11	**Retained Earnings Allocated to Preferred Stock, Jan. 1, 19X5, Co. S**		
12	Common Stock ($10 par), Co. S		(100,000)
13	Retained Earnings, Jan. 1, 19X5, Co. S		(130,000)
14			
15	Sales	(450,000)	(200,000)
16	Cost of Goods Sold	200,000	150,000
17	Expenses	100,000	25,000
18	Subsidiary Income	(15,200)	
19		0	0
20	Combined Net Income		
21	To Minority Interest (see distribution schedule)		
22	Balance to Controlling Interest (see distribution schedule)		
23	Total Minority Interest		
24	Retained Earnings, Controlling Interest, Dec. 31, 19X5		
25			

Eliminations and Adjustments:
(1) Distribute the beginning-of-the-period subsidiary retained earnings into the portions allocable to common and preferred stock. The typical procedure would be to consider the stated subsidiary retained earnings as applicable to common and to remove the preferred portion. This distribution reflects 4 years of arrearage (as of January 1, 19X5) at $6,000 per year.

None Owned by Parent
Subsidiary Company S
Financial Statements
December 31, 19X5

WORKSHEET 8–4

Eliminations & Adjustments				Consolidated Income Statement	Minority Interest	Controlling Retained Earnings	Consolidated Balance Sheet	
Dr.		Cr.						
							409,600	1
							650,000	2
		(2)	15,200					3
		(3)	164,800					4
		(4)	15,600					5
(4)	15,600	(5)	4,680				10,920	6
							(195,000)	7
							(200,000)	8
(5)	3,120					(336,880)		9
					(100,000)			10
		(1)	24,000		(24,000)			11
(3)	80,000				(20,000)			12
(1)	24,000				(21,200)			13
(3)	84,800							14
				(650,000)				15
				350,000				16
(5)	1,560			126,560				17
(2)	15,200							18
	224,280		224,280					19
				(173,440)				20
				9,800	(9,800)			21
				163,640		(163,640)		22
					(175,000)		(175,000)	23
						(500,520)	(500,520)	24
							0	25

(2) Eliminate the parent's entry recording its share of subsidiary current income.
(3) Eliminate the pro rata subsidiary common stockholders' equity at the beginning of the period against the investment account. This step includes elimination of the 80% of subsidiary retained earnings applicable to common stock.
(4) Distribute the excess of cost according to the determination and distribution of excess schedule.
(5) Amortize the goodwill for the past two years and the current year.

(continued)

Subsidiary Company S Income Distribution

Internally generated net income (no adjustments)	$25,000
Less preferred cumulative claim to minority	**(6,000*)**
Common stock income...............	$19,000
Minority share...........................	20%
Minority interest in common income	$ 3,800
Total minority interest ($6,000* + $3,800)................................	$ 9,800

Parent Company P Income Distribution

Amortization of goodwill ....(5) $1,560	Internally generated net income............................. $150,000
	80% × Co. S adjusted income on common stock of $19,000........................ 15,200
	Controlling interest................................... $163,640

Worksheet 8–5 (see page 465)

Subsidiary Preferred
Company P and
Worksheet for Consolidated
For Year Ended

(Credit balance amounts are in parentheses.)

		Trial Balance	
		Company P	Company S
1	Current Assets	194,600	150,000
2	Property, Plant, and Equipment (net)	400,000	250,000
3	Investment in Company S Common Stock	195,600	
4			
5			
6	**Investment in Company S Preferred Stock**	**75,800**	
7			
8	Goodwill		
9	Liabilities	(150,000)	(45,000)
10	Common Stock, Co. P	(200,000)	
11	**Paid-In Capital, Co. P**		
12	Retained Earnings, Jan. 1, 19X5, Co. P	(347,200)	
13	Preferred Stock ($100 par), Co. S		(100,000)
14	Retained Earnings Allocated to Preferred Stock, Jan. 1, 19X5, Co. S		
15	Common Stock ($10 par), Co. S		(100,000)
16	Retained Earnings, Jan. 1, 19X5, Co. S		(130,000)
17			
18	Sales	(450,000)	(200,000)
19	Cost of Goods Sold	200,000	150,000
20	Expenses	100,000	25,000
21	Subsidiary Income—Common	(15,200)	
22	**Subsidiary Income—Preferred**	**(3,600)**	
23		0	0
24	Combined Net Income		
25	To Minority Interest (see distribution schedule)		
26	Balance to Controlling Interest (see distribution schedule)		
27	Total Minority Interest		
28	Retained Earnings, Controlling Interest, Dec. 31, 19X5		
29			

Eliminations and Adjustments:

(1–5)   Same as Worksheet 8–4; the common stock investment elimination procedures are unaffected by the investment in preferred stock.

(6)   Eliminate the entry recording the parent's share of income allocable to preferred stock. If declared, intercompany preferred dividends also would have been eliminated. This adjustment restores the investment account to its beginning-of-the-period equity balance.

Stock Owned by Parent
Subsidiary Company S
Financial Statements
December 31, 19X5

WORKSHEET 8–5

Eliminations & Adjustments		Consolidated Income Statement	Minority Interest	Controlling Retained Earnings	Consolidated Balance Sheet	
Dr.	**Cr.**					
					344,600	1
					650,000	2
	(2) 15,200					3
	(3) 164,800					4
	(4) 15,600					5
	(6) 3,600					6
	(7) 72,200					7
(4) 15,600	(5) 4,680				10,920	8
					(195,000)	9
					(200,000)	10
	(7) 2,200				(2,200)	11
(5) 3,120				(344,080)		12
(7) 60,000			(40,000)			13
(7) 14,400	(1) 24,000		(9,600)			14
(3) 80,000			(20,000)			15
(1) 24,000			(21,200)			16
(3) 84,800						17
		(650,000)				18
		350,000				19
(5) 1,560		126,560				20
(2) 15,200						21
(6) 3,600						22
302,280	302,280					23
		(173,440)				24
		6,200	(6,200)			25
		167,240		(167,240)		26
			(97,000)		(97,000)	27
				(511,320)	(511,320)	28
					0	29

(7)   The parent's ownership portion of the par value and beginning-of-the-period retained earnings applicable to preferred stock is eliminated against the balance in the investment in preferred stock account. The difference in this case was an increase in equity, and it was carried to the controlling paid-in capital.

(continued)

Subsidiary Company S Income Distribution

Internally generated net income (no adjustments)	$25,000
Less preferred cumulative claim:	
to minority, 40% × $6,000	(2,400*)
to controlling, 60% × $6,000	**(3,600)**
Common stock income................	$19,000
Minority share..........................	20%
Minority interest in common income	$ 3,800
Total minority interest ($2,400* + $3,800)...............................	$ 6,200

Parent Company P Income Distribution

Amortization of goodwill ....(5)	$1,560	Internally generated net income.............................	$150,000
		60% × Co. S income attributable to preferred stock.............	**3,600**
		80% × Co. S adjusted income on common stock of $19,000.........	15,200
		Controlling interest.....................	$167,240

Worksheet 8–6 (see page 474)

Sale of Subsidiary Interest
Company P and
Worksheet for Consolidated
For Year Ended

(Credit balance amounts are in parentheses.)

		Trial Balance	
		Company P	Company S
1	Investment in Company S (60%)	244,500	
2			
3			
4	Equipment	600,000	100,000
5	Accumulated Depreciation—Equipment	(100,000)	(60,000)
6	Other Assets	581,500	305,000
7	Goodwill		
8	Common Stock, Co. P	(500,000)	
9	Retained Earnings, Jan. 1, 19X3, Co. P	(700,000)	
10			
11	Common Stock, Co. S		(100,000)
12	Retained Earnings, Jan. 1, 19X3, Co. S		(215,000)
13	Sales	(500,000)	(200,000)
14	Cost of Goods Sold	350,000	140,000
15	Expenses	50,000	30,000
16			
17			
18	**Gain on Sale of Subsidiary Stock, Co. P**	**(6,475)**	
19	Subsidiary Income	(19,525)	
20			
21	**Income Sold to Minority (second 20% block)**		
22		0	0
23	Combined Net Income		
24	To Minority Interest (see distribution schedule)		
25	Balance to Controlling Interest (see distribution schedule)		
26	Total Minority Interest		
27	Retained Earnings, Controlling Interest, Dec. 31, 19X3		
28			

During Period; No Loss of Control
Subsidiary Company S
Financial Statements
December 31, 19X5

WORKSHEET 8–6

Eliminations & Adjustments		Consolidated Income Statement	Minority Interest	Controlling Retained Earnings	Consolidated Balance Sheet	
Dr.	Cr.					
	(2) 18,000					1
	(3) 189,000					2
	(4) 37,500					3
					700,000	4
(4) 15,000	(5) 9,000				(154,000)	5
					886,500	6
(4) 22,500	(6) 6,750				15,750	7
					(500,000)	8
(5) 6,000				(689,500)		9
(6) 4,500						10
(3) 60,000			(40,000)			11
(3) 129,000			(86,000)			12
		(700,000)				13
		490,000				14
(1) 875		86,125				15
(5) 3,000						16
(6) 2,250						17
		(6,475)				18
(1) 1,525						19
(2) 18,000						20
	(1) 2,400		(2,400)			21
262,650	262,650					22
		(130,350)				23
		9,600*	(9,600)			24
		120,750*		(120,750)		25
			(138,000)		(138,000)	26
				(810,250)	(810,250)	27
					0	28

(continued)

Eliminations and Adjustments:

(1) The income earned by the parent on the 20% interest sold on July 1, though earned by the controlling interest, now belongs to the minority interest. The minority interest owns 20% of the reported subsidiary income for the half year ($12,000), which is $2,400. The minority is unaffected by amortizations resulting from a previous price paid by the parent. Note that step (1) credits the account, Income Sold to Minority, to accomplish the transfer of the income to the minority interest. The offsetting debits are explained as follows:

20% of subsidiary income for the first six months, adjusted for one-fourth of the parent's half-year amortization of excess) or (20% × $12,000) − [1/4 × 1/2 × ($4,000 + $3,000)]	$1,525
Depreciation adjustment (1/4 × 1/2 × $4,000)	500
Goodwill amortization (1/4 × 1/2 × $3,000)	375
Total debits	$2,400

Amortizations based on an 80% interest for the first half of the year are proper, since the consolidation involves an 80% controlling interest for the first half of the year and a 60% controlling interest for the second half of the year.

(2) Eliminate the parent's entry recording its 60% share of subsidiary net income of $30,000. This step restores the 60% interest to its simple-equity-adjusted cost at the beginning of the year, so that the investment can be eliminated against subsidiary equity balances at the beginning of the year.

(3) Eliminate 60% of the subsidiary equity balances at the beginning of the year against the investment account. An excess cost of $37,500 remains. This amount is three-fourths (60% ÷ 80%) of the original excess shown on page 467, since only a 60% interest is retained, as compared to an original investment of 80%.

(4) Since only three-fourths of the original investment remains, 75% of the excesses shown in the original determination and distribution of excess schedule on page 467 are recorded.

(5) 75% of the original $4,000 annual depreciation adjustments are recorded for the past two years and the current year. Note that the remaining depreciation adjustments applicable to the interest sold are recorded already.

(6) 75% of the original $3,000 annual goodwill amortization is recorded for the past two years and the current year. Again, amortizations of goodwill applicable to the interest sold have been recorded already.

Subsidiary Company S Income Distribution

	Internally generated net income...	$ 30,000
	Adjusted income	$ 30,000
	Minority share............................	40%
	Minority interest for full year	$ 12,000
	Less income purchased (20% × $12,000, first 6 months)............	2,400
	Minority interest........................	$ 9,600*

Parent Company P Income Distribution

Depreciation adjustment on 60% interest....................................(5) $3,000 Goodwill amortization on 60% interest....................................(6) 2,250	Internally generated net income.............................	$100,000
	Adjusted income	$ 94,750
	60% × Company S income of $30,000....................................	18,000
	20% × Company S income for first 6 months (net of amortization)	1,525
	Gain on sale of subsidiary interest.................................	6,475
	Controlling interest.....................	$120,750*

Worksheet 8–7 (see page 477)   **Balance**
                                                      Company P and
                                                      Worksheet for
(Credit balance amounts are in parentheses.)   December

		Balance Sheet	
		Company P	Company S
1	Cash	61,936	106,535
2	Accounts Receivable	80,000	200,000
3	Inventory, Dec. 31, 19X4	60,000	150,000
4	Land	300,000	250,000
5	Building	800,000	600,000
6	Accumulated Depreciation — Building	(400,000)	(100,000)
7	Equipment	120,000	95,000
8	Accumulated Depreciation — Equipment	(70,000)	(30,000)
9	Investment in Company S Bonds	90,064	
10	Investment in Company S Stock	750,000	
11			
12	Goodwill		
13	Accounts Payable	(92,000)	(75,000)
14	Bonds Payable		(100,000)
15	Discount on Bonds Payable		3,465
16	Common Stock, Co. P	(500,000)	
17	Retained Earnings, Dec. 31, 19X4, Co. P	(1,200,000)	
18			
19			
20			
21	Common Stock, Co. S		(200,000)
22	Retained Earnings, Dec. 31, 19X4, Co. S		(900,000)
23			
24		0	0
25	Total Minority Interest		
26			

Eliminations and Adjustments:
(C) Investment in Company S Stock is converted to the simple equity method *as of December 31, 19X4,* as follows: 80% × $300,000 increase in retained earnings = $240,000.
(1) 80% of the subsidiary equity balances are eliminated against the investment in stock account.
(2) The $110,000 excess of cost is distributed according to the determination and distribution of excess schedule.
(3) The excess attributable to the building is amortized for four years at $3,000 per year.
(4) The excess attributable to goodwill is amortized for four years at $4,000 per year.
(5) The intercompany trade balance is eliminated.

Sheet Only
Subsidiary Company S
Consolidated Balance Sheet
31, 19X4

WORKSHEET 8–7

Eliminations & Adjustments				Minority Interest	Consolidated Balance Sheet	
Dr.		Cr.				
					168,471	1
		(5)	35,000		245,000	2
		(6)	16,000		194,000	3
					550,000	4
					1,400,000	5
(2)	30,000	(3)	12,000		(482,000)	6
		(7)	5,000		210,000	7
(7)	3,000				(97,000)	8
		(8)	90,064			9
(C)	240,000	(1)	880,000			10
		(2)	110,000			11
(2)	80,000	(4)	16,000		64,000	12
(5)	35,000				(132,000)	13
(8)	100,000					14
		(8)	3,465			15
					(500,000)	16
(3)	12,000	(C)	240,000		(1,402,377)	17
(4)	16,000					18
(6)	12,800	(8)	5,177			19
(7)	2,000					20
(1)	160,000			(40,000)		21
(1)	720,000	(8)	1,294	(178,094)		22
(6)	3,200					23
	1,414,000		1,414,000			24
				(218,094)	(218,094)	25
					0	26

(6) The gross profit of $16,000 (40% × $40,000) recorded by Company S and applicable to merchandise in Company P's ending inventory is deferred by reducing the inventory and retained earnings. Since the sale was made by Company S, the adjustment is allocated to the minority and controlling retained earnings.

(7) As of December 31, 19X4, $2,000 (2/5) of the profit on the equipment sale still is to be deferred. Since the sale was made by Company P, the controlling retained earnings absorbs this adjustment, and the equipment and accumulated depreciation accounts are adjusted.

(8) Investment in Company S Bonds is eliminated against the net book value of the bonds. The net gain on the worksheet retirement is allocated to the minority and controlling retained earnings, since the subsidiary originally issued the bonds.

CHAPTER 9

SUBSIDIARY EQUITY TRANSACTIONS; INDIRECT AND MUTUAL HOLDINGS

This chapter deals with additional issues involving the recording and subsequent elimination of the parent's account, Investment in Subsidiary. Accounting issues resulting from equity transactions of the subsidiary are considered first. These transactions include the subsidiary issuances of stock dividends, subsidiary sales of additional shares, and subsidiary stock purchases of its own common stock. Such transactions may affect the parent ownership percentage and the value of the controlling interest.

This chapter also deals with multilevel affiliate holdings. This topic includes subsidiaries that are, in turn, parent companies with respect to another subsidiary and subsidiaries that own shares of their parent company.

SUBSIDIARY STOCK DIVIDENDS

A subsidiary may issue stock dividends in order to convert retained earnings into paid-in capital. The minimum amount to be removed from retained earnings is the par value or stated value of the shares distributed. However, according to accounting principles, when the distribution does not exceed 20% to 25% of the previously outstanding shares, an amount equal to the market value of the shares should be removed from retained earnings and transferred to paid-in capital. The recording of stock dividends at market value is defended by the following statement from ARB No. 43:

> ... a stock dividend does not, in fact, give rise to any change whatsoever in either the corporation's assets or its respective shareholders' proportionate interests therein. However, it cannot fail to be recognized that, merely as a consequence of the expressed purpose of the transaction and its characterization as a dividend in related notices to shareholders and

the public at large, many recipients of stock dividends look upon them as distributions of corporate earnings and usually in an amount equivalent to the fair value of the additional shares received.[1]

Unfortunately, accounting theory is not consistent when it comes to recording the receipt of dividends by an investor. Even though the false impression of the "typical" investor is sufficient reason to allow the issuing corporation to record the market value of the shares distributed, the investor is not permitted to do likewise. In fact, the investor must not record income when stock dividends are received, but must acknowledge the true impact of the transaction, which is that nothing of substance has been given or received. Thus, the investor merely makes a memo entry indicating that the cost of the original investment now is allocated to a greater number of shares. The revised number of shares is important in computing cost per share if there is a subsequent partial sale of the investment.

To review the recording of a stock dividend and to provide a basis for worksheets, assume that Company P acquired an 80% interest in Company S on January 1, 19X1, at which time the following determination and distribution of excess schedule was prepared:

Price paid		$200,000
Less interest acquired:		
Common stock ($10 par)...	$100,000	
Retained earnings..	80,000	
Total stockholders' equity.......................................	$180,000	
Interest acquired...	80%	144,000
Excess of cost over book value attributed to goodwill		
(10-year life)..		$ 56,000

On January 2, 19X3, Company S declared and distributed a 10% stock dividend. Prior to declaration of the dividend, its stockholders' equity appeared as follows:

Common stock ($10 par)	$100,000
Retained earnings	120,000
Total stockholders' equity	$220,000

In the following entry to record the stock dividend, Company S acknowledged the $25 market value of the 1,000 shares distributed:

Retained Earnings (or Stock Dividends Declared)		
($25 market value × 1,000 shares)...........................	25,000	
Common Stock ($10 par × 1,000 shares.......................		10,000
Additional Paid-In Capital from Stock Dividend		
(1,000 shares × $15 excess over par).......................		15,000

---

[1]*Accounting Research and Terminology Bulletins, No. 43,* "Restatement and Revision of Accounting Research Bulletins" (New York: American Institute of Certified Public Accountants, 1961), Ch. 7, Sec. B, par. 10.

PARENT USING THE SIMPLE EQUITY METHOD

Continuing the example, on January 1, 19X3, Company P has a simple-equity-adjusted balance of $232,000 in its investment in Company S account, derived as follows:

Original cost..		$200,000
Share of undistributed income:		
Company S retained earnings, January 1, 19X3................	$120,000	
Company S retained earnings, January 1, 19X1................	80,000	
Increase in retained earnings....................................	$ 40,000	
Ownership interest...	80%	32,000
Simple-equity-adjusted balance, January 1, 19X3.................		$232,000

During 19X3, Company S earned $20,000 and made no other dividend declarations. Company P would make the following entries under the simple equity method:

Receipt of stock dividend:

Jan. 2, 19X3   Memo: Investment in Company S now includes 800 added shares for a total of 8,800 shares. The parent's interest remains at 80%.

Recording of equity income:

Dec. 31, 19X3   Investment in Company S...................... 16,000
                             Subsidiary Income............................. 16,000
                             To record the 80% interest in Company S $20,000 reported net income for 19X3.

The following partial worksheet lists the investment in Company S account at the December 31, 19X3 simple-equity-adjusted cost of $248,000:

	Partial Trial Balance		Eliminations & Adjustments	
	Company P	Company S	Dr.	Cr.
Investment in Co. S	248,000			(1) 16,000
				(2) 176,000
				(3) 56,000
Goodwill			(3) 56,000	(4) 16,800
Common Stock, Co. P	(500,000)			
Retained Earnings, Co. P	(420,000)		(4) 11,200	
Common Stock ($10 par), Co. S		(110,000)	(2) 88,000	
Additional Paid-In Capital from Stock Dividend, Co. S		(15,000)	(2) 12,000	
Retained Earnings, Co. S (reduced $25,000 for stock dividend)		(95,000)	(2) 76,000	
Subsidiary Income	(16,000)		(1) 16,000	
Expenses	30,000	18,000	(4) 5,600	

Eliminations and Adjustments:
(1) Eliminate the parent's entry recording its share of subsidiary income for the current year. There is no complication caused by the stock dividend, since it does not constitute income to Company P.
(2) Eliminate 80% of Company S equity balances as restructured by the stock dividend. If the subsidiary recorded the stock dividend with a debit to Stock Dividends Declared, 80% of that account would be eliminated in this step.
(3) Distribute the excess cost to the goodwill account as required by the determination and distribution of excess schedule.
(4) Amortize the goodwill for three years. Amortization for the two prior years reduces the controlling interest in retained earnings, while the current-year amortization reduces current combined net income.

Note that the partial worksheet includes the redistributed capital structure of Company S which results from the stock dividend. It should be clear that the complications arising from stock dividends pertain primarily to their recording by the separate affiliated firms. There is only a minimal effect on the consolidated worksheet.

PARENT USING THE COST METHOD

In the preceding example, if the parent, Company P, had used the cost method to record its investment in Company S, no adjustments would have been made to the investment account. The investment in Company S still would be carried at its original cost of $200,000 on the December 31, 19X3 worksheet.

The declaration of a stock dividend by a subsidiary requires a more difficult process for the conversion of the parent's investment account from a cost to a simple equity basis. The conversion must reflect all the changes in subsidiary retained earnings since acquisition, including the retained earnings transferred to paid-in capital as a result of a stock dividend. The correct simple equity conversion would be made as follows for the preceding example:

Retained earnings, January 2, 19X3 (after stock dividend)........................	$95,000
Retained earnings, January 1, 19X1	80,000
Change in retained earnings balance...	$15,000
Retained earnings transferred to paid-in capital ($25 × 1,000 shares) as a result of stock dividend...	25,000
Total change in retained earnings	$40,000
Ownership interest...	80%
Simple equity conversion...	$32,000

A faster approach to the simple equity conversion is to consider the change in total subsidiary stockholders' equity as follows:

Subsidiary equity, January 1, 19X3..	$220,000
Subsidiary equity, January 1, 19X1..	180,000
Net change	$ 40,000
Ownership interest...	80%
Simple equity conversion..	$ 32,000

Normally, a parent will maintain a permanent file with the needed information for this adjustment. This faster method, however, could be useful in later years, if facts surrounding the stock dividend were not readily available. The faster procedure will work well, provided there have been no other changes in subsidiary paid-in capital, such as a subsidiary sale or retirement of its shares, in the interim periods.

The $32,000 simple equity conversion would be the first step on a worksheet when the cost method is used for the subsidiary investment. This step converts the investment in subsidiary account to its simple equity balance at the beginning of 19X3. The entry would be:

Investment in Company S... 32,000
    Retained Earnings (January 1, 19X3)............................   32,000

The remaining worksheet procedures would not include the elimination of the current year's subsidiary income, but otherwise would be identical to steps (2) through (4) of the preceding partial worksheet.

SUBSIDIARY SALE OF ITS OWN COMMON STOCK

A parent's investment in a subsidiary is affected by a common stock sale by the subsidiary, whether or not the parent participates in the transaction. The total equity of the subsidiary is increased, and the parent's ownership percentage may be reduced. The impact of the sale on the controlling interest must be calculated, and, in most cases, an equity adjustment will be needed either as part of the use of the equity method or as part of the conversion technique employed for parents using the cost method.

SALE OF SUBSIDIARY STOCK TO MINORITY SHAREHOLDERS

A parent may allow a subsidiary to sell additional shares of stock in order to raise equity funds. A sale of stock by the subsidiary to its minority shareholders results in an increase in the total stockholders' equity against which the controlling interest has a claim. However, the effect of increasing the number of subsidiary shares in the hands of minority stockholders is to lower the controlling interest ownership percentage. Thus, the controlling ownership receives a smaller portion of a larger subsidiary equity. The net effect on the value of the controlling interest depends on the price at which the shares are sold.

A subsidiary stock sale may appear to create a gain or loss to the parent, since there is an effect on the value of the controlling interest. The traditional theory for such a transaction is that, from a single entity viewpoint, this gain or loss is the result of a transaction between the consolidated firm and its shareholders. As a result, such a gain is treated as additional paid-in capital of the parent. A loss is an offset to paid-in capital, unless none exists, in which case the loss is removed from the parent's retained earnings.

In 1980, the AICPA Accounting Standards Executive Committee released an issues paper supporting the recognition of gains and losses on some of these types of transactions, and in 1983 the SEC issued Staff Bulletin 51, which endorsed the gain or loss treatment if the stock is sold in a public offering and is not part of a broader reorganization that will involve other capital transactions. The recognition of a gain or loss is supported on the grounds that it should not matter whether the parent decreases its interest by selling shares (in which case a gain or loss is recognized) or whether the parent decreases its interest by directing the subsidiary to issue additional shares. The public offering requirement assures that a gain or loss is not created arbitrarily but instead relies on a well-defined market value. This text will use the gain/loss approach only for public offerings (to comply with SEC requirements) but will retain the use of the adjustment of paid-in capital for other sales.

Parent Using the Equity Method. A parent company using either the simple or sophisticated equity method usually will need to make an adjustment to its investment account when its subsidiary sells additional shares of stock to minority shareholders. To illustrate, assume that Company P has a 90% interest in Company S. The interest was purchased on January 1, 19X1, at which time the following determination and distribution of excess schedule was prepared:

Price paid		$140,000
Less interest acquired:		
Common stock ($10 par)..	$100,000	
Retained earnings, January 1, 19X1............................	50,000	
Total stockholders' equity......................................	$150,000	
Interest acquired...	90%	135,000
Excess of cost over book value attributed to goodwill		
(10-year life)...		$ 5,000

On January 1, 19X4, 2,000 shares of previously unissued common stock are sold to the minority interest. As a result, the parent's interest is reduced to 75% (9,000/12,000). An analysis of the controlling interest before and after the sale of 2,000 new subsidiary shares to minority shareholders follows. The analysis shows the three possibilities: shares sold at book value (Case 1), at more than book value (Case 2), and at less than book value (Case 3).

	Case 1	Case 2	Case 3
Sale price per share...	$24	$30	$20
Company S shareholders' equity prior to sale............................	$240,000	$240,000	$240,000
Add to common stock, $10 par × 2,000 shares.........................	20,000	20,000	20,000
Add to paid-in capital in excess of par.....................................	28,000	40,000	20,000
Company S shareholders' equity subsequent to sale	$288,000	$300,000	$280,000
Controlling interest subsequent to sale (75%)	$216,000	$225,000	$210,000
Prior controlling interest (90% × $240,000)	216,000	216,000	216,000
Net increase (decrease) in controlling interest	$ 0	$ 9,000	($ 6,000)

Based on the results of the three cases within the above table, it should be noted that no change in controlling interest occurs when a subsidiary sells new stock to minority shareholders at book value. An increase occurs when the stock is sold above book value, and a decrease results when the stock is sold below book value.

Assuming the shares were not sold in a public offering, no gain or loss would be recognized. The parent would adjust its investment in subsidiary account to record the effect on controlling interest in each of the three cases as follows:

Case 1:   Memo entry only to record a change from a 90% to a 75% interest.

Case 2:   Investment in Company S.................................. 9,000
              Paid-In Capital in Excess of Par 9,000
              To record increase in ownership interest.

Case 3:   Retained Earnings.. 6,000
              Investment in Company S.............................. 6,000
              To record decrease in ownership interest. It is assumed that no parent additional paid-in capital exists to offset the decrease.

Note that these entries would be made directly on the books of the parent; they are not worksheet adjustments.

To illustrate the effect of Case 2 on consolidation, assume that subsidiary income for 19X4 was $40,000 and that no dividends were declared. The investment account balance under the simple equity method would be determined as follows:

Original cost...	$140,000
Simple equity income adjustments, 19X1 through 19X3,	
90% × $90,000 increase in retained earnings	81,000
Increase from stock sale to minority on January 1, 19X4	9,000
Simple equity adjustment for 19X4 subsidiary income,	
75% × $40,000 income..	30,000
Balance, December 31, 19X4	$260,000

In the following partial worksheet for the year ended December 31, 19X4, the trial balances of Company P and Company S reflect the sale of 2,000 additional shares at $30 per share (Case 2):

Company P and Subsidiary Company S
Partial Worksheet (Simple Equity Method, No Gain or Loss Recorded)
For Year Ended December 31, 19X4

	Trial Balance		Eliminations & Adjustments	
	Company P	Company S	Dr.	Cr.
Investment in Co. S (75%)	260,000			(1) 30,000
				(2) 225,000
				(3) 5,000
Goodwill			(3) 5,000	(4) 2,000
Common Stock, Co. P	(400,000)			
Paid-In Capital in Excess of Par, Co. P	(9,000)			
Retained Earnings, Co. P	(320,000)		(4) 1,500	
Common Stock, Co. S		(120,000)	(2) 90,000	
Paid-In Capital in Excess of Par, Co. S		(40,000)	(2) 30,000	
Retained Earnings, Co. S		(140,000)	(2) 105,000	
Subsidiary Income	(30,000)		(1) 30,000	
Expenses	40,000	27,000	(4) 500	

Eliminations and Adjustments:
(1) Eliminate the parent's entry recording subsidiary income for the current year. The parent's share is now 75% of the subsidiary undistributed net income. If the sale had occurred *during the year,* the *old* percentage of ownership would be applied to income earned prior to the sale date.
(2) Eliminate the parent's 75% share of subsidiary equity balances at the beginning of the year against the investment account.
(3) Distribute to the goodwill account the original excess of cost over book value as required by the January 1, 19X1 determination and distribution of excess schedule.
(4) Amortize the goodwill for the past three years and the current year.

If the shares were sold in a public offering, a gain or loss could be recognized based on the market value of the shares sold. The gain/loss approach takes the position that the parent has sold indirectly a portion of its interest. This means that the portion of any excess of cost or book value applicable to the interest sold should be adjusted for that interest sold, just as it would be if the parent sold a portion of its interest directly. In the preceding example, the parent's ownership interest decreased from 90% to 75% as a result of the subsidiary stock sale. Of the total original goodwill of $5,000, 1/6[(90% − 75%) ÷ 90%] or $833 is applicable to the interest sold and must be removed from the investment account. Goodwill has been amortized over 3 years of its 10-year life; thus, $250 [($833 ÷ 10) × 3] of the goodwill applicable to the interest sold already has been amortized on the consolidated worksheets. Since the 15% interest no longer will be consolidated, it is necessary to adjust the parent's retained earnings for the $250 of amortizations. The net or remaining goodwill applicable to the interest is $583 ($833 − $250) which should be deducted from the increase or added to the decrease in controlling interest resulting from the stock sale. The same procedure would be used for any other excesses of cost or book value applicable to identifiable assets. The net impact of the subsidiary stock sale at the three alternative prices is:

	Case 1	Case 2	Case 3
Sale price per share...	$24	$30	$20
Net increase (decrease) in controlling interest	$ 0	$9,000	($6,000)
Adjustment for net goodwill applicable to interest sold	(583)	(583)	(583)
Gain (loss) on interest sold.....................................	($583)	$8,417	($6,583)

The parent would record the effect on the controlling interest in each case as follows:

Case 1:	Retained Earnings (3 years' amortization on 1/6 of $5,000 goodwill)...	250	
	Loss on Sale of Subsidiary Stock..........................	583	
	Investment in Company S (1/6 of $5,000 goodwill)..		833
	To record loss on subsidiary stock sale.		
Case 2:	Investment in Company S ($9,000 − $833 goodwill)...	8,167	
	Retained Earnings...	250	
	Gain on Sale of Subsidiary Stock		8,417
	To record gain on subsidiary stock sale.		
Case 3:	Retained Earnings...	250	
	Loss on Sale of Subsidiary Stock..........................	6,583	
	Investment in Company S ($6,000 + $833 goodwill)...		6,833
	To record loss on subsidiary stock sale.		

To illustrate the effect of Case 2 on consolidation, assume that subsidiary income for 19X4 was $40,000 and that no dividends were declared. The investment account balance under the simple equity method would be determined as follows:

Original cost...	$140,000
Simple equity income adjustments, 19X1 through 19X3, 90% × $90,000 increase in retained earnings	81,000
Increase from stock sale to minority on January 1, 19X4......................................	8,167
Simple equity adjustment for 19X4 subsidiary income, 75% × $40,000 income	30,000
Balance, December 31, 19X4	$259,167

In the Case 2 partial worksheet for the year ended December 31, 19X4, the trial balances of Company P and Company S reflect the sale of 2,000 additional shares at $30 per share where the gain is to be recognized:

Company P and Subsidiary Company S
Partial Worksheet (Simple Equity Method, Gain or Loss Recorded)
For Year Ended December 31, 19X4

	Trial Balance		Eliminations & Adjustments	
	Company P	Company S	Dr.	Cr.
Investment in Co. S (75%)	259,167			(1) 30,000
				(2) 225,000
				(3) 4,167
Goodwill			(3) 4,167	(4) 1,668
Common Stock, Co. P	(400,000)			
Paid-In Capital in Excess of Par, Co. P	(9,000)			
Retained Earnings, Co. P	(320,000)		(4) 1,251	
Common Stock, Co. S		(120,000)	(2) 90,000	
Paid-In Capital in Excess of Par, Co. S		(40,000)	(2) 30,000	
Retained Earnings, Co. S		(140,000)	(2) 105,000	
Subsidiary Income	(30,000)		(1) 30,000	
Gain on Sale of Subsidiary Stock	(8,417)			
Expenses	40,000	27,000	(4) 417	

Eliminations and Adjustments:
(1) Eliminate the parent's entry recording subsidiary income for the current year. The parent's share is now 75% of the subsidiary undistributed net income. If the sale had occurred *during the year,* the *old* percentage of ownership would be applied to income earned prior to the sale date.
(2) Eliminate the parent's 75% share of subsidiary equity balances at the beginning of the year against the investment account.
(3) Distribute to the goodwill account the remaining (5/6) excess of cost over book value that was shown on the original determination and distribution of excess schedule.
(4) Amortize the remaining goodwill for the past three years and the current year (5/6 × 500 per year = $417).

The consolidated worksheet may require the adjustment of both the controlling and minority interests in beginning retained earnings for intercompany transactions originating in previous periods. When such adjustments are necessary, the current, not the original, ownership interest percentages are used.

Parent Using the Cost Method. A parent using the cost method records only dividends received from a subsidiary. Usually, no adjustment is made for any other changes in the subsidiary stockholders' equity, including changes caused by sales of subsidiary stock. As a result, the entry to convert from the cost method to the equity method on future worksheets must consider not only the equity adjustments for the subsidiary undistributed income, but also adjustments caused by subsidiary stock sales. A parent using the cost method still would list the subsidiary investment at its original cost.

The following partial worksheet demonstrates the consolidation procedures needed for Case 2 when the cost method is used. This example further assumes that the sale of subsidiary stock was a private offering and that no gain needs to be recognized.

Company P and Subsidiary Company S
Partial Worksheet (Cost Method, No Gain or Loss Recorded)
For Year Ended December 31, 19X4

	Trial Balance		Eliminations & Adjustments			
	Company P	Company S	Dr.		Cr.	
Investment in Co. S (75%)	140,000		(C)	90,000	(1)	225,000
					(2)	5,000
Goodwill			(2)	5,000	(3)	2,000
Common Stock, Co. P	(400,000)					
Paid-In Capital in Excess of Par, Co. P					(C)	9,000
Retained Earnings, Co. P ($81,000 less since no equity income was recorded)	(239,000)		(3)	1,500	(C)	81,000
Common Stock, Co. S		(120,000)	(1)	90,000		
Paid-In Capital in Excess of Par, Co. S		(40,000)	(1)	30,000		
Retained Earnings, Co. S		(140,000)	(1)	105,000		
Expenses	40,000	27,000	(3)	500		

Eliminations and Adjustments:
(C) The simple equity conversion is recorded:

Undistributed income:
   90% of change in retained earnings of Company S from
     January 1, 19X1, to January 1, 19X4, 90% × $90,000............ $81,000
Adjustment to paid-in capital:
   Controlling interest in Company S equity subsequent to sale
     on January 1, 19X4, 75% × $300,000.................................. $225,000
   Controlling interest in Company S equity prior to sale on
     January 1, 19X4, 90% × $240,000.......................................   216,000
     Net increase in paid-in capital...   9,000
Total increase in the investment account................................. $90,000

(1) Eliminate 75% of the subsidiary equity balances at the beginning of the year against the investment account.
(2) Distribute the excess of cost to the goodwill account as shown by the original determination and distribution of excess schedule.
(3) Amortize the goodwill for the past three years and the current year.

To review this process, the cost-to-simple-equity conversion amount for Case 2 is determined as it would apply to the December 31, 19X5 worksheet:

Undistributed income:
90% of change in retained earnings of Company S from January 1, 19X1, to January 1, 19X4, 90% × $90,000.....		$ 81,000
75% of change in retained earnings of Company S from January 1, 19X4, to January 1, 19X5, 75% × $40,000.....		30,000
Increase in Company P retained earnings		$111,000
Adjustment to paid-in capital:		
Controlling interest in Company S equity subsequent to sale on January 1, 19X4, 75% × $300,000	$225,000	
Controlling interest in Company S equity prior to sale on January 1, 19X4, 90% × $240,000...........................	216,000	
Net increase in paid-in capital....................................		9,000
Total increase in investment account		$120,000

A dangerous shortcut might be attempted, whereby the net change in the controlling ownership interest is calculated by comparing 90% of the total subsidiary equity on January 1, 19X1, to 75% of the total subsidiary equity on January 1, 19X5. This shortcut will produce the correct adjustment to the investment in subsidiary account, but it will *not* provide the analysis needed to distribute the adjustment to the parent's paid-in capital and retained earnings.

A unique situation arises for a firm using the cost method that wishes to record a gain or loss on a subsidiary stock sale. In order to record the gain or loss, the equity-adjusted cost must be calculated on the date of the transaction, and the investment account must be adjusted for the gain or loss. This means that, when consolidating, the investment account is adjusted for the impact of the subsidiary stock sale but not for the parent's share of subsidiary earned income. In the previous example, it would be necessary to do a cost-to-equity adjustment based on a 90% interest prior to the subsidiary stock sale and a 75% interest subsequent to the sale. This approach does have the advantage of making the adjustment only once on the parent's books rather than repeating it on each year's worksheet.

PARENT PURCHASE OF NEWLY ISSUED SUBSIDIARY STOCK

When a subsidiary issues new stock, a parent may exercise its preemptive right and purchase additional shares in proportion to its original ownership interest. When this occurs, the investment account is increased by the price paid for the newly purchased stock. For example, Company P of the previous examples would make the following entry if it maintained its 90% interest by purchasing 90% of the 2,000 newly issued Company S shares for $30 each:

Investment in Company S (1,800 shares × $30)...............	54,000	
Cash..		54,000

Company S would make the following entry to record the sale of the entire 2,000 shares for $30 each:

Cash..	60,000	
Common Stock ($10 × 2,000 shares)		20,000
Paid-In Capital in Excess of Par....................................		40,000

The consolidation process will eliminate 90% of all subsidiary equity, including the above increment. Thus, $54,000 of the $60,000 addition will be eliminated. No new excess is created, and the original disparity between the investment account and the underlying equity is not altered. As a result, *no additional equity adjustment is needed when the parent maintains its ownership interest and when the same price is paid by all buyers.* Future equity adjustments and eliminations continue, based on a 90% interest.

The parent might purchase more than 90% of the newly issued shares. In this situation, an additional excess of cost or book value may be created. The stock purchased in excess of that needed to preserve the original ownership interest must be treated as a new block for which a separate determination and distribution of excess schedule is prepared. For example, if the parent purchased all 2,000 shares at $30 per share, the schedule would be prepared as follows for the 200 shares acquired in excess of those needed to preserve the original 90% interest:

Price paid (200 × $30)...		$6,000
Less interest acquired:		
Total as shown in Case 2 (page 538).............................	$300,000	
Incremental interest (200 ÷ 12,000)................................	$1\frac{2}{3}\%$	5,000
Excess of cost over book value attributed to goodwill		
(to be amortized over 10 years).......................................		$1,000

Future eliminations would be based on a $91\frac{2}{3}\%$ ownership interest (11,000 ÷ 12,000). The $1,000 excess would require separate distribution and amortization on future worksheets.

If the parent buys fewer shares than needed to preserve its original ownership percentage, it must make an equity adjustment for the change in its interest caused by the increased minority ownership. Assume that Company P purchased 1,000 of the 2,000 newly issued shares for $30 per share. The parent then would own 10,000 of the 12,000 total subsidiary shares, or 5/6. Consequently, future eliminations would be based on an $83\frac{1}{3}\%$ (5/6) ownership interest. As a result of the subsidiary stock issuance, the parent would calculate an equity adjustment as follows:

Total shareholder equity subsequent to sale........................	$300,000	
Controlling interest..	$83\frac{1}{3}\%$	$250,000
Prior interest adjusted for purchase of new shares:		
Ownership interest prior to sale, 90% × $240,000............	$216,000	
Add cost of new shares, 1,000 × $30	30,000	246,000
Net increase in ownership interest.....................................		$ 4,000

In addition to recording the purchase, the parent then would make the following entry:

Investment in Company S...	4,000	
Paid-In Capital in Excess of Par.......................................		4,000

If the stock sale was a public offering and the parent chose to record a gain on the transaction, a gain account would be credited. However, it would be necessary to adjust for the excess attributable to the interest involved. In this case, the adjustment would be immaterial since the interest lost is only $7\frac{2}{5}\%$ [(90% − $83\frac{1}{3}\%$) ÷ 90%] of the original interest.

SUBSIDIARY PURCHASE OF ITS OWN COMMON STOCK

A subsidiary's acquisition of its own shares held by the minority interest is considered to be an indirect purchase of an additional interest in the subsidiary by its parent company.[2] From a consolidated viewpoint, the subsidiary is acting as an agent of the parent which desires the additional interest in the subsidiary. This means that another block of stock has been purchased which will require a determination and distribution of excess schedule. Typically, the subsidiary would record the purchase of the shares as treasury stock at cost. On subsequent consolidated worksheets, the treasury stock account would be eliminated against the underlying equity it represents.

Some consolidated firms still may practice what could be termed the *retirement method*. This method has the subsidiary retire the minority shares purchased. The parent company then adjusts its subsidiary investment account for the impact of the retirement on its interest in the subsidiary.[3] The continued use of this method can be defended only on the basis of materiality.

---

[2]*Accounting Interpretations of APB Opinion No. 16*, (New York: American Institute of Certified Public Accountants, 1972), par. 26.

[3]To illustrate the retirement method, consider this example. A subsidiary has 10,000 shares outstanding and has a total stockholders' equity of $240,000. The parent company owns 7,000 shares prior to the purchase of 2,000 minority shares by the subsidiary for $52,000. The purchase increases the parent to a 7/8 interest. The parent's change in equity would be calculated as follows:

Parent interest prior to retirement, 70% × $240,000 equity.................................	$168,000
Parent interest after retirement, 7/8 × ($240,000 − $52,000)	164,500
Adjustment	$ 3,500

The adjustment in the investment account is accompanied by an adjustment in the parent company paid-in capital in excess of par since the decrease in interest results from a stock transaction.

PURCHASE OF SHARES AS TREASURY STOCK

To illustrate a subsidiary treasury stock purchase, assume that the parent, Company P, owned a 70% interest in Company S. On January 1, 19X1, Company S had the following stockholders' equity:

Capital stock ($10 par)	$100,000
Paid-in capital in excess of par	50,000
Retained earnings	90,000
Total stockholders' equity	$240,000

On this date, the subsidiary purchased 2,000 of its 10,000 outstanding shares. The following entry then was recorded by Company S as a result of this purchase from minority shareholders at a cost of $26 each:

Treasury Stock (at cost)	52,000	
Cash		52,000

As a result of the purchase, Company S had the following stockholders' equity:

Capital stock ($10 par)	$100,000
Paid-in capital in excess of par	50,000
Retained earnings	90,000
Total	$240,000
Less treasury stock (at cost)	52,000
Total stockholders' equity	$188,000

Although the subsidiary views the investment as treasury stock, the consolidated viewpoint treats the investment as an additional interest purchased by the parent. This is the first time an investment on the books of the subsidiary should be eliminated against subsidiary equity. Assuming that no assets or liabilities had market values different from book values, the parent's determination and distribution of excess schedule would be prepared as follows:

Price paid		$52,000
Less interest acquired in Company S:		
Common stock ($10 par)	$100,000	
Paid-in capital in excess of par	50,000	
Retained earnings, January 1, 19X1	90,000	
Total stockholders' equity	$240,000	
Interest acquired	**20%**	48,000
Excess of cost over book value attributed to goodwill (with a 40-year life)		$ 4,000

The parent's additional 20% investment caused by the subsidiary treasury stock purchase will have the following ramifications on subsequent worksheets:

1. The subsidiary will maintain the investment in treasury stock at cost and would have no reason to make equity adjustments to the cost. This means that a cost-to-equity conversion entry will be required for the investment on the worksheet. The adjustment to the investment account will require an adjustment to the controlling retained earnings.
2. The treasury stock account, which is treated as an additional investment in the subsidiary on the worksheet, will be eliminated against the *subsidiary equity accounts* like any other investment in subsidiary account. The excess will be distributed and amortized. All previous years' amortizations are, as always, adjustments to controlling retained earnings only.
3. All eliminations of intercompany profits will be based on a 90% (original 70% plus new 20%) interest as of January 1, 19X1.
4. The adjusted internally reported income of the subsidiary now will be distributed 90% to the controlling interest and 10% to the minority interest.

RESALE OF SHARES HELD IN TREASURY

The purchase and resale of treasury stock by a subsidiary would be handled as two separate events using the previously described methods. There may be alternative procedures which could be used if there is the intent to resell the treasury shares in the near future. When, for example, the treasury stock is purchased and resold within the consolidated firm's fiscal period, a shortcut is possible. Since there would be no change in the parent's percentage of ownership by the end of the period, the parent only needs to make an adjustment equal to its ownership interest multiplied by the subsidiary's increase or decrease in equity as a result of the treasury stock transaction. This adjustment should be carried to the additional paid-in capital of the parent and is not viewed as an operating gain or loss since it results from dealings with the firm's own shareholders. Using the same reasoning, a decrease in equity reduces parent retained earnings only when no additional paid-in capital is available.

This procedure also might be justified for treasury stock transactions crossing over fiscal periods. It is only necessary that the subsidiary treasury stock account be left on the consolidated worksheet at cost and that eliminations be made according to the parent's ownership percentage, unadjusted for the number of treasury shares. When the treasury shares are resold, the parent would adjust its accounts in the same manner as was done for a treasury stock purchase and resale within a fiscal period.

If a parent is using the cost method and did not adjust for subsidiary treasury stock transactions, an adjustment can be made as part of the cost-to-equity conversion process.

INDIRECT HOLDINGS

A parent company may own a controlling interest in a subsidiary, which, in turn, owns a controlling interest in another firm. For example, Company A may own a 75% interest in Company B, which, in turn, owns an 80% interest in Company C. Thus, A has indirect holdings in C. This situation could be diagrammed as follows:

Level 1		Level 2	
owns 75%		owns 80%	
A ————————→	B	————————→	C

The treatment of the *level one* investment in B and the *level two* investment in C can be mastered with the theory that has been discussed, but the procedures must be applied carefully. The procedures are applied easily to indirect holdings when the level one investment already exists at the time of the level two purchase. Complications arise in preparing the determination and distribution of excess schedule for the new investment when the level two investment exists prior to the time that the parent achieves control over the subsidiary (level one investment). These complications result because the level two investment held by the subsidiary represents one of the subsidiary's assets that may require adjustment to market value on the determination and distribution of excess schedule prepared at the time of the parent's level one acquisition. The use of separate and distinct determination and distribution of excess schedules for each level of investment should facilitate the maintaining of proper accounting when two or more levels are involved.

LEVEL ONE HOLDING
ACQUIRED FIRST

Assume that Company A purchased a 75% interest in Company B on January 1, 19X1, at which time the following determination and distribution of excess schedule was prepared:

Price paid		$400,000
Less interest acquired in Company B:		
Common stock ($10 par)..	$200,000	
Retained earnings, January 1, 19X1............................	100,000	
Total stockholders' equity..	$300,000	
Interest acquired...	75%	225,000
Excess of cost over book value attributed to building		
and equipment (10-year life)		$175,000

On January 1, 19X2, the subsidiary, Company B, purchased an 80% interest in Company C, and the following schedule was prepared:

Price paid		$270,000
Less Company B's interest acquired in Company C:		
Common stock ($10 par)..	$100,000	
Retained earnings, January 1, 19X2............................	120,000	
Total stockholders' equity..	$220,000	
Interest acquired...	80%	176,000
Excess of cost over book value attributed to goodwill		
(20-year life)...		$ 94,000

Equity adjustments must be made carefully. Company A must be sure that Company B has included its equity income from Company C in its net income before Company A records its percentage share of Company B income.

Assume the following internally generated net incomes:

	Company A	Company B	Company C
19X1..............	$100,000	$100,000	$20,000
19X2..............	70,000	76,000	30,000
19X3..............	90,000	100,000	30,000

On this basis, the following simple equity adjustments would be required:

	Company B's Books		Company A's Books	

19X1 Dec. 31	None (interest in Company C not yet acquired).		Investment in Company B...... 75,000
			  Subsidiary Income ....
			    To adjust for 75% of
			    Company B reported
			    income.
				75,000

19X2 Dec. 31	Investment in Company C 24,000
	  Subsidiary Income.............
	    To adjust for 80% of
	    Company C reported
	    income.
		24,000	Investment in Company B...... 75,000
			  Subsidiary Income ....
			    To adjust for 75% of
			    Company B total income
			    ($76,000 plus $24,000
			    subsidiary income).
				75,000

19X3 Dec. 31	Investment in Company C 24,000
	  Subsidiary Income.............
	    To adjust for 80% of
	    Company C reported
	    income.
		24,000	Investment in Company B...... 93,000
			  Subsidiary Income ....
			    To adjust for 75% of
			    Company B total income
			    ($100,000 plus $24,000
			    subsidiary income).
				93,000

Worksheet 9–1, pages 580–583, is based on the trial balances of the three separate firms on December 31, 19X3. The investment account balances reflect the equity adjustments previously shown. The following additional information for 19X3 is assumed:

	Intercompany Sales by B to A	Intercompany Sales by C to B
Selling company goods in buyer's January 1, 19X3 inventory..............	$ 8,000	$ 6,000
Sales during 19X3	50,000	40,000
Selling company goods in buyer's December 31, 19X3 inventory	10,000	10,000
Gross profit on all sales......................	25%	30%

The investment accounts must be handled carefully when any eliminations are made in order to insure that the minority interest accounts are available to receive amortizations of excesses. It is suggested that the level one investment be eliminated first, thereby reducing Company B retained earnings to the minority interest. Then it will be possible to allocate the amortizations of excess resulting from the level two (Company C) holding to the controlling interest (Company A) and the Company B minority interest. Since Company B owns the interest in Company C, the Company B minority interest must share in the amortizations of excess resulting from the investment in Company C.

In Worksheet 9–1, the combined net income is $196,100, which must be distributed to the two minority interests and to the controlling interest. Distribution must proceed from the *lowest* level (level two) to insure proper distribution. Company B adjusted income includes 80% of Company C adjusted income. Thus, the Company C income distribution schedule must be completed first, followed by the distribution schedules for Companies B and A. These schedules accompany Worksheet 9–1.

If the cost method was used in the previous example, the investment account balances still would contain the January 1, 19X1 $400,000 cost of the Company B investment and the January 1, 19X2 $270,000 cost of the Company C investment. Conversion entries would be made on the consolidated worksheet to update both investment accounts to their January 1, 19X3 simple equity balances. It is advisable to make equity adjustments at the *lowest* level of investment first, because the retained earnings of the midlevel firm must be adjusted for its share of investment income before the parent can adjust for the change in its subsidiary's retained earnings. The following simple equity conversion entry would be made first for Company B's investment in Company C:

```
Investment in Company C ...........................................   24,000
    Retained Earnings (Company B)...................................            24,000
        80% of $30,000 increase in Company C retained
        earnings between January 1, 19X2, and January 1, 19X3.
```

The following conversion entry then would be made for Company A's investment in Company B:

```
Investment in Company B .........................................   150,000
    Retained Earnings (Company A)...............................            150,000
        75% of $200,000 increase in Company B retained
        earnings (including previous equity adjustment for
        Company B) between January 1, 19X1, and
        January 1, 19X3.
```

Eliminations and adjustments would be made as on Worksheet 9–1, except that there would be no need to eliminate the current year's equity adjustment.

LEVEL TWO HOLDING EXISTS AT TIME OF PARENT'S PURCHASE

When a parent acquires a controlling interest in another parent company, the determination and distribution of excess schedule must be based on the acquired firm's *consolidated* balance sheet. For example, assume that Company Y purchased an 80% interest in Company Z on January 1, 19X1, and that Company X purchased a 70% interest in Company Y on January 1, 19X3. Also assume that on January 1, 19X3, Company Y owns equipment which is undervalued by $40,000 and that Company Z (the subsidiary) has equipment which is undervalued by $100,000. Company X would prepare the following determination and distribution of excess schedule based on the controlling interest in Company Y:

Price paid		$700,000
Less interest acquired:		
Company Y common stock...	$400,000	
Company Y controlling interest in consolidated retained earnings..	320,000	
Total Company Y stockholders' equity	$720,000	
Interest acquired..	70%	504,000
Excess of cost over book value		$196,000
Excess of cost attributable to Company Y equipment:		
70% × $40,000 undervaluation	**$ 28,000**	
Excess of cost attributable to Company Z equipment:		
70% × 80% × $100,000 undervaluation.......................	**56,000**	84,000
Goodwill (20-year life)..		$112,000

Note the following features of the preceding schedule:

1. Company Y consolidated equity is multiplied by the parent's (Company X) ownership interest to arrive at the excess of cost over book value.
2. When a Company Y (level one investment) asset is to be adjusted, it should be adjusted for the parent's ownership portion (70%) of the value discrepancy.
3. When a Company Z (level two investment) asset is to be adjusted, it should be adjusted for only the Company X ownership share of the Company Y share (70% × 80%, or 56%) of the value discrepancy.
4. Resulting goodwill is based on the consolidated asset values for Companies Y and Z.

When the simple equity method is used for the investments, the procedures illustrated in Worksheet 9–1 apply without modification. When the cost method is used, simple equity conversion adjustments again proceed from the lowest level. Be sure to note, however, that in this example Company X would convert to the equity basis for the change in Company Y retained earnings after January 1, 19X3.

CONNECTING AFFILIATES

A business combination involving connecting affiliates exists when a parent firm has a direct (level one) investment in a company and an indirect (level two) investment in the same company sufficient to result in control. For example, the following diagram illustrates a connecting affiliate structure:

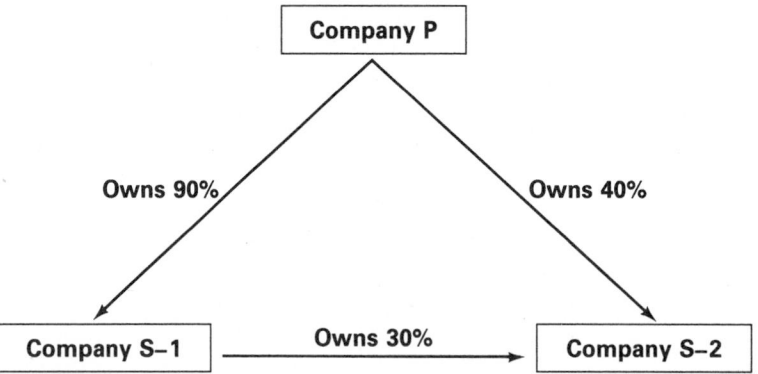

Not only does Company P have a 90% interest in Company S–1, but it also has, in effect, a 67% interest in Company S–2, calculated as follows:

Direct...	40%
Indirect (90% × 30%)......................................	27%
Total	67%

This type of structure is consolidated more readily once the determination and distribution of excess schedule has been prepared. Caution must be used in the schedule preparation because of differing dates for each investment. Referring to the diagram, the special concerns in consolidating connecting affiliates are as follows:

1. Company S-2 generally is not included in the consolidation process until the total percentage of S-2 shares held by the parent and its subsidiaries (70% in this example) exceeds 50%. Prior to that time, an investment of 20% or more is treated according to APB Opinion No. 18, and a lesser investment is accounted for under the cost method.
2. Any amortizations of excess resulting from the 30% investment of Company S-1 in Company S-2 are distributed to the controlling and S-1 minority interests in retained earnings on a 90/10 basis.

3. Any adjustments to retained earnings caused by Company S-2 generated transactions are distributed 30% to minority S-2, 3% (10% × 30%) to minority S-1, and 67% [40% + (90% × 30%)] to the controlling interest.

4. Income distributions would begin with Company S-2: 30% of its income would go to minority S-2, 30% would flow to the Company S-1 distribution schedule, and 40% would flow to the Company P schedule. Company P will receive 90% of the Company S-1 adjusted income (including the 30% share of Company S-2).

5. When either equity method is used, Companies P and S-1 each must adjust for its interest in Company S-2, even though neither firm's interest by itself would merit consolidation techniques.

6. When the cost method is used, each investment is converted to the simple equity method from the purchase date forward. Again, equity conversions must begin at the lowest level. For example, the Company S-1 investment in Company S-2 must be converted first, so that Company S-1 retained earnings is updated before the Company P investment in Company S-1 is converted to the simple equity method.

MUTUAL HOLDINGS

A mutual holding structure exists when the subsidiary owns any percentage of the parent company common stock. Such an investment must be eliminated in the consolidation process. There are two methods through which such holdings may be consolidated. The first and more popular method is called the *treasury stock method*. From a consolidated viewpoint, the subsidiary acquisition of parent shares is viewed as a retirement of the shares or as a temporary treasury stock purchase where there is an intent to resell the shares. Under both approaches to the treasury stock method, the shares are *off the market* and have *no claim to income*. The other method is termed the *reciprocal method*, which allocates to the minority interest a percentage of the parent income. This method requires simultaneous equations and becomes even more complicated when there are excesses of cost or book value applicable to each set of investments and/or intercompany profit transactions. The method will be explained in its simplest state, but it is considered to be obsolete and theoretically unsound in that it views parent shares held by the subsidiary as being alive and entitled to a share of combined net income.

TREASURY STOCK METHOD

The treasury stock method does not view parent shares held by the subsidiary as outstanding. When it is intended that the shares are to be reissued, they are viewed as treasury shares and are recorded at cost. When resold, an excess received over cost is carried to additional paid-in capital. If cost exceeds proceeds on resale, the difference is offset against existing paid-in capital. If there is no paid-in capital, retained earnings is reduced. When it is not intended that the shares be reissued, the stock is retired on the worksheet using the original investment cost as the retirement price. Regardless of the approach used, the resulting capital account adjustments fall entirely upon the parent. The subsidiary is viewed as an agent accomplishing the transaction. An important requirement of either of the treasury stock approaches is that the subsidiary investment in the parent be *maintained at its original cost*. Since the stock is not to be viewed as outstanding, it has no claim on income. If equity adjustments have been made by error, they must be reversed on the consolidated worksheet.

To illustrate the treasury stock method, consider the following example. Suppose that Company P acquired an 80% interest in Company S on January 1, 19X1, at which time the following determination and distribution of excess schedule was prepared:

Price paid		$200,000
Less interest acquired:		
Common stock ($10 par)...	$100,000	
Retained earnings..	50,000	
Total stockholders' equity..	$150,000	
Interest acquired...	80%	120,000
Excess of cost over book value attributed to equipment		
(20-year remaining life)		$ 80,000

Further assume that on January 1, 19X3, Company S purchases a 10% interest in the parent for $80,000. There would be no need for a determination and distribution of excess schedule for the subsidiary investment, since no excess of cost or book value is acknowledged or distributed. For 19X3, the parent will make the normal simple equity adjustment to acknowledge its 80% interest in subsidiary income of $20,000:

Investment in Company S...	16,000	
Subsidiary Income...		16,000
To record 80% of subsidiary reported income of		
$20,000.		

There is no equity adjustment for the Company S investment in the parent since it must remain at cost.

The trial balances of the two firms on December 31, 19X3, are contained in the first two columns of Worksheet 9–2 on pages 584–587. The investment in Company S account on Worksheet 9–2 is computed as follows:

Original cost........................	$200,000
80% × 19X1 and 19X2 undistributed income of $40,000......................	32,000
19X3 simple equity adjustment...	16,000
Balance, December 31, 19X3	$248,000

Examination of the formal statements of the consolidated firm reveals that the treasury shares are held by the consolidated firm and that no income accrues to them. These statements, based on Worksheet 9–2, are as follows:

Company P and Subsidiary Company S
Consolidated Income Statement
For Year Ended December 31, 19X3

Sales..	$500,000
Less cost of goods sold...	300,000
Gross profit...	$200,000
Less expenses...	144,000
Combined net income...	$ 56,000
Minority interest of Company S	4,000
Consolidated net income...	$ 52,000

Company P and Subsidiary Company S
Retained Earnings Statement
For Year Ended December 31, 19X3

	Minority Interest	Controlling Interest
Balance, January 1, 19X3......................................	$18,000	$192,000
Net income...	4,000	52,000
Balance, December 31, 19X3.................................	$22,000	$244,000

Company P and Subsidiary Company S
Consolidated Balance Sheet
December 31, 19X3

Assets		Stockholders' Equity		
Equipment.............	$868,000	Minority interest		$ 42,000
Less accumulated		Controlling interest:		
depreciation........	162,000	Common stock	$500,000	
		Retained earnings	244,000	744,000
		Total....................................		$786,000
		Less treasury stock		
		(at cost)		80,000
Total assets............	$706,000	Net stockholders' equity		$706,000

RECIPROCAL METHOD

To understand the objections to the reciprocal method, it is necessary to examine the procedures required by the method. This will be done using the same example as was used for the treasury stock method. The same determination and distribution of excess schedule would be prepared for the parent company investment in the subsidiary. But, unlike the treasury stock method, a separate determination and distribution of excess schedule must be prepared for the subsidiary investment in the parent firm.

On January 1, 19X3, Company S purchases a 10% interest in Company P. The determination and distribution of excess schedule for this investment is prepared as follows:

Price paid		$80,000
Less interest acquired:		
Common stock..	$500,000	
Retained earnings..	200,000	
Total stockholders' equity..	$700,000	
Ownership interest...	**10%**	70,000
Excess of cost over book value attributed to goodwill		
(10-year life)..		$10,000

Typically, the determination and distribution of excess schedule will be based only on Company P equity and not on the total controlling interest. The excess could be distributed to the separate assets of Company P (including the investment in Company S), but, based on materiality, it usually would be distributed only to goodwill. The parent and the subsidiary may use either the cost method or the equity method to account for intercompany investments. In Worksheet 9–3 on pages 588–591, both firms are assumed to be using the simple equity method. Company P has recorded subsidiary income of $16,000 (80% × Company S reported income of $20,000), and Company S has recorded investment income of $4,000 (10% × Company P internal income of $40,000).

In Worksheet 9–3, the combined net income is distributed to Company P and Company S by solving simultaneously the following equations which are based on each company's *adjusted internally generated income:*

Let P = Company P income
Let S = Company S income

$$P = \$36,000 + .8S$$
$$S = \$19,000 + .1P$$

Solution:
$$P - .8S = \$36,000$$
$$-.1P + \quad S = \$19,000$$

Multiply the first solution equation by .1 and then add the equations:

$$.1P - \quad .08S = \$ \ 3,600$$
$$+ -.1P + 1.00S = \$19,000$$
$$.92S = \$22,600$$
$$S = \$24,565$$

Substitute for S in the first equation:

$$P = \$36,000 + .8(\$24,565)$$
$$P = \$55,652$$

To minority interest: 20% × Company S income of $24,565 = $ 4,913

To controlling interest: 90% × Company P income of $55,652 = $50,087

The treasury stock method usually is more practical to use than the reciprocal method and is supported by ARB No. 51, which states "Shares of the parent held by a subsidiary should not be treated as outstanding stock in the consolidated balance sheet."[4] Further support comes from an American Accounting Association publication, which states:

Shares of the controlling company's capital stock owned by a subsidiary before the date of acquisition of control should be treated in consolidation as treasury stock. Any subsequent acquisition or sale by a subsidiary should likewise be treated in the consolidated statements as though it had been the act of the controlling company.[5]

QUESTIONS

1. What effect does a subsidiary stock dividend have on consolidation procedures (a) when the equity method is used? (b) when the cost method is used?
2. Indicate how one calculates the dollar impact on the parent company's investment account of a sale of additional common stock by a subsidiary to minority shareholders only.
3. Assume that a subsidiary issues additional shares of common stock, but that the parent buys none of these shares. Further assume that the parent's interest (in dollars) increases as a result of the transaction. What are the alternative theories of dealing with the increase and under what circumstances might each be appropriate?
4. State how to adjust the parent's investment account for a subsidiary stock sale at more than book value in a public market offering assuming that:
   (a) The parent purchased all the shares.
   (b) The parent purchased the same percentage of new shares as it previously owned.
   (c) The parent purchased a lower percentage of new shares than it previously owned.

---

[4]*Accounting Research Bulletin No. 51*, "Consolidated Financial Statements" (New York: American Institute of Certified Public Accountants, 1959), par. 13.

[5]*Accounting and Reporting Standards for Corporate Financial Statements and Preceding Statements and Supplements* (Columbus: American Accounting Association, 1957), 44.

5. What is the applicable general accounting theory for the purchase of treasury shares by a subsidiary? How should the investment be recorded on the subsidiary's books, and what are the consolidated worksheet procedures for the treasury stock?

6. What special procedures are necessary when making equity adjustments to record subsidiary income when an indirect holding situation exists?

7. What new procedures are needed on the determination and distribution of excess schedule when a parent acquires a controlling interest in a subsidiary company which, at the time of the acquisition, also owns a controlling interest in another firm?

8. What is a connecting affiliate, and how is income distributed to the parent calculated?

9. Describe a mutual holding and the alternative methods used to consolidate such holdings.

10. Why might the reciprocal method of accounting for mutual holdings be considered theoretically unsound?

11. Under the treasury stock method of accounting for mutual holdings, intent determines the exact treatment of the parent shares owned by the subsidiary. Explain the different treatments available under the treasury stock method.

EXERCISES

Exercise 1. On January 1, 19X7, Paton Industries purchased 80% of the outstanding stock of Banjo Controls for $420,000. At the time of the acquisition, Banjo Controls had the following stockholders' equity:

Common stock ($10 par)............................	$300,000
Paid-in capital in excess of par...................	90,000
Retained earnings......................................	110,000
Total stockholders' equity.......................	$500,000

It was determined that Banjo Controls' book values approximated market as of the purchase date. Any excess of cost over book value was attributed to goodwill and given a 40-year life.

On July 1, 19X7, Banjo Controls distributed a 10% stock dividend when the market value of its common stock was $15 per share. A cash dividend of $.50 per share was distributed on December 31, 19X7. Banjo Controls' net income for 19X7 amounted to $40,000 and was earned evenly throughout the year.

(1) Prepare the entry required on Banjo Controls' books to reflect the stock dividend distributed on July 1, 19X7. Prepare the stockholders' equity section of Banjo Controls' balance sheet as of December 31, 19X7.
(2) Prepare the simple equity method entries that Paton Industries would make during 19X7 to record its investment in Banjo Controls.
(3) Prepare the eliminations that would be made on the December 31, 19X7 consolidated worksheet. (Assume the use of the simple equity method.)

Exercise 2. Barnco Corporation had the following stockholders' equity on January 1, 19X8:

Common stock ($10 par).............................	$200,000
Paid-in capital in excess of par...................	100,000
Retained earnings.....................................	150,000
Total stockholders' equity.......................	$450,000

Grand Company purchased 75% of the outstanding common stock of Barnco Corporation for $300,000 on January 1, 19X7, at which time Barnco had a retained earnings balance of $100,000. Also on that date, there was no difference between the price paid and the interest acquired in Barnco.

On July 1, 19X8, Barnco Corporation sold 5,000 shares of stock in a public offering. Grand Company purchased none of the shares. Barnco had net income of $50,000 for the first half of 19X8 and $40,000 for the second half. Barnco has never distributed cash dividends.

(1) Prepare the entries on Grand Company's books, using the simple equity method, to reflect the investment in Barnco Corporation. Assume that the stock was sold to the public at (a) $22 per share, (b) $25 per share, and (c) $30 per share.
(2) Comment on how the entries would differ if the shares were sold in a private sale.

Exercise 3. Assume the same facts as in Exercise 2, except that Grand Company accounts for its investment in Barnco Corporation by the cost method.

Prepare the entry that would be needed on the 19X9 worksheet to convert the investment account to its simple equity balance as of January 1, 19X9. Prepare the entry based on each of the following prices for the 5,000 shares issued July 1, 19X8: (a) $22 per share, (b) $25 per share, and (c) $30 per share.

Exercise 4. On January 1, 19X8, Tobin Company purchased an 80% interest in Carter Company for $300,000. On the purchase date, Carter Company had the following stockholders' equity:

Common stock ($5 par).............................	$150,000
Paid-in capital in excess of par...................	120,000
Retained earnings.....................................	105,000
Total stockholders' equity.......................	$375,000

Carter Company had net income of $40,000 for 19X8. No dividends were paid or declared during 19X8.

On January 1, 19X9, Carter Company sold 10,000 shares of common stock at $15 per share in a public offering.

Assuming that the parent uses the simple equity method, prepare all parent company entries required for the issuance of the shares. Also prepare a new determination and distribution of excess schedule for the investment if it is needed. Assume the following alternative situations:

(1) Tobin Company purchased 5,000 shares.
(2) Tobin Company purchased 8,000 shares.
(3) Tobin Company purchased 9,000 shares.

Exercise 5. The following comparative statements of stockholders' equity were prepared for Nolte Corporation:

	Jan. 1, 19X3	Jan. 1, 19X5	Jan. 1, 19X8
Common stock ($10 par)................	$300,000	$300,000	$300,000
Paid-in capital in excess of par.......	60,000	60,000	60,000
Retained earnings........................	—	42,000	120,000
Total......................................	$360,000	$402,000	$480,000
Less treasury stock (at cost)...........	—	(75,000)	(75,000)
Total stockholders' equity...........	$360,000	$327,000	$405,000

Tarman Corporation purchased 60% of Nolte Corporation common stock for $12 per share on January 1, 19X3, when the latter corporation was formed.

On December 31, 19X4, Nolte Corporation purchasd 5,000 shares of its own common stock from minority interests for $15 per share. These shares were accounted for as treasury stock at cost.

Nolte had $50,000 of net income in 19X8 and never has declared a cash dividend.

Assuming that Tarman Corporation uses the cost method to record its investment in Nolte Corporation, prepare the necessary cost-to-simple-equity conversion and the eliminations and adjustments required on the consolidated worksheet as of December 31, 19X8. Include all pertinent supporting calculations in good form. Any excess of cost over book value is considered to be goodwill with a 10-year life.

Exercise 6. You have secured the following information for Companies A, B, and C concerning their internally generated net incomes (excluding subsidiary income) and dividends paid:

		A	B	C
19X5	Internally generated net income...............	$30,000	$20,000	$10,000
	Dividends declared and paid....................	10,000	5,000	—
19X6	Internally generated net income...............	50,000	30,000	25,000
	Dividends declared and paid....................	10,000	5,000	5,000
19X7	Internally generated net income...............	40,000	40,000	30,000
	Dividends declared and paid....................	10,000	5,000	5,000

(1) Assume that Company A purchased an 80% interest in Company B on January 1, 19X5, and that Company B purchased a 60% interest in Company C on January 1, 19X6. Prepare the simple equity method adjusting entries made by Companies A and B for subsidiary investments for the years 19X5 through 19X7.

(2) Assume that Company B acquired a 70% interest in Company C on January 1, 19X5, and that Company A acquired a 90% interest in Company B on January 1, 19X7. Prepare the simple equity method adjusting entries made by Companies A and B for subsidiary investments for the years 19X5 through 19X7.

Exercise 7.   Companies D, E, and F produced the following separate internally generated net incomes during 19X9:

	D	E	F
Sales	$320,000	$375,000	$100,000
Less cost of goods sold	200,000	300,000	60,000
Gross profit	$120,000	$ 75,000	$ 40,000
Expenses	50,000	30,000	10,000
Internally generated net income	$ 70,000	$ 45,000	$ 30,000

Company D purchased a 60% interest in Company E on January 1, 19X6, and Company E purchased a 70% interest in Company F on January 1, 19X7. Each investment was acquired at a price equal to the book value of the stock purchased.

Additional information:

(a) Company E sold a machine to Company F on January 1, 19X8, for $20,000, when the machine had a book value of $15,000. The machine is being depreciated on a straight-line basis over five years.

(b) Company D purchased goods billed at $30,000 from Company F during 19X9. The price includes a $66\frac{2}{3}$% markup on cost. One-half of the goods are held in Company D's year-end inventory.

(c) Company E purchased goods billed at $30,000 from Company D during 19X9. Company D always bills Company E for cost plus 50%. Company E had $6,000 of Company D goods in its beginning inventory and $2,400 of Company D goods in its ending inventory.

(d) Company F purchased goods billed at $15,000 from Company E during 19X9. Company E bills Company F at cost plus 25%. At year end, $7,500 of the goods remain unsold. The goods were inventoried at $5,000, under the lower-of-cost-or-market procedure.

Prepare the consolidated income statement for 19X9, including the distribution of combined net income supported by distribution schedules.

Exercise 8.   On January 1, 19X6, Hinsdale Company purchased an 80% interest in Kork Company for $110,000. The purchase price represented a $10,000 excess over book value, which was attributed to goodwill and given a 10-year life. The investment is recorded under the simple equity method.

On January 1, 19X8, Goning Company purchased a 60% interest in Hinsdale Company for $350,000. Goning Company believes that the goodwill remaining on the investment by Hinsdale in Kork is stated correctly. Comparative equities of Hinsdale Company and Kork Company immediately prior to the purchase revealed:

Stockholders' Equity	Hinsdale Company	Kork Company
Common stock ($5 par)...	$200,000	—
Common stock ($10 par)..	—	$100,000
Paid-in capital in excess of par....................................	100,000	20,000
Retained earnings...	150,000	80,000
Total stockholders' equity..	$450,000	$200,000

An analysis of the separate accounts of Hinsdale and Kork on January 1, 19X8, revealed that Kork's inventory was undervalued by $20,000 and that Hinsdale's equipment with a 5-year future life was undervalued by $30,000. All other book values approximated market values for Hinsdale and Kork.

Prepare the determination and distribution of excess schedule for Goning's purchase of Hinsdale Company on January 1, 19X8.

Exercise 9.   The following diagram depicts the investment affiliations between Companies X, Y, and Z:

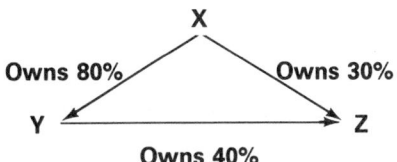

The following facts apply to 19X3 operations:

	X	Y	Z
Internally generated net income.........................	$120,000	$80,000	$50,000
Dividends declared and paid.............................	50,000	20,000	10,000

All investments were made at a price equal to book value.
(1) Prepare the simple equity method adjustments that would be made for the investments owned by Companies X and Y during the year 19X3.
(2) Assume that Company Z sold a piece of equipment to Company Y on January 1, 19X3, for $32,000. The book value of the machine was $20,000, and it had an 8-year remaining life. Straight-line depreciation is used. Using the facts given, determine the combined net income and indicate the interest of each ownership group. Income distribution schedules may be used for support.

Exercise 10.   Myles Corporation and its subsidiary, Dowling Corporation, had the following trial balances as of December 31, 19X8:

	Myles Corporation	Dowling Corporation
Current Assets..	400,000	182,000
Investment in Dowling Corporation	398,000	—
Investment in Myles Corporation..........................	—	150,000
Property, Plant, and Equipment (net)	850,000	400,000
Liabilities...	(200,000)	(100,000)
Common Stock ($10 par).....................................	(1,000,000)	(500,000)
Retained Earnings, Jan. 1, 19X8	(400,000)	(100,000)
Sales..	(800,000)	(350,000)
Dividend Income	—	(2,000)
Subsidiary Income...	(18,000)	—
Cost of Goods Sold..	600,000	240,000
Expenses..	150,000	80,000
Dividends Declared..	20,000	—
Total..	0	0

Myles Corporation purchased its 60% interest in Dowling Corporation for $350,000 on January 1, 19X6. At that time, Dowling retained earnings balance was $50,000. Any excess of cost over book value was attributed to goodwill and given a 20-year life.

Dowling Corporation purchased a 10% interest in Myles Corporation on January 1, 19X8, for $150,000. Myles' book values approximated market values at the time of the purchase. Any resulting goodwill is being amortized over 20 years.

No intercompany transactions occurred during 19X8.

(1) Prepare determination and distribution of excess schedules for the intercompany investments.

(2) Prepare the 19X8 consolidated income statement, including the combined net income distribution, using the reciprocal method for mutual holdings.

(3) Prepare the 19X8 consolidated income statement, including the combined net income distribution, using the treasury stock method for mutual holdings. Prepare the supporting income distribution schedules.

(4) State how the investment in Myles stock will appear on the consolidated balance sheet under the two alternative methods of accounting for mutual holdings.

PROBLEMS

Problem 9–1. On January 1, 19X7, Zorn Corporation purchased 8,000 shares of Tessman Company stock and 18,000 shares of Sargant Company stock for $200,000 and $250,000, respectively. The excess of cost over book value on each investment was attributed to goodwill and given a 10-year life.

Tessman Company and Sargant Company had the following stockholders' equities immediately prior to Zorn's purchases:

	Tessman Company	Sargant Company
Common stock ($5 par)	$ 50,000	—
Common stock ($10 par)...	—	$300,000
Paid-in capital in excess of par......................................	100,000	—
Retained earnings...	50,000	100,000
Total stockholders' equity..	$200,000	$400,000

Additional information:

(a) Net income for Tessman Company and Sargant Company for 19X7 and 19X8 follows (income is assumed to be earned evenly throughout the year):

	19X7	19X8
Tessman Company	$30,000	$40,000
Sargant Company........................	50,000	40,000

(b) No cash dividends were paid or declared by Tessman or Sargant during 19X7 and 19X8.

(c) Tessman Company distributed a 10% stock dividend on December 31, 19X7. Tessman stock was selling at $20 per share when the stock dividend was declared.

(d) On July 1, 19X8, Tessman Company sold 2,750 shares of stock at $30 per share in a public offering. Zorn Corporation purchased none of these shares.

(e) Sargant Company sold 5,000 shares of stock on July 1, 19X7, at $20 per share. Zorn Corporation purchased 3,000 of these shares.

(f) On January 1, 19X8, Sargant Company purchased 5,000 shares of its common stock from minority interests at $12 per share. These shares were sold on January 5, 19X8, at $18 per share. Zorn Corporation did not purchase any of these shares.

Required:

Assume that Zorn Corporation uses the simple equity method. Record each of the adjustments required during 19X7 and 19X8. Provide all supporting calculations in good form.

Suggestion: Since the Tessman sale of stock was a public offering, the parent should recognize an income statement gain. However, it is necessary to reduce the parent's investment account for the interest in the excess of cost which has been lost. The treasury stock purchase and resale by Sargant occurred in the same reporting period; thus the parent may make one entry to record the net impact of the treasury stock transaction.

Problem 9–2. On January 1, 19X6, Barstow Corporation acquired a 60% interest in Kantor Company and an 80% interest in Saeger Company. The purchase prices were $200,000 and $250,000, respectively. The excess of cost over book value for each investment was considered to be goodwill with a 10-year life. Neither subsidiary is trading its stock publicly.

Immediately prior to the purchases, Kantor Company and Saeger Company had the following stockholders' equities:

	Kantor Company	Saeger Company
Common stock ($10 par)..	$200,000	—
Common stock ($20 par)	—	$200,000
Paid-in capital in excess of par..................................	50,000	—
Retained earnings..	100,000	100,000
Total stockholders' equity.......................................	$350,000	$300,000

Additional information:

(a) Kantor Company and Saeger Company had the following net incomes for 19X6 through 19X8 (incomes were earned evenly throughout the year):

	19X6	19X7	19X8
Kantor Company	$50,000	$60,000	$60,000
Saeger Company..	40,000	30,000	55,000

(b) Kantor Company had the following equity-related transactions for the first three years after it became a subsidiary of Barstow Corporation:

July 1, 19X6	Sold 5,000 shares of its own stock at $20 per share. Barstow purchased 3,000 of these shares.
December 31, 19X7	Paid a cash dividend of $1 per share.
July 1, 19X8	Purchased 5,000 shares of minority-owned stock as treasury shares at $25 per share.

(c) Saeger Company had the following equity-related transactions for the first three years after it became a subsidiary of Barstow Corporation:

December 31, 19X6	Issued a 10% stock dividend. The estimated market value of Saeger common stock was $30 per share on the declaration date.
October 1, 19X7	Sold 4,000 shares of its own stock at $25 per share. Of these shares, 200 were purchased by Barstow.

(d) Barstow Corporation has $200,000 of additional paid-in capital on December 31, 19X8.

Required:

Barstow Corporation uses the cost method to account for its investments in subsidiaries. Convert its investments to the simple equity method as of December 31, 19X8, and provide adequate support for the entries. Assume that the 19X8 nominal accounts are closed.

Suggestion: Since the stock sales were not public offerings, no gain or loss is recognized; instead, the adjustment is to the paid-in capital of the parent company.

Problem 9–3. On January 1, 19X6, Parson Company purchased 80% of the outstanding common stock of Schell Company for $650,000.

On January 1, 19X8, Schell Company sold 25,000 shares of common stock to the public at $9 per share. Parson Company did not purchase any of these shares. It is considered appropriate for the parent to record a gain or loss on the subsidiary stock sale; however, no entry has been made by the parent. Schell Company had the following stockholders' equity at the end of 19X5 and 19X7:

| | December 31 | |
	19X5	19X7
Common stock ($2 par)	$200,000	$200,000
Paid-in capital in excess of par	400,000	400,000
Retained earnings	100,000	180,000
Total stockholders' equity	$700,000	$780,000

On the January 1, 19X6 acquisition date, Schell Company's book values approximated market values, except for a building that was undervalued by $60,000. The building had an estimated future life of 20 years. Any additional excess was attributed to goodwill and given a 10-year life.

Trial balances of the two firms as of December 31, 19X8, are as follows:

	Parson Company	Schell Company
Cash	229,040	30,000
Accounts Receivable (net)	280,000	190,000
Inventory	325,000	175,000
Investment in Schell Company	650,000	—
Property, Plant, and Equipment	2,450,000	1,400,000
Accumulated Depreciation	(1,256,000)	(536,000)
Liabilities	(750,000)	(210,000)
Common Stock ($10 par)	(1,500,000)	—
Common Stock ($2 par)	—	(250,000)
Paid-In Capital in Excess of Par	—	(575,000)
Retained Earnings, Jan. 1, 19X8	(375,000)	(180,000)
Sales	(1,600,000)	(750,000)
Subsidiary Dividend Income	(23,040)	—
Cost of Goods Sold	1,120,000	450,000
Other Expenses	405,000	220,000
Dividends Declared	45,000	36,000
Total	0	0

During 19X8, Schell Company sold $200,000 of merchandise to Parson Company at cost plus 25%. This was the first intercompany sale between the two firms. $50,000 of the goods remain in Parson's ending inventory.

Required:

Prepare the worksheet necessary to produce the consolidated financial statements of Parson Company and its subsidiary as of December 31, 19X8.

Include the determination and distribution of excess and income distribution schedules.

Problem 9–4. On January 1, 19X7, Wisco Corporation purchased a 60% interest in Flanner Company for $162,000. Flanner stockholders' equity on the purchase date was as follows:

Common stock ($5 par)	$100,000
Paid-in capital in excess of par	70,000
Retained earnings	60,000
Total stockholders' equity	$230,000

At the purchase date, it was determined that the book values of Flanner's assets and liabilities approximated market values, except for a piece of equipment that was undervalued by $40,000. The equipment had an estimated remaining life of 10 years and is being depreciated on a straight-line basis.

On January 1, 19X8, Flanner Company sold 5,000 shares of common stock in a public offering at $15 per share. Wisco Company purchased 4,000 shares. Any excess of cost over book value on the additional interest was attributed to goodwill and given a 10-year life.

The following schedule summarizes the intercompany merchandise sales for 19X8:

	Wisco Corporation	Flanner Company
Merchandise in buyer's inventory, Jan. 1, 19X8	$ 5,000	$ 6,000
Intercompany sales for 19X8	30,000	20,000
Merchandise in buyer's inventory, Dec. 31, 19X8	2,000	8,000
Gross profit on sales	40%	30%

No intercompany debt remained as of December 31, 19X8.

Wisco's investment in Flanner Company balance was determined as follows:

Original cost	$162,000
60% of Flanner 19X7 income ($40,000 × 60%)	24,000
Subtotal	$186,000
Less 60% of Flanner dividends declared in 19X7 (60% × $8,000)	(4,800)
Subtotal	$181,200
Cost to acquire additional shares (new issue)	60,000
64% of Flanner 19X8 income ($50,000 × 64%)	32,000
Subtotal	$273,200
Less 64% of Flanner dividends declared in 19X8 (64% × $10,000)	(6,400)
Investment balance, December 31, 19X8	$266,800

Flanner has paid a quarterly $.10 dividend per outstanding common share since the second quarter of 19X6.

The trial balances of the two firms as of December 31, 19X8, are as follows:

	Wisco	Flanner
Cash	28,800	38,500
Accounts Receivable	205,000	60,000
Inventory	350,000	80,000
Investment in Flanner Company	266,800	—
Property, Plant, and Equipment	1,800,000	360,000
Accumulated Depreciation	(600,000)	(89,500)
Accounts Payable	(180,000)	(64,000)
Other Current Liabilities	(26,000)	(8,000)
Bonds Payable	(500,000)	—
Common Stock ($10 par)	(1,000,000)	—
Common Stock ($5 par)	—	(125,000)
Paid-In Capital in Excess of Par	—	(120,000)
Retained Earnings, Jan. 1, 19X8	(212,600)	(92,000)
Sales	(1,950,000)	(600,000)
Subsidiary Income	(32,000)	—
Cost of Goods Sold	1,170,000	420,000
Other Expenses	630,000	130,000
Dividends Declared	50,000	10,000
Total	0	0

Required:

Prepare the worksheet necessary to produce the consolidated financial statements of Wisco Corporation and its subsidiary as of December 31, 19X8. Include the determination and distribution of excess and income distribution schedules.

Problem 9–5. The audit of Barns Company and its subsidiaries for the year ended December 31, 19X2, was completed. The working papers contain the following information:

(a) Barns Company acquired 4,000 shares of Webb Company common stock for $320,000 on January 1, 19X1. Webb Company purchased 500 shares of its own stock as treasury shares for $48,000 on January 1, 19X2.
(b) Barns Company acquired all 8,000 outstanding shares of Elcho Company stock on January 1, 19X1, for $600,000. On January 1, 19X2, Elcho Company issued through a private sale 2,000 additional shares to new minority shareholders at $85 per share. Barns has no investments other than the stock of Webb and Elcho.
(c) Elcho Company originally issued $200,000 of 10-year, 8% mortgage bonds at 98, due on January 1, 19X5. On January 1, 19X2, Webb Company purchased $150,000 of these bonds in the open market at 98. Interest on the bonds is paid each June 30 and December 31.

(d) Condensed balance sheets of Webb and Elcho on January 1, 19X1, and January 1, 19X2, are as follows:

	Webb Company		Elcho Company	
	1/1/X2	1/1/X1	1/1/X2	1/1/X1
Current assets	$225,000	$195,000	$205,000	$280,400
Property, plant, and equipment	350,000	305,000	623,800	613,000
Unamortized bond discount	—	—	1,200	1,600
Total	$575,000	$500,000	$830,000	$895,000
Current liabilities	$125,000	$100,000	$105,000	$ 95,000
Bonds payable	—	—	200,000	200,000
Capital stock ($50 par)	250,000	250,000	400,000	400,000
Retained earnings	200,000	150,000	125,000	200,000
Total	$575,000	$500,000	$830,000	$895,000

(e) Total dividends declared and paid during 19X2 were as follows:

Barns Company	$24,000
Webb Company	25,000
Elcho Company	10,000

In addition to the dividend payments, Barns Company and Webb Company each had declared dividends of $1 per share payable in January, 19X3.

(f) On June 30, 19X2, Barns sold equipment with a book value of $8,000 to Webb for $10,000. Webb depreciates equipment by the straight-line method based on a 10-year life.

(g) Barns Company consistently sells to its subsidiaries at prices which realize a gross profit of 25% on sales. Webb and Elcho Companies sell to each other and to Barns Company at cost. Prior to 19X2, intercompany sales were negligible; but the following sales were made during 19X2:

	Total Sales	Included in Purchaser's Inventory at December 31, 19X2
Barns Company to Webb Company	$172,000	$20,000
Barns Company to Elcho Company	160,000	40,000
Webb Company to Elcho Company	25,000	5,000
Webb Company to Barns Company	28,000	8,000
	$385,000	$73,000

(h) At December 31, 19X2:

Barns Company owed Webb Company	$24,000
Webb Company owed Elcho Company	16,000
Elcho Company owed Barns Company	12,000
Total	$52,000

(i)   The following trial balances as of December 31, 19X2, were prepared:

	Barns	Webb	Elcho
Cash	110,000	23,500	165,200
Accounts Receivable	85,000	73,500	105,000
Inventories	138,000	163,000	150,000
Investment in Webb Company Stock	320,000	—	—
Investment in Elcho Company Stock	600,000	—	—
Investment in Elcho Company Bonds	—	148,000	—
Property, Plant, and Equipment	700,000	525,000	834,000
Accumulated Depreciation	(402,000)	(325,000)	(240,000)
Accounts Payable	(202,000)	(150,500)	(86,900)
Dividends Payable	(12,000)	(5,000)	—
Bonds Payable	(400,000)	—	(200,000)
Unamortized Bond Discount	—	—	800
Capital Stock ($50 par)	(600,000)	(250,000)	(500,000)
Paid-In Capital in Excess of Par	—	—	(70,000)
Retained Earnings, Jan. 1, 19X2	(278,200)	(170,000)	(115,000)
Treasury Stock (at cost)	—	48,000	—
Gain on Sale of Equipment	(2,000)	—	—
Sales	(2,950,000)	(1,550,000)	(1,750,000)
Interest Income on Bonds	—	(13,000)	—
Dividend Income	(28,000)	—	—
Cost of Goods Sold	2,500,000	1,200,000	1,400,000
Operating Expenses	405,000	280,000	290,500
Interest Expense	16,200	2,500	16,400
Total	0	0	0

Required:

Prepare the worksheet necessary to produce the consolidated financial statements of Barns Company and its subsidiaries for the year ended December 31, 19X2. Include the determination and distribution of excess and income distribution schedules. Any excess of cost over book value is attributable to goodwill with a 10-year life. All bond discounts are assumed to be amortized on a straight-line basis.   (AICPA adapted)

Suggestion: The treasury stock represents a separate block of stock to be eliminated. The impact of the subsidiary sale of shares should not be reflected as an income statement gain or loss.

Problem 9–6.   The following diagram depicts the relationships between Mary Company, Jack Company, and Jill Company on December 31, 19X8:

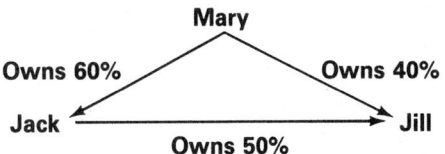

Mary Company purchased its interest in Jack Company on January 1, 19X6, for $200,000. Jack Company purchased its interest in Jill Company on January 1, 19X7, for $75,000. Mary Company purchased its interest in Jill Company on January 1, 19X8, for $72,000.

The following stockholders' equities are available:

	Jack Company December 31, 19X5	Jill Company December 31, 19X6	Jill Company December 31, 19X7
Common stock ($10 par).......................	$150,000	—	—
Common stock ($20 par)	—	$100,000	$100,000
Paid-in capital in excess of par..............	75,000	—	—
Retained earnings..............................	75,000	50,000	80,000
Total equity.....................................	$300,000	$150,000	$180,000

On January 2, 19X8, Jill Company sold a machine to Mary Company for $20,000. The machine had a book value of $10,000 with an estimated life of five years and is being depreciated on a straight-line basis.

Jack Company sold $20,000 of merchandise to Jill Company during 19X8 to realize a gross profit of 30%. Of this merchandise, $5,000 remained in Jill Company's December 31, 19X8 inventory. Jill owes Jack $3,000 on December 31, 19X8, for merchandise delivered during 19X8.

Trial balances of the three firms prepared from general ledger account balances on December 31, 19X8, are as follows:

	Mary	Jack	Jill
Cash...	66,500	60,000	30,000
Accounts Receivable	200,000	55,000	30,000
Inventory	360,000	80,000	50,000
Investment in Jack Company	266,000	—	—
Investment in Jill Company	86,000	107,500	—
Property, Plant, and Equipment..................	2,250,000	850,000	350,000
Accumulated Depreciation.........................	(938,000)	(377,500)	(121,800)
Intangibles..	15,000	—	—
Accounts Payable	(215,500)	(61,000)	(22,000)
Accrued Expenses	(12,000)	(4,000)	(1,200)
Bonds Payable	(500,000)	(300,000)	(100,000)
Common Stock ($5 par)............................	(500,000)	—	—
Common Stock ($10 par)...........................	—	(150,000)	—
Common Stock ($20 par)...........................	—	—	(100,000)
Paid-In Capital in Excess of Par..................	(700,000)	(75,000)	—
Retained Earnings, Jan. 1, 19X8	(290,000)	(130,000)	(80,000)
Sales...	(1,800,000)	(500,000)	(300,000)
Gain on Sale of Equipment........................	—	—	(10,000)
Subsidiary Income...................................	(58,000)	(20,000)	—
Cost of Goods Sold..................................	1,170,000	350,000	180,000
Other Expenses.......................................	525,000	100,000	90,000
Dividends Declared..................................	75,000	15,000	5,000
Total...	0	0	0

Required:

Prepare the worksheet necessary to produce the consolidated financial statements of Mary Company and its subsidiaries as of December 31, 19X8. Include the determination and distribution of excess and income distribution schedules. Any excess of cost is assumed to be attributable to goodwill with a 20-year life.

Problem 9–7.   On January 1, 19X6, Irving Company purchased an 80% interest in Jason Company for $500,000. The following determination and distribution of excess schedule was prepared at that time:

Price paid		$500,000
Less interest acquired:		
Common stock ($20 par)	$500,000	
Retained earnings...	100,000	
Total stockholders' equity......................................	$600,000	
Interest acquired...	80%	480,000
Excess of cost over book value		$ 20,000
Excess of cost attributable to inventory, 80% × $10,000....	$ 8,000	
Excess of cost attributable to equipment (8-year life),		
80% × $15,000	12,000	20,000
Goodwill..		$ 0

All of the undervalued inventory was sold by Jason Company during 19X6.
On January 1, 19X7, Jason Company purchased a 60% interest in Kelsie Company for $100,000. The following determination and distribution of excess schedule was prepared at that time.

Price paid		$100,000
Less interest acquired:		
Common stock ($10 par)..	$100,000	
Retained earnings...	50,000	
Total stockholders' equity......................................	$150,000	
Interest acquired...	60%	90,000
Excess of cost over book value		$ 10,000
Excess of cost attributable to building (15-year life),		
60% × $10,000		6,000
Goodwill (20-year amortization)		$ 4,000

The following intercompany sales transactions occurred during 19X7:

	Irving to Jason	Kelsie to Irving
Seller's goods in buyer's January 1,		
19X7 inventory.......................................	$ 5,000	—
Sales during 19X7......................................	20,000	$10,000
Seller's goods in buyer's December 31,		
19X7 inventory.......................................	4,000	2,000
Gross profit on sales..................................	25%	30%

On December 31, 19X7, Irving Company owed Kelsie Company $1,000 for merchandise received in 19X7. Jason Company had no outstanding liabilities to Irving Company on December 31, 19X7.

Trial balances of the three firms as of December 31, 19X7, follow:

	Irving Company	Jason Company	Kelsie Company
Cash..	103,000	40,000	15,000
Accounts Receivable.............................	170,000	70,000	35,000
Inventory...	250,000	105,000	53,000
Prepaid Expenses.................................	6,000	1,500	—
Investment in Jason Company.................	500,000	—	—
Investment in Kelsie Company................	—	100,000	—
Land..	300,000	140,000	25,000
Building..	500,000	275,000	140,000
Accumulated Depreciation — Building.......	(200,000)	(100,000)	(50,000)
Equipment...	650,000	380,000	100,000
Accumulated Depreciation — Equipment ...	(350,000)	(73,500)	(70,000)
Accounts Payable.................................	(150,000)	(70,000)	(70,000)
Other Liabilities...................................	(20,000)	(8,000)	(3,000)
Bonds Payable.....................................	(400,000)	(200,000)	—
Common Stock ($20 par)........................	(1,000,000)	(500,000)	—
Common Stock ($10 par)........................	—	—	(100,000)
Retained Earnings, Jan. 1, 19X7..............	(300,000)	(125,000)	(50,000)
Sales..	(1,500,000)	(700,000)	(400,000)
Subsidiary Dividend Income....................	(4,000)	—	—
Cost of Goods Sold...............................	1,125,000	510,000	280,000
Other Expenses....................................	275,000	150,000	95,000
Dividends Declared...............................	45,000	5,000	—
Total..	0	0	0

Required:

Prepare the worksheet necessary to produce the consolidated financial statements of Irving Company and its subsidiaries as of December 31, 19X7. Include the income distribution schedules.

Problem 9–8. The following diagram depicts the relationships between Ackley Company, Biernat Company, and Cromwell Company on December 31, 19X7:

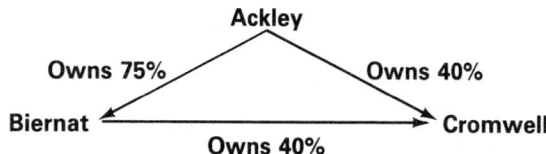

Information regarding the preceding investments follows:

(a) Ackley Company purchased its 40% interest in Cromwell Company on December 31, 19X3, for $50,000. On that date, Cromwell Company's book values approximated market values. Cromwell's plant assets consisted of several pieces of equipment that were being depreciated on a straight-line basis with estimated future lives of ten years.

(b) On January 1, 19X6, Ackley Company purchased a 75% interest in Biernat Company for $400,000. The following determination and distribution of excess schedule was prepared at that time:

Price paid		$400,000
Less interest acquired:		
Common stock ($5 par)	$300,000	
Paid-in capital in excess of par...................................	100,000	
Retained earnings..	30,000	
Total stockholders' equity.......................................	$430,000	
Interest acquired...	75%	322,500
Excess of cost over book value		$ 77,500
Excess of cost attributable to building (20-year life),		
75% × $40,000		30,000
Goodwill (10-year life)		$ 47,500

(c) On January 1, 19X7, Biernat Company acquired a 40% interest in Cromwell Company for $92,000. Cromwell's book values approximated market values at this date.

(d) The following stockholders' equities have been made available:

	Cromwell Company December 31 19X3	Cromwell Company December 31 19X6	Biernat Company December 31 19X5
Noncumulative $6 preferred stock ($100 par and liquidating value)	—	—	$ 50,000
Common stock ($5 par)	—	—	300,000
Common stock ($10 par).................	$200,000	$200,000	—
Paid-in capital in excess of par.........	—	—	100,000
Retained earnings (deficit)	(50,000)	30,000	30,000
Total equity.................................	$150,000	$230,000	$480,000

(e) The following is information regarding intercompany merchandise sales in 19X7:

	Ackley to Cromwell	Cromwell to Biernat
Seller's merchandise in buyer's December 31, 19X6 inventory	$ 2,000	—
19X7 sales	16,000	$5,000
Seller's merchandise in buyer's December 31, 19X7 inventory	1,000	1,000
Intercompany receivable/payable on December 31, 19X7	3,000	500
Gross profit on sales	30%	40%

Trial balances of the three firms as of December 31, 19X7, are as follows:

	Ackley Company	Biernat Company	Cromwell Company
Cash	117,800	49,300	20,000
Accounts Receivable (net)	200,000	100,000	44,000
Inventory	277,000	206,000	58,000
Investment in Cromwell Company	50,000	92,000	—
Investment in Biernat Company	400,000	—	—
Property, Plant, and Equipment	2,800,000	1,500,000	220,000
Accumulated Depreciation	(1,120,000)	(593,000)	(90,000)
Accounts Payable	(206,000)	(112,000)	(4,000)
Bonds Payable	(1,000,000)	(700,000)	—
Preferred Stock	—	(50,000)	—
Common Stock ($5 par)	(500,000)	(300,000)	—
Common Stock ($10 par)	—	—	(200,000)
Paid-In Capital in Excess of Par	(700,000)	(100,000)	—
Retained Earnings, Jan. 1, 19X7	(270,000)	(61,000)	(30,000)
Sales	(1,500,000)	(850,000)	(400,000)
Subsidiary Dividend Income	(18,800)	(800)	—
Cost of Goods Sold	1,050,000	552,500	240,000
Other Expenses	350,000	240,000	140,000
Preferred Dividends Declared	—	3,000	—
Common Dividends Declared	70,000	24,000	2,000
Total	0	0	0

Required:

Prepare the worksheet necessary to produce the consolidated financial statements of Ackley Company and its subsidiaries as of December 31, 19X7. Include the determination and distribution of excess and income distribution schedules.

Problem 9–9.   Packard Corporation purchased an 80% interest in Stutz Company for $600,000 on January 1, 19X7. The following determination and distribution of excess schedule was prepared:

Price paid		$600,000
Less interest acquired:		
Common stock ($15 par)..	$450,000	
Retained earnings...	200,000	
Total stockholders' equity......................................	$650,000	
Interest acquired..	80%	520,000
Excess of cost over book value attributable to goodwill		
(20-year life)...		$ 80,000

On January 1, 19X8, Stutz Company purchased 10% of Packard Corporation common stock on the open market for $150,000. After the purchase, the following determination and distribution of excess schedule was prepared:

Price paid		$150,000
Less interest acquired:		
Common stock ($5 par)..	$ 375,000	
Paid-in capital in excess of par...............................	600,000	
Retained earnings...	350,000	
Total stockholders' equity......................................	$1,325,000	
Interest acquired..	10%	132,500
Excess of cost over book value attributable to building		
and equipment (10-year life), 10% × $175,000............		$ 17,500

Packard Corporation has paid a $.15 per share quarterly dividend since January, 19X3, while Stutz Company has paid a $.10 per share quarterly dividend since mid-19X5.

Trial balances of the two firms as of December 31, 19X8, are as follows:

	Packard Corporation	Stutz Company
Current Assets..	253,200	185,000
Investment in Stutz Company	646,400	—
Investment in Packard Corporation........................	—	150,000
Property, Plant, and Equipment.............................	1,900,000	1,000,000
Accumulated Depreciation....................................	(717,600)	(332,500)
Liabilities...	(680,000)	(290,000)
Common Stock ($5 par).......................................	(375,000)	—
Common Stock ($15 par)......................................	—	(450,000)
Paid-In Capital in Excess of Par............................	(600,000)	—
Retained Earnings, Jan. 1, 19X8	(350,000)	(230,000)
Sales...	(2,200,000)	(900,000)
Investment Income	(32,000)	(4,500)
Cost of Goods Sold..	1,540,000	630,000
Other Expenses..	570,000	230,000
Dividends Declared..	45,000	12,000
Total...	0	0

Required:

(1) Prepare the worksheet necessary to produce the consolidated financial statements of Packard Corporation and its subsidiary as of December 31, 19X8, using the treasury stock method. Include the income distribution schedules.

(2) Prepare the formal consolidated balance sheet for December 31, 19X8.

Problem 9–10.   Using the data of Problem 9–9, (1) prepare the 19X8 consolidated worksheet of Packard Corporation and its subsidiary using the reciprocal method. The distribution of combined net income should be determined by solving simultaneous equations. (2) Prepare the formal consolidated balance sheet for December 31, 19X8.

Problem 9–11.   On January 1, 19X6, Heckert Company purchased a controlling interest in Allen Company. The following information is available:

(a) Heckert Company purchased 1,600 shares of Allen Company outstanding stock on January 1, 19X5, for $48,000 and purchased an additional 1,400 shares on January 1, 19X6, for $52,000.

(b) An analysis of the stockholders' equity accounts at December 31, 19X5, and 19X4, follows:

	Heckert Company December 31		Allen Company December 31	
	19X5	19X4	19X5	19X4
Common stock ($10 par)...............	$150,000	$150,000	—	—
Common stock ($5 par)................	—	—	$ 20,000	$ 20,000
Paid-in capital in excess of par......	36,000	36,000	10,000	10,000
Retained earnings........................	378,000	285,000	112,000	82,000
Total......................................	$564,000	$471,000	$142,000	$112,000

(c) Allen Company's marketable securities consist of 1,500 shares of Heckert Company stock purchased on June 15, 19X6, in the open market for $18,000. The securities were purchased as a temporary investment and were sold on January 15, 19X7, for $25,000.

(d) On December 10, 19X6, Heckert Company declared a cash dividend of $.50 per share, payable January 10, 19X7, to stockholders of record on December 20, 19X6. Allen Company paid a cash dividend of $1 per share on June 30, 19X6, and distributed a 10% stock dividend on September 30, 19X6. The stock was selling for $15 per share ex-dividend on September 30, 19X6. Allen Company paid no dividends in 19X5.

(e) Allen Company sold machinery, with a book value of $4,000 and a remaining life of five years, to Heckert Company for $4,800 on December 31, 19X6. The gain on the sale was credited to the other income account.

(f) Allen Company includes all intercompany receivables and payables in its trade accounts receivable and trade accounts payable accounts.

(g) During 19X6, the following intercompany sales were made:

	Net Sales	Included in Purchaser's Inventory at December 31, 19X6
Heckert Company to Allen Company	$ 78,000	$24,300
Allen Company to Heckert Company	104,000	18,000
	$182,000	$42,300

Heckert Company sells merchandise to Allen Company at cost. Allen Company sells merchandise to Heckert at the regular selling price to make a normal profit margin of 30%. There were no intercompany sales in prior years.

The trial balances of the two firms at December 31, 19X6, are as follows:

	Heckert Company	Allen Company
Cash..	37,900	29,050
Marketable Securities...	33,000	18,000
Trade Accounts Receivable	210,000	88,000
Allowance for Doubtful Accounts	(6,800)	(2,300)
Intercompany Receivables..	24,000	—
Inventories...	275,000	135,000
Machinery and Equipment..	514,000	279,000
Accumulated Depreciation.......................................	(298,200)	(196,700)
Investment in Allen Company (at cost).......................	100,000	—
Patents..	35,000	—
Dividends Payable	(7,500)	—
Trade Accounts Payable	(195,500)	(174,050)
Intercompany Payables	(8,000)	—
Common Stock ($10 par)	(150,000)	—
Common Stock ($5 par)..	—	(22,000)
Paid-In Capital in Excess of Par	(36,000)	(14,000)
Retained Earnings..	(370,500)	(102,000)
Sales and Services...	(850,000)	(530,000)
Dividend Income	(3,000)	—
Other Income	(9,000)	(3,700)
Cost of Goods Sold..	510,000	374,000
Depreciation Expense..	65,600	11,200
Administrative and Selling Expenses	130,000	110,500
Total..	0	0

Required:

Prepare the worksheet necessary to produce the consolidated financial statements of Heckert Company and its subsidiary for the year ended December 31, 19X6. Include the determination and distribution of excess and income distribution schedules. Assume any excess of cost over book value is attributable to goodwill with a 20-year life. For any mutual holdings, use the treasury stock method. (AICPA adapted)

Worksheet 9–1 (see page 549)

Indirect Holdings;
Company A and
Worksheet for Consolidated
For Year Ended

(Credit balance amounts are in parentheses.)

		Trial Balance		
		Company A	Company B	Company C
1	Inventory, Dec. 31, 19X3	80,000	20,000	30,000
2				
3	Other Assets	60,000	146,000	130,000
4	Building and Equipment	300,000	200,000	150,000
5	Accumulated Depreciation	(100,000)	(60,000)	(30,000)
6	Investment in Company B	643,000		
7				
8				
9	Investment in Company C		318,000	
10				
11				
12	Goodwill			
13	Common Stock ($10 par), Co. A	(300,000)		
14	**Retained Earnings, Jan. 1, 19X3, Co. A**	**(500,000)**		
15				
16				
17				
18	Common Stock ($10 par), Co. B		(200,000)	
19	**Retained Earnings, Jan. 1, 19X3, Co. B**		**(300,000)**	
20				
21				
22				
23	Common Stock ($10 par), Co. C			(100,000)
24	**Retained Earnings, Jan. 1, 19X3, Co. C**			**(150,000)**
25				
26	Sales	(400,000)	(300,000)	(150,000)
27	Cost of Goods Sold	250,000	160,000	80,000
28				
29				
30	Expenses	60,000	40,000	40,000
31				
32	Subsidiary Income	(93,000)	(24,000)	
33				
34		0	0	0
35	Combined Net Income			
36	To Minority Interest, Company C (see distribution schedule)			
37	To Minority Interest, Company B (see distribution schedule)			
38	To Controlling Interest (see distribution schedule)			
39	Total Minority Interest			
40	Retained Earnings, Controlling Interest, Dec. 31, 19X3			
41				

Intercompany Sales
Subsidiary Companies B and C
Financial Statements
December 31, 19X3

WORKSHEET 9–1

Eliminations & Adjustments		Consolidated Income Statement	Minority Interest	Controlling Retained Earnings	Consolidated Balance Sheet	
Dr.	Cr.					
	(11) 2,500				124,500	1
	(13) 3,000					2
					336,000	3
(3) 175,000					825,000	4
	(4) 52,500				(242,500)	5
	(1) 93,000					6
	(2) 375,000					7
	(3) 175,000					8
	(5) 24,000					9
	(6) 200,000					10
	(7) 94,000					11
(7) 94,000	(8) 9,400				84,600	12
					(300,000)	13
(4) 35,000				(458,895)		14
(8) 3,525						15
(10) 1,500						16
(12) 1,080						17
(2) 150,000			(50,000)			18
(2) 225,000			(72,965)			19
(8) 1,175						20
(10) 500						21
(12) 360						22
(6) 80,000			(20,000)			23
(6) 120,000			(29,640)			24
(12) 360						25
(9) 90,000		(760,000)				26
(11) 2,500	(9) 90,000	401,700				27
(13) 3,000	(10) 2,000					28
	(12) 1,800					29
(4) 17,500		162,200				30
(8) 4,700						31
(1) 93,000						32
(5) 24,000						33
1,122,200	1,122,200					34
		(196,100)				35
		5,760*	(5,760)			36
		29,460*	(29,460)			37
		160,880*		(160,880)		38
			(207,825)		(207,825)	39
				(619,775)	(619,775)	40
					0	41

(continued)

Eliminations and Adjustments:

(1)   Eliminate the entry made by Company A to record its share of Company B income. This step returns the investment in Company B account to its January 1, 19X3 balance to aid the elimination process.

(2)   Eliminate 75% of the January 1, 19X3 Company B equity balances against the investment in Company B.

(3)   Distribute the $175,000 excess of cost to the building and equipment account according to the determination and distribution of excess schedule applicable to the level one investment.

(4)   Amortize the excess (added depreciation) according to the determination and distribution of excess schedule. This step requires adjustment of Company A retained earnings for 19X1 and 19X2, plus adjustment of 19X3 expenses.

(5)   Eliminate the entry made by Company B to record its share of Company C income. This returns the investment in Company C account to its January 1, 19X3 balance to aid elimination.

(6)   Eliminate 80% of the January 1, 19X3 Company C equity balances against the investment in Company C.

(7)   Distribute the $94,000 excess of cost to goodwill according to the determination and distribution of excess schedule applicable to the level two investment.

(8)   Amortize the excess (goodwill amortization) according to the determination and distribution of excess schedule. Since created by actions of subsidiary Company B, the 19X2 amortization must be prorated 25% ($1,175) to the Company B minority interest and 75% ($3,525) to the controlling interest. Note that the Company B minority interest appears on the worksheet only after the first level investment has been eliminated, again pointing to the need to eliminate the level one investment first.

(9)   Eliminate intercompany sales to prevent double counting in the consolidated sales and cost of goods sold.

(10) Eliminate the Company B profit contained in the beginning inventory. Since Company B generated the sale, the correction of beginning retained earnings is split 75% to the controlling interest and 25% to the minority interest. The cost of goods sold is decreased since the beginning inventory was overstated.

(11) The cost of goods sold is adjusted and the ending inventory is reduced by the $2,500 of Company B profit contained in the ending inventory.

(12) Eliminate the Company C profit contained in the beginning inventory. Since Company C generated the retained earnings adjustment, it is apportioned as follows:

To minority interest in Company C (20%)	$ 360
To minority interest in Company B (25% of 80%)	360
To controlling interest (75% of 80%)	1,080
Total	$1,800

(13) The cost of goods sold is adjusted and the ending inventory is reduced by the $3,000 of Company C profit contained in the ending inventory.

Company C Income Distribution

Ending inventory profit ....(13)	$ 3,000	Internally generated income	$ 30,000
		Beginning inventory profit.... **(12)**	1,800
		Adjusted income	$ 28,800
		Company B share, 80%	23,040
		Company C minority interest, 20%	$ 5,760*

Company B Income Distribution

Ending inventory profit ....(11)	$ 2,500	Internally generated income	$100,000
Amortization of goodwill resulting from purchase of investment in Company C .... **(8)**	4,700	Beginning inventory profit.... (10)	2,000
		80% of Company C adjusted income....................	23,040
		Adjusted income	$117,840
		Company A share, 75%..............	88,380
		Company B minority interest, 25%	$ 29,460*

Company A Income Distribution

Building and equipment depreciation resulting from investment in Company B ...... (4)	$17,500	Internally generated income	$ 90,000
		75% of Company B adjusted income....................	88,380
		Controlling interest	$160,880*

Worksheet 9–2 (see page 554)

(Credit balance amounts are in parentheses.)

Mutual Holdings,
Company P and
Worksheet for Consolidated
For Year Ended

		Trial Balance	
		Company P	Company S
1	Investment in Company S (80%)	248,000	
2			
3			
4	**Investment in Company P (10%), at cost**		**80,000**
5	Equipment	608,000	180,000
6	Accumulated Depreciation	(100,000)	(50,000)
7	Common Stock, Co. P	(500,000)	
8	Retained Earnings, Jan. 1, 19X3, Co. P	(200,000)	
9	Common Stock, Co. S		(100,000)
10	Retained Earnings, Jan. 1, 19X3, Co. S		(90,000)
11	Sales	(300,000)	(200,000)
12	Cost of Goods Sold	180,000	120,000
13	Expenses	80,000	60,000
14	Subsidiary Income	(16,000)	
15	**Treasury Stock (at cost)**		
16		0	0
17	Combined Net Income		
18	To Minority Interest (see distribution schedule)		
19	Balance to Controlling Interest (see distribution schedule)		
20	Total Minority Interest		
21	Retained Earnings, Controlling Interest, Dec. 31, 19X3		
22			

Eliminations and Adjustments:
(1) Eliminate the entry made by the parent during the current year to record its share of Company S income.
(2) Eliminate 80% of the January 1, 19X3 subsidiary equity balances against the investment in Company S account.
(3) Distribute the excess of cost over book value to the equipment account as specified by the determination and distribution of excess schedule.
(4) Amortize the excess of $80,000 for the past two years and the current year.
(5) The investment in Company P must be at cost. If any equity adjustments have been made, they must be reversed and the investment in the parent returned to cost. If the shares are to

Treasury Stock Method
Subsidiary Company S
Financial Statements
December 31, 19X3

WORKSHEET 9–2

Eliminations & Adjustments		Consolidated Income Statement	Minority Interest	Controlling Retained Earnings	Consolidated Balance Sheet	
Dr.	Cr.					
	(1) 16,000					1
	(2) 152,000					2
	(3) 80,000					3
	(5) 80,000					4
(3) 80,000					868,000	5
	(4) 12,000				(162,000)	6
					(500,000)	7
(4) 8,000				(192,000)		8
(2) 80,000			(20,000)			9
(2) 72,000			(18,000)			10
		(500,000)				11
		300,000				12
(4) 4,000		144,000				13
(1) 16,000						14
(5) 80,000					80,000	15
340,000	340,000					16
		(56,000)				17
		4,000*	(4,000)			18
		52,000*		(52,000)		19
			(42,000)		(42,000)	20
				(244,000)	(244,000)	21
					0	22

be reissued, as is the case in this example, the investment then is transferred to the treasury stock account, a contra account to total consolidated stockholders' equity.

As an alternative to step 5, the cost of the treasury shares could be used to retire them on the worksheet as follows:

Common Stock, Company P..	50,000	
Retained Earnings, Company P...	30,000	
Investment in Company P..		80,000

(continued)

Subsidiary Company S Income Distribution

	Internally generated net income...	$20,000
	Adjusted income	$20,000
	Minority share............................	20%
	Minority interest........................	$ 4,000*

Parent Company P Income Distribution

Amortization of excess cost—depreciation ....(4)	$4,000	Internally generated net income...	$40,000
		80% × Company S adjusted income of $20,000	16,000
		Controlling interest	$52,000*

Worksheet 9–3 (see page 556)

Mutual Holdings,
Company P and
Worksheet for Consolidated
For Year Ended

(Credit balance amounts are in parentheses.)

		Trial Balance	
		Company P	Company S
1	Investment in Company S (80%)	248,000	
2			
3			
4	**Investment in Company P (10%)**		**84,000**
5			
6			
7	Equipment	608,000	180,000
8	Accumulated Depreciation	(100,000)	(50,000)
9	Goodwill		
10	**Common Stock, Co. P**	**(500,000)**	
11	**Retained Earnings, Jan. 1, 19X3, Co. P**	**(200,000)**	
12			
13	Common Stock, Co. S		(100,000)
14	Retained Earnings, Jan. 1, 19X3, Co. S		(90,000)
15	Sales	(300,000)	(200,000)
16	Cost of Goods Sold	180,000	120,000
17	Expenses	80,000	60,000
18			
19	**Subsidiary (or Investment) Income**	(16,000)	**(4,000)**
20			
21		0	0
22	Combined Net Income		
23	**To Minority Interest (see solution to simultaneous equations, page 556)**		
24	**Balance to Controlling Interest (see solution to simultaneous equations)**		
25	Total Minority Interest		
26	Retained Earnings, Controlling Interest, Dec. 31, 19X3		
27			

Eliminations and Adjustments:
(1–4) Same as entries 1–4 of Worksheet 9–2.
   (5) Eliminate the entry made by Company S to record its share of Company P income.
   (6) Eliminate 10% of the January 1, 19X3 parent equity balances against the investment in Company P account. Note that 10% of the original January 1, 19X3 Company P retained earnings is eliminated without regard to the $8,000 amortization of excess adjustment, since

Reciprocal Method
Subsidiary Company S
Financial Statements
December 31, 19X3

WORKSHEET 9–3 ||||||||||||||||||||||||||

Eliminations & Adjustments Dr.	Eliminations & Adjustments Cr.	Consolidated Income Statement	Minority Interest	Controlling Retained Earnings	Consolidated Balance Sheet	
	(1) 16,000					1
	(2) 152,000					2
	(3) 80,000					3
	(5) 4,000					4
	(6) 70,000					5
	(7) 10,000					6
(3) 80,000					868,000	7
	(4) 12,000				(162,000)	8
(7) 10,000	(8) 1,000				9,000	9
(6) 50,000					(450,000)	10
(4) 8,000				(172,000)		11
(6) 20,000						12
(2) 80,000			(20,000)			13
(2) 72,000			(18,000)			14
		(500,000)				15
		300,000				16
(4) 4,000		145,000				17
(8) 1,000						18
(1) 16,000						19
(5) 4,000						20
345,000	345,000					21
		(55,000)				22
		4,913	**(4,913)**			23
		50,087		**(50,087)**		24
			(42,913)		(42,913)	25
				(222,087)	(222,087)	26
					0	27

this adjustment was not included in the original determination and distribution of excess schedule.

(7) Distribute the excess of cost over book value to the goodwill account as specified by the determination and distribution of excess schedule.

(8) Amortize the excess for the current year.

(continued)

Company S Adjusted Internally Generated Income (see page 556)

Amortization of excess cost—goodwill amortization.....(8)	$1,000	Unadjusted internally generated income......................	$20,000
		Adjusted..	$19,000

Company P Adjusted Internally Generated Income (see page 556)

Amortization of excess cost — depreciation .... (4)	$4,000	Unadjusted internally generated income	$40,000
		Adjusted	$36,000

Note: If intercompany profit adjustments existed, they would be entered in the income distribution schedule.

CHAPTER   10

SPECIAL APPLICATIONS OF CONSOLIDATION PROCEDURES

This chapter explores the application of consolidation procedures to additional areas, starting with the preparation of a statement of cash flows for a consolidated firm. The special procedures necessary to compute earnings per share for a consolidated firm then will be analyzed. Following these topics, the taxation of a consolidated firm is discussed. Members of a group subject to consolidation procedures may be taxed as separate entities or, in some cases, may be taxed as a single, consolidated firm.

The application of the sophisticated equity method, which is required by APB Opinion No. 18 for certain unconsolidated investments, is considered. Basically, the Opinion requires the application of the same sort of procedures used in consolidations, so that the net income of the investor using the sophisticated equity method will be similar to the net income that would result if actual consolidation procedures were used.

This chapter also applies purchase accounting procedures to what usually is termed a leveraged buyout (LBO). A leveraged buyout occurs when a group of investors (often employees) purchases an existing firm (often a subsidiary firm of the parent company). The leveraged aspect of the transaction is the borrowing by the investors of a large portion of the funds needed to purchase the subsidiary stock from the parent.

The appendix to this chapter applies consolidation procedures to the firm which has chosen to decentralize its accounting so as to create various separate accounting units. While individual reporting for the created units meets internal reporting needs, the separate statements must be combined for external reporting purposes.

CONSOLIDATED STATEMENT OF CASH FLOWS

FASB Statement of Financial Accounting Standards No. 95 requires that a statement of cash flows accompany a firm's published income statement and balance sheet. The process of preparing a consolidated statement of cash flows is similar to that which is used for a single firm, a topic covered in depth in intermediate accounting texts. Since the analysis of changes in cash of a consolidated entity begins with consolidated statements, intercompany transactions will have been eliminated already and thus will not cause any complications. However, because of the parent-subsidiary relationship, there are some situations that require special consideration. These situations are discussed in the following paragraphs.

CASH ACQUISITION OF CONTROLLING INTEREST

The cash purchase of a controlling interest in a firm is considered an *investing activity* and would appear as a cash outflow in the cash flows from investing activities section of the statement of cash flows. It also is necessary to explain the total increase in consolidated assets and the addition of the minority interest to the consolidated balance sheet. This is a result of the requirement that the statement of cash flows disclose investing and *financing activities* which affect the firm's financial position even though they do not impact cash.

To illustrate the disclosure required, consider an example of a cash purchase of an 80% interest in a firm. Assume that Company S had the following balance sheet on January 1, 19X1, when Company P acquired an 80% interest for $540,000 in cash:

Assets		Liabilities and Equity	
Cash and cash equivalents	$ 50,000	Long-term liabilities	$150,000
Inventory	60,000	Common stock ($10 par)	200,000
Equipment (net)	190,000	Retained earnings	350,000
Building (net)	400,000		
Total assets	$700,000	Total liabilities and equity	$700,000

Assuming that the market values of the inventory, equipment, and building are $60,000, $250,000, and $425,000, respectively, and that any remaining excess of cost is attributed to goodwill with a 20-year life, the following determination and distribution of excess schedule would be prepared:

Price paid		$540,000
Less interest acquired:		
Common stock ($10 par)	$200,000	
Retained earnings	350,000	
Total stockholders' equity	$550,000	
Interest acquired	80%	440,000
Excess of cost over book value		$100,000
Excess of cost attributable to long-lived assets:		
Equipment, 80% × $60,000	$ 48,000	
Building, 80% × $25,000	20,000	68,000
Goodwill (20-year amortization)		$ 32,000

The effect of the purchase on the balance sheet accounts of the consolidated firm for 19X1 would be as follows:

	Debit	Credit
Cash ($540,000 paid − $50,000 subsidiary cash)		490,000
Inventory...	60,000	
Equipment ($190,000 book value + $48,000 excess)..............	238,000	
Building ($400,000 book value + $20,000 excess).................	420,000	
Goodwill..	32,000	
Long-term liabilities		150,000
Minority interest (20% × $550,000 subsidiary equity)..............		110,000
Total	750,000	750,000

The disclosure of the purchase on the statement of cash flows would be summarized as follows:

Under the heading "Cash flows from investing activities":

Payment for purchase of Company S, net of cash
    acquired .... ($490,000)

In the supplemental schedule of noncash financing and investing activity:

Company P purchased 80% of the common stock of Company S for $540,000. In conjunction with the acquisition, liabilities were assumed and a minority interest was created as follows:

Adjusted value of assets acquired	
($700,000 book value + $100,000 excess)..........................	$800,000
Cash paid for common stock	540,000
Balance	$260,000
Liabilities assumed	$150,000
Minority interest..	$110,000

NONCASH ACQUISITION OF CONTROLLING INTEREST

Suppose that, instead of paying cash for its controlling interest, Company P issued 10,000 shares of its $10-par stock for the controlling interest. Further assume that the shares had a market value of $54 each. Since the acquisition price is the same ($540,000) the determination and distribution of excess schedule would not change. The analysis of balance sheet account changes would be as follows:

	Debit	Credit
Cash ($50,000 subsidiary cash)..	50,000	
Inventory..	60,000	
Equipment ($190,000 book value + $48,000 excess)...............	238,000	
Building ($400,000 book value + $20,000 excess)..................	420,000	
Goodwill..	32,000	
Long-term liabilities		150,000
Minority interest (20% × $550,000 subsidiary equity).............		110,000
Common stock, $10 par, Company P...................................		100,000
Paid-in capital in excess of par, Company P.........................		440,000
Total...	800,000	800,000

The disclosure of the purchase on the statement of cash flows would be summarized as follows:

Under the heading "Cash flows from investing activities":

Cash acquired in purchase of Company S..................... $50,000

In the supplemental schedule of noncash financing and investing activity:

Company P acquired 80% of the common stock of Company S in exchange for 10,000 shares of Company P common stock valued at $540,000. In conjunction with the acquisition, liabilities were assumed and a minority interest was created as follows:

Adjusted value of assets acquired
  ($700,000 book value + $100,000 excess)........................... $800,000

Common stock issued.. $540,000

Liabilities assumed $150,000

Minority interest... $110,000

When an acquisition qualifies as a pooling of interests, all prior financial statements are consolidated retroactively which requires that cash flow analyses proceed from a comparison of the consolidated balance sheets of the current and previous periods. Due to the retroactive application of the pooling of interests, there will be no difference between the comparative statements as a result of the pooling. The impact of the pooling on the consolidated stockholders' equity is disclosed in the period the pooling is consummated.

ADJUSTMENTS RESULTING FROM BUSINESS COMBINATIONS

A business combination will have ramifications on the statements of cash flows prepared in subsequent periods. A purchase may create amortizations of excess deductions (noncash items) which need to be adjusted. In addition, there may be impact resulting from additional purchases of subsidiary shares and/or dividend payments by the subsidiary. Intercompany bonds and nonconsolidated investments also need to be considered for their impact.

Amortization of Excesses. Income statements prepared for periods including or following a purchase of another firm will include the amortization of the excesses that are shown on the determination and distribution of excess schedule as well as book value depreciation and amortization recorded by both the parent and subsidiary. These amortizations of the excesses, while reflected in consolidated net income, do not require the use of cash and thus must be included as an adjustment to consolidated net income to arrive at cash flows from operating activities. For example, if the building and equipment of Company S have useful lives of 20 years and 5 years, respectively, the following adjustments would appear on the cash flows statement for 19X1:

Cash from operating activities:
    Consolidated net income.. $XXXXX
    Add amortizations resulting from business combination:
        Depreciation [(1/5 × $48,000) + (1/20 × $20,000)].................... 10,600
        Goodwill amortization (1/20 × $32,000)................................... 1,600

In addition, cash from operating activities would be adjusted for depreciation and amortizations of book value recorded by the constituent firms on their separate books.

Purchase of Additional Subsidiary Shares. The purchase of additional shares directly from the subsidiary results in no added cash flowing into the consolidated firm. The transfer of cash within the consolidated firm would not appear in the consolidated statement of cash flows. However, the purchase of additional shares from the minority does result in an outflow of cash. From a consolidated viewpoint it is the equivalent of purchasing treasury shares. Thus it would be listed under financing activities.

Subsidiary Dividends. Dividends paid by the subsidiary to the parent are a transfer of cash within the consolidated entity and thus would not appear in the consolidated statement of cash flows. However, dividends paid by the subsidiary to minority shareholders represent a flow of cash to parties outside the consolidated group and would appear as an outflow under the cash flows from financing activities heading of the consolidated statement of cash flows.

Purchase of Intercompany Bonds. The purchase of intercompany bonds effects a cash flow from one member of the consolidated group to parties outside the consolidated entity. Recall that the purchase of intercompany bonds is viewed as a retirement of the bonds on the consolidated worksheet. The consolidated statement of cash flows also treats the purchase of the bonds as a retirement of the consolidated firm's debt and includes the cash outflow under the caption, cash flows from financing activities. Since the process of constructing a cash flows statement starts with the consolidated income statement and balance sheet, intercompany interest payments and amortizations of premiums and/or discounts already are eliminated and will not enter into the analysis of consolidated cash flows. Only cash interest payments to bondholders outside the consolidated entity are important to the analysis and should be included in cash flows from operating activities.

Nonconsolidated Investments. Investments in the stock of firms not included in the consolidated group result in income to the consolidated entity. Where the investment is accounted for under the cost method, cash dividends received are included in cash flows from operating activities. However, where the equity method is applied, only that portion of the income received in cash may be included in cash from operating activities. For example, the investee may report income of $50,000 and pay dividends of $10,000. Assume further that the consolidated firm paid $20,000 more than book value for its 30% interest and regards the excess as attributable to goodwill with a 40-year life. Investment income under the equity method would be calculated as follows:

30% of reported income of $50,000	$15,000
Less amortization of excess cost ($20,000 ÷ 40)	500
Equity income	$14,500

Only $3,000 (30% × $10,000) was received in the form of cash dividends; thus the $14,500 of income would be reduced to only $3,000 of cash from operating activities. The $11,500 of undistributed income would be adjusted out of net income to arrive at cash from operating activities.

PREPARATION OF CONSOLIDATED STATEMENT OF CASH FLOWS

A complete example of the process of preparing a consolidated statement of cash flows is presented in this section. Assume that Company P originally purchased a 70% interest in Company S on January 1, 19X1, and purchased another 10% interest on January 1, 19X3, the beginning of the current year. In addition, Company P purchased a 20% interest in Company E on January 2, 19X2, and accounts for the investment under the sophisticated equity method. The following determination and distribution of excess schedules were prepared for each investment.

For the January 1, 19X1, 70% investment in subsidiary Company S:

Price paid		$335,000
Less interest acquired:		
Common stock	$ 50,000	
Paid-in capital in excess of par	150,000	
Retained earnings	100,000	
Total equity	$300,000	
Interest acquired	70%	210,000
Excess of cost over book value		$125,000
Excess of cost attributable to equipment (5-year life)		25,000
Goodwill (10-year life)		$100,000

For the January 1, 19X3, 10% investment in subsidiary Company S:

Price paid		$56,000
Less interest acquired:		
Common stock...	$ 50,000	
Paid-in capital in excess of par....................................	150,000	
Retained earnings..	160,000	
Total equity...	$360,000	
Interest acquired..	10%	36,000
Excess of cost over book value attributed to goodwill		
(10-year life)...		$20,000

For the January 1, 19X2, 20% investment in nonconsolidated Company E:

Price paid		$55,000
Less interest acquired:		
Common stock...	$100,000	
Retained earnings..	150,000	
Total equity...	$250,000	
Interest acquired..	20%	50,000
Excess of cost over book value attributed to goodwill		
(10-year life)...		$ 5,000

The following consolidated statements were prepared for Company P and its subsidiary, Company S, for 19X3:

Company P and Subsidiary Company S Consolidated Income Statement For Year Ended December 31, 19X3		
Sales..		$900,000
Less cost of goods sold...		525,000
Gross profit..		$375,000
Less expenses:		
General and administrative....................................	$150,500	
Depreciation..	70,000[a]	
Goodwill amortization..	12,000[b]	232,500
Operating income..		$142,500
Investment income (equity method)		15,500[c]
Combined net income of Companies P and S............		**$158,000**
Less minority interest...		**11,200**
Consolidated net income...		**$146,800**

[a]Includes $5,000 of depreciation resulting from the excess of the subsidiary equipment's market value over book value on January 1, 19X1, the date on which the 70% interest was acquired.

[b]Consists of the $10,000 goodwill amortization on the 70% interest acquired January 1, 19X1, and the $2,000 goodwill amortization on the 10% interest acquired January 1, 19X3.

[c]20% of Company E net income of $80,000 less $500 amortization of goodwill. (Dividends received were $2,000.)

Company P and Subsidiary Company S
Consolidated Retained Earnings Statement
For Year Ended December 31, 19X3

	Minority	Controlling
Retained earnings, January 1, 19X3	$32,000*	$420,000
Add distribution of combined net income	11,200	146,800
Less dividends declared	(4,000)	(50,000)
Balance, December 31, 19X3	$39,200	$516,800

*The retained earnings balance for Company S on January 1, 19X3, was $160,000; $32,000 represents the minority's 20% remaining interest subsequent to Company P's 10% interest acquired on January 1, 19X3.

Company P and Subsidiary Company S
Consolidated Balance Sheet
December 31, 19X2 and 19X3

Assets	19X3	19X2
Cash and cash equivalents	$ 179,000	$ 160,000
Inventory	210,000	180,000
Accounts receivable	100,000	120,000
Property, plant, and equipment	1,330,000	1,250,000
Accumulated depreciation	(370,000)	(300,000)
Goodwill	168,000	160,000
Investment in Company E (20%)	333,500	320,000
Total assets	$1,950,500	$1,890,000

Liabilities and Stockholders' Equity	19X3	19X2
Accounts payable	$ 202,500	$ 210,000
Bonds payable	300,000	300,000
Minority interest	79,200	108,000*
Controlling interest:		
Common stock, par	200,000	200,000
Paid-in capital in excess of par	652,000	652,000
Retained earnings	516,800	420,000
Total liabilities and stockholders' equity	$1,950,500	$1,890,000

*Represents the 30% interest as of December 31, 19X2; interest was reduced to 20% on January 1, 19X3.

The following additional facts are available to aid in the preparation of a consolidated statement of cash flows:

1. Company P purchased a new piece of equipment during 19X3 for $80,000.
2. In 19X3 Company P declared and paid $50,000 in dividends, and Company S declared and paid $20,000 in dividends.

Illustration 10–1 is a worksheet approach to calculating a statement of cash flows under the *indirect method*. Explanations 1 through 8 use changes in balance sheet accounts to analyze cash from operations. This information is taken from the income statement and is implied from changes in current assets and current liabilities. Explanation 9 reflects the only investing activity in this example. Explanations 10 through 12 show the financing activities. The worksheet provides the information needed to develop the statement of cash flows located on page 601.

If the *direct method* of disclosing cash from operating activities is used, the cash flows from operating activities section of the statement of cash flows would be prepared as follows:

Cash flows from operating activities:
  Cash from customers
    ($900,000 sales + $20,000 decrease in accounts receivable) $920,000
  Cash from investments (dividends received)............................... 2,000
  Cash to suppliers ($525,000 cost of goods sold + $30,000
    inventory increase + $7,500 decrease in accounts payable)........ (562,500)
  Cash for general and administrative expenses........................... (150,500)
    Net cash provided by operating activities............................... $209,000

Illustration 10–1
Company P and Subsidiary Company S
Worksheet for Analysis of Cash: Indirect Method
For Year Ended December 31, 19X3

	Account Change		Explanations			
	Debit	Credit		Debit	Credit	Balance
Inventory...............................	30,000		6)	30,000		0
Accounts receivable.................		20,000			5) 20,000	0
Property, plant, and equipment...	80,000		9)	80,000		0
Accumulated depreciation		70,000			3) 70,000	0
Goodwill...............................	8,000		10)	20,000	4) 12,000	0
Investment in						
Company E (20%).................	13,500		8)	13,500		0
Accounts payable....................	7,500		7)	7,500		0
Bonds payable						0
Minority interest.....................	28,800		10)	36,000	2) 11,200	
			12)	4,000		0
Controlling interest:						
Common stock, par						0
Paid-in capital in						
excess of par						0
Retained earnings................		96,800	11)	50,000	1) 146,800	0
	167,800	186,800		241,000	260,000	
Net change in cash..................	19,000	0		19,000	0	

Cash from Operations:		Explanations	
		Debit	Credit
Consolidated net income...	1)	146,800	
Minority interest in combined net income...............	2)	11,200	
Depreciation expense..	3)	70,000	
Amortization of goodwill..	4)	12,000	
Decrease in accounts receivable............................	5)	20,000	
Increase in inventory	6)		30,000
Decrease in accounts payable................................	7)		7,500
Equity income in excess of dividends.....................	8)		13,500
Net cash provided by operating activities................		209,000	
Cash from Investing:			
Purchase of equipment	9)		80,000
Net cash used in investing activities.......................			80,000
Cash from Financing:			
Purchase of 10% minority interest..........................	10)		56,000
Dividend payment to controlling interest	11)		50,000
Dividend payment to minority interest.....................	12)		4,000
Net cash used in financing activities.......................			110,000
Net cash provided		19,000	

Company P and Subsidiary Company S
Consolidated Statement of Cash Flows
For Year Ended December 31, 19X3

Cash flows from operating activities:		
Consolidated net income..		$146,800
Adjustments to reconcile net income to net cash:		
Minority interest in combined net income...................................	$11,200	
Depreciation expense..	70,000	
Amortization of goodwill...	12,000	
Decrease in accounts receivable...	20,000	
Increase in inventory..	(30,000)	
Decrease in accounts payable..	(7,500)	
Equity income from Company E in excess of dividends received...	(13,500)	
Total adjustments...		62,200
Net cash provided by operating activities...............................		$209,000
Cash flows from investing activities:		
Purchase of equipment		(80,000)
Cash flows from financing activities:		
Acquisition of 10% minority interest.......................................	($56,000)	
Dividend payments to controlling interests.................................	(50,000)	
Dividend payments to minority interest	(4,000)	
Net cash used in financing activities....................................		(110,000)
Net increase in cash and cash equivalents		$ 19,000
Cash and cash equivalents at beginning of year		160,000
Cash and cash equivalents at year end		$179,000

CONSOLIDATED EARNINGS PER SHARE

The computation of consolidated earnings per share (EPS) observes all of the guidelines regarding income and share adjustments discussed in Chapter 2. (For the purpose of this discussion, all calculations will be made only on an annual basis.) The calculation of EPS is not altered when applied to the consolidated firm providing that the subsidiary firm has *no dilutive securities*. As long as no such securities exist, the consolidated net income is divided by the number of outstanding parent company shares, and numerator and denominator adjustments caused by parent company dilutive securities can be considered in the normal manner. When the subsidiary has dilutive securities, the calculation of consolidated EPS becomes a two-stage process. First, the EPS of the subsidiary must be calculated. Then the consolidated EPS is calculated using as a component of the calculation the adjusted EPS of the subsidiary. This two-stage process handles subsidiary dilutive securities which require the possible issuance of subsidiary company shares. A further complication occurs when the subsidiary has outstanding dilutive options, warrants, and/or convertible securities which may require the issuance of parent company shares.

First consider the calculation of consolidated EPS when the subsidiary has outstanding dilutive securities which may require the issuance of subsidiary company shares only. The basic model by which to compute consolidated EPS in this situation is as follows:

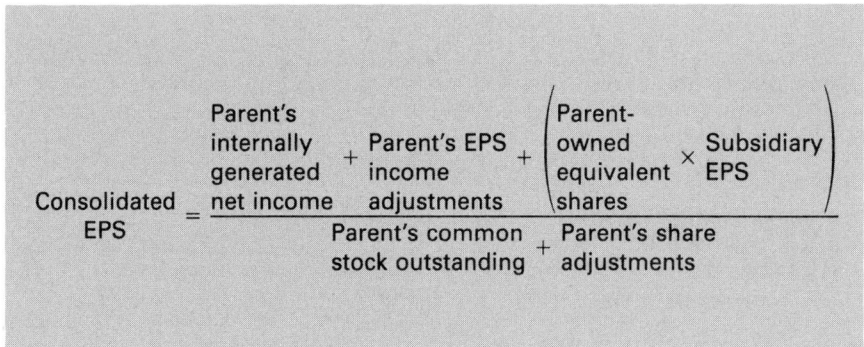

$$\text{Consolidated EPS} = \frac{\begin{array}{l}\text{Parent's}\\\text{internally}\\\text{generated}\\\text{net income}\end{array} + \begin{array}{l}\text{Parent's EPS}\\\text{income}\\\text{adjustments}\end{array} + \left(\begin{array}{l}\text{Parent-}\\\text{owned}\\\text{equivalent}\\\text{shares}\end{array} \times \begin{array}{l}\text{Subsidiary}\\\text{EPS}\end{array}\right)}{\begin{array}{l}\text{Parent's common}\\\text{stock outstanding}\end{array} + \begin{array}{l}\text{Parent's share}\\\text{adjustments}\end{array}}$$

This model may be used to compute either primary or fully diluted EPS. The parent's internally generated net income should be adjusted for unrealized profits recorded during the current period and for realization of profits deferred from previous periods. Likewise, the income used to compute the subsidiary EPS must be adjusted for intercompany transactions. To illustrate, assume the following data concerning the subsidiary:

Net income (adjusted for intercompany profits).................................	$22,000
Preferred stock dividend..	$ 2,000
Interest on convertible bonds...	$ 3,000
Common stock shares outstanding...	5,000
Warrants to purchase one share of common stock...........................	1,000
Warrants held by parent	500
Convertible bonds outstanding	
(convertible into ten shares of common stock)	200
Convertible bonds held by parent...	180

$$\frac{\text{Subsidiary}}{\text{Primary EPS}} = \frac{\overset{(1)}{\$22,000} - \$2,000 + \overset{(2)}{\$3,000}}{\underset{(3)}{5,000} + 2,000 + \underset{(4)}{500}} = \$3.07$$

(1) Dividend on nonconvertible preferred stock, none of which is owned by the parent.
(2) Income adjustment for convertible debentures which are considered a common stock equivalent.
(3) Share adjustment associated with convertible debentures, 200 bonds × 10 shares per bond.
(4) Share adjustment (treasury stock method) associated with the warrants. It is assumed that, using the average market value of the stock, 500 shares could be purchased with the proceeds of the sale and that 500 additional new shares would be issued.

Assume that the parent owns 80% of the subsidiary and has internally generated net income of $40,000 and 10,000 shares of common stock outstanding. Also assume that the parent has dilutive bonds outstanding which are convertible into 3,000 shares of common stock. The consolidated primary EPS would be computed as follows:

$$\frac{\text{Consolidated}}{\text{Primary EPS}} = \frac{\overset{(1)}{\$40,000} + \$5,000 + \overset{(2)}{\$18,574}}{\underset{(3)}{10,000 + 3,000}} = \$4.89$$

(1) Income adjustment from interest on parent company convertible bonds.
(2) Subsidiary common shares owned by parent

(80% × 5,000)...	4,000
Parent-owned equivalent shares applicable to convertible debentures (90% × 2,000).......................	1,800
Parent-owned equivalent shares applicable to warrants (50% × 500)	250
Total parent-owned equivalent shares........................	6,050
Parent's interest in subsidiary income (6,050 shares × $3.07 subsidiary PEPS)....................	$18,574

(3) Shares assumed to be issued in exchange for parent company convertible bonds.

If the dilutive subsidiary securities enable the holder to acquire common stock of the parent, these securities are not included in the computation of subsidiary EPS. However, these securities must be included in the parent's share adjustment in computing consolidated EPS. The basic model by which to compute consolidated EPS in this situation is as follows:

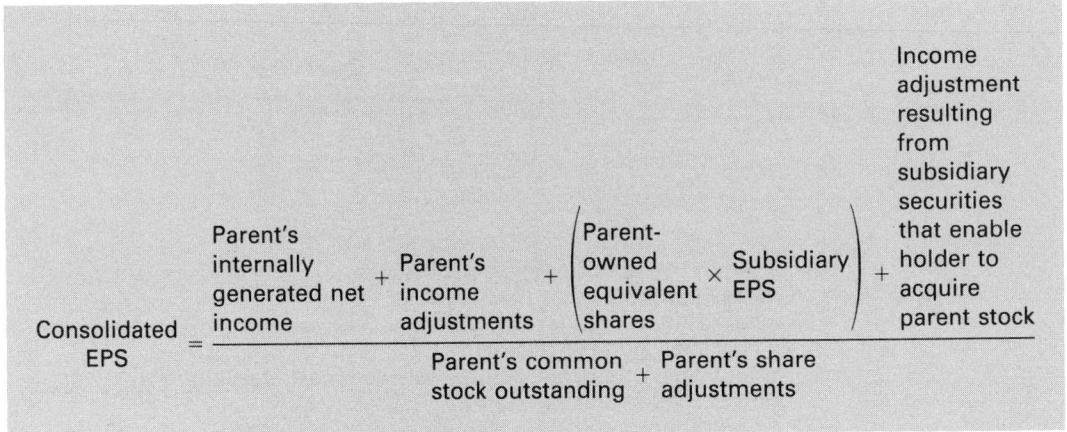

To illustrate, assume the following facts for a parent owning 90% of the outstanding subsidiary shares:

Parent internally adjusted net income	$20,000
Parent company common stock shares outstanding	10,000
Parent company dilutive convertible bonds:	
Interest expense..	$ 1,000
Shares to be issued in conversion...	2,000
Subsidiary net income...	$ 7,000
Subsidiary common stock shares outstanding	4,000
Subsidiary preferred stock convertible into parent common stock:	
Dividend requirement..	$ 1,200
Number of preferred shares..	1,000
Number of parent company common shares required.........................	2,000
Subsidiary common stock warrants to acquire 100 parent shares.............	100

The first step is to calculate the subsidiary's EPS as follows:

$$\frac{\text{Subsidiary}}{\text{EPS}} = \frac{\$7,000 - \$1,200 \text{ preferred dividends}}{4,000 \text{ outstanding shares}} = \$1.45$$

Note that the subsidiary convertible preferred stock and stock warrants are not satisfied with subsidiary shares and thus are not considered converted for the purpose of calculating subsidiary EPS. The consolidated primary EPS would be computed as follows:

$$\frac{\text{Consolidated}}{\text{Primary EPS}} = \frac{\overset{(1)}{\$20,000} + \overset{(2)}{\$1,000} + (3,600 \times \$1.45) + \overset{(3)}{\$1,200}}{\underset{(4)}{10,000 + (2,000 + 2,000 + 50)}} = \$1.95$$

(1) $1,000 income adjustment associated with the parent company convertible security.

(2) The parent's share of subsidiary EPS. Again, since the subsidiary's preferred stock and warrants are not convertible into subsidiary shares, the total parent-owned equivalent shares is 90% × 4,000.

(3) Income adjustment representing the dividend on subsidiary preferred shares that would not be paid if the shares were converted into common stock of the parent. Note that 100% of the adjustment is added back, even though the parent's interest in the subsidiary is less than 100%.

(4) The parent's share adjustment consisting of 2,000 shares traceable to the parent company convertible security; 2,000 shares traceable to the subsidiary preferred stock that is convertible into parent common stock; and 50 incremental shares traceable to the subsidiary warrants to acquire parent common stock. It is assumed that 50 of the 100 shares required to satisfy the warrants can be purchased with the proceeds of the exercise and that 50 new shares must be issued.

Special analysis is required in computing consolidated EPS when an acquisition occurs during a reporting period. When the acquisition is a pooling of interests, the computation of EPS includes subsidiary income and securities for the entire period. However, when the acquisition is a purchase, only subsidiary income since the acquisition date is included, and the number of subsidiary shares is weighted for the partial period.

TAXATION OF CONSOLIDATED FIRMS

Consolidated firms that do not meet the requirements to be an *affiliated group,* as defined by the tax law, must pay their taxes as separate entities. The tax definition of an affiliated group is less inclusive than that used in accounting theory. The Tax Reform Act of 1984 does not allow two or more corporations to file a consolidated return or to be considered an affiliated group for tax purposes unless the parent owns:

1. 80% of the voting power of all classes of stock and
2. 80% of the fair market value of all the outstanding stock of the other corporation.

For these provisions, stock must be (1) entitled to vote, (2) convertible, and (3) not limited and preferred as to dividends and as to redemption and liquidation rights. Comparison of these criteria with those required for consolidated financial reporting should make it obvious that many consolidated firms have no choice but to submit to separate taxation of the member firms.

Consolidated firms that meet the tax-law requirements to be an affiliated group may elect to be taxed as a single entity or as separate entities. Once the election is made to file as a single entity, the permission of the Internal Revenue Service is required before the firms can be taxed separately again. Firms that elect to be taxed as a single entity file a consolidated tax return which may provide several tax advantages. For example, a consolidated return permits the offset of operating profits and losses and of capital gains and losses. Also, intercompany profits are not taxed until realized in later periods.

When affiliated firms elect not to file a consolidated return, each legal entity within the group computes and pays its tax independently. These separate returns may provide several tax advantages. For example, affiliated firms that file separate tax returns are not required to use the same tax year or accounting methods. It also may be advantageous to file separate returns when there are intercompany losses; however, most such losses are disallowed under tax law.

CONSOLIDATED TAX RETURN

When an affiliated group elects to be taxed as a single entity, combined income as determined on the worksheet is the basis for the tax calculation. The affiliated firms should not record a provision for income tax based on their own separate incomes. Rather, the income tax expense is calculated as part of the consolidated worksheet process. Once calculated, the tax provision may be recorded on the books of the separate firms.

As an example of an affiliated group choosing to be taxed as a single entity, assume that Company P purchased an 80% interest in Company S on January 1, 19X1, at which time the following determination and distribution of excess schedule was prepared:

Price paid		$800,000
Less interest acquired:		
Common stock..	$500,000	
Retained earnings, January 1, 19X1............................	400,000	
Total stockholders' equity..	$900,000	
Interest acquired..	80%	720,000
Excess of cost over book value attributed to goodwill		
with a 40-year life...		$ 80,000

The following income statements are for Companies P and S for 19X3. Since the firms desire to file a consolidated tax return, neither firm has recorded a provision for income tax. The corporate tax rate is 30%.

	Company P	Company S
Sales..	$600,000	$400,000
Less cost of goods sold..	350,000	200,000
Gross profit..	$250,000	$200,000
Less operating expenses	100,000	100,000
Operating income..	$150,000	$100,000
Subsidiary income..	80,000	—
Income before tax...	$230,000	$100,000

On January 1, 19X2, Company P sold a piece of equipment, with a book value of $40,000, to Company S for $60,000. The equipment is depreciated by Company S on a straight-line basis over a 5-year life.

The following applies to intercompany merchandise sales to Company P by Company S:

Intercompany sales in beginning inventory of Company P......................	$ 50,000
Intercompany sales in ending inventory of Company P.........................	70,000
Sales to Company P during 19X3	100,000
Gross profit rate..	50%

Worksheet 10–1, pages 662–665, contains the trial balances of Companies P and S on December 31, 19X3. Since the income tax is to be calculated on the worksheet, no provision exists on the separate books. If separate provisions appear in the trial balances, they should be eliminated as an initial procedure in consolidating.

The balance of the account Investment in Company S results from the use of the simple equity method. Steps (1) through (9) are similar to the steps prepared in previous worksheets; step (10) is the only new procedure. In step (10), the provision for income tax is calculated by multiplying the combined taxable income by the tax rate. The combined taxable income is determined by adding the goodwill amortization to the combined income before tax. As mentioned in Chapter 3, in most purchase situations the amortizations of excess resulting from the investment are not tax deductible.[1] The tax provision is the amount recorded for financial reporting purposes and may differ from the liability reported on the tax return itself.

The final complexity caused by a consolidated return involves the distribution of combined income. In the schedules that accompany Worksheet 10–1, the income distributions start with internally generated income before taxes. All adjustments to the worksheet are entered before tax effects. This procedure results in an adjusted income before tax for each firm.

The income tax expense of the member firms then is calculated. The income distribution schedules allocate the income tax expense and proceed to calculate each firm's adjusted net income. The subsidiary adjusted net income is distributed to the controlling and minority interests according to ownership percentages.

It will be necessary for each member firm to record its share of the tax provision on its own books. The subsidiary, Company S, would record the following:

Provision for Income Tax	27,000	
Income Tax Payable..		27,000
To record the allocated portion of the tax provision.		

---

[1] When there are nondeductible amortizations of excess cost, there also may be a recorded deferred tax liability. Recall that an excess of market value over cost relative to an identifiable asset requires the recording of a deferred tax liability for the amount of the tax rate times the excess. This deferred tax liability would be amortized to tax expense in proportion to the amortization of the excess.

The parent, Company P, would record the following:

Subsidiary Income (80% × $27,000 tax provision)..............   21,600
   Investment in Company S...   21,600
      To adjust Subsidiary Income for the tax expense
      recorded by Company S.

Provision for Income Tax   46,200
   Income Tax Payable..   46,200
      To record the allocated portion of the tax provision.

In review, consolidated returns are consistent with consolidated reporting procedures and do not alter in any way the procedures that have been discussed in previous chapters. It is necessary only to add new procedures to the worksheet to provide for income taxes.

SEPARATE TAX RETURNS

When a separate return is required or elected to be filed, each member of the consolidated group must base its tax calculation on its separate income. In determining their taxable income, corporations generally are allowed a deduction of 80%[2] of the dividends received from nonaffiliated, taxable, domestic corporations in order to reduce multiple taxation of the same income. Affiliated firms filing separate returns may deduct 100% of such dividends. In the illustrations that follow, 20% of the dividends received are subject to income taxes. Since each firm calculates its tax separately, each trial balance on the consolidated worksheet should include the provision for income tax and the related liability.

The major complication in the computation of taxes for the individual firms is that the provision for tax is based on the separate firm's reported income prior to its adjustment for intercompany transactions. Thus, the majority of intercompany transactions create *timing differences* that will require adjustments to the amounts provided for applicable taxes. This complication leads to a need for interperiod tax allocation when companies are consolidated. For example, assume that a parent sells a piece of equipment, with a book value of $25,000, to a subsidiary for $45,000 on January 1, 19X1. The asset has a 5-year life, and straight-line depreciation is used. Assuming a 30% tax rate, the parent will record a $20,000 gain and $6,000 in taxes in the period in which the equipment is sold. However, from a consolidated viewpoint, the gain should be prorated over the 5-year life, requiring the $6,000 tax provision to be allocated over 5 years at a rate of $1,200 per year. On December 31, 19X1, the following entry for tax applicable to the sale would be made on the consolidated worksheet:

Deferred Tax Expense* (4 years × $1,200).........................   4,800
   Provision for Income Tax   4,800
    *Entry is made assuming adequate deferred tax liability for offset in the future.

---

[2]The exclusion rate is determined by current tax law and is subject to change.

In each subsequent period, the tax applicable to the period would be recognized and the remaining deferred tax established on the worksheet. The following entry would be made on the December 31, 19X2 consolidated worksheet:

Deferred Tax Expense (3 remaining years × $1,200) 3,600
Provision for Income Tax (for 19X2) 1,200
    Retained Earnings — Parent Company (adjustment for 4
    years, expensed by the parent in 19X1)..................... 4,800

The use of separate tax returns for a consolidated group leads to a complicated application of interperiod tax allocation techniques. The calculations may become cumbersome even when only intercompany sales of plant assets and merchandise are involved. To illustrate, assume that Company P purchased a 75% interest in Company S on January 1, 19X1, at which time the following determination and distribution of excess schedule was prepared:

Price paid		$285,000
Less interest acquired:		
Common stock...	$100,000	
Retained earnings, Jan. 1, 19X1	250,000	
Total stockholders' equity.......................................	$350,000	
Interest acquired...	75%	262,500
Excess of cost over book value attributed to		
goodwill with a 20-year life..		$ 22,500

On January 1, 19X3, Company S sold equipment, with a book value of $60,000, to Company P for $100,000. Company P is depreciating the asset over 5 years on a straight-line basis.

During 19X4, Companies P and S reported the following operating incomes before tax:

	Company P	Company S
Sales...	$430,000	$240,000
Less cost of goods sold......................................	280,000	150,000
Gross profit...	$150,000	$ 90,000
Less operating expenses	70,000	30,000
Operating income before tax	$ 80,000	$ 60,000

A 30% corporate tax rate is assumed for both firms. The following data apply to intercompany merchandise sales to Company S by the parent, Company P:

Intercompany sales in beginning inventory of Company S.....................	$ 60,000
Intercompany sales in ending inventory of Company S.........................	40,000
Sales to Company S during 19X4	100,000
Gross profit rate...	40%

Taxation of Separate Entities. Before Companies P and S can be consolidated, it is necessary to calculate their separate tax liabilities since the 80% test of an affiliated group for tax purposes is not met. The tax provision of the subsidiary is $18,000 (30% × $60,000 Company S income before tax). Company S would record its tax provision as follows:

Provision for Income Tax 18,000
    Income Tax Payable   18,000

The tax provision for Company P requires consideration of the tax status of subsidiary income. When the conditions for an affiliated group are not met the parent company must include in its taxable income 20% of the dividends it receives from a subsidiary. When an affiliated group *elects* separate taxation, no dividends are included and no additional tax needs to be calculated. According to APB Opinion No. 23, subsidiary income included in the pretax income of a parent leads to a timing difference between the earning of the income and its inclusion in the tax return as dividend income.[3] APB Opinion No. 23 presumes that all subsidiary income will be transferred to the parent unless:

1. There are definite plans on the part of the parent to reinvest the undistributed earnings of the subsidiary, which will allow indefinite postponement of their remittance to the parent; or
2. The earnings will be remitted as part of a tax-free liquidation.

These exceptions were retained by FASB Statement No. 96. Assuming that these exceptions do not apply, Company P must provide for tax expense equal to its tax rate times 20% of its share of the total subsidiary net income. This tax may be viewed as a *secondary tax* since it is the second taxation of subsidiary income. For 19X4, this tax liability would be calculated as follows:

Subsidiary net income $42,000
Controlling interest, 75% × $42,000   31,500
Provision for tax on subsidiary income, 30% × (20% × $31,500)   1,890

Company P would add this amount to the tax it has provided for its internally generated income to arrive at its total tax provision for the period:

Tax on internally generated income, 30% × $80,000 .... $24,000
Secondary tax provision for subsidiary income   1,890
    Total Company P provision for tax $25,890

Since Company P has not received its share of the income of Company S, the secondary tax is not immediately payable, and a deferred tax liability for $1,890 is created. Assuming that the tax on internally generated income is currently payable, Company P would make the following entry to record its 19X4 tax provision:

Provision for Income Tax 25,890
    Income Tax Payable   24,000
    Deferred Tax Liability   1,890

---

[3]*Opinions of the Accounting Principles Board, No. 23,* "Accounting for Income Taxes—Special Areas" (New York: American Institute of Certified Public Accountants, 1971), pars. 9–12.

If dividends had been paid by the subsidiary, the secondary tax applicable to the dividends received by Company P would be included in the current tax liability.

Worksheet Procedures. Worksheet 10–2, pages 666–669, includes the trial balances of Companies P and S. Several observations should be made regarding the amounts listed:

1. The balance in Investment in Company S is computed according to the simple equity method, as follows:

Original cost...		$285,000
Subsidiary income, 19X1–19X3 *(after tax)*:		
Company S retained earnings, Jan. 1, 19X4	$350,000	
Company S retained earnings, Jan. 1, 19X1	100,000	
Net increase..	$250,000	
Controlling interest...	75%	187,500
Controlling interest in subsidiary net income, 19X4		
(75% × $42,000)		31,500
Equity-adjusted balance, Dec. 31, 19X4.......................		$504,000

2. Since the parent's share of subsidiary undistributed income has been recorded from the date of acquisition, a deferred tax liability has been recorded by Company P each year to recognize the secondary tax provision. The total deferred tax liability on December 31, 19X4, is calculated as follows:

Deferred tax liability on 19X1–19X3 income	
(20% × 30% × $187,500 19X1–19X3 undistributed income)	$11,250
Current year's additional deferment (20% × 30% × $31,500)............	1,890
Total deferred tax liability...	$13,140

3. The trial balances of both companies include their separate provisions for income tax and the current tax liabilities. *These provisions do not reflect adjustments for intercompany transactions.*

Worksheet steps (1) through (9) are identical to those that would be prepared in the absence of any consideration of taxes. The first special procedure to consider is step (10). Its purpose is to adjust for the tax impact of the adjustments that affect beginning retained earnings. Step (5) reduced retained earnings for the intercompany profit on the equipment sale. Now it is necessary to increase retained earnings for the deferred tax expense already recorded by the separate firms concerning this profit. Not only has a tax provision relative to this sale been recorded by the subsidiary, but the parent also has recorded the secondary tax applicable to the sale. Both sets of taxes are viewed now as deferred (prepaid). Since the taxes have been expensed previously, they also are removed from retained earnings. In addition, step (10) defers the tax that has been recorded by Company P relative to the intercompany inventory profit at the start of the year. Since the sale was made and the tax recorded by the parent company, there is no secondary tax.

Step (11) deals with the tax impact of adjustments to the current-year income. Since part of the intercompany profit on the equipment sale will be recognized this year, the deferred tax (including the secondary tax) now is expensed. Likewise, the tax deferred relative to the beginning inventory profit is expensed. It then becomes necessary to defer the tax applicable to the intercompany profit in the ending inventory. Again, since the inventory profit was recorded by the parent and not the subsidiary, there is no secondary tax.

When the steps in Worksheet 10–2 are completed, the resulting combined net income is $105,933, which is distributed to the controlling and minority interests. The distribution schedules start with internally generated net income *after tax*, since the tax expense is calculated by each firm separately. Thus, each adjustment must be on an aftertax basis when made to the internally generated net income.

EQUITY METHOD FOR UNCONSOLIDATED INVESTMENTS

Prior to the 1971 issuance of APB Opinion No. 18, "The Equity Method of Accounting for Investments in Common Stock," investors could freely choose between the equity and cost methods to recognize income on their investments. When the equity method was used, it tended to be a simple equity method that recognized only a pro rata share of the investee's income, without any attempt to amortize an excess of cost or book value on the investment or to defer intercompany gains and losses. The choice between these two divergent methods is not significant when consolidation is required since the investment and investment income accounts are eliminated in the consolidation process. However, the accounting profession did become concerned with the use of the cost method for major investments not subject to consolidation. The APB reasoned that, in such cases, the investor may have significant influence over the investee's dividend policy and that the payment of dividends often would be unrelated to the investee's income during a given period. For example, dividend payments would be level over a period of years during which income varied significantly. This reasoning led the APB to state:

> The equity method tends to be most appropriate if an investment enables the investor to influence the operating or financial decisions of the investee. The investor then has a degree of responsibility for the return on its investment, and it is appropriate to include in the results of operations of the investor its share of earnings or losses of the investee. Influence tends to be more effective as the investor's percent of ownership in the voting stock of the investee increases. Investments of relatively small percentages of voting stock of an investee tend to be passive in nature and

enable the investor to have little or no influence on the operations of the investee.[4]

APB Opinion No. 18 requires the use of the sophisticated equity method for the following types of investments:

1. *Influential investments.* The APB defines influence as "representation on the board of directors, participation in policy-making processes, material intercompany transactions, interchange of managerial personnel, or technological dependency."[5] When the investor holds 20% or more of the voting shares of an investee, influence is assumed, and the sophisticated equity method is required unless the investor takes on the burden of proof to show that influence does not exist, in which case the cost method would be used.[6] When the investment falls below 20%, the presumption is that influence does not exist, and the cost method is to be used unless the investor can show that influence does exist despite the low percentage of ownership. Since the most common use of the sophisticated equity method is for influential (20% to 50%) investments, such investments are used in subsequent illustrations.

2. *Corporate joint ventures.* A corporate joint venture is a separate, specific project organized for the benefit of several corporations. An example would be a research project undertaken jointly by several members of a given industry. The member firms typically participate in the management of the venture and share the gains and losses. Since such an arrangement does not involve passive investors, the sophisticated equity method is required.

3. *Unconsolidated subsidiaries.* A parent may own over 50% of the shares of a subsidiary, but may meet one of the exceptions (control is temporary or does not rest with the majority owner) to the requirement that subsidiaries be consolidated. However, if influence does exist, the sophisticated equity method would be used for the investment.

As defined by APB Opinion No. 18, the use of the equity method requires that the investment in common stock appear as a single, equity-adjusted amount on the balance sheet of the investor. The investor's income statement will include the investor's share of the investee ordinary income as a single amount in the ordinary income section. The investor's share of investee discontinued operations, extraordinary items, and cumulative effects of changes in accounting principles will appear as single amounts in

---

[4]*Opinions of the Accounting Principles Board, No. 18,* "The Equity Method of Accounting for Investments in Common Stock" (New York: American Institute of Certified Public Accountants, 1971), par. 12.

[5]*Ibid.,* par. 17.

[6]For examples of situations that may overcome the presumption of influence, see FASB Interpretation No. 35, "Criteria for Applying the Equity Method of Accounting for Investments in Common Stock" (Stamford: Financial Accounting Standards Board, 1981).

the sections of the investor's income statement that correspond to the placement of these items in the investee's statement.

CALCULATION OF EQUITY INCOME

In its basic form, the equity method requires the investor to recognize its pro rata share of investee reported income. Dividends, when received, do not constitute income, but are viewed instead as a partial liquidation of the investment. In reality, however, the price paid for the investment usually will not agree with the underlying book value of the investee, which requires that any amortization of an excess of cost or book value be treated as an adjustment of the investor's pro rata share of investee income. It is very likely that the reported income of the investee will include gains and losses on transactions with the investor. As was true in consolidations, these gains and losses cannot be recognized until they are confirmed by a transaction between the affiliated group and unrelated parties. The proper application of the sophisticated equity method will mean that the income recognized by the investor will be the same as it would be under consolidation procedures. In fact, the sophisticated equity method sometimes is referred to as "one-line consolidation."

In the next two sections, the sophisticated equity method will be presented without consideration of the tax implications. Following that the tax effect on such an investment will be addressed.

Amortization of Excesses. A determination and distribution of excess schedule is prepared for a sophisticated equity method investment just as it would be if the investment was to be consolidated. For example, assume that the following schedule was prepared by Excel Corporation for a 25% interest in Flag Company acquired on January 1, 19X1:

Price paid		$300,000
Less interest acquired:		
Common stock ($10 par)..	$200,000	
Retained earnings, January 1, 19X1............................	600,000	
Total stockholders' equity..	$800,000	
Interest acquired..	25%	200,000
Excess of cost over book value		$100,000
Less excess attributable to equipment with a 5-year		
remaining life and undervalued by $80,000,		
25% × $80,000		20,000
Goodwill (40-year life)...		$ 80,000

As a practical matter, APB Opinion No. 18 states that it may not be possible to relate the excess to specific assets, in which case the entire excess may be considered goodwill. However, an attempt should be made to allocate the excess in the same manner as would be done for the purchase of a controlling interest in a subsidiary.

The determination and distribution of excess schedule indicates the pattern of amortization to be followed. The required amortizations must be made directly through the investment account since the distributions shown on the schedule are not recorded in the absence of consolidation procedures. Assuming that Flag Company reported income of $50,000 for 19X1, Excel Corporation would make the following entry for 19X1:

Investment in Flag Company...	6,500	
Investment Income		6,500

Income is calculated as follows:

25% × Flag reported income of $50,000...............................		$12,500
Less amortizations of excess cost:		
Equipment, $20,000 ÷ 5	$4,000	
Goodwill, $80,000 ÷ 40	2,000	6,000
Investment income, net of amortizations................................		$ 6,500

If an investment is acquired for less than book value, the excess of book value over cost would be amortized over a period not to exceed 40 years. This procedure would increase investment income in the years of amortization.

Intercompany Transactions by Investee. The investee may sell inventory to the investor. As would be true if the investment were consolidated, the share of the investee's profit on goods still held by the investor at the end of a period cannot be included in income of that period. Instead, the profit must be deferred until the goods are sold by the investor. Since the two firms are separate reporting entities, the intercompany sales and related debt cannot be eliminated. Only the investor's share of the investee's profit on unsold goods in the hands of the investor is deferred. In a like manner, the investor may have plant assets that were purchased from the investee. The investor's share of the investee's gains and losses on these sales also must be deferred and allocated over the depreciable lives of the assets. Profit deferments should be handled in an income distribution schedule similar to that used for consolidated worksheets. To illustrate, assume the following facts for the example of the 25% investment in Flag by Excel. Again, note that income tax is not being considered in this illustration:

1. Excel had the following merchandise acquired from Flag Company in its ending inventories:

Year	Amount	Gross Profit of Flag Company
19X1	$30,000	40%
19X2	40,000	45

2. Excel purchased a truck from Flag Company on January 1, 19X1, for $20,000. The truck is being depreciated over a 4-year life on a straight-line basis with no salvage value. The truck had a net book value of $16,000 when it was sold by Flag.

3. Flag Company had an income of $50,000 in 19X1 and $70,000 in 19X2.
4. Flag declared and paid $10,000 in dividends in 19X2.

Based on these facts, Excel Corporation would prepare the following income distribution schedules:

19X1 Income Distribution for Investment in Flag Company

Gain on sale of truck, to be amortized over 4 years..............	$ 4,000	Reported income of Flag Company..............	$50,000
Profit in Excel ending inventory, 40% × $30,000	12,000	Realization of 1/4 of profit on sale of truck	1,000
		Adjusted income of Flag Company..............	$35,000
		Ownership interest, 25%...	$ 8,750
		Less amortization of excess cost:	
		Equipment................ $4,000	
		Goodwill................... 2,000	6,000
		Investment income, net of amortizations......	$ 2,750

19X2 Income Distribution for Investment in Flag Company

Profit in Excel ending inventory, 45% × $40,000	$18,000	Reported income of Flag Company..............	$70,000
		Profit in Excel beginning inventory, 40% × $30,000	12,000
		Realization of 1/4 of profit on sale of truck....	1,000
		Adjusted income of Flag Company..............	$65,000
		Ownership interest, 25%...	$16,250
		Less amortization of excess cost:	
		Equipment................ $4,000	
		Goodwill................... 2,000	6,000
		Investment income, net of amortizations......	$10,250

The schedules would lead to the following entries to record investment income:

19X1	Investment in Flag Company	2,750	
	Investment Income...		2,750
19X2	Investment in Flag Company	10,250	
	Investment Income...		10,250

In addition, the following entry would be made in 19X2 to record dividends received:

Cash...	2,500	
Investment in Flag Company......................................		2,500

It should be noted that only the investor's share of intercompany gains and losses is deferred. The investee's remaining stockholders are not affected by Excel Corporation's investment.

TAX EFFECTS OF EQUITY METHOD

The investor not meeting the requirements of affiliation as defined by the tax law pays income taxes on dividends received. In the case of a domestic corporation, 20% of the dividends are includable in taxable income. However, a timing difference is created through the use of the equity method for financial reporting.[7] As a result, *the provision for tax must be based on the equity income, and a deferred tax liability must be created for undistributed investment income.* The provision may be based on the assumption that investment income either will be distributed in dividends or will be realized via the sale of the investment. In the latter case, it is likely that the income would be taxed in the form of a capital gain. The assumption used will determine the tax rate to be applied to the undistributed income. The provision for tax is based on the investment income after adjustments and amortizations. However, amortizations of excess cost are not tax deductible, so they must be added back to the investment income to compute the tax.

The following illustration is based on the previous example of Flag Company and Excel Corporation. Now, as a consideration of tax, it is assumed that each firm is subject to a 30% income tax. Excel Corporation's share of Flag Company *net* income would be calculated as follows:

	19X1	19X2
Adjusted income of Flag Company, before tax*.....................	$35,000	$65,000
Tax provision (30%)...	10,500	19,500
Adjusted net income of Flag Company.............................	$24,500	$45,500
Ownership interest in adjusted net income (25%).................	$ 6,125	$11,375
Less amortizations of excess	6,000	6,000
Income from investment	$ 125	$ 5,375

*See the income distribution schedules in the previous section.

---

[7]*Opinions of the Accounting Principles Board, No. 24,* "Accounting for Income Taxes— Investments in Common Stock Accounted for by the Equity Method (Other than Subsidiaries and Corporate Joint Ventures)" (New York: American Institute of Certified Public Accountants, 1972), par. 7.

Note that the tax provision calculated by the investor will not agree with the provision for tax on the books of the investee. This is due to the adjustments made in the income distribution schedules to recognize the profit deferrals.

The 19X1 and 19X2 entries to record investment income and the applicable tax provision would be:

19X1	Investment in Flag Company	125	
	Investment Income...		125
	Provision for Income Tax [20% × 30% × ($125 investment income + $6,000 nondeductible amortizations of excess)]	368	
	Deferred Tax Liability.......................................		368
19X2	Investment in Flag Company	5,375	
	Investment Income...		5,375
	Cash	2,500	
	Investment in Flag Company		2,500
	Provision for Income Tax [20% × 30% × ($5,375 investment income + $6,000 nondeductible amortizations of excess)]	683	
	Income Tax Payable (20% × 30% × $2,500 dividends)...................		150
	Deferred Tax Liability ($683 − $150)		533

UNUSUAL EQUITY ADJUSTMENTS

There are several unusual situations involving the investee that require special procedures for the proper recording of investment income. These situations are described in the following paragraphs.

Investee with Preferred Stock. In the absence of consolidation, an investment in preferred stock does not require elimination. However, the existence of preferred stock in the capital structure of the investee requires that the investor's equity adjustment be based on only that portion of investee income available for common stockholders. Dividends declared on preferred stock must be subtracted from income of the investee. When the preferred stock has cumulative or participation rights, the claim of preferred stockholders must be subtracted from the investee income each period to arrive at the income available for common stockholders. The procedures for calculating this income are contained in Chapter 8. This income would be the basis for the equity adjustment.

Investee Stock Transactions. The investee corporation may engage in transactions with its common stockholders, such as issuing additional shares, retiring shares, or engaging in treasury stock transactions. Each of these transactions affects the investor's equity interest. The dollar effect is calculated in the same manner as for subsidiary stock transactions in Chapter 9. The equity of the investor is calculated immediately prior to and subsequent to the investee transaction. The net change calculated is treated as investment income (loss) in the case of an investor-investee relationship. Recall, from Chapter 9, that a parent corporation would not necessarily treat such a change in its equity as an income statement gain or loss since the change results from stockholder transactions rather than from transactions with outside parties.

Write-Down to Market Value. The investment in another firm is subject to reduction to a lower market value if it appears that a relatively permanent fall in value has occurred. The fact that the current market value of the shares is temporarily less than the equity-adjusted cost of the shares is not sufficient cause for a write-down. When the sophisticated equity method is used and a permanent decline in value occurs, a reduction would be made to the equity-adjusted cost. The equity method would continue to be applied subsequent to the write-down. There can be no subsequent write-ups, however, other than through normal equity adjustments.

Zero Investment Balance. It is possible that an investee will suffer losses to the extent that the continued application of the equity method would produce a negative balance in the investment account. Equity adjustments are to be discontinued when the investment balance becomes zero.[8] Further losses are acknowledged only by memo entries, which are needed to maintain the total unrecorded share of losses. If the investee again becomes profitable, the investor must not record income on the investment until its subsequent share of income equals the previously unrecorded share of losses.

To illustrate these procedures, assume that Grate Corporation has a 35% investment in Dittmar Company, with a sophisticated-equity-adjusted cost of $30,000 on January 1, 19X1, and that Dittmar reports the following results:

Period	Income (loss)
19X1	($80,000)
19X2	(50,000)
19X3	(20,000)
19X4	90,000

The following T account summarizes entries for 19X1 through 19X4 (taxes are ignored):

---

[8]According to APB Opinion No. 18 (par. 19i), any net advance to the investee which the investor may have on its books also is available to offset the investor's share of investee losses until the receivable is reduced to a zero balance.

Investment in Dittmar Company

Equity-adjusted balance,
  Jan. 1, 19X1 ....
	$30,000	Equity loss for 19X1,
		  35% × $80,000 Dittmar loss........
			$28,000

		Recorded equity loss for 19X2,
		  35% × $50,000 Dittmar
		  loss = $17,500; loss limited to
		  investment balance...................
			2,000

Balance	$ 0	Memo entries: Unrecorded 19X2 loss,	

Memo entry:
  Unrecorded share of 19X4
    Dittmar income ....
	22,500	$17,500 − $2,000	$15,500

		Unrecorded loss for 19X3, 35% × $20,000 Dittmar loss.....	7,000

Actual entries resumed:
  Recorded equity income, 19X4,
    35% × $90,000 Dittmar
    income, less amount to cover
    unrecorded losses
    ($15,500 + $7,000) ....
	$ 9,000		

Balance, Dec. 31, 19X4	$ 9,000		

Intercompany Transactions by Investor. An investor may sell merchandise and/or plant assets to an investee at a gain or loss. When influence is deemed to exist, it might seem appropriate to defer the entire gain or loss until the asset is resold or depreciated by the investee. However, an interpretation of APB Opinion No. 18 requires the entire gain or loss to be deferred only when the transaction is with a controlled (over 50%-owned) investee and is not at arm's length. In all other cases, it is appropriate to defer only a gain or loss that is in proportion to the investor's ownership interest.[9]

To illustrate, assume that Grate Corporation, which owns a 35% interest in Dittmar Company, sold $50,000 of merchandise to Dittmar at a gross profit of 40%. Of this merchandise, $20,000 is still in Dittmar's 19X1 ending inventory. Grate needs to defer only profit equal to the $8,000 (40% × $20,000) unrealized gross profit multiplied by its 35% interest, or $2,800. Grate would make the following entry on December 31, 19X1:

Sales	2,800	
Deferred Gross Profit on Sales to Investee		2,800

Assuming that the investor recorded the provision for income tax prior to this adjustment, the tax applicable to the unrealized gain would be deferred by the following entry, which is based on a 30% tax rate:

Deferred Tax Expense (30% × $2,800)	840	
Provision for Income Tax		840

---

[9]*Accounting Interpretations,* "The Equity Method of Accounting for Investments in Common Stock: Accounting Interpretations of APB Opinion No. 18" (New York: American Institute of Certified Public Accountants, 1971), par. 1.

The deferred gross profit and the related tax deferment would be realized in the period in which the goods are sold to outside parties. The deferred profit and related tax effects on plant asset sales would be realized in proportion to the depreciation recorded by the investee company.

It may occur that the investor will purchase outstanding bonds of the investee. Unlike consolidation procedures, the bonds are not assumed to be retired since the investor and investee are separate reporting entities. Similarly, a purchase of investor bonds by the investee is not a retirement of the bonds. Thus, no adjustments to income are necessary as a result of intercompany bondholdings.

Gain or Loss of Influence. An investor may own less than a 20% interest in an investee, in which case the cost method ordinarily would be used to record investment income. If the investor subsequently buys sufficient additional shares to have its total interest equal or exceed 20%, the investor must apply retroactively the sophisticated equity method to the total holding period of the investment. APB Opinion No. 18 requires a correction of retained earnings for the period prior to the time the 20% interest is achieved.

It is possible that an investor will own 20% or more of the voting shares of the investee, but will sell a portion of the shares so that the ownership interest falls below 20%. In such a case, the sophisticated equity method is discontinued as of the sale date. However, there is no adjustment back to the cost method. The balance of the investment account remains at its equity-adjusted balance on the sale date. Should influence be attained again, a retroactive ("catch-up") equity adjustment would be made.

When all or part of an investment recorded under the sophisticated equity method is sold, the gain or loss is based on the equity-adjusted balance as of the sale date. An adjustment also would be necessary for deferred tax balances applicable to the investment.

DISCLOSURE REQUIREMENTS

Since a significant portion of the investor's income may be derived from investments, added disclosures are required in order to inform properly the readers of the financial statements. For investments of 20% or more, the investor must disclose the name of each investee, the percentage of ownership in each investee, and the disparity between the cost and underlying book value for each investment. If the sophisticated equity method is not being applied, the reasons must be given. When investments are material with respect to the investor's financial position or income, the financial statements of the investees should be included as supplemental information.

When a market value for the investment is available, it should be disclosed. However, if the investor owns a relatively large block of a subsidiary's shares, quoted market values would have little relevance because the sale of an entire controlling interest would involve different motivations and would result in a unique value.

LEVERAGED BUYOUT

It has become a common occurrence to form a skeleton corporation for the sole purpose of acquiring a controlling interest in an existing corporation. Frequently, the management of the corporation to be acquired are the instigators of the acquisition. A successful example of a leveraged buyout is offered by Harley Davidson Corporation, the only American manufacturer of motorcycles. Once a separate corporation, Harley Davidson was acquired by AMF Corporation. After several years of being a subsidiary, the Harley Davidson division was purchased by new investors, including employees, and again became a separate corporation.

Properly structured, a leveraged buyout follows the principles of purchase accounting which allows the market values of the assets and liabilities of the acquired corporation to be recorded. There are some guidelines which must be met. These guidelines were issued by the Emerging Issues Task Force of the FASB in 1987.[10] First, it is necessary that the controlling interest in voting common shares pass to a new controlling investor or group of investors. It is not required that there be a single controlling investor; it is sufficient to have a group of investors with a common interest act as a control group. Second, in order for all the shares acquired to be recognized at their market value, at least 80% of the consideration given to the former shareholders who are not part of the new controlling group must be monetary (cash or debt). If this test is not met, only the shares acquired for monetary consideration are recorded at market value, and those acquired for stock are recorded at book value. Shares of the former corporation that were owned by members of the new control group are not recorded at market value; instead, they are recorded at the equity-adjusted cost of the owner. Unless it can be demonstrated to the contrary, members of the former firm's management that receive shares of the new firm are assumed to be part of the new control group. In essence, these shares are treated as a prior block purchase and will be valued at their original cost plus equity adjustments. If the equity-adjusted cost is not determinable, they are recorded at book value.

The value at which the acquired shares are recorded may be summarized as follows:

1. All shares previously purchased by the new control group are at their equity-adjusted cost.
2. Shares acquired by the new control group from an old control group:
   a. All shares are at market value if 80% or more of the consideration is monetary.
   b. Only those shares acquired for monetary consideration are at market value if less than 80% of the total consideration is monetary. The remaining shares are at book value.

---

[10]*Highlights of Financial Reporting Issues*, "Leveraged Buyouts: Emerging Issues Task Force Consensus Issue No. 86–16" (Stamford: Financial Accounting Standards Board, October, 1987).

ACQUISITION MEETING 80% TEST

As an example of a leveraged buyout meeting the 80% test, assume that Former Company has the following balance sheet on the date that it is acquired by a new ownership group, New Company:

Assets		Liabilities and Equity	
Current assets...................	$100,000	Liabilities..........................	$ 80,000
Land and buildings (net)....	200,000	Common stock	
Equipment (net)................	50,000	(10,000 shares, $2 par) ...	20,000
		Paid-in capital in	
		excess of par.................	70,000
		Retained earnings.............	180,000
Total assets......................	$350,000	Total liabilities and equity ...	$350,000

The market values of Former's assets and liabilities agree with book values, except for the land and buildings which have a fair market value of $300,000. New Company was formed by selling 2,000 shares of no-par stock for $20 each and by borrowing $300,000. The market value of Former Company shares is $40 each. Payment for the 10,000 shares of Former Company is made as follows:

1. 1,000 shares owned by parties who are members of the new control group are acquired in exchange for 2,000 shares of New Company stock. The equity-adjusted cost per share is $35 for these owners.
2. 500 shares owned by parties not a part of the new control group are acquired in exchange for 1,000 New Company shares.
3. The remaining 8,500 shares are purchased from parties not a part of the new control group for $340,000 in cash.

The monetary consideration given to parties not a part of the new control group is 94.4% (8,500 shares ÷ 9,000 shares) of the total consideration. Since this exceeds the required 80% test, the entire interest acquired from this group should be recorded at *market value*. The value to be assigned to the net assets acquired is calculated:

9,000 noncontrolling group shares at their $40 market value..................	$360,000
1,000 controlling group shares at their $35 adjusted cost	35,000
Total	$395,000

The $395,000 total price would be assigned to accounts as follows:

Price paid		$395,000
Allocate to:		
Current assets..	$100,000	
Land and buildings	300,000	
Equipment..	50,000	
Liabilities	(80,000)	370,000
Goodwill..		$ 25,000

Theoretically, it would be more correct to prepare a separate distribution schedule for the prior investment in 1,000 shares by the new control group. However, it is simpler to "roll" the equity-adjusted cost of the prior investment into the cost of the new investment and to prepare a single distribution schedule. In most cases, this should not have a material impact on the values assigned.

The entries to record the formation of New Company and to acquire Former Company are as follows:

Formation of New Company:

Cash..	40,000	
Common Stock, no par		40,000

Borrowing of $300,000:

Cash..	300,000	
Long-term Debt		300,000

Acquisition of Former Company:

Current Assets	100,000	
Land and Buildings...	300,000	
Equipment...	50,000	
Goodwill...	25,000	
Liabilities		80,000
Cash...		340,000
Common Stock, no par		
[(500 shares × $40) + (1,000 shares × $35)]...........		55,000

ACQUISITION NOT MEETING 80% TEST

Revising the previous example, assume that less than 80% of the consideration given to the noncontrol group is in a monetary form. This will limit further the extent to which market values of the acquired firm may be recognized. The facts are changed as follows:

1. $240,000 is borrowed by New Company instead of $300,000.
2. 2,000 shares of Former Company are acquired from parties that are not a part of the new control group in exchange for 4,000 New Company shares.

Now only 77.8% (7,000 ÷ 9,000) of the shares acquired from parties not a part of the control group are purchased for monetary consideration. Thus, only the shares acquired for monetary consideration will be recorded at market value. The value to be assigned to the net assets acquired is calculated:

7,000 noncontrolling group shares acquired for cash at $40 per share		$280,000
2,000 noncontrolling group shares exchanged for New Company stock at **book value** of $27 ($270,000 equity ÷ 10,000 shares)...................		54,000
1,000 controlling group shares at their $35 adjusted cost		35,000
Total		$369,000

Since 20% of the interest acquired is to be recorded at book value, 20% of each asset's book value also is recorded, and only 80% of each asset's market value is recorded. Again, the equity-adjusted cost of the previously purchased 1,000 shares is combined with the cost of the 7,000 shares acquired later for cash and is used to adjust accounts to 80% of market value. The $369,000 total price would be assigned to accounts as follows:

Price paid			$369,000
Allocate to:			
Current assets (book = market value)...........		$100,000	
Land and buildings:			
20% × $200,000 book value....................	$ 40,000		
80% × $300,000 market value.................	240,000	280,000	
Equipment (book = market value)................		50,000	
Liabilities (book = market value)		(80,000)	350,000
Goodwill..			$ 19,000

The entries to record the formation of New Company and to acquire the Former Company are as follows:

Formation of New Company:

Cash...	40,000	
Common Stock, no par		40,000

Borrowing of $240,000:

Cash...	240,000	
Long-term Debt		240,000

Acquisition of Former Company:

Current Assets	100,000	
Land and Buildings..	280,000	
Equipment..	50,000	
Goodwill...	19,000	
Liabilities		80,000
Cash..		280,000
Common Stock, no par		
[(2,000 shares × $27) + (1,000 shares × $35)]		89,000

Special procedures are required if shares are purchased from members of the new control group for monetary consideration. It is necessary to record the shares at their equity-adjusted cost. This means that all shares received from the control group members are recorded at their equity-adjusted cost, and the cash paid for the shares is carried as a *contra-equity* account in the same manner as treasury stock at cost.

APPENDIX: BRANCH ACCOUNTING

Thus far in the text, consolidation procedures have been used to prepare combined statements for affiliates that are separate legal entities. Consolidation procedures also may be used to combine the separate statements of segments of a single firm. A large firm may divide itself into separate reporting units for internal management purposes, using the separate statements of these units to provide the information needed for decentralized decision making. As useful as these statements might be, they are limited to internal reporting purposes and may *not* be used *for external financial reporting*. Therefore, segment statements must be combined into a single set of statements that reflect the economic entity. The following sections discuss the accounting procedures used to prepare separate statements for segments and to combine these statements.

PREPARATION OF SEGMENT STATEMENTS

A commonly used type of segment reporting involves a home office with decentralized sales branches. Accounting principles for home office and branch accounting are well defined and are used to illustrate segmental accounting. Typically, the home office will keep a perpetual record of its investment in a branch office. The account *Investment in Branch* includes the original funds given to a branch to start operations. Subsequent advances also are included, as well as billings for merchandise and other assets provided to the branch. The investment account receives equity-method adjustments to recognize the reported income of the branch, and the account is reduced by payments received from the branch. Payments may include the satisfaction of trade debt or remittance of profits. The home office also uses special procedures to record shipments of merchandise to a branch. Since no actual sale has occurred, shipments are recorded in the account *Shipments to Branch* at the cost of the goods shipped. When shipments are billed to the branch at a price in excess of the home office cost, it is common to record the markup in an *unrealized intercompany inventory profit account* that is available for later analysis. Profit on merchandise sold by the branch during the period may be recognized, while profit applicable to unsold goods in the branch's ending inventory must be deferred.

The branch usually accounts for its operations as if it was a separate entity. It records its own purchases, sales, asset acquisitions, and expenses. Merchandise acquisitions are separated into purchases from outside firms and shipments from the home office. The branch also maintains an account called *Home Office Equity*, in which its cumulative liability to the home office for all funds, merchandise, and other assets received is recorded. The account is reduced for remittances to the home office. The income calculated each period is credited to the home office equity account on the branch's books.

When all entries are recorded properly, the account recorded by the home office, Investment in Branch, and the reciprocal account recorded by the branch, Home Office Equity, should agree. Likewise, the amounts representing intercompany merchandise transfers, as recorded in Shipments to Branch and the reciprocal account, *Shipments from Home Office,* should agree. These reciprocal accounts may require adjustments on both sets of books to account for merchandise and/or cash in transit in order to bring them into agreement. Equality of the reciprocal accounts, while not necessary for separate statements, is required for the consolidation process.

The income reported by a branch typically is not its correct operating income. Merchandise may be sold by the home office to the branch at a profit. The profit realized on home office shipments sold by the branch must be added to the branch's income to arrive at the branch's real impact on corporate income. It also is possible that the home office incurred expenses which were attributable to the branch but not billed to the branch. For example, a building used by the branch may be carried on the home office records. Depreciation on the building might not be billed to the branch on the theory that the branch manager has no discretion in the amount of the expense. Expenses attributable to the branch but not billed to it must be subtracted from its reported income. In summary, a T account for *Branch Income* could be envisioned as follows:

Branch Income

Depreciation on branch office not billed to branch.......................... $6,000	Reported operating income of branch $20,000
	Profit on merchandise transferred to branch, realized by branch sale... 4,000
	Branch income................. $18,000

Following is a typical set of transactions and entries as they would be recorded on the home office and branch books.

1. The home office sends $100,000 to a newly formed branch so that it may begin operations.

Home Office

| Investment in Branch... | 100,000 | |
| Cash... | | 100,000 |

Branch

| Cash... | 100,000 | |
| Home Office Equity... | | 100,000 |

2. The branch purchases inventory and equipment from outside firms.

    Home Office

    No entry

    Branch

Equipment	50,000	
Purchases	40,000	
Cash		90,000

3. The home office, which is using a periodic inventory system, transfers goods with a cost of $40,000 to the branch for $50,000. The unrealized profit on the sale is isolated by the parent in a separate account.

    Home Office

Investment in Branch	50,000	
Shipments to Branch		40,000
Unrealized Intercompany Inventory Profit		10,000

    Branch

Shipments from Home Office	50,000	
Home Office Equity		50,000

4. The branch sells goods for $110,000.

    Home Office

    No entry

    Branch

Cash	110,000	
Sales		110,000

5. The home office pays $2,000 for insurance applicable to the branch and charges the branch.

    Home Office

Investment in Branch	2,000	
Cash		2,000

    Branch

Selling and Administrative Expense	2,000	
Home Office Equity		2,000

6. The home office records but does not charge the branch for depreciation on the branch office.

    Home Office

Depreciation Expense—Branch	10,000	
Accumulated Depreciation—Buildings		10,000

    Branch

    No entry

7. The branch records depreciation on equipment it purchased.

Home Office

No entry

Branch

Depreciation Expense — Equipment	5,000	
Accumulated Depreciation — Equipment		5,000

8. Remaining expenses incurred by the branch are recorded.

Home Office

No entry

Branch

Selling and Administrative Expense	20,000	
Cash		20,000

9. The branch remits $45,000 to the home office.

Home Office

Cash	45,000	
Investment in Branch		45,000

Branch

Home Office Equity	45,000	
Cash		45,000

10. The branch prepares the following trial balance, which is the basis for the branch's closing entries and which will be used in the preparation of combined home office and branch statements:

Cash	55,000
Equipment	50,000
Accumulated Depreciation — Equipment	(5,000)
Purchases	40,000
Shipments from Home Office	50,000
Depreciation Expense — Equipment	5,000
Selling and Administrative Expense	22,000
Sales	(110,000)
Home Office Equity	(107,000)
Total	0

Assuming that the branch has $20,000 of goods in its ending inventory, of which $10,000 was acquired from the home office, the branch records the cost of goods sold.

Home Office

No entry

Branch

Inventory	20,000	
Cost of Goods Sold..	70,000	
Purchases..		40,000
Shipments from Home Office................................		50,000

The branch then closes its operating income to the home office equity account and reports its income to the home office.

Home Office

Investment in Branch...	13,000	
Branch Income..		13,000

Branch

Sales..	110,000	
Cost of Goods Sold..		70,000
Depreciation Expense — Equipment..........................		5,000
Selling and Administrative Expense..........................		22,000
Home Office Equity		13,000

After the branch closes its nominal accounts, it prepares its separate internal statements based on these entries. The branch's separate income statement and balance sheet follow.

Branch
Income Statement
For Year Ended December 31, 19X1

Sales		$110,000
Less cost of goods sold		70,000
Gross profit..		$ 40,000
Less expenses:		
Selling and administrative	$22,000	
Depreciation...	5,000	27,000
Branch operating income before taxes.....................		$ 13,000

Branch
Balance Sheet
December 31, 19X1

Assets			Liabilities and Equity	
Cash.........................		$ 55,000	Home office equity....	$120,000
Inventory..................		20,000		
Equipment...............	$50,000			
Less accumulated depreciation...........	5,000	45,000		
			Total liabilities and	
Total assets..............		$120,000	equity	$120,000

11. The home office adjusts the branch's reported income for the gross profit realized on the branch's sale of shipments received from the

home office. Of the original shipments, 80% are sold, and thus 80% of the intercompany profit is realized.

Home Office

| Unrealized Intercompany Inventory Profit | 8,000 | |
| Branch Income | | 8,000 |

Branch

No entry

12. The home office adjusts branch income for depreciation expense incurred for, but not charged to, the branch.

Home Office

| Branch Income | 10,000 | |
| Depreciation Expense — Branch | | 10,000 |

Branch

No entry

As a result of these adjustments, the home office will disclose adjusted branch income of $11,000 on its separate internal statements.

PREPARATION OF COMBINED STATEMENTS

With separate home office and branch statements prepared for internal purposes, a single set of combined statements for the entire firm must be prepared next. The separate trial balances of the home office and its branch become the basis for a combined worksheet. Before the accounts are combined, the reciprocal accounts (Investment in Branch and Home Office Equity as well as Shipments to Branch and Shipments from Home Office) must have equal balances. If there is inequality, adjusting entries must be made on the separate records of the home office and its branch.

Worksheet 10–3, pages 670–671 is a combined financial statement worksheet for 19X1, based on the preceding home office and branch example. The pre-closing trial balance of the branch, page 629, is combined with a pre-closing home office trial balance. The home office trial balance is prepared prior to recording the branch income in entries 11 and 12. This worksheet deviates from a consolidated worksheet for a parent and subsidiary as follows:

1. A summarized cost of goods sold account is not used in the trial balances. To avoid any error, the reciprocal merchandise shipment accounts should appear on the worksheet. Thus, the ending inventory of the single firm should be entered as an adjusting entry on the worksheet. As a result, a Cost of Goods Sold column is added to the worksheet.

2. There is never a minority interest; thus, there is no distribution of income and no Minority Interest column.
3. The account Home Office Equity replaces the usual subsidiary company stockholders' equity accounts.

Worksheet 10-3 is the basis for the following formal combined statements:

Home Office and Branch		
Income Statement		
For Year Ended December 31, 19X1		
Sales..		$260,000
Less cost of goods sold...............................		122,000
Gross profit......................................		$138,000
Less expenses:		
Selling and administrative expense	$47,000	
Depreciation expense—buildings.....................	22,000	
Depreciation expense—equipment	10,000	79,000
Net income		$ 59,000

Home Office and Branch	
Retained Earnings Statement	
For Year Ended December 31, 19X1	
Balance, January 1, 19X1.............................	$300,000
Net income for 19X1.................................	59,000
Balance, December 31, 19X1..........................	$359,000

Home Office and Branch
Balance Sheet
December 31, 19X1

Assets		Stockholders' Equity	
Cash.............................	$ 96,000	Common stock..............	$200,000
Inventory......................	68,000	Retained earnings	359,000
Buildings	400,000		
Less accumulated			
depreciation...............	(120,000)		
Equipment....................	130,000		
Less accumulated			
depreciation...............	(15,000)		
		Total stockholders'	
Total assets...................	$559,000	equity	$559,000

The only complication in subsequent periods is the unrealized inter-company inventory profit applicable to the branch's beginning inventory. The branch's beginning inventory includes such profit and thus is overstated for combined reporting purposes. To illustrate the additional worksheet pro-cedures, the previous example is continued into 19X2. The branch has $10,000 of merchandise in its December 31, 19X1 inventory, and the home office has $2,000 of unrealized intercompany inventory profit remaining on December 31, 19X1. Assume that during 19X2, the home office transfers goods with a cost of $60,000 to the branch at a billed price of $75,000 (25% markup on cost). The following entries are made:

Home Office

Investment in Branch	75,000	
Shipments to Branch		60,000
Unrealized Intercompany Inventory Profit		15,000

Branch

| Shipments from Home Office | 75,000 | |
| Home Office Equity | | 75,000 |

The following partial worksheet illustrates the steps required as a result of the intercompany merchandise transactions in 19X2:

Home Office and Branch
Partial Worksheet for Combined Financial Statements
For Year Ended December 31, 19X2

| | Trial Balance | | Eliminations & Adjustments | |
	Home	Branch	Dr.	Cr.
Inventory, Jan. 1, 19X2	50,000	20,000*		(1) 2,000
Shipments to Branch	(60,000)		(2) 60,000	
Shipments from Home Office		75,000		(2) 75,000
Unrealized Intercompany Inventory Profit	(17,000)		(1) 2,000	
			(2) 15,000	

*$10,000 was acquired from the home office.

Eliminations and Adjustments:
(1) Reduce the beginning inventory held by the branch to cost by removing the $2,000 of 19X1 unrealized intercompany profit applicable to it. The unrealized profit of $2,000 plus the unreal-ized profit on 19X2 shipments is the balance of the unrealized intercompany inventory profit account.
(2) Eliminate the cost of the 19X2 shipments to the branch and the $15,000 unrealized profit appli-cable to them against Shipments from Home Office. All remaining procedures would continue as in Worksheet 10–3.

It is possible that other types of transactions, such as sales of plant assets, could occur between the home office and branch. In each case, the usual procedures applicable to consolidations of parent-subsidiary firms are applied. Other than the existence of unique reciprocal accounts, branch accounting is simply the consolidation of a 100%-owned subsidiary acquired at a cost equal to book value.

QUESTIONS

1. During the current period, a firm acquired an 80% interest in another company. What are the implications of the transaction on the consolidated cash flows statement (a) if cash was paid for the interest? (b) if stock of the parent was issued as consideration?
2. What is the impact on the consolidated statement of cash flows of a business combination accounted for as a purchase which occurred in a prior period?
3. Which of the following items would be included in a consolidated statement of cash flows and, if they are included, in what section would they appear?
   (a) Amortization of excesses relative to the investment.
   (b) Parent company investment in subsidiary bonds purchased directly from the subsidiary.
   (c) Parent company acquisition that meets the pooling criteria.
   (d) Cash acquisition of remaining interest in a subsidiary following a pooling of interests.
   (e) Minority interest in subsidiary equity in year of acquisition.
   (f) Parent company sale of a part of its interest in a subsidiary.
   (g) Cash dividends paid by a 90%-owned subsidiary.
4. Indicate how the computation of consolidated earnings per share is influenced by the minority interest in a subsidiary's equity.
5. In calculating the tax provision for an affiliated group, what adjustments must be made to combined income to arrive at combined taxable income? Explain why the adjustments are necessary.
6. Discuss the need for interperiod tax allocation as a part of the consolidation process when members of a consolidated group file separate tax returns.
7. Company S has operating income of $100,000 before tax. Company P has a 70% ownership interest in Company S. Assuming that Companies P and S are taxed as separate entities, what provision for tax must P make for its share of S income? Assume a 30% tax rate for both companies.
8. Briefly describe when the APB Opinion No. 18 sophisticated equity method must be used in accounting for an investment.

9. Why is the APB Opinion No. 18 sophisticated equity method viewed as requiring a "one-line" consolidation?

10. Is it possible for the investment account to have a negative balance under the sophisticated equity method?

11. Horvath Corporation owns a 25% interest in Candle Company. Determine how much profit should be deferred if (a) Horvath sold merchandise to Candle during the year and $1,000 of unrealized profit from the sale remains in Candle's year-end inventory; (b) Candle sold to Horvath merchandise during the year and $1,000 of unrealized profit remains in Horvath's year-end inventory.

12. Discuss the use of lower-of-cost-or-market values in regard to investments carried under the APB Opinion No. 18 equity method.

13. Describe the accounting procedures for (a) an investor who owns less than a 20% interest in an investee and subsequently purchases enough stock to exceed 20%, and (b) an investor whose ownership interest exceeds 20%, but who subsequently sells a portion of the investment to cause the interest to fall below 20%.

14. What disclosures concerning material investments must be made on the financial statements?

15. A single leveraged buyout transaction may result in three different types of values being recorded as part of the cost of the interest acquired. What are these values and under what circumstances are they recorded?

16. Is it necessary that one entity establish control over a firm in order to record a leveraged buyout? Is it required or permissible to include former owners of a controlling interest in the new control group?

EXERCISES

Exercise 1.   Parson Corporation purchased 90% of Sanders Corporation outstanding common stock for $480,000 on January 1, 19X3. Any excess of cost over book value is attributed to goodwill with a 10-year life. Part of the purchase price was provided by Parson's January 1, 19X3 issuance of $200,000 in bonds at face value. The balance of the $480,000 was paid in cash. Sanders' balance sheet at that date showed the following:

Assets		Liabilities and Stockholders' Equity	
Cash................................	$ 20,000	Current liabilities	$110,000
Inventory	140,000	Bonds payable	100,000
Property, plant, and		Common stock.................	350,000
equipment (net).............	550,000	Retained earnings.............	150,000
Total assets.....................	$710,000	Total liabilities and equity ...	$710,000

Consolidated net income for 19X3 was $119,000, net of the minority's interest of $8,000. Parson Corporation declared and paid dividends of $10,000, and Sanders declared and paid dividends of $5,000.

Based on the following balance sheet information, prepare the consolidated statement of cash flows using the indirect method for Parson Corporation and its subsidiary for the year ended December 31, 19X3. Any supporting schedules should be in good form.

	Parson Corporation December 31, 19X2	Consolidated December 31, 19X3
Cash...	$ 60,000	$ 81,500
Inventory......................................	260,000	337,000
Property, plant, and equipment (net)	800,000	1,265,000
Goodwill.......................................	—	27,000
Current liabilities	(160,000)	(284,000)
Bonds payable	(200,000)	(500,000)
Minority interest............................	—	(57,500)
Controlling common stock..............	(500,000)	(500,000)
Controlling retained earnings..........	(260,000)	(369,000)
Total...	$ 0	$ 0

Exercise 2. Keller Corporation acquired 70% of the outstanding common stock of Ney Company on January 1, 19X0. An appraisal on that date showed that Ney's assets included equipment that had a 5-year remaining life and was overvalued $25,000, and a building that had a 20-year life and was undervalued $40,000. In 19X3, Keller reported income of $100,000 (exclusive of subsidiary income), and Ney reported income of $45,000. Ney's ending inventory included $30,000 of goods purchased in 19X3, the sale of which had yielded a 25% gross profit to Keller.

Prepare the cash flow from operations section of the consolidated statement of cash flows using the indirect method for Keller and Ney for the year ended December 31, 19X3. Base this section solely on the information given. Ignore tax considerations.

Exercise 3. Johnstone Company purchased 70% of the 10,000 outstanding shares of Gleason Company common stock on March 1, 19X0, and wants to increase its ownership interest to 80% as of January 1, 19X2. Compare the effects that the following alternatives would have on the 19X2 consolidated statement of cash flows:

(1) An additional 1,000 common shares are purchased by Johnstone from the minority stockholders.

(2) Johnstone succeeds in purchasing 9,000 shares of Gleason's new 10,000-share common stock issuance.

Assume that there is no excess under either alternative.

Exercise 4. On January 1, 19X8, Rodgers Industries purchased an 80% interest in Conley Supply Company for $450,000. No excess of cost or book value resulted from the purchase. Separate income statements of the two firms for 19X8 are as follows:

	Rodgers Industries	Conley Supply Company
Sales...	$1,000,000	$620,000
Less cost of goods sold.....................................	650,000	400,000
Gross profit...	$ 350,000	$220,000
Less other expenses	200,000	150,000
Operating income...	$ 150,000	$ 70,000
Subsidiary dividend income................................	8,000	—
Income before tax...	$ 158,000	$ 70,000

Since the firms desire to file a consolidated tax return, neither firm has recorded a provision for income tax.

Assuming a 30% corporate tax rate, prepare the 19X8 consolidated income statement with a provision for tax. Include a schedule computing the provision for tax to be allocated to the separate firms. Assume that there were no intercompany transactions.

Exercise 5.   On July 1, 19X7, Darl Company purchased a 70% interest in Dole Company for $395,000. The following determination and distribution of excess schedule was prepared:

Price paid		$395,000
Less interest acquired:		
Common stock ($10 par).............................	$350,000	
Retained earnings....................................	100,000	
Total stockholders' equity........................	$450,000	
Interest acquired......................................	70%	315,000
Excess of cost over book value attributable to goodwill		
(40-year life)...		$ 80,000

The companies had the following income statements for 19X8:

	Darl Company	Dole Company
Sales...	$800,000	$600,000
Less cost of goods sold...............................	420,000	300,000
Gross profit...	$380,000	$300,000
Less other expenses	250,000	130,000
Operating income......................................	$130,000	$170,000
Subsidiary income.....................................	119,000	—
Income before tax......................................	$249,000	$170,000
Provision for income tax (30%)	74,700	51,000
Net income...	$174,300	$119,000

Since the firms do not meet the requirements to be taxed as a single entity, each firm pays its taxes separately (30% tax rate). It is assumed that all subsidiary income eventually will be distributed as dividends.

Prepare the December 31, 19X8, consolidated income statement of Darl Company and its subsidiary. Include the distribution of combined net income. Assume that there were no intercompany transactions. Any supporting calculations and schedules should be in good form.

Exercise 6. On May 1, 19X6, Kardinal Company purchased a 70% interest in Bostrom Company for $350,000. The following determination and distribution of excess schedule was prepared:

Price paid		$350,000
Less interest acquired:		
Common stock ($12 par)...	$300,000	
Retained earnings..	100,000	
Total stockholders' equity..	$400,000	
Interest acquired..	70%	280,000
Excess of cost over book value attributable to goodwill		
(20-year life)...		$ 70,000

Kardinal Company and Bostrom Company had the following separate income statements for the year ended December 31, 19X8:

	Kardinal Company	Bostrom Company
Sales...	$750,000	$550,000
Less cost of goods sold..	440,000	357,500
Gross profit..	$310,000	$192,500
Less other expenses	200,000	140,000
Income before dividends..	$110,000	$ 52,500
Dividends received	17,500	—
Income before tax..	$127,500	$ 52,500

During 19X8, Bostrom Company paid cash dividends of $1 per share of common stock.

Prepare the entry to record income tax payable on each firm's books. Assume a 30% corporate income tax rate.

Exercise 7. The separate income statements of Casper Company and its 60%-owned subsidiary, Varsity Company, for the year ended December 31, 19X7, are as follows:

	Casper Company	Varsity Company
Sales...	$520,000	$300,000
Less cost of goods sold..	350,000	180,000
Gross profit..	$170,000	$120,000
Less operating expenses	100,000	90,000
Operating income..	$ 70,000	$ 30,000
Subsidiary income..	12,600	—
Income before tax..	$ 82,600	$ 30,000
Provision for income tax	21,756	9,000
Net income...	$ 60,844	$ 21,000

The following additional information is available:

(a) Casper Company purchased its interest in Varsity Company on July 1, 19X5. There was no excess of cost or book value associated with the original purchase.

(b) Varsity Company sold a piece of equipment to Casper Company on December 31, 19X6, for $10,000. This piece of equipment had a book value of $5,000 and an estimated future life of four years at the purchase date. Straight-line depreciation is assumed.

(c) Casper Company sold $15,000 worth of merchandise to Varsity Company during 19X7. Casper sells its merchandise at a price that enables it to realize a gross profit of 30%.

(d) Varsity Company had $2,000 worth of this merchandise in its ending inventory.

(e) A corporate income tax rate of 30% is assumed.

Prepare the worksheet adjustments pertaining to the intercompany transactions, and prepare the interperiod tax allocations that result from the elimination of the intercompany transactions.

Exercise 8.   Tailor Corporation purchased a 25% interest in Libby Company for $100,000 on January 1, 19X7. The following determination and distribution of excess schedule was prepared:

Price paid		$100,000
Less interest acquired:		
Common stock ($10 par)...	$200,000	
Retained earnings..	100,000	
Total stockholders' equity..	$300,000	
Interest acquired..	25%	75,000
Excess of cost over book value		$ 25,000
Less excess attributable to equipment, 25% × $40,000		
(10-year life)...		10,000
Goodwill (20-year life)..		$ 15,000

Libby Company earned income of $16,000 in 19X7 and $24,000 in 19X8. Libby Company declared a 25-cent per share cash dividend on December 22, 19X8, payable January 12, 19X9, to stockholders of record on December 30, 19X8.

Prepare the equity adjustment required by APB Opinion No. 18 on Tailor's books on December 31, 19X7, and December 31, 19X8, to account for its investment in Libby Company. Assume that Tailor Corporation makes no adjustment except at the end of each calendar year. Ignore income tax considerations.

Exercise 9.   On January 1, 19X7, Petero Corporation purchased a 30% interest in Yancy Company for $220,000. The following determination and distribution of excess schedule was prepared:

Price paid		$220,000
Less interest acquired:		
Common stock ($5 par)................................	$200,000	
Paid-in capital in excess of par....................	320,000	
Retained earnings.....................................	130,000	
Total stockholders' equity........................	$650,000	
Interest acquired.......................................	30%	195,000
Excess of cost over book value attributable to goodwill		
(10-year life)..		$ 25,000

The following information relates to intercompany merchandise sales:

	Petero to Yancy	Yancy to Petero
Sales for 19X7..	$40,000	$20,000
Seller inventory in buyer's December 31, 19X7 inventory ...	2,000	5,000
Sales for 19X8..	35,000	30,000
Seller inventory in buyer's December 31, 19X8 inventory ...	3,000	2,000
Gross profit on sales...	25%	30%

The following schedule summarizes Yancy's income and dividends paid in 19X7 and 19X8:

	19X7	19X8
Income..	$40,000	$35,000
Dividends paid	12,000	12,000

Prepare the equity adjusting entries required by APB Opinion No. 18 for Petero Corporation's investment in Yancy Company on December 31, 19X7, and December 31, 19X8. Assume that Petero Corporation adjusts its investment account only at the end of each calendar year. Ignore income tax considerations, and provide any supporting schedules in good form.

Exercise 10. Spancode Corporation acquired a 30% interest in the outstanding stock of Wurl Corporation on January 1, 19X6. At that time, the following determination and distribution of excess schedule was prepared:

Price paid		$120,000
Less interest acquired:		
Common stock...	$150,000	
Retained earnings.....................................	165,000	
Total stockholders' equity........................	$315,000	
Interest acquired.......................................	30%	94,500
Excess of cost over book value attributable to goodwill		
(10-year life)..		$ 25,500

During 19X6, Wurl reported net income of $90,000. On December 31, 19X6, Spancode purchased $30,000 of inventory from Wurl. Wurl's gross profit rate is 30%. Spancode also purchased a machine from Wurl for $15,000 on January 1, 19X6. The machine had a book value of $10,000 and a 5-year remaining life. Wurl paid $20,000 in dividends during 19X6.

Prepare an income distribution schedule for Wurl and record the entries to adjust the investment in Wurl account.

Exercise 11. Hanson Corporation purchased a 10% interest in Novic Company on January 1, 19X6, and an additional 15% interest on January 1, 19X8. These investments cost Hanson Corporation $80,000 and $110,000, respectively.

The following stockholders' equities of Novic Company are available:

	December 31, 19X5	December 31, 19X7
Common stock ($10 par).................	$500,000	$500,000
Retained earnings..........................	250,000	300,000
Total equity................................	$750,000	$800,000

Any excess of cost over book value on the original investment was attributed to goodwill and given a 5-year life. Any excess on the second purchase is attributable to equipment with a 4-year life.

Novic Company had income of $30,000, $30,000, and $40,000, for 19X6, 19X7, and 19X8, respectively. Novic paid dividends of $.20 per share in 19X7 and in 19X8.

Ignore income tax considerations, and assume that adjusting entries are made at the end of the calendar year only.

(1) Prepare the equity "catch-up" entry, as required by APB Opinion No. 18, on January 1, 19X8, when Hanson's investment in Novic Company first exceeded 20%. Any supporting schedules should be in good form.
(2) Prepare the December 31, 19X8 equity adjustment on Hanson's books. Provide supporting calculations in good form.

Exercise 12. On January 1, 19X7, Lind Corporation purchased a 30% interest in Soder Realty Company for $175,000. Soder Realty Company had the following stockholders' equity at that time:

Common stock ($6 par)............................	$120,000
Paid-in capital in excess of par...................	100,000
Retained earnings.....................................	180,000
Total stockholders' equity.......................	$400,000

Any excess of cost over book value in the purchase price was attributed to goodwill and given a 10-year life.

The following schedule summarizes Soder Realty's income and dividends paid in 19X7 and 19X8:

	19X7	19X8
Income..	$60,000	$85,000
Dividends declared and paid.........	30,000	30,000

On January 1, 19X9, Lind Corporation sold its interest in Soder Realty Company for $250,000.

Prepare the entry to record the sale of Lind Corporation's interest in Soder Realty Company. Assume that all equity adjustments were made properly. Ignore tax considerations, and provide any supporting schedules in good form.

Exercise 13. On January 1, 19X7, Pandel Company purchased a 20% interest in Bornco Industries for $200,000. Bornco Industries had the following stockholders' equity at that time:

Common stock ($1 par)	$100,000
Paid-in capital in excess of par	500,000
Retained earnings	300,000
Total stockholders' equity	$900,000

On the purchase date, Bornco Industries' book value approximated market value. Any excess of cost over book value was attributed to goodwill with a life of five years.

Bornco Industries earned $60,000 (net of tax) in 19X7, and paid dividends of $.20 per share.

Prepare the equity adjusting entries on December 31, 19X7, as required by APB Opinion No. 18, for Pandel Company's investment in Bornco Industries. Assume a 30% tax rate and that all of Bornco's income eventually will be distributed as dividends. Any supporting schedules and calculations should be in good form.

Exercise 14. Modern Corporation was formed on January 1, 19X1 by issuing 4,000 shares of $10 par stock for $20 per share. Modern Corporation is going to engage in a leveraged buyout of Antique Company. Antique Company had the following stockholders' equity on January 1, 19X1:

Common stock ($10 par, 10,000 shares outstanding)	$100,000
Paid-in capital in excess of par	150,000
Retained earnings	80,000
Total equity	$330,000

The market value of Antique Company shares is $40 each. 2,000 Antique shares will be acquired from members of Antique Company's control group in exchange for 4,000 Modern Corporation shares. The equity-adjusted cost of the control group's shares is $25 per share. Calculate the total cost of Antique Company under each of the following assumptions:
 (a) Modern Corporation borrows $240,000 and purchases for $40 each the remaining 8,000 shares held by parties outside the control group of Antique Company.
 (b) Modern Corporation borrows $200,000 and purchases 7,000 noncontrol group shares for $40 each. Modern issues 2,000 of its shares in exchange for 1,000 Antique Company shares held by noncontrol group members.
 (c) Modern Corporation borrows $160,000 and purchases 6,000 noncontrol group shares for $40 each. Modern issues 4,000 of its shares in exchange for 2,000 Antique Company shares held by noncontrol group members.

Exercise 15. Old Time Company has the following balance sheet on January 1, 19X1, when it is the target of a leveraged buyout by Hercules Corporation:

Assets		Stockholders' Equity	
Cash...............................	$ 50,000	Common stock	
Inventory..........................	100,000	($5 par, 10,000 shares)....	$ 50,000
Property and plant............	200,000	Paid-in capital in excess	
		of par...........................	160,000
		Retained earnings.............	140,000
Total assets......................	$350,000	Total equity......................	$350,000

The property and plant have a market value of $230,000.

Hercules Corporation incorporated by issuing 3,000 shares of $10 par common stock for $40 each. The company also borrowed $160,000 from long-term lenders. The leveraged buyout was accomplished as follows:

1,000 shares exchanged on a 1-to-1 basis with members of the old control group. The equity-adjusted cost per share for these shares was $31.

2,000 shares exchanged on a 1-to-1 basis with noncontrol group members.

7,000 shares of Old Time purchased from noncontrol group members for $40 per share.

Prepare the balance sheet of Hercules Corporation immediately after the leveraged buyout. Provide supporting calculations in good form.

Appendix Exercise. The December 31, 19X8 trial balances of a home office and its branch are as follows:

	Home Office	Branch
Cash..	25,000	21,000
Inventory (Jan. 1, 19X8)..	80,000	—
Buildings...	200,000	—
Accumulated Depreciation—Buildings........................	(60,000)	—
Equipment..	100,000	20,000
Accumulated Depreciation—Equipment	(20,000)	(2,000)
Investment in Branch..	45,000	—
Common Stock ($10 par)...	(250,000)	—
Retained Earnings, Jan. 1, 19X8	(74,500)	—
Home Office Equity..	—	(45,000)
Sales...	(300,000)	(60,000)
Purchases..	250,000	30,000
Shipments to Branch	(15,000)	—
Shipments from Home Office......................................	—	20,000
Unrealized Intercompany Inventory Profit...................	(5,000)	—
Selling and Administrative Expense............................	10,000	14,000
Depreciation Expense...	12,000	2,000
Depreciation Expense—Branch..................................	2,500	—
Total...	0	0

On December 31, 19X8, the home office had merchandise of $50,000 on hand, and the branch had merchandise of $10,000, including $5,000 of merchandise received from the home office.

(1) Prepare the eliminations that would be needed on a worksheet for all combined statements.

(2) Prepare the combined income statement for 19X8.

PROBLEMS

Problem 10–1. Rausch Industries purchased an 80% interest in the outstanding common stock of Arb Company on January 1, 19X0. The determination and distribution of excess schedule prepared at the date of acquisition was based on a purchase price of $568,000, a total Arb equity of $650,000, and a $22,500 undervaluation of equipment with a 3-year life. Any remaining excess was attributed to goodwill and given a 10-year life.

Comparative consolidated balance sheet data are as follows:

	December 31, 19X0	December 31, 19X1
Cash...	$ 80,000	$ 127,500
Inventory.....................................	120,000	260,000
Accounts receivable.......................	200,000	300,000
Property, plant, and equipment.......	3,000,000	3,050,000
Accumulated depreciation..............	(1,080,000)	(1,280,000)
Investment in Chester Corp. (30%)...	—	216,500
Goodwill......................................	27,000	24,000
Accounts payable..........................	(117,000)	(200,000)
Bonds payable	(100,000)	(200,000)
Minority interest...........................	(138,000)	(151,000)
Controlling interest:		
Common stock, par.....................	(1,000,000)	(1,000,000)
Additional paid-in capital.............	(650,000)	(650,000)
Retained earnings.......................	(342,000)	(497,000)
Total..	$ 0	$ 0

The following additional information concerning Rausch and Arb is available for 19X1:

(a) Arb purchased equipment for $50,000 in cash.

(b) On January 1, 19X1, Rausch purchased 30% of the outstanding common stock of Chester Corporation for $200,000. No excess resulted from this transaction. Chester earned an $80,000 net income in 19X1 and paid $25,000 in dividends.

(c) In December, 19X1, Arb issued $100,000 of bonds at face value to help finance a building addition on which construction is slated to begin in January.

(d) Consolidated net income (controlling interest) for 19X1 was $255,000; the minority interest in net income was $16,000. Rausch paid $100,000 in dividends in 19X1, and Arb paid $15,000.

Required:

Prepare the consolidated statement of cash flows to accompany the other financial statements of Rausch Industries and its subsidiary for the year ended December 31, 19X1. The indirect method format may be used. Any supporting calculations and schedules should be in good form.

Problem 10–2. Bird Enterprises purchased 90% of the common stock of Robin Corporation on January 1, 19X0, for an agreed price of $450,000. Bird issued 1,500 shares of common stock, with a $10 par value and $50 market value per share, to the stockholders of Robin Company to partially pay for the acquisition; the balance of the price was paid in cash by year end. Robin's balance sheet on the purchase date was as follows:

Assets		Liabilities and Equity	
Cash................................	$ 60,000	Accounts payable	$ 45,000
Accounts receivable..........	95,000	Long-term liabilities..........	120,000
Plant assets (net)..............	460,000	Common stock ($10 par)....	150,000
		Retained earnings.............	300,000
Total assets......................	$615,000	Total liabilities and equity...	$615,000

Any excess cost was attributed to equipment with a 5-year life.

Consolidated net income (controlling interest) for 19X0 was $162,000, and the minority interest in net income was $30,000.

Comparative balance sheet data are as follows:

	December 31, 19W9 (Parent only)	December 31, 19X0 (Consolidated)
Cash..	$ 82,000	$ 95,000
Accounts receivable.......................	120,000	161,000
Plant assets (net)..........................	870,000	1,276,000
Accounts payable	(52,000)	(80,000)
Long-term liabilities.......................	(80,000)	(200,000)
Minority interest............................	—	(75,000)
Common stock ($10 par).................	(200,000)	(215,000)
Additional paid-in capital................	(300,000)	(360,000)
Retained earnings..........................	(440,000)	(602,000)
Total..	$ 0	$ 0

No plant assets were purchased or sold during the period.

Required:

Prepare the consolidated statement of cash flows (indirect method) for the year ended December 31, 19X0, for Bird Enterprises and its subsidiary. Any supporting schedules should be in good form.

Problem 10–3.   Presented below are the consolidated workpaper balances of Bush Inc. and its subsidiary, Dorr Corporation, as of December 31, 19X6 and 19X5:

Assets	19X6	19X5	Net Change Incr. (Decr.)
Cash...	$ 313,000	$ 195,000	$118,000
Marketable equity securities (at cost).........................	175,000	175,000	—
Allowance to reduce marketable equity securities to market...	(13,000)	(24,000)	11,000
Accounts receivable (net)	418,000	440,000	(22,000)
Inventories..	595,000	525,000	70,000
Land..	385,000	170,000	215,000
Plant and equipment...	755,000	690,000	65,000
Accumulated depreciation	(199,000)	(145,000)	(54,000)
Goodwill (net)	57,000	60,000	(3,000)
Total assets...	$2,486,000	$2,086,000	$400,000

Liabilities and Stockholders' Equity			
Current portion of long-term note	$ 150,000	$ 150,000	—
Accounts payable and accrued liabilities......................	595,000	474,000	$121,000
Note payable, long-term..	300,000	450,000	(150,000)
Deferred income taxes	44,000	32,000	12,000
Minority interest in net assets of subsidiary	179,000	161,000	18,000
Common stock ($10 par)...	580,000	480,000	100,000
Additional paid-in capital..	303,000	180,000	123,000
Retained earnings..	335,000	195,000	140,000
Treasury stock (at cost)	—	(36,000)	36,000
Total liabilities and stockholders' equity..................	$2,486,000	$2,086,000	$400,000

Additional information:
(a) On January 20, 19X6, Bush Inc. issued 10,000 shares of its common stock for land having a fair market value of $215,000.
(b) On February 5, 19X6, Bush reissued all of its treasury stock for $44,000.
(c) On May 15, 19X6, Bush paid a cash dividend of $58,000 on its common stock.
(d) On August 8, 19X6, equipment was purchased for $127,000.
(e) On September 30, 19X6, equipment was sold for $40,000. The equipment cost $62,000 and had a net book value of $34,000 on the date of the sale.
(f) On December 15, 19X6, Dorr Corporation paid a cash dividend of $50,000 on its common stock.
(g) Deferred income taxes represent timing differences relating to the use of accelerated depreciation methods for income tax reporting and the straight-line method for financial reporting.
(h) Net income for 19X6 was as follows:

Controlling interest in combined net income......................	$198,000
Dorr Corporation...	110,000

(i) Bush Inc. owns 70% of Dorr Corporation. There was no change in ownership interest in Dorr during 19X5 and 19X6. There were no intercompany transactions other than the dividend paid to Bush by its subsidiary.

Required:

Prepare the statement of cash flows for the consolidated firm using the indirect method. A cash analysis worksheet should be prepared to aid in the development of the statement. Any other supporting schedules should be in good form.

Problem 10–4.   On January 1, 19X2, Peabody Corporation acquired an 80% interest in Summers Corporation. Information regarding the income and equity structure of the two companies as of the year ended December 31, 19X4, is as follows:

	Peabody	Summers
Internally generated net income	$50,500	$56,000
Common shares outstanding during the year	20,000	12,000
Warrants to acquire Peabody stock, outstanding during the year	2,000	1,000
5% convertible $100 par preferred shares outstanding during the year	—	800
Nonconvertible preferred shares outstanding	1,000	—

Additional information is as follows:
(a) The warrants to acquire Peabody stock were issued in 19X3. Each warrant can be exchanged for one share of Peabody common stock at an exercise price of $12 per share. The three-month test was met in 19X3.
(b) Each share of convertible preferred stock can be converted into two shares of Summers common stock. The preferred stock pays an annual dividend totaling $4,000. When issued in 19X2, the Aa bond yield was 6%. Peabody owns 60% of the convertible preferred stock.
(c) The nonconvertible preferred stock was issued on July 1, 19X4, and paid a six-month dividend totaling $500.
(d) Relevant market prices per share of Peabody common stock during 19X4 are as follows:

	Average	Ending
1st Quarter	$10	$11
2d Quarter	12	14
3d Quarter	13	15
4th Quarter	16	15

Required:

Compute the primary and fully diluted consolidated EPS for the year ended December 31, 19X4.

Problem 10–5.   On January 1, 19X8, Dorn Company exchanged 12,000 shares of its common stock, with a market value of $15 per share (par value,

$10), for 80% of the outstanding stock of Moore Inc. Moore had the following stockholders' equity on that date:

Common stock ($2 par).............................	$ 20,000
Paid-in capital in excess of par...................	50,000
Retained earnings.....................................	80,000
Total equity..	$150,000

At the time of the purchase, equipment with an 8-year remaining life was undervalued by $20,000. Any remaining excess was attributed to goodwill and given a 20-year life.

Intercompany merchandise transactions during 19X8 were as follows:

	Dorn to Moore	Moore to Dorn
Sales...	$12,000	$16,000
Markup on cost	25%	40%

Dorn had $2,100 of Moore's goods in its ending inventory, and Moore had $1,500 of Dorn's goods in its ending inventory.

Moore and Dorn qualify as an affiliated group for tax purposes and thus will file a consolidated tax return. A 30% tax rate is assumed.

Dorn uses the cost method to record its investment in Moore. Since Moore paid no dividends in 19X8, Dorn has recorded no income on its investment in Moore. The two firms prepared the following separate income statements for 19X8:

	Dorn	Moore
Sales...	$980,000	$600,000
Less cost of goods sold.............	800,000	375,000
Gross profit...........................	$180,000	$225,000
Less expenses..........................	80,000	185,000
Income before tax..................	$100,000	$ 40,000

Required:

Prepare the 19X8 consolidated income statement in schedule form, including eliminations and adjustments. Provide the schedules showing the distribution of combined net income to the minority and controlling interests.

Problem 10–6.   Powell Company purchased a 90% interest in Styza Company for $220,000 on January 2, 19X2. Any excess of cost over book value was attributed to goodwill and given a 10-year life.

Additional information:

(a) The stockholders' equity of Styza Company was as follows:

	1/2/X2	1/1/X5
Common stock ($10 par)............	$100,000	$100,000
Paid-in capital in excess of par...	50,000	50,000
Retained earnings.....................	75,000	150,000
Total equity...........................	$225,000	$300,000

(b) Styza sold 5,000 shares of newly issued common stock in a private placement for $40 per share on January 2, 19X5. Powell purchased none of the shares. The impact of this sale on Powell is not taxable.

(c) Trial balances of Powell Company and its subsidiary, Styza Company, as of December 31, 19X7, are as follows:

	Powell Company	Styza Company
Other Current Assets...	112,000	285,000
Inventory..	150,000	40,000
Investment in Styza Company.....................................	220,000	—
Plant Assets..	300,000	360,000
Accumulated Depreciation..	(150,000)	(80,000)
Current Liabilities	(50,000)	(10,000)
Common Stock ($10 par)...	(200,000)	(150,000)
Paid-In Capital in Excess of Par.................................	(50,000)	(200,000)
Retained Earnings, Jan. 1, 19X7	(242,360)	(220,000)
Sales...	(500,000)	(300,000)
Cost of Goods Sold..	300,000	220,000
Other Expenses..	80,000	30,000
Dividend Income	(6,000)	—
Provision for Income Tax...	36,360	15,000
Dividends Declared..	—	10,000
Total..	0	0

(d) Both firms are taxed as separate entities at a 30% tax rate during all years included in the facts.

(e) On January 2, 19X4, Powell sold a machine to Styza for $40,000. The machine cost $32,500. Styza is depreciating the machine over 5 years using the sum-of-the-years-digits method.

(f) During 19X7, Styza sold $60,000 of merchandise to Powell. As in the past, the price provides for a 25% markup on cost. Powell had $16,000 of Styza goods in its beginning inventory and $12,000 of Styza goods in its ending inventory.

Required:

Prepare the worksheet necessary to produce the consolidated financial statements of Powell Company and its subsidiary as of December 31, 19X7. Include the income distribution schedules.

Problem 10–7. On January 1, 19X7, Pippins Company purchased a 70% interest in Simmons Company for $253,000. Any excess of cost over book value was attributed to goodwill with a 5-year life. At the time of the purchase, Simmons Company retained earnings was $100,000.

The following additional information is available:

(a) Pippins Company sold a machine to Simmons for $13,000 on July 1, 19X7. At the purchase date, the machine had a book value of $9,000 and an estimated future life of ten years. Straight-line depreciation is used by both companies for all their equipment. For income tax purposes, the gain on the sale of the equipment was taxable in the year of the sale.

(b) The following information applies to intercompany merchandise sales by Simmons Company to Pippins during 19X8:

19X8 sales	$25,000
Intercompany merchandise in January 1, 19X8 inventory	2,000
Intercompany merchandise in December 31, 19X8 inventory.........	4,000
Gross profit on sales...	30%

(c) Simmons paid cash dividends of $.20 per share during 19X8. The 19X8 dividends were the first paid in the company's history.

(d) A 40% tax rate is applicable to both firms. The firms do not qualify as an affiliated group for tax purposes.

(e) Trial balances of the two companies as of December 31, 19X8, are as follows:

	Pippins Company	Simmons Company
Cash...	117,120	67,000
Accounts Receivable	310,000	95,000
Inventory	340,000	110,000
Investment in Simmons Company........................	309,000	—
Land...	400,000	200,000
Buildings and Equipment	1,750,000	750,000
Accumulated Depreciation....................................	(940,000)	(260,000)
Liabilities	(800,000)	(500,000)
Common Stock ($1 par)......................................	(100,000)	—
Common Stock ($2 par)......................................	—	(100,000)
Paid-In Capital in Excess of Par...........................	(900,000)	(150,000)
Retained Earnings, Jan. 1, 19X8	(380,000)	(142,000)
Sales..	(2,000,000)	(700,000)
Subsidiary Income...	(33,600)	—
Cost of Goods Sold...	1,300,000	400,000
Other Expenses	580,000	220,000
Provision for Income Tax.....................................	50,016	32,000
Income Tax Payable...	(48,420)	(32,000)
Deferred Tax Liability	(4,116)	—
Dividends Declared...	50,000	10,000
Total...	0	0

Required:

Prepare the worksheet necessary to produce the consolidated financial statements of Pippins Company and its subsidiary as of December 31, 19X8. Include the determination and distribution of excess and income distribution schedules.

Problem 10–8. On January 1, 19X6, Pankow Company purchased an 80% interest in Johnson Company for $420,000. Pankow Company prepared the following determination and distribution of excess schedule for its investment:

Price paid		$420,000
Less interest acquired:		
Common stock ($10 par)..	$100,000	
Paid-in capital in excess of par.................................	150,000	
Retained earnings...	200,000	
Total stockholders' equity.....................................	$450,000	
Interest acquired..	80%	360,000
Excess of cost over book value		$ 60,000
Less excess attributable to building, 80% × $30,000		
undervaluation (20-year life)		24,000
Goodwill (5-year life)...		$ 36,000

Additional information:

(a) On July 1, 19X6, Pankow sold a machine to Johnson Company for $40,000. The machine had a net book value of $24,000 and an estimated future life of 8 years as of the sale date. Straight-line depreciation is assumed.

(b) Pankow and Johnson have had intercompany merchandise sales since January 1, 19X6. A summary of the 19X8 intercompany merchandise sales follows:

	Pankow to Johnson	Johnson to Pankow
Seller's merchandise in buyer's		
January 1, 19X8 inventory	$ 3,000	$ 1,000
19X8 sales..	20,000	30,000
Seller's merchandise in buyer's		
December 31, 19X8 inventory..........................	2,000	3,000
Outstanding intercompany payables,		
December 31, 19X8	1,500	2,000
Gross profit on sales......................................	25%	30%

(c) Trial balances of the two firms as of December 31, 19X8, are as follows:

	Pankow Company	Johnson Company
Cash..	112,600	35,000
Accounts Receivable	180,000	84,000
Inventory	200,000	100,000
Investment in Johnson Company	420,000	—
Property, Plant, and Equipment	1,800,000	750,000
Accumulated Depreciation	(1,180,000)	(365,500)
Accounts Payable	(136,000)	(68,000)
Other Liabilities	(46,000)	(6,000)
Common Stock ($10 par)	(1,000,000)	(100,000)
Paid-In Capital in Excess of Par	—	(150,000)
Retained Earnings, Jan. 1, 19X7	(260,000)	(250,000)
Sales...	(1,200,000)	(400,000)
Subsidiary Dividend Income	(10,000)	—
Cost of Goods Sold..	800,000	250,000
Other Expenses	259,400	108,000
Dividends Declared	60,000	12,500
Total..	0	0

(d) Neither firm has provided for income tax. The firms qualify as an affiliated group and thus will file a consolidated tax return based on a 30% corporate tax rate.

Required:

(1) Prepare a consolidated worksheet based on the trial balances. Include a provision for income tax and include the income distribution schedules.
(2) Record the provisions for tax on the books of the separate firms.

Problem 10–9. On January 1, 19X6, Parker Company purchased a 25% interest in Thomas Company for $300,000. Thomas Company stockholders' equity immediately prior to the purchase was as follows:

Common stock ($10 par)...........................	$ 750,000
Retained earnings....................................	250,000
Total stockholders' equity.....................	$1,000,000

Thomas Company's book values approximated market values, except for a building that was undervalued by $40,000. The building had an estimated future life of 20 years and is being depreciated on a straight-line basis. Any additional excess was attributed to goodwill and given a 10-year life.

The following additional information is available.

(a) On July 1, 19X6, Thomas sold a machine to Parker Company for $24,000. At the sale date, the machine had a book value of $16,000 and an estimated future life of 10 years. Straight-line depreciation is being used.
(b) Parker has provided specialized management services to Thomas Company since January, 19X6. Parker charges Thomas $15,000 per year for these services. Thomas Company always has paid $7,500 of this fee on July 15 and the remaining $7,500 on January 15 of the following year.
(c) The following chart summarizes intercompany merchandise transactions:

	19X6		19X7		19X8	
	P to T	T to P	P to T	T to P	P to T	T to P
Seller's merchandise in buyer's beginning inventory......................	—	—	$ 1,000	—	$ 4,000	$ 2,000
Yearly sales.....................................	$10,000	—	30,000	$10,000	25,000	25,000
Seller's merchandise in buyer's ending inventory	1,000	—	4,000	2,000	2,000	3,000
Gross profit on sales......................	30%	—	30%	25%	30%	25%

(d) Parker Company's and Thomas Company's income and dividends paid in 19X6–19X8 were as follows (tax effects are ignored):

| | 19X6 | | 19X7 | | 19X8 | |
	Parker	Thomas	Parker	Thomas	Parker	Thomas
Income............	$100,000	$48,000	$60,000	$50,000	$75,000	$65,000
Dividends paid	60,000	30,000	50,000	30,000	50,000	35,000

Required:

Prepare all entries necessitated by Parker Company's investment in Thomas Company (as required by APB Opinion No. 18) for 19X6 through 19X8. Supporting schedules should be in good form. Ignore income tax.

Problem 10–10.   On January 1, 19X6, Arlan Company purchased a 30% interest in Champion Company for $120,000. Arlan Company prepared the following determination and distribution of excess schedule:

Price paid		$120,000
Less interest acquired:		
Common stock ($5 par)...	$100,000	
Paid-in capital in excess of par...................................	100,000	
Retained earnings...	100,000	
Total stockholders' equity..	$300,000	
Interest acquired..	30%	90,000
Excess of cost over book value		$ 30,000
Less excess attributable to equipment, 30% × $20,000		
(10-year life)...		6,000
Goodwill (20-year life)...		$ 24,000

The following additional information is available:
(a) Arlan Company sold a machine to Champion Company for $20,000 on July 1, 19X7. At this date, the machine had a book value of $10,000 and an estimated future life of ten years. Straight-line depreciation (to the nearest month) is being used. For income tax purposes, the gain on the sale was taxable in the year of the sale.
(b) The following applies to Champion Company merchandise sales to Arlan for 19X7 and 19X8:

	19X7	19X8
Intercompany merchandise in beginning inventory	—	$ 2,500
Sales for the year	$10,000	15,000
Intercompany merchandise in ending inventory............	2,500	5,000
Gross profit on sales...	40%	30%

(c) Internally generated net incomes (after taxes) for the two firms are as follows:

	19X6	19X7	19X8
Arlan Company	$40,000	$50,000	$55,000
Champion Company	25,000	30,000	25,000

(d) Champion paid dividends of $5,000, $10,000, and $10,000, in 19X6, 19X7, and 19X8, respectively.

(e) The corporate income tax rate is 30%.

Required:

Prepare all adjustments to Arlan Company's investment in Champion Company account, as required by APB Opinion No. 18, on December 31, 19X6, 19X7, and 19X8. Consider income tax implications. (Only the incremental taxes applicable to the intercompany investment needs to be considered.) Supporting calculations and schedules should be in good form.

Problem 10–11. Bastian Inc., a domestic corporation having a fiscal year ending June 30, has purchased common stock in several other domestic corporations. As of June 30, 19X8, the balance in Bastian's investment account was $870,600, the total cost of stock purchased less the cost of stock sold. Bastian Inc. wishes to restate the investment account to reflect the provisions of APB Opinion No. 18.

Data concerning the investments follow:

		Hupp Inc.	Geer Inc.	Cargo Inc.
Shares of common stock outstanding................		3,000	32,000	100,000
Shares purchased by Bastian	(a)	300	8,000	30,000
	(b)	810		
Date of purchase	(a)	July 1, 19X5	June 30, 19X6	June 30, 19X7
	(b)	July 1, 19X7		
Cost of shares purchased	(a)	$ 49,400	$46,000	$670,000
	(b)	142,000		

Balance sheet at date indicated:

Assets	Hupp Inc. July 1, 19X7	Geer Inc. June 30, 19X6	Cargo Inc. June 30, 19X7
Current assets..	$ 362,000	$ 39,600	$ 994,500
Property, plant, and equipment (net of depreciation)......................................	1,638,000	716,400	3,300,000
Patent (net of amortization)	—	—	148,500
Total assets...	$2,000,000	$756,000	$4,443,000

Liabilities and Equity	Hupp Inc. July 1, 19X7	Geer Inc. June 30, 19X6	Cargo Inc. June 30, 19X7
Liabilities..	$1,500,000	$572,000	$2,494,500
Common stock...	260,000	80,000	1,400,000
Retained earnings..	240,000	104,000	548,500
Total liabilities and equity................................	$2,000,000	$756,000	$4,443,000

Additional information:

	Hupp Inc.	Geer Inc.	Cargo Inc.
Changes in common stock since July 1, 19X5....................	None	None	None
Average remaining life of plant assets at date of balance sheet (above)...	12 years	9 years	22 years
Analysis of retained earnings:			
Balance, July 1, 19X5...	$234,000		
Net income, July 1, 19X5, to June 30, 19X6..................	53,400		
Dividend paid—April 1, 19X6	(51,000)		
Balance, June 30, 19X6	$236,400	$104,000	
Net income (loss), July 1, 19X6, to June 30, 19X7	55,600	(2,000)	
Dividend paid—April 1, 19X7	(52,000)	—	
Balance, June 30, 19X7	$240,000	$102,000	$548,500
Net income, July 1, 19X7, to June 30, 19X8..................	25,000	18,000	330,000
Dividends paid:			
December 31, 19X7..	—	—	(150,000)
June 1, 19X8..	—	(5,600)	—
Balance, June 30, 19X8	$265,000	$114,400	$728,500

Bastian's first purchase of Hupp stock was made because of the high rate of return expected on the investment. All later purchases of stock were made to gain substantial influence over the operations of the various companies.

In December, 19X7, changing market conditions caused Bastian to reevaluate its relation to Geer. On December 31, 19X7, Bastian sold 6,400 shares of Geer for $54,400.

For Hupp and Geer, the fair market values of the net assets did not differ materially from the book values shown in the balance sheets. For Cargo, fair market values exceeded book values only with respect to the patent, which had a market value of $300,000 and a remaining life of 15 years as of June 30, 19X7.

At June 30, 19X8, Bastian's inventory included $48,600 of items purchased from Cargo during May and June at a 20% markup over Cargo's cost.

Required:

Prepare a worksheet to calculate the balance of Bastian's investment account as of June 30, 19X8, and its investment income by year for the three years then ended. Transactions should be listed in chronological order, and supporting computations and schedules should be in good form. Ignore income taxes. Amortization of goodwill, if any, is to be over a 40-year period. Use the following columnar headings for the worksheet:

		Investments			Investment Income For Year Ended June 30			Other Accounts	
Date	Descrip-tion	Hupp Dr. (Cr.)	Geer Dr. (Cr.)	Cargo Dr. (Cr.)	19X6 Cr. (Dr.)	19X7 Cr. (Dr.)	19X8 Cr. (Dr.)	Name	Amount Dr. (Cr.)

(AICPA adapted)

Problem 10–12. Newtech Company was formed on January 1, 19X5. The shareholder group issued 4,000 shares of $10 par common stock for $25 per share. The company was formed by an employee group to purchase Oldtech (a subsidiary of Gigantic Corporation) which had the following balance sheet on the January 3, 19X5 acquisition date:

Assets		Liabilities and Stockholders' Equity	
Cash.................................	$ 60,000	Bonds payable	$150,000
Inventory..........................	130,000	Common stock ($10 par)....	100,000
Accounts receivable..........	40,000	Paid-in capital in excess	
Equipment.......................	75,000	of par...........................	120,000
Building (net)	120,000	Retained earnings.............	85,000
Land................................	30,000		
		Total liabilities and	
Total assets.....................	$455,000	stockholders' equity.......	$455,000

The market values differed from book values in the case of the inventory, equipment, and building which were appraised at $150,000, $100,000, and $200,000, respectively. The market value of Newtech stock is $25 per share. 2,000 Newtech shares were exchanged with parties who were part of the control group of Oldtech for 1,000 Oldtech shares. The equity-adjusted cost of the shares held by Oldtech's control group was $35 per share. These individuals also will be part of the control group of Newtech. The 9,000 remaining shares of Oldtech were acquired from parties that are not part of Newtech's control group.

Required:

(1) Assume that Newtech borrowed $250,000 on a long-term note. Newtech then paid $50 per share for 7,000 shares of Oldtech and issued 4,000 of its shares in exchange for 2,000 Oldtech shares. Prepare all entries to record the formation of Newtech Corporation, the borrowing, and the buyout of Oldtech. Include a support schedule for the values assigned to the accounts.

(2) Assume that Newtech borrowed $300,000 on a long-term note. Newtech then paid $50 per share for 8,000 shares of Oldtech and issued 2,000 of its shares in exchange for 1,000 Oldtech shares. Prepare all entries to record the formation of Newtech Corporation, the borrowing, and the buyout of Oldtech. Include a support schedule for the values assigned to the accounts.

Suggestion: Be sure to determine if the 80% test is met in each case before proceeding to assign values to the accounts.

APPENDIX PROBLEMS

Problem 10A-1.   The following series of transactions refer to the first year of operation for a newly formed branch:
(a) The home office sends $60,000 to a newly formed branch to start operations.
(b) The home office transfers merchandise, with a cost of $30,000, to the branch for $40,000. The unrealized profit is isolated by the home office in a separate account.
(c) The branch purchases $40,000 worth of merchandise from outside suppliers.
(d) The home office transfers machinery, with a book value of $50,000, to the branch for $40,000. The asset will be depreciated over 10 years using the straight-line method with no salvage value. The market value of the machinery is $56,000. Transportation charges of $2,000 are paid by the home office.
(e) The branch sells $75,000 worth of merchandise.
(f) The home office pays $3,500 of expenses applicable to the branch but does not charge the branch for them.
(g) The branch records depreciation of $4,000 on the machinery.
(h) The branch incurs and records $15,000 of selling and administrative expense.
(i) The branch remits $35,000 to the home office.

Required:

Journalize the preceding transactions on the books of the home office and branch. Both the home office and the branch use a periodic inventory system.

Problem 10A-2.   On October 1, 19X7, O'Reilly Company opened a branch office. Transactions affecting the branch office for the fiscal year ending September 30, 19X8, follow:
(a) The home office sent $50,000 to the branch so that operations could begin.
(b) The home office billed the branch $48,000 for merchandise shipments. The billed amount included a 20% markup on cost. The home office uses an unrealized intercompany inventory profit account.
(c) The branch office purchased $20,000 of merchandise from outside suppliers.
(d) Branch office sales amounted to $75,000, all on credit.
(e) Branch receivables of $15,000 were outstanding at September 30, 19X8. The branch office deemed $2,000 worth of these receivables uncollectible and set up an allowance account.

(f) The home office paid $2,000 of branch expenses but did not charge the branch.

(g) The branch office paid $8,000 of expenses during the fiscal year. Of these expenses, $2,000 related to home office activities and was charged to the home office.

(h) Included in the expenses of the home office are $5,000 of depreciation for the building and equipment and $2,000 of selling and administrative expenses, applicable to the branch office. The branch was not notified of these expenses.

(i) The branch office remitted $50,000 to the home office. The home office acknowledged receipt on September 29, 19X8.

(j) A branch office physical inventory on September 30, 19X8, indicated merchandise on hand of $5,500, of which $3,000 was received from the home office.

A trial balance for the home office of O'Reilly Company, as of September 30, 19X8, is as follows:

Cash	69,000
Accounts Receivable	75,000
Inventory, October 1, 19X7	35,000
Investment in Branch	46,000
Plant and Equipment	800,000
Accumulated Depreciation	(250,000)
Liabilities	(70,000)
Common Stock	(400,000)
Retained Earnings, October 1, 19X7	(227,000)
Sales	(405,000)
Purchases	300,000
Shipments to Branch	(40,000)
Unrealized Intercompany Inventory Profit	(8,000)
Selling and Administrative Expense	48,000
Selling and Administrative Expense — Branch	2,000
Depreciation Expense	20,000
Depreciation Expense — Branch	5,000
Total	0

The home office September 30, 19X8 inventory amounted to $30,000.

Required:

(1) Prepare the entries on the branch office books to record the transactions for the year ended September 30, 19X8. Do not close the books. Both the home office and the branch use a periodic inventory system.

(2) Prepare the pre-closing trial balance of the branch office as of September 30, 19X8. Then prepare the closing entries.

(3) Prepare the branch's internal income statement.

(4) Calculate the branch income that would be shown on the home office noncombined statements.

(5) Prepare the worksheet necessary to produce the combined financial statements of O'Reilly Company and the branch office as of September 30, 19X8.

(6) Prepare the formal combined income statement and combined balance sheet of O'Reilly Company as of September 30, 19X8.

Problem 10A–3. The general ledger trial balances at December 31, 19X8, for Midwest Sales Company and its Ohio branch office are as follows:

	Home	Branch
Cash	40,000	8,000
Accounts Receivable	31,000	12,000
Inventory—Home Office, Jan. 1, 19X8	70,000	—
Inventory—Branch Office, Jan. 1, 19X8	—	15,000
Property, Plant, and Equipment	120,000	—
Accumulated Depreciation	(30,000)	—
Investment in Branch	20,000	—
Accounts Payable	(36,000)	(14,500)
Accrued Expenses	(14,000)	(2,500)
Home Office Equity	—	(8,000)
Common Stock ($10 par)	(50,000)	—
Retained Earnings, Jan. 1, 19X8	(45,000)	—
Home Office:		
Sales	(440,000)	—
Purchases	290,000	—
Expenses	44,000	—
Branch Office:		
Sales	—	(95,000)
Purchases	—	24,000
Purchases from Home Office	—	45,000
Expenses	—	16,000
Total	0	0

An audit disclosed the following:

(a) On December 23, the branch office manager purchased $5,000 of furniture and fixtures but failed to notify the home office. The bookkeeper, knowing that all plant assets are carried on the home office books, recorded the proper entry on the branch office records. It is the company's policy not to take any depreciation on assets acquired in the last half of the year.

(b) On December 27, a branch office customer erroneously paid an account of $2,000 to the home office. The bookkeeper made the entry on the home office books but did not notify the branch office.

(c) On December 30, the branch office remitted cash of $5,000, which was received by the home office in January, 19X9.

(d) On December 31, the branch office erroneously recorded the December allocated expense from the home office as $500 instead of $1,500.

(e) On December 31, the home office shipped merchandise billed at $3,000 to the branch office. The merchandise was received in January, 19X9.

(f) Depreciation for the year, not yet recorded, is $8,000 on home office assets and $4,000 on branch assets.

(g) The entire beginning inventory of the branch office had been purchased from the home office. Home office 19X8 shipments to the branch were purchased by the home office in 19X8. The physical inventories at December 31, 19X8, excluding the shipment in transit, are:

Home Office....... $55,000 (at cost)
Branch Office ..... 20,000 (comprised of $18,000 from the home office and $2,000 from outside vendors)

(h) The home office consistently bills shipments to the branch office at 25% above cost. The sales account is billed for the invoice price.

Required:

Prepare the combined statement worksheet with columns for Trial Balance, Eliminations and Adjustments, Cost of Goods Sold, Net Income, Retained Earnings, and Balance Sheet. (Disregard income taxes.)

(AICPA adapted)

Problem 10A–4. The trial balances of the home office and branch office of LaFore Company at December 31, 19X8, are as follows:

	Home	Branch
Cash...	17,000	200
Inventory, Jan. 1, 19X8...	23,000	11,550
Sundry Assets...	200,000	48,450
Investment in Branch	60,000	—
Sundry Liabilities..	(35,000)	(3,500)
Common Stock..	(200,000)	—
Retained Earnings, Jan. 1, 19X8	(31,000)	—
Home Office Equity..	—	(51,500)
Sales..	(155,000)	(140,000)
Purchases...	190,000	—
Shipments to Branch	(110,000)	—
Shipments from Home Office..	—	105,000
Allowance for Markup in Branch Inventory......................	(1,000)	—
Freight-In from Home Office	—	5,250
Sundry Expenses...	42,000	24,550
Total..	0	0

The audit at December 31, 19X8, disclosed the following:

(a) The branch office deposits all cash receipts in a local bank for the account of the home office. The audit working papers for the cash cutoff revealed the following information:

Amount	Deposited by Branch	Recorded by Home Office
$1,050	December 27, 19X8	December 31, 19X8
1,100	December 30, 19X8	January 2, 19X9
600	December 31, 19X8	January 3, 19X9
300	January 2, 19X9	January 6, 19X9

(b) The branch office pays expenses incurred locally from an imprest bank account that is maintained with a balance of $2,000. Checks are drawn once a week on this imprest account, and the home office is notified of the amount needed to replenish the account. At December 31, an $1,800 reimbursement check was mailed to the branch office.

(c) The branch office receives all of its goods from the home office. The home office bills the goods at a markup of 10% of cost. At December 31, a shipment with a billing value of $5,000 was in transit to the branch. Freight costs are typically 5% of billed values. Freight costs are considered to be inventoriable costs.

(d) The trial balance beginning inventories are shown at their respective costs to the home office and to the branch office. The inventories at December 31, excluding the shipment in transit, are:

Home office, at cost.....................................	$30,000
Branch office, at billing value.......................	10,400

Required:

Prepare the combined statement worksheet for LaFore Company and its branch, with columns for Trial Balance, Eliminations and Adjustments, Cost of Goods Sold, Net Income, Retained Earnings, and Balance Sheet. (Disregard income taxes.) (AICPA adapted)

Worksheet 10–1 (see page 607)

(Credit balance amounts are in parentheses.)

		Trial Balance	
		Company P	Company S
1	Cash	200,000	380,000
2	Inventory, Dec. 31, 19X3	150,000	120,000
3	Plant and Equipment	900,000	1,100,000
4	Accumulated Depreciation	(440,000)	(150,000)
5			
6	Investment in Company S	1,120,000	
7			
8			
9	Goodwill		
10	Liabilities		(150,000)
11	Common Stock, Co. P	(800,000)	
12	Retained Earnings, Jan. 1, 19X3, Co. P	(900,000)	
13			
14			
15	Common Stock, Co. S		(500,000)
16	Retained Earnings, Jan. 1, 19X3, Co. S		(700,000)
17			
18	Sales	(600,000)	(400,000)
19	Cost of Goods Sold	350,000	200,000
20			
21	Expenses	100,000	100,000
22	Subsidiary Income	(80,000)	
23		0	0
24	**Combined Income Before Tax**		
25	**Provision for Income Tax**		
26	**Income Tax Payable**		
27			
28	Combined Net Income		
29	To Minority Interest (see distribution schedule)		
30	Balance to Controlling Interest (see distribution schedule)		
31	Total Minority Interest		
32	Retained Earnings, Controlling Interest, Dec. 31, 19X3		
33			

Consolidated Income Tax Return
Subsidiary Company S
Financial Statements
December 31, 19X3

WORKSHEET 10–1 ||||||||||||||||||||||||

Eliminations & Adjustments Dr.		Eliminations & Adjustments Cr.		Consolidated Income Statement	Minority Interest	Controlling Retained Earnings	Consolidated Balance Sheet	
							580,000	1
		(9)	35,000				235,000	2
		(5)	20,000				1,980,000	3
(5)	4,000						(582,000)	4
(6)	4,000							5
		(1)	80,000					6
		(2)	960,000					7
		(3)	80,000					8
(3)	80,000	(4)	6,000				74,000	9
							(150,000)	10
							(800,000)	11
(4)	4,000					(860,000)		12
(5)	16,000							13
(8)	20,000							14
(2)	400,000				(100,000)			15
(2)	560,000				(135,000)			16
(8)	5,000							17
(7)	100,000			(900,000)				18
(9)	35,000	(7)	100,000	460,000				19
		(8)	25,000					20
(4)	2,000	(6)	4,000	198,000				21
(1)	80,000							22
								23
				(242,000)				24
(10)	**73,200**			73,200				25
		(10)	**73,200**				(73,200)	26
1,383,200		1,383,200						27
				(168,800)				28
				12,600	(12,600)			29
				156,200		(156,200)		30
					(247,600)		(247,600)	31
						(1,016,200)	(1,016,200)	32
							0	33

(continued)

Eliminations and Adjustments:

(1) Eliminate the parent's entry recording its share of the current year's subsidiary income. This step returns the investment account to its balance on January 1, 19X3.

(2) Eliminate 80% of the January 1, 19X3 subsidiary equity balances against the investment in Company S.

(3) Distribute the $80,000 excess of cost to the goodwill account.

(4) Amortize the goodwill at an annual amount of $2,000 for the past two years and for the current year.

(5) Remove from retained earnings the undepreciated gain at the beginning of the year on the sale of the equipment. Since the sale was by the parent, the entire adjustment is removed from the controlling interest in retained earnings.

(6) Adjust accumulated depreciation and the current year's depreciation expense for the $4,000 overstatement of depreciation caused by the original $20,000 intercompany gain.

(7) Eliminate intercompany merchandise sales of $100,000 to avoid double counting.

(8) Reduce the cost of goods sold by the $25,000 of intercompany profit included in the beginning inventory. Since the sale was made by the subsidiary, the reduction to retained earnings is borne 80% by the controlling interest and 20% by the minority interest.

(9) Reduce the ending inventory to its cost to the consolidated firm by decreasing it $35,000, and increase the cost of goods sold by $35,000.

(10) Record the provision for income tax, calculated as follows:

Combined income before tax	$242,000
Add back goodwill deduction not allowed as tax deduction	2,000
Combined taxable income	$244,000
Tax liability (30% × $244,000)	$ 73,200

Subsidiary Company S Income Distribution

		Internally generated income before tax..........................	$100,000
Gross profit on ending inventory (50% × $70,000)..(9)	$35,000	Gross profit on beginning inventory (50% × $50,000)........................(8)	25,000
		Adjusted income before tax...	$ 90,000
		Company S share of taxes (30% × $90,000).......... (10)	**27,000**
		Company S net income.........	$ 63,000
		Minority share......................	20%
		Minority interest...................	$ 12,600

Parent Company P Income Distribution

		Internally generated income before tax..........................	$150,000
Amortization of goodwill......(4)	$ 2,000	Realized profit on equipment ($20,000 × 20%)............(6)	4,000
		Adjusted income before tax...	$152,000
		Company P share of taxes (30% × $154,000*) ...... (10)	**46,200**
		Company P net income.........	$105,800
		Share of subsidiary net income (80% × $63,000).....	50,400
		Controlling interest...............	$156,200

*The parent's share of taxes is based on its adjusted income before tax, $152,000, plus the $2,000 nondeductible goodwill amortization.

Worksheet 10–2 (see page 611)

(see page 611)

Nonaffiliated
Company P and
Worksheet for Consolidated
For Year Ended

(Credit balance amounts are in parentheses.)

		Trial Balance	
		Company P	Company S
1	Cash	19,200	80,000
2	Inventory, Dec. 31, 19X4	170,000	150,000
3	Plant and Equipment	600,000	550,000
4	Accumulated Depreciation	(410,000)	(120,000)
5			
6	Investment in Company S	504,000	
7			
8			
9	Goodwill		
10	Common Stock, Co. P	(250,000)	
11	Retained Earnings, Jan. 1, 19X4, Co. P	(510,450)	
12			
13			
14	Common Stock, Co. S		(250,000)
15	Retained Earnings, Jan. 1, 19X4, Co. S		(350,000)
16			
17	Sales	(430,000)	(240,000)
18	Cost of Goods Sold	280,000	150,000
19			
20	Expenses	70,000	30,000
21	**Provision for Income Tax**	**25,890**	**18,000**
22	Subsidiary Income	(31,500)	
23	**Income Tax Payable**	**(24,000)**	**(18,000)**
24	**Deferred Tax Liability**	**(13,140)**	
25		0	0
26	Combined Net Income		
27	To Minority Interest (see distribution schedule)		
28	Balance to Controlling Interest (see distribution schedule)		
29	Total Minority Interest		
30	Retained Earnings, Controlling Interest, Dec. 31, 19X4		
31			

Group for Tax Purposes
Subsidiary Company S
Financial Statements
December 31, 19X4

WORKSHEET 10–2 ||||||||||||||||||||||||

Eliminations & Adjustments Dr.		Eliminations & Adjustments Cr.		Consolidated Income Statement	Minority Interest	Controlling Retained Earnings	Consolidated Balance Sheet	
							99,200	1
		(9)	16,000				304,000	2
		(5)	40,000				1,110,000	3
(5)	8,000						(514,000)	4
(6)	8,000							5
		(1)	31,500					6
		(2)	450,000					7
		(3)	22,500					8
(3)	22,500	(4)	4,500				18,000	9
							(250,000)	10
(4)	3,375					(474,483)		11
(5)	24,000							12
(8)	24,000	(10)	15,408					13
(2)	187,500				(62,500)			14
(2)	262,500				(81,900)			15
(5)	8,000	(10)	2,400					16
(7)	100,000			(570,000)				17
		(7)	100,000	322,000				18
(9)	16,000	(8)	24,000					19
(4)	1,125	(6)	8,000	93,125				20
(11)	**5,052**			48,942				21
(1)	31,500							22
							(42,000)	23
(10)	**17,808**	**(11)**	**5,052**				(384)	24
	719,360		719,360					25
				(105,933)				26
				11,900	(11,900)			27
				94,033		(94,033)		28
					(156,300)		(156,300)	29
						(568,516)	(568,516)	30
							0	31

(continued)

Eliminations and Adjustments:
(1) Eliminate the parent's entry recording its share of subsidiary income for the current year. This entry now includes the parent's share of the subsidiary income *after tax*, since the firms are taxed as separate entities.
(2) Eliminate 75% of the January 1, 19X4 subsidiary equity balances against the investment in Company S.
(3) Distribute the $22,500 excess of cost in the investment account to the goodwill account.
(4) Amortize the goodwill for the current year and the three previous years at $1,125 per year.
(5) Eliminate the unamortized intercompany profit on the equipment sale by Company S as of January 1, 19X4. This elimination includes a $40,000 reduction in the asset account, an $8,000 decrease in accumulated depreciation, and a $32,000 (*before-tax*) decrease in beginning retained earnings. Since the sale was by the subsidiary, the retained earnings adjustment is allocated 75% to the controlling interest and 25% to the minority interest.
(6) Adjust the current year's depreciation expense and accumulated depreciation by the $8,000 current year's portion of the intercompany profit on the equipment sale.
(7) Eliminate intercompany merchandise sales of $100,000 to avoid double counting.
(8) Remove the gross profit on intercompany sales recorded by Company P in 19X3 from its January 1, 19X4 retained earnings. The beginning inventory of Company S included $60,000 of goods sold by Company P with a gross profit of 40%, or $24,000. On a consolidated basis, the cost of goods sold is overstated, and this step removes $24,000 from the consolidated cost of goods sold.
(9) Remove the $16,000 gross profit from the ending inventory and increase the cost of goods sold by the same amount. The Company S ending inventory includes $40,000 of goods sold by Company P with a gross profit of 40%.
(10) Adjust the beginning retained earnings balances for the tax effects of previous adjustments, as follows:

| | Retained Earnings Increase | | |
	Total	25% Minority Interest	75% Controlling Interest
Prepaid tax on $32,000 unamortized intercompany equipment gain of step (5), paid by Company S (30% × $32,000)...........	$ 9,600	$2,400	$ 7,200
Prepaid tax on $32,000 unamortized intercompany gain of step (5), paid by Company P (30% tax on 20% **taxable portion** of 75% share of aftertax gain of $22,400*)...	1,008	—	1,008
Prepaid tax relating to Company P gross profit on goods in Company S beginning inventory, step (8) (30% × $24,000)	7,200	—	7,200
Total increase in retained earnings.................	$17,808	$2,400	$15,408

*70% × $32,000 = $22,400

Step (10) increases the minority share of January 1, 19X4 retained earnings by $2,400 and increases the controlling share of January 1, 19X4 retained earnings by $15,408. The deferred tax liability is decreased by the total, $17,808.
(11) Adjust the current-year tax provision for the tax effects of previous adjustments to the current year's income, as follows:

| | Increase in Provision for Income Tax | | |
	Total	25% Minority Interest	75% Controlling Interest
Expiration of prepaid tax on equipment gain of step (6), paid by Company S (30% × $8,000)...	$2,400	$600	$1,800
Expiration of prepaid tax on equipment gain of step (6), paid by Company P (30% tax on 20% **taxable portion** of 75% share of the aftertax realized gain of $5,600*).................	252	—	252
Expiration of prepaid tax relating to gross profit on Company P goods in Company S beginning inventory, step (8) (30% × $24,000)......................................	7,200	—	7,200
Prepaid tax originating on gross profit on Company P goods in Company S ending inventory, step (9) (30% × $16,000)	(4,800)	—	(4,800)
Total increase in provision for income tax.......	$ 5,052	$600	$ 4,452

*70% × $8,000 = $5,600

No adjustment results from the amortization of goodwill since it is not tax deductible.

Subsidiary Company S Income Distribution

	Internally generated net income **after tax** (70% × $60,000)..................	$42,000
	Realized gain on depreciable asset sale ($8,000 − $2,400 tax) ...(6) **(11)**	5,600
	Adjusted net income...............	$47,600
	Minority share.........................	25%
	Minority interest......................	$11,900

Parent Company P Income Distribution

Ending inventory profit ($16,000 − $4,800 tax).(9) **(11)**	$11,200	Internally generated net income **after tax** (70% × $80,000).............................	$56,000
Goodwill amortization, not tax deductible ....(4)	1,125	Beginning inventory profit ($24,000 − $7,200 tax).(8) **(11)**	16,800
		75% of subsidiary adjusted income less tax [(75% × $47,600) − (30% tax × 20% **taxable portion** × 75% × $47,600)]..................	33,558
		Controlling interest..................	$94,033

Worksheet 10–3 (see page 631)

(Credit balance amounts are in parentheses.)

		Trial Balance	
		Home	Branch
1	Cash	41,000	55,000
2	Inventory, Jan. 1, 19X1	60,000	
3	Buildings	400,000	
4	Accumulated Depreciation—Buildings	(120,000)	
5	Equipment	80,000	50,000
6	Accumulated Depreciation—Equipment	(10,000)	(5,000)
7	**Investment in Branch**	107,000	
8	Common Stock	(200,000)	
9	Retained Earnings, Jan. 1, 19X1	(300,000)	
10	**Home Office Equity**		(107,000)
11	Sales	(150,000)	(110,000)
12	Purchases	90,000	40,000
13	**Shipments to Branch**	(40,000)	
14	**Shipments from Home Office**		50,000
15	**Unrealized Intercompany Inventory Profit**	(10,000)	
16	Selling and Administrative Expense	25,000	22,000
17	Depreciation Expense—Buildings	12,000	
18	Depreciation Expense—Equipment	5,000	5,000
19	Depreciation Expense—Branch	10,000	
20		0	0
21	**Inventory, Dec. 31, 19X1**		
22			
23	Cost of Goods Sold		
24	Net Income		
25	Retained Earnings, Dec. 31, 19X1		
26			

Eliminations and Adjustments:
(1) Eliminate the reciprocal accounts, Investment in Branch and Home Office Equity. In essence, these accounts are intercompany receivable/payable accounts.
(2) Eliminate Shipments to Branch plus Unrealized Intercompany Inventory Profit against Shipments from Home Office. This entry eliminates intercompany sales.
(3) Merge the separate branch expense accounts on the home office books with home office expenses.

and Branch
Combined Financial Statements
December 31, 19X1

WORKSHEET 10-3

Eliminations & Adjustments		Cost of Goods Sold	Net Income	Retained Earnings	Balance Sheet	
Dr.	Cr.					
					96,000	1
		60,000				2
					400,000	3
					(120,000)	4
					130,000	5
					(15,000)	6
	(1) 107,000					7
					(200,000)	8
				(300,000)		9
(1) 107,000						10
			(260,000)			11
		130,000				12
(2) 40,000						13
	(2) 50,000					14
(2) 10,000						15
			47,000			16
(3) 10,000			22,000			17
			10,000			18
	(3) 10,000					19
						20
(4) 68,000	(4) 68,000	(68,000)			68,000	21
235,000	235,000					22
		122,000	122,000			23
			(59,000)	(59,000)		24
				(359,000)	(359,000)	25
					0	26

(4) Enter the ending inventory twice: as a debit that is extended to the Balance Sheet column and as a credit that is extended to the Cost of Goods Sold column. The amount of inventory entered is net of intercompany profit. In this case, the amount is calculated as follows:

Home office inventory (arbitrary)		$50,000
Branch inventory acquired from outside parties		10,000
Branch inventory from home office	$10,000	
Less unrealized home office profit (20%)	2,000	8,000
Combined inventory, December 31, 19X1		$68,000

PART THREE

MULTINATIONAL ACCOUNTING

O ur global economy influences not only how business is conducted but also the accounting for multinational transactions. Many companies engage in a variety of transactions with foreign parties. If these transactions require settlement in a currency other than that of the domestic entity, special accounting principles must be applied. A growing number of companies are investing in foreign entities for a variety of reasons. Reporting the financial statements of a foreign investee in the currency of the investor provides more readily usable information for investment decision making. The process of translating financial statements measured in a foreign currency into statements measured in the investor's domestic currency requires specialized accounting procedures.

CHAPTER 11

ACCOUNTING FOR FOREIGN CURRENCY TRANSACTIONS

The extent of international activity by U.S. corporations has increased significantly since World War II. The number and the importance of foreign subsidiaries have been impressive and have resulted in the emergence of multinational business on a large scale. Such business investment provides opportunities for product diversification, increased profits, and enhanced corporate status. It also aids in elevating the standard of living in under-developed foreign countries and contributes to the balance of international payments. However, foreign investment exposes the parent corporation to a wide range of business risks and competitive disadvantages. For example, firms engaged in foreign operations may be affected by foreign cultural and political values, possible discrimination and interference by foreign host nations, and competition from established foreign firms. For U.S. corporations, these disadvantages generally are outweighed by the advantages.

Domestic companies transact business with foreign entities in a variety of ways. In some instances, these activities constitute foreign currency transactions and may involve sales or purchases of goods and services, lending or borrowing of funds, and a variety of other transactions. The exporting and importing of merchandise represent a major level of activity between the U.S. and other countries. These activities, in billions of dollars, are as follows:

U.S. Merchandise Exports and Imports

	1982	1983	1984	1985	1986	1987
Exports	211.2	201.8	219.9	215.9	224.0	249.6
Imports	247.6	268.9	332.4	338.1	368.5	409.9

Source: Department of Commerce, Bureau of Economic Analysis

It is important to note the major trade deficit that has been characteristic of our foreign activities. The above statistics are only for merchandise and do not include U.S. military activity, receipts or payments of income from U.S./foreign investment activity, or other services. The accounting implications of these foreign currency transactions are discussed in this chapter.

Domestic entities also have investment interests in foreign operations which take various forms. For example, a foreign operation may be a branch, division, subsidiary, joint venture, or equity investment of a domestic company. The U.S. investment abroad has increased significantly over time along with the related investment income as indicated by the following statistics (in billions of dollars):

	U.S. Investment Abroad					
	1982	1983	1984	1985	1986	1987
Annual increase in investment abroad	121.2	49.8	22.3	32.6	98.0	76.0
Investment Income	83.5	77.3	85.9	88.8	90.1	103.8

Source: Department of Commerce, Bureau of Economic Analysis

These foreign operations most often prepare financial statements in a currency other than the reporting currency of the domestic entity. The process of translating these foreign financial statements into the currency of the domestic entity is discussed in the following chapter. Regardless of the form in which international business or economic globalization occurs, the volatility of currency exchange rates results in significant risk which must be addressed by appropriate management strategies.

FOREIGN CURRENCY TRANSACTIONS AND EXCHANGE RATES

Transactions between a domestic entity and a foreign entity often may be denominated in a currency other than the domestic entity's reporting currency. Such transactions are referred to as *foreign currency transactions*. The currency required to settle a transaction is referred to as the *denominated currency*. This settlement amount is fixed in terms of the currency and does not respond to changes in the exchange rate. For example, if an American company sells goods to a French company and the receivable is to be paid in dollars, the transaction is said to be denominated in dollars. However, if the receivable is to be paid in French francs, the transaction is denominated in francs. The settlement in francs constitutes a foreign currency transaction because the denominated currency is different than the domestic reporting currency (dollars). All further discussions will assume that the domestic reporting currency is the U.S. dollar.

It becomes readily apparent that if a transaction is denominated in a currency other than the dollar, the denominated amount must be expressed in dollars for domestic reporting purposes. This process is accomplished through the use of an exchange rate, which represents the amount of one currency that can be exchanged for another at a particular point in time. The expression of amounts in an entity's reporting currency which are denominated or measured in a different currency is referred to as *foreign currency translation.*

In most nations, foreign currency is a commodity that is traded actively on organized exchanges, resulting in the establishment of exchange rates between various currencies. Exchange rates that vary over time as a result of market conditions are referred to as *free market or floating rates.* The market conditions affecting exchange rates are reflective of economic, political, inflationary, and international conditions. Some governments establish *official or fixed exchange rates* and only permit the free market rate to vary within a limited range. In some cases, special rates are established for certain types of transactions, such as import and export sales and dividend payments, to accomplish desired political and economic objectives. For example, to encourage exports and to discourage capital withdrawal, a foreign government may establish favorable official exchange rates for export sales and less favorable exchange rates for the payment of dividends to investors in other countries. The forces of supply and demand, however, occasionally make it difficult for a government to maintain an official exchange rate, and, in response, the government either devalues or revalues its currency.

The exchange rate that applies to the immediate delivery of a currency is referred to as a *spot rate.* Most foreign currencies are traded at two spot rates. A *buying rate* is the rate used to exchange foreign currency for domestic currency (e.g., pesos for dollars). A *selling rate* is the rate used to exchange domestic currency for foreign currency (e.g., dollars for pesos). The difference or spread between the buying and selling rates represents the gross profit accruing to the broker in foreign currency. Spot rates are quoted either directly or indirectly. A *direct quotation* (foreign currency in dollars) indicates the amount of domestic currency to be exchanged for one unit of foreign currency. For example, quotes of France 0.1638 and Britain 1.7265 indicate that one French franc is equal to approximately 16 cents and a British pound is equal to approximately $1.73. This is a familiar means of quotation when traveling in foreign countries. An *indirect quotation* (dollar in foreign currency) indicates the amount of foreign currency to be exchanged for one unit of domestic currency. For example, one dollar equals approximately six French francs or 0.58 British pounds. (Illustrations in this chapter will employ direct quotation exchange rates.) What does it mean when the dollar strengthens? A strengthening of the domestic currency means that it may be exchanged for a greater number of the foreign currency units. Therefore, the strengthening currency would be evidenced by a reduction in the directly quoted amount and an increase in the indirectly quoted amount. The opposite would be true for a weakening of the domestic currency.

In addition to exchange rates governing the immediate delivery of a currency, *forward rates* apply to the exchange of different currencies at a future point in time, such as in sixty or ninety days. The agreement to exchange currencies at a future date is contained in a *forward exchange contract*, which is designed to hedge against future changes in spot rates. The forward exchange contract specifies the future exchange date and the forward rate of exchange. For example, the forward rate on a British pound is $1.7187. This means that, after the specified time from the contract date has elapsed, one pound will be exchanged for $1.7187. The accounting for foreign currency transactions, which is discussed next, demonstrates the importance of both spot and forward exchange rates.

ACCOUNTING FOR FOREIGN CURRENCY TRANSACTIONS

Assume that a U.S. company sells mining equipment to a British company and that the equipment must be paid for in thirty days with U.S. dollars. This transaction is denominated in dollars and also will be measured by the U.S. company in dollars. Changes in the exchange rate between the U.S. dollar and the British pound from the transaction date to the settlement date will not expose the U.S. company to any risk or gain. Now assume that the same transaction occurs except that the transaction is to be settled in British pounds. Because this transaction is denominated in pounds and will be measured by the U.S. company in dollars, changes in the exchange rate subsequent to the transaction date could expose the U.S. company to risk or gain. For example, if the U.S. dollar strengthens relative to the pound (one receives more pounds per dollar), settlement of the receivable will result in collecting a fixed amount of British pounds which are worth fewer dollars, and the U.S. company will experience a loss due to exchange rate changes. If the dollar weakens, the opposite effect would be experienced, as the U.S. company would receive a gain due to exchange rate changes. To summarize, *changes in exchange rates do not affect transactions which are both denominated and measured in the reporting entity's currency.* Therefore, these transactions require no special accounting treatment. However, *if a transaction is denominated in a foreign currency and measured in the reporting entity's currency, changes in the exchange rate do result in a gain or loss to the reporting entity.* These gains or losses are referred to as *transaction gains or losses,* and their recognition requires special accounting treatment.

Two methods have been proposed for the treatment of exchange gains or losses arising from foreign currency transactions. One method treats the transaction and subsequent settlement as *one transaction* or event. Proponents of this method view the subsequent gain or loss as an adjustment of the original transaction. This method suggests that the original transaction and the effects of any subsequent exchange gains or losses should be viewed together in such a way that the final domestic cash flow associated with the event determines the dollar basis of the transaction. Applying this to the example regarding the mining equipment sale denominated in British pounds, an exchange gain or loss would be accounted for as an adjustment to the sales proceeds and would affect the related gross profit.

The other method of accounting for foreign currency transaction gains or losses is the *two-transaction method*, which suggests that a deferred settlement of the transaction gives rise to a gain or loss. Therefore, the initial transaction is recorded independently of the settlement transaction. This method is required by the FASB and is consistent with accepted accounting techniques, which normally account for the financing of a transaction as a separate and distinct event. (Unless otherwise stated, the two-transaction method will be used throughout the chapter.) Returning to the example regarding the mining equipment sale denominated in pounds, an exchange gain or loss would be accounted for separately from the sales transaction and would not affect the related gross profit. This exchange gain or loss is not viewed as an extraordinary item, but should be included in determining net income from operations for the period and should be disclosed in the financial statements or in a note to the statements.[1]

To illustrate the concepts presented, assume that the U.S. company sells the mining equipment on June 1, 19X9, with the corresponding receivable to be paid or settled on July 1, 19X9. The equipment has a selling price of $306,000 and a cost of $250,000. On June 1, 19X9, the British pound is worth $1.70 and on July 1, 19X9, the pound is worth $1.60. Entries to record the transaction under various assumptions are demonstrated in the following tables:

Transaction Denominated in Dollars

U.S. Company (dollars)			British Company (pounds)		
June 1, 19X9					
Accounts Receivable...........	306,000		Equipment.........................	180,000*	
Sales Revenue...............		306,000	Accounts Payable		180,000
			*($306,000 ÷ $1.70 = 180,000)		
Cost of Goods Sold	250,000				
Inventory.......................		250,000			
July 1, 19X9					
Cash...............................	306,000		Accounts Payable	180,000	
Accounts Receivable........		306,000	Exchange Loss..................	11,250	
			Cash............................		191,250*
			*($306,000 ÷ $1.60 = 191,250)		

Note: The U.S. company experienced no exchange gain or loss because its transaction was both denominated and measured in dollars. However, the British company did experience an exchange loss because its transaction was measured in pounds and denominated in dollars.

---

[1] *Statement of Financial Accounting Standards*, No, 52, "Foreign Currency Translation" (Stamford: Financial Accounting Standards Board, 1981), par. 30.

Transaction Denominated in Pounds: One-Transaction Method

U. S. Company (dollars)			British Company (pounds)		

June 1, 19X9

Accounts Receivable...........	306,000		Equipment........................	180,000	
Sales Revenue................		306,000	Accounts Payable		180,000
Cost of Goods Sold	250,000				
Inventory		250,000			

July 1, 19X9

Cash..............................	288,000		Accounts Payable	180,000	
Sales Revenue.................	18,000*		Cash............................		180,000
Accounts Receivable........		306,000			

*[180,000 × ($1.60 − $1.70)] = $18,000

Note: The U.S. company experienced an exchange loss because the transaction was denominated in pounds and measured in dollars. The loss, under the one-transaction method, resulted in an adjustment to sales revenue. The British company experienced no exchange gain or loss because its transaction was both denominated and measured in pounds.

Transaction Denominated in Pounds: Two-Transaction Method

U.S. Company (dollars)			British Company (pounds)		

June 1, 19X9

Accounts Receivable...........	306,000		Equipment........................	180,000	
Sales Revenue................		306,000	Accounts Payable		180,000
Cost of Goods Sold	250,000				
Inventory		250,000			

July 1, 19X9

Cash..............................	288,000		Accounts Payable	180,000	
Exchange Loss*.................	18,000		Cash............................		180,000
Accounts Receivable........		306,000			

*The *decrease* in the value of the British pound from $1.70 to $1.60 results in a *loss* to the U.S. firm since the pounds it *received* are less valuable than they were at the transaction date.

Note: The recording of the transactions is the same as for the one-transaction method except for the recording of the exchange loss. The loss is considered to be part of a financing decision and unrelated to the original sales transaction.

UNSETTLED FOREIGN CURRENCY TRANSACTIONS

If a foreign currency transaction is unsettled at year end, a gain or loss should be recognized to reflect the change in the exchange rate occurring between the transaction date and year end. This treatment focuses on accrual accounting and the fact that exchange gains and losses occur over time rather than only at the date of settlement or payment.

To illustrate the accounting for unsettled transactions, assume that a U.S. company purchases goods from a foreign firm on November 1, 19X1. The purchase in the amount of 1,000 foreign currencies (FC) is to be paid for on February 1, 19X2. To record or measure the transaction, the domestic company would make the following entry, assuming that 1 FC = $1:

| Inventory | 1,000 | |
| Accounts Payable | | 1,000 |

Purchase of inventory for 1,000 FC when the exchange
rate is 1 FC = $1.

Assuming that the exchange rate on the December 31, 19X1 year end is
1 FC = $1.04, the following entry would be necessary:

| Exchange Loss* [1,000 × ($1.04 − $1.00)] | 40 | |
| Accounts Payable | | 40 |

To accrue the exchange loss on the unperformed portion of the
foreign currency transaction when 1 FC = $1.04.

*The *increase* in the value of each FC from $1.00 to $1.04 results in a *loss* to the domestic
firm since, as of year end, the firm would have to pay *out* more dollars than originally
recorded in order to eliminate the liability.

Assuming that 1 FC equals $1.10 on the settlement date, the domestic entity
would make the following entry to record the settlement:

Accounts Payable ($1,000 + $40)	1,040	
Exchange Loss [1,000 × ($1.10 − $1.04)]	60	
Cash		1,100

To record payment of liability for 1,000 FC when
1 FC = $1.10.

The December 31 entry implies that, if the transaction had been settled at
year end, the domestic firm would have had to expend $1,040 to acquire
1,000 FC. Therefore, a loss of $40 is traceable to the unperformed portion of
the transaction. Some theorists have suggested that an exchange gain or loss
should not be recognized prior to settlement because the gain or loss has not
been "realized" through settlement. This position fails to recognize the merits
of accrual accounting and is in conflict with the position of the FASB, which
is stated as follows:

> At each balance sheet date, recorded balances that are denominated in a
> currency other than the functional currency of the recording entity shall
> be adjusted to reflect the current exchange rate.[2]

HEDGING WITH FORWARD EXCHANGE CONTRACTS

Hedging is a form of risk reduction management in response to fluctuating
currency exchange rates. To avoid exposure to changes in future exchange
rates when a foreign transaction is denominated in a foreign currency, it is
possible to agree currently to buy or sell the foreign currency at a preestablished rather than an uncertain rate of exchange. This would be accomplished

---

[2]*Ibid.*, par. 16.

through the use of a forward exchange contract, which, as previously mentioned, is an agreement to buy or sell a foreign currency at a specified forward (future) date at a preestablished forward rate. The forward contract allows one to hedge against any exchange losses that may arise since the contract fixes the future rate of exchange. For example, in the previous illustration of a foreign currency transaction, the U.S. company experienced a $100 exchange loss because it had to settle a liability denominated in 1,000 FC at a settlement date rate of 1 FC = $1.10, rather than at the original transaction date rate of 1 FC = $1. However, if a forward contract had provided for the delivery of the needed foreign currency at a forward rate of 1 FC = $1.04, the exchange loss would have been reduced by $60 since the transaction could have been settled with currency acquired at a rate of 1 FC = $1.04 rather than 1 FC = $1.10.

The forward rate specified in a contract will differ from the current spot rate. The difference between the forward rate and the spot rate at the date of the contract's inception is referred to as a *contract premium or discount* and generally is amortized over the life of the contract. A premium occurs when the forward rate is higher than the existing spot rate, and a discount occurs when the forward rate is lower than the existing spot rate. These differences between the forward rate and the spot rate normally are small and are due to interest differentials between the two currencies involved.

Forward contracts are purchased from foreign currency brokers, who measure the *interest differentials* between holding an investment in foreign currency and holding an investment in domestic currency. For example, if a broker sold a contract to deliver foreign currency in 30 days, the interest differential would be the difference between:

1. The interest earned on investing foreign currency for the 30 days prior to delivery date and
2. The 30 days of interest lost on the domestic currency that was not invested but was used to acquire the foreign currency needed for delivery.

Brokers dealing in forward contracts reduce their risks by extensive trading in contracts. For example, assume that a company has a contract to sell 1,000 FC in 90 days to a broker at a forward rate of 1 FC = $1. If the spot rate in 90 days is 1 FC = $.80, the broker would experience a loss of $200. However, if the broker originally could have found a company wanting to buy 1,000 FC in 90 days at a forward rate of 1 FC = $1.10, the broker would have been able to cover the $200 loss and actually experience an overall gain of $100.

Forward exchange contracts are used in foreign currency transactions in one of two ways. First, a forward contract may be used to hedge against either the exposed position created by a single transaction or the net exposed position created by several transactions. An *exposed net asset position* exists when a foreign currency transaction or a series of such transactions results in assets denominated in the foreign currency exceeding liabilities denominated in the foreign currency.

A second use of a forward contract with respect to foreign currency transactions is in response to an identifiable foreign currency commitment. In this instance, the forward contract is acquired as a hedge because there is an existing commitment that will result in a future transaction denominated in a foreign currency. This hedge is in response to an exposed position that will arise via the commitment rather than an exposed position that has arisen already via existing foreign currency transactions.

Hedge on Exposed Position. Forward contracts are similar to purchase commitments in that both are forms of executory contracts in which future exchange rates have been established. Typically, executory contracts are not recorded until at least partial performance has taken place by one of the parties to the contract. The fact that forward contracts may be sold after inception indicates that they are economic resources and is the basis for suggestions that unperformed forward contracts should be recorded as assets stated at market price. The FASB views an unperformed forward exchange contract as an asset for which changes in value due to exchange rate fluctuations should be recognized as a component of current operating income. The FASB states that:

> *A gain or loss (whether or not deferred) on a forward contract . . . shall be computed by multiplying the foreign currency amount of the forward contract by the difference between the spot rate at the balance sheet date and the spot rate at the date of inception of the forward contract (or the spot rate last used to measure a gain or loss on that contract for an earlier period).*[3]

If a forward contract represents a hedge on an exposed position resulting from an existing foreign currency transaction, the gain or loss on the contract is recognized currently rather than deferred. To illustrate, assume the following:

1. On November 1, 19X1, a U.S. firm buys inventory from a foreign company, payable on February 1, 19X2, in the amount of 1,000 FC.
2. On November 1, 19X1, the U.S. firm purchases a 90-day forward contract to buy 1,000 FC at a forward rate of 1 FC = $1.012.
3. Spot rates on selected dates are as follows:

Date	Rate
November 1, 19X1	1 FC = $1.00
December 31, 19X1	1 FC = 1.04
February 1, 19X2	1 FC = 1.10

The following entries reflect the proper accounting for these facts:

---

[3]*Ibid.*, par. 18.

19X1

Nov. 1 Inventory... 1,000
             Accounts Payable 1,000
                 Purchase of inventory for 1,000 FC when 1 FC = $1.

         Foreign Currency Due from Broker 1,000
         Deferred Contract Premium..................................... 12
             Dollars Due to Broker.. 1,012
                 Purchase of 1,000 FC to be delivered in 90 days
                 when the forward rate is 1 FC = $1.012.[4]

Dec. 31 Exchange Loss... 40
             Accounts Payable 40
                 To accrue the exchange loss on the unperformed
                 portion of the foreign currency transaction when
                 1 FC = $1.04.

         Contract Expense 8
             Deferred Contract Premium.................................... 8
                 To amortize the forward contract premium
                 ($12 × 2/3).

         Foreign Currency Due from Broker 40
             Exchange Gain.. 40
                 To record the gain on the forward contract when the
                 year-end spot rate is FC = $1.04. At year end,
                 the 1,000 FC is worth $1,040 versus the $1,000
                 recorded initially.[5]

19X2

Feb. 1 Dollars Due to Broker............................... 1,012
         Investment in Foreign Currency.................... 1,100
             Foreign Currency Due from Broker 1,040
             Cash 1,012
             Exchange Gain... 60
                 To record the settlement of the forward contract
                 when 1 FC = $1.10.

         Contract Expense 4
             Deferred Contract Premium.................................... 4
                 To amortize the balance of the forward contract
                 premium.

         Accounts Payable 1,040
         Exchange Loss... 60
             Investment in Foreign Currency............................... 1,100
                 To record the settlement of the liability when
                 1 FC = $1.10.

---

[4]An alternative for this entry would be a memo entry to describe the commitment resulting from the contract. Such treatment emphasizes the executory nature of the contract.

[5]If the contract is not recorded initially, exchange gains or losses would be recognized and an allowance for exchange gains or losses would be employed. For example, in the illustration the entry would be:

Allowance for Exchange Gains or Losses 40
    Exchange Gain... 40

Changes in the spot exchange rate affecting the hedging transaction are reflected in the account *Foreign Currency Due from (to) Broker* only. Notice that the account representing dollars due to (from) the broker is fixed in amount and does not change given exchange rate fluctuations. The previous entries reflect the objective of a forward contract, which is to hedge against exchange losses. The exchange loss which would have been experienced without the hedge had been offset effectively as illustrated below:

	Without the Hedge	With the Hedge
Exchange gain (loss) on foreign currency transaction [1,000 FC × ($1.10 − $1.00)]	($100)	($100)
Exchange gain (loss) on hedge [1,000 FC × ($1.10 − $1.00)]	—	100
Contract expense	—	(12)
Net income effect	($100)	($12)

Unfortunately not all hedging transactions are as effective in reducing foreign currency transaction exchange losses. For instance, a forward contract may not cover the entire period between transaction date and settlement date. Therefore, a portion of the time frame is not hedged effectively and exchange losses may occur. In addition, when a forward contract establishes a forward rate, it is possible that changes in the spot rate may not move in the same direction. Considering the previous transactions, assume the same facts except that the spot rates are as follows:

Date	Rate
November 1, 19X1	1 FC = $1.00
December 31, 19X1	1 FC = 0.98
February 1, 19X2	1 FC = 0.96

In effect, the hedge eliminated potential exchange gains as follows:

	Without the Hedge	With the Hedge
Exchange gain (loss) on foreign currency transaction [1,000 FC × ($.96 − $1.00)]	$40	$40
Exchange gain (loss) on hedge [1,000 FC × ($.96 − $1.00)]	—	(40)
Contract expense	—	(12)
Net income effect	$40	($12)

It is important to note that forward contracts also may be used to sell foreign currencies at a more favorable rate than the spot rate existing at the settlement date. To illustrate, assume that a domestic company sells goods to a foreign purchaser for 1,000 FC when the spot rate is 1 FC = $1, and assume that the receivable is to be paid in sixty days in foreign currency. If the spot rate at the settlement date was 1 FC = $.95, the domestic company would have an exchange loss of $50 [1,000 FC × ($.95 − $1)]. A forward exchange contract to sell the 1,000 FC at a forward rate of 1 FC = $.98, or $980 (1,000 FC × $.98), would have reduced the exchange loss to a net amount of $20 [1,000 FC × ($.98 − $1)].

Hedge on Identifiable Foreign Currency Commitment. In the illustration on the preceding pages, the forward contract was acquired at the transaction date. However, it is possible to acquire a forward contract prior to the transaction date. For example, a domestic firm may enter into a noncancelable commitment with a foreign supplier to deliver goods in two months. The purchase transaction would not be recorded until the goods are delivered. However, at the time of the commitment, the U.S. company knows that exchange losses could be experienced if the dollar weakens relative to the foreign currency. In order to help reduce this potential risk and maintain the dollar basis of the transaction, the domestic firm could enter into a forward contract to receive foreign currency in two months. During the period between the commitment date and the transaction date, rate changes may give rise to gains or losses on such forward contracts. Of concern is whether these gains or losses should be recognized prior to the transaction date or be deferred until that date.

The dollar basis of a foreign currency transaction is established at the transaction date, not at the commitment date. To recognize a gain or loss on a forward contract during the commitment period would result partially in establishing the dollar basis of the transaction prior to the transaction date. Recognizing a gain or loss during the commitment period also could benefit (penalize) one period's net income and penalize (benefit) a subsequent period's net income. After considering the views of concerned parties, the FASB concluded that a gain or loss on a forward contract that met certain conditions should be deferred until the transaction date. At the transaction date, the deferred gain or loss would be considered in determining the dollar basis of the transaction. This treatment of the deferred gain or loss, in essence, follows the one-transaction method discussed earlier for foreign currency transactions. However, a loss should not be deferred if such deferral would result in an overall transaction loss being recognized at a later date.

To be considered a hedge on an identifiable foreign currency commitment, a foreign currency transaction must meet *both* of the following conditions:

(a) *The foreign currency transaction is designated as, and is effective as, a hedge of a foreign currency commitment.*
(b) *The foreign currency commitment is firm.*[6]

It is important to note that these two conditions relate to a foreign currency transaction. Although identifiable foreign currency commitments are

---

[6]*Statements of Financial Accounting Standards*, No. 52, op. cit., par. 21.

hedged frequently through the use of forward contracts, they also may be hedged with transactions that are not forward contracts. For example, if a foreign currency loan is to be repaid with the proceeds of an identifiable foreign currency sales transaction, the loan would be accounted for as a hedge on an identifiable foreign currency commitment. Application of the first condition technically is possible only after it is known whether the hedge offsets the transaction gain or loss.

Although the conditions previously discussed may be satisfied, the hedging transaction may exceed the amount of the related foreign currency commitment or extend beyond the time at which the transaction is settled. In these situations, the gain or loss on the transaction should be accounted for as follows:

1. The gain or loss traceable to the portion of the hedging transaction in excess of the commitment should be deferred to the extent that the transaction provides an aftertax hedge. The gain or loss so deferred should be included as an offset to the related tax effects in the period such tax effects are recognized.
2. That portion of a gain or loss on a hedging transaction in excess of the amount that provides a hedge on an aftertax basis should not be deferred.
3. The gain or loss traceable to the time period after the transaction date of the commitment should not be deferred.[7]

If a hedge on an identifiable foreign currency commitment is terminated before the transaction date of the commitment, any deferred gain or loss as of the termination date should continue to be deferred until the transaction date of the commitment.

To illustrate a hedge on an identifiable foreign currency commitment, assume the following:

1. The conditions necessary for the deferral of exchange gains or losses prior to the transaction date have been satisfied.
2. On January 1, 19X1, a domestic firm agrees to sell goods to a foreign customer, with delivery to be made on March 1, 19X1. The goods, valued at 1,000 FC and having a cost of $800, are to be paid for 60 days after delivery.
3. On January 1, 19X1, the domestic firm purchased a 120-day forward contract to sell 1,000 FC at a forward rate of 1 FC = $0.99.
4. Spot rates on selected dates are as follows:

Date	Rate
January 1, 19X1	1 FC = $1.00
March 1, 19X1	1 FC = 0.98
May 1, 19X1	1 FC = 0.96

---

[7]*Ibid.*

The following entries reflect the proper accounting for these facts:

19X1

Jan. 1	Dollars Due from Broker...	990	
	Deferred Contract Discount.......................................	10	
	Liability to Broker		1,000
	Purchase of the contract to sell 1,000 FC in 120 days		
	when the forward rate is 1 FC = $0.99.		

Mar. 1	Liability to Broker	20	
	Deferred Exchange Gain..		20
	To record the deferred gain on the forward contract		
	when the spot rate is 1 FC = $0.98.		

	Accounts Receivable..	980	
	Deferred Exchange Gain..	20	
	Sales..		1,000
	To record the sale when the spot rate is 1 FC = $0.98,		
	and to recognize the deferred gain on the forward		
	contract as an adjustment to sales.		

	Cost of Goods Sold..	800	
	Inventory		800
	To record the cost of goods sold.		

	Contract Expense...	5	
	Deferred Contract Discount.....................................		5
	To recognize the amortization of the contract discount		
	($10 × 60/120).[8]		

May 1	Foreign Currency..	960	
	Exchange Loss..	20	
	Accounts Receivable...		980
	To record the collection of the receivable when the		
	spot rate is 1 FC = $0.96.		

	Liability to Broker	980	
	Exchange Gain...		20
	Foreign Currency...		960
	To record the transfer of FC to the broker when the		
	spot rate is 1 FC = $0.96.		

	Cash..	990	
	Dollars Due from Broker.......................................		990
	To record the receipt of cash from the broker at the		
	established forward rate of 1 FC = $0.99.		

	Contract Expense...	5	
	Deferred Contract Discount.....................................		5
	To recognize the remaining amortization of the		
	contract discount.		

At the commitment date, the seller anticipated a gross profit of $200, which is the difference between the $800 inventory cost and the sales value

---

[8]As an alternative, the premium or discount amortization may be included in the determination of the dollar basis of the transaction, which would have been achieved by debiting Sales rather than Contract Expense.

of $1,000 (1,000 FC × spot rate of 1 FC = $1 at the commitment date). The hedge on the commitment was employed to preserve this anticipated gross profit on the sale. Extending the hedge past the transaction date was done to reduce the risk of exchange fluctuations affecting the collection value of the account receivable. The effect of the hedge on the foreign currency commitment is illustrated below:

	Desired Position	Without Hedge	With Hedge
Sales price	$1,000	$980*	$1,000
Cost of goods sold	(800)	(800)	(800)
Gross profit	$ 200	$180	$ 200
Exchange gain (loss) on foreign currency transaction	—	(20)**	(20)
Exchange gain (loss) on hedge	—	—	20
Contract expense	—	—	(10)
Net income effect	$ 200	$160	$ 190

*This represents the 1,000 FC at the March 1, 19X1 exchange rate of 1 FC = $0.98.
**This represents the 1,000 FC receivable originally recorded at $980 but collected for $960 when the exchange rate was 1 FC = $0.96.

If the risk of adverse exchange rate changes during the commitment period had not been hedged, the actual gross profit on the sale would have been reduced to $180. However, the hedge was effective in maintaining the original anticipated dollar basis of the transaction and allowed for the recognition of a $200 gross profit. Furthermore, extending the hedge beyond the transaction date resulted in offsetting the subsequent exchange rate loss. Once again, the direct cost to manage these risks was the contract expense of $10, which represented the difference between the original spot rate and the forward rate.

Although the illustration ignored the tax impact of the transactions, the FASB, as previously stated, provides for hedging on an aftertax basis. A hedge on an aftertax basis recognizes that there may be a tax impact associated with the foreign currency commitment itself and a separate tax impact associated with the gain or loss on the forward contract. In the illustration, for example, there is a tax impact associated with the sale of inventory and a tax impact associated with the gain on the forward contract to hedge the foreign currency commitment. The desired objective is for the gain (loss) on such a hedge less the net related tax impact to equal the exchange loss (gain) associated with the settlement of the foreign currency commitment.

Forward Contracts as Means of Speculation. In addition to employing forward contracts as a means of hedging an exposed position or a foreign currency commitment, they may be employed as a means of speculating in foreign currencies. Foreign currencies are traded actively as commodities and thus provide opportunities for speculation. For example, a U.S. investor might purchase a forward contract to sell foreign currency at a given forward rate. The investor may not even possess the foreign currency, but subsequently will attempt to sell the contract at a gain. A gain or loss on a contract held in speculation should be determined by:

. . . multiplying the foreign currency amount of the forward contract by the difference between the forward rate available for the remaining maturity of the contract and the contracted forward rate (or the forward rate last used to measure a gain or loss on that contract for an earlier period).[9]

In addition to the different basis for measuring a gain or loss on a speculative contract, no separate recognition is given to the premium or discount on the contract. To illustrate the accounting for a speculative contract, assume the following:

1. On November 1, 19X2, a calendar-year investor purchased a 90-day forward contract to buy 1,000 FC at a forward rate of 1 FC = $1.01, when the spot rate was 1 FC = $1.
2. On December 31, 19X2, the forward rate for a 30-day forward contract was 1 FC = $1.02.
3. On February 1, 19X3, the investor paid the broker and received the foreign currency. The spot rate was 1 FC = $1.03.

The following entries reflect the proper accounting for these facts:

19X2
Nov. 1   Foreign Currency Due from Broker 1,010
           Dollars Due to Broker..   1,010
                 To record the purchase of the forward contract when
                 the forward rate is 1 FC = $1.01.

Dec. 31 Foreign Currency Due from Broker   10
           Exchange Gain...   10
                 To recognize the speculation gain based on the
                 difference between the forward rate available for the
                 remaining maturity and the original forward rate
                 [1,000 FC × ($1.02 − $1.01)].

19X3
Feb. 1   Dollars Due to Broker... 1,010
           Cash   1,010
                 To record the payment to the broker at the agreed
                 rate of 1 FC = $1.01.

           Foreign Currency... 1,030
           Foreign Currency Due from Broker   1,020
           Exchange Gain...   10
                 To record the receipt of 1,000 FC when the spot
                 rate was 1 FC = $1.03.

Note that the investor's exchange gain prior to maturity was measured by the difference between forward rates and that no separate recognition was given to the contract premium. The total exchange gain of $20 is based on the difference between the spot rate at the maturity of the contract and the original forward rate [1,000 FC × ($1.03 − $1.01)].

Although the illustration assumed that the investor took delivery of the foreign currency, in a more typical situation an investor would not hold a

---

[9]*Statement of Financial Accounting Standards, No. 52, op. cit.*, par. 19.

forward contract to maturity but would sell the contract to another party. Assuming the same facts except that the investor sold the contract for $10 on December 31, 19X2, the following entry would have been made on December 31, in addition to the other November 1 and December 31 entries:

```
19X2
Dec. 31  Cash.............................................................    10
         Dollars Due to Broker.............................................  1,010
            Foreign Currency Due from Broker........................              1,020
```

As mentioned previously, the special treatment given forward contracts held for speculation also is required for other forward contracts to the extent they exceed:

1. That amount required to cover an exposed net asset or liability position, and/or
2. That amount needed to hedge on an aftertax basis an identifiable foreign currency commitment.

Summary. The presence of free or floating exchange rates and the accompanying volatility in such rates has affected significantly how domestic companies do business abroad. In addition, foreign currencies are viewed as commodities to be traded actively. This chapter has discussed the accounting for foreign currency transactions and several of the risk management actions which may be taken in response to exchange rate fluctuations. The various hedging transactions discussed are summarized as follows:

	Hedge on an Exposed Position	Hedge on an Identifiable Commitment	Speculative Hedge
Basic Purpose of Forward Contract	Reduce exchange rate risk between the transaction and settlement dates.	Maintain the anticipated dollar basis of the transaction by reducing exchange rate risk between the commitment and transaction dates.	Speculate on the changing value of the currencies.
Recognition of Gain or Loss on Forward Contract	Recognize on an accrual basis as a component of net income.	Defer gain or loss experienced between the commitment and transaction dates. Adjust the dollar basis of the transaction by the deferred amount. Gains or losses subsequent to the transaction date are recognized on an accrual basis as a component of net income.	Recognize on an accrual basis as a component of net income.

	Hedge on an Exposed Position	Hedge on an Identifiable Commitment	Speculative Hedge
Measurement Basis for Gain or Loss on Forward Contract	Difference between the spot rates over the life of the contract.	Difference between the spot rates on the commitment and transaction dates for the deferred amount. Difference between the spot rates on the transaction and settlement dates for the amount included as a component of net income.	Difference between the forward rates over the life of the contract.
Accounting for Contract Premium or Discount	Recognize over the life of the contract as a financing expense.	Recognize over the life of the contract as a financing expense. As an alternative, adjust the dollar basis of the transaction for the premium or discount amortization between the commitment and transaction dates.	No separate recognition but rather becomes part of the investment basis.

QUESTIONS

1. Explain how a spot rate differs from a forward rate.
2. Explain how the direct and indirect exchange rates are affected when the U.S. dollar strengthens against the Japanese yen.
3. Assuming a British company buys inventory from a U.S. company, what conditions must exist in order for an exchange gain to be experienced by the U.S. company?
4. A domestic company is purchasing inventory abroad, and the dollar is expected to strengthen relative to the foreign currency. Would the

domestic company prefer to have the transaction denominated in dollars or in the foreign currency?

5. How is the difference between the spot rate and the forward rate accounted for in a hedge of an exposed liability position?

6. Under what conditions would a hedge on an exposed asset position result in offsetting exchange gains?

7. What are the criteria for a hedge on an identifiable foreign currency commitment?

8. Explain how the gain or loss on a hedge on an identifiable foreign currency commitment should be accounted for if the amount of the hedge exceeds the amount of the commitment.

9. What is the proper accounting for a contract discount or premium on a hedge held for speculative purposes?

EXERCISES

Exercise 1. Hartford Industries purchases component parts from a variety of Japanese suppliers and then assembles the parts in the United States. The finished goods are sold primarily to Canadian companies. On June 1, 19X8, Hartford purchased units from a Japanese vendor for 2,000,000 yen denominated in dollars. An additional 3,000,000 yen of goods were purchased on June 10, 19X8, with the transaction being denominated in yen. Hartford paid both invoices on July 10, 19X8. These units were assembled and sold to a Canadian firm on July 15, 19X8, for 80,000 Canadian dollars, to be settled on July 30, 19X8, in Canadian dollars. Relevant direct exchange rates are as follows:

	Foreign Currency in U.S. Dollars	
Date	Japanese Yen	Canadian Dollars
June 1, 19X8	$0.0076	$0.83
June 10, 19X8	0.0077	0.83
June 30, 19X8	0.0075	0.85
July 10, 19X8	0.0081	0.85
July 15, 19X8	0.0081	0.86
July 30, 19X8	0.0084	0.87

Prepare the journal entries to record all the transactions of Hartford Industries assuming monthly statements are prepared on an accrual basis.

Exercise 2. Given the facts of Exercise 1, assume that Hartford had decided to purchase a forward contract on June 10, 19X8, for purchasing yen. Hartford wants the forward contract to offset the net effect on income of both the Japanese and Canadian transactions. Define the contract terms so that there would be no overall net exchange gain or loss including contract expenses.

Exercise 3. On October 1, 19X8, Jem Company delivered goods to a West German company. The invoice amount of 300,000 deutsche marks (DM) is payable on January 31, 19X9, in DM. On November 1, 19X8, Jem purchased a 90-day forward contract to sell 300,000 DM at a forward rate of $0.56. Direct spot rates are as follows:

| October 1, 19X8 | $0.54 | December 31, 19X8 | $0.53 |
| November 1, 19X8 | 0.55 | January 31, 19X9 | 0.52 |

Assuming Jem's year end is December 31, prepare the journal entries necessary for Jem to account for all the transactions.

Exercise 4. Batiste Designers contracted to purchase fine quality silk from a Far Eastern country on February 1, 19X2. Batiste agreed to purchase 300 yards at 90 FC per yard, with delivery to be made on May 1, 19X2. Payment is due in foreign currency 30 days after delivery. Batiste acquires forward contracts to buy and sell foreign currency on a regular basis to prevent possible losses due to changes in the value of the foreign currency and as a means of speculation. They acquired such a contract on February 1, 19X2, for the purchase of 40,000 FC on June 1, 19X2. Exchange rates are as follows:

Date	Spot Rate	Forward Rate for Remaining Maturity of Contract
February 1, 19X2	1 FC = $.123	1 FC = $.127
May 1, 19X2	1 FC = .128	1 FC = .130
June 1, 19X2	1 FC = .126	—

Prepare the journal entries necessary for Batiste Designers to record the purchase and the forward contract activity. Ignore all tax implications.

Exercise 5. Maxwell Enterprises purchases forward exchange contracts for a variety of reasons. Determine the effect on 19X8 net income of each of the following hedging transactions.

(1) Forward Contract A was purchased on November 1, 19X8, for speculative purposes at a forward rate of 1 FC = $1.45 when the spot rate was $1.50. This 90-day contract to buy 100,000 FC has a forward rate of $1.43 on December 31, 19X8.

(2) Forward Contract B was purchased on September 1, 19X8, as a hedge against a commitment to take delivery of equipment on December 1, 19X8. The equipment will be used by Maxwell in its manufacturing division and has a cost of 100,000 FC. Maxwell must settle the transaction in FC on February 1, 19X9. The 150-day forward contract to buy 80,000 FC had a forward rate of $1.47. The spot rates on September 1, 19X8, December 1, 19X8, and December 31, 19X8, were $1.49, $1.48, and $1.475, respectively.

(3) Forward Contract C was purchased on October 1, 19X8, to cover an exposed asset position when the spot and forward rates were $1.48 and $1.49, respectively. The contract to sell 30,000 FC expired on December 1, 19X8, when the spot rate was $1.48.

(4) Forward Contract D was purchased for speculation and had terms identical to Contract C. Maxwell sold the contract on November 1, 19X8, for $250 net of commissions.

‖‖‖

PROBLEMS

Problem 11-1.   Milwaukee Specialty Foods Inc. is a large purveyor of sausage and other processed meat products. The majority of Milwaukee Specialty's sales and purchase transactions are with U.S. firms. In recent years, however, the firm has sold its products and, to a lesser extent, purchased supplies in West Germany. As an accommodation to German customers and suppliers, all of these transactions are denominated in deutsche marks.

To eliminate any possibility of losses due to a fall in the value of the German currency, Milwaukee Specialty always hedges its net creditor position in deutsche marks by writing forward contracts to deliver that currency to brokers. These hedges are on existing transactions rather than identifiable commitments. The most recent forward contract was entered into on December 15, 19X2, and called for the firm to deliver 400,000 deutsche marks in 90 days.

In addition to the transactions related to German activities, Milwaukee Specialty is involved in two other forward contracts. The first of these, a contract to purchase 1,000,000 Canadian dollars, originally was entered into on July 1, 19X1, as a hedge against possible exchange losses on a loan from a Montreal bank, which is to be repaid in Canadian dollars on June 30, 19X3. The other forward contract that Milwaukee Specialty held was a commitment to purchase 1,000,000 Mexican pesos on March 1, 19X3. This contract was entered into on December 1, 19X2, with the intention of earning a profit on excess funds that the firm's treasurer forecasted for early 19X3.

The following table presents relevant rates for the forward contracts:

Date	Type of Rate	Rate in U.S. Dollars
Deutsche Marks		
December 15, 19X2	Spot	1 = $.40
December 15, 19X2	Forward	1 = .42
December 31, 19X2	Spot	1 = .38
December 31, 19X2	Forward	1 = .40
Canadian Dollars		
July 1, 19X1	Spot	1 = .90
July 1, 19X1	Forward	1 = .92
December 31, 19X1	Spot	1 = .88
December 31, 19X2	Spot	1 = .90
December 31, 19X2	Forward	1 = .92
Mexican Pesos		
December 1, 19X2	Spot	1 = .04
December 1, 19X2	Forward	1 = .05
December 31, 19X2	Spot	1 = .03
December 31, 19X2	Forward	1 = .04

Required:

Compute the gain or loss on each of Milwaukee Specialty's forward contracts for the year ended December 31, 19X2. Do not attempt to compute the total foreign exchange gain or loss.

Problem 11–2.   Austin Engineering Corporation assembles small pocket calculators, which it sells primarily in domestic markets. However, Austin has been developing sales markets in France and has been purchasing subassemblies from a Japanese manufacturer. Selected transactions for 19X8 are as follows:

(a) On March 1, Austin purchased 6,000 calculator subassemblies from the Japanese manufacturer for a total price of $9,600, to be paid in dollars on April 20, 19X8. On March 1, the exchange rate was 1 yen = $.37.

(b) On May 5, Austin sold 22,000 calculators to a French importer for a total selling price of 1,350,000 francs. At the time of the sale, the exchange rate was 1 franc = $.18; however, when payment was received in francs on May 26, 19X8, the exchange rate was 1 franc = $.22.

(c) On July 2, 19X8, Austin purchased more subassemblies from the Japanese manufacturer; however, due to changing economic conditions, the entire purchase price of $36,900 was to be paid in yen on September 1. The relevant exchange rates were:

July 2..   1 yen = $.41
September 1 ....   1 yen = $.44

On July 2, to hedge against future currency devaluations, Austin purchased a 60-day forward contract to buy yen at a forward rate of 1 yen = $.43.

(d) Another major sale for 1,000,000 francs was made to the French importer on September 8, 19X8, when the exchange rate was 1 franc = $.23. On September 25, when the exchange rate was 1 franc = $.22, Austin purchased a 30-day forward contract to sell 1,000,000 francs at a forward rate of 1 franc = $.19. When payment in francs was received from the importer on October 25, 19X8, the exchange rate was 1 franc = $.18.

(e) A final 19X8 purchase of subassemblies took place on December 16, when the exchange rate was 1 yen = $.40. The purchase price of 200,000 yen was to be paid on January 25, 19X9. At the time of the purchase, Austin acquired a 30-day forward contract to buy the yen at a forward rate of 1 yen = $.42.

(f) To plan properly for a noncancelable commitment to purchase subassemblies for delivery on March 25, 19X9, Austin acquired on December 26, 19X8, a 90-day forward exchange contract to buy yen at a forward rate of 1 yen = $.45. On December 26, the exchange rate was 1 yen = $.41. The forward exchange contract was for 210,000 yen, all of which will be used to cover the noncancelable commitment.

(g) The following exchange rates are in effect on December 31, 19X8:

1 yen   = $.42
1 franc = $.17

Required:

Assuming that Austin's year end is December 31, prepare the 19X8 journal entries to account for all of Austin's transactions.

Problem 11–3.   On November 1, 19X8, Allis Fashions, which has a calendar year end, agreed to purchase inventory from a French designer for 1,700,000 French francs (FF). The inventory is to be delivered on December 15, 19X8. The goods have a sales value of $300,000. The shipment must be paid for on January 31, 19X9, in FF. In order to maintain the anticipated gross profit on the merchandise, Allis purchased a forward contract on November 1, 19X8, to buy FF at a forward rate of $0.175. The forward contract, which expires on February 28, 19X9, is designated as a hedge on the purchase commitment and is expected to be effective as such. Assume that the inventory is sold subsequently for $250,000 on January 15, 19X9, and that selected direct spot rates are as follows:

November 1, 19X8	$0.170	January 15, 19X9	$0.182
December 15, 19X8	0.175	January 31, 19X9	0.185
December 31, 19X8	0.180	February 28, 19X9	0.187

Required:
(1) Prepare all the necessary journal entries for Allis to record the previous transactions.
(2) Prepare a schedule which calculates the net income effect of (a) the desired position, (b) the position without the hedge, and (c) the position with the hedge.

Problem 11–4.   Jenner Corporation recently has begun to expand its international markets and has engaged in several foreign currency transactions. In one particular series of transactions, the company purchased components from a French manufacturer on October 1, 19X8. The components cost 800,000 French francs (FF), and Jenner anticipated that the components could be assembled at its Kentucky plant for an additional cost of $40,000. Upon receipt of the goods on October 20, 19X8, Jenner entered into an agreement with a British company to purchase the finished goods for $224,900, to be settled in British pounds. The goods will be shipped on November 30, 19X8, with payment to be received on January 20, 19X9.

Required:
(1) Assuming that the liability to the French vendor becomes due before the payment from the British company is received, how can Jenner protect itself against fluctuations in the respective foreign currencies?
(2) Assuming that the payment to the French vendor is due subsequent to the receipt of pounds from the British company, how can Jenner guard against foreign currency fluctations relative to the dollar?
(3) Assume that on October 20, 19X8, Jenner purchases a forward contract to sell British pounds for 800,000 French francs on January 20, 19X9. Assume that the payment to the French vendor may be paid on or after

January 20, 19X9. Given the following rates, calculate the contract premium or discount on the forward contract.

Spot rates as of October 20, 19X8:

1 pound = $1.73
1 pound = 17.3 francs
1 franc = 0.058 pounds
1 franc = $0.10

Forward rate as of October 20, 19X8, for delivery on January 20, 19X9:

1 pound = 16 francs

(4) Assume the same spot and forward rates as given in (3) and that the following additional forward rates are available:

Forward rates as of October 20, 19X8, for delivery on January 20, 19X9:

1 pound = $1.72
1 dollar = 9.5 francs

Calculate whether Jenner is better off (a) using one forward contract of 50,000 pounds for 800,000 francs to settle the amount due the French vendor or (b) buying two contracts: one to sell 50,000 pounds for dollars and the other to sell dollars for 800,000 francs.

Problem 11–5.   Wollner Manufacturing Inc. began purchasing inventory from a foreign supplier. Its first purchase was delivered on October 1, 19X8, with payment due on October 31, 19X8. The inventory with a cost of 100,000 foreign currencies (FC) was denominated in dollars. A second purchase of materials was delivered on October 15, 19X8, with payment due in FC on November 15, 19X8, in the amount of 150,000 FC. Due to major volatility in the exchange rates, management decided to hedge the exposed liability by securing a forward exchange contract on October 15, 19X8. The contract to purchase 170,000 FC at a forward rate of $1.72 expires on November 15, 19X8. Late in October, it became apparent that inventory shortages were developing. So the company signed a commitment on October 31, 19X8, to purchase 200,000 FC of inventory to be delivered on November 30, 19X8. The purchase is denominated in FC with payment due on January 31, 19X9. In order to secure the gross profit anticipated on the future sale of the goods, Wollner decided to hedge the FC commitment by purchasing on October 31, 19X8, a contract to buy FC to be delivered on January 31, 19X9. This contract for 200,000 FC had a forward rate of $1.74. Assume that contract premium or discount on the hedge of an identifiable commitment will not be deferred.

Required:
Assuming that Wollner has a calendar year end, prepare all the necessary journal entries for Wollner to record the previously described events. Selected direct spot rates are as follows:

October 1, 19X8	$1.710	November 30, 19X8	$1.737
October 15, 19X8	1.720	December 31, 19X8	1.750
October 31, 19X8	1.725	January 31, 19X9	1.754
November 15, 19X8	1.731		

Problem 11–6.   Assume the same facts as given in Problem 11–5 but with the following different spot rates:

October 1, 19X8	$1.710	November 30, 19X8	$1.660
October 15, 19X8	1.705	December 31, 19X8	1.650
October 31, 19X8	1.683	January 31, 19X9	1.642
November 15, 19X8	1.670		

Required:

Prepare a schedule to calculate the net income effect of Wollner's transactions.

CHAPTER 12

TRANSLATION OF FOREIGN CURRENCY FINANCIAL STATEMENTS

The previous chapter identified a variety of transactions which may occur between a domestic (U.S.) company and a foreign entity. These transactions were not dependent on the domestic company having any type of ownership interest in the foreign entity. However, many domestic companies do have an ownership interest in or control of foreign companies, and accounting for these interests presents special problems. The accounting treatments of domestic and foreign entity relationships which involve some degree of control are summarized as follows:

Domestic Entity	Foreign Entity	Accounting Treatment
Home Office	Branch	Branch accounting
Parent	Subsidiary	Consolidated financial statements or separate financial statements
Investor	Investee	Investment in foreign entity at cost or equity

DEVELOPMENT OF ACCOUNTING AND TRANSLATION PRINCIPLES

The financial statements of the foreign investee or branch must be presented in such a way that they can be consolidated or combined with the domestic financial statements. Two special problems occur when the domestic company invests in a foreign operation. First, it is possible that the foreign statements have been prepared on a basis other than generally accepted accounting principles (GAAP) and, therefore, must be adjusted accordingly. Second, the foreign financial statements typically are prepared in a foreign currency which must be translated into the domestic entity's reporting currency. Only after dealing with these two complications will the foreign financial statements be compatible with the domestic financial statements.

DIFFERENCES IN ACCOUNTING PRINCIPLES

Various factors have influenced the development of accounting principles in different countries. Among these factors are: (1) the degree of self-regulation by the accounting profession, (2) business customs, (3) tax legislation, (4) legal traditions, and (5) inflationary factors. These elements have contributed to the development of accounting principles which are different than GAAP. For instance, tax allocation and Lifo inventory methods are not common to many foreign countries. In addition, the tax systems found in some foreign countries are significantly different than that of the U.S. In order to show more specifically the differences in accounting principles between countries, the following examples are presented:

> Inventory Accounting—Lower of cost or market is required in the Philippines, Spain, Australia, and South Africa. Lifo cannot be used in Brazil, Denmark, or Sweden. In West Germany, Italy, the Netherlands, and South Africa, Lifo is acceptable provided that the current value of the ending inventory is disclosed.

> Property and Depreciation—Property may be revalued in several countries, including the British Isles, Spain, Australia, the Philippines, and France. In the United Kingdom, intangibles normally are not amortized. Only straight-line depreciation is recognized for audit purposes in Canada.

> Capitalization of Leases—The capitalization of leases is not recognized in West Germany, Japan, France, or the United Kingdom.

> Accounting for Goodwill—Italy allows either the capitalization and amortization of goodwill or the immediate write-off of goodwill against stockholders' equity or income. Similar alternatives are available in the British Isles, the Netherlands, and West Germany.

> Accounting for Changes in Accounting Principles—Statements of prior years must be adjusted retroactively in Canada, the British Isles, and South Africa. The effect of a change must be included in the current year's income in France, Germany, and Italy.

The significant growth in international markets and investment opportunities has led to a global economy in which more uniform financial reporting is being sought. Managers of international companies need to compare the operating results of segments located in different foreign areas. Such comparability is possible only if all segments employ similar principles which are not affected by local differences. Investment opportunities now are available on an international scale, and investors need comparable financial information regardless of the country in which the investment is located. In recent years, considerable effort has been devoted to the development of international accounting standards. In 1973, the members of the Accountants' International Study Group (AISG) established the International Accounting Standards Committee (IASC), which has issued Statements of International Accounting Standards dealing with a variety of financial reporting topics. The members of the IASC are encouraging their respective countries to conform their standards to those of the IASC and to disclose any departures from established IASC standards. Similar efforts are being undertaken by the European Economic Community (EEC) and the International Federation of Accountants (IFAC), which was established in 1977. The international accounting standards being generated by these organizations have been extremely valuable in furthering the financial reporting systems of many companies and eliminating less useful alternative accounting methods. Because of the need to appeal to a broad range of participating countries, the standards which are developed tend to be more general and less sophisticated than GAAP in the U.S.

To provide useful information, the financial statements of foreign entities must be adjusted to conform to GAAP. This conformity of accounting principles is required by the U.S. accounting profession, the Securities and Exchange Commission, and the Internal Revenue Service. Many foreign subsidiaries initially are required by their parent companies to develop accounting systems which produce financial information in conformity with GAAP; therefore, the need to adjust foreign statements is eliminated.

PREVIOUS APPROACHES TO TRANSLATION

For entities doing business in several currencies, the need to convert or translate such amounts into a single reporting currency is an obvious practical necessity. As previously defined, translation is the process of expressing amounts denominated or measured in foreign currencies into amounts measured in the reporting currency (dollars) of the domestic (U.S.) entity. However, the development of a rational and acceptable translation method has been difficult because several issues are involved in the translation process. For example, a decision must be made as to whether current or historical exchange rates should be employed. In addition, the translation method must specify which accounts will be translated at the various rates. If different accounts are translated at different rates, the basic balance sheet equation will not balance, and the necessary balancing amount must be accounted for and interpreted.

In the following paragraphs, the translation methods that have been used in the past will be discussed briefly. A review of these methods will highlight the various theories that have been applied to the issues involved in the translation process.

Current-Noncurrent Method. The *current-noncurrent method* was presented in Chapter 12 of Accounting Research Bulletin No. 43 and for many years was viewed as the established method of translation. According to this method, the balance sheet classification of assets and liabilities determines which exchange rate should be employed in translation. Current items would be translated at the current exchange rate, while noncurrent items would be translated at the historical rate that existed when the asset or liability was recorded originally. The translation of current and noncurrent items at different rates results in an inequality that represents the gain or loss due to exchange rate fluctuations (exchange gain or loss).

Opponents of this method point out that the balance sheet classification of an item, versus the attribute of the item being measured, determines its translation rate. The treatments of inventory and long-term debt frequently are cited as examples of how the strict application of the current-noncurrent method fails to achieve the objectives of translation. For example, if a foreign subsidiary incurred a long-term debt, originally stated at 1,000 FC, when the exchange rate was 1 FC = $1 and if the current exchange rate is 1 FC = $1.10, the debt would be translated to $1,000. If the debt was settled currently, however, it would require an expenditure of 1,000 FC, or $1,100 if paid in dollars. Thus, the current-noncurrent method fails to recognize the current equivalent claim on domestic currency. Furthermore, the translation of inventory, a current item stated at historical cost, produces a measure that departs from historical cost but does not reflect current replacement cost or selling price.

ARB No. 43 applied a realization test for recognition of exchange gains and losses. Only realized gains were recognized, while both realized and unrealized losses were charged against income. Unrealized gains were deferred except to the extent that they offset previous unrealized losses in total.[1] Unfortunately, realization criteria were not established, and a cash transaction test was not used to distinguish between realized and unrealized items. Realization often was associated with the payment of dividends from the foreign unit to the domestic entity. The absence of sound criteria made the application of this section of ARB No. 43 impracticable.

The deficiencies of the current-noncurrent method were reduced as a result of certain exceptions prescribed in Chapter 12 of ARB No. 43. For example, if long-term debt or capital stock were issued in order to acquire long-lived assets shortly before exchange rates changed substantially and permanently, the related exchange gain or loss was to be accounted for as an adjustment to the basis of the acquired assets.

Monetary-Nonmonetary Method. APB Opinion No. 6, which modified Chapter 12 of ARB No. 43, permitted the use of the *monetary-nonmonetary method*. According to this method, the selection of an appropriate exchange

---

[1]*Accounting Research Bulletins, No. 43,* "Restatement and Revision of Accounting Research Bulletins" (New York: American Institute of Certified Public Accountants, 1961), Ch. 12, pars. 10–11.

rate is based on the characteristics of assets and liabilities. Monetary assets and liabilities are those which represent a fixed number of foreign currency units, while all other items are viewed as nonmonetary. Monetary items are translated at the current exchange rate, while other items are converted at the exchange rate that existed when the assets and liabilities were recorded originally. For example, inventory stated at replacement cost would be viewed as nonmonetary and, therefore, would be translated at the historical exchange rate. Thus, under this method the measurement of an item at current values has no effect on the exchange rate to be used. Exchange gains or losses generally would be accounted for in the same way as under the current-noncurrent method.

1971 Exposure Draft. In 1971, the Accounting Principles Board issued an exposure draft in response to significant currency realignments. The draft proposed that companies using the monetary-nonmonetary method defer exchange gains or losses that did not exceed the gains or losses related to long-term debt. The deferred items then would be amortized over the remaining life of the debt. Further action on the exposure draft was never taken; however, some companies adopted the principles of the draft.

Statement of Financial Accounting Standards, No. 1. Prior to 1973, domestic firms could employ any of the translation methods discussed previously. This situation prompted the FASB in 1973 to issue Statement of Financial Accounting Standards, No. 1, "Disclosure of Foreign Currency Translation Information." The Statement did not express a preference for any particular translation method, but it did require disclosure of the following information:

   a. *A statement of translation policies including identification of: (1) the balance sheet accounts that are translated at the current rate and those translated at the historical rate, (2) the rates used to translate income statement accounts (e.g., historical rates for specified accounts and a weighted average rate for all other accounts), (3) the time of recognition of gain or loss on forward exchange contracts, and (4) the method of accounting for exchange adjustments (and if any portion of the exchange adjustment is deferred, the method of disposition of the deferred amount in future years).*
   b. *The aggregate amount of exchange adjustments originating in the period, the amount thereof included in the determination of income and the amount thereof deferred.*
   c. *The aggregate amount of exchange adjustments included in the determination of income for the period, regardless of when the adjustments originated.*
   d. *The aggregate amount of deferred exchange adjustments, regardless of when the adjustments originated, included in the balance sheet*

(e.g., such as in a deferral or in a "reserve" account) and how this amount is classified.

e. *The amount by which total long-term receivables and total long-term payables translated at historical rates would each increase or decrease at the balance sheet date if translated at current rates.*

f. *The amount of gain or loss which has not been recognized on unperformed forward exchange contracts at the balance sheet date.*[2]

Statement of Financial Accounting Standards, No. 8. As a result of expanding activities of U.S. firms in foreign markets, changes in the international monetary system, and the existence of alternative translation methods, the FASB began an extensive study of foreign currency translation in 1973. This effort produced Statement of Financial Accounting Standards, No. 8, "Accounting for the Translation of Foreign Currency Transactions and Foreign Currency Financial Statements," which superseded sections of previous pronouncements dealing with foreign operations and translation (ARB No. 43, APB Opinion No. 6, and FASB Statement No. 1). The Statement emphasized that the translation process should change the unit of measure from foreign currency to dollars without changing the accounting principles. Therefore, the foreign entity's measurement bases and principles of revenue/expense recognition that conform to generally accepted accounting principles should not be affected by the translation process. The Statement evaluated alternative translation methods and recognized the temporal method as being most compatible with its objectives.

Under the *temporal method*, particular attention is paid to whether an accounting principle measures an asset or liability in terms of current values or past values. According to this method, the current exchange rate should be employed if the attribute measured represents the current command over foreign currency as portrayed by current values. If the attribute measured represents past foreign money prices (historical costs), however, the exchange rates that prevailed at that time should be employed. Therefore, the measurement of an attribute in foreign currency is translated into a measurement in dollars, while the foreign statement measurement base (current cost/historical cost) is retained. For example, money and receivables and payables presented in foreign currency statements represent the current amount of foreign money owned or promised. The attribute to be measured in terms of domestic currency is the command over domestic currency represented by those foreign monies. This temporal attribute can be measured by converting foreign monies owned or promised into domestic currency, using the current spot exchange rate that exists at the balance sheet date. Likewise, inventory stated at replacement cost would be translated at the current exchange rate.

---

[2]*Statement of Financial Accounting Standards, No. 1,* "Disclosure of Foreign Currency Translation Information" (Stamford: Financial Accounting Standards Board, 1973), par. 6.

In most instances, the use of the temporal method coincidentally produces the same results as would be achieved if the monetary-nonmonetary method were employed. However, the monetary-nonmonetary method focuses on the classification of items, while the temporal method focuses on the measurement bases (current or past monetary prices) used to measure the attributes of assets and liabilities. The most obvious difference in applying the two methods is that the temporal method uses the current exchange rate to translate nonmonetary items recorded at current value (e.g., inventory measured at market prices).

According to FASB Statement No. 8, exchange gains and losses that resulted from translation and foreign currency transactions should be included in the determination of net income for the period. The total exchange gain or loss should be disclosed either in the financial statements or in a related footnote. The FASB reasoned that gains and losses due to changes in the exchange rate are objectively measured historical facts and relate to the time period in which the rate change occurs.

STATEMENT OF FINANCIAL ACCOUNTING STANDARDS, NO. 52

Following its promulgation in 1975, Statement No. 8 became the subject of considerable controversy. When the Statement was applied, multinational corporations reported significant fluctuations in profits as a result of foreign currency exchange rate variations and the presentation of translation losses as a component of reported income. Statement No. 8 was criticized for its failure to reflect the underlying economic realities of foreign operations and rate changes and for its reporting requirements that resulted in data being volatile due to rate changes rather than operating factors. For example, assume a U.S. company has a British subsidiary whose only asset is an investment in securities of various British companies. The securities are valued at current values and have been acquired through the use of equity capital only. Assuming that the dollar weakens relative to the pound, translation into dollars under the temporal method would have resulted in the recognition of a translation loss. However, because the securities ultimately will be liquidated into pounds, the exchange rate between the pound and dollar has no bearing on the profitability of the British company.

In late 1981, after considering two exposure drafts in response to these criticisms, the FASB issued Statement of Financial Accounting Standards, No. 52, "Foreign Currency Translation." Statement No. 52 adopted a *functional currency* approach which should satisfy the following objectives in the translation process:

a. *Provide information that is generally compatible with the expected economic effects of a rate change on an enterprise's cash flows and equity.*

b. *Reflect in consolidated statements the financial results and relationships of the individual consolidated entities as measured in their* functional currencies *in conformity with U.S. generally accepted accounting principles.*[3]

The first objective of Statement No. 52 recognizes that exchange rate fluctuations may not have any real bearing on a foreign entity. The previous example of the British company owning securities demonstrates this point. The ultimate value of the securities to the entity will not be affected, regardless of how much the rate of exchange between the pound and dollar fluctuates. However, if the securities held were of U.S. companies which ultimately would be exchanged for dollars, exchange rate fluctuations would affect the British company's cash flows and equity.

The second objective recognizes that foreign companies may be rather autonomous and often operate in an environment which is significantly different than that of the U.S. The financial relationships and patterns which result from this different environment should not be changed by a translation process if the underlying environment has not changed. For example, if a foreign subsidiary, which operates exclusively in that foreign country, has a current ratio of 2.3:1, the current ratio after translation should remain 2.3:1. Certainly in this case the process of translation should not be able to change a company's current ratio.

Adoption of a translation method that fails to reflect properly the economic effects of rate changes may produce misleading results. FASB Statement No. 8 was subject to the major criticism that it resulted in the recognition of major translation losses that distorted earnings and had no effect on cash flows. The functional currency approach does not remeasure foreign operations as though they originally had been conducted in the domestic reporting currency. Rather, the functional currency approach retains the financial results and relationships that were influenced by the economic environment in which the foreign entity operates. Rate changes that do not have a current economic impact but do have a remote or uncertain implication for the enterprise should be excluded from net income.

IDENTIFYING THE FUNCTIONAL CURRENCY

In order to achieve the objectives of Statement No. 52, it is critical to identify the economic environment in which a foreign entity operates. The economic environment is identified by determining the currency in which the entity primarily generates and expends cash. The identified currency is referred to as the *functional currency*. For example, a West German company acquires factors of production (material, labor, equipment, etc.) from German sources to manufacture a product. The finished product is sold throughout West

---

[3]*Statement of Financial Accounting Standards, No. 52,* "Foreign Currency Translation" (Stamford: Financial Accounting Standards Board, 1981), par. 4.

Germany. Acquiring the necessary factors of production requires the expenditure of deutsche marks (DM) and sales revenues also are collected in DM. Given these facts, the deutsche mark would be identified as the functional currency because the company's operations are self-contained and integrated within West Germany. The identification of the functional currency is not always so clear, thereby requiring the use of professional judgment. If the German company sold its finished goods primarily in Japan and received payment in yen, a decision must be made as to whether the DM or the yen is the functional currency. It also is possible that a foreign entity might have more than one functional currency. This would occur if the entity had separable divisions or branches which are operated in different economic environments requiring cash flows in different currencies.

Identification of the functional currency is not subject to definitive criteria. However, certain basic economic factors should be considered in making this identification.[4] Some of these factors are summarized as follows:

Factors Suggesting the Functional Currency

Indicator	Foreign Currency as Functional Currency	Parent's Currency as Functional Currency
Cash flows	Cash flows are primarily in the foreign currency. Such flows do not impact the parent's cash flows.	Cash flows directly impact the parent's cash flows and are readily available to the parent.
Sales price	Sales prices are influenced by local factors rather than exchange rates.	Sales prices are influenced by international factors and exchange rate changes.
Sales market	There is an active and primarily local market.	The sales market is primarily in the parent's country.
Expenses	Goods and services are acquired locally and denominated in local currencies.	Goods and services are acquired from the parent's country.
Financing	Financing is secured locally and denominated in local currencies. Debt is serviced through local operations.	Financing is secured primarily from the parent or is denominated in the parent's currency.
Intercompany transactions and arrangements	Intercompany transaction volume is low. Major interrelationships between foreign and parent operations do not exist.	Intercompany transaction volume is high. There are major interrelationships between entities. Foreign entity holds major assets and obligations of the parent.

These factors should be considered both individually and collectively in order to identify the functional currency. The selection of a functional currency should be applied consistently over time, unless significant changes suggest that the functional currency has changed. Changes in the functional currency should not be accounted for on a retroactive basis or as a cumulative effect.

---

[4]*Ibid.*, par. 42.

BASIC TRANSLATION PROCESS: FUNCTIONAL CURRENCY TO REPORTING CURRENCY

Once a foreign entity's functional currency has been identified, it must be translated into the domestic entity's reporting currency (dollars for U.S. companies) using an appropriate exchange rate. In studying the problems associated with foreign currency translation, the FASB concluded that the results and relationships presented in functional currency financial statements would be retained if the translation was based exclusively on the current rate of exchange between the functional currency and the reporting currency. Generally, this *current rate* method is governed by the following procedures:

1. All assets and liabilities are translated at the current exchange rate at the date of translation.
2. Elements of income are translated at the current exchange rates that existed at the time that the revenues and expenses were recognized. As a practical consideration, income elements may be translated at a weighted average exchange rate for the period.
3. Equity accounts other than retained earnings are translated at historical exchange rates. If the domestic parent's investment in a foreign company has been acquired as a purchase (versus pooling of interests), the historical rate on the date of acquisition is used to translate equity accounts. If a pooling of interests has occurred, the original historical rate in effect when the foreign company experienced the equity transaction is used for translation purposes.
4. Translated retained earnings generally is equal to:
    a. the translated retained earnings at the end of the prior period plus
    b. the translated income (see item 2) less
    c. the value of dividends translated at the appropriate historical exchange rates.
    If the domestic company has acquired an interest in a foreign company during the current period, the retained earnings balance at the date of acquisition should be translated using the rate at that time. Only after the year of acquisition will retained earnings be translated as the sum of items a. through c.
5. Components of the statement of cash flows are translated at the exchange rates in effect at the time of the cash flows. Operations are translated at the rate used for income elements. The reconciliation of the change in cash and cash equivalents during the period should include the effect of exchange rate changes on cash balances.

In all translations that follow, it will be assumed that purchase accounting, rather than pooling of interests accounting, is appropriate unless otherwise stated.

ACCOUNTING FOR TRANSLATION ADJUSTMENTS

Translation adjustments result from the process of translating foreign financial statements from their functional currency into the domestic entity's reporting currency. Because various exchange rates (current, historical, and weighted average) are used in the translation process, the basic equality of the balance sheet equation is not preserved. Therefore, from a mechanical viewpoint, the translation adjustment is an amount necessary to balance a translated entity's trial balance. Translation adjustments do not have a direct effect on reporting currency cash flows. However, they do have an indirect effect on the net investment in the foreign entity but not on the operations of the foreign entity. The indirect effect is considered to be so remote and/or uncertain that translation adjustments should be accumulated as a separate component of equity and thereby excluded from the determination of earnings. Since translation adjustments may be realized upon the sale, complete liquidation, or substantially complete liquidation of the investment in the foreign entity, the indirect effect on the net investment is realized as a part of the gain or loss on disposal of the investment.[5]

Although the translation adjustment is a balancing amount necessary to satisfy the balance sheet equation, the current period's adjustment may be calculated directly as follows:

1. The change in exchange rates during the period multiplied by the amount of net assets (i.e., owners' equity) held by the domestic investor at the beginning of the period, plus
2. The difference between the weighted average exchange rate used in translating income elements and the end-of-period exchange rate multiplied by the increase or decrease in net assets for the period, excluding capital transactions, plus (minus)
3. The increase (decrease) in net assets as a result of capital transactions, including investments by the domestic investor during the period (e.g., stock issuances and retirements and dividends), multiplied by the difference between the end-of-period exchange rate and the exchange rate at the time of the transaction.

DEMONSTRATING THE TRANSLATION PROCESS

The principles of translation previously discussed will be applied to the preparation of foreign subsidiary or branch statements for consolidation or

---

[5]See *FASB Interpretation No. 37*, "Accounting for Translation Adjustments upon Sale of Part of an Investment in a Foreign Entity" (Stamford: Financial Accounting Standards Board, 1983) and *Statement of Financial Accounting Standards, No. 52, op. cit.*, pars. 110 and 119.

combination with domestic entity or home office statements. One of the primary criteria established to determine if consolidation is appropriate deals with the extent of control the parent corporation exercises over the subsidiary. With respect to foreign subsidiaries, effective control is determined, in part, by currency restrictions and the possibility of nationalization of the operation by foreign governments. Assuming that consolidation is appropriate, the financial statements of the foreign entity must be translated into dollars according to the principles expressed in FASB Statement No. 52. Then intercompany eliminations are made, and the statements are consolidated according to the principles of consolidation discussed earlier in this text.

Unconsolidated foreign investments also must be translated. Unconsolidated subsidiaries are accounted for according to either the cost method or the equity method. The method used depends upon whether certain criteria established in APB Opinion No. 18 are satisfied.

Under the cost method, the investment in the subsidiary is carried at its original cost plus additional investments less the cost of securities sold. With respect to translation, this method does not present any specific difficulties if payments in foreign currency are translated into dollars at the appropriate exchange rate. If factors existing in the environment of a foreign country suggest a permanent impairment in the value of the investment, the basis of the investment should be reduced appropriately.

Foreign statements of an investee accounted for by the equity method first should be translated into dollars before the equity method is applied. As in the case of the cost method, if a permanent impairment in the value of the investment occurs, the basis of the investment should be reduced appropriately. The use of the equity method will be demonstrated later in the chapter.

Illustration 12–1, which is an example of a foreign subsidiary translation, is based on the following facts:

1. Fori Corporation began operations on January 1, 19X0. On January 1, 19X1, when net assets totaled 100,000 foreign currencies (FC), 90% of Fori stock was acquired by Dome Corporation. Fori's functional currency is the foreign currency, and it maintains its records in the functional currency.
2. Sales to Dome are billed in the foreign currency, and all receivables from Dome have been collected, except for the amount shown in the account *Due from Dome*. All other sales are billed in the foreign currency as well. The level of sales and purchases was constant over the year.
3. Selected exchange rates between the functional currency and the dollar are as follows:

Date	Rate
January 1, 19X0	1 FC = $0.98
January 1, 19X1	1 FC = 1.00
December 31, 19X1	1 FC = 1.05
19X1 average	1 FC = 1.03

Illustration 12–1
Fori Corporation
Trial Balance Translation
December 31, 19X1

Account	Balance in Functional Currency	Relevant Exchange Rate ($/FC)	Balance in Dollars
Cash	10,000 FC	1.05	$ 10,500
Accounts Receivable..........................	20,000	1.05	21,000
Due from Dome	15,000	1.05	15,750
Inventory (at cost)	30,000	1.05	31,500
Prepaid Insurance............................	3,000	1.05	3,150
Land (acquired March 1, 19X1)...........	25,000	1.05	26,250
Depreciable Assets	120,000	1.05	126,000
Cost of Goods Sold	180,000	1.03	185,400
Depreciation Expense	13,000	1.03	13,390
Income Tax Expense.........................	30,000	1.03	30,900
Other Expenses (including interest)....	20,000	1.03	20,600
Total debits..................................	466,000 FC		$484,440
Accounts Payable.............................	20,000 FC	1.05	$ 21,000
Taxes Payable.................................	30,000	1.05	31,500
Accrued Interest Payable..................	1,000	1.05	1,050
Mortgage Payable—Land	20,000	1.05	21,000
Common Stock	80,000	1.00	80,000
Retained Earnings	20,000	Note A	20,000
Sales—Dome	80,000	1.03	82,400
Sales—Other..................................	200,000	1.03	206,000
Gain on Sale of Depreciable Assets....	2,000	1.03	2,060
Allowance for Doubtful Accounts.......	1,000	1.05	1,050
Accumulated Depreciation.................	12,000	1.05	12,600
Cumulative Translation Adjustment (to balance).................................	—	—	5,780
Total credits.................................	466,000 FC		$484,440

Note A—The beginning balance of retained earnings normally is equal to the translated value of the previous period's ending retained earnings. However, since 19X1 is the first year Dome has owned Fori, the beginning balance is set equal to the January 1, 19X1 (acquisition date) balance of retained earnings in foreign currency translated at the January 1, 19X1 spot rate. The balance sheet for 19X1 would show a translated value for retained earnings equal to the translated beginning balance of retained earnings plus the translated value of net income less dividends translated at the rate existing on the declaration date.

(continued)

Recomputation of Translation Adjustment

Net assets owned by the investor at beginning of period multiplied by the change in exchange rates during the period [0 × ($1.05 − $1.00)]..	$ 0
Increase in net assets (excluding capital transactions) multiplied by the difference between the current rate and the average rate used to translate income [39,000 FC × ($1.05 − $1.03)].................	780
Increase in net assets due to capital transactions (including investments by the domestic investor) multiplied by the difference between the current rate and the rate at the time of the capital transaction [100,000 FC × ($1.05 − $1.00)]	5,000
Translation adjustment..	$5,780

Note that the recomputation measures only the $5,780 translation adjustment traceable to 19X1. After the first year of operation, the annual translation adjustments will be accumulated and presented as a component of equity. For example, if Fori Corporation has a translation adjustment of $4,400 traceable to 19X2, the equity section of the balance sheet at the end of 19X2 will show a cumulative adjustment of $10,180 ($5,780 + $4,400).

The translation demonstrated in Illustration 12–1 has accomplished the objectives of translation as presented in FASB Statement No. 52. The economic effect of the exchange rate change (i.e., translation adjustment) has been presented as an increase in stockholders' equity. The spot rate had increased from a beginning-of-the-year rate of 1 FC = $1.00 to an end-of-period rate of 1 FC = $1.05. This change indicates that the foreign currency strengthened relative to the dollar. Therefore, the domestic company's investment in the net assets of the foreign subsidiary has increased in accounting value as evidenced by the increase in stockholders' equity. The translated financial statements also reflect the same financial results and relationships of the foreign company as originally measured in its functional currency. For example, the following ratios indicate that the original relationships have been preserved after translation.

Ratio	Before Translation	After Translation
Current	1.53 (78,000 ÷ 51,000)	1.53 (81,900 ÷ 53,550)
Debt-to-equity	0.51 (71,000 ÷ 139,000)	0.51 (74,550 ÷ 145,950)
Gross profit %	36% (100,000 ÷ 280,000)	36% (103,000 ÷ 288,400)

CONSOLIDATING THE FOREIGN SUBSIDIARY

After a foreign entity's financial statements have been translated into the domestic reporting currency (dollars), they are used in preparing consolidated or combined financial statements or in accounting for the investment by the equity method. Preparation of consolidated financial statements also requires that certain eliminating entries be prepared.

In order to demonstrate the consolidated process, the facts of Illustration 12–1 will be discussed further. Assume that Dome Corporation paid 105,000 FC for its 90% interest in Fori Corporation, and recall that at the time of acquisition (January 1, 19X1) Fori equity consisted of 80,000 FC of common stock and 20,000 FC of retained earnings. Upon acquisition of Fori, Dome recorded its investment as follows:

Investment in Fori	105,000	
Cash (105,000 × $1.00)		105,000

The acquisition cost of 105,000 FC exceeds by 15,000 FC the 90,000 FC [90% × (80,000 FC + 20,000 FC)] book value of the net assets acquired. This excess of cost over book value is assumed to be traceable to undervalued equipment which is depreciated by the straight-line method and has a ten-year useful life. The initial difference between cost and book values should be calculated in the foreign currency and then translated into dollars using the rate of exchange at the date of acquisition.

Because the foreign subsidiary is to be consolidated, the simple equity method would be used. Therefore, the parent company would record its interest in the current-period income and declared dividends of the foreign subsidiary. However, Dome would not recognize the current-period amortization of the excess of cost over book value component of its investment. The 19X1 income for Fori and Dome's equity share are calculated as follows:

Account	Balance in Functional Currency	Relevant Exchange Rate ($/FC)	Balance in Dollars
Sales — Dome	80,000	1.03	$ 82,400
Sales — Other	200,000	1.03	206,000
Cost of Goods Sold	(180,000)	1.03	(185,400)
Gain on Sale of Depreciable Assets	2,000	1.03	2,060
Depreciation Expense	(13,000)	1.03	(13,390)
Income Tax Expense	(30,000)	1.03	(30,900)
Other Expenses (including interest)	(20,000)	1.03	(20,600)
Net Income	39,000		$ 40,170
Dome's share			90%
Dome's interest in Fori net income (in dollars)			$ 36,153

The parent's entry to record its interest in the foreign subsidiary's undistributed income would be as follows:

Investment in Fori	36,153	
Subsidiary Income		36,153

Worksheet 12–1, pages 714–716, shows the consolidated financial statements of Dome and Fori Corporations. The trial balance amounts for Dome are assumed and Fori's balances are based on Illustration 12–1. Steps (1) and (2) of the worksheet follow the usual procedures of eliminating the current-

Worksheet 12–1

Consolidating the
Dome Corporation and
Worksheet for Consolidated
For Year Ended

(Credit balance amounts are in parentheses.)

		Trial Balance	
		Dome Corp.	Fori Corp.
1	Cash	56,800	10,500
2	Accounts Receivable	112,000	21,000
3	Allowance for Doubtful Accounts	(5,600)	(1,050)
4	Inventory, Dec. 31, 19X1	154,700	31,500
5	Prepaid Insurance	9,050	3,150
6	Due from Dome		15,750
7	Investment in Fori Corporation	141,153	
8			
9			
10	Land	125,000	26,250
11	Depreciable Assets	500,000	126,000
12	Accumulated Depreciation	(100,000)	(12,600)
13	Accounts Payable	(112,000)	(21,000)
14	Taxes Payable	(150,000)	(31,500)
15	Accrued Interest Payable	(16,000)	(1,050)
16	Mortgage Payable—Land	(105,000)	(21,000)
17	Common Stock	(350,000)	(80,000)
18	Paid-In Capital in Excess of Par	(100,000)	
19	Retained Earnings, Jan. 1, 19X1	(116,000)	(20,000)
20	**Cumulative Translation Adjustment—Fori**		**(5,780)**
21	**Cumulative Translation Adjustment—Dome**		
22			
23	Sales—Dome		(82,400)
24	Sales—Other	(908,600)	(206,000)
25	Gain on Sale of Depreciable Assets	(8,600)	(2,060)
26	Cost of Goods Sold	703,850	185,400
27	Depreciation Expense	45,600	13,390
28	Income Tax Expense	108,000	30,900
29	Other Expenses (including interest)	51,800	20,600
30	Subsidiary Income	(36,153)	
31		0	0
32	Combined Net Income		
33	To Minority Interest		
34	Balance to Controlling Interest		
35	Total Minority Interest		
36	Retained Earnings, Controlling Interest, Dec. 31, 19X1		
37			

Foreign Subsidiary
Subsidiary Fori Corporation
Financial Statements (in dollars)
December 31, 19X1

WORKSHEET 12-1

Eliminations & Adjustments		Consolidated Income Statement	Minority Interest	Controlling Retained Earnings	Consolidated Balance Sheet	
Dr.	**Cr.**					
					67,300	1
					133,000	2
					(6,650)	3
					186,200	4
					12,200	5
	(5) 15,750					6
	(1) 36,153					7
	(2) 90,000					8
	(4) 15,000					9
					151,250	10
(4) 15,750					641,750	11
	(4) 1,575				(114,175)	12
(5) 15,750					(117,250)	13
					(181,500)	14
					(17,050)	15
					(126,000)	16
(2) 72,000			(8,000)		(350,000)	17
					(100,000)	18
(2) 18,000			(2,000)	(116,000)		19
(3) 5,202			(578)			20
	(3) 5,202				(5,922)	21
	(4) 720					22
(6) 82,400						23
		(1,114,600)				24
		(10,660)				25
	(6) 82,400	806,850				26
(4) 1,545		60,535				27
		138,900				28
		72,400				29
(1) 36,153						30
246,800	246,800					31
		(46,575)				32
		4,017	(4,017)			33
		42,558		(42,558)		34
		(14,595)			(14,595)	35
				(158,558)	(158,558)	36
					0	37

Eliminations and Adjustments:
(1) Eliminate the entries in the subsidiary income account against the investment in Fori account to record the parent's 90% controlling interest in the subsidiary.
(2) Eliminate 90% of the subsidiary's January 1, 19X1 equity balances against the balance of the investment account.
(3) Distribute the cumulative translation adjustment between controlling and minority interests.
(4) Distribute the excess of cost over book value of 15,000 FC and record appropriate amortization.
(5) Eliminate the intercompany trade balances.
(6) Eliminate the intercompany sales assuming that none of the goods purchased from Fori remain in Dome's ending inventory.

Subsidiary Fori Corp. Income Distribution

	Internally generated net income.....	$40,170
	Adjusted income	$40,170
	Minority share............................	10%
	Minority interest.........................	$ 4,017

Parent Dome Corp. Income Distribution

Equipment depreciation $1,545	Internally generated net income.....	$ 7,950
	Share of subsidiary income (90% × $40,170)........................	36,153
	Controlling interest......................	$42,558

period entry recording the parent's share of the subsidiary net income and its share of the subsidiary equity accounts as of the beginning of the period. Steps (5) and (6) follow the usual worksheet eliminations and adjustments for intercompany transactions. Step (3) allocates 90% of Fori's cumulative adjustment to the controlling interest.

Step (4) recognizes that the excess of cost over book value of 15,000 FC must be translated at the exchange rate existing at year end. However, the amortization of this excess must be translated at the average exchange rate for the period. These rates result in the following translated amounts for the worksheet entry:

Depreciable assets (15,000 FC × $1.05)..	$15,750
Accumulated depreciation (15,000 FC ÷ 10 × $1.05)............................	1,575
Depreciation expense (15,000 FC ÷ 10 × $1.03)	1,545

The cumulative adjustment included in step (4) results from changes in exchange rates which have occurred:

1. Since the excess at the beginning of the period was translated,
2. Since the accumulated amortization at the beginning of the period was translated, and
3. Since the current period's amortization of the excess was translated.

Because the excess of cost over book value is not recorded by the foreign subsidiary (assuming push-down accounting is not applied), the effect of such rate changes on this excess has not been included previously in the cumulative translation adjustment. The $720 additional cumulative adjustment traceable to the excess of cost over book value is determined as follows:

	Exchange Rate Used		
	Beginning or Average	End of Period	Difference
1. Excess at beginning of period...................	$15,000	$15,750	$750
2. Less accumulated amortization at beginning of period...............................	—	—	—
3. Less current amortization expense.............	(1,545)	(1,575)	(30)
Net balance...	$13,455	$14,175	$720

The consolidation procedures just discussed also are applicable to periods subsequent to the first year of acquisition. Although the methodology is the same, the following should be noted:

1. The parent must continue to recognize its interest in the amortization of any original excess of cost over book value.
2. Any additional cumulative adjustment traceable to the excess of cost over book value should continue to be recognized.

If the parent's interest in the foreign subsidiary is between 20 percent and 49 percent, the subsidiary will not be consolidated and the sophisticated equity method should be employed. The sophisticated equity method requires that subsidiary income or loss be adjusted for the amortization of differences between book and market values of the investment and any intercomany profits or losses. The application of the sophisticated equity method to an investment in a foreign entity will be demonstrated using the facts of Illustration 12–1.

Assume that Dome Corporation paid 35,000 FC ($35,000) for a 30% interest in Fori Corporation on January 1, 19X1, when Fori's equity was 100,000 FC. Any excess of cost is considered traceable to undervalued equipment which is depreciated by the straight-line method and has a ten-year remaining useful life. Dome's interest in the adjusted net income of Fori is calculated as follows:

Fori net income translated into dollars...	$40,170
Dome's share..	30%
Dome's interest in Fori net income...	$12,051
Amortization of excess related to the equipment [(35,000 FC − (30% × 100,000 FC)) ÷ 10 years × $1.03 average rate]...............................	(515)
Dome's equity share of Fori net income adjusted for amortization of excess...	$11,536

The investor also must recognize its interest in the cumulative translation adjustment for 19X1, calculated as follows:

Cumulative translation adjustment (from Illustration 12–1) $5,780
Dome's share 30%
Dome's interest in the cumulative translation adjustment $1,734

The following entries are to record Dome's interest in the foreign entity under the sophisticated equity method:

```
19X1
Jan.  1    Investment in Fori Corporation ........................   35,000
               Cash .....................................................        35,000
                  To record the initial investment of 35,000 FC
                  when the spot rate was 1 FC = $1.00.

Dec. 31    Investment in Fori Corporation ........................   13,270
               Subsidiary Income ....................................        11,536
               Cumulative Translation Adjustment ...............         1,734
                  To record share of net income adjusted for
                  the amortization of excess and share of
                  cumulative translation adjustment.
```

Notice that under the sophisticated equity method the investor recorded both the amortization of the excess of cost over book value and its share of the cumulative translation adjustment.

SPECIAL TRANSLATION ISSUES

The current rate approach to translation is not appropriate in cases where it does not capture adequately the economic effect of exchange rate changes on the reporting entity. These situations are described in the following paragraphs. The alternative translation method used in these situations is the temporal method, which was discussed previously and was adopted originally by FASB Statement No. 8.

Books of Record Not Maintained in Functional Currency. The translation process just illustrated was based on the assumption that the foreign entity maintained its records in the functional currency. It is possible that a foreign entity may maintain its records in a currency that is not its functional currency. For example, assume that a French company purchases materials from British vendors with amounts due payable in British pounds. The materials are assembled in France and then returned to England for resale. Sales revenues are collected in pounds. Considering the factors used to identify the functional currency, the pound would be the French company's functional currency. However, the French company maintains its books of record (accounting records) in French francs even though its functional currency is the British pound. Now assume that the French company had purchased its materials in the U.S., payable in dollars, and then sold the finished goods in the U.S., collectible in dollars. The company's functional currency would have been the dollar although it maintained its books of record in French francs.

When a foreign company's books of record are not maintained in the functional currency, remeasurement of the financial statements into the functional currency is required before translation can occur. The objective of remeasurement is to insure that the foreign entity's records and statements reflect the activities of the entity as transacted in its functional currency. Therefore, the remeasurement process is designed to produce records as though they had been maintained originally in the functional currency. This process requires the use of the temporal method.

The translation adjustment resulting from remeasurement is to be included as a component of the foreign entity's income. After the remeasurement process is complete, the functional currency statements are translated into the domestic reporting currency using the functional currency approach. However, if the functional currency is the dollar, remeasurement into the dollar eliminates the need for translation.

Under the temporal method, both current and historical exchange rates should be used. These exchange rates represent the relationship between the books of record currency and the functional currency. Examples of accounts that should be translated at historical rates are as follows:

> Marketable securities carried at cost:
>> Equity securities
>> Debt securities not intended to be held until maturity
> Inventories carried at cost
> Prepaid expenses such as insurance, advertising, and rent
> Property, plant, and equipment
> Accumulated depreciation on property, plant, and equipment
> Patents, trademarks, licenses, and formulas
> Goodwill
> Other intangible assets
> Deferred charges and credits, except deferred income taxes and policy
>> acquisition costs for life insurance companies
> Deferred income
> Common stock
> Preferred stock carried at issuance price
> Examples of revenues and expenses related to nonmonetary items:
>> Cost of goods sold
>> Depreciation of property, plant, and equipment
>> Amortization of intangible items such as goodwill, patents, licenses, etc.
>> Amortization of deferred charges or credits except deferred income taxes
>>> and policy acquisition costs for life insurance companies[6]

---

[6]*Statement of Financial Accounting Standards, No. 52, op. cit.*, par. 48.

A special remeasurement rule is necessary for inventory (and other assets, such as marketable securities) when the rule of cost or market, whichever is lower, is applied. Before the rule is applied, the inventory cost and market amounts must be expressed in the functional currency. A possible result is for an inventory write-down to occur in the functional currency, even though no write-down is suggested in the books of record currency. It also is possible for a write-down in the books of record currency to be no longer appropriate in the functional currency.

The remeasurement into a functional currency is demonstrated in Illustration 12–2, which is based on the following facts:

1. Clancy Corporation began operations on January 1, 19X1, as a wholly-owned foreign subsidiary of Drake Inc., a U.S. company.
2. Inventory in the books of record currency (BR) is carried at market, even though its historical cost is 16,000 BR. Inventory was acquired uniformly throughout the year. The weighted-average cost method is used to determine the cost of sales.
3. Depreciable assets were acquired (sold) on the following dates:

Date	Cost
January 1, 19X1	100,000 BR
May 1, 19X1	30,000 BR
July 1, 19X1	(10,000) BR

The asset sold was acquired on January 1, 19X1. The selling price of this asset was 11,000 BR.
4. Depreciation is based on the straight-line method and a 10-year useful life.
5. Relevant direct exchange rates are as follows:

Date	FC/BR	$/FC
January 1, 19X1	1 BR = 2.0 FC	1 FC = $1.40
May 1, 19X1	1 BR = 2.1 FC	1 FC = 1.30
July 1, 19X1	1 BR = 2.4 FC	1 FC = 1.10
December 31, 19X1	1 BR = 2.8 FC	1 FC = 1.00
19X1 average	1 BR = 2.5 FC	1 FC = 1.25

Highly Inflationary Economies. When an entity's financial statements are expressed in the functional currency, the statements are translated directly into the reporting currency. However, this procedure is not followed for a foreign entity with a functional currency of a country that has a highly inflationary economy. The FASB defines such an economy as one that has a cumulative inflation rate of approximately 100 percent or more over a 3-year period. Other factors, such as the trend of inflation, also may suggest a highly inflationary economy.[7] Currently, a number of third world nations have economies which meet the definition of highly inflationary.

---

[7]Ibid., par. 11.

Illustration 12–2
Clancy Corporation
Trial Balance Translation
December 31, 19X1

Account	Balance in BR	Relevant Exchange Rate (FC/BR)	Balance in FC	Relevant Exchange Rate ($/FC)	Balance in Dollars
Cash	10,000 BR	2.80	28,000 FC	1.00	$ 28,000
Accounts Receivable	28,000	2.80	78,400	1.00	78,400
Inventory (at market)*	15,000	Note A	40,000	1.00	40,000
Prepaid Expenses	5,000	2.50	12,500	1.00	12,500
Depreciable Assets	120,000	Sch. A	239,000	1.00	239,000
Cost of Goods Sold	145,000	2.50	362,500	1.25	453,125
Depreciation Expense	11,500	Sch. A	23,200	1.25	29,000
Other Expenses	27,000	2.50	67,500	1.25	84,375
Income Tax Expense	16,500	2.80	46,200	1.25	57,750
Exchange Loss (to balance)	0	—	57,700	1.25	72,125
Total debits	378,000 BR		955,000 FC		$1,094,275
Accounts Payable	7,500 BR	2.80	21,000 FC	1.00	$ 21,000
Accrued Expenses	12,000	2.80	33,600	1.00	33,600
Notes Payable	84,000	2.80	235,200	1.00	235,200
Common Stock	40,000	2.00	80,000	1.40	112,000
Cumulative Translation Adjustment	0	—	0	—	(32,075)
Retained Earnings	0	Note B	0	—	0
Sales	220,000	2.50	550,000	1.25	687,500
Gain on Sale of Depreciable Asset	1,500	Note C	7,400	1.25	9,250
Allowance for Doubtful Accounts	2,000	2.80	5,600	1.00	5,600
Accumulated Depreciation	11,000	Sch. A	22,200	1.00	22,200
Total credits	378,000 BR		955,000 FC		$1,094,275

*In more complex instances, the remeasurement of ending inventory and cost of sales will depend on the inventory valuation method used. For example, Lifo ending inventory will consist of the (1) beginning inventory multiplied by the applicable exchange rate(s) plus (2) unsold current purchases multiplied by the applicable exchange rate(s).

Note A— The historical cost and market value of the ending inventory must be remeasured into the functional currency before the rule of cost or market, whichever is lower, may be applied.

Historical cost (16,000 × 2.50) 40,000
Market value (15,000 × 2.80) 42,000

Because the historical cost in functional currency is less than the market value in functional currency, historical cost will be the carrying basis.

Note B— The remeasured value of zero for retained earnings represents the beginning-of-the-period value. The balance sheet for 19X1 would show a remeasured value for retained earnings equal to the remeasured value of undistributed net income. This value also would represent the remeasured value for beginning retained earnings in the 19X2 trial balance.

(continued)

Note C—The remeasured value of the gain must be inferred, based on the following entry to record the
sale of the asset:

Cash (11,000 × 2.40)	26,400	
Accumulated Depreciation (500 × 2.00)....................................	1,000	
Depreciable Assets (10,000 × 2.00)...		20,000
Gain on Sale of Depreciable Asset...		7,400

Schedule A
Remeasurement of Depreciable Assets, Depreciation Expense, and Accumulated Depreciation

	Balance in BR	Exchange Rate (FC/BR)	Balance in FC
Depreciable assets:			
January 1, 19X1 acquisition............................	100,000 BR	2.00	200,000 FC
May 1, 19X1 acquisition	30,000	2.10	63,000
July 1, 19X1 disposition	(10,000)	2.40	(24,000)
	120,000 BR		239,000 FC
Depreciation expense:			
January 1, 19X1 acquisition............................	9,000 BR	2.00	18,000 FC
	500	2.00	1,000
May 1, 19X1 acquisition	2,000	2.10	4,200
	11,500 BR		23,200 FC
Accumulated depreciation:			
Annual expense	11,500 BR	see above	23,200 FC
Asset disposed..	(500)	2.00	(1,000)
	11,000 BR		22,200 FC

If a foreign entity's currency has lost its utility as a measure of a store
of value and lacks stability, it probably would not serve as a useful functional currency. To ignore this situation in subsequent translations might
produce misleading results. The translation of noncurrent assets of a foreign
company in a highly inflationary economy at current rates of exchange produces curious results. The translated amounts may not represent reasonable
dollar equivalent measures of such assets' historical costs. For example, assume that a foreign company acquires a fixed asset for a cost of 100,000 FC
when the exchange rate is 1 FC = $1.00. Since that time, the foreign country
has experienced a cumulative rate of inflation of 270%, and the current rate
of exchange is 1 FC = $0.40. If the fixed asset was translated using the cur-
rent rate method, the translated value of the asset would be $40,000 versus
its original translated cost of $100,000. One proposed solution to this curious
result would be to adjust the foreign financial statements for inflation rates
since acquisition and then apply the current rate method. The inflation-
adjusted value of the fixed asset would be 270,000 FC (100,000 FC × 270%),
and its translated value at current rates would be $108,000 (270,000 FC ×
$0.40). This translated amount is more meaningful than the $40,000 value
previously determined. The FASB decided against adjusting foreign amounts
for inflationary effects and instead decided that the domestic currency

(dollars) should serve as the foreign entity's functional currency. Thus, the foreign entity's statements should be remeasured into the functional currency (U.S. dollars) using the temporal method. Applying the temporal method to the fixed asset example would require the use of the original historical rate of exchange and results in a translated value of $100,000 (100,000 FC × $1.00). This value is more meaningful than the $40,000 value previously determined and also does not commingle historical and inflation-adjusted values into the same set of financial statements. It is important to note that using the temporal approach will result in the remeasurement of the statements into dollars and that any further translation will not be necessary. Also note that the use of the temporal method will result in an exchange gain or loss that should be included in the income for the period.

Special Consolidation Procedures for Remeasured Financial Statements. The example of consolidation procedures in Worksheet 12–1 is based on foreign financial statements which have been translated using the current rate method. In those instances where the functional currency is the dollar or the foreign economy is highly inflationary, the foreign financial statements are remeasured directly into dollars using the temporal method. The use of this method affects the consolidation process as follows:

1. The translation adjustment is recognized as a component of subsidiary net income rather than a component of stockholders' equity.
2. The dollar amount of any excess of cost over book value remains the same over time and does not result in an additional translation adjustment. This is the case because historical rates (which do not change), rather than current rates, are used to remeasure the excess. Thus, the dollar amount of the amortization of excess also does not change from period to period.

GAINS AND LOSSES EXCLUDED FROM INCOME

The separate component of equity in which cumulative translation adjustments are reported also should include gains and losses attributable to:

(a) *Foreign currency transactions that are designated as, and are effective as, economic hedges of a net investment in a foreign entity, commencing as of the designation date.*

(b) *Intercompany foreign currency transactions that are of a long-term investment nature (that is, settlement is not planned or anticipated in the foreseeable future), when the entities to the transaction are consolidated, combined, or accounted for by the equity method in the reporting enterprise's financial statements.*[8]

---

[8]*Ibid.*, par. 20.

A foreign currency transaction that is a hedge of a net investment in a foreign entity should be accounted for in the same way as the effect of rate changes on the net investment. For example, a domestic corporation with an investment in a French subsidiary, in which the franc is the functional currency, might borrow francs and identify the transaction as a hedge on the net investment in the French subsidiary. Because the loan is a liability and the net investment is an asset, a rate change will have opposite effects on the loan and the translation adjustment. Therefore, the foreign currency transaction is a hedge of the net investment and will offset the translation adjustment. However, if the gain (loss) on the hedge (after tax effects) is greater than the corresponding translation loss (gain), the excess transaction gain (loss) must be included in the determination of net income.

EXCHANGE RATES AND INTERCOMPANY PROFITS

It is fairly common for a foreign country to have more than one exchange rate, such as a commercial rate and a financial rate. Therefore, the FASB stated that the following exchange rates should be used in the translation process:

(a) *Foreign Currency Transactions—The applicable rate at which a particular transaction could be settled at the transaction date shall be used to translate and record the transaction. At a subsequent balance sheet date, the current rate is that rate at which the related receivable or payable could be settled at that date.*

(b) *Foreign Currency Statements—In the absence of unusual circumstances, the rate applicable to conversion of a currency for purposes of dividend remittances shall be used to translate foreign currency statements.* [9]

If an exchange rate between the functional currency and the reporting currency is lacking temporarily, the first subsequently available exchange rate should be used. However, if the absence of an exchange rate is other than temporary, consolidation or equity method accounting may not be appropriate.

Once a foreign entity's financial statements have been translated into the reporting currency, certain eliminations and adjustments due to intercompany transactions generally will be required. With regard to the exchange rate that should be used to translate such transactions, the FASB concluded that all intercompany balances, except for intercompany profits and losses, should be translated at the rates used for all other accounts. Intercompany

[9]*Ibid.*, par. 27.

profits and losses should be translated using the exchange rate that existed at the date of the sale or transfer. As a practical matter, however, average rates or approximations may be used to translate such profits and losses.

INCOME TAX ALLOCATION

Interperiod tax allocation is appropriate when gains or losses resulting from foreign currency transactions are included in income in a different period for accounting purposes than for tax purposes. The gains or losses on certain types of foreign currency transactions are presented as a component of equity rather than as a component of income. According to the principles of intraperiod tax allocation, the income taxes related to such items also should be allocated to equity. With respect to translation adjustments, the FASB decided that deferred taxes should not be provided for translation adjustments attributable to an investment in a foreign entity for which deferred taxes are not recognized on unremitted earnings. However, if deferred taxes are recognized on unremitted earnings, deferred taxes should be provided, along with the translation adjustment, as a separate component of stockholders' equity.

DISCLOSURE REQUIREMENTS

Statement No. 52 requires that foreign currency transaction and hedging gains and losses included in the determination of net income be disclosed in the financial statements or the accompanying notes. An analysis of the separate component of equity affected by certain foreign currency transactions and hedges and translation adjustments should be presented. The analysis may be in a separate statement, in a note to the financial statements, or as part of the statement of changes in equity. At a minimum, the analysis should disclose:

(a) *Beginning and ending amount of cumulative translation adjustments.*

(b) *The aggregate adjustment for the period resulting from translation adjustments and gains and losses from certain hedges and intercompany balances.*

(c) *The amount of income taxes for the period allocated to translation adjustments.*

(d) *The amounts transferred from cumulative translation adjustments and included in determining net income for the period as a result of the sale or complete or substantially complete liquidation of an investment in a foreign entity.* [10]

---

[10]*Ibid.*, par. 31.

Although the various effects of rate changes subsequent to the end of the period normally are not disclosed, their effects on unsettled balances arising from foreign currency transactions should be disclosed if significant.

QUESTIONS

1. Discuss how the use of accounting principles other than GAAP by a foreign subsidiary affects the process of preparing consolidated financial statements.
2. Specify the basic objectives in translating foreign currency financial statements.
3. Define the term functional currency and describe several instances in which a foreign entity's currency may not be the functional currency.
4. Discuss how manufacturing equipment and the related depreciation expense measured in a foreign company's functional currency would be translated under the temporal method assuming that:
    (a) purchase accounting was used.
    (b) pooling of interests accounting was used.
5. Discuss the accounting treatment of translation adjustments under the temporal and current rate (FASB Statement No. 52) methods.
6. Under what circumstances might the gain/loss on a foreign currency transaction receive the same treatment as a translation adjustment under the current rate method?
7. Discuss why the current rate method may not be applied to a foreign entity whose functional currency is that of a country whose economy is highly inflationary.
8. If a foreign entity maintains its records in a currency that is not the functional currency, explain the methodology for translating such information into the parent's reporting currency.
9. What rates should be used to translate and eliminate the balances resulting from a sale of inventory to a foreign subsidiary by a domestic parent?
10. Under what circumstances might the cumulative translation adjustment be removed from stockholders' equity?

EXERCISES

Exercise 1.   Select the best answer for each of the following questions that relate to accounting for foreign operations and transactions.

(1) Maggy Company translated foreign currency amounts at December 31, 19X5. At that time, Maggy had foreign subsidiaries with 1,500,000 local currency units (LCU) in long-term receivables and 2,400,000 LCU in long-term debt. The rate of exchange in effect when the specific transactions occurred involving those foreign currency amounts was 2 LCU to $1. The rate of exchange in effect at December 31, 19X5, was 1.5 LCU to $1. The translation of the foreign currency amounts into dollars would result in long-term receivables and long-term debt, respectively, of:
a. $750,000 and $1,200,000.   c. $1,000,000 and $1,200,000.
b. $750,000 and $1,600,000.   d. $1,000,000 and $1,600,000.

(2) A company is translating account balances from another currency into dollars for its December 31, 19X5 statement of financial position and for its calendar year 19X5 retained earnings statement and statement of cash flows. The average exchange rate for the year 19X5 should be used to translate:
a. Cash at December 31, 19X5.
b. Land purchased in 19X3.
c. Retained earnings at January 1, 19X5.
d. Sales for 19X5.

(3) Dease Company owns a foreign subsidiary with 3,600,000 local currency units (LCU) of property, plant, and equipment at December 31, 19X5, before accumulated depreciation is deducted. Of this amount, 2,400,000 LCU were acquired in 19X3 when the rate of exchange was 1.6 LCU to $1, and 1,200,000 LCU were acquired in 19X4 when the rate of exchange was 1.8 LCU to $1. The rate of exchange in effect at December 31, 19X5, was 2 LCU to $1. The weighted average of exchange rates in effect during 19X5 was 1.92 LCU to $1. Assuming that the property, plant, and equipment are depreciated using the straight-line method over a ten-year period with no salvage value, how much depreciation expense relating to the foreign subsidiary's property, plant, and equipment should be charged in Dease's income statement for 19X5?
a. $180,000.   c. $200,000.
b. $187,500.   d. $216,667.

(4) Clark Company owns a foreign subsidiary that had net income for the year ended December 31, 19X5, of 4,800,000 local currency units (LCU), which was translated appropriately into $800,000. On October 15, 19X5, when the rate of exchange was 5.7 LCU to $1, the foreign subsidiary paid Clark a dividend of 2,400,000 LCU. The dividend represented the net income of the foreign subsidiary for the six months ended June 30,

19X5, during which time the weighted average of exchange rates was 5.8 LCU to $1. The rate of exchange in effect at December 31, 19X5, was 5.9 LCU to $1. What rate of exchange should be used to translate the dividend for the December 31, 19X5 financial statements?

a. 5.7 LCU to $1.   c. 5.9 LCU to $1.
b. 5.8 LCU to $1.   d. 6.0 LCU to $1.

(5) When combined or consolidated financial statements for a domestic and a foreign company are prepared, the account balances expressed in the foreign currency must be translated into the domestic currency. The objective of the translation process is to obtain currency valuations that:

a. Are conservative.
b. Reflect current monetary equivalents.
c. Are expressed in domestic units of measure and are in conformity with domestic generally accepted accounting principles.
d. Reflect the translated account at its unexpired historical cost.

(6) Lochlann Company used U.S. dollars to purchase all the outstanding common stock of Dey Company, a Canadian corporation. At the date of purchase, a portion of the investment account was allocated appropriately to goodwill. One year later, after an exchange rate decrease (U.S. dollars have become less valuable), the goodwill should be shown in the consolidated balance sheet at what amount?

a. An increased amount, less amortization.
b. The same amount, less amortization.
c. A lesser amount, less amortization.
d. An increased or lesser amount, depending on management policy, less amortization.   (AICPA adapted)

Exercise 2.   Ecola Enterprises is a wholly-owned subsidiary of a U.S. company. Ecola's functional currency is the French franc (FF), and its December 31, 19X9 trial balance in French francs is as follows:

	Debit	Credit
Current Assets	3,480,000	
Manufacturing Equipment	6,170,000	
Manufacturing Plant	2,240,000	
Accumulated Depreciation		3,680,000
Land	1,020,000	
Current Liabilities		1,927,000
Mortgage and Loans Payable		3,110,000
Common Stock		1,000,000
Paid-In Capital in Excess of Par		200,000
Retained Earnings, Jan. 1, 1989		1,263,000
Sales Revenue		10,880,000
Cost of Goods Sold	7,320,000	
Selling, General, and Administrative Expenses	1,830,000	
Total	22,060,000	22,060,000

Sales and related expenses occur uniformly throughout the year. The common stock originally was issued to the parent on January 1, 19X6, with the exception of 200,000 FF of stock which was sold on February 1, 19X8, to the parent at a 13% premium above par value.

Subsidiary net incomes since the beginning of operations are as follows:

19X6...	410,000 FF
19X7...	530,000
19X8...	760,000

Subsidiary dividend declarations are as follows:

March 1, 19X7	80,000 FF
March 1, 19X8	120,000
March 1, 19X9	237,000

Relevant direct spot rates ($/FF) are as follows:

January 1, 19X6...................	$0.130	March 1, 19X8.....................	$0.162
19X6 average	0.138	19X8 average	0.164
March 1, 19X7	0.142	December 31, 19X8..............	0.167
19X7 average	0.153	March 1, 19X9.....................	0.170
December 31, 19X7..............	0.158	19X9 average	0.172
February 1, 19X8	0.160	December 31, 19X9..............	0.175

Prepare the December 31, 19X9 translated trial balance of Ecola Enterprises. Supporting notes should be in good form.

Exercise 3.   Given the facts presented in Exercise 2:
(1) Calculate the translation adjustment traceable to 19X8 and 19X9 by direct computation.
(2) Assume that the 19X9 translation adjustment for Ecola was a $30,000 debit. Define the terms of a foreign currency loan that would serve as a hedge against the translation adjustment. Assume that the loan was initiated on March 1, 19X9.
(3) Discuss how the translation adjustment would be accounted for if the parent company sold 80% of its interest in the foreign subsidiary.

Exercise 4.   On January 1, 19X8, Boyer Developments purchased 90% of the stock in a foreign company specializing in hotel construction. At the time of the acquisition, the foreign company equity consisted of the following balances in foreign currency (FC):

Common stock......................................	300,000 FC
Paid-in capital in excess of par................	80,000
Retained earnings.................................	120,000
Total equity..	500,000 FC

Boyer paid 600,000 FC for its 90% interest, with the excess over book value being attributable to undeveloped land held by the foreign subsidiary. On July 1, 9X8, the subsidiary declared a 20,000 FC dividend, payable on August 1, 19X8. The foreign company reported 100,000 FC of net income during 19X8. The December 31, 19X8 cumulative translation adjustment is $33,000. Selected direct exchange rates ($/FC) are as follows:

January 1, 19X8...	$1.00
July 1, 19X8...	1.02
August 1, 19X8...	1.03
December 31, 19X8..	1.05
19X8 average	1.02

Prepare all the journal entries related to Boyer's investment in the foreign subsidiary and all the necessary eliminating and adjusting entries upon consolidation assuming use of the simple equity method.

Exercise 5.   Shaid Corporation is a wholly-owned subsidiary of Hawkes Inc. Shaid, a South American company, was organized on July 1, 19X5, when the general price-level index in its country was 400. The price-level index is 1,000 at December 31, 19X6. The general price-level index in the U.S., where Hawkes is incorporated, has gone from 110 to 121 during the same time period.

Shaid's accounting records contain the following information:

(a) Inventory is accounted for by the Lifo inventory method on a periodic basis. The 19X6 beginning inventory is composed entirely of purchases made on July 1, 19X5. Inventory information for 19X6 is as follows:

Date	Account	Amount in Foreign Currency
January 1, 19X6	Beginning Inventory	30,000 FC
April 1, 19X6	Purchases	18,000
June 1, 19X6	Purchases	25,000
October 1, 19X6	Purchases	40,000
November 1, 19X6	Purchases	20,000
December 31, 19X6	Ending Inventory	52,000

(b) Equipment was acquired and sold as detailed in the following schedule. There were no intercompany equipment transactions.

Date	Cost Acquired (Sold)
July 1, 19X5	120,000 FC
April 1, 19X6	50,000
October 1, 19X6	(16,000)

The selling price of the equipment sold was 13,200 FC. This equipment was acquired on July 1, 19X5.

(c) Depreciation is computed using the straight-line method over an 8-year life. Salvage value is ignored. A half year of depreciation is taken in the years of acquisition and disposition.

(d) The November 1 inventory purchase in part (a) was acquired from Hawkes Inc., with payment due in foreign currency in 90 days. On November 1, Hawkes purchased a 90-day forward contract to sell the 20,000 FC to a broker at a forward rate of 1 FC = $1.27.

(e) Relevant exchange rates are as follows:

Date	Rate
July 1, 19X5	1 FC = $1.19
April 1, 19X6	1 FC = 1.23
June 1, 19X6	1 FC = 1.22
October 1, 19X6	1 FC = 1.25
November 1, 19X6	1 FC = 1.26
December 31, 19X6	1 FC = 1.28
19X6 average	1 FC = 1.24

Calculate the translated value of the following accounts:
(1) Cost of goods sold for 19X6.
(2) Gain or loss on the October 1, 19X6 equipment sale.
(3) Hawkes' liability to broker associated with the forward contract, as of December 31, 19X6.

Exercise 6.   For each of the following independent cases, determine the translated value of the relevant accounts.

Case A: A foreign subsidiary has inventory accounted for by the lower-of-cost-or-market rule. The 1987 ending inventory, with a cost of 180,000 FC, was written down to a market value of 176,000 FC. The cost of the inventory is traceable to an October 1, 19X7 purchase of 150,000 FC and a December 15, 19X7 purchase of 30,000 FC. The foreign company's functional currency is the U.S. dollar. Relevant exchange rates on October 1, 19X7, December 15, 19X7, and December 31, 19X7, are 1 FC = $1.76, 1 FC = $1.72, and 1 FC = $1.82, respectively. Calculate the translated value of the December 31, 19X7 ending inventory.

Case B: A foreign subsidiary purchased inventory for 380,000 FC from its U.S. parent on November 1, 19X7. The parent's cost of the inventory sold was $500,000. As of December 31, 19X7, the subsidiary has 60% of the inventory on hand. The subsidiary's functional currency is the foreign currency. Relevant exchange rates on November 1, 19X7, and December 31, 19X7, are 1 FC = $2.00 and 1 FC = $2.10, respectively. Calculate the translated value of the subsidiary's December 31, 19X7 inventory after eliminating the intercompany profit.

Case C: A foreign subsidiary acquired depreciable assets measured in foreign currency A (FCA) over several years. The subsidiary's functional currency is foreign currency B (FCB). All assets are depreciable on a straight-line basis over a 10-year useful life. Relevant asset costs and exchange rates are as follows:

	Asset Cost	1 FCA =	1 FCB =
January 1, 19X6	380,000	2.10 FCB	$1.10
March 1, 19X6	710,000	1.98	1.08
July 1, 19X6	216,000	1.92	1.06
December 1, 19X6	30,000	2.01	1.04
19X6 average		2.03	1.05

Calculate the translated value of the 19X6 depreciation expense.

PROBLEMS

Problem 12–1.   On January 1, 19X3, Dudwil Corporation acquired a foreign subsidiary, Holman Company, by paying cash for all of the outstanding common stock of Holman. Both companies continued to operate as separate entities. On the purchase date, Holman Company's accounts were stated fairly in local currency units (FC). Subsequent sales of Holman common stock have been purchased by Dudwil in order to maintain its 100% ownership.

Holman's trial balance, in functional currency units (same as the local currency units), at December 31, 19X7, follows:

	Debit	Credit
Cash..	58,400	
Marketable Securities...	32,500	
Accounts Receivable (net)...	51,370	
Inventories...	108,000	
Surrender Value of Life Insurance.................................	7,200	
Intangible Assets..	123,900	
Property, Plant, and Equipment....................................	636,000	
Accumulated Depreciation...		93,850
Accounts Payable...		74,000
Accrued Interest Payable..		7,120
Notes Payable...		52,000
Bonds Payable..		80,000
Capital Stock..		83,000
Paid-In Capital in Excess of Par....................................		190,300
Retained Earnings...		390,400
Sales...		936,300
Cost of Goods Sold...	762,000	
Interest Expense..	7,120	
Depreciation Expense..	39,350	
Amortization Expense—Intangibles...............................	3,100	
Other Expenses...	84,230	
Gain on Sale of Equipment...		2,400
Other Income..		3,800
Total..	1,913,170	1,913,170

The following additional information is available:
(a) Holman uses the Lifo inventory method to account for its inventory. Purchases took place uniformly throughout 19X7. There were no intercompany sales during 19X7.
(b) During 19X7, Holman declared and paid a dividend of 7,000 FC at the end of each calendar quarter.
(c) The balances in the contributed capital accounts resulted from the following transactions:

Date	Capital Stock	Paid-In Capital in Excess of Par
January 1, 19X3	40,000 FC	80,000 FC
June 30, 19X5	40,000	104,300
January 1, 19X6	10,000	20,000
August 1, 19X6	(7,000)	(14,000)
	83,000 FC	190,300 FC

(d) The January 1, 19X7 balance in retained earnings resulted from the following:

19X3 net income..................................	50,000 FC
19X4 net income.................................	173,000
February 1, 19X5 dividend.....................	(40,000)
19X5 net income.................................	206,400
January 1, 19X6 stock dividend.............	(30,000)
February 1, 19X6 dividend....................	(90,000)
19X6 net income	149,000
	418,400 FC

(e) The notes payable in Holman's trial balance represents a loan from Dudwil Corporation. The loan was made on January 1, 19X7, and is to be repaid in foreign currency. However, the loan does not bear interest and is of a long-term investment nature because settlement of the debt is not anticipated in the foreseeable future.

(f) The balance in the account Other Income represents consulting fees charged to Dudwil during 19X7. The reciprocal account on the parent company's books shows the fees at $2,300.

(g) Selected translation rates are as follows:

Date	Rate
January 1, 19X3	1 FC = $.30
19X3 average	1 FC = .32
19X4 average	1 FC = .38
February 1, 19X5	1 FC = .42
June 30, 19X5	1 FC = .45
19X5 average	1 FC = .45
January 1, 19X6	1 FC = .50
February 1, 19X6	1 FC = .52
August 1, 19X6	1 FC = .60
December 31, 19X6	1 FC = .61
19X6 average	1 FC = .56
March 31, 19X7	1 FC = .63
June 30, 19X7	1 FC = .66
September 30, 19X7	1 FC = .70
December 31, 19X7	1 FC = .75
19X7 average	1 FC = .70

Required:

(1) Prepare a schedule to convert the December 31, 19X7 trial balance of Holman Company from local currency units to dollars. The schedule should show the unconverted trial balance, the conversion rates, and the converted trial balance. (Do not extend the trial balance to statement columns. Supporting schedules should be in good form.)

(2) Prepare a schedule that details the direct computation of the 19X7 adjustment resulting from translation. Supporting calculations should be in good form.

(3) Calculate the foreign currency transaction gain or loss experienced by Dudwil with respect to the note payable. Discuss the accounting treatment of this gain or loss.

Problem 12–2.   On January 1, 19X6, On-Time Corporation purchased a 25% interest in Glarus Watches, Inc., a foreign manufacturer of men's and ladies' watches. On-Time purchased the investment for $55,000, which included payment for goodwill that is being amortized over 20 years.

The following information is available regarding Glarus Watches:

(a) Sales occurred and inventory was purchased evenly throughout the year.

(b) Dividends of 2.5 FC per share were declared on July 1 of each year except 19X3, the first year of operation.

(c) Sales were made to On-Time in 19X6 and 19X7. The 19X7 beginning inventory held by On-Time included watches that had been purchased from Glarus, with a value of 15,000 FC. On-Time's ending inventory includes 15% of the 19X7 purchases from Glarus. Glarus charged On-Time 25% over cost for these sales.

(d) Net income for 19X6 was 58,000 FC.

(e) Relevant exchange rates are as follows:

Date	Rate
January 1, 19X6	1 FC = $.39
July 1, 19X6	1 FC = .37
December 31, 19X6	1 FC = .40
19X6 average	1 FC = .38
January 1, 19X7	1 FC = .41
July 1, 19X7	1 FC = .44
December 31, 19X7	1 FC = .43
19X7 average	1 FC = .42

(f) The investment in Glarus Watches is accounted for by the sophisticated equity method.

(g) The 19X6 translation adjustment was a $7,600 credit.

The trial balance of Glarus Watches Inc. on December 31, 19X7, is as follows:

	Debit	Credit
Cash	35,000	
Accounts Receivable	90,000	
Inventory	260,000	
Prepaid Rent	6,000	
Property, Plant, and Equipment	425,000	
Land	115,000	
Cost of Goods Sold	324,000	
Depreciation Expense	35,000	
Selling and Administrative Expense	232,000	
Interest Expense	40,000	
Other Expenses	88,000	
Accounts Payable		75,000
Accrued Interest Payable		12,000
Income Taxes Payable		44,000
Wages Payable		16,000
Notes Payable		150,000
Common Stock (20 FC par)		200,000
Paid-In Capital in Excess of Par		145,000
Retained Earnings		82,000
Sales — On-Time		115,000
Sales — Other		675,000
Accumulated Depreciation		136,000
Total	1,650,000	1,650,000

Required:
(1) Prepare a schedule to compute the 19X7 translation adjustment.
(2) Determine the December 31, 19X7 carrying value of On-Time's investment in Glarus. Supporting schedules should be in good form.

Problem 12–3.   Divall is a French company whose functional currency is the French franc (FF). The company was founded on July 1, 19X7, with the sale of stock for 11,880,000 FF, of which 10,000,000 FF represented par value. On January 1, 19X9, a U.S. company purchased for cash all of the stock of Divall for 14,000,000 FF when the retained earnings balance of Divall was 1,200,000 FF. The excess paid over book value is attributable to undervalued depreciable property which had a remaining useful life of 12 years at the date of acquisition.

Divall's unadjusted trial balance in FF on December 31, 19X9, is as follows:

	Debit	Credit
Cash and Receivables	2,210,000	
Inventory..	5,700,000	
Prepaid Assets	122,000	
Property, Plant, and Equipment..............................	7,533,000	
Accumulated Depreciation.....................................		817,000
Other Assets	1,200,000	
Accounts and Notes Payable...................................		2,984,000
Dividends Payable (declared on December 1, 19X9)		320,000
Common Stock..		10,000,000
Paid-In Capital in Excess of Par		1,880,000
Retained Earnings..		880,000
Sales Revenue..		8,954,000
Cost of Goods Sold...	6,060,000	
Selling, General, and Administrative Expenses	3,010,000	
Total...	25,835,000	25,835,000

The trial balance has not been adjusted to reflect gains and losses on the following transactions:

(a) Inventory includes materials purchased from a West German company in the amount of 230,000 FF. At the date of purchase, 1 FF = 0.35 deutsche marks (DM) and at December 31, 19X9, 1 FF = 0.38 DM. The purchase, which is denominated in DM, is payable in early January of the next year.

(b) Notes payable includes a loan from a U.S. bank in the amount of 700,000 FF. The loan was received on August 1, 19X9, when 1 FF = $0.14. The loan is denominated in dollars.

The December 31, 19X9 ending inventory includes 430,000 FF of goods, which is a portion of the amount purchased from the U.S. parent on October 1, 19X9. The original purchase, which was denominated in FF, had a value of $130,000 and a cost to the parent of $104,000.

Relevant direct exchange rates ($/FF) are as follows:

July 1, 19X7	$0.140
January 1, 19X9...	0.170
August 1, 19X9..	0.173
October 1, 19X9...	0.180
December 1, 19X9..	0.179
December 31, 19X9.......................................	0.178
19X9 average	0.174

Required:

(1) Prepare for Divall the December 31, 19X9 adjusted trial balance in FF and the translated value of the account balances in dollars. Supporting schedules should be in good form.

(2) Prepare the parent's journal entries related to the investment in the foreign subsidiary and all necessary eliminating and adjusting entries upon consolidation assuming use of the simple equity method. Supporting schedules should be in good form.

Problem 12–4. On April 1, 19X9, Wagner Manufacturing purchased for cash an 80% interest in a West German company. At the time of the purchase, the foreign company's equity in deutsche marks (DM) consisted of the following:

Common stock.................................	10,000,000 DM
Paid-in capital in excess of par...........	2,720,000
Retained earnings............................	5,960,000
Total equity..................................	18,680,000 DM

Wagner paid 15,100,000 DM for its interest in the foreign subsidiary. The amount paid in excess of the underlying book value is attributable to the following items measured in DM:

Inventory...	16,000 DM
Building..	50,000
Land..	90,000

The building had a 20-year remaining useful life as of the acquisition date. The appreciated inventory on April 1, 19X9, subsequently has been sold.

On August 1, 19X9, Wagner sold inventory to the foreign subsidiary, payable in dollars. The inventory had a sales value of $80,000 and a cost of $60,000. As of December 31, 19X9, one-third of the inventory remains on hand. On November 1, 19X9, Wagner lent the subsidiary $200,000, payable in dollars in three months with interest accruing at 10%. On September 1, 19X9, the subsidiary declared a 200,000 DM dividend. The foreign subsidiary reported net income for the nine-month period ending December 31, 19X9, of 2,730,000 DM.

Relevant direct exchange rates ($/DM) for 19X9 are as follows:

March 31	$0.50	November 1.........................	$0.46
August 1.............................	0.49	March to December average ..	0.47
September 1	0.48	December 31........................	0.44

Required:
(1) Directly calculate the translation adjustment for the nine-month period ending December 31, 19X9.
(2) Prepare all necessary eliminating and adjusting entries for Wagner in regards to its investment in the foreign subsidiary assuming use of the simple equity method.

Problem 12–5. Reslin Corporation is a New York-based manufacturer of photographic supplies. On August 1, 19X3, Reslin expanded its network of operations by opening a branch office in Great Britain. The following information is available regarding accounts of the home office and branch for the year ended December 31, 19X5:

(a) On December 22, 19X5, the home office shipped merchandise billed at $12,600 to the branch office. The merchandise was received in January, 19X6.

(b) The branch office received all of its beginning inventory and 40% of its ending inventory from the home office. The home office bills the goods at cost plus a markup of 12% of cost. Purchases are made uniformly throughout the year, and branch inventory is accounted for by the Fifo method. The 19X5 beginning inventory of the branch office is £86,000. The current cost of ending inventories at December 31, 19X5, excludes the shipment in transit.

(c) A photographer on location in Great Britain purchased film on account from the branch office. Upon returning to the U.S., however, the photographer erroneously paid the account to the New York office on December 30, 19X5. The bookkeeper recorded the $1,300 payment on the books of the home office but did not notify the branch office.

(d) On December 30, the branch office authorized a remittance of £4,400 to be made to the home office. Payment was received by the home office on January 2, 19X6.

(e) On December 31, the branch office recorded the December allocated general and administrative expense from the home office as £570 instead of £750.

(f) The annual insurance premium is paid by the branch office on March 31 of each year.

(g) As of May 1, 19X5, the rate of exchange is £1 equals $1.60. The previous rate, which had been in effect since 19X2, was £1 equals $1.75. The average annual rate of exchange was £1 equals $1.65.

Trial balances at December 31, 19X5, for the home office and its branch are as follows. No adjustments required by home office accounting procedures have been recorded.

	Branch Office Trial Balance (in pounds)	Home Office Trial Balance (in dollars)
Cash	65,000	140,000
Accounts Receivable	100,000	205,000
Inventory, Dec. 31, 19X5	131,250	650,000
Prepaid Insurance	1,500	—
Customer Deposits (refundable)	680	2,300
Property, Plant, and Equipment	950,000	2,710,000
Investment in Branch	—	23,940
Cost of Goods Sold	1,424,750	3,780,000
Selling Expenses	41,000	113,000
General and Administrative Expense	92,500	366,000
Depreciation Expense	120,000	250,000
Accounts Payable	(130,000)	(290,000)
Customer Deposits (refundable)	(680)	(2,300)
Mortgage Payable on Building	(203,000)	(512,000)
Accumulated Depreciation	(380,000)	(995,000)
Home Office Equity	(3,320)	—
Capital Stock ($2 par)	—	(320,000)
Retained Earnings, Jan. 1, 19X5	—	(510,000)
Sales	(2,209,680)	(4,750,940)
Shipments to Branch (at retail)	—	(860,000)
Total	0	0

Required:

Prepare a columnar worksheet to present the combined income statement and combined balance sheet of Reslin Corporation and its foreign branch office, with all amounts stated in U.S. dollars. Key and explain worksheet eliminations and adjustments, and show supporting computations in good form. Ignore income taxes.

Problem 12–6.   Master Gaskets (MG) was formed on July 1, 19X7, as a wholly-owned subsidiary of Crane Industries, a U.S. based company. MG is located in Great Britain and primarily purchases inventory from the parent for resale in the U.S. MG's functional currency is the U.S. dollar although its December 31, 19X8 trial balance is in pounds as follows:

	Debit	Credit
Cash and Receivables	1,483,000	
Inventory	1,210,000	
Office Equipment	280,000	
Accumulated Depreciation		42,000
Accounts Payable		1,509,000
Loans Payable		416,000
Common Stock		100,000
Paid-In Capital in Excess of Par		30,000
Retained Earnings		75,000
Sales		4,104,000
Cost of Goods Sold	2,320,000	
Interest Expense	16,000	
Other Expenses	967,000	
Total	6,276,000	6,276,000

The office equipment was acquired on July 1, 19X7, and is being depreciated over a ten-year life by the straight-line method. The resulting depreciation expense is included in Other Expenses. The ending inventory value, under the lower-of-cost-or-market rule, has been determined by comparing the cost of £1,325,000 to the market value of £1,210,000. The inventory on hand at year end represents costs incurred uniformly throughout the last two months of 19X8. It is assumed that the cost of goods sold has been incurred uniformly throughout the year.

The loan payable balance represents a loan from a British bank. Although the functional currency is the dollar, the loan is denominated in pounds. MG obtained the loan on September 1, 19X8, in the amount of £400,000. The trial balance amount includes £16,000 of accrued interest recognized uniformly over the four months since September 1, 19X8. Unfortunately, MG's trial balance does not reflect any transaction gain or loss associated with this loan.

The common stock account includes £10,000 traceable to a stock dividend declared on July 1, 19X8, when the fair market value of the stock was £14,000. The remeasured value of the December 31, 19X7 retained earnings balance was $144,180.

Relevant direct exchange rates ($/£) are as follows:

July 1, 19X7	$1.60	19X8 average	$1.54
June 1, 19X8	1.55	Average for last 2 months	
July 1, 19X8	1.53	of 19X8............................	1.48
September 1, 19X8	1.51	Average for last 4 months	
December 31, 19X8	1.47	of 19X8............................	1.50

Required:

Prepare the translated trial balance of MG for the year ended December 31, 19X8. Supporting schedules should be in good form.

Problem 12–7. Vulcan Systems, a Swiss company, was formed on July 1, 19X3, when it issued 100,000 shares of common stock to Nordrex Inc., a U.S. corporation. Vulcan acquires certain subassemblies from Nordrex, but acquires most of its materials in West Germany. The materials are processed and assembled in West Germany and sold throughout Europe. Sales contracts are denominated in German deutsche marks. Vulcan maintains its books of record in Swiss francs and has the following trial balance, in Swiss francs, on December 31, 19X5:

	Debit	Credit
Cash..	120,000	
Accounts Receivable (net)...	1,480,000	
Inventory (at cost)...	1,215,000	
Prepaid Expenses	284,000	
Property, Plant, and Equipment.................................	4,880,000	
Cost of Goods Sold..	8,760,000	
Depreciation Expense..	382,000	
Other Expenses...	2,540,000	
Income Tax Expense	1,240,000	
Accounts Payable		860,000
Due to Nordrex		180,000
Accrued Expenses		64,000
Taxes Payable		280,000
Notes Payable		1,860,000
Loan Payable to Nordrex...		1,400,000
Common Stock..		1,300,000
Paid-In Capital in Excess of Par.		45,000
Retained Earnings..		282,000
Sales..		13,800,000
Accumulated Depreciation..		830,000
Total...	20,901,000	20,901,000

The following additional information is available:
(a) The rule of cost or market, whichever is lower, is applied to the ending inventory. The inventory had a market value of 1,320,000 German deutsche marks.
(b) Vulcan uses Fifo to determine inventory cost. The cost of goods sold, in Swiss francs, was determined as follows:

Beginning inventory (acquired in 4th quarter, 19X4)........................	860,000
Purchases—1st quarter, 19X5...	2,450,000
Purchases—2d quarter, 19X5...	2,690,000
Purchases—3d quarter, 19X5...	2,130,000
Purchases—4th quarter, 19X5..	1,845,000
Total available..	9,975,000
Ending inventory...	1,215,000
Cost of goods sold..	8,760,000

(c) The property, plant, and equipment consists of the following items, measured in Swiss francs:

Item	Cost	Acquisition Date
Land	840,000	July 1, 19X3
Equipment	1,760,000	July 1, 19X3
Equipment	1,840,000	January 1, 19X4
Equipment	440,000	July 1, 19X5
	4,880,000	

Depreciable assets have a useful life of ten years and no salvage value. The straight-line depreciation method is employed.

(d) The account Due to Nordrex represents amounts due for purchases of subassemblies. The subassemblies had an equivalent cost to Nordrex of 135,000 Swiss francs. All of the subassemblies had been sold by Nordrex as of year end.

(e) The loan payable to Nordrex represents a long-term loan made on July 1, 19X4. Settlement of the loan is not anticipated in the foreseeable future.

(f) The 10-Swiss franc par common stock was issued as follows:

Date	Par Value	Excess of Par
July 1, 19X3	1,000,000	—
July 1, 19X4	300,000	45,000
	1,300,000	45,000

Dividends of one Swiss franc per share have been declared on September 1 of each year since 19X4.

(g) All other expenses were incurred uniformly throughout the year.

(h) The retained earnings balance, in Swiss francs, consists of the following:

19X3 net loss	(370,000)
19X4 net income.......................................	912,000
19X4 dividend	(130,000)
19X5 dividend	(130,000)
	282,000

(i) Assume the translated values of the 19X3 net loss and 19X4 net income are (407,000) DM and 1,103,520 DM, respectively.

(j) Relevant direct exchange rates are as follows:

Date	Deutsche Marks/Franc	Dollars/Deutsche Mark
July 1, 19X3	1.00 deutsche marks	$.40
19X3 average	1.10	.42
January 1, 19X4	1.18	.44
July 1, 19X4	1.20	.43
September 1, 19X4	1.22	.43
19X4—4th quarter	1.24	.41
19X4 average	1.21	.42
19X5—1st quarter	1.26	.40
19X5—2d quarter	1.30	.37
19X5—3d quarter	1.32	.35
19X5—4th quarter	1.34	.31
July 1, 19X5	1.30	.36
September 1, 19X5	1.34	.33
December 31, 19X5	1.36	.30
19X5 average	1.31	.35

Required:

(1) Translate Vulcan's December 31, 19X5 trial balance into the domestic reporting currency. All supporting schedules should be in good form.

(2) Discuss how the long-term loan by Nordrex affects combined income.

Problem 12–8. Global Mining Corporation is a U.S. manufacturer of heavy mining equipment. The equipment is manufactured from subassemblies that are acquired from both domestic and foreign suppliers.

At the beginning of 19X8, Global arranged for 3,000,000 deutsche marks of financing in the U.S. and contributed another 2,000,000 deutsche marks to organize a wholly-owned subsidiary in West Germany for manufacturing subassemblies. A condensed trial balance of the West German subsidiary for December 31, 19X8, is as follows, in deutsche marks:

	Debit	Credit
Cash	150,000	
Accounts Receivable	450,000	
Inventories	175,000	
Property, Plant, and Equipment (net)	4,525,000	
Other Assets	300,000	
Cost of Goods Sold	1,225,000	
Depreciation Expense	475,000	
Other Expenses	300,000	
Accounts Payable		100,000
Long-Term Debt		3,000,000
Common Stock		500,000
Paid-In Capital in Excess of Par		1,500,000
Sales		2,500,000
Total	7,600,000	7,600,000

The equipment is depreciated on a straight-line basis over ten years, and acquisitions occurred as follows:

January 1, 19X8	4,000,000 deutsche marks
April 1, 19X8	1,000,000
Total	5,000,000 deutsche marks

The ending inventory consists of goods manufactured uniformly throughout November and December, 19X8. The cost of goods sold represents production that occurred uniformly throughout the prior ten months. Unless otherwise stated, all other elements of income occurred uniformly throughout the year. Because the West German subsidiary is a direct and integral component of Global's operations, its functional currency is the U.S. dollar.

Although the majority of Global's purchases of subassemblies are denominated in the U.S. dollar, the following transactions were denominated in foreign currencies:

(a) On June 1, 19X8, Global purchased inventory from a British vendor. The cost of 40,000 pounds was paid on July 15, 19X8.

(b) On September 1, 19X8, Global purchased inventory from a West German vendor. The cost of 60,000 deutsche marks was paid on November 1, 19X8. At the date of purchase, Global also acquired a 60-day forward contract to buy deutsche marks at the forward rate of 1 deutsche mark = $.52.

(c) On December 1, 19X8, Global entered into a firm commitment to acquire subassemblies from a French vendor. The cost of the subassemblies that were to be delivered on February 1, 19X9, was 124,000 francs. On December 15, 19X8, Global acquired a 45-day forward contract to buy the French francs at a forward rate of 1 franc = $.17. The forward contract was purchased as a hedge on the commitment to the French vendor.

On August 1, 19X8, Global sold one-fourth of its 80% interest in a Mexican tin mine for $100,000. The net assets of the Mexican subsidiary were 4,200,000 pesos and 4,980,000 pesos on January 1, 19X8, and August 1, 19X8, respectively. Net income during the first seven months of 19X8 was 900,000 pesos, and the only capital transaction taking place during this period was a cash dividend of 120,000 pesos. The dividend was declared on June 30, 19X8, and paid on July 15, 19X8. On January 1, 19X8, the cumulative translation adjustment was $23,000.

Relevant exchange rates are as follows:

		Dollars per Unit of Foreign Currency
Deutsche marks:	January 1, 19X8	$ .47
	April 1, 19X8	.49
	September 1, 19X8	.50
	November 1, 19X8	.54
	December 31, 19X8	.55
Pounds:	June 1, 19X8	2.30
	July 15, 19X8	2.40
	December 31, 19X8	2.35
Francs:	December 1, 19X8	.17
	December 15, 19X8	.16
	December 31, 19X8	.18
Pesos:	January 1, 19X8	.06
	June 30, 19X8	.08
	July 15, 19X8	.09
	August 1, 19X8	.10

Required:

Translate the December 31, 19X8 trial balance of the West German subsidiary into dollars, and provide any supporting schedules in good form. Then calculate the effect on Global's 19X8 income as a result of the events described. All average exchange rates should be calculated, using a simple average for the period involved.

Problem 12–9.   Klug Manufacturing Company is a West German subsidiary of a U.S. company. Klug records its operations and prepares financial statements in deutsche marks (DM). However, its functional currency is the British pound (£). Klug was organized and acquired by the U.S. company on June 1, 19X6. The cumulative translation adjustment as of December 31, 19X8, was $79,860. The value of the subsidiary retained earnings expressed in British pounds and U.S. dollars as of December 31, 19X8, was £365,000 and $618,000, respectively. On March 1, 19X9, Klug declared a dividend of 120,000 DM. The trial balance of Klug in DM as of December 31, 19X9, is as follows:

	Debit	Credit
Cash	240,000	
Accounts Receivable (net)	2,760,000	
Inventory (at cost)	3,720,000	
Marketable Securities (at cost)	2,040,000	
Prepaid Insurance	210,000	
Depreciable Assets	8,730,000	
Accumulated Depreciation		1,417,000
Cost of Goods Sold	17,697,000	
Selling, General, and Administrative Expenses	4,762,000	
Sales Revenue		26,430,000
Investment Income		180,000
Accounts Payable		2,120,000
Unearned Sales Revenue		960,000
Loans and Mortgage Payable		5,872,000
Common Stock		1,500,000
Paid-In Capital in Excess of Par		210,000
Retained Earnings		1,470,000
Total	40,159,000	40,159,000

The marketable securities were acquired on November 1, 19X8, and the prepaid insurance was acquired on December 1, 19X9. The cost of goods sold and the ending inventory are calculated by the weighted-average method. The underlying costs have been incurred uniformly throughout the year. 60% of the depreciable assets existed at June 1, 19X6, and the balance was acquired on March 1, 19X8. The depreciable assets are amortized over a ten-year period by the straight-line method. Of the total depreciation expense, 80% is traceable to the cost of goods sold and the balance is in general expenses. On November 1, 19X8, Klug received a prepayment by a customer valued at 3,000,000 DM. On February 1, 19X9, 2,040,000 DM of the prepayment was earned. The balance remains unearned as of December 31, 19X9.

Relevant exchange rates are as follows:

	1 DM =	1 £ =
June 1, 19X6	£0.310	$1.600
March 1, 19X8	0.300	1.640
November 1, 19X8	0.305	1.650
December 31, 19X8	0.310	1.680
February 1, 19X9	0.302	1.670
March 1, 19X9	0.300	1.660
December 1, 19X9	0.290	1.640
December 31, 19X9	0.288	1.640
19X9 average	0.297	1.660

Required:

Translate Krug's trial balance into dollars as of December 31, 19X9. Supporting schedules should be in good form.

PART FOUR

SPECIAL REPORTING CONCERNS

An important quality of accounting information is its timeliness. In order to achieve timeliness, financial statements often are presented on an interim basis, which requires some modification of the accounting principles used to prepare annual statements. Another special reporting concern arises when a company's activities consist of several segments or lines of business. The financial statements of such conglomerates combine a variety of business activities. In order to make these statements more understandable, special disclosures should report financial information by operating segments.

Many companies are subject to the reporting and disclosure requirements of the Securities and Exchange Commission. These requirements are very extensive and call for a variety of special forms to be filed with the SEC.

CHAPTER 13

INTERIM REPORTING AND SEGMENTAL DATA

This chapter focuses on two areas of significance to most large, publicly held companies: interim reporting and segmental disclosure. The relevance of financial information is enhanced if the information is provided on a timely basis. Interim financial reporting addresses the need for timely information and provides users with relevant data which may be used to evaluate the present and help to project future results. The division of an annual reporting period into shorter interim periods results in some unique accounting problems which are addressed in this chapter. Segmental data also is concerned with providing relevant information which enhances interfirm comparability. Many companies consist of operating units which differ significantly from each other in terms of products, markets served, and manufacturing methods. Therefore, it becomes difficult to compare these diverse entities to other entities which may not have such diversity. In order to resolve this apparent lack of comparability, diverse companies are divided into segments which reflect the unique components of the company's business. Not only does segmental data improve comparability, but it also allows users to better understand how economic conditions may affect various segments of a business. The criteria for segmental disclosures are discussed in this chapter along with the specific content of such disclosures.

INTERIM REPORTING

To satisfy the need for timely financial information, many business entities have developed interim reporting models that provide financial information on a monthly or quarterly basis or at other defined intervals. These interim data may consist of statements of financial position, income statements, and statements of cash flows. However, primary emphasis is placed on the public disclosure of interim income data.

A substantial amount of empirical research has been devoted to an examination of the utility of publicly disclosed interim financial reports. This research has identified significant stock market reaction to the issuance of interim reports and has noted the influence of interim reports on actual investment decisions. Interim reports provide such an important basis for the prediction of annual income that the demand for these reports nearly parallels the demand for annual reports.

The established utility of interim data emphasizes the importance of applying generally accepted accounting principles, including the principle of adequate disclosure, to interim reports. Therefore, the American Institute of Certified Public Accountants, the National Association of Accountants, the Financial Executives Institute, the Financial Analysts Federation, the Securities and Exchange Commission, and the principal stock exchanges have directed efforts toward the development and improvement of interim financial reporting.

APPROACHES TO REPORTING INTERIM DATA

Earlier forms of interim reporting provided the user of such data with various disclosures other than the computation of net income. However, as the importance of interim income statements became more apparent, different views of the interim period developed. One view of the interim period is that it represents a distinct, independent accounting period, separate from the annual accounting period. Therefore, interim net income should be determined by using the same principles and estimations as would be used if the interim period was an annual accounting period. For example, annual repair expenditures incurred during the interim period should be expensed in that period, rather than deferred to future interim periods.

Another view of the interim period is that it is an integral part of the annual period and, therefore, does not stand as a distinct, independent period. Thus, deferrals, accruals, and estimations at the end of the interim period should depend upon estimates of annual revenue and expense relationships. Although this viewpoint requires estimates not required by the independent period viewpoint, it may result in interim data that are more indicative of annual values and that are more useful for predictive and comparative purposes.

Based on this latter viewpoint, a portion of annual repair expenditures described previously should be deferred to the year's subsequent interim periods that are benefited. For example, if the annual repair of $12,000 occurred in the first quarter, the data might be used to predict incorrectly an annual repair expense of $48,000. Thus, a quarterly allocation of the $12,000 expenditure (i.e., $3,000 expensed in the first quarter) might provide the best basis for the projection of annual expenses.

OPINIONS OF THE ACCOUNTING PRINCIPLES BOARD, NO. 28

In 1973, the Accounting Principles Board issued Opinion No. 28, "Interim Financial Reporting," which applies to both internally and externally issued reports. This Opinion was in response to the growing interest in the credibility of interim data and to the apparent need for an authoritative statement from the accounting profession regarding generally accepted accounting principles for such data. The Opinion also may have been influenced by the interim reporting requirements of the SEC.

APB Opinion No. 28 is based on the conclusion that an interim period should be viewed as *an integral part of the annual period,* not as a distinct, independent period. The Opinion reflects the APB's concern for the consistent application of principles by stating that financial statements for each interim period should be based on the *same accounting principles and practices* that are used for the preparation of annual financial statements. However, certain modifications of these principles and practices that relate to costs and expenses may be necessary so that the reported results of an interim period more closely relate to the annual income statement.

Modifications for Costs and Expenses. Those costs that are directly related or allocated to products sold or to services rendered for annual reporting purposes should be given similar treatment for interim reporting purposes. However, the following modifications are acceptable in the area of inventory costing:

1. The gross profit method or other methods that are not used for annual purposes may be used for interim purposes in those instances where taking an interim physical inventory would be too costly or where perpetual inventory records are lacking or unreliable. The inventory method used for interim purposes should be disclosed. Significant differences between estimates of the inventory and the annual physical inventory also should be disclosed.
2. Use of the Lifo method for interim purposes may result in inventory liquidations that will be replaced by year end. To compensate for these interim liquidations, the interim cost of goods sold should include the *replacement cost* of liquidated inventory.
3. The use of lower of cost or market may suggest inventory losses for the interim period. Recoveries of these losses in subsequent periods should be recognized as gains to the extent of the losses previously recognized in interim periods within the same fiscal year. An exception to this rule is that temporary market declines need not be recognized for the interim period.
4. The use of standard costs for determining inventory should be applied on the same basis as is required for annual purposes. Material price vari-

ances and volume variances that are planned and expected to be absorbed by year end ordinarily should be deferred until year end.[1]

In order to illustrate the special treatment given interim liquidations, assume that a company's Lifo inventory available for sale during the second quarter consisted of beginning inventory of 1,000 units at a cost of $20 each and current purchases of 2,000 units at a cost of $30 each. Assume 2,500 units were sold during the quarter with the expectation that they would be replaced for $32 a unit. If management anticipates that the annual ending inventory will be 900 units, the interim cost of sales would be calculated as follows:

$$
\begin{array}{ll}
\text{2,000 units @ \$30} = & \text{\$60,000} \\
\text{400 units @ \$32} = & \text{12,800} \\
\text{100 units @ \$20} = & \underline{\text{2,000}} \\
\text{Cost of sales} \quad = & \underline{\underline{\text{\$74,800}}}
\end{array}
$$

Notice that the liquidation of 500 units from the beginning inventory resulted in using the $32 replacement cost, rather than the $20 cost, for the 400 units that were expected to be replaced by year end.

In reporting costs and expenses that are not allocated to products sold or to services rendered, but are charged against income in the interim period, the following standards apply:

(a) *Costs and expenses other than product costs should be charged to income in interim periods as incurred, or be allocated among interim periods based on an estimate of time expired, benefit received or activity associated with the periods. Procedures adopted for assigning specific cost and expense items to an interim period should be consistent with the bases followed by the company in reporting results of operations at annual reporting dates. However, when a specific cost or expense item charged to expense for annual reporting purposes benefits more than one interim period, the cost or expense item may be allocated to those interim periods.*

(b) *Some costs and expenses incurred in an interim period, however, cannot be readily identified with the activities or benefits of other interim periods and should be charged to the interim period in which incurred. Disclosure should be made as to the nature and amount of such costs unless items of a comparable nature are included in both the current interim period and in the corresponding interim period of the preceding year.*

(c) *Arbitrary assignment of the amount of such costs to an interim period should not be made.*

[1]*Opinions of the Accounting Principles Board, No. 28,* "Interim Financial Reporting" (New York: American Institute of Certified Public Accountants, 1973), par. 14.

(d)   Gains and losses that arise in any interim period similar to those that would not be deferred at year end should not be deferred to later interim periods within the same fiscal year.[2]

To illustrate the above concepts, assume that the following expenditures have occurred at the beginning of the second quarter:

1.   A twelve month insurance premium was paid in the amount of $1,200.
2.   Research costs in the amount of $18,000 were paid and are expected to benefit the company over the next 18 months.
3.   A contribution in the amount of $1,000 was made although the benefits to subsequent quarters is uncertain.

The expenses to be recognized in the second quarter are as follows:

Insurance expense ($1,200 ÷ 12 × 3 months)	$ 300
Research costs ($18,000 ÷ 3 quarters—not to be deferred beyond year end)	6,000
Contribution expense	1,000
	$7,300

Certain costs and expenses of an entity are subject to year-end adjustments, such as inventory shrinkage, allowance for uncollectible accounts, and year-end bonuses. These adjustments should not be recognized totally in the final interim period if they relate to activities of other interim periods. Therefore, to generate interim financial reports that contain a reasonable portion of annual expenses, a portion of estimated year-end adjustments should be allocated to each interim period on the basis of a revenue or a cost relationship. For example, a company that estimates an expected material year-end adjustment to its perpetual inventory, based on a physical inventory, should allocate a portion of that estimated adjustment to each interim period.

The costs and expenses as well as revenues of some businesses are subject to seasonal variations. Since interim reports for such businesses must be considered as representative of the annual period, APB Opinion No. 28 states that:

> . . . such businesses should disclose the seasonal nature of their activities, and consider supplementing their interim reports with information for twelve-month periods ended at the interim date for the current and preceding years.[3]

Adjustments Related to Prior Interim Periods. By the definitions set forth in FASB Statement No. 16, "Prior Period Adjustments," many items that were viewed previously as prior period adjustments became elements

---

[2]*Ibid.*, par. 15.
[3]*Ibid.*, par. 18.

of current operating income. However, certain items are given special treatment in interim reports. For example, an adjustment or settlement of litigation or of income taxes should *not* affect current interim income, provided that *all* of the following criteria are met:

(a) *The effect of the adjustment or settlement is material in relation to income from continuing operations of the current fiscal year or in relation to the trend of income from continuing operations or is material by other appropriate criteria, and*

(b) *All or part of the adjustment or settlement can be specifically identified with and is directly related to business activities of specific prior interim periods of the current fiscal year, and*

(c) *The amount of the adjustment or settlement could not be reasonably estimated prior to the current interim period but becomes reasonably estimable in the current interim period.*[4]

If such an item occurs in other than the first interim period of the current fiscal year and if all or part of the item is an adjustment related to prior interim periods of the current fiscal year, it should be reported as follows:

(a) *The portion of the item that is directly related to business activities of the enterprise during the current interim period, if any, shall be included in the determination of net income for that period.*

(b) *Prior interim periods of the current fiscal year shall be restated to include the portion of the item that is directly related to business activities of the enterprise during each prior interim period in the determination of net income for that period.*

(c) *The portion of the item that is directly related to business activities of the enterprise during prior fiscal years, if any, shall be included in the determination of net income of the first interim period of the current fiscal year.*[5]

It should be noted that the FASB recently has been considering eliminating the special treatment given prior period adjustments in interim financial statements.

ACCOUNTING FOR INCOME TAXES IN INTERIM STATEMENTS

To be representative of annual net income, interim income should include the effect of income taxes. Accounting for income taxes in interim financial statements is based on the application of principles established in APB Opinion Nos. 23 and 24, FASB Interpretation No. 18, and FASB Statement No. 96. In addition, the following guidelines are applicable to the establish-

---

[4]*Statement of Financial Accounting Standards, No. 16, "Prior Period Adjustments"* (Stamford: Financial Accounting Standards Board, 1977), par. 13.
[5]*Ibid.*, par. 14.

ment of an effective tax rate for interim purposes that is representative of the estimated annual effective tax rate:

1. The effective tax rate for the entire current fiscal period must be estimated at the end of each interim period and applied to interim income. The interim tax expense or benefit should be the difference between (a) the year-to-date tax expense or benefit and (b) the amounts of tax reported in previous interim periods of the current year.
2. The estimated effective tax rate should reflect tax planning alternatives, such as capital gains rates, permanent differences, and tax credits. The tax effect of operating loss carryforwards, however, should be recognized only to the extent that a deferred tax liability is reduced.
3. Nonordinary items of income or loss (unusual *or* infrequently occurring items, extraordinary items, discontinued operations, and the cumulative effect of changes in accounting principles) are *not* included in the computation of the estimated effective tax rate, nor are these items prorated over the balance of the fiscal period.
4. Changes in tax legislation are to be accounted for in interim periods subsequent to the effective date of the legislation.[6]

The first guideline is designed to insure that the interim income tax rate is representative of the tax rate applicable to the entire fiscal period. For example, if income from continuing operations during the first interim period is $25,000, under a graduated taxing system the effective tax rate at this level of income might be 15%. However, if the annual ordinary income is expected to be $335,000, the effective annual tax rate might be 34%. Therefore, the latter rate should be used as the interim tax rate.

As stated in the second guideline, the estimated effective tax rate also should reflect tax planning alternatives. If necessary, the rate should be revised each interim period in order to reflect changed expectations. Both the first and fourth guidelines indirectly emphasize that changes in the estimated annual effective tax rate should be accounted for as a change in estimate. Therefore, such changes in the tax rate from period to period should be reflected in the tax expense or benefit of the current period in which the change occurs.

The computation of the estimated effective tax rate is presented in Cases A and B of Illustration 13–1. Case C demonstrates the determination of the tax expense traceable to interim income and the handling of a change in the estimated effective tax rate.

Interim Operating Losses. In some instances, an interim operating loss may be present. Given this loss, a question arises as to the potential tax benefit associated with the loss. The potential tax benefit is a function of the following three factors:

---

[6]*Opinions of the Accounting Principles Board, No. 28, op. cit.*, pars. 19–20.

Illustration 13–1
Case A

Annual operating income is expected to be $200,000. It is anticipated that a tax credit of $13,250 will be available. Assume that corporate income is taxed as follows: first $50,000 at 15%; $50,001—$75,000 at 25%; and over $75,000 at 34%. A surtax of 5% is imposed on income over $100,000 up to $335,000. The effective tax rate is computed as follows:

Item	Amount	Tax Rate	Tax Expense
Ordinary income:			
First..	$ 50,000	15%	$ 7,500
Next..	25,000	25	6,250
Next..	125,000	34	42,500
	$200,000		
Surtax amount..............................	$100,000	5	5,000
Tax credit			(13,250)
			$48,000

Effective tax rate: $48,000 ÷ $200,000 = 24%

Case B

Expected annual operating income of $120,000 includes $10,000 of goodwill amortization which is not deductible for tax purposes (i.e., a permanent difference). Assume that the statutory tax rate is 40%. Therefore, taxes payable will be equal to the taxable income of $130,000 ($120,000 + $10,000) multiplied by the rate of 40%, or $52,000 of taxes payable.

Effective tax rate: $52,000 ÷ $120,000 = 43%

Case C
Income in All Interim Periods—Change in Effective Tax Rate

Interim Period (Quarter)	Ordinary Income		Effective Tax Rate	Tax Expense (Benefit)		
	Current Period	Year-to-Date		Year-to-Date	Previously Reported	Current Period
First	$30,000	$ 30,000	40%	$12,000	—	$12,000
Second	40,000	70,000	40	28,000	$12,000	16,000
Third	20,000	90,000	45	40,500	28,000	12,500
Fourth	50,000	140,000	45	63,000	40,500	22,500

1. The extent to which the year-to-date (YTD) operating loss may be offset by income in later interim periods of the *current* fiscal year.
2. The extent to which the YTD operating loss may be offset by income of *prior* fiscal years included in a carryback period.
3. The extent to which the YTD operating loss would reduce deferred tax liabilities in *future* years included in the carryforward period.

The basic concern addressed by these factors is whether the operating loss is able to be offset against operating income and therefore result in a tax benefit. If the facts suggest that such a benefit is assured, then the benefit should be recognized in the calculation of the effective annual tax rate. Each of the three factors will be discussed in the following paragraphs.

The first factor suggests that the benefit associated with a YTD operating loss should be recognized if the loss will be offset against income in later interim periods of the fiscal year. APB Opinion No. 28 states that:

> *An established seasonal pattern of loss in early interim periods offset by income in later interim periods should constitute evidence that realization is assured beyond reasonable doubt, unless other evidence indicates the established seasonal pattern will not prevail. The tax effects of losses incurred in early interim periods may be recognized in a later interim period of a fiscal year if their realization, although initially uncertain, later becomes assured beyond reasonable doubt. When the tax effects of losses that arise in the early portions of a fiscal year are not recognized in that interim period, no tax provision should be made for income that arises in later interim periods until the tax effects of the previous interim losses are utilized.*[7]

The offset of an established seasonal loss by subsequent interim income is demonstrated in Case A of Illustration 13–2, shown on pages 758 and 759. Case B of this illustration demonstrates a YTD loss whose tax benefit is not certain initially but later becomes recognizable.

In certain instances, a current YTD interim loss may not be offset by income in later interim periods. However, as suggested by the second factor, the tax benefit of the YTD loss should be recognized to the extent that the loss may be carried back against the prior three years of income. Loss carrybacks must begin with the earliest of the prior three years and then proceed to the next earliest year. The tax benefit traceable to the loss, therefore, is a function of the tax rate applied to a prior year's income. Case C of Illustration 13–2 involves the carryback of a YTD loss. Note that in this case the loss is not offset completely against prior income. However, the tax benefit is recognized to whatever extent possible.

The same carryback principles apply if an annual loss is anticipated. For example, if a company has a YTD loss of $40,000 and an anticipated annual loss of $100,000, the amount of tax benefit would be dependent upon the extent to which the $100,000 loss may be carried back. These principles are demonstrated in Case D of Illustration 13–2.

According to the third factor, to the extent that losses are not absorbed by income in later interim periods and/or the prior three years of income, tax benefits still may be recognized currently. Losses not offset already may be

---

[7]*Ibid.*, par. 20.

carried forward against deferred tax credits which would reverse in the next 15 years. Recall that deferred tax credits result from temporary differences between accounting income and taxable income. These differences will result in taxable amounts in future years. For example, the use of an accelerated depreciation method for tax purposes and straight-line depreciation for financial purposes represents a temporary difference. Initially, this difference will result in accounting income being greater than taxable income. This difference times the present tax rate is recognized as a deferred tax credit or liability. Assume that a company has a $150,000 asset with a 5-year useful life to be depreciated by the sum-of-the-years-digits method for tax reporting and by the straight-line method for financial reporting. Depreciation expense in the first year is $50,000 and $30,000 for tax and financial purposes, respectively. The difference times an assumed present statutory tax rate of 30% would result in a deferred tax credit of $6,000 [($50,000 − $30,000) × 30%]. In future years, the difference will begin to reverse as the depreciation expense for tax purposes becomes less than the depreciation expense for financial purposes. Therefore, the deferred tax credit will be paid. However, if the current period has operating losses which cannot be offset by subsequent interim income and/or carryback provisions, these losses can be used to offset or reduce the deferred tax credits which otherwise would have become payable. It is important to note that the 15-year carryforward is only applicable if there are deferred tax credits which would reverse during that period of time. Any projections of subsequent annual income during the 15-year period against which the losses might be offset are *not* considered. The carryforward principles are demonstrated in Case E of Illustration 13–2.

If present net operating losses cannot be offset totally by any of the options discussed (subsequent interim income, carrybacks, or carryforwards), the recognized tax benefit is reduced accordingly. However, those losses which are not offset may be offset subsequently against future years' recognized income or additional deferred tax credits which may arise in the carryforward period. When the tax benefit associated with these remaining losses is recognized, it is classified the same as the item against which the losses were offset. For example, if the remaining losses were offset against subsequent income from continuing operations, the benefit would become a component of income from continuing operations. However, if the remaining losses were offset against a subsequent extraordinary item, the tax benefit would be classified as extraordinary. To demonstrate these principles, consider the facts of Case E in Illustration 13–2. In this instance, the annual anticipated loss of $80,000 was used to offset $40,000 of prior years' income and $8,000 of deferred tax credits representing the tax on $20,000 of temporary differences ($8,000 ÷ 40%) reversing in the next 15 years. Therefore, the equivalent of $60,000 ($40,000 + $20,000) of the loss was offset in order to generate the $24,000 tax benefit. The remaining loss of $20,000 (original $80,000 − $60,000 offset) may offset future income or deferred tax credits arising in the 15-year carryforward period. Assuming that the subsequent year has a recognized pretax income from continuing operations of $25,000 which would be taxed at 40%, a tax benefit of $8,000 ($20,000 × 40%), representing the offsetting of the remaining $20,000 loss against the income from continuing operations, would be recognized. The subsequent year's net tax expense on the continuing income would be $2,000, for an effective tax rate of 8% ($2,000 ÷ $25,000). The net tax expense results from the tax expense of $10,000 on the $25,000 of income reduced by the $8,000 tax benefit.

Illustration 13–2
Case A
Seasonal YTD Loss Offset by Subsequent Interim Income

Interim Period (Quarter)	Ordinary Income		Effective Tax Rate	Tax Expense (Benefit)		
	Current Period	Year-to-Date		Year-to-Date	Previously Reported	Current Period
First	($30,000)	($30,000)	40%	($12,000)	—	($12,000)
Second	20,000	(10,000)	40	(4,000)	($12,000)	8,000
Third	40,000	30,000	40	12,000	(4,000)	16,000
Fourth	40,000	70,000	40	28,000	12,000	16,000

Case B
YTD Loss where Tax Benefit is Uncertain Initially

Interim Period (Quarter)	Ordinary Income		Effective Tax Rate	Tax Expense (Benefit)		
	Current Period	Year-to-Date		Year-to-Date	Previously Reported	Current Period
First	($30,000)	($30,000)	0%	—	—	—
Second	20,000	(10,000)	0	—	—	—
Third	40,000	30,000	40	$12,000	—	$12,000
Fourth	40,000	70,000	40	28,000	$12,000	16,000

Case C
YTD Loss with No Assurance of Subsequent Interim Income;
$30,000 of Prior Three Years' Income Taxed at 50%

Interim Period (Quarter)	Ordinary Income		Effective Tax Rate	Tax Expense (Benefit)		
	Current Period	Year-to-Date		Year-to-Date	Previously Reported	Current Period
First	($40,000)	($40,000)	50%	($15,000)[a]	—	($15,000)
Second	10,000	(30,000)	50	(15,000)	($15,000)	—
Third	35,000	5,000	40[b]	2,000	(15,000)	17,000
Fourth	30,000	35,000	40	14,000	2,000	12,000

[a]Only $30,000 of the $40,000 loss can be offset against the prior years' income, resulting in a tax benefit of $15,000.
[b]The current-year statutory tax rate is 40%.

Case D
YTD and Anticipated Annual Loss with $60,000 of Prior Three Years' Income Taxed at 50%

| Interim Period (Quarter) | Ordinary Income | | Effective Tax Rate | Tax Expense (Benefit) | | |
	Current Period	Year-to-Date		Year-to-Date	Previously Reported	Current Period
First	($40,000)	($40,000)	30%ᶜ	($12,000)	—	($12,000)
Second	(30,000)	(70,000)	30	(21,000)	($12,000)	(9,000)
Third	5,000	(65,000)	30	(19,500)	(21,000)	1,500
Fourth	(35,000)	(100,000)	30	(30,000)	(19,500)	(10,500)

ᶜThe effective tax rate of 30% is based on a $30,000 tax benefit ($60,000 × 50%) expressed as a percentage of the $100,000 anticipated annual loss.

Case E
YTD and Anticipated Annual Loss with Carrybacks and Carryforwards Available

| Interim Period (Quarter) | Ordinary Income | | Effective Tax Rate | Tax Expense (Benefit) | | |
	Current Period	Year-to-Date		Year-to-Date	Previously Reported	Current Period
First	($20,000)	($20,000)	30%ᵈ	($6,000)	—	($6,000)
Second	15,000	(5,000)	30	(1,500)	($6,000)	4,500
Third	(35,000)	(40,000)	30	(12,000)	(1,500)	(10,500)
Fourth	(40,000)	(80,000)	30	(24,000)	(12,000)	(12,000)

ᵈThe calculation of the effective tax rate is based on the following:

Prior 3 years of income of $40,000 taxed at a prior rate of 40%	$16,000
Deferred tax credits reversing in the next 15 years based on the current tax rate of 40%	8,000
Total tax benefit	$24,000

The effective tax rate of 30% is based on the $24,000 total tax benefit expressed as a percentage of the $80,000 anticipated annual loss.

Nonordinary Items of Income or Loss. Certain elements making up an entity's net income are reported separately or shown net of tax. These elements include discontinued operations, extraordinary items, and cumulative effects of changes in accounting principles. As previously stated, these items are not included in the determination of the estimated effective tax rate applied to ordinary income. Therefore, the tax effect of these nonordinary items must be determined independently on an incremental basis. If *one* nonordinary item exists, the incremental income tax is the *difference* between:

1. The income tax expense (benefit) traceable to the estimated annual ordinary income, and
2. The income tax expense (benefit) traceable to the *total* of the estimated annual ordinary income plus the incremental nonordinary item.

If *several* nonordinary items exist, the incremental tax is the *difference* between:

1. The income tax expense (benefit) traceable to the *total* of the estimated annual ordinary income plus the *first* incremental nonordinary item, and
2. The income tax expense (benefit) traceable to the *total* of the estimated annual ordinary income plus the *first and second* incremental nonordinary items.

This process is repeated until all incremental items have been considered in the order in which they appear in the income statement. For example, the tax on discontinued operations is determined before the tax on extraordinary items. In Case A of Illustration 13–3, the incremental tax is calculated for a company with a nonordinary income of $20,000 (Item A) and a nonordinary loss of $10,000 (Item B).

If there is a nonordinary loss, the tax benefit of the loss should be recognized if it can be offset by other existing YTD elements of income and projected income for the balance of the year which is virtually certain. If projected income is not virtually certain, the nonordinary loss must be evaluated against YTD ordinary income. If offset by YTD income is not possible,

Illustration 13–3
Case A
Calculation of Incremental Tax

	Income	Cumulative Income Including	
		Item A	Items A & B
Ordinary Income:			
Year-to-date income......................	$100,000		
Projected income...........................	50,000		
Total ordinary income.................	$150,000	$150,000	$150,000
Nonordinary income:			
Item A..		20,000	20,000
Item B..			(10,000)
Total cumulative income		$170,000	$160,000
Tax expense:			
At statutory rate of 40%..................	$ 60,000	$ 68,000	$ 64,000
Less tax credit...............................	15,000	15,000	15,000
Total tax.....................................	$ 45,000	$ 53,000	$ 49,000
Previous tax on income.....................		(45,000)	(53,000)
Incremental tax expense (benefit):			
Item A..		$ 8,000	
Item B..			($ 4,000)

Case B
Extraordinary Loss with Carryback Assured

| Interim Period (Quarter) | Ordinary Income | | Extra-ordinary Item | Effective Tax Rate | Current Period Tax Expense (Benefit) | |
	Current Period	Year-to-Date			Ordinary Income	Extraordinary Income
First	$20,000	$20,000	—	40%	$ 8,000	—
Second	10,000	30,000	($40,000)	40	4,000	($16,000)
Third	20,000	50,000	—	40	8,000	—
Fourth	40,000	90,000	—	40	16,000	—

Case C
Extraordinary Loss with Carryback or Carryforward Not Possible

| Interim Period (Quarter) | Ordinary Income | | Extra-ordinary Item | Effective Tax Rate | Current Period Tax Expense (Benefit) | |
	Current Period	Year-to-Date			Ordinary Income	Extraordinary Income
First	$20,000	$20,000	—	40%	$ 8,000	—
Second	10,000	30,000	($40,000)	40	4,000	($12,000)*
Third	20,000	50,000	—	40	8,000	(4,000)
Fourth	40,000	90,000	—	40	16,000	—

*The tax benefit of the extraordinary loss is limited to the extent that it offsets ordinary income recognized already.

the principles discussed previously regarding carrybacks and carryforwards would be applicable. In both Cases B and C of Illustration 13–3, it is assumed that projected income is not virtually certain. Case B demonstrates the treatment of an extraordinary loss which is not entirely offset by YTD income. The YTD income is $30,000 and, therefore, $10,000 of the extraordinary loss cannot be currently offset. However, it is assumed that a carryback of the remaining loss is possible. Case C demonstrates an extraordinary loss which is not entirely offset by YTD income and which is not able to be carried back or forward against other income or deferred tax credits. Therefore, the tax benefit on the extraordinary loss is recognized only to the extent that it offsets YTD income.

Discontinued Operations. The accounting effects of a discontinued segment should be reflected in an income statement as two distinct components: (1) income or loss from operations of the discontinued segment prior to the measurement date and (2) income or loss on disposal of the discontinued segment. (Chapter 2 provides additional coverage of discontinued operations.) Both of these items should be presented net of tax. When interim statements are prepared, a problem arises in that income or loss from operations of the discontinued segment, recognized in an interim period prior to the measurement date, will have been included in ordinary income of the prior period(s) and in the determination of the effective tax rate of the prior period(s). Once the measurement date has been established, the total taxes of the prior periods must be reallocated between ordinary income (loss) traceable to continuing operations and ordinary income (loss) traceable to the discontinued operations. This allocation of the previously reported tax involves the following steps:

1. The original year-to-date and balance-of-the-year projections used to calculate the estimated effective tax rate are allocated between the continuing and discontinued operations.
2. The original tax planning alternatives, permanent differences, and tax credits used to calculate the tax rate are allocated between the continuing and discontinued operations.
3. The projected items being allocated in (1) and (2) are the originally reported amounts. That is, the projections relating to the balance of the year are not changed or revised but remain the same as in the prior interim periods. To permit the revision of an earlier projection would have the effect of accounting for a change in estimate on a retroactive basis, which is not acceptable.
4. The amounts now allocated to continuing operations are used to calculate a new effective tax rate traceable to continuing operations. The tax on the continuing operations of the prior interim period(s) also is recalculated.
5. The new tax on the continuing operations of the prior interim period(s) is compared to the originally reported tax (which included both the continuing and discontinued operations), with the difference representing the tax traceable to the discontinued operations.

From the measurement date forward, the discontinued operations will not be commingled with the continuing operations. Thus, the tax effect of the discontinued items is calculated on an incremental basis as is the case with other nonordinary items of income. The interim effect of a discontinued operation is demonstrated in Illustration 13–4.

Change in Accounting Principle. APB Opinion No. 28 indicates that, in general, a change in accounting principle during an interim period should be accounted for in accordance with APB Opinion No. 20, "Accounting Changes." To simplify the accounting for such changes, the APB encouraged management to adopt accounting changes in the first interim period of the current fiscal year. Nevertheless, the APB recognized that changes would continue to be made in other than the first interim period and, therefore, prescribed special procedures. However, these procedures were amended in 1974 by FASB Statement No. 3, "Reporting Accounting Changes in Interim Financial Statements."

When interim reports are prepared, the proper accounting for a change in an accounting principle depends on (a) whether the change requires the determination of a cumulative effect and (b) whether the change takes place in the first interim period of the fiscal year. A change requiring retroactive

Illustration 13–4
Discontinued Operations

Facts:

After issuing first-quarter interim data, the company adopted in the second quarter a formal plan calling for the disposal of one of its segments. Ordinary income reported in the first quarter included a $10,000 loss traceable to the segment being discontinued. It is assumed that any loss traceable to the discontinued segment will have tax benefits and that the estimated effective tax rate of 40% on income from continuing operations, used in the first quarter, is to be revised to 45% and applied to the remaining continuing segments.

Analysis:

The following schedule illustrates the retroactive restatement of previously issued interim data in order to disclose separately both continuing and discontinued operations.

Interim Period (Quarter)	Ordinary Income		Discontinued Segment		Effective Tax Rate	Current Period Tax Expense (Benefit) Applicable to		
	Current Period	Year-to-Date	Operating Income	Estimated Loss on Disposal		Continuing Segments	Discontinued Segment	
							Operations	Loss on Disposal
First	$40,000	$ 40,000	—	—	40%	$16,000	—	—
First—								
Restated	50,000	50,000	($10,000)	—	45	22,500	($6,500)[a]	—
Second	30,000	80,000	5,000	($60,000)	45	13,500	4,250[b]	($27,000)[b]
Third	50,000	130,000	—	—	45	22,500	—	—
Fourth	60,000	190,000	—	—	45	27,000	—	—

[a]The $6,500 tax benefit traceable to the operations of the discontinued segment is the result of comparing the tax of $22,500 traceable to continuing operations with the $16,000 of tax previously recognized as being traceable to continuing operations, which at that time included the results of the now discontinued segment. Therefore, the difference between the two tax amounts relates to the exclusion and inclusion, respectively, of the results traceable to the discontinued segment. Notice that the total tax expense presented for the first period, restated, totals $16,000, which is the tax originally reported for the first quarter.
[b]These amounts represent the incremental tax traceable to the discontinued segment less amounts reported in previous interim periods. For example, the $4,250 represents the difference between (1) the tax benefit on the loss to date traceable to the discontinued segment's operations (45% × $5,000) and (2) the tax benefit of $6,500 traceable to the discontinued segment's operating loss recognized in prior periods.

restatement of previously issued annual financial statements, rather than the determination of the cumulative effect, will require the restatement of previously issued interim financial information. If such a change occurs in other than the first interim period, such restatement also will involve the restatement of taxes to reflect the estimated effective tax rate, which is based on annual ordinary income (or loss) as determined in accordance with the newly adopted accounting principle. The restatement of the previous tax rate is affected only by the change in principle and, therefore, does not allow for any revisions of projected data that were used to calculate the earlier tax rate. This treatment is consistent with the principle that changes in estimates should not be accounted for on a retroactive basis.

If a cumulative effect-type change takes place in the first interim period of the fiscal year, the cumulative effect of the change on retained earnings as of the beginning of the year should be included in net income of the first interim period. However, if the cumulative effect-type change is made in other than the first interim period, it is assumed for accounting purposes that it took place in the first interim period. Therefore, the change should be accounted for as follows:

1. Financial statements for all interim periods in the current fiscal year should be restated to reflect the adoption of the new principle, and
2. The cumulative effect of the change on retained earnings as of the beginning of the current fiscal year should be included in the restated net income of the first interim period rather than in the interim period in which the change was adopted.[8]

Accounting for the cumulative effect of a change in principle may result in a restated tax rate for the interim periods prior to the change. As is the case with all other restatements of earlier tax rates, only the effect of the *nonordinary* income items should be considered. Therefore, the tax on the cumulative effect should be computed on an *incremental* basis, as previously illustrated, and the tax previously reported for the pre-change interim periods should be restated as follows:

> *The restated tax (or benefit) shall reflect the year-to-date amounts and annual estimates originally used for the pre-change interim periods, modified only for the effect of the change in accounting principle on those year-to-date and estimated annual amounts.*[9]

A cumulative effect-type change in principle also requires the following disclosures:

(a) *In financial reports for the interim period in which the new accounting principle is adopted, disclosure shall be made of the nature of and justification for the change.*

(b) *In financial reports for the interim period in which the new accounting principle is adopted, disclosure shall be made of the effect of the change on income from continuing operations, net income, and related per share amounts for the interim period in which the change is made. In addition, when the change is made in other than the first interim period of a fiscal year, financial reports for the period of change shall also disclose (i) the effect of the change on income from continuing operations, net income, and related per share amounts for each pre-change interim period of that fiscal year and (ii) income*

---

[8]*Statement of Financial Accounting Standards, No. 3,* "Reporting Accounting Changes in Interim Financial Statements" (Stamford: Financial Accounting Standards Board, 1974), par. 10.
[9]*FASB Interpretation No. 18,* "Accounting for Income Taxes in Interim Periods" (Stamford: Financial Accounting Standards Board, 1977), par. 64.

from continuing operations, net income, and related per share amounts for each pre-change interim period restated. . . .

(c) *In financial reports for the interim period in which the new accounting principle is adopted, disclosure shall be made of income from continuing operations, net income, and related per share amounts computed on a pro forma basis for (i) the interim period in which the change is made and (ii) any interim periods of prior fiscal years for which financial information is being presented. If no financial information for interim periods of prior fiscal years is being presented, disclosure shall be made, in the period of change, of the actual and pro forma amounts of income from continuing operations, net income, and related per share amounts for the interim period of the immediately preceding fiscal year that corresponds to the interim period in which the change is made. . . .*

(d) *In year-to-date and last-twelve-months-to-date financial reports that include the interim period in which the new accounting principle is adopted, the disclosures specified in the first sentence of subparagraph (b) above and in subparagraph (c) above shall be made.*

(e) *In financial reports for a subsequent (post-change) interim period of the fiscal year is which the new accounting principle is adopted, disclosure shall be made of the effect of the change on income from continuing operations, net income, and related per share amounts for that post-change interim period.* [10]

In a change to the Lifo inventory method, the disclosures for a cumulative effect-type change are required, except that the cumulative effect of the change on retained earnings and pro forma amounts should not be determined. If the change is made in other than the first interim period, all pre-change interim statements must be restated to reflect the adoption of the new accounting principle. The beginning inventory computed by the previous inventory method is assumed to be the beginning measure of base stock for purposes of applying Lifo.

DISCLOSURES OF SUMMARIZED INTERIM DATA

To maintain the timeliness of interim data, companies frequently report summarized interim data rather than complete financial statements. When publicly traded companies report summarized interim data, the following disclosures are required at a minimum:

(a) *Sales or gross revenues, provision for income taxes, extraordinary items (including related income tax effects), cumulative effect of a change in accounting principles or practices, and net income.*

---

[10]*Statement of Financial Accounting Standards, No. 3, op. cit.,* par. 11.

(b) *Primary and fully diluted earnings per share data for each period presented, determined in accordance with the provisions of APB Opinion No. 15, "Earnings per Share."*

(c) *Seasonal revenue, costs or expenses.*

(d) *Significant changes in estimates or provisions for income taxes.*

(e) *Disposal of a segment of a business and extraordinary, unusual or infrequently occurring items.*

(f) *Contingent items.*

(g) *Changes in accounting principles or estimates.*

(h) *Significant changes in financial position.* [11]

In addition to providing this data for the current quarter, such data should be provided for the current year to date or the last twelve months to date, plus comparable data for the preceding year.

Frequently, companies do not issue separate fourth-quarter reports or provide fourth-quarter disclosure of summarized data because annual audited statements will be forthcoming. In such cases, a note to the annual financial statements should disclose the effect of the following items for the fourth quarter: disposals of a segment, extraordinary items, unusual or infrequently occurring items, and changes in accounting principles. Disclosure in the annual financial statements also should include the aggregate effect of year-end adjustments that are material to the fourth-quarter results.

REPORTING FOR BUSINESS SEGMENTS OF AN ENTERPRISE

As discussed in Chapter 1, the concept of an accounting entity is indispensable because it defines the boundaries of the activity that is the subject matter of accounting. Typically, the accounting entity is defined for external reporting purposes as the entire enterprise. However, many modern enterprises are so diversified that disclosure of the financial activity of various components or segments of the enterprise is most useful in some instances.

IMPORTANCE OF SEGMENTAL REPORTING

The significance of reporting for segments is related closely to the corporate merger activity that took place during the 1960s. Prior to this time, merger activity could be characterized as either horizontal or vertical integration. *Horizontal integration* refers to the acquisition of companies in similar or closely related businesses, while *vertical integration* refers to acquisitions that would improve the production and/or marketing efforts of the acquiring

---

[11]*Opinions of the Accounting Principles Board, No. 28, op. cit.,* par. 30.

company. However, due to increased legal and governmental pressure, the merger activity of the 1960s departed from earlier patterns and was characterized by the acquisition of companies with activities that primarily were unrelated to the activities of the acquiring company. These mergers resulted in what generally are referred to as *conglomerates* or diversified companies. To adapt to the competitive pressures of these companies, many other firms began to diversify internally rather than through business acquisitions.

It soon became apparent that disclosure of the aggregate activities of diversified companies in the form of consolidated financial statements no longer would satisfy the informational needs of various parties. In the mid 1960s, professional business groups, governmental agencies, and investors began to emphasize the importance of disclosing the business activities of the unrelated segments that composed a diversified company. While differing on the means and extent of implementing the desire for additional information, the concept of segmental reporting has been endorsed by the American Institute of Certified Public Accountants, the Financial Executives Institute, the Financial Analysts Federation, the National Association of Accountants, the Securities and Exchange Commission, and the Federal Trade Commission.

Although total enterprise financial statements provide users with a basis for evaluating the performance of an enterprise as a whole, total performance is a function of the performance of the various segments that constitute the enterprise. Therefore, an analysis of a segment's investment opportunities, risks indicated by its profitability, its growth potential, and its production and marketing processes provides interested parties with an excellent basis for evaluating present and future performance of the segment and the enterprise as a whole. Segmental information also may provide users with an improved basis for making interenterprise comparisons between companies that have a single industry or product affiliation and segments of a similar nature within diversified companies.

There is a strong body of empirical research that supports the position that segmental data have utility. This research and the prominence of diversified companies effectively have established the importance of segmental data for maintaining an efficient capital market. For example, studies have suggested that segmental data can lead to more accurate predictions of enterprise earnings and changes in earnings levels. In addition, surveys have shown that sophisticated users, such as financial analysts, find the use of segmental data to be a significant factor in the area of security valuation.

STATEMENT OF FINANCIAL ACCOUNTING STANDARDS, NO. 14

Prior to 1976, diversified companies were free to determine the extent of segmental information to be disclosed in their financial reports to the public.

These disclosures frequently concentrated on information concerning segmental revenues and profit contributions. In 1976, the Financial Accounting Standards Board issued Statement No. 14, "Financial Reporting for Segments of a Business Enterprise," which deals with the following topics:

1. The qualifications of a reportable segment,
2. The specific segmental data that must be disclosed and how such data should be disclosed.
3. The additional data that must be disclosed concerning foreign operations, export sales, and sales to major customers.

The Statement sets forth minimum disclosure requirements for all companies composed of reportable segments. Reporting companies also are encouraged to provide additional disclosures when relevant. However, the minimum disclosures need to be presented only when a public enterprise issues a complete set of annual financial statements that presents financial position, results of operations, and cash flows in conformity with generally accepted accounting principles.[12]

Definition of a Segment. A major issue involved in segmental reporting is the determination of a business segment. Theoretically, a segment should be defined in response to the informational needs of user groups. For example, an equity investor may find the definition of segments in terms of product lines to be most useful, while the needs of another user may suggest that segments be defined in terms of broad geographical areas served by the company. Approaches to the definition of a segment have focused on such variables as geographical markets, product lines, broad industry groups, and/or profit centers employed for internal planning and control. Established classification systems for segmental reporting, such as the Standard Industrial Classification and the Enterprise Standard Industrial Classification, have been used in certain instances. However, research has suggested that such systems may not be the most appropriate means of defining business segments.

The FASB elected to define a segment as:

> ...a component of an enterprise engaged in providing a product or service or a group of related products and services primarily to unaffiliated customers (i.e., customers outside the enterprise) for a profit.[13]

Although more decisive guidelines for the definition of a segment could have been established, the FASB recognized that no single set of segment criteria would be applicable to all companies. Therefore, the FASB concluded

---

[12]*FASB Statement No. 18*, "Financial Reporting for Segments of a Business Enterprise — Interim Financial Statements," removed the former requirement that interim financial statements include segmental information.

[13]*Statement of Financial Accounting Standards, No. 14*, "Financial Reporting for Segments of a Business Enterprise" (Stamford: Financial Accounting Standards Board, 1976), par. 10.

that the definition of a segment should be left to the discretion of management. However, the following factors should be considered when determining segments:

(a) The nature of the product. *Related products or services have similar purposes or end uses. Thus, they may be expected to have similar rates of profitability, similar degrees of risk, and similar opportunities for growth.*

(b) The nature of the production process. *Sharing of common or interchangeable production or sales facilities, equipment, labor force, or service group or use of the same or similar basic raw materials may suggest that products or services are related. Likewise, similar degrees of labor intensiveness or similar degrees of capital intensiveness may indicate a relationship among products or services.*

(c) Markets and marketing methods. *Similarity of geographic marketing areas, types of customers, or marketing methods may indicate a relationship among products or services. . . . The sensitivity of the market to price changes and to changes in general economic conditions may also indicate whether products or services are related or unrelated.* [14]

If practicable, these factors should be applied on a worldwide basis. If not practicable, foreign operations may be viewed as a single segment.

Given a defined industry segment, segmental data do not need to be disclosed unless the segment qualifies as a reportable segment by satisfying *one or more* of the following criteria:

(a) *Its revenue (including both sales to unaffiliated customers and intersegment sales or transfers) is 10 percent or more of the combined revenue (sales to unaffiliated customers and intersegment sales or transfers) of all of the enterprise's industry segments.*

(b) *The absolute amount of its operating profit or operating loss is 10 percent or more of the greater, in absolute amount, of:*
  (i) *The combined operating profit of all industry segments that did not incur an operating loss, or*
  (ii) *The combined operating loss of all industry segments that did incur an operating loss.*

(c) *Its identifiable assets are 10 percent or more of the combined identifiable assets of all industry segments.* [15]

Certain exceptions to these criteria are permitted. For example, if a segment currently fails to satisfy one or more of the criteria, but has done so in the past or is expected to do so in the future, segmental disclosures should be presented so that the comparability of past and future reporting periods is preserved. Alternatively, if a segment currently happens to satisfy one or

---

[14]*Ibid.,* par. 100.
[15]*Ibid.,* par. 15.

more of the criteria, but normally does not, it may be best to view the segment as nonreportable. However, in this situation, appropriate reasons for not reporting segmental activities should be disclosed. Illustration 13–5 demonstrates the application of the criteria for determining whether a segment is reportable.

Other practical limitations concerning the number of reportable segments are identified as follows:

1. As the number of reportable segments increases above 10, serious consideration should be given as to whether the volume of segmental data begins to diminish the utility of segmental reporting.
2. The reportable segments, in the aggregate, should represent a substantial portion of the total enterprise's activities. The substantial portion test is

---

Illustration 13–5

**Reportable Segments:
Demonstration of Criteria**

Facts:

Whalen Corporation has classified its operations into industry segments and has provided the following data for each segment:

| | Revenues | | | | |
Segment:	Unaffiliated Customers	Intersegment Sales	Total	Operating Profit (Loss)	Identifiable Assets
A	$100,000	$15,000	$115,000	$ 45,000	$ 280,000
B	20,000	—	20,000	(10,000)	80,000
C	230,000	40,000	270,000	130,000	1,100,000
D	45,000	5,000	50,000	(60,000)	320,000
E	37,000	8,000	45,000	25,000	295,000
F	140,000	14,000	154,000	85,000	760,000
	$572,000	$82,000	$654,000	$215,000	$2,835,000
Corporate level	60,000	—	60,000	20,000	705,000
Total	$632,000	$82,000	$714,000	$235,000	$3,540,000

Analysis:

The determination of which segments are reportable requires the following evaluation, in which only combined data relating to the segments (not including corporate-level activity) are employed:

1. Total sales to unaffiliated customers $572,000
   Total intersegment sales 82,000
   Combined revenue $654,000

   Segment revenue required to satisfy criterion (a):
                        $654,000 × 10% = $65,400

2. | Segment | Operating Profit | Operating Loss |
|---------|-----------------|----------------|
| A | $ 45,000 | |
| B | | $10,000 |
| C | 130,000 | |
| D | | 60,000 |
| E | 25,000 | |
| F | 85,000 | |
| Total | $285,000 | $70,000 |

Portion of absolute amount of the greater of the operating profit or the operating loss to satisfy criterion (b):

$$\$285,000 \times 10\% = \$28,500$$

3. Segment identifiable assets required to satisfy criterion (c):
$$\$2,835,000 \times 10\% = \$283,500$$

Whether the criteria are satisfied is summarized as follows:

	Criterion Satisfied			
Segment	Revenue	Operating Profit (Loss)	Identifiable Assets	Segment Reportable
A	Yes ($115,000 > $65,400)	Yes ($ 45,000 > $28,500)	No ($ 280,000 < $283,500)	Yes
B	No ($ 20,000 < $65,400)	No ($ 10,000 < $28,500)	No ($ 80,000 < $283,500)	No
C	Yes ($270,000 > $65,400)	Yes ($130,000 > $28,500)	Yes ($1,100,000 > $283,500)	Yes
D	No ($ 50,000 < $65,400)	Yes ($ 60,000 > $28,500)	Yes ($ 320,000 > $283,500)	Yes
E	No ($ 45,000 < $65,400)	No ($ 25,000 < $28,500)	Yes ($ 295,000 > $283,500)	Yes
F	Yes ($154,000 > $65,400)	Yes ($ 85,000 > $28,500)	Yes ($ 760,000 > $283,500)	Yes

All of the segments are reportable except for Segment B.

satisfied if the combined revenue from *sales to unaffiliated customers* of all *reportable* segments is at least 75 percent of the combined revenue from *sales to unaffiliated customers* of all *industry* segments. If this test is not satisfied, additional segments should be classified as reportable until the test is satisfied, subject to the practical limitation discussed in item (1).

3. If a single reportable segment accounts for a "dominant portion" of the total enterprise's activities, segmental reporting is not required, although the nature of this dominant segment should be disclosed. A dominant segment is one whose "revenue, operating profit or loss, and identifiable assets each constitute more than 90 percent of related combined totals for all industry segments, and no other industry segment meets any of the 10-percent tests..."[16]

Based on the basic facts presented in Illustration 13–5, the practical limitations regarding the number of reportable segments have been satisfied.

---

[16]*Ibid.*, par. 20.

There are no more than ten reportable segments, no segment is dominant, and the reportable segments represent a substantial portion of the enterprise's activities, determined as follows:

Sales to unaffiliated customers of all reportable segments (all segments except Segment B):

$$\$572,000 - \$20,000 = \$552,000$$

Minimum level of sales to unaffiliated customers of all industry segments:

$$\$572,000 \times 75\% = \$429,000$$

The sales to unaffiliated customers of all reportable segments exceed the minimum level needed to satisfy the substantial portion limitation.

Content of Segment Disclosure. For each segment that has been determined to be reportable, the nature of the segment's products and services and its respective revenue, operating profit or loss, and identifiable assets must be disclosed. In addition, certain other disclosures are required.

The revenue to be disclosed by each of the reporting segments should include an amount for sales to unaffiliated customers and a separate amount for sales to other segments (intersegment sales). With respect to intersegment sales, the method of pricing these sales (transfer pricing) should be disclosed, and any change in methods should be discussed fully in terms of the nature and effect of the change.

Although a specific transfer pricing method is not required by FASB Statement No. 14, several methods are available. Alternative methods range from pricing based on incremental costs incurred to pricing based on negotiations that are intended to simulate actual market conditions. In the opinion of the authors, the objectives and utility of segmental reporting are best served by a transfer pricing method which, when possible, approximates the actual selling price that would have been experienced if the sale had involved an unaffiliated customer.

The reported revenue of each segment also should include interest earned from outside sources and interest earned on intersegment trade receivables. However, interest earned on advances or loans to other segments should not be included in revenues unless the lending segment's principal operations are of a financial nature.

Since operating profit is of primary interest to users of segmental data, each reportable segment must disclose its operating profit or loss, which represents the revenues discussed previously, including intersegment sales, less the operating expenses traceable to the revenues. Operating expenses that are not directly traceable to one segment but are common or traceable to several segments should be allocated among the benefiting segments on a reasonable basis. The allocation method selected should be disclosed as well as the nature and effect of any changes in methods.

A variety of expense allocation methods have been used, ranging from sophisticated modeling techniques to arbitrary methods that have not captured the true relationship between cost incurrence and segment performance. Theoretically, the allocation of common costs should be based on a cause and effect approach, since the costs would not be incurred if ultimately they did not benefit the segments. However, a controversy has focused on whether allocation is practical and whether it produces comparability among companies. As a result, an acceptable alternative approach avoids allocation altogether by disclosing only directly traceable costs. This alternative, however, presents the problem of having to distinguish clearly between directly traceable costs and allocable costs.

The operating profit or loss of each reportable segment should not include the effects of any of the following: general corporate expenses, interest expense on nontrade advances or loans from other segments (except in the case of a segment that has borrowed from another segment whose operations are mainly financial in nature), domestic and foreign income taxes, equity in the profits or losses of unconsolidated subsidiaries and investees, gains or losses on discontinued operations, extraordinary items (not including items that are unusual or infrequently occurring), the cumulative effect of changes in accounting principles, and minority interests. The nature of the items excluded from the operating profit or loss should be disclosed and an analysis of how the items relate to each segment should be provided. In addition to the disclosure of operating profit or loss, management may disclose other measures of segmental profit, such as profit contribution (segment revenue less directly traceable costs), if the nature of the profit measure is disclosed adequately.

To evaluate segmental profitability more fully, FASB Statement No. 14 requires disclosure of each reportable segment's identifiable assets that were employed to generate the revenue and operating profit or loss of that segment. Therefore, the tangible and intangible assets used exclusively by the segment and the allocated portion of shared assets are presented net of their related valuation allowances, such as accumulated depreciation and allowances for uncollectible accounts. Excluded from the measure of identifiable assets are those assets not used in the operations of a segment, such as corporate-level assets. Advances or loans to other segments should be excluded as well, unless the lending segment's operations are primarily financial in nature.

The information required to be disclosed by reportable segments also must be presented in the aggregate for the segments that do not qualify as reportable segments. Revenues, profits, and identifiable assets presented separately for each reportable segment and in the aggregate for all nonreportable segments must be reconciled to the related amounts appearing in the financial statements for the enterprise as a whole. To accomplish this reconciliation, certain adjustments and eliminations for intersegment transactions must be presented and explained in the accompanying footnotes. For example, sales between segments are included in segmental revenues but must be eliminated from the financial statements of the whole enterprise in order to present the consolidated revenues.

In addition to the previous disclosures, the following related disclosures are required:

(a) *Disclosure shall be made of the aggregate amount of depreciation, depletion, and amortization expense for each reportable segment.*

(b) *Disclosure shall be made of the amount of each reportable segment's capital expenditures, i.e., additions to its property, plant, and equipment.*

(c) *For each reportable segment disclosure shall be made of the enterprise's equity in the net income from and investment in the net assets of unconsolidated subsidiaries and other equity method investees whose operations are vertically integrated with the operations of that segment. Disclosure shall also be made of the geographic areas in which those vertically integrated equity method investees operate.*

(d) *Paragraph 17 of APB Opinion No. 20 requires that the effect on income of a change in accounting principle be disclosed in the financial statements of an enterprise in the period in which the change is made. Disclosure shall also be made of the effect of the change on the operating profit of reportable segments in the period in which the change is made.*[17]

The segmental disclosures required by FASB Statement No. 14 must be presented within the body of the financial statements, entirely in the footnotes to the financial statements, or in separate schedules that are included as an integral part of the financial statements. An example of the disclosure format appears in Illustration 13–6.

Disclosure of Foreign Operations. To this point, the reporting requirements associated with segments have been defined primarily around product or service lines. In addition to this disclosure, enterprises are required to disclose key financial data for each significant foreign geographical area, which is an area whose revenue from sales to *unaffiliated* customers or whose identifiable assets account for 10 percent or more of the respective *consolidated* amounts.

An enterprise's foreign operations are defined as:

... *those revenue-producing operations (except for unconsolidated subsidiaries and other unconsolidated investees) that (a) are located outside of the enterprise's home country and (b) are generating revenue either from sales to unaffiliated customers or from intraenterprise sales or transfers between geographic areas.*[18]

---

[17]*Ibid.*, par. 27.
[18]*Ibid.*, par. 31.

Illustration 13–6

Segmental Report

For Year Ended December 31, 19X8

	Reportable Segments		Other Segments	Adjustments and Eliminations*	Consolidated
	A	B			
Revenues:					
From unaffiliated customers....................	$10,000	$12,000	$5,000	—	$27,000
From intersegment sales...	3,000	—	2,000	($5,000)	—
Total	$13,000	$12,000	$7,000	($5,000)	$27,000
Operating profit..................	$ 3,000	$ 1,000	$ 500	($ 400)	$ 4,100
Equity in income of Co. X.....					300
General corporate expenses...					(600)
Interest expense.................					(200)
Income from continuing operations before income taxes					$ 3,600
Identifiable assets at 12/31/X8.......................	$20,000	$17,000	$8,000	($ 350)	$44,650
Investment in net assets of Co. X............................					6,350
Corporate assets					5,000
Total assets at 12/31/X8....					$56,000

*The nature of these adjustments and eliminations would be discussed in the notes accompanying this segmental report.

Information about a company's foreign operations and domestic operations must be disclosed if *one or both* of the following criteria are satisfied:

    (a) *Revenue generated by the enterprise's foreign operations from sales to unaffiliated customers is 10 percent or more of consolidated revenue as reported in the enterprise's income statement.*

    (b) *Identifiable assets of the enterprise's foreign operations are 10 percent or more of consolidated total assets as reported in the enterprise's balance sheet.* [19]

If one or both of these criteria are satisfied, the foreign operations may be divided into geographical areas, such as Western Europe and Asia or Germany and Japan. If the foreign operations consist of more than one significant geographical area, it may be more useful to disclose information about the different foreign geographical areas rather than disclosing the foreign operations as a whole.

---

[19]*Ibid.*, par. 32.

When the foreign operations of an enterprise satisfy the necessary criteria and when foreign geographical areas are significant, the enterprise must disclose the following information for domestic operations, for each significant foreign geographical area, and for the aggregate of foreign geographical areas deemed not to be significant:

1. Revenue as defined for segment disclosure, including sales between geographical areas,
2. Operating profit or loss as defined for segment disclosure, or net income or some other measure of profitability, and
3. Identifiable assets as defined for segment disclosure.

This information should be reconciled to the respective consolidated totals in a manner similar to that demonstrated in Illustration 13–6.

Export Sales and Sales to Major Customers. When an enterprise's domestic operations contain sales to *unaffiliated* foreign customers, these export sales must be disclosed if they account for 10% or more of total enterprise revenue from sales to unaffiliated customers. When an enterprise has sales to major customers or governmental agencies, sales to any single customer should be disclosed if these sales account for 10% or more of total enterprise revenue. For purposes of this disclosure, a group of entities under common control is considered to be a single customer. Federal, state, local, and foreign governments or agencies each should be considered a single customer.

When disclosure about major customers is appropriate, the nature and amount of the major sales and the identity of the segments making the sales should be disclosed. However, the names of the customers do not need to be disclosed.[20]

The segmental disclosure information from the 1987 annual report of Harnischfeger Industries, Inc. is presented in Exhibit 1. Notice that the required disclosures are made for both business and geographical segments as well as for export sales and sales to major customers.

Exhibit 1

Note 17— Segment Information

The Company designs, manufactures and markets products structured into five industry segments.

Integrated Material Handling Systems (Harnischfeger Engineers, Inc.) designs, engineers and integrates automated material

handling systems for manufacturing, distribution and warehousing applications and provides related engineering services.

Defense-Related Computer Systems (Syscon Corporation), acquired on December 30, 1986, evaluates, develops and manages

---

[20]*Statement of Financial Accounting Standards, No. 30*, "Disclosure of Information about Major Customers" (Stamford: Financial Accounting Standards Board, 1979), par. 6.

computer software systems and hardware/ software products primarily for the Department of Defense and other United States government agencies.

The Material Handling Equipment Division (Harnischfeger Corporation) designs, manufactures and markets for a wide variety of users, lines of overhead cranes, electric wire rope and chain hoists, automated monorail systems, standard components for independent regional overhead crane manufacturers, modernization of existing cranes, engineered products and a line of industrial electrical components for use in a variety of industries and applications.

The Mining Equipment Division (Harnischfeger Corporation) produces and market

electric mining shovels, electric and diesel-electric draglines, and hydraulic mining excavators for the surface mining and quarrying industries.

Papermaking Machinery and Systems (Beloit Corporation), acquired on March 31, 1986, is a leading manufacturer of papermaking machinery and allied equipment for the forest products and pulp and paper industries.

Intersegment sales are not significant. Inter-area sales are recorded at discounted market prices. Common operating plants have been allocated to the respective segments. Corporate assets include, principally, cash, cash equivalents and administration facilities.

Segments of business by industry are presented below:

BUSINESS SEGMENT	Total Sales	Operating Income	Depreciation and Amortization	Capital Expenditures	Identifiable Assets
1987					
Integrated Material Handling Systems..................................	$ 80,782	$ 1,981	$ 192	$ 814	$ 31,144
Defense-Related Computer Systems.................................	113,171	13,646	(2,002)	1,901	120,553
Material Handling Equipment........	98,057	(6,995)	2,100	1,605	74,887
Mining Equipment.......................	173,498	19,136	2,621	3,305	127,013
Papermaking Machinery and Systems.................................	492,038	33,497	12,818	19,473	552,670
Total business segments...........	957,546	61,265	15,729	27,098	906,267
Corporate....................................		(17,947)	1,579	256	53,706
Discontinued operations					90,954
Investment in affiliates.................					19,733
Consolidated total	$957,546	$ 43,318	$17,308	$27,354	$1,070,660
1986					
Integrated Material Handling Systems..................................	$ 62,704	$ (6,227)	$ —	$ —	$ 18,450
Material Handling Equipment........	107,381	(3,128)	2,922	1,615	86,041
Mining Equipment.......................	197,683	24,548	2,870	3,220	134,407
Papermaking Machinery and Systems.................................	345,917	40,937	7,673	6,193	528,591
Total business segments...........	713,685	56,130	13,465	11,028	767,489
Corporate....................................		(16,220)	1,540	306	116,072
Discontinued operations				439	64,968
Investment in affiliates.................					18,395
Consolidated total	$713,685	$ 39,910	$15,005	$11,773	$ 966,924

(continued)

BUSINESS SEGMENT	Total Sales	Operating Income	Depreciation and Amortization	Capital Expenditures	Identifiable Assets
1985					
Integrated Material Handling Systems...................	$ 59,527	$ 2,249	$ —	$ —	$ 20,997
Material Handling Equipment........	108,369	5,926	3,489	2,587	100,280
Mining Equipment.......................	199,446	31,565	2,786	2,458	135,285
Total business segments............	367,342	39,740	6,275	5,045	256,562
Corporate....................................		(10,459)	1,368	950	229,465
Discontinued operations				597	140,630
Investment in affiliates.................					13,545
Consolidated total	$367,342	$ 29,281	$ 7,643	$ 6,592	$ 640,202

Sales to agencies of the government of the United States approximated 15% of net sales in 1987. Approximately 95% of the Defense-Related Computer Systems group's sales resulted from contracts with the United States Government. The changes in accounting for pensions as described in Note 2 decreased 1986 operating income of the Mining Equipment Division, Material Handling Equipment Division and Integrated Material Handling Systems by $1,392, $1,245 and $658, respectively.

Geographical segment information is presented below:

	Total Sales	Interarea Sales	Sales to Unaffiliated Customers	Operating Income	Identifiable Assets
1987					
Unites States......................................	$684,966	$(44,842)	$640,124	$50,791	$602,475
Foreign	340,077	(22,655)	317,422	11,151	348,198
Interarea Eliminations.........................	(67,497)	67,497	—	(677)	(44,406)
	$957,546	$ —	$957,546	$61,265	$906,267
1986					
United States...................................	$545,760	$(41,389)	$504,371	$40,906	$495,665
Foreign	236,581	(27,267)	209,314	17,860	303,658
Interarea Eliminations.........................	(68,656)	68,656	—	(2,636)	(31,834)
	$713,685	$ —	$713,685	$56,130	$767,489
1985					
United States...................................	$304,890	$(28,298)	$276,592	$35,244	$235,018
Foreign	95,129	(4,379)	90,750	4,198	34,337
Interarea Eliminations.........................	(32,677)	32,677	—	298	(12,793)
	$367,342	$ —	$367,342	$39,740	$256,562

Exports of U.S. produced products were approximately $108,000, $145,000 and $131,000 in 1987, 1986 and 1985, respectively, and their destinations were as follows:

Sales of mining shovels and related parts to an agency of the government of Turkey approximated 13% of net sales in 1985.

	1987	1986	1985
North America	38%	24%	18%
South America	25	22	17
Asia	22	32	51
Europe	13	14	6
Africa	1	7	5
Australia	1	1	3
	100%	100%	100%

QUESTIONS

1. Define the account Allowance for Lifo Replacement Cost. Where would such an account appear on financial statements and under what conditions?
2. If a company expensed annual promotional fees, how would it account for such fees if they were incurred in the first quarter of the year?
3. Discuss how the taxes traceable to a second-quarter extraordinary item are determined.
4. If a change in accounting principle occurs in the third quarter of the year, how should it be disclosed in the interim statement?
5. How does the application of the lower-of-cost-or-market rule differ between interim and annual data?
6. If a company typically accrues bonuses for officers at year end, how should such bonuses be reflected in interim statements?
7. If a third-quarter estimate of annual tax credits is different than an earlier quarter's estimate, how does such a change affect the earlier quarter's reported taxes?
8. Why does segmental data improve interfirm comparability?
9. What factors should be considered in the determination of what constitutes a segment?
10. What criteria must be satisfied in order for an identified segment to be considered a reportable segment?
11. How does the sale of merchandise between significant segments affect the reported amounts of segmental operating profit or loss?

12. A manufacturing segment earned interest from another segment. One-half of the interest is traceable to a trade receivable and the balance is traceable to a loan receivable. How should such interest be reported?

EXERCISES

Exercise 1. The following data represents the accounting results and projections of four separate cases for the year ended September 30, 19X9, with year-to-date totals as of May 31, 19X9.

	Case A	Case B	Case C	Case D
Statutory tax rate....................	34%	34%	28%	28%
Year-to-date realized pretax income (loss)	$100,000	($260,000)	($120,000)	$160,000
Pretax income (loss) projected for the remainder of the year..........................	85,000	(320,000)	180,000	(245,000)
Annual tax credit available	6,000	21,000	3,000	3,000

The following additional information is available:

Case B: Pretax income was $145,000 in 19X6, $190,000 in 19X7, and $110,000 in 19X8. The effective tax rate was 30% in each of these years.

Case C: A total deduction of $15,000 for the amortization of goodwill is included in the 19X9 figures. Such amortization is not deductible for income tax purposes. Established seasonal patterns assure the realization of the tax benefit associated with the year-to-date loss and the $3,000 available tax credit.

Case D: Year-to-date income includes interest income of $25,000 on tax-free municipal bonds and interest expense of $7,000 on a loan for the purchase of these bonds. Pretax income (loss) was $80,000 in 19X6, ($20,000) in 19X7, and $60,000 in 19X8. The effective tax rate was 35% in each of these years.

Calculate the effective annual tax rate for each case.

Exercise 2. The following is a list of account titles found on the books of Seymour Corporation:

(a) Inventory Shrinkage
(b) Research and Development Costs
(c) Inventory
(d) Prepaid Expenses
(e) Unfavorable Materials Usage Variance

Discuss the methods of evaluating each account for presentation in interim financial statements of the corporation. Indicate any deviation from normal accounting procedure that is required for presentation. If there are alternatives, discuss each separately.

Exercise 3. Reimer Industries reported a pretax income from continuing operations of $110,000 for the first quarter of 19X9 and projected income of $475,000 for the remainder of the year. The statutory tax rate is 34%. In the second quarter, Reimer Industries decided to change from the straightline method of depreciation to an accelerated method for some of its equipment. The cumulative effect of this change is to decrease income in the first quarter by $30,000 and decrease the income of prior years by $70,000. Due to this change, Reimer projected the remainder of 19X9's income to be $55,000 less than previously estimated. Reimer also concluded that some of its equipment should have a 5-year useful life rather than a 10-year life. Had Reimer been using a 5-year life, the first quarter of 19X9 would have had additional depreciation expense of $10,000, and the past years' depreciation expense would have increased by $35,000. The effect of this change would be to reduce projected income for the remainder of 19X9 by an additional $40,000.

Prepare in good form the calculation of the original and restated interim income (loss) and tax expense (benefit) for Reimer Industries' first quarter of 19X9.

Exercise 4. Wert Company has sought assistance in preparing its second quarter income statement for 19X2. Figures for sales revenue, selling expenses, and general and administrative expenses are $860,000, $68,000, and $117,000, respectively.

For each of the following situations, determine the cost of goods sold and prepare an interim income statement in good form for the three months ended June 30, 19X2.

(1) Wert uses a standard cost accounting system for inventory and product costs. Net unfavorable cost variances for the second quarter total $2,600 and represent the difference between actual and standard production costs. Management considers such variances as a manufacturing cost and includes them in the income statement above the gross profit line. It is expected that an unfavorable purchase price variance of $900 will be absorbed by December 31, 19X2.

Production for the second quarter at standard cost was $600,000. Beginning and ending finished goods inventories (standard cost) were $71,000 and $98,000, respectively.

(2) The Lifo cost of goods sold was $596,000 and includes sales of 15,000 units costed out at their 19X1 base layer cost of $7 per unit. The current replacement cost of these units is $11 per unit. It is expected that the 19X2 year-end inventory will be 2,000 units less than the 19X1 year-end inventory.

(3) Beginning inventory of $52,000 reflects a first quarter write-down of $2,200 due to the application of the lower-of-cost-or-market rule. Through a market price recovery in the second quarter, inventory increased in value by $3,750. Wert purchased 18,000 units of inventory ($28 per unit) in the second quarter. Ending inventory (Fifo basis) was $60,500.

Exercise 5.   Weiss Corporation reported $65,000 of pretax income from continuing operations during the first quarter of 19X9. Projected income for the remainder of 19X9 was $140,000, of which $110,000 was traceable to continuing operations. Estimated annual tax credits were $5,000. The statutory tax rate is 34%. Second-quarter pretax income from continuing operations was $42,000, with anticipated income from continuing operations for the remainder of 19X9 of $60,000.

During the second quarter, Weiss Corporation decided to discontinue a segment. Prior to the measurement date, amounts traceable to the discontinued segment included a $4,000 income for the first quarter and a $5,500 loss for the second quarter. The discontinued segment had a second-quarter, post-measurement date loss of $8,000. The segment estimated additional losses prior to disposition to be $30,000 plus estimated gain on disposal of the assets of $10,000. The company revised its estimated tax credits traceable to annual continuing operations to $8,000.

Prepare in good form the calculation of the original and restated interim income (loss) and tax expense (benefit) for Weiss Corporation's first two quarters of 19X9. Include a supporting schedule showing the calculation of the estimated effective tax rates.

Exercise 6.   Various users of financial data recognize that there are certain factors, such as the availability of alternative accounting principles (e.g., Lifo, Fifo), that in general reduce intercompany comparability. However, segmental reporting has been suggested as a means of improving comparability between single-industry companies and diversified companies.

Limiting your response to the unique aspects of segmental reporting, identify those factors that would tend to reduce the intercompany comparability of segmental data.

Exercise 7.   The following partial trial balance as of December 31, 19X8, is given for Wordan Company:

	Segment			
	A*	B	C	Corporate
Cost of Goods Sold	N/A	145,000	210,000	
Selling and General Expenses	105,000	20,000	108,000	30,000
Interest Expense on:				
Trade Payables	N/A	15,000	8,000	
Loan Payables to A	—	20,000	10,000	
Income Tax Expense	—	—	—	
Sales Revenue:				
Outside Sales	N/A	150,000	500,000	120,000
Intersegment Sales	N/A	20,000	48,000	
Interest Income	400,000	—	3,000	
Extraordinary Gain	—	50,000	—	

*Segment A is a bank.

Determine which segment(s) would be reportable based on operating profit or loss.

Exercise 8. The following information is given for the seven segments of Staven Supplies:

Segment	Revenues	Operating Profit (Loss)	Identifiable Assets
1..	$1,540,000	$ 602,000	$1,600,000
2..	805,000	(208,000)	870,000
3..	1,948,000	530,000	1,250,000
4..	1,070,000	375,000	1,800,000
5..	760,000	220,000	965,000
6..	980,000	402,000	1,400,000
7..	1,071,000	(106,000)	1,380,000
Corporate-level items........................	820,000	170,000	560,000
	$8,994,000	$1,985,000	$9,825,000
Intercompany adjustments and eliminations............................	(278,300)	(75,000)	(305,000)
Consolidated total............................	$8,715,700	$1,910,000	$9,520,000

10% of the revenues of segments 2, 4, and 5 are traceable to intersegment sales.

(1) Determine which segments are reportable.

(2) Determine whether a substantial portion of Staven's total operations is represented by reportable segments.

(3) Determine which segments would qualify as significant geographical areas, assuming the following geographical classifications:

Location	Segments
Central America	1, 2, 3
Middle East	4, 5
Western Europe	6, 7

Exercise 9. Badger Industries is a large international company with extremely diversified activities. These activities include:

(a) Food processing operations in Chicago, Tulsa, and Louisville. Processed foods under several labels are sold to independent grocers throughout the Midwest and Southwest. Cans used in the operation are manufactured by Krystal Can Company, a wholly-owned subsidiary.

(b) Seven citrus groves in central Florida. Approximately 70% of a harvest is trucked to the company's Louisville food processing operation, the balance of the harvest is processed, on location, into frozen juice concentrates.

(c) A Cleveland operation that manufactures packaging for perishable food products and cardboard packaging for transporting equipment components, such as engines and transmissions.

(d) Four large resort hotels, three of which are located along the eastern seaboard and one of which is located in the Bahamas.

(e) A chain of travel agencies in the New York and Boston areas.

(f) A paper products division that manufactures napkins, paper plates, paper towels, and greeting cards. These products are sold to grocery stores and variety stores.

Determine how the activities of Badger should be classified into segments for external reporting purposes.

PROBLEMS

Problem 13–1. Pintex Corporation prepares quarterly financial statements for its shareholders. In the first quarter of 19X9, Pintex experienced a $90,000 pretax loss. Due to the seasonal nature of its products, the company projected total annual income of $380,000. Annual tax credits were estimated at $8,000. The statutory tax rate is 34%.

During the second quarter, Pintex had pretax income of $145,000. At the beginning of the second quarter, Pintex changed depreciation methods from accelerated to straight-line. The cumulative effect of this change on prior years is an increase in pretax income of $26,000. The effect on the first quarter would be to offset $8,000 of the loss. The change in depreciation methods would have caused the annual income estimated at the end of the first quarter to be $410,000. At the end of the second quarter, estimated annual income was $450,000.

In the third quarter, the company experienced an extraordinary loss of $45,000. Pretax income from operations remained strong for the third quarter at $210,000. Expected income for the remainder of 19X9 was $160,000. The amount of annual tax credits was revised to $6,000.

Required:

Prepare in good form the calculation of each quarter's income (loss) and tax expense (benefit). Include restated quarters for the cumulative effect of the change in accounting principle. Also provide a supporting schedule showing the calculation of the estimated effective tax rates.

Problem 13–2. Paxton Company has sought assistance in preparing its third quarter income statement for 19X8. Pertinent data for the third quarter are as follows:

(a) The estimated effective tax rate has been revised in the third quarter to 40% as compared to management's earlier estimate of 30%. This new rate also is to be used to restate prior periods due to the decision to discontinue operations.

(b) Income before taxes from all operations was $1,420,000.

(c) The cost of goods sold from all operations was determined by the Lifo inventory method as follows:

	Total	Average Cost Per Unit
Beginning inventory.........	$ 500,000	$50
Purchases......................	1,800,000	60
Goods available..............	$2,300,000	
Ending inventory.............	100,000	
	$2,200,000	

It is expected that the annual 19X8 ending inventory will be $400,000 and that the replacement cost of inventory will be $65 per unit during the fourth quarter of 19X8.

(d) Included in the revenues is a rather unusual, first-time sale of marketable securities that were acquired in an earlier year as part of an investment portfolio. The securities sold during the third quarter had a basis of $210,000 and were sold for $185,000.

(e) During the third quarter, management adopted a plan calling for the discontinuation of its engineering consulting segment. The performance of this segment, excluding disposals of assets, is as follows:

	Quarter			
	1	2	3	4 (Expected)
Revenue...	$800,000	$ 400,000	$200,000	$300,000
Depreciation...	(25,000)	(20,000)	(18,000)	(18,000)
Other operating expenses.......................	(700,000)	(1,100,000)	(622,000)	(632,000)
Income before taxes	$ 75,000	($ 720,000)	($440,000)	($350,000)

Approximately 90% of all third-quarter revenue and expenses relate to the period prior to the measurement date. It is expected that the operations of the segment during 19X9 prior to final disposal will result in a pretax loss of $100,000.

Some of the assets of the discontinued segment were sold prior to the measurement date for a loss of $50,000. The balance of the segment's assets will be disposed of in 19X9 for an estimated gain of $500,000.

(f) Revenue for the third quarter also includes $160,000 of revenue resulting from the settlement of a rate dispute traceable to the first quarter of 19X8. The amount of the settlement could not be estimated previously.

Previously issued interim income statements reported pretax net losses of $950,000 for the first two quarters of 19X8. At that time, only $400,000 of the losses were carried back to prior years (at a prior-year rate of 30%), with no assurance that the balance of the losses had tax benefits (i.e., could be carried forward).

Required:

Prepare in good form a partial income statement for the third quarter of 19X8 and all necessary supporting schedules.

Problem 13–3.   Mikelson Company, a California corporation listed on the Pacific Coast Stock Exchange, budgeted activities for 19X5 as follows:

	Amount	Units
Net sales	$6,000,000	1,000,000
Cost of goods sold..	3,600,000	1,000,000
Gross profit..	$2,400,000	
Selling, general, and administrative expenses	1,400,000	
Operating income...	$1,000,000	
Nonoperating revenue and expenses.........................	—	
Income before income taxes.................................	$1,000,000	
Estimated income taxes (current and deferred)............	550,000	
Net income...	$ 450,000	
Earnings per share of common stock.........................	$4.50	

Mikelson has operated profitably for many years and has experienced a seasonal pattern of sales volume and production. For 19X5, sales volume is expected to follow a quarterly pattern of 10%, 20%, 35%, and 35%, respectively, because of the seasonality of the industry. Also, due to production and storage capacity limitations, it is expected that production will follow a pattern of 20%, 25%, 30%, and 25% per quarter, respectively.

At the end of the first quarter of 19X5, the controller of Mikelson prepared and issued the following interim report for public release:

	Amount	Units
Net sales	$600,000	100,000
Cost of goods sold..	360,000	100,000
Gross profit..	$240,000	
Selling, general, and administrative expenses	275,000	
Operating loss...	($ 35,000)	
Loss from warehouse fire....................................	(175,000)	
Loss before income taxes....................................	($210,000)	
Estimated income taxes	—	
Net loss...	($210,000)	
Loss per share of common stock..............................	($2.10)	

The following additional information is available for the first quarter, but was not included in the public information released:

(a) The company uses a standard cost system in which standards are set at currently attainable levels on an annual basis. At the end of the first quarter, there was an underapplied fixed factory overhead (volume variance) of $50,000 that was treated as an asset at the end of the quarter. Production during the quarter was 200,000 units, of which 100,000 were sold.

(b) The selling, general, and administrative expenses were budgeted on a basis of $900,000 fixed expenses for the year plus $.50 variable expenses per unit of sales.

(c) Assume that the warehouse fire loss met the conditions of an extraordinary loss. The warehouse had an undepreciated cost of $320,000; $145,000 was recovered from insurance on the warehouse. No other gains or losses are anticipated this year from similar events or transactions, nor has Mikelson had any similar losses in preceding years; thus, the full loss will be deductible as an ordinary loss for income tax purposes.

(d) The effective income tax rate, for federal and state taxes combined, is expected to average 55% of income before income taxes during 19X5. There are no permanent differences between pretax accounting income and taxable income.

Required:

(1) Without reference to the specific situations described in this problem, what are the standards of disclosure for interim financial data (published interim financial reports) for publicly traded companies? Explain.

(2) Identify the weaknesses in form and content of Mikelson's interim report without reference to the additional information.

(3) For each of the four items of additional information, indicate the preferable treatment for interim reporting purposes and explain why that treatment is preferable.

(AICPA adapted)

Problem 13–4.   At the end of the first quarter of 19X9, Spirex Company reported pretax income from continuing operations of $45,000 and projected $110,000 of income for the remainder of 19X9. Estimated tax credits for the year were $9,000.

During the second quarter, Spirex Company decided to make two changes. The first involved a re-evaluation of the useful lives of certain depreciable assets. If the change in useful lives had been made earlier, first-quarter income would have decreased by $4,000, and projected income for the remainder of the year would have been $11,000 less.

The second decision was a change in depreciation methods. Depreciation expense for prior years would have been reduced by $21,000. The effect on the first quarter from this change was a decrease in pretax income of $5,500. The first quarter projection of income for the remainder of 19X9 was revised to $98,000 due to this change.

The pretax income from continuing operations for the second quarter was a loss of $50,000 after the change in depreciation methods and useful lives. Projected income for the last half of 19X9 was $60,000. The estimated annual tax credits were reduced to $5,200. Realization of any tax benefits and tax credits is assumed due to the seasonal nature of the business.

Due to poor results in the first half of the year, a decision was made in the third quarter to discontinue a segment. Income and losses traceable to the discontinued segment prior to the measurement date were as follows: a $12,000 income, a $34,000 loss, and a $7,000 loss for the first three quarters, respectively. The post-measurement date effect of the decision was an $8,000 loss. The effects on earlier projections due to the discontinued operations were as follows: no change in the projection made at the end of the first quarter and a $7,000 decrease in the projected income made at the end of the second quarter.

The third-quarter pretax income from continuing operations is $28,000, with projected income of $14,000 for the fourth quarter. Pretax income (loss) as reported originally for the prior three years was ($22,000), ($8,000), and $36,000, respectively. The statutory tax rate for prior years and the present year is 30%.

Required:
(1) Prepare in good form the calculation of the income (loss) and tax expense (benefit) for the first three quarters of 19X9. Include restated quarters as needed, and provide a supporting schedule showing the calculation of the effective tax rates.
(2) Recompute the third quarter results given the following changed information:
   (a) Assume that the post-measurement date effect of the discontinued operations was a $63,000 loss and,
   (b) Pretax income (loss) for the prior three years was as follows:

19X8	($25,000)
19X7	30,000
19X6	15,000

The tax rate for these years was 35%. There was no income or loss for years prior to 19X6.

Problem 13–5.   Doyle Corporation reported pretax income from continuing operations of $80,000 for the first six months of 19X4, with projected income of $40,000 for the next six months. Associated tax expense for the first six months was based on a statutory rate of 40%.

In the third quarter of 19X4, Doyle Corporation reported a pretax loss of $120,000 from continuing operations. This amount included the effects of a change in accounting principle that occurred during the quarter. The pretax effect of the change was a decrease of $40,000 in the first six months' income and a decrease of $10,000 in 19X3 income. If the principle adopted in the third quarter had been in effect during the first six months of 19X4, the projected income at that time would have been $30,000 for the second six months rather than the previously estimated $40,000. Although the third-quarter results were a disappointment, the company projected a fourth-quarter pretax income from continuing operations of $20,000. Any losses could be partially carried back against previous years' cumulative pretax income of $15,000, which was taxed at 40%.

The fourth quarter produced a pretax income from the now continuing operations of $30,000. A decision was made in the fourth quarter to discontinue a segment, the significance of which is summarized as follows:

Income (loss) prior to measurement date:

Traceable to quarter 4, 19X4	($ 5,000)
Traceable to quarter 3, 19X4	(60,000)
Traceable to quarters 1 and 2, 19X4..	—
Income (loss) from measurement date to year end	(18,000)
Anticipated gain subsequent to year end	15,000

The third-quarter projection of fourth-quarter income included $40,000 traceable to continuing operations. The fourth-quarter tax expense or benefit traceable to continuing operations is based on the assumption that any operating loss carryforward is not assured beyond a reasonable doubt.

Although 19X4 was a difficult year, management's decisions began to pay off, as evidenced by a first-quarter, 19X5 pretax income from continuing operations of $40,000, with an annual projected income of $120,000 and a projected 19X5 tax credit of $12,000.

Required:

Prepare in good form the calculation of the income (loss) and tax expense (benefit) for each interim period of 19X4 and the first quarter of 19X5. Include restated quarters as needed. A supporting schedule showing the calculation of the estimated effective tax rates should be provided.

Problem 13–6. Kersten Corporation began operations in 19X8 and reported a pretax income of $8,000 when the statutory tax rate was 30%. There were no permanent differences in this first year of operations. In the first quarter of 19X9, the company reported pretax income of $30,000. The income included $2,000 of goodwill amortization which represented one-fourth of the annual amount. This amortization is not deductible for income tax purposes. In the first quarter only, the income did not include the effects of the following items:

(a) Annual bonuses to officers estimated to be $32,000 and
(b) Research and development costs of $30,000 that were incurred in the quarter and that are expected to benefit the next four years of operations.

Projected pretax income for the balance of the year was estimated to be $40,000, and energy tax credits in the amount of $4,000 were estimated to be earned in the first nine months.

In the second quarter of 19X9, the company experienced a pretax loss of $34,000, including the amortization of goodwill. This loss also included the Lifo cost of goods sold in the amount of $12,000, traceable to the liquidation of a product line. It is expected that the inventory will be replaced in the third quarter at a cost of $15,000 and that a similar liquidation will not occur. Due to the severity of economic conditions, it is estimated that subsequent quarters will generate a pretax loss of $20,000. A temporary difference which occurred in 19X8 resulted in a deferred tax credit (liability) of $2,000 which is expected to be reversed in 19X9.

During the third quarter of 19X9, the company decided to restructure itself. It sold off certain assets, acquired a new operating division, and revalued goodwill. These actions resulted in a modest pretax income of $12,000 including goodwill amortization of $1,500 for the quarter. However, it is expected that the restructuring will result in a fourth-quarter pretax income of $18,000.

Required:

Assuming a 19X9 statutory tax rate of 40%, prepare in good form the calculation of each quarter's income (loss) and tax expense (benefit). Provide a supporting schedule showing the calculation of the estimated effective tax rates.

Problem 13–7. At the end of the first quarter of 19X9, Interco reported pretax income from continuing operations of $30,000 and projected another $60,000 of income for the balance of the year. It was estimated that certain tax credits totaling $6,000 would be available during the year.

Midway through the second quarter, the company decided to change its method of computing depreciation. The change had the following effects:

	Incremental Impact on Pretax Income
Prior years	$25,000
First quarter	7,000
First half of second quarter	4,000
First-quarter projection for the balance of the year	22,000

The second quarter resulted in a pretax loss of $80,000 which was based on the newly adopted depreciation method. Unfortunately, a loss of $2,000 was projected for the balance of the year. The estimated amount of annual tax credits was reduced to zero.

Due to the poor results in the first half of the year, a decision was made in the third quarter to discontinue an operation. The discontinued operation had the following profits and losses:

	Income/(loss)
Pre-measurement date realized effects traceable to the discontinued operation:	
First quarter	($20,000)
Second quarter	(60,000)
Third quarter	(10,000)
Portion of earlier projections traceable to the discontinued operation:	
First-quarter projection	(15,000)
Second-quarter projection	(62,000)
Post-measurement date effects traceable to the discontinued operation:	
Third quarter	(8,000)
Fourth-quarter estimate	(50,000)
Subsequent-year estimate	70,000

The third-quarter pretax income from continuing operations was $30,000, with a projected income of $20,000 for the balance of the year. It was estimated that tax credits of $2,000 would be available to the company in the fourth quarter.

Pretax income from continuing operations in the prior three years totaled $10,000 as originally reported. The statutory tax rate for the prior and current years is 30%.

Required:

Prepare in good form the calculation of the income (loss) and tax expense (benefit) for the first three quarters of 19X9. Include restated quarters as needed, and prepare a schedule showing the calculation of the effective tax rates.

Problem 13–8. Tress Corporation is a rapidly growing company that has diversified into a number of different segments. The following partial trial balance which includes the effect of intercompany transactions is for the year ended December 31, 19X9:

Net Sales..	(14,332,250)
Cost of Goods Sold..............................	7,180,000
General and Administrative Expenses.....	1,620,000
Gain on Sale of Fixed Asset...................	(100,000)
Investment Income	(315,000)
Interest Income	(162,000)
Extraordinary Loss................................	230,000
Discontinued Operations:	
Loss from Operations........................	781,000
Loss from Disposal of Assets..............	481,000
Income Tax Expense	940,000

Tress Corporation has 5 distinct segments (A–E) in addition to corporate operations. Net sales are allocated to the segments as follows:

Segment	Net Sales
A	$ 4,023,500
B...	2,749,000
C...	574,500
D	6,185,250
E...	800,000
Total	$14,332,250

Ten percent of D's sales are made to A, and 7% of B's sales are made to C. The cost of the goods sold to A by D is $200,000, and the cost of the goods sold to C by B is $144,000. The total cost of goods sold is allocated to the segments by the following percentages: A 30%, B 29%, C 6%, D 24%, and E 11%. Of the items C purchased from B, 25% are included in C's ending inventory.

Of the general and administrative expenses, 20% are traceable to corporate operations. The balance is allocated in proportion to segment revenues, including interest income and the gain on the sale of the fixed asset.

Investment income is traceable to corporate operations.

Interest income is traceable directly to the segments and the corporate level as follows:

Segment A...	$48,000
Segment B...	19,000
Segment C...	—
Segment D...	60,000
Segment E...	12,000
Corporate level.......................................	23,000

Segment B's (a manufacturing segment) interest income includes $9,000 traceable to a short-term, $100,000 loan to C.

Unconsolidated assets are identifiable as follows:

	A	B	C	D	E	Corporate
Current assets.....	$ 912,000	$ 681,000	$ 305,000	$ 309,000	$ 389,000	$ 115,000
Property, plant, and equipment (net)...............	7,136,000	4,643,000	1,480,000	4,181,000	1,543,000	1,737,000

Included in B's property, plant, and equipment is a machine that B purchased at the beginning of the year from A for $300,000. Segment A originally purchased the machine for $250,000, two years prior to this sale. Accumulated depreciation (straight-line method) on the machine was $50,000 at the time of the sale. Segment B recorded $30,000 of depreciation on the machine for the year based on the straight-line method. The gain on the sale of the machine is included in A's revenue.

Required:

Develop a schedule that will report the revenues, operating profits, and identifiable assets of the reportable segments and other segments and will reconcile these items to the December 31, 19X9 consolidated amounts.

Problem 13–9. Thel Corporation is a highly diversified company composed of four industry segments. Segment A involves the production of commercial fishing equipment, Segment B manufactures health aids, Segment C consists of several pulp and paper mills, and Segment D produces recreational vehicles. Thel has prepared the consolidated income statement at the top of the next page and has asked for assistance in the preparation of segmental data.

Of the total annual sales, 20% are to foreign customers, most of whom are located in certain Scandinavian countries. The revenues generated by segments during 19X3 were as follows: $125,000 by A, $23,000 by B, $21,000 by C, and $71,000 by D. An additional transaction occurring in 19X3, but not considered in the segment sales figures, was a sale by Segment D to Segment C. Goods costing $7,500 were sold for $10,000, and 30% of these goods remain in C's inventory at year end.

Thel Corporation
Consolidated Income Statement
For Year Ended December 31, 19X3

Sales		$240,000
Cost of goods sold	$168,250	
General and administrative expenses	22,000	
Selling expenses	14,000	204,250
Operating income		$ 35,750
Other income and expenses:		
Interest income	$ 3,500	
Equity in income of unconsolidated investees	8,750	
Interest expense	(4,500)	7,750
Income from continuing operations before income taxes		$ 43,500
Provision for income taxes		13,050
Income from continuing operations		$ 30,450
Discontinued operations:		
Loss from operations of Florida plant (net of income tax effect)	($ 6,500)	
Gain on disposal of Florida plant (net of income tax effect)	10,300	3,800
Income before extraordinary item		$ 34,250
Extraordinary loss (net of income tax effect)		(2,600)
Net income		$ 31,650

The cost of goods sold by segment is:

Segment A...	$72,000		Segment C...	$14,000
Segment B...	15,500		Segment D...	76,000

The general and administrative expenses are analyzed as follows:

Directly traceable to the corporate level	$7,400
Directly traceable to Segment A	3,700
Directly traceable to Segment B	2,200
Directly traceable to Segment C	1,900
Directly traceable to Segment D	2,800

The balance of these expenses and the selling expenses are allocated to the segments based on sales (including intersegment sales).

The interest income of $3,500 represents the earnings on marketable securities controlled by corporate headquarters. The gain on discontinued operations is traceable to Segment A, while the extraordinary loss is traceable to operations in Segment B.

Consolidated assets (net of appropriate contra assets) total $601,000 and are identifiable as follows:

Corporate level	$ 89,000
Segment A	251,000
Segment B	37,000
Segment C	43,000
Segment D	158,000
Investment in unconsolidated subsidiaries...	23,000

Eliminated from total assets is a $9,000 loan receivable held by Segment A against Segment B.

Required:

(1) Develop a schedule that will report the revenues, operating profits, and identifiable assets of the reportable segments and other segments and will reconcile these items with the related consolidated amounts. Be sure to provide support for the determination of reportable segments.

(2) Write the footnote that would accompany the reports generated in (1).

Problem 13–10.   Agri-Tech Company is composed of six segments. The revenues, operating profit, and identifiable assets of each segment for the year ended December 31, 19X3, are as follows:

Segment:	Revenues	Operating Profit (Loss)	Identifiable Assets
A	$ 20,000	$ 5,000	$ 25,000
B	280,000	90,000	210,000
C	15,000	(7,000)	30,000
D	175,000	20,000	70,000
E	35,000	12,000	60,000
F	45,000	15,000	45,000
Corporate level	—	—	20,000
	$570,000	$135,000	$460,000

Segments A through C are domestic segments; Segments D through F are foreign geographical areas.

The cost of goods sold for domestic segments is equal to 30% of revenues, including interest income. The cost of goods sold for foreign operations is 25% of the sales price.

Corporate expenses account for $23,250 of the general, administrative, and selling expenses, which total $300,000.

The provision for income tax for 19X3 is $25,500. Interest expense on corporate-level debt is $12,000. All revenues are to unaffiliated customers except:

(a) A sale of goods from domestic Segment C to foreign Segment D. The goods were transferred at a price of $3,000. As of year end, 20% of these goods remain in D's inventory.

(b) At midyear, domestic Segment B advanced to foreign Segment D the sum of $5,000, which is to be repaid with interest in one year at an annual interest rate of 10%. Domestic Segment B is a financial institution.

(c) A sale identical to that described in (a) was made by Segment B to Segment C.

Required:

Develop a segmental report for Agri-Tech Company based on geographical areas. Be sure to include support for the determination of reportable foreign operations by geographical area.

CHAPTER 14

THE SECURITIES AND EXCHANGE COMMISSION

This chapter is intended to provide a brief overview of the Securities and Exchange Commission (SEC). The Commission's history and organizational structure will be discussed. In addition, a number of acts administered by the SEC will be identified, with particular attention given to the Securities Act of 1933 and the Securities Exchange Act of 1934 and their related disclosure requirements. The effect of the SEC on standard setting, professional ethics, and professional liability also will be discussed. Volumes have been devoted to examining the role and impact of the SEC. Therefore, one must note that this chapter only scratches the surface of a very large topic.

ORIGIN OF THE SEC

The growth of the industrial revolution brought about an increasing number of corporations characterized by separation of management and ownership. As the industrial base grew, capital markets expanded, and organized securities exchanges developed. In order for such markets to function properly, a system of full and fair disclosure was necessary. Unfortunately, such a system of disclosure was slow to develop.

Prior to the formation of the SEC, several unsuccessful attempts were made to provide for federal regulation dealing with financial disclosure. A number of states enacted securities laws known as "Blue Sky" laws, in reference to some security schemes which had no more basis than a piece of blue sky. These state statutes often were ineffective due to the existence of legal exceptions to the laws and a lack of enforcement. Another problem was that state laws did not address the sale of securities through instruments of interstate commerce.

The early 1900s saw a number of deceptive trading and exporting practices. Some traders engaged in "wash" sales, which involved the selling and subsequent repurchase of stock. This practice resulted in inflating trade volumes and artificially increasing security prices. The securities market also suffered from a lack of financial disclosure. Managements of publicly traded companies often used "inside" (undisclosed) information to their advantage. Certain critical values, such as sales, cost of goods sold, and depreciation were not presented clearly. One study documenting inadequate disclosure was conducted by Lawrence Sloan using 1927 financial reports. The study found that 43% of the gross incomes were not reported by 57% of the companies studied and that only 40% of the companies disclosed the amount of depreciation and depletion.[1] In addition to inadequate disclosure, fraudulent reporting went undetected and, in turn, affected the securities market.

The stock market crash of 1929 and the subsequent declining market through 1932 was viewed by many as being directly related to the inadequate and false financial reporting practices of publicly traded companies. It became apparent that some type of federal involvement was necessary in order to curb the abuses of the past. The Securities Act of 1933 and the Securities Exchange Act of 1934 were in direct response to this need. In 1934, by an act of Congress as part of the Securities Exchange Act of 1934, the SEC was created as an independent regulatory agency of the U.S. government. At that time, the SEC assumed a quasi-judicial role in controlling the distribution and trading of securities. In addition, the Commission became responsible for developing a system of full and fair financial disclosure so that investors would have the necessary information to make informed investment decisions. This disclosure-oriented focus was not designed to remove speculative or risky securities from the market place, but rather to provide the necessary information to evaluate risk and perform comparisons to other investments. Since its inception, the SEC has made major contributions toward the standardization of financial reporting and the assurance of full and fair disclosure, goals which may not have been achieved by a voluntary disclosure system.

ORGANIZATION AND AUTHORITATIVE SOURCES OF THE SEC

The SEC consists of five commissioners who are appointed by the President of the United States. The President also selects one of these commissioners to act as chairman. No more than three of the commissioners may be from the same political party, and commissioners serve a five-year staggered term. Principal offices of the SEC are located in Washington D.C. and there are nine additional regional offices, some of which have their own regional branch offices. The organizational chart of the SEC is presented in Illustration 14–1.

---

[1]Joel Seligman, "The SEC and Accounting: A Historical Perspective," *The SEC and Accounting: The First 50 Years*, eds. Robert H. Mundheim and Noyes E. Leech (Amsterdam: North Holland, 1986), 6–7.

Illustration 14-1

U.S. SECURITIES AND EXCHANGE COMMISSION

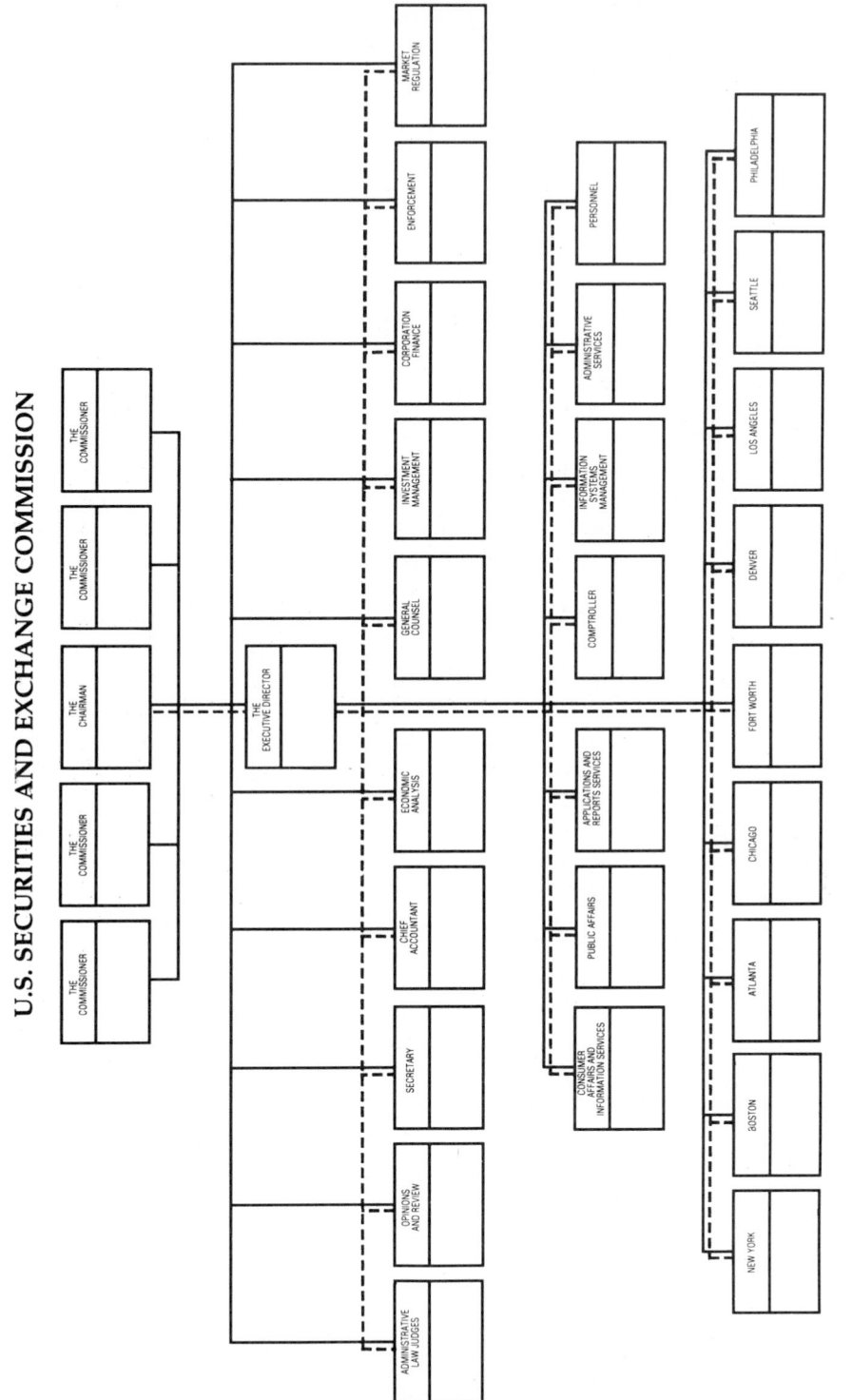

LINES OF POLICY AND JUDICIAL AUTHORITY

LINES OF BUDGET AND MANAGEMENT AUTHORITY

Source: Commerce Clearing House, Inc. (February, 1988).

OPERATING DIVISIONS

The Commission consists of four divisions whose functions are highlighted briefly in this section.

1. *Division of Corporation Finance.* This division has a significant impact on the accounting profession. Of major concern to this unit are the Securities Act of 1933 and the Securities Exchange Act of 1934. Providing disclosure standards for and conducting reviews of registration statements filed in conjunction with the public offering of securities are two of its primary functions. The division also examines the annual filings and proxy solicitations under those Acts for which it establishes disclosure requirements. Through its administrative interpretations of the Securities Act, this division provides an advisory service to accountants, attorneys, underwriters, and others associated with the various filings.

   Reports concerning insider trading by officers and directors of registered companies are reviewed here, as are various types of reports that are completed along industry lines and serve as the basis for comments to filers and recommendations for improved disclosures. The division also is concerned with indentures covering debt securities under the Trust Indenture Act of 1939. Excluded from its jurisdiction are investment companies registered under the Investment Company Act of 1940. These companies are overseen by another division.

   In addition, certain offices have operating and staff functions within the division, such as the Office of Tender Offers, Office of International Corporate Finance, and the Office of Small Business Policy. The division also has been responsible for overseeing the development of EDGAR (Electronic Data Gathering, Analysis and Retrieval), which is a computerized filing and retrieval system.

   From the tremendous responsibility given to the Division of Corporation Finance, it is clear that many issues concerning financial disclosure and accounting for new transactions are identified in this division. These items often are referred to the Office of the Chief Accountant. As the Commissioners' principal accounting adviser, the Chief Accountant considers accounting and auditing issues along with issues affecting the form and content of filings. Policies concerning the qualifications and independence of public accountants also are handled in the office of this adviser.

2. *Division of Investment Management.* Among other concerns, this division administers the Investment Company Act of 1940 and the Investment Advisers Act of 1940 and oversees the execution of the Public Utility Holding Company Act of 1935. Registered investment companies and pooled investment funds or accounts are in this division's jurisdiction.

3. *Division of Enforcement.* This division is responsible for enforcing the various acts administered by the Commission. Potential violators are investi-

gated by the division, and an investigation may result in administrative and injunctive cooperation with the Office of the General Counsel.

4. *Division of Market Regulation.* This division regulates security exchanges and over-the-counter markets. Brokers and dealers are required to register with the SEC and are subject to periodic inspections by the division. Through its activities, the division attempts to identify fraudulent, manipulative, deceptive, and unusual trading activities.

SOURCES OF SEC REQUIREMENTS

Compliance with the various acts administered by the SEC requires affected companies to file certain financial and nonfinancial information with the Commission. The rules and regulations dealing with accounting issues are contained in several sources, each of which are discussed next.

Filing Forms. Various forms are required to be filed with the SEC, and a company, with advice from its legal counsel, must select the appropriate form. The applicable forms identify the type of information to be provided and either give detailed instructions or refer to other SEC regulations for the instructions. For example, Form S–18, which is a statement used for the registration of securities whose aggregate offering price does not exceed $7.5 million, requires the filer to provide, among other items, the following information:

> Item 4.   Use of Proceeds — Information required by Item 504
>   of Regulation S-K is to be furnished.
> Item 9.   Legal Proceedings — Information required by Item 103
>   of Regulation S-K is to be furnished.

Although these two items refer to other SEC regulations for guidance, the instructions for some items are contained in the form itself. For instance, Item 17, Description of Property, contains its own instructions regarding the physical location and general character of plants and other important physical assets.

Regulation S-X. This regulation is the primary accounting regulation, as it provides the minimum requirements for the form and content of financial statements and their footnotes and supplemental schedules. Since the regulation provides only minimum standards, the filer must disclose any additional information deemed necessary in order to make the financial information not materially misleading. Although the basis for this regulation is Generally Accepted Accounting Principles (GAAP), presentations and disclosures not required by GAAP may be needed. The regulation is divided into twelve articles that are summarized next.

ARTICLES OF REGULATION S-X

Article	Subject	Summary of Contents
1	Application of Regulation S-X	Specifies the registration statements and reports to which Regulation S-X is applicable and defines terminology used in the Regulation.
2	Qualifications and Reports of Accountants	Contains the requirements as to the qualifications (independence) of accountants and the contents of their reports.
3	General Instructions for Financial Statements	Sets forth instructions for (a) the nature of financial statements required and the persons, dates, and periods they must cover and (b) the age of interim financial statements required to be included in registration and proxy statements.
3A	Consolidated and Combined Financial Statements	Contains the requirements for the presentation of consolidated and combined financial statements.
4	Rules of General Application	Contains the rules for form, order, and terminology and for certain of the footnotes required to be furnished as part of the financial statements.
5	Commercial and Industrial Companies	Sets forth the information to be included in balance sheet and statement of income captions for commercial and industrial companies. Also specifies the schedules that are to be filed.
5A	Companies in the Development Stage	Contains the additional disclosure requirements for companies in the development stage.
6	Registered Investment Companies	
6A	Employee Stock Purchase, Savings and Similar Plans	These articles set forth the information to be included in financial statements of special types of entities.
7	Insurance Companies	
8	Committees Issuing Certificates of Deposit	
9	Bank Holding Companies	
10	Interim Financial Statements	Sets forth the form and content of interim financial statements and the periods for which such statements must be presented in Form 10-Q.
11	Pro Forma Financial Information	Specifies the form and content of pro forma financial disclosures and when such disclosures are required. Also provides guidance for the presentation of financial forecasts that may be furnished in lieu of pro forma disclosures.
12	Form and Content of Schedules	Sets forth the form and content of schedules required in accordance with Rule 5-04 (and certain other rules for special types of entities).

Source: SEC Manual (New York: Coopers & Lybrand, 1987), 286.

Regulation S-K. This regulation is concerned with certain information not contained in basic financial statements. Adopted in 1977, the regulation standardizes the disclosure requirements for the various forms to be filed with the SEC primarily under the Securities Act of 1933 and the Securities Exchange Act of 1934. The items making up the regulation are summarized in the following table:

SUBJECTS COMPRISING REGULATION S-K

Items	Content
Sec 229–10 (a)–(c)	Applicability of Regulation S-K. Commission's views on factors to be considered in formulating and describing financial projections.
101–105	Description of the business and subsidiaries over the past five years. Description of physical plant and other important physical assets in regards to suitability, adequacy, productive capacity, and extent of utilization. Description of material pending legal procedures other than routine litigation incidental to the business.
201–202	Description of markets in which common equity is traded, along with market price and dividends per share for the last two fiscal years and any subsequent interim periods.
301–304	Description of securities to be registered. Selected financial information presented in columnar form for the last five fiscal years. Selected quarterly data for the last two fiscal years and any subsequent interim periods. Management's discussion and analysis of financial conditions and operations. Also included is a discussion of changes in and disagreements with outside auditors that have taken place within 24 months prior to, or in any period subsequent to, the date of the most recent financial statements.
401–404	Identification of directors, executive officers, promoters, and control persons. Description of all compensation paid to the company's five most highly compensated executives and to all executive officers as a group. A detailing of the company voting securities owned by certain beneficial owners and management. Disclosure of certain material related to party transactions.
501–512	Information dealing with a registration statement and prospectus provisions, including the following: Content on front and back pages of prospectus Summary information, risk factors, and earnings ratios Use of proceeds Determination of offering price Dilution of book value Selling security holders who will be offered stock Plan of distribution through underwriters Interests of named expert and counsel Disclosure of Commission position on indemnification for Securities Act liabilities Expenses of issuance and distribution other than underwriter's discounts and commissions Undertakings as to filings and disclosure
601	Details of various exhibits to be presented.
701–702	Description of securities sold that were not registered. Effect of indemnification of controlling persons, directors, or officers.
801–802	Listing of industry guides calling for specific disclosures.

Annual Report Requirements. Companies registered under Section 12 of the Securities Exchange Act of 1934 are required to send annual reports to shareholders in connection with annual meetings at which directors are elected, regardless of whether or not proxies are solicited. The content of the reports are specified in Rule 14a-3 and Rule 14c-3 of the 1934 Act. These rules refer, in part, to the requirements of Regulation S-X and Regulation S-K. Therefore, annual reports to shareholders normally contain a significant portion of the information required by Regulations S-X and S-K. As part of the SEC's integrated disclosure system, these annual reports may be integrated by reference with certain forms required to be filed by various acts administered by the SEC. Integrating the reporting requirements of the securities acts and the annual report provides more complete and consistent information and reduces the cost of compliance with the various acts.

Other SEC Sources. The SEC also issues Financial Reporting Releases (FRRs) and Accounting and Auditing Enforcement Releases (AAERs), both of which have codified and replaced the previously issued Accounting Series Releases (ASRs). The FRRs contain the SEC's position on accounting and auditing principles and cover a wide variety of topics, from interim reporting to the disclosure of compensating balances. The accounting principles contained in the FRRs reflect the SEC's position that accounting principles for which there is substantial authoritative support are generally acceptable for SEC reporting purposes. Statements and Interpretations issued by the Financial Accounting Standards Board, Opinions of the Accounting Principles Board, and Accounting Research Bulletins issued by the Committee on Accounting Procedure are recognized by the SEC as having substantial authoritative support. The AAERs present SEC enforcement actions against accountants with regard to accounting and/or auditing issues. Therefore, the AAERs provide accountants with insight into what may not constitute acceptable practice before the SEC.

In 1976, the SEC began to issue Staff Accounting Bulletins (SABs), which are published jointly by the Office of the Chief Accountant and the Division of Corporation Finance. The SABs represent informal interpretations regarding accounting and disclosure principles. Normally, they take the format of questions of fact followed by an interpretative response. The SABs are not official rules or interpretations which have been approved by the SEC. However, filings which are in conflict with a SAB probably would not be approved by the Commission.

ACTS ADMINISTERED BY THE SEC

A number of acts are administered by the SEC. The securities acts of 1933 and 1934 are of major importance to the accounting profession and represent a major force in the movement toward full and fair disclosure. The following sections discuss these securities acts along with other acts administered by the SEC.

SECURITIES ACT OF 1933

During the New Deal era of President Franklin D. Roosevelt, the Securities Act of 1933 (hereafter referred to as the 1933 Act) was passed in response to many of the trading abuses and the stock market crash discussed earlier. The

1933 Act is a full-disclosure act that generally requires the filing of a registration statement by companies seeking to make a public distribution of securities through the instruments of interstate commerce. However, exemption from the registration process is available in the following instances provided certain conditions are met:

Private, noninvestment-company offerings up to $500,000 in any twelve-month period.

Noninvestment-company offerings up to $5 million in any twelve-month period, provided that there are no more than 35 unaccredited investors, even though the number of accredited investors (banks, insurance companies, investment companies, and certain individuals) is not limited.

Private offerings or placements in unlimited amounts that are not publicly advertised or solicited, provided that there are no more than 35 unaccredited investors, even though the number of accredited investors is not limited.

Intrastate transactions involving only offerings of local companies to state residents.

Offerings solely to accredited investors if the amount is not in excess of $5 million in any twelve-month period.

Offerings up to $1.5 million in any twelve-month period under SEC Regulation A.

Securities of charitable, governmental, and certain financial organizations.

Securities issued exclusively to the issuer's existing shareholders to facilitate stock dividends, splits, etc.

Securities issued in connection with a corporate reorganization due to bankruptcy.

Certain other securities involving commercial paper and specialized transactions.

The registration statement is designed to provide potential investors with full and fair disclosure concerning the issuing company so that they may make informed investment decisions. As previously mentioned, the SEC does not assume the role of judging the investment merits of a public offering of securities.

Registration Forms. There are over fifteen forms which may be used to register a public offering of securities. The choice of the proper form is generally a function of the type of issuing company, the intended use of the securities, and the previous experience of the issuer with SEC filings. Some of the more common filing choices are as follows:

General Description of Common 1933 Act Forms

S-1   General form for securities of all issuers for which no other form is prescribed, except that Form S-1 may not be used by foreign governments.

S-2   Short form for issuers meeting specified criteria.

S-3   Short form for issuers meeting specified criteria and certain transaction requirements.

S-4   For registration of securities in connection with business combination transactions; replaces Forms S-14 and S-15.

S-5   For unit investment trusts registered on Form N-8B-2.

S-8   For securities to be offered to employees under any stock option or other employee benefit plan.

S-11   For registration of securities of real estate investment trusts or other companies whose primary business is holding real estate.

S-18   An abbreviated S-1 form available for use by companies with less than $5 million in assets and fewer than 500 stockholders for an initial security offering of up to $7.5 million.

1-A.   Form used to notify the SEC of an offering to be made pursuant to Regulation A.

Source: K. Fred Skousen, *An Introduction to the SEC* (Cincinnati: South-Western Publishing Co., 1987), 44.

Form S-1 is one of the more common forms used to register securities, and it includes much of the same information found in other forms applicable to the 1933 Act. The major items to be included in Form S-1 are as follows:

PART I: INFORMATION REQUIRED IN PROSPECTUS

Item

1   Forepart of the registration statement and outside front cover page of prospectus
2   Inside front and outside back cover pages of prospectus
3   Summary information, risk factors, and ratio of earnings to fixed charges
4   Use of proceeds
5   Determination of offering price
6   Dilution
7   Selling security holders
8   Plan of distribution
9   Description of securities to be registered
10   Interests of named experts and counsel
11   Information with respect to the registrant
     (a)   Description of business
     (b)   Description of property
     (c)   Legal proceedings
     (d)   Market price of and dividends on the registrant's common equity and related stockholder matters, if common equity securities are being offered
     (e)   Financial statements
     (f)   Selected financial data
     (g)   Supplementary financial information
     (h)   Management's discussion and analysis of financial condition and results of operations
     (i)   Disagreements with accountants on accounting and financial disclosure

Item
___

      (j)   Directors and executive officers
      (k)   Executive compensation
      (l)   Security ownership of certain beneficial owners and management
      (m) Certain relationships and related transactions
  12   Disclosure of Commission position on indemnification for Securities Act liabilities

PART II: INFORMATION NOT REQUIRED IN PROSPECTUS

Item
___

  13   Other expenses of issuance and distribution
  14   Indemnification of directors and officers
  15   Recent sales of unregistered securities
  16   Exhibits and financial statement schedules
  17   Undertakings

Source: *SEC Manual* (New York: Coopers & Lybrand, 1987), 206–207.

Aside from Items 11(e) and 16, the requirements for all other items are found in Regulation S-K. The financial statements required by Item 11(e) of Form S-1 include in part:

1. Audited balance sheets for the two most recent fiscal year ends;
2. Audited statements of income and cash flows (previously changes in financial position) for the three most recent fiscal year ends;
3. Unaudited interim balance sheets and statements of income and cash flows, depending on how many days after year end the registration statement becomes effective; and
4. An analysis of the changes in each caption of the stockholders' equity presented in the balance sheet for each period covered by an income statement.

The exhibits and financial statement schedules required by Item 16 include, in part, information on investments, short-term borrowing, related party transactions, and property, plant, and equipment.

Activities Subsequent to Filing. After filing a registration form (such as Form S-1), the filing is reviewed by the SEC staff and a letter of comment is sent to the issuer which notes any deficiencies or items needing clarification. Although a registration may become effective within twenty days of filing, the issuer's response to comment letters and staffing pressures at the SEC result in most filings becoming effective much later than the twenty days after filing. Prior to the effective date of registration, underwriters and/or dealers may identify prospective buyers who are interested in the securities to be issued. Interested parties normally are made aware of the potential offering through the use of a preliminary ("red herring") prospectus or "tombstone" advertisements. However, prior to the effective date no securities can be sold nor can offers to buy be accepted. Also prior to the effective date, the issuer and the underwriter must agree on the offering price of the security, the underwriter's discounts and commissions, and the net proceeds. This information is provided to the SEC in the form of a *pricing amendment*. This amendment usually is filed just before the registration statement becomes effective.

Because underwriters are associated with the registration of securities, they must act with *due diligence*. Of particular importance is any information which may affect the value of the securities to be issued. In order to satisfy partially this due diligence requirement, an underwriter may secure from an independent accountant a *comfort letter* which provides certain negative assurances regarding the form and fairness of unaudited interim statements and events.[2] This comfort letter is not required by the 1933 Act, but rather is provided exclusively for the benefit of the underwriter. Assuming that the comfort letter is satisfactory and that the SEC has declared the registration statement effective, the underwriter and dealer then are free to sell and distribute the securities. Ten to fourteen days after the effective date the *closing date* usually occurs. At this time, the issuer releases the securities to the underwriter in exchange for the proceeds. The independent accountant must update the comfort letter to cover the period to within five days of the closing date.

Advantages/Disadvantages of Going Public. Obviously, the ability to secure capital on a national scale is the major goal of registering under the 1933 Act. An established market created for the stock makes easier the transferring of ownership to the owner's family, company employees (through stock ownership plans), or other companies to affect a business combination. The subsequent need to attract additional capital is accomplished more easily if the company already is traded publicly. However, these advantages do not come without costs. The filing of a registration statement is time consuming and involves the efforts of management, independent accountants, attorneys, and underwriters. Responding to the comment letter(s) from the SEC also requires the time of these parties. All of this commitment results in management incurring significant professional fee expenses. As will be discussed shortly, publicly traded companies must continue to file with the SEC certain information that, in turn, results in increased costs. Due to the public availability of SEC filings, a public company no longer enjoys the confidentiality that is characteristic of nonpublic firms. This increased exposure allows competitors, regulators, and investors seeking control greater insight into the company's operations and finances. Often such exposure results in increased competition for market share, more restrictions on management's activities, and less control over the operations of the company.

---

[2]For additional information on the content of a comfort letter see Statement on Auditing Standards No. 49 (AU 634), "Letters for Underwriters."

SECURITIES EXCHANGE ACT OF 1934

The 1933 Act is concerned primarily with the initial distribution of securities. However, the Securities Exchange Act of 1934 (hereafter referred to as the 1934 Act) is concerned largely with the subsequent trading of securities, the regulation of securities markets, and the periodic reporting of information by affected companies.

Regulating the Trading of Securities. The 1934 Act regulates the trading of securities on national exchanges or on the over-the-counter market in several ways. Wash sales, insider trading, or any other deceptive or fraudulent practices which are designed to manipulate the market volume or price of a security are prohibited by the 1934 Act. The Federal Reserve Board regulates the use of credit (margin accounts) for purchasing securities, but the SEC through the 1934 Act enforces the use of credit. The 1934 Act also requires a form to be filed within 10 days of one's becoming a director, officer, or more-than-10% stockholder or beneficial owner. In addition, reports must be filed within 10 days after the end of a month in which a change in beneficial ownership occurs.

National securities exchanges are required by the 1934 Act to register with the SEC. The registered exchanges periodically must report information regarding their rules and operations. Brokers and dealers are required under the 1934 Act to report their financial condition and annual income and expenses. Minimum capital and recording requirements for brokers and dealers also are established by the SEC.

Proxy Solicitations. The 1934 Act regulates the trading of securities by overseeing proxy and tender offer solicitations. Certain information must be provided to shareholders if proxies are being sought or if annual meetings are being held. The information required in these two instances is basically the same; therefore, the content of a proxy statement serves to illustrate the information requirements. The scope of information to be included in a proxy statement pursuant to Section 14(a) of the 1934 Act is presented in the following table. Parties soliciting proxies in opposition to management also are required by the 1934 Act to submit certain information.

CONTENTS OF PROXY STATEMENT

Item	Subject
1	Date, time, and place information
2	Revocability of proxy
3	Dissenters' right of appraisal
4	Persons making the solicitation
5	Interest of certain persons in matters to be acted upon
6	Voting securities and principal holders thereof
7	Directors and executive officers
8	Compensation of directors and executive officers
9	Independent public accountants
10	Compensation plans

(continued)

Item	Subject
11	Authorization or issuance of securities otherwise than for exchange
12	Modification or exchange of securities
13	Financial and other information
14	Mergers, consolidations, acquisitions, and similar matters
15	Acquisition or disposition of property
16	Restatement of accounts
17	Action with respect to reports
18	Matters not required to be submitted
19	Amendment of charter, bylaws, or other documents
20	Other proposed action
21	Vote required for approval

Source: *SEC Manual* (New York: Coopers & Lybrand, 1987), 122–123.

If directors are to be elected at the annual meeting, proxy statements must be accompanied by an annual report whose content is specified by the SEC as part of its integrated disclosure system. Buyers making a tender offer must file certain information regarding their background, purpose, and financing.

Periodic Reporting Under the 1934 Act. A major portion of the 1934 Act deals with the registration of traded companies along with a periodic reporting requirement. Companies traded on national exchanges or over the counter that have assets greater than $3 million and have 500 or more shareholders are required to file Form 10, which is a registration statement. This statement is not as complete as the registration required under the 1933 Act, but there are a number of common features. On a continuing basis, required companies must file a number of periodic reports. Although there are several reports which may be required for a given situation, only the most common report forms will be discussed.

Form 10-K. Form 10-K is an annual report that must be filed within 90 days after the end of the fiscal year. However, specified schedules may be filed within 120 days after the end of the fiscal year. Also, certain information may be incorporated by reference from data contained in proxy statements and annual reports to shareholders. The items of information to be included in Form 10-K are contained in the following table:

INFORMATION CONTAINED IN FORM 10-K

PART I

Item	
1	Business
2	Properties
3	Legal proceedings
4	Submission of matters to a vote of security holders

PART II

Item

5   Market for registrant's common equity and related stockholder matters
6   Selected financial data
7   Management's discussion and analysis of financial condition and results of operations
8   Financial statements and supplementary data
9   Disagreements on accounting and financial disclosure

PART III

Item

10   Directors and executive officers of the registrant
11   Executive compensation
12   Security ownership of certain beneficial owners and management
13   Certain relationships and related transactions

PART IV

Item

14   Exhibits, financial statement schedules, and reports on Form 8-K

Source: *SEC Manual* (New York: Coopers & Lybrand, 1987), 122–123.

Requirements for Items 8 and 14 also are contained in Regulation S-K. The financial statements and schedules required by these two items include:

1. Balance sheet as of the end of each of the two latest fiscal years;
2. Statements of income, cash flows, and changes in stockholders' equity for each of the three latest fiscal years; and
3. Financial statement schedules as needed to support the statements or as required by Regulation S-X.

All of these statements and schedules must be audited for each period they are required.

Form 10-Q. Companies required to file Form 10-K also must file a quarterly report on Form 10-Q for each of the first three quarters of the fiscal year. Form 10-Q consists of two parts, a financial report and a special events report, that must be filed within 45 days after the end of each of the three quarters.

The financial report portion of the form requires the following condensed statements:

1. An interim balance sheet as of the end of the most recent quarter and a balance sheet as of the end of the prior fiscal year;
2. An interim statement of income for the most recent quarter, for the year-to-date period, and for the corresponding periods (quarter and year-to-date) of the prior fiscal year; and
3. A statement of cash flows for the current year-to-date and the corresponding period of the prior fiscal year.

There is no requirement that these statements or their accompanying notes to audited or reviewed by an independent public accountant. However, the SEC is considering a requirement that all quarterly statements be reviewed. As in the case of Form 10-K, certain information may be incorporated by reference from data contained in a quarterly shareholders' report. In addition to the statements, management's discussion and analysis of financial condition and results of operations are required by Item 303 of Regulation S-K.

The special events information required by Part II of Form 10-Q includes the following items whose content is more fully described by Regulation S-K:

Item 1. Legal proceedings
Item 2. Changes in securities
Item 3. Defaults upon senior securities
Item 4. Submission of matters to a vote of security holders
Item 5. Other information
Item 6. Exhibits and reports on Form 8-K

Form 8-K. If certain significant events or other events of which a prudent investor should be informed occur, a Form 8-K must be filed. The reportable significant events are as follows:

Item 1. Changes in control of the registrant
Item 2. Acquisition or disposition of assets
Item 3. Bankruptcy or receivership
Item 4. Changes in registrant's certifying accountants
Item 5. Other events
Item 6. Resignations of registrant's directors

All items except Item 5 must be reported within 15 days of their occurrence. Item 5 is optional and therefore has no time requirement. The acquisition or disposition of assets in Item 2 is necessary only if a significant amount of assets (defined in Form 8-K) are involved. If so, an Item 7 of Form 8–K is required to present certain financial information and statements regarding the acquisition or disposition.

Item 4 is extremely important to accountants, especially the new certifying accountant. The content of this disclosure provides insight into accounting issues facing the registrant:

(a) *State the date of such resignation (or declination to stand for reelection), dismissal, or engagement.*

(b) *State whether in connection with the audits of the two most recent fiscal years and any subsequent interim period preceding such resignation, dismissal, or engagement there were any disagreements with the former accountant on any matter of accounting principles or practices, financial statement disclosure, or auditing scope or procedure, which disagreements if not resolved to the satisfaction of the former accountant would have caused him to make reference in connection with his report to the subject matter of the disagreement(s);*

also, describe each such disagreement. The disagreements required to be reported in response to the preceding sentence include both those resolved to the former accountant's satisfaction and those not resolved to the former accountant's satisfaction. Disagreements contemplated by this rule are those which occur at the decision-making level (i.e., between personnel of the registrant responsible for presentation of its financial statements and personnel of the accounting firm responsible for rendering its report).

(c) *State whether the principal accountant's report on the financial statements for any of the past two years contained an adverse opinion or a disclaimer of opinion or was qualified as to uncertainty, audit scope, or accounting principles; also describe the nature of each adverse opinion, disclaimer of opinion, or qualification.*

(d) *The registrant shall request the former accountant to furnish the registrant with a letter addressed to the Commission stating whether he agrees with the statements made by the registrant in response to this item and, if not, stating the respects in which he does not agree. The registrant shall file a copy of the former accountant's letter as an exhibit to the report on this form. If the former accountant's letter is unavailable at the time of filing, it shall be filed within thirty days thereafter.*

(e) *State whether the decision to change accountants was recommended or approved by:*

  (1) *Any audit or similar committee of the Board of Directors, if the issuer has such a committee; or*

  (2) *The Board of Directors, if the issuer has no such committee.*[3]

In 1988, the SEC adopted measures to expand the disclosure required by Item 4 of Form 8-K to include the following:

• *Certain "reportable events." These include situations in which the former accountant had expressed concerns about the adequacy of the company's internal controls, the reliability of management's representations, or an unwillingness to be associated with the financial statements. As such reportable events are to be reported in a manner similar to disagreements.*

• *Certain prior consultations with the newly engaged accountant within two years prior to the change. Disclosure is required in either of two situations. In the first, the consultation is such that the consulted accountant must deal with it in accordance with the requirements of Statement on Auditing Standards No. 50, "Reports on the Application of Accounting Principles." That covers situations in which the accountant believes the advice is important to the company's decision on an accounting, auditing, or financial reporting issue. In the second situ-*

---

[3]*Op. cit.,* 189–190.

ation requiring disclosure, the consultation is related to a disagreement or a reportable event between the company and the former accountant. In either of these two situations, the Form 8-K must describe the newly engaged accountant's views, state whether the former accountant was consulted and, if so, state his views.

- *Whether any disagreement or reportable event was discussed with the company's audit committee.*
- *Whether the company authorized the former accountant to respond fully to questions the newly engaged accountant asked about disagreements with the company.*
- *Whether the former accountant resigned, declined to stand reelection, or was dismissed.* [4]

The SEC is proposing to reduce from 15 days to 5 days the time allowed a company to report a change in auditors as well as other significant events. The time the former auditor has to respond to the Item 4 report would be reduced from 30 days to 10 days. In addition, the proposal would require the auditor's response to be forwarded to the SEC within two days of its receipt.

OTHER ACTS ADMINISTERED BY THE SEC

Although the 1933 and 1934 Acts are extremely important to many accountants, the SEC administers several other important acts. These acts are summarized as follows:

Public Utility Holding Company Act of 1935 — Companies holding 10% or more of the voting stock of electric or gas utilities must register with the SEC and report annually. The annual reports must contain audited financial statements prepared by specialized principles required by the SEC. The SEC regulates the securities issued by holding companies and is responsible for simplifying the capital structure of these companies.

Trust Indenture Act of 1939 — Companies issuing debt securities, subject to certain exemptions, may do so only if a trust indenture and an independent trustee have been approved by the SEC.

Investment Company Act of 1940 — The SEC regulates the activities and composition of investment companies. Such companies are required to file a registration statement with the SEC along with periodic reports. Audited financial statements are required.

---

[4]*Financial Reporting & Accounting: 1988 Update* (New York: Arthur Young, 1988), 28–29.

Investment Advisors Act of 1940—Certain parties who are engaged in the business of investment advice must register with the SEC. The SEC monitors the background, qualifications, and activities of the advisors.

Securities Investor Protection Act of 1970—This act has established a fund to help protect investors up to certain monetary limits. Fees are collected from brokers, dealers, and members of the national securities exchanges by the Securities Investor Protection Corporation (SIPC) and are used to finance the protection fund.

Foreign Corrupt Practices Act of 1977—This act contains two main provisions. The first provision makes it unlawful for a company or representative to make payments to foreign political parties, officials, or candidates for the purpose of securing business. This provision applies to any company, not just public companies. The second provision requires public companies to maintain a system of internal accounting control in order to satisfy control objectives. Companies also are required to maintain detailed records which will portray "accurately and fairly" a company's financial activities. This act imposes significant responsibility on the accounting profession in terms of discovering and reporting prohibited payments. The responsibility for developing and reporting on control systems is significant.

Insider Trading Sanctions Act of 1984—This act increases the criminal penalties and punitive damages associated with profiting from the illegal use of insider information.

SEC INFLUENCE ON ACCOUNTING PROFESSION

The SEC has influenced and will continue to influence the accounting profession in a variety of ways. Several of the more significant ways in which the SEC has affected the accounting profession are discussed in the following paragraphs.

DEVELOPMENT OF ACCOUNTING PRINCIPLES

The development of accounting principles has been influenced by the SEC in an unusual and indirect way. The SEC has the statutory power to prescribe the accounting principles to be used in filings under the 1933 and 1934 Acts as well as several other acts. Certainly, the Commission has exercised its authority through Regulation S-X, accounting requirements for investment advisors, Staff Accounting Bulletins, and Financial Reporting Releases. However, the SEC traditionally has encouraged the accounting profession, rather than the government, to be the official promulgator of generally accepted accounting principles.

The Commission has not been passive in the standard-setting process, but rather has been a persistent force behind the establishment of principles. For example, in several instances the SEC has required an accounting treatment or disclosure before the profession has. Normally, the result has been the adoption by the accounting profession of appropriate principles, as was the case with inflation accounting and accounting for computer software costs. In a few instances, however, the SEC's position has resulted in a major conflict with the profession, as seen in the areas of oil and gas producers and the preferability of principles in the context of accounting changes. Accounting for the investment tax credit represents an area where the SEC took a position that the profession's stance was too narrow for SEC purposes.

Today the SEC is involved heavily with the FASB and the AICPA and is a strong influencing factor in standard setting. The SEC's contribution to the standardization of financial statements and textual items has been significant and has served to accelerate the promulgation of accounting principles.

DEVELOPMENT OF AUDITING STANDARDS

Although the SEC's authority to establish auditing standards and procedures technically is limited to brokers, dealers, and investment companies, it still has been an important factor in the development of such standards. The 1941 amendment to Regulation S-X required auditors to state whether examinations were in accordance with *generally accepted auditing standards*. Shortly thereafter, the auditing profession adopted ten generally accepted auditing standards. Current filing requirements of the SEC have been a factor in expanding the attest function and the recent development of attestation standards. Through its enforcement activities, the SEC has identified areas of concern, thereby suggesting the need for new audit approaches and procedures. Standards on related party transactions, communication between newly engaged and former auditors, and management representation letters are partly in response to SEC enforcement actions. The recent Treadway Commission report on fraudulent financial reporting has made several recommendations that will affect the SEC and the auditing profession in the following areas: change of auditors, audit committees, management reports on financial statement and internal control responsibility, and review of quarterly data.[5]

---

[5]*Report of the National Commission on Fraudulent Financial Reporting* (National Commission on Fraudulent Financial Reporting, 1987).

IMPOSITION OF LEGAL LIABILITY

The independent auditor, as an expert associated with filing before the SEC, is exposed to a significant amount of potential liability. Section 11(a) of the 1933 Act imposes liability for material misstatements or omissions of fact in a registration statement. Any purchaser of the security may sue the auditor if a loss occurs and a defect in the statement is present. The plaintiff does not have to rely on the statement or the privy to the contract with the auditor. The burden of proof is thrust upon the defendant, the auditor. Adding to the risk of liability is the fact that the auditor's responsibility for the discovery of subsequent events extends to the effective date of the registration statement. In addition to the civil liabilities that can be imposed, criminal liability can be imposed under Section 24 of the 1933 Act.

Independent auditors also may be exposed to liability under the provisions of the 1934 Act. Section 18(a) of the 1934 Act addresses potential liability to both buyers and sellers of securities resulting from statements that were materially false and/or misleading. This section is similar to common law liability in that it requires reliance by the plaintiff and a causal connection between the misstatement and the plaintiff's loss. Applicable sections of this act do not thrust the burden of proof on the auditor, nor do they require active responsibility for events past the date of the audit report. Generally, liability will be imposed only for gross negligence or fraud.

Section 10(b) and Rule 10b-5 of the 1934 Act are anti-fraud provisions extending to both buyers and sellers of securities. The 1976 Hochfelder case[6] resulted in a U.S. Supreme Court decision which held that the auditor must have intended to deceive, manipulate, or defraud the buyer in order for liability to arise. However, subsequent cases have held that reckless disregard or absent knowledge of a falsity may be cause for action under the section. Criminal penalties against auditors may be imposed by Section 32 of the 1934 Act.

INDEPENDENCE OF AUDITORS

Rule 2.01 of Regulation S-X addresses the qualifications of public accountants (auditors) necessary in order to practice before the SEC. The Commission requires auditors to be independent in both fact and appearance. As ethical standards regarding independence developed, the SEC always emphasized independence in appearance even though the AICPA at times placed more emphasis on independence in fact. The AICPA's Code of Conduct as it relates to independence basically is accepted by the SEC. However, the SEC believes that independence is impaired in certain situations that are considered acceptable from the viewpoint of the AICPA. Therefore, a more restrictive position is taken by the SEC.

[6]421 U.S. 909 (1975).

For example, the performance of accounting/bookkeeping services by an auditor for a client whose audited financial statements are submitted to the SEC is not acceptable to the SEC. However, the AICPA does not prohibit such services for audit clients, provided that certain conditions are satisfied. Regarding prospective financial information, the SEC has taken a position that CPAs who prepare or assist clients in the preparation of prospective financial information impair their own audit independence for all periods covered by the prospective data. This position is in contrast to that of the AICPA and has serious implications for auditors of companies that in the future may become SEC registrants.

QUESTIONS

1. What are several of the forces that may have contributed to the passage of the Securities Act of 1933?
2. What are the primary responsibilities of the Chief Accountant of the SEC?
3. Regulation S-X is an important regulation involving several acts administered by the SEC. What is the primary function of this regulation?
4. What sources of accounting principles developed outside of the SEC are considered to have substantial authoritative support by the SEC?
5. How does the integrated disclosure system affect the content of a company's annual report?
6. What is the purpose of a registration statement as required by the Securities Act of 1933?
7. Why would an underwriter seek a comfort letter from an independent accountant?
8. Although new companies go public every year, what are some of the disadvantages of doing so?
9. Where might an interested party find information relating to officers of a public company?
10. Form 8-K requires certain significant events to be reported to the SEC. What are some examples of such events?
11. Aside from the 1933 and 1934 Securities Acts, what other acts are administered by the SEC?
12. What are the basic provisions of the Foreign Corrupt Practices Act of 1977?
13. How does the element of reliance on the registration statements in the context of accountants' legal liability differ between the 1933 and 1934 Securities Acts?

EXERCISES

Exercise 1. The reporting and disclosure requirements of the SEC are very extensive. The requirements are communicated in a variety of ways. Identify and briefly discuss the primary sources of these requirements.

Exercise 2. A registration statement, as required by the Securities Act of 1933, is designed to provide potential investors with full and fair disclosure.
(1) State the exemptions from the registration process.
(2) Discuss what logic supports the exemption relating to offerings involving sophisticated investors.
(3) Assuming a publicly traded company was to acquire a private company by the issuance of securities, identify the appropriate registration statement to be filed.

Exercise 3. Form S-1 contains certain information to be included in a prospectus.
(1) Identify the specific financial statements that must be included in the prospectus.
(2) Identify the nature of the other information with respect to the registrant that must be included in the prospectus.

Exercise 4. Form 8-K under the Securities Exchange Act of 1934 requires a registrant to report changes in its independent (certifying) accountants within a period of time.
(1) Discuss why a change in independent accountants represents such a significant event.
(2) Discuss the basis types of information that must be reported by the registrant when a change occurs.
(3) Identify what information the preceding (former) independent accountant must provide.

Exercise 5. Forms 10-K and 10-Q are both required under the Securities Exchange Act of 1934. These forms are important to the process of full and fair disclosure. Compare and contrast these forms with respect to: the types of financial statements included, the involvement of independent accountants, the frequency of filing, and the content of the forms.

Exercise 6. The development of accounting principles and auditing standards are influenced by many factors. The accounting profession has assumed significant responsibility, but not without the involvement of the SEC. Discuss the role of the SEC in this standard-setting environment.

PART FIVE

PARTNERSHIPS

P artnerships are a common form of organization for many entities. The characteristics of a partnership are significantly different from the corporate form of organization and, in turn, result in certain accounting principles that are unique to partnerships. A critical part of accounting for a partnership deals with the allocation of profits and losses among the partners. Special methods also may be employed to account for the admission or withdrawal of partners. The liquidation of a partnership is influenced by legal concepts that must be adhered to in order to achieve an equitable termination of the business. Accountants often are asked to assist clients in the liquidation process and, therefore, must understand the underlying concepts.

CHAPTER 15

PARTNERSHIPS: NATURE, FORMATION, AND DIVISION OF INCOME

In a majority of states, the legal nature and functioning of partnerships is governed by the Uniform Partnership Act (UPA), which deals with the nature of a partnership, relations with persons dealing with a partnership, the rights of partners, and the dissolution and termination of a partnership. In Section 6 of this act, a *partnership* is defined as "an association of two or more persons to carry on as co-owners a business for profit." Such associations were dominant forms of business organization prior to the industrial revolution and still remain a popular form of organization for many small and medium-size businesses.

CHARACTERISTICS OF A PARTNERSHIP

Partnerships normally are classified as either general or limited. A *general partnership* consists of several general partners who may act publicly on behalf of the firm and who are personally liable for obligations of the partnership. A *limited partnership* consists of one or more general partners and one or more limited or special partners who contribute capital but do not participate in management of the firm. The limited partners' liability for partnership obligations is restricted to a stated amount, usually equal to their interest in the partnership.

RELATIONSHIP OF PARTNERS

A partnership represents a voluntary association of individuals to carry out a business purpose. In this association, a fiduciary relationship exists between the partners, requiring them to exercise good faith, loyalty to the firm, and sound business judgment in conducting the firm's business. An individual partner is viewed as a co-owner of partnership property, creating a *tenancy in partnership*. When specific assets are contributed by a partner, they lose their identity as to source and become the shared property of the partnership. Without the consent of all partners, such property cannot be utilized by any partner for personal purposes.

The relationship between partners also is characterized as one of *mutual agency*, which means that each partner is an agent for the other partners and the partnership when transacting partnership business. Therefore, in carrying on the business of the partnership, the acts of every partner bind the partnership itself, even when a partner commits a wrongful act or a breach of trust. However, if a partner has no authority to act for the partnership and the party with whom the partner is dealing knows this, the partnership is not bound by the partner's actions.

A general partnership is characterized by *unlimited liability*, in that all partners are liable, jointly and severally, for acts that bind the partnership. This liability is not limited to the partners' interests in the partnership, but may extend to their personal net worth. However, newly admitted partners, who are personally liable for partnership debts incurred subsequent to their admission, are liable for debts of the previous partnership only to the extent of their interest in the partnership.

PARTNERSHIP DISSOLUTION

Although a partnership is formed easily and does not need state approval, its life is limited and it may be dissolved much more easily than a corporation. *Dissolution* is defined in Section 29 of the UPA as "the change in the relation of the partners caused by any partner ceasing to be associated in the carrying on as distinguished from the winding up of the business." Generally, a partnership is dissolved upon the death, withdrawal, or bankruptcy of an individual partner (owner). The admission of a new partner also results in the dissolution of the former partnership. Thus, any change in the association of the individual partners is termed dissolution.

Although dissolution occurs when there is a change in a partner's association with the other partners, it does not result necessarily in the termination of the basic business function. Therefore, a change in the ownership structure dissolves the former partnership, but often this change results in the formation of a new partnership to carry on the business purpose of the original partnership.

TAX IMPLICATIONS OF A PARTNERSHIP

The partnership is not viewed as a separate taxable entity, but rather as a conduit through which taxable items pass to the partners. Therefore, the taxable income (or loss) generated by partnership operations is allocated to the individual partners and reported by them on their personal tax returns. Elements of partnership revenue and expense maintain their special tax status on the returns of the individual partners.

Another result of viewing a partnership as a conduit for tax purposes is that assets contributed by the partners retain the same tax basis that they had prior to contribution to the partnership. For example, if assets with a tax basis of $12,000 and a fair market value of $20,000 are contributed to a partnership, the tax basis for partnership purposes will remain at $12,000. The conduit concept also results in defining the tax basis of a partner's personal interest in the partnership as the sum of:

1. The tax basis of individual assets contributed to the partnership, *plus*
2. The value of other partners' liabilities assumed by the individual partner, *less*
3. The value of the individual partner's liabilities assumed by the other partners.

To illustrate, assume that partners A and B contribute assets with tax bases of $30,000 and $15,000, respectively. Liabilities associated with these assets are $10,000 and $5,000, respectively. The partners agree to accept equal liability for the obligations associated with the contributed assets. The tax basis for each partner's interest, calculated as follows, may be used to determine the personal tax effects of a subsequent sale or liquidation of the interest.

	Partner A	Partner B
Tax basis of assets contributed..	$30,000	$15,000
Tax basis of other partner's liabilities assumed (1/2 of $5,000 for A and 1/2 of $10,000 for B)...........................	2,500	5,000
Tax basis of liabilities assumed by other partners (1/2 of $10,000 for A and 1/2 for $5,000 for B).........................	(5,000)	(2,500)
Tax basis of partner's interest...	$27,500	$17,500

It is important to note that the sum of the tax bases of partners' interests ($27,500 + $17,500) must equal the sum of the tax bases of assets contributed by the partners ($30,000 + $15,000).

PARTNERSHIP VS. CORPORATION

The nature of a partnership may be better understood by comparing a partnership with a corporation. Many of the nontax-related differences between these two forms of organization are summarized on page 823. Of these differences, one of the most significant is the partnership characteristic of unlimited liability. In a corporation, the liability of shareholders is limited to either capital contributed or legal capital, depending on the state of incorporation. Another difference is that the corporate assumption of continuing life is not as applicable to a partnership.

SIGNIFICANT NONTAX-RELATED DIFFERENCES
BETWEEN A PARTNERSHIP AND A CORPORATION

	Partnership	Corporation
Continuity	Has a limited life and normally is dissolved when any change occurs in the ownership structure of the firm. However, the partnership need not be liquidated and may continue its original purpose.	Has a life that theoretically is defined as infinite. Changes in the ownership structure of the firm do not result in termination of the entity's life.
Formality	Little formality necessary for partnership formation. Relatively free from public supervision.	A corporation is created with the approval of the state from which its powers are derived, and therefore it must function within limits prescribed by the state.
Liability	Unlimited liability, i.e., each individual general partner is personally liable for the debts of the partnership.	The capital contributed by a shareholder is the extent of the individual shareholder's liability for debts of the corporation. Original shareholders also may be liable for the amount of any discounts that result from the initial issuance of stock.
Management	General partners are active in the management of the business and exert a high degree of direct control over the business.	Corporations are characterized by absentee ownership, which means that shareholders normally are not active in management. Shareholders elect a board of directors that exercises direct control over the business. Under this arrangement, individual shareholders exercise indirect control over the business.
Ability to Attract Capital	Theoretically, a partnership may have greater borrowing power than a corporation because creditors may have access to the personal assets of partners. However, the small ownership base of a partnership makes it difficult to raise capital. The fact that ownership in a partnership is not transferred easily also restricts the firm's ability to attract capital.	The limited liability associated with a corporate investment should enhance the attractiveness of such investments. However, in smaller corporations it is common for shareholders to personally guarantee the debts of the corporation. Ease of transferability of ownership also improves the firm's ability to attract capital.

Major differences also exist between a corporation and a partnership in the area of taxation. These tax-related differences, which are summarized as follows, are based on the concept of the corporation as a taxable entity, separate from its shareholders. The primary result of this concept is that the corporation is taxed when the income is earned, and the individual shareholders are taxed when the income is distributed as dividends. This characteristic is referred to as *double taxation,* and its significance depends on the extent to which dividends are distributed and on the tax rates to which the owners are subject. The effect of double taxation may be minimized if employee-shareholders do not receive dividends, but are rewarded in the form of salaries, which are deductible expenses. However, the Internal Revenue Service must be satisfied that the amount of such salaries is reasonable. A corporation also may attempt to avoid double taxation by accumulating earnings or by electing to be taxed as a partnership.

SIGNIFICANT TAX-RELATED DIFFERENCES BETWEEN A PARTNERSHIP AND A CORPORATION

	Partnership	Corporation
Taxable	Not a separate taxable entity, but rather a conduit through which taxable items are passed on to the owners (partners).	Is a separate, distinct taxable entity apart from the shareholder. Therefore, income is taxed once at the corporate level and again at the shareholder level when such income is distributed, i.e., double taxation.
Tax Rates	The individual partners are taxed on their shares of partnership income, whether distributed or not, at the progressive tax rates applicable to individuals.	The corporation is taxed at the rate of 15% on the first $50,000 of taxable income, 25% on the next $25,000, 34% on the next $25,000, 39% on the next $235,000, and 34% on taxable income over $335,000.
Maintaining the Identity of Various Elements of Taxable Income	Elements making up a partnership's income maintain their special tax status on the returns of the individual partners; e.g., if a partnership has tax-exempt income, it retains its identity in the preparation of the individual partners' tax returns as tax-exempt income.	Elements making up corporate income do not maintain their special status when distributed to shareholders in the form of a dividend; e.g., if corporate income includes some tax-exempt income, that income will be taxed to the shareholders when distributed in the form of a dividend.
Other Tax Items	The tax advantages associated with certain fringe benefits are much greater for employee-shareholders than they would be if the employees were partners in a firm. Such fringe benefits may involve profit-sharing plans, pension plans, medical reimbursement and insurance plans, group life insurance, and death benefits.	

Accumulation of Earnings. Rather than distributing taxable dividends, the corporation may retain income so that the shareholders are not taxed on that income. However, if the shareholders sell their stock in the corporation and if the stock sells at a price that exceeds its tax basis, the gain on the sale would be taxed at the rate applied to capital gains.

It should be noted, however, that the retention of income may not be practical because of the accumulated earnings tax. This tax is a penalty imposed on a corporation that accumulates its earnings to avoid the income tax that would have been incurred by the shareholders if dividends had been distributed. The intent to avoid taxes may be established by demonstrating that the corporation has accumulated earnings in excess of the reasonable needs of the business. Reasonable needs of the business would include such items as plant expansion, asset replacement, debt retirement, stock retirement, customer-supplier loans, and working capital.

Subchapter S Corporations. The disadvantage associated with double taxation may be eliminated if a corporation elects to be taxed as a Subchapter S corporation. Under this election, the corporation is treated as a partnership for tax purposes. The corporate entity itself pays no tax, and the shareholders pay tax on their share of corporate income, whether or not it is distributed to them. This special treatment is based on the view that certain corporations, in substance, are the same as a partnership. This analogy is appropriate for nonpublic corporations, in which major shareholders act in the same capacity as partners in a partnership.

The corporation electing to be taxed as a Subchapter S corporation must meet certain requirements. For example, the corporation must have only one class of stock owned by thirty-five or fewer stockholders. Certain technical procedures also are employed with respect to the determination and classification of taxable income.

UNDERLYING EQUITY THEORIES

As discussed in Chapter 1, the theoretical framework of accounting consists, in part, of various theories that explain the nature of the equities making up a particular business entity. This entire body of theories, known as equity theory, provides support for the accounting, reporting, and legal characteristics of a business entity. Thus, an understanding of these characteristics is aided by the identification of the supporting theory. Some of the characteristics of a partnership may be traced to the proprietary theory, for example, while other characteristics may be traced to the entity theory. The fact that partnerships are influenced by both the proprietary and entity theories has resulted in accounting methods that are unique to partnerships. The following summary of various partnership characteristics relates them to the appropriate underlying equity theory.

Partnership Characteristics Traceable to the Proprietary Theory

Interest on debt is viewed as a component of the income calculation.

Salaries to partners are viewed as a distribution of income versus a component of the income calculation.

A personal relationship exists between owners and management.

The concept of unlimited liability suggests that the amount by which partnership liabilities exceed partnership assets could be satisfied by a partner's net personal assets (the amount by which personal assets exceed personal liabilities). Therefore, unsatisfied partnership liabilities could be viewed as debts of the individual owners versus the distinct partnership entity.

The partnership is not viewed as a distinct taxable entity, but rather as a conduit through which income passes to the owners, at which point it is taxed.

The tax basis of assets contributed to a partnership is the same as the basis when held by the individual partners, thereby suggesting the absence of a distinct business entity.

(continued)

Unlike corporations, there is no breakdown of the sources of owners' equity on a partnership balance sheet.

The continuity of the original partnership generally is dissolved upon the admission or withdrawal of a partner.

Changes in the ownership structure of the partnership are used to suggest revaluations of partnership assets, thereby emphasizing the measurement of the partners' wealth.

Partnership Characteristics Traceable to the Entity Theory

The partnership may enter into contracts in its own name and in some states may sue and be sued in its own name.

Property contributed to the partnership becomes the property of the partnership, and the contributing partner no longer retains a claim to the specific assets contributed.

The *marshaling of assets* doctrine recognizes that the debts of the partnership and individual partners are separate and distinct. Upon liquidation, partnership liabilities represent claims against the assets of the partnership, and the partner's personal liabilities represent claims against the partner's personal assets. (This doctrine will be discussed more fully in Chapter 16.)

If there is a change in the relation of the partners caused by the exit of any partner or the entrance of a new partner, the partnership is not necessarily liquidated and may continue its original purpose. Also, the assignment of a partner's interest to another does not dissolve the partnership.

ACCOUNTING FOR PARTNERSHIP ACTIVITIES

The remainder of this chapter discusses the accounting for a partnership's ongoing activities and the allocation of partnership profits or losses. Changes in the ownership structure of a partnership and the liquidation of a partnership are covered in the following chapter. Accounting for a partnership's activities is influenced by both the proprietary and entity theory, as discussed earlier, and to a large extent by the intent of the partners.

A partnership may come into existence without having to receive formal, legal, or state approval and may result even from the actions of the parties involved. To capture properly the intent of the parties involved, it is most advisable to develop a written partnership agreement. This written agreement, referred to as the *articles of partnership*, will govern significantly the activities of the partnership. At a minimum, it should include the following provisions:

1. Partnership name and address.
2. Partners' names and addresses.
3. Effective date of partnership.
4. A description of the general business purpose and the limited duration of such purpose, if applicable.
5. Powers and duties of partners.
6. Procedures governing the valuation of assets invested.

7. Procedures governing the admission of a new partner(s).
8. Procedures governing the distribution of profits and losses.
9. Procedures governing the payment or receipt of interest on loans (versus capital contributions) with partners.
10. Salaries to be paid to partners.
11. Withdrawals of capital to be allowed each partner and the determination of what constitutes excess withdrawals.
12. Procedures governing the death of a partner and the determination of the decedent's equity in the partnership.
13. Procedures governing the retirement of a partner and the determination of the partner's equity in the partnership.
14. Matters requiring the consent of all partners.
15. The date when the profits are divided and the partnership books are closed.

As the accounting for a partnership is developed more fully in this text, it will become apparent that the articles of partnership provide crucial guidance. Even though the UPA covers certain topics found in the articles of partnership, it is important to note that many sections of the UPA are applicable only in the absence of a partnership agreement. Legal and accounting issues affecting a partnership are resolved best by evaluating the intent of the partners as set forth in a partnership agreement, rather than looking to the UPA.

ONGOING ACTIVITIES OF A PARTNERSHIP

Except for transactions with the partners, in ongoing activities of a partnership, for the most part, are accounted for in the same way as for a corporation. Activities of a partner typically are accounted for through the use of three special accounts: a drawing account, a capital account, and a partner's loan account.

A drawing account is established for each partner and is debited and credited for the following transactions:

Drawing Account	
Debit	**Credit**
Periodic withdrawals of partnership assets	Partner's share of partnership profits
Payments made by the partnership on behalf of an individual partner	
Partner's share of partnership losses	

The debit or credit balance is closed to the capital account.

The amount and timing of a partner's withdrawal of partnership assets should be addressed in the articles of partnership. These articles may stipulate that a withdrawal in excess of a prescribed amount be considered a withdrawal of invested capital, which should be debited immediately to the partner's capital account rather than to the drawing account.

After the determination of the partnership profit or loss, each partner's share is closed to the respective drawing account. The debit or credit balance in the drawing account is then closed to the respective capital account. The drawing account is a temporary account and only the balance in a partner's capital account is presented in a partnership balance sheet. It is important to note that a partnership balance sheet does not present separately initial invested capital and earnings retained in the partnership, as would be the case in a corporation balance sheet.

Each partner's interest in the net assets of the partnership is measured at book value in the capital account established for that partner. This account indicates the destination of capital (claims to net assets) upon dissolution of the partnership. In contrast, the sources of capital for a corporation are stressed by using several capital accounts, such as capital stock, paid-in capital in excess of par, and retained earnings.

A partner's capital account is debited and credited for the following transactions:

Capital Account

Debit	Credit
Withdrawals in excess of a specified amount	Initial and subsequent investments of capital
Closing of a net debit balance in the partner's drawing account	Closing of a net credit balance in the partner's drawing account

As is the case with all entities, the investment of capital in a partnership should be measured at the fair market value of all tangible and intangible assets contributed. An individual partner's liabilities that have been assumed by the partnership also should be recorded at fair market value. This valuation of the investment at fair market value contrasts with the tax basis of a partner's investment, which, as noted previously, does not reflect fair market value. The proper valuation of each partner's net investment of capital is extremely important. For example, if an asset invested by a partner is undervalued by the partnership and is sold immediately for a gain, all the partners share in the realized gain, which properly should have accrued to the original investing partner.

The post-closing balances in the capital accounts of the various partners represent each partner's interest in the net assets of the partnership. A partner's interest in the partnership is often different from the partner's interest in the profits and losses of the partnership. To illustrate, assume that partners A and B have capital balances of $200 and $400, respectively. A's balance reflects a $33\frac{1}{3}$% interest in the partnership capital. If A and B agree to divide a $400 profit equally, the capital balances of A and B will be $400 and $600, respectively. A's balance now reflects a 40% interest in the partnership.

Occasionally, partners will loan assets to the partnership, or the partnership will loan assets to partners. It is important from a legal standpoint to differentiate between a loan and an additional investment of capital, especially when the liquidation of a partnership takes place (Chapter 15). The nature of such transactions should be made clear by examining the intent of the individual partner or the partnership. If the contribution by a partner is really an additional investment of capital, it should be accounted for in the partner's capital account. However, if the transaction is truly a loan, it should be accounted for in a separate loan account for the partner, and provision for the payment of interest on the loan should be made.

The following entries reflect the nature and use of the various partnership accounts:

Event	Entry		
Partner A contributes cash to the partnership. Partner B contributes inventory and office equipment, and the partnership assumes the liability associated with the equipment.	Cash............................ Inventory...................... Office Equipment........... Note Payable.............. Partner A, Capital........ Partner B, Capital........	10,000 5,000 4,000	2,000 10,000 7,000
Partner B loans the partnership $3,000 to be repaid in one year at a stated annual interest rate of 6%.	Cash............................ Partner B, Loan...........	3,000	3,000
A personal debt owed by Partner A is paid by the partnership.	Partner A, Drawing......... Cash........................	500 a	500
Partners A and B withdraw cash of $500 and $1,200, respectively. Drawings in excess of $1,000 are viewed as excessive withdrawals and are charged against capital.	Partner A, Drawing......... Partner B, Drawing......... Partner B, Capital........... Cash........................	500 a 1,000 b 200	1,700
The net income of the partnership is divided equally between the partners.	Income Summary........... Partner A, Drawing...... Partner B, Drawing......	10,000	5,000 a 5,000 b
The partners' drawing accounts are closed to their respective capital accounts.	Partner A, Drawing......... Partner B, Drawing......... Partner A, Capital........ Partner B, Capital........	4,000 a 4,000 b	4,000 4,000

DIVISION OF PROFITS AND LOSSES

An important process to be outlined in the articles of partnership is the manner in which profits and losses are to be divided among the partners. There are several alternative methods of allocating profits and losses. However, if the articles of partnership are silent on this point, Section 18 of the UPA states that profits and losses are to be divided equally among the partners.

The division of partnership income should be based on an analysis of the correlation between the capital and labor committed to the firm by individual partners and the income that subsequently is generated. As a result, profits might be divided in one or more of the following ways:

1. According to a ratio,
2. According to the capital investments of the partners, and/or
3. According to the labor (or service) rendered by the partners.

Profit and Loss Ratios. Partnership agreements frequently call for the division of profits and losses according to some ratio. Normally, the ratio designed for the division of profits also is used for the division of losses, unless a specific provision to the contrary exists. This method obviously provides a simplified way of dividing profits and, if approached properly, may provide an equitable division as well. Theoretically, the ratio should attempt to combine into one base the capital and service contributions made by the respective partners. Again, it is important to note that a partner's interest in profits and losses is often different from the partner's interest in total partnership capital (net assets).

To illustrate this method, assume that the articles of partnership state that partnership profits and losses should be divided between partners A and B in the ratio of 60:40. Partnership income of $20,000 would be divided as follows:

	Partner A	Partner B
Income to partners:		
A: $20,000 × 60%...............	$12,000	—
B: $20,000 × 40%...............	—	$8,000

Capital Investments of Partners. The capital investments of the partners, represented by the balances in their respective capital accounts, may be employed as a basis for dividing a portion of the profits. The division is accomplished by imputing interest on the invested capital at some specified rate. This interest is not viewed as a partnership expense, but rather as a means of allocating profits and losses among the partners. Typically, the balance of profits not allocated on the basis of invested capital is allocated according to some profit and loss ratio.

When the partners' capital investments are to be used as the basis for allocating profits, the partnership agreement should specify:

1. Whether the respective partners' capital balances are to be determined before or after the partners' year-to-date withdrawals recorded in their drawing accounts are offset against their capital accounts.
2. Whether the amount of capital investment for allocation purposes is to be:

a.   capital at the beginning of the accounting period,
b.   capital at the end of the accounting period, or
c.   weighted average capital during the accounting period.
3.   The rate of interest to be imputed on the invested capital.

With respect to the first point, it is important that the partnership agreement clearly establish how invested capital is to be determined. Since each partner's equity is a combination of capital and drawing account balances, partners' drawings may be offset against the balances in their respective capital accounts for purposes of allocating income based on invested capital. However, a partnership agreement may state that only withdrawals above a certain limit are to be viewed as offsets against capital balances. It also is possible for a partnership agreement to call for interest to be imputed only if the amount of invested capital exceeds some prescribed limit or average amount.

To illustrate the use of invested capital as a basis for allocating partnership profits, assume that:

1.   Partnership profit is $20,000.
2.   Interest on invested capital is to be imputed at the rate of 10%.
3.   Profits not allocated on the basis of invested capital are to be allocated equally among the partners.
4.   The capital accounts of Partners A and B, just prior to the closing of their drawing accounts, are as follows:

Partner A, Capital			
10/1/X1	30,000	1/1/X1	100,000
		7/1/X1	10,000

Partner B, Capital			
10/1/X1	10,000	1/1/X1	60,000

If interest is to be imputed on the partners' invested capital at the beginning of the period (1/1/X1), the partnership profit of $20,000 would be allocated as follows:

	Partner A	Partner B	Total
Interest on beginning capital:			
A: 10% × $100,000	$10,000	—	$10,000
B: 10% × $ 60,000	—	$6,000	6,000
			$16,000
Balance per ratio (equally)...............................	2,000	2,000	4,000
Allocation of profit..	$12,000	$8,000	$20,000

If interest is to be imputed on the partners' invested capital at the end of the period, the partnership profit of $20,000 would be allocated as follows:

	Partner A	Partner B	Total
Interest on ending capital:			
A: 10% × $80,000..........................	$ 8,000	—	$ 8,000
B: 10% × $50,000..........................	—	$5,000	5,000
			$13,000
Balance per ratio (equally)..............	3,500	3,500	7,000
Allocation of profit......................	$11,500	$8,500	$20,000

If interest is to be imputed on the partners' weighted average invested capital during the period, the partnership profit of $20,000 would be allocated as follows:

	Partner A	Partner B	Total
Interest on weighted average capital:			
A: 10% × $97,500 (Schedule A)............	$ 9,750	—	$ 9,750
B: 10% × $57,500 (Schedule B)............	—	$5,750	5,750
			$15,500
Balance per ratio (equally)..............	2,250	2,250	4,500
Allocation of profit......................	$12,000	$8,000	$20,000

Schedule A
Weighted Average Capital of Partner A

(1) Amount Invested	(2) Number of Months Invested	(1) × (2) Weighted Dollars
$100,000	6	$ 600,000
110,000	3	330,000
80,000	3	240,000
	12	$1,170,000

Weighted average capital: $1,170,000 ÷ 12 = $ 97,500

Schedule B
Weighted Average Capital of Partner B

(1) Amount Invested	(2) Number of Months Invested	(1) × (2) Weighted Dollars
$60,000	9	$540,000
50,000	3	150,000
	12	$690,000

Weighted average capital: $690,000 ÷ 12 = $ 57,500

Services Rendered by Partners. A partner's labor or service to the firm may be a primary force in the generation of revenue. Normally, the profit and loss agreement recognizes variations in effort by calling for a portion of income to be allocated to partners as salary. Such salaries, like interest on capital investments, are viewed as a means of allocating income rather than as an expense. It is important to note that this treatment of partners' salaries differs from the treatment of employee/shareholder salaries in a corporation, and the difference should be considered when the performance of a partnership is compared with that of a competing corporation.

When dealing with a profit and loss agreement that employs salaries as a means of allocating income, it is important not to confuse such salaries with partners' drawings. For example, a partner withdrawing $1,000 a month from the partnership, may suggest that $12,000 of partnership income is being distributed to the partner as an annual salary or that these withdrawals may be ignored for purposes of dividing profits. Generally, a partner's drawing is not viewed as a salary but as a withdrawal of assets that reduces the partner's equity. For clarification purposes, the partnership agreement should state whether regular withdrawals of specific amounts should be viewed as salary for purposes of allocating income among the partners.

Bonuses to partners also may be used as a means of recognizing a partner's service to the firm. Such bonuses usually are figured as a percentage of partnership income either before or after the bonus. When the bonus is to be a percentage of income before the bonus, the calculation is straightforward. If the bonus is to be figured as a percentage of income after the bonus, the following formula is used:

$$\text{Bonus} = X\% \,(I - \text{Bonus})$$

Where: X% is the bonus percentage

I is the income before bonus

For example, if partner A is to receive a bonus of 10% of partnership income after the bonus, the bonus is calculated as follows, assuming that income before the bonus is $110,000:

(a) Bonus = 10% ($110,000 − Bonus)   (c) 110% (Bonus) = $11,000

(b) Bonus = $11,000 − 10% (Bonus)   (d)   Bonus = $10,000

Multiple Bases of Allocation.   In many cases, income is allocated to the respective partners by combining several allocation techniques. To illustrate, assume that a profit and loss agreement of the ABC partnership contains the following provisions:

1.   Interest of 6% is to be paid on that portion of a partner's ending capital balance in excess of $100,000.
2.   Partner C is to receive a bonus equal to 10% of partnership income after the bonus.
3.   Salaries of $10,000 and $12,000 are to be paid to partners A and C, respectively.
4.   The balance of income is to be distributed in the ratio of 1:2:1 to A, B, and C, respectively.

Assuming a partnership income of $33,000 and ending capital balances of $80,000, $150,000, and $110,000 for partners A, B, and C, respectively, income is distributed to the partners as shown in Illustration 15–1.

Illustration 15–1
Profit Allocation: Multiple Bases

	Partner A	Partner B	Partner C	Total
Interest on excess capital balance	—	$3,000	$ 600	3,600
Bonus	—	—	3,000*	3,000
Salaries...................................	$10,000	—	12,000	22,000
Subtotal	$10,000	$3,000	$15,600	$28,600
Remaining profit	1,100	2,200	1,100	4,400
Income allocation................	$11,100	$5,200	$16,700	$33,000

*Bonus = 10% (I − Bonus)
Bonus = 10% ($33,000 − Bonus)
(110%) Bonus = $3,300
Bonus = $3,000

Allocating Profit Deficiencies and Losses. In the previous examples of profit allocations, the partnership income was sufficient in amount to satisfy all of the provisions of the profit and loss agreement. However, if the income is not sufficient or an operating loss exists, one of the two following alternatives may be employed:

1. Completely satisfy all provisions of the profit and loss agreement and use the profit and loss ratios to absorb any deficiency or additional loss caused by such action.
2. Satisfy each of the provisions to whatever extent is possible.

To illustrate these alternatives, assume the same information used in Illustration 15–1 for the ABC partnership, except that the partnership income is $22,000. In Illustration 15–2, the income is divided by using the first alternative.

Normally, the first method also is used when the partnership has an overall loss. For example, given a partnership loss of $2,400, the methodology in Illustration 15–2 would be employed, except that a bonus would not be recognized. The deficiency to be allocated among the partners, in the ratio of 1:2:1, would be $28,000 (subtotal of $25,600 plus the loss of $2,400).

The second alternative, which is used less frequently, requires that the provisions of the profit and loss agreement be ranked by order of priority. Assuming that the components listed in Illustration 15–2 are already in order of priority, a partnership income of $22,000 would be distributed as follows:

$ 3,600	for interest on excess capital balances
2,000	for bonus
16,400	for salaries
$22,000	

Illustration 15–2

Profit Allocation: Deficiency Allocated in Profit and Loss Ratio

	Partner A	Partner B	Partner C	Total
Interest on excess capital balance	—	$3,000	$ 600	$ 3,600
Bonus	—	—	2,000*	2,000
Salaries	$10,000	—	12,000	22,000
Subtotal	$10,000	$3,000	$14,600	$27,600
Deficiency	(1,400)	(2,800)	(1,400)	(5,600)
Income allocation	$ 8,600	$ 200	$13,200	$22,000

*Bonus = 10% (I − Bonus)
  Bonus = 10% ($22,000 − Bonus)
(110%) Bonus = $2,200
  Bonus = $2,000

The salaries of $16,400 would be allocated to partners A and C according to the ratio suggested by their normal salaries of $10,000 and $12,000, respectively. Therefore, A would receive 10/22 of the $16,400, or $7,455, while C would receive 12/22, or $8,945. Using this alternative, the partners' share of the $22,000 income would be $7,455, $3,000, and $11,545, respectively.

Special Allocation Procedures. A partnership profit and loss agreement may include special provisions for handling items that represent (a) corrections of prior years' income or (b) current-period, nonoperating gains or losses. Even though a correction of prior years' income may not satisfy the criteria for a prior-period adjustment, as defined by the Financial Accounting Standards Board, it may be more equitable to allocate the item among the partners according to the profit and loss agreement for the relevant prior period rather than the current period. For example, assume that partners A, B, and C, who previously shared profits equally, currently share profits in the ratio of 2:2:1. Also assume that in the current year, the partnership incurs a loss of $10,000 due to the settlement of litigation involving a matter arising in a prior period. Rather than allocating the loss according to the current profit ratios, it may be more equitable to base the allocation on the prior ratios.

A similar procedure may be adopted for the current-period realization of nonoperating gains or losses. Rather than allocating a gain on the sale of a plant asset according to the partners' current profit-sharing ratios, it may be more equitable to use the ratios that existed during the period when unrealized appreciation actually took place. To illustrate, assume that land with a basis of $40,000 has been held for three years and is sold for $60,000 in the current period. Based on the assumed profit-sharing ratios of prior periods, the $20,000 gain would be allocated to partners A, B, and C as follows:

Year	Profit Ratios	Appreciation	Profit Allocation		
			A	B	C
1	1:1:2	$ 4,000	$1,000	$1,000	$2,000
2	2:1:2	10,000	4,000	2,000	4,000
3	2:2:2	6,000	2,000	2,000	2,000
		$20,000	$7,000	$5,000	$8,000

If the partnership had not established special provisions for handling such items, the gain of $20,000 would have been allocated equally among the partners according to their current profit ratio of 2:2:2.

QUESTIONS

1. List four characteristics of a partnership which indicate that it is not a separate, distinct entity.
2. In theory, why might a partnership have the ability to attract more capital than a corporation?
3. How does viewing a partnership by the proprietary theory explain its tax treatment?
4. A restaurant organized as a partnership has three partners, one of whom is involved in the day-to-day operations of the business. What are the consequences of having articles of partnership that do not address specifically the allocation of profits?
5. What are the possible explanations for a post-closing debit balance in a partner's capital account?
6. What adjustments are necessary in order to compare the income of a business organized as a partnership to that of a similar business organized as a corporation?
7. Identify the basic activities or transactions that affect a partner's capital account.
8. If the income of a partnership is not sufficient to cover all elements of a profit and loss agreement, how should the income be divided?
9. Under what circumstances might a salary or bonus be more appropriate than interest on capital balances as a means of allocating profits?
10. Discuss why a profit and loss agreement that includes interest as a percentage of year-end capital may not be equitable.
11. A partner receives $1,000 a month from the partnership. What is the significance of viewing the payment as a withdrawal versus a salary?

EXERCISES

Exercise 1. Adams, Baker, and Clark formed a partnership by contributing the following assets and associated liabilities:

	Assets	Liabilities
Adams.....................................	$75,000	$30,000
Baker......................................	50,000	24,000
Clark	25,000	12,000

Each of the asset amounts is equal to the tax basis of that asset. The interest in the assets and debts of the partnership of Adams, Baker, and Clark are 3:2:1, respectively.
(1) Calculate the tax basis in the partnership for each partner.
(2) Calculate the accounting basis in the partnership for each partner.

Exercise 2. In 19X1, a new partnership purchased land on the edge of the town of Otisville. The partners erected a building and opened a furniture and appliance store under the name of Furniture Fair. The partnership agreement specified that profits or losses should be shared equally after the allocation of partners' salary allowances and interest on average capital balances.

Otisville has grown considerably, and the store is now one of the most prominent stores in a fashionable suburban area. Good management, imaginative merchandising, and the general growth in the economy have made Furniture Fair the leading and most profitable firm of its type in the Otisville trade area.

Now the partners wish to admit another investor and incorporate the business. The original partners will purchase at par an amount of preferred stock equal to the book value of their interest in the partnership and common stock equal to that portion of fair market value that exceeds their book value. The new investor will purchase, at a ten percent premium over par value, common and preferred stock equal to one-third of the total number of shares purchased by the original partners. The corporation then will purchase the Furniture Fair partnership at its fair market value from the partners. After the consummation of the partners' plan, the corporation will acquire the partnership assets, assume the liabilities, and employ the partners to manage the corporation.
(1) List and explain the differences in terms and valuations that would be expected in comparing the assets that appear on the balance sheet of the proposed corporation and the assets that appear on the partnership balance sheet.
(2) List and explain the differences that would be expected in a comparison of an income statement prepared for the proposed corporation and an income statement prepared for the partnership.   (AICPA adapted)

Exercise 3.   Drake, Forrest, and Gibbons own a video rental store that is organized as a partnership. Their partnership agreement includes the following:

(a) Drake is to receive a salary of $15,000 and a bonus of 2.5% of income before the bonus.

(b) Forrest is to receive a salary of $10,000 and a bonus of 5% of income before the bonus.

(c) All partners are to receive 10% interest on their average capital invested. The average capital balances are as follows:

Drake	$ 30,000
Forrest...	45,000
Gibbons..	100,000

(d) Any residual amounts are to be divided equally.

(1) Determine how a before-bonus profit of $80,000 would be allocated among the partners.

(2) Determine how a loss of $17,500 would be allocated among the partners.

Exercise 4.   Newman and Mason are partners in a car rental business. Included in their partnership agreement is a provision for interest to be paid on the weighted average capital balance for each partner at a rate of 10%. Periodic withdrawals by a partner will not affect the capital balance until the accumulated annual withdrawals exceed $4,000. The current year's withdrawal and investment information for each partner is as follows:

	Newman	Mason
Beginning capital balance, January 1, 19X9......................	$30,000	$24,000
Withdrawal of capital, February 1, 19X9..........................	(3,000)	(1,000)
Capital investment, May 1, 19X9	—	3,000
Withdrawal of capital, August 1, 19X9............................	(4,000)	(500)
Withdrawal of capital, November 1, 19X9........................	—	(3,500)

Determine the interest to be allocated to each partner as provided in the partnership agreement.

Exercise 5.   Xavier, Yates, and Zale are partners in a dry cleaning business. Their partnership agreement provides that the partners shall receive interest on their respective average yearly capital balances at the rate of 8%. Any residual profits or losses shall be divided equally among the partners.

The following information is available for the second year of operations:

(a) Partners' capital balances as of January 1, 19X2:

Xavier	$24,000
Yates...	17,500
Zale..	13,000

(b) Additional investments were made during the year as follows:

Xavier	$4,500 on April 1, 19X2
Zale................	$2,000 on July 1, 19X2, and $15,000 on September 1, 19X2

(c) The drawing accounts of the partners have the following debit balances at the end of 19X2:

Xavier	$1,000
Yates..	1,000
Zale...	500

(d) Partnership income for the year is $21,100.

(1) Discuss the advantages and disadvantages of using the weighted average capital balance as the base for determining interest on capital contributed.
(2) Determine the interest on weighted average capital balances that partners Xavier, Yates, and Zale should receive for the year 19X2. Assume that the partners' withdrawals are not to influence the capital balances for purposes of computing interest.
(3) Determine the capital account balances for Xavier, Yates, and Zale after all closing entries have been journalized and posted at the end of 19X2. Supporting schedules should be in good form.

Exercise 6. Jackson, Karner, and Lawson are partners in a lumber company. Their partnership agreement provides for the following profit and loss distributions:

(a) Jackson, Karner, and Lawson are to receive salaries of $20,000, $18,000, and $6,825, respectively. Jackson is to receive a bonus equal to 10% of income before the bonus.
(b) Each partner is to receive 10% interest on the weighted average capital balance.
(c) Withdrawals are considered to be reductions of capital for purposes of interest calculations.
(d) Any remaining profits or losses are to be divided equally among the partners.

Capital balance information for 19X9 is as follows:

	Jackson	Karner	Lawson
Beginning capital balance, January 1, 19X9........	$5,000	$3,000	$20,000
Withdrawal of capital, April 1, 19X9...................	(500)	—	(1,000)
Capital investment, July 1, 19X9........................	1,000	2,000	7,500
Withdrawal of capital, October 1, 19X9	(500)	(1,000)	—

Assume that Jackson's share of the allocated profits is to be withdrawn. Determine how much profit the partnership must earn to allow Jackson to withdraw exactly $30,500 excluding previous withdrawals. Supporting schedules should be in good form.

Exercise 7. Burns and Egen formed a partnership on January 6, 19X1. At that time, Burns contributed capital of $25,000. Egen contributed no capital, but has a specialized expertise and manages the firm full time. There were no withdrawals by either party during the year. The partnership agreement provides for the following:

(a) Capital accounts are to be credited annually with interest at 5% of the beginning capital balance.
(b) Egen is to be paid a salary of $1,400 per month.
(c) Egen is to receive a bonus of 20% of before-bonus income calculated before the partners' interest and salary are deducted.
(d) Profits are to be divided between Burns and Egen in the ratio of 9:1, respectively.
(e) Bonuses, interest, and Egen's salary are to be considered partnership expenses.

The partnership 19X1 income statement is as follows:

Revenue	$101,250
Expenses (including salary, interest, and bonus)	(54,500)
Income	$ 46,750

Assuming that Egen withdraws one-half of the salary at year end, determine Egen's bonus and Burns' and Egen's capital balances at year end.
(AICPA adapted)

PROBLEMS

Problem 15–1. On January 1, 19X4, the partnership of Barber, Robly, and Tessen decided to merge with another partnership. The partners agreed that, prior to the merger, the records of the partnership should be revised to put all past transactions on the accrual basis following current accounting theory. Additional information is as follows:
(a) Barber and Tessen originally formed a law practice on January 1, 19X1, sharing profits and losses equally. Robly was admitted as a new partner on January 1, 19X2. The new partnership shared profits and losses as follows: Barber, 40%; Robly, 20%; and Tessen, 40%.
(b) Barber, Robly, and Tessen have followed accrual accounting, but the following errors have been discovered:
  (1) A $5,000 advance payment on April 4, 19X1, credited to earned revenue, was unearned as of December 31, 19X1; it should have been recognized on February 15, 19X2.
  (2) Law books worth $3,000 were loaned by Barber to the partnership on January 1, 19X1, and were to be returned after five years. The partnership depreciated the books evenly over the years, but they never were recorded as a partnership asset.
  (3) On December 20, 19X3, the partnership received a $2,000 advance from a client, which was credited to earned revenue.
(c) The Barber, Robly, and Tessen partnership always has treated salaries as a direct reduction of capital; but as part of the new partnership agree-

ment, the salaries are to be treated as a distribution of income, and retroactive correction of the accounts is to be made. The following schedule indicates the salaries received by the individual partners and the income earned by the partnership for 19X1, 19X2, and 19X3:

| Year | Salaries Received | | | Income Before Salaries |
	Barber	Robly	Tessen	
19X1	$15,000	—	$15,000	$25,000
19X2	20,000	$15,000	25,000	50,000
19X3	25,000	15,000	25,000	70,000

(d) A condensed balance sheet as of December 31, 19X3, for the Barber, Robly, and Tessen partnership is as follows:

Assets		Liabilities and Capital	
Cash	$ 5,000	Liabilities.........................	$ 5,000
Receivables (net).............	22,000	Barber, capital.................	25,000
Books (net)	14,000	Robly, capital	15,000
Other assets...................	24,000	Tessen, capital	20,000
		Total liabilities	
Total assets...................	$65,000	and capital..................	$65,000

Required:
(1) Prepare a schedule to compute the 19X1, 19X2, and 19X3 corrected incomes of the partnership on the accrual basis. (Any depreciation should be computed on the straight-line basis. Ignore tax implications.)
(2) Prepare a schedule to show how these corrected incomes of the partnership are allocated to the individual partners.
(3) Prepare a schedule to correct the partners' capital accounts as of December 31, 19X3. Include the effects of the prior income distributions and the revised income distributions.

Problem 15–2.   Manning and Peterson have agreed to form a partnership, both contributing assets and associated liabilities. They have agreed to assume equal responsibility for the obligations of those assets. A schedule of the assets and liabilities contributed to the partnership is as follows:

	Book Basis	Tax Basis	Fair Market Value
Manning:			
Cash.................................	$28,000	$28,000	$28,000
Land.................................	30,000	30,000	60,000
Building, net	50,000	42,000	74,000
Mortgage on building	41,000	41,000	41,000
Peterson:			
Inventory.........................	19,000	17,000	19,000
Equipment, net.................	44,000	39,000	44,000
Note payable, equipment	7,000	7,000	7,000
Truck, net.........................	8,000	4,000	3,000
Note payable, truck...........................	6,000	6,000	6,000
Accrued liabilities	15,000	15,000	15,000

Required:

(1) Calculate the tax basis of each partner.

(2) Calculate each partner's capital balance per books.

Problem 15-3. Case, Harvey, and Richards were CPAs who agreed to consolidate their individual practices as of January 1, 19X7. The partnership agreement includes the following features:

(a) Each partner's capital contribution is the net amount of the assets and liabilities taken over by the partnership, which are as follows:

	Case	Harvey	Richards
Cash......	$ 5,000	$ 5,000	$ 5,000
Accounts receivable......	14,000	6,000	16,000
Furniture and library......	4,300	2,500	6,200
Accumulated depreciation...	(2,400)	(1,500)	(4,700)
Accounts payable......	(300)	(1,400)	(700)
Capital contribution......	$20,600	$10,600	$21,800

The partners guaranteed the collectibility of their receivables.

(b) Richards had leased office space with a monthly rental of $600 and was bound by the lease until June 30, 19X7. The partners agree to pay the rent and to occupy Richards' office space until the expiration of the lease. However, the partners expressed concern that the rent was too high and that a fair rental value would be $450 per month. The excess rent is to be charged to Richards at year end. On July 1, the partners moved to new quarters with a monthly rent of $500.

(c) No salaries are to be paid to the partners. The individual partners are to receive 20% of the gross fees billed to their respective clients during the first year of the partnership. After operating expenses are deducted, the balance of the fees billed is to be credited to the partners' capital accounts in the following ratios: Case, 40%; Harvey, 35%; Richards, 25%.

(d) On April 1, 19X7, Williams was admitted to the partnership. Williams is to receive 20% of the fees from new business obtained after April 1, after expenses applicable to that new business are deducted. Expenses are to be apportioned to the new business in the ratio of total expenses (other than bad debt losses) to total gross fees.

The following information pertains to the partnership's activities for the first year of operations:

(a) Fees were billed as follows:

Case's clients	$22,000
Harvey's clients	12,000
Richards' clients	11,000
New business:	
Prior to April 1	3,000
After April 1	12,000
Total......	$60,000

(b) Total expenses, excluding depreciation and uncollectible accounts expense, were $19,350, including the amount actually paid for rent. Depreciation is to be computed each year at the rate of 10% of the original asset cost. Depreciable assets purchased during the year, on which one-half year's depreciation is to be taken, totaled $5,000.

(c) Individual cash drawings during the year were as follows:

Case..	$ 5,200
Harvey..	4,400
Richards	5,800
Williams	2,500
	$17,900

(d) Of Case's and Harvey's receivables, $1,200 and $450, respectively, proved to be uncollectible. A new client, billed in March for $1,600, had been adjudicated bankrupt, and a settlement of fifty cents on the dollar was made.

Required:

Prepare a statement of the partners' capital accounts for the year ended December 31, 19X7. Supporting computations should be in good form. (Disregard income taxes.)   (AICPA adapted)

Problem 15–4.   Howard, White, and Young have formed a partnership. Their partnership agreement contains the following provisions regarding the allocation of profits and losses:

(a) Howard and White are to receive salaries of $11,500 and $15,800, respectively.

(b) Young is to receive a bonus of 10% of partnership income after the bonus.

(c) All partners are to receive interest of 6% on their weighted average capital balances. Withdrawals are to be considered reductions in capital for purposes of calculating the interest.

(d) Any remaining amounts will be allocated as follows: Howard, 20%; White, 40%; and Young, 40%.

Investment and withdrawal information for each partner is as follows:

	Howard	White	Young
Beginning capital balance, January 1, 19X9......	$30,000	$45,000	$27,000
Withdrawal of capital, April 1, 19X9.................	(3,000)	(6,000)	—
Withdrawal of capital, May 1, 19X9..................	—	—	(9,000)
Capital investment, July 1, 19X9.....................	2,000	—	6,000
Withdrawal of capital, October 1, 19X9	(3,000)	(4,000)	—

Required:

For each of the following independent situations, prepare a schedule allocating the profit among the partners:

(1) Partnership income is $55,000 for 19X9.

(2) Partnership income is $22,000 for 19X9.

Supporting schedules should be in good form.

Problem 15–5.   Bryant-Domer Company is a partnership that sells appliances to the retail trade and also sells wholesale to builders and contractors. The partnership agreement provides for a 14% imputed interest rate on invested capital; salaries of $12,000 and $16,000 for Bryant and Domer, respectively; and a 10% bonus for Domer. Changes in the 19X8 capital accounts of both partners, excluding normal withdrawals, were as follows:

Bryant, Capital				Domer, Capital		
12/1/X8	5,500	1/1/X8	85,000	4/1/X8	3,000	1/1/X8	96,800
		2/1/X8	2,000			7/1/X8	6,500
		9/1/X8	1,500			10/1/X8	4,500

Required:

For each of the following independent situations, prepare the profit allocation schedule for Bryant-Domer Company. Supporting calculations should be in good form.

(1) Interest on invested capital is based on ending capital balances after deducting year-to-date withdrawals of $8,000 for Bryant and $6,300 for Domer. The bonus is a percentage of partnership income before the bonus; 19X8 income was $39,942. The provisions of the partnership agreement are to be satisfied to whatever extent possible in the following order: interest, salaries, and bonus. Any remaining partnership income is to be allocated 60% to Bryant and 40% to Domer.

(2) Interest on invested capital is based on weighted average capital balances. The bonus is a percentage of partnership income after the bonus; 19X8 income was $66,000. All provisions of the partnership agreement are to be satisfied completely, and any remaining income or deficiency created is to be allocated 75% to Bryant and 25% to Domer.

(3) Interest is based on ending capital balances in excess of $62,000. The bonus is a percentage of partnership income after the bonus; 19X8 income after salaries and bonus was $8,000. All provisions of the partnership agreement are to be satisfied completely. The articles of partnership are silent on the matter of profit and loss division between the partners.

Problem 15–6.   Carson, Dowman, and Evans own an office automation and consulting business organized as a partnership. Evans is considering retirement from the partnership. In order to more fairly measure Evans' interest in capital, an audit of the company's first two years of operations was performed in early 19X9. The original partnership agreement called for Carson to receive a 10% bonus on income after the bonus, with the remaining profits or losses to be divided as follows: Carson, 30%; Dowman, 30%; and Evans, 40%. Reported income for 19X7 was $44,000.

In the second year of operations, the agreement was modified to reflect Evans' decision to become less involved in the business. The new agreement called for Carson still to receive a 10% bonus on income after the bonus, but altered the allocation of remaining amounts as follows: Carson, 35%; Dowman, 35%; and Evans, 30%. Reported income for 19X8 was $42,000.

The partners always had agreed that any adjustment to reported amounts would be allocated based on the profit and loss agreement in effect during the period to which the adjustment relates. The audit indicated that the following items were not accounted for properly:

(a) 19X7:
    (1) Failed to amortize the business name contributed by Carson. The fair market value of the intangible was $50,000 and should have been amortized over a ten-year life using straight-line amortization.
    (2) Failed to defer prepaid insurance premiums of $3,000.
    (3) A capital withdrawal of $5,000 made by Carson on July 1, 19X7, was classified incorrectly as a Note Receivable.
    (4) Failed to accrue $2,000 of employee wages on December 31, 19X7.
    (5) Failed to record consulting fees of $8,400 earned in 19X7 but billed in 19X8.
(b) 19X8:
    (1) Ending inventory included a computer invoiced on December 31, 19X8, for $4,000 but not yet received. Terms were F. O. B. destination.
    (2) Failed to accrue $8,600 of rent expense of December 31, 19X8.
    (3) Failed to reverse $3,000 of interest income properly accrued at the end of 19X7, resulting in income recognition in both years.

Required:

Assume the following unadjusted December 31, 19X8 capital account balances: Carson, $25,000; Dowman, $30,000; and Evans, $28,000. Prepare a schedule to reflect the adjusted capital balances as of December 31, 19X8. Supporting calculations should be in good form.

CHAPTER 16

PARTNERSHIPS: OWNERSHIP CHANGES AND LIQUIDATION

The Uniform Partnership Act (UPA) defines dissolution as "the change in the relation of the partners caused by any partner ceasing to be associated in the carrying on as distinguished from the winding up of the business." Sections 31 and 32 of the UPA identify the various causes of dissolution and suggest that the admission or withdrawal of a partner results in dissolution. Although dissolution ends the association of partners for their original purpose, it does not result necessarily in the termination of the partnership's basic business function. The remaining partners may continue to operate the business, or they may decide to terminate or liquidate the business. It is important for contemplated partnership changes to be well planned, so that either the continuation or the liquidation of the partnership may proceed smoothly and equitably.

This chapter focuses on partnership dissolution due to ownership changes resulting from the admission and/or withdrawal of a partner and the related accounting implications. The winding up or liquidation of a partnership also is discussed.

OWNERSHIP CHANGES

Changes in the ownership structure of a corporation are everyday occurrences, as evidenced by the activity of security exchanges. These changes typically involve transactions between existing and prospective shareholders and, therefore, create no special accounting problems for the corporate entity, other than updating its listings of stockholders. In the case of a partnership, however, changes in ownership structure are events that require special accounting treatment.

Accounting for changes in the ownership of a partnership is influenced heavily by the legal concept of dissolution. When there is a change in the ownership structure, the original partnership is dissolved and most often a new partnership is created. This dissolution and subsequent creation of a partnership indicates that a new legal entity has been created and that accounting should measure properly the initial contributions of capital being made to the new partnership. The proprietary theory, as discussed in Chapter 1, also influences the accounting for changes in the ownership structure of a partnership. Under this theory, primary attention is focused on measuring the wealth of the individual proprietors or partners. Changes in ownership involve exchanges of consideration that reflect the current value of a partnership interest. Therefore, changes in ownership provide a basis for currently measuring partnership wealth or value.

Because of the influence of the dissolution concept and proprietary theory, ownership changes often are viewed as reliable exchanges, which may indicate that:

1. The existing assets of the original partnership should be revalued,
2. Previously unrecorded intangible assets exist that are traceable to the original partnership, and/or
3. Goodwill exists that is traceable to a new partner.

The extent to which such value changes are recorded should be evaluated against the information standards presented in Chapter 1 and established principles governing the recording of ownership changes.

ADMISSION OF A NEW PARTNER

The admission of a new partner requires the approval of the existing partners, although a partner's interest may be assigned to someone outside the partnership without the consent of the other partners. However, assigning an interest does not dissolve the partnership, and it does not allow the assignee to participate in the management of the partnership or to review transactions and records of the partnership. The assignee receives only the agreed portion of the assigning partner's profit or loss.

Assuming that a new partner has been approved by the existing partners, the new partner normally will experience the same general risks and rights of ownership as do the other existing partners. However, creditors presenting claims against the partnership that were incurred prior to admission of the new partner cannot attach the personal assets of the new partner for settlement of their claims. Therefore, the level of liability of a new partner is less than that of an existing partner. Section 17 of the UPA states that:

> *A person admitted as a partner into an existing partnership is liable for all the obligations of the partnership arising before his admission as though he had been a partner when such obligations were incurred, except that this liability shall be satisfied only out of partnership property.*

Contribution of Assets to Existing Partnership. One method of gaining admission to an existing partnership involves contributing assets directly to the partnership entity itself. In this case, the exchange represents an arm's-length transaction between the entity and the incoming partner. If the book value of the original partnership's net assets approximates fair market value, the incoming partner's contribution would be expected to be equal to the portion of the equity that the new partner is acquiring. For example, if an incoming partner is to acquire a one-fourth interest in a partnership that has a book value and a fair market value of $60,000, the original $60,000 now would represent a three-fourths interest in the new partnership. Therefore, the total partnership capital must be $80,000, of which $60,000 is traceable to the old partners and $20,000 is traceable to the assets contributed by the new partner.

An incoming partner also may acquire an interest in the partnership for a price in excess of that indicated by the book value of the original partnership's net assets. This situation would suggest the existence of:

1. Unrecorded appreciation on identifiable net assets of the original partnership, and/or
2. Unrecorded goodwill that also is traceable to the original partnership.

However, it is possible that an incoming partner may acquire an interest in the partnership at a price less than that indicated by the book value. This situation would suggest the existence of:

1. Unrecorded depreciation or write-downs on the identifiable net assets of the original partnership, and/or
2. A contribution by the incoming partner of some intangible asset (goodwill) in addition to a measured contribution.

When an incoming partner's contribution is different from that indicated by the book values of the original partnership, the admission of the partner typically is recorded by either the *bonus method* or the *goodwill method*. These two methods are mutually exclusive of each other. Both methods permit the assumption that there is unrecorded goodwill to be recognized. However, the use of either method does not prevent the recognition of differences between the book value and fair market value of recorded net assets.

Bonus Method. The bonus method of recording the admission of a partner accounts for partnership capital at recorded book values. The proper application of this method will result in the following conditions:

1. Total capital of the new partnership will be equal to the book value of the existing partners' capital plus the recorded value of the incoming partner's investment, and

2. Upon admission, the incoming partner's capital will be determined by multiplying the total capital of the new partnership by the acquired percentage interest in capital. The previous partners' capital balances will be reallocated to the extent of the bonus.

Bonus to Old Partners. When an incoming partner's contribution indicates the existence of unrecorded net asset appreciation and/or unrecorded goodwill, the bonus method does not record these previously unrecorded items, but rather grants a "bonus" to the old partners. The bonus, which increases the capital accounts of the old partners, is made possible by recording in the new partner's capital account only a portion of the actual contribution to the partnership.

To illustrate this method, assume the following:

		Percentage Interest in	
Existing Partners	Capital Balance	Capital	Profit
Partner A	$30,000	40%	50%
Partner B	45,000	60	50

Then assume that C invests $27,000 in the partnership in exchange for a 20% interest in capital and a one-third interest in profits. Since the total capital of the new partnership equals $102,000 ($30,000 + $45,000 + $27,000) and since the new partner is acquiring a 20% interest in capital, it seems reasonable that the incoming partner's capital account initially should reflect 20% of the total capital, or $20,400. The $6,600 difference between C's contribution and the interest recorded for C indicates the existence of unrecorded intangibles (goodwill) or unrecorded appreciation on existing assets. Regardless of the identity of the $6,600, the value must be allocated to the appropriate parties. If the unrecorded value had been realized through a sale, the resulting profit would have been divided between the old partners in accordance with their profit and loss agreement. Therefore, assuming that the $6,600 is identified as a bonus to the old partners and is divided between them according to their profit and loss ratio, the entry to record C's investment is as follows:

Assets	27,000	
A, Capital..		3,300
B, Capital..		3,300
C, Capital..		20,400

Bonus to New Partner. When the new partner invests some intangible asset, such as business acumen or an established clientele, it is possible to have a bonus credited to the new partner. For example, given the same basic facts as in the previous illustration, assume that C invests $10,000 for a 20% interest in capital and a one-third interest in profits. Total capital of the partnership would be $85,000 ($30,000 + $45,000 + $10,000) and C's share of the total capital would be 20%, or $17,000. Partner C is acquiring a $17,000 interest in capital in exchange for an investment of $10,000, and the old partners are transferring $7,000 of their capital to C in exchange for unrecorded intangible assets invested by C. Partner C's admission is recorded by the following entry:

Assets	10,000	
A, Capital..	3,500	
B, Capital..	3,500	
C, Capital...		17,000

Partner C's bonus may be viewed as a cost incurred to acquire C's goodwill. Since all costs to acquire assets eventually affect income and are allocated among the partners, C's bonus is allocated to A and B according to their profit and loss ratio.

The recording of a bonus traceable to the incoming partner was based on the assumption that the new partner was contributing an intangible asset in addition to other assets valued at $10,000. However, the substance of the transaction may indicate that no intangibles are being contributed and that the existing assets of the old partnership are overvalued. For example, in the previous illustration, C invested $10,000 in return for a 20% interest in the new partnership's total capital. Therefore, the total capital of the new partnership may be interpreted from C's investment to be equal to $50,000 ($10,000 ÷ 20%). Of this total, $10,000 is traceable to the new partner, and the balance of $40,000 represents the fair market value of the old partners' capital. Assuming that this is a proper interpretation of the substance of the transaction between the new partner and the partnership, C's admission to the partnership is recorded as follows:

A, Capital..	17,500	
B, Capital..	17,500	
Assets		35,000
To record the write-down of the original partners' capital from a book value of $75,000 ($30,000 + $45,000) to its implied fair market value of $40,000.		
Assets	10,000	
C, Capital...		10,000
To record C's contribution of assets to the partnership.		

After these entries are posted, the total capital of the new partnership is $50,000 ($30,000 + $45,000 − $35,000 + $10,000), of which C's share is $10,000 (20% × $50,000), as initially represented by the balance in C's capital account.

Goodwill Method. The goodwill method emphasizes the legal significance of a change in the ownership structure of a partnership. From a legal viewpoint, the entrance of a new partner results in the dissolution of the previous partnership and the creation of a new legal entity. Since a new entity has resulted, the assets transferred to this entity should be recorded at their current fair market value. After a complete analysis, both tangible and intangible assets acquired by the new entity, including goodwill created by the previous partnership, should be recorded.

Goodwill Traceable to Old Partners. When the bonus method is used to account for the admission of a new partner, the total capital of the new entity equals the book value of the previous partners' capital plus the incoming partner's investment. When the goodwill method is employed, however, the total capital of the new partnership must approximate the fair market value of the entity.

To illustrate the goodwill method, assume the following:

| | | Percentage Interest in | |
Existing Partners	Capital Balance	Capital	Profit
Partner A	$30,000	40%	50%
Partner B	45,000	60	50

If C invests $27,000 in the partnership in exchange for a 20% interest in capital and a one-third interest in profit, such an investment implies that the entity has a fair market value of $135,000 ($27,000 ÷ 20%). However, the book value of the new partnership equals only $102,000 when the former partners' capital balances of $75,000 are added to C's $27,000 investment. Thus, $33,000 must be added to the existing book value.

Another interpretation of the transaction would be that, given the $102,000 book value of the new partnership, a 20% interest should have cost $20,400 ($102,000 × 20%). The new partner paid an extra $6,600 ($27,000 − $20,400) for a 20% interest in the difference between the implied fair market value and the book value of the new entity. Therefore, the total difference must be $33,000 ($6,600 ÷ 20%).

The difference between the higher fair market value and the book value of the new entity, as previously discussed, may be traceable to unrecorded appreciation and/or unrecorded goodwill. Each of these possible explanations should be analyzed thoroughly to account properly for a change in the ownership structure of a partnership. If differences between the fair market value and the book value of recorded assets are identifiable, appropriate adjustments to asset balances should be considered. Since a change in ownership structure creates a new, distinct legal entity, every attempt should be made to identify differences between fair market and book values. However, the absence of objective and independent valuations often prevents such an analysis. For example, fair market values are not readily available for certain specialized assets, and the alternative of engaging an independent appraiser could become an expensive option. Furthermore, estimating fair market values with the use of specific price-level indexes is often difficult because of the absence of relevent indexes. Another reason for not recording changes in market values is that the resulting differences between the bases for tax purposes and the bases for book purposes would require more complex records.

Unrecorded goodwill also may be identifiable. In the previous example, assuming that there are no differences between the fair market value and book value of recorded assets, the new partner's willingness to pay more than the proportionate book value of the new entity indicates that goodwill existed prior to the new partner's admission. If this intangible asset could have been sold prior to the admission of the partner, the realized profit would have been allocated to the old partners. Therefore, the goodwill is recorded and allocated to the old partners according to their profit and loss ratio. The investment by C is recorded under the goodwill method as follows:

Assets	27,000	
Goodwill	33,000	
A, Capital		16,500
B, Capital		16,500
C, Capital		27,000

It is important to note that the new partner's capital account balance represents a 20% interest in the total capital of the new partnership, as verified by the following computation:

Original capital	$ 75,000
C's investment	27,000
Goodwill	33,000
	$135,000
C's interest	× 20%
C's capital balance	$ 27,000

The recognition of goodwill traceable to the previous partners is criticized by some accountants. If the concept of a new legal entity is cast aside, some would argue that the goodwill is self-created and, therefore, should not be recognized. APB Opinion No. 17, "Intangible Assets," prohibits the recognition of goodwill unless it has been purchased from another entity. To argue that the new partnership is in substance a continuation of the previous partnership would prevent the recognition of goodwill traceable to the old partnership.

It also may be argued that the difficulties associated with the measurement of the fair market value of existing assets unjustifiably forces the recognition of goodwill for lack of a more precise analysis. However, the argument that the fair market value of a new partnership, as indicated by the new partner's investment, is not objectively or independently determined overlooks the basic nature of the transaction. Negotiations between previous partners and a new partner would be described as arm's length, since both parties involved are seeking independently a fair price.

Goodwill Traceable to New Partner. It is possible for goodwill to be attributable to the new partner. For example, given the same basic facts as in the previous illustrations, assume that C invests $10,000 to acquire a 20% interest in the partnership of A and B. C's investment implies a fair market value of the new entity equal to $50,000 ($10,000 ÷ 20%). However, the book value of the new partnership equals $85,000, consisting of the old partners' capital balances of $75,000 plus C's investment of $10,000. This difference between the fair market value and the higher book value indicates the existence of unrecorded write-downs and/or goodwill contributed by the incoming partner. Assuming that net assets should not be written down, the amount of the unrecorded goodwill may be computed as the difference between:

1. The amount that should have been paid by the new partner, as indicated by the book value of the previous partnership (calculated by dividing the original book value of the partnership by the total percentage interest of the original partners in the new partnership, and subtracting the original book value), and
2. The amount actually paid by the new partner.

In this example, the $75,000 original book value would represent 80% of the new partnership capital, or $93,750 ($75,000 ÷ 80%). Therefore, it appears that the new partner should have paid $18,750 ($93,750 less the original $75,000 book value) for a 20% interest in the partnership; however, the partner actually paid only $10,000. The difference between what should have been paid ($18,750) and the amount actually paid ($10,000) represents the goodwill traceable to the incoming partner. The investment by C would be recorded under the goodwill method as follows:

Assets	10,000	
Goodwill	8,750	
C, Capital		18,750

Note that the new partner's capital account balance represents a 20% interest in the total capital of the new partnership, as shown by the following computation:

Original capital	$75,000
C's investment	10,000
Goodwill	8,750
	$93,750
C's interest	× 20%
C's capital balance	$18,750

The fact that a new legal entity is created supports the recognition of goodwill and other contributed assets at their fair market value. If the concept of a new entity is set aside, the goodwill may be viewed as being purchased by the previous partnership in exchange for partnership equity. Accounting theory and current practice support the recording of goodwill acquired or purchased from other entities.

Methodology for Determining Goodwill. An analysis of the previous examples reveals that goodwill may be traceable to either the original partners or the incoming partner. To apply the goodwill method properly, the following methodology may be helpful in identifying the origin of the goodwill and its amount:

1. Determine the entity's fair market value, as indicated by the new partner's investment (new partner's investment divided by the percentage interest acquired in the partnership).
2. If the fair market value determined is:
   (a) Greater than the book value of the new partnership, implied goodwill is traceable to the old partners and is allocated among them according to their profit ratios. The amount of goodwill is equal to the difference between (1) the fair market value indicated by the new partner's investment and (2) the book value of the new partnership.
   (b) Less than the book value of the new partnership, implied goodwill is traceable to the new partner. The amount of goodwill is equal to the difference between (1) the amount that should have been paid by the new partner to acquire an interest in the book value of the partnership and (2) the actual amount paid.
3. The initial capital balance of the new partner always is equal to the new partner's interest in the total capital of the new partnership after goodwill is recognized.

Comparison of Bonus and Goodwill Methods. The bonus method adheres to the historical cost concept and often is used in accounting practice. It is objective in that it establishes total capital of the new partnership at an amount based on actual consideration received from the new partner. The bonus method indirectly acknowledges the existence of goodwill by giving a bonus to either old or new partners.

The goodwill method results in the recognition of an asset implied by a transaction rather than recognizing an asset actually purchased. Historically, goodwill has been recognized only when purchased so that a more objective measure of its value is established. Therefore, opponents of the goodwill method contend that goodwill is not determined objectively and that other factors may have influenced the amount of investment required from the new partner. Also, certain recipients of partnership financial statements may question the valuation of goodwill, since increasing total assets may result in an understatement of the return on total assets or equity.

Use of the goodwill method also could produce inequitable results if either of the following conditions exist:

1. The new partner's interest in profits does not equal the new partner's initial interest in capital.
2. Former partners do not share profits and losses in the same relationship to each other as they did before the admission of a new partner.

The importance of these concepts can be illustrated using the following facts:

	Old Partners		New Partner
	A	B	C
Original capital..	$30,000	$45,000	
Original profit and loss percentage..................	50%	50%	
New partner's capital.....................................			$27,000
New profit and loss percentage.....................	$33\frac{1}{3}\%$	$33\frac{1}{3}\%$	$33\frac{1}{3}\%$
New partner's interest in capital.....................			20%

The new capital balances that result from using the goodwill method and the bonus method are as follows:

	Old Partners		New Partner
	A	B	C
Goodwill method:			
Goodwill allocation	$16,500	$16,500	
New capital balances.................................	46,500	61,500	$27,000
Bonus method:			
Bonus allocation..	3,300	3,300	
New capital balances.................................	33,300	48,300	20,400

Assuming that the recorded goodwill proves to be worthless (or assuming that goodwill is amortized in total), the decline in asset value would reduce the partners' capital balances according to their profit and loss ratio as follows:

	Partner			
	A	B	C	Total
Capital balances if goodwill method used...................	$46,500	$61,500	$27,000	$135,000
Goodwill write-off (amortization)..............................	(11,000)	(11,000)	(11,000)	(33,000)
Capital balances after write-off	$35,500	$50,500	$16,000	$102,000
Capital balances if bonus method used......................	33,300	48,300	20,400	102,000
Differences...	$ 2,200	$ 2,200	($ 4,400)	$ 0

The capital balances that result from using the two methods are different because the new partner's interest in profits and interest in capital are not equal. In this illustration, C acquired a 20% capital interest and a $33\frac{1}{3}\%$ interest in profits. Therefore, C paid for 20% of the implied goodwill but had to absorb $33\frac{1}{3}\%$ of the goodwill amortization.

To further illustrate the concepts, assume the same facts, except that the new profit and loss percentages are 50%, 30%, and 20% for partners A, B, and C, respectively. If the recorded goodwill proves to be worthless, the decline in asset value would affect the partners' capital balances as follows:

	Partner			
	A	B	C	Total
Capital balances if goodwill method used	$46,500	$61,500	$27,000	$135,000
Goodwill write-off (amortization).............................	(16,500)	(9,900)	(6,600)	(33,000)
Capital balances after write-off	$30,000	$51,600	$20,400	$102,000
Capital balances if bonus method used	33,300	48,300	20,400	102,000
Differences	($ 3,300)	$ 3,300	$ 0	$ 0

In this case, partners A and B shared equally in the initial recording of goodwill, but unequally in the subsequent amortization of goodwill.

Now assume the same facts, except that the new profit and loss percentages are 40%, 40%, and 20% for partners A, B, and C, respectively. After the amortization of goodwill, the capital balances would be identical to those achieved under the bonus method, as indicated in the following table:

	Partner			
	A	B	C	Total
Capital balances if goodwill method used	$46,500	$61,500	$27,000	$135,000
Goodwill write-off (amortization).............................	(13,200)	(13,200)	(6,600)	(33,000)
Capital balances after write-off	$33,300	$48,300	$20,400	$102,000
Capital balances if bonus method used	$33,300	$48,300	$20,400	$102,000

The equality between the capital balances is achieved because neither of the two conditions that produce inequities exist. If these conditions do exist, preference is given typically to the bonus method because of the possible inequities that may result from the write-off of goodwill.

Contribution of Assets to Existing Partners. A new partner also may be admitted to the partnership by acquiring all or part of the capital interest of one or more existing partners in exchange for some consideration (assets). In this case, the new partner deals directly with an existing partner or partners rather than with the partnership entity. Therefore, the acquisition price is paid to the selling partner(s) and not to the partnership itself. The partnership records the redistribution of capital interests by transferring all or a portion of the seller's capital to the new partner's capital account, but does not record the transfer of any assets.

To illustrate, assume the following facts:

		Percentage Interest in	
Existing Partners	Capital Balance	Capital	Profit
Partner A	$30,000	40%	50%
Partner B	45,000	60	50

Now assume that new partner C purchased 50% of A's interest in capital and 50% of B's interest in capital in exchange for $50,000. This purchase resulted in C having a 50% interest in the total partnership capital.

There are several alternative ways of recording the contribution of assets by C to the existing partners. If the consideration paid by the incoming partner is not used to impute the fair market value of the partnership, the transaction would be recorded by the partnership entity as follows:

A, Capital (50% × $30,000)	15,000	
B, Capital (50% × $45,000)	22,500	
C, Capital		37,500

The $50,000 actually paid by C was not used as a basis for the entry because it represents consideration paid to the individual partners personally rather than to the partnership entity. This accounting treatment frequently is compared to that of a corporation when a stockholder sells shares or an interest in corporate capital to another investor in the corporation. The corporation does not record the transaction or use it as a basis for revaluing corporate assets but merely acknowledges the changing identity of its shareholders.

An alternative but less frequently used method of recording this transaction would be to impute the fair market value of the partnership entity from the consideration paid by the new partner. For example, if C paid $50,000 to acquire a 50% interest in the capital of the partnership vis-a-vis the individual partners, then the total implied current value of the partnership would be $100,000 ($50,000 ÷ 50%). The difference between the imputed value of $100,000 and the partnership's previous book value of $75,000 ($30,000 + $45,000) is interpreted to represent undervalued existing assets and/or goodwill traceable to the old partnership. This alternative interpretation would result in recording the transaction as follows:

Assets and/or Goodwill	25,000	
A, Capital		12,500
B, Capital		12,500
To record the previously unrecognized increase in value of the partnership.		
A, Capital [50% × ($30,000 + $12,500)]	21,250	
B, Capital [50% × ($45,000 + $12,500)]	28,750	
C, Capital		50,000
To record the transfer of the original partners' adjusted capital to incoming partner C.		

Normally, this alternative method is not employed because (1) the transaction was not between the partnership and the incoming partner, but rather between individual partners, and (2) the consideration paid by the incoming partner may not provide a reliable indicator of the partnership entity's current value. However, the method may provide useful information for deciding how to allocate the acquisition price between the selling partners. The selling partners' original capital plus their share of any imputed value increments may indicate the current values for which the incoming partner was paying. For example, the purchase price of $50,000 may be allocated to partners A and B as follows:

| | Partner | | |
	A	B	Total
Original capital..	$30,000	$45,000	$ 75,000
Share of value increment...................................	12,500	12,500	25,000
Total imputed value	$42,500	$57,500	$100,000
Percentage acquired by new partner....................	50%	50%	50%
Total purchase price.......................................	$21,250	$28,750	$ 50,000

WITHDRAWAL OF A PARTNER

When a partner withdraws, the partnership agreement should be consulted to determine if any guidelines have been established that would influence the procedure. The withdrawal of a partner requires a determination of the fair market value of the partnership entity and a measurement of partnership income to the date of withdrawal. Also, in many cases, the equity of the retiring partner may not be equal to the partner's capital balance as a result of (1) the existence of accounting errors, (2) differences between the fair market value and the recorded book value of assets, and/or (3) unrecorded assets such as goodwill.

If accounting errors are discovered, they should be treated as prior-period adjustments and corrected by adjusting the capital balances of the partners. Theoretically, an error should be allocated to partners' capital balances according to the profit and loss ratio that existed when the error was committed. Therefore, it is necessary to identify the period to which the error is traceable. This practice can become complicated, and a well-designed partnership agreement should include procedures for dealing with the correction of errors.

Recognizing differences between book value and fair market value may be as appropriate when an individual withdraws from the partnership as when an individual is admitted. If accounting recognition of such differences is not desired, however, these differences nevertheless should influence the amount to be paid to the withdrawing partner.

Selling an Interest to Existing Partners. As is the case with the admission of a partner, the withdrawal of a partner may involve (1) a transaction with existing partners or a new partner, or (2) a transaction with the partnership entity itself. In the first case, the equity of the withdrawing partner will be purchased with the personal assets of existing or new partners rather than with the assets of the partnership.

To illustrate, assume the following:

| | Partner | | |
	A	B	C
Capital balance	$30,000	$50,000	$20,000
Profit and loss percentage	40%	40%	20%
Percentage interest in capital	30%	50%	20%

Now assume that partner A withdraws from the partnership and that C purchases A's interest at its current value of $36,000. If the price paid by C is not used to impute the value of the entity, the transaction would be recorded as follows:

A, Capital	30,000	
C, Capital		30,000

As previously discussed, an alternative treatment would be to recognize any value increment indicated by the transaction and then transfer the adjusted capital balances.

Selling an Interest to the Partnership. When a withdrawing partner sells an interest to the partnership rather than to an individual partner, the bonus or goodwill methods may be employed. The bonus method is used most frequently, but the choice between methods should be based on a thorough analysis of the transaction.

Using the same facts as in the previous illustration and assuming the use of the bonus method, the purchase of A's equity by the partnership would be recorded as follows:

A, Capital	30,000	
B, Capital	4,000	
C, Capital	2,000	
Cash		36,000

The entry indicates that the remaining partners granted a bonus to A, measured by the difference between the recorded capital and the fair market value of A's equity. The bonus is charged to the remaining partners according to their profit and loss ratio.

The goodwill method focuses on the payment to the withdrawing partner as an indication of the fair market value of the partnership. If the imputed goodwill or undervalued assets were disposed of, the partners would divide the gain according to their profit and loss ratio. Assuming that existing assets are properly valued, the $36,000 payment to A consists of A's capital balance of $30,000 plus a $6,000 share of the unrecorded goodwill. Therefore, the $6,000 represents A's 40% interest in total goodwill of $15,000 ($6,000 ÷ 40%).

Two alternatives are now available: (1) recognize only the goodwill that is traceable to the retiring partner, or (2) recognize the amount of goodwill traceable to the entire entity. The first alternative stresses the importance of recognizing only the amount of goodwill that actually is purchased from the withdrawing partner. Using this alternative, A's withdrawal would be recorded as follows:

Goodwill	6,000	
A, Capital		6,000
A, Capital	36,000	
Cash		36,000

If the amount of goodwill traceable to the entire entity is recognized, the goodwill would be allocated to the partners according to their profit and loss ratio, as reflected in the following entries to record A's withdrawal:

Goodwill	15,000	
A, Capital		6,000
B, Capital		6,000
C, Capital		3,000
A, Capital	36,000	
Cash		36,000

Whether part or all of the goodwill is recognized, opponents of this procedure contend that transactions between partners should not be viewed as arm's length; therefore, the measure of goodwill may not be determined objectively. Also, inequitable results may be produced if the remaining partners subsequently change their profit and loss ratio.

Effects of a Partner's Withdrawal. When the interest of a withdrawing partner is acquired by the remaining partners or the partnership, serious demands upon the liquidity of the partners and the partnership may result. If withdrawal is due to the death of the partner, funds may be provided from the proceeds of life insurance policies taken out by the partnership itself or by individual partners. For example, if partner A takes out a life insurance policy on partner B and B subsequently dies, the proceeds payable to A may be used to acquire B's interest.

The UPA, in Section 42, states that a retiring or deceased partner's estate may receive interest as an ordinary creditor on that portion of the withdrawing partner's capital interest that remains in the partnership (i.e., has not been disbursed yet). In lieu of interest, the UPA states that the profits attributable to the use of the withdrawing partner's capital still retained in the partnership may be received. Once again, a partnership agreement that addresses the valuation of a withdrawing partner's interest and the means of payment is a valuable aid in properly accounting for the withdrawal of a partner.

PARTNERSHIP LIQUIDATION

The process of liquidation consists of the conversion of partnership assets into a distributable form and the distribution of these assets to creditors and owners. To achieve an orderly and legally sound liquidation, some fundamental guidelines need to be identified.

LIQUIDATION GUIDELINES

The underlying theme in accounting for partnership liquidation is the equitable distribution of the assets. To be equitable, a distribution should recognize the legal rights of the partnership creditors and individual partners. All liquidation expenses and gains or losses from conversion of partnership assets also must be allocated to the partners before assets actually are distributed to the individual partners. Failure to consider these factors may result in the premature or incorrect distribution of assets to a partner. If a premature or incorrect distribution of assets cannot be recovered, the partnership fiduciary who authorized the distribution may be held liable.

Ranking of Partnership Liabilities. The UPA establishes rules governing the priority in which partnership assets are distributed to creditors and partners. Subject to any agreement to the contrary, the following sequence of payments should be observed:

1. Amounts owed to creditors other than partners.
2. Amounts owed to partners other than for capital and profits, i.e., partners' loans to the partnership.
3. Amounts owed to partners as capital.
4. Amounts owed to partners as profits not currently closed to partners' capital accounts.

Although loans from partners have a higher legal priority than amounts owed as capital and profits, the doctrine of *right of offset* sets aside this ranking in favor of procedural and economic considerations that facilitate the actual liquidation process. The effect of this doctrine is that loans due to partners are used to offset actual or anticipated debit balances in partners' capital accounts. Amounts owed to partners as capital and profits are viewed typically as one element rather than two separate priority levels. Therefore, items 2, 3, and 4 may be combined without destroying the fairness of a distribution.

Liability for Debit Capital Balances. The UPA, in Section 40, states that partners should contribute assets to the partnership to the extent of their debit balances. However, if such a contribution is not possible because of special personal or legal considerations, the debit balance will be viewed as a realization loss and allocated according to the remaining partners' profit and loss ratio. For example, assume that partners A, B, and C share in profits and losses in the ratio of 1:2:1, respectively. If C is unable to contribute any asset to eliminate a debit capital balance, that balance would be allocated to A and B in the ratio of 1:2. Partners who absorb other partners' debit capital balances have a legal claim against the deficient partner. However, the collectibility of such a claim depends on the personal wealth of the deficient partner.

Marshaling of Assets. The provisions that call for the contribution of personal assets to a liquidating partnership illustrate the characteristic of unlimited liability discussed in Chapter 15. However, such personal liability depends on the legal doctrine of *marshaling of assets*. This doctrine, which is applied when the partnership and/or one or more of the partners are insolvent, states that:

1. Partnership assets are first available for the payment of partnership debts. Any excess assets are available for payment of the individual partner's debts, but only to the extent of the partner's interest in the capital of the partnership.
2. Personal assets of a partner are applied against personal debts, ranked in order of priority as follows:
   (a) Amounts owed to personal creditors.
   (b) Amounts owed to partnership creditors.
   (c) Amounts owed to partners by way of contribution.

Amounts owed to partners by way of contribution refers to amounts owed the partnership as represented by the partner's debit capital balance. This amount is viewed by the UPA as separate from the amounts owed to personal creditors. For example, if a partner has personal assets of $12,000, personal liabilities of $8,000, and a debit capital balance of $16,000, personal assets would be distributed as follows:

Payable to personal creditors...........................	$ 8,000
Payable to partnership for debit capital balance...	4,000
Total personal assets	$12,000

Under common law and federal bankruptcy law, which may be applicable when the UPA has not been adopted, amounts owed to partners by way of contribution are on an equal basis (*pari passu*) with personal creditors of the partner. According to this rule, the $12,000 of personal assets would be distributed as follows:

Payable to personal liabilities [($8,000 ÷ $24,000) × $12,000]..................	$ 4,000
Payable to partnership for debit capital balance [($16,000 ÷ $24,000) × $12,000]...	8,000
Total personal assets	$12,000

The legal doctrine of marshaling of assets is demonstrated by the following cases:

Case A — Insolvent Partners

The partnership is solvent, with total assets of $16,000 and total liabilities of $9,000. Information relating to the individual partners is as follows:

	Partner A	Partner B
Total personal assets	$10,000	$15,000
Total personal liabilities...........	13,000	18,000
Partnership capital balances	5,000	2,000

Analysis: Unsatisfied personal creditors may attach a partner's interest in the solvent partnership, but only to the extent of the partner's capital balance. Thus, unsatisfied personal creditors could seek recourse as follows:

	Partner A	Partner B
Unsatisfied personal creditors...	$3,000	$3,000
Interest in partnership capital available to personal creditors...	(3,000)	(2,000)
Personal liabilities not satisfied......................................	$ 0	$1,000

Case B — Insolvent Partnership

The partnership is insolvent, with total assets of $23,000 and total liabilities of $25,000. Information relating to individual partners is as follows:

	Partner A	Partner B
Total personal assets	$10,000	$8,000
Total personal liabilities...........	6,000	7,000
Partnership capital balances	500	(2,500)

Analysis: Unsatisfied partnership creditors may seek recourse from the individual partners in accordance with a proper marshaling of assets, as reflected in Illustration 16–1.

Illustration 16–1
Distribution of Assets — Insolvent Partnership

	Partner A		Partner B		AB Partnership			
	Assets	Liab.	Assets	Liab.	Assets	Liab.	A, Capital	B, Capital
Beginning balances[1].......	$10,000	$6,000	$8,000	$7,000	$23,000	$25,000	$ 500	($2,500)
Payment of liabilities	(6,000)	(6,000)	(7,000)	(7,000)	(23,000)	(23,000)		
	$ 4,000	0	$1,000	0	0	$ 2,000	$ 500	($2,500)
Payment of partnership creditors[2].......	(2,000)					(2,000)	2,000	
	$ 2,000	0	$1,000	0	0	0	$2,500	($2,500)
Payment toward debit capital balance[3]			(1,000)		$ 1,000			1,000
	$ 2,000	0	0	0	$ 1,000	0	$2,500	($1,500)
Capital distribution to A....	1,000				(1,000)		(1,000)	
Balances[4]	$ 3,000	0	0	0	0	0	$1,500	($1,500)

[1]Beginning asset balances represent realizable values.
[2]Unsatisfied partnership creditors may claim the net personal assets of a solvent partner, regardless of the amount of the partner's interest in the capital of the partnership. A's capital interest is increased by the payment of partnership liabilities.
[3]If the payment toward the debit capital balance had preceded B's payment of personal liabilities, a proper marshaling of assets would not have been achieved and B's personal creditors would not have been satisfied.
[4]If B later pays the debit capital balance, the funds would be distributed to A. However, if B cannot pay, the loss will be borne by A.

Case C—Insolvent Partner and Partnership

The partnership is insolvent, with total assets of $20,000 and total liabilities of $25,000. Information relating to individual partners is as follows:

	Partner A	Partner B
Total personal assets	$13,000	$12,000
Total personal liabilities...........	10,000	15,000
Partnership capital balances	(7,000)	2,000

Analysis: Partner B is solvent also, and the recourse B's personal creditors have against the partnership depends upon A's future contribution to the partnership. Illustration 16–2 reflects the distribution of assets in accordance with the marshaling concept.

Illustration 16–2

Distribution of Assets—Insolvent Partner and Partnership

	Partner A		Partner B		AB Partnership			
	Assets	Liab.	Assets	Liab.	Assets	Liab.	A, Capital	B, Capital
Beginning balances[1]	$13,000	$10,000	$12,000	$15,000	$20,000	$25,000	($7,000)	$2,000
Payment of liabilities	(10,000)	(10,000)	(12,000)	(12,000)	(20,000)	(20,000)		
	$ 3,000	0	0	$ 3,000	0	$ 5,000	($7,000)	$2,000
Payment of partnership creditors.....	(3,000)					(3,000)	3,000	
Balances[2]	0	0	0	$ 3,000[3]	0	$ 2,000	($4,000)	$2,000

[1]Beginning asset balances represent realizable values.
[2]If A later pays $4,000 to the partnership to eliminate the debit capital balance, the payment will be allocated first to the partnership liabilities and then to B. However, if A is not able to make a payment, claims against the partnership by the creditors and B will be totally uncollectible.
[3]The unsatisfied personal creditors of B are unable to seek recovery against the credit capital balance of B because the partnership itself is not solvent.

LUMP SUM LIQUIDATIONS

The guidelines discussed in the preceding section are important factors influencing the procedural and legal aspects of a partnership liquidation. Upon liquidation of a partnership, the amount of assets ultimately to be distributed to the individual partners is determined through the use of either a lump sum liquidation schedule or an installment liquidation schedule.

A lump sum liquidation requires that all assets be realized before a distribution is made to partners, thus avoiding the possibility of a premature distribution. To illustrate a lump sum liquidation, assume the following:

1.   Asset, liability, loan, and capital balances are as shown in Illustration 16–3, after books for the final operational period are closed.
2.   Profit and loss percentages for partners A, B, and C are 40%, 40%, and 20%, respectively.
3.   Personal assets and debts of the partners are as follows:

	A	B	C
Total personal assets	$30,000	$40,000	$20,000
Total personal liabilities....	10,000	37,200	24,000

4.   Sales of assets are as follows:

Date	Book Value	Selling Price	Gain (Loss)
February 15	$50,000	$60,000	$10,000
March 2	30,000	10,000	(20,000)
March 7	40,000	20,000	(20,000)

5.   Total liquidation expenses of $2,000 are paid on March 4.

Illustration 16–3 presents the lump sum distribution and demonstrates the following concepts that were discussed previously:

1.   Gains and losses on realization are allocated according to the partners' profit and loss ratio.

Illustration 16–3
Lump Sum Liquidation Statement

	Cash	Noncash Assets	Liabilities	Loan from A	Capital Balances A	B	C
Beginning balances...	$10,000	$120,000	$80,000	$9,000	$25,000	$10,000	$6,000
February 15, sale of assets at a gain.....	60,000	(50,000)			4,000	4,000	2,000
March 2, sale of assets at a loss	10,000	(30,000)			(8,000)	(8,000)	(4,000)
Payment of liquidation expenses.............	(2,000)				(800)	(800)	(400)
March 7, sale of assets at a loss	20,000	(40,000)			(8,000)	(8,000)	(4,000)
Balances	$98,000	0	$80,000	$9,000	$12,200	($ 2,800)	($ 400)
Payment of liabilities	(80,000)		(80,000)				
Balances	$18,000	0	0	$9,000	$12,200	($ 2,800)	($ 400)
B's contribution........	2,800					2,800	
Balances	$20,800	0	0	$9,000	$12,200	0	($ 400)
Absorption of C's balance					(400)		400
Balances	$20,800	0	0	$9,000	$11,800	0	0
Payment to A..........	(20,800)			(9,000)	(11,800)		
Final balances..........	0	0	0	0	0	0	0

2. Claims against the partnership are paid in the proper order.
3. The marshaling of assets doctrine is followed to determine the disposition of B's and C's debit balances in their capital accounts. That is, a partner's personal assets first are used to satisfy personal liabilities. Then, to the extent possible, remaining assets are contributed to the partnership to eliminate debit capital balances.
4. C's debit capital balance is charged against A, the only personally solvent partner.
5. Partner A will have a claim against C's personal assets for the debit balance that was absorbed.

INSTALLMENT LIQUIDATIONS

The complete liquidation process easily might extend over several months or longer, and it may not be possible to postpone payments to creditors and partners until all assets have been realized. Therefore, payments may be made on an installment basis to creditors and partners during the liquidation process. To avoid the problem associated with premature payments, installment payments may be made to partners only after anticipating all liabilities, possible losses, and liquidation expenses. To provide a proper solution to installment liquidations, either a schedule of safe payments is prepared as amounts become available for distribution or a predistribution plan is used to direct the distribution of any available sum.

Schedule of Safe Payments. The possibility of premature payments to partners is reduced by using a schedule of safe payments, which reflects a conservative approach to liquidation. The schedule indicates how available funds should be distributed to partners. It is based on the anticipation of all possible liabilities and expenses, including those expected to be incurred in the process of liquidation. The effect of these items on partnership capital is allocated among the partners according to their profit and loss agreement.

In keeping with the conservative approach, the schedule also is based on the assumption that all noncash assets will be worthless; therefore, the assumed loss is allocated among the partners according to their profit and loss ratio. The allocation of the assumed loss could produce debit balances in partners' capital accounts, and these balances are treated as being uncollectible. Therefore, the assumed debit capital balances are allocated to those partners with credit balances according to their profit and loss ratio. When the allocation of estimated liabilities, expenses, liquidation losses, and debit balances is completed, assets may be distributed safely to the partners in amounts equal to the resulting credit capital balances.

A new schedule of safe payments is prepared each time a distribution to partners is scheduled. These schedules support an installment liquidation statement, which summarizes changes in real account balances as the liquidation proceeds. When the partners' capital balances are in the profit and loss ratio, all partners will share in a given distribution. All future distributions to partners will be allocated automatically according to their profit ratio, thus eliminating the need for another schedule of safe payments.

To illustrate the use of schedules of safe payments in conjunction with an installment liquidation, assume the following:

1. Asset, liability, loan, and capital balances are shown in Illustration 16–4 (pages 868 and 869), after books for the final operational period are closed.
2. Profit and loss percentages for partners A, B, and C are 40%, 40%, and 20%, respectively.
3. Sales of assets are as follows:

Date	Book Value	Selling Price	Gain (Loss)
February 15	$60,000	$40,000	($20,000)
March 2	30,000	15,000	(15,000)
March 17	10,000	20,000	10,000
April 1	20,000	24,000	4,000

4. Liquidation expenses are estimated to be $10,000. Cash is to be restricted in that amount until expenses are paid.
5. Installment distributions of unrestricted cash are made on February 17, March 5, March 18, and April 2.
6. Total liquidation expenses of $8,000 are paid on March 4.

Illustration 16–4 is based on these facts and demonstrates the following concepts:

1. Gains and losses on realization are allocated according to the partners' profit and loss ratio.
2. Unsold noncash assets are assumed to be worthless for purposes of determining the safe payments to partners.
3. Loan balances are combined with capital balances according to the right of offset doctrine. This offset can result in partners receiving distributions of capital before other partners' loan accounts have been paid (as in the February 17 distribution in Illustration 16–4). However, such distributions may be placed in escrow until it is certain that debit balances will not develop in these partners' capital accounts.
4. Distributions are applied to a partner's loan balance before they are applied to the partner's capital balance.
5. Typically, the doctrine of marshaling of assets is ignored until all assets have been realized, at which time debit balances in partners' capital accounts may be satisfied through contributions of personal assets.
6. A schedule of safe payments is an iterative process that will cease when the schedule indicates that a given distribution will be shared among all partners. Further distributions will be allocated among the partners according to their profit and loss ratio. For example, when the March 5 distribution in Schedule A indicates that all partners will receive a por-

tion of the distribution, the distribution on March 18 would be made in the profit and loss ratio, with results identical to those that would be indicated by continuing the schedule of safe payments:

Partner	(1) Total Distri- bution to All Partners	(2) Partner's Profit and Loss Percentage	(1) × (2) Amount To Be Distributed	Amount To Be Distributed per Schedule of Safe Payments
A	$20,000	40%	$ 8,000	$ 8,000
B	20,000	40	8,000	8,000
C	20,000	20	4,000	4,000
			$20,000	$20,000

7. The partner with the greatest ability to absorb anticipated losses (i.e., preserves a credit capital balance after allocating anticipated losses) will be the first to receive a safe payment.

Illustration 16–4

Installment Liquidation Statement

	Cash	Noncash Assets	Liabilities	Loan from A	Capital Balances A	B	C
Beginning balances...	$10,000	$120,000	$30,000	$5,000	$25,000	$55,000	$15,000
February 15, sale of assets	40,000	(60,000)			(8,000)	(8,000)	(4,000)
Balances	$50,000	$ 60,000	$30,000	$5,000	$17,000	$47,000	$11,000
Payment of liabilities...	(30,000)		(30,000)				
February 17, distribution (Schedule A)..........	(10,000)					(10,000)	
Balances	$10,000	$ 60,000	0	$5,000	$17,000	$37,000	$11,000
March 2, sale of assets	15,000	(30,000)			(6,000)	(6,000)	(3,000)
Payment of liquidation expenses..............	(8,000)				(3,200)	(3,200)	(1,600)
Balances	$17,000	$ 30,000	0	$5,000	$ 7,800	$27,800	$ 6,400
March 5, distribution (Schedule A)..........	(17,000)			(800)		(15,800)	(400)
Balances	0	$ 30,000	0	$4,200	$ 7,800	$12,000	$ 6,000
March 17, sale of assets	$20,000	(10,000)			4,000	4,000	2,000
Balances	$20,000	$ 20,000	0	$4,200	$11,800	$16,000	$ 8,000
March 18, distribution (Schedule A)..........	(20,000)			(4,200)	(3,800)	(8,000)	(4,000)
Balances	0	$ 20,000	0	0	$ 8,000	$ 8,000	$ 4,000
April 1, sale of assets	$24,000	(20,000)			1,600	1,600	800
Balances	$24,000	0	0	0	$ 9,600	$ 9,600	$ 4,800
Final distribution.......	(24,000)				(9,600)	(9,600)	(4,800)
Balances	0	0	0	0	0	0	0

Schedule A—Schedule of Safe Payments

	A	B	C	Total
Profit and loss percentage...	40%	40%	20%	100%
February 17 Distribution				
Combined capital and loan balances before distribution...	$22,000	$47,000	$11,000	$80,000
Estimated liquidation expenses	(4,000)	(4,000)	(2,000)	(10,000)
Balances	$18,000	$43,000	$ 9,000	$70,000
Maximum loss possible...	(24,000)	(24,000)	(12,000)	(60,000)
Balances	($ 6,000)	$19,000	($ 3,000)	$10,000
Allocation of debit capital balances.............................	6,000	(9,000)	3,000	0
Safe payment	0	$10,000	0	$10,000
March 5 Distribution				
Combined capital and loan balances before distribution...	$12,800	$27,800	$ 6,400	$47,000
Maximum loss possible...	(12,000)	(12,000)	(6,000)	(30,000)
Safe payments..	$ 800	$15,800	$ 400	$17,000
March 18 Distribution (schedule not required)				
Combined capital and loan balances before distribution...	$16,000	$16,000	$ 8,000	$40,000
Maximum loss possible...	(8,000)	(8,000)	(4,000)	(20,000)
Safe payments..	$ 8,000	$ 8,000	$ 4,000	$20,000

Predistribution Plan. Schedules of safe payments provide a means of guaranteeing the propriety of installment distributions to partners, especially in complex situations. However, a predistribution plan provides a less tedious means of determining distributions to partners. The predistribution plan is prepared in advance of actual distributions and provides the user with information regarding the order and amount of all future distributions. As was the case with schedules of safe payments, the predistribution plan (1) combines partners' loan balances with their capital balances; (2) anticipates all possible liabilities, losses on realization, and liquidation expenses; and (3) recognizes that the partner with the greatest ability to absorb anticipated losses will be the first partner to receive safe payments.

To prepare the predistribution plan, all anticipated but unrecorded liabilities and liquidation expenses are allocated to the various partners' capital balances according to their profit and loss ratio. The resulting capital balances then are evaluated to determine the maximum loss from realization that could be absorbed by the partners before a debit balance is created in their respective capital accounts. As suggested by the schedule of safe payments, the partner who maintains a credit capital balance after assuming that all noncash assets are worthless is the partner with the greatest ability to absorb realization losses. Therefore, that partner will be the first to receive an actual distribution of assets.

The maximum loss a partner could absorb (*maximum loss absorbable*), before a debit balance in the partner's capital account is created, is determined by the following calculation:

$$\text{Maximum Loss Absorbable (MLA)} = \frac{\text{Partner's Capital Balance}}{\text{Partner's Profit and Loss Percentage}}$$

Since the partner with the largest MLA will be the first to receive an actual distribution, the MLAs are used to indicate the order in which partners will receive distributions. However, it should be noted that the MLAs do not indicate the amounts of the distributions. To illustrate, assume that a partnership consists of three partners (A, B, and C) who have capital balances, before the realization of noncash assets, of $70,000, $60,000, and $40,000, respectively, and profit and loss percentages of 35%, 25%, and 40%, respectively. The maximum losses absorbable by partners A, B, and C are determined as follows:

Partner	(1) Capital Balance	(2) Profit and Loss Percentage	(1) ÷ (2) Maximum Loss Absorbable	Rank
A	$70,000	35%	$200,000	Second
B	60,000	25	240,000	First
C	40,000	40	100,000	Third

If all partners had identical maximum losses absorbable, then all partners would share in any given distribution. Therefore, the amount of any distribution to be paid to a particular partner can be determined by calculating the distributions needed ultimately to give all partners the same maximum loss absorbable. In the present example, if B's capital balance was reduced to $50,000 as the result of an actual distribution of $10,000, B's new maximum loss absorbable would be equal to A's original maximum loss absorbable, as follows:

Partner	(1) Capital Balance	(2) Profit and Loss Percentage	(1) ÷ (2) Maximum Loss Absorbable
A	$70,000	35%	$200,000
B	50,000	25	200,000
C	40,000	40	100,000

Therefore, the first $10,000, or any portion thereof, that is available for distribution to partners should be paid entirely to partner B.

If A's capital balance was reduced to $35,000 and B's capital balance was reduced to $25,000 as the result of actual distributions of $35,000 and $25,000, respectively, to these partners, all partners then would have equivalent maximum losses absorbable. Thus, the predistribution plan suggests that the next $60,000, or any portion thereof, that is available for distribution to partners should be paid to partners A and B according to the profit ratio of 35:25 and that all further distributions should be divided among all partners according to their respective profit ratio.

The process of preparing the predistribution plan is summarized as follows:

1. Calculate each partner's maximum loss absorbable.
2. Rank partners in descending order according to the amounts of their maximum losses absorbable.
3. Determine what amount must be paid to the partner ranked first to achieve equality between the maximum losses absorbable of that partner and the second-ranked partner. This amount represents the safe payment that can be paid to the first-ranked partner.
4. Determine what amount must be paid in total to those partners having equivalent maximum losses absorbable so that their new maximum losses absorbable would be equal to that of the next-highest-ranked partner. This amount would be divided among the partners receiving the distribution according to the relationship that their profit percentages have to each other.
5. Continue step 4 until all partners have equivalent maximum losses absorbable.
6. When all partners have equal maximum losses absorbable, distributions would be allocated according to the partners' profit ratio.

To demonstrate this entire process, the following facts are used as the basis for the predistribution plan in Illustration 16–5 (page 872):

	Partner		
	A	B	C
Profit and loss percentage	30%	50%	20%
Combined capital and loan balance	$33,000	$45,000	$14,000

Total liabilities of the partnership equal $20,000.
Total liquidation expenses are expected to be $10,000.

To relate the predistribution plan in Illustration 16–5 to an actual distribution, assume that distributions are made as follows:

Date	Amount	Purpose
February 15	$20,000	Pay liabilities
March 1	5,000	Pay partners
March 15	8,000	Pay liquidation expenses
March 27	9,000	Pay partners
April 4	30,000	Pay partners

Illustration 16–5

Predistribution Plan
Computation of Payments to Partners

	Capital Balances			Maximum Loss Absorbable		
	A	B	C	A	B	C
(1) Profit and loss percentage..........	30%	50%	20%			
Capital and loan balance............	$33,000	$45,000	$14,000			
Allocate expected liquidation expenses.............................	(3,000)	(5,000)	(2,000)			
(2) Balances	$30,000	$40,000	$12,000			
Maximum loss absorbable (MLA) [(2) ÷ (1)].....................				$100,000	$80,000	$60,000
(3) Amount needed to reduce highest-ranked MLA to next-highest-ranked MLA				(20,000)		
New MLAs				$ 80,000	$80,000	$60,000
(4) Reduction in capital (payment) needed to achieve reduction in MLA [(3) × (1)].....................	(6,000)					
(5) New capital balance [(2) − (4)] ...	$24,000	$40,000	$12,000			
(6) Amount needed to reduce highest-ranked MLAs to next-highest-ranked MLA				(20,000)	(20,000)	
New MLAs				$ 60,000	$60,000	$60,000
(7) Reduction in capital (payment) needed to achieve reduction in MLA [(6) × (1)]...................	(6,000)	(10,000)				
(8) New capital balance [(5) − (7)] ...	$18,000	$30,000	$12,000			

When MLAs are equal, future distributions are allocated to all partners according to their profit and loss percentages.

			Payable to			
Level	Amount	Liabilities	Estimated Liquidation Expenses	A	B	C
I	First $20,000	$20,000				
II	Next $10,000		$10,000			
III	Next $ 6,000			100%		
IV	Next $16,000			37.5% (3/8)	62.5% (5/8)	
V	Any additional payments			30%	50%	20%

Rather than constructing numerous schedules of safe payments to determine the recipients of these distributions, the predistribution plan indicates the following distribution:

| | | | | Payable to | | | Level |
| | | Lia- | Liquidation | | | | per Plan |
Date	Amount	bilities	Expenses	A	B	C	(Illus. 16–5)
Feb. 15	$20,000	$20,000					I
Mar. 1	5,000			$ 5,000			III
Mar. 15	8,000		$8,000				II
Mar. 27	9,000			1,000			III
				3,000	$ 5,000		IV
Apr. 4	30,000			3,000	5,000		IV
				6,600	11,000	$4,400	V
	$72,000	$20,000	$8,000	$18,600	$21,000	$4,400	

Several aspects of this distribution need to be emphasized. First of all, notice that actual payments to partners precede the payment of the liquidation expenses. This action is acceptable because the computations in Illustration 16–5 already had allowed for liquidation expenses of $10,000. However, if liquidation expenses exceed the estimated amount of $10,000, previous payments to partners could prove to be premature and ultimately could require repayments from partners to the partnership. Another important feature is that all payments required by a specific level of the plan shown in Illustration 16–5 must be satisfied to whatever extent possible before another level of the plan is entered. Finally, when a particular distribution is divided among several partners, the amount is allocated to the sharing partners according to their respective profit ratio.

QUESTIONS

1. Why does the withdrawal of a partner result in a dissolution but not necessarily a liquidation of the partnership?
2. If an incoming partner acquires an interest in the partnership for less than book value, what factors must be identified to determine whether or not the recognition of goodwill may be appropriate?
3. A student of accounting comments that: "The bonus method of accounting for changes in ownership is employed in only those cases where goodwill or unrealized appreciation is absent." Discuss the student's comment.
4. How is the amount of goodwill traceable to either old or new partners determined?
5. Why is the bonus method of accounting for ownership changes more widely used in practice?
6. Why doesn't the admission of a partner through a direct purchase of an existing partner's interest normally result in the recognition of goodwill or a bonus, assuming more than book value is paid?

7. After all liabilities have been paid, how does an installment liquidation insure that distributions are not made to partners prematurely?
8. In calculating a schedule of safe payments, how should costs associated with the disposing of assets be considered?
9. Explain the right of offset and its significance in the liquidation process.
10. What is the doctrine of marshaling of assets, and when is it applicable to a partnership?
11. Under the doctrine of marshaling of assets, why do unsatisfied partnership creditors have more flexibility to become satisfied than do unsatisfied personal creditors?
12. What is the impact on partnership creditors of applying common law, rather than the Uniform Partnership Act, in the marshaling of assets?

EXERCISES

Exercise 1.   Davis and Irving are business partners who share in profits and losses at the rates of 40% and 60%, respectively. Johnson is investing $20,000 in the partnership for a 20% interest. Prior to the admission of Johnson, the capital balances of the existing partners were: Davis, $25,000; and Irving, $40,000.

(1) Calculate the amount of bonus to be recognized by the previous partners if the bonus method is employed.
(2) Calculate the amount of goodwill to be recognized by the previous partners if the goodwill method is employed.
(3) Assuming that the goodwill is deemed worthless and that the partners share profits and losses equally, calculate the inequity of using the goodwill method rather than the bonus method.

Exercise 2.   Red, White, and Blue are partners in a business and share in its profits at the respective rates of 50%, 30%, and 20%. At the beginning of the new fiscal year, they admit Green, who is to invest in the firm sufficient cash to have a one-third interest in the partnership and profits.

The following trial balance is taken from the original partnership's records:

Cash..	100,000	
Marketable Securities....................	75,000	
Accounts Receivable.....................	225,000	
Accounts Payable		50,000
Long-Term Notes Payable.............		30,000
Red, Capital		175,000
White, Capital..............................		100,000
Blue, Capital................................		45,000
Total.......................................	400,000	400,000

The securities have a market value of $50,000, and an allowance of $25,000 is expected to cover collection losses on the receivables. No other adjustments of the net assets are considered necessary; however, the three partners among themselves must bring the balances in their capital accounts into agreement with their interest in profits.

(1) What amount must be invested by Green?
(2) What settlement is made among the partners?
(3) Prepare the entry to adjust the capital accounts.
(4) What are the balances in the partners' capital accounts after Green's admission?

Exercise 3.   Anderson, Garner, Mason, and Sanders are business partners who have capital balances of $27,000, $36,000, $45,000, and $32,000, respectively. Their partnership agreement calls for the allocation of profits and losses at the rates of 20%, 30%, 30%, and 20%, respectively. Sanders is withdrawing from the partnership.

(1) Assuming Sanders' interest in the partnership is sold for $37,000, calculate the remaining partners' capital balances under both the bonus and goodwill methods.
(2) Assuming Sanders' interest in the partnership is sold for $25,000, calculate the remaining partners' capital balances under both the bonus and goodwill methods.

Exercise 4.   The following information relates to Pfarr and Williams, who are partners in a business being liquidated:

	Pfarr	Williams
Partnership balances:		
Loan payable—Williams	—	$ 5,000
Capital balance (deficit)	$20,000	($14,000)
Profit and loss percentage	70%	30%
Personal assets (including partnership loan payable)	$30,000	$22,000
Personal liabilities	$15,000	$21,000

(1) After applying the right of offset doctrine, indicate how each partner's personal assets would be distributed assuming that the Uniform Partnership Act (UPA) is applicable.
(2) Determine the effect on the calculations in (1) if the right of offset doctrine was ignored.
(3) After applying the right of offset doctrine, indicate how each partner's personal assets would be distributed assuming that common law is applicable.

Exercise 5.   JKL Construction Company, a partnership, has total assets of $149,000 and total liabilities of $165,000. The following information relates to the individual partners:

	Jason	Kelly	Linden
Total personal assets	$52,000	$41,500	$28,000
Total personal liabilities	47,000	33,500	34,000
Partnership capital balance (deficit)	7,000	3,000	(26,000)
Profit and loss percentage	50%	30%	20%

If Linden inherits $16,000 after liquidation of the JKL partnership, what will be the priority and amount of claims existing against the $16,000? What claims (who and how much) will remain unsatisfied?

Exercise 6.   The following balance sheet is for the partnership of Thomas, James, and Carson, who share profits and losses in the ratio of 4:3:1, respectively:

Assets		Liabilities and Capital	
Cash	$ 45,000	Liabilities	$ 92,000
Other assets	297,000	Thomas, capital	160,000
		James, capital	65,000
		Carson, capital	25,000
Total assets	$342,000	Total liabilities and capital	$342,000

(1) Assume that the assets and liabilities are valued fairly and that the partnership wishes to admit Rollo as a new partner with a one-fifth interest in capital. Without recording goodwill or bonus, determine what Rollo's contribution should be.
(2) If Rollo contributes $88,000, prepare the journal entries to record Rollo's contribution and the new capital balance using (a) the bonus method and (b) the goodwill method.
(3) If the partnership decides to liquidate the business rather than admit Rollo, determine the cash distribution to each partner if the other assets are sold for $249,000. Use a lump sum liquidation schedule for these determinations.

Exercise 7.   The partnership of W, J, and T has cash of $15,000, other assets of $47,000, and liabilities of $21,000. Partners W and J have capital balances of $30,000 and $16,000, respectively, and partner T has a deficit of $5,000. On September 1, 19X5, the partnership begins to liquidate by selling equipment with a book value of $23,000 for $17,000. Liquidation expenses incurred were $2,000, with another $1,600 of expenses estimated to be incurred. On September 20, 19X5, $12,000 of assets were sold for $15,000. Additional liquidation expenses of $900 were incurred, with future liquidation costs estimated to be $1,300.

Assuming that the partners share profits and losses equally, determine how the available cash would be distributed on September 1 and September 15, 19X5. Schedules of safe payments should be prepared in conjunction with this installment liquidation process.

Exercise 8. The TLC Company is a partnership in which Tellier, Larsen, and Collins each have an interest. Information relating to each of the partners is as follows:

	Tellier	Larsen	Collins
Partnership:			
Capital balance...	$ 30,000	$47,000	($15,000)
Loan payable to:	—	5,000	—
Profit and loss percentage...........................	30%	50%	20%
Personal:			
Assets	$100,000	$60,000	$17,000
Liabilities..	120,000	84,000	10,000

The partnership has cash, other assets, and other liabilities of $12,000, $68,000, and $13,000, respectively. The partners have agreed to liquidate the partnership. However, the partnership has agreed to purchase Tellier's interest for $23,000 prior to beginning the liquidation. The bonus method is used to record this transaction, and Tellier is held without recourse regarding any liabilities of the partnership.

Assuming that the other assets are sold for $54,000, indicate how much cash Larsen will receive after liquidating the partnership.

Exercise 9. Delaney, Gray, and Sullivan are considering the liquidation of their partnership, which has assets of $110,000 and liabilities, including a $10,000 loan from Sullivan, of $30,000. Delaney and Gray each have capital balances of $33,000. Profits and losses are shared 30%, 30%, and 40% for Delaney, Gray, and Sullivan, respectively.

Prepare a predistribution plan to govern the possible liquidation, assuming liquidation expenses of $10,000.

PROBLEMS

Problem 16–1. Buckner and Pressey are partners in a dry cleaning business in which profits and losses are shared equally. Buckner and Pressey have capital balances of $40,000 and $60,000, respectively.

Required:

For each of the six situations presented next, prepare the necessary entries for the partnership records.

	Situation		
	(1)	(2)	(3)
Admission of new partner:			
Entering partner	Nelson	Nelson	Nelson
Purchase price.............................	$60,000	$30,000	$40,000
Interest in capital acquired.............	30%	20%	30%
Paid to..	Partnership	Partnership	Pressey
Method used................................	Bonus	Goodwill	N/A
	(4)	(5)	(6)
Withdrawal of previous partner:			
Exiting partner	Buckner	Buckner	Buckner
Selling price................................	$48,000	$25,000	$39,000
Interest in capital sold...................	40%	20%	30%
Paid by.......................................	Partnership	Partnership	Partnership
Method used................................	Bonus	Goodwill traceable to exiting partner	Goodwill traceable to all partners

Problem 16–2. The partnership of Baker, Carlson, and Dill is adjusting its accounting reports to convert them uniformly to the accrual basis in anticipation of admitting Thompson as a new partner. Some accounts are on the accrual basis and others are on the cash basis. The partnership's books were closed, and the following trial balance was prepared as of December 31, 19X6:

Cash...	10,000	
Accounts Receivable	40,000	
Inventory	26,000	
Land..	9,000	
Building..	50,000	
Accumulated Depreciation—Building		2,000
Equipment...	56,000	
Accumulated Depreciation—Equipment		6,000
Goodwill..	5,000	
Accounts Payable		55,000
Allowance for Future Inventory Losses		3,000
Baker, Capital		40,000
Carlson, Capital...		60,000
Dill, Capital		30,000
Total..	196,000	196,000

Inquiries disclosed the following:

(a) The partnership was organized on January 1, 19X5, with no provision in the partnership agreement for the distribution of profits and losses. During 19X5, profits were distributed equally among the partners. The partnership agreement was amended effective January 1, 19X6, to provide for the following profit and loss percentages: Baker, 50%; Carlson, 30%; and Dill, 20%. The amended partnership agreement also stated that the accounting records were to be maintained on the accrual basis and that any adjustments necessary for 19X5 should be allocated according to the 19X5 distribution of profits.

(b) The following amounts were not recorded as prepayments or accruals:

	December 31	
	19X5	19X6
Prepaid insurance..............................	$ 650	$700
Advances from customers..................	1,100	200
Accrued interest expense	450	

The advances from customers were recorded as sales in the year cash was received.

(c) In 19X6, the partnership recorded a provision of $3,000 for an anticipated decline in inventory prices. The provision was unnecessary and inconsistent with good accounting procedure and should be reversed.

(d) The partnership expensed equipment that was purchased for $4,400 on January 7, 19X6. This equipment has an estimated life of ten years and an estimated salvage value of $400. The partnership depreciates its capitalized equipment under the declining-balance method at twice the straight-line depreciation rate.

(e) The partners agreed to establish an allowance for doubtful accounts at 2% of current accounts receivable and 5% of past due accounts. At December 31, 19X5, the partnership had $54,000 of accounts receivable, of which only $4,000 were past due. At December 31, 19X6, 15% of accounts receivable were past due, of which $4,000 represented sales made in 19X5, although they were considered collectible. The partnership had written off uncollectible accounts in the year the accounts became worthless, as follows:

	Account Written Off In	
	19X6	19X5
19X6 account	$ 800	—
19X5 account	1,000	$250

(f) Goodwill was recorded on the books in 19X6 and credited to the partners' capital accounts in the profit and loss ratio in recognition of an increase in the value of the business resulting from improved sales volume. The partners agreed to write-off the goodwill before admitting the new partner.

Required:

(1) Prepare a worksheet for the partnership showing the adjustments and the adjusted trial balance on the accrual basis at December 31, 19X6. All adjustments affecting income should be made directly to the partners' capital accounts. Supporting calculations should be in good form.

(2) On December 31, 19X6, Thompson invested $55,000 in the partnership. Assuming that the total capital for Baker, Carlson, and Dill is $140,000,

compute the amount of goodwill to be allocated to each partner under each of the following alternative agreements:

(a) Thompson is to be granted a one-fourth interest in the partnership. The original partners will share profits and losses in the same proportion as they had before the admission of Thompson.

(b) The partnership expects to continue to earn an annual return of 15% on invested capital. The normal rate of return for a comparable partnership is 10%. The expected earnings of the new partnership in excess of the normal rate of return are to be capitalized as goodwill at the rate of 20%. The partners are to share profits and losses as follows: Baker, 40%; Carlson, 30%; Dill, 20%; and Thompson, 10%.

(AICPA adapted)

Problem 16–3. Young, Black, and O'Sullivan had capital balances on January 1, 19X8, of $18,000, $34,000, and $4,000, respectively. The partners shared profits equally. Since January 1, 19X8, the following events have occurred:

(a) Totsky purchased Black's interest in the partnership for $40,000 on July 1, 19X8, after the partnership reported a loss of $18,000.

(b) To improve sales, the partnership merged with another company owned by Loren. Loren acquired a 40% interest in profits and losses and a 60% interest in capital for $42,000. The goodwill method is employed for admissions and withdrawals of partners.

(c) The partnership reported a loss of $8,000 in the second half of 19X8.

(d) To improve liquidity, O'Sullivan was asked to contribute cash toward the reduction of a debit capital balance. O'Sullivan, who has filed for personal bankruptcy, has personal liabilities of $36,000 and personal assets of $33,000. O'Sullivan remained in the partnership and made the maximum contribution under federal bankruptcy law.

(e) Income for the year 19X9 was $50,000.

(f) O'Sullivan began to borrow heavily from the partnership during 19X9 and, as of year end, had a loan balance of $4,000. The partnership agreed to buy out O'Sullivan's net interest for $7,400. Shortly thereafter, Young bought Totsky's partnership interest for $35,000.

Required:

Prepare a schedule to reflect the changes in the capital balances of the partners since January 1, 19X8. Supporting calculations should be in good form.

Problem 16–4. The balance sheet of Alamo Trucking as of December 31, 19X8, is as follows:

Assets		Liabilities and Capital	
Cash..............................	$ 15,000	Accounts payable	$ 32,000
Accounts receivable, net....	85,000	Loans payable...................	240,000
Equipment, net.................	210,000	Duke, capital	16,000
Land..............................	60,000	Johnson, capital	22,000
Securities, at cost	20,000	Olsen, capital	80,000
Total assets.....................	$390,000	Total liabilities and capital...	$390,000

Earnings for the first quarter of 19X9 were $32,000. The partnership agreement calls for a monthly salary of $2,000 for both Duke and Johnson. Olsen is to receive interest of 20% on his/her quarterly beginning capital balance. Remaining profits or losses are to be allocated equally among the partners.

At the beginning of the second quarter, Meyers acquired a one-fourth interest in the partnership for $45,000. The partnership agreed to record the investment by the goodwill method and to modify the profit and loss agreement as follows:

	Duke	Johnson	Olsen	Meyers
Monthly salary	$2,000	$2,000	—	$1,000
Bonus as a percentage of earnings after the bonus	—	—	—	10%
Interest on beginning quarterly capital	—	—	20%	—
Profit and loss percentage	30%	20%	40%	10%

Second-quarter earnings were $22,000.

At the beginning of the third quarter, Olsen's interest in capital and profits was sold to Zeller for $92,000. The third quarter had reported earnings of $44,000.

At the beginning of the fourth quarter, Duke's interest in capital and profits was sold to the partnership for $30,000. This transaction was to be recorded by the goodwill method, recognizing goodwill traceable to the exiting partner only. The remaining partners retained their proportionate profit and loss ratio.

After Duke's retirement, Mitchell agreed to purchase a 50% interest in the partnership for $225,000. The recording of this investment was to be made using the goodwill method and was to reflect the differences between the book value and market value of certain assets as of the transaction date. Their values as of October 1, 19X9, were as follows:

	Book Value	Market Value
Accounts receivable (net)	$92,000	$73,000
Land	60,000	72,000

Required:

Prepare a schedule analyzing the changes in partners' capital balances since December 31, 19X8. Supporting calculations should be in good form.

Problem 16–5. Book value and market value information for the public accounting firm of Davis, Baker, and Winslow as of December 31, 19X9, is shown at the top of the next page.

In recent years, the partnership experienced serious disagreement over a variety of business issues. Liquidating the partnership has become a very real, but rather lengthy alternative. Baker is impatient with the process of liquidation and offers to sell his/her interest in the partnership to Davis and Winslow for $70,000. The remaining partners would use the bonus method to record the transaction and then proceed with the liquidation. Winslow is anxious to proceed with the liquidation because his/her personal assets of $80,000 barely cover personal liabilities of $72,000.

	Book Value	Market Value
Cash..	$ 78,000	$ 78,000
Receivables, net	43,000	32,000
Furniture and fixtures, net	22,000	18,000
Technical library, net..	14,000	17,000
Securities, at cost	16,000	21,000
Other assets..	2,000	—
Total..	$175,000	$166,000
Accounts payable	$ 4,500	
Wages and salaries payable...............................	5,400	
Notes payable..	20,100	
Loans payable, Davis	12,000	
Davis, capital..	64,000	
Baker, capital..	80,000	
Winslow, capital	(11,000)	
Total..	$175,000	

Required:

Assuming that liquidation expenses are estimated to be $6,000, would Davis and Winslow be well advised to accept Baker's offer or to just proceed directly with the liquidation of the firm? Supporting calculations should be in good form.

Problem 16–6. Head, Purtell, and Wigdale, who share profits and losses in the ratio of 2:5:3, respectively, have decided to liquidate their real estate investment company. The balance sheet of the company prior to liquidation is as follows:

Assets		Liabilities and Capital	
Cash................................	$ 18,000	Mortgages payable...........	$ 70,000
Loan receivable		Purtell, loan.....................	17,000
from Head	13,000	Head, capital....................	30,000
Real estate......................	121,000	Purtell, capital..................	50,000
		Wigdale, capital	(15,000)
Total assets.....................	$152,000	Total liabilities and capital...	$152,000

On July 18, 19X9, real estate having a book value of $91,000 and a $55,000 mortgage was sold for $71,000 after incurring expenses of $5,000. It was expected that the remaining property could be sold for a profit after incurring brokerage fees of $4,000. In actuality, the remaining real estate was sold for $18,000 over book value, and associated brokerage fees were $3,000.

Excluding distributions from the partnership, the personal net worth of each of the partners, including loans to or from the partnership, is as follows:

	Head	Purtell	Wigdale
Assets	$20,000	$87,000	$64,000
Liabilities..	49,000	42,000	53,000

The Uniform Partnership Act (UPA) is governing in cases of insolvency.

Required:
(1) Prepare an installment liquidation schedule with all necessary supporting schedules.
(2) Calculate the minimum net amount that must be realized from the sale of assets so that Head's personal creditors will be satisfied. Assume that partners with debit balances will be able to contribute toward these balances to the extent allowed by the UPA.

Problem 16–7.   The BLD partnership has assets of $268,000, including a $22,000 loan receivable from Bartels, one of the firm's three partners. Liabilities of the firm total $113,000, including a $12,000 loan payable to Darby, another partner of the firm. The partners, Bartels, Darby, and Lockwood, have capital balances of $85,000, $82,000, and ($12,000), respectively. The partnership agreement allocates profits and losses as follows:

	Annual Salary	Bonus as a Percentage of Partnership Income	Profit and Loss Percentage
Bartels.............................	$30,000	10%	60%
Darby.............................	42,000	—	10%
Lockwood........................	36,000	—	30%

The partners have agreed to liquidate the business and have estimated liquidation expenses of $10,000.

Required:
(1) Prepare a predistribution plan that may be used to determine how liquidation proceeds would be distributed to the partners.
(2) If the $101,000 of liabilities, net of the loan payable, were settled and the next $30,000 were distributed to Bartels, calculate how any remaining funds should be distributed.

Problem 16–8.   Justin, Sullivan, and Weiss formed a partnership several years ago. Unfortunately, the company has experienced a downturn in sales and profits and has decided to liquidate the partnership. The partnership has assets of $732,000 and liabilities of $280,000, including a $30,000 loan from Sullivan. Prior to the allocation of an $80,000 loss in the last quarter of 19X8, the partners' capital balances were as follows:

Justin, capital..	$210,000
Sullivan, capital.......................................	352,000
Weiss, capital	(30,000)

Each of the partners is to be allocated a quarterly salary of $15,000, and remaining profits and losses are to be shared in the following percentages: Justin, 20%; Sullivan, 60%; and Weiss, 20%.

The partnership is liquidated over the first two months of 19X9 as follows:
January, 19X9:
(1) Liquidation expenses were estimated to be $15,000.
(2) Assets with book values totaling $300,000 were sold for $220,000.
(3) Cash of $50,000 was contributed toward Weiss' debit capital balance.

February, 19X9:

(1) Assets with book values totaling $220,000 were sold for $250,000.
(2) Equipment with a book value of $80,000 and a market value of $70,000 was transferred to Justin, whose capital balance was reduced accordingly.
(3) An unrecorded trade receivable of $20,000 was discovered.
(4) Remaining assets were sold for $40,000.
(5) Actual liquidation expenses were $10,000.
(6) All available cash was distributed.

Required:

Prepare a schedule showing how assets of the partnership are distributed during liquidation.

Problem 16–9.   Wall, Hurd, Bemis, and Lenz are considering dissolving their partnership. They plan to sell the assets gradually so that losses will be minimized. Liquidation expenses of $12,000 are anticipated. The partners share profits and losses as follows: Wall, 40%; Hurd, 30%; Bemis, 20%; and Lenz, 10%. The partnership's trial balance as of May 1, 19X2, the date on which liquidation begins, is as follows:

Cash...	500	
Receivables....................................	18,800	
Inventory, May 1, 19X2....................	45,500	
Equipment (net).............................	32,200	
Accounts Payable		3,500
Wall, Loan.....................................		4,000
Hurd, Loan.....................................		9,000
Wall, Capital..................................		25,000
Hurd, Capital.................................		21,000
Bemis, Capital...............................		23,500
Lenz, Capital		11,000
Total...	97,000	97,000

Required:
(1) Prepare a schedule for a predistribution plan as of May 1, 19X2, showing how cash may be distributed among partners by installments as it becomes available.
(2) On May 31, 19X2, if cash of $19,400 became available for creditors, liquidation expenses, and partners, how would the cash be distributed?
(3) If, instead of being dissolved, the partnership continues operations and earns a profit of $31,500, how should that profit be distributed, assuming that, in addition to the aforementioned profit-sharing arrangement, it was provided that Lenz receive a bonus of 5% of income from operations after treating such a bonus as an expense?   (AICPA adapted)

Problem 16–10. Part I: The partnership of Aikens, Barnes, and Clinton is winding up its affairs. The following information has been gathered:
(a) The trial balance of the partnership at June 30, 19X7, is as follows:

Cash..	6,000	
Accounts Receivable	22,000	
Inventory...	14,000	
Property, Plant, and Equipment (net)	99,000	
Aikens, Loan	12,000	
Clinton, Loan..	7,500	
Accounts Payable		17,000
Aikens, Capital		67,000
Barnes, Capital		45,000
Clinton, Capital..		31,500
Total..	160,500	160,500

(b) The partners share profits and losses as follows: Aikens, 50%; Barnes, 30%; and Clinton, 20%.

(c) The partners are considering an offer of $100,000 for the accounts receivable, inventory, and plant assets as of June 30. The $100,000 would be paid to the partners in installments, but the number and amounts are to be negotiated.

Required:

Prepare a predistribution plan schedule as of June 30, 19X7, showing how the $100,000 would be distributed as it becomes available.

Part II: Assume the same facts as in Part 1, except that the partners have decided to liquidate their partnership instead of accepting the offer of $100,000. Cash is distributed to the partners at the end of each month.

A summary of liquidation transactions follows:

July:

  $16,500 — collected on accounts receivable; balance is uncollectible

  $10,000 — received from sale of entire inventory

  $ 1,000 — liquidation expenses paid

  $ 8,000 — cash retained in the business at the end of month

August:

  $1,500 — liquidation expenses paid

  — Clinton's capital was reduced when Clinton accepted a piece of special equipment that had a book value of $4,000. The partners agreed that a value of $10,000 should be placed on the machine for liquidation purposes.

  $2,500 — cash retained in the business at the end of month

September:

  $75,000 — received on sale of remaining plant assets

  $ 1,000 — liquidation expenses paid

  No cash was retained in the business.

Required:

Prepare a schedule of cash payments as of September 30, 19X7, showing how the cash actually was distributed. Supporting calculations should be in good form.   (AICPA adapted)

Problem 16–11.   The partnership agreement of Smith, Bailey, Davis, Williams, and Perry contained a buy and sell agreement, among numerous other provisions, which would become operative in case of the death of any partner. Some provisions contained in the buy and sell agreement were as follows:

1. Purposes of the buy and sell agreement:
    (a) The partners mutually desire that the business shall be continued by the survivors without interruption or liquidation upon the death of one of the partners.
    (b) The partners also mutually desire that the deceased partner's estate shall receive the full value of the partner's interest in the partnership, and that the estate shall share in the earnings of the partnership until the deceased partner's interest is fully purchased by the surviving partners.
2. Purchase and sale of deceased partner's interest:
    (a) Upon the death of a partner, the partnership shall continue to operate.
    (b) Upon the partner's death, the survivors shall purchase, and the executor or administrator of the deceased partner's estate shall sell to the surviving partners, the deceased partner's interest in the partnership for the price and upon the terms and conditions hereinafter set forth.
    (c) The deceased partner's estate shall retain the deceased partner's interest until the amount specified in the next paragraph is paid in full by the surviving partners.
    (d) The partners agree that the purchase price for the partnership interest shall be an amount equal to the deceased partner's capital account at the date of death. Said amount shall be paid to the legal representative of decedent as follows:
        (1) The first installment of 30 percent of said capital account shall be paid within 60 days from the date of death of the partner, or within 30 days from the date on which the personal representative of decedent becomes qualified by law, whichever date is later, and
        (2) The balance shall be due in four equal installments, which shall be payable annually on the anniversary date of said death.
3. Decreased partner's estate's share of the earnings:
    (a) The partners mutually desire that the deceased partner's estate shall be guaranteed a share in the earnings of the partnership over the period said estate retains an interest in the partnership. Said estate shall not be deemed to have an interest in the partnership after the final installment for the deceased partner's capital account is paid, even though a portion of the guaranteed payments specified below may be unpaid and may be due and owing.
    (b) The deceased partner's estate's guaranteed share of the earnings of the partnership shall be determined from two items and shall be paid at different times as follows:
        (1) First, interest shall be paid on the unpaid balance of the deceased partner's capital account at the same date that the installment on

the purchase price is paid. The amount to be paid shall be an amount equal to accrued interest at the rate of 6 percent per annum on the unpaid balance of the purchase price for the deceased partner's capital account.

(2) Second, the partners agree that the balance of the guaranteed payment from the partnership earnings shall be an amount equal to 25 percent of the deceased partner's share of the aggregate gross receipts of the partnership for the full 36 months preceding the month of the partner's death. Said amount shall be payable in 48 equal monthly installments without interest, and the first payment shall be made within 60 days following the death of the partner or within 30 days from the date on which the personal representative of the deceased becomes qualified, whichever date is later, provided, however, that the payment so made under this provision during any twelve-month period shall not exceed the highest annual salary on a calendar-year basis received by the partner for the three calendar years immediately preceding the date of the partner's death. In the event that said payment would exceed said salary, then an amount per month shall be paid that does not so exceed said highest monthly salary, and the term over which payment shall be paid to the beneficiary shall be lengthened beyond the said 48 months in order to complete said payment.

Smith and Perry were killed simultaneously in an automobile accident on January 10, 19X7. The surviving partners notified the executors of both estates that the first payment due under the buy and sell agreement would be paid on March 10, 19X7, and that subsequent payments would be paid on the tenth day of each month as due.

The following information was determined from the partnership records:

Partner	Profit and Loss Percentage	Capital Accounts on 1/10/X7	Annual Salaries to Partners		
			19X4	19X5	19X6
Smith	30%	$25,140	$16,500	$17,000	$17,400
Bailey	25	21,970	15,000	15,750	16,500
Davis	20	4,780	12,000	13,000	14,000
Williams	15	5,860	9,600	10,800	12,000
Perry	10	2,540	8,400	9,600	10,800

The partnership gross receipts for the three prior years were:

19X4..	$296,470
19X5..	325,310
19X6..	363,220

Required:

Prepare a schedule of the amount to be paid to the Smith Estate and to the Perry Estate in March, 19X7; December, 19X7; and January, 19X8. The schedule should identify the amounts attributable to earnings, to interest in the guaranteed payments, and to capital. Supporting calculations should be in good form.   (AICPA adapted)

PART SIX

Governmental and Not-For-Profit Accounting

Whereas management in the private sector devotes its energy and talent to maximize profits, governmental units and not-for-profit organizations focus on service. The recipients often do not pay in proportion to services received. For example, the costs of fire or police protection, education, park systems, environmental conservation, welfare, and other governmental or not-for-profit services are borne by the general population.

The primary objective of external financial reporting for governmental units and not-for-profit organizations is accountability. However, there is no "bottom-line" amount or earnings per share figure to judge success. Instead, there is the elusive factor of service. To control activities and measure service, variations in the accounting and reporting process are introduced. Budgets have far greater power for control, particularly when they are entered formally into the accounting records in order to provide close comparisons with actual results. With financial resources being derived from many different sources, some with specific restrictions as to their consumption, fund accounting provides a medium to display proper use for intended purposes.

CHAPTER 17

GOVERNMENTAL ACCOUNTING: GENERAL FUND AND THE ACCOUNT GROUPS

The federal accounting system with its myriad of agencies, each with peculiar reporting requirements, is an extensive topic. Although accounting students are not expected to demonstrate knowledge of federal governmental accounting in CPA examinations, they should have some knowledge of accounting for the smaller governmental divisions, such as states, counties, cities, and school districts. These smaller divisions are the primary areas of study in this chapter and in the chapter that follows. However, since the accounting procedures for these smaller units have followed the development of accounting for the federal goverment, this chapter begins with a discussion of the history of federal governmental accounting.

BRIEF HISTORY OF FEDERAL GOVERNMENTAL ACCOUNTING

In a democracy, the elected members of the legislative branch have governing authority, which includes the powers to levy and collect taxes and to borrow money. The Constitution of the United States assigned to Congress the control of the federal government's financial affairs and stipulated that the Treasury could spend only money that had been appropriated by Congress. Congress soon relinquished that control by passing the Treasury Act of 1789, which created the Department of the Treasury as an agency of the executive branch and gave the Department the authority to determine whether expenditures were legal and proper. Although the Act required the Treasury to make an annual report of public money receipts and disbursements, Congress surrendered direct control over fiscal administration to the executive branch, which, in essence, audited its own actions.

With the exceptional growth in federal expenditures resulting from World War I, Congress realized that the legislative branch should review expenditures independently. Thus, Congress passed the Budget and Accounting Act of 1921, which was the first action to return control over federal fiscal policy to the legislative branch. Among other changes, this act created the Bureau of the Budget, which now is the Office of Management and Budget, and the General Accounting Office. The director of the Office of Management and Budget is to aid the President in the creation of the annual federal budget, which must be submitted to Congress for approval. The duties assigned to the General Accounting Office (GAO) include the establishment and review of accounting systems and procedures to be used by all agencies of the federal government.

During the next three decades, various acts and commissions attempted to respond to a general dissatisfaction with the efficiency and economy of federal operations. In the Supplemental Appropriations Act of 1956, for example, the use of accrual accounting was required for governmental operations:

> As soon as practicable after August 1, 1956, the head of each executive agency shall, in accordance with principles and standards prescribed by the Comptroller General, cause the accounts of such agency to be maintained on an accrual basis to show the resources, liabilities, and costs of operations of such agency with a view to facilitating the preparation of cost-based budgets.

Persons in authority have been reluctant to insist on the implementation of accrual accounting, even though it supposedly is illegal for federal agencies not to use the accrual system. In 1973, for example, a commission recommended to the President that there be indefinite postponement of the project to place the federal budget on an accrual basis, since only a minority of the agencies used it for reporting purposes.

State and local governments and governmental utilities, hospitals, colleges, and universities are not permitted such latitude of choice as to an accounting basis. These units must measure the flow of financial resources using an accrual or modified accrual basis of accounting.

ACCOUNTING STANDARDS FOR GOVERNMENTAL UNITS — THE GASB

Much of the early development of governmental accounting and reporting may be attributed to the authoritative work of the National Council on Governmental Accounting (NCGA) of the Municipal Finance Officers Association and its predecessor bodies. This group attempted to establish principles within the parameters of varying statutes and enormous political pressures.

In 1968, it produced the book, *Governmental Accounting, Auditing, and Financial Reporting*. In March, 1979, a revised and condensed summary was published as Statement 1, *Governmental Accounting and Financial Reporting Principles*, along with Statement 2, *Grant, Entitlement, and Shared Revenue Accounting and Reporting by State and Local Governments*. In August, 1980, the AICPA issued Statement of Position 80–2, "Accounting and Financial Reporting by Governmental Units." It declared that financial statements presented in accordance with Statement 1 are in conformity with generally accepted accounting principles. In 1988, the NCGA released its second revision of *Governmental Accounting, Auditing, and Financial Reporting (GAAFR)*, an invaluable guide in this area of study.

Since 1979, the accounting profession and groups representing state, county, and local governments have attempted to develop a new structure for setting governmental accounting standards. The primary issue was whether accounting standards for governmental units should be promulgated by the Financial Accounting Standards Board (FASB) or by a separate body. Early in 1984, the Financial Accounting Foundation, through which the FASB is organized and funded, announced the approval of a five-member Governmental Accounting Standards Board (GASB), with the Financial Accounting Foundation exercising oversight responsibility over the GASB, as it does over the FASB. The GASB was organized with the understanding that it would establish financial reporting standards for the activities and transactions of state and local governmental entities and that the FASB would establish standards for the activities of all other entities. In the absence of a GASB standard for a particular activity, governmental entities would be expected to follow FASB standards. The GASB replaces the National Council on Governmental Accounting, which had been the primary body setting accounting standards for governmental units. However, the National Council's statements remain in force until replaced or modified by the GASB. Authoritative accounting and financial reporting guidance for state and local governmental entities is provided by the GASB in its publication, *Codification of Governmental Accounting and Financial Reporting Standards*.

PRINCIPLES AND PROCEDURES OF GOVERNMENTAL ACCOUNTING

The fundamental purpose of accounting is the communication of financial information to assist in the evaluation of prior performance and current financial position and in the planning of future action. Therefore, both governmental and commercial units adhere to the generally accepted accounting standards of relevance, reliability, neutrality, comparability, and full disclosure, and both use the double-entry system.

The accounting and reporting procedures for a governmental unit differ in some respects, however, from those of a commercial unit because governmental and commercial units have different purposes and operate in different environments. For example, while the primary purpose of a commercial unit is the maximization of profit within the limits of socially acceptable action, the primary purpose of a governmental unit is to provide services. Also, the conduct of governmental units is more severely limited by legal requirements and regulations. Although governmental accounting should be based on principles and techniques that promote economy and efficiency in accounting for public funds, it also must demonstrate compliance with applicable legal provisions.

Powerful pressures are being brought to bear by bond rating firms, such as Standard and Poor's Corporation, to force state and local governments to improve their accounting systems to conform to generally accepted accounting principles. Failure to do so would have a negative impact on the ratings assigned to a governmental unit's bond offering, and the unit would not be rated at all if its reporting is inadequate or untimely. Therefore, an increasing number of state and local governmental units undergo an audit by independent accountants. If the auditor's opinions are to be unqualified, the financial statements presented must be timely and in conformity with generally accepted accounting principles.

FUNDS IN A GOVERNMENTAL UNIT

In a profit organization, the total business constitutes the accounting entity. For a governmental unit, accounting and reporting are designed to permit each major activity to be accounted for independently with its own self-balancing set of accounts. The activities might include constructing major assets, paying long-term debt, providing goods or services for a fee, functioning as a trustee, and conducting day-to-day operations. Each of these activities would be accounted for as a separate entity, referred to as a *fund*, which records its assets, related liabilities, and equity balances as well as accounts for changes in these balances over a fiscal period. Funds are designed to prove that resources obtained for a specific purpose are used for that purpose. The number of funds established depends on the nature and volume of activity, the degree of control desired, and the legal requirements. However, confusion may result if too many funds are established. In general, it is best to have the minimum number of funds necessary to meet legal and operational requirements.

There are three broad categories or types of funds:

1. *Governmental funds* account for those activities that provide citizens with services that are financed primarily by taxes and intergovernmental grants. It is unfortunate that the term "governmental funds" was adopted, since it refers to only one of the three categories of funds used in governmental accounting. To remove as much confusion as possible, this text will refer to the category as *governmental-type funds.*

2. *Proprietary funds* account for business-type activities that derive their revenue from charges to users of goods or services. They follow the commercial accounting model in measuring net income. An example would be a publicly-owned utility.
3. *Fiduciary funds* account for resources for which the governmental unit acts as a trustee or agent.

ACCOUNTING FOR GOVERNMENTAL-TYPE FUNDS

Operations of a state, county, or large city are very diverse. Trying to account for operations in one governmental-type fund would result in relaxation of financial control and confusing financial reports. Four major activities are accounted for separately in their own funds if the quantity of activity warrants segregation. These four governmental-type funds are:

1. *General Fund* — accounts for resources that have no specific restrictions and are available for operational expenditures not relegated to one of the other governmental-type funds. Since it accounts for general operations, it is the most essential fund. Every governmental unit has a General Fund.
2. *Special Revenue Funds* — account for resources that legally are restricted to expenditure for specific operational purposes, such as a toll tax levied to be used for road maintenance.
3. *Capital Projects Funds* — account for resources to be used for the construction or acquisition of major capital facilities.
4. *Debt Service Funds* — account for resources to be used for payment of general long-term debt and interest.

MEASUREMENT FOCUS AND BASIS

Measurement focus in accounting indicates *what* is being measured. The measurement focus of governmental-type funds is the flow of financial resources. The basis of accounting dictates *when* the items to be measured are recognized. Under the cash basis of accounting, revenue is recognized when cash is received, and expenditures are recognized when paid. The cash basis is subject to manipulation and is inappropriate for governmental accounting.

The GASB stipulated that governmental-type funds should recognize revenues and expenditures on the modified accrual basis. Revenues are inflows from external parties of financial resources that do not require repayment. Revenues are recognized in the period in which they are measurable and become available to finance expenditures. In public finance, some revenue elements lend themselves to pure accrual, such as the levy of property taxes, where the liability of a taxpayer is established and where collectibility is assured or losses can be estimated. However, sometimes it is not practical to use an accrual basis for other revenue items. For example, local income taxes or sales taxes are not accrued, since the revenue from specific taxpayers is unknown until payment is received. Such revenue elements are best recognized when cash is received.

Expenditures are outflows of financial resources to external parties. They are recognized when goods or services are received and a related liability is incurred. Even the purchase of a fixed asset by the General Fund is an expenditure of that fund because the action reduces its financial resources. Depreciation is not recognized in a governmental-type fund, since it does not involve a flow of resources. Note that governmental-type funds do not have *expenses*, but instead have *expenditures*. There are no "expenses" in these funds because income determination is not an issue.

Fixed assets are not carried in governmental-type funds because they are not financial resources available for expenditure. To include them would change the measurement focus and cause confusion in the minds of readers of financial statements. Instead, the fixed assets are recorded in their own group. The change in nomenclature from fund to group is intentional. A *group* is not a fiscal entity. It does not report changes over a period of time, but is merely an inventory. The General Fixed Assets Account Group lists the general capital assets of the governmental body, excluding those of proprietary or fiduciary funds.

Applying a financial resources measurement focus on an accrual or modified accrual basis improves *interperiod equity measurement*, which determines whether or not current-year revenues were adequate to cover current-year cost of services provided. If not, part of the burden must be covered by net financial resources accumulated during past periods or must be shifted to future periods. If citizens are able to understand that concept, governmental financial reporting will have made progress in meeting its primary objective of accountability.

This chapter will discuss accounting for the General Fund, the General Fixed Assets Account Group, and the General Long-Term Debt Account Group. The next chapter will deal with the remaining governmental-type funds, as well as the proprietary and fiduciary funds.

USE OF BUDGETARY ACCOUNTING

A governmental unit prepares an operational budget that indicates the estimated inflows and outflows of resources. The budget of every major unit is reviewed by a legislative body. When the budget is approved and enacted, it becomes law and the unit has authority to generate revenues and to proceed with expenditures.

In governmental accounting, all budgetary accounts, as well as revenue and expenditure accounts recording actual transactions, are control accounts that oversee the detail maintained in subsidiary records. Even a city of moderate size may have a dozen major sources of revenue (property taxes, sales taxes, licenses, permits, fines, etc.). It easily may have twenty major types of expenditures (police and fire departments, highways, finance, personnel, sanitation, education, etc.) To conserve space and to present a better overview of the accounting process, only the control accounts will be used. They will be designated with the word "Control" in parentheses. The technique also will serve as a reminder that the supporting detail would be entered simultaneously into the appropriate subsidiary records.

In a business, ultimate achievement and control are reflected by its net income or net loss. This control feature is missing in governmental-type funds, which need a method of exercising financial control over revenues and expenditures by comparing them with annual budgetary projections. The task is accomplished by introducing into the accounting system a budgetary account as a counterpart for each control account in which the actual inflow and outflow of resources are recorded. Actual inflows of resources are recorded either as revenues or as *other financing sources*. The latter includes operational transfers in from other funds, proceeds from general long-term debt, and proceeds from the sale of fixed assets up to their original cost. A transfer in from another fund of the same governmental unit is not considered revenue, since it is not received from an outside source. Proceeds from general long-term debt are not considered revenue because they must be repaid. Actual outflows of resources in governmental-type funds are recorded either as expenditures or as *other financing uses*. The latter consists mainly of operational transfers to other funds.

The control accounts for other financing sources and for other financing uses were developed to prevent the same amount of revenue or expenditure from being recorded twice. For example, the General Fund will record taxes levied as revenue and may regularly transfer tax collection to other funds, which should not record the same item again as revenue. Instead, the recipient fund records resources received by crediting Other Financing Sources (Control), while the General Fund enters the transfer by debiting Other Financing Uses (Control). In this way, revenue is reported by the donor fund when it originally received the resources. The expenditure is recorded by the recipient fund when the resources are expended. Such movements of resources between funds are referred to as *operating transfers*.

The following summary indicates the names of the budgetary accounts used to record estimates, as well as the equivalent accounts used to record actual inflows and outflows of resources:

Item Recorded	Budgetary Accounts	Equivalent Accounts for Actual Events
Inflows of resources	Estimated Revenues (Control) Estimated Other Financing Sources (Control)	Revenues (Control) Other Financing Sources (Control)
Outflows of resources	Appropriations (Control) Estimated Other Financing Uses (Control)	Expenditures (Control) Other Financing Uses (Control)

Note that the account titles are very similar, except for the budgetary estimate for expenditures, which is recorded in Appropriations (Control). At any time during the fiscal year, it is possible to determine what percentage of estimated revenues and estimated other financing sources has been received and what proportion of the appropriations and estimated other financing uses has been committed. Unless the estimates are altered materially, no other entries are recorded in budgetary accounts until the end of the period, when they are closed.

ACCOUNTING FOR THE GENERAL FUND

The General Fund is the most important fund. It is used to account for unrestricted resources, mostly of a current nature, involved in the unit's operations. Even the smallest governmental unit will have a General Fund, which accounts for the major portion of revenue. Revenues result from property, income, gasoline, and sales taxes, as well as fines, penalties, permits, licenses, and grants from other governmental units.

To visualize the accounting process of the General Fund and the flow of information that produces the financial reports, the activities of Geiser City will be examined for the fiscal year ended September 30, 19X4. The General Fund trial balance on September 30, 19X3, is as follows:

Geiser City
General Fund Trial Balance
September 30, 19X3

Cash..	235,000	
Taxes Receivable — Delinquent...	30,000	
Allowance for Uncollectible Delinquent Taxes.....................		20,000
Vouchers Payable		170,000
Fund Balance — Reserved for Encumbrances		20,600
Fund Balance — Unreserved, Undesignated........................		54,400
	265,000	265,000

RECORDING THE BUDGET

The city council and the mayor have approved the budget for the following year, with estimated revenues of $1,350,000, appropriations of $1,300,000, and an estimated transfer of $30,000 to be made during the year to the Debt Service Fund. Again, transfers to other funds are not expenditures and in the budgetary entry are segregated from the estimated expenditures (appropriations) in a budgetary account labeled Estimated Other Financing Uses (Control). The budgetary entry permits isolation of estimated amounts from actual amounts so that the two may be compared. A convenient technique for remembering how to record the budget is to follow the logic that estimated revenues are forecasts of asset inflows and should be debited. Appropriations, as estimated authorizations to spend, and transfers to other funds will result in future asset outflows and should be credited. If the estimates of inflows and outflows are not equal in amount, the difference is recorded in the account Budgetary Fund Balance — Unreserved. The entry to record Geiser City's budget for its General Fund is:

Estimated Revenues (Control)	1,350,000	
Appropriations (Control)......................................		1,300,000
Estimated Other Financing Uses (Control)..............		30,000
Budgetary Fund Balance — Unreserved		20,000

Almost all of the accounts in governmental accounting are control accounts, requiring the details of their composition to be maintained in subsidiary records. To support total estimated revenues of $1,350,000, a breakdown of sources should be provided in the explanation of the budget entry or in a separate schedule. In practice, there could be as many as one hundred or more revenue items. For purposes of illustration, however, the number of revenue items is condensed, as shown in the following schedule of estimated revenues:

Geiser City
General Fund Estimated Revenues
For Year Ending September 30, 19X4

General property taxes...	$ **882,500**
Licenses and permits	125,500
Revenue from state grants...	200,000
Other revenues...	142,000
Total estimated revenues..	$1,350,000

Just as the total projected income is debited to Estimated Revenues (Control) in the general ledger, so each of the detailed estimated sources is debited to its own account in the subsidiary revenue ledger. The following subsidiary account for general property taxes illustrates the procedure of posting to subsidiary records:

Revenue Ledger

ACCOUNT	General Property Taxes		ACCOUNT NO.	
DATE	**ITEM**	**DEBIT** (Estimate)	**CREDIT** (Actual)	**BALANCE** (DR.) CR.
Oct. 1	Budget estimate	**882,500**		(882,500)

Not only must the accounting system provide for control of revenues, but it also must accommodate expenditures. To provide a basis for comparison between expected and actual expenditures, budgetary as well as actual expenditures accounts are an integral part of the accounting system. In the entry to record Geiser City's budget for its General Fund, the credit to Appropriations (Control) represents the estimate of the expenditures of $1,300,000 for the coming year. In support of the appropriations total, a summary of approved estimated expenditures by departments or activities might appear as follows:

Geiser City
Department or Activity Appropriations
For Year Ending September 30, 19X4

General government: legislative, judicial, and executive.................	$ 129,000
Public safety	277,300
Education	591,450
Highways and streets...	94,500
Sanitation and health...	97,750
Welfare...	51,000
Culture and recreation..	59,000
Total appropriations..	$1,300,000

Each of these departments or activities must submit detailed appropriation requests on the basis of subfunctions and object of expenditure. The Education Division, for example, might present the following estimate of expenditures:

Geiser City
Education Division
Request for Appropriation
For Year Ending September 30, 19X4

Supplies	**$160,000**
Salaries	350,000
Equipment...	60,000
Professional fees	21,450
Total..	$591,450

One approach to controlling expenditures is to establish subsidiary accounts by division or department. If this approach is followed by Geiser City, each of the expenditure items for the Education Division would have its own subsidiary account, such as the one that follows for supplies. Each expenditure account would be designed to show the original appropriation, the encumbrances (amounts committed), the expenditures (amounts spent), and the remaining unencumbered balance.

Education Division Expenditure Ledger

ACCOUNT	Supplies						ACCOUNT NO.
			ENCUMBRANCES			EXPENDITURES	UNEN-CUMBERED
DATE	ITEM	DEBIT	CREDIT	BALANCE	ITEM	TOTAL	BALANCE
Oct. 1	Budget appropriation						**160,000**

RECORDING ACTUAL REVENUES AND TRANSFERS

Property taxes are a major source of revenue for Geiser City's General Fund and are used to illustrate the recording of revenues. The property tax roll provides ownership information, legal descriptions, and amounts of gross tax levies, which support a debit to Taxes Receivable—Current. The estimated collectible amount is credited to Revenues (Control) and entered in the subsidiary revenue ledger. The following entry records the levy of the property tax and makes provision for the estimated uncollectibles:

Taxes Receivable—Current	919,000	
Revenues (Control)...		**881,300**
Allowance for Uncollectible Current Taxes		37,700

Both the revenues (control) account in the general ledger and the general property taxes account in the subsidiary revenue ledger are credited for the actual revenue. After the preceding entry is posted, General Property Taxes appears as follows:

Revenue Ledger

ACCOUNT	General Property Taxes			ACCOUNT NO.	
DATE	ITEM	DEBIT (Estimate)	CREDIT (Actual)	BALANCE (DR.) CR.	
Oct. 1	Budget estimate	882,500		(882,500)	
1	Tax levy		**881,300**	(1,200)	

During the fiscal period, a debit balance in a subsidiary revenue account usually represents additional revenue expected in the future. At the end of the fiscal period, a debit balance indicates a deficiency of actual revenue as compared to estimated revenue, while a credit balance shows an excess of actual over estimated revenues.

Cash inflows from property tax or income tax collections peak near the due dates for payment. Prior to their receipt, a governmental unit may have obligations that must be paid. Local banks usually provide short-term financing, using as security the taxing power of the unit, which is required to sign an instrument referred to as a *tax anticipation note*. Receipt of cash from such notes would be recorded in the General Fund with the following entry:

Cash...	XXX	
Tax Anticipation Notes Payable...............................		XXX

Later, as cash inflows from taxes provide resources, the following entry would record the payment of the notes and the interest, with the interest recorded as an expenditure:

Tax Anticipation Notes Payable....................................	XXX	
Expenditures (Control) (for interest)	XXX	
Cash...		XXX

During the year, the following additional events related to revenue are recorded in the General Fund of Geiser City, whose trial balance is shown on page 897.

Event	Entry		

Of the total delinquent taxes of $30,000 carried over from the prior period, $14,000 is collected. The balance is uncollectible.	Cash..
	Allowance for Uncollectible
	    Delinquent Taxes........................
	    Taxes Receivable—Delinquent..........
		14,000
		
		16,000
			
			30,000

The excess allowance for uncollectible delinquent taxes is transferred to Revenues (Control).	Allowance for Uncollectible
	    Delinquent Taxes........................
	    Revenues (Control)........................
		
		4,000
			
			4,000

Of current taxes receivable, $850,000 is collected during the year and $12,700 is written off as uncollectible.	Cash..
	Allowance for Uncollectible
	    Current Taxes...........................
	    Taxes Receivable—Current.............
		850,000
		
		12,700
			
			862,700

During the year, cash was collected from the following sources:
   Licenses and permits.............. $320,000
   Other revenues..................... 150,000
   Total............................... $470,000
	Cash..
	    Revenues (Control)........................
	    (with credit posting to each subsidiary
	    revenue account)
		470,000	
			470,000

At year end, property taxes not collected are classified as delinquent, as are the estimated uncollectible allowances.	Taxes Receivable—Delinquent..............
	    Taxes Receivable—Current
	    ($919,000 − $862,700).................
		56,300	
			
			56,300

	Allowance for Uncollectible
	    Current Taxes...........................
	Allowance for Uncollectible
	Delinquent Taxes
	    ($37,700 − $12,700).....................
		25,000	
			
			25,000

As indicated in the second entry, a revision of the estimated amount of uncollectible current and delinquent taxes and tax liens is treated as a change in accounting estimate through Revenues (Control). Only adjustments of confirmed errors of prior periods are recorded directly in the account Fund Balance—Unreserved, Undesignated.

Tax Liens. The law outlines the procedures to be followed in posting a lien or claim against property when property tax payments remain delinquent after a specified time period. The following entry records the exercise of such a lien for a hypothetical county:

Tax Liens Receivable	31,000	
Allowance for Uncollectible Delinquent Taxes................	12,000	
Taxes Receivable—Delinquent................................		31,000
Allowance for Uncollectible Tax Liens		12,000

Although the governmental unit may retain property against which foreclosure proceedings have been completed, it is customary to sell the property, in which case the entry is:

Cash..	11,000	
Allowance for Uncollectible Tax Liens (for any loss on		
disposition)	5,000	
Tax Liens Receivable		16,000

Adjustment for an inadequate or excessive allowance for uncollectibles is recorded as a change in accounting estimate through the revenues (control) account.

Transfers from Other Governmental Units (Intergovernmental Transfers). Resources to be received from federal, state, or local governmental units should be recognized as revenue in the General Fund when the resources are measurable and available. Such resources may be in the form of grants, entitlements, or shared revenues for operational purposes normally financed through the General Fund. For example, if a City has been notified by the federal government that it is to receive $75,000 within a short period of time to assist in the operation of its child-care program and $25,000 in the second quarter of the next year, the following entry would be made in the General Fund:

Due from Federal Government	100,000	
Revenues (Control)...		75,000
Deferred Revenue...		25,000

Grants to a governmental unit may carry strong restrictions on their use. For example, the federal government may be willing to give a locality a grant, providing it builds a bridge over a river and connects its main road to the federal highway. In this case, the restricted grant should be recognized as revenue only to the extent that expenditures have been made, with the remainder of the grant revenue recorded as deferred. This type of restricted grant sometimes is called an *expenditure-driven* grant.

RECORDING ENCUMBRANCES AND ACTUAL EXPENDITURES

To prevent overexpenditure, the General Fund uses an encumbrance system. Under this system, whenever a purchase order or other commitment is approved, an entry is made to record the estimated cost of the commitment. For example, an approved purchase order for school supplies, estimated to cost $10,000, is recorded as follows:

| Encumbrances (Control) .... | 10,000 | |
| Budgetary Fund Balance—Reserved for Encumbrances .. | | 10,000 |

The entry is posted to the general ledger, where Encumbrances (Control) is a quasi-expenditure account and where Budgetary Fund Balance—Reserved for Encumbrances is a form of restriction of the fund balance. The entry also is entered in the encumbrances section of the supplies account of the subsidiary expenditure ledger for the Education Division, reducing the unencumbered balance, as follows:

Education Division Expenditure Ledger

ACCOUNT	Supplies						ACCOUNT NO.
		ENCUMBRANCES			EXPENDITURES		UNEN-CUMBERED
DATE	ITEM	DEBIT	CREDIT	BALANCE	ITEM	TOTAL	BALANCE
Oct. 1	Budget appropriation						160,000
4	Purchase order	**10,000**		10,000			150,000

When the invoice is received for the purchase of items or services, the encumbrance entry is reversed, and the encumbrance is lifted to permit the deduction of the actual amount. Note that it is always the amount of the original estimate and not the actual cost that is used in the reversing entry. Assuming that the invoice for supplies amounts to $10,200, the two entries to record the invoice are:

Budgetary Fund Balance—Reserved for Encumbrances......   10,000
     Encumbrances (Control)   10,000
          To reverse entry for encumbrance at estimated cost.

Expenditures (Control)..   10,200
     Vouchers Payable..   10,200
          To record invoice at actual cost.

The supplies account in the subsidiary expenditure ledger appears as follows:

Education Division Expenditure Ledger

ACCOUNT	Supplies						ACCOUNT NO.
		ENCUMBRANCES			EXPENDITURES		UNEN-CUMBERED
DATE	ITEM	DEBIT	CREDIT	BALANCE	ITEM	TOTAL	BALANCE
Oct. 1	Budget appropriation						160,000
4	Purchase order	10,000		10,000			150,000
Nov. 7	Invoice received		**10,000**	-0-	**10,200**	10,200	149,800

When the encumbrance and the actual amount are identical, the unencumbered balance is not changed. However, when the amounts are not identical, the net effect is an adjustment of the unencumbered balance to reflect the amount of the actual expenditure. Thus, at any time, the subsidiary ledgers provide a continuing record of the unencumbered balances and of how closely the actual expenditures match encumbrances. The following equation is derived from an examination of the supplies account:

Unencumbered balance

= Appropriations − Expenditures total − Encumbrances balance

For internal expenditures, such as salaries, which are subject to little variation and to additional internal controls, it is not customary to involve the encumbrance accounts. When salaries are paid, they are recorded directly as expenditures and reduce the unencumbered balance of the salaries account in the subsidiary expenditure ledger.

ENCUMBRANCES OF A PRIOR PERIOD

It is not unusual to have encumbrances for approved purchase orders recorded one year and the actual invoices received in the following year. When the encumbrances were recorded initially, estimated amounts were used as projections of what was likely to occur. These budgetary accounts with their estimated amounts should not be in the same journal entry with accounts and amounts reflecting actual events. The simplest way to dispose of year-end budgetary account balances is to reverse the entry that created them. Such is the procedure recommended to clear budgetary account balances related to outstanding encumbrances at year end. On September 30, 19X3, Geiser City would have made the entry:

Budgetary Fund Balance — Reserved for Encumbrances..	20,600	
Encumbrances (Control)		20,600
To cancel year-end encumbrances for outstanding purchase orders.		

To display in the balance sheet equity section that the government has potential commitments on purchase orders, a reservation of the fund balance is recorded. The entry also serves to reduce the amount of net resources indicated in the unreserved fund balance as being available for additional commitment. On September 30, 19X3, Geiser City would have made the entry:

Fund Balance — Unreserved, Undesignated..................	20,600	
Fund Balance — Reserved for Encumbrances		20,600
To reclassify fund balance for year-end outstanding purchase orders.		

Both entries are reversed at the start of the subsequent year, since the unreserved fund balance account will be reduced by that year's actual expenditures. The usual budgetary entry then is made, reinstating the encumbrances that will be honored in the coming year:

Encumbrances (Control)	20,600	
Budgetary Fund Balance — Reserved for Encumbrances...		20,600
To reinstate outstanding encumbrances.		

In accordance with these procedures, on October 1, 19X3, Geiser City would return the reserve shown in the opening trial balance on page 897 to the unreserved fund balance as follows:

Fund Balance—Reserved for Encumbrances   20,600
  Fund Balance—Unreserved, Undesignated...............   20,600
    To reverse year-end reclassification entry.

The following events relate to Geiser City's expenditures and transfers during the year.

Event	Entry		

Throughout the year, encumbrances totaling $738,000 were recorded, including those from prior year end of $20,600.	Encumbrances (Control) ....
	  Budgetary Fund Balance—
	    Reserved for Encumbrances .....
		738,000	738,000

Vouchers were approved, liquidating $700,000 of encumbrances for:	Budgetary Fund Balance—Reserved
	    for Encumbrances ....
	  Encumbrances (Control) ....
		700,000	700,000

Supplies .... $300,000 Building............................. 200,000 Other expenditures................ 272,000	Inventory of Supplies .... Expenditures (Control).................... Vouchers Payable......................	300,000 472,000	772,000
Total $772,000			
Vouchers were approved for the following non-encumbered items:	Expenditures (Control).................... Vouchers Payable......................	518,000	518,000
Salaries .... $490,000 Other expenditures................ 28,000			
Total $518,000			
Vouchers totaling $1,400,000 were paid.	Vouchers Payable......................... Cash.....................................	1,400,000	1,400,000
Transfer of $30,000 is made to the Debt Service Fund.	Other Financing Uses (Control)........ Cash.....................................	30,000	30,000
Supplies totaling $260,000 were consumed.	Expenditures (Control).................... Inventory of Supplies	260,000	260,000

Adjust Fund Balance—Reserved for Inventory of Supplies to equal inventory. (See discussion below.)	Fund Balance—Unreserved,
	    Undesignated........................
	  Fund Balance—Reserved for
	    Inventory of Supplies..............
		40,000	40,000

The amount of unreserved fund balance represents net financial resources available for future periods. But one of those assets for Geiser City is the inventory of supplies, which will not be converted into cash and will not be available to meet future commitments. Therefore, the unreserved fund balance must be restricted by an amount equal to the inventory on the financial statement date. In this case, the amount of the inventory at year end is $40,000 ($300,000 − $260,000). Thereafter, the account Fund Balance—Reserved for Inventory of Supplies will be kept equal to the inventory amount by periodic adjustment through the unreserved fund balance account.

Corrections of previous years' errors in nominal accounts are made directly through the account Fund Balance—Unreserved, Undesignated. For example, Geiser City failed to record invoiced expenditures for last year of $30,600 that were not encumbered. Of this amount, $10,100 was paid this year and incorrectly debited to Expenditures (Control). The unpaid portion of $20,500 was to be vouchered. The entry would be:

Fund Balance—Unreserved, Undesignated......................	30,600	
Expenditures (Control)...		10,100
Vouchers Payable...		20,500
To correct error for failure to record expenditures chargeable to last year.		

The fund balance accounts require further clarification. The equity fund balance accounts are either reserved or unreserved. Reserved fund balances indicate that those amounts are not available for future appropriation or expenditure or are legally segregated for a specific future use, such as the Fund Balance—Reserved for Inventory of·Supplies. The unreserved fund balance may be designated, usually by legislative action, to reflect tentative, future management plans for which there will be resource utilization, such as a Fund Balance—Designated for Equipment Replacement. The remainder of the unreserved fund balance is labeled "unreserved, undesignated" and indicates the amount of net financial resources totally uncommitted.

SPECIAL ASSESSMENTS

GASB Statement No. 6, *Accounting and Financial Reporting for Special Assessments*, issued in January of 1987, eliminated the Special Assessments Fund, formerly a governmental-type fund. The elimination was expected to remedy inconsistencies in accounting for special assessments, which resembled events already being accounted for in other funds.

There are two kinds of special assessments:

1. *Service-type special assessments* cover operating activities, such as snow plowing, that do not result in increases in fixed assets. Payment for service special assessments seldom is arranged on an installment basis. A single charge is added to the property tax bill. Service assessments are accounted for in the fund type that best reflects the nature of the transaction, usually in the General Fund, Special Revenue Funds, or an Enterprise Fund.
2. *Capital improvement special assessments* result in additions or improvements to a government's fixed assets—for example, streets, gutters, or sidewalks. If the improvement provides capital assets that become part of an enterprise activity, such as water main construction for a utility, accounting would be done in Enterprise Funds. If the improvement results in a general fixed asset, accounting would be in the Capital Projects Fund or the General Fund, using the same basis as for any other capital improvement. Capital Project and Enterprise Fund accounting are covered in the next chapter.

FINANCIAL REPORTS OF THE GENERAL FUND

Several major changes in governmental accounting resulted from the incorporation of Statement 1 in the 1980 and 1988 versions of GAAFR. The 1968 version stated that it was inappropriate to issue a set of combined financial statements for a governmental unit. It recommended segmented reports by individual funds and groups, since multiple accounting and reporting variations are permitted for various funds. The resulting reports caused confusion and did not promote understanding of governmental accounting.

Statement 1 requires that all funds be accounted for either as governmental funds or as proprietary funds. Fiduciary funds, if they are expendable, are accounted for as governmental funds, while nonexpendable and pension trust funds are accounted for as proprietary funds. The simplification of accounting procedures makes it possible to present financial statements in columnar form for all fund types and account groups, with a combined total column, permitting an overview of the total governmental unit's operation. Existing standards require a governmental unit to issue annual combined financial statements covering all of its funds and account groups as its minimum general purpose financial statements for compliance with generally accepted accounting principles. Greater detail, including comparative data, may be provided by supplemental reports for individual funds and groups. Both combined and individual fund and group reports will be illustrated when appropriate.

To illustrate the recommended form of the financial statements, the year-end reports of Geiser City's General Fund are developed from the following year-end trial balance. These reports consist of a balance sheet and a statement of revenues, expenditures, and changes in fund balances.

Geiser City
General Fund Trial Balance
September 30, 19X4

Cash	139,000	
Taxes Receivable — Delinquent	56,300	
Allowance for Uncollectible Delinquent Taxes		25,000
Inventory of Supplies	40,000	
Vouchers Payable		90,700
Fund Balance — Reserved for Inventory of Supplies		40,000
Fund Balance — Unreserved, Undesignated		4,400
Revenues (Control)		1,355,300
Expenditures (Control)	1,250,100	
Other Financing Uses (Control)	30,000	
Encumbrances (Control)	38,000	
Budgetary Fund Balance — Reserved for Encumbrances		38,000
Estimated Revenues (Control)	1,350,000	
Appropriations (Control)		1,300,000
Estimated Other Financing Uses (Control)		30,000
Budgetary Fund Balance — Unreserved		20,000
	2,903,400	2,903,400

Balance Sheet. The General Fund year-end balance sheet for Geiser City, shown in Illustration 17–1, differs substantially from its private business counterpart. First, it deals almost exclusively with current assets and current liabilities, and the difference between these two amounts appears as the fund balance—either reserved (committed) or unreserved. Second, the long-term classifications of assets and liabilities usually are absent, since the general fixed assets are included in the General Fixed Assets Account Group, and the general long-term debt is carried in the General Long-Term Debt Account Group.

Illustration 17–1

Geiser City
General Fund Balance Sheet
September 30, 19X4

Assets

Cash		$139,000
Taxes receivable—delinquent.....................................	$56,300	
Less allowance for uncollectible delinquent taxes......	25,000	31,300
Inventory of supplies		40,000
Total assets..		$210,300

Liabilities and Fund Equity

Liabilities:		
Vouchers payable		$ 90,700
Fund balances:		
Reserved for encumbrances	$38,000	
Reserved for inventory of supplies.........................	40,000	
Unreserved, undesignated....................................	41,600	
Total fund equity		119,600
Total liabilities and fund equity		$210,300

Statement of Revenues, Expenditures, and Changes in Fund Balances.

The statement of revenues, expenditures, and changes in fund balances is to be interpreted as an operating statement and is prepared on an all-inclusive basis, disclosing all elements that contributed to the change in fund balances. The statement should contain details on the major revenue sources and on expenditures by function or program. Other financing sources or uses and any corrections that altered the fund balance also should be presented. For governmental-type funds for which an annual budget legally is adopted, the statement of revenues, expenditures, and changes in fund balances must show both budgeted and actual amounts in order to be in compliance with generally accepted accounting principles. A variance column showing the difference between budgeted and actual amounts is advisable. Normally such data would be shown only for the General Fund and Special Revenue Funds in the financial reports of the individual funds.

The statement of revenues, expenditures, and changes in fund balances for Geiser City, shown in Illustration 17–2, omits the comparative figures for the preceding period, although normally they would be of assistance in a financial evaluation. The statement reflects estimated and actual amounts of revenues, expenditures, and other changes that relate to this year. The beginning fund balance and ending fund balance amounts are the total of unreserved and reserved fund balances. The final actual fund balances amount ($119,600) must agree with the total fund equity shown on the balance sheet.

Illustration 17–2

Geiser City
General Fund
Statement of Revenues, Expenditures, and Changes in Fund Balances—
Budget and Actual
For the Fiscal Year Ended September 30, 19X4

	Budget	Actual	Variance— Favorable (Unfavorable)
Revenues:			
General property taxes............	$ 882,500	$ 885,300	$ 2,800
Licenses and permits..............	125,500	120,000	(5,500)
Intergovernmental revenues....	200,000	200,000	-0-
Miscellaneous revenues..........	142,000	150,000	8,000
Total revenues	$1,350,000	$1,355,300	$ 5,300
Expenditures:			
General government..............	$ 129,000	$ 120,305	$ 8,695
Public safety	277,300	252,795	24,505
Highways and streets.............	94,500	86,100	8,400
Sanitation and health.............	97,750	87,750	10,000
Welfare.................................	51,000	46,000	5,000
Culture and recreation	59,000	53,400	5,600
Education	591,450	603,750	(12,300)
Total expenditures..............	$1,300,000	$1,250,100	$49,900
Excess of revenues over expenditures..................	$ 50,000	$ 105,200	$55,200
Other financing sources (uses)....	(30,000)	(30,000)	-0-
Excess of revenues and other sources over expenditures and other uses......................	$ 20,000	$ 75,200	$55,200
Fund balances, October 1, 19X3...	75,000	75,000	-0-
Correction of prior year's expenditures.........................	-0-	(30,600)	(30,600)
Fund balances, September 30, 19X4................	$ 95,000	$ 119,600	$24,600

Interim Reports. Interim reports are prepared primarily for internal use and should be designed to assist in managerial control by revealing areas of strength or weakness. The reports may be prepared on a monthly or quarterly basis, comparing actual results to budgetary estimates when useful and including data for the year to date. Interim balance sheets of governmental funds using budgetary accounts require three modifications to make them useful. First, following the total assets, a section labeled *Resources* is introduced to show the amount of estimated revenues not yet received that will become available later in the year. Second, the fund equity section is expanded to show appropriations still available. Third, the Budgetary Fund Balance — Unreserved amount is combined with the Fund Balance — Unreserved, Undesignated balance, thus indicating what the unreserved balance would be if all budgetary projections actually materialized. Using hypothetical amounts, a partial interim balance sheet highlighting the three necessary modifications would appear as follows:

City of X
General Fund Interim Balance Sheet
July 31, 19X1

Assets and Resources

Total assets...................................		$300,000
Resources:		
Estimated revenues	$1,350,000	
Less revenues to date	750,000	600,000
Total assets and resources................		$900,000

Liabilities and Fund Equity

Total liabilities.................................		$115,000
Fund equity:		
Appropriations		$1,300,000
Less: Expenditures	$670,000	
Encumbrances..........................	230,000	900,000
Available appropriations..................		$ 400,000
Budgetary fund balance — reserved		
for encumbrances..........................		230,000
Reserved for inventory of supplies		55,000
Unreserved, Undesignated		100,000
Total fund equity		785,000
Total liabilities and fund equity		$900,000

CLOSING THE GENERAL FUND

The simplest closing process is first to reverse the budgetary entries and then to close the actual revenue and expenditure accounts, including the other financing sources and uses accounts, into the Fund Balance — Unreserved, Undesignated account. Closing entries for Geiser City would appear as follows:

Appropriations (Control)..	1,300,000	
Estimated Other Financing Uses (Control)................	30,000	
Budgetary Fund Balance — Unreserved	20,000	
Estimated Revenues (Control)		1,350,000
To reverse entry recording budget.		

Budgetary Fund Balance — Reserved for		
Encumbrances..	38,000	
Encumbrances (Control)		38,000
To close budgetary accounts related to		
encumbrances.		

At this point it is wise to make the entry to reserve an amount of the fund balance equal to the encumbered purchase orders, as follows:

Fund Balance — Unreserved, Undesignated..............	38,000	
Fund Balance — Reserved for Encumbrances		38,000

The final closing entry would be:

Revenues (Control)..	1,355,300	
Expenditures (Control)......................................		1,250,100
Other Financing Uses (Control)		30,000
Fund Balance — Unreserved, Undesignated...........		75,200

ACCOUNTING FOR THE GENERAL FIXED ASSETS ACCOUNT GROUP

Fixed assets of a proprietary fund or a fiduciary fund are accounted for within those funds and often are referred to as *fund capital assets*. All other fixed assets are considered *general fixed assets* and are accounted for in the General Fixed Assets Account Group. This account group, which was created to control fixed assets that are not resources of any fund, may be thought of as an inventory record of fixed assets for the purpose of assigning responsibility for custody and proper use. Five fixed asset categories are recommended: land, buildings, improvements other than buildings, machinery and equipment, and construction in progress. Each category should have a control account in the ledger and should be substantiated by supporting detailed records.

There is one class of fixed assets that governmental units may omit from their General Fixed Assets Account Group. These assets are the public domain or *infrastructure* fixed assets, such as sidewalks, streets, curbs, and bridges. Their inclusion in formal reports is recommended but not required. Whatever policy is adopted, however, must be followed consistently. If they are formally included in the General Fixed Assets Account Group, they should be recorded in Improvements Other Than Buildings. Most governmental units do not record them, but maintain separate descriptive records on infrastructure fixed assets.

The acquisition of a general fixed asset is recorded in the General Fixed Assets Account Group by a debit to one of the five specific asset accounts. The credit indicates the source of the asset, selected from the following recommended titles:

> Investment in General Fixed Assets —
> Capital Projects Funds
> General Fund
> Special Revenue Funds
> Donations

To illustrate this procedure, a building acquired with General Fund revenues would require the following entries:

Fund or Group in Which Recorded	Entry		
General Fund	Expenditures (Control).........................	200,000	
	Vouchers Payable.............................		200,000
	(This entry is part of the entry on page 905, which records vouchers of $772,000.)		
General Fixed Assets Account Group	Buildings	200,000	
	Investment in General Fixed Assets — General Fund		200,000

The basis of a fixed asset is cost or, if the asset is donated, appraised market value at time of receipt. Subsequent to the acquisition of a fixed asset, capital and maintenance expenditures must be distinguished, as they are in commercial accounting, since maintenance expenditures should not increase the accountability of the General Fixed Assets Account Group.

When a governmental unit disposes of a general fixed asset, the original cost of the asset is removed from the General Fixed Assets Account Group. In the General Fund, proceeds from the sale up to the original cost are recorded with a credit to Other Financing Sources (Control). In the rare case of a sale at more than the asset's original cost, the gain is credited to Revenues (Control). For example, if a governmental unit sells equipment for $110,000, carried in the General Fixed Assets Account Group at $100,000, the following entries would be made:

Fund or Group in Which Recorded	Entry		
General Fund	Cash..	110,000	
	Other Financing Sources (Control)......		100,000
	Revenues (Control).........................		10,000
General Fixed Assets Account Group	Investment in General Fixed		
	Assets — General Fund	100,000	
	Machinery and Equipment		100,000

Instead of selling the equipment, assume that the governmental unit traded it for a larger model costing $235,000, with an allowance of $110,000 for the smaller unit. Statement 1 indicates that fixed asset costs should be recorded using the *net* method—(total purchase price less any trade-in allowance). Thus, the entries would be:

Fund or Group in Which Recorded	Entry		
General Fund	Expenditures (Control).........................	125,000	
	Vouchers Payable...........................		125,000
General Fixed Assets Account Group	Investment in General Fixed		
	Assets — General Fund	100,000	
	Machinery and Equipment		100,000
	Machinery and Equipment...................	125,000	
	Investment in General Fixed		
	Assets — General Fund		125,000

Stewardship responsibility for general fixed assets would be improved if the new assets were recorded at their total cost, with the trade-in value functioning as a reduction in the amount to be paid. This is the *gross* method recommended in the 1988 GAAFR. The entries then would be:

Fund or Group in Which Recorded	Entry		
General Fund	Expenditures (Control).........................	235,000	
	Vouchers Payable...........................		125,000
	Other Financing Sources (Control)......		110,000
General Fixed Assets Account Group	Investment in General Fixed		
	Assets — General Fund	100,000	
	Machinery and Equipment		100,000
	Machinery and Equipment...................	235,000	
	Investment in General Fixed		
	Assets — General Fund		235,000

Either method conforms with generally accepted accounting principles. The gross method seems preferable because it monitors the value of the new asset, rather than the amount of the cash outlay.

Leasing affords the opportunity to acquire the service of a fixed asset with a reduced immediate outlay and without increasing bonded debt. As resources become more limited, long-term leasing by governmental units becomes more widespread.

Governmental units should adhere to the FASB statements regarding leasing. When long-term noncancelable lease arrangements resemble a purchase, the leased general fixed asset should be recorded in the General Fixed Assets Account Group. The liability for the long-term lease is recorded in the General Long-Term Debt Account Group, similar to the procedure for handling a serial bond issue, which is discussed later in this chapter and in the chapter that follows.

Notice that there is no accumulated depreciation involved in the typical recording of the sale or exchange of a general fixed asset. When net income is determined, as in proprietary funds, or when capital maintenance is important, as in some fiduciary funds, depreciation expense must be recognized. But governmental-type funds are not concerned with either of these elements. Emphasis is on expenditures, rather than on expenses. According to the NCGA, recording depreciation expense of general fixed assets in governmental-type funds is improper:

> To record depreciation expense in governmental funds would inappropriately mix two fundamentally different measurements, expenses and expenditures. General fixed asset acquisitions require the use of governmental fund financial resources and are recorded as expenditures. General fixed asset sale proceeds provide governmental fund financial resources. Depreciation expense is neither a source nor a use of governmental fund financial resources, and thus is not properly recorded in the accounts of such funds.[1]

If it is desired to indicate asset usage or consumption to date, accumulated depreciation may be recorded in the General Fixed Assets Account Group by debiting the appropriate investment in general fixed asset account and crediting the accumulated depreciation account. Entries for the disposition of a general fixed asset would remove the related accumulated depreciation.

To illustrate the financial statements of the General Fixed Assets Account Group, a schedule of general fixed assets for the City of Martinsville is shown in Illustration 17–3. This basic statement shows the total amount for each category of fixed assets (Land, Buildings, etc.). The counter-balancing equity indicates the sources of the assets. When each of the asset categories is summarized in one amount, it is also desirable to provide a schedule that indicates the function or activity to which the fixed assets were assigned.

Governmental units generally comply with legal regulations in accounting for fixed assets. However, supporting records in a governmental unit are often incomplete and fail to provide the data that should be the output of a properly functioning system of asset control. It is unfortunate that the law does not require adherence to the same principles and procedures that are used by commercial accounting in its treatment of plant assets. Not

---

[1]Statement 1, *Governmental Accounting and Financial Reporting Principles* (Chicago: Municipal Finance Officers Association of the United States and Canada, March, 1979), 10.

Illustration 17–3

City of Martinsville
Schedule of General Fixed Assets
December 31, 19X2

General fixed assets:	
Land	$1,259,500
Buildings	2,855,500
Improvements other than buildings	1,036,750
Machinery and equipment	452,500
Construction in progress	1,722,250
Total general fixed assets	$7,326,500
Investments in general fixed assets by source:	
Capital projects funds	$5,879,100
General fund	562,400
Special revenue funds	309,500
Donations	575,500
Total investment in general fixed assets	$7,326,500

only would the citizenry be better informed by these procedures, but the financial management of the governmental unit would be more efficient.

ACCOUNTING FOR THE GENERAL LONG-TERM DEBT ACCOUNT GROUP

When long-term debt will be met by the resources of a specific fund, it is shown as a liability of that fund, as in the case of proprietary funds and fiduciary funds. All other long-term debt is labeled *general long-term debt* and is accounted for in the General Long-Term Debt Account Group. This account group, which was designed to monitor long-term debt that is not the responsibility of any particular fund, furnishes a record of the unmatured principal of all general long-term obligations of the governmental unit. Referring to a long-term obligation as "general" indicates that the community can use its taxing power to pay debt principal and interest. Interest is not accounted for in the General Long-Term Debt Account Group. To maintain the self-balancing nature of the account group, the issuance of long-term obligations is recorded by debiting Amount To Be Provided for Payment of (properly identified) Debt and crediting a liability account.

The proposed statement of the GASB, *Measurement Focus and Basis of Accounting — Governmental Funds,* would change the treatment for non-capital-related debt. Such debt is incurred to cover an operational deficit or in anticipation of future revenues. Even if long-term in nature, such non-capital-related debt providing financial resources to, and expected to be repaid from, the assets of a governmental-type fund would be recorded as a liability of that fund rather than in the General Long-Term Debt Account Group.

To illustrate the entries for the General Long-Term Debt Account Group, assume that a unit incurs a general long-term obligation in the form of term bonds of $1,000,000 to acquire property.[2] The price at which the bonds are sold will not affect the entry to record the issuance of the bonds. As shown in the following entry, the bonds are recorded in the General Long-Term Debt Account Group at the face value to be redeemed at maturity.

Amount To Be Provided for Payment of Term Bonds..	1,000,000	
Term Bonds Payable..		1,000,000

Payment of both principal and interest is handled by the Debt Service Fund, where "service" is synonymous with "payment," but the General Long-Term Debt Account Group records all amounts that become available in the Debt Service Fund for retirement of general long-term debt principal. Assuming that the Debt Service Fund receives an annual appropriation of $80,000 to provide for the eventual retirement of the term bonds, the following entry is recorded in the General Long-Term Debt Account Group:

Amount Available in Debt Service Funds — Term Bonds...	80,000	
Amount To Be Provided for Payment of Term Bonds...		80,000

In the combined balance sheet of a governmental unit, balances in the accounts, Amount Available and Amount To Be Provided, are shown as debits.

If sound actuarial practices have been employed, the Debt Service Fund will retire the obligation at the appropriate time, and the General Long-Term Debt Account Group will make the following entry:

Term Bonds Payable..	1,000,000	
Amount Available in Debt Service Funds — Term Bonds...		1,000,000

The report provided by this account group is the schedule of general long-term debt, which is composed of two sections. The first section shows the amounts available in the Debt Service Fund for repayment of general

---

[2]A term bond is one in which the entire principal is due on one date. A serial bond issue is redeemed in periodic payments. Term bonds are rare, but better illustrate entries in the General Long-Term Debt Account Group.

long-term debt and the amounts still to be provided for their retirement. The second section lists the total term and serial bond debt payable and other possible commitments. In this schedule, the amount already available plus the amount to be provided always must equal the maturity value of the long-term debt. Illustration 17–4 displays a hypothetical schedule of general long-term debt for the City of Martinsville:

Illustration 17–4

City of Martinsville
Schedule of General Long-Term Debt
December 31, 19X2

Amount Available and To Be Provided
for the Payment of General Long-Term Debt

Term bonds:		
Amount available in debt service funds	$ 196,205	
Amount to be provided	203,795	
Total — term bonds		$ 400,000
Serial bonds:		
Amount available in debt service funds	$ 14,005	
Amount to be provided	2,385,995	
Total — serial bonds		2,400,000
Other general long-term liabilities:		
Amount to be provided for payment of special		
assessment debt*		200,000
Total available and to be provided		$3,000,000

General Long-Term Debt

Term bonds payable	$ 400,000
Serial bonds payable	2,400,000
Special assessment debt with governmental commitment*	200,000
Total general long-term debt payable	$3,000,000

*These items are discussed in Chapter 18.

REVIEW OF ENTRIES FOR THE GENERAL FUND AND ACCOUNT GROUPS

The following example will provide a comprehensive review of the General Fund, the General Fixed Assets Account Group, and the General Long-Term Debt Account Group. The General Fund balance sheet for Junction City, as of December 31, 19X2, is as follows:

Junction City
General Fund Balance Sheet
December 31, 19X2

Assets

Cash..		$100,000
Taxes receivable—delinquent-19X2.................................	$50,000	
Less allowance for uncollectible delinquent taxes-19X2...	20,000	30,000
Tax liens receivable-19X1	$25,000	
Less allowance for uncollectible tax liens-19X1..............	5,000	20,000
Inventory of supplies		20,000
Total assets...		$170,000

Liabilities and Fund Equity

Liabilities:		
Vouchers payable		$ 30,000
Fund balances:		
Reserved for encumbrances-19X2................................	$40,000	
Reserved for inventory of supplies	20,000	
Unreserved, undesignated..	80,000	
Total fund equity		140,000
Total liabilities and fund equity		$170,000

During 19X3, the following entries are recorded in the General Fund of Junction City. If an event also requires that an entry be made in one of the account groups, the necessary entry is indicated as part of the event.

Event	Entry in the General Fund		
The budget is approved. Estimated inflows are from:	Estimated Revenues (Control)	614,000	
	Estimated Other Financing Sources		
Revenues $600,000	(Control)	360,000	
General long-term debt	Appropriations (Control).....................		860,000
issuance........................... 200,000	Estimated Other Financing Uses		
Transfers from other funds 60,000	(Control)		50,000
Sales of fixed assets carried at $100,000 (amount received above carrying value is	Budgetary Fund Balance— Unreserved...............................		64,000
recorded as revenue)........... 114,000			
Estimated outflows are for:			
Expenditures......................... $860,000			
Transfers to other funds 50,000			
Property taxes of $500,000 are levied, of which $30,000 is estimated to be uncollectible.	Taxes Receivable—Current	500,000	
	Allowance for Uncollectible Current		
	Taxes...		30,000
	Revenues (Control)..........................		470,000
Collection of taxes and related interest for the year:	Cash...	495,000	
	Taxes Receivable—Current		450,000
Current taxes $450,000	Taxes Receivable—Delinquent-19X2...		32,000
Delinquent taxes-19X2 32,000	Tax Liens Receivable-19X1................		10,000
Interest on delinquent taxes..... 2,000	Revenues (Control)..........................		3,000
Tax liens-19X1 10,000			
Interest on tax liens-19X1 1,000			
Total $495,000			

Event	Entry in the General Fund		

The amount of the Fund Balance — Reserved for Encumbrances was returned to the unreserved fund balance.

Fund Balance — Reserved for Encumbrances-19X2	40,000	
Fund Balance — Unreserved, Undesignated		40,000

Property against which there are unpaid tax liens for 19X1 is sold for $7,000. (The loss is an adjustment of current revenue, since it represents a change in estimate.)

Cash	7,000	
Allowance for Uncollectible Tax Liens-19X1	5,000	
Revenues (Control)	3,000	
Tax Liens Receivable-19X1		15,000

Tax liens totaling $18,000 are issued against 19X2 delinquent taxpayers.

Tax Liens Receivable-19X2	18,000	
Taxes Receivable — Delinquent-19X2		18,000

Allowance for Uncollectible Delinquent Taxes is reclassified and is reduced, so as not to exceed the related tax liens receivable of $18,000. As a change in estimate, the credit is made to Revenues (Control).

Allowance for Uncollectible Delinquent Taxes-19X2	20,000	
Allowance for Uncollectible Tax Liens-19X2		18,000
Revenues (Control)		2,000

Uncollected current taxes are declared delinquent and the related allowance is reclassified.

Taxes Receivable — Delinquent-19X3	50,000	
Taxes Receivable — Current		50,000
Allowance for Uncollectible Current Taxes	30,000	
Allowance for Uncollectible Delinquent Taxes-19X3		30,000

Cash received for licenses, fees, and fines totals $70,000.

Cash	70,000	
Revenues (Control)		70,000

To acquire land, a general long-term $200,000 serial bond issue is sold for 102. The premium will be transferred to another fund. This event requires an entry in the General Long-Term Debt Account Group:

Cash	204,000	
Other Financing Sources (Control)		200,000
Due to Other Funds		4,000

Amount To Be Provided for Payment of Serial Bonds	200,000	
Serial Bonds Payable		200,000

Other funds transfer $60,000 to the General Fund.

Cash	60,000	
Other Financing Sources (Control)		60,000

Total amount encumbered for approved purchase orders was $600,000, including $40,000 of previous year-end encumbrances.

Encumbrances (Control)	600,000	
Budgetary Fund Balance — Reserved for Encumbrances		600,000

The following vouchers were approved:

General expenditures	$760,000
Purchase of equipment	40,000
Purchase of supplies (a perpetual inventory system is used)	70,000
Total	$870,000

Expenditures (Control)	800,000	
Inventory of Supplies	70,000	
Vouchers Payable		870,000

Event	Entry in the General Fund		
Of this total, $510,000 was encumbered. The following entry is required in the General Fixed Assets Account Group:	Budgetary Fund Balance — Reserved for Encumbrances .... Encumbrances (Control)	510,000	510,000
Machinery and Equipment........... 40,000 Investment in General Fixed Assets — General Fund.................. 40,000			
$50,000 was transferred from the General Fund to other funds.	Other Financing Uses (Control) .... Cash...	50,000	50,000
Vouchers totaling $880,000 were paid.	Vouchers Payable............................. Cash...	880,000	880,000
The year-end supplies inventory amounted to $26,000.	Expenditures (Control)......................... Inventory of Supplies ($20,000 + $70,000 − $26,000)	64,000	64,000
Fund Balance — Reserved for Inventory of Supplies is adjusted to agree with the inventory of supplies.	Fund Balance — Unreserved, Undesignated............................. Fund Balance — Reserved for Inventory of Supplies ($26,000 − $20,000).....................	6,000	6,000
Equipment carried at $100,000 in the General Fixed Assets Account Group is sold for $114,000. The following entry is required in the General Fixed Assets Account Group:	Cash... Other Financing Sources (Control) ...... Revenues (Control).........................	114,000	100,000 14,000
Investment in General Fixed Assets — General Fund................ 100,000 Machinery and Equipment........ 100,000			

QUESTIONS

1. Explain the financial advantage for a governmental unit to adhere to generally accepted accounting principles.
2. Define a fund as the term is used in governmental accounting in contrast to how the term is used in commercial accounting.
3. What is meant by the measurement focus in accounting? What is the measurement focus for governmental-type funds?
4. Why is interperiod equity measurement important in governmental-type fund accounting?
5. The use of four governmental-type funds has been recommended. Identify the fund described in each of the following cases:
   (a) The fund that accounts for charges levied against properties directly benefited by a major capital improvement.

(b) The fund that accounts for revenues from a city sales tax legally restricted to finance new construction.

(c) The fund that accounts for payment of principal and interest on general long-term debt.

(d) The fund that accounts for proceeds from a bond issue to be used to construct a central library.

(e) Every governmental unit should have this fund to account for day-to-day operations.

6. Define revenues and expenditures as the terms apply to governmental-type funds.

7. List the advantages of introducing budgetary accounts into the accounting system.

8. Discuss the significance of the encumbrance system.

9. What is the purpose of establishing the account Fund Balance—Reserved for Inventory in the General Fund?

10. Describe the relationship between revenues and expenditures for a period in a governmental-type fund.

11. Indicate which fund is most likely to record the following special assessments:

(a) For a major general fixed asset improvement.

(b) To cover heavy sanding of streets during winter.

(c) For capital equipment for a utility.

12. What events would involve a debit or credit to Fund Balance—Unreserved, Undesignated in the General Fund?

13. Explain the three differences between the interim and year-end balance sheets of the General Fund.

14. Contrary to general procedure, proprietary funds account for their own fixed assets. Why is this deviation tolerated?

15. Discuss the purpose of the General Long-Term Debt Account Group.

EXERCISES

Exercise 1. Select the best answer for each of the following multiple-choice questions.

1. In a governmental-type fund, which one of the following constitutes revenue?

a. Cash received from another fund of the same unit.

b. Bond proceeds.

c. Property taxes.

d. Refund on an invoice for fuel.

2. In a governmental-type fund, which one of the following is considered an expense?
   a. The purchase of a capital asset.
   b. The purchase of supplies.
   c. Salaries earned.
   d. None of the above.

3. In a governmental-type fund, the purchase of equipment is debited to:
   a. Expenditures (Control).
   b. Appropriations (Control).
   c. Equipment.
   d. General Fixed Assets.

4. When a portion of property tax proceeds recorded in the General Fund is transferred to another fund, the account to be debited in the General Fund is:
   a. Expenditures (Control).
   b. Revenues (Control).
   c. Estimated Revenues (Control).
   d. Other Financing Uses (Control).

5. In the recording of a city's budget, which one of the following accounts is debited?
   a. Appropriations (Control).
   b. Estimated Revenues (Control).
   c. Estimated Other Financing Uses (Control).
   d. Encumbrances (Control).

Exercise 2.   Select the best answer for each of the following multiple-choice questions.

1. On the schedule of general fixed assets, accumulated depreciation:
   a. May not be shown.
   b. May be shown, if depreciation is charged to Other Financing Uses (Control).
   c. May be shown, if depreciation is charged to Expenditures (Control).
   d. May be shown, if an Investment in General Fixed Assets account correspondingly is reduced.

2. The General Long-Term Debt Account Group reflects:
   a. All long-term debt of a governmental unit.
   b. General long-term debt and other commitments.
   c. All long-term debt and accrued interest thereon.
   d. Only general long-term debt and accrued interest thereon.

3. In the General Long-Term Debt Account Group records, the following correct entry appears:

Amount Available in Debt Service Funds XXX
   Amount To Be Provided for Payment of Bonds XXX

An acceptable explanation for this entry would be that it records the:
a. Issuance of bonds.
b. Receipt of resources by a fund to cover bond redemption.
c. Maturing of a bond issue.
d. Redemption of a bond issue.

4. A general fixed asset is purchased by the General Fund. The invoice is recorded in the General Fund by debiting:
a. Expenditures (Control).
b. Appropriations (Control).
c. Encumbrances (Control).
d. The fixed asset account.

5. Years ago the city purchased land for $10,000. The council approved its sale for $120,000. In the General Fund, the gain on the sale would be credited to:
a. Revenues (Control).
b. Other Financing Sources (Control).
c. Fund Balance—Unreserved, Undesignated.
d. Fund Balance—Reserved for Fixed Assets.

Exercise 3.   Prepare the entries to record the following General Fund transactions for the Village of Vale for the year ended September 30, 19X2:
(a) Revenues are estimated at $250,000; expenditures are estimated at $240,000.
(b) A tax levy is set at $250,000, of which 1% will likely be uncollectible.
(c) Purchase orders amounting to $140,000 are authorized.
(d) Tax receipts total $180,000.
(e) Invoices totaling $125,000 are received and vouchered for orders originally estimated at $123,000.
(f) Salaries amounting to $73,000 are approved for payment.
(g) A state grant-in-aid of $50,000 is received.
(h) Fines and penalties of $5,000 are collected.
(i) Property for a wildlife sanctuary is purchased, costing $45,000. No encumbrance had been made for this item.
(j) A generous citizen has donated the property adjacent to the sanctuary. The fair market value of the property is $38,000.
(k) Amounts of $6,000 due to other village funds are approved for payment. (Credit: Due to Other Funds)
(l) The village's share of sales tax due from the state is $15,000.
(m) Vouchers totaling $175,000 are paid.
(n) Accounts are closed at year end.

Exercise 4.   The trial balance prepared for the City of Figie for its fiscal year ended June 30, 19X5, is as follows:

Cash...	110,000	
Receivables (net)..	40,000	
Vouchers Payable..		65,000
Budgetary Fund Balance—Reserved for Encumbrances....		60,000
Fund Balance—Unreserved, Undesignated...................		18,000
Budgetary Fund Balance—Unreserved.........................	5,000	
Estimated Revenues (Control).....................................	600,000	
Revenues (Control)...		610,000
Appropriations (Control)...		605,000
Expenditures (Control)..	543,000	
Encumbrances (Control)..	60,000	
	1,358,000	1,358,000

(1) Prepare a balance sheet as of June 30, 19X5.
(2) Prepare a statement of revenues, expenditures, and changes in fund balances, using budget and actual amounts with variances for the fiscal year ended June 30, 19X5, and reflecting the total fund equity.

Exercise 5.   A city purchased land, costing $50,000, for park development. The amount had been encumbered at $55,000. Ten years later, because of a population shift, the park is no longer practical. The city sells the land for $117,000. Prepare journal entries to record the purchase and subsequent sale of the land, indicating in what fund or group each entry would be made. Use this format:

<u>Event</u>   <u>Fund or Group</u   <u>Entry</u>

Exercise 6.   For the following transactions, prepare the entries that would be recorded in the General Fixed Assets Account Group for the City of Lansing:
(a) From Special Revenue Funds resources, the city purchased property costing $800,000, with three-fourths of the cost allocated to a building.
(b) A mansion belonging to the great-granddaughter of the city's founder was donated to the city. The land cost the original owner $600, and the house was built for an additional $50,000. At the time of donation, the property had an estimated market value of $400,000, of which $220,000 was allocable to the land. The property was accepted and is to be used as a park and as a museum.
(c) A central fire station, financed by general obligation bonds, was two-thirds completed at year end, with costs to date of $700,000.
(d) A new fire engine was purchased with a list price of $131,000. The city traded a used fire engine originally purchased for $100,000. The trade-in value was $21,000. Both engines were purchased from general property tax revenues. Lansing uses the net method.
(e) A new street was completed at a cost of $250,000, which is to be charged, through Capital Projects Funds special assessments, against property owners in the vicinity. The city follows GASB recommendations relative to infrastructures.

Exercise 7.   Prepare the entries that would be made in the General Long-Term Debt Account Group for the following events:

(a) To finance the construction of an art center, $1,300,000 of general obligation term bonds were sold for $1,100,000.

(b) The General Fund allocated $130,000 to a Debt Service Fund to begin to provide for retirement of the bonds in (a) at maturity.

(c) To help finance the construction of a health center, $2,000,000 of 6%, 10-year serial bonds were sold at 101. An expenditure of $320,000 was recorded in the General Fund to transfer to the Debt Service Fund resources to cover the annual interest and the first serial redemption.

(d) Serial bonds of $200,000 matured and were retired through the Debt Service Fund.

PROBLEMS

Problem 17–1.   Select the best answer for each of the following multiple-choice questions.

1. The measurement focus for governmental-type funds is the:
    a. Flow of cash.
    b. Flow of resources.
    c. Amount of gross revenue.
    d. Matching of revenues and expenditures.

2. The accounting basis for governmental-type funds is the:
    a. Accrual basis.
    b. Modified accrual basis.
    c. Cash basis.
    d. Modified cash basis.

3. Interperiod equity measurement for governmental-type funds determines whether:
    a. There is a positive cash flow.
    b. There is a profit.
    c. Current-period revenues cover cost of services provided.
    d. Actual amounts exceed budgeted amounts.

4. The proceeds of a long-term bond issue were used by a county to acquire general fixed assets. The long-term liability is recorded:
    a. Only in the General Long-Term Debt Account Group.
    b. Only in the General Fund.
    c. Both in the General Fund and in the General Long-Term Debt Account Group.
    d. In the appropriate governmental-type fund, depending on the nature of the asset involved.

(continued)

5. A general fixed asset would be found:
   a. Only in the General Fund.
   b. In any of the governmental-type funds.
   c. On the asset side of the General Long-Term Debt Account Group.
   d. In none of the governmental-type funds.

Problem 17–2.   Select the best answer for each of the following multiple-choice questions.

1. Lacking sufficient cash for operations, a city borrows money from a bank, using as collateral the expected receipts from levied property taxes. Upon receipt of cash from the bank, the General Fund would credit:
   a. Revenues (Control).
   b. Other Financing Sources (Control).
   c. Tax Anticipation Notes Payable.
   d. Taxes Receivable — Delinquent.

2. The recorded amount for uncollectible taxes was overstated. To revise the estimate during the same fiscal period, the journal entry would credit:
   a. Expenditures (Control).
   b. Revenues (Control).
   c. Allowance for Uncollectible Delinquent Taxes.
   d. Fund Balance — Unreserved, Undesignated.

3. If not expenditure-driven, a grant approved by the federal government to assist in a city's welfare program during the current year should be credited to:
   a. Revenues (Control).
   b. Fund Balance — Reserved for Welfare Programs.
   c. Fund Balance — Unreserved, Undesignated.
   d. Other Financing Sources (Control).

4. Which one of the following equations will yield the appropriations available balance in an expenditure subsidiary ledger account?
   a. Appropriations − expenditures total.
   b. Appropriations − encumbrances balance.
   c. Appropriations − expenditures total − encumbrances balance.
   d. Appropriations − expenditures total + encumbrances balance.

5. In a county's interim balance sheet for its General Fund, the amount of the Unreserved Fund Balance equals:
   a. A budgetary amount.
   b. An actual amount.
   c. A combination of budgetary and actual amounts.
   d. The excess of the revenues over expenditures for the interim period.

Problem 17–3.   Omitting amounts, prepare journal entries in the General Fund to record the following selected events:

(a) The budget is approved. The city will float a bond issue and transfer some resources to other funds. Inflows of resources are expected to exceed outflows.

(b) Property taxes are levied, of which some percentage will be uncollectible.
(c) Some of the delinquent property taxes from last year are collected. Others are written off as uncollectible, using the available allowance account.
(d) Purchase orders are approved.
(e) Payroll for the month is vouchered. Ignore payroll deductions.
(f) An invoice is vouchered for an amount less than its encumbrance.

Problem 17–4.   A summary of the General Fund transactions for the City of Whitby for the year ended December 31,19X7, is as follows:
(a) A budget was approved, showing estimated revenues of $900,000, appropriations of $875,000, transfers in of $27,000 from other funds, and required transfers of $20,000 to other funds.
(b) Property taxes in the amount of $550,000 were levied. In past years, 1% of the property taxes levied proved uncollectible.
(c) Encumbrances for $25,000 had not been liquidated by the end of 19X6. Invoices for all these items were received in 19X7 and totaled $24,000. An account Fund Balance—Reserved for Encumbrances-19X6 for $25,000 existed. The encumbrances had not been reinstated in 19X7.
(d) Collections from property taxes totaled $544,000, of which $20,000 represented collections on delinquent taxes. Delinquent taxes of $8,000 remain uncollected, on which a $3,000 allowance is carried. Remaining taxes receivable—current and taxes receivable—delinquent were converted into taxes receivable—delinquent and tax liens receivable, respectively.
(e) Purchase orders totaling $600,000 were issued. Subsequently, invoices were received amounting to $585,000 for items estimated to cost $580,000.
(f) Included in the recorded expenditures are $10,000 of supplies. An ending inventory of supplies amounted to $2,000, for which the fund balance should be reserved.
(g) A tract of land was purchased for $250,000. Payment was made from the General Fund, in whose appropriations the item had been included. The amount had not been encumbered.
(h) Whitby received $300,000 as its part of federal revenue-sharing programs. Grants-in-aid of $60,000 due from the state government are recorded. None of the grants is expenditure-driven.
(i) Required transfers of $20,000 are made to other funds.
(j) An offer was received from a land developer who will pay $380,000 for the land acquired by the city in (g). The sale is approved. The developer remits $100,000 with a note due in 90 days, bearing 8% interest.
(k) Transfers received from other funds amount to $23,000.
(l) The developer in (j) remits payment for the note plus interest.

Required:
(1) Prepare journal entries to record the General Fund transactions.
(2) Prepare closing entries for the General Fund. Create a reserve for encumbrances from the unreserved fund balance.

(continued)

(3) Prepare a statement of revenues, expenditures, and changes in fund balances, using the preferred form and incorporating budgetary items. On January 1, 19X7, the unreserved fund balance showed a debit balance (deficit) of $180,000.

Problem 17–5. The General Fund trial balance of the City of Olna at December 31, 19X2, was as follows:

Cash...	62,000	
Taxes Receivable—Delinquent....................................	46,000	
Estimated Uncollectible Taxes—Delinquent.......................		8,000
Stores Inventory...	18,000	
Vouchers Payable		28,000
Fund Balance—Reserved for Stores...............................		18,000
Fund Balance—Reserved for Encumbrances.......................		12,000
Fund Balance—Unreserved, Undesignated........................		60,000
	126,000	126,000

Collectible delinquent taxes are expected to be collected within 60 days after the end of the year. Olna uses the purchase method to account for stores inventory. The following data pertain to 19X3 General Fund operations:
(a) Budget adopted:

Revenues and other financing sources:	
Taxes	$220,000
Fines, forfeits, and penalties	80,000
Miscellaneous revenues	100,000
Share of bond issue proceeds.................	200,000
	$600,000
Expenditures and other financing uses:	
Program operations..............................	$300,000
General administration..........................	120,000
Stores	60,000
Capital outlay.......................................	80,000
Transfer to Debt Service Fund.................	20,000
	$580,000

The fund balance reserved for encumbrances is returned to the unreserved fund balance.
(b) Taxes were assessed at an amount that would result in revenues of $220,800, after deduction of 4% of the tax levy as uncollectible.
(c) Orders placed for:

Program operations.................................	$176,000
General administration.............................	80,000
Capital outlay...	60,000
	$316,000

(d) The city council designated $20,000 of the unreserved fund balance for possible appropriation for capital outlay.
(e) Cash collections and transfer:

Delinquent taxes (balance is uncollectible)	$ 38,000
Current taxes	226,000
Refund of overpayment on equipment invoice..........................	4,000
Fines, forfeits, and penalties	88,000
Miscellaneous revenues	90,000
Share of bond issue proceeds...	200,000
Transfer of discontinued capital project fund balance	18,000
	$664,000

(f) Encumbrances approved for payment:

	Estimated	Actual
Applicable to prior year but reinstated....................	$ 12,000	$ 12,000
Program operations	144,000	154,000
General administration..	84,000	80,000
Capital outlay...	62,000	62,000
	$302,000	$308,000

(g) Additional vouchers approved, not previously encumbered:

Program operations....................................	$188,000
General administration...............................	38,000
Capital outlay...	18,000
Transfer to Debt Service Fund....................	20,000
	$264,000

(h) A taxpayer overpaid 19X3 taxes by $2,000. The taxpayer applied for a $2,000 credit against 19X4 taxes. The city council granted the request. The council instructed the city controller to adjust the estimated uncollectible current taxes to cover the remaining uncollected balance.

(i) Vouchers paid amounted to $580,000.

(j) Stores inventory on December 31, 19X3, amounted to $12,000.

Required:

Using control accounts, prepare journal entries to record the foregoing data. Omit explanations.   (AICPA adapted)

Problem 17–6.   An inexperienced accounting clerk made the following summary journal entries in the General Fund of the Town of St. Francis. Using control accounts, prepare the entries that should have been made in the General Fund to record the events. Also prepare any entries needed in the account groups. Upon submission of these new entries, those of the clerk will be destroyed.

(a) Unrealized Revenues	300,000	
Estimated Bond Proceeds....................................	100,000	
Estimated Bills		380,000
Surplus..		20,000
To record the budget.		

(b) Made this memo as a record that $280,000 of property taxes were levied, but no cash was received. The Mayor said about 5% would be uncollectible.

(c) Cash... 255,000
   Bad Debts (uncollectible taxes)............................ 5,000
      Taxes Income...   260,000
            To record cash collections and no-good debt.

(d) Purchases of Supplies 19,000
   Land (for possible parking lot)............................ 40,000
   General Expenses 81,000
      Cash...   100,000
      Vouchers Payable   40,000
            To record payments made and bills owed. I'm
            expecting $32,000 of more bills to come in for
            orders placed.

(e) Supplies Still on Hand 7,000
      Surplus...   7,000
            To record year-end inventory.

(f) Cash... 94,000
      Bonds Payable   94,000
            To record sale of $100,000 of bonds due in
            5 years. Should be used to start constructing
            the parking lot.

Problem 17–7. The following schedule of general fixed assets was obtained from the records of the City of Ocala:

City of Ocala
Schedule of General Fixed Assets
December 31, 19X7

General fixed assets:
Land..	$1,000,000
Buildings	2,150,000
Improvements other than buildings............................	1,400,000
Machinery and equipment......................................	800,000
Construction in progress	250,000
Total general fixed assets	$5,600,000

Investments in general fixed assets from:
Capital projects funds:
Serial bonds...	$1,900,000
Federal grants...	800,000
State grants	450,000
General fund revenues..	1,250,000
Special revenue funds revenues................................	1,200,000
Total investment in general fixed assets.....................	$5,600,000

A summary of fixed asset transactions for 19X8 follows:

(a) Construction on the new school, a capital project started during 19X7, was completed at a total cost of $850,000, which was financed by a serial bond issue. No other construction was in progress at the beginning of 19X8.

(b) A citizen donated 400 acres of land to the city to be used as a park. The land had a fair market value of $140,000 when donated.

(c) The municipal water works constructed a new pumping plant at a cost of $120,000. The plant was financed from the water utility revenues.

(d) The fire department traded in an old fire engine and $105,000 cash for a new model. The old equipment originally had cost $65,000, and $15,000 was allowed on the trade-in. (Record in conformance with Statement 1, using the net method.)

(e) The city hall was refurbished at a cost of $40,000, which was paid from General Fund revenues. The refurbishing constituted a capital improvement.

(f) Road use taxes of $30,000 were collected by a Special Revenue Fund, of which $20,000 has been used for improvements other than buildings.

Required:

(1) Prepare journal entries only for those transactions that are to be accounted for in the General Fixed Assets Account Group. Use the city's account titles.

(2) Prepare a schedule of general fixed assets as of December 31, 19X8.

Problem 17–8. The City of Foster was incorporated on January 1, 19X2. On December 31, 19X7, a careful study of the city's records revealed the following information regarding long-term debt:

(a) General obligation bonds in the amount of $1,500,000 were authorized and issued at face value on July 1, 19X2, to finance the construction of a school. The 6% bonds pay interest semiannually on January 1 and July 1 and mature 10 years from the issuance date.

(b) Serial bonds of $1,000,000 were sold at 99 on January 1, 19X4, to help finance a new city hall and cultural center. An additional $750,000 was received from an anonymous benefactor. The 5% serial bonds were to be redeemed in annual amounts of $100,000, beginning on January 1, 19X7. A sinking fund was established on January 2, 19X4, to provide for the retirement of the serial bonds. Deposits of $70,000 were to be made on January 2 of each year, beginning in 19X4. All amounts deposited were invested immediately at a net yield of 8%.

(c) Property owners were assessed $750,000, to be paid in 5 equal annual installments, to finance construction of a storm sewer system and repaving of the affected roadways. To have cash when needed to pay for the construction, $600,000 of 5%, 5-year bonds were issued at face value by the storm sewer proprietary fund.

(d) Term bonds totaling $400,000 were sold at face value on January 1, 19X5, to finance construction. The 10-year, 5% bonds pay interest semiannually on January 1 and July 1. Each year, starting with January 1, 19X5,

$40,000 was to be set aside in a sinking fund to provide for retirement of the bonds at maturity. Any income earned by the sinking fund was to be applied to the semiannual interest payments.

Required:

(1) Prepare only the journal entries for the transactions that would be recorded in the General Long-Term Debt Account Group through December 31, 19X7.

(2) Prepare a schedule of general long-term debt for the City of Foster as of December 31, 19X7.

Problem 17–9.   Enter the January 2, 19X8 trial balance of Aubrey Township on a worksheet, using these columnar headings:

Accounts	Trial Balance Dr.	Trial Balance Cr.	Interim Entries Dr.	Interim Entries Cr.	Revenues and Expenditures Dr.	Revenues and Expenditures Cr.	Balance Sheet Dr.	Balance Sheet Cr.
Cash..	90,000							
Taxes Receivable—Delinquent........................	20,000							
Allowance for Uncollectible Delinquent Taxes...................		2,000						
Tax Liens Receivable................................	4,000							
Allowance for Uncollectible Tax Liens................		1,000						
Due from Parks Fund	2,000							
Inventory of Supplies................................	5,000							
Vouchers Payable		43,000						
Due to Utility Fund		4,000						
Deferred Revenues from Prepaid Taxes..............		15,000						
Fund Balance—Reserved for Supplies Inventory		5,000						
Fund Balance—Unreserved, Undesignated		51,000						
	121,000	121,000						

The following events occurred during the first six months of 19X8:

(a) The adopted budget showed:

Estimated expenditures.............................	$600,000
Transfers to other funds............................	27,000
Estimated revenues	635,000

(b) Property taxes of $430,000 were levied, with 2% of the gross levy considered uncollectible. The gross levy includes the prepaid taxes.

(c) Tax liens proved uncollectible. The property was foreclosed and sold for $2,500.

(d) Amounts encumbered totaled $250,000.

(e) Cash collected:

All delinquent property taxes......................	$ 20,000
Current taxes	290,000
Due from Parks Fund	1,000
Fines and penalties.................................	13,000
	$324,000

(f) Items vouchered totaled $186,000, representing $183,000 of encumbrances. Included in both were $26,000 for supplies, for which a perpetual inventory system is maintained.

(g) Cash payments:

Vouchered items..	$151,000
Nonvouchered items that were not encumbered........................	39,000
Due to Utility Fund	4,000
	$194,000

(h) Supplies inventory on June 30 was $21,000.

Required:

(1) Complete the General Fund interim worksheet for the six months ended June 30, 19X8. Ignore entries for any other fund or group. Label entries on the worksheet according to their corresponding events. Formal journal entries are not required.

(2) Prepare the interim balance sheet as of June 30, 19X8.

Problem 17-10.   You have been engaged by the Town of Ego to examine its June 30, 19X8 balance sheet. You are the first CPA to be engaged by the town, and you find that acceptable methods of municipal accounting have not been employed. The town clerk stated that the books had not been closed and presented the following trial balance of the General Fund as of June 30, 19X8:

Cash...	150,000	
Taxes Receivable—Current Year.......................................	59,200	
Allowance for Estimated Losses—Current Year Taxes Receivable..		18,000
Taxes Receivable—Prior Year...	8,000	
Allowance for Estimated Losses—Prior Year Taxes Receivable..		10,200
Estimated Revenues...	310,000	
Appropriations		348,000
Donated Land..	27,000	
Expenditures—Building Addition Constructed...................	50,000	
Expenditures—Serial Bonds Paid....................................	16,000	
Other Expenditures...	280,000	
Revenues..		354,000
Accounts Payable		126,000
Fund Balance—Unreserved, Undesignated........................		44,000
	900,200	900,200

Additional information:

(a) The estimated losses of $18,000 for current year taxes receivable were determined to be a reasonable estimate, but for the prior year they should not exceed 100%.

(b) Included in the revenues account is a credit of $27,000 representing the value of land donated by the state for construction of a municipal park.

(c) The Expenditures—Building Addition Constructed balance is the cost of an addition to the Town Hall building. This addition was constructed and completed in June, 19X8. The General Fund recorded the payment as authorized.

(d) The Expenditures—Serial Bonds Paid balance reflects the transfer to the Debt Service Fund that accounts for serial bond retirement and interest payments. Transfer of interest payments of $7,000 for this bond issue is included in Other Expenditures.

(e) Operating supplies ordered in the prior fiscal year and chargeable to that year were received and consumed in June, 19X7. The outstanding purchase orders for these supplies, which were not recorded in the accounts at June 30, 19X7, amounted to $8,800. The vendors' invoices for these supplies were charged to Other Expenditures when paid in July of 19X7.

(f) Outstanding purchase orders at June 30, 19X8, for operating supplies totaled $2,100. These purchase orders were not recorded on the books.

(g) The balance in Revenues includes credits for $20,000 for a note issued to a bank to obtain cash in anticipation of tax collections and for $1,000 for the sale of scrap iron from the town's water plant. The note was still outstanding at June 30, 19X8. Operations of the water plant are accounted for in the Water Fund, which is to receive the proceeds from the scrap sale.

(h) At year end, current taxes are to be reclassified as delinquent.

Required:

(1) Prepare the adjusting entries for the General Fund for the fiscal year ended June 30, 19X8. Account titles should be respected if acceptable, even though different.

(2) Prepare formal adjusting journal entries for the General Fixed Assets Account Group and for the General Long-Term Debt Account Group.

(AICPA adapted)

CHAPTER 18

GOVERNMENTAL ACCOUNTING: SPECIAL FUNDS

Special funds are self-balancing funds that are used to record events and to exhibit results for a specific area of responsibility. In a small town, there may not be enough activity to warrant more than a General Fund, but the larger the governmental unit and the more diverse the activities with which it is involved, the greater the necessity to introduce special funds.

SPECIAL REVENUE FUNDS

When revenue is to be devoted to a specified current operating purpose or to the acquisition of relatively minor fixed assets and when the revenue received is unrelated to the value of services rendered, its accounting is assigned to a *Special Revenue Fund*. An example of an activity that would be accounted for in a Special Revenue Fund would be the levy of a hotel room tax earmarked to promote tourism. In a Special Revenue Fund, the accounting must be designed to permit close scrutiny of activities. If more resources were produced than were anticipated, the project must not be permitted to expand beyond the original authorization, nor should money be permitted to accumulate beyond reasonable needs. However, sufficient resources should be generated to permit the activity to be completed successfully.

The desired control may be accomplished by using the same accounting procedures as those used by the General Fund. The budget, for example, is recorded by using the appropriate budgetary control accounts and their related subsidiary records. Commitments are recorded by using an encumbrance and expenditure system. Since both the accounting procedures and the financial statements for Special Revenue Funds parallel so closely those of the General Fund, they will not be illustrated.

A governmental unit having both a General Fund and a Special Revenue Fund would prepare a combined statement of revenues, expenditures, and changes in fund balances—budget and actual—for the two funds. The format would be similar to that illustrated on page 909. Its structure would show the following columnar amount headings, with totals as an optional feature:

General Fund			Special Revenue Funds			Total		
Budget	Actual	Variance—Favorable (Unfavorable)	Budget	Actual	Variance—Favorable (Unfavorable)	Budget	Actual	Variance—Favorable (Unfavorable)

CAPITAL PROJECTS FUNDS

Capital Projects Funds account for the construction of major *general* fixed assets, which excludes construction of capital facilities by proprietary funds. Each project should be accounted for separately in subsidiary records to demonstrate compliance with legal and contractual provisions.

Resources for capital projects result from transfers received from the General Fund or some other fund, proceeds of general obligation bonds, grants from another governmental unit, or special assessments levied against property owners who benefit from the project. Grants from another governmental unit and special assessments levied are recorded as revenues. Bond proceeds (because they must be repaid) and transfers from other funds (because they previously were recognized as revenue) are accounted for as other financing sources.

Statement 1, Governmental Accounting and Financial Reporting Principles, coordinated the accounting and financial reporting treatments for all governmental-type funds. As a result, it shifted emphasis for Capital Projects Funds from a project-reporting basis to an annual or other budget-period basis. When the capital projects are expected to take several years to complete and will involve large amounts of money, budgetary control is advisable. The operating budget is prepared on an *annual* basis and, therefore, includes the expected revenues, estimated other financing sources, and estimated expenditures for only the current fiscal year. The following entry records the annual budget:

Estimated Other Financing Sources (Control)*	XXX	
Estimated Revenues (Control)**	XXX	
Appropriations (Control)		XXX
Budgetary Fund Balance—Unreserved (either debited or credited)		XXX

*Resources from the General Fund or other funds and the sale of general obligation bonds.
**Resources from county, state, or federal grants and from special assessments.

When resources result from bond issuance, total proceeds are credited to the other financing sources (control) account. Any premium on the sale of the bonds should be transferred to the Debt Service Fund, reducing the amount to be accumulated in that fund to meet interest payments. When the bonds are sold at a discount, however, legal and practical restrictions prevent the opposite movement. The discount merely reduces the amount shown as other financing sources.

Adopting the annual reporting period permits the accounting for many events to be the same as for other governmental-type funds. The entries to record the budget, to record encumbrances upon issuing approved purchase orders, to reverse the encumbrance entry upon receipt of invoices, and to close accounts at year end are the same as the entries discussed in the preceding chapter for the General Fund.

Capital Projects Funds have the authority through annually approved budgets to continue expenditures within prescribed limits until a project is completed. Although a project may not be completed at the end of a fiscal period, typical closing entries are recorded. Annual closing permits the actual activity to be compared with the legally adopted annual operating budget. Also, in the closing process, the credit to Expenditures (Control) provides the amount of capitalizable expenditures to be recorded in the General Fixed Assets Account Group for Construction in Progress.

The actual cost of a capital project probably will differ from its estimated cost. A deficiency usually is covered by a transfer from the General Fund. If an excess of resources exists upon completion of the project, it generally is returned to the General Fund or to the Debt Service Fund. Such a transfer is called a *residual equity transfer* and is reported as an addition to or deduction from the beginning fund balance of governmental-type funds. Upon completion of the project, it is customary to withhold part of the payment until final inspection and approval. The liability is recorded in the account Contracts Payable—Retained Percentage.

To illustrate accounting for Capital Projects Funds, assume that the City of Berryville plans to build a $300,000 addition to its municipal auditorium. The project will begin in 19X1 and is to be completed in 19X2. The following entries record the events that occur during construction:

Event	Entry		
The project budget is $300,000, to be financed by a general bond issue. The 19X1 operating budget is based on 1/3 of the work being completed that year. The city uses an other financing sources (control) account.	Estimated Other Financing Sources (Control)	300,000	
	Appropriations (Control)		100,000
	Budgetary Fund Balance— Unreserved		200,000
A $300,000, 8% general bond issue is floated at 101.	Cash...	303,000	
	Other Financing Sources (Control)		303,000
The bond premium is transferred to the Debt Service Fund.	Other Financing Uses (Control)	3,000	
	Cash...		3,000
A contract is signed for the auditorium construction at an estimated cost of $270,000.	Encumbrances (Control)	270,000	
	Budgetary Fund Balance—Reserved for Encumbrances		270,000

Event	Entry		

The architect's bill for $10,650 is received, of which $7,650 is paid. Upon final building approval, the balance is due. The item was not encumbered.

Expenditures (Control).........................	10,650		
Cash...		7,650	
Vouchers Payable............................		3,000	

A partial billing is received from the contractor for $60,000, equal to the amount encumbered for these items. The account Contracts Payable is credited for the liability to the principal contractor. (If the amount of equivalent encumbrance is not specified, the encumbrance entry is reversed for the amount of the billing.)

Expenditures (Control).........................	60,000		
Contracts Payable		60,000	
Budgetary Fund Balance — Reserved			
for Encumbrances........................	60,000		
Encumbrances (Control)		60,000	

The contractor is paid $60,000.

Contracts Payable	60,000		
Cash...		60,000	

Books for 19X1 are closed. The credit to Expenditures (Control) is the basis for the following entry in the General Fixed Assets Account Group:

Budgetary Fund Balance — Unreserved ..	200,000		
Appropriations (Control).......................	100,000		
Estimated Other Financing Sources			
(Control)		300,000	

Construction in		Other Financing Sources (Control)	300,000
Progress.............. 70,650		Expenditures (Control)......................	70,650
Investment in		Fund Balance — Unreserved,	
General Fixed		Undesignated	229,350
Assets — Capital			
Projects Funds...... 70,650			

Budgetary Fund Balance — Reserved			
for Encumbrances........................	210,000		
Encumbrances (Control)		210,000	

A reserve is established equal to the unexpended encumbrances at year end.

Fund Balance — Unreserved,			
Undesignated.............................	210,000		
Fund Balance — Reserved for			
Encumbrances............................		210,000	

At the beginning of 19X2, the reserve is returned to the unreserved fund balance.

Fund Balance — Reserved for			
Encumbrances............................	210,000		
Fund Balance — Unreserved,			
Undesignated.............................		210,000	

The encumbrances are reinstated.

Encumbrances (Control)	210,000		
Budgetary Fund Balance — Reserved			
for Encumbrances........................		210,000	

The operating budget for 19X2 is recorded; completion is estimated to cost an additional $215,000, including the amount encumbered in the previous year.

Budgetary Fund Balance — Unreserved ..	215,000		
Appropriations (Control)....................		215,000	

The contract is completed in 19X2. Additional cost is $227,000, of which $10,000 is withheld in a separate account until final inspection and approval.

Expenditures (Control)..........................	227,000		
Contracts Payable		217,000	
Contracts Payable — Retained			
Percentage		10,000	
Budgetary Fund Balance — Reserved			
for Encumbrances........................	210,000		
Encumbrances (Control)		210,000	

Excluding the retained percentage, the contractor is paid.

Contracts Payable	217,000		
Cash...		217,000	

Event	Entry		
Books for 19X2 are closed. The credit to Expenditures (Control) is the basis for the following entry in the General Fixed Assets Account Group:	Appropriations (Control)......................	215,000	
	Budgetary Fund Balance— Unreserved..............................		215,000
Buildings 297,650	Fund Balance—Unreserved,		
Construction in Progress.............. 70,650	Undesignated............................	227,000	
Investment in General Fixed Assets—Capital Projects Funds...... 227,000	Expenditures (Control).....................		227,000

CAPITAL IMPROVEMENT SPECIAL ASSESSMENTS

Capital Projects Funds include in their domain the recording of major capital improvements, such as sewers, that primarily benefit a limited number of property owners against whom special assessments are levied. The initiative for such projects often is taken by the property owners who request the improvement. However, authorization must be approved through appropriate channels. Once the project is approved, the estimates for the budget period (not the total project budget) are recorded.

To ease the burden and promote successful collection from property owners, collections of special assessments are arranged on an installment basis. Initial costs are covered by collection of the current installment, which may be recorded directly in the Capital Projects Fund. However, payments to contractors cannot await collections of the deferred installments. To meet construction costs, a bond issue often is floated, with proceeds approximately equal to the amount of the deferred installments. In the Capital Project Fund, bond proceeds are credited to Other Financing Sources (Control). Any premium generally is transferred to the Debt Service Fund by a debit to Other Financing Uses (Control).

When the collections of the deferred special assessments are to be used to repay the related debt, they are accounted for in a Debt Service Fund. Assessments currently due are segregated from those due in future fiscal periods, as revenues and deferred revenues are recorded in the Debt Service Fund:

Special Assessments Receivable—Current	100,000	
Special Assessments Receivable—Deferred..................	400,000	
Revenues (Control)...		100,000
Deferred Revenues		400,000

Details of the assessments are entered in a subsidiary ledger, where the levy against each owner and its collections are indicated. At the end of the fiscal year, a deferred installment due within the next year is reclassified as revenue, and the deferred receivable is reclassified as current. In the illustration, if annual installments are $100,000, the reclassification entries are:

Special Assessments Receivable — Current	100,000	
Special Assessments Receivable — Deferred...............		100,000
Deferred Revenues	100,000	
Revenues (Control)...		100,000

When the bonds are to be repaid from the collection of the related special assessments, the governmental unit usually is obligated in some way in case of default by the property owners. In this situation, the entry in the General Long-Term Debt Account Group reveals the commitment:

Amount To Be Provided for Payment of Special Assessment Debt....	XXX	
Special Assessment Debt with Governmental Commitment.........		XXX

In some cases, the governmental unit has the primary responsibility for repayment of the bonds. In these situations, they are recorded in the General Long-Term Debt Account Group with the same entry used to record any other general obligation debt:

Amount To Be Provided for Payment of Special Assessment Debt....	XXX	
Special Assessment Bonds Payable..		XXX

In the rare case in which the governmental unit is not liable in any manner whatsoever, the special assessment bond liability is not shown in the General Long-Term Debt Account Group, but should appear in the notes to the financial statements. Debt servicing is reported in an Agency Fund, rather than in a Debt Service Fund. Accounting for the construction phase in a Capital Projects Fund is the same as for other capital projects.

The construction phase of the project is recorded in the Capital Projects Funds, using an encumbrance system and the other accounts typically used in recording a capital improvement. At year end, the capitalizable costs of an unfinished special assessment project are entered in the General Fixed Assets Account Group:

Construction in Progess	XXX	
Investment in General Fixed Assets — Capital Projects Funds		
(Special Assessments)		XXX

Annual closing of books is recommended. The completion of the special assessment project is recorded in the General Fixed Assets Account Group with the customary entry:

(Proper Fixed Asset Account)	XXX	
Construction in Progress		XXX
Investment in General Fixed Assets — Capital Projects Funds		
(Special Assessments)		XXX

When a governmental unit has more than one capital project, combining financial statements are prepared. In these statements, a separate column is provided for each project. To show the structure of such statements,

Illustration 18–1 is a combining balance sheet for the City of Berryville's Capital Projects Funds. It presents the auditorium project for which entries were provided, plus another project for the installation of sewers under a special assessment plan.

The combining statement of revenues, expenditures, and changes in fund balances will show as revenues those resources obtained by special assessment, by grant, or from some other governmental unit. Transfers from other funds within the same governmental unit or proceeds of a bond issue are presented as other financing sources. The form used in Illustration 18–2 on page 942 is the one currently preferred, with the final amount representing the total of both reserved and unreserved fund balances.

Illustration 18–1

City of Berryville
Capital Projects Funds
Combining Balance Sheet
December 31, 19X1

Assets	Municipal Auditorium	Sewer Special Assessment	Total
Cash..	$232,350	$102,000	$334,350
Special assessments receivable.........		160,000	160,000
Investments		40,000	40,000
Total assets....................................	$232,350	$302,000	$534,350
Liabilities and Fund Balances			
Vouchers payable	$ 3,000	$157,000	$160,000
Retained percentage	–0–	50,000	50,000
Total liabilities.................................	$ 3,000	$207,000	$210,000
Fund balances:			
Reserved for encumbrances...........	$210,000	$ 90,000	$300,000
Unreserved, undesignated.............	19,350	5,000	24,350
Total fund balances.......................	$229,350	$ 95,000	$324,350
Total liabilities and fund balances......	$232,350	$302,000	$534,350

DEBT SERVICE FUNDS

As discussed in Chapter 17, the function of the General Long-Term Debt Account Group is to provide a record of the unredeemed principal of long-term liabilities incurred to acquire general fixed assets. Closely related to this account group are *Debt Service Funds*, whose primary function is to account for

City of Berryville
Capital Projects Funds
Combining Statement of Revenues, Expenditures, and Changes in Fund
Balances For the Year Ended December 31, 19X1

	Municipal Auditorium	Sewer Special Assessment	Total
Revenues......................................	–0–	$118,000	$118,000
Expenditures................................	$ 70,650	157,000	227,650
Excess (deficiency) of revenues over expenditures......................	($ 70,650)	($ 39,000)	($109,650)
Other financing sources (uses):			
Proceeds of bonds.....................	$300,000	$196,000	$496,000
Payments to Debt Service............	–0–	(62,000)	(62,000)
Total other financing sources (uses).....................................	$300,000	$134,000	$434,000
Excess (deficiency) of revenues and other sources over expenditures and other uses........	$229,350	$ 95,000	$324,350
Fund balances at beginning of year	–0–	–0–	–0–
Fund balances at end of year..........	$229,350	$ 95,000	$324,350

cash accumulation to cover the payment of principal and interest on those obligations shown in the General Long-Term Debt Account Group.

As in other governmental-type funds, the modified accrual basis is used for recognizing revenues, other financing sources, and expenditures in Debt Service Funds. Interest on general long-term debt is an item for which the accrual basis is modified. For example, assume that a governmental unit has a fiscal year ending June 30, with interest on long-term debt to be paid on July 31. Since expenditures are authorized by appropriations, it is essential that expenditures be recorded in the same period as the appropriations. Thus, the interest will not be accrued on June 30, because the appropriation to cover the interest will not be provided until the budget for the next period is recorded on July 1.

The most popular method of raising long-term resources is by the issuance of serial bonds, which are redeemed in a series of installments. Term bonds, whose total face value becomes due at one time, are now extremely rare. When serial bonds are issued, there is no substantial accumulation of cash in a sinking fund for redemption of the principal, unless the first series will not mature for several fiscal periods and contributions for retirement are to begin immediately. Instead, the budget for the year of payment provides for interest and principal redemption. In Debt Service Funds, an entry to record the budget seldom is used, because expenditures for principal and interest are known and there is no need to compare them with budgetary amounts.

Resources to cover expenditures may come from several sources. A portion of a property tax levy may be authorized to be recorded directly in a Debt Service Fund. The entries would be similar to those made in the General Fund to record a tax levy. The net amount of taxes estimated to be collected is credited to Revenues (Control), since the resources are received from outsiders. Transfers received by the Debt Service Fund from funds that already have recorded the resources as revenues are credited to Other Financing Sources (Control). As discussed in Chapter 17, this procedure prevents Revenues (Control) from being credited in two funds for the same resources — once in the originating fund (in this case, the General Fund) and again in the recipient fund (in this case, a Debt Service Fund).

Prior to redemption, the bond liability for unmatured general debt is not recorded in a Debt Service Fund, but is entered in the General Long-Term Debt Account Group. However, when a serial bond matures and when payment of interest is due, the following entry is recorded in a Debt Service Fund:

Expenditures (Control)	XXX	
Matured Bonds Payable		XXX
Matured Interest Payable		XXX

An entry to record payment of these matured items then would be made. Simultaneously, an entry to record reduction of the bond principal is made in the General Long-Term Debt Account Group. Many governmental units employ the services of financial institutions to conduct actual payments for interest and serial redemptions. When cash is released to such a fiscal agent, the account debited is Cash with Fiscal Agent. Upon notification by the agent that actual payments have been made, the Debt Service Fund entry is:

Matured Bonds Payable	XXX	
Matured Interest Payable	XXX	
Cash with Fiscal Agent		XXX

The following entries would be made in a Debt Service Fund for the indicated events that relate to a serial bond issue. As demonstrated by these entries, the interplay between funds and groups is especially prevalent in accounting for general bond issues.

Event	Entry		
An 8%, $300,000 general serial bond issue for bridge construction is sold at 101. The premium is transferred from the Capital Projects Fund to the Debt Service Fund. (An entry also is made in the Capital Projects Fund and the General Long-Term Debt Account Group.)	Cash	3,000	
	Other Financing Sources (Control)		3,000

Event	Entry		
Of the property taxes, $50,000 is levied specifically to cover debt service on these bonds; 1% of the taxes levied is estimated to be uncollectible.	Taxes Receivable — Current	50,000	
	Allowance for Uncollectible Current Taxes		500
	Revenues (Control)		49,500
All property taxes are collected, except for $400 that is written off. The difference between estimated and actual uncollectible taxes is recorded in Revenues (Control).	Cash	49,600	
	Allowance for Uncollectible Current Taxes	500	
	Taxes Receivable — Current		50,000
	Revenues (Control)		100
The fund receives $7,000 of its $9,000 share of state gasoline taxes, the balance to be received late in the next period.	Cash	7,000	
	Due from State	2,000	
	Revenues (Control)		7,000
	Deferred Revenues		2,000
A transfer of $30,000 is received from the General Fund.	Cash	30,000	
	Other Financing Sources (Control)		30,000
Cash is transmitted to a fiscal agent for payment of the first $60,000 of maturing bonds and $24,000 of interest due on the last day of the fiscal period.	Cash with Fiscal Agent	84,000	
	Cash		84,000
The matured bonds and interest are recorded.	Expenditures (Control)	84,000	
	Matured Bonds Payable		60,000
	Matured Interest Payable		24,000
The fiscal agent reports that all payments have been made, except for $1,000 of interest.	Matured Bonds Payable	60,000	
	Matured Interest Payable	23,000	
	Cash with Fiscal Agent		83,000
Books are closed at year end.	Revenues (Control)	56,600	
	Other Financing Sources (Control)	33,000	
	Expenditures (Control)		84,000
	Fund Balance — Reserved for Debt Service		5,600

Assets transferred to a Debt Service Fund must be used to redeem bonds or to pay interest. There are no unreserved assets. Any excess of assets over liabilities is reserved for debt service. Therefore, at year end, the accounts are closed to Fund Balance — Reserved for Debt Service, rather than to an unreserved fund balance.

Debt Service Funds employ two financial statements for reporting purposes: a balance sheet and a statement of revenues, expenditures, and changes in fund balances. Illustration 18–3 is a combining balance sheet for Vernon Town. This balance sheet has a column for the Bridge Construction Debt Service Fund, for which the entries have been presented, and a column for a Health Center Debt Service Fund.

The notes to the financial statements would explain that the money to cover the final matured bonds and interest for the Health Center Debt Service Fund has been forwarded to a fiscal agent. Once word is received that these payments have been made, that fund will be closed.

The combining statement of revenues, expenditures, and changes in fund balances for Vernon Town's Debt Service Funds is shown in Illustration 18–4 on page 946. This statement itemizes revenues by source and ex-

Illustration 18–3

Vernon Town
Debt Service Funds
Combining Balance Sheet
December 31, 19X2

Assets	Bridge Construction	Health Center	Total
Cash...	$5,600	—	$ 5,600
Cash with fiscal agents........................	1,000	$102,000	103,000
Due from state	2,000	—	2,000
Total assets.....................................	$8,600	$102,000	$110,600
Liabilities and Fund Balance			
Liabilities:			
Matured interest payable..................	$1,000	$ 2,000	$ 3,000
Matured bonds payable....................	—	100,000	100,000
Deferred revenue............................	2,000	—	2,000
Fund balance:			
Reserved for debt service.................	5,600	—	5,600
Total liabilities and fund balance....	$8,600	$102,000	$110,600

penditures by nature, and it summarizes the causes of changes in fund balances during the period.

PROPRIETARY FUNDS

The funds discussed to this point have been governmental-type funds. The second category of funds—*proprietary funds*—now will be discussed. By definition, the term "proprietary" means pertaining to a proprietor and implies that users of goods or services will be charged on the basis of consumption, similar to the practice in private industries. Usually charges are set to recover as much as possible of the total cost, including depreciation. Whatever is not recovered must be subsidized.

All proprietary funds are involved with providing goods or services. If they serve the general public, their activities are accounted for in *Enterprise Funds*. If they serve other departments of the same governmental unit or a different governmental unit, their activities are accounted for in *Internal Service Funds*.

The accounting emphasis for governmental-type funds is on available, spendable resources and their expenditure, employing the modified accrual basis of accounting. The accounting for proprietary funds, however, emphasizes expenses, rather than expenditures, and is similar to that for a private enterprise. Proprietary funds measure net income, focusing on the total cost

Illustration 18–4

Vernon Town
Debt Service Funds
Combining Statement of Revenues, Expenditures,
and Changes in Fund Balances
For the Year Ended December 31, 19X2

	Bridge Construction	Health Center	Total
Revenues:			
Taxes	$49,600	—	$ 49,600
Intergovernmental[1]	7,000	$ 46,000	53,000
Miscellaneous	—	3,000	3,000
Total revenues........................	$56,600	$ 49,000	$105,600
Expenditures:			
Principal retirement	$60,000	$100,000	$160,000
Interest charges...........................	24,000	2,000	26,000
Total expenditures....................	$84,000	$102,000	$186,000
Excess (deficiency) of revenues over expenditures..............................	($27,400)	($ 53,000)	($ 80,400)
Other financing sources (uses):			
Operating transfers in	33,000	—	33,000
Excess (deficiency) of revenues and other financing sources over expenditures...............................	$ 5,600	($ 53,000)	($ 47,400)
Fund balances at beginning of year...	—	53,000	53,000
Fund balances at end of year...........	$ 5,600	–0–	$ 5,600

of services and the amounts of cost recovered by revenue. Proprietary funds are accounted for with a capital maintenance measurement focus, using the accrual basis of accounting. They account for their own assets (including fixed assets and depreciation) and liabilities (including long-term debt), and they differentiate between contributed and earned equity, just as a corporation would.

One of the rare times that amounts due from another fund are treated as revenue is in the case of proprietary funds furnishing goods or services to other funds. For example, a computer center accounted for in an Internal Service Fund may provide service to the General Fund. This transaction is quasi-external, because the item would have been treated as revenue if it had been billed to an outsider. Therefore, the billing represents revenue to the Internal Service Fund. Such treatment is necessary for the proper determination of a proprietary fund's operation and for rate setting. If the fund receiving the goods or services is proprietary, it debits an expense account; if it is a governmental-type, it debits an expenditures account.

---

[1]Intergovernmental revenues are amounts from other governmental units.

ENTERPRISE FUNDS

Enterprise Funds account for goods or services provided by a governmental unit to the general public. The user is charged for these goods or services, based on consumption. For example, the operations of utilities, public housing, public parking, and airports would be covered by Enterprise Funds. These funds continue indefinitely and are self-supporting, depending upon the amounts charged to cover part or all of the costs of operation, debt service, and maintenance of capital facilities. Net income is accumulated in an account labeled Unreserved Retained Earnings. To remain self-sustaining, the fund must deduct depreciation expense in the determination of net income. Losses eventually would require either an increase in charges or a contribution from some other source.

At the inception of an Enterprise Fund (or Internal Service Fund), capital must be provided either by issuance of long-term debt or by transfer from some other source, such as a municipality's General Fund. In the latter case, the amount received is credited to an account labeled Capital Contribution from Municipality. Note the similarity to the paid-in capital account of a corporation. As a measure of original asset sources, the contribution remains in the fund indefinitely or until the fund is terminated. If operations are profitable and arrangements specify that profits shall be shared with the General Fund, an amount analogous to a dividend is charged against Unreserved Retained Earnings.

Contributed capital also is increased when capital assets financed by special assessments are acquired by an Enterprise Fund. When special assessments are levied, instead of crediting Revenues (Control) as is done in governmental-type funds, Contributed Capital from Special Assessments is credited. Upon acquisition or completion of the capital asset, its cost is capitalized in the Enterprise Fund.

An Enterprise Fund's operational effectiveness may be monitored in part by the net income or net loss figure. As in commercial operations, budgets are prepared. However, budgets are not recorded formally in the accounts, perhaps because the fund's self-supporting nature requires a high degree of operational freedom, but more likely because fixed budgetary amounts would be of much less value when there is a variable demand by the public for goods and services.

Control accounts for revenues and expenses commonly are used, with details in supporting records. In accounting for revenues, two control accounts are used: Operating Revenues (Control) for charges for services and Nonoperating Revenues (Control) for grants received, interest and rent earned, or other miscellaneous financial revenues. A similar breakdown is used to account for expenses: Operating Expenses (Control) for expenses directly related to goods or services produced, such as salaries, depreciation, heat, light, materials, and taxes, and Nonoperating Expenses (Control) for financial expenses, such as bond interest. Except for the use of these four nominal control accounts, journal entries for revenues and expenses, including adjustments, are much the same as in private enterprise accounting.

One of the unusual features of accounting for Enterprise Funds is the introduction of restricted assets and the current liabilities to be paid therewith. *Restricted assets* are assets (cash and investments) upon which some limitation has been imposed that makes them available only for designated purposes. Examples of restricted assets are amounts of customer deposits subject to refund and cash turned over to a fiscal agent for payment of bond interest or principal redemption.

Restricted assets and their related current liabilities must be recorded in specially designated accounts so that the segregation of these items is ensured. For example, if a water utility receives deposits covering meter installations for customers and these deposits are refundable, they would be recorded as follows:

Restricted Assets—Customers' Deposits Cash.......................... XXX
    Customers' Deposits Payable from Restricted Assets..............   XXX

If the deposits are invested, the entry to record the investment would be:

Restricted Assets—Customers' Deposits Investments............... XXX
    Restricted Assets—Customers' Deposits Cash......................   XXX

When a computer is used, it may be programmed to earmark the restricted accounts. In this case, the restriction in the account title may be omitted.

The appearance of restricted assets and their related current liabilities is especially common when an Enterprise Fund is accounting for a public utility. A major source of funding for utilities is the sale of revenue bonds, which are floated to permit the construction of, or an addition to, a facility. Since payments for these bonds depend on the existence of operating income, the bond indenture usually includes several restrictions. For example, it may require that the bond proceeds be expended only for construction, making the proceeds a restricted asset. The following entry would be required:

Restricted Assets—Revenue Bond Construction Cash XXX
    Revenue Bonds Payable...   XXX

As amounts are committed, the liability would be identified as payable from a restricted asset:

Construction in Process... XXX
    Construction Contracts Payable from Restricted Assets   XXX

Payment of the liability would be recorded with the following entry:

Construction Contracts Payable from Restricted Assets XXX
    Restricted Assets—Revenue Bond Construction Cash   XXX

If a municipality received approval to expand its utility facilities by issuing a combination of special assessment bonds and revenue bonds, the following entry would be required in an Enterprise Fund:

Restricted Assets — Construction Cash	XXX	
Special Assessment Bonds Payable.....................................		XXX
Revenue Bonds Payable...		XXX

Note that the redemption and servicing of both the revenue bonds and the special assessment bonds is the financial responsibility of the utility Enterprise Fund. Therefore, neither liability appears in the General Long-Term Debt Account Group or in the Debt Service Funds. As pointed out in Statement No. 6 by the GASB:

> *Special assessment debt for which the government is obligated in some manner . . . should be reported in the General Long-Term Debt Account Group, except for the portion, if any, that is a direct obligation of an enterprise fund, or that is expected to be repaid from operating revenues of an enterprise fund.* [2]

The balance sheet of a commercial utility may begin with its fixed assets because they are extremely important. However, the combining of the balance sheet of a government-owned utility with the balance sheets of other governmental funds is simplified if the customary sequence is followed. The balance sheet for the Clermont County Water and Sewer Fund, in Illustration 18–5 on pages 950 and 951, adheres to such a presentation, with restricted assets following the regular current assets and preceding the fixed assets. Note also that current liabilities are segregated to show amounts payable from regular current assets and amounts payable from restricted assets.

Most revenue bonds for enterprise funds are serial bonds that require the earmarking of monies for the payment of interest and for the establishment of a fund for principal redemption. These resources would be restricted assets, while the current interest and serial installment payable would be recorded as current liabilities payable from restricted assets. To further protect the bondholder, at least psychologically, many serial revenue bonds require that unreserved retained earnings be restricted in an amount equal to the excess of restricted assets related to the bond issue over the current liability for interest and principal. If the amounts in the Water and Sewer Fund balance sheet (Illustration 18–5) are compared with assumed amounts at the end of the previous year, the additional amount to be reserved would be determined as follows:

---

[2]Statement 6, *Accounting and Financial Reporting for Special Assessments* (Stamford: Governmental Accounting Standards Board, January, 1987), 7.

	Dec. 31, 19X2	Dec. 31, 19X1 (assumed)
Restricted assets related to revenue bonds:		
Cash with fiscal agent for bond service.........	$ 80,444	$ 87,200
Revenue bond debt service cash	5,000	3,000
Revenue bond fund	124,155	93,975
Total	$209,599	$184,175
Current liabilities related to revenue bonds:		
Accrued revenue bond interest payable.........	$ 32,444	$ 37,200
Matured revenue bonds payable	48,000	50,000
Total	$ 80,444	$ 87,200
Excess of bond-related restricted assets over bond-related current liabilities	$129,155	$ 96,975

Illustration 18–5

Clermont
Water and
Balance
December

Assets

Current assets:		
Cash..	$ 257,036	
Receivables (net)	33,480	
Inventories and prepaid expenses	24,230	
Total current assets..		$ 314,746
Restricted assets:		
Cash with fiscal agent for bond service......................................	$ 80,444	
Revenue bond construction cash...	17,760	
Revenue bond debt service cash	5,000	
Revenue bond fund:		
Cash.. $ 10,355		
Investments 113,800	124,155	
Customers' deposits:		
Investments .... $ 63,000		
Interest receivable on investments 650	63,650	
Total restricted assets		291,009
Property, plant, and equipment:		
Land..	$ 211,100	
Buildings .... $ 447,700		
Less accumulated depreciation 90,718	356,982	
Improvements other than buildings....................... $3,887,901		
Less accumulated depreciation 348,944	3,538,957	
Machinery and equipment..................................... $1,841,145		
Less accumulated depreciation 201,138	1,640,007	
Construction in process...	22,713	
Total property, plant, and equipment................		5,769,759
Total assets...		$6,375,514

If the bond indenture requires that the reserves be increased to equal the bond-related restricted assets that are not offset by bond-related current liabilities, the following entry becomes necessary:

Retained Earnings—Unreserved ($129,155 − $96,975).......	32,180	
Retained Earnings—Reserved for Bond Debt Service ($5,000 − $3,000)		2,000
Retained Earnings—Reserved for Bond Retirement ($124,155 − $93,975)		30,180

The statement of revenues, expenses (not expenditures), and changes in retained earnings for an Enterprise Fund, as shown in Statement 1, focuses on total retained earnings, both reserved and unreserved. Such a

---

Enterprise Fund

County
Sewer Fund
Sheet
31, 19X2

Liabilities and Fund Equity

Liabilities:		
Current liabilities (payable from current assets):		
Vouchers payable	$ 195,071	
Accrued wages and taxes payable.......................	2,870	
Construction contracts payable	8,347	$ 206,288
Current liabilities (payable from restricted assets):		
Construction contracts payable	$ 17,760	
Accrued revenue bond interest payable	32,444	
Matured revenue bonds payable	48,000	
Customer deposits..	63,000	161,204
Total current liabilities......................................		$ 367,492
Long-term liabilities:		
Revenue bonds payable		2,448,000
Total liabilities...		$2,815,492
Fund equity:		
Contributed capital:		
Contribution from municipality		$1,392,666
Retained earnings:		
Reserved for bond debt service..........................	$ 5,000	
Reserved for bond retirement	124,155	
Total reserved	$ 129,155	
Unreserved..	2,038,201	
Total retained earnings......................................		2,167,356
Total fund equity		$3,560,022
Total liabilities and fund equity		$6,375,514

statement for the Clermont County Water and Sewer Fund is shown in Illustration 18–6.

Illustration 18–6
Enterprise Fund

Clermont County
Water and Sewer Fund
Statement of Revenues, Expenses, and Changes in Retained Earnings
For the Year Ended December 31, 19X2

Operating revenues:		
Charges for services		$ 727,150
Operating expenses:		
Personal services (salaries and fees)...................	$306,100	
Materials and supplies	106,580	
Depreciation..	103,600	
Heat, light, power, and taxes.............................	47,900	
Total operating expenses..................................		564,180
Operating income..		$ 162,970
Nonoperating revenues (expenses):		
Operating grants	$ 5,000	
Interest revenue	2,830	
Rental income...	1,000	
Interest expense	(92,988)	
Total nonoperating revenues (expenses).............		(84,158)
Net income...		$ 78,812
Retained earnings at beginning of year (reserved and unreserved)...		2,088,544
Retained earnings at end of year (reserved and unreserved)...		$2,167,356

In 1989, the GASB issued Statement No. 9, *Reporting Cash Flows of Proprietary and Nonexpendable Trust Funds and Governmental Entities That Use Proprietary Fund Accounting.* It stipulated that a statement of cash flows for such funds should show movements of combined unrestricted and restricted cash and cash equivalents for the reported period, segregated into four categories:

1. Cash flows from operating activities, which would include cash received from sales of goods or services and cash paid to suppliers, employees, and providers of services.
2. Cash flows from noncapital financing activities, which would include proceeds from borrowings not related to capital asset acquisition and repayments thereon, as well as operating grants or transfers not related to capital asset acquisition.

3. Cash flows from capital and related financing activities to acquire or dispose of capital assets, which would include grants or transfers related to capital asset acquisition.
4. Cash flows from investing activities.

The statement of cash flows should report net cash provided or used for each of the four categories. This objective can be accomplished by using the direct method, as shown in Illustration 18–7A for a hypothetical electric utility. The GASB recommends the use of this method. In addition, a reconciliation of net *operating* income to net cash flow from operating activities (Category 1) must be provided in a separate schedule to accompany the cash flows statement or in the notes to the financial statements. Such a reconciliation is presented in Illustration 18–7B on page 954.

Illustration 18–7A

Zenith City Electric Utility Fund
Statement of Cash Flows for the Year Ended June 30, 19X9
Increase (Decrease) in Cash and Cash Equivalents

Cash flows from operating activities:		
Cash received from customers..............................	$456,000	
Cash paid to suppliers and employees...................	(400,300)	
Other operating revenues.....................................	7,500	
Net cash provided by operating activities............		$ 63,200
Cash flows from noncapital financing activities:		
Net repayments under revolving loan arrangement.	($ 10,700)	
Operating grants received	50,000	
Operating transfers out to other funds...................	(37,500)	
Net cash provided by noncapital financing activities..		1,800
Cash flows from capital and related financing activities:		
Proceeds from sale of capital bonds......................	$125,000	
Principal and interest paid on capital bonds...........	(100,000)	
Acquisition and construction of capital assets.........	(75,000)	
Proceeds from sale of equipment.........................	70,000	
Net cash provided by capital and related financing activities..		20,000
Cash flows from investing activities:		
Purchases of investment securities.......................	($ 62,500)	
Proceeds from sale and maturities of securities......	36,500	
Interest and dividends received on investments......	3,000	
Net cash used in investing activities...................		(23,000)
Net increase in cash and cash equivalents		$ 62,000
Cash and cash equivalents at beginning of year		100,000
Cash and cash equivalents at end of year		$162,000

Illustration 18–7B

Zenith City Electric Utility Fund
Reconciliation of Net Operating Income to Net Cash Provided by
Operating Activities
For the Year Ended June 30, 19X9

Net operating income (loss)......................................		($ 49,800)
Adjustments to reconcile net operating income to net cash provided by operating activities:		
Depreciation..	$122,000	
Provision for uncollectible accounts......................	1,000	
Changes in assets and liabilities:		
Increase in accounts receivable.........................	(15,000)	
Decrease in inventory	2,000	
Decrease in prepaid expenses...........................	500	
Increase in accounts payable	2,500	
Total adjustments...		113,000
Net cash provided by operating activities...................		$ 63,200

INTERNAL SERVICE FUNDS

Internal Service Funds are similar to Enterprise Funds in that they are self-sustaining, depend on amounts charged for services rendered, and receive start-up resources. The difference is that users of their services are other departments of the same governmental unit or other governmental units. A computer center, a central purchasing department, or a central garage would be accounted for in Internal Service Funds.

Since they do not deal with the general public and usually do not issue bonds that result in restrictions, Internal Service Funds do not have restricted assets. Their accounting procedures resemble those for a commercial business even more closely than do those of Enterprise Funds. Internal Service Funds must recover their costs, including depreciation, or be subsidized. Therefore, they maintain records of fixed assets and use the accrual basis of accounting. Budgetary accounts are not used, although budget forecasts facilitate the calculation of overhead rates to be applied in determining charges.

The financial statements of Internal Service Funds consist of the balance sheet, the statement of revenues, expenses, and changes in retained earnings, and the statement of cash flows. These statements closely resemble commercial financial statements and will not be illustrated.

FIDUCIARY FUNDS: TRUST AND AGENCY FUNDS

As mentioned in Chapter 17, fiduciary funds account for resources for which a governmental unit is acting as a trustee or agent. This category of funds includes Expendable Trust Funds, Nonexpendable Trust Funds, Pension Trust Funds, and Agency Funds.

TRUST FUNDS

Assets held by a governmental unit that functions as a trustee may be donated by a corporation or by an individual for the educational or cultural benefit of the community. The accounting for these assets and the operation of the Trust Fund depend on the document that created the fund. If both the assets contributed (the principal) and the earnings may be expended, the fund is an *Expendable Trust Fund*, which is accounted for in much the same manner as a General Fund, using a modified accrual basis. Budgetary accounts are essential for monitoring expenditures of the principal and income. Since they are similar to governmental-type funds, Expendable Trust Funds will not be reviewed.

If earnings but not principal may be expended, the fund is a *Nonexpendable Trust Fund*. Nonexpendable Trust Funds, frequently referred to as Endowment Funds, result from the acceptance of assets that are invested to produce earnings for a designated purpose. For example, a donor might contribute real property and investments, designating that earnings be used to enhance a city's art collection. Depreciation on real property included in the principal of the trust would be recognized in order to protect that principal. It also would be essential to differentiate between principal items and revenue items. The most complete segregation will result if two Endowment Funds are established—one to record principal items and another to record revenues and expenditures. The procedure becomes especially useful if bonds are purchased at a premium as part of the trust fund. Cash flows and available revenue are not identical because of the amortization of the premium. The segregation process protects the principal.

When donors establish a nonexpendable trust, the assets donated are credited to Revenues (Control) in the Endowment Principal Fund. Revenues earned also are credited to Revenues (Control). A liability to the Endowment Revenues Fund for the period's net income is established by debiting Other Financing Uses (Control). In the closing process, that portion of Revenues (Control) representing donated assets is closed into Fund Balance—Reserved for Endowments, emphasizing that principal assets are to remain intact.

The only source of assets for the Endowment Revenues Fund is the net earnings transferred from the Endowment Principal Fund. These earnings are credited to Other Financing Sources (Control). Distributions of such revenues are recorded as expenditures. In the year-end closing process of the Endowment Revenues Fund, any difference between the amounts received from the principal fund and total expenditures is closed to Fund Balance— Reserved for Endowments, which indicates that the undistributed assets are restricted.

The procedures for both the Endowment Principal Fund and the Endowment Revenues Fund for Cedar City are illustrated by the events and entries shown below.

The financial statements for a Nonexpendable Trust Fund are a balance sheet, a statement of revenues, expenditures, and changes in fund balances, and a statement of cash flows. These statements isolate principal and revenue components, which may be presented on separate statements or on one statement, with self-balancing sections or columns labeled "As to Principal" and "As to Revenue." The last two statements follow the usual format and will not be shown, but a columnar balance sheet for Cedar City's Governmental Accounting Scholarship Fund is shown in Illustration 18–8.

Event

Cedar City receives an endowment of $50,000 to establish a Nonexpendable Trust Fund whose revenue is to be used to encourage students to study governmental accounting.

9% bonds with a face value of $40,000 are purchased at 101, maturing in 10 years.

Bond interest of $3,600 is received. Premium is amortized pro rata.

The liability to Endowment Revenues Fund for net revenue is recorded.

Cash due is remitted.

A grant of $3,000 is given to a student.

Books are closed at year end.

Illustration 18–8

Cedar City
Balance Sheet
Governmental Accounting Scholarship Endowment Fund
December 31, 19X2

Assets	As to Principal	As to Revenue	Total
Cash..	$ 9,640	$560	$10,200
Investments	40,000	—	40,000
Unamortized premium	360	—	360
Total assets...	$50,000	$560	$50,560

Liabilities and Fund Balances			
Liabilities..	—	—	—
Fund balances:			
Reserved for endowments........................	$50,000	$560	$50,560
Total liabilities and fund balances...............	$50,000	$560	$50,560

Entries in Endowment Principal Fund			Entries in Endowment Revenues Fund		
Cash..	50,000		No entry.		
Revenues (Control).................		50,000			
Investments.............................	40,000		No entry.		
Unamortized Premium	400				
Cash....................................		40,400			
Cash.......................................	3,600		No entry.		
Unamortized Premium		40			
Revenues (Control).................		3,560			
Other Financing Uses (Control).....	3,560		Due from Endowment Principal		
Due to Endowment Revenues			Fund	3,560	
Fund...................................		3,560	Other Financing Sources (Control) ..		3,560
Due to Endowment Revenues			Cash	3,560	
Fund...................................	3,560		Due from Endowment Principal		
Cash....................................		3,560	Fund		3,560
No entry.			Expenditures (Control)	3,000	
			Cash		3,000
Revenues (Control)......................	53,560		Other Financing Sources (Control)....	3,560	
Other Financing Uses (Control) ..		3,560	Expenditures (Control)		3,000
Fund Balance — Reserved for			Fund Balance — Reserved for		
Endowments......................		50,000	Endowments		560

PENSION TRUST FUNDS

Public employees retirement system funds are accounted for in *Pension Trust Funds*. In no other area of accounting is actuarial assistance so vital. Abiding by the requirements of the retirement plan and considering the employee population as to age, sex, marital status, and the myriads of other variables that affect working lives and retirement, actuaries must estimate the amount of resources necessary as of a given date to meet retirement commitments. To protect the employees' interests, Pension Trust Funds should use a full accrual basis of accounting.

Contributions to a retirement plan may be from both employer and employees (a contributory plan) or from employer only (a noncontributory plan). Employees who resign usually have the option to withdraw their own contributions (but not the employer's contributions) or to leave them in the plan as vested amounts, providing certain requirements are met. The amounts belong to the employee, who will have access to them upon meeting prescribed retirement conditions.

Increases in the resources of Pension Trust Funds result from contributions and investment earnings and are recorded as operating revenues. Decreases in resources result from payments to retired employees and from refunds and are treated as operating expenses.

All assets of a pension trust belong to the employees, and these assets are reflected in either the liabilities or the restricted reserves. To indicate that there is a restriction against all resources, journal entries record reservations of all of the trust fund balance. The reserved fund balances represent resources supporting the various stages of the retirement plan. There are four reserves commonly used in Pension Trust Funds:

1. Fund Balance—Member Contributions represents the amount of accumulated contributions made by nonretired participating employees, plus earnings on these contributions.
2. Fund Balance—Employer Contributions represents the amount of accumulated contributions made by the employer pertaining to nonretired participating employees, plus earnings on these contributions. The account is increased for any unfunded liability resulting from actuarial valuation.
3. Fund Balance—Benefit and Disability Reserve represents amounts transferred from the first two reserves upon the retirement or disability of an employee, plus earnings on amounts transferred.
4. Fund Balance—Undistributed Investment Earnings Reserve represents amounts earned on assets attributable to the first three reserves, but not yet allocated to them.

To demonstrate the accounting process for a Pension Trust Fund, the journal entries recording each event and its effect on the reserves for Desert City's Pension Trust Fund for employees' retirement are shown on pages 960 and 961. All entries illustrated are made in one trust fund and represent amounts for the entire year. The journal entries on page 960 record asset inflows and outflows and are similar to entries shown previously for other funds. The entries in the reserve accounts, shown on page 961, are made periodically, usually at year end, in order to update the status of the reserves that represent the assets. In this example, however, the reserve entries are recorded when the original events are recorded in order to better illustrate the flow from one reserve to another.

The two entries for reinstatement to the unreserved fund balance of $20,500 and $9,000, respectively, need further explanation. Payments to retired employees or payments to employees who resign and withdraw their contributions are debited to Operating Expenses (Control). Amounts equal to these payments no longer need to be reserved from the fund balance. They are returned to the unreserved fund balance by reversing the entry that created them, using the amount of the payment and the appropriate reserve.

The balance sheet for Desert City's Pension Trust Fund as of December 31, 19X2, is shown below. The fund has been operating for several years. A feature of the balance sheet is the presence of four reserve accounts,

---

Illustration 18–9

Desert City
Balance Sheet
Employees' Retirement Trust Fund
December 31, 19X2

Assets

Cash	$ 76,152
Investments	1,109,549
Interest receivable on investments	1,200
Total assets	$1,186,901

Liabilities and Fund Balances

Liabilities:	
Due to resigned employees	$ 2,700
Benefits payable	1,500
Total liabilities	$ 4,200
Fund balances:	
Reserved for:	
Member contributions	$ 338,564
Employer contributions	763,155
Benefits and disability	320,782
Undistributed investment earnings	3,200
Total reserved for employees' retirement system	$1,425,701
Unreserved, undesignated	(243,000)
Total fund balances	$1,182,701
Total liabilities and fund balances	$1,186,901

Event		Journal Entry for Original Event		

Cash contributions are received from:

Employees............................	$ 60,000	Cash..	150,000	
Employer.............................	90,000	Operating Revenues		
Total	$150,000	(Control)		150,000

Earnings of $84,000 on investments are received and $1,200 is accrued.

Cash..	84,000	
Interest Receivable on		
Investments..............................	1,200	
Operating Revenues		
(Control)		85,200

Payments of $19,000 are made to retired employees and $1,500 is payable.

Operating Expenses (Control)................	20,500	
Cash..		19,000
Benefits Payable		1,500

Refunds of $6,300 were made and $2,700 is due to employees who resigned and withdrew their contributions.

Operating Expenses (Control)................	9,000	
Cash..		6,300
Due to Resigned		
Employees................................		2,700

Books are closed at year end.

Operating Revenues (Control)	235,200	
Operating Expenses		
(Control)		29,500
Fund Balance — Unreserved,		
Undesignated		205,700

---

which is understandable because all assets are reserved for the benefit of employees. Also, the account Fund Balance—Unreserved, Undesignated typically has a debit balance, representing the shortage of net assets to cover the total amount reserved for the retirement system.

Changes in the retirement reserves of a pension trust are so revealing that an analysis of changes in each of the reserves for the year should be

Event	Journal Entry Involving Fund Balances		
Amounts are reserved, based on contributions.	Fund Balance — Unreserved, Undesignated	150,000	
	Fund Balance — Member Contributions		60,000
	Fund Balance — Employer Contributions		90,000
Amounts are reserved, based on allocated investment earnings:	Fund Balance — Unreserved, Undesignated	85,200	
Employees' contributions......... $23,000	Fund Balance — Member Contributions		23,000
Employer's contributions 37,000	Fund Balance — Employer Contributions		37,000
Benefit and disability.............. 22,000	Fund Balance — Benefit and Disability Reserve...................		22,000
Undistributed earnings 3,200	Fund Balance — Undistributed Investment Earnings Reserve........................		3,200
Total $85,200			
For retiring employees, transfer from contribution reserves to benefit reserve:	Fund Balance — Member Contributions	6,000	
Of employees........................ $ 6,000	Fund Balance — Employer Contributions	10,000	
Of employer......................... 10,000	Fund Balance — Benefit and Disability Reserve........................		16,000
Total $16,000			
Reinstatement to the unreserved fund balance of amount equal to payments and related liability. (See discussion of this entry on page 959.)	Fund Balance — Benefit and Disability Reserve........................	20,500	
	Fund Balance — Unreserved, Undesignated.............................		20,500
Reinstatement to the unreserved fund balance of amount equal to refunds and related liability. (See discussion of this entry on page 959.)	Fund Balance — Member Contributions	9,000	
	Fund Balance — Unreserved, Undesignated.............................		9,000
Adjust balance of employer contribution reserve to reflect revised unfunded liability of $3,000 per periodic actuarial valuation.	Fund Balance — Unreserved, Undesignated	3,000	
	Fund Balance — Employer Contributions		3,000

prepared. It should be structured with a column for each reserve and a total, showing beginning balances, additions, deductions, and final balances.

The statement of revenues, expenses, and changes in fund balances adheres to the all-inclusive approach, whereby the net income is added to the total of all fund balances at the beginning of the period to yield their total at the end of the period.

Public employee retirement systems and pension trusts that follow procedures outlined in the National Council of Governmental Accounting's Statement No. 6, *Pension Accounting and Financial Reporting,* are not required to present a statement of changes in financial position or of cash flows. Such data are available in the analysis of changes in the various reserves of the Pension Trust Fund.

AGENCY FUNDS

An *Agency Fund* is required when money collected or withheld, such as deductions from government employees' salaries for social security or for hospitalization premiums, must be forwarded to the proper destination. Agency Funds frequently have no end-of-period balances because money is transferred prior to the end of the period. When the money has not been forwarded, a liability to the ultimate recipient is shown. There is no fund balance, and the only financial statement would be a balance sheet listing the assets held and the related liabilities, supported by a statement of changes in assets and liabilities. The latter statement shows for each asset and liability its beginning balance, any additions or deletions, and the final balance. If the Agency Fund is to receive a fee for its services, the amount usually is recorded as a liability to the General Fund of the governmental unit, which records it as revenue when received. For example, state law may give a county the responsibility for collecting property taxes levied within its boundaries, with the county receiving a fee to cover its administration of the plan. The county, as well as each political subdivision, would record its share of taxes receivable in its General Fund. The Tax Agency Fund of Zee County would make the following series of entries for the events described:

Event	Entry in Tax Agency Fund		
Gross taxes receivable to be collected for all units are as follows:	Taxes Receivable for All Units.......	1,000,000	
	Due to Other Governmental		
Zee County........................ $ 300,000	Units.................................		1,000,000
X City.............................. 600,000			
T Town............................. 100,000			
Total $1,000,000			
Taxes are collected.	Cash....................................	1,000,000	
	Taxes Receivable for		
	All Units		1,000,000
The liability to each unit is recorded, net of 2% fee earned by the county for collection and processing for other units. (The county would not charge itself a fee.) The fee is to be remitted to the county General Fund.	Due to Other Governmental		
	Units.................................	1,000,000	
	Due to Zee County General		
	Fund.................................		314,000
	Due to X City		588,000
	Due to T Town		98,000

Event	Entry in Tax Agency Fund		
Cash is released to each governmental unit.	Due to Zee County General Fund		314,000	
	Due to X City	588,000	
	Due to T Town	98,000	
	Cash		1,000,000

The General Fund of X City records the receipt of cash from the Tax Agency Fund, net of the fee, as follows:

Cash (for net proceeds)	588,000	
Expenditures (Control) (for fee charged)	12,000	
Taxes Receivable—Current		600,000

Agency Funds also are used in the case of a capital project undertaken by a governmental unit in which special assessment bonds were issued, but for which the unit has no financial responsibility in case of nonpayment. The unit functions as an agent, a financial conduit between the bondholders and the owners of the assessed property. When collections from assessed property owners are received by the Agency Funds, this entry is made:

Cash	XXX	
Due to Special Assessment Bondholders for Interest Payment..		XXX
Due to Special Assessment Bondholders for Principal Redemption		XXX

Upon payment to the bondholders, the entry is reversed. Neither the liability for principal repayment nor the debt service expenditures is recorded in any other fund or group because the governmental unit was not obligated in any manner.

GOVERNMENTAL ACCOUNTING—A REVIEW

In governmental accounting, each fund or group is a separate accounting entity, entrusted to record only a limited phase of an event. Complete recording, as shown in Chapters 17 and 18, often involves more than one fund or group. To serve as a reference and to review governmental accounting, Illustration 18–10 on pages 964 and 965 is a matrix of selected events that are recorded in more than one fund or group. Used in the matrix are the four governmental-type funds (General, Special Revenue, Debt Service, Capital Projects), the two types of proprietary funds (Enterprise, Internal Service), a Trust and Agency Fund, and the two account groups for general fixed assets and general long-term debt.

To illustrate the interplay between funds and groups, the entries to record the events related to the issuance of general obligation bonds for financing the cost of constructing a civic center are presented in Illustration 18–11 on pages 964 through 967.

Illustration 18–10 **Matrix of Selected Events**

Events To Be Recorded

1. Purchase of equipment with General Fund resources
2. Issuance of general obligation serial bonds at a premium for city hall construction
3. Transfer by General Fund to meet matured serial bonds and interest payments

4. Payment of bond interest and matured serial bonds
5. Completion of special assessment construction project
6. Levy of property taxes by General Fund against city's utility

7. Billing of General and Special Revenue Funds for central computer service
8. Contribution made by city to a nonexpendable endowment fund
9. Remittance of city's share of pension fund costs for current period

10. Recording of depreciation
11. Redemption of final serial of general obligation bonds, with deficiency covered by General Fund
12. Closing entry for Capital Projects Fund involving a partially completed project

Illustration 18–11 **Interplay Between Funds and Groups To Record General**

Event	General Fund	Capital Projects Fund	
General obligation serial bonds sold at a premium to cover cost of civic center project. Premium will be transferred to Debt Service Fund.		Cash...................... XX	
		Other Financing Sources (Control)	XX
		Other Financing Uses (Control) XX	
		Due to Debt Service Fund	XX
Serial bond premium is transferred to Debt Service Fund.		Due to Debt Service Fund XX	
		Cash....................	XX

Requiring Entry in More Than One Fund or Group

Governmental-Type Funds				Proprietary Funds		Fiduciary Fund	Account Groups		
General	Special Revenue	Debt Service	Capital Projects	Enterprise	Internal Service	Trust and Agency	General Fixed Assets	General Long-Term Debt	
X	—	—	—	—	—	—	X	—	1.
—	—	X	X	—	—	—	—	X	2.
X	—	X	—	—	—	—	—	X	3.
—	—	X	—	—	—	—	—	X	4.
—	—	—	X	—	—	—	X	—	5.
X	—	—	—	X	—	—	—	—	6.
X	X	—	—	—	X	—	—	—	7.
X	—	—	—	—	—	X	—	—	8.
X	—	—	—	—	—	X	—	—	9.
—	—	—	—	X	X	X	—	—	10.
X	—	X	—	—	—	—	—	X	11.
—	—	—	X	—	—	—	X	—	12.

Obligation Serial Bonds for a Capital Project

Debt Service Fund		General Long-Term Debt Account Group		General Fixed Assets Account Group
Due from General Fund	XX	Amount To Be Provided for Payment of Serial Bonds..............	XX	
Other Financing Sources (Control)	XX	Serial Bonds Payable	XX	

Cash......................	XX			
Due from General Fund	XX			

(continued)

Event	General Fund	Capital Projects Fund
Contractor completes civic center started this period and is paid, except for 10% payment withheld until final approval.		Expenditures (Control)........... XX Contracts Payable. XX Contracts Payable— Retained Percentage........ XX Contracts Payable.... XX Cash................... XX
Bond serial and interest mature.		
General Fund transfers to Debt Service Fund amount to cover matured principal and interest.	Other Financing Uses (Control).......... XX Cash.................. XX	
Debt Service Fund pays matured serial and interest.		

ANNUAL FINANCIAL REPORTING

The principal role of financial reporting is to provide information. A comprehensive annual financial report should be prepared by every governmental unit in order to demonstrate that it has complied with the provisions of the law. The comprehensive annual financial report includes at least two sets of financial statements, along with their notes and any additional data that may be considered necessary. These two sets are (1) the general purpose combined financial statements and (2) combining statements by fund type. General purpose combined financial statements furnish in columnar form an overview of the financial position of all funds and account groups and of the operating results of all funds. The headings of a combined balance sheet and

Debt Service Fund		General Long-Term Debt Account Group		General Fixed Assets Account Group	
				Buildings	XX
				Investment in General Fixed Assets—Capital Projects Fund (General Obligation Bonds).............	XX
Expenditures (Control)	XX				
Matured Serial Bonds Payable ..	XX				
Matured Interest Payable	XX				
Cash.......................	XX	Amount Available in Debt Service Fund—Serial Bonds...............	XX		
Other Financing Sources (Control)	XX	Amount To Be Provided for Payment of Serial Bonds..............	XX		
Matured Serial Bonds Payable	XX	Serial Bonds Payable	XX		
Matured Interest Payable	XX	Amount Available in Debt Service Fund—Serial Bonds...............	XX		
Cash..................	XX				

combined statement of revenues, expenditures, and changes in fund balances follow:

Combined Balance Sheet—All Fund Types and Account Groups
December 31, 19X7

	Governmental-Type Funds				Proprietary Funds		Fiduciary Funds	Account Groups		Totals (Memorandum Only)	
ASSETS	General	Special Revenue	Debt Service	Capital Projects	Enterprise	Internal Service	Trust and Agency	General Fixed Assets	General Long-Term Debt	December 31, 19X7	December 31, 19X6
Cash	$258,500	$101,385	$ 43,834	$431,600	$257,036	$29,700	$ 216,701	—	—	$1,338,756	$1,258,909
Cash with fiscal agent	—	—	102,000	—	—	—	—	—	—	102,000	—
Investments at cost or amortized cost	65,000	37,200	160,990	—	—	—	1,239,260	—	—	1,502,450	1,974,354

Combined Statement of Revenues, Expenditures, and Changes in Fund Balances
All Governmental-Type Funds and Expendable Trust Fund
For the Fiscal Year Ended December 31, 19X7

| | | | | | Fiduciary Fund | Totals (Memorandum Only) | |
| | Governmental-Type Funds | | | | | Year Ended | |
	General	Special Revenue	Debt Service	Capital Projects	Expendable Trust	December 31, 19X7	December 31, 19X6
Revenues:							
Taxes	$881,300	$189,300	$79,177	—	—	$1,149,777	$1,137,900
Special assessments levied	—	—	—	$240,000	—	240,000	250,400
Licenses and permits	103,000	—	—	—	—	103,000	96,500

A complete set of general purpose combined financial statements would include a:

1. Combined balance sheet for all fund types and account groups.
2. Combined statement of revenues, expenditures, and changes in fund balances for all governmental-type funds and Expendable Trust Funds.
3. Combined statement of revenues, expenditures, and changes in fund balances for the General and Special Revenue Funds—both budget and actual.
4. Combined statement of revenues, expenditures or expenses, and changes in retained earnings or fund balances for all proprietary funds, Nonexpendable Trust Funds, and Pension Trust Funds.
5. Combined statement of cash flows for all proprietary funds and Nonexpendable Trust Funds.

These five combined statements constitute the minimum financial statements necessary for fair presentation in accordance with generally accepted accounting principles.

For a comprehensive annual financial report, greater detail is necessary. More detail is provided by the combining statements, which give data for all funds of a similar type. For example, the combined balance sheet shows that Capital Projects Funds have a cash balance of $431,600. A breakdown of this amount is shown in the following combining balance sheet for all Capital Projects Funds:

Capital Projects Funds
Combining Balance Sheet
December 31, 19X7

| | City Hall Project | Gas Pipeline Project | Stadium Project | Totals | |
				19X7	19X6
Assets:					
Cash................	$240,000	$108,000	$83,600	$431,600	$237,000

In addition to the five combined financial statements, a comprehensive annual financial report would include the following items:

1. Combining statements for each fund type where there is more than one fund of that type, such as the Capital Projects Funds illustrated.
2. Individual fund or account group statements where there is only one fund of that type, or if it is necessary to present prior-year or budgetary comparisons or detail to assure sufficient disclosure.
3. Schedules presenting additional data necessary for fair presentation in conformity with generally accepted accounting principles, such as data related to a bond issue or to a leasing agreement.

In its Statement 1, the National Council on Governmental Accounting provided an excellent pyramid of financial reporting,[3] with which some liberties have been taken:

PYRAMID OF FINANCIAL REPORTING

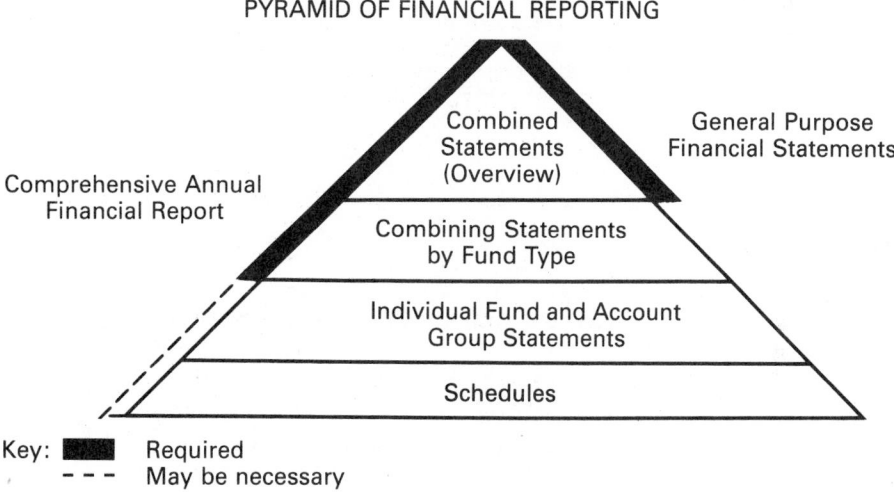

With greater detail in each descending level, the pyramid gives the basis for a governmental unit to decide just how far down to go in order to provide adequate disclosure for its reporting needs.

As a final review of governmental accounting and reporting principles, the following summary is provided:

---

[3]Statement 1, *Governmental Accounting and Financial Reporting Principles* (Chicago: Municipal Finance Officers Association of the United States and Canada, March, 1979), 20.

Summary of Governmental Accounting

Characteristic	Governmental-Type Funds
Basis of accounting	Modified accrual
Measurement focus	On flow of current financial resources
Formal recording of the budget: General and Special Revenue Funds	Mandatory
Capital Projects Funds operating on an annual budget	Discretionary (based on complexity)
Debt Service Funds	No
Other funds	
Maintains record of fixed assets used in operations	No
Maintains record of long-term debt	No

QUESTIONS

1. Discuss the similarities between a Special Revenue Fund and a General Fund.
2. Why are fixed asset acquisitions from proceeds of general obligation bonds not accounted for in the General Fund?
3. If a Capital Projects Fund has authority to continue operations over several fiscal periods, why is it desirable to close its records at the end of each period?
4. Explain the necessity to introduce a deferred revenues account in the levy of capital special assessments.
5. Give the entry in the General Long-Term Debt Account Group to record the issuance of bonds related to construction of general fixed assets from special assessments where the governmental unit has assumed responsibility for payment in case of default. Explain the purpose of the entry.
6. The Debt Service Fund does not use budgetary accounts. What is the logic for not doing so?
7. When a Debt Service Fund receives resources, it might credit Revenues (Control) or Other Financing Sources (Control). Under what circumstances would each of these credits be used?

and Reporting Principles

Expendable Trust Funds	Proprietary, Non-expendable Trust, and Pension Trust Funds	Agency Funds
Modified accrual	Accrual	Modified accrual
On flow of financial resources	On net income and capital maintenance	On assets entrusted, wherein assets = liabilities
Yes	No	No
No	Yes	No
No	Yes	No

8. What is the characteristic that determines whether an activity should be accounted for in a Special Revenue Fund or in an Enterprise Fund?
9. In what ways does accounting for an Enterprise Fund closely resemble accounting for a commercial enterprise?
10. What is the purpose of a capital contribution account in an Enterprise Fund?
11. A city levies capital special assessments against property owners. Indicate what the credit accounts would be to record the event in a governmental-type fund and in a proprietary fund. Justify the difference in treatment.
12. Explain the nature of restricted assets in an Enterprise Fund.
13. Four fund balance reserve accounts generally are required in accounting for an employee Pension Trust Fund. Identify the four reserves and briefly describe the nature of the balance in each account.
14. Explain why Agency Funds have no fund balance accounts.

EXERCISES

Exercise 1.   Select the best answer for each of the following multiple-choice items.

1. Accounting for Special Revenue Funds closely resembles the accounting for:
   a. General Funds.
   b. Capital Projects Funds.
   c. Enterprise Funds.
   d. Agency Funds.

2. Bonds are issued at a premium by a Capital Project Fund. The premium should be:
   a. Retained in the Capital Projects Fund.
   b. Credited directly to the unreserved fund balance of the Capital Project Fund.
   c. Transferred to the Debt Service Funds.
   d. Used to reduce the net cost of the project involved.

3. Bonds are issued at a discount by a Capital Projects Fund. The discount should be:
   a. Covered by an immediate transfer from the General Fund.
   b. Debited directly to the unreserved fund balance of the Capital Project Fund.
   c. Charged against the Debt Service Funds.
   d. Reflected in the smaller amount credited to the account Other Financing Sources (Control).

4. At the beginning of a fiscal period, unexpended encumbrances at the previous year end related to an incomplete project in the Capital Projects Funds generally are reinstated by crediting:
   a. Unreserved Fund Balance.
   b. Budgetary Fund Balance—Reserved for Encumbrances.
   c. Encumbrances (Control).
   d. Expenditures (Control).

5. At year end, the following correct entry is made in the appropriate fund or account group:

   Construction in Progress.. XXX
      Investment in General Fixed Assets—Capital Projects
       Funds XXX

   The amount for the entry may be found in the Capital Projects Fund's:
   a. Entry closing budgetary account balances.
   b. Entry closing actual account balances.
   c. Fixed Asset in Process account.
   d. Fund Balance Reserved for Construction account.

Exercise 2.   Select the best answer for each of the following multiple-choice items.
1. Resources for a capital improvement are provided by special assessments. At the start of the second year of the project, a reclassification

entry in the Debt Service Fund that debits Deferred Revenues would credit:
a. Special Assessments Receivable—Deferred.
b. Revenues (Control).
c. Unreserved Fund Balance.
d. Fund Balance Reserved for Special Assessments.

2. If a governmental unit makes no guarantees regarding repayment of a capital improvement special assessment bond issue, the liability for the bonds would:
a. Not appear in the financial statements or in their notes.
b. Not appear in the financial statements, but would appear in the notes to the financial statements.
c. Appear in the Capital Projects Funds.
d. Appear in the General Long-Term Debt Account Group.

3. The following is a correct entry:

Construction in Progress..	XXX	
Investment in General Fixed Assets—Capital Projects		
Funds		XXX

The entry would be found in the:
a. Capital Projects Funds.
b. Enterprise Funds.
c. General Fund.
d. General Fixed Assets Account Group.

4. Which one of the following is least likely to make a formal entry for its budget?
a. General Fund.
b. Special Revenues Funds.
c. Capital Projects Funds.
d. Debt Service Funds.

5. The following correct entry appears in a Debt Service Fund:

Matured Bonds Payable..	XXX	
Matured Interest Payable	XXX	
Cash with Fiscal Agent..		XXX

An appropriate explanation would be, "To record:
a. Direct payment to bondholders."
b. The matured bonds and interest."
c. Payments made by a fiscal agent to bondholders."
d. Payments made to a fiscal agent."

Exercise 3. Select the best response for each of the following multiple-choice questions that refer to transactions of Brockton City.

1. In preparing the General Fund budget of Brockton City for the forthcoming fiscal year, the city council appropriated a sum greater than expected revenues. This action of the council will result in:
   a. A cash overdraft during that fiscal year.
   b. An increase in encumbrances by the end of that fiscal year.
   c. A debit to Budgetary Fund Balance—Unreserved.
   d. A necessity for compensatory offsetting action in the Debt Service Fund.

2. Brockton City's water utility, which is an Enterprise Fund, submits a bill for $9,000 to the General Fund for water service supplied to city departments and agencies. Submission of this bill would result in:
   a. Creation of balances that will be eliminated on the city's combined balance sheet.
   b. Recognition of revenue by the Water Utility Fund and of an expenditure by the General Fund.
   c. Recognition of an encumbrance by both the Water Utility Fund and the General Fund.
   d. Creation of balances that will be eliminated on the city's combined statement of changes in fund balances.

3. What would be the effect on the General Fund of recording a $15,000 purchase of a new fire truck in the current fiscal year, using General Fund resources for which a $14,600 encumbrance had been recorded in the General Fund in the previous year?
   a. Increase Expenditures (Control) by $15,000.
   b. Increase Expenditures (Control) by $14,600.
   c. Increase Expenditures (Control) by $400.
   d. Have no effect on the General Fund.

4. What will be the balance sheet effect of recording $50,000 of depreciation in the accounts of a utility, an Enterprise Fund, owned by Brockton City?
   a. Reduce total assets of the Utility Fund and the General Fixed Assets Account Group by $50,000.
   b. Reduce total assets of the Utility Fund by $50,000, but have no effect on the General Fixed Assets Account Group.
   c. Reduce total assets of the General Fixed Assets Account Group by $50,000, but have no effect on assets of the Utility Fund.
   d. Have no effect on total assets of either the Utility Fund or the General Fixed Assets Account Group.   (AICPA adapted)

Exercise 4. Prepare journal entries to record the following events. Identify the fund or group of accounts in which each entry is made.
(a) The city authorized the construction of a city hall to be financed by $200,000 from the General Fund and the proceeds of a $2,000,000 general obligation serial bond issue, which is sold at 99.
(b) The General Fund remits the $200,000 to the recipient fund.

(c) A contract is signed with Galen Construction Company for the construction of the city hall at an estimated cost of $2,100,000.

(d) The project is one-half complete at year end. A liability is recorded at $1,000,000, and related to encumbrances of $980,000. Work in progress is entered at $1,050,000.

Exercise 5. In 19X3, the Town of Ryan authorized the construction of concrete roadways on Mark and Marion Avenues. The public works department estimates the cost of the project at $220,000. The General Fund contributed $20,000 to be used for construction. To help pay for the project, $200,000 of 4-year, 6% special assessment bonds are sold at par on July 1, 19X3. Interest payment dates are January 1 and July 1 of each year. Purchase orders totaling $40,000 are issued, and a contract is signed at an estimated additional cost for the project of $180,000. Invoices for all purchase orders total $38,000, while the actual contract cost amounts to $185,000. Liabilities for these amounts are entered. Except for $20,000 withheld on the contract until final approval, all liabilities related to the completed construction are paid. Ryan does not use budgetary accounts for these smaller projects. Prepare entries in the Capital Projects Fund for these events.

Exercise 6. Prepare journal entries required by a Debt Service Fund to record the following transactions:

(a) On January 2, a $1,000,000, 6%, 10-year general obligation serial bond issue is sold at 99. Interest is payable annually on December 31, along with one-tenth of the original principal.

(b) At year end, the first serial of bonds matures, along with interest on the bond issue.

(c) The General Fund transfers cash to meet the matured items.

(d) A check for the matured items is sent to Lehigh Bank, the agent handling the payments.

(e) Later, the bank reports that the first serial has been redeemed. One check for interest of $400 was returned by the post office because the bond owner had moved. The bank will search for the new address.

Exercise 7. Prepare journal entries to record the following events in the City of Bakersfield's Water Commission, a utility operated as an Enterprise Fund:

(a) From its General Fund revenues, the city transferred $300,000, which is restricted for the drilling of additional wells.

(b) Billings for water consumption for the month totaled $287,000, including $67,000 billed to other funds.

(c) Billing amounts collected from other funds was $42,000 and from other users, $190,000.

(d) To raise additional funds, the utility issued $700,000 of 5%, 10-year revenue bonds at face value. Proceeds are restricted to the development of wells.

(e) The contract with the well driller showed an estimated cost of $930,000.

(continued)

(f) At year end, the contractor sent a bill for $360,000 for work done to date. The amount was approved for payment.

(g) A check for $300,000 was issued to the contractor.

PROBLEMS

Problem 18–1. Select the best answer for each of the following multiple-choice items.

1. In the final year of a capital project that took several years to complete, the total cost of the project would be shown in the Capital Projects Fund as the balance in:
   a. The Expenditures (Control) account.
   b. The Construction in Progress account.
   c. The Fund Balance — Reserved for Encumbrances account.
   d. No account.

2. A bond issue is floated to provide resources for a major capital improvement whose cost is to be met by special assessments against benefited property owners. Generally, the amount of the bond proceeds is approximately equal to:
   a. The estimated total cost of the project.
   b. The amount of the deferred special assessments.
   c. The total of all special assessments on the project.
   d. The amount debited to Expenditures (Control) over the life of the project.

3. A governmental unit assumes responsibility in case of default for the bond debt related to a special assessment capital project for a general fixed asset. In this case, the bond liability is reflected in the:
   a. General Long-Term Debt Account Group.
   b. Capital Projects Funds.
   c. Debt Service Funds.
   d. General Fund.

4. Measurement focus for Enterprise Funds is on:
   a. The flow of resources.
   b. The assets entrusted.
   c. Net income and capital maintenance.
   d. The unreserved fund balance.

5. When special assessments are levied by an Enterprise Fund for capital asset acquisition, the account credited in the journal entry is:
   a. Revenues (Control).
   b. Other Financing Sources (Control).
   c. Contributed Capital from Special Assessments.
   d. Fund Balance Reserved for Special Assessments.

Problem 18–2.   Select the best answer for each of the following multiple-choice items.

1. A successful computer center operated as an Internal Service Fund is sharing its profits by remitting cash to the General Fund. The account to be debited in the Internal Service Fund to record the remittance is:
   a. Other Financing Uses (Control).
   b. Expenditures (Control).
   c. Financial Expense.
   d. Retained Earnings—Unreserved

2. Bonds are issued to expand a city's water utility. The bond liability is recorded in the:
   a. Enterprise Funds.
   b. Capital Projects Funds.
   c. Debt Service Funds.
   d. General Long-Term Debt Account Group.

3. An electric utility has a debit balance account called "Customers' Deposits Refundable." It is an illustration of a(n):
   a. Appropriated asset.
   b. Restricted asset.
   c. Reserved asset.
   d. Funded asset.

4. The following correct entry is found in a county's Pension Trust Fund:

   Fund Balance—Benefit and Disability Reserve   XXX
       Fund Balance—Unreserved, Undesignated   XXX

   An acceptable explanation is that the entry records a:
   a. Contribution by employees to their pension fund.
   b. Contribution by the employer to the pension fund.
   c. Reversal of a previous entry, using the amount of pension payments.
   d. Reversal of a previous entry, using the amount of pension contributions withdrawn by terminated employees.

5. A capital project for a general fixed asset is undertaken for which special assessment serial bonds are issued. The governmental unit has absolutely no financial responsibility in case of default. As a serial matures, the entry for repayment is made in the:
   a. General Long-Term Debt Account Group.
   b. Capital Projects Funds.
   c. Debt Service Funds.
   d. Agency Funds.

Problem 18–3.   Select the best response for each of the following multiple-choice questions.

Items 1 and 2 are based on the following information:

During the year ended December 31, 19X1, Leyland City received a restricted (expenditure-driven) state grant of $500,000 to finance the purchase of buses for the handicapped and an additional grant of $100,000 to aid in the financing of bus operations in 19X1. Only $300,000 of the capital grant was used in 19X1 for the purchase of buses, but the entire operating grant of $100,000 was spent in 19X1:

1. If Leyland City's bus transportation system is accounted for as part of the city's General Fund, how much should Leyland City report as grant revenues for the year ended December 31, 19X1?
    a. $100,000.   b. $300,000.   c. $400,000.   d. $500,000.

2. If Leyland City's bus transportation system is accounted for as an Enterprise Fund, how much should Leyland City report as grant revenues for the year ended December 31, 19X1?
    a. $100,000.   b. $300,000.   c. $400,000.   d. $500,000.

Items 3 and 4 are based on the following information:

On December 31, 19X1, Madrid Township paid a contractor $2,000,000 for the total cost of a new firehouse built in 19X1 on township-owned land. Financing was by means of a $1,500,000 general obligation bond issue sold at face amount on December 31, 19X1, with the remaining $500,000 transferred from the General Fund.

3. What should be reported on Madrid Township's 19X1 financial statements for the Capital Projects Fund?
    a. Revenues, $1,500,000; expenditures, $1,500,000.
    b. Revenues, $1,500,000; other financing sources, $500,000; expenditures, $2,000,000.
    c. Revenues, $2,000,000; expenditures, $2,000,000.
    d. Other financing sources, $2,000,000; expenditures, $2,000,000.

4. What should be reported on Madrid Township's 19X1 financial statements for the General Fund?
    a. Expenditures, $500,000.
    b. Other financing uses, $500,000.
    c. Revenues, $1,500,000; expenditures, $2,000,000.
    d. Revenues, $1,500,000; other financing uses, $2,000,000.

5. The following balances are included in the subsidiary records of Burwood Village's Parks Department:

Appropriations—supplies	$7,500
Expenditures—supplies	4,500
Encumbrances—supply orders	750

    How much does the department have available for additional commitment for supplies?
    a. 0.   b. $2,250.   c. $3,000.   d. $6,750.

Items 6 and 7 are based on the following information:

The following events relating to the City of Albury's Debt Service Funds occurred during the year ended December 31, 19X1:

Debt principal matured...	$2,000,000
Unmatured (accrued) interest on outstanding debt at January 1, 19X1...	50,000
Interest on matured debt..	900,000
Unmatured (accrued) interest on outstanding debt at December 31, 19X1...	100,000
Interest revenue from investments	600,000
Cash transferred from General Fund for retirement of debt principal	1,000,000
Cash transferred from General Fund for payment of matured interest..	900,000

All principal and interest due in 19X1 were paid on time.

6. What is the total amount of expenditures that Albury's Debt Service Funds should record for the year ended December 31, 19X1?
   a. $900,000.   b. $950,000   c. $2,900,000.   d. $2,500,000.

7. How much revenue should Albury's Debt Service Funds record for the year ended December 31, 19X1?
   a. $600,000.   b. $1,600,000.   c. $1,900,000.   d. $2,500,000.

8. The following assets are among those owned by the City of Foster:

Apartment building (part of the principal of a nonexpendable trust fund)...	$ 200,000
City hall...	800,000
Three fire stations...	1,000,000
City streets and sidewalks	5,000,000

   How much should be included in Foster's General Fixed Assets Account Group?
   a. Either $1,800,000 or $6,800,000.
   b. Either $2,000,000 or $7,000,000.
   c. $6,800,000.
   d. $7,000,000.

9. Ariel Village issued the following bonds:

Revenue bonds to be repaid from admission fees collected by the Ariel Zoo Enterprise Fund..	$200,000
General obligation bonds issued for the Ariel Water Enterprise Fund, which will service the debt	300,000

   How much of these bonds should be accounted for in Ariel's General Long-Term Debt Account Group?
   a. 0.   b. $200,000.   c. $300,000.   d. $500,000.

(AICPA adapted)

Problem 18-4.   The City of Helena authorized the construction of a museum and sale of general obligation term bonds to finance its construction. Budgetary accounts are employed in the city's Capital Projects Funds. The following transactions relating to the museum project occurred during the fiscal year ended June 30, 19X7:

(a) The museum project budget is $4,000,000. It is expected that 70% of the work will be done during this fiscal year. The project will be completed next year. Until they are committed, proceeds from the bond sale are expected to earn $120,000, with earnings remaining in the Museum Capital Projects Fund.

(b) On July 1, 19X6, the city issued $4,000,000 of 30-year, 7% general obligation bonds for $4,100,000. Semiannual interest dates are December 31 and June 30. The premium of $100,000 was transferred to the Debt Service Funds.

(c) On July 3, 19X6, the Museum Capital Projects Fund invested $3,500,000 of the bond proceeds in short-term commercial paper at face value with no accrued interest.

(d) On July 15, 19X6, the city signed a contract with BZ Construction Company to build the museum for $3,960,000.

(e) On December 15, 19X6, the Museum Capital Projects Fund received $2,050,000 from the maturing of part of the short-term paper purchased on July 3. The cost of these notes was $2,000,000.

(f) On December 20, 19X6, an additional $40,000 was transferred to the Debt Service Funds, which paid the semiannual bond interest on December 28. The city does not capitalize interest.

(g) On January 20, 19X7, BZ Construction billed the city $3,000,000 for work to date. The contract calls for 10% retention until acceptance of the building. The amount previously encumbered is approximately equal to the billing. A check for $2,000,000 was sent to the contractor.

(h) On June 30, 19X7, an adjusting entry for accrued interest of $40,000 was made. The interest will be received by the Museum Capital Projects Fund on July 1.

(i) On June 30, 19X7, the Museum Capital Projects Fund transferred $140,000 for the semiannual bond interest payment to the Debt Service Funds, which paid the interest.

(j) On June 30, 19X7, closing entries were made for the Museum Capital Projects Fund. The fund balance was reserved for outstanding encumbrances.

Required:
(1) Prepare journal entries to record the events in the Museum Capital Projects Fund, using the appropriate letters (a) through (j).
(2) Prepare any necessary journal entries for the other funds and groups, using the appropriate letters (a) through (j).
(3) Prepare a balance sheet for the City of Helena's Museum Capital Projects Fund as of June 30, 19X7.

Problem 18–5. A selected list of transactions for the City of Baylor for the fiscal year ending June 30, 19X8, follows:
(a) The city government authorized a budget with estimated revenues of $2,500,000 and appropriations of $2,450,000.
(b) The city's share of state gasoline taxes is estimated to be $264,500. These taxes are to be used only for highway maintenance. Appropriations are authorized in the amount of $250,000.

(c) Property taxes of $1,400,000 are levied by the city. In the past, uncollectible taxes have averaged 2% of the gross levy.

(d) A $1,000,000 term bond issue for construction of a school is authorized and sold at 102. The bond premium is transferred to the Debt Service Fund.

(e) Contracts are signed for the construction of the school at an estimated cost of $1,000,000.

(f) The school is constructed at a cost of $990,000.

(g) The Debt Service Fund will need $150,000 from the General Fund for estimated interest and principal payments for the year.

(h) A cash contribution of $100,000 is made by the General Fund to the Debt Service Fund.

(i) Earnings of the Debt Service Fund amount to $3,050. Interest of $45,000 is paid.

(j) Land with a fair market value of $100,000 is donated to the city.

(k) The city received $205,000 in partial payment of its share of state gasoline taxes, with an additional $60,000 due from the state government at an unspecified future time.

(l) Vouchers totaling $210,000, which represent highway labor maintenance costs, are approved for payment by the Special Revenue Fund.

Required:

For each of the events described, prepare the journal entries for all of the funds and groups of accounts involved, using the following format:

Fund or Group	Journal Entry

Problem 18–6.   The City of Palo Verde operates a central computer center through an Internal Service Fund. The Computer Internal Service Fund was established by a contribution of $800,000 from the General Fund on July 1, 19X6, at which time a building was acquired at a cost of $200,000 cash. A used computer was purchased for $500,000. The post-closing trial balance of the fund at June 30, 19X8, was as follows:

Cash	150,000	
Due from General Fund	120,000	
Inventory of Materials and Supplies	80,000	
Land	60,000	
Building	200,000	
Allowance for Depreciation — Building		10,000
Computer Equipment	556,000	
Allowance for Depreciation — Computer Equipment		228,000
Vouchers Payable (to Outsiders)		38,000
Contributions from General Fund		800,000
Retained Earnings — Unreserved		90,000
	1,166,000	1,166,000

The following information applies to the year ended June 30, 19X9:

(a) Materials and supplies were purchased on account for $74,000.

(b) The inventory of materials and supplies at June 30, 19X9, was $58,000.

(c) Salaries paid totaled $230,000, including related costs.

(d) A billing from the Utility Enterprise Fund for $30,000 was paid.

(e) Depreciation on the building and on the equipment was $5,000 and $114,000, respectively.

(f) Billings to other departments for service were as follows:

General Fund	$362,000
Water and Sewer Fund	84,000
Special Revenue Fund	32,000

(g) Unpaid interfund receivable balances at June 30, 19X9, were:

General Fund	$106,000
Special Revenue Fund	16,000

(h) Vouchers payable at June 30, 19X9, were $14,000.

Required:

(1) For the period July 1, 19X8, through June 30, 19X9, prepare journal entries to record the transactions in the Computer Internal Service Fund. The city uses control accounts for revenues and expenses.

(2) Prepare closing entries at June 30, 19X9.

Problem 18–7.   Each of the following transactions is independent of the others. They represent practical situations encountered in accounting for municipal governments.

(a) The city council of Butler adopted a general operating budget in which revenues are estimated at $795,000 and anticipated expenditures are $750,000.

(b) Taxes of $260,000 are levied for the Special Revenue Funds of Whitewater. One percent is estimated to be uncollectible.

(c) On July 25, 19X7, office supplies estimated to cost $42,390 are ordered for the General Fund of the City of York, which operates on a calendar-year basis and does not use a perpetual inventory system. The supplies are received on August 9, accompanied by an invoice for $42,500, which is vouchered.

(d) On October 10, 19X7, the General Fund of Maple Bluff repaid to the Utility Fund a loan of $1,000 plus $40 interest. The loan had been made earlier in the fiscal year.

(e) A leading citizen died and left undeveloped land to Reno for a future school site. The donor's cost was $35,000; fair market value at the date of death was $90,000.

(f) On March 1, 19X4, Dallas issued 4% special assessment bonds at 96, payable on March 1, 19X9, at face value of $400,000. Interest is payable annually. Dallas will use the proceeds to finance a street curbing project and guarantees debt repayment.

(g) A citizen of Cheyenne donated common stock valued at $52,000 to the city. Under terms of an agreement, the principal amount is not to be expended, and income must be used for college scholarships. Later, dividends of $3,100 are received and transferred to the Endowment Revenues Funds.

(h) On February 1, 19X3, the City of Portland, which operates on a calendar-year basis, issued 5% general obligation bonds with a face value of $500,000. Proceeds were $518,000. The premium was transferred to the Debt Service Funds for ultimate payment of principal. The bond issue was floated to finance the construction of a city hall addition estimated to cost $500,000. On December 3, 19X3, the addition was completed at a cost of $497,000, all of which was paid.

Required:

For each of the transactions described, prepare the journal entries for all of the funds and groups of accounts involved, using the following format:

Fund or Group	Journal Entry

(AICPA adapted)

Problem 18–8. In compliance with a newly enacted state law, Hayes County assumed the responsibility of collecting all property taxes levied within its boundaries as of July 1, 19X7. The following composite property tax rate per $100 of net assessed valuation was developed for the fiscal year ending June 30, 19X8:

Hayes County General Fund	$ 6.00
Dane City General Fund	3.00
Newark Township General Fund	1.00
	$10.00

All property taxes are due in quarterly installments and, after being collected, are distributed to the governmental units represented in the composite rate. To administer the collection and distribution of such taxes, Hayes County has established a Tax Agency Fund.

Additional information:

(a) To reimburse itself for estimated administrative expenses of operating the Tax Agency Fund, the county is to deduct 2% from the tax collections for Dane City and Newark Township. The total amount deducted is to be remitted to the Hayes County General Fund.

(b) Current-year tax levies to be collected by the Tax Agency Fund are as follows:

	Gross Levy	Estimated Amount To Be Collected
Hayes County	$3,600,000	$3,500,000
Dane City	1,800,000	1,740,000
Newark Township	600,000	560,000
	$6,000,000	$5,800,000

(c) In its original computation of the gross levy, Newark Township made an error that will reduce both the gross and estimated amounts to be collected by $10,000.

(d) As of September 30, 19X7, the Tax Agency Fund has received $1,440,000 in first-quarter payments. On October 1, the Agency Fund made a distribution to the three governmental units on the basis of the composite property tax rate.

Required:

For the period July 1, 19X7, through October 1, 19X7, prepare journal entries to record the preceding transactions, using the following format:

	Hayes County Tax Agency Fund		Hayes County General Fund		Dane City General Fund		Newark Township General Fund	
Accounts	Debit	Credit	Debit	Credit	Debit	Credit	Debit	Credit

(AICPA adaped)

Problem 18–9. The following trial balance of the Employees' Retirement System Fund for Redford City was prepared by a clerk who used only balance sheet accounts in recording the events for the fiscal year ended December 31, 19X2:

Cash...	28,000	
Investments	496,000	
Due to Resigned Employees........		2,000
Annuities Payable.......................		3,000
Surplus......................................		519,000
	524,000	524,000

An investigation uncovered the following activity in the surplus account:

	Contributions		Retired Employees' Annuities	Total
	Employee	Employer		
Balances on January 1, 19X2.............................	$100,000	$200,000	$159,000	$459,000
Events during 19X2: Amounts received (city still owes $4,000 at year end)	16,000	32,000	—	48,000
Payments to retired employees.....................	—	—	(13,000)	(13,000)
Annuities payable at year end	—	—	(3,000)	(3,000)
Annuities established for current retirees..............	(12,000)	(17,000)	29,000	—
Investment earnings received (accrued earnings of $5,000 have not been recorded at year end)	8,000	13,000	9,000	30,000
Due to resigned employees for their contributions	(2,000)	—	—	(2,000)
Balances on December 31, 19X2	$110,000	$228,000	$181,000	$519,000

An actuarial report indicates that as of January 1, 19X2, there was an actuarially computed deficiency of $117,000 to fund plan requirements. As of December 31, 19X2, the deficiency is $104,000.

Required:
(1) Prepare journal entries to correct the balance sheet accounts as of January 1, 19X2, including the recording of the computed deficiency.
(2) Prepare journal entries to record the events transpiring during 19X2 as they should have been recorded originally.
(3) Prepare a balance sheet of the Employees' Retirement System Fund as of December 31, 19X2.

Problem 18–10.   In response to a petition signed by the property owners of Carriage Hills Subdivision, the City of Newton will oversee the installation of sidewalks, curbs, and gutters in the subdivision, to be accounted for in the city's Capital Projects Fund. Newton reports on a calendar-year basis. Construction is estimated to cost $900,000 and will be financed by a $100,000 county grant, a $50,000 transfer from the city's General Fund, and special assessments of $750,000 to be levied against subdivision property owners. One-third of the levy is to be due on February 1 of each year, starting with 19X1. The first $250,000 installment will be received by the Capital Projects Fund directly. The remaining installments will be used to service the related bond debt. The project is to begin on January 15, 19X1 and is to take 18 months to complete. It is estimated that 70% of the work will be completed during 19X1.

To cover construction costs, a 6%, $500,000 special assessment serial bond issue will be floated on March 1, 19X1. Interest is to be paid semiannually on September 1 and March 1. One-fifth of the principal will be redeemed on March 1 of each year, starting with 19X2. Since interest earned on special assessments will offset bond interest cost, the city will not accrue interest.

Although the special assessments will provide cash to redeem the bond principal and pay the bond interest, Newton has pledged its full faith and credit as security for the bond obligation.

The following events happen during 19X1:
(a) On January 2, the city council adopted the annual budget for the Carriage Hills project in the Capital Projects Fund.
(b) On January 2, the receivables from the General Fund and the county were recorded.
(c) On January 5, special assessments were levied in accordance with the plan, with one-third due on February 1.
(d) On January 9, amounts due from the General Fund and the county were received.
(e) On January 10, encumbrances for the year were recorded at $675,000.
(f) By February 1, the first special assessment installment was collected.
(g) On March 1, bonds with a $500,000 face value were sold at 101. Except for the price, other conditions remained in accordance with the bond

plan. The premium was to be transferred to the Debt Service Fund later in the year.

(h) On March 1, $600,000 was invested in a 5% money market account by the Capital Projects Fund.

(i) On August 31, $15,000 for interest payment was transferred by the Capital Projects Fund to the Debt Service Fund. The amount included the premium on the bond sale.

(j) On September 1, the semiannual bond interest was paid.

(k) On December 15, the contractor submitted an invoice for $600,000 that was approved for payment, except for a 10% amount to be paid on completion and acceptance of the project. Related encumbrances totaled $595,000.

(l) On December 29, $400,000 was withdrawn from the money market investment. Interest of $16,600 was received.

(m) On December 30, the contractor was mailed a check for $540,000. In addition, vouchers for $76,600 were prepared and paid for items on the project that were not encumbered.

(n) The next assessment installment was reclassified upon special direction of the city council.

(o) An amount equal to project expenditures to date was capitalized.

Required:

For each of the preceding events, prepare the journal entries for all of the funds and groups of accounts involved, using the following format:

Fund or Group   Entry

Problem 18–11. The pre-closing, year-end trial balance for a Capital Projects Fund of the City of Newton as of December 31, 19X1, follows:

Cash	90,000	
Investments	200,000	
Special Assessments Receivable—Current	250,000	
Special Assessments Receivable—Deferred	250,000	
Contracts Payable—Retained Percentage		60,000
Deferred Revenues—Special Assessments		250,000
Revenues (Control)		616,600
Other Financing Sources (Control)		550,000
Expenditures (Control)	676,600	
Other Financing Uses (Control)	10,000	
Encumbrances (Control)	80,000	
Budgetary Fund Balance—Reserved for Encumbrances		80,000
Estimated Revenues (Control)	350,000	
Estimated Other Financing Sources (Control)	550,000	
Appropriations (Control)		630,000
Estimated Other Financing Uses (Control)		15,000
Budgetary Fund Balance—Unreserved		255,000
	2,456,600	2,456,600

Required:

(1) Prepare the year-end statement of revenues, expenditures, and changes in fund balances for this project that began on January 2, 19X1.

(2) Prepare the balance sheet as of December 31, 19X1.

(3) Prepare closing entries as of December 31, 19X1. Restrict the unreserved fund balance for the outstanding encumbrances.

Problem 18–12. You are given the following post-closing trial balance for one of the capital projects of the City of Newton as of January 1, 19X2. The project was started last year and should be completed in June of 19X2.

Cash..	90,000	
Investments	200,000	
Special Assessments Receivable—Current..........	250,000	
Special Assessments Receivable—Deferred........	250,000	
Contracts Payable—Retained Percentage............		60,000
Deferred Revenues—Special Assessments		250,000
Fund Balance—Reserved for Encumbrances.......		80,000
Fund Balance—Unreserved, Undesignated.........		400,000
	790,000	790,000

Events occurring during 19X2 follow:

(a) On January 2, the city adopted an operating budget for the project for 19X2. Revenues were estimated at $267,000, expenditures at $223,400, and other financing uses at $115,000.

(b) The amount reserved for encumbrances was reversed on January 2. These encumbrances, along with $138,000 of additional encumbrances, were booked on January 5.

(c) By February 1, $220,000 of special assessments were collected, along with interest of $17,600. Interest of $2,400 was billed on the uncollected current special assessments, which were reclassified as delinquent.

(d) On February 28, $115,000 was transferred to the Debt Service Fund for payment of $100,000 of principal and $15,000 of interest on the related bond issue that has matured.

(e) March 1 payments to bondholders were made by the Debt Service Fund. Although payments to bondholders were to be made from collections of special assessments, the city had guaranteed repayment of bond obligations in case of default by the property owners.

(f) By March 14, delinquent special assessments and interest thereon of $2,650 were collected.

(g) By May 1, expenditures of $220,000 were vouchered to Contracts Payable. The usual 10% retained percentage was entered. The project now was complete at a total cost of $896,600.

(h) A check for $100,000 was issued to the contractor on May 10.

Required:

Prepare journal entries to record each of the preceding events in the proper funds and groups of accounts, using the following format:

Fund or Group	Entry

CHAPTER 19

ACCOUNTING FOR NOT-FOR-PROFIT UNIVERSITIES AND PROVIDERS OF HEALTH CARE SERVICES

Not-for-profit activities are a significant portion of the economy of the United States. In this chapter, the not-for-profit organizations discussed are colleges and universities (herein collectively referred to as "universities") and providers of health care services. Chapter 20 details the accounting for voluntary health and welfare organizations and briefly covers other not-for-profit organizations.

GENERAL CHARACTERISTICS

Both governmental units and not-for-profit organizations have as their primary purpose the rendering of service without profit motivation. With their devotion to service rather than to profits, the success of not-for-profit organizations is difficult to evaluate because of the lack of objective measures of "service." Furthermore, the lack of the profit motive is reflected in weaknesses in accounting and reporting. For example, accrual accounting might not be used and, therefore, cost procedures might not be incorporated into an organization's accounting system. With no built-in cost system, the benefits of variance analysis are not available. Recently, institutions such as universities and health care providers have begun a thorough analysis of the cost of their services.

THE BUDGET

In many not-for-profit organizations, the budget is prepared perfunctorily and reviewed haphazardly, if at all. As a direct result of failing to view the budget as an essential tool for control and direction of the organization, some not-for-profit organizations, such as educational and religious groups, racquet and golf clubs, and fraternal organizations, constantly are confronted with financial difficulties.

As in a commercial enterprise, the budgeting process should involve the establishment of goals, the measurement of actual performance, and the comparison of actual with projected performance to evaluate results. This process requires the input of persons who can determine what resources will become available, what the group desires to achieve with those resources, and how the resources should be applied to yield the greatest benefit. If the organization or program is well established, a useful starting point is the previous year's budget and its variances, adjusted for any changes in objectives. If the group or program is new, the preparation of an effective operating budget requires careful research to produce realistic estimates of both revenues and expenditures.

Expenditures should be planned to maximize service output without producing either a surplus or deficit. A sizable excess of revenues over expenditures implies that more or better service could be provided. A deficit may indicate the need to curtail future services, since future funds may have to be committed to cover past deficits.

In accounting for universities and providers of health care services, it is not as common to find budgetary amounts formally entered into principal ledger accounts as it is in governmental accounting. Often, detailed budgetary amounts are entered directly in appropriate subsidiary records, and encumbrances are entered directly in an encumbrance column in the expenditures subsidiary record. Although subsidiary records are not supported by principal ledger control accounts when this procedure is followed, some degree of control is achieved by comparing the subsidiary records with actual revenues and expenditures.

If a budgetary entry is recorded, it would be similar to the one used in governmental accounting, and it would be reversed at year end. Assuming that estimated revenues exceed estimated expenditures and allocations, the budgetary entry would be:

Estimated Revenues..	XXX	
Estimated Expenditures (or Budget Allocations for		
Expenditures)		XXX
Unallocated Balance		XXX

PLEDGES

The lifeblood of many not-for-profit organizations is the promised contribution, or *pledge*. In most cases, to encourage pledges of larger amounts, donors are permitted to pay their pledges over a period of time. As a result, organizations are confronted with the accounting problem of whether to recognize revenue when the pledge commitment is made or as cash is received.

As is the case with most receivables, the longer the time interval over which payment is spread, the stronger will be the probability that a pledge will not be collected. Furthermore, a pledge may not be legally enforceable, and suits to collect pledges are rare because unfavorable public reaction could be disastrous for an organization. Nevertheless, when pledges due within a one-year period are a material portion of revenue, the accrual basis should be used so that revenue is recognized when the signed pledge is received. If property other than cash is pledged, its market value or appraisal value is recognized as revenue. An Allowance for Uncollectible Pledges should be created also, with the amount dependent upon the organization's historical experience with collections.

If the payment period extends beyond annual limits, the technique of deferring recognition of revenue is recommended. For example, assume that individuals pledge $30,000 to a hospital. Of this amount, one-third is to be collected in the current year. The remainder is collectible in equal annual installments, with 5% estimated to be uncollectible. This pledge is recorded as follows:

Pledges Receivable	30,000	
Nonoperating Revenue—Contributions		10,000
Deferred Pledge Revenue		19,000
Allowance for Uncollectible Pledges		1,000

FUND ACCOUNTING

Accounting processes are influenced by the nature of an organization and its goals and available resources. Since not-for-profit organizations, as with governmental units, must insure that resources are expended for the purposes intended, fund accounting is used.

AUDIT GUIDES

Until recently, there were no accounting opinions, standards, or guidelines that applied directly to the approximately one-half million not-for-profit organizations in the United States. Prior to 1972, there was no uniformity in reporting, and few rules were acknowledged universally. Since that time, however, the American Institute of Certified Public Accountants has issued five audit guides applicable to this group:

> Audits of Colleges and Universities (Revised, 1975)
> Audits of Voluntary Health and Welfare Organizations (Revised, 1974)
> Audits of State and Local Governmental Units (Revised, 1986)
> Audits of Certain Nonprofit Organizations (1981)
> Audits of Providers of Health Care Services (1989)

These guides give direction to accountants in their examinations of not-for-profit and governmental organizations. Each guide includes appropriate accounting principles that are based on the philosophy that the reader of not-for-profit financial reports needs information about the organization's service to the public and the cost of that service.

ACCOUNTING FOR NOT-FOR-PROFIT UNIVERSITIES

The responsibilities of a not-for-profit university may be classified as academic, financial, student services, and public relations. Academic functions include instruction, research, and public service. The financial sphere covers the management and reporting of business and financial affairs as well as auxiliary enterprises, such as housing, food service, and student union operation. Student services includes all student activities not directly classified as academic or financial, such as admissions, records, health, counseling, and publications. Public relations involves the communication and establishment of goodwill with academic and administrative staff, alumni, and the community.

The effectiveness with which a university accomplishes its objectives in these four areas depends upon the resources at its disposal. A university levies tuition fees, but these fees do not cover total operational costs. Therefore, other sources of revenue are essential. These sources include gifts, income from endowment funds, grants from governmental units or foundations, and, for public universities, appropriations from state legislatures.

ACCOUNTING SYSTEM AND FINANCIAL STATEMENTS

The day-to-day activities of a university are recorded in its current funds, which consist of two self-balancing subfunds. The *Unrestricted Current Fund* represents amounts that are available for any current activity commensurate with the university's objectives. The *Restricted Current Fund* accounts for those resources available only for an externally specified purpose. The segregation of Unrestricted Current Funds from Restricted Current Funds is necessary to substantiate that the limitations placed on restricted funds by outside sources have been observed. *Plant Funds* account for capital assets and for resources to be used to acquire additional capital assets or to retire indebtedness related to capital assets. Plant Funds consist of several subgroups, each of which is designed to record a certain phase of activity related to fixed assets. *Endowment and Similar Funds* account for endowments received. In addition, a university may employ Loan Funds, Annuity Funds, and Agency Funds. Each fund may have its own accounting records, or, if the university is large, all funds may be integrated into one record system.

In this situation, electronic data processing equipment probably would be used to produce reports for each fund.

Operating or current funds record revenues and expenditures in nominal accounts. In the other funds, Fund Balance may be credited directly for resources received and debited directly for resource outflows. As a result, only the current funds present a statement of revenues and expenditures. Except for depreciation, the accrual basis is used in university accounting.

Starting in 1987, an interesting battle for turf developed between the AICPA and the GASB regarding the recording of depreciation by a governmental university (city, county, or state). The AICPA pronouncement, *Audits of Colleges and Universities* (Revised, 1975), stipulated that depreciation should not be shown in operating statements. In August of 1987, the AICPA changed its position when it issued FASB Statement No. 93, "Recognition of Depreciation by Not-for-Profit Organizations," which required such organizations to recognize depreciation in their general purpose external financial statements. About 80 universities said that they would rather accept qualified opinions on their financial statements than comply with FASB No. 93. To substantiate their position, the universities explained that since service, rather than profit, is their objective, accounting and reporting should concentrate on resources received and expended. Depreciation should not be recognized because that would duplicate amounts previously recorded as expenditures when the asset was acquired.

In January of 1988, the GASB came to their rescue by issuing Statement No. 8, "Applicability of FASB Statement No. 93 to Certain State and Local Governmental Entities." It specified that governmental universities should *not* change their accounting and reporting for depreciation of capital assets, but were not precluded from depreciating capital assets. Under an option offered by the audit guide, they could show an allowance for depreciation in the balance sheet. Since the proclamations of the GASB in the area of setting standards of accounting and reporting for state and local governmental entities take precedence over those of the FASB, governmental universities need not report depreciation. Reacting to the opposition, the FASB voted in 1988 to delay the effective date of Statement No. 93. Instead of being effective for financial statements issued for fiscal years beginning after May 15, 1988, it was moved forward to fiscal years beginning on or after January 1, 1990, by FASB Statement No. 99, "Deferral of the Effective Date of Recognition of Depreciation by Not-for-Profit Organizations." Only time will tell whether or not the GASB position will be a true victory.

The fact that depreciation need not be reported in its external financial statements does not prevent its computation and use in independent determinations of the total cost of operating the university. Such cost computations are useful in establishing charges for auxiliary enterprise services, which include dormitories, bookstores, cafeterias and restaurants, medical service, and the student union. Especially for services provided to the general public, amounts charged should include depreciation considerations, even though depreciation is not recorded formally. A part of the amount that a university receives from grants reimburses it for overhead, which should include depreciation. The only university fund in which a provision for depreciation must be entered is in the unusual case that fixed assets are a part of a nonexpendable endowment fund, which must protect its principal.

As with financial statements of all not-for-profit organizations, the financial statements of a university should reveal resources received and committed rather than net income. The three principal financial statements for a university are:

1. The statement of current funds revenues, expenditures, and other changes, which provides detail on revenues, expenditures, transfers, and other changes in fund balances for the period.
2. The combined balance sheet, which is a side-by-side presentation of the balance sheets indicating the financial position of each fund.
3. The statement of changes in fund balances—the most important of the three financial statements—which provides a summary of activities for the period in each fund and their impact on each fund balance account.

Each of these statements is explained and illustrated at appropriate points in the discussion that follows.

UNIVERSITY CURRENT FUNDS— UNRESTRICTED

The Unrestricted Current Fund of a university is similar to the General Fund of a governmental unit in that it accounts for current assets available to cover current operational costs and resulting current liabilities. No outside limitations apply to its resources.

A university might establish one master control account for unrestricted revenues, with details as to major sources recorded in subsidiary records. More commonly, separate revenue accounts are established, using the following scheme for the three major groups of revenues, as suggested in the audit guide:

Educational and general revenues group, with accounts for:
  Student tuition and fees (recognized when due or billed, with appropriate allowance for uncollectibles)
  Governmental appropriations (detailed as to federal, state, and local)
  Governmental grants and contracts (detailed as to federal, state, and local)
  Gifts and private grants
  Endowment income
  Other sources

Auxiliary enterprises revenues

Expired term endowment revenues

In the interest of full disclosure, operating revenues are recorded in these accounts. Auxiliary enterprises revenues are segregated to permit the evaluation of performance and the degree of self-support. Expired term endowment income represents dollar amounts of term endowments on which the restriction has lapsed, freeing them to become unrestricted resources.

Unrestricted Current Fund expenditures are the costs incurred to conduct the university's daily operations using unrestricted resources. Expenditures may be classified in a number of ways, depending on the purpose. In financial reports, the audit guide recommends classification by function for two major groupings, which are the same as the first two used to classify revenues. The resulting expenditure accounts are as follows:

Educational and general expenditures group, with accounts for:
Instruction (expenditures for credit and noncredit courses)
Research (expenditures to produce research results)
Public support (expenditures for noninstructional services, including conferences, seminars, and consulting)
Academic support (expenditures supporting instruction and public services, such as libraries, galleries, audiovisual services, and academic deans)
Student services (expenditures for student admission and registration and cultural and athletic activities)
Institutional support (expenditures for central administration)
Operation and maintenance of plant
Student aid (expenditures for scholarships, fellowships, tuition remissions, and outright grants)
Auxiliary enterprises expenditures

In addition to expenditures, the Unrestricted Current Fund Balance is affected by transfers. *Discretionary* or *nonmandatory transfers*, such as transfers to a loan fund or a plant fund, are transfers of unrestricted resources to other funds at the discretion of the university's governing authority. *Mandatory transfers* are required transfers of resources to other funds. Some mandatory transfers, such as amounts set aside for debt retirement and interest payment, result from binding legal contracts. Other mandatory transfers arise from the acceptance of a grant or donation that requires the university to match some or all of the amounts received. Although the source of mandatory transfers may be either Unrestricted or Restricted Current Funds, it is more commonly Unrestricted Funds.

Discretionary transfers are recorded by debiting either Unrestricted Current Fund Balance or a temporary equity account, such as Transfer to Loan Fund. The temporary equity account would be closed to Unrestricted Current Fund Balance at year end. Mandatory transfers, however, are recorded by debiting the account Mandatory Transfers. These transfers, which may relate to either educational and general activities or to auxiliary enterprises, are segregated on financial reports.

To illustrate the accounting process in the Unrestricted Current Fund, assume that Rogers University maintains separate records for each of its funds. It uses detailed revenue and expenditure accounts recommended by the audit guide, rather than broad control accounts, and the budget is recorded formally. Encumbrance items are entered directly into subsidiary records, but no formal entries for them are made. The summarized events for Rogers University are described and recorded as follows:

Event		Entry		
The following budget is approved:		Estimated Revenues......................	3,300,000	
Estimated revenues...........	$3,300,000	Estimated Expenditures..............		3,000,000
Estimated expenditures......	3,000,000	Unallocated Balance		300,000
Unallocated balance..........	$ 300,000			
Educational and general revenue is earned or billed:		Accounts Receivable.....................	3,000,000	
		Revenues—Student Tuition and Fees....................................		1,680,000
Student tuition and fees (of which $20,000 is considered uncollectible)...	$1,700,000	Revenues—Governmental Appropriations		750,000
Governmental appropriations...............	750,000	Revenues—Private Gifts and Grants.................................		250,000
Private gifts and grants	250,000	Revenues—Endowment Income ...		50,000
Endowment income	50,000	Revenues—Other Income..........		250,000
Other income..................	250,000	Allowance for Uncollectibles		20,000
Total	$3,000,000			
Of the total revenues, $2,800,000 is collected.		Cash.......................................	2,800,000	
		Accounts Receivable..................		2,800,000
Revenue billed for dormitories (an auxiliary enterprise) is $400,000, of which $20,000 is not yet received.		Cash.......................................	380,000	
		Accounts Receivable.....................	20,000	
		Revenues—Auxiliary Enterprises ...		400,000
Purchases of materials and supplies total $400,000, of which $25,000 is not yet paid.		Inventory of Materials....................	400,000	
		Cash.......................................		375,000
		Accounts Payable......................		25,000
Expenditures are paid and assigned to:		Expenditures—Instruction..............	1,050,000	
		Expenditures—Research..............	100,000	
Instruction	$1,050,000	Expenditures—Academic Support ...	150,000	
Research.........................	100,000	Expenditures—Student Services	200,000	
Academic support	150,000	Expenditures—Institutional Support...	200,000	
Student services...............	200,000	Expenditures—Operation and Maintenance of Plant.....................	400,000	
Institutional support...........	200,000	Expenditures—Student Aid	40,000	
Operation and maintenance of plant	400,000	Expenditures—Auxiliary Enterprises	260,000	
Student aid	40,000	Cash.......................................		2,400,000
Auxiliary enterprises	260,000			
Total	$2,400,000			
Materials and supplies used:		Expenditures—Instruction..............	268,000	
		Expenditures—Student Services	22,000	
Instruction	$ 268,000	Expenditures—Auxiliary Enterprises...	90,000	
Student services...............	22,000	Inventory of Materials.................		380,000
Auxiliary enterprises	90,000			
Total	$ 380,000			

Event	Entry		
Cash is transferred to Plant Funds for:	Fund Balance (or Transfer to Plant Funds)................................	147,000	
	Mandatory Transfers for Principal Payment............................	20,000	
Addition to plant (discretionary)............... $ 147,000	Cash..		167,000
Payment of mortgage (mandatory).................. 20,000			
Total .... $ 167,000			
The Board of Trustees has agreed to transfer $3,000 to the Loan Fund on the first day of the next fiscal year.	Fund Balance (or Transfer to Loan Fund)...................................	3,000	
	Due to Other Funds....................		3,000
Aid is granted to students:	Expenditures — Student Aid	175,000	
	Accounts Receivable....................		140,000
Remission of tuition........... $ 140,000	Cash..		35,000
Cash scholarships 35,000			
Total .... $ 175,000			
The Board of Trustees authorizes an immediate transfer of $150,000 to the Endowment Fund.	Fund Balance (or Transfer to Endowment Fund)	150,000	
	Cash..		150,000
Term endowments expired, making $20,000 cash available. (Term endowments are discussed on page 1002.)	Cash..	20,000	
	Revenues — Expired Term Endowments..........................		20,000
The budgetary entry is reversed.	Unallocated Balance	300,000	
	Estimated Expenditures.................	3,000,000	
	Estimated Revenues....................		3,300,000
The books are closed, with a separate closing entry for Auxiliary Enterprises to demonstrate the degree of success.	Revenues — Student Tuition and Fees....................................	1,680,000	
	Revenues — Governmental Appropriations	750,000	
	Revenues—Private Gifts and Grants ..	250,000	
	Revenues — Endowment Income.....	50,000	
	Revenues — Other Income..............	250,000	
	Revenues — Expired Term Endowments..........................	20,000	
	Expenditures — Instruction...........		1,318,000
	Expenditures — Research.............		100,000
	Expenditures—Academic Support ..		150,000
	Expenditures — Student Services ..		222,000
	Expenditures — Institutional Support		200,000
	Expenditures — Operation and Maintenance of Plant..............		400,000
	Expenditures — Student Aid		215,000
	Fund Balance		395,000
	Revenues — Auxiliary Enterprises.....	400,000	
	Expenditures — Auxiliary Enterprises		350,000
	Fund Balance		50,000
	Fund Balance	20,000	
	Mandatory Transfers for Principal Payment................................		20,000

Event	Entry		
If separate transfer accounts were used to record discretionary transfers, they would be closed at this point.	Fund Balance	300,000	
	Transfer to Plant Funds		147,000
	Transfer to Loan Fund		3,000
	Transfer to Endowment Fund		150,000

UNIVERSITY CURRENT FUNDS — RESTRICTED

For an activity to enter the Restricted Current Fund of a university, some limitation placed by an external entity on the resources received must exist. The same revenue and expenditure accounts used in the Unrestricted Current Fund are available, but Restricted Current Fund revenues arise primarily from governmental grants and contracts, private gifts, and endowment income. Expenditures generally are relegated to instruction, research, and student aid.

Unless the restriction placed upon contributed resources is respected, these resources may have to be returned to the donor. Until they are expended properly, they should not be considered as revenue. As a consequence, expenditures govern the recognition of revenue. These resources are expenditure-driven, similar to such items in governmental accounting. This situation requires the following entries in a Restricted Current Fund:

Event	Entry		
Resources are contributed by a corporation for scholarships to minorities.	Assets Contributed	XXX	
	Fund Balance		XXX
Expenditures are made in compliance with restrictions; revenue is recognized	Expenditures — Student Aid	XXX	
	Cash		XXX
	Fund Balance	XXX	
	Revenues — Private Gifts and Grants		XXX

Fund Balance is increased at the time of the receipt of the resources. Revenue is not recognized until resources are expended and then in the exact amount of the expenditures. As a result, revenues always will equal expenditures in the Restricted Current Fund.

The following events affected the Restricted Current Fund of Rogers University. Only one fund balance account is maintained. Data on sources, purposes, and applications of restricted resources are recorded in subsidiary records.

Event	Entry		
A restricted gift of $70,000 is received to assist library operations.	Cash...................... Fund Balance	70,000	70,000
Endowment income of $8,000 is received, restricted to Student Aid activities.	Cash...................... Fund Balance	8,000	8,000

Of the following expenditures, all but $4,000 are paid:

For library operations	$67,000
For student aid	6,000
Total	$73,000

	Expenditures — Academic Support..... Expenditures — Student Aid .... Cash.................... Accounts Payable....	67,000 6,000	69,000 4,000
Revenues are recorded to the extent of expenditures.	Fund Balance .... Revenues — Private Gifts and Grants... Revenues — Endowment Income.......	73,000	67,000 6,000
The books are closed. Since revenues equal expenditures, Fund Balance is not involved.	Revenues — Private Gifts and Grants... Revenues — Endowment Income....... Expenditures — Academic Support..... Expenditures — Student Aid	67,000 6,000	67,000 6,000

STATEMENT OF REVENUES, EXPENDITURES, AND OTHER CHANGES

The statement of revenues, expenditures, and other changes is provided by only the current funds, since the other funds record changes in resources directly through their fund balances. This statement shows the current funds revenues by source, expenditures by function, and other changes, such as mandatory and discretionary transfers. In the design recommended by the audit guide, the statement does not attempt to show net income or net loss, since this amount is not of primary concern to a not-for-profit unit. Instead, the final amount is the net increase or decrease in the Unrestricted and Restricted Fund Balances, which also is shown in the statement of changes in fund balances. The recommended form, presented in Illustration 19–1, shows columns for the Unrestricted Current Fund, the Restricted Current Fund, and the total.

Note that in the Restricted Current Fund column the total revenues equal the total expenditures. Also note in this column the amount labeled

Illustration 19–1

Rogers University
Statement of Current Funds Revenues, Expenditures, and Other Changes
For the Year Ended June 30, 19X0

	Unrestricted	Restricted	Total
Revenues:			
Educational and general:			
Student tuition and fees...........	$1,680,000		$1,680,000
Governmental appropriations ...	750,000		750,000
Private gifts and grants............	250,000	$67,000	317,000
Endowment income.................	50,000	6,000	56,000
Other income..........................	250,000		250,000
Total educational and general revenues..........................	$2,980,000	$73,000	$3,053,000
Auxiliary enterprises..................	400,000		400,000
Expired term endowments...........	20,000		20,000
Total revenues......................	$3,400,000	$73,000	$3,473,000
Expenditures and mandatory transfers:			
Educational and general:			
Instruction	$1,318,000		$1,318,000
Research................................	100,000		100,000
Academic support....................	150,000	$67,000	217,000
Student services......................	222,000		222,000
Institutional support.................	200,000		200,000
Operation and maintenance of plant	400,000		400,000
Student aid.............................	215,000	6,000	221,000
Total educational and general expenditures.....................	$2,605,000	$73,000	$2,678,000
Mandatory transfers for principal payment...............................	20,000		20,000
Total......................................	$2,625,000	$73,000	$2,698,000
Auxiliary enterprises expenditures..........................	350,000		350,000
Total expenditures and mandatory transfers..............	$2,975,000	$73,000	$3,048,000
Other transfers and additions (deductions):			
Excess of restricted receipts over transfers to revenues		$ 5,000	$ 5,000
Transfers to other funds.............	($ 300,000)		(300,000)
Net increase in fund balances.........	$ 125,000	$ 5,000	$ 130,000

Excess of restricted receipts over transfers to revenues. As shown in the entries recorded by the Restricted Current Fund, a total of $78,000 in restricted resources was received this period, but only $73,000 was expended, producing $5,000 of resources received and not expended. This item must be introduced on the statement of revenues, expenditures, and other changes in order to produce the correct net increase in Fund Balance.

An exceptionally high degree of accounting sophistication is required to interpret the statement of revenues, expenditures, and other changes in its present form. Its primary value is the detail it provides for revenues, expenditures, and transfers. However, if the primary emphasis is on resources made available (revenues) and resources applied (expenditures), a useful figure would be their difference, which is not furnished. The difference between total revenues and the sum of expenditures and mandatory transfers also is not provided, but it would have managerial value. The only net figure is the final amount of change in the fund balances. A superficial glance at the change of $125,000 in the Unrestricted Current Fund could lead the unwary to conclude incorrectly that the fund grew by only this amount. In reality, the increase in the fund is $425,000, which is the excess of total revenues ($3,400,000) over total expenditures and mandatory transfers ($2,975,000). The discretionary transfers of $300,000 to various other funds reduced the change to $125,000.

BALANCE SHEET

The audit guide presents a combined balance sheet for all funds, with separate, self-balancing totals for each fund as shown in Illustration 19–3 on pages 1012 and 1013. To facilitate the presentation and discussion of the balance sheet for Rogers University, a separate balance sheet for each fund will be presented immediately after the discussion of that fund. The current funds balance sheet, subdivided as to unrestricted and restricted items, is shown in Illustration 19–2, Part 1.

LOAN FUNDS

Loan Funds are established to account for resources that are available for loans primarily to students and possibly to faculty and staff. Loan Funds are revolving (self-perpetuating), with repayments of principal and the excess of interest collected over costs incurred becoming the base for additional loans. Both principal and earnings must be available for loan purposes. If only the income from a gift or grant may be used for loan purposes, the principal should not be in the Loan Fund but in the Endowment Fund.

Illustration 19–2, Part 1

Rogers University
Partial Balance Sheet
June 30, 19X0

Current Funds

Assets		Liabilities and Fund Balances	
Unrestricted:		**Unrestricted:**	
Cash...................................	$ 260,000	Accounts payable	$ 230,000
Investments	450,000	Due to other funds...............	198,000
Accounts receivable (net)	306,000	Fund balance	726,000
Inventory of materials	110,000		
Prepaid expenses	28,000		
Total unrestricted...............	$1,154,000	Total unrestricted..................	$1,154,000
Restricted:		**Restricted:**	
Cash...................................	$ 153,000	Accounts payable	$ 18,000
Investments	247,000	Fund balance	450,000
Accounts receivable (net)	68,000		
Total restricted	$ 468,000	Total restricted	$ 468,000
Total current funds	$1,622,000	Total current funds	$1,622,000

The resources of Loan Funds consist mainly of gifts restricted for loan purposes and Unrestricted Current Fund resources transferred by authorization of the governing board. Although assets are not segregated by restriction, the fund balance must reveal its restricted and unrestricted portions. No revenue or expenditure accounts are used. Additions to the Loan Fund are recorded directly in the restricted or unrestricted fund balance, while expenditures and losses are deducted directly from the fund balance.

The following entries are recorded in the Loan Fund of Rogers University. The balance sheet section for the Loan Fund appears in Illustration 19–2, Part 2, on page 1002.

Event	Entry		
A donation of $25,000 is received from an alumnus for student loan purposes.	Cash... Fund Balance — Restricted.................	25,000	25,000
Investments costing $5,000 are sold for $5,500. Gain is restricted.	Cash... Investments.................................... Fund Balance — Restricted.................	5,500	5,000 500
Loans totaling $24,000 are made to students. Collections from other loans of restricted funds total $20,000 plus $1,000 of interest.	Loans Receivable............................... Cash...	24,000	24,000
	Cash... Loans Receivable............................. Fund Balance — Restricted.................	21,000	20,000 1,000

Event	Entry		
A $500 student loan made from restricted funds is uncollectible.	Fund Balance — Restricted.................... Loans Receivable	500	500
The board approved the transfer of $3,000 from the Unrestricted Current Fund, to be made on July 1, 19X0.	Due from Unrestricted Current Fund....... Fund Balance — Unrestricted..........	3,000	3,000

Illustration 19–2, Part 2

Rogers University
Partial Balance Sheet
June 30, 19X0

Loan Fund

Assets		Fund Balance	
Cash...............................	$29,500	Fund balance:	
Investments	5,000	Restricted	$82,500
Loans receivable..............	58,500	Unrestricted	13,500
Due from Unrestricted Current Fund.................	3,000		
Total loan fund.................	$96,000	Total loan fund.................	$96,000

ENDOWMENT AND SIMILAR FUNDS

The following types of endowment funds, each having its own fund balance account, are included in the category of Endowment and Similar Funds for a university:

1. *Regular or pure endowments* are funds whose principal has been specified by the donor as nonexpendable. The resources are invested, and the earnings are available for expenditure, usually by the Unrestricted Current Fund.

2. *Term endowments* are funds whose principal is expendable after a specified time period or after a designated event, at which point the resources are added to the Unrestricted Current Fund, unless the original donor has specified some other application.

3. *Quasi-endowments* are funds set aside by the board or controlling body, usually from Unrestricted Current Funds. Restricted Current Funds also may be set aside if the donor's limitations are not violated. Since these funds are discretionary, technically they do not belong to the endowment category, hence the addition to the title of "and Similar Funds."

Accounting should be detailed sufficiently in subsidiary records to demonstrate compliance with the restrictions of each endowment fund. In the balance sheet, the assets are not segregated, but the fund balance section shows the endowment, term endowment, and quasi-endowment components for which separate accounts are established.

As gifts and bequests are received, either the account Fund Balance—Endowment or Fund Balance—Term Endowment is credited. Assets received as a result of discretionary transfers are credited to Fund Balance—Quasi-Endowment. Gains or losses on the disposition of endowment assets are recorded directly in the appropriate fund balance account. Note that gains or losses are considered changes in principal and not as income or expense, unless otherwise specified by the donor.

The resources for endowment funds often are pooled for investment purposes, with the various fund balances sharing proportionally in the outcome based on the market values of investments at the time of pooling or at specified future dates. Procedures for investment pooling are discussed in Chapter 20. Income from restricted endowment resources should be transferred immediately to and recorded directly in the fund balance of the Restricted Current Fund, the Loan Fund, the Endowment Fund, or the Plant Fund, depending upon which fund the donor has specified should reap the benefits. Income on which there is no restriction should be transferred to and recorded directly in the Unrestricted Current Fund, where it is credited to Endowment Income. If, for some reason, there is a delay in making the transfer, the income received should be recorded in the Endowment Fund, with a credit to a liability to the proper fund. The costs of managing endowment funds should be borne by the university's Unrestricted Current Fund, which benefits from the income from unrestricted endowment investments.

To illustrate some of the accounting techniques, the following series of events is recorded, and the portion of the balance sheet devoted to Endowment and Similar Funds is shown in Illustration 19–2, Part 3, on page 1004.

Event	Entry		
The board of trustees transferred $150,000 from the Unrestricted Current Fund.	Cash.. Fund Balance—Quasi-Endowment...	150,000	150,000

Endowment Fund investments carried at $200,000 are sold for $260,000. Investment earnings of $40,000 are received, shared equally by the current funds.	Cash..
	    Investments..............................
	    Fund Balance—Endowment..........
	    Due to Other Funds.....................
		300,000	200,000
			60,000
			40,000

Common stock with a market value of $120,000 is received as a pure endowment donation.	Investments................................. Fund Balance—Endowment..........	120,000	120,000
Term endowments expired, resulting in $20,000 being released to the Unrestricted Current Fund.	Fund Balance—Term Endowment..... Cash...	20,000	20,000

Illustration 19–2, Part 3

Rogers University
Partial Balance Sheet
June 30, 19X0

Endowment and Similar Funds

Assets		Liabilities and Fund Balances	
Cash............................	$ 460,000	Liabilities:	
Investments	1,270,000	Due to other funds.....	$ 40,000
		Fund balances:	
		Endowment	790,000
		Term endowment......	460,000
		Quasi-endowment	440,000
Total endowment and		Total endowment and	
similar funds.............	$1,730,000	similar funds.............	$1,730,000

Although most universities report their investments on a cost basis, the audit guide permits the use of market value, provided this basis is used for all investments of all funds. Under the market value method, unrealized gains and losses are recognized and are accounted for as if realized.

ANNUITY AND LIFE INCOME FUNDS

Resources may be accepted by a university under the stipulation that periodic payments are to continue as an annuity to the donor or other designated beneficiary for an indicated time period. These resources should be accounted for in an *Annuity Fund* at their market value on the date of receipt. A liability for the actuarially computed present value of expected total annuity payments is recorded, with the excess credited to Annuity Fund Balance. As each payment is made, the difference between the actual payment and its original present value is charged directly to Annuity Fund Balance. For example, assume that a retired administrator donated $50,000 to a university. The administrator is to receive annuity payments of $3,000 per year for life; thereafter, the principal is to be used for student aid. The present value of the annuity is actuarially computed to be $22,000. The entry to record receipt of the donation is:

Cash — Annuity	50,000	
Annuities Payable		22,000
Annuity Fund Balance		28,000

At the end of the first year, the administrator is mailed a check for $3,000. The present value of the first payment included in the $22,000 figure is $2,830. The entry to record the payment is:

Annuities Payable	2,830	
Annuity Fund Balance	170	
Cash — Annuity		3,000

A *Life Income Fund* is used if all income received on contributed assets is to be paid to the donor or other specified recipient for life. When the original contributed assets are recorded at market value, the corresponding credit is to Life Income Fund Balance. As income is received, a liability for its payment is established immediately.

When the annuity payments or the life income payments cease, the principal is transferred to the donor-specified fund group or to the Unrestricted Current Fund revenue if no principal restriction exists. Also, unless otherwise specified, gains or losses on the sale of investments are treated as changes in principal and are recorded directly in the appropriate fund balance account.

Events that affected the ongoing Annuity and Life Income Funds of Rogers University are described and recorded as follows. The balance sheet section for these funds appears in Illustration 19–2, Part 4, on page 1006.

Event	Entry		
Cash of $12,000 from Life Income Fund investments and $18,000 from Annuity Fund investments is received. (Separate accounts are maintained for life income cash and annuity cash.)	Cash — Life Income	12,000	
	Life Income Payable		12,000
	Cash — Annuity	18,000	
	Annuity Fund Balance		18,000
A retired professor donated $100,000. The professor is to receive $6,000 per year for life. Thereafter, the principal is to be used for student aid. The present value of the annuity is actuarially computed to be $44,000.	Cash — Annuity	100,000	
	Annuities Payable		44,000
	Annuity Fund Balance		56,000
Payments are made to:	Annuities Payable	27,000	
	Annuity Fund Balance	4,000	
Annuitants (originally recorded present values, $27,000) $31,000	Cash — Annuity		31,000
Life income beneficiaries.... 12,000	Life Income Payable	12,000	
	Cash — Life Income		12,000
Annuity fund investments with a book value of $50,000 are sold for $59,500.	Cash — Annuity	59,500	
	Investments — Annuity		50,000
	Annuity Fund Balance		9,500

Illustration 19–2, Part 4

Rogers University
Partial Balance Sheet
June 30, 19X0

Annuity and Life Income Funds

Assets		Liabilities and Fund Balances	
Annuity funds:		Annuity funds:	
Cash..........................	$109,500	Annuities payable........	$232,000
Investments	326,000	Fund balance	203,500
Total annuity funds......	$435,500	Total annuity funds......	$435,500
Life income funds:		Life income funds:	
Cash..........................	$ 2,500	Life income payable.....	$ 1,500
Investments	204,500	Fund balance	205,500
Total life income funds..	$207,000	Total life income funds..	207,000
Total annuity and life income funds...........	$642,500	Total annuity and life income funds...........	$642,500

If a university has a substantial amount of Annuity and Life Income Funds, two separate funds could be established, removing the necessity to identify each component of an entry. The typical financial reports of these funds would display only the financial condition (balance sheet) and the changes in fund balances.

PLANT FUNDS

Plant Funds include four separate, self-balancing subgroups:

1. *Unexpended Plant Fund* accounts for resources that are to be used to acquire properties. Such resources may be received as a gift or grant restricted to plant acquisition, in which case Fund Balance — Restricted is credited. Assets may be transferred by university authorities from the current funds or other funds, requiring a credit to Fund Balance — Unrestricted to record their receipt. When cash is expended to acquire existing capital assets, the appropriate fund balance account is debited as Cash is credited. The assets acquired are recorded in the Investment in Plant subgroup, discussed on page 1007, with a credit to Net Investment in Plant. For a major construction project, a bond issue usually is floated. The proceeds and bond liability are recorded in the Unexpended Plant Fund, preferably until the construction is completed. As work is

begun, costs are debited to a construction in progress account. Upon completion, the total cost is transferred to the Investment in Plant subgroup, along with the related bond liability, with any difference between the two amounts recorded in Fund Balance—Unrestricted. If financing was achieved with a mortgage, the accounting procedure would be the same except for the designation of the liability as a mortgage payable.

2. *Plant Fund for Renewals and Replacements* accounts for resources that are available to keep the physical plant in operating condition. Such expenditures seldom lead to capitalization. Resources transferred to this subgroup as a result of discretionary action by the governing board are recorded by crediting the account Fund Balance—Unrestricted. Resources received from outside sources which specified that the amounts must be used for renewals and replacements are credited to Fund Balance—Restricted. When expenditures are made, the proper fund balance is debited, and the cash or a liability account is credited. The amount remaining in the two fund balance accounts represents the unexpended resources available for renewals and replacements.

3. *Plant Fund for Retirement of Indebtedness* corresponds to the Debt Service Fund of a governmental unit. This fund accounts for the resources accumulated for the payment of interest and principal of Plant Fund indebtedness. Since the liabilities are included in the Investment in Plant subgroup, payments of either interest or principal are recorded as direct reductions of the Retirement of Indebtedness Fund Balance.

4. The *Investment in Plant* subgroup controls all plant assets except those found in the Endowment Fund. This subgroup is similar to a combination of the General Fixed Assets and General Long-Term Debt Account Groups of a governmental unit. Assets are acquired as a result of transfers from the Unexpended Plant Fund subgroup, donations, and expenditures of the current funds. For a university, the costs of books and other library items are considered major outlays and are classified as plant assets. Liabilities related to the Investment in Plant also are shown in this subgroup. When principal is paid by the Plant Fund for Retirement of Indebtedness subgroup, the liability is reduced in the Investment in Plant subgroup, with a corresponding increase in Net Investment in Plant. Upon completion of a construction project whose costs were accumulated in the Unexpended Plant Fund, the Investment in Plant subgroup debits the asset completed, credits any remaining related liability, such as Bonds Payable or Mortgage Payable, and credits the difference to the account Net Investment in Plant.

The entries unique to the Plant Funds of Rogers University are presented on pages 1008 and 1009, with an indication of which of the four subgroups is recording the event. The Plant Funds section of the balance sheet is shown in Illustration 19–2, Part 5, on page 1010.

Event

Stock with a market value of $90,000 is received from an art patron to
finance an art gallery addition.

Cash is transferred from the Unrestricted Current Fund to cover:
   Additions to plant.. $147,000
   Payment on mortgage carried in Plant Funds 20,000

Payment of $100,000 is made on the mortgage related to completed plant.

A collection of first editions, appraised at $30,000, is donated to the
university.

An $800,000 bond issue is sold at face value to finance a business school
wing.

Construction of the wing is one-fourth completed.

Contract is completed at additional cost of $640,000 and is paid in full.

Completed building costs are transferred to Investment in Plant subgroup.

Land valued at $160,000 is donated by an alumnus.

Building repairs constituting a renewal of $50,000 are paid, of which $5,000
is from restricted resources.

Restricted earnings received on investments of:
   Unexpended Fund.. $ 40,000
   Renewals and Replacements Fund... 5,000

Plant Fund Subgroup	Entry		
Unexpended	Investments..	90,000	
	Fund Balance—Restricted...		90,000
Unexpended	Cash..	147,000	
	Fund Balance—Unrestricted..		147,000
Retirement of Indebtedness	Cash..	20,000	
	Fund Balance—Unrestricted..		20,000
Retirement of Indebtedness	Fund Balance—Unrestricted..	100,000	
	Cash..		100,000
Investment in Plant	Mortgage Payable...	100,000	
	Net Investment in Plant..		100,000
Investment in Plant	Library Books..	30,000	
	Net Investment in Plant..		30,000
Unexpended	Cash..	800,000	
	Bonds Payable...		800,000
Unexpended	Construction in Progress...	200,000	
	Contracts Payable..		200,000
Unexpended	Construction in Progress...	640,000	
	Contracts Payable..	200,000	
	Cash..		840,000
Unexpended	Bonds Payable...	800,000	
	Fund Balance—Unrestricted..	40,000	
	Construction in Progress...		840,000
Investment in Plant	Buildings...	840,000	
	Bonds Payable...		800,000
	Net Investment in Plant..		40,000
Investment in Plant	Land..	160,000	
	Net Investment in Plant..		160,000
Renewals and Replacements	Fund Balance—Restricted...	5,000	
	Fund Balance—Unrestricted..	45,000	
	Cash..		50,000
Unexpended	Cash..	40,000	
	Fund Balance—Restricted...		40,000
Renewals and Replacements	Cash..	5,000	
	Fund Balance—Restricted...		5,000

Illustration 19–2, Part 5

Rogers University
Partial Balance Sheet
June 30, 19X0

Plant Funds

Assets		Liabilities and Fund Balances	
Unexpended:		Unexpended:	
Cash...	$ 275,000	Accounts and notes payable ..	$ 110,000
Investments	1,285,000	Bonds payable	400,000
Due from other funds...........	150,000	Fund balances:	
		Restricted	1,000,000
		Unrestricted	200,000
Total unexpended...............	$ 1,710,000	Total unexpended...............	$ 1,710,000
Renewals and replacements:		Renewals and replacements:	
Cash..................................	$ 10,000	Fund balances:	
Investments	150,000	Restricted	$ 25,000
Deposits	100,000	Unrestricted	235,000
Total renewals.....................	$ 260,000	Total renewals....................	$ 260,000
Retirement of indebtedness:		Retirement of indebtedness:	
Cash..................................	$ 50,000	Fund balances:	
Deposits	250,000	Restricted	$ 185,000
		Unrestricted	115,000
Total.................................	$ 300,000	Total.................................	$ 300,000
Investment in plant:		Investment in plant:	
Land..................................	$ 500,000	Notes payable	$ 790,000
Land improvements.............	1,000,000	Bonds payable	1,400,000
Buildings	20,000,000	Mortgage payable...............	1,200,000
Equipment..........................	15,000,000	Net investment in plant........	38,210,000
Library books	5,100,000		
Total investment in plant.........	$41,600,000	Total investment in plant.........	$41,600,000
Total plant funds	$43,870,000	Total plant funds	$43,870,000

AGENCY FUNDS

Agency Funds account for resources which are not the property of the university but which are held in the university's custody. An example of such resources is assets belonging to student organizations. The total amount of these resources represents a liability. As a result, there is no fund balance, and Agency Funds would not appear in the analysis of changes in fund balances. The balance sheet section for the Agency Funds of Rogers University is shown in Illustration 19–2, Part 6.

Illustration 19–2, Part 6

Rogers University
Partial Balance Sheet
June 30, 19X0

Agency Funds			
Assets		**Liabilities**	
Cash............................	$ 50,000	Deposits held for others ..	$110,000
Investments	60,000		
Total agency funds	$110,000	Total agency funds	$110,000

COMBINED BALANCE SHEET

The individual balance sheets of the funds are placed in sequence to form a composite balance sheet. The current funds are shown first, and the other balance sheets are shown in the sequence given in this chapter. Although this form appears to be the preference of the audit guide, the composite balance sheet does not give the reader a conception of the university's total financial position and activities for the year. A distinct weakness in the composite balance sheet is that Rogers University's cash appears in nine different places and its investments in eight, and there are fifteen various fund balances. One alternative would be to present a combined balance sheet with a column for each fund and perhaps the total. The audit guide cautions, however, that "in the balance sheet, columnar fund group figures should not be crossfooted in a total column, to reflect an overall financial position of the institution, unless all necessary disclosures are made."[1] Combining such items as cash into one total could be misleading since all cash is not available for discretionary spending but is, in part, restricted. With sufficient and careful disclosure, however, the alternative form could be advantageous. A columnar balance sheet for Rogers University is shown in Illustration 19–3 on pages 1012 and 1013.

STATEMENT OF CHANGES IN FUND BALANCES

The most revealing financial report for a university is the statement of changes in fund balances. It is a statement of the university's total activities for the period. In condensed form, it reveals for each fund (except Agency

---

[1]*Audits of Colleges and Universities* (New York: American Institute of Certified Public Accountants, Revised, 1975), 57.

Illustration 19–3

Rogers
Combined
June

	Current Funds		Loan Funds	Endowment and Similar Funds
	Unrestricted	Restricted		
Assets				
Cash...	$ 260,000	$153,000	$29,500	$ 460,000
Deposits				
Due from other funds..............................			3,000	
Investments	450,000	247,000	5,000	1,270,000
Receivables (net)	306,000	68,000	58,500	
Inventories of materials..........................	110,000			
Prepaid expenses	28,000			
Land..				
Land improvements..............................				
Buildings				
Equipment				
Library books.......................................				
Total assets..	$1,154,000	$468,000	$96,000	$1,730,000
Liabilities				
Notes and accounts payable....................	$ 230,000	$ 18,000		
Due to other funds.................................	198,000			$ 40,000
Deposits held for others.........................				
Life income payable...............................				
Annuities payable..................................				
Bonds payable				
Mortgages payable................................				
Total liabilities.....................................	$ 428,000	$ 18,000		$ 40,000
Fund balances (See Illustration 19–4):				
Unrestricted......................................	$ 726,000		$13,500	$ 440,000
Restricted		$450,000	82,500	1,250,000
Net investment in plant.......................				
Total fund balances...............................	$ 726,000	$450,000	$96,000	$1,690,000
Total liabilities and fund balances............	$1,154,000	$468,000	$96,000	$1,730,000

Funds) the revenues and other additions to fund balances, expenditures and other deductions from fund balances, and transfers between funds, both mandatory and discretionary. It concludes with the net increase or decrease in each fund balance, which is combined with the beginning balance to pro-

Alternate Form

University
Balance Sheet
30, 19X0

Annuity and Life Income Funds	Plant Funds				Agency Funds	Total
	Unexpended	Renewals and Replacements	Retirement of Indebtedness	Investment in Plant		
$112,000	$ 275,000	$ 10,000	$ 50,000		$ 50,000	$ 1,399,500
		100,000	250,000			350,000
	150,000					153,000
530,500	1,285,000	150,000			60,000	3,997,500
						432,500
						110,000
						28,000
				$ 500,000		500,000
				1,000,000		1,000,000
				20,000,000		20,000,000
				15,000,000		15,000,000
				5,100,000		5,100,000
$642,500	$1,710,000	$260,000	$300,000	$41,600,000	$110,000	$48,070,500
	$ 110,000			$ 790,000		$ 1,148,000
						238,000
					$110,000	110,000
$ 1,500						1,500
232,000						232,000
	400,000			1,400,000		1,800,000
				1,200,000		1,200,000
$233,500	$ 510,000			$ 3,390,000	$110,000	$ 4,729,500
	$ 200,000	$235,000	$115,000			$ 1,729,500
$409,000	1,000,000	25,000	185,000			3,401,500
				$38,210,000		38,210,000
$409,000	$1,200,000	$260,000	$300,000	$38,210,000		$43,341,000
$642,500	$1,710,000	$260,000	$300,000	$41,600,000	$110,000	$48,070,500

duce the ending fund balance as shown in the balance sheet. The Agency Funds are excluded since they have no fund balances.

The columnar format is illustrated in the audit guide, but with the customary warning that columns should not be crossfooted unless care is taken to provide full disclosure about the restricted nature of some items. A columnar statement of changes in fund balances for Rogers University is shown in Illustration 19–4 below.

Although most items in the statement of changes in fund balances are straightforward, a few should be noted. When the Retirement of Indebted-

Illustration

Rogers
Statement of Changes
For Year Ended

	Current Funds	
	Unrestricted	Restricted
Revenues and other additions:		
Educational and general revenues...	$2,980,000	
Auxiliary enterprises revenues..	400,000	
Expired term endowment revenues..	20,000	
Gifts and bequests— restricted		$ 70,000
Investment income—restricted...		8,000
Gains on sale of investments—restricted		
Gains on sale of investments—unrestricted..............................		
Retirement of indebtedness		
Expended on plant facilities...		
Total revenues and other additions..	$3,400,000	$ 78,000
Expenditures and other deductions:		
Educational and general expenditures	$2,605,000	$ 73,000
Auxiliary enterprises expenditures...	350,000	
Loan cancellations and write-offs		
Expired term endowments..		
Adjustment of actuarial liability..		
Retirement of indebtedness		
Expenditures for plant facilities..		
Expenditures for plant maintenance		
Total expenditures and other deductions....................................	$2,955,000	$ 73,000
Transfers among funds—additions (deductions):		
Mandatory principal payment..	$ (20,000)	
Other transfers...	(300,000)	
Total transfers..	$ (320,000)	–0–
Net increase (decrease) for the year	$ 125,000	$ 5,000
Fund balance—beginning of the year..	601,000	445,000
Fund balance—end of the year..	$ 726,000	$450,000

ness subgroup is reduced by principal payments on plant obligations, the Investment in Plant subgroup is increased correspondingly. Similarly, the Unexpended Plant Fund subgroup's expenditures for plant assets increase the Investment in Plant subgroup. As mentioned previously, most of the resources for payment come from the Unrestricted Current Fund, whose fund

19–4

University
in Fund Balances
June 30, 19X0

Loan Funds	Endowment and Similar Funds	Annuity and Life Income Funds	Plant Funds			
			Unexpended	Renewals and Replacements	Retirement of Indebtedness	Investment in Plant
$25,000	$ 120,000	$ 56,000	$ 90,000			$ 190,000
1,000		18,000	40,000	$ 5,000		
500						
	60,000	9,500				
						100,000
						40,000
$26,500	$ 180,000	$ 83,500	$ 130,000	$ 5,000	–0–	$ 330,000
$ 500						
	$ 20,000					
		$ 4,000				
					$100,000	
			$ 40,000			
				$ 50,000		
$ 500	$ 20,000	$ 4,000	$ 40,000	$ 50,000	$100,000	–0–
					$ 20,000	
$ 3,000	$ 150,000		$ 147,000			
$ 3,000	$ 150,000	–0–	$ 147,000	–0–	$ 20,000	–0–
$29,000	$ 310,000	$ 79,500	$ 237,000	$ (45,000)	$ (80,000)	$ 330,000
67,000	1,380,000	329,500	963,000	305,000	380,000	37,880,000
$96,000	$1,690,000	$409,000	$1,200,000	$260,000	$300,000	$38,210,000

balance was reduced when amounts were transferred to one of the plant subgroups. When payments actually are made, there is a shifting of amounts within the subgroups, but no additional net reduction. The other noteworthy item is that the section relating to transfers between funds is self-balancing — what increases one fund balance through mandatory or discretionary transfers reduces some other fund by the same amount.

FUTURE OF ACCOUNTING FOR UNIVERSITIES

The needs of administrators and trustees to know cost per credit hour of instruction, to determine overhead charges as a part of grant requests, and to approach break-even points for auxiliary enterprise services call for inclusion of all costs, including depreciation. Although the audit guide states an optional approach allowing recognition of an allowance for depreciation, clearly the AICPA and the GASB have not yet settled on this matter.

Financial reports for various colleges of a university and their educational programs are prepared primarily for internal planning and seldom are issued to the general public. Without data on program costs, revenues, and achievements, a citizen cannot make a valid decision about whether or not a university is operating wisely.

Some authorities believe that present financial reports would be improved greatly by structuring them with only three columns that show unrestricted, restricted, and total amounts. Their claim is that readers would be able to see the total activity without the intervention of confusing detail. The primary objective of financial reports is communication, which will come about only if readers understand what reports are saying. There is still more work to be done before that objective is reached.

ACCOUNTING FOR PROVIDERS OF HEALTH CARE SERVICES

Advancement in medical practice and health care services has increased the median age of the United States population. Expenditures for medical care now equal more than ten percent of the gross national product. Health care entities include hospitals, clinics, continuing care retirement communities, health maintenance organizations, home health agencies, and nursing homes. Classified by sponsorship or equity structure, health care units fall into three categories:

1. Investor-owned health care entities (or proprietary entities), which are privately owned and operated for a profit.
2. Governmental health care entities (or public entities), which are operated by a governmental unit and accounted for as an enterprise fund, such as a veterans' hospital.
3. Voluntary not-for-profit health care entities, including those with a religious affiliation, which are organized and sustained by members of a community.

The remainder of this chapter deals with accounting for voluntary not-for-profit health care entities. Accounting guidelines for these entities are set forth in the AICPA's *Audits of Providers of Health Care Services* (1989). Although this audit guide was prepared by the AICPA to assist auditors of such entities, it serves as an excellent source of information for resolving problems that relate to accounting procedures for those organizations.

A modern health care provider may be a complex entity with medical, surgical, research, teaching, and public service aspects. One very unusual element about health care operations is the manner of payment for services. A significant portion of the fees for health care service is paid by a third party, such as Medicare, Medicaid, Blue Cross, or some other insurance provider. Health care entities are reimbursed not on the basis of listed prices, but on the basis of the cost of providing services, as that cost is defined by the third-party payor. A cost determination must be made according to formulas agreed upon in the law (Medicare and Medicaid) or in the contract (other insurance providers). Cost determination requires allocation of overhead, including depreciation. Thus, not-for-profit health care organizations follow the accrual basis of accounting, permitting comparison of results with profit-oriented health care units.

With the many restrictions resulting from donations, endowments, insurance company contracts, and government regulations for reimbursement, the activities of a health care provider lend themselves to fund accounting. The audit guide recommends the use of two classes of funds:

1. *Donor-restricted funds,* which account for resources whose use has been limited and defined by an outsider. This class is subdivided into Specific-Purpose Funds, Plant Replacement and Expansion Funds, Endowment Funds, and other such donor-restricted funds as required by activities.
2. *General Funds,* which account for resources available for general operations, with no restrictions placed upon those resources by an outsider. This class includes assets whose use is limited and property and equipment related to general operations.

Each fund consists of a set of self-balancing accounts designed to reflect activities within its domain.

DONOR-RESTRICTED FUNDS

Health care providers receive bequests, gifts, and grants that are restricted by the donor as to use for (1) specific operating purposes, (2) additions to plant, (3) endowments, or (4) annuities or life incomes. A donor-restricted fund is established for accumulating resources in each of these categories until the resources become available for expenditure by the General Funds. As feeders to the General Funds, donor-restricted funds need no revenue or expense accounts. When restricted assets are received, they are recorded in the proper donor-restricted fund with a credit to the appropriate fund balance account. When the donor-restricted assets are to be used for their intended purpose, they may be recorded as a transfer or, more commonly, as a direct debit to the appropriate fund balance account.

The *Specific-Purpose Fund* records donor-restricted resources available for current but specified operations. When the expenditure is to be made in accordance with the donor's wishes, a transfer is recorded to the General Funds, which credits Other Operating Revenue upon its receipt. The *Plant Replacement and Expansion Fund* accounts for resources that must be used to purchase property or equipment. These restricted resources are considered to be capital contributions. When the expenditure for plant is made by the General Funds in compliance with the wishes of the donor, a cash transfer is recorded by reducing the fund balance account of the Plant Replacement and Expansion Fund and increasing the fund balance account of the General Funds. The *Endowment Fund* accounts for resources that are received to create permanent endowments (whose income only may be expended) or term endowments (whose principal eventually will become available for expenditure). Some health care providers maintain a separate fund balance for each of these endowment types; others combine them into one fund balance account, with supporting records maintaining identity. As term endowment funds or revenues from permanent endowments become available for general operations, the General Funds record them by crediting Nonoperating Revenue. Should the term endowments be restricted further, for example, to purchase equipment, they are transferred to the appropriate donor-restricted fund. It is possible that other donor-restricted funds, such as annuity funds or loan funds, may become necessary, depending upon the activities of the organization.

GENERAL FUNDS

The General Funds is one fund that accounts for unrestricted resources and liabilities not relegated to one of the donor-restricted funds. Its assets comprise three distinct segments: current assets, assets whose use is limited, and property and equipment. The General Funds' assets and liabilities are classified as current or noncurrent according to generally accepted accounting principles.

Assets whose use is limited include assets set aside by the governing board for a specific purpose, sometimes referred to as *board-designated assets*. For example, the board may authorize that $10,000 be set aside for capital improvements, which would be recorded as follows:

Cash — Limited in Use for Capital Expansion 10,000
    Cash 10,000

The limitation is internal and, therefore, belongs in the General Funds. This segment also includes assets resulting from an operational agreement entered into by the board, such as the proceeds of a bond issue limited in use as stipulated by the bond indenture. Assets set aside to provide for self-insurance or to meet depreciation fund requirements with third-party payors belong to this segment as well.

Property and equipment include the physical properties used in operations, along with their accumulated depreciation and related liabilities. Note the difference between this procedure and that followed by universities, which segregate their fixed assets in a separate Plant Fund and do not record depreciation. Do not confuse this property and equipment with the donor-restricted Plant Replacement and Expansion Funds. The latter are resources being accumulated to permit future acquisitions of fixed assets by the General Funds.

Operating versus Nonoperating Classification. Revenues and expenses are considered *operating* if they relate to the principal activity of providing health care services. Revenues, expenses, gains, or losses from activities that are incidental to the providing of health care services or from events beyond the entity's control are classified as *nonoperating*. Operating and nonoperating revenues and expenses are recorded only in the General Funds, not in any of the donor-restricted funds.

With the desired detail incorporated in subsidiary support records, the following operating revenue control accounts are available:

1. *Patient Service Revenue*, the major revenue account for a hospital, in which the gross revenues earned are recorded on an accrual basis at established rates for:
   a. Routine services (room and board, general nursing, and home health care).
   b. Other nursing services (in operating, recovery, and delivery rooms).
   c. Professional services (physician's care, lab work, pharmacy, blood bank, radiology, dialysis, and physical therapy).
2. *Resident Service Revenue*, the major revenue account for a nursing home or continuing care retirement community. It records rental fees earned from residents or amortization of their advance payment of fees.
3. *Other Operating Revenue*, which records revenue from services other than health care provided to patients and residents. Also recorded is revenue

from sales or services to persons other than patients. Thus, Other Operating Revenue would include:

a. Revenue from educational programs, such as nursing school tuition.
b. Revenue from specific-purpose gifts and grants to the extent that the related expenditures are included in operations, another example of expenditure-driven revenue recognition.
c. Revenue from sales of medical or pharmacy supplies to employees or physicians.
d. Revenue from sale of cafeteria meals to employees, medical staff, and visitors.
e. Revenue from snack bars, gift shops, parking lots, and other service facilities.

The control account, *Nonoperating Revenue,* records revenue not related directly to an entity's principal operations. These items are primarily financial in nature and include unrestricted pledges, gifts, or grants, unrestricted income from endowment funds, maturing of term endowment funds, income and gains from investments of General Funds, and gains on sales of hospital property.

Patient Service Revenue is recorded on a gross charge basis. A third-party payor, such as Blue Cross, may reimburse a hospital on the basis of predetermined amounts that are less than the original gross charges for described services. The difference between the gross revenue and the amount expected to be collected from the third party is referred to as the *contractual adjustment.* It is deducted from the gross patient service revenue on the hospital's statement of revenues and expenses. Also deducted are adjustments for charitable services to indigent patients from whom collection will not be possible, courtesy allowances granted to hospital employees, and estimated uncollectible amounts. These four deductions from gross patient service revenue may be grouped into one debit account, Provision for Adjustments and Uncollectibles, as the contra account for allowances is credited. The objective of grouping these items is to be able to show the net patient service revenue on the statement of revenues and expenses.

Payments made to a health care unit by third parties include reimbursement for depreciation. Often this portion of the payment is limited in use to replacing or adding to property, plant, or equipment. Total billings are included in revenue of the General Funds to permit matching of total revenues and expenses. When collected, the restricted portion is transferred to a special account with the entry:

Cash—Assets Whose Use is Limited by Agreement with
    Third-Party Payors for Funded Depreciation........................   XXX
    Cash..   XXX

Titles given to operating expenses of a health care facility may differ, depending upon the nature of its activities. Specific expenses may be recorded in one of two ways. The first method collects data based upon the type of service provided by the expense. With supporting details in subsidiary records, the following control accounts under this method are common to many health care organizations:

1. *Nursing Services Expense,* for the cost of nursing services directly related to the patient or resident.
2. *Other Professional Services Expense,* for professional services indirectly related to the patient or resident, such as lab fees or pharmacy costs. Note that some hospitals combine the two accounts, Nursing Services Expense and Other Professional Services Expense, into one account labeled Professional Care of Patients Expense.
3. *General Services Expense,* for costs of the cafeteria, food service, and housekeeping. Where food services constitute a major cost, some hospitals prefer to segregate them into the account Dietary Services Expense.
4. *Fiscal Services Expense,* for admitting, cashiering, and accounting costs.
5. *Administrative Services Expense,* for insurance, taxes, and personnel costs.
6. *Depreciation Expense,* if not already allocated.
7. *Interest Expense,* if not already allocated.

For example, to record salaries earned, a debit would be made to each of the first five control accounts, with subsidiary records indicating that the charge was for salaries. The statement of revenues and expenses of the General Funds would show the total for each service, such as Nursing Services Expense, but not the nature of that total (salaries, supplies, etc.).

Some health care units prefer to use a different classification, one that is based on the nature of the expense, such as salaries, supplies, etc. The decision as to which classification system to use depends upon various elements, including the size of the entity, the talents of its staff and management, and its reporting requirements. Although the audit guide uses the functional classification of expenses in its illustration for a hospital, one should be familiar with both systems of treating expenses.

Malpractice Claims. The current environment in relation to medical malpractice claims has caused insurance companies to raise premiums to health care providers dramatically or to limit the amount of risk they are willing to insure. To find a health care provider that is fully insured against medical malpractice losses is a rarity. Many have dropped their malpractice insurance or have adopted other approaches for protection. Some pay losses as they occur. Others establish trust funds with a trustee.

The accounting issue is to determine when the costs of malpractice claims should be recognized. An AICPA statement stipulates that:

The ultimate costs of malpractice claims, which include costs associated with litigating or settling claims, should be accrued when the incidents occur that give rise to the claims, if it can be determined that it is probable that liabilities have been incurred and if the amounts of the losses can be reasonably estimated.[2]

If the health care provider is covered by insurance, the premiums applicable to the reporting period are expensed, plus an amount for estimated claim costs for the reporting period not covered by the insurance arrangement. The entry to record claim costs is:

Medical Malpractice Costs (or Administrative Services Expense) ..   XXX
    Cash (or Unexpired Premiums)   XXX
    Estimated Additional Malpractice Liability   XXX

Even hospitals that report expenses on a functional basis sometimes segregate the medical malpractice costs from the other administrative services costs to emphasize their critical nature.

As a result of the large settlements granted in malpractice cases, some health care organizations became self-insured, establishing a trust account with an outside trustee who determines funding requirements. Two entries are necessary. The first establishes the estimated claim costs and liability:

Medical Malpractice Costs (or Administrative Services Expense) ..   XXX
    Estimated Malpractice Liability..   XXX

The second entry records the contribution to the trustee:

Cash — Limited in Use Under Malpractice Funding Arrangement ..   XXX
    Cash..   XXX

The amount in the trust account is reported in the balance sheet of the General Funds as an asset whose use is limited. Claims expected to be paid during the next operating cycle are classified as current liabilities, while the remainder of the liability balance is shown as noncurrent.

Whether the health care provider is covered by insurance, pays losses as they occur, or has a trust fund arrangement, the amount of the expense should reflect the best estimate of ultimate costs of malpractice claims related to incidents that occurred during the reporting period.

Donated Items. Activities of health care providers are enhanced by volunteers who donate their time and abilities. Donated services should be

---

[2]*Statement of Position 87–1*, "Accounting for Asserted and Unasserted Medical Malpractice Claims of Health Care Providers and Related Issues" (New York: American Institute of Certified Public Accountants, March 16, 1987), par. 21.

recorded only if an employer-employee relationship exists and if there is some objective basis for assigning value for services rendered. Thus, most voluntary service by senior citizens, candy stripers, and others is not recorded. However, when an institution is operated by a religious group whose members receive token payment or no payment at all, the value of donated services should be charged to the proper expense account and credited to Nonoperating Revenue. This account also is used to record unrestricted contributions of cash and other noncapital assets.

In the case of donations of sizable amounts of supplies by drug firms or associations of doctors, their estimated purchase costs should be treated as inventory and credited to Nonoperating Revenue. As mentioned, unrestricted donations of property, plant, or equipment are treated as capital contributions and are debited to the fixed asset account in the General Funds and credited directly to its fund balance account at estimated market value. If donations of property are donor-restricted, as in the case of property donated to an Endowment Fund, the same entry is made but in the appropriate fund, in this case, the Endowment Fund.

Illustrative Entries for General Funds. To illustrate the recording of events for a hospital, the year's affairs of Fitale Hospital's General Funds are summarized next. The illustrative entries employ broad categories of control accounts and natural expense classification.

Event		Entry		
Gross charges to patients are for:		Accounts Receivable.....................	5,200,000	
		Patient Service Revenue..............		5,000,000
Daily patient services...........	$3,200,000	Other Operating Revenue...........		200,000
Other nursing services.........	500,000			
Professional services...........	1,300,000			
Other nonmedical				
services.........................	200,000			
Total	$5,200,000			
Estimates are made for:		Provision for Adjustments and		
		Uncollectibles........................	402,000	
Contractual adjustments........	$ 380,000	Allowance for Adjustments		
Uncollectibles.....................	22,000	and Uncollectibles..................		402,000
Total	$ 402,000			
An analysis of accounts receivable shows:		Cash..	4,000,000	
		Allowance for Adjustments and		
		Uncollectibles........................	290,000	
Cash collected....................	$4,000,000	Accounts Receivable..................		4,290,000
Contractual adjustments with third-party				
payors..........................	200,000			
Uncollectible	90,000			
Total	$4,290,000			
Inventory purchases amounted to $700,000; payments totaled $690,000.		Inventories.................................	700,000	
		Cash.......................................		690,000
		Accounts Payable.....................		10,000

Event	Entry		
Drugs and supplies costing $720,000 are requisitioned.	Drugs and Supplies Used .... Inventories................................	720,000	720,000
Salaries earned (ignore payroll deductions) amounted to $3,000,000, of which $2,950,000 is paid.	Wages, Salaries, and Benefits .... Cash....................................... Accrued Expenses.....................	3,000,000	2,950,000 50,000
Outside professional fees of $300,000 are paid.	Purchased Services .... Cash.......................................	300,000	300,000

Payments are made on:

Current installment of long-term debt	$ 80,000
Notes payable	200,000
Interest expense...................	66,000
Total	$346,000

	Current Installment of Long-Term Debt .... Notes Payable .... Interest Expense......................... Cash.......................................	80,000 200,000 66,000	346,000
Equipment costing $110,000 is purchased for cash.	Property and Equipment................. Cash.......................................	110,000	110,000
Received $50,000 cash from Specific-Purpose Fund to cover current operations.	Cash... Other Operating Revenue...........	50,000	50,000
A transfer of $200,000 is made from the Plant Replacement and Expansion Fund for purchase of a coronary monitoring device.	Cash... Transfers from Plant Replacement and Expansion Fund	200,000	200,000
Coronary monitoring device is purchased and payment is made.	Property and Equipment................. Cash.......................................	200,000	200,000
Unrestricted earnings of $540,000 are received from the Endowment Fund.	Cash... Nonoperating Revenue...............	540,000	540,000
Depreciation expense provision for the year is $400,000.	Depreciation Expense.................... Accumulated Depreciation	400,000	400,000
Transfer of $250,000 is made to Plant Replacement and Expansion Fund, as required by third-party payor revenues restricted in use to plant replacement.	Transfers to Plant Replacement and Expansion Fund .... Cash.......................................	250,000	250,000

The current portion of long-term debt is reclassified as current from:

Bonds payable.......................	$50,000
Mortgage note payable	30,000
Total	$80,000

	Bonds Payable............................ Mortgage Note Payable................. Current Installment of Long-Term Debt	50,000 30,000	80,000
A provision for medical malpractice costs of $450,000 is recorded. The hospital is self-insured.	Medical Malpractice Costs............. Estimated Malpractice Liability......	450,000	450,000
A malpractice self-insurance trust at Third Bank is increased by $230,000.	Cash—Limited in Use Under Malpractice Funding Arrangement.......................... Cash.......................................	230,000	230,000

FINANCIAL STATEMENTS OF A HEALTH CARE PROVIDER

Since revenue and expense accounts normally do not appear in donor-restricted funds, the statement of revenues and expenses is prepared only for the General Funds. The form is straightforward, showing operating revenues minus operating expenses as income or loss from operations. The non-operating revenue is added to this amount. To avoid the concept of profits, a not-for-profit health care entity labels its final line *Excess (Deficiency) of revenues over expenses,* as shown in Illustration 19–5A. In practice, comparative financial statements would be presented. To conserve space, the results of only one year's activity will be illustrated.

Illustration 19–5A

Fitale Hospital
Statement of Revenues and Expenses of the General Funds
For the Year Ended December 31, 19X1

Patient service revenue	$5,000,000
Provision for contractual adjustments and uncollectibles	402,000
Net patient service revenue	$4,598,000
Other operating revenue	250,000
Total operating revenue	$4,848,000
Operating expenses:	
Wages, salaries, and benefits	$3,000,000
Drugs and supplies used	720,000
Purchased services	300,000
Medical malpractice costs	450,000
Depreciation	400,000
Interest	66,000
Total operating expenses	$4,936,000
Loss from operations	($ 88,000)
Nonoperating revenue:	
Unrestricted revenue from Endowment Fund	$ 540,000
Excess of revenues over expenses	$ 452,000

At year end, the following closing entry for the General Funds would be prepared:

Patient Service Revenue	5,000,000	
Other Operating Revenue	250,000	
Nonoperating Revenue	540,000	
Provision for Adjustments and Uncollectibles		402,000
Wages, Salaries, and Benefits		3,000,000
Drugs and Supplies Used		720,000
Purchased Services		300,000
Medical Malpractice Costs		450,000
Depreciation Expense		400,000
Interest Expense		66,000
Fund Balance		452,000

If Fitale Hospital preferred to report its expenses using a functional classification, the statement of revenues and expenses of the General Funds might appear as shown in Illustration 19–5B.

In addition to the statement of revenues and expenses of the General Funds, a voluntary hospital provides a balance sheet, a statement of changes in fund balances, and a statement of cash flows of the General Funds.

The balance sheet form shown in the audit guide follows the same format as for a university, wherein the individual fund balance sheets are stacked one upon the other. The sequence begins with the General Funds, whose assets are segregated into the segments: current assets, assets whose use is limited, property and equipment, and possibly other assets. Also shown are the current and other liabilities of the General Funds and a single Fund Balance amount. The balance sheets of the donor-restricted funds follow in this sequence: Specific-Purpose Funds, Plant Replacement and Expansion Funds, Endowments Funds, and any other restricted funds that may have been adopted, as shown in Illustration 19–6 on pages 1028–1029.

In support of the balance sheet, a statement of changes in fund balances is prepared. All items that changed fund balances, including transfers, are shown in the same sequence of funds as in the balance sheet, but in columnar form, as shown in Illustration 19–7 on page 1030.

The statement of cash flows is provided only for the General Funds. Recall that all donor-restricted funds are feeders to the General Funds. The audit guide encourages the use of the direct method to present cash flows, although it does accept the indirect method. The guide suggests that the provisions of FASB Statement No. 95, "Statement of Cash Flows," also should be applied to not-for-profit health care entities. The direct method will require a reconciliation of excess of revenues over expenses to net cash provided by operating activities and nonoperating revenue. As shown in Illustration 19–8A on page 1031, the cash flows statement closely follows its commercial counterpart. A few differences do arise. In the section labeled, *Cash flows from investing activities,* the total amount of cash outflow for property and equipment is reduced by the amount financed by the donor-

Illustration 19–5B

Fitale Hospital
Statement of Revenues and Expenses of the General Funds
For the Year Ended December 31, 19X1

Patient service revenue	$5,000,000
Provision for contractual adjustments and uncollectibles	402,000
Net patient service revenue	$4,598,000
Other operating revenue	250,000
Total operating revenues	$4,848,000
Operating expenses:	
Nursing services	$1,674,000
Other professional services	1,070,000
General services	870,000
Fiscal services	168,000
Administrative services	238,000
Medical malpractice costs	450,000
Depreciation	400,000
Interest	66,000
Total operating expenses	$4,936,000
Loss from operations	($ 88,000)
Nonoperating revenue:	
Unrestricted revenue from Endowment Fund	$ 540,000
Excess of revenues over expenses	$ 452,000

restricted assets. In addition, a transfer to another fund by the General Funds is shown as a use of cash. Items on the statement of cash flows and its accompanying reconciliation (Illustration 19–8B, page 1031) with an amount of zero ordinarily would not appear; they are inserted to provide guidance as to their location if they did exist.

Assets

GENERAL FUNDS

Current assets:

Cash...	$105,000	
Receivables (net)	900,000	
Due from Specific-Purpose Funds................................	100,000	
Inventories (at Lifo or market, whichever is lower).........	135,000	
Prepaid expenses	60,000	
Total current assets..		$1,300,000
Assets whose use is limited:		
Cash—limited under malpractice funding arrangement.................	$440,000	
Investments limited for capital items	60,000	
Total assets whose use is limited		500,000
Property and equipment (net)		6,000,000
		$7,800,000

DONOR-RESTRICTED FUNDS

Specific-Purpose Funds:

Cash...	$ 1,500
Investments (at cost, which approximates market).........................	204,500
	$ 206,000

Plant Replacement and Expansion Funds:

Cash...	$ 15,000
Investments (at cost, which approximates market).........................	700,000
Pledges receivable (net)	35,000
	$ 750,000

Endowment Funds:

Cash...	$ 80,000
Investments (at cost, which approximates market).........................	4,020,000
	$4,100,000

19–6

Hospital
Sheet
31, 19X1

Liabilities and Fund Balances

GENERAL FUNDS

Current liabilities:

Notes and accounts payable	$420,000	
Current installments of long-term debt	80,000	
Advances from third-party payors	200,000	
Accrued expenses	100,000	
Malpractice claims	90,000	
Total current liabilities		$ 890,000
Estimated malpractice costs		640,000
Long-term debt, excluding current installments		1,170,000
Fund balance		5,100,000
		$7,800,000

DONOR-RESTRICTED FUNDS

Specific-Purpose Funds:

Due to General Funds	$ 100,000
Fund balance	106,000
	$ 206,000

Plant Replacement and Expansion Funds:

Fund balance	$ 750,000
	$ 750,000

Endowment Funds:

Fund balance	$4,100,000
	$4,100,000

Illustration 19–7

Fitale Hospital
Statement of Changes in Fund Balances
For the Year Ended December 31, 19X1

	General Funds	Donor-Restricted Funds		
		Specific-Purpose Funds	Plant Replacement and Expansion Funds	Endowment Funds
Balances at beginning of year...	$4,698,000	$109,000	$610,000	$3,180,000
Additions:				
Excess of revenues over expenses	$ 452,000			
Gifts, grants, and bequests....		$ 30,000	$ 40,000	$1,000,000
Investment income		15,000	50,000	270,000
Gain on sale of investments ..		2,000		190,000
Transfer to finance property and equipment additions....	200,000		(200,000)	
Transfer to reflect third-party payor revenue restricted to property and equipment replacement......................	(250,000)		250,000	
	$ 402,000	$ 47,000	$140,000	$1,460,000
Deductions:				
Transfer to other operating revenue..........................		($ 50,000)*		
Transfer to nonoperating revenue..........................				($ 540,000)*
Balances at end of year............	$5,100,000	$106,000	$750,000	$4,100,000

*These transfers are not added to the General Funds column because they were recorded by the General Funds as revenue and, therefore, are included in the line, *Excess of revenues over expenses.*

Illustration 19–8A

Fitale Hospital
Statement of Cash Flows of the General Funds
For the Year Ended December 31, 19X1

Cash flows from operating activities and nonoperating revenue:	
Cash received from patients and third-party payors	$4,000,000
Other receipts from operations	50,000
Receipts from unrestricted gifts and bequests	540,000
Interest and dividends received...	–0–
Cash paid to employees and suppliers................................	(4,220,000)
Interest paid (net of amount capitalized)	(66,000)
Net cash provided by operating activities and nonoperating revenue.....................................	$ 304,000
Cash flows from investing activities:	
Purchase of property and equipment.................................	($ 310,000)
Transfer from donor-restricted fund for purchase of property and equipment..	200,000
Cash outflows for property and equipment	($ 110,000)
Cash transfer to assets whose use is limited	(230,000)
Cash transfer to Plant Replacement and Expansion Fund.......	(250,000)
Net cash used by investing activities	($ 590,000)
Cash flows from financing activities:	
Repayment of long-term debt..	–0–
Net cash used by financing activities.............................	–0–
Net increase (decrease) in cash and cash equivalents..............	($ 286,000)
Cash and cash equivalents at beginning of year	391,000
Cash and cash equivalents at end of year	$ 105,000

Illustration 19–8B

Fitale Hospital
Reconciliation of Excess of Revenues Over Expenses
To Net Cash Provided by Operating Activities and Nonoperating Revenue
For the Year Ended December 31, 19X1

Excess of revenues over expenses	$452,000
Adjustments to reconcile excess of revenues over expenses to net cash provided by operating activities and nonoperating revenue:	
Depreciation...	400,000
Noncash gifts and bequests...	–0–
Increase in liability for estimated malpractice costs..............	450,000
Net increase in receivables and inventory	(968,000)
Net decrease in accounts payable and accrued expenses.......	(30,000)
Net cash provided by operating activities and nonoperating revenue...	$304,000

QUESTIONS

1. Without the built-in monitor of a profit motive, weaknesses have developed in accounting and reporting for not-for-profit organizations. Itemize these weaknesses.
2. Why is it unwise for a not-for-profit unit to have a large excess or deficiency of revenue over expenditures?
3. Describe the function of the two subfunds of a university's current funds.
4. Interpret the following closing entry for a university:

Revenues — Auxiliary Enterprises	500,000	
Expenditures — Auxiliary Enterprises		480,000
Fund Balance..		20,000

5. Of the various funds used in university accounting, indicate which is probably the most complex and explain why.
6. Why do assets whose use is limited constitute a part of the General Funds of a health care provider rather than a part of donor-restricted funds?
7. Explain a hospital's rigid adherence to gross revenue determination.
8. Name three of the four items that are grouped in the account Provision for Adjustments and Uncollectibles. Briefly describe the function of the account.
9. A donation of medical supplies to a provider of health care is credited to a different account than an unrestricted donation of property. Name the accounts that are credited and explain the difference in treatment.
10. What is the major difference in accounting for the Unrestricted Current Fund of a university and the General Funds of a health care provider?
11. Name three different procedures that providers of health care follow to cover the cost of malpractice claims. In all procedures, what should the amount of the cost represent?
12. Explain why transfers from a provider of health care's Endowment Fund or Specific-Purpose Fund to its General Funds do not appear in the General Funds section of the statement of changes in fund balances.

EXERCISES

Exercise 1.   Select the best answer for each of the following multiple-choice questions.

Items 1 through 3 are based on the following data:

For its summer session, Durham University collected in cash $750,000 for tuition and fees, refunded $30,000 for cancelled classes and drops, granted $60,000 in scholarships, and allowed $20,000 for tuition remission for children of faculty. There are $50,000 of uncollected tuition and fees, of which $15,000 is deemed uncollectible.

1. Student tuition and fees revenue for the summer session are:
   a. $880,000.   b. $860,000.   c. $800,000.   d. $770,000.

2. Total Expenditures — Student Aid for the summer session is:
   a. $95,000.   b. $80,000.   c. $60,000.   d. $20,000.

3. On the statement of current funds revenues and expenditures, the amount of revenue from "Student tuition and fees" is:
   a. $800,000.   b. $785,000.   c. $770,000.   d. $755,000.

4. The following correct entry is found on a university's accounting records:

   Fund Balance   XXX
       Mandatory Transfers for Principal Payment..............   XXX

   An acceptable explanation for the entry would be: "To record
   a. The closing of the mandatory transfers account."
   b. A reserve for mandatory transfers."
   c. A liability for mandatory transfers."
   d. An amount due from another fund to cover mandatory transfers."

5. A university had Endowment and Similar Funds. The addition of the phrase, "and Similar Funds," indicates the presence of:
   a. Pure endowments.
   b. Term endowments.
   c. Quasi-endowments.
   d. Expended endowments.

Exercise 2.   A hospital has three revenue controlling accounts: Patient Service Revenue, Other Operating Revenue, and Nonoperating Revenue.
(a) State in general terms the type of revenue found in each controlling account.
(b) Indicate into which of the three controlling accounts each of the following would be placed by using the symbols PS for Patient Service Revenue, OO for Other Operating Revenue, and N for Nonoperating Revenue:

   1. Tuition for entry to the nursing school   ____
   2. An unrestricted gift of cash   ____
   3. General nursing fees charged to patients   ____
   4. Charges for physicians' care   ____
   5. A restricted grant used for research on genes   ____
   6. Dividends from General Funds' investments   ____
   7. Revenue from gift shop sales   ____
   8. Patient room and board charges   ____
   9. Proceeds from sales of cafeteria meals   ____
   10. Recovery room fees   ____

Exercise 3. Record the following events that affect the Unrestricted Current Fund of Jordan University, which uses the typical control accounts for its revenues and expenditures. Omit explanations.

(a) Student fees of $300,000 were assessed, of which $250,000 have been collected and $3,000 are estimated to be uncollectible.

(b) The book store operates in rented space and is run on a break-even basis. Revenues totaled $90,000, of which 80% was collected to date. Salaries of $30,000 and rent of $10,000 are paid. Other operating expenses amount to $45,000, of which $5,000 have not been paid.

(c) A mandatory transfer of $50,000 was made for a payment due on the gymnasium building mortgage.

(d) The Student Aid Committee report showed:

Cash scholarships issued............................	$7,500
Remission of tuition....................................	3,000

(e) A check for $7,000 and a pledge for $3,000 are received from the local medical society to cover part of the cost of research on drug effects, one of the university's educational programs.

Exercise 4. Record the following events that affect the Restricted Current Fund of Jordan University. Omit explanations.

(a) A private grant of $50,000 was received, to be used exclusively for defraying costs of holding conferences on the topic of genes.

(b) By year end, $45,000 of the grant mentioned in (a) had been applied to the purpose stipulated.

(c) The grant provided that amounts not awarded by year end are to be transferred to the Endowment Fund. The liability to that fund is recorded.

(d) An alumnus, a former athlete, contributed $15,000 to assist in the search for a basketball coach.

Exercise 5. Record the following events that affect the Loan Fund of Jordan University. Omit explanations.

(a) An alumnus donates $200,000 to establish a student loan fund. Students are charged a 5% annual interest rate.

(b) Loans of $180,000 are made to students.

(c) The remaining $20,000 is deposited in the University Credit Union, which pays a current interest rate of 7%.

(d) Loans of $20,000 are repaid, plus $800 of interest.

(e) Interest of $900 is received from the University Credit Union.

(f) A student who had borrowed $1,000 was in a serious bike accident and withdrew from school. The university wrote off the loan as uncollectible.

Exercise 6. Record the following events that affect Jordan University's Annuity and Life Income Funds.

(a) On July 1, 19X0, J. H. March, Emeritus Professor of Accounting, moved out of the state. March donated to the university common stock with a cost basis of $50,000 and a market value of $90,000. March is to receive an annuity of $5,000 a year for life; at death, the securities are to be sold and the remaining cash balance is to be transferred to the Student Loan Fund. At a 10% annual rate and a life expectancy of 12 years, the present value of the annuity payments is $34,000.

(b) The stock paid $5,400 in dividends each twelve-month period.

(c) One year later, a payment of $5,000 is made to Professor March. The present value of that payment included in the $34,000 figure was $4,545.

(d) A second payment was made a year later. Its present value included in the $34,000 was $4,132.

(e) A month later, Professor March died, eliminating the liability for future annuity payments.

(f) The common stock was sold for $97,000. The cash balance was transferred to the Student Loan Fund.

Exercise 7. Record the following events that affect the Unexpended Plant Fund of Jordan University.

(a) A transfer of $200,000 is made from the Unrestricted Current Fund to the Unexpended Plant Fund to finance an addition to the Fine Arts Building.

(b) Work on the Fine Arts addition is in progress. At year end, costs of construction total $80,000, of which $20,000 is unpaid. The university vice-president for finance prefers that transfers to the Investment in Plant subgroup be made only upon completion of any project.

(c) The project is completed during the next year at an additional cost of $140,000. Unpaid contract costs now total $35,000.

(d) Transfer of the Fine Arts addition is made to the Investment in Plant subgroup.

Exercise 8. Record the following events that affect Jordan University's Investment in Plant subgroup.

(a) A partial payment of $5,000 is made from the Unrestricted Current Fund on the gymnasium building mortgage, which is carried as a liability in the Investment in Plant subgroup.

(b) New gymnasium equipment costing $30,000 is purchased from the portion of the Unexpended Plant Fund donated by a former Olympic medal winner for that purpose.

(c) The Fine Arts Building addition is completed at a total cost of $220,000, of which $35,000 in contract costs is unpaid.

(d) During a celebration after a basketball victory, $2,000 of gym equipment disappeared.

Exercise 9. Record the following events in the General Funds of Curative Hospital.

(a) Patients were billed for the following gross charges:

Room and board	$470,000
Physicians' care......................................	220,000
Laboratory and radiology	110,000

(b) Revenues were reported from:

Newsstand and snack bar.........................	$16,000
Parking lot charges.................................	3,200
Vending machines..................................	9,800

(c) A charity allowance of $13,000 was granted indigent patients.
(d) Contractual adjustments granted to patients for Medicare charges totaled $48,000.
(e) The hospital increased its allowance for adjustments and uncollectibles by $26,000.

Exercise 10. Ambulance Service is a not-for-profit health care provider. Prepare the reconciliation of excess of expenses over revenues to net cash provided by operating activities and nonoperating revenue that would accompany its statement of cash flows under the direct method for the year ended December 31, 19X4.

Excess of expenses over revenues	($ 93,000)
Noncash items: Depreciation....................	117,000
Amortization of bond premium......................	22,000
Cash paid for acquisition of property........	10,000
Payment to settle long-term note payable	63,000
Net decrease in receivables and supplies..	38,000
Net increase in current payables	10,000

PROBLEMS

Problem 19–1. Select the best answer for each of the following multiple-choice items: (AICPA adapted)

1. For the summer session of 19X7, Ariba University assessed its students $1,700,000 (net of refunds), covering tuition and fees for educational and general purposes. However, only $1,500,000 was expected to be realized since scholarships totaling $150,000 were granted to students and since tuition remissions of $50,000 were allowed to faculty members' children attending Ariba. What amount should Ariba include in the Unrestricted Current Fund as revenues from student tuition and fees?
   a. $1,500,000.   b. $1,550,000.   c. $1,650,000.   d. $1,700,000.

2. Park College is sponsored by a religious group. Volunteers from this religious group regularly contribute their services to Park and are paid nominal amounts to cover their commuting costs. During 19X6, the total amount paid to these volunteers was $12,000. The gross value of services

performed by them, as determined by reference to lay-equivalent salaries, amounted to $300,000. What amount should Park record as expenditures in 19X6 for these volunteers' services?

a. $312,000. b. $300,000. c. $12,000. d. $0.

3. Abbott University's Unrestricted Current Fund comprised the following:

Assets $5,000,000
Liabilities (including deferred revenues of $100,000) 3,000,000

The fund balance of Abbott's Unrestricted Current Fund was:

a. $1,900,000. b. $2,000,000. c. $2,100,000. d. $5,000,000.

4. The following receipts are among those recorded by Curry College during 19X9:

Unrestricted gifts $500,000
Restricted current funds (expended for current operating
  purposes)... 200,000
Restricted current funds (not yet expended) 100,000

The amount that should be included in current funds revenues is:

a. $800,000. b. $700,000. c. $600,000. d. $500,000.

5. Palma Hospital's patient service revenues for services provided in 19X8, at established rates, amounted to $8,000,000 on the accrual basis. For internal reporting, Palma uses the discharge method. Under this method, patient service revenues are recognized only when patients are discharged, with no recognition given to revenues accruing for services to patients not yet discharged. Patient service revenues at established rates using the discharge method amounted to $7,000,000 for 19X8. According to generally accepted accounting principles, Palma should report patient service revenues for 19X8 of:

a. Either $8,000,000 or $7,000,000, at the option of the hospital.
b. $8,000,000.
c. $7,500,000.
d. $7,000,000.

6. During 19X5, Shaw Hospital purchased medicines for hospital use totaling $800,000. Included in this $800,000 was an invoice of $10,000 that was cancelled in 19X5 by the vendor because the vendor wished to donate this medicine to Shaw. This donation of medicine should be recorded as:

a. A $10,000 reduction of medicine expense.
b. An increase in nonoperating revenue of $10,000.
c. A direct $10,000 credit to the General Funds balance.
d. A $10,000 credit to the restricted funds balance.

7. In 19X6, Pyle Hospital received a $250,000 pure endowment grant. Also in 19X6, Pyle's governing board designated, for special uses, $300,000 which had originated from unrestricted gifts. What amount of these resources should be accounted for as part of the General Funds?

a. $0. b. $250,000. c. $300,000. d. $550,000.

(continued)

8. Cura Hospital's property, plant, and equipment, net of depreciation, amounted to $10,000,000, with related mortgage liabilities of $1,000,000. What amount should be included in the donor-restricted fund grouping?
   a. $0.   b. $1,000,000.   c. $9,000,000.   d. $10,000,000.

Problem 19–2. Select the best answer for each of the following multiple-choice items: (AICPA adapted)

1. On March 1, 19X8, A. C. Rowe established a $100,000 endowment fund, the income from which is to be paid to Elm Hospital for general operating purposes. Elm does not control the fund's principal. Rowe appointed West National Bank as trustee of this fund. What journal entry is required by Elm to record the establishment of the endowment?
   a. Cash $100,000
          Nonexpendable Endowment Fund $100,000
   b. Cash   100,000
          Endowment Fund Balance   100,000
   c. Nonexpendable Endowment Fund   100,000
          Endowment Fund Balance   100,000
   d. Memorandum entry only.

2. In 19X8, Wells Hospital received an unrestricted bequest of common stock with a market value of $50,000 on the date of receipt of the stock. The testator had paid $20,000 for this stock in 19X6. Wells should record this bequest as:
   a. Nonoperating revenue of $50,000.
   b. Nonoperating revenue of $30,000.
   c. Nonoperating revenue of $20,000.
   d. A memorandum entry only.

3. Cedar Hospital has a marketable equity securities portfolio that is included appropriately in noncurrent assets in unrestricted funds. The portfolio has an aggregate cost of $300,000. It had an aggregate market value of $250,000 at the end of 19X7 and $290,000 at the end of 19X6. If the portfolio was reported properly in the balance sheet at the end of 19X6, the change in the valuation allowance at the end of 19X7 should be:
   a. $0.
   b. A decrease of $40,000.
   c. An increase of $40,000.
   d. An increase of $50,000.

4. Ross Hospital's accounting records disclosed the following information:

   Net resources invested in plant assets $10,000,000
   Board-designated funds...   2,000,000

   What amount should be included as part of the General Funds?
   a. $12,000,000.   b. $10,000,000.   c. $2,000,000.   d. $0.

5. For the 19X7 summer session, Selva University assessed its students $300,000 for tuition and fees. However, the net amount realized was only $290,000 because of the following reductions:

Tuition remissions granted to faculty members' families................. $3,000
Class cancellation refunds 7,000

How much Unrestricted Current Funds revenues from tuition and fees should Selva report for the period?

a. $290,000.   b. $293,000.   c. $297,000.   d. $300,000.

6. The following information was available from Forest College's accounting records for its current funds for the year ended March 31, 19X3:

Restricted gifts received:
    Expended.. $100,000
    Not expended... 300,000
Unrestricted gifts received:
    Expended.. 600,000
    Not expended... 75,000

What amount should be included in current funds revenues for the year ended March 31, 19X3?

a. $600,000.   b. $700,000.   c. $775,000.   d. $1,000,000.

7. The following expenditures were among those incurred by Cheviot University during 19X7:

Administrative data processing .... $ 50,000
Scholarships and fellowships... 100,000
Operation and maintenance of physical plant 200,000

The amount to be included in the functional classification "Institutional Support" expenditures account is:

a. $50,000.   b. $150,000.   c. $250,000.   d. $350,000.

Problem 19–3.   A partial balance sheet of Rapapo State University as of the end of its fiscal year, July 31, 19X2, is as follows:

Rapapo State University
Current Funds Balance Sheet
July 31, 19X2

Assets		Liabilities and Fund Balances	
Unrestricted:		Unrestricted:	
Cash............................	$200,000	Accounts payable	$100,000
Accounts receivable		Due to other funds.........	40,000
(net of $15,000		Deferred revenue—	
allowance)	360,000	tuition and fees	25,000
Prepaid expenses	40,000	Fund balance	435,000
Total unrestricted........	$600,000	Total unrestricted........	$600,000
Restricted:		Restricted:	
Cash............................	$ 10,000	Accounts payable	$ 5,000
Investments	210,000	Fund balance	215,000
Total restricted	$220,000	Total restricted	$220,000
Total current funds	$820,000	Total current funds	$820,000

The following information pertains to the year ended July 31, 19X3:

(a) Cash collected from students' tuition totaled $3,000,000. Of this amount, $362,000 represented accounts receivable outstanding at July 31, 19X2;

$2,500,000 was for current-year tuition; and $138,000 was for tuition applicable to the semester beginning in August, 19X3.

(b) Deferred revenue at July 31, 19X2, was earned during the year ended July 31, 19X3.

(c) Accounts receivable at July 31, 19X2, that were not collected during the year ended July 31, 19X3, were determined to be uncollectible and were written off against the allowance account. At July 31, 19X3, the allowance account was estimated at $10,000.

(d) During the year, an unrestricted appropriation of $60,000 was made by the state, to be paid to Rapapo sometime in August, 19X3.

(e) During the year, unrestricted cash gifts of $80,000 were received from alumni. Rapapo's board of trustees allocated $30,000 of these gifts to the student loan fund.

(f) During the year, restricted fund investments costing $25,000 were sold for $31,000. Restricted fund investments were purchased at a cost of $40,000. Restricted fund investment income of $18,000 was earned and collected during the year.

(g) Unrestricted general expenses of $2,500,000 were recorded in the voucher system. At July 31, 19X3, the unrestricted accounts payable balance was $75,000.

(h) The restricted accounts payable balance at July 31, 19X2, was paid. The restricted fund paid $10,000 from its investment income for costs of an ongoing research project.

(i) The $40,000 due to other funds at July 31, 19X2, was paid to the plant fund as required.

(j) One quarter of the prepaid expenses at July 31, 19X2, expired during the current year and pertained to general education expense. There was no addition to prepaid expenses during the year.

Required:

(1) Prepare journal entries in summary form to record the foregoing transactions for the year ended July 31, 19X3. Letter each entry to correspond with the letter indicated in the description of its respective transaction, and omit explanations. Use the following format:

| | | Current Funds | | | |
| | | Unrestricted | | Restricted | |
Entry Letter	Accounts	Debit	Credit	Debit	Credit

(2) Prepare a statement of current funds revenues, expenditures, and other changes, including a total column, for the year ended July 31, 19X3, and conclude with the fund balances at year end.   (AICPA adapted)

Problem 19–4.   The current funds balance sheet of Burnsville University as of the end of its fiscal year, June 30, 19X7, is as follows:

Burnsville University
Current Funds Balance Sheet
June 30, 19X7

Assets			Liabilities and Fund Balances		
Unrestricted:			Unrestricted:		
Cash..........................	$210,000		Accounts payable	$ 45,000	
Accounts receivable—			Deferred revenues	66,000	
student tuition and			Fund balances...............	515,000	$626,000
fees less allowance					
for doubtful					
accounts of $9,000..	341,000				
State appropriations					
receivable	75,000	$626,000			
Restricted:			Restricted:		
Cash..........................	$ 7,000		Fund balances...........		67,000
Investments	60,000	67,000			
Total current funds ..		$693,000	Total current funds ..		$693,000

The following transactions occurred during the fiscal year ended June 30, 19X8:

(a) On July 7, 19X7, a gift of $100,000 was received from an alumnus. The alumnus requested that one-half of the gift be used for the purchase of books for the university library and that the remainder be used for the establishment of a scholarship fund. The alumnus further requested that the income generated by the scholarship fund be used annually to award a scholarship to a qualified disadvantaged student. On July 20, 19X7, the board of trustees resolved that the funds of the newly established scholarship fund would be invested in savings certificates. On July 21, 19X7, the savings certificates were purchased.

(b) Revenue from student tuition and fees applicable to the year ended June 30, 19X8, amounted to $1,900,000. Of this amount, $66,000 was collected in the prior year and $1,686,000 was collected during the year ended June 30, 19X8. In addition, at June 30, 19X8, the university had received cash of $158,000 representing fees for the session beginning July 1, 19X8.

(c) During the year ended June 30, 19X8, the university had collected $349,000 of the outstanding accounts receivable at the beginning of the year. The remainder was determined to be uncollectible and was written off against the allowance account. At June 30, 19X8, the allowance account was increased by $3,000.

(d) During the year, interest charges of $6,000 were earned and collected on late student fee payments.

(e) During the year, the state appropriation was received. An additional unrestricted appropriation of $50,000 was made by the state, but had not been paid to the university as of June 30, 19X8.

(f) An unrestricted gift of $25,000 cash was received from alumni of the university.

(g) During the year, investments of $21,000 were sold for $26,000. Investment income amounting to $1,900 was received.

(h) During the year, unrestricted operating expenses of $1,777,000 were recorded. At June 30, 19X8, $59,000 of these expenses remained unpaid.

(i) Restricted current funds of $13,000 were spent for authorized purposes during the year.

(j) The accounts payable at June 30, 19X7, were paid during the year.

(k) During the year, $7,000 interest was earned and received on the savings certificates purchased in accordance with the board of trustees' resolution, as discussed in (a).

Required:

(1) Prepare journal entries to record the transactions in the Unrestricted and Restricted Current Funds and the Endowment Fund. Letter journal entries to correspond with the transactions, using the following format:

Event	Fund	Journal Entry
(a)		

(2) Prepare a statement of changes in fund balances for the year ended June 30, 19X8, using a column for each of the three funds, but no total column.

Problem 19–5. The following events occurred as part of the operations of Volz State University:

(a) To construct a new computer complex, the university floated at par a $20,000,000, 7% serial bond issue on October 1, paying interest on June 30 and December 31. Accrued interest is to be transferred to the Retirement of Indebtedness Plant Fund when construction begins. Construction costs are to be accumulated in the Unexpended Plant Fund until the unit is completed.

(b) Since construction has begun, the accrued interest, which must be used to assist in meeting bond interest payments, is transferred. Payments for construction to date total $5,000,000.

(c) On December 31, a mandatory transfer of $350,000 is made from the Unrestricted Current Fund to cover the remainder of the interest due on December 31 on the bond issue.

(d) The bond interest due on December 31 is paid.

(e) Construction of the complex is completed at an additional cost of $15,000,000. Payment is made.

(f) Cost of the completed complex is transferred.

(g) A required transfer of $2,700,000 is made from the Unrestricted Current Fund to cover redemption of the first bond serial of $2,000,000 plus interest.

(h) Payments are made for the items in (g).

(i) A gift of land and a building was received, appraised at $200,000 and $350,000, respectively. The state's leading industrialist made the gift on condition that the university would assume a $90,000 mortgage on the property.

(j) The donor's relative contributed $100,000 in cash for the acquisition of rare first editions for the university library.

(k) The director of the library located a collection of first editions that was available for $150,000. The university board transferred $50,000 from the Unrestricted Current Fund to cover the difference.

(l) The first edition collection is purchased and payment is made.

Required:

Prepare journal entries to record the events, indicating in which funds the entries are made. Use the following format:

Event	Fund	Journal Entry
(a)		

Problem 19–6.   The following selected events relate to the 19X4 activities of Better Care Nursing Home, Inc., a not-for-profit agency:

(a) Gross patient service revenue totaled $2,300,000. The provision for uncollectible accounts was estimated at $92,000. The allowance for contractual adjustments was increased by $140,000.

(b) After a conference with representatives of Red Star Insurance Company, differences between the amounts accrued and subsequent settlements reduced receivables by $60,000.

(c) A grateful patient donated securities with a cost of $10,000 and a market value at date of donation of $75,000. The donation was restricted to expenditure for modernization of equipment. The donation was accepted.

(d) Cash of $37,000 that had been restricted by a donor for operating purposes was used during the year.

(e) The board transferred $50,000 of cash to add to the resources held for capital improvements.

(f) Pledges of $80,000 and cash of $20,000 were received to increase an endowment fund. Of the pledges, 5% are considered uncollectible. Term endowments of $10,000 matured and were released to cover operations.

(g) Equipment costing $250,000 was purchased on account. Restricted resources held for that purpose were transferred to the General Funds.

(h) The nursing home uses functional operating expense control accounts. Expenses for the year were for:

Nursing services	$1,080,000
Dietary services	228,000
Maintenance services	112,000
Administrative services	273,000
Interest	160,000
Subtotal (of which $253,000 is unpaid)	$1,853,000
Depreciation	67,000
Total	$1,920,000

Required:

(1) Omitting explanations, prepare journal entries for all of the funds affected by the foregoing events. Use the following format:

Letter	Fund	Journal Entry
(a)		

(2) Prepare a statement of revenues and expenses of the General Funds for the year ended December 31, 19X4.

Problem 19–7. The following nominal accounts were extracted from the December 31, 19X3 adjusted trial balance of the General Funds of Dade County Hospital:

Gross patient service revenue..................................	$11,049,200
Restricted research grant revenue to the extent expended..	361,000
Revenue from sale of cafeteria meals to guests and employees..	108,000
Unrestricted gifts and grants..................................	100,200
Unrestricted income from endowment funds...........	12,000
Revenue from parking lot......................................	31,000
Revenue from vending machines	68,000
Income on investments whose use is limited by the board for capital improvements	207,000
Provision for medical malpractice costs	$ 112,500
Provision for contractual adjustments under third-party reimbursement programs...........................	1,328,500
Provision for uncollectibles and charity cases...........	556,100
Wages, salaries, and benefits.................................	6,589,100
Supplies used	1,511,200
Purchased professional services.............................	838,300
Depreciation and amortization	478,200
Interest expense..	142,200
Loss on sale of General Funds investments..............	5,300

Required:

Prepare a statement of revenues and expenses of the General Funds for the year ended December 31, 19X3.

Problem 19–8. During the calendar year 19X6, the following events occurred at Marcus Hospital, a voluntary hospital:
(a) Gross charges for hospital services were debited to Accounts Receivable. The hospital controller wishes to use separate revenue accounts for:

Room and board charges	$780,000
Charges for other professional services	320,000
Other nursing services	140,000

(b) Deductions from gross billings were as follows:

Contractual adjustments..	$50,000
Provision for uncollectible receivables	30,000
Charity services..	15,000

The accounting system uses a single allowance account.
(c) Charity services accounts receivable of $15,000 were written off.
(d) During the year, the following contributions were received:

From C. Marcus for future acquisition of a new x-ray machine $25,000
From J. Sago for an emergency fund to be used if special
   assistance for burn care services is required 60,000
From various sources, with no restrictions as to use 79,000

(e) In the Endowment Fund, various unrestricted investment earnings total-ing $23,000 have been collected. They are to be accumulated in the ac-count Due to General Funds. Periodically, transfers are made to the General Funds, which do not accrue the amounts since the time of trans-fer is unpredictable. Transfers of $21,000 of such earnings are made.

(f) A new x-ray machine costing $36,000 is acquired. A transfer of cash is made from the Plant Replacement Fund, including Marcus's contribu-tion plus other available cash. There is a 30-day trial period before pay-ment is due. The invoice was vouchered.

(g) The old x-ray machine is sold for $8,000. It cost $27,000 and had a book value of $6,000 when sold. The gain is unrestricted.

(h) The following data are provided regarding accounts receivable collections:

Gross billings.. $980,000
Less: Contractual adjustments 40,000
       Uncollectible accounts written off................................. 11,000
Cash collected.. $929,000

Cash collected includes reimbursement by third-party payors for depre-ciation of $63,000, which must be accumulated to update facilities.

(i) Vouchers totaling $1,190,000 were issued for the following items:

Administrative services expense $120,000
Fiscal services expense... 94,000
General services expense... 225,000
Nursing services expense... 520,000
Other professional services expense 165,000
Supplies (perpetual inventory is used)..................................... 60,000
Expenses accrued at December 31, 19X5 6,000

(j) Cash payments on vouchers payable during the year were $925,000.

(k) Supplies of $37,000 were issued to nursing services.

(l) Plant Replacement and Expansion Fund investments earned $7,000, of which $6,000 was received. Earnings are restricted for plant expansion.

(m) Depreciation for the year amounts to $155,000.

(n) Included in the vouchered items was a bill for burn care services of $10,000. A transfer is made to the General Funds from Sago's contribution.

(o) A payment of $27,000 is made, covering $15,000 of mortgage bonds re-tired at face value and $12,000 for the annual interest. The hospital records interest as a part of Administrative Services Expense.

(p) The Endowment Fund contains only permanent endowments. Invest-ments of that fund costing $50,000 were sold for $61,000. Gains must remain in the fund.

Required:

Prepare journal entries to record events, using the following format:

Event	Fund	Journal Entry
(a)		

Problem 19-9.   Using the data from Problem 19-8, prepare a statement of revenues and expenses for Marcus Hospital for the year ended December 31, 19X6.

Problem 19-10.   You are provided with a summarized version of the cash account of the General Funds for Parkside Hospital, a not-for-profit organization. Prepare a statement of cash flows of the General Funds, using the direct method, for the year ended December 31, 19X6.

Cash Account — General Funds

	Debit	Credit
Cash balance, January 1, 19X6.....................................	275,900	
Cash received from: Patients	2,061,900	
Third-party payors........................	6,500,000	
Operation of gift shop...................	517,700	
Unrestricted gifts...........................	323,500	
Transfer from donor-restricted fund for purchase of		
property and equipment...	43,000	
Transfer to assets whose use is limited.........................		228,000
Early repayment of long-term debt..............................		242,300
Cash paid to: Employees...		1,151,000
Suppliers..		6,200,000
Providers of consultation services............		800,000
Bank for interest......................................		147,000
Contractor for purchase of property and		
equipment...		501,200
Cash balance, December 31, 19X6...............................	452,500	

Problem 19-11.   Using data from Problem 19-10 and the following additional information, prepare a reconciliation of excess of revenues over expenses to net cash provided by operating activities and nonoperating revenue that would accompany Parkside Hospital's statement of cash flows for the General Funds for the year ended December 31, 19X6.

The following condensed statement of revenues and expenses of the General Funds for the year ended December 31, 19X6, shows:

Total operating revenues..........................	$9,283,300
Total operating expenses	8,780,100
Income from operations........................	$ 503,200
Nonoperating revenue	360,100
Excess of revenues over expenses	$ 863,300

Included in the condensed statement of revenue and expenses were:

Depreciation and amortization	$432,500
Noncash gifts and bequests.......................	17,500
Increase in expense and liability for	
estimated malpractice costs....................	12,300

An analysis of comparative balance sheet items showed the following changes in balances during 19X6:

Increase in patient accounts receivable.......	$227,400
Decrease in supplies inventory...................	11,800
Increase in accounts payable	30,100

(AICPA adapted)

Problem 19–12. Esperanza Hospital's post-closing trial balance at December 31, 19X6, is as follows:

Cash..	60,000	
Investment in U.S. Treasury Bills...............................	400,000	
Investment in Corporate Bonds.................................	500,000	
Interest Receivable..	10,000	
Accounts Receivable	50,000	
Inventory	30,000	
Land...	100,000	
Building...	800,000	
Equipment..	170,000	
Allowance for Depreciation......................................		410,000
Accounts Payable		20,000
Notes Payable...		70,000
Endowment Fund Balance.......................................		520,000
Other Fund Balances..		1,100,000
	2,120,000	2,120,000

Esperanza, which is a not-for-profit hospital, did not maintain its books in conformity with the principles of hospital fund accounting. Effective January 1, 19X7, Esperanza's board of trustees voted to adjust the December 31, 19X6 general ledger balances and to establish separate funds for the General Funds, the Endowment Fund, and the Plant Replacement and Expansion Fund.

Additional account information:
(a) Investment in Corporate Bonds pertains to the amount required to be accumulated under a board policy to invest cash equal to accumulated depreciation until the funds are needed for asset replacement. The $500,000 balance at December 31, 19X6, is less than the full amount required because of errors in computation of building depreciation for past years. Included in the allowance for depreciation is a correctly computed amount of $90,000 applicable to equipment.
(b) Endowment Fund Balance has been credited with the following:

Donor's bequest of cash..	$300,000
Gains on sales of securities	100,000
Interest and dividends earned in 19X4, 19X5, and 19X6	120,000
Total..	$520,000

The terms of the bequest specify that the principal, plus all gains on sales of investments, are to remain fully invested in U.S. government or corporate securities. At December 31, 19X6, $400,000 was invested in

U.S. Treasury bills. The bequest further specifies that interest and dividends earned on investments are to be used for payment of current operating expenses.

(c) Land comprises the following:

Donation of land 40 years ago, at appraised value......................	$ 40,000
Appreciation in value of land as determined by an independent appraiser 5 years ago..	60,000
Total...	$100,000

(d) Building comprises the following:

Hospital building completed 40 years ago when operations were started (useful life of 50 years), at cost...................................	$720,000
Installation of elevator 20 years ago (estimated useful life of 20 years), at cost	80,000
Total...	$800,000

Required:

Enter the post-closing trial balance on a worksheet. Use the following columnar headings with a debit and credit column for each: Trial Balance, Adjustments, General Funds, Endowment Fund, and Plant Replacement and Expansion Fund.

Enter the adjustments necessary to restate the general ledger account balances properly. Distribute the adjusted balances to establish the separate funds accounts, and complete the worksheet. Formal journal entries are not required, but supporting computations should be referenced to the worksheet adjustments.

CHAPTER 20

ACCOUNTING FOR VOLUNTARY HEALTH AND WELFARE ORGANIZATIONS

This chapter discusses accounting and financial reporting for voluntary health and welfare organizations. To qualify as this type of not-for-profit organization, two criteria must be met. First, a primary source of revenue should be contributions from donors who do not themselves directly benefit from the organization's programs. A community symphony orchestra would not qualify because it derives a large share of its revenue from box office receipts. Second, the program must be in the area of health, welfare, or community service, such as care for the elderly, the indigent, or the handicapped, or projects to protect the environment.

FUNDS

Although most contributions are made with no restrictions attached, some donations specify the purpose for which they must be expended. To segregate resources and to demonstrate compliance with restrictions, fund accounting is used. The funds that are practical for most voluntary health and welfare organizations are:

Unrestricted: Current Unrestricted Fund
Restricted: Current Restricted Fund
Land, Building, and Equipment Fund (or Plant Fund)
Endowment Fund
Custodian Fund

Although these funds are similar to the funds used in university accounting—two current funds consisting primarily of current assets and current liabilities, a separate plant fund (but without subgroups), and an endowment fund—all voluntary health and welfare organization funds (except custodian funds) record revenues and expenses. In accounting for universities, only the two current funds have revenue and expense accounts, while the other funds record changes directly through their fund balance accounts.

CURRENT UNRESTRICTED FUND

The *Current Unrestricted Fund* accounts for resources that have no external restrictions and that are available for current operations at the discretion of the governing board. The board, however, may place its own restrictions on the fund balance. In the same manner that industry appropriates retained earnings, the board of directors of a health and welfare organization may designate a portion of its fund balance for a special project. To reflect such an action, the fund balance consists of two accounts. One is Fund Balance — Designated, which corresponds to an appropriated retained earnings account. The other account is Fund Balance — Undesignated, which resembles the free or unappropriated retained earnings balance. The designated fund balance may be created only from, and ultimately must be returned to, the undesignated fund balance, just as appropriated retained earnings come from and return to the free retained earnings balance.

CURRENT RESTRICTED FUND

The *Current Restricted Fund* accounts for assets received from outside sources for a current operating purpose specified by the donor. The distinguishing feature between unrestricted and restricted funds is whether or not an externally imposed restriction exists. A contribution received by a health agency to conduct sex education classes is an example of a restricted resource. In the Current Restricted Fund, a separate fund balance account may be established for each program. A more common procedure is to use one fund balance account as a control over supporting records that provide detailed segregation and identification. Specifically excluded from this fund are contributions of endowments or contributions restricted to the acquisition of plant assets, which are recorded in other appropriate funds.

LAND, BUILDING, AND EQUIPMENT FUND (OR PLANT FUND)

The *Plant Fund* accounts for the activity related to fixed assets, including the accumulation of resources to acquire or replace them, the liabilities related to them, as well as their acquisition, their disposal, and their depreciation. To determine the total cost of rendering service, depreciation of assets employed in providing that service must be recorded in the Plant Fund, with the typical depreciation entry debiting Depreciation Expense and crediting Accumulated Depreciation.

Two fund balance accounts are used in the Plant Fund. The first is labeled Fund Balance — Unexpended, which represents the net assets in the fund not yet committed. The second is Fund Balance — Expended, which shows the net amount invested in plant assets, equal to the gross fixed assets minus accumulated depreciation and minus any liabilities directly related to those assets, such as a mortgage. Each time there is a change in the net amount invested in fixed assets as defined, there must be a change in the respective fund balance accounts. For example, assume that there is a payment on a mortgage liability from Plant Fund cash. In addition to the payment entry, a second entry is necessary because the reduction of the mortgage liability increases the net investment in plant and the cash payment reduces the unexpended assets. The additional entry needed is:

Fund Balance — Unexpended	XXX	
Fund Balance — Expended		XXX

This entry also would be necessary if fixed assets were purchased using Plant Fund cash.

Fixed assets may be acquired by the expenditure of Current Unrestricted Fund cash. To show the increase in the net investment in plant, the following entry is recorded in the Plant Fund:

Land, Building, and Equipment	XXX	
Fund Balance — Expended		XXX

In the Current Unrestricted Fund, the expenditure could be recorded with a debit to the account Transfer to Plant Fund or debited directly to Fund Balance — Undesignated, as Cash is credited. As long as the records provide data for the financial statements, either method is acceptable. Since the unrestricted fund is the one most often involved in making transfers to other funds, this text will follow the procedure of using a separate account to record a transfer in the unrestricted fund, while handling transfers in other funds directly through the appropriate fund balance account.

If fixed assets are sold, the usual entry is made in the Plant Fund, with the gain or loss recorded in a miscellaneous revenue or miscellaneous expense account. A second entry is necessary to show the change in the respective fund balance accounts equal to the *book value* of the asset sold. At year end, the gain or loss on the sale will increase or decrease Fund Balance — Unexpended through the closing process. For example, assume that equipment costing $6,000, with $4,000 of accumulated depreciation, is sold for $3,100. The entries in the Plant Fund are:

Cash	3,100	
Accumulated Depreciation	4,000	
Land, Building, and Equipment		6,000
Miscellaneous Revenue		1,100
To record equipment sale.		

Fund Balance — Expended...	2,000	
Fund Balance — Unexpended		2,000
To record decrease in net investment in plant equal to		
book value of asset sold.		

Although the unexpended net assets increased by $3,100, the portion equal to the gain of $1,100 will increase Fund Balance — Unexpended at year end, when the revenue accounts are closed.

ENDOWMENT FUND

The *Endowment Fund* accounts for gifts or bequests with the legal restriction that the principal be maintained in perpetuity or until the occurrence of a specified event. Various conditions are possible, depending upon the desires of the contributor. Unless otherwise specified, net gains or losses on the sale of Endowment Fund assets are increases or decreases of the fund principal.

Endowment Fund investment revenue may be restricted or unrestricted. When the investment revenue is identical to the cash flow, as in the case of cash dividends, the income may be recorded directly in the fund that is to receive it. Such income not subject to any restrictions by the principal donor may be recorded directly in the Current Unrestricted Fund as investment revenue. If the revenue is subject to a restriction, it would be recorded directly in the appropriate restricted fund. An alternative process would be to record the cash received in the Endowment Fund, with a credit to a liability to the ultimate recipient fund. This approach would require another entry to record the cash transfer between funds, at which time the liability and receivable accounts would be reduced. For example, if a cash dividend on Endowment Fund investments is received and there are no restrictions on the revenue, the entries in the respective funds, under the alternative method, are:

Endowment Fund:

Cash...	XXX	
Due to Current Unrestricted Fund		XXX

Current Unrestricted Fund:

Due from Endowment Fund..	XXX	
Investment Revenue...		XXX

Where the cash flow and the revenue to be recognized are not equal, as in the case of interest received on bonds purchased at a premium or discount, the latter approach of making entries in both funds is preferable. It permits tighter control over cash flows, all of which are recorded first in the Endowment Fund. A liability is recorded for the cash to be transferred to other funds. For example, assume that $100,000 of 14%, 10-year bonds are purchased at 110 on an annual interest payment date, with interest to go to the Current Unrestricted Fund. The entry to record their purchase in the Endowment Fund is:

Investment in 14% Bonds	100,000	
Premium on Bonds Purchased	10,000	
Cash		110,000

A year later, a check for $14,000 is received. If the total $14,000 is entered as revenue in the Current Unrestricted Fund, eventually the principal of the Endowment Fund will be reduced by $10,000, since the Endowment Fund will receive upon bond maturity only $100,000 for its $110,000 cash outlay. To prevent such an erosion of principal, a portion of the interest equal to the premium amortization is retained as principal of the Endowment Fund and a liability for the net amount available to the Current Unrestricted Fund is established. Under straight-line amortization, the entries would be:

Endowment Fund:

Cash	14,000	
Premium on Bonds Purchased		1,000
Due to Current Unrestricted Fund		13,000
To retain as principal the straight-line amortization of premium on bonds purchased ($10,000 ÷ 10 years).		

Current Unrestricted Fund:

Due from Endowment Fund	13,000	
Investment Revenue		13,000

If bonds are purchased at a discount, the entry to record the discount accumulation in the Endowment Fund depends upon the arrangements with the donor or the decision of the controlling board. If only the immediate cash flow from the investment is available to the recipient fund, the discount accumulation is credited to Investment Revenue in the Endowment Fund. If total revenue, including discount accumulation, must be available to the fund designated as the recipient, a liability to that fund for the total is credited.

To illustrate, assume that $100,000 of 10%, 10-year bonds are purchased at 95 on an annual interest payment date, with interest to go to the Current Unrestricted Fund. The entry to record the purchase in the Endowment Fund is:

Investment in 10% Bonds	100,000	
Discount on Bonds Purchased		5,000
Cash		95,000

Most endowments make only the immediate cash flow available, in which case the following entries based on straight-line accumulation are recorded one year later:

Endowment Fund:

Cash	10,000	
Discount on Bonds Purchased	500	
Due to Current Unrestricted Fund		10,000
Investment Revenue		500

Current Unrestricted Fund:
    Due from Endowment Fund... 10,000
        Investment Revenue...   10,000

In the rare case where the donor would require total revenue, including discount accumulation, to be available, the entries would be:

Endowment Fund:
    Cash.. 10,000
    Discount on Bonds Purchased....................................   500
        Due to Current Unrestricted Fund   10,500

Current Unrestricted Fund:
    Due from Endowment Fund... 10,500
        Investment Revenue...   10,500

CUSTODIAN FUND

A *Custodian Fund* is somewhat similar to the Agency Funds of other not-for-profit organizations, in that the assets do not belong to the organization holding them. There is a more technical distinction as pointed out in the audit guide, which states "Custodian Funds are established to account for assets received by an organization to be held or disbursed only on instructions of the person or organization from whom they were received."[1]

Assets are recorded in Custodian Funds when received, along with a liability to the donor. Only when they are released by the contributor will the assets be recorded as revenue in the appropriate fund. For most organizations, Custodian Funds do not exist. If they do exist, Custodian Funds should be shown on the balance sheet, but should not be combined with amounts of other funds.

ACCOUNTING PRINCIPLES AND PROCEDURES

The full accrual basis of accounting should be used in accounting and reporting for voluntary health and welfare organizations if the reports are to be considered as prepared in accordance with generally accepted accounting principles. All funds (except Custodian Funds) use revenue and expense accounts.

The audit guide for voluntary health and welfare organizations states that, if available for expenditure, current restricted gifts and other revenue should be reported when received. This procedure is in direct contrast to that used for hospitals and universities, for which the respective audit guides recommend that revenues in restricted funds be recognized only when expended for their intended purposes. Thus, if a donor makes a

---

[1] *Audits of Voluntary Health and Welfare Organizations* (New York: American Institute of Certified Public Accountants, 1974), 3.

$10,000 contribution to a voluntary health and welfare organization for a current restricted program, but only $8,000 is expended, the organization must recognize $10,000 as revenue in order to be in compliance with the audit guide.

A significant aspect of accounting and reporting for voluntary health and welfare organizations is that financial reports must show expenses on a program basis. As a result of this requirement, the costs of each program and supporting service are available, and the effectiveness with which the organization's resources have been managed can be measured.

The dependence upon public support for the majority of its resources influences the accounting for a voluntary health and welfare organization. Two major categories are used to record and communicate inflows of resources: public support and revenue. *Public support* is the inflow of resources from voluntary donors who receive no direct, personal benefit from the organization's usual programs in exchange for their contributions. *Revenues* are inflows of resources resulting from a charge for service or from financial activities.

PUBLIC SUPPORT

The following accounts, which may be found in all funds (except Custodian Funds), are used to record receipts of assets in the public support category:

> Contributions
> Special Events Support
> Legacies and Bequests
> Received from Federated and Nonfederated Campaigns

Contributions. Cash collections that do not involve a previous pledge are credited to the account Contributions. Voluntary health and welfare organizations also receive pledges for contributions, which are recorded at the gross amount as Pledges Receivable, with a credit to Contributions. A provision and an allowance for estimated uncollectible pledges are established, based on historical collection experience. The provision for uncollectible pledges is a contra account to Contributions on the operating statement, while the allowance is a contra account to Pledges Receivable on the balance sheet.

Securities and other property received should be entered in the appropriate fund at their market value at the time of receipt. These assets are most likely to be received as restricted contributions to the Plant Fund or to the Endowment Fund. The donor may restrict not only the purpose but also the timing of use. If the donation is not available until some future fiscal period, a deferred credit account, Contributions Designated for Future Periods, is introduced. The amount is transferred to Contributions in the period when it becomes available.

Common to voluntary health and welfare organizations is the donation of materials to be used in providing service or to be processed for subsequent sale. These materials should be recorded as inventory, with a credit to Contributions at their market value when received, provided that they are substantial in amount and that a measurable value for them can be established, either by sale shortly thereafter or by appraisal. An example would be the donation of clothing or household goods to Goodwill Industries.

Occasionally, a voluntary health and welfare organization will be permitted to use building facilities rent free. In this situation, both the contribution and the rent expense should be recorded at the amount that normally would be charged for rent. Donated fixed assets for which title is received, such as equipment or land and building, should be entered as a contribution at market value in the Plant Fund, if the fixed asset is to be used by the organization. If the donated fixed asset is accepted with the intent to sell within the near future, it is recorded with a credit to Contributions in the Unrestricted Fund or in one of the restricted funds, depending upon the donor's stipulations.

Although the range of personal services that volunteers donate varies between organizations, these services should be recorded if they are significant and if all three of the following criteria are met:

1. Services provided would have to be performed by salaried personnel, were it not for the volunteer.
2. Duties of the volunteer are controlled by the organization.
3. The value of the volunteer's services is measurable and material. The amount paid salaried personnel for equivalent services would be a useful measure of value.

If the three tests are met, donated services are recorded with a debit to an expense account, such as Salary Expense, and a credit to Contributions. The audit guide specifically excludes from donated services the assistance of volunteers for concentrated fund drives because of the difficulty of enforcing the second criterion of control over the volunteers.

Special Events Support. Another subdivision of the public support category covers an organization's special fund-raising events, in which the participant has the opportunity to receive something of value in exchange for a contribution. Raffles, dinners, bingo games, and bake sales are examples of special events. The gross inflow of resources is credited to the account Special Events Support in the fund that is to benefit. Direct costs of the event, excluding promotional costs, are charged to the account Cost of Special Events. Comparing these two balances permits one to judge the effectiveness of the event. Promotional costs, such as advertising or the salaries of employees involved in the event, are charged against the account Fund-Raising Expense. The audit guide requires that the portion of the budget consumed by fund raising be revealed.

Legacies and Bequests. Every voluntary health and welfare organization hopes that its programs will be so deserving that they will encourage donors to make major contributions of personal property or real property through their wills. Since these items tend to be more substantial in amount, the audit guide recommends that such contributions be shown as a separate item of public support under the account Legacies and Bequests. They are entered as a credit to that account when the organization is reasonably certain of the amount to be received.

Received from Federated and Nonfederated Campaigns. The final item considered as public support is the amount received from federated (associated) and nonfederated organizations. This amount is credited to the account Received from Federated and Nonfederated Campaigns. An amount allocated by United Way to a health and welfare organization would be an example of support received from a federated organization. An amount raised by independent professional fund-raising groups would be an illustration of resources received from nonfederated campaigns.

REVENUES

In addition to public support, resources may be received that are classified as revenue. These resources would include fees charged for services and investment transaction revenue. In the first group (fees charged for services) would be the following accounts:

1. Membership Dues Revenue for dues charged members to join and to use facilities or to receive publications.
2. Program Services Fees for amounts charged clients for services of the organization, such as consulting, testing, or advising.
3. Sales of Publications and Supplies for proceeds from the sales of these items.

The second group (investment transaction revenue) could include the following accounts:

1. Investment Revenue for interest, dividends, and other earnings.
2. Realized Gain on Investment Transactions for gains from the sale or exchange of investments.
3. Net Increase (or Decrease) in Carrying Value of Investments for the unrealized appreciation (or depreciation) of investments if they are carried at market value.

Each of the items of revenue would be recorded in the fund that is entitled to its use. Thus, the unrestricted revenue from the Endowment Fund would be recorded directly in the Current Unrestricted Fund with a credit to Investment Revenue. Restricted investment revenue is reported directly in the fund that is entitled to it in compliance with the donor's wishes.

The audit guide permits voluntary health and welfare organizations to carry their investments either at cost or at market value, but the same basis must be applied to all the investments of all the funds. Cost includes not only the total cost of purchased investments but also the market value at the date of receipt of donated investments. When there is a relatively permanent reduction in market value, the impairment to cost should be recorded. If all investments are reflected at market value, the unrealized appreciation (or depreciation) is shown separately in Net Increase (or Decrease) in Carrying Value of Investments. Although gaining in acceptance, this alternative has been adopted by few organizations, partially as the result of the reluctance of accountants to recognize unrealized gains.

If an organization is fortunate enough to accumulate substantial investments in its various funds, pooling may be advisable. *Pooling of investments* is the process of combining the investments of various funds into one group or pool to provide greater flexibility at lower cost and to provide diversification to spread the risk. Once pooled, individual investments lose their identity as to fund. Each contributing fund merely maintains in its investment account an amount representing its portion of the pool. Before any additions or withdrawals may be made, the market value of the total portfolio must be determined. Realized gains and losses (and unrealized, if investments are carried at market value rather than cost) are allocated to each participating fund on the basis of its share of the total market value at the previous valuation date. The proportion of each fund's market value may be expressed in terms of units or in terms of percentages of the total. The latter method is more flexible and is used in Illustration 20–1, which shows changes in pooled investments over a period of time as explained in the narrative that follows the illustration.

Illustration 20–1
Pooling of Investments

Fund	(1) Cash and/or MV of Securities	(2) Original Equity Percent	(3) Total Pool December 31, 19X0 Cost	(4) Total Pool December 31, 19X0 Market	(5) Mkt. Value Including $50,000	(6) Revised Equity Percent	(7) After Withdrawal of $25,000	(8) New Equity Percent
Unrestricted.	$ 36,000	20%	$ 40,000	$ 50,000	$ 50,000	16.67%	$ 25,000	9.09%
Plant..........	54,000	30	60,000	75,000	75,000	25.00	75,000	27.27
Endowment.	90,000	50	100,000	125,000	175,000	58.33	175,000	63.64
Total........	$180,000	100%	$200,000	$250,000	$300,000	100.00%	$275,000	100.00%

The investments of the Current Unrestricted Fund, the Plant Fund, and the Endowment Fund of a voluntary health and welfare organization were pooled as of January 2, 19X0. The investment accounts are maintained at market. Cash and/or market value of the securities pooled are shown in Column (1). The percentage of the total contributed by each fund is shown in Column (2). During the ensuing year, net realized gains retained by the investment pool amounted to $20,000. Based on its equity percentage, each fund records its share of the gain. Thus, the Current Unrestricted Fund's entry for 20% of the $20,000 gain would be:

Pooled Investments..	4,000	
Realized Gain on Investment Transactions		4,000

The $20,000 increase in the pool results in a revised cost basis as of December 31, 19X0, shown in Column (3). On December 31, 19X0, the Endowment Fund receives a contribution of securities, which have a market value of $50,000 and which are to be pooled with the other investments whose market value on that date also must be determined if the process is to be equitable. The total market value of the other investments is determined to be $250,000, which is allocated to each fund, as shown in Column (4), on the basis of the percentage previously computed. After acceptance of the additional $50,000 of Endowment Fund securities, the total market value is $300,000, as shown in Column (5), from which revised equity percentages are determined, shown in Column (6).

Immediately after each addition to or withdrawal from the pool, new equity percentages must be determined. To avoid numerous computations, it is common practice to permit changes only at the end of a calendar quarter. Assume that on December 31, 19X0, the Current Unrestricted Fund needs $25,000 to meet expenses and that the amount is withdrawn from the investment pool. Since each fund already has recorded its share of the unrealized gains, the entry in the Unrestricted Fund would be:

Cash..	25,000	
Pooled Investments...		25,000

With this redemption, the new market value of remaining pool investments is $275,000, shown in Column (7), with the revised equity percentages listed in Column (8).

When investments are pooled, each fund involved initiates an account, Pooled Investments, that should be carried at market value to reflect directly its equity in the pool. To illustrate the entries for the Endowment Fund in the previous illustration when investments are carried at market value, the following entries are presented:

Pooled Investments..	90,000	
Cash..		90,000
To record original investment as of January 2, 19X0.		
Pooled Investments..	10,000	
Realized Gain on Investment Transactions		10,000
To record realized gain on investment transactions for 19X0 (50% × $20,000).		
Pooled Investments..	25,000	
Net Increase in Carrying Value of Investments		25,000
To record increase in market value over cost at year end (50% × $50,000).		

Investments (or Securities)	50,000	
Contributions...		50,000
To record securities received as a contribution.		
Pooled Investments..	50,000	
Investments (or Securities)		50,000
To record transfer of contributed securities to pool at market value.		

After the series of entries has been posted, the balance in Pooled Investments in the Endowment Fund is $175,000. This amount represents the market value of its equity in the pool at year end.

PROGRAM AND SUPPORTING SERVICES COSTS

The audit guide emphasizes that voluntary health and welfare organizations exist to render service or to conduct programs. Their operating statements will not show typical expenses, such as salaries or rent, but will show the cost of each program or service the organization provides—the costs in which the general public, the contributors, and the controlling agencies primarily are interested. For example, the operating statement of an environmental protection association might show the cost of conducting a program to reduce river pollution or to provide an animal and bird sanctuary. These projects fall in an expense grouping called *Program Services*. The other expense grouping shown on an operating statement is referred to as *Supporting Services*, which includes fund-raising costs and management and general costs for the overall direction of the organization.

Individual expenses, such as salaries or rent, are recorded in the respective expense accounts of the appropriate funds, in much the same way that they would be recorded in the accounts of profit entities. Most of the expenses will be recorded in the unrestricted fund, since it is the principal operating fund; but some expenses, such as depreciation, may be recorded in the restricted funds. At the end of the fiscal year, the expenses recorded in each fund are allocated to the programs conducted and to the supporting services of management and fund raising. Allocation of joint costs should be on some rational basis, such as assigning salaries on the basis of time expended, allotting rental charges on the basis of floor space, or apportioning supplies expense on the basis of consumption. However, it is not always simple to allocate costs.

The public has been deluged with informational materials that attempt to educate the reader about proper health habits to avoid disease or infection, about birth control and other family planning issues, and about the need to protect endangered species or the environment. Included in much of this material is a fund-raising appeal. A question arises as to whether the total cost of sending such literature should be charged to the program publicized or to fund raising, or whether it should be allocated between them. Since board members, donors, and the general public pay particular attention to the percentages of revenue consumed by administrative and fund-raising purposes, the desire to keep those percentages at a minimum is understandable.

There has been controversy over this issue mostly because of the conflicting guidance from the AICPA. Its audit guide for voluntary health and welfare organizations (1966) supported allocation in some paragraphs and charged total joint costs to the primary category of activity (primary purpose rule) in others. In 1974, its revised *Standards of Accounting and Financial Reporting for Voluntary Health and Welfare Organizations* stated that if multiple-purpose activities include an appeal for financial support as an essential part, the entire costs should be charged to fund raising. In 1987, the issue was resolved when the AICPA stated that:

> *If it can be demonstrated that a bona fide program or management and general function has been conducted in conjunction with the appeal for funds, joint costs should be allocated between fund raising and the appropriate program or management and general function.*[2]

CLOSING ENTRIES

After all expenses have been assigned, an entry is made in each fund to close the expense accounts and charge each of the expenses to the programs and supporting services. For the environmental protection association used earlier as an example, the following entry might be recorded in the Current Unrestricted Fund:

River Pollution Program	XXX	
Animal and Bird Sanctuary Program	XXX	
Management and General Services	XXX	
Fund-Raising Services	XXX	
Salary Expense, Supplies Expense, etc.		XXX

The final closing entries close each fund's support and revenue accounts, as well as the program and services accounts, to the appropriate fund balance. The closing entry for the Current Unrestricted Fund of the environmental protection association might be:

Contributions	XXX	
Legacies and Bequests	XXX	
Membership Dues Revenue	XXX	
Investment Revenue	XXX	
River Pollution Program		XXX
Animal and Bird Sanctuary Program		XXX
Management and General Services		XXX
Fund-Raising Services		XXX
Fund Balance — Undesignated		XXX

[2]Statement of Position 87-2, *Accounting for Joint Costs of Informational Materials and Activities of Not-for-Profit Organizations That Include a Fund-Raising Appeal* (New York: American Institute of Certified Public Accountants, 1987), par. 15.

If the board of directors should decide to designate a specified sum of the Current Unrestricted Fund for a future program to reduce air pollution, the undesignated fund balance is appropriated as follows:

```
Fund Balance — Undesignated.............................................   XXX
      Fund Balance — Designated for Air Pollution Program..............         XXX
```

FINANCIAL STATEMENTS

The audit guide requires three financial statements for voluntary health and welfare organizations: an operating statement, which is referred to formally as a statement of support, revenue, and expenses and changes in fund balances; a statement of functional expenses; and a balance sheet. These statements are illustrated later in the chapter.

An operating statement can be prepared after the expense allocation entry has been recorded in each fund. It is structured with a column for each fund (except the Custodian Fund) to show how effectively the organization operated during the period.

Since program costs and not the typical expenses, such as salaries, are shown in an operating statement, a summary of expenses by nature is provided in a separate statement. This statement of functional expenses, as required by the audit guide, supplements the operating statement. It disregards individual funds and presents the total of each expense for all funds combined and the allocation of each expense to the various programs and services.

A balance sheet is prepared either in columnar form with a column for each fund or with individual fund balance sheets layered one upon the other. The latter form is followed in the audit guide.

ILLUSTRATION OF ACCOUNTING FOR A VOLUNTARY HEALTH AND WELFARE ORGANIZATION

To illustrate the recording of events and the preparation of financial reports for a voluntary health and welfare organization, assume that the People's Environmental Protection (PEP) Association, a voluntary community organization, has three programs: Valley Air Pollution, Keep Fish in the Lakes, and Flood Control. The trial balances of the various funds of PEP on January 1, 19X5, are as follows:

People's Environmental Protection (PEP) Association
Fund Trial Balances
January 1, 19X5

	Current Funds		Plant Fund	Endowment Fund
	Unrestricted	Restricted		
Cash...............................	40,000	12,500	2,000	9,000
Pledges Receivable...........	24,000	600	—	—
Allowance for				
Uncollectible Pledges.....	(3,000)	(100)	—	—
Investments.....................	61,000	—	—	244,000
Land, Building, and				
Equipment...................	—	—	92,700	—
Accumulated Depreciation..	—	—	(16,700)	—
Totals.........................	122,000	13,000	78,000	253,000
Accounts Payable.............	33,000	4,000	—	—
Fund Balances:				
Designated...................	25,000	—	—	—
Undesignated...............	64,000	—	—	—
Restricted....................	—	9,000	—	253,000
Expended....................	—	—	76,000	—
Unexpended................	—	—	2,000	—
Totals.........................	122,000	13,000	78,000	253,000

The following events occur during the calendar year 19X5. They are summarized to conserve space and minimize duplication. Entries are shown following each transaction, with the designation of the fund in which each entry is recorded appearing above the amounts for the entry.

1. As a result of its fund-raising program, cash contributions and pledges were received.

	Unrestricted		Restricted	
Cash...	235,000		90,000	
Pledges Receivable..........................	80,000		20,000	
Contributions.................................		315,000		110,000

2. Based on past experience, 5% of the pledges were estimated to be uncollectible.

	Unrestricted		Restricted	
Provision for Uncollectible Pledges.......	4,000		1,000	
Allowance for Uncollectible Pledges..		4,000		1,000

3. During the year, cash was collected from some pledges, while others were written off as uncollectible.

	Unrestricted		Restricted	
Cash...	78,000		17,500	
Allowance for Uncollectible Pledges.....	5,000		600	
Pledges Receivable........................		83,000		18,100

4. A cash donation of $40,000 was received, on condition that it be used to acquire equipment that will assist in water quality improvement.

	Plant	
Cash...	40,000	
Contributions..		40,000

5. With the donor's approval, the $40,000 served as a partial payment on the purchase of a weed cutter costing $50,000. A note was signed for the unpaid balance.

	Plant	
Land, Building, and Equipment	50,000	
Cash...		40,000
Notes Payable on Equipment		10,000
Fund Balance—Unexpended	40,000	
Fund Balance—Expended..		40,000

6. The following bequests were received: $100,000 unrestricted and $20,000 as a permanent Endowment Fund whose earnings are unrestricted.

	Unrestricted		Endowment	
Cash...	100,000		20,000	
Legacies and Bequests		100,000		20,000

7. PEP held a special summer event to promote its activities, the net proceeds of which were unrestricted. Gross revenues totaled $9,000, with direct costs for the event amounting to $2,000.

	Unrestricted	
Cash...	9,000	
Special Events Support		9,000
Cost of Special Events.......................	2,000	
Cash...		2,000

8. An annual membership to PEP is $100, permitting members and their families to use lake facilities for swimming, sailing (no motors allowed), or fishing. The proceeds are not restricted.

	Unrestricted	
Cash...	118,000	
Membership Dues Revenue.............		118,000

9. The local PEP unit receives unrestricted cash of $16,000 as its share of a campaign run by its national affiliate.

	Unrestricted	
Cash...	16,000	
Received from Federated and Nonfederated Campaigns		16,000

10. The Endowment Fund reports investment revenue of $28,000, of which $21,000 is not restricted and $7,000 is restricted to publication of pamphlets on flood control. Earnings of the Endowment Fund are recorded directly in the fund that is entitled to them.

	Unrestricted		Restricted	
Cash..	21,000		7,000	
Investment Revenue......................		21,000		7,000

11. PEP carries its investments in all funds at market value. The Endowment Fund sold investments for $27,000. They had a cost of $20,000 and a carrying value of $25,000 in the investment account.

	Endowment	
Cash..	27,000	
Investments (at market)		25,000
Gain on Sale of Investments		2,000

12. The Endowment Fund purchased additional investments costing $46,000.

	Endowment	
Investments..	46,000	
Cash...		46,000

13. The investments of the Current Unrestricted Fund have shown no material change in market value over the year. At year end, the market value of investments in the Endowment Fund has increased from $265,000 to $294,000.

	Endowment	
Investments..	29,000	
Net Increase in Carrying Value of Investments........................		29,000

14. A special recreational building and dock costing $96,000 were purchased with Unrestricted Fund cash.

	Unrestricted	
Transfer to Plant Fund (or Fund Balance — Undesignated)..............	96,000	
Cash...		96,000

	Plant	
Land, Building, and Equipment	96,000	
Fund Balance — Expended		96,000

15. Accounts payable and expenses were paid or established.

	Unrestricted	Restricted
Accounts Payable (January 1).............	33,000	4,000
Salaries Expense............................	180,000	20,000
Payroll Taxes..................................	24,000	6,000
Mailing and Postage Expense.............	40,000	10,000
Rent Expense..................................	23,000	5,000
Telephone Expense	5,000	1,000
Research Expense............................	165,000	50,000
Professional Services: Legal and Audit..	27,000	7,000
Supplies Expense............................	10,000	3,000
Miscellaneous Expense.....................	4,000	1,000
Accounts Payable..........................	31,000	1,000
Cash..	480,000	106,000

16. Depreciation for the year amounted to $22,000.

	Plant
Depreciation Expense	22,000
Accumulated Depreciation	22,000

17. Early in the year, cash contributions for current operations were received, but they cannot be used until late in the following year.

	Unrestricted	Restricted
Cash...	2,000	3,000
Contributions Designated for Future Periods.....................................	2,000	3,000

18. At year end, the expenses of each fund were allocated to the various programs and supporting services. The Endowment Fund has no expenses to allocate. For the two current funds, the following entry closed the expenses and recorded the allocation:

	Unrestricted	Restricted
Valley Air Project..............................	117,000	13,000
Fish in the Lakes Program	131,000	49,000
Flood Control Program	204,000	31,000
Management and General Services	22,000	8,000
Fund-Raising Services	4,000	2,000
Salaries Expense............................	180,000	20,000
Payroll Taxes.................................	24,000	6,000
Mailing and Postage Expense...........	40,000	10,000
Rent Expense................................	23,000	5,000
Telephone Expense	5,000	1,000
Research Expense..........................	165,000	50,000
Professional Services: Legal and Audit.......................................	27,000	7,000
Supplies Expense...........................	10,000	3,000
Miscellaneous Expenses	4,000	1,000

The Plant Fund has only one expense to allocate—depreciation.

	Plant
Valley Air Project	2,000
Fish in the Lakes Program	3,000
Flood Control Program	16,000
Management and General Services	1,000
Depreciation Expense	22,000

In the allocation process and in the closing entries, two expense items were not included because they are shown on the operating statement as direct deductions from public support resources. One is the provision for estimated uncollectible pledges, which is subtracted from the gross contributions amount. The other is the direct cost of a special event, which is subtracted from the gross proceeds of that event. These two items would be closed when the accounts to which they relate are closed.

With expenses allocated to programs and supporting services, it is now possible to prepare the statement of support, revenue, and expenses and changes in fund balances (Illustration 20–2, on page 1068). The sequence of items is suggested by the title. Inflows of resources from public support and revenues are listed first, followed by the expense totals for each program and supporting service, taken directly from the closing and allocation entries. The next items shown are changes in fund balances other than those resulting from operational revenue and expenses, such as corrections for prior periods or transfers to or from other funds. The beginning balance for each fund is added, resulting in the fund balance at the end of the period.

The final entry at year end for each fund closes the support and revenue accounts, as well as the program and supporting services expenses, into the appropriate fund balance accounts. Using the statement of support in Illustration 20–2, the following entry closes the current funds accounts, including the provision for uncollectible pledges and cost of special events accounts and their related resource inflow accounts:

	Unrestricted	Restricted
Contributions	315,000	110,000
Special Events Support	9,000	
Legacies and Bequests	100,000	
Received from Federated and Nonfederated Campaigns	16,000	
Membership Dues Revenue	118,000	
Investment Revenue	21,000	7,000
Fund Balance—Undesignated	1,000	
Provision for Uncollectible Pledges	4,000	1,000
Cost of Special Events	2,000	
Valley Air Project	117,000	13,000
Keep Fish in the Lakes Program	131,000	49,000
Flood Control Program	204,000	31,000
Management and General Services	22,000	8,000
Fund-Raising Services	4,000	2,000
Transfer to Plant Fund	96,000	
Fund Balance		13,000

Illustration 20–2

People's Environmental Protection (PEP) Association
Statement of Support, Revenue, and Expenses and Changes in Fund Balances
For the Year Ended December 31, 19X5

	Current Funds		Plant Fund	Endowment Fund	Total All Funds
	Unrestricted	*Restricted*			
Public support and revenue:					
Public support:					
Contributions (net of provision for uncollectible pledges for current funds of $4,000 and $1,000 respectively)	$311,000	$109,000	$ 40,000	—	$460,000
Special events (net of direct costs of $2,000)	7,000	—	—	—	7,000
Legacies and bequests	100,000	—	—	$ 20,000	120,000
Received from federated and nonfederated campaigns	16,000	—	—	—	16,000
Total public support..............	$434,000	$109,000	$ 40,000	$ 20,000	$603,000
Revenue:					
Membership dues...................	$118,000	—	—	—	$118,000
Investment revenue	21,000	$ 7,000	—	—	28,000
Net increase in carrying value of investments*	—	—	—	$ 29,000	29,000
Realized gain on investments....	—	—	—	2,000	2,000
Total revenue	$139,000	$ 7,000		$ 31,000	$177,000
Total support and revenue.....	$573,000	$116,000	$ 40,000	$ 51,000	$780,000
Expenses:					
Program services:					
Valley air project....................	$117,000	$ 13,000	$ 2,000	—	$132,000
Keep fish in the lakes...............	131,000	49,000	3,000	—	183,000
Flood control...........................	204,000	31,000	16,000	—	251,000
Total program services..........	$452,000	$ 93,000	$ 21,000	—	$566,000
Supporting services:					
Management and general.........	$ 22,000	$ 8,000	$ 1,000	—	$ 31,000
Fund raising............................	4,000	2,000	—	—	6,000
Total supporting services.......	$ 26,000	$ 10,000	$ 1,000	—	$ 37,000
Total expenses	$478,000	$103,000	$ 22,000	—	$603,000
Excess of public support and revenue over expenses	$ 95,000	$ 13,000	$ 18,000	$ 51,000	$177,000
Other changes in fund balances:					
Plant acquired from unrestricted funds......................................	(96,000)	—	96,000	—	—
Fund balances, January 1, 19X5	89,000	9,000	78,000	253,000	429,000
Fund balances, December 31, 19X5 ...	$ 88,000	$ 22,000	$192,000	$304,000	$606,000

*PEP has adopted the market value method for carrying its investments. The method requires that unrealized appreciation of investments be recognized.

In the Plant Fund, contributions are closed to the account Fund Balance — Unexpended:

	Plant Fund	
Contributions...	40,000	
Fund Balance — Unexpended		40,000

For the Plant Fund, one item that deserves special attention in the closing process is depreciation. The balance in the account Fund Balance — Expended, representing the net investment in plant, should equal gross fixed assets minus accumulated depreciation minus related liabilities. In the entry that recorded depreciation, the credit to Accumulated Depreciation will require a decrease in Fund Balance — Expended. Since the depreciation expense account was eliminated when it was assigned to specific programs and services, Fund Balance — Expended must be reduced by the depreciation amount assigned. The reduction is accomplished in the following closing entry:

	Plant Fund	
Fund Balance — Expended (for depreciation assigned)......	22,000	
Valley Air Project...		2,000
Keep Fish in the Lakes Program		3,000
Flood Control Program		16,000
Management and General Services		1,000

The final closing entry for the Endowment Fund consists of debiting accounts that show resource inflows, crediting loss or expense accounts, and clearing the difference through Fund Balance. The entry is as follows:

	Endowment	
Legacies and Bequests	20,000	
Net Increase in Carrying Value of Investments................	29,000	
Gain on Sale of Investments	2,000	
Fund Balance		51,000

Since the investments account of the Endowment Fund is carried at market value, it is entirely possible that the carrying value may decrease. If this situation occurs, the account Net Decrease in Carrying Value of Investments is debited and the investments account is credited. The closing entry would credit Net Decrease in Carrying Value of Investments.

The operating statement of a voluntary health and welfare organization provides valuable data on the total cost per period of each program and of supporting services. To provide the reader of its financial statements with additional information, the audit guide states that a statement of functional expenses should be included in the reports. This statement shows the allocation of each expense (salaries, rent, etc.) and reveals the cost by function of carrying on the organization's activities. The statement of functional expenses for PEP is shown in Illustration 20–3 on page 1070.

Illustration 20–3

People's Environmental Protection (PEP) Association
Statement of Functional Expenses
For the Year Ended December 31, 19X5

	Total All Services	Program Services				Supporting Services		
		Valley Air Project	Fish in the Lakes	Flood Control	Total Programs	Management and General	Fund Raising	Total Supporting
Salaries.............	$200,000	$ 36,000	$ 60,000	$ 80,000	$176,000	$20,000	$4,000	$24,000
Payroll taxes......	30,000	5,400	9,000	12,000	26,400	3,000	600	3,600
Mailing and postage..........	50,000	10,000	20,000	19,700	49,700	—	300	300
Rent	28,000	8,000	5,000	11,600	24,600	3,000	400	3,400
Telephone	6,000	1,500	1,300	2,500	5,300	—	700	700
Research...........	215,000	35,000	80,000	100,000	215,000	—	—	—
Professional: legal and audit..............	34,000	24,000	2,000	4,000	30,000	4,000	—	4,000
Supplies...........	13,000	10,100	—	2,900	13,000	—	—	—
Miscellaneous....	5,000	—	2,700	2,300	5,000	—	—	—
Total expenses before depreciation ...	$581,000	$130,000	$180,000	$235,000	$545,000	$30,000	$6,000	$36,000
Depreciation of buildings and equipment......	22,000	2,000	3,000	16,000	21,000	1,000	—	1,000
Total expenses...	$603,000	$132,000	$183,000	$251,000	$566,000	$31,000	$6,000	$37,000

The balance sheet for PEP on December 31, 18X5, is given in Illustration 20–4. It follows the form shown in the audit guide by stacking the individual balance sheets of the various funds.

As is true in reporting for profit enterprises, financial statements of voluntary health and welfare organizations would be prepared with comparative figures for the preceding year. The statements also should be accompanied by notes that would summarize significant accounting policies.

ACCOUNTING FOR OTHER NOT-FOR-PROFIT ORGANIZATIONS

In 1981, the AICPA issued the audit guide, *Audits of Certain Nonprofit Organizations*, which provides direction for the application of generally accepted accounting principles to not-for-profit organizations that presently are not covered by other audit guides. For example, it declares that to be in conformity with generally accepted accounting principles, financial reports must use the accrual basis of accounting. However, the organization's books may be maintained on some other basis and adjusted at year end, since a cash

Illustration 20–4

People's Environmental Protection (PEP) Association
Balance Sheets
December 31, 19X5

Assets		Liabilities and Fund Balances	

CURRENT FUNDS

Unrestricted

Assets		Liabilities and Fund Balances	
Cash...	$ 41,000	Accounts payable	$ 31,000
Investments (at market, which		Contributions designated for	
approximates cost)	61,000	future periods	2,000
Pledges receivable (less allowance		Total liabilities and deferred	
for uncollectibles of $2,000)	19,000	revenues...........................	$ 33,000
		Fund balances:	
		Designated for long-term	
		investments	$ 25,000
		Undesignated...........................	63,000
		Total fund balances..............	88,000
Total.................................	$121,000	Total.................................	$121,000

Restricted

Assets		Liabilities and Fund Balances	
Cash...	$ 24,000	Accounts payable	$ 1,000
Pledges receivable (less		Contributions designated for	
allowance for uncollectibles of		future periods	3,000
$500).....................................	2,000	Total liabilities and deferred	
		revenues...........................	$ 4,000
		Fund balance (restricted).............	22,000
Total.................................	$ 26,000	Total.................................	$ 26,000

PLANT FUND (OR LAND, BUILDING, AND EQUIPMENT FUND)

Assets		Liabilities and Fund Balances	
Cash...	$ 2,000	Notes payable on equipment	$ 10,000
Land, building, and equipment		Fund balances:	
(less accumulated depreciation		Expended	$190,000
of $38,700).............................	200,000	Unexpended	2,000
		Total fund balances..............	$192,000
Total.................................	$202,000	Total.................................	$202,000

ENDOWMENT FUND

Assets		Liabilities and Fund Balances	
Cash...	$ 10,000	Fund balance	$304,000
Investments at market (cost,			
$210,000)	294,000		
Total.................................	$304,000	Total.................................	$304,000

basis is more practical for maintaining the records of many of these organizations. Entities that have restricted resources should use fund accounting for reporting purposes to demonstrate compliance with externally imposed restrictions. Financial statements to be provided are a balance sheet, a statement of operations and changes in fund balances, and a statement of changes in financial position, along with notes for appropriate disclosures of policy.

Among the not-for-profit entities that are affected by this audit guide are the following:

Cemetery organizations
Civic and fraternal organizations
Labor unions
Libraries and museums
Performing arts and other cultural organizations
Political parties
Private and community foundations

Private elementary and secondary schools
Professional associations
Public broadcasting stations
Religious organizations
Research and scientific organizations
Social and country clubs
Trade associations
Zoological and botanical societies

NEED FOR COMMUNICATION

The performance of not-for-profit organizations cannot be judged with a profit yardstick. Their activities usually are not subject to direct competition from similar units in the community. Those who have the need or the authority must insist that financial reporting be reviewed constantly to ensure that understandable financial statements are available. Only then can resource providers evaluate how effectively stewardship responsibilities have been discharged, the quality of the service and programs, and whether additional resources should be contributed for their future support.

QUESTIONS

1. Name the two criteria that must be met for an entity to qualify as a voluntary health and welfare organization.
2. Differentiate between the accounts Fund Balance—Designated and Fund Balance—Undesignated in the Current Unrestricted Fund of a voluntary health and welfare organization.
3. Defend the statement that accounting for voluntary health and welfare organizations closely resembles accounting for universities. What are two major differences in accounting for these types of not-for-profit entities?

4. Indicate in which fund the following entry would appear, and identify an event that would require the entry:

Fund Balance—Expended... XXX
         Fund Balance—Unexpended XXX

5. Differentiate between public support and revenue as sources of assets.
6. A university and a voluntary health and welfare organization both receive a contribution of $25,000 for restricted current operations. By the end of the fiscal period, both spend $5,000 of the contribution. State the amount that each recognizes as revenue, and give the journal entries that each would make to record the events.
7. Explain the logic (not the process) of pooling of investments.
8. Why does the operating statement of a voluntary health and welfare organization not show expenses by their natural classification, such as salary expense?
9. Explain the purpose of the account Cost of Special Events.
10. What was the primary purpose rule in relation to joint-cost allocation? What is the currently recommended procedure?

EXERCISES

Exercise 1. Select the best answer for each of the following multiple-choice items.

The following information is the basis for the first four items:

A voluntary health organization received equipment donated by a local citizen, who imposed no restrictions on its use.

1. Assume the equipment will be retained by the organization for use in its office. The donation should be recorded in the:
   a. Current Unrestricted Fund.
   b. Current Restricted Fund.
   c. Plant Fund.
   d. Endowment Fund.

2. Under the assumption in item 1, the entry to be made in the appropriate fund would credit the account:
   a. Fund Balance—Unexpended.
   b. Fund Balance—Expended.
   c. Revenue.
   d. Contributions.

(continued)

3. Assume the equipment is to be sold within the near future. The donation should be recorded in the:
   a. Current Unrestricted Fund.
   b. Current Restricted Fund.
   c. Plant Fund.
   d. Endowment Fund.

4. Under the assumption in item 3, the entry to be made in the appropriate fund would credit the account:
   a. Fund Balance — Unexpended.
   b. Fund Balance — Expended.
   c. Revenue.
   d. Contributions.

5. Upon her death, a resident left a substantial sum of money to a voluntary welfare organization. To record its receipt, the account to be credited if there were no restrictions is:
   a. Fund Balance — Unrestricted.
   b. Contributions.
   c. Legacies and Bequests.
   d. Revenue.

Exercise 2.   Select the best answer for each of the following multiple-choice items.

The following data apply to the first two questions:

A voluntary health organization conducted a drive. One large cash donation specified that the sum was to be used to acquire a computer as soon as possible.

1. The amount received should be recorded in the:
   a. Current Unrestricted Fund.
   b. Current Restricted Fund.
   c. Plant Fund.
   d. Endowment Fund.

2. To record the cash received, the account to be credited is:
   a. Fund Balance — Restricted.
   b. Revenue.
   c. Legacies and Bequests.
   d. Contributions.

The following data apply to the next two questions:

A voluntary welfare organization received a substantial pledge with the condition that the amount be matched by other contributions before the combined amounts could be expended for a new building. It is expected that it will take several years to match the pledge.

3. The pledge should be recorded in the:
   a. Plant Fund.
   b. Current Restricted Fund.
   c. Endowment Fund.
   d. Custodian Fund.

4. To record the pledge, the account to be credited is:
   a. Fund Balance — Restricted.
   b. Deferred Revenue.
   c. Contributions.
   d. Legacies and Bequests.

5. Resources received by a voluntary health and welfare organization are classified into two major categories as either:
   a. Public support or revenue.
   b. Contributions or special events support.
   c. Fees charged or investment transaction revenue.
   d. Program service fees or membership dues revenue.

Exercise 3.   On January 2, 19X1, the available cash in the following funds was placed into an investment pool:

Fund	Cash Pooled
Current Unrestricted	$ 40,000
Current Restricted.........	30,000
Plant	10,000
Endowment	20,000
Total	$100,000

During the next year, no additional cash was placed into the pool, nor was any amount withdrawn. At the end of the year, the pooled investments had a basis of $120,000, representing original contributions plus $20,000 of realized gains that remained in the investment pool. At year end, the market value of the pool amounted to $130,000.
(1) Prepare a schedule reflecting pooling activities for the year 19X1.
(2) Prepare the journal entry to record the Endowment Fund's share of the realized and unrealized gains. If the Plant Fund wished to withdraw its holdings in the pool, how much would it receive at year end?

Exercise 4.   By placing a check mark in the appropriate column, indicate in which fund of a voluntary health and welfare organization the following events normally would be recorded. (Note: An event may require entries in more than one fund.)

| | Current Funds | | | Endow- |
Event	Unre-stricted	Re-stricted	Plant Fund	ment Fund
(a) Receipt of donated securities, revenue from which is to be used for both unrestricted and specified current activities...........................	_____	_____	_____	_____
(b) Revenue from donated securities in (a) is received ...	_____	_____	_____	_____
(c) Receipt of donated fixed assets, which are to be sold, with no restrictions on proceeds	_____	_____	_____	_____
(d) Depreciation is recorded	_____	_____	_____	_____
(e) The board of directors makes an appropriation of the undesignated fund balance	_____	_____	_____	_____
(f) An adjustment is made to Fund Balance— Unexpended	_____	_____	_____	_____

Exercise 5.   Record the following events that involved the Current Unrestricted Fund of the Mental Health Clinic, a voluntary health and welfare organization:

(a) Cash contributions of $18,000 and pledges for $32,000 were received.

(b) It is estimated that 10% of the pledges will prove uncollectible.

(c) A fund-raising dinner grossed $6,300 from the sale of 420 tickets. The catered dinner cost $7 per plate for the 360 people who attended, plus $180 for rental of the dining room. Payment for costs was made.

(d) To expand the services of the clinic, a professional fund-raising group was hired to undertake a 9-month campaign. At the end of that time, the group submitted the following report:

Cash collected..	$ 70,000
Pledges (should be 95% collectible)............	30,000
Total proceeds.......................................	$100,000
Less 20% fund-raising fee.........................	20,000
Net proceeds from drive.........................	$ 80,000

Exercise 6.   Record the following events that involved the Land, Building, and Equipment (Plant) Fund of the Mental Health Clinic, a voluntary health and welfare organization:

(a) A contribution of $10,000 was received and is to be used for the purchase of equipment, but not until an addition to the building is constructed. This event is not likely to occur during the next two years.

(b) Equipment costing $17,000, with a book value of $8,000, was sold for $10,000. The proceeds are to remain in the Land, Building, and Equipment Fund.

(c) Depreciation of $9,000 is recorded on various plant items.

(d) Equipment was purchased for $12,000, with payment due in 30 days.

(e) The liability for the equipment purchased in (d) was paid.

Exercise 7.   Record the following events that involved the Endowment Fund of Mercy Health Clinic, a voluntary health and welfare organization:

(a) In a will, a leading citizen left a bequest of $100,000 to the clinic. Stipulations were that the amount was to become the corpus of a permanent endowment. Any income received would be used first to cover any loss of principal, with the remaining revenue to be used for an educational program on mental problems. The total amount was received and invested in 8% municipal bonds purchased at face value on an interest date.

(b) Investments were carried at cost. Later in the year, half of the bond investment was sold at 98, plus $3,000 of accrued interest. A liability to the recipient fund was recorded.

(c) Other Endowment Fund investments earned $11,000. The amount is not subject to any limitations and is recorded directly in the recipient fund.

Exercise 8.   Using the balance sheets of the individual funds shown in Illustration 20–4:

(1) Prepare a columnar balance sheet, with a column for each fund and a total column.

(2) Indicate what difficulties in physical construction are encountered in the process of preparing the columnar balance sheet.

(3) Discuss the advantages and disadvantages for the reader of the columnar form versus the layered form followed by the AICPA as illustrated in the chapter.

Exercise 9.   The characteristics of voluntary health and welfare organizations differ in certain respects from the characteristics of state or local governmental units. As an example, voluntary health and welfare organizations derive their revenues primarily from voluntary contributions from the general public, while governmental units derive their revenues from taxes and from services provided to their jurisdictions.

(1) Describe fund accounting and discuss whether its use is consistent with the concept that an accounting entity is an economic unit that has control over resources, accepts responsibilities for making and carrying out commitments, and conducts economic activity.

(2) Discuss how methods used to account for fixed assets differ between voluntary health and welfare organizations and governmental units.

(AICPA adapted)

PROBLEMS

Problem 20–1.   Select the best answer for each of the following multiple-choice items.

1. Aviary Haven, a voluntary welfare organization funded by contributions from the general public, received unrestricted pledges of $500,000 during 19X6. It was estimated that 12% of these pledges would be uncollectible. By the end of 19X6, $400,000 of the pledges had been collected, and it was expected that $40,000 more would be collected in 19X7, with the balance of $60,000 to be written off as uncollectible. Donors did not specify any periods during which the donations were to be used. What amount should Aviary include under public support in 19X6 for net contributions?

   a. $500,000.   b. $452,000.   c. $440,000.   d. $400,000.

Items 2 and 3 are based on the following information pertaining to the sale of equipment by Nous Foundation, a voluntary health and welfare organization:

Sales price	$12,000
Cost	14,000
Carrying amount	10,000

Nous made the correct entry to record the $2,000 gain on sale.

2. The additional entry that Nous should record in connection with this sale is:

	Debit	Credit
a.	Fund Balance — Expended	Fund Balance — Unexpended
b.	Fund Balance — Unexpended	Fund Balance — Expended
c.	Excess Revenues (Control)	Sale of Equipment
d.	Current Unrestricted Fund	Fund Balance — Undesignated

3. The amount that should be debited and credited for the additional entry in connection with this sale is:

   a. $2,000.   b. $10,000.   c. $12,000.   d. $14,000.

4. The following expenditures were among those incurred by a voluntary welfare society during 19X7:

Printing of annual report	$10,000
Unsolicited merchandise sent to encourage contributions	20,000

   What amount should be classified as fund-raising costs in the society's activity statement?

   a. $0.   b. $10,000.   c. $20,000.   d. $30,000.

5. Apex Inc. donated a computer to Bird Shelter, a voluntary organization. The computer cost Apex $40,000. On the date of donation, it had a book

value of $25,000 and a market value of $20,000. The Bird Shelter's depreciation expense should be based on:

a. $40,000.   b. $25,000.   c. $20,000.   d. $15,000.

(AICPA adapted)

Problem 20–2.   Select the best answer for each of the following multiple-choice questions.

1. Donor-restricted contributions that have been given to a voluntary health and welfare organization for the purpose of purchasing fixed assets should be recorded in the:
   a. Current Unrestricted Fund.
   b. Current Restricted Fund.
   c. Land, Building, and Equipment Fund (Plant Fund).
   d. Endowment Fund.

2. The journal entry debiting Fund Balance—Unexpended and crediting Fund Balance—Expended would appear in which one of the following funds of a voluntary health and welfare organization?
   a. Current Unrestricted Fund.
   b. Current Restricted Fund.
   c. Land, Building, and Equipment Fund (Plant Fund).
   d. Endowment Fund.

3. The following correct entry is found on the books of a voluntary health and welfare organization:

   Fund Balance—Undesignated XXX
       Fund Balance—Designated for AIDS Research   XXX

   From the entry, one should conclude that the board of directors has:
   a. Designated a portion of the Current Unrestricted Fund Balance for a future AIDS research program.
   b. Designated a portion of the Current Restricted Fund Balance for a future AIDS research program.
   c. Transferred resources to an AIDS research program.
   d. Directed that unused resources previously assigned to an AIDS research program be returned to Fund Balance.

4. To protect the principal of an Endowment Fund of a voluntary health and welfare organization, unrestricted cash interest received on bond investments purchased at a premium should be transferred to the Current Unrestricted Fund:
   a. In an amount equal to net earnings after premium amortization.
   b. In an amount equal to the gross cash interest received.
   c. Only when the interest received equals the total premium paid.
   d. Only upon the maturity of the bonds.

5. The investments of various funds of a voluntary health and welfare organization are pooled and carried at market value. At the end of the period, there is a decrease in total market value. One of the funds involved in the

pool is the Endowment Fund. Its share of the market value decrease should:

a. Not be recorded until the loss is realized.

b. Be debited to Realized Loss on Pooled Investments.

c. Be debited to Endowment Fund Balance.

d. Be debited to Net Decrease in Carrying Value of Investments.

Problem 20–3. Listed are four independent transactions or events that relate to a local government and to a voluntary health and welfare organization:

(a) $25,000 was disbursed from the General Fund (or its equivalent) for the cash purchase of new equipment.

(b) An unrestricted cash gift of $100,000 was received from a donor.

(c) Listed common stocks with a total carrying value of $50,000 were sold by an endowment fund for $55,000 before any dividends were earned on these stocks.

(d) $1,000,000 (face amount) of general obligation bonds payable were sold at par, with the proceeds required to be used solely for construction of a new building. This building was completed at a total cost of $1,000,000, and the total amount of bond issue proceeds was disbursed in payment.

Required:

(1) For each of the listed transactions or events, prepare journal entries, without explanations, specifying the affected funds and account groups and showing how these transactions or events should be recorded by a local government whose debt is serviced by general tax revenues.

(2) For each of the listed transactions or events, prepare journal entries, without explanations, specifying the affected funds and showing how these transactions or events should be recorded by a voluntary health and welfare organization that maintains a separate plant fund.

(AICPA adapted)

Problem 20–4. The Laurel Cancer Institute, a voluntary health organization, has the following funds:

Fund Number	Fund
100	Current Unrestricted Fund
200	Unrestricted Investment Fund
300	Fund Restricted for Specified Purposes
400	Plant Fund
500	Endowment Fund

The following events occurred during the year:

(a) A badly needed electronic microscope with a market value of $38,000 was donated and accepted.

(b) A $20,000 payment was made by the Plant Fund on a building mortgage.

(c) The Endowment Fund received $2,500 in earnings, of which $2,000 is unrestricted and $500 is restricted to the purchase of drugs for cancer research. Cash transfers are made only at the end of each month. Unrestricted earnings came from bond investments on which applicable amortization of premium is $400. Endowment Fund principal is not to be diluted.

(d) An unrestricted gift of $4,000 is received. The board of trustees has decided that the amount should be transferred to the Unrestricted Investment Fund.

(e) A gift of $40,000 has been accepted. It must be used for research on the drug, interferon. The institute follows the procedure recommended by the audit guide. To date, $35,000 has been spent on the project.

(f) The board of trustees has decided to designate $100,000 of the Current Unrestricted Fund Balance for future study of interferon.

(g) Equipment costing $10,000 is purchased. Current Unrestricted Fund cash of $7,000 and Plant Fund cash of $3,000 were used to make the payment.

Required:

Prepare journal entries for the preceding events, using the following format. (Note: An item may require entries in more than one fund.) Omit explanations.

Event	Fund Number	Journal Entry
(a)		

Problem 20–5. The Senior Citizens Agency is a voluntary health and welfare organization. The following events affect its Land, Building, and Equipment Fund (Plant Fund). The agency uses one control account for its fixed assets, with supporting subsidiary records.

(a) Property was purchased for $200,000. A down payment of $40,000 was made, and a 14% mortgage was signed for the remainder. The down payment included $25,000 transferred to the Plant Fund from the Current Unrestricted Fund.

(b) Office furniture was purchased for $9,000 on open account.

(c) A local corporation donated and installed room partitions. The value of the donated items and services was $4,000.

(d) At year end, a payment was made covering mortgage interest for one year, plus a $10,000 payment on the principal.

(e) Office equipment costing $3,000, with a book value of $1,000, was sold for $1,800 cash.

(f) Fully depreciated equipment costing $7,000 was written off. There was no scrap value.

(g) A depreciation schedule was prepared, showing annual depreciation expense of $46,000, which was recorded.

(h) Two years ago, the will of an agency volunteer·granted $50,000 for the acquisition and installation of theater equipment, providing the organization acquired a new building. The amount now was expended in accordance with the stipulations of the will, and payment of $50,000 was made.

(i) The account payable of $9,000 mentioned in item (b) was paid.

Required:

Prepare journal entries to record the preceding events in the Plant Fund. (Note: Pay particular attention to any event requiring an entry that changes the net investment in plant assets. Such an event also will require an entry to change the respective fund balance accounts.)

Problem 20–6.   Following are the adjusted current funds trial balances of Community Association for Handicapped Children, a voluntary welfare organization, at June 30, 19X4:

Community Association for Handicapped Children
Adjusted Current Funds Trial Balances
June 30, 19X4

	Unrestricted		Restricted	
Cash..	40,000		9,000	
Bequest Receivable...............................			5,000	
Pledges Receivable..............................	12,000			
Accrued Interest Receivable...................	1,000			
Investments (at cost, which approximates market)..	100,000			
Accounts Payable and Accrued Expenses..		50,000		1,000
Deferred Revenue................................		2,000		
Allowance for Uncollectible Pledges.......		3,000		
Fund Balances, July 1, 19X3:				
Designated.......................................		12,000		
Undesignated...................................		26,000		
Restricted				3,000
Transfers of Endowment Fund Revenue..		20,000		
Contributions		300,000		15,000
Membership Dues		25,000		
Program Service Fees		30,000		
Investment Revenue		10,000		
Deaf Children's Program.......................	120,000			
Blind Children's Program......................	150,000			
Management and General Services	45,000		4,000	
Fund-Raising Services..........................	8,000		1,000	
Provision for Uncollectible Pledges.........	2,000			
	478,000	478,000	19,000	19,000

Required:
(1) Prepare a statement of support, revenue, and expenses and changes in fund balances, separately presenting each current fund and their total for the year ended June 30, 19X4.
(2) Prepare a separate balance sheet for each of the current funds as of June 30, 19X4.   (AICPA adapted)

Problem 20–7.   Thirty years ago, a group of civic-minded merchants in Albury City organized the "Committee of 100" for the purpose of establishing the Community Sports Club, a not-for-profit sport organization for local youth. Each of the Committee's 100 members contributed $1,000 toward the Club's capital and, in turn, received a participation certificate. In addition, each participant agreed to pay dues of $200 a year for the Club's operations. All dues have been collected in full by the end of each fiscal year ending March 31. Members who have discontinued their participation have been replaced by an equal number of new members through transfer of the participation certificates from the former members to the new ones. Following is the Club's trial balance at April 1, 19X2:

Cash..	9,000	
Investments (at market, equal to cost)	58,000	
Inventories...	5,000	
Land...	10,000	
Building...	164,000	
Accumulated Depreciation—Building		130,000
Furniture and Equipment...	54,000	
Accumulated Depreciation—Furniture and Equipment..		46,000
Accounts Payable		12,000
Participation Certificates (100 at $1,000)		100,000
Cumulative Excess of Revenue over Expenses............		12,000
	300,000	300,000

Transactions and adjustment data for the year ended March 31, 19X3, are as follows:
(a) Collections from participants for dues totaled $20,000.
(b) Snack bar and soda fountain sales amounted to $28,000.
(c) Interest and dividends totaling $6,000 were received.
(d) The following additions were made to the voucher register:

House expense..	$17,000
Snack bar and soda fountain	26,000
General and administrative..........................	11,000

(e) Vouchers totaling $55,000 were paid.
(f) Assessments for capital improvements not yet incurred totaled $10,000. The assessments were made on March 20, 19X3, and were to be collected during the year ending March 31, 19X5.

(g) An unrestricted bequest of $5,000 was received.

(h) Investments are valued at market, which amounted to $65,000 at March 31, 19X3. There were no investment transactions during the year.

(i) Depreciation for the year is as follows:

Building..	$4,000
Furniture and equipment............................	8,000

Depreciation is allocated to:

House expense...	$9,000
Snack bar and soda fountain	2,000
General and administrative.........................	1,000

(j) The actual physical inventory, which was $1,000 at March 31, 19X3, pertains to the snack bar and fountain.

Required:

(1) On a functional basis, record the transactions and adjustments in journal entry form for the year ended March 31, 19X3. Omit explanations, but letter the entries to correspond to the data given.

(2) Prepare the statement of revenue, expenses, and changes in cumulative excess of revenue over expenses for the year ended March 31, 19X3.

(AICPA adapted)

Problem 20–8. The Abuse Clinic, a voluntary health and welfare organization, conducts two programs: Alcohol and Drug Abuse and Outreach to Teens. It has the typical supporting services of management and fund raising. The trial balances of its various funds as of January 1, 19X2, are as shown at the top of the next page.

During 19X2, the following events related to the clinic occurred. To minimize repetition, similar events for the year are combined.

		Unrestricted	Restricted
(a)	Contribution pledges received	$396,000	$162,000
(b)	Estimated uncollectible pledges	20,000	6,000
(c)	Cash collected on pledges.........................	380,000	148,000
	Pledges written off as uncollectible............	18,000	5,000
(d)	Investment revenue received (including accrued)..	9,000	1,000
(e)	Items paid:		
	Accounts payable as of January 1, 19X2....	14,000	
	Salaries and payroll taxes........................	60,000	23,000
	Rent expense		10,000
	Telephone and miscellaneous expenses....	10,000	2,000
	Nursing and medical fees	70,000	50,000
	Educational seminars expenses	38,000	20,000
	Research expenses	137,000	16,000
	Medical supplies (perpetual inventory is used)	71,000	29,000

Abuse Clinic
Trial Balances
January 1, 19X2

Debits	Current Funds		Plant Fund	Endowment Fund
	Unrestricted	Restricted		
Cash...	53,000	5,000	12,000	1,000
Investments (at cost)........................	120,000	7,000	45,000	200,000
Accrued Investment Revenue.............	6,000	—	—	—
Pledges Receivable...........................	45,000	—	—	—
Grants Receivable.............................	—	16,000	—	—
Inventories of Educational Materials...	11,000	—	—	—
Inventories of Medical Supplies	12,000	—	—	—
Land, Building, and Equipment	—	—	173,000	—
Total..	247,000	28,000	230,000	201,000

Credits				
Allowance for Uncollectible Pledges...	9,000	—	—	—
Accumulated Depreciation.................	—	—	22,000	—
Accounts Payable	14,000	—	—	—
Contributions Designated for Future Periods..	22,000	—	—	—
10% Mortgage Payable......................	—	—	40,000	—
Fund Balances:				
Designated for Research.................	50,000	—	—	—
Designated for Long-Term Investments	40,000	—	—	—
Undesignated..............................	112,000	—	—	—
Restricted	—	28,000	—	201,000
Expended	—	—	111,000	—
Unexpended	—	—	57,000	—
Total..	247,000	28,000	230,000	201,000

(f) The residence of a leading citizen was bequeathed in a will to the clinic. After the person's death, it was found that the building was not suitable for clinical use, and it would be sold as soon as possible. The residence was appraised at $92,000. The will stipulated that proceeds from the sale must be used to expand the clinical building. The will also provided $30,000 in cash to create a fund, the revenue from which must be devoted to an alcohol abuse program.

(g) During the year, a dinner was held to raise additional funds for the clinical building. Gross cash proceeds were $48,000, of which $18,000 was paid for direct costs.

(h) Bids for construction of a wing for the clinical building were sought. The contract was let at a cost of $250,000. The residence received from the citizen was sold for $100,000, which was used as a partial payment on the contract, along with the net proceeds from the dinner mentioned in (g). The wing was completed. A 12%, 20-year mortgage was signed for the remaining $120,000.

(i)   A grant of $16,000 from the state government, awarded last year for a special drug abuse program, was received. The item originally was recorded as a grant receivable.

(j)   At year end, a physical inventory shows $3,000 of educational materials and $18,000 of medical supplies in the Unrestricted Fund and $7,000 of medical supplies in the Restricted Fund.

(k)   Annual depreciation amounts to $20,000.

(l)   A payment of $5,000 was made against the 10% mortgage payable, plus a payment of $4,000 for interest was made.

(m) Plant Fund investment revenue was $4,000, of which $3,000 was received. Revenue must be used for plant purposes.

(n)   Endowment Fund investment revenue received amounted to $16,000. There is no restriction on $10,000 of the revenue. The remaining $6,000 must be devoted to alcohol abuse programs. Items are entered directly in recipient funds.

(o)   Half of the contributions designated for future periods in the Unrestricted Fund became available.

(p)   The board of directors has decided to increase the Fund Balance Designated for Research from $50,000 to $90,000.

(q)   Unpaid items in the Unrestricted Fund on December 31, 19X2, consist of $3,000 for accrued salaries and $10,000 for educational materials that are maintained on a perpetual inventory basis.

(r)   Endowment Fund investments costing $40,000 were sold for $65,000. The gain remains a part of the fund principal.

Required:

(1)   Prepare journal entries to record the events, using the following format:

Event	Fund	Journal Entry
(a)		

(2)   Prepare pre-allocation trial balances, reflecting balances immediately after the preceding entries are posted, in the same format as the trial balances at the beginning of the problem.

Problem 20–9. The Abuse Clinic, a voluntary health and welfare organization, conducts two programs: Alcohol and Drug Abuse and Outreach to Teens. It has the typical supporting services of management and fund raising. The condensed pre-allocation trial balances of its four funds as of December 31, 19X2, are as follows:

Abuse Clinic
Condensed Pre-Allocation Trial Balances
December 31, 19X2

Debits	Current Funds Unrestricted	Current Funds Restricted	Plant Fund	Endowment Fund
Assets (net)................................	235,000	48,000	433,000	256,000
Salaries and Payroll Taxes..............	63,000	23,000	—	—
Telephone and Miscellaneous Expenses................................	10,000	2,000	—	—
Nursing and Medical Fees..............	70,000	50,000	—	—
Educational Seminars Expenses......	46,000	20,000	—	—
Research Expense........................	137,000	16,000	—	—
Medical Supplies Expense..............	65,000	22,000	—	—
Rent Expense.............................	—	10,000	—	—
Interest Expense.........................	—	—	4,000	—
Depreciation Expense....................	—	—	20,000	—
Provision for Uncollectible Pledges..	20,000	6,000	—	—
Cost of Special Events...................	—	—	18,000	—
Total......................................	646,000	197,000	475,000	256,000

Credits	Current Funds Unrestricted	Current Funds Restricted	Plant Fund	Endowment Fund
Liabilities...................................	24,000	—	155,000	—
Fund Balances:				
Designated.............................	130,000	—	—	—
Undesignated..........................	72,000	—	—	—
Restricted...............................	—	28,000	—	201,000
Expended...............................	—	—	226,000	—
Unexpended............................	—	—	(58,000)	—
Contributions.............................	407,000	162,000	92,000	—
Legacies and Bequests..................	—	—	—	30,000
Special Events Support..................	—	—	48,000	—
Investment Revenue......................	13,000	7,000	4,000	—
Gain on Sale of Investments...........	—	—	8,000	25,000
Total......................................	646,000	197,000	475,000	256,000

In preparation for the allocation of expenses to programs and supporting services, a study was conducted to determine an equitable manner for assigning each expense. The study resulted in the table for percentage allocations presented at the top of the next page.

Required:
(1) Using a total of allocable expenses of the Current Restricted Fund, prepare a journal entry to assign those expenses to the programs.
(2) With the following format, prepare a schedule to show the assignment of the Current Unrestricted Fund's allocable expenses to the various pro-

Percentage of Allocations

Expenses To Be Allocated	Programs		Supporting Services	
	Alcohol and Drug Abuse	Outreach to Teens	Management	Fund Raising
All expenses of the restricted fund	60%	40%	—	—
Expenses of the unrestricted fund:				
Salaries and payroll taxes.............	30	20	30%	20%
Telephone and miscellaneous........	20	20	15	45
Nursing and medical fees.............	70	30	—	—
Educational seminars...................	30	60	—	10
Research....................................	60	40	—	—
Medical supplies.........................	90	10	—	—
Expenses of the Plant Fund:				
Interest......................................	50	10	30	10
Depreciation...............................	50	10	30	10

grams and supporting services, using the percentages provided by the problem:

Abuse Clinic
Allocation of Expenses of Current Unrestricted Fund
For the Year Ended December 31, 19X2

Expense Allocated	Total Amount	Programs		Supporting Services	
		Alcohol and Drug Abuse	Outreach to Teens	Management	Fund Raising

(3) Using the schedule from requirement (2), prepare a journal entry to record the allocation and closing of expenses of the Current Unrestricted Fund.

(4) Prepare a journal entry to record the allocation and closing of the expenses of the Plant Fund.

Problem 20–10.   The Abuse Clinic, a voluntary health and welfare organization, conducts two programs: Alcohol and Drug Abuse and Outreach to Teens. It has the typical supporting services of management and fund raising. The condensed trial balances of its four funds after allocable expenses have been assigned are presented at the top of the next page.

Required:

(1) Prepare a statement of support, revenue, and expenses and changes in fund balances in the format shown in Illustration 20–2 on page 1068. Fund balance amounts as of January 1, 19X2, are shown in Problem 20–8.

(2) Prepare closing entries for each fund.

Abuse Clinic
Condensed Post-Allocation Trial Balances
December 31, 19X2

Debits	Current Funds		Plant Fund	Endowment Fund
	Unrestricted	Restricted		
Assets (net)...................................	235,000	48,000	433,000	256,000
Alcohol and Drug Abuse Program...	224,400	85,800	12,000	—
Outreach to Teens Program............	124,500	57,200	2,400	—
Management and General Services...	20,400	—	7,200	—
Fund-Raising Services....................	21,700	—	2,400	—
Provision for Uncollectible Pledges..	20,000	6,000	—	—
Cost of Special Events...................	—	—	18,000	—
Totals......................................	646,000	197,000	475,000	256,000

Credits	Unrestricted	Restricted	Plant Fund	Endowment Fund
Liabilities.....................................	24,000	—	155,000	—
Fund Balances:				
Designated..............................	130,000	—	—	—
Undesignated...........................	72,000	—	—	—
Restricted	—	28,000	—	201,000
Expended	—	—	246,000	—
Unexpended	—	—	(78,000)	—
Contributions	407,000	162,000	92,000	—
Special Events Support	—	—	48,000	—
Legacies and Bequests..................	—	—	—	30,000
Investment Revenue	13,000	7,000	4,000	—
Gain on Sale of Investments...........	—	—	8,000	25,000
Totals......................................	646,000	197,000	475,000	256,000

Problem 20–11. From the condensed pre-allocation trial balances and allocation schedule shown in Problem 20–9, prepare a statement of functional expenses for the Abuse Clinic for the year ended December 31, 19X2.

Problem 20–12. From the pre-allocation trial balances prepared as a solution for Problem 20–8, prepare the balance sheets in the format recommended by the audit guide as illustrated in the chapter. Verify that totals of the fund balances for each fund agree with the final amounts shown in the statement of support prepared as part of the solution for Problem 20–10.

PART SEVEN

FIDUCIARY ACCOUNTING

A fiduciary relationship is created when the property of one party is transferred to another who then becomes responsible for its care. Upon the death of an individual, assets come under the jurisdiction of the executor or administrator of the decedent's estate. A grantor may turn over assets to a trustee for the benefit of others. When an organization becomes insolvent financially, a trustee may be appointed to manage its affairs. In each of these situations, the legal process places a designated party in a position of trust or confidence. The provisions of law stipulate methods of providing for the accountability of that party by requiring specialized reports that summarize the actions taken by the fiduciary.

CHAPTER 21

ESTATES AND TRUSTS

An *estate* consists of the net assets owned by a person at the time of death and may include both real property and personal property. Historically, the distinction between these two kinds of property developed through legal processes. For example, redress for trespass or dispossession of immovable and indestructible property, such as land, was sought by taking action to recover the property. The action was labeled a "real action," and property involved in such action became known as real property. If movable or destructible property was damaged, action to recover for the damage was taken against the person responsible, and such property was referred to as personal property. The distinction between real and personal property is pertinent to an estate, since title or right to real property passes directly to the recipient, while the right to personal property passes to the estate administrator or executor until it is distributed.

An estate ceases to exist when all the property has been distributed according to the terms of a valid will or the stipulations of law. This distribution may include a transfer of property to a *trust*, which holds the property for the benefit of others. Since both an estate and a trust consist of property that may be under the control of someone other than the owner, the accounting procedures for the two entities are quite similar. These procedures and related legal aspects are discussed in this chapter.

ESTATE PLANNING

Tax planning may be defined as an effort to reduce the cost of living by minimizing income taxes. Estate planning may be defined as an effort to reduce the cost of dying by minimizing estate and inheritance taxes. All tax planning should be done well in advance of the imposition of the tax. Likewise, estate planning must be done well in advance of death.

This chapter is only an introduction to a complicated subject. Estate planning is complex because the circumstances differ for each individual. The larger the estate, the more complex will be the planning and the greater will be the necessity for involving an estate planning specialist, a lawyer, and an accountant, one of whom should be a tax expert. One point on which all will agree is not to die without a valid will.

Only with a valid will may the wishes of the decedent be known and fulfilled. With no such will, assets will be distributed in accordance with the fairly impersonal provisions of the law. Existing wills should be reexamined in light of the dramatic changes resulting from the 1981, 1984, and 1986 tax acts. Among other considerations, family estate planning would involve:

1. Maximizing benefits of the marital deduction.
2. Making gifts during one's lifetime.
3. Taking actions to accomplish a step-up in property basis.
4. Taking actions to benefit from a loss in property values.
5. Maneuvering with charitable deductions.
6. Planning estate liquidity.

To be protected, an estate must have a certain amount of liquid assets to pay death taxes and the probate costs of establishing the validity of the will. Otherwise, a forced sale of estate assets might result. Some form of insurance is recommended to provide liquidity and flexibility.

FEDERAL ESTATE TAXATION

Significant changes regarding gratuitous transfers of property resulted from the *Tax Reform Act of 1976.* Prior to its enactment, transfers of property during the owner's lifetime were subject to the federal gift tax, while property passing as a result of death was subject to the federal estate tax. The rules and rates for these taxes were different. Most of the distinction was removed by the Tax Reform Act, which substituted a unified transfer tax, commonly referred to as the *federal estate tax,* for life and death transfers made after 1976.

The computation of the federal estate tax may be summarized as follows:

Gross estate	XX
Less deductions allowed	− XX
Taxable estate	XX
Add post-1976 taxable gifts	+ XX
Tax base	XX
Tentative tax on total transfers	XX
Less tax credits	− XX
Estate tax due	XX

The starting point for the computation of the federal estate tax is the determination of the gross estate, which includes the fair market value of property owned by the decedent at date of death, regardless of the nature of the property. Whether it is real or personal, tangible or intangible, business or nonbusiness, the property is includable. Then the taxable estate is determined by subtracting the total of the following allowable deductions:

1. Allowable expenses, such as funeral expenses and costs of administrating the estate;
2. Indebtedness against property included in the gross estate, such as a mortgage and other debts of the decedent;
3. Unpaid property and income taxes of the decedent to date of death;
4. Losses from casualty or theft of estate assets during the period of settlement;
5. Transfers to charity specified by the will; and
6. Marital deduction, which is unlimited in amount, for estate property that passes to the surviving spouse.

The *Revenue Act of 1978* required that the taxable estate be increased by any taxable gifts made after 1976. Gifts would be taxable to the donor if their fair market value per donee for the tax year exceeded $3,000 ($6,000 for consenting spouse gifts) through 1981. For gifts after 1981, taxable gifts result if they exceed $10,000 ($20,000 for consenting spouse gifts) per donee per year. After taxable gifts are added to the taxable estate, the tax rates found in the *unified rate schedule* are applied to the tax base. The resulting tentative tax then is reduced by a *unified credit,* which exempts estates of $600,000 or less from taxation. The amount of the property exempted from tax is called the *exemption equivalent.* For an individual who dies after 1986, the maximum unified credit is $192,800, which exempts $600,000 of property in an estate from taxation. Also deducted are state death taxes and taxes already paid on taxable gifts made after 1976. The result is the estate tax due.

Progressive estate tax rates range from 18% to 55%. The *Deficit Reduction Act of 1984* established a 55% maximum rate on total taxable transfers of more than $3,000,000. The maximum rate was scheduled to drop to 50% in 1988, but Congress decided to retain the top rate through 1992.

MARITAL DEDUCTION

In the computation of the taxable estate, recall that a marital deduction is allowed for the value of qualifying property passing to a surviving spouse. The amount of the deduction is unlimited. No matter how large the estate, a bequest of all property to one's surviving spouse will eliminate completely federal estate taxes for the decedent. That statement is technically correct, but incomplete. It also should state that the deduction may defer estate taxes only until the death of the other spouse. At that point, it may be discovered that use of the unlimited deduction actually increased the overall estate tax. This can result because the tax rates are progressive (the higher the tax base, the higher the rates) and because the effect of the unlimited marital deduction is to channel all assets into the estate of the surviving spouse.

To illustrate, assume that John Bates dies in 19X9 and is survived by his wife, Sara, and one child. His will stipulates that Sara is to receive all his property, worth $1,500,000. His debts amount to $150,000; funeral and administrative costs total $50,000. The following year, Sara dies, with the estate assets still intact. Her deductions include $80,000 of debts and $20,000 of funeral and administrative costs. With an unlimited marital deduction, their estate tax computations are as follows:

	John		Sara	
Gross estate		$1,500,000		$1,300,000
Less deductions:				
Debts	$ 150,000		$80,000	
Funeral and administrative costs	50,000		20,000	
Marital deduction	1,300,000	1,500,000	–0–	100,000
Taxable estate		$ –0–		$1,200,000
Estate tax before credits				$ 427,800
Less unified credit				192,800
Estate tax due				$ 235,000

As an alternate strategy, John's will could have stipulated that an amount equal to the exemption equivalent ($600,000) be placed in a trust, with Sara as the income beneficiary. If properly designed, the trust would not be included in Sara's estate upon her death. The remainder of John's net assets ($700,000) could go directly to her and qualify for the marital deduction. Now their estate tax computations would be:

	John		Sara	
Gross estate		$1,500,000		$700,000
Less deductions:				
Debts	$150,000		$80,000	
Funeral and administrative costs	50,000		20,000	
Marital deduction	700,000	900,000	–0–	100,000
Taxable estate		$ 600,000		$600,000
Estate tax before credits		$ 192,800		$192,800
Less unified credit		192,800		192,800
Estate tax due		$ –0–		$ –0–

Failure to do some estate planning cost the Bates family $235,000.

ESTATE REDUCTION WITH GIFTS

Estate planning is essential to achieve the maximum benefit provided in the law, especially when the impact of continued inflation is considered. One simple way to reduce an estate is to make gifts annually. Currently, the first $10,000 ($20,000 for consenting spouse gifts) to any one person during any calendar year is excluded in determining taxable gifts. This is an annual exclusion. Consenting spouses who participate for ten years in an annual gift program involving six recipients would be able to transfer $1,200,000 ($20,000 × 6 × 10) without incurring any gift tax. Spouses also can make gifts to each other. No matter what the amount, such gifts between spouses are free of gift taxes.

One might ask, "What is the maximum total gift a husband and wife may give to one individual at one time without incurring any tax?" For gift tax purposes, a gift made by one person to someone other than his or her spouse is considered as having been made one-half by each spouse. Each spouse is entitled to a unified credit of $192,800, or an exemption equivalent gift of $600,000, plus the annual $10,000 exclusion. Therefore, a husband and wife could give $1,220,000 (2 × $610,000) to one person without incurring a tax. The unified credit may be used only one time by each spouse. Once used, a unified transfer tax would be due on gifts above the annual exclusion and eventually on their total remaining taxable estate.

VALUATION OF ESTATE ASSETS

Fair market value must be established for assets included in an estate. Some valuations, such as the values of stocks and bonds traded on recognized exchanges, pose no problems. For other assets, such as property, jewelry, art objects, or antiques, a competent appraisal in writing should be obtained. Assets are included in the estate at their fair market value on the date of death or on an alternate valuation date, if the executor or administrator so elects. If the alternate valuation date is elected, all estate property must be valued as of six months after the decedent's death, except for property sold, distributed, or otherwise disposed of during the six-month period. Such property is valued as of the date of disposition. The alternate valuation date may be used only if it would reduce the total gross estate and decrease the estate tax liability. The alternate valuation date protects estates if there should be a significant decrease in property values during the six-month interval.

Formerly, it would have been possible for an executor, knowing that there would be no estate tax to pay, to select the alternate valuation date if assets increased in value, thereby giving the heirs a higher basis for their inherited property, at no cost to the estate. To prevent this windfall, Congress took an action that permitted election of the alternate valuation date only if it would reduce the total gross estate and decrease the estate tax liability.

Congress felt it was being sufficiently generous by permitting a stepped-up basis. Recall that, to the recipient, the basis of property acquired from a decedent is market value on the date of death or alternate valuation date. That regulation may result in a step-up of basis. For example, assume that Karen Owens held stock with a cost of $100,000. At the date of her death, it was worth $500,000 and was willed to her nephew, whose basis now becomes $500,000. A subsequent sale by him for $500,000 would result in no taxable gain. Although the value of the stock must be included in the inventory of the estate, which would be subject to the unified transfer tax only if the estate is large enough, the $400,000 gain would escape *federal income taxation* because of the step-up in basis. If Karen had sold the stock before her death, the gain would have been subject to income tax. Tax planning would suggest that, if possible, property that has appreciated substantially in value should be held as part of an estate because of the advantage of the step-up in basis. The opposite is true if there is a substantial decline in value. If Karen's stock had a value of $5,000 on the valuation date, that would become the basis to her nephew. Neither he nor the estate would derive any benefit from the $95,000 loss in value. If Karen had sold the stock prior to death, benefits resulting from the deductibility of the loss for income tax purposes would have materialized.

INCOME TAXATION OF ESTATES AND TRUSTS

Under the tax code, estates and trusts are separate tax entities. The code requires the filing of an estate tax return (Form 706), in which the unified transfer tax is computed. This return must be filed within nine months after the death of the decedent, providing the taxable estate exceeds the applicable exemption equivalent. In addition, income tax returns for the estate or trust must be filed. Although there are some exceptions and special provisions, the taxable income of an estate or trust is computed on Form 1041 (U.S. Fiduciary Income Tax Return) in a manner similar to that for an individual. Generally, income from estate or trust assets will be taxed either to the estate or trust or to the beneficiary, but not to both. Income from property normally is taxed to the holder of its title. Since title to real property passes directly to the heir at date of death, income from such property is taxed to the heir and not to the estate.

An estate may function merely as a conduit, as in the case of receiving income designated for a specific beneficiary. Such income retains its identity when it passes to the beneficiary. If the income received is nontaxable, such as interest on municipal bonds, it will remain tax free upon distribution to the beneficiary.

SETTLING AN ESTATE

When a person dies *intestate* (leaving no valid will), the probate court appoints an administrator to handle the settling of the estate according to applicable state laws. These laws vary between states. Although a *Uniform Probate Code* was drafted in 1969 and approved by the American Bar Association, it has been adopted with revisions by less than half of the states. Nevertheless, the provisions of the Code are treated as the majority position in this text.

In an intestate situation, real property is distributed according to the laws of descent of the state where the property is located, while personal property is distributed according to the laws of distribution of the decedent's home state, called the *state of domicile*. In general, only a spouse or blood relative may receive an intestate distribution. As shown in the following diagram, the spouse or blood relative may be described as an heir or as next of kin, depending on the kind of property distributed.

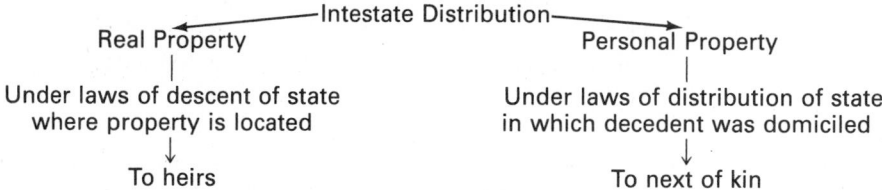

If a person dies *testate* (leaving a valid will), the probate court must establish the validity of the will. Property then may be distributed according to the terms of the will by an executor who is nominated in the will, subject to approval of the court. The executor may be one or more persons or an institution, such as a bank. If the named executor is unable or has no desire to function in that capacity, the court will appoint an administrator.

In a testate situation, a distribution of real property is a *devise,* and the recipient of the property is the *devisee*. Distributions of personal property are called bequests or *legacies,* and the recipient of personal property is called the *legatee*. The following diagram identifies the recipients of a testate distribution:

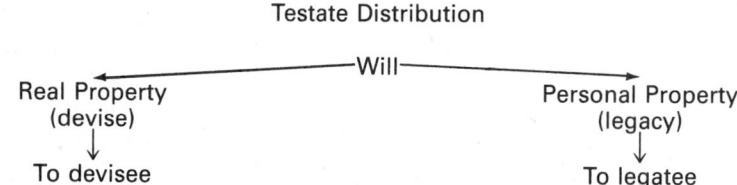

A devise is usually a distribution of a specific piece of property. In contrast, legacies may include one or more of the following types:

1. A *general legacy* is a gift of an indicated amount or quantity of something: five thousand dollars or 20 bottles of wine.
2. A *specific legacy* is a gift of a particular, specified thing, distinguishable from others: my three-carat diamond ring or the 20 bottles of Romanee Conti Burgundy 1961 on the north wall of my wine cellar.

3. A *demonstrative legacy* is a gift of an amount from a specific source, with the will stipulating that, if the amount cannot be satisfied from that source, it shall be satisfied from the general estate: $50,000 from several identified insurance policies. If proceeds are inadequate to meet the amount, the difference shall constitute a general legacy.
4. A *residuary legacy* is composed of all estate property remaining after assigning the general, specific, and demonstrative legacies.
5. A *pecuniary legacy* is any legacy of money. It could be a general, specific, or demonstrative legacy, but it must be money.

Administrators and executors are referred to as personal representatives or *fiduciaries* because they function as stewards of the estate. Their duty is to safeguard property, which includes the interim management of any business in which the decedent functioned in a managerial capacity.

One of the first responsibilities of the fiduciary is to determine the *homestead allowance* and the *family allowance*, which are exempt from claims against the estate. Most states provide for these rights, which are described in the Uniform Probate Code as follows:

> *A surviving spouse of a decedent . . . is entitled to a homestead allowance of $5,000. If there is no surviving spouse, each minor child and each dependent child of the decedent is entitled to a homestead allowance amounting to $5,000 divided by the number of minor and dependent children of the decedent.*[1]

> *. . . the surviving spouse and minor children whom the decedent was obligated to support . . . are entitled to a reasonable allowance in money out of the estate for their maintenance during the period of administration.*[2]

The family allowance consists of intimate objects of the deceased and an amount of cash or productive property to provide funds for the surviving family until matters are settled. What constitutes a "reasonable allowance" depends upon the circumstances in each case, but the fiduciary may not grant more then $500 per month for one year. If a greater allowance is deemed necessary, a special court order must be obtained.

After the immediate needs of the family are satisfied, the fiduciary takes a complete inventory of the estate and files a report with the court. The fiduciary also publishes a notice to creditors, requesting that all claims against the estate be filed. These claims are reviewed as to amount and authenticity. Accepted claims are paid, a schedule of planned distribution of estate property is prepared and filed, and the distribution is accomplished. The settlement process is completed when the fiduciary accounts to the court for the period of stewardship.

---

[1] *Uniform Probate Code (U.L.A.)* (St. Paul: West Publishing Company, 1974), Sec. 2–401.
[2] *Ibid.*, Sec. 2–403.

If funds are not adequate to satisfy all accepted claims, state laws provide a priority for settlement. Although the sequence may differ from state to state, the most common order is:

1. Claims having a special lien against property, but not to exceed the value of the property.
2. Funeral and administrative expenses.
3. Taxes: income, estate, and inheritance.
4. Debts due the United States and various states.
5. Judgments of any court of competent jurisdiction.
6. Wages due domestic servants for a period of not more than one year prior to date of death and medical claims for the same period.
7. All other claims.

Within a class, each claim is satisfied on a pro rata basis if funds are inadequate to accomplish total payment for that class.

ACCOUNTING FOR ESTATES

Estate accounting is designed to facilitate reporting to the court for the term of the fiduciary's accountability. This accountability is increased by an inflow of assets and reduced by an outflow of assets. Therefore, accounting procedures for an estate should accommodate these inflows and outflows.

Accounting for an estate also is based on a distinction between principal and income. This distinction is essential because a will usually provides for the spouse and/or other beneficiaries to share in income earned subsequent to the date of death. Furthermore, income may be assigned to an income beneficiary for a stipulated period, after which time the assets may be distributed to a party called the *remainderman*. For example, income from a group of assets may be granted to the spouse for life (a *life tenant*), and upon the spouse's death, the assets are distributed to the children (the remaindermen). The distinction between principal and income also must be respected because certain expenses and claims may be paid only from principal, while others may be paid only from income.

To account for the distinction between principal and income, two control accounts are used: Estate Principal and Estate Income. The balances of these accounts must be equal to the total of the assets that belong to each group after closing entries are posted. In addition to the two control accounts, two cash accounts are used: Cash—Principal and Cash—Income.

The inventory of property owned by the decedent on the date of death and subject to the administration of the executor or administrator constitutes the initial *principal* or *corpus* (body) of the *probate* estate. The total of the probate estate may be less than that of the gross estate because the former consists only of property of the decedent that passes to heirs under a will or the law of intestacy. For example, proceeds to a designated beneficiary from a life insurance policy to which the deceased has relinquished control are not part of the probate estate but must be included in the gross estate. Although title to real property goes directly to the devisee, many fiduciaries prefer to include such property in the listing of assets to make it complete and in agreement with the amount of the gross estate. Subsequently, an entry showing the transfer of such property to the devisee is made.

Included in principal would be accruals of income to the date of death, providing that the accruals were available on that date. Thus, interest on bond investments accrued to the date of death would be included, since it was available and could have been received by sale of the bonds. Interest on a money market certificate that is available only upon maturity of the certificate would not be accrued. Interest that is not accrued as a part of principal is treated as income when received. Cash dividends generally are accrued as of the date of death if the dividends were declared prior to death. Stock dividends remain a part of principal. Rents receivable at the date of death become a part of principal in most states, with rents earned after death considered income.

When the initial inventory of estate assets has been completed, a copy is filed with the probate court. The fiduciary records the inventory by debiting each asset for its fair market value at the date of death or the alternate valuation date and crediting the account Estate Principal. If principal assets are discovered subsequent to the filing of the inventory, the court must be notified. An entry is made by the fiduciary, debiting the discovered assets at their fair market value on the date of death or on the alternate valuation date and crediting the account Assets Subsequently Discovered. Gains on the sale or other disposition of principal assets increase principal, while losses on disposition reduce principal.

Liabilities are not recorded until paid since the accountability of the fiduciary is reduced only by payment. After claims have been proved and accepted, the source of payment, whether principal or income, must be determined. The payment of such expenses as interest, rent, and other payables accrued to the date of death is charged against principal. The payment of expenses incurred after death is charged against income. In most states, whether property taxes are charged against principal or income depends on the date the taxes become a lien against the property. If they become a lien prior to the date of death, they are charged totally against principal. If they become a lien after death, they are charged against income. A few states allow proration.

The elements of the estate or trust relating to principal are self-balancing, as are the income elements. It would be possible to set up two sets of books — one for principal and one for income — but this procedure seldom is followed. Instead, journal entries are designed to have equal debits and credits that affect principal accounts or equal debits and credits that affect income accounts. Even in a compound entry affecting both principal and income, the entry must not destroy the self-balancing nature of the two categories of elements in an estate or a trust.

The items that are usually chargeable against principal and the account debited when each item is recorded are as follows:

Item	Account Debited
Debts of the decedent incurred prior to death	Debts of Decedent Paid
Funeral and administrative expenses	Funeral and Administrative Expenses
Costs incurred in probating the will	Funeral and Administrative Expenses
Final income taxes of decedent	Debts of Decedent Paid
Federal estate tax[3] and any state inheritance tax	Funeral and Administrative Expenses
Legal and other professional fees to preserve estate principal	Funeral and Administrative Expenses
Charges applicable to principal property that produces no income	Expenses Chargeable Against Principal
Distributions of legacies or devises in a testate distribution	Legacies Distributed **or** Devises Distributed } often combined in the first account
Distributions to heirs or next of kin in an intestate distribution	Distributions to Heirs **or** Distributions to Next of Kin } often combined in the first account
Disposition of estate assets at a loss	Loss on Realization of Principal Assets (a gain would be credited to Gain on Realization of Principal Assets, with total proceeds on any sale of a principal asset debited to Cash — Principal)

When income cash is received, Estate Income is credited and, if the estate is large, a subsidiary ledger is maintained which details the types of income.

The items for which income cash usually is disbursed and the account debited when each item is recorded are as follows:

Item	Account Debited
Expenses incurred to protect income flow	Expenses Chargeable Against Income
Ordinary repairs to income-producing property	Expenses Chargeable Against Income
Distributions of income cash to beneficiaries	Distributions to Income Beneficiaries

ILLUSTRATIVE ENTRIES AND REPORTS

To illustrate the accounting for an estate, assume that Todd Shortlife, a bachelor, died on June 30, 19X1. In his will, Shortlife named Mary Doyle as

---

[3]The Uniform Probate Code provides that where the will does not stipulate treatment of estate taxes, they are to be prorated to the recipients of estate assets on the basis of the value of the asset received relative to the aggregate value of all estate assets subject to tax.

the executrix of his estate. The events that occurred after the death of Short-life are described and recorded as follows:

Event	Entry		
June 30, 19X1: An inventory of estate assets is taken:	Cash — Principal..............................	70,000	
	9% X Co. Bonds	97,000	
	Accrued Interest on X Co. Bonds	1,500	
Cash in bank .... $ 70,000	Q Corp. Stock.................................	100,000	
9% X Co. bonds, $100,000 face value; interest dates of May 1 and November 1; fair market value (FMV) 97,000	Dividends Receivable......................... Estate Principal.............................	4,000	272,500
Q Corporation stock (FMV)....... 100,000			
Dividend on Q Corp. stock, declared June 10, payable July 10............................. 4,000			
July 10: The dividend is received.	Cash — Principal.............................. Dividends Receivable.......................	4,000	4,000
July 15 to November 30: The following items are paid:	Funeral and Administrative Expenses ($3,800 + $5,000)........................	8,800	
	Debts of Decedent Paid	41,200	
Funeral expenses................... $ 3,800	Cash — Principal.............................		50,000
Administrative fees, $100 of which are chargeable against income............................ 5,100	Expenses Chargeable Against Income.... Cash — Income	100	100
Income tax to date of death..... 30,000			
Debts incurred prior to death.... 11,200			
Nov. 1: Bond interest is received. (Note how this compound entry maintains the equality of principal and income elements.)	Cash — Principal..............................	1,500	
	Cash — Income................................	3,000	
	Estate Income		3,000
	Accrued Interest on X Co. Bonds		1,500
Nov. 1: X Co. Bonds are sold for $101,000.	Cash — Principal..............................	101,000	
	9% X Co. Bonds		97,000
	Gain on Realization of Principal Assets		4,000
Nov. 8: Fiduciary discovers a safety deposit box with $8,000 cash.	Cash — Principal.............................. Assets Subsequently Discovered	8,000	8,000
Dec. 1: The following legacies are distributed:	Legacies Distributed	60,000	
	Q Corp. Stock................................		50,000
To Todd's brother, one-half of Q Corp. stock To Todd's church, $10,000	Cash — Principal............................		10,000
Dec. 10: A dividend of $1,500 is received on Q Corp. stock.	Cash — Income................................ Estate Income	1,500	1,500
Dec. 15: Todd's nephew is to receive 3/4 of any income cash available on December 31 of each year until a trust becomes operative. The money is paid.	Distributions to Income Beneficiaries..... Cash — Income (3/4 × $4,400)..........	3,300	3,300

A review of the journal entries in the example substantiates the self-balancing nature of the entries involving principal and those related to income. Thus, a double trial balance may be prepared for the estate — one as to principal and one as to income — as follows:

Estate of Todd Shortlife
Mary Doyle, Executrix
Trial Balance
December 31, 19X1

	As to Principal		As to Income	
Cash—Principal	124,500			
Cash—Income			1,100	
Q Corp. Stock.................................	50,000			
Assets Subsequently Discovered........		8,000		
Gain on Realization of Principal Assets		4,000		
Funeral and Administrative Expenses......................................	8,800			
Debts of Decedent Paid....................	41,200			
Legacies Distributed.........................	60,000			
Estate Principal................................		272,500		
Expenses Chargeable Against Income.....................................			100	
Distributions to Income Beneficiaries			3,300	
Estate Income				4,500
	284,500	284,500	4,500	4,500

Periodically, the fiduciary will prepare a report to the court, summarizing the results during the period of stewardship. This report is called a *charge and discharge statement*. The preparation of the report is simplified if a double trial balance has been prepared, since the charge and discharge statement is divided into two parts—one as to principal and one as to income. The statement for the estate of Todd Shortlife on December 31, 19X1, is at the top of the next page.

In a more complex estate, each of the items in the charge and discharge statement would be supported by a schedule providing detail. For example, a supporting schedule for gains and losses on realization of principal assets might appear as follows:

Schedule of Gains and Losses on Realization
of Principal Assets

Asset	Inventory Value	Proceeds on Realization	Loss	Gain
Geiser Corp. stock	$ 80,000	$ 60,000	($20,000)	
Glory bonds............................	90,000	120,000		$30,000
Land.......................................	10,000	50,000		40,000
Totals.................................	$180,000	$230,000	($20,000)	$70,000

The final clause of Shortlife's will involves the establishment of a trust for his nephew. The will indicates that, when the trust becomes operative, the nephew shall receive all income from the trust until he is 25 years of age,

Estate of Todd Shortlife
Mary Doyle, Executrix
Charge and Discharge Statement
For the Period June 30, 19X1, to December 31, 19X1

As to Principal

I charge myself with:

Assets per original inventory	$272,500	
Assets subsequently discovered............................	8,000	
Gain on realization of principal assets....................	4,000	
Total charges		$284,500

I credit myself with:

Funeral and administrative expenses......................	$ 8,800	
Debts of decedent paid	41,200	
Legacies distributed...	60,000	
Total credits..		110,000

Balances as to estate principal, consisting of:

Cash — principal	$124,500	
Q Corp. stock......................................	50,000	$174,500

As to Income

I charge myself with:

Estate income		$ 4,500

I credit myself with:

Expenses chargeable against income......................	$ 100	
Distributions to income beneficiaries......................	3,300	
Total credits..		3,400

Balance as to estate income, consisting of:

Cash — income..		$ 1,100

at which time the principal of the trust will be released to him. To account for the fulfillment of this clause, the fiduciary would prepare entries to transfer all of the assets to the trust. However, adjustment to a pure accrual basis would be necessary only if it would alter the amounts to be distributed to different parties.

The entries to transfer the Shortlife assets to the trust as of December 31, 19X1, are as follows:

Principal Assets Transferred to First National Trust Company...	174,500	
Cash — Principal..		124,500
Q Corp. Stock...		50,000
Income Assets Transferred to First National Trust Company...	1,100	
Cash — Income..		1,100

When the duties of the fiduciary cease, the estate records are closed. Estate Principal and Estate Income are the clearing accounts, as shown in the following entries:

Estate Principal...	98,000	
Assets Subsequently Discovered	8,000	
Gain on Realization of Principal Assets.........................	4,000	
Funeral and Administrative Expenses.........................		8,800
Debts of Decedent Paid		41,200
Legacies Distributed		60,000
Estate Principal...	174,500	
Principal Assets Transferred to First National Trust Company...		174,500
Estate Income..	3,400	
Expenses Chargeable Against Income.......................		100
Distributions to Income Beneficiaries........................		3,300
Estate Income..	1,100	
Income Assets Transferred to First National Trust Company...		1,100

BOND PREMIUM AND DISCOUNT

When bonds are a part of the estate at the time of death, the premium or discount for bonds acquired by the decedent before death usually is not amortized. If the bonds are held to maturity and face value is received, the excess or deficiency is treated as a gain or loss on realization of principal assets.

The same procedure is followed if the bonds are sold prior to maturity. For example, the $100,000 bonds in the Shortlife estate were recorded at $97,000, which was their fair market value at the date of death. When the bonds were sold for $101,000 on November 1, the gain on the sale was the $4,000 difference between the selling price and the fair market value at the date of death, with no adjustment for discount accumulation.

A different approach must be used if bonds are purchased by the fiduciary for either an estate or a trust. Generally, premium should be amortized, but discount should not be accumulated. To illustrate the logic in this rule, assume that a $1,000, 9% bond is purchased by a fiduciary for $1,100 on an interest payment date. The bond matures in five years. The following entry records the purchase:

Bond Investment	1,000	
Premium on Bond Purchased	100	
Cash — Principal..		1,100

If the premium is not amortized when the first six-months' interest check is received, the interest would be recorded as follows:

Cash — Income...	45	
Estate Income...		45

When the bond matures, there would be a return to principal of only the $1,000 face value. Principal would be reduced, while income would benefit. Since the 9% contract interest was received only because of the premium paid when the bond was purchased, income should be entitled to market interest, while principal is granted an amount equal to the premium amortization. Therefore, the correct entry to record the interest received and the straight-line amortization of premium would be:

```
Cash — Income...................................................................    35
Cash — Principal [1/2 × ($100 ÷ 5)] .................................    10
    Estate Income ..............................................................         35
    Premium on Bond Purchased .........................................         10
```

As another example, assume that a 7% bond is purchased by a fiduciary at 95 on an interest date, five years before maturity. The following entry records the purchase:

```
Bond Investment .............................................................  1,000
    Cash — Principal...........................................................        950
    Discount on Bond Purchased ..........................................         50
```

If a pro rata portion of the discount is accumulated when the six-months' interest check is received, the following entry would result:

```
Cash — Income...................................................................    35
Discount on Bond Purchased [1/2 × ($50 ÷ 5)]....................     5
    Estate Income ..............................................................         40
```

The credit to Estate Income exceeds the cash received, which suggests that more income is available for distribution than actually exists. Thus, accumulation of discount on purchased bonds is improper. At maturity, the discount is recognized as a gain on realization of a principal asset. These procedures are necessary if estate principal is to be protected and excessive distributions to income beneficiaries are to be prevented.

TAXES

Unless the will contains instructions to the contrary, the decedent's final income tax and the estate tax are chargeable against principal. The federal government offers an unusual opportunity to pay federal estate taxes at a discount through the purchase of certain U.S. Treasury bonds, referred to as "flower" bonds. Flower bonds have an effective yield that is considerably below market interest rates. They are sold at a discount, but the government will accept them at par value to pay federal estate taxes if the bonds were owned by the decedent at the date of death. Thus, the discount bonds "flower" into par value upon redemption in payment of estate taxes. The bonds should be purchased as late as possible because of their low effective yield. The Internal Revenue Service is amazingly cooperative since it accepts the trade date, rather than the later settlement date, as the acquisition date of the bonds.

When death is near, a purchase of flower bonds in the name of the dying individual may be made by a party having a power of attorney. For example, Tom Jensen is seriously ill. Upon the advice of his tax counselor, he purchases flower bonds with a face value of $200,000 at 73, or $146,000. A week later, he dies. The executor of his estate may redeem the bonds at $200,000 to pay federal estate taxes. Although the $200,000 is includable in his estate, the beneficiaries will receive an additional $54,000, reduced by any estate tax due on that amount.

For the period subsequent to the date of death, the estate also is subject to income taxes, which must be allocated between principal and income. Estate income tax on gains on principal assets realized is charged against principal, while income taxes on interest earned and dividends declared and received after the date of death are a reduction of income. Property taxes generally are not accrued, but are recorded as of the date they become a lien against the property.

DEPRECIATION AND DEPLETION

Unless the will requires it, the common procedure is not to make any charge against income for depreciation. If the decedent wishes to protect principal for the depreciation factor, there should be a statement in the will that depreciation should be charged against income and that an amount equal to the depreciation should be transferred from income to principal. For depletion on wasting assets, the general rule is that income should be charged for the depletion because of the possibility of total consumption of principal.

TRUSTS

The primary reason for the creation of a trust is that the owner does not wish the property to be released to the heirs, at least not for a period of time. The need for trusts has been described as follows:

> A trust is designed to supply one or more elements lacking in a given person's character or ability or taste which are essential to the proper care, management, and use of property. These elements are physical capacity, mental competence, thrift, interest, maturity, experience, and prudence. If a testator decides that any individual to whom he would make a gift under his will lacks any one of these elements, he should consider putting that gift in trust instead of making it outright.[4]

A trust is particularly significant when the heir is a minor or a spouse who is not knowledgeable about money matters or who has no experience in financial affairs. Too often, a spouse has received large amounts of insur-

---

[4]Gilbert Thomas Stephenson, *Estates and Trusts* (New York: Appleton-Century-Crofts, Inc., 1965), 81.

ance settlements, for example, that are channeled into unwise investments or distributed too generously, with the result that the spouse experiences financial hardship. To prevent this situation, a life insurance trust could be created, under which a trust is made the beneficiary of the insurance proceeds, with the trustee investing and protecting the assets, while distributing income to the designated beneficiaries.

There is no limit to the number and variations of trust arrangements, but all trusts have the basic advantage that legal title and responsibilities of ownership and management are granted to one party, while the benefits flow to another, who need do nothing but enjoy them. Trusts may become operative while the grantor is still alive (an *inter vivos,* or *living trust*) or may be created through a will to become effective upon death (a *testamentary trust*). If a will creates a testamentary trust, the will still must be probated before property may be released by the fiduciary to the trustee.

The *trustee* may be an individual, or the trustee may be a bank, since every major bank has a trust department whose services are available for a fee. The primary duties of a trustee are to carry out the terms of the trust, to protect the property, and to be fair and impartial on matters affecting the income beneficiaries and remaindermen. Care should be exercised in the choice of a trustee; for once title to the property is transferred, the trustee cannot be removed except for proven illegal or unwise actions.

ACCOUNTING FOR TRUSTS

The accounting procedures for a trust and an estate are very similar. For both, there must be separation of principal and income. For both, charge and discharge statements are used as the medium for reporting. The following entries briefly illustrate the accounting for a trust and the similarity to estate entries. These entries would be recorded by the trustee for the Shortlife trust (page 1105) when the assets from the fiduciary of the Shortlife estate are accepted. Thereafter, the journal entries for a trust are patterned closely after those of an estate.

Cash — Principal	124,500	
Q Corp. Stock	50,000	
Trust Principal		174,500
Cash — Income	1,100	
Trust Income		1,100

To demonstrate adherence to the terms of the trust, the trustee must provide annual, confidential reports to income beneficiaries and remaindermen. For a testamentary trust, a report also must be rendered to the probate court of the county in which the will was admitted to probate. The nature of the report is dependent upon the statutory requirement of the relevant state. Generally within 30 days after the end of each year, a report must be filed that shows:

1. The trust principal on hand at the beginning of the period.
2. Changes in the trust principal during the period, such as asset acquisitions or dispositions.
3. The trust principal on hand at the end of the period, its composition, and the estimated market values of all investments.

As to trust income, the report shows:

1. The trust income on hand at the beginning of the period.
2. Trust income received during the period, detailing the sources and amounts.
3. Distributions of trust income made during the period to income beneficiaries.
4. The trust income on hand at the end of the period and how it is invested.

These requirements may be met by the periodic filing of a charge and discharge statement, provided that sufficient detail as to principal and as to income is incorporated into the report. At the time of submitting the statements to the court, many trustees prefer to close trust books to have them correspond to the annual time frame used in filing reports. Trust Principal and Trust Income are the clearing accounts used in the closing process, paralleling the procedures for closing an estate.

A procedure followed by trustees is to accrue income or expense only when it is necessary to protect the rights of the parties involved. If a trust is established in which the income beneficiary is also the remainderman, generally nothing is achieved by making accrual adjustments at year end prior to preparing necessary reports. An occasion when it would be appropriate to accrue is one in which the trust agreement states that income beneficiaries are entitled to income until their death. Upon the demise of one of the income beneficiaries, accrual basis adjustments would be made to the date of death in order to compute the amount of income entitlement.

The trust will terminate when all trust property is distributed in accordance with the trust arrangement. For example, a trust may have been created to provide a beneficiary with income until a certain age is reached, at which time trust principal is released. The trustee's final report will take the same form as the periodic reports but, in addition, will itemize total distribution of trust principal and income to indicate termination of stewardship.

TAX PLANNING WITH TRUSTS

Trusts are useful devices that serve three functions. Trusts can (1) provide a method to manage assets, (2) exempt part or all of an estate from probate, and (3) reduce or even eliminate estate taxes.

An inter vivos trust that is revocable still provides orderly management of assets in case of incapacity or incompetence of the grantor. An inter vivos trust that is irrevocable eliminates assets from probate, and such assets will not be subject to estate taxes. A testamentary trust assures that assets will be managed in a designated manner. These are the basic kinds of trusts, each with many possible variations.

A charitable remainder trust could be used to illustrate one of the variations. A charitable remainder trust pays its income to one or more beneficiaries for life. With the death of the last income beneficiary, the assets of the trust go to the remainderman, which must be a charitable organization. Under such an arrangement, a charitable contribution deduction is available to the grantor when the trust is created. The income from trust assets is allocated to the beneficiaries, who may be in a lower tax bracket or have no tax to pay. Upon death of the grantor, the property is excluded from the estate, thereby escaping estate taxes.

Many opportunities for tax planning are available for individuals, businesses, and fiduciaries. The rules are complex and require careful study, but the effort to reduce taxes can be exciting and rewarding.

QUESTIONS

1. What is the legal distinction between real and personal property? What relevance does the distinction have for estate planning?
2. Define unified credit. What relationship does it have to the exemption equivalent?
3. State the maximum gratuitous transfer of property (gift) for years after 1981, so as not to incur any federal gift tax (a) for a married couple and (b) for a single taxpayer.
4. Is it true that federal estate taxes for a married couple may be eliminated completely by use of the unlimited marital deduction? Is the adoption of such a procedure always wise? Explain.
5. State the rule that establishes the alternative valuation date for estate tax purposes.
6. Briefly explain how an estate asset may receive a stepped-up basis. What is the advantage of a stepped-up basis?
7. After providing for the special reservation of assets because of the state's family allowance and homestead allowance, the estate does not have sufficient assets to settle all accepted claims. The fiduciary informs the funeral director who handled final arrangements that the funeral expenses will have to be paid on a pro rata basis with all other claims. Is the statement of the fiduciary correct?

8. In accounting for estates or trusts, why is there no account titled Cash?
9. In estate accounting, when is accrual accounting used?
10. What is the double trial balance found in estate accounting and what is its purpose?
11. Outline the steps that are followed to settle the estate of a decedent who left a valid will.
12. On an essay examination on estate accounting, a student submitted the following statement: "On bonds that constitute a part of the estate principal, premium should not be amortized but discount should." Identify the errors in the statement and submit a corrected statement.
13. What purpose would be served by recognizing depreciation on estate plant assets?
14. Someone once said, "A trust is established because people have weaknesses or are ignorant." Do you agree?

EXERCISES

Exercise 1.   Select the best answer for each of the following multiple-choice questions.

1. You have been informed that, under your late aunt's will, you are a legatee. Technically, this means that you will receive:
   a. Cash.
   b. Real property.
   c. Personal property.
   d. The face value of a life insurance policy.

2. Tim Mietrich, a single man, has accumulated a considerable amount of assets. He wishes to reduce his ultimate estate tax. Over the next twelve years, the maximum total gifts that he could make without incurring any gift tax or consumption of the unified credit is:
   a. $10,000 × 12.
   b. $20,000 × 12.
   c. $10,000 × 12 × 10.
   d. Not determinable from the facts provided.

3. Carlota Lopez wishes to donate $10,000 to her church this year. Her estate is large and will be subject to estate tax. She is undecided whether to give $10,000 in cash, donate shares of stock that cost $40,000 with a current market value of $10,000 and little hope of recovery, or sell these shares and donate the proceeds. Considering only these facts, she should:

a. Sell the stock and donate the proceeds.
b. Donate $10,000 cash and keep the stock.
c. Donate the shares of stock.
d. Make no donation until the market value of the shares has recovered.

Items 4 and 5 are based on the following information:

A trustee purchased with principal cash five 14%, $1,000 bonds on July 1 at 102 for a trust. Interest is payable semiannually on January 1 and July 1. Bonds mature in ten years.

4. The correct entry to record the purchase is:

a. Bond Investment... 5,100
   Cash 5,100
b. Bond Investment... 5,000
   Premium on Bonds Purchased............................. 100
   Cash — Principal 5,100
c. Bond Investment... 5,000
   Premium on Bonds Purchased............................. 100
   Cash — Principal 5,000
   Cash — Income 100
d. Bond Investment... 5,000
   Accrued Interest on Bonds Purchased 100
   Cash — Principal 5,100

5. The correct entry to record the receipt of the first interest check is:

a. Cash — Income 345
   Cash — Principal 5
   Trust Income 345
   Premium on Bonds Purchased............................. 5
b. Cash — Income 350
   Trust Income 350
c. Cash — Income 350
   Trust Income 345
   Premium on Bonds Purchased............................. 5
d. Cash — Principal 350
   Trust Principal 5
   Trust Income 345

Exercise 2. Select the best answer for each of the following multiple-choice items.

1. Julio Doro received 400 shares of stock from his mother as a result of her death on February 1. Her basis for the stock was $12,000. The stock had a market value of $20,000 on February 1, $23,000 six months later, and $25,000 when the estate tax return was filed. The alternate valuation date was not applicable. Julio's basis for the stock is:
   a. $25,000.   b. $23,000.   c. $20,000.   d. $12,000.

2. Which one of the following statements in regard to the maximum marital deduction is correct?
   a. Its use could increase the overall estate tax.
   b. It should not be combined with a gift program.
   c. It is of greater tax benefit to the surviving spouse than to the deceased.
   d. It is of greater benefit to taxable estates of $600,000 or less.

3. The valid will of Ginger Hill said, "I leave my friend Chien Yang $10,000." This is an illustration of a:
   a. Specific legacy.
   b. General legacy.
   c. Demonstrative legacy.
   d. Residuary legacy.

4. In most cases, the basis for effective estate planning is dependent upon:
   a. Having a valid and available will.
   b. Using the maximum marital deduction.
   c. Selling securities with a stepped-up basis before death.
   d. Putting the only copy of your will in a safety deposit box.

5. John and Mary, a married couple with no children, hold all of their property jointly. Neither has a will. John is killed in an accident. Mary dies three months later. The estate would be:
   a. Divided one-third to John's family and two-thirds to Mary's family.
   b. Divided equally between John's family and Mary's family.
   c. Inherited by John's family.
   d. Inherited by Mary's family.

Exercise 3.   The following events related to an estate require specific control accounts for their proper recording. Excluding the two cash accounts, provide the title of the control account necessary to record each of the events.
(a) Recording the original assets of the estate.
(b) Locating additional assets after the initial inventory was filed.
(c) Paying debts incurred by the decedent.
(d) Distributing personal property in accordance with the will.
(e) Distributing income earned and received after date of death.

Exercise 4.   The following transactions are typical of those incurred by an estate:
(a) Recording of the original assets of the estate.
(b) Sale of capital stock in the original estate at a gain.
(c) Recording receipt of interest (partly accrued at date of death) on bonds in the original estate.
(d) Recording assets subsequently discovered.
(e) Purchase of bonds at a premium, along with accrued interest.
(f) Receipt of first interest check on bonds in (e).
(g) Payment of property taxes on a rental apartment. The taxes became a lien after the date of death.

Assuming that no stipulation to the contrary is made in the will, indicate whether the typical accounting treatment of each of the items would affect principal accounts only, income accounts only, or both. Use the following columnar format for your answers, placing an "X" in the appropriate column.

	Would Affect		
Letter of Item	Principal Only	Income Only	Principal and Income

Exercise 5. Each of the following situations concerns the making of gifts as it relates to estate planning:

(a) Mr. and Mrs. Herman have two married daughters, an unmarried son, and four grandchildren. During the next six years, they wish to make the maximum total gifts possible to their descendents (including spouses) without incurring any federal gift tax or consuming their unified credit. What would this total amount be for the six years?

(b) Mrs. Gehrig, a widow, has three married children and two grandchildren. What is the maximum amount she can give each year to her descendents and their spouses without incurring any federal gift tax or consuming her unified credit?

(c) Frank Martin, who is single, has two nieces and one nephew. What is the maximum amount he can give each year to these relatives without incurring any federal gift tax or consuming his unified credit?

Exercise 6. Casey Jones died testate on May 1, 19X0. As the approved executor, prepare journal entries to record the following activities related to the estate:

(a) The assets are inventoried, and the following listing is filed with the probate court:

Cash...	$ 60,000
Stock of Trains Inc.	40,000
Zip Railroad 10% bonds, interest payable March 1 and	
September 1, at face value (also market value)....................	120,000
Accrued interest on Zip bonds	2,000
Personal and household effects..	30,000
Total..	$252,000

(b) Funeral expenses paid, $2,800.

(c) Dividends were declared on May 10 by Trains Inc., and the check for $800 was received on June 1.

(d) Interest on Zip Railroad bonds was collected on September 1.

(e) Half of the Zip Railroad bonds were sold on October 1 at 103 plus accrued interest.

(f) Casey was a bachelor. The will stipulates that his personal and household effects be given to his housekeeper, Karen Kay. The executor released the items to her.

(g) On December 1, the executor's fee of $3,000 was approved by the court and paid. Of the total amount, $200 is to be charged against income of the estate.

Exercise 7.   Prepare a charge and discharge statement from the following double trial balance prepared from the estate records of Casey Jones:

	As to Principal		As to Income	
Cash—Principal	118,200			
Cash—Income			5,100	
Stock of Trains Inc.	40,000			
Zip Railroad Bonds	60,000			
Gain on Realization of Principal Assets		1,800		
Funeral and Administrative Expenses.....................................	5,600			
Legacies Distributed.........................	30,000			
Estate Principal...............................		252,000		
Expenses Chargeable Against Income			200	
Estate Income				5,300
	253,800	253,800	5,300	5,300

Exercise 8.   The will of Casey Jones stipulated that, when feasible, all remaining assets should be used to establish a trust at State National Bank, the income from which is to be given to charity.
(1) Prepare journal entries to transfer to the trust the estate principal and income assets shown in the double trial balance in Exercise 7.
(2) Prepare journal entries to close the executor's records.

PROBLEMS

Problem 21–1.   Select the best answer for each of the following multiple-choice items.

1. The federal unified estate and gift tax is a(an):
    a. Progressive tax.
    b. Regressive tax.
    c. Fixed tax.
    d. Excise tax.

2. Where the filing of an estate tax return is required, it must be filed:
    a. Within 6 months after the date of death.
    b. Within 9 months after the date of death.
    c. Within 12 months after the date of death.
    d. By the end of the calendar year in which the person died.

3. Assets discovered subsequent to the date of death usually are:
    a. Prorated equally between estate income and principal.
    b. Turned over to the state of domicile.
    c. Added to estate income.
    d. Added to estate principal.

4. Peter Plum died, leaving his estate to his sister, Polly. The alternate valuation date was elected properly by the administrator. Peter's estate included 1,000 shares of K Corp. stock. Peter's basis for the stock was $20,000. Polly received the stock 10 months after Peter's death. Market values of the stock were:

At the date that Peter died	$29,000
Six months after Peter died	36,000
Ten months after Peter died	39,000

Polly's basis for this stock is:
a. $20,000.　　　b. $29,000.　　　c. $36,000.　　　d. $39,000.

Problem 21–2. Select the best answer for each of the following multiple-choice questions.

1. If bonds were acquired before death and became a part of the initial estate:
   a. Premium is amortized but discount is not.
   b. Discount is amortized but premium is not.
   c. Neither premium nor discount is amortized.
   d. Both premium and discount are amortized.

2. If bonds are purchased at a premium or discount by a fiduciary for an estate or a trust:
   a. Premium is amortized but discount is not.
   b. Discount is amortized but premium is not.
   c. Neither premium nor discount is amortized.
   d. Both premium and discount are amortized.

3. The following entry is found in the accounting records for an estate:

Assets Transferred to State Trust Company	296,400	
Cash — Principal		80,000
Cash — Income		10,000
Zeus Corporation Bond Investment		206,400

A proper conclusion would be that:
   a. The fiduciary has decided not to continue to conduct the affairs of the estate and has transferred the estate to a trust company.
   b. The person making the entry is not very knowledgeable about accounting for estates and trusts.
   c. Principal and income assets were merged to simplify accounting.
   d. The bonds were purchased at a premium with trust principal cash.

4. Under the Deficit Reduction Act of 1984, the election to use the alternate valuation date for estate asset valuation may be made only if:
   a. The estate is not subject to the unified tax.
   b. The value of the estate increased but was still not subject to the unified tax.
   c. The value of the estate increased and is subject to tax.
   d. It would reduce the gross estate and the tax liability.

(continued)

5. A legacy of money is always a:
   a. General legacy.
   b. Pecuniary legacy.
   c. Demonstrative legacy.
   d. Specific legacy.

Problem 21–3.   Early in 1990, Alex Bowe dies, leaving a gross estate of $1,400,000. He had outstanding debts of $50,000. Administrative expenses of the estate amounted to $50,000. Later that year, his wife dies, leaving an estate of $250,000, in addition to the property left to her by her husband. Administrative expenses on Mrs. Bowe's estate were $60,000.

You are provided with the following partial unified estate and gift tax table:

Exceeding (A)	Not Exceeding (B)	Tax on Amount in Column (A)	Rate of Tax on Excess over Amount in Column (A)
$ 500,000	$ 750,000	$155,800	37%
750,000	1,000,000	248,300	39
1,000,000	1,250,000	345,800	41
1,250,000	1,500,000	448,300	43

Required:
(1) Ignoring state gift and estate taxes, determine the amount of federal estate tax on both estates:
   (a) If Mr. Bowe left his total estate to his wife, exercising the unlimited marital deduction.
   (b) If Mr. Bowe left his wife an estate that will equate his taxable estate with the maximum unified credit.
(2) What does the estate tax computation demonstrate relative to exercising the unlimited marital deduction?

Problem 21–4.   The following selected events occurred after the death of Gloria Scott on January 31, 19X1:
(a) The inventory of estate assets as of the date of death included Oklahoma City 5% bonds, paying interest annually on September 1. The face value of the bonds was $100,000. On the date of death, the market value of the bonds was 95. (The journal entry should show how the bonds and interest would be recorded as part of the original estate.)
(b) On May 31, the fiduciary sold the bonds for 94 plus accrued interest.
(c) An apartment building was part of the estate. The property originally cost the decedent $260,000, of which $20,000 was applicable to the land. The building was 30% depreciated as of the date of death, based on a 40-year estimated life, zero salvage value, and the straight-line depreciation method. The fiduciary agrees with the originally estimated life. Market

value of the property as of the date of death is $320,000, of which $40,000 is applicable to the land. (The journal entry should show how the property would be recorded as part of the inventory of the estate.)

(d) Scott's will stipulated that, in regard to the property discussed in (c), the principal of the estate should be protected by assigning rental income equal to depreciation directly to principal. For the ensuing year, gross apartment rentals collected were $60,000. Expenses paid amounted to $17,000.

(e) After the deduction of expenses, the net rental income from the apartment building is to be released to Scott's nephew, but the amount shall not exceed $25,000 per year. The maximum annual amount was paid to the income beneficiary.

Required:

Prepare journal entries to record each of these events.

Problem 21–5.   Laurel Rose has been the executrix of her brother's estate since his death on February 1, 19X6. The following events occurred during her administration.

(a) Included in the principal assets were 40, $1,000, 8% City of Pittsburgh bonds, paying interest on January 1 and July 1. The bonds had a market value of 101 on February 1, 19X6. Rose sold the bonds at 103, plus accrued interest, on March 1, 19X6.

(b) On March 1, 19X6, Rose purchased 50, $1,000, 5% City of Detroit bonds at 98, plus accrued interest. The bonds pay interest on April 1 and October 1. The bonds mature on April 1, 19X8.

(c) On March 1, 19X6, she also purchased $10,000 (face value) of 7% City of Newark bonds at 102, plus accrued interest. The bonds pay interest on June 1 and December 1. The bonds mature on December 1, 19X7.

(d) On April 1, 19X6, she received a check for the interest on the Detroit bonds.

(e) On June 1, 19X6, she received a check for the interest on the Newark bonds.

(f) On September 1, 19X6, she sold the Detroit bonds at 101, plus accrued interest.

Required:

Prepare journal entries to record each of these events. Use straight-line method of amortization where applicable.

Problem 21–6.   Sheri Shannon died on June 1, 19X3, leaving a valid will that named her friend, Steve Chevalier, the executor of the estate.

(a) Steve prepared the following inventory of assets, listing their market values as of June 1:

Cash..	$31,000
1,000 shares of Pal Corp. common stock...................................	60,000
2,000 shares of BVD Corp. common stock.................................	40,000
Rapid Transit Corp. (RTC) 8% bonds, interest payable April 1 and October 1, $30,000 face amount...	30,300
Time-share condominium unit at Lake Tahoe, used for her two-week vacations..	10,000
Sheri's one-half interest in the Sheri Limo Service Co.	70,000

(b) On June 15, after filing the inventory of assets with the probate court, Steve discovered Sheri's gold-coin collection that was appraised at $18,000.

(c) On June 20, a $250 check was received from Pal Corporation for dividends declared on May 10, 19X3, to owners on record as of May 30.

(d) Steve sold the time-share condominium for $14,000 on July 7.

(e) The following items were paid between June 1 and July 31:

Sheri's charge card purchases..	$1,900
Funeral costs...	6,000
Lawyer's fee to probate the will	800
Cost to paint condominium prior to sale	1,100
Payment to executor approved by the court	1,700

(f) On July 5, a $15,000 check was received for Sheri's portion of partnership earnings for the quarter ended June 30. Earnings are fairly constant from one month to the next and are available for withdrawal on a monthly basis if a partner so desires. Otherwise, payments are made quarterly.

(g) Sheri's partner offered Steve $90,000 for her interest in the partnership. Steve accepted the offer and received full payment.

(h) On October 1, a check for interest was received from Rapid Transit Corp.

(i) On December 1, Steve completed Sheri's final income tax return, paying the additional tax due of $18,200.

Required:
(1) Prepare journal entries to record the events.
(2) Prepare a charge and discharge statement as of December 31, 19X3.

Problem 21-7. On the top of the following page, you are given the trial balance of the estate of Sheri Shannon as of December 31, 19X3. Her will stipulated that the executor should be granted $30,000 from principal cash. The remainder of the estate's principal assets and its income asset are to be transferred to Community Bank, which will act as trustee of an endowment fund. Income from trust assets shall be used for scholarships for accounting majors at a local university.

Required:
(1) Record the payment to the executor and the transfer of all remaining assets to the trustee.

Cash—Principal	115,950	
Cash—Income	5,800	
Pal Corp. Stock..	60,000	
BVD Corp. Stock...	40,000	
Rapid Transit Corp. Bonds....................................	30,300	
Coin Collection..	18,000	
Estate Principal...		241,700
Estate Income		5,800
Assets Subsequently Discovered..................................		28,250
Gain on Realization of Principal Assets		24,000
Funeral and Administrative Expenses	8,500	
Debts of Decedent Paid..	20,100	
Expenses Chargeable Against Principal..........................	1,100	
	299,750	299,750

(2) Prepare journal entries to close the executor's records.

(3) Prepare journal entries to record receipt of assets by the trustee. Explain why it was unnecessary to accrue the interest on the Rapid Transit Corp. bonds to the date of actual transfer.

Problem 21–8.   The probate court is dissatisfied with the procedures followed by the executor of the estate of Jean O'Brien and demands the records. The executor submits the following:

Journal Entries for the Estate of Jean O'Brien — Died, May 1, 19X6

May	8	Bank Checking Account..	14,100	
		Insurance Policy at Cash Surrender Value (face of policy is $100,000 and is payable to the estate)	18,000	
		Shannon Corporation 12% Bonds (interest is payable April 1 and October 1; face value, $100,000; fair market value at date of death, $106,000; recorded at Jean's cost)	124,000	
		O'Brien Corporation Common Stock (10,000 shares of $10 par. Stock was quoted at $18 when Jean died. These shares were a gift from her father, the founder of the corporation, so I've entered them at $1, just to make a record.)	1	
		Condominium (Her condo is just like mine, which cost me $96,000 a week before she died. Her cost was $73,000.)...	73,000	
		Paintings (I don't understand these, but a dealer says they are worth $25,000. They cost Jean $9,000.)	25,000	
		Gain on Paintings...		16,000
		Total Estate...		238,101
		This is a list of the assets I found so far. I made a copy of this entry and filed it with the court. I omitted a Silver Cloud Rolls-Royce, worth about $30,000. I'll keep the car instead of asking for a fee. Jean always said she wanted me to have it. She must have forgotten it when she made out her will.		
May	9	Cash	2,000	
		O'Brien Corporation Dividend....................................		2,000
		Received a check for a dividend declared April 2 to holders of record on April 25.		

June 1   Cash   100,000
              Insurance Policy at Cash Surrender Value   18,000
              Gain on Loss of Jean O'Brien   82,000
                  This is the check from the insurance company.

        5   Expenses...   44,000
              Cash   44,000
                  I issued checks to cover:
                  Funeral expenses .... $ 5,100
                  Jean's medical bills   300
                  Final income tax payments...................   17,900
                  Jean's charges on American Express......   700
                  Partial payment on estate tax. The will
                    says it should be charged against
                    principal, whatever that means...........   20,000
                        Total $44,000

       30   Expenses...   25,000
              Paintings   25,000
                  Turned paintings over to Art Institute, as the will
                    said I should do.

Sept. 10   Loss on O'Brien Corporation Common Stock...................   1
              O'Brien Corporation Common Stock..........................   1
                  The will stated that the stock should be returned to
                    the corporation, so I did it.

Oct.   1   Cash   6,000
              Interest Received...   6,000
                  To record check received from Shannon
                    Corporation.

        1   Cash   90,000
              Condominium   73,000
              Gain on Sale of Condominium.................................   17,000
                  To record sale of condo. The will says the proceeds
                    should be used to establish a Jean O'Brien
                    Scholarship Endowment Fund at State University,
                    her alma mater.

        3   Cash Turned over to State University   90,000
              Cash   90,000
                  I sent a check to the university for the scholarship
                    endowment fund.

       31   Expenses...   3,000
              Cash   3,000
                  The court relieved me as executor and said I could
                    not have the Rolls-Royce. This payment to me is to
                    be charged to principal. I don't think what they did
                    is fair to me.

Required:
(1) The probate judge is disgusted with the records, terminates the executor's responsibilities, and appoints you as the replacement. Prepare a correct set of entries to date.
(2) Prepare a charge and discharge statement. No supporting schedules are necessary.

Problem 21–9.   Arthur Taine died in an accident on May 31, 19X6. His will, dated February 28, 19X4, provided that all just debts and expenses be paid and that his property be disposed of as follows:

Personal residence is devised to Bertha Taine, widow.

U.S. Treasury bonds and Puritan Company stock are to be placed in trust. All income is to go to Bertha Taine during her lifetime.

Seneca Company mortgage notes are bequeathed to Elaine Taine Langer, daughter.

A cash bequest of $10,000 is to be made to David Taine, son.

The remainder of the estate is to be divided equally between the two children, Elaine Taine Langer and David Taine.

The will further provided that, during the administration period, Bertha Taine is to be paid $300 a month out of estate income. Estate and inheritance taxes are to be borne by the principal of the estate. David Taine was named as executor and trustee.

An inventory of the decedent's property was prepared. The fair market value of all items as of the date of death was determined. The preliminary inventory, before the computation of any appropriate income accruals on inventory items, follows:

Personal residence..	$ 45,000
Jewelry — diamond ring	9,600
York Life Insurance Company — term life insurance policy on life of Arthur Taine, with Bertha Taine designated as beneficiary	120,000
Granite Trust Co. — 5% savings bank account, in trust for Philip Langer (grandchild), interest credited January 1 and July 1; balance May 31	400
Fidelity National Bank checking account balance...........................	143,000
$100,000 U.S. Treasury bonds, 3%, interest payable March 1 and September 1	100,000
$9,700 Seneca Co. first mortgage notes, 6%, interest payable May 31 and November 30...	9,900
800 shares Puritan Company common stock	64,000
700 shares Meta Manufacturing common stock	70,000

The executor opened an estate bank account, to which he transferred the decedent's checking account balance. Other deposits, through July 1, 19X7, were as follows:

Interest collected on U.S. Treasury bonds:	
September 1, 19X6	$ 1,500
March 1, 19X7	1,500
Dividends received on Puritan Company stock:	
June 15, 19X6, declared May 7, 19X6, payable to holders of record May 27, 19X6	800
September 15, 19X6...	800
December 15, 19X6...	1,200
March 15, 19X7...	800
June 15, 19X7...	800
Net proceeds of June 19, 19X6 sale of 700 shares of Meta Manufacturing common stock...	68,810

Payments were made from the estate's checking account through July 1, 19X7, for the following:

Funeral expenses..	$ 2,000
Assessments for additional 19X4 federal and state income taxes ($1,700) plus interest ($110) to May 31, 19X6	1,810
19X6 income taxes of Arthur Taine for the period January 1 through May 31, 19X6, in excess of amounts paid by the decedent on Declaration of Estimated Tax	9,100
Federal and state fiduciary income taxes, fiscal year ending June 30, 19X6 ($75), and June 30, 19X7 ($1,400).....................................	1,475
Federal and state estate taxes..	58,000
Monthly payments to Bertha Taine: 13 payments of $300 each	3,900
Attorney's and accountant's fees...	25,000

The executor waived his commission. However, he desired to receive his father's diamond ring in lieu of the $10,000 specific legacy. All parties agreed to this in writing, and the court's approval was secured. All other specific legacies were delivered by July 15, 19X6. On July 2, 19X7, final distributions of the residuary legacies were made to Elaine and David, the latter continuing to function as trustee, establishing separate records for the trust.

Required:

Prepare journal entries to record all events related to the estate of Arthur Taine, including transfer to the trust and final closing entries for the estate.

(AICPA adapted)

Problem 21–10. Using the information detailed in Problem 21–9, prepare a charge and discharge statement and supporting schedules for the period May 31, 19X6, through July 1, 19X7. The following supporting schedules should be included:

Schedule 1—Original principal of the estate
2—Gains and losses on realization of principal assets
3—Funeral and administrative expenses
4—Debts of decedent paid
5—Legacies distributed
6—Principal assets on hand, July 1, 19X7
7—Proposed plan of distribution of estate assets as of July 1, 19X7
8—Income collected
9—Expenses chargeable to income
10—Distributions to income beneficiary   (AICPA adapted)

Problem 21–11. The will of William Kraus, deceased, provided that as soon as possible a trust be established to assist his daughter, Sandy, in continuing voice lessons in New York City in preparation for a career in opera. Providing her progress is satisfactory, she shall receive $1,000 on the first day of each month. An additional $5,000 shall be made available during the summer if she is accepted at a recognized school for opera singers. Payments to Sandy shall be charged against trust income during the year. If income for the year is inadequate to cover expenses chargeable against income and income distributions, the deficiency shall be covered by principal, with no need for reimbursement from later income. If within six years Sandy has made a successful debut, the remaining assets shall be released to her. If she has not made her debut within that period, the payments shall cease, with any remaining assets turned over to UWM University for music scholarships.

The following events occurred that involved the trust:

(a) The will specified that principal and income assets of the estate retain their identity when transferred to the trust. The following assets were accepted by the trustee on January 2, 19X3:

As to principal: Cash..	$40,000	
AMD common stock	15,000	
Parrot 6% preferred stock...............	30,000	
Rental property	80,000	$165,000
As to income: Cash		4,000

(b) A $20,000, six-month money market certificate was purchased with principal cash on February 10, when the annual rate was 14%.

(c) On March 15, a dividend of $1,200 was received on the AMD common stock. By year end, the value of the stock increased from $15,000 to $18,000.

(d) Rental income of $4,200 for the first six months of 19X3 was received. Ordinary property expenses of $1,200 were paid. The trustee believed that the net return was not adequate to justify retaining the property in the trust. It was sold for $73,000 on July 1, 19X3.

(e) On July 1, principal cash was invested in 15% industrial bonds with a face value of $80,000, purchased at 105 plus accrued interest from May 1, the last semiannual interest payment date. The bonds mature on November 1, 19X6.

(f) Sandy was notified that she was accepted for the summer session master classes in voice at the La Scala School for Voice in Italy. On July 3, a payment of $5,000 was made to her in accordance with the will.

(g) On August 12, a check for the interest on the money market certificate was received. The trustee renewed the certificate for another six months.

(h) The annual dividend of $1,800 on the Parrot 6% preferred was received on September 2. The trustee believed that the return was minimal. When a takeover bidder offered $42,000 for the stock, the trustee sold. Most of the proceeds were invested in $36,000 (face value) of City of Madison 10% bonds, purchased at 96 and accrued interest on October 1. Semiannual interest payment dates are June 1 and December 1. The bonds mature on December 1, 19X9.

(i) Interest on the industrial bonds was received on November 1. When necessary, the trustee uses pro rata amortization techniques on interest collection dates only. Since Sandy is the only income beneficiary, the trustee does not accrue at calendar year end, an acceptable procedure under the circumstances.

(j)   On December 1, interest on the City of Madison 10% bonds was received.

(k)   During the year, twelve monthly payments of $1,000 were made to Sandy. (Make one entry for the twelve payments.)

(l)   The trustee's fee of $4,000, which is to be charged against principal, was paid.

(m) Since trust income was inadequate to meet expenses chargeable against income and income distributions, an entry was to be made to cover the deficiency.

Required:

(1)   Prepare journal entries to record the events for the year.

(2)   Prepare a charge and discharge statement for the trust for the year ended December 31, 19X3.

CHAPTER 22

INSOLVENCY

In 1988, Dun and Bradstreet reported that one percent of the U.S. firms in its database failed in the previous year, with total liabilities exceeding $35 billion. There has been an acceleration in bankruptcy filings as an aftermath of deflation, sluggish consumer demand, and increased foreign competition. For example, in the mid 1980s, business bankruptcy filings increased 75% in one year in the Southern District of Texas. Billions of dollars of assets have been and are being administered through increasingly crowded bankruptcy courts. If business management has not learned to plan effectively, to organize efficiently, and to recognize problems fairly quickly, it may be confronted with a situation of *insolvency* — not being able to meet financial obligations as they become due.

An example of this situation is Chrysler Corporation. In 1979, oil prices doubled after the Shah of Iran was deposed. At a time when the public wanted smaller cars, Chrysler continued to make large ones. The oil situation and the economic downturn in the early 1980s resulted in year after year of losses until the company seemed doomed. There was negative cash flow. Banks were demanding payment and would not extend further credit. Chrysler's stock had dropped so low that it would have been impossible to raise sufficient equity through stock offerings. Management considered filing a petition for bankruptcy. However, a sterling performance by Lee Iacocca convinced Congress that, unless it came to Chrysler's rescue, massive unemployment would occur, with a great drain on government resources resulting from welfare and unemployment payments and loss of tax revenue. Iacocca won. Chrysler was revived by a financial transfusion of borrowed funds guaranteed by the federal government.

This chapter will discuss various relief procedures that do not involve court actions, as well as the legal procedures available under the Bankruptcy Reform Act of 1978 and the 1986 Bankruptcy Code amendments.

RELIEF PROCEDURES NOT REQUIRING COURT ACTION

When a business becomes insolvent, the simplest procedure is to arrange an *agreement with creditors*, which grants an extension of time for meeting obligations. This approach could be useful when the debtor has suffered only a temporary financial setback and previously has demonstrated successful operational capabilities. Another approach is the *composition agreement*, by which creditors agree to a scaling down of the amounts owed by the debtor. For example, each creditor might be willing to accept $.80 per dollar of debt if resorting to other processes would result in receiving less. These two procedures are possible without court action.

Another available relief procedure is a *troubled debt restructure*, under which the creditors grant to the debtor concessions that they normally would not consider. Such concessions usually result in a gain to the debtor and a loss to the creditors, who agree to the restructuring of debt on the likelihood that they ultimately will receive more than by pursuing other courses of action. Troubled debt restructure is a topic covered in intermediate accounting textbooks.

A corporation may not be insolvent, but may have accumulated a relatively large deficit as a result of such problems as an excessive investment in plant assets or inventory, or management's inability to recognize and influence market demands. If management is replaced and if profits result from new policies, most state laws still will not permit declaration of dividends until the deficit is eliminated. The turn-about period and deficit elimination may take so long that the investors' interest in the company vanishes, and capital acquisition becomes difficult. To overcome such a handicap, the corporation might seek a *quasi-reorganization*.

Quasi-reorganization does not require court action, nor does it require the consent of creditors since creditor interests are not altered. However, the procedure is described in state laws, many of which require a quasi-reorganization to be approved by two-thirds of the stockholders.

The primary purpose of a quasi-reorganization is to eliminate a large deficit and to take such action as will permit successful operations in the future. Excessive plant capacity and equipment may be sold. Plant assets that are retained may be revalued to reflect a lower but fair value, thereby reducing depreciation charges allocated to future periods. For example, as part of the quasi-reorganization process, a corporation's board of directors reduces plant assets from a cost of $1,000,000 to a more realistic fair value of $400,000 and reduces accumulated depreciation from $200,000 to $80,000. Future annual depreciation charges will be reduced from $50,000 to $20,000. The entry to record the revaluation would be:

Accumulated Depreciation	120,000	
Retained Earnings	480,000	
Property, Plant, and Equipment		600,000

It should be noted that the write-down of the assets increases the deficit, which then will be eliminated by subsequent changes in the capital structure.

The deficit is eliminated by charges against the existing paid-in capital in excess of par or stated values. If no such paid-in capital exists, it may be created by altering the capital structure and substituting stock with lower par value or lower stated value for existing shares. To illustrate the manner in which the owners' equity section in the balance sheet is revised by a quasi-reorganization, assume the following stockholders' equity:

Common stock ($10 par, 12,000 shares outstanding)	$120,000
Retained earnings (deficit)	(45,000)
Total stockholders' equity	$ 75,000

On March 1, 19X0, the stockholders approve a reduction in par value to $1. Note that such a maneuver has absolutely no effect on the proportionate interests of each stockholder.

The entries to record the quasi-reorganization are as follows:

Common Stock ($10 par)	120,000	
Common Stock ($1 par)		12,000
Paid-In Capital from Reduction in Stock Par Value (or		
Reorganization Capital)		108,000
To record the reduction in par value.		
Paid-In Capital from Reduction in Stock Par Value	45,000	
Retained Earnings		45,000
To eliminate the deficit.		

Immediately following the quasi-reorganization, the owners' equity section would show:

Common stock ($1 par, 12,000 shares outstanding)	$12,000
Paid-in Capital from reduction in stock par value	63,000
Retained earnings (subsequent to March 1, 19X0)	–0–
Total stockholders' equity	$75,000

In future financial statements, retained earnings must be dated to indicate the starting point of new accumulations. The process of dating retained earnings should be continued for as long a period of time as is deemed advisable, but rarely does it exceed ten years.

BANKRUPTCY REFORM ACT OF 1978 AND THE 1986 BANKRUPTCY CODE AMENDMENTS

If a satisfactory solution cannot be reached under the procedures described in the previous paragraphs, the legal proceedings for bankruptcy may be initiated. Attitudes toward bankruptcy have changed considerably from the time of the Romans, when unpaid creditors were permitted to kill the debtor and divide the body among themselves. Modern bankruptcy procedures attempt to give a debtor a fresh start, unburdened by former obligations, while simultaneously accomplishing an equitable distribution of the debtor's property among creditors.

In an attempt to modernize an antiquated system existing under the Bankruptcy Act of 1898, as amended by the Chandler Act of 1938, Congress passed the *Bankruptcy Reform Act of 1978* (Title 11 of the U.S. Code), which became effective on October 1, 1979. Under the former acts, U.S. District Courts were given the responsibility of functioning as courts of bankruptcy. The office of *referee* was created, granting it jurisdiction over bankruptcy proceedings. Later, referees were assigned the title of *bankruptcy judge.* As cases became more complicated, it was sometimes difficult to determine whether an issue should be settled under the Rules of Bankruptcy Procedure governing the courts of bankruptcy or under the Rules of Civil Procedure used by the District Courts.

The Bankruptcy Reform Act of 1978 (hereafter referred to as the Act) initiated an interesting experiment whose objective was to expedite the formulation and handling of administrative procedures for bankruptcy cases. It established a five-year pilot program that relieved bankruptcy judges of most administrative duties and permitted them to concentrate on the resolution of substantive matters. In each of the eighteen experimental judicial districts created by the Act, a U.S. trustee was appointed under the supervision of the U.S. Assistant Attorney General. The U.S. trustees were responsible for: (1) monitoring the performance of the private trustees that they appointed to bankruptcy cases, (2) functioning as trustees when private trustees were unable or unwilling to serve, and (3) overseeing the general administration of bankruptcy cases.

In 1982, the U.S. Supreme Court ruled that the section of the Act giving bankruptcy judges the power to consider and rule on issues that were not directly part of the bankruptcy proceedings was unconstitutional. Under the Act, bankruptcy judges had the power to consider any issue arising in or related to bankruptcy cases. Thus, if a company had filed in bankruptcy court and another company had a damage suit against it, the damage claim could have been heard in bankruptcy court instead of in a federal district or state court. Under the Supreme Court's decision, bankruptcy judges now must limit their rulings to issues directly related to bankruptcy proceedings. In June, 1984, Congress passed a bill to overhaul the bankruptcy system. The bill limited the powers of bankruptcy judges to comply with the 1982 Supreme Court decision and created 85 new federal trial and appellate judgeships to assist with cases that spill out of bankruptcy courts. The other provisions of the Act remained operative.

Bankruptcy rules were modified effective August 1, 1987, by Bankruptcy Code amendments as detailed in the *Bankruptcy Judges, U.S. Trustees, and Family Farmer Bankruptcy Act of 1986.* The act authorized 52 additional bankruptcy judges to break up the log jam of cases awaiting disposition. It made the U.S. Trustee system permanent and nationwide, under the control of the U.S. Attorney General. Supervisory and administrative duties of the U.S. Trustee were broadened and even include the reporting of any potential crimes to the Attorney General.

A bankruptcy case may be filed under one of the following operative chapters of the code:

Chapter 7: Liquidation. A nonbusiness debtor or any business not wishing to remain in operation, except a railroad, governmental unit, bank, insurance company, or savings and loan association, may file a petition under this chapter. Filing of a joint case by a debtor and spouse is permissible.

Chapter 9: Adjustments of Debts of a Municipality is not covered in this text.

Chapter 11: Reorganization. The purpose of Chapter 11 is to assist a company or individual to remain in possession of the business during the judicial process of reorganization, without the appointment of a trustee and without the harassment of creditors. This chapter is used primarily by corporate or partnership debtors. Although the chapter may be used by an individual proprietor, the procedures are more cumbersome and more expensive than those of Chapter 13. Only individuals with substantial assets and liabilities resort to Chapter 11 proceedings.

Chapter 13: Adjustments of Debts of an Individual with Regular Income. This chapter is limited exclusively to individuals, including sole proprietors, with less than $100,000 in unsecured debt and less than $350,000 in secured debt. A joint case of debtor and spouse is permissible if their combined debt does not exceed the two limitations.

There are provisions for the movement or conversion of a case from one chapter to another, such as converting an unsuccessful reorganization (Chapter 11) to a liquidation (Chapter 7).

COMMENCEMENT OF A BANKRUPTCY CASE

The Act states that a debtor must be a person (individual, partnership, or corporation) residing in or having a domicile, business, or property in the United States, or be a municipality. If a debtor initiates the action of filing a petition with the court of bankruptcy under the appropriate chapter of the Act, it is a *voluntary* case. A voluntary petition may seek relief under Chapters 7, 9, 11, or 13. Filing constitutes an *order for relief,* which represents a stay of action by prohibiting commencement or continuation of legal action against the debtor to recover a claim.

If the petition is filed by someone other than the debtor, an *involuntary* proceeding results. Such proceedings may be filed under Chapter 7 (Liquidation) or Chapter 11 (Reorganization), but not under Chapter 13, where the individual debtor is willing to make payments to creditors. Involuntary proceedings may not be initiated against a farmer or a charitable organization. Under Chapters 7 and 11, if a debtor has twelve or more creditors, three or more of them may file an involuntary petition, providing the total of their noncontingent, unsecured claims is $5,000 or more. If there are less than twelve creditors, one or more of them may initiate an involuntary case, but the same limit of $5,000 applies. In an involuntary case, the claims must have arisen before the order for relief was issued. The court will issue such an order if the debtor files no answer to the involuntary petition. If an answer is filed by the debtor, the court will hold a hearing, following which it either will dismiss the case, issue an order for relief, or postpone the decision pending receipt of additional information.

CHAPTER 7—LIQUIDATION

The commencement of a voluntary or involuntary case under Chapter 7 (Liquidation) creates an estate that consists of the assets of the debtor, who must file an inventory of debts and property on a form called the Statement of Assets and Liabilities. This form consists of the following schedules:

1. Schedule A—Statement of All Liabilities of Debtor
    Schedule A–1—Creditors Having Priority (with amount of claim)
    Schedule A–2—Creditors Holding Security (with market value of
    security and amount of claim)
    Schedule A–3—Creditors Having Unsecured Claims Without Priority
    (with amount of claim)
2. Schedule B—Statement of All Property of Debtor
    Schedule B–1—Real Property (with market values)
    Schedule B–2—Personal Property (with market values)
    Schedule B–3—Property Not Otherwise Scheduled (includes property
    transferred for benefit of creditors within four
    months prior to filing of the petition)
    Schedule B–4—Property Claimed as Exempt (with reference to the
    statute creating the exemption and value claimed as
    exempt)

A debtor who is an individual must file a list of property claimed as exempt. Such property is to be retained by the debtor in order to achieve financial survival without becoming a public charge. Exempt property normally may not be attached to satisfy claims. To determine what property is exempt, the debtor may follow either the applicable state law or the itemization under the Act, which exempts the following:

1. A homestead equity, not to exceed $7,500 in value.
2. An equity in one motor vehicle, not to exceed $1,200.

3. Household furnishings, wearing apparel, appliances, books, animals, crops, or musical instruments held primarily for use of the debtor or dependents, not to exceed $200 in value in any particular item.
4. An equity in family jewelry, not to exceed $500 in value.
5. An equity in any property up to $400, plus any unused amount of the $7,500 household exemption in (1). This provision offers additional protection for the debtor who does not own a home.
6. An equity in implements, professional books, or tools used in the trade of the debtor or dependents, not to exceed $750 in value.
7. Any unmatured life insurance contract owned by the debtor.
8. Debtor's right to receive social security benefits, unemployment benefits, veterans benefits, or disability benefits.

If a case is properly structured, the debtor may retain a substantial portion of property because of the exemptions. Since a debtor may use either the state or federal exemptions, a couple filing jointly may enjoy the better features of each. One spouse may use the federal list, which is more generous in regard to personal property, while the other selects the state list, which may be more liberal in regard to real property. For example, Wisconsin law permits a debtor to retain a $25,000 equity in a homestead, in contrast to the $7,500 equity permitted by the federal law. If the debtor has a homestead worth $100,000, with a $75,000 mortgage, Wisconsin law allows retention of the $25,000 equity and, therefore, of the home. The retainable equity interest may be increased to $32,500 under a joint filing if advantage of the federal law is retained by one spouse, who selects the $7,500 federal household equity exemption. These features have caused some to comment that the Act is unduly generous to the debtor at the expense of creditors.

As soon as possible after issuing the order for relief, the court appoints an interim trustee to take charge until a permanent trustee is selected, and then a meeting of creditors is called. Creditors either may elect a permanent trustee or have the interim trustee serve in that capacity. If desired, creditors may elect a committee of 3 to 11 creditors to assist and advise the trustee in the administration of the estate. Only creditors who have filed a written proof of claim at or before the meeting are entitled to vote. Proofs of claim are examined by the trustee, who may accept them or, if they are improper, disallow them. To be considered in the settlement, a claim normally must be filed within six months after the date set for the first meeting of creditors.

The debtor is required to be present at the meeting of creditors in order to be subject to examination by the creditors or the trustee and must cooperate with the trustee in the preparation of an inventory of property, the examination of proofs of claim, and the general administration of the estate. To assist the trustee, a debtor files a *statement of affairs,* consisting of answers to a series of stated questions about the identity of the debtor's records and books, transactions, and events affecting the financial condition of the debtor, including any prior bankruptcy proceedings. This *legal* statement of affairs is not to be confused with the *accounting* statement of affairs discussed later in the chapter.

Duties of Trustee. The trustee shall:

1. Collect and reduce to money the nonexempt property of the estate.
2. Account for all money and property received, maintaining a record of cash receipts and disbursements.
3. Investigate the financial affairs of the debtor, including a review of the forms filed by the debtor.
4. Examine proofs of claim and disallow any improper claim.
5. Furnish information reasonably requested by a party of interest.
6. Operate the business of the debtor, if any, when so authorized by the court if such operation is in the best interest of the estate and consistent with its orderly liquidation.
7. Pay dividends to creditors as promptly as practicable, with regard for priorities. (The law applies the term "dividend" to any payment made to a creditor.)
8. File reports of progress, with the final report accompanied by a detailed statement of receipts and disbursements.

Disposition of Property. One duty of the trustee is to dispose of property, even if another entity has an allowed claim secured by a lien on the property. The claim is secured to the amount of the value of the property. For example, if a creditor has an allowed claim of $20,000, with a sole lien against real property whose market value is $30,000, the claim is fully secured. Upon realization of the property, the excess of $10,000 would be available to meet unsecured claims in the order of priority. If the creditor in the example has an allowed claim of $35,000, there is a secured claim of $30,000 and an unsecured claim of $5,000.

Priorities for Unsecured Claims. An order of priority to receive distributions from amounts available to meet unsecured claims has been established by the Act. Each rank must be paid in full or provided for before any amount is paid to the next lower rank. When the amount is inadequate to pay all claims of a given rank, the amount is distributed on a pro rata basis within that rank. When the amount is sufficient to pay the claims of all ranks, which is highly unlikely, the excess amount is returned to the debtor. The order of priority for allowed unsecured claims is as follows:

1. Expenses to administer the estate. Those who administer the estate should be assured of payment; otherwise, competent attorneys and accountants would not be willing to participate.
2. Debts incurred after the commencement of a case of involuntary bankruptcy but before the order for relief or appointment of a trustee. These items are granted priority in order to permit the business to carry on its operations during the period of legal proceedings.
3. Wages up to $2,000 per individual, earned within 90 days before the filing of the petition or the cessation of the debtor's business, whichever occurs first.

4. Unpaid contributions to employee benefit plans to the extent of $2,000 per employee covered by the plan, less any amount paid to participating employees under priority 3.
5. Deposits up to $900 each for goods or services never received from the debtor.
6. Tax claims of a governmental unit. Since these taxes are nondischargeable (i.e., they still must be met by the debtor after the termination of the case), the arrangement favors the debtor. Whatever funds are available for this priority will reduce the amount the debtor will have to pay later. For this reason, if a governmental unit fails to file a claim for taxes, the Act permits the debtor to do so.
7. Claims of general creditors not granted priority. All remaining unsecured claims fall into this category.

For a successful case under Chapter 11 (Reorganization) or Chapter 13 (Individual), the sequence of priority also has significance. In a Chapter 11 case, the plan of reorganization will not be confirmed unless the court has determined that creditors will receive at least as much as they would under Chapter 7. The same idea is used for Chapter 13 cases, for which the Code states that the court will approve the plan only if the value of the property to be distributed on account of each allowed unsecured claim is not less than the amount that would be paid under Chapter 7.

Discharge of Debtor. After the trustee has issued the final report, the court will grant a discharge of indebtedness, provided that the debtor is an individual and has not committed any act that would deny discharge, such as fraud, lack of cooperation, or having been granted a discharge within the past six years. The discharge absolves the debtor from debts that arose before the order for relief and voids any action to recover on such debts. Certain debts survive discharge and continue to be the responsibility of the debtor. These debts are referred to as *nondischargeable debts* and include the following:

1. Tax claims of a governmental unit.
2. Debts resulting from obtaining property or services under false pretenses.
3. Claims known by the debtor but not listed, unless the creditor had ample notice to file.
4. A claim against the debtor for larceny, embezzlement, or fraud.
5. Alimony and child support payments.
6. Debts for willful and malicious injury by the debtor to another entity or to property.
7. Fines and penalties payable to a governmental unit.
8. Most debts for educational loans, unless they first became due more than five years before the date of the petition.
9. Debts declared nondischargeable in an earlier bankruptcy proceeding.

Except for the claims listed, the discharge accomplishes the primary purpose of bankruptcy proceedings—granting the debtor a fresh start by providing relief from indebtedness.

CHAPTER 11—REORGANIZATION

The ultimate purpose of an action under Chapter 11, either voluntary or involuntary, is to formulate and have confirmed a plan of reorganization that will permit continued operation of the business. Generally, the debtor remains in charge. A trustee may be appointed, but only for just cause, such as proven fraud or the debtor's inability to manage. Whether the debtor remains in possession or a trustee is appointed, the same legal statement of affairs must be filed, as in the case of a liquidation. A decision must be made on the wisdom of continuing the business operation. In addition, a plan of reorganization must be designed and approved, or a recommendation to convert to a liquidation under Chapter 7 or a debt adjustment plan under Chapter 13 must be made.

After the filing of the petition, the law provides that the debtor shall not be harassed by creditors or stockholders in order to afford the debtor the opportunity to devote full energy to the reorganization. For the first 120 days, the debtor has the exclusive right to file a plan of reorganization. Thereafter, a plan may be filed by any party of interest. The court appoints a committee of the creditors holding the seven largest claims against the debtor. A committee of equity security holders also may be appointed. Their primary functions are to consult with the debtor in possession (or the trustee) about the administration of the case and to assist in the formulation of a plan of reorganization.

Companies have used Chapter 11 procedures to gain court protection for a broad spectrum of purposes. In 1982, front-page headlines announced that Manville Corporation, the largest asbestos company in the world, filed a petition for reorganization and protection. At the time, it ranked 181st in *Fortune's* list of the nation's leading industrial corporations. Amazing was the fact that, with net assets of over $2 billion, it was a financially healthy company. However, lawsuits at the rate of 500 a month were being brought against the company by workers who allegedly had developed lung cancer and other diseases as a result of their exposure to asbestos. Its chairperson, John A. McKinney, estimated that, at the going settlement rate of $40,000 per case, a reserve fund of at least $2 billion would have to be created, virtually wiping out its net worth and crippling operations. The board of directors filed under Chapter 11 to establish an effective method for handling the asbestos claims.

In April, 1987, Texaco filed under Chapter 11. Thus began the largest bankruptcy case to date. Texaco had assets of $34 billion and liabilities of $20 billion. It filed to delay and possibly reduce the history-making $10.5 billion judgment against it awarded to Pennzoil Company in 1985. Texaco had been found guilty of improper and illegal action when it disrupted the merger pact that was in process between Pennzoil and Getty Oil. Texaco was trying to prevent possible panic among its creditors if it had to commit billions of dollars of assets as security for payment while it sought relief from the enormous damage award.

In May, 1988, LTV Corporation unveiled a Chapter 11 reorganization plan to pay $6.2 billion in debt. This sum did not include $2 billion for underfunding of its pension plans. LTV claimed that it was the responsibility of the federal agency, Pension Benefit Guaranty Corporation, to safeguard the pensions of workers of a failing company. The agency maintained that LTV was capable of funding its retirement plans. The company responded that, if it was forced to do so, it would have to sell its aerospace and defense units, thereby jeopardizing possible recovery. So important was the decision that U.S. District Judge Robert W. Sweet ordered a full trial to enable both parties to garner and present more evidence.

Generally, Chapter 11 is not successful in protecting assets outside of the United States. Foreign courts typically do not recognize the concept of bankruptcy reorganization. *Business Week* made the comment that, to foreign creditors, reorganization means "grab the assets."[1] When U.S. Lines, Inc., with its fleet of 27 ships, filed for protection from creditors in 1986, the following events occurred:

Belgium — Local courts placed Lines' Belgium assets under a trustee.
England — British courts froze company assets and bank accounts.
Italy — Courts placed company assets in Italy in receivership.
Hong Kong — Creditors seized four ships and auctioned them for $16 million. The ships cost U.S. Lines $184 million.
Netherlands — Dutch creditors seized Lines' European headquarters building and filed involuntary bankruptcy proceedings.[2]

Recent events have strengthened the position of those who are critical of the manner in which Chapter 11 has been manipulated. It was designed to assist those in difficulty under the conventional interpretation of indebtedness. On the docket of bankruptcy courts have been companies who have filed in order to protect themselves from mass tort litigations (Manville, with its asbestos products, and A. H. Robins Inc., with its Dalkon Shield contraceptive device), to ward off enforcement of huge judgments (Texaco), or to escape funding of pension plans (LTV Corporation). It is doubtful that Congress intended bankruptcy laws to be an umbrella of corporate protection with such serious public consequences. One congressman referred to such court decisions as "a puzzling misreading of congressional intent."

Plan of Reorganization. The plan of reorganization must detail the methods and means by which it will achieve its objectives. Possible arrangements will involve eliminating some debt, reducing debt principal and/or interest,

---

[1]Todd Vogel, "There's No Word for Chapter 11 in Dutch," *Business Week* (November 30, 1987): 62.
[2]*Ibid.*

reducing interest rates, postponing payment, and exchanging an equity interest for creditor claims or exchanging a lower ranking for a higher equity interest, such as substitution of common stock for preferred stock. The plan identifies the various classes of claims (secured versus unsecured) and classes of interests (stockholders or limited partners). It indicates the claims or interests that are not impaired, as well as the treatment to be accorded those that are impaired. A class is impaired if the plan alters its legal or contractual rights.

If a class is not impaired, it is considered to have accepted the plan. The holder of a claim or interest impaired by the plan may accept or reject it. If at least two-thirds in amount and more than one-half in number of a class of claims and if at least two-thirds in amount of a class of interests accept a plan, it may be confirmed by the court. Before confirmation, the court verifies that each holder of a claim or interest will receive or retain under the plan property of a value that is not less than the amount such holder would receive under a Chapter 7 liquidation.

Once a plan is confirmed by the court, its provisions are binding on the debtor and on all creditors and equity security holders, whether or not they accepted the plan. Confirmation vests property of the estate in the debtor in possession or trustee. Such property is free of all claims of creditors and interests of equity holders, except as stipulated in the provisions of the plan. Under Chapter 11, once a plan is confirmed, the payment obligation of the debtor is fixed, regardless of any subsequent increase in the debtor's net cash inflow. If the reorganization is not accomplishing its intended objectives during the period outlined in the plan, a request for modification may be submitted to the court for approval, or a request may be filed to convert to a Chapter 7 liquidation or to a Chapter 13 adjustment of debts, whichever will be in the best interest of the parties involved. Subsequent procedures must follow those applicable to the appropriate chapter.

Accounting for a Reorganization. In accounting for a reorganization, it is useful to introduce the account, Reorganization Capital, in which to collect the results of changes in the interests of various parties. To illustrate, various portions of an approved plan of reorganization are described and recorded as follows:

Reorganization Plan	Entry		
100,000 shares of $50 par common are replaced by 100,000 shares of $10 par common.	Common Stock ($50 par).......	5,000,000	
	Common Stock ($10 par)		1,000,000
	Reorganization Capital........		4,000,000
Preferred stockholders relinquish undeclared dividends in arrears of $160,000.	No entry is made, since dividends are undeclared and would appear only in the notes to the financial statements.		
Bondholders will not collect $100,000 of unpaid interest.	Accrued Interest Payable.......	100,000	
	Reorganization Capital........		100,000

Reorganization Plan	Entry		
Plant and equipment is to be reduced by $2,000,000, decreasing future depreciation charges and reflecting fair, but not unduly conservative, amounts.	Reorganization Capital........... Plant and Equipment (or Accumulated Depreciation).................	2,000,000	2,000,000
Unsecured creditors reflected in Vouchers Payable will receive 40 cents on the dollar for the $1,000,000 owed.	Vouchers Payable................. Reorganization Capital........	600,000	600,000
The deficit of $2,100,000 is to be eliminated.	Reorganization Capital........... Retained Earnings............	2,100,000	2,100,000

At this point, Retained Earnings shows no balance, and the account should be dated, as in the case of quasi-reorganizations. If the plan has been accomplished fully, the balance of $600,000 in Reorganization Capital would be shown on future balance sheets as a part of paid-in capital rather than retained earnings.

CHAPTER 13—ADJUSTMENT OF DEBTS OF AN INDIVIDUAL WITH REGULAR INCOME

Cases under Chapter 13 have become more numerous under the new law. Formerly, the individual had to be a wage earner, which excluded single proprietors. The Act now permits any individual whose income is sufficiently stable to meet payments under a proposed plan to request financial comfort under Chapter 13, provided that unsecured claims against the debtor do not exceed $100,000 and secured claims do not exceed $350,000. Only the debtor may file a plan to meet obligations under Chapter 13. There is no involuntary approach; debtors cannot be forced into a plan under this chapter. Upon the voluntary filing of a plan by the debtor, a trustee is appointed, whose primary responsibilities are to be present at any hearings and to advise and assist the debtor in carrying out the plan. If a business is involved, the debtor remains in charge, with the trustee reviewing its operation.

To be confirmed, the debtor's plan must provide for the transmission of all or such part of the future earnings as will permit its successful execution. The plan may modify the rights of secured claim holders or of unsecured claims, with the following restrictions:

1. That each secured claim holder has accepted the plan, or provision is made for transfer of the property securing such claim to its holder.
2. That unsecured claims entitled to priority (pages 1134 and 1135) will be paid in full under a deferred payment arrangement.
3. That other unsecured claims shall be treated equitably and shall receive

not less than they would under a Chapter 7 liquidation. No approval by unsecured claim holders is required.

After due notice, the court will hold a hearing and issue a confirmation of the plan if there is no unresolved objection and no violation of the chapter. The plan normally should not extend beyond three years except by specific approval of the court, in which case it may be extended, but not to exceed two additional years. Once confirmed, the plan binds the debtor and claimants. However, under Chapter 13, a creditor or the trustee may compel a postconfirmation modification of the plan if the debtor's income increases beyond expectation during the term of the plan. The debtor remains in possession of all property of the estate, including earnings from the debtor's services from the inception of the case until discharge. At any time, a debtor voluntarily may request a conversion from this chapter to another chapter under the Act. If the debtor fails to comply with the plan or displays unusual delay prejudicial to carrying out its requirements, any party in interest may request the court for a conversion to Chapters 7 or 11 if such action is in the best interest of the parties concerned.

When conditions of the plan have been met and payments have been completed, the court will issue a discharge, relieving the debtor of obligations provided for by the plan. A discharge may be granted by the court after a hearing, even if plan payments have not been completed, if failure to make payments is the result of circumstances over which the debtor did not have control, as in the case of a natural catastrophe that destroys the debtor's assets.

ACCOUNTING STATEMENT OF AFFAIRS

Earlier in this chapter, a reference was made to the legal statement of affairs, which consists of responses to questions regarding a debtor's financial condition. The other report with the same name is the accounting statement of affairs, which is discussed in this section of the chapter. Under both a reorganization and an adjustment of the debts of an individual, the plans will not be confirmed by the court unless creditors will receive at least as much as they would under a liquidation. It is mandatory, therefore, that the estimated amounts to be received by all parties be determined. The primary purpose of the accounting statement of affairs is to approximate the estimated amounts available to each class of claims. It thereby assists all concerned parties in reaching a decision as to what insolvency action is preferable. It is a balance sheet of a potentially liquidating concern rather than of a going concern. Thus, it shifts the emphasis for assets from historical cost to estimated realizable values and the allocation of proceeds to creditors and stockholders.

In the past, the preparation and the format of the statement of affairs have been cumbersome and confusing. Thus, a revised form is recommended, in which the statement of affairs is split into two sections, one dealing with the assets and the other with the liabilities and the owners' equity. Before the statement of affairs is prepared, however, the account balances should be adjusted fully, an income statement should be prepared, and owners' equity should be adjusted to include the net profit or net loss to date.

The asset portion of the statement of affairs in revised form would have the following columnar headings:

Assets	Book Values	Shrinkage or (Excess)	Estimated Realizable Value	Assignable to	
				Secured	Unsecured

The asset account titles and their adjusted book values are entered in the first two columns. Working with net balances is helpful since the elimination of contra accounts, such as Allowance for Doubtful Accounts or Accumulated Depreciation, permits the direct calculation of the shrinkage or excess on realization.

The equity section is designed with the following columnar headings:

Liabilities and Owners' Equity	Book Values		Claims of		
	Owners' Equity	Liabili- ties	Secured	Unsecured	
				Class 1–6	Class 7

Equity accounts are listed and their adjusted balances are entered in either the Owners' Equity or the Liabilities column. Since the last three columns represent the reclassification of liabilities into legal categories, the process is easier if all liabilities appear in the adjacent column. After the amounts are entered in the book value columns, the combined sum of the Owners' Equity and Liabilities columns should equal the total of the asset Book Values column.

For each asset, the net realizable value must be estimated, using whatever information is available. For example, receivables would exclude unrealizable amounts; marketable securities would be based on current market reports; and real estate would reflect current market appraisals. Some assets, such as goodwill, may have no realizable value. The estimated realizable values are entered in the third amount column to facilitate assignment to the two categories that follow. For each asset, the difference between realizable value and book value is entered as a shrinkage or an excess. Total shrinkage or excess and total amount realizable are determined. These totals are verifiable since total book values plus net excess or minus net shrinkage must equal total realizable values of the assets.

Estimated realizable amounts are allocated so that the amounts can be identified with the appropriate type of claim. When the amount realizable from pledged assets exceeds the claim, an amount equal to the claim is entered in the Secured column of the asset section, and any excess is entered in the Unsecured column. At the same time, in the equity section, the corresponding liability is classified as Secured. If the estimated realizable value of pledged assets is less than the claim, the entire amount expected to be realized is entered in the Secured column of the asset section, the same amount is entered in the equity section in the Secured column, and the unsecured portion of the liability is extended as a Class 7 unsecured claim, as described on page 1134.

The simultaneous completion of the asset and equity sections of the statement of affairs is limited to secured portions of claims. The estimated proceeds from assets on which there is no lien are entered in the Unsecured column of the asset section, and no related entry is made in the equity section. When all estimated asset proceeds have been extended, the accuracy of the assignment of the assets should be checked by verifying that the combined totals of the amounts assigned to the Secured and Unsecured columns equal the Estimated Realizable Value column total.

In the equity section, any remaining liabilities that have not been classified must be unsecured. The six classes having a priority are grouped to determine if their total claims can be met. Class 7 claims are shown separately. The combined totals of the three columns of claims must equal the total of the Liabilities column.

The total of unsecured claims that have priority (Classes 1 through 6) is subtracted from the total realizable amount available for unsecured creditors in the asset section. The resulting difference represents the amount available to Class 7 general creditors. If the amount available for these creditors is less than their claims, there is a deficiency. If the amount available is greater than their claims, the general creditors may expect payment in full, and the excess would become available for the owners. The estimated amount available for the unsecured creditors may be inadequate to cover unsecured claims with priority in Classes 1 through 6. In this situation, the sequence of priority stipulated in the Act must be followed.

To illustrate the preparation of a statement of affairs, assume the following data for Troubled Corporation:

1. Cash includes $300 of uncollectible IOU memos.
2. Receivables are estimated to produce $14,000.
3. Marketable securities have a market value of $9,000.
4. Sale of inventories should yield $11,000.
5. Land and buildings can be sold for $12,000 cash, with the buyer assuming the mortgage and its unpaid interest.

6. The machinery will realize $4,000, of which $3,000 must be assigned to a creditor (account payable) who is owed $3,800.
7. All salaries qualify for priority.

The following fully adjusted balance sheet for Troubled Corporation is the basis for the statement of affairs on page 1144.

Troubled Corporation
Balance Sheet
February 28, 19X0

Assets

Current assets:

Cash		$ 4,000
Accounts receivable	$20,000	
Less allowance for doubtful accounts	2,000	18,000
Marketable securities		8,000
Inventories		40,000	$ 70,000

Property, plant, and equipment:

	Cost	Accumulated Depreciation	Book Value	
Land	$ 10,000	—	$10,000	
Buildings	70,000	$20,000	50,000	
Machinery	30,000	16,000	14,000	
Total	$110,000	$36,000		74,000

Goodwill	6,000
Total assets	$150,000

Liabilities and Stockholders' Equity

Current liabilities:

Accounts payable	$45,000	
Accrued income taxes	4,000	
Accrued interest on mortgage payable	2,000	
Accrued salaries	13,000	$ 64,000

Long-term liability:

Mortgage payable	50,000
Total liabilities	$114,000

Stockholders' equity:

Common stock	$54,000	
Additional paid-in capital	6,000	
Deficit	(24,000)	36,000
Total liabilities and stockholders' equity		$150,000

Troubled Corporation
Statement of Affairs
February 28, 19X0

Assets	Book Values	Shrinkage or (Excess)	Estimated Realizable Value	Assignable to Secured	Assignable to Unsecured
Cash	$ 4,000	$ 300	$ 3,700		$ 3,700
Accounts receivable (net).................	18,000	4,000	14,000		14,000
Marketable securities..........	8,000	(1,000)	9,000		9,000
Inventories...........	40,000	29,000	11,000		11,000
Land	10,000 ⎫	(4,000)	64,000	$52,000	12,000
Buildings (net).......	50,000 ⎭				
Machinery (net).....	14,000	10,000	4,000	3,000	1,000
Goodwill..............	6,000	6,000	–0–		
Total	$150,000	$44,300	$105,700	$55,000	$50,700
Less unsecured claims with priority (Class 1 through 6)					17,000
Available for Class 7 unsecured claims					$33,700
Class 7 unsecured claims					(42,000)
Deficiency to unsecured creditors in Class 7...................................					($ 8,300)

Liabilities and Owners' Equity	Book Values Owners' Equity	Book Values Liabilities	Claims of Secured	Claims of Unsecured Class 1-6	Claims of Unsecured Class 7
Accounts payable		$ 45,000	$ 3,000		$42,000
Accrued items:					
Income taxes		4,000		$ 4,000	
Interest on mortgage payable		2,000	2,000		
Salaries		13,000		13,000	
Mortgage payable		50,000	50,000		
Common stock..............	$54,000				
Additional paid-in capital	6,000				
Deficit	(24,000)				
Total	$36,000	$114,000	$55,000	$17,000	$42,000

Since the amount of owners' equity functions as a financial cushion for creditors, the deficiency of $8,300 for Troubled Corporation is verified as follows:

Net shrinkage of assets per statement of affairs....................................	$44,300
Less stockholders' equity	36,000
Deficiency...	$ 8,300

Of interest to the unsecured creditors in Class 7 and the bankruptcy court is a ratio that is referred to as the *dividend* to general unsecured creditors. This ratio is computed as follows:

$$\text{Dividend} = \frac{\text{Net proceeds available to unsecured creditors in Class 7}}{\text{Total claims of unsecured creditors in Class 7}}$$

The dividend is an estimate of how much will be received by Class 7 unsecured creditors for each dollar owed to them, and it is expressed either in absolute amount or in percentage form.

The approximate dividend to Class 7 unsecured creditors of Troubled Corporation will be:

$$\frac{\$33,700}{\$42,000} = \$.80 \text{ on } \$1, \text{ or } 80\%$$

The secured portion of claims receives 100 cents on the dollar. Since some claims are in part fully secured and in part unsecured, they may receive different percentages of their claim, depending upon the proportion that is secured. For example, one of the accounts payable of $3,800 had a lien on machinery that is expected to realize $3,000. For the remaining $800, the amount realizable is 80%, or $640. Thus, the creditor may expect to receive $3,640, or approximately 96% of the $3,800 claim.

In a manufacturing organization, where inventories are in various stages of completion, the preparation of the statement of affairs is simplified if inventories are entered at estimated book values based on projected actions. For example, assume that the following inventory amounts appear in the trial balance of a manufacturing company:

Finished goods	$110,000
Work in process	200,000
Materials	77,000

The plant manager estimates that the work in process in its present stages of completion would realize only $30,000 as scrap. However, if the work in process is completed by adding $27,000 of materials now on hand and by incurring $40,000 of additional labor and overhead, an estimated $180,000 can be realized. Thus, by investing $67,000 of additional materials, labor, and overhead, $150,000 may be gained.

If the book value of materials is realized, if $120,000 is realized for goods already completed, and if the decision is made to complete work in process, one method to show the inventories in the statement of affairs would be based on the estimated cash inflow, reduced by any required cash outlay, as follows:

Assets	Book Values	Shrinkage or (Excess)	Estimated Realizable Value
Finished goods	$110,000	($10,000)	$120,000
Work in process	200,000	60,000	140,000*
Materials	77,000	27,000	50,000

*Realizable value of $180,000 less $40,000 additional labor and overhead cost.

This portrayal is inaccurate, however, since the total book value of materials would be realized either by requisition to complete the work in process or by sale. The labor and overhead cost probably would not be met from the proceeds of the sale of inventory, but from whatever cash is available. Furthermore, it is not the work in process inventory that will be realized, but that inventory converted to its finished state. Therefore, a better procedure would be to adjust the inventory balances to reflect the amounts that would result if suggested actions were consummated. The amounts are determined as shown in the following T accounts, using a cost completion approach:

	Materials		Work in Process		Finished Goods	
Beginning balances...	77,000		200,000		110,000	
Transfer of materials ..		27,000	27,000			
Additional labor and overhead ..			40,000			
Transfer to finished goods				267,000	267,000	
Balances for statement of affairs...	50,000		0		377,000	

The revised inventories would appear in the statement of affairs as follows:

Assets	Book Values	Shrinkage or (Excess)	Estimated Realizable Value
Finished goods	$377,000	$77,000	$300,000
Work in process...........................	–0–		–0–
Materials	50,000	–0–	50,000

With this procedure, it is apparent that no shrinkage resulted from the realization of materials, that work in process inventory was completed, and that finished goods would yield $300,000. The additional labor and overhead of $40,000 must appear in the equity section as accrued liabilities and would rank as a Class 2 unsecured claim.

In addition to its use in an insolvency situation, the statement of affairs would be useful when a company is seeking additional capital and wishes to demonstrate the strength of its financial position. The statement would be especially helpful when a company's assets have appreciated substantially. Another potential user of the statement is a company that anticipates the sale of a bond issue. If such a company prepared a pro forma statement of affairs, potential buyers of the bonds could be shown what conditions might be if the bonds were sold and the proceeds were applied to the intended project.

FIDUCIARY ACCOUNTING AND REPORTING

A fiduciary relationship is established whenever one person is entrusted with the property of another and must account for and report on its stewardship to the interested parties. In Chapter 7 liquidation cases, a fiduciary (the trustee) is responsible for specified assets, including those involved in the operation of the debtor's business until it is sold. Although the debtor usually remains in possession of the business in Chapter 11 reorganizations, a trustee may be appointed if there is evidence of mismanagement, fraud, or incompetence.

ACCOUNTING RECORDS AND PROCEDURES

To illustrate fiduciary accounting resulting from the Act, assume that a trustee has been appointed under a Chapter 11 corporate reorganization, requiring partial liquidation of a mismanaged segment of operations, after which control is returned to a new group of officers. The fiduciary may continue with the accounting records already in existence or may initiate a new set, the latter procedure being more common because it isolates results more clearly. If new accounting records are to be established, the assets accepted by the fiduciary are debited at their book values, with a credit to an account called X Corporation in Trusteeship. On the corporate books, the transfer of assets is recorded by debiting an account to charge the fiduciary, such as E. Schenker, Trustee. These new accounts are reciprocal and represent the accountability of the trustee.

The fiduciary is not responsible for commitments made by the corporation prior to the period of stewardship. Therefore, those liabilities remain on the corporate books. However, the courts may direct payment of such liabilities. In this case, the trustee either may debit X Corporation in Trusteeship directly or create a temporary account, such as Accounts Payable—X Corporation, which periodically is closed into the major reciprocal account. The corporation would reflect payment with a debit to Accounts Payable and a credit to the account E. Schenker, Trustee.

The usual accounting procedures are followed by the trustee to record revenues and expenses. At the end of the year or at termination of the period of stewardship, the profit or loss on the trustee's books is closed into the accountability account, X Corporation in Trusteeship. On the corporate books, net income is recorded with a debit to the trustee account and a credit to Retained Earnings, while a net loss is recorded by the reverse procedure. When control is returned to the owners, the trustee eliminates all account balances, including the X Corporation in Trusteeship balance. The corporation records these accounts and eliminates the trustee account.

While the trustee is in control, the corporation's financial story is contained partly in the records of the trustee and partly in those of the corporation. The two records must be combined in order to prepare financial statements. The following skeleton worksheet is designed to accomplish the objective of reuniting the two sets of financial information:

X Corporation in Trusteeship
E. Schenker, Trustee
Worksheet for Combined Trial Balance
For Year Ended June 30, 19X1

Account Title	Trial Balance Trustee	Trial Balance Corporation	Adjustments and Eliminations		Combined Trial Balance
Debits: E. Schenker, Trustee		90,000		(a)90,000	
Total debits	500,000	420,000			
Credits: X Corp. in Trusteeship	90,000		(a)90,000		
Total credits	500,000	420,000			

The worksheet begins with the trial balances of the trustee's records and the corporation's records. These trial balances should be adjusted fully before they are entered on the worksheet. Any additional adjustments discovered subsequently are entered, and the two reciprocal account balances are eliminated. The items then are combined to produce a trial balance from which financial statements may be prepared.

REALIZATION AND LIQUIDATION ACCOUNT

After a trustee is appointed, the court expects to receive periodic reports on the status of the fiduciary's activities. The special report for this purpose is a legal form, called the *realization and liquidation account*. The conventional realization and liquidation account derives the title "account" from its structure, which resembles a T account. The statement consists of three main sections: assets, liabilities, and revenues and expenses.

The assets section is divided into four parts, as follows:

Realization and Liquidation Account
Assets

Assets to be realized: (Itemized assets originally accepted by fiduciary)	Assets realized: (Itemized proceeds of assets realized by fiduciary)
Assets acquired (or discovered): (Itemized assets subsequently acquired by fiduciary)	Assets not realized: (Itemized)

In the Assets To Be Realized section, assets accepted by the fiduciary are itemized at book value amounts. Cash is excluded from the assets section since it already is "realized." As an adjunct to the report, however, the court is provided with a duplication of the cash account, which shows the beginning balance of cash as well as all receipts and disbursements. Supplementary detail also is furnished for the owners' equity. Neither the supplementary cash schedule nor the owners' equity detail is considered a part of the formal realization and liquidation account.

Additional noncash assets acquired by the fiduciary through normal activities, such as receivables resulting from sales on open account, are presented under Assets Acquired. Also included in this section are assets discovered by the fiduciary, such as additional inventory. The combination of assets to be realized and assets acquired represents the total noncash asset responsibility of the fiduciary.

Under the usual procedure, the proceeds from any asset realized are shown in the Assets Realized section. The book values of assets still unrealized at the end of the period are listed in the final section, Assets Not Realized. This procedure, however, has some weaknesses, one of which is the treatment of the gain or loss on realization of an asset. For example, if land that is carried in Assets To Be Realized at $10,000 is sold for $15,000, the entire $15,000 proceeds usually would be shown in Assets Realized, without specifically identifying the gain. If book values, rather than proceeds, are listed in Assets Realized and if the gain is presented in the revenues and expenses section, tighter control is possible since the following relationship will result:

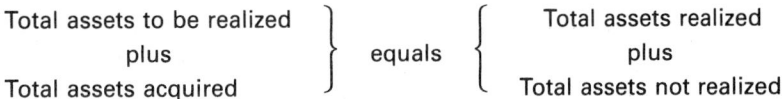

Total assets to be realized plus Total assets acquired equals Total assets realized plus Total assets not realized

Another example of the weakness of the gross proceeds approach is the treatment of the sale of merchandise. The proceeds of the sale would appear in the Assets Realized section and also would appear either as an increase in cash in the supplementary cash schedule or as an asset acquired in the form of receivables. Nowhere would the gross profit or loss appear. If the typical accounting approach was followed, however, the sales revenue and cost of sales would be shown in the revenues and expenses section.

Although the same net income or net loss will result from either procedure, the recommended approach seldom is found. To date, courts have been reluctant to adopt the book value approach for reflecting disposition of assets, as normally is done in accounting. Therefore, most of the discussion that follows will adhere to the conventional legal format in spite of its limitations.

The conventional report also is peculiar in its treatment of depreciation. For example, equipment accepted by the fiduciary at a net book value of $6,000, which is not yet realized and which has depreciated $1,000 at the time of the report, typically is shown in the respective sections of the realization and liquidation account as follows:

Partial Realization and Liquidation Account	
Assets	
Assets to be realized:	
Equipment (net)............ $6,000	
	Assets not realized:
	Equipment (net)........ $5,000

The $1,000 of depreciation is not shown explicitly. If it is desired to maintain the equality of the four divisions of the assets category, the depreciation could be shown as an expense and as an asset realized, as follows:

Partial Realization and Liquidation Account	
Assets	
Assets to be realized:	Assets realized:
Equipment (net)............ $6,000	Equipment depreciation.. $1,000
	Assets not realized:
	Equipment (net)........ $5,000

The liabilities section of the realization and liquidation account also is segmented into four parts, as follows:

Realization and Liquidation Account (continued)	
Liabilities	
Liabilities liquidated:	Liabilities to be liquidated:
(Itemized)	(Itemized)
Liabilities not liquidated:	Liabilities incurred:
(Itemized)	(Itemized)

The Liabilities To Be Liquidated section includes the liabilities that existed when the fiduciary was appointed. Additional liabilities arising after that time are listed under Liabilities Incurred. At the end of the period, either the liabilities will be paid or they remain "to be liquidated."

Book values are used more commonly in the liabilities section than in the assets section. Thus, the following relationship exists:

$$\left.\begin{array}{c}\text{Liabilities liquidated}\\ \text{plus}\\ \text{Liabilities not liquidated}\end{array}\right\} \text{equals} \left\{\begin{array}{c}\text{Liabilities to be liquidated}\\ \text{plus}\\ \text{Liabilities incurred}\end{array}\right.$$

When settlement of a liability is made at less than its book value, it is recommended that the gain on the settlement be shown in Supplementary Revenues, so that this relationship is maintained.

The revenues and expenses section of the realization and liquidation account lists the expenses incurred by the fiduciary and the revenues earned during the period of stewardship, as follows:

Realization and Liquidation Account (continued)	
Revenues and Expenses	
Supplementary expenses: (Itemized)	Supplementary revenues: (Itemized)

The quantity and nature of the supplementary expenses and revenues included will depend on the manner in which asset and liability movements are portrayed. If book values are used, the gains and losses on these movements are listed with the expenses or the revenues, and the net income or net loss is produced within the revenues and expenses section itself. If presentation is based on gross proceeds, there are fewer items in this section, and the section is less revealing because none of the gains or losses is shown. To determine the net income or net loss under the conventional gross proceeds method, it is necessary to add all debits and all credits for the three sections involved—assets, liabilities, and revenues and expenses. The difference between the two totals equals the net income or net loss for the reporting period.

To illustrate the preparation of a realization and liquidation account, assume that Troubled Corporation on pages 1142–1145 is insolvent. Under Chapter 7, a trustee is appointed. All liabilities are liquidated, except the Class 7 claims and the $2,000 fee of the trustee. Assets realized the following amounts during the next ten months:

Assets	Book Value	Amount Realized
Accounts receivable.........	$ 9,000	$ 7,000
Marketable securities.......	4,000	5,000
Inventories.....................	40,000	11,000 sold on account
Land and buildings...........	60,000	12,000 cash plus assumption of mortgage and interest
Machinery.....................	14,000	4,000
Goodwill.......................	6,000	–0–

The realization and liquidation account under the conventional form of presentation appears in Illustration 22–1 on page 1152. The supplementary schedules of cash and owners' equity appear on page 1153.

Illustration 22–1

Conventional Approach

Troubled Corporation
Realization and Liquidation Account
For the Ten Months Ended December 31, 19X0
Submitted by J. Hart, Trustee

Assets

Assets to be realized:			**Assets realized:**		
Accounts receivable (net)—old	$18,000		Accounts receivable— old	$ 7,000	
Marketable securities	8,000		Marketable securities	5,000	
Inventories...............	40,000		Inventories..............	11,000	
Land........................	10,000		Land }	64,000	
Buildings (net)..........	50,000		Buildings }		
Machinery (net)	14,000		Machinery...............	4,000	$ 91,000
Goodwill..................	6,000	$146,000			
Assets acquired:			**Assets not realized:**		
Accounts receivable— new (from sale of inventory)		11,000	Accounts receivable —old	$ 9,000	
			—new..................	11,000	
			Marketable securities	4,000	24,000

Liabilities

Liabilities liquidated:			**Liabilities to be liquidated:**		
Accounts payable	$ 3,000		Accounts payable	$45,000	
Accrued income taxes...................	4,000		Accrued income taxes	4,000	
Accrued interest on mortgage payable..	2,000		Accrued interest on mortgage payable..	2,000	
Accrued salaries.......	13,000		Accrued salaries.......	13,000	
Mortgage payable.....	50,000	72,000	Mortgage payable.....	50,000	114,000
Liabilities not liquidated:			**Liabilities incurred:**		
Accounts payable	$42,000		Trustee's fee payable		2,000
Trustee's fee payble ..	2,000	44,000			

Revenues and Expenses

Supplementary expenses:			**Supplementary revenues:**		
Trustee's fee		2,000	(none)		
Subtotal................		$275,000	Subtotal................		$231,000
			Net loss................		44,000
		$275,000			$275,000

Supplementary Schedules

Cash

Beginning balance.........................	$ 4,000	Cash IOUs written off...................	$ 300
Proceeds from:		Payment of: Accounts payable......	3,000
Accounts receivable..................	7,000	Accrued income taxes.	4,000
Marketable		Accrued salaries........	13,000
securities.............................	5,000		
Land and buildings..................	12,000		
Machinery.............................	4,000		
Subtotal......................................	$32,000	Subtotal......................................	$20,300
		Balance	11,700
	$32,000		$32,000
Ending balance............................	$11,700		

Owners' Equity

		Common stock............................	$54,000
		Additional paid-in capital.............	6,000
		Deficit..	(24,000)
Write-off of cash IOUs..................	$ 300	Beginning balance........................	$36,000
Net loss per realization and			
liquidation account	44,000		
Subtotal......................................	$44,300		$36,000
		Balance	8,300
	$44,300		$44,300
Ending balance............................	$ 8,300		

Before the realization and liquidation account is submitted to the court, a condensed balance sheet should be prepared in order to verify that the major elements are still in balance. The condensed balance sheet for Troubled Corporation is as follows:

Troubled Corporation
Condensed Balance Sheet
December 31, 19X0

Cash................................	$11,700	Liabilities not liquidated....	$44,000
Assets not realized..........	24,000	Owners' equity	(8,300)
	$35,700		$35,700

A verification of net loss or net gain statement has been promoted as a substitution for the realization and liquidation account, because the verification statement is less awkward and is a more effective medium for communicating results, especially to nonaccountants. In this statement, the net loss of $44,000 is verified by comparing the book values of assets realized with their proceeds and adding the trustee's fee to the resulting loss, as follows:

	Verification of Net Loss As Presented in Realization and Liquidation Account		
	Book Value	Proceeds	Loss (Gain)
Accounts receivable—old	$ 9,000	$ 7,000	$ 2,000
Marketable securities	4,000	5,000	(1,000)
Inventories	40,000	11,000	29,000
Land and buildings	60,000	64,000	(4,000)
Machinery	14,000	4,000	10,000
Goodwill	6,000	–0–	6,000
Subtotal	$133,000	$91,000	$42,000
Trustee's fee			2,000
Net loss			$44,000

The necessity for a verification of net loss or net gain statement supports the position that the conventional approach is not informative. Illustration 22–2 presents a realization and liquidation account resulting from the adoption of the book value technique. Three points in particular should be noted: (1) use of book values in the Assets Realized section, (2) the self-balancing nature of the assets and liabilities sections, and (3) production of the $44,000 net loss exclusively in the revenues and expenses section. The supplementary schedules of cash and owners' equity would remain the same.

Illustration 22–2

Alternate Book Value Approach
Realization and Liquidation Account
For the Ten Months Ended December 31, 19X0
Submitted by J. Hart, Trustee

Assets

Assets to be realized:			Assets realized:		
Accounts receivable (net)—old	$18,000		Accounts receivable—old	$ 9,000	
Marketable securities	8,000		Marketable securities	4,000	
Inventories	40,000		Inventories	40,000	
Land	10,000		Land and buildings	60,000	
Buildings (net)	50,000		Machinery	14,000	
Machinery (net)	14,000		Goodwill	6,000	$133,000
Goodwill	6,000	$146,000			
Assets acquired:			Assets not realized:		
Accounts receivable—new (from sale of inventory)		11,000	Accounts receivable —old	$ 9,000	
			—new	11,000	
			Marketable securities	4,000	24,000
		$157,000			$157,000

Liabilities

Liabilities liquidated:			Liabilities to be liquidated:		
Accounts payable	$ 3,000		Accounts payable	$45,000	
Accrued income taxes	4,000		Accrued income taxes	4,000	
Accrued interest on mortgage payable..	2,000		Accrued interest on mortgage payable..	2,000	
Accrued salaries	13,000		Accrued salaries	13,000	
Mortgage payable.....	50,000	$ 72,000	Mortgage payable.....	50,000	$114,000
Liabilities not liquidated:			Liabilities incurred:		
Accounts payable	$42,000		Trustee's fee payable		2,000
Trustee's fee payable	2,000	44,000			
		$116,000			$116,000

Revenues and Expenses

Supplementary expenses:			Supplementary revenues:		
Loss on realization of:			Sales of inventory.....	$11,000	
Accounts receivable —old	$ 2,000		Gain on sale of marketable securities	1,000	
Machinery.............	10,000		Gain on sale of land and buildings	4,000	$ 16,000
Goodwill..............	6,000		Net loss.....................		44,000
Cost of inventory sold.....................	40,000				
Trustee's fee............	2,000	$ 60,000			
		$ 60,000			$ 60,000

In the realization and liquidation account, several items have possible alternative treatments. For example, the write-off of the worthless IOUs in the cash balance could be shown as a supplementary expense, rather than as a direct debit to owners' equity. The sale of inventory on account could be shown as a supplementary revenue, rather than as an asset realized. If book values are maintained in the Assets Realized section, the write-off of goodwill could be shown as a supplementary expense and as an asset realized.

Variations in treatment are more significant in the preparation of a realization and liquidation account for a fiduciary who continues to operate a company while attempting to resolve its problems. Since the fiduciary prepares periodic statements of income in which nominal elements of revenue and expense are presented in their customary form, it would seem advisable to manipulate the realization and liquidation account so that these elements can be transferred easily to the revenues and expenses section. Thus, depreciation and other write-offs, as well as gains and losses on realizations, would be entered as supplementary expenses or revenues. This process would be logical for accountants since they would be basing their report on standard accounting procedures and entries. For example, the purchase of inventory and the sale of goods under a perpetual inventory system would require the normal entries and would be reported in the realization and liquidation account, as follows:

Event	Entry
Purchase of inventory	Inventory (Assets acquired) Accounts Payable (Liabilities incurred)
Cost of sales	Cost of Goods Sold (Supplementary expenses) Inventory (Assets realized)

Although the courts generally require reports to be based on the perpetual system, a periodic system could be used. Under such a system, the same events would be presented as follows:

Event	Entry
Purchase of inventory	Purchases (Supplementary expenses) Accounts Payable (Liabilities incurred)
Cost of sales	No entry for cost of sales

The totals of the realization and liquidation account will be influenced automatically by the cost of goods sold as a result of reporting the following items:

Debits	Credits
Beginning inventory (Assets to be realized) Purchases (Supplementary expenses)	Ending inventory (Assets not realized)

In reports of stewardship, the fiduciary must follow the wishes of the court. However, communication and reporting techniques could be improved by a cooperative effort between the legal and accounting professions.

QUESTIONS

1. Of the various procedures available to an insolvent debtor, which is the simplest? Under what conditions would the procedure be accepted by creditors?
2. What are the four operative chapters of the Bankruptcy Reform Act of 1978, and what area does each one cover?
3. Distinguish between a voluntary and an involuntary case under the Bankruptcy Reform Act.

4. Under a Chapter 7 liquidation, what procedure should a debtor follow to maximize the amount of property claimed as exempt?

5. What are the responsibilities of a debtor under a Chapter 7 liquidation once a trustee has been appointed?

6. What did one congressman mean when he referred to bankruptcy court decisions as "a puzzling misreading of congressional intent?"

7. Under the Bankruptcy Reform Act, do all unsecured creditors share pro rata in funds as they become available? Explain.

8. Define nondischargeable debts and give several illustrations.

9. What is the primary difference between a full and a quasi-reorganization?

10. What purpose is served by the account Reorganization Capital?

11. Explain the requirement for dating retained earnings after a reorganization.

12. Differentiate between the legal statement of affairs and the accounting statement of affairs.

13. When an accounting statement of affairs is prepared by the method illustrated in the chapter, five checkpoints are available to monitor whether equalities are being maintained. List the five equality checkpoints.

14. What is the nature of the dividend as typically computed from the accounting statement of affairs? Will all creditors receive this percentage of their claims?

15. Describe the preferred procedure for dealing with work in process inventory in the accounting statement of affairs when the intention is to complete the inventory to maximize the amount to be realized.

16. Describe the nature of a fiduciary relationship.

17. Explain the relationship between the accounts Carter Corporation in Trusteeship and J. Haertel, Trustee.

18. Explain why it often is necessary to use a worksheet to produce a combined trial balance for a company in trusteeship.

19. What function does the realization and liquidation account serve? Explain the nature of its three principal segments.

20. Discuss variations in the treatment of items that might be included in a realization and liquidation account.

EXERCISES

Exercise 1. Select the best answer for each of the following multiple-choice items.

1. Upon completion of an accounting statement of affairs for a corporation, the dividend was computed at 110%. One correctly may conclude that:

a. It was a waste of time and money to prepare the statement.

b. Creditors would receive 10% more than the book value of their debts.

c. Creditors could expect to receive payment in full, with an amount remaining for the stockholders.

d. The statement of affairs was prepared incorrectly.

2. The primary difference between a balance sheet and an accounting statement of affairs is that:

a. A balance sheet reflects book values, while a statement of affairs emphasizes realization values.

b. Assets are arranged in a different sequence.

c. Liabilities are arranged in a different sequence.

d. Owners' equity is not considered in the statement of affairs.

3. An accounting statement of affairs of a corporation in financial difficulty indicates that unsecured creditors would receive 40 cents on the dollar. Which one of the following assets is most likely to realize the smallest percentage of its book value?

a. Accounts receivable.

b. Inventories.

c. Plant and equipment.

d. Goodwill.

4. An accounting statement of affairs includes:

a. Only asset and liability accounts.

b. Only real accounts.

c. Both real and nominal accounts.

d. Only nominal accounts.

5. If a dividend of 80% is allocable to Class 7 unsecured creditors based on an accounting statement of affairs, it correctly may be concluded that:

a. All unsecured claims will receive the same percentage of return.

b. All unsecured claims will be paid in full.

c. Class 1 through 6 unsecured claims will be paid in full.

d. Stockholders will receive 20% of their equity.

Exercise 2.   Select the best answer for each of the following multiple-choice questions.

1. Immediately after the recording of a quasi-reorganization, there will be no balance in the account:

a. Accumulated Depreciation.

b. Capital Stock.

c. Paid-In Capital from Reorganization.

d. Retained Earnings.

2. An arrangement for creditors to accept an amount less than the amount owed to them is referred to as a:
   a. Charge and discharge agreement.
   b. Composition agreement.
   c. Bankruptcy agreement.
   d. Chandler agreement.

3. Nondischargeable debts are debts:
   a. Secured by assets that will realize less than the amount of the debt.
   b. That are unsecured.
   c. That remain the responsibility of the debtor even after a discharge of indebtedness.
   d. That arise after the order for relief has been issued.

4. In a liquidation proceeding, if the proceeds on the realization of an asset exceed the lien against that asset, the excess is assigned to:
   a. The holder of the lien.
   b. Other lien holders whose assets will not realize a sufficient amount to cover their liens.
   c. Meet the claims of the unsecured creditors.
   d. The stockholders of the corporation.

5. Under the Bankruptcy Reform Act, if the plan calls for the allocation of an individual's future earnings, it is most likely a proceeding under:
   a. Chapter 7.   b. Chapter 9.   c. Chapter 11.   d. Chapter 13.

Exercise 3.   The stockholders of Vegas Corporation have authorized the company to conduct a quasi-reorganization in order to revise asset valuations and eliminate its deficit. A condensed balance sheet at October 1, 19X5, just prior to the quasi-reorganization, is as follows:

Assets		Liabilities and Equity	
Current assets...............	$ 400,000	Liabilities	$ 600,000
Property and equipment		Capital stock ($10 par)..	2,200,000
(net)..........................	2,000,000	Deficit.........................	(400,000)
		Total liabilities and	
Total assets.................	$2,400,000	equity	$2,400,000

Additional data:
(a) Inventories have been overvalued by $80,000.
(b) Plant assets have been appraised at $1,500,000.
(c) Stockholders have approved a reduction in the par value of capital stock to $5 per share.

(1) Prepare journal entries to record the quasi-reorganization.
(2) Prepare a balance sheet for immediately after the quasi-reorganization.

Exercise 4. Kline Corporation received the necessary approval of two-thirds of its stockholders to undergo a quasi-reorganization. A condensed current balance sheet at June 1, 19X8, follows:

Assets

Current assets:
Cash..	$ 40,000	
Accounts receivable (net)	120,000	
Inventories..	100,000	
Total current assets..................................		$260,000

Property, plant, and equipment:
Land..		$200,000	
Plant and equipment................................	$500,000		
Less accumulated depreciation	150,000	350,000	550,000
Total assets..			$810,000

Liabilities and Stockholders' Equity

Current liabilities	$150,000	
8% Bonds payable	300,000	
Total liabilities..		$450,000
Preferred stock (cumulative 6%, $100 par; dividends are three years in arrears)..........	$200,000	
Common stock ($20 par)	400,000	
Deficit..	(240,000)	360,000
Total liabilities and stockholders' equity........		$810,000

The plan of quasi-reorganization calls for the following procedures:
(a) Plant and equipment are to be reduced to a book value of $300,000 through an adjustment to the accumulated depreciation account.
(b) For each share of 6%, $100 par, cumulative preferred stock, holders are to receive 2 shares of 8%, $40 par, noncumulative preferred stock. Dividends in arrears are to be sacrificed
(c) The par value of common stock is to be reduced to $5 per share.
(1) Prepare the journal entries to reflect the quasi-reorganization.
(2) Prepare a balance sheet after giving effect to the reorganization.

Exercise 5. J. Wachs, CPA, has prepared a statement of affairs. Assets against which there are no claims or liens are expected to produce $70,000, which must be allocated to unsecured claims of all classes totaling $105,000. The following are some of the claims outstanding:
(a) Accounting fees for Wachs, $1,500.
(b) An unsecured note for $1,000, on which $60 of interest has accrued, held by S. Bart.
(c) A note for $3,000, secured by $4,000 of receivables, estimated to be 60% collectible, held by J. Gamble.
(d) A $1,500 note, on which $30 of interest has accrued, held by B. Land. Property with a book value of $1,000 and a market value of $1,800 is pledged to guarantee payment of principal and interest.
(e) Unpaid income taxes of $3,500.

From this information, determine:

(1) The total amount allocable to unsecured claims with priority.

(2) The dividend per each dollar of Class 7 unsecured claims.

(3) The amount each of the claimants may expect to realize.

Exercise 6. Power Manufacturing Corporation is in financial difficulty. The following information relative to its inventories has been provided:

(a) Current balances:

Materials	$ 40,000
Work in process	60,000
Finished goods	100,000

(b) Unused materials will realize $.50 on the dollar.

(c) All finished goods are expected to realize 120% of cost.

(d) No liens exist on any inventories.

(e) To complete work in process, it is estimated that $26,000 of the materials in stock will be added and $24,000 of other costs will be incurred.

Using the cost completion approach and supporting T accounts for the three inventories, show how the inventories would appear in the assets section of the accounting statement of affairs.

Exercise 7. Under Chapter 7 of the Bankruptcy Reform Act, Martin Company is to proceed with liquidation. A trustee has been appointed, and the following transactions have occurred:

(a) Receivables collected amount to $9,000. Uncollectible accounts of $1,500 are written off.

(b) Accrued wages of $1,200 are paid.

(c) Bonds payable of $100,000 face value, originally sold at face value, are retired at 85, plus accrued interest of $3,000.

(d) Securities costing $8,000 are sold for $7,500, less brokerage fee of $210.

(e) Depreciation on machinery is $600.

(f) Payments on accounts payable total $6,500.

(g) A machine that originally cost $15,000 and has a book value of $5,000 is sold for $6,000.

Using the preferred accounting approach, indicate how each of the transactions would be shown on the realization and liquidation account and on the supplementary schedules.

Example:
Inventory with a book value of $9,000 was sold for
$10,000, of which $2,500 was collected in cash.
Solution:

Cash (in Cash Schedule)	2,500	
Assets Acquired—Receivables	7,500	
Supplementary Revenues—Sales		10,000
Supplementary Expenses—Cost of Goods Sold	9,000	
Assets Realized—Inventory		9,000

Exercise 8. The partially completed assets section of a realization and liquidation account is as follows:

Rainbow Company
Realization and Liquidation Account
For the Six Months Ended June 30, 19X2
Submitted by M. Mares, Trustee

Assets

Assets to be realized:		Assets realized:	
Receivables (net)—old.....	$40,000		
Marketable securities.......	8,000		
Inventory.......................	?	Inventory.......................	$30,000
Land.............................	30,000		
Building (net)..................	20,000		
Equipment (net)..............	40,000		

Assets acquired:	Assets not realized:	
	Receivables (net)—old.....	$ 8,000

Additional information:
(a) All of the inventory was sold on account at 20% above cost.
(b) Of the old receivables, $4,000 were written off as uncollectible. Of the new receivables, 60% were collected.
(c) The marketable securities consisted of 100 shares of Day Industries stock. These shares were sold at $60 each. Brokerage commissions and fees were $180.
(d) The land and building were sold for $55,000.
(e) The equipment was sold for $30,000 on terms of 1/3 down and a six-month, 8% note accepted for the remainder.

Complete the assets section of the realization and liquidation account, using net proceeds for assets realized rather than book values.

PROBLEMS

Problem 22–1. Select the best answer for each of the following multiple-choice questions.

1. A corporate quasi-reorganization is one that affects the interests of:
   a. The owners only.
   b. Short-term creditors only.
   c. Both short-term and long-term creditors.
   d. Creditors and owners.

2. The plan of reorganization under Chapter 11 of the Bankruptcy Reform Act will not be confirmed unless:

  a. The debtor first has completed required actions under Chapter 7 of the Act.
  b. The debtor can prove that there will be regular income in the future with which to meet obligations.
  c. Creditors will suffer no loss.
  d. Creditors will receive at least as much as they would under Chapter 7.

3. The accountant for a corporation undergoing a Chapter 11 reorganization uses a reorganization capital account to adjust the interests of parties involved. Upon completion of the reorganization, this account should:
  a. Be closed to Retained Earnings.
  b. Remain on the books as part of contributed capital.
  c. Be dated for a reasonable length of time.
  d. Be shown as an extraordinary item on the income statement.

4. An accounting statement of affairs for a corporation showed a credit balance in Retained Earnings. On the statement, the amount should be allocated to:
  a. Secured creditors.
  b. Class 1–6 unsecured creditors.
  c. Class 7 unsecured creditors.
  d. None of the creditors.

5. An accountant was preparing an accounting statement of affairs for a corporation whose land and building had a book value of $700,000 and a net realizable value of $500,000. The mortgage lien on the property was $400,000. On the statement of affairs, the accountant should allocate:
  a. $500,000 to the mortgage holder.
  b. $400,000 to the mortgage holder and $100,000 to the partially secured creditor group.
  c. $400,000 to the mortgage holder and $100,000 to the unsecured creditor group.
  d. $400,000 to the mortgage holder and $100,000 to Retained Earnings.

Problem 22–2. Select the best answer for each of the multiple-choice items, based on the following data.

The post-closing trial balance of a manufacturing company shows inventories of:

Raw materials	$ 60,000
Work in process	100,000
Finished goods	140,000

Work in process would realize only $18,000 as scrap. It can be completed by adding $15,000 of raw material on hand and incurring $32,000 of additional labor. It then will be worth $200,000.

1. The amount of the financial advantage of completing the work in process, rather than selling it as scrap, is:
  a. $182,000.   b. $135,000.   c. $53,000.   d. $29,000.

2. The additional labor cost to complete the work in process is ranked as:
   a. An unsecured claim with priority.
   b. A class 7 unsecured claim.
   c. A partially secured claim.
   d. A secured claim.

3. If raw material available after completion of the work in process can realize $.70 on the dollar, the amount realizable from raw material is:
   a. $60,000.   b. $46,500.   c. $42,000.   d. $31,500.

4. If the cost completion method of inventory presentation is employed on the accounting statement of affairs, the amount realizable from work in process is shown as:
   a. $0.   b. $53,000.   c. $168,000.   d. $200,000.

5. If the cost completion method of inventory presentation is employed on the accounting statement of affairs, the book value amount for finished goods is shown as:
   a. $140,000.   b. $147,000.   c. $187,000.   d. $287,000.

Problem 22–3.   Select the best answer for each of the following multiple-choice questions regarding a realization and liquidation account for a corporation in trusteeship.

1. The available cash balance when the trustee took over stewardship would be shown in the:
   a. Assets To Be Realized section.
   b. Assets Acquired section.
   c. Assets Not Realized section.
   d. Supplementary cash schedule.

2. If the gross proceeds approach is used as the basis for recording the realization of an asset, the amount of the gain or loss on disposition is:
   a. Not shown in the realization and liquidation account.
   b. Shown in the Assets To Be Realized section.
   c. Shown in the Assets Realized section.
   d. Shown in the revenues and expenses section.

3. If the book value approach is used as the basis for recording the realization of an asset, the amount of the gain or loss on disposition is:
   a. Not shown in the realization and liquidation account.
   b. Shown in the Assets To Be Realized section.
   c. Shown in the Assets Realized section.
   d. Shown in the revenues and expenses section.

4. The liquidation of a liability incurred by the corporation prior to the trustee's stewardship but paid by the trustee is:
   a. Not shown in the realization and liquidation account.
   b. Shown in the Liabilities Liquidated section.
   c. Shown in the Liabilities Incurred section.
   d. Shown in the revenues and expenses section.

5. The liquidation of a liability incurred by the trustee is:
   a. Not shown in the realization and liquidation account.
   b. Shown in the Liabilities Liquidated section.
   c. Shown in the Liabilities Incurred section.
   d. Shown in the revenues and expenses section.

Problem 22-4. The audit of Shaky Corporation for the year ended December 31, 19X6, has just begun. The president indicates that the company is insolvent and may require liquidation unless a large loan can be obtained immediately. A lender who is willing to advance $450,000 to the company has been located, but the loan will be subject to the following conditions:

(a) A $700,000, 8% mortgage, along with three months' accrued interest, will be canceled in exchange for 5,000 shares of $100 par, 6% cumulative, nonparticipating preferred stock.

(b) The $450,000 loan will require that a 12% mortgage be placed on the land and buildings as security. The 12% mortgage principal is payable in equal installments over 15 years.

(c) On May 1, 19X5, the company's trade creditors accepted $360,000 in notes, payable on demand, at 6% interest in settlement of all past due accounts. No payment has been made to date. The company will offer either to settle these liabilities at $.75 per $1 owed or to replace the notes payable on demand with new notes payable for the full amount of the indebtedness, including accrued interest. The new notes would pay interest at 8% and mature in five years. It is estimated that $200,000 of the demand notes will be exchanged for the longer-term notes and that the other creditors will accept the offer of a reduced cash settlement.

(d) A new issue of 1,000 shares of $100 par, 5% noncumulative, nonparticipating preferred stock will replace 1,000 outstanding shares of $100 par, 7% cumulative, participating preferred stock. Preferred stockholders will repudiate all claims to $14,000 of dividends in arrears. The company never has declared the dividends formally.

(e) A new issue of 600 shares of $50 par, class A common stock will replace 600 outstanding shares of $100 par, class A common stock.

(f) A new issue of 650 shares of $40 par, class B common stock will replace 650 outstanding shares of $100 par, class B common stock.

(g) The deficit is to be eliminated.

The president of Shaky Corporation requests that the auditor determine the effect of the foregoing on the company and furnishes the following condensed account balances, which the auditor believes are presented fairly:

Bank overdraft	$ 15,000
Other current assets	410,000
Property, plant, and equipment (net)	990,000
Trade accounts payable	235,000
Other current liabilities	85,000
Paid-in capital in excess of par on 7% cumulative preferred	125,000
Retained earnings (deficit)	(345,000)

Required:

(1) Prepare pro forma journal entries to give effect to the foregoing as of January 1, 19X7. Key entries to lettered information.

(2) Prepare a pro forma balance sheet as of January 1, 19X7, as if the reorganization had been consummated.

(AICPA adapted)

Problem 22–5. A proposal for the reorganization of Duke Corporation has been presented to the court. To aid the court in deciding on the merit of the proposal, an accountant has been asked to examine it and to prepare comparative balance sheets before and after the proposed reorganization. The following balance sheet is provided:

Duke Corporation
Balance Sheet
October 31, 19X1

Assets

Cash	$ 287,500
Other current assets	1,437,500
Bond sinking fund	625,000
Land	1,350,000
Plant and equipment	9,000,000
Accumulated depreciation	(5,000,000)
Total assets	$7,700,000

Liabilities and Stockholders' Equity

Preferred dividends payable	$ 45,000
Bond interest payable	424,760
Other current liabilities	44,400
Mortgage bonds payable—11%	2,500,000
Mortgage bonds payable—8%	1,872,000
Discount on 8% bonds payable	(212,500)
Preferred stock, $6 cumulative, no par, 7,500 shares issued	843,750
Preferred stock, $7.50 noncumulative, no par, 20,000 shares issued	2,125,000
Common stock, no par, 50,000 shares issued	781,250
Deficit	(723,660)
Total liabilities and stockholders' equity	$7,700,000

Details of the reorganization proposal are as follows:

(a) The preferred dividends payable constitute an illegal dividend declaration because of the deficit. The dividends are to be eliminated.

(b) Consolidated first mortgage 10% bonds of $3,750,000, dated November 1, 19X1, and redeemable on November 1 ten years hence, are to be sold on December 1, 19X1, at 95 plus accrued interest.

(c) Outstanding 8% and 11% bonds are to be redeemed on December 1,

19X1, at their November 1, 19X1 book values plus accrued interest for 6 months only.

(d) The $6 preferred stock is to be replaced by 6%, $100 par preferred stock.

(e) New $5 par common stock is to be exchanged on the following basis: 20 shares of new common for each share of $7.50 preferred stock; 2 shares of new common for each share of old, no-par common stock.

Required:

On 4-column journal paper, indicate the revisions in the present balance sheet and produce a pro forma balance sheet resulting from the plan of reorganization. Suggested headings for the amount columns are:

Column 1—Balance Sheet before Reorganization
    2 and 3—Reorganization Entries
    4—Balance Sheet after Reorganization

Problem 22–6. Creditors of Lap Company are concerned because payments are not being met. On March 15, 19X4, the following balance sheet was prepared:

Assets

Cash..		$ 10,000
Notes receivable (net of discounted notes)......................		15,000
Accounts receivable (no allowance for uncollectibles)		24,000
Inventory..		20,000
Prepaid expenses		1,000
Land...		16,000
Buildings	$50,000	
Less accumulated depreciation	20,000	30,000
Machinery..	$30,000	
Less accumulated depreciation	18,000	12,000
Goodwill...		4,000
Total assets..		$132,000

Liabilities and Stockholders' Equity

Notes payable..		$ 15,000
Accounts payable		20,000
Accrued interest on notes payable................................		450
Accrued interest on mortgage payable.............................		700
Accrued wages payable..		6,100
Taxes payable		2,200
Mortgage payable...		25,000
Total liabilities...		$ 69,450
Capital stock	$80,000	
Deficit..	(17,450)	62,550
Total liabilities and stockholders' equity.....................		$132,000

Additional information:

(a) Customers' notes receivable of $7,000 were discounted at the bank with recourse. These notes were due March 10, 19X4. No payments have been made to the bank, nor is the liability reflected in the balance sheet. Accrued interest and protest fees on the dishonored notes will amount to $550. In addition, $11,000 of notes receivable have been pledged to one of the creditors for an account payable of $12,000. All nondiscounted notes are collectible.

(b) Accounts receivable are classified as follows:

	Book Value	Estimated Realization
Good accounts	$ 9,000	$ 9,000
Doubtful accounts............................	10,000	7,000
Bad accounts	5,000	–0–
Total...	$24,000	$16,000

Good accounts receivable of $4,000 have been pledged to the holder of a $3,000 note payable on which there is $100 of accrued interest.

(c) The mortgage payable held by the bank is secured by a lien upon the land and buildings. Lap Company has received an offer to purchase the land and buildings for $36,000.

(d) Machinery will realize about $9,000. Inventory can be sold at 80% of cost. Nothing is realizable from prepaid expenses.

(e) Liquidation expenses are expected to be $1,000, plus a trustee's fee of $2,000.

(f) Wages payable include $2,400 of unpaid salary to the company president. All wages were earned within the preceding 90-day period.

Required:

(1) Prepare a statement of affairs. (Suggestion: Adjust or create any real accounts necessary, based on the data provided, before entering book values in the statement of affairs.)

(2) Determine the dividend to Class 7 unsecured claims.

Problem 22–7. Carbo Corporation, a subsidiary of Darren Manufacturing Company, is undergoing liquidation, with the prospect of paying its creditors at the rate of $.30 on the dollar. Darren Manufacturing Company is thereby in financial difficulty, and its creditors call for a statement of affairs and a deficiency statement.

The balance sheet of Darren Manufacturing Company as of August 31, 19X7, is as follows:

Assets

Current assets:			
Cash..		$ 660	
Notes receivable......................................		5,500	
Accrued interest on notes receivable		44	
Accounts receivable..................................	$33,440		
Less allowance for doubtful accounts	275	33,165	
Inventories: Finished goods.........................	$ 6,050		
Work in process........................	7,150		
Materials	14,300	27,500	
Prepaid expenses		540	$ 67,409
Investments:			
Carbo Corporation stock.............................		$52,800	
Advance to Carbo Corporation......................		22,000	74,800
Property, plant, equipment, and intangibles:			
Land..		$ 9,900	
Buildings	$38,500		
Less accumulated depreciation	6,600	31,900	
Machinery and equipment...........................	$30,000		
Less accumulated depreciation	4,590	25,410	
		13,200	80,410
Goodwill..			
Total assets...			$222,619

Liabilities and Stockholders' Equity

Current liabilities:			
Notes payable		$49,500	
Accounts payable		44,000	
Wages payable.......................................		880	
Taxes payable		825	
Mortgage interest payable...........................		440	
Note interest payable.................................		220	$ 95,865
Long-term liabilities:			
8% Mortgage payable on land and			
buildings			11,000
Total liabilities..			$106,865
Stockholders' equity:			
Common stock ($10 par)..............................		$66,000	
Retained earnings:			
Appropriated for expansion	$16,500		
Unappropriated balance	33,254	49,754	115,754
Total liabilities and stockholders' equity.............			$222,619

The following additional information is available:

(a) Estimated realizable values of:

Land..	$11,000
Buildings	16,500
Machinery and equipment............................	17,600
Finished goods...	4,400
Work in process	2,200
Materials	8,800

(b) In the cash drawer are found $60 of uncollectible IOUs included in the cash account balance.

(c) Notes receivable and interest are collectible.

(d) Accounts receivable are expected to realize the following amounts:

	Book Value	Realizable Value
Good accounts	$13,200	$13,200
Doubtful accounts....................................	11,000	4,965
Bad accounts	9,240	–0–
Total...	$33,440	$18,165

(e) Prepaid expenses have no realizable value.

(f) Notes payable consist of:

A note for $9,900, secured by notes receivable of $1,100 and by warehouse receipts for materials having a book value of $3,850 and an estimated realizable value of $3,300.

A note for $7,150, which is unsecured.

A note for $2,750, on which $33 of interest has accrued, secured by notes receivable of $3,330.

A note for $29,700, with accrued interest of $187. The holder of the note also holds Carbo Corporation stock as collateral.

(g) All wages payable qualify as priority items.

Required:

(1) Prepare a statement of affairs.

(2) Prepare a deficiency statement.

Problem 22–8. A creditor's committee of Carlton Company has obtained the March 31, 19X5 balance sheet shown at the top of the next page.

An analysis of the company's accounts disclosed the following:

(a) Carlton Company started business on April 1, 19X0, with authorized stock of $100 par. Of the 1,000 authorized shares, 750 were paid for in full at par, and 250 were subscribed at par, with a required 20% down payment and the balance payable upon call. All of the subscriptions receivable is due from W. Krueger, president of the company, and is fully collectible.

(b) Marketable securities include the $25,000 cost of U.S. Treasury bonds and 25 shares of Groves Company common stock, costing $2,750, with a market value of $3,300. Treasury stock also is included in the marketable securities, at a cost of $1,000 for the 40 shares.

(c) The land originally cost $10,000, and the building was erected at a cost of $102,500. Of the accumulated depreciation, $30,000 is applicable to the building. The realizable value of the real estate is $75,000.

(d) Notes receivable were endorsed with recourse when discounted and are expected to be dishonored. Of the accounts receivable, $3,000 are considered collectible.

Assets

Current assets:

Cash...		$ 11,250	
Marketable securities		28,750	
Notes receivable...................................	$ 10,000		
Less notes receivable discounted	10,000	–0–	
Accounts receivable.................................	$ 15,000		
Less allowance for doubtful accounts..	1,000	14,000	
Subscriptions receivable...........................		20,000	
Inventories:			
Finished goods.....................................	$ 27,500		
Work in process....................................	11,250		
Materials	15,000	53,750	
Total current assets...............................			$127,750
Property, plant, and equipment:			
Land and building...................................	$112,500		
Equipment..	60,000	$172,500	
Less accumulated depreciation		50,000	
Total property, plant, and equipment....			122,500
Total assets...			$250,250

Liabilities and Stockholders' Equity

Current liabilities:			
Notes payable		$ 87,500	
Accounts payable		60,000	
Salaries payable....................................		2,650	
Property tax payable...............................		1,150	
Total current liabilities.........................		$151,300	
Long-term liabilities:			
First mortgage payable	$ 37,500		
Second mortgage payable........................	50,000	87,500	
Total liabilities.......................................			$238,800
Stockholders' equity:			
Common stock, $100 par (1,000 shares authorized)			
750 shares issued		$ 75,000	
250 shares subscribed...........................		25,000	
Total...		$100,000	
Retained earnings (deficit)........................		(88,550)	
Total stockholders' equity...........................			11,450
Total liabilities and stockholders' equity.........			$250,250

(e) Inventories are shown at cost. Any finished goods are expected to yield 110% of cost. If scrapped, goods in process have a realizable value of only $2,200. It is estimated, however, that the work in process can be completed by the addition of $3,000 of present materials and an expenditure of $3,500 for labor. The materials deteriorate rapidly and will realize only 20% of cost. (Use the cost completion method illustrated in the text.)

(f) Equipment is estimated to have a realizable value of $12,000.

(g) Notes payable include a $25,000 note to Aerotex Company and a $62,500 note to B. Williams. Aerotex holds $15,000 of U.S. Treasury bonds as security for its loans. It also holds the first mortgage of $37,500 on the company's real estate, interest on which is paid through March 31, 19X5. The note payable to Williams is secured by a chattel mortgage on factory equipment. Interest on the note has been paid through March 31, 19X5. Williams also holds the second mortgage on the real estate.

(h) Any expenses not specifically mentioned need not be considered. All salaries qualify for priority, including labor to complete the work in process.

Required:

(1) Prepare a statement of affairs for Carlton Company.

(2) Prepare a schedule indicating the percentage of recovery by each creditor.

Problem 22–9. Mayne Manufacturing Co. has incurred substantial losses for several years and has become insolvent. On March 31, 19X5, Mayne petitioned the court for protection from creditors and submitted the following statement of financial position.

Mayne Manufacturing Co.
Statement of Financial Position
March 31, 19X5

Assets	Book Value	Liquidation Value
Accounts receivable..	$100,000	$ 50,000
Inventories..	90,000	40,000
Plant and equipment...	150,000	160,000
Totals...	$340,000	$250,000

Liabilities and Equity		
Accounts payable—general creditors........................	$600,000	
Common stock outstanding.....................................	60,000	
Deficit..	(320,000)	
Total..	$340,000	

Mayne's management informed the court that the company has developed a new product. A prospective customer is willing to sign a contract for the purchase of 10,000 units of this product during the year ending March 31, 19X6, 12,000 units of this product during the year ending March 31, 19X7, and 15,000 units of this product during the year ending March 31, 19X8, all at a price of $90 per unit. This product can be manufactured using Mayne's present facilities. Monthly production with immediate delivery is expected to be uniform within each year. Receivables are expected to be collected during the calendar month following sales.

Unit production costs of the new product are expected to be as follows:

Direct materials...	$20
Direct labor...	30
Variable overhead...	10

Fixed costs (excluding depreciation) will amount to $130,000 per year.

Purchases of direct materials will be paid during the calendar month following purchase. Fixed costs, direct labor, and variable overhead will be paid as incurred. Inventory of direct materials will be equal to 60 days' usage. After the first month of operations, 30 days' usage of direct materials will be ordered each month.

The general creditors have agreed to reduce their total claims to 60% of their March 31, 19X5 balances, under the following conditions:

(a) Existing accounts receivable and inventories are to be liquidated immediately, with the proceeds turned over to the general creditors.

(b) The balance of reduced accounts payable is to be paid as cash is generated from future operations, but in no event later than March 31, 19X7. No interest will be paid on these obligations.

Under this proposed plan, the general creditors would receive $110,000 more than the current liquidation value of Mayne's assets. The court has engaged you to determine the feasibility of this plan.

Required:

Ignoring any need to borrow and repay short-term funds for working capital purposes, prepare a cash budget for the years ending March 31, 19X6 and 19X7, showing the cash expected to be available to pay the claims of the general creditors, payments to general creditors, and the cash remaining after payment of claims. Support the cash budget with two schedules showing collections from customers and disbursements for direct materials.

Problem 22–10. You have been appointed trustee for Tara Industries Inc. because of a serious disagreement between major stockholders. The following balance sheet was prepared as of July 1, 19X7, the effective date of your appointment:

Assets

Current assets:		
Cash..	$ 12,000	
Receivables (net)	28,000	
Inventory	44,000	$ 84,000
Property, plant, and equipment:		
Land..	$ 40,000	
Building (net)	36,000	
Equipment (net)..	48,000	124,000
Total assets..		$208,000

Liabilities and Stockholders' Equity

Current liabilities:		
Notes payable	$ 24,000	
Accounts payable	36,000	
Taxes payable	8,000	
Accrued mortgage interest	1,000	$ 69,000
Long-term liabilities:		
Mortgage payable...		50,000
Total liabilities..		$119,000
Stockholders' equity:		
Common stock ($100 par)....................................	$120,000	
Retained earnings (deficit)	(31,000)	89,000
Total liabilities and stockholders' equity.............		$208,000

Transactions for July are summarized as follows:

Cash receipts:		
Sales for cash	$ 36,000	
Collection of receivables....................................	16,000	
Sale of equipment	8,000	
	$ 60,000	

Cash disbursed for payment of:		
Accounts payable	$ 12,000	
Mortgage interest...	1,000	
Taxes	8,000	
Salaries	2,000	
	$ 23,000	

Inventory sold for cash during July cost $28,000.
Receivables of $3,000 were written off during July.
Equipment sold had a book value of $10,000.
Depreciation on the building and equipment for July was $300 and $640, respectively.

Required:

Prepare a realization and liquidation account for July, using the conventional gross proceeds approach. Include proper supplementary schedules.

Problem 22–11. On petition of creditors, CB Radio Corporation was placed in trusteeship by order of a district court in an attempt to reinstate it on a sound financial base. As of January 1, 19X1, the trustee took over all of the corporate assets shown in the balance sheet, but would record only payments of liabilities previously incurred by the corporation. Gains and losses on the disposition of assets acquired by the corporation are to be attributed to the corporation rather than to the trustee.

CB Radio Corporation
Balance Sheet
December 31, 19X0

Assets

Current assets:			
Cash..................................		$ 24,000	
Accounts receivable........................	$210,000		
Less allowance for doubtful accounts....................................	10,000	200,000	
Notes receivable............................	$ 80,000		
Less notes receivable discounted ...	50,000	30,000	
Marketable securities		60,000	
Finished goods.............................		110,000	
Work in process............................		10,000	
Materials		40,000	
Prepaid insurance..........................		3,000	$477,000

	Cost	Accumulated Depreciation	Book Value	
Property, plant, and equipment:				
Land..............................	$ 30,000	—	$ 30,000	
Building........................	100,000	$ 12,000	88,000	
Machinery and equipment	120,000	40,000	80,000	
Office equipment.............	20,000	4,000	16,000	
Total..........................	$270,000	$ 56,000		214,000

Other assets:		
Goodwill.......................................		100,000
Total assets......................................		$791,000

Liabilities and Stockholders' Equity

Current liabilities:		
Accounts payable	$250,000	
Notes payable	200,000	
Wages payable...............................	20,000	
Taxes payable	10,000	
Mortgage interest payable................	2,500	$482,500
Long-term liability:		
10% Mortgage payable....................		25,000
Total liabilities.....................................		$507,500
Stockholders' equity:		
Common stock, no par, 4,000 shares authorized, 1,500 shares outstanding................................	$300,000	
Deficit...	(16,500)	283,500
Total liabilities and stockholders' equity...		$791,000

Additional data to be considered:

(a) Old accounts receivable amounting to $13,000 were written off. On the new accounts receivable, a provision to cover estimated uncollectible accounts of $2,000 is made.

(b) Depreciation expense for 19X1 was 12% on machinery and equipment, 4% on buildings (80% to factory and 10% each to selling and administrative), and 10% on office equipment.

(c) Prepaid insurance as of January 1, 19X1, should be charged as follows: $2,000 to manufacturing, $600 to selling, and $400 to administrative expenses.

(d) The following summary of transactions occurring during 19X1 was prepared:

Sales on account, $500,000
Purchases of materials on account, $150,000
Cash receipts include:

Collection on old accounts receivable	$197,000
Collection on old notes receivable	30,000
Collection on new accounts receivable	400,000
Net proceeds from sale of all securities	80,000
Proceeds from sale of additional 1,500 shares of no-par common stock	90,000
	$797,000

Cash disbursements include:
  Payments of the following old corporate liabilities approved by the court:

Accounts payable	$250,000
Mortgage interest payable	2,500
Wages payable	20,000
Taxes payable	10,000
Notes payable	200,000
	$482,500

Payments of items incurred during the period of trusteeship:

Accounts payable	$ 90,000
Mortgage interest	2,500
Direct labor	80,000
Manufacturing expenses	39,000
Selling expenses	58,000
Administrative expenses	36,000
Insurance premium	4,000
	$309,500

(e) Ending inventories as of December 31, 19X1, are:

Finished goods	$40,000
Work in process	20,000
Materials	30,000
Prepaid insurance	4,000

(f) All discounted notes receivable were paid to the bank by the makers.
(g) The books of the trustee were closed as of December 31, 19X1, since a court order had been received to return the CB Radio Corporation operations to its former management. The trustee's fee of $15,000 was approved for payment by the court on January 3, 19X2.

Required:
(1) Prepare journal entries to record the events on the books of the trustee and on the books of the corporation.
(2) Prepare an income statement in accordance with the wishes of the court.
(3) Prepare a realization and liquidation account, using book values, as recommended in the chapter.

PRESENT VALUE TABLES

Present Value of $1 Due in n Periods

$$PV = A\left[\frac{1}{(1+i)^n}\right] = A(PVF_{\overline{n}|i})$$

n	2%	3%	4%	5%	6%	8%	10%	12%	16%	20%
1	0.9804	0.9709	0.9615	0.9524	0.9434	0.9259	0.9091	0.8929	0.8621	0.8333
2	0.9612	0.9426	0.9246	0.9070	0.8900	0.8573	0.8264	0.7972	0.7432	0.6944
3	0.9423	0.9151	0.8890	0.8638	0.8396	0.7938	0.7513	0.7118	0.6407	0.5787
4	0.9238	0.8885	0.8548	0.8227	0.7921	0.7350	0.6830	0.6355	0.5523	0.4823
5	0.9057	0.8626	0.8219	0.7835	0.7473	0.6806	0.6209	0.5674	0.4761	0.4019
6	0.8880	0.8375	0.7903	0.7462	0.7050	0.6302	0.5645	0.5066	0.4104	0.3349
7	0.8706	0.8131	0.7599	0.7107	0.6651	0.5835	0.5132	0.4523	0.3538	0.2791
8	0.8535	0.7894	0.7307	0.6768	0.6274	0.5403	0.4665	0.4039	0.3050	0.2326
9	0.8368	0.7664	0.7026	0.6446	0.5919	0.5002	0.4241	0.3606	0.2630	0.1938
10	0.8203	0.7441	0.6756	0.6139	0.5584	0.4632	0.3855	0.3220	0.2267	0.1615
11	0.8043	0.7224	0.6496	0.5847	0.5268	0.4289	0.3505	0.2875	0.1954	0.1346
12	0.7885	0.7014	0.6246	0.5568	0.4970	0.3971	0.3186	0.2567	0.1685	0.1122
13	0.7730	0.6810	0.6006	0.5303	0.4688	0.3677	0.2897	0.2292	0.1452	0.0935
14	0.7579	0.6611	0.5775	0.5051	0.4423	0.3405	0.2633	0.2046	0.1252	0.0779
15	0.7430	0.6419	0.5553	0.4810	0.4173	0.3152	0.2394	0.1827	0.1079	0.0649
16	0.7284	0.6232	0.5339	0.4581	0.3936	0.2919	0.2176	0.1631	0.0930	0.0541
17	0.7142	0.6050	0.5134	0.4363	0.3714	0.2703	0.1978	0.1456	0.0802	0.0451
18	0.7002	0.5874	0.4936	0.4155	0.3503	0.2502	0.1799	0.1300	0.0691	0.0376
19	0.6864	0.5703	0.4746	0.3957	0.3305	0.2317	0.1635	0.1161	0.0596	0.0313
20	0.6730	0.5537	0.4564	0.3769	0.3118	0.2145	0.1486	0.1037	0.0514	0.0261
25	0.6095	0.4776	0.3751	0.2953	0.2330	0.1460	0.0923	0.0588	0.0245	0.0105
30	0.5521	0.4120	0.3083	0.2314	0.1741	0.0994	0.0573	0.0334	0.0116	0.0042
40	0.4529	0.3066	0.2083	0.1420	0.0972	0.0460	0.0221	0.0107	0.0026	0.0007
50	0.3715	0.2281	0.1407	0.0872	0.0543	0.0213	0.0085	0.0035	0.0006	0.0001

Present Value of an Annuity of $1 per Period

$$PV_n = R\left[\frac{1 - \frac{1}{(1+i)^n}}{i}\right] = R(PVAF_{\overline{n}|i})$$

n	2%	3%	4%	5%	6%	8%	10%	12%	16%	20%
1	0.9804	0.9709	0.9615	0.9524	0.9434	0.9259	0.9091	0.8929	0.8621	0.8333
2	1.9416	1.9135	1.8861	1.8594	1.8334	1.7833	1.7355	1.6901	1.6052	1.5278
3	2.8839	2.8286	2.7751	2.7232	2.6730	2.5771	2.4869	2.4018	2.2459	2.1065
4	3.8077	3.7171	3.6299	3.5460	3.4651	3.3121	3.1699	3.0373	2.7982	2.5887
5	4.7135	4.5797	4.4518	4.3295	4.2124	3.9927	3.7908	3.6048	3.2743	2.9906
6	5.6014	5.4172	5.2421	5.0757	4.9173	4.6229	4.3553	4.1114	3.6847	3.3255
7	6.4720	6.2303	6.0021	5.7864	5.5824	5.2064	4.8684	4.5638	4.0386	3.6016
8	7.3255	7.0197	6.7327	6.4632	6.2098	5.7466	5.3349	4.9676	4.3436	3.8372
9	8.1622	7.7861	7.4353	7.1078	6.8017	6.2469	5.7590	5.3282	4.6065	4.0310
10	8.9826	8.5302	8.1109	7.7217	7.3601	6.7101	6.1446	5.6502	4.8332	4.1925
11	9.7868	9.2526	8.7605	8.3064	7.8869	7.1390	6.4951	5.9377	5.0286	4.3271
12	10.5753	9.9540	9.3851	8.8633	8.3838	7.5361	6.8137	6.1944	5.1971	4.4392
13	11.3484	10.6350	9.9856	9.3936	8.8527	7.9038	7.1034	6.4235	5.3423	4.5327
14	12.1062	11.2961	10.5631	9.8986	9.2950	8.2442	7.3667	6.6282	5.4675	4.6106
15	12.8493	11.9379	11.1184	10.3797	9.7122	8.5595	7.6061	6.8109	5.5755	4.6755
16	13.5777	12.5611	11.6523	10.8378	10.1059	8.8514	7.8237	6.9740	5.6685	4.7296
17	14.2919	13.1661	12.1657	11.2741	10.4773	9.1216	8.0216	7.1196	5.7487	4.7746
18	14.9920	13.7535	12.6593	11.6896	10.8276	9.3719	8.2014	7.2497	5.8178	4.8122
19	15.6785	14.3238	13.1339	12.0853	11.1581	9.6036	8.3649	7.3658	5.8775	4.8435
20	16.3514	14.8775	13.5903	12.4622	11.4699	9.8181	8.5136	7.4694	5.9288	4.8696
25	19.5235	17.4131	15.6221	14.0939	12.7834	10.6748	9.0770	7.8431	6.0971	4.9476
30	22.3965	19.6004	17.2920	15.3725	13.7648	11.2578	9.4269	8.0552	6.1772	4.9789
40	27.3555	23.1148	19.7928	17.1591	15.0463	11.9246	9.7791	8.2438	6.2335	4.9966
50	31.4236	25.7298	21.4822	18.2559	15.7619	12.2335	9.9148	8.3045	6.2463	4.9995

INDEX

CHECK FIGURES FOR SELECTED PROBLEMS

PROB.	CHECK FIGURES
1-2	(1) Constant cost and current cost/constant dollar gross profits are $17,018 and $15,273, respectively (3) Increase due to changes in purchasing power is $1,200
2-1	19X8 net loss on discontinued operations, $93,000; 19X8 cumulative effect of the change, $225,000
2-2	Case a - loss from discontinued operations, $11,880 Case c - income from discontinued operations, $5,280
2-3	(1) Effect of change, $130,000
2-4	Situation A, 19X4 net income, $128,200; Situation D, 19X4 net income, $100,000
2-5	Alternative (b), 19X5 SA = $13,125 for PEPS; Alternative (e), 19X5 IA = $400,000 for FDEPS
2-7	PEPS, $2.1890
2-8	PEPS, $18.897; FDEPS, $14.735
2-9	PEPS, $2.436; FDEPS, $2.466
2-10	PEPS, $1.500; FDEPS, $1.494
2-11	PEPS, $14.01
3-1	Goodwill, $215,000
3-2	Paid-in capital in excess of par, $220,000; Retained earnings, $590,000
3-3	(1) Present value of bonds; Co. A $371,152, Co. B $234,742; Goodwill: Co. A $22,920, Co. B $19,646
3-4	(a) Goodwill, $60,000; (b) Land, $20,000; (c) Deferred credit, $20,000
3-5	(1) (a) Goodwill, $90,000; (b) Gain on sale of business, $40,000 (2) (a) Land, $55,200; (b) Loss on sale of business, $124,000
3-6	Net investment in direct financing lease, $710,605; Goodwill, $82,678
3-7	(1) Deferred tax liability, $54,000; (2) Adjustment to deferred tax liability, $31,500
3-8	(1) (a) Goodwill, $165,000; (b) Additional goodwill, $50,000 (2) (a) Goodwill, $215,000; (b) Decrease paid-in capital, $10,000
3-9	(1) Paid-in capital in excess of par, $440,000; (2) Paid-in capital in excess of par, $120,000; (3) Retained earnings, $610,000
3-10	(1) Paid-in capital in excess of par, $1,950,000; (2) Goodwill, $4,665,000
3-11	(1) Allowance for doubtful accounts, $5,300; Retained Earnings, $535,700 (2) Net income, 19X5, $340,000; 19X6, $394,700
3-12	(1) 870 shares issued for 250 Martin shares; (2) Paid-in capital in excess of par, $48,300
3-13	(2) Property B, $450,000; Income on investment, $95,000
4-1	(2) Remaining goodwill, $18,000
4-2	(1) Increase goodwill for Bristol, $50,000; decrease goodwill for Costello, $20,000 (2) Decrease goodwill for Bristol, $50,000; Decrease goodwill for Costello, $20,000
4-3	Total assets: (1) $3,560,000, (2) $3,440,000, (3) $2,840,000
4-4	(1) Goodwill, $60,800; (2) Excess cost attributable to fixed assets and deferred tax expense, $8,800
4-5	Total value available for long lived assets, $799,000
4-6	(1) Goodwill, $125,000; (2) Increase in paid-in capital in excess of par, $50,000
4-7	(1) Goodwill, $24,000; (2) Minority interest, $270,000
4-8	Present value of bonds, $371,152; Total value assigned to long-lived assets, $503,922
4-9	Goodwill, $336,000
4-10	Total assets, $4,150,000
4-11	(1) Goodwill, $526,500; (2) Retained earnings recorded at acquisition, $102,600; Minority interest $96,400
4-12	(1) (b) Increase in paid-in capital in excess of par, $265,000; (2) (a) Goodwill, $3,000
4-13	Goodwill, $44,680; Minority interest, $27,320

CHECK FIGURES

PROB.	
5-1	(3) Cost to equity conversion; Barns +$32,000, Charms -$9,000
	(4) Minority interest: Barns $47,000, Charms $12,000
5-2	Consolidated net income, $80,950; Minority interest, $120,000
5-3	Consolidated net income, $81,600; Minority interest, $57,000
5-4	Balance sheet, Goodwill $92,500; Retained earnings, $297,500
5-5	Retained earnings, $545,000
5-6	Consolidated net income, $70,700; Minority interest, $41,000
5-7	Consolidated net income, $73,700; Minority interest, $45,000
5-8	Equity conversion, $36,000; Minority interest, $62,000
5-9	Consolidated net income, $45,000; Retained earnings, $175,000
5-10	Goodwill recorded, $72,000; Consolidated net income, $39,500; Minority interest, $31,400
5-11	Consolidated net income, $34,800; Minority interest, $45,000
5-12	Goodwill recorded, $186,000; Combined net income, $310,200
5-13	Goodwill on balance sheet, $4,900; Combined net income, $243,650; Minority interest, $90,000
5-14	Net increase on goodwill, $610,000; Controlling interest, $19,124; Minority interest, $769,960
5-15	Trial balance figures: Goodwill, $1,347,500; Accumulated depreciation--machinery and equipment, $11,126,000
5A-1	Controlling interest, $150,600; Minority interest, $164,000
5A-2	Controlling interest, $106,600; Minority interest, $70,000
6-1	Income distribution: minority, $8,990; controlling, $76,740
6-2	Cost of goods sold, $7,368,000; Combined net income, $1,262,000
6-3	Cost of goods sold, $1,594,075; Combined net income, $269,925
6-4	Controlling interest, $991,448; Controlling retained earnings, $2,671,400
6-5	Cost of goods sold, $873,000; Controlling interest, $194,480
6-6	Controlling interest, $206,710; Controlling retained earnings, $610,760
6-7	Balance sheet construction in progress, $784,298; Controlling interest, $392,138; Controlling retained earnings, $1,655,838
6-8	Balance sheet construction in progress, $1,232,000; Combined net income, $146,525; Controlling retained earnings, $305,836
6-9	Cost of goods sold, $165,000; Controlling interest, $72,800
6-10	Cost of goods sold, $1,348,670; Controlling interest, $147,064; Controlling retained earnings, $710,064
6-11	Cost of goods sold, $457,500; Controlling interest, $55,300; Controlling retained earnings, $73,400
6-12	Cost of goods sold, $188,000; Controlling interest, $75,766; Controlling retained earnings, $756,208
6-13	Cost of goods sold, $1,151,500; Controlling interest, $148,300; Controlling retained earnings, $773,300
6A-1	Cost of goods sold, $1,888,000; Combined net income, $334,000; Controlling retained earnings, $586,000
6A-2	Cost of goods sold, $210,000; Controlling interest, $611,700; Controlling retained earnings, $1,452,950
7-1	Loss on bond retirement on Jan. 1, 19X6, $2,440; Combined net income, $803,639
7-2	Gain on bond retirement on Jan. 1 19X6, $6,056; Controlling interest, $209,342
7-3	Loss on bond retirement on July 2, 19X3, $3,087; Controlling interest, $222,769
7-4	Loss on bond retirement on Jan. 1, 19X6, $15,000; Controlling interest, $1,499,400
7-5	Extraordinary loss on bond retirement, $5,535; Controlling interest, $64,478; Controlling retained earnings, $1,874,478
7-6	Loss on bond retirement on Jan. 1, 19X6, $15,592; Controlling interest, $119,203; Controlling retained earnings, $341,346
7-7	Extraordinary gain on bond retirement, $50,188; Controlling interest, $409,812; Controlling retained earnings, $989,112
7-8	Gain on bond retirement on Jan. 1, 19X6, $7,023; Controlling interest, $60,412; Controlling retained earnings, $627,709
7-9	Combined net income, $1,021,000; Controlling retained earnings, $1,932,350
7-10	Controlling interest, $288,000; Minority interest, $316,200; Controlling retained earnings, $718,400
7-11	Controlling interest, $154,125; Minority interest, $91,587; Controlling retained earnings, $426,725
7-12	Controlling interest, $344,656; Minority interest $249,607; Controlling retained earnings, $1,065,515
7-13	Controlling interest, $3,403; Minority interest $128,326; Controlling retained earnings, $365,777

PROB.	CHECK FIGURES

CHECK FIGURES

8-1   Controlling interest, $133,250; Minority interest, $40,000; Controlling retained earnings, $257,000

8-2   Controlling interest, $138,100; Minority interest, $46,000; Controlling retained earnings, $423,300

8-3   Controlling interest, $132,950; Minority interest, $175,000; Controlling retained earnings, $432,950

8-4   Controlling interest, $615,819; Minority interest, $284,920; Controlling retained earnings, $3,585,389

8-5   Gain on sale of subsidiary, $6,600

8-6   Equity conversion, $59,200; Controlling interest, $354,520

8-7   Gain on bond retirement on Jan. 1, 19X5, $7,877; Controlling interest, $69,009; Controlling retained earnings, $433,398

8-8   Gain on sale of 1/9 interest, $11,950; loss on sale of 8/9 interest, $24,000

8-9   Purchased income, $5,000; Cost of goods sold, $1,783,000; Controlling interest, $226,250

8-10   Extraordinary gain on bond retirement, $1,500; Controlling interest, $71,040; Controlling retained earnings, $200,640

8-11   (1) Controlling interest, $46,010; Minority interest, $42,560;
(2) Gain on sale of subsidiary interest, $8,090

8-12   Gain on sale of investment, $16,000; Controlling interest, $861,600; Minority interest, $285,200

8A-1   Minority interest, $90,000; Controlling retained earnings, $3,004,900

8A-2   Minority interest, $25,200; Controlling retained earnings, $487,217

8A-3   Retained earnings, $4,290,000

9-1   Gain on sale of Tessman stock, $6,000

9-2   Net increases: Investment in Kantor, $87,000; Treasury stock, $6,000; Investment in Saeger, $70,000

9-3   Gain on sale of stock, $5,160; Controlling interest, $119,680; Minority interest, $374,040

9-4   Cost of goods sold, $1,539,900; Controlling interest, $179,224; Controlling retained earnings, $336,064

9-5   Controlling interest, $121,650; Minority interest, $192,250; Controlling retained earnings, $364,850

9-6   Controlling interest, $155,500; Minority interest, $182,500; Controlling retained earnings, $368,500

9-7   Controlling interest, $141,982; Minority interest, $204,568; Controlling retained earnings, $406,232

9-8   Controlling interest, $149,645; Minority interest, $224,355; Controlling retained earnings, $401,045

9-9   Controlling interest, $118,000; Minority interest, $141,600; Controlling retained earnings, $423,500

9-10   Controlling interest, $114,065; Minority interest, $143,785; Controlling retained earnings, $384,565

9-11   Controlling interest, $176,975; Minority interest, $42,450; Controlling retained earnings, $560,065

10-1   Cash provided by operating activities, $300,500

10-2   Cash provided by operating activities, $328,000

10-3   Cash provided by operating activities, $384,000

10-4   Consolidated Primary EPS, $4.57; Consolidated fully diluted EPS, $4.54

10-5   Provision for tax, $41,730

10-6   Total conversion to equity, $139,500; Controlling interest, $103,006; Minority interest, $237,328

10-7   Controlling interest, $101,987.12; Minority interest, $128,784; Controlling retained earnings, $427,870.24

10-8   Controlling interest, $118,379; Minority interest, $103,236; Controlling retained earnings, $334,789

10-9   Net share of income: 19X6, $5,600; 19X7, $8,075

10-10   Net share of income: 19X6, $5,700; 19X7, $6,990; 19X8, $5,595

10-11   Investment account balances: Hupp, $201,075; Geer, $9,550; Cargo, $717,540

10-12   (1) Goodwill, $41,000; (2) Goodwill, $55,000

10A-1   Depreciation expense, $4,000

10A-2   Branch income: Reported by Branch, $4,500; Reported by Home office, $3,000; Total net income, $77,000

10A-3   Net income, $91,800

10A-4   Net income, $44,170

11-1   Deutsche marks gain, $8,000; Pesos loss, $10,000

11-3   (2) Net income effect with hedge, $5,900

11-4   (3) Contract discount, $6,500; (4) Two contracts are preferred

11-6   Net income effect, 19X8, $8,850; 19X9, $3,800

12-1   (2) Translation adjustment, $97,353; (3) Exchange gain, $7,280

12-2   (2) Carrying value, $65,689